SOMETHING ABOUT THE AUTHOR®

Something about the Author *was named an* **"Outstanding Reference Source,"** *the highest honor given by the American Library Association Reference and Adult Services Division.*

ISSN 0276-816X

SOMETHING ABOUT THE AUTHOR®

Facts and Pictures about Authors
and Illustrators of Books for Young People

volume 209

GALE
CENGAGE Learning™

Detroit • New York • San Francisco • New Haven, Conn • Waterville, Maine • London

GALE
CENGAGE Learning

Something about the Author, Volume 209

Project Editor: Lisa Kumar

Editorial: Laura Avery, Pamela Bow, Jim Craddock, Amy Fuller, Andrea Henderson, Margaret Mazurkiewicz, Tracie Moy, Jeff Muhr, Kathy Nemeh, Mary Ruby, Mike Tyrkus

Permissions: Leitha Etheridge-Sims, Jacqueline Flowers, Kelly Quin

Imaging and Multimedia: Leitha Etheridge-Sims, John Watkins

Composition and Electronic Capture: Amy Darga

Manufacturing: Drew Kalasky

Product Manager: Janet Witalec

For product information and technology assistance, contact us at **Gale Customer Support, 1-800-877-4253.**
For permission to use material from this text or product, submit all requests online at **www.cengage.com/permissions.**
Further permissions questions can be emailed to **permissionrequest@cengage.com**

Gale
27500 Drake Rd.
Farmington Hills, MI, 48331-3535

LIBRARY OF CONGRESS CATALOG CARD NUMBER 62-52046

ISBN-13: 978-1-4144-4222-8
ISBN-10: 1-4144-4222-X

ISSN 0276-816X

This title is also available as an e-book.
ISBN-13: 978-1-4144-6441-1
ISBN-10: 1-4144-6441-X
Contact your Gale, Cengage Learning sales representative for ordering information.

Printed in the United States of America
1 2 3 4 5 6 7 14 13 12 11 10

Contents

Authors in Forthcoming Volumes vii

Introduction ix

SATA Product Advisory Board xi

Illustrations Index 205

Author Index 239

A

B

Bataille, Marion 1963- 1

Beake, Lesley 1949- 1

Bluemle, Elizabeth 4

Bouwman, Heather M.
  See Bouwman, H.M. 6

Bouwman, H.M. 6

Bowler, Tim 1953- 7

Brittney, L. 11

Broda, Ron 1954- 12

Brooks, Laurie 14

Bulion, Leslie 1958- 15

Busby, John 1942- 17

C

Carrillo, Patricia S.
  See Carrillo, P.S. 19

Carrillo, P.S. 19

Carter, Anne Laurel 1953- 19

Case, Chris 1976- 22

Catt, Louis
  See French, Vivian 47

Chichester Clark, Emma 1955- 24

Clayton, Elaine 1961- 30

D

Davis, Eleanor 1983(?)- 33

Delacre, Lulu 1957- 34

Donofrio, Beverly 1950- 38

Drummond, Allan 1957- 40

E

Ellison, Elizabeth Stow 1970- 43

Emerson, Kevin 44

F

Farr, Richard 1960- 45

Fontenot, Mary Alice 1910-2003
  Obituary Notice 46

French, Vivian 47

Funke, Cornelia 1958- 55

Funke, Cornelia Caroline
  See Funke, Cornelia 55

G

Gifaldi, David 1950- 62

Gilmore, Rachna 1953- 64

Gonsalves, Rob 1959- 68

Guay, Rebecca 69

Guay-Mitchell, Rebecca
  See Guay, Rebecca 69

H

Hearn, Diane Dawson 1952- 70

Hegamin, Tonya C. 1975- 73

Herrick, Steven 1958- 74

Hines, Anna Grossnickle 1946- 78

Hoppe, Paul 84

Hubbard, Crystal 86

K

Kimmel, Elizabeth Cody 88

Kingfisher, Rupert 91

Kissel, Richard 92

Knudson, Mike 1965- 93

Koertge, Ron 1940- 93

Kozjan, Drazen 99

L

Larkspur, Penelope
  See Wyatt, Valerie 203

Lessac, Frané 1954- 101

Lewis, Richard 1956- 107

Lewis, Rose 108

Lewis, Rose A.
  See Lewis, Rose 108

Ludwig, Trudy 1959- 109

Lynch, Chris 1962- 112

M

Mara, Rachna
  See Gilmore, Rachna 64

McCall, Bruce 1935- 118

McCauley, Adam 1965- 120

McLaughlin, Lauren 123

Montanari, Eva 1977- 124

N

Naylor, Phyllis Reynolds 1933- 126

Nicholls, Sally 1983- 136

O

Odone, Jamison 1980- 137

O'Donnell, Liam 1970- 138

Orlean, Susan 1955- 140

P

Paul, Ann Whitford 1941- 144

Preller, James 1961- 148

Preus, Margi 151

R

Rolston, Steve 1978- 153

Rosoff, Meg 1956- 154

Ruelle, Karen Gray 1957- 158

S

Sanchez, Anita 1956- 162

Smith, Andrew 1959- 162

Smith, Andrew Anselmo
  See Smith, Andrew 162

Smucker, Anna Egan 1948- 164

Snyder, Laurel 1974- 165

Staake, Bob 1957- 167

Stampler, Ann Redisch 170

Stevens, Helen 172

Stewart, Melissa 1968- 172

Strickland, Shadra 178

Stuchner, Joan Betty 179

Sue, Majella Lue 181

Swanson, Susan Marie 1955- 182

T

Takahashi, Hideko 186

Tedesco, P.R.
  See Naylor, Phyllis Reynolds 126

Tubb, Kristin O'Donnell 1971- 188

W

Weber, Jill 1950- 189

Weston, Robert Paul 192

Widener, Terry 1950- 193

Willard, Elizabeth Kimmel
  See Kimmel, Elizabeth Cody 88

Williams, Alex 1969- 197

Winters, Katharine
  See Winters, Kay 198

Winters, Kay 1936- 198

Wyatt, Valerie 203

Authors in Forthcoming Volumes

Below are some of the authors and illustrators that will be featured in upcoming volumes of *SATA*. These include new entries on the swiftly rising stars of the field, as well as completely revised and updated entries (indicated with *) on some of the most notable and best-loved creators of books for children.

*Steve Augarde ▮ Well known as an illustrator and a paper engineer for children's books, Augarde was awarded a bronze medal in the 2003 Nestlé Smartie Book Prizes for his debut young-adult novel, *The Various*. Part one of the "Touchstone Trilogy," *The Various* was followed by *Celandine* and *Winter Wood*, which tell a fanciful story about a girl's efforts to rescue a tribe of local fairies.

Royce Buckingham ▮ Attorney-turned-screenwriter and novelist Buckingham began his writing career while working as a county prosecutor in his home state of Washington. The author of *Demonkeeper* and other horror fiction, he has also created a number of award-winning short films and screenplays.

Jack E. Davis ▮ Davis is a highly regarded illustrator of children's books whose quirky cartoon art adds an extra dose of humor to books such as Daniel Pinkwater's *The Picture of Morty and Ray* and John Lithgow's *Marsupial Sue*. A self-trained artist who works primarily in acrylics and pencils, Davis began his career as a designer and art director for an advertising agency before turning to freelance work. He counts among his influences painters Charles Bragg and Fernando Botero.

*Will Hillenbrand ▮ Based in Cincinnati, Ohio, Hillenbrand is an award-winning author and illustrator whose works include dozens of picture books for young readers. In addition to his self-illustrated titles, such as *Down by the Station, Fiddle-I-Fee,* and *My Book Box,* he has also illustrated stories by noted writers Eric A. Kimmel, Phyllis Root, Judy Sierra, Judith St. George, and David A. Adler, among a host of others.

Mary Hogan ▮ Hogan began her career as an editor at *Teen* magazine, and she fictionalizes her experiences there in her "Susanna" series about a fifteen-year-old intern at a popular gossip magazine. Typical teen issues are also the focus of *The Serious Kiss, Perfect Girl,* and *Pretty Face,* all of which focus on dating, best friends, and school and family worries.

Walter Lyon Krudop ▮ Krudop is an award-winning author, illustrator and animator. Living and working in New York City, he published his first picture book, *Blue Claws*, in 1993, and has followed it with several other self-illustrated stories of close family relationships. In addition, Krudop has created artwork for numerous books by other writers, among them Robert Burleigh's critically acclaimed *Black Whiteness: Admiral Byrd Alone in the Antarctic* and Kathryn Lasky's picture-book biography *Born in the Breezes: The Seafaring Life of Joshua Slocum.*

*Daniel Pinkwater ▮ Celebrated as an original, imaginative, and versatile writer for children and young adults, the prolific Pinkwater creates stories that illustrate the absurdity of adult reality while treating young readers to plenty of laughs. Whether they are tubby preadolescent boys or mischievous polar bears, his characters ultimately shine in books such as *Pickle Creature, The Wuggie Norple Story, Fat Camp Commandos,* and *Looking for Bobowicz: A Hoboken Chicken Story,* the last illustrated by his wife, Jill Pinkwater.

Sergio Ruzzier ▮ An Italian-born illustrator who produced his first original picture book in 1999, Ruzzier has become known for his unique, sometimes monstrous characters. In addition to creating art for children's books such as the poetry collection *Moon, Have You Met My Mother?* by Karla Kuskin and Lore Segal's *Why Mole Shouted and Other Stories,* he has produced award-winning original self-illustrated stories that include *The Little Giant* and *Amandina.* Sometimes compared to noted illustrator Maurice Sendak, Ruzzier has been cited for his subtle use of color and his sketchy yet exacting line drawings.

Francisco X. Stork ▮ Stork is the author of the young-adult novels *Marcelo in the Real World* and *Behind the Eyes,* both of which feature Mexican-American characters who draw on the strengths of family and culture while making their way in a sometimes difficult world. Based on its author's own experiences, the award-winning *Behind the Eyes* finds a studious Chicano teen seeking revenge following his brother's murder, while an autistic boy learns to cope through his work with injured horses in *Marcelo in the Real World.*

*Janet S. Wong ▮ A poet whose works employ a variety of voices and styles, Wong explores her heritage as an American born of Korean-Chinese parents. In addition to verse collections such as *Good Luck Gold and Other Poems,* Wong treats younger readers to her evocative rhymes in picture books such as *Alex and the Wednesday Chess Club, The Dumpster Diver,* and *Apple Pie Fourth of July,* while her writing and advocacy on behalf of literacy has earned her numerous awards and other recognition.

Introduction

Something about the Author (*SATA*) is an ongoing reference series that examines the lives and works of authors and illustrators of books for children. *SATA* includes not only well-known writers and artists but also less prominent individuals whose works are just coming to be recognized. This series is often the only readily available information source on emerging authors and illustrators. You'll find *SATA* informative and entertaining, whether you are a student, a librarian, an English teacher, a parent, or simply an adult who enjoys children's literature.

What's Inside *SATA*

SATA provides detailed information about authors and illustrators who span the full time range of children's literature, from early figures like John Newbery and L. Frank Baum to contemporary figures like Judy Blume and Richard Peck. Authors in the series represent primarily English-speaking countries, particularly the United States, Canada, and the United Kingdom. Also included, however, are authors from around the world whose works are available in English translation. The writings represented in *SATA* include those created intentionally for children and young adults as well as those written for a general audience and known to interest younger readers. These writings cover the entire spectrum of children's literature, including picture books, humor, folk and fairy tales, animal stories, mystery and adventure, science fiction and fantasy, historical fiction, poetry and nonsense verse, drama, biography, and nonfiction. Obituaries are also included in *SATA* and are intended not only as death notices but also as concise overviews of people's lives and work. Additionally, each edition features newly revised and updated entries for a selection of *SATA* listees who remain of interest to today's readers and who have been active enough to require extensive revisions of their earlier biographies.

Autobiography Feature

Beginning with Volume 103, many volumes of *SATA* feature one or more specially commissioned autobiographical essays. These unique essays, averaging about ten thousand words in length and illustrated with an abundance of personal photos, present an entertaining and informative first-person perspective on the lives and careers of prominent authors and illustrators profiled in *SATA*.

Two Convenient Indexes

In response to suggestions from librarians, *SATA* indexes no longer appear in every volume but are included in alternate (odd-numbered) volumes of the series, beginning with Volume 57.

SATA continues to include two indexes that cumulate with each alternate volume: the Illustrations Index, arranged by the name of the illustrator, gives the number of the volume and page where the illustrator's work appears in the current volume as well as all preceding volumes in the series; the Author Index gives the number of the volume in which a person's biographical sketch, autobiographical essay, or obituary appears in the current volume as well as all preceding volumes in the series.

These indexes also include references to authors and illustrators who appear in *Gale's Yesterday's Authors of Books for Children, Children's Literature Review,* and *Something about the Author Autobiography Series.*

Easy-to-Use Entry Format

Whether you're already familiar with the *SATA* series or just getting acquainted, you will want to be aware of the kind of information that an entry provides. In every *SATA* entry the editors attempt to give as complete a picture of the person's life and work as possible. A typical entry in *SATA* includes the following clearly labeled information sections:

PERSONAL: date and place of birth and death, parents' names and occupations, name of spouse, date of marriage, names of children, educational institutions attended, degrees received, religious and political affiliations, hobbies and other interests.

ADDRESSES: complete home, office, electronic mail, and agent addresses, whenever available.

CAREER: name of employer, position, and dates for each career post; art exhibitions; military service; memberships and offices held in professional and civic organizations.

MEMBER: professional, civic, and other association memberships and any official posts held.

AWARDS, HONORS: literary and professional awards received.

WRITINGS: title-by-title chronological bibliography of books written and/or illustrated, listed by genre when known; lists of other notable publications, such as plays, screenplays, and periodical contributions.

ADAPTATIONS: a list of films, television programs, plays, CD-ROMs, recordings, and other media presentations that have been adapted from the author's work.

WORK IN PROGRESS: description of projects in progress.

SIDELIGHTS: a biographical portrait of the author or illustrator's development, either directly from the biographee—and often written specifically for the *SATA* entry—or gathered from diaries, letters, interviews, or other published sources.

BIOGRAPHICAL AND CRITICAL SOURCES: cites sources quoted in "Sidelights" along with references for further reading.

EXTENSIVE ILLUSTRATIONS: photographs, movie stills, book illustrations, and other interesting visual materials supplement the text.

How a *SATA* Entry Is Compiled

SATA editors examine a wide variety of published sources to gather information for an entry. Biographical and bibliographic sources are consulted, as are book reviews, feature articles, published interviews, and material sometimes obtained from the biographee's family, publishers, agent, or other associates. Whenever possible, the author or illustrator is sent a copy of the entry to check for accuracy and completeness.

Entries that have not been verified by the biographees or their representatives are marked with an asterisk (*).

Contact the Editor

We encourage our readers to examine the entire *SATA* series. Please write and tell us if we can make *SATA* even more helpful to you. Give your comments and suggestions to the editor:

Editor
Something about the Author
Gale, Cengage Learning
27500 Drake Rd.
Farmington Hills MI 48331-3535

Toll-free: 800-877-GALE
Fax: 248-699-8070

Something about the Author Product Advisory Board

The editors of *Something about the Author* are dedicated to maintaining a high standard of excellence by publishing comprehensive, accurate, and highly readable entries on a wide array of writers for children and young adults. In addition to the quality of the content, the editors take pride in the graphic design of the series, which is intended to be orderly yet inviting, allowing readers to utilize the pages of *SATA* easily and with efficiency. Despite the longevity of the *SATA* print series, and the success of its format, we are mindful that the vitality of a literary reference product is dependent on its ability to serve its users over time. As literature, and attitudes about literature, constantly evolve, so do the reference needs of students, teachers, scholars, journalists, researchers, and book club members. To be certain that we continue to keep pace with the expectations of our customers, the editors of *SATA* listen carefully to their comments regarding the value, utility, and quality of the series. Librarians, who have firsthand knowledge of the needs of library users, are a valuable resource for us. The *Something about the Author* Product Advisory Board, made up of school, public, and academic librarians, is a forum to promote focused feedback about *SATA* on a regular basis. The nine-member advisory board includes the following individuals, whom the editors wish to thank for sharing their expertise:

Eva M. Davis
Director,
Canton Public Library,
Canton, Michigan

Joan B. Eisenberg
Lower School Librarian,
Milton Academy,
Milton, Massachusetts

Francisca Goldsmith
Teen Services Librarian,
Berkeley Public Library,
Berkeley, California

Susan Dove Lempke
Children's Services Supervisor,
Niles Public Library District,
Niles, Illinois

Robyn Lupa
Head of Children's Services,
Jefferson County Public Library,
Lakewood, Colorado

Victor L. Schill
Assistant Branch Librarian/Children's Librarian,
Harris County Public Library/Fairbanks Branch,
Houston, Texas

Caryn Sipos
Community Librarian,
Three Creeks Community Library,
Vancouver, Washington

Steven Weiner
Director,
Maynard Public Library,
Maynard, Massachusetts

something ABOUT the AUthor

BATAILLE, Marion 1963-

Personal

Born 1963, in France. *Education:* École Supérieure d'Arts Graphiques, degree.

Addresses

Home—Paris, France.

Career

Graphic artist and illustrator.

Writings

Op-up (pop-up book), Les Trois Ourses (Paris, France), 2006, published as *ABC3D*, Roaring Brook Press (New York, NY), 2008.

Contributor to periodicals, including *Le Monde*.

Adaptations

Op-up was the focus of a short film.

Biographical and Critical Sources

PERIODICALS

Horn Book, November-December, 2008, Lolly Robinson, review of *ABC3D*, p. 688.
Kirkus Reviews, September 15, 2008, review of *ABC3D*.
New York Times Book Review, November 9, 2008, Becca Zerkin, review of *ABC3D*, p. 22.
Publishers Weekly, August 18, 2008, "Top of the Pops," p. 62.
Washington Post Book World, September 7, 2008, Kristi Jemtegaard, review of *ABC3D*, p. 12.

ONLINE

Livres Animes Web site (in French), http://www.livres animes.com/ (December 15, 2009), interview with Bataille.*

*   *   *

BEAKE, Lesley 1949-

Personal

Born 1949, in Scotland; married. *Education:* Earned teacher's certificate at Rhodes University.

Addresses

Home—16 Forest Hill, Simon's Town, 7975 South Africa. *E-mail*—lesley@wine.co.za.

Career

Author, editor, and educator. Has taught in South Africa; freelance travel writer; editor of educational book series for South African publishers. Cofounder of Vil-

lage Schools Project, Nyae Nyae, Namibia; member of Parliamentary Millennium Project in South Africa, 2006. *Winescape* magazine, former editor; editor of winenews.co.za for eight years; has also served as editor of periodicals, including *Reflections, Savanna,* and *Souvenir.*

Awards, Honors

Young Africa Award for children's literature, 1987, and Sir Percy Fitzpatrick Award for best children's book, 1988, both for *The Strollers;* third prize, Young Africa Award, 1988, for *Traveller;* Cosmopolitan Award for woman of achievement, 1989; third prize, Young Africa Award, 1989, J & B Rare Achievers Award for outstanding success in the field of literature, 1989, Sir Percy Fitzpatrick Award for best children's book, 1990, and M-Net Book Prize, 1991, all for *A Cageful of Butterflies; Fair Lady* Travel Writing award, 1990; South African Children's Book Forum honors award, 1991, Notable Children's Book designation, American Library Association (ALA), 1993, Best Book for Young Adults designation, ALA, 1994, and gold medal for Best Children's Book in English, Namibian Children's Book Forum, 1995, all for *Song of Be;* honorable mention, Namibian Children's Book Forum Awards in English Prose, 1991, for *Tjojo and the Wild Horses;* Children's Book Forum Honours selection, 1992, for *The Race;* Asahi Reading Award, International Board on Books for Young People, 1996, for *One Dark Night;* Highlights Foundation scholarship, 1997; premio Mundial de Literatura José Marti nomination, 1997; Hans Christian Andersen Award nomination, South African Children's Book Forum, 2004; Astrid Lindgren Award nomination, 2005.

Writings

Detained at Her Majesty's Pleasure: The Journal of Peter David Hadden, Tafelberg (Cape Town, South Africa), 1986.

The Strollers, Maskew Miller Longman (Cape Town, South Africa), 1987.

A Cageful of Butterflies, Maskew Miller Longman (Cape Town, South Africa), 1988.

Traveller, Maskew Miller Longman (Cape Town, South Africa), 1988.

Merino, Maskew Miller Longman (Cape Town, South Africa), 1988.

Rainbow, Maskew Miller Longman (Cape Town, South Africa), 1988.

Harry Went to Paris, Penguin, 1989.

Serena's Story, Maskew Miller Longman (Cape Town, South Africa), 1990.

Tjojo and the Wild Horses, De Jager-HAUM Publishers (Pretoria, South Africa), 1990.

Mandi's Wheel, illustrated by Joe Madisia, Build a Book Collective/New Namibia Books (Windhoek, Namibia), 1990.

Song of Be, Maskew Miller Longman (Cape Town, South Africa), 1991, Holt (New York, NY), 1993.

Bau and the Baobab Tree, Tafelberg (Cape Town, South Africa), 1992.

One Dark Night, Little Library, 1993.

The Race, Oxford University Press (Oxford, England), 1993.

Lamma Adventure, Macmillan (Hong Kong), 1993.

Café Thunderball, De Jager-HAUM Publishers (Pretoria, South Africa), 1993.

The Story-telling Day, Maskew Miller Longman (Cape Town, South Africa), 1994.

Who's There?, Maskew Miller Longman (Cape Town, South Africa), 1994.

Desert Hero, Maskew Miller Longman (Cape Town, South Africa), 1994.

Z456 to the Rescue, Maskew Miller Longman (Cape Town, South Africa), 1994.

Looking for Me, Maskew Miller Longman (Cape Town, South Africa), 1994.

Jakey, Tafelberg (Cape Town, South Africa), 1997.

(With Tina Schouw) *Tina's Song,* illustrated by Elizabeth Andrew, Cambridge University Press (Cape Town, South Africa), 1999.

Home Now, illustrated by Karin Littlewood, Frances Lincoln (London, England), 2006, Charlesbridge (Watertown, MA), 2007.

Author's work has been published in African languages, including Silozi, Ateso, Icibemba, Lunda, Kiikaonde, Luganda, Hausa, and Shona, as well as in Dutch, Italian, Norwegian, and French. Contributor to periodicals, including *Fair Lady, Femina, Cosmopolitan, House and Leisure, Reader's Digest,* and *Wildside.*

"ZEBRA BOOKS" SERIES

Hello? Hello?, Kagiso Publishers (Pretoria, South Africa), 1995.

The Library Book, Kagiso Publishers (Pretoria, South Africa), 1995.

The Last Minute, Kagiso Publishers (Pretoria, South Africa), 1995.

Sidima's Goal, Kagiso Publishers (Pretoria, South Africa), 1995.

An Ordinary Barking Dog, Kagiso Publishers (Pretoria, South Africa), 1995.

Lisiwe's Long Walk, Kagiso Publishers (Pretoria, South Africa), 1995.

Nomisa Waits, Kagiso Publishers (Pretoria, South Africa), 1995.

Stop Making That Noise!, Kagiso Publishers (Pretoria, South Africa), 1995.

Our House, Kagiso Publishers (Pretoria, South Africa), 1995.

The Chase, Kagiso Publishers (Pretoria, South Africa), 1995.

Dizzie Lizzie, Disco Dancer, Kagiso Publishers (Pretoria, South Africa), 1995.

Diamonds, Kagiso Publishers (Pretoria, South Africa), 1995.

Free to Be Me, Kagiso Publishers (Pretoria, South Africa), 1995.

Also served as series editor, with Ann Walton.

"SUNBIRD BOOKS" SERIES

Esi Hates School, PPS Publishers, 1997.
Dorsla and the Stolen Gold, PPS Publishers, 1997.
Faqu's Goats, PPS Publishers, 1997.
Julie and the New Shoes, PPS Publishers, 1997.

Also served as series editor, with Ann Walton.

"STARS OF AFRICA" SERIES

Hare Helps, Maskew Miller Longman (Cape Town, South Africa), 2000.
Frog and Dog, Maskew Miller Longman (Cape Town, South Africa), 2001.
Bad John, Maskew Miller Longman (Cape Town, South Africa), 2001.
Kubi the Star, Maskew Miller Longman (Cape Town, South Africa), 2002.
Lindal's Little Cow, Maskew Miller Longman (Cape Town, South Africa), 2002.
My Mother Hates Television, Maskew Miller Longman (Cape Town, South Africa), 2002.
Waiting for Rain, Maskew Miller Longman (Cape Town, South Africa), 2003.
Grandfather Remembers, Maskew Miller Longman (Cape Town, South Africa), 2003.
The Bead Book, Maskew Miller Longman (Cape Town, South Africa), 2003.

Also served as series editor.

Sidelights

Award-winning author, editor, and educator Lesley Beake has published numerous works for children, including *Song of Be* and *Home Now.* All of her titles are set in Africa, where the author makes her home. The books "express my love of the landscape and the places that I care about and reflect the experiences I have shared with children here," as Beake noted on her home page.

Born and raised in Scotland, Beake later moved to South Africa, where she earned a teaching certificate at Rhodes University. During her teaching career, Beake traveled around South Africa, becoming familiar with both the Western and Eastern Capes. She also worked in Namibia during that nation's transition to an independent government, and she was involved in a host of educational projects that benefited the Ju/'hoansi people of Eastern Bushmanland. "It is these experiences that inform my stories for young people," the author remarked.

A noted travel writer, Beake has enjoyed a varied career. She has contributed articles to such publications as *Fairlady* and *Femina,* and she served as a correspon-

dent to the radio show *Woman's World.* She has also edited *Savanna,* a magazine about southern Africa, and *Winescape,* a periodical devoted to wine tourism. "My life is spent reading and writing, with a fair amount of travel happening simultaneously," the author remarked.

Beake published her first book for young readers, *Detained at Her Majesty's Pleasure: The Journal of Peter David Hadden,* in 1986. Since that time, she has written some fifty works for children and young adults, and she has edited around 200 books, including several for adults. In the late 1990s, the author began focusing her efforts on developing educational titles for underprivileged children, including the "Zebra Books" and "Stars of Africa" series. Some of the works have been published outside of Africa, a development that "makes me very happy because our stories are important and the children of this continent have much to share with children elsewhere," as she noted.

Song of Be, one of Beake's best-known works, is a coming-of-age tale set in Namibia as that nation prepares for its first democratic elections. The work centers on Be, a Ju/'hoan Bushman girl who has left her ancestral lands to journey with her mother to Ontevrede, the farm where her grandfather works. Be is taught to read and write by Min, the farmer's wife, and soon realizes that Western texts often misrepresent her people's history. Be also becomes aware of her grandfather's painful history of enforced slavery as well as her mother's relationship with the farm owner, and she falls in love with Khu, a Bushman who encourages her family to vote.

Song of Be garnered strong reviews. Because of its strongly developed characters, observed a *Publishers Weekly* contributor, "the story is never overwhelmed by its political message and by the copious amount of information it conveys." According to Stephenie Yearwood, writing in the *ALAN Review,* Beake's "novel is marked by its beauty and simplicity of style, inventiveness of structure, and an emotionally intense plotscape." Yearwood continued, "*Song of Be* is a story which fulfills the promise of the best of multicultural literature, both a foray into the alienness of cultures and an affirmation of shared human truths and emotions. Readers cannot understand Be without learning something of her remarkable society and its history, yet we can understand her situation and indeed see parallels to it in our own experience."

Home Now, a highly regarded picture book, concerns Sieta, a young African girl who moves to her aunt's village after the death of her parents. Burdened with sad memories, Sieta finds it difficult to adjust to the unfamiliar environment. During a class trip to a park, Sieta makes a special connection with an orphaned baby elephant named Satara, and the youngster returns to the park again and again to visit her new companion. "This subtle depiction of loss is moving and painful but ultimately a story of survival," a *Kirkus Reviews* critic

wrote of *Home Now,* and a London *Sunday Times* reviewer noted that Beake's "lyrical and hopeful text tempers the tale with gentle humanity."

Describing her philosophy on the Charlesbridge Publishers Web site, Beake stated: "I believe in the universality of children's experience." She added, "I believe that the place to bring these issues to their attention is through the most powerful medium of all . . . the written word."

Biographical and Critical Sources

PERIODICALS

ALAN Review, spring, 1997, Stephenie Yearwood, "Emerging into Independence: The Self and the Culture in Lesley Beake's *Song of Be.*"

Bookbird, September, 2004, Patricia E. Bandre, "Lesley Beake: Author, South Africa," p. 58.

Booklist, February 1, 2007, Julie Cummins, review of *Home Now,* p. 60.

Guardian (London, England), January 9, 2007, Kate Agnew, review of *Home Now,* p. 7.

Kirkus Reviews, December 15, 2006, review of *Home Now,* p. 1264.

Publishers Weekly, November 22, 1993, review of *Song of Be,* p. 64.

School Librarian, November, 1993, review of *The Race,* p. 147; February, 1996, review of *A Cageful of Butterflies,* p. 29; spring, 2007, Angela Redfem, review of *Home Now,* p. 17.

School Library Journal, March, 2007, review of *Home Now,* p. 151.

Sunday Times (London, England), November 19, 2006, review of *Home Now.*

Times Educational Supplement, July 7, 1995, review of *The Strollers,* p. R8.

ONLINE

Lesley Beake Home Page, http://michelle.wine.co.za/Michelle-Clients/Lesley (March 1, 1998).*

* * *

BLUEMLE, Elizabeth

Personal

Born in Phoenix, AZ; daughter of an actress and a magician. *Education:* University of California, Berkeley, B.A.; Bank Street College of Education, M.Ed.; Vermont College, M.A. (writing for children and young adults).

Addresses

Home and office—VT. *E-mail*—ehb@elizabethbluemle.com.

Career

Bookseller and writer. Flying Pig Bookstore, founder and co-owner, 1996—. Worked as a creative writer/producer in Hollywood, CA; former editorial director at a book packager; formerly worked as assistant teacher and head school librarian in New York, NY.

Writings

My Father, the Dog, illustrated by Randy Cecil, Candlewick Press (Cambridge, MA), 2006.
Dogs on the Bed, illustrated by Anne Wilsdorf, Candlewick Press (Cambridge, MA), 2008.
How Do You Wokka-Wokka?, illustrated by Randy Cecil, Candlewick Press (Cambridge, MA), 2009.

Sidelights

Elizabeth Bluemle grew up in a family that shared a love of words; her mother was an actress, and her older sister also performed in theater at a young age. As a child, Bluemle lived in Arizona and California, and she began her early career in Los Angeles, working as a creative writer and producer in Hollywood. Eventually deciding that she did not want a career in television, Bluemle traveled through Europe before moving to San Francisco, then New York, and eventually to Vermont. There, together with a good friend, she decided to open a bookstore for children, and she completed a M.A. in writing for children and young adults at Vermont College.

Bluemle's first book for children, *My Father, the Dog,* focuses on a young narrator who is convinced that her father is really a pooch. Like the family pet, her father scratches himself in the morning, can clear a room with a "toot," growls if he is roused from a nap, and shows great loyalty to the family. In *School Library Journal* Piper L. Nyman found the book to be "ideal for storytimes or one-on-one sharing," and a contributor to *Kirkus Reviews* dubbed Bluemle's story "tail-wagging hilarity that's simply doggone funny." A *Publishers Weekly* critic considered *My Father, the Dog* to be an "appealingly flippant debut," and concluded that "young dog lovers will lap this up."

In *Dogs on the Bed* a human family of four sleeps with six dogs on the large family bed. However, the dogs are restless, squirming and barking at things that their two-legged bed-mates cannot see. Eventually, all ten bed-sharers find a place on the bed where each can catch a few hours of comfortable sleep. According to a contributor to *Kirkus Reviews,* Bluemle's "rollicking, rhyming text" for this book features "exuberant descriptions and details of the dogs' antics." Piper Nyman, writing for *School Library Journal,* wrote that the author's "exuberant, rhyming text delights the ear" and Shelle Rosenfeld commented in *Booklist* that the "rousing rhymes and frequent refrains" in *Dogs on the Bed* "provide continuous, peppy entertainment."

Elizabeth Bluemle's humorous picture book **My Father, the Dog** *features Randy Cecil's colorful cartoon art.* (Illustration copyright © 2006 by Randy Cecil. All rights reserved. Reproduced by permission of Candlewick Press, Inc., Somerville, MA.)

Multi-ethnic young children living in an urban neighborhood demonstrate their silly walks and dances in *How Do You Wokka-Wokka?* The title is full of nonsense rhymes that Marge Loch-Wouters suggested in her *School Library Journal* review may encourage young readers and listeners to make up their own. "This bouncy book is a joy as a read-aloud," Loch-Wouters added, while Rosenfeld explained that Bluemle's "peppy prose incorporates wordplay, repetition, and bouncy sounds." Also praising the rhyming text in *How Do You Wokka-Wokka?*, a *Publishers Weekly* contributor cited the story's "strong and catchy beat."

Biographical and Critical Sources

PERIODICALS

Booklist, May 15, 2006, Randall Enos, review of *My Father, the Dog,* p. 48; November 15, 2008, Shelle Rosenfeld, review of *Dogs on the Bed,* p. 49; September 1, 2009, Shelle Rosenfeld, review of *How Do You Wokka-Wokka?,* p. 98.

Kirkus Reviews, April 1, 2006, review of *My Father, the Dog,* p. 342; September 1, 2008, review of *Dogs on the Bed;* July 1, 2009, review of *How Do You Wokka-Wokka?*

Publishers Weekly, May 8, 2006, review of *My Father, the Dog,* p. 64; July 6, 2009, review of *How Do You Wokka-Wokka?,* p. 50.

School Library Journal, July, 2006, Piper L. Nyman, review of *My Father, the Dog,* p. 68; January, 2009, Piper Nyman, review of *Dogs on the Bed,* p. 72; August, 2009, Marge Loch-Wouters, review of *How Do You Wokka-Wokka?,* p. 70.

ONLINE

Elizabeth Bluemle Home Page, http://www.elizabeth bluemle.com (December 17, 2009).*

BOUWMAN, Heather M.
See BOUWMAN, H.M.

* * *

BOUWMAN, H.M.
(Heather M. Bouwman)

Personal

Children: two. *Education:* Calvin College, B.A.; University of Illinois, M.A., Ph.D. *Hobbies and other interests:* Traditional Korean martial arts.

Addresses

Home and office—St. Paul, MN. *Office*—JRC 341, University of St. Thomas, 2115 Summit Ave., Saint Paul, MN 55105-1096. *E-mail*—hmbouwman@gmail.com; hmbouwman@stthomas.edu.

Career

Author and educator. University of St. Thomas, St. Paul, MN, professor of English, 2001—. Member, The Loft Literary Center.

Member

Society of Children's Book Writers and Illustrators, Children's Literature Network, National Council of Teachers of English, Society of Early Americanists.

Writings

The Remarkable and Very True Story of Lucy and Snowcap, Marshall Cavendish (Tarrytown, NJ), 2008.

Sidelights

An educator and writer, H.M. Bouwman did not become serious about writing prose until after the birth of her second child. After a move to St. Paul, Minnesota, to work as a professor of English at St. Thomas University, Bouwman began connecting with other writers. She joined the Society of Children's Book Writers and Illustrators and took classes, also participating in the mentor program at The Loft Literary Center, a Minneapolis-based writing initiative that helps authors to connect and learn from each other.

Many of the ideas in Bouwman's first novel tie into her academic work: similar to Australia, the Americas were a place to where the British shipped their criminals, and the author studied this facet of American history while researching her graduate thesis. Taking place during the late 1700s, *The Remarkable and Very True Story of Lucy and Snowcap* is set on a series of imaginary is-

lands off the coast of New England. The characters of Lucy, a descendent of a family of original island inhabitants who were forced from their homes by British colonizers, and Snowcap, the daughter of British convicts, are both based on bits of history. Lucy and Snowcap, each considered special by her respective culture, must overcome their differences in order to keep all of the men from Lucy's island from turning to stone. A *Kirkus Reviews* contributor hailed *The Remarkable and Very True Story of Lucy and Snowcap* as "an original, remarkable and very true debut," and described Bouwman's tale as "beautifully written, fully realized, [and] fast-paced."

Biographical and Critical Sources

PERIODICALS

Kirkus Reviews, August 1, 2008, review of *The Remarkable and Very True Story of Lucy and Snowcap.*
School Library Journal, November, 2008, Necia Blundy, review of *The Remarkable and Very True Story of Lucy and Snowcap,* p. 115.

Cover of H.M. Bouwman's middle-grade novel The Remarkable and Very True Story of Lucy and Snowcap, *featuring artwork by Nicoletta Ceccoli.* (Marshall Cavendish Children, 2008. Illustration © by Nicoletta Ceccoli. Reproduced by permission.)

H.M. Bouwman Home Page, http://www.hmbouwman.com (December 17, 2009).

St. Thomas University Web site, http://www.stthomas.edu/ (December 17, 2009), "Heather Bouwman."*

* * *

BOWLER, Tim 1953-

Personal

Born November 14, 1953, in Leigh-on-Sea, Essex, England; married; wife a teacher. *Education:* East Anglia University, degree (Swedish). *Hobbies and other interests:* Squash, rugby, swimming, sailing, basketball, soccer, yoga, reading, poetry, music.

Addresses

Home—Devon, England. *Agent*—Caroline Walsh, David Higham Associates, Ltd., 5-8 Lower John St., Golden Square, London W1F 9HA, England. *E-mail*—info@ timbowler.co.uk.

Career

Writer and novelist. Worked variously in forestry and timber trade; teacher of foreign languages and of English as a second language, then head of modern languages, for seven years at school in Newton Abbot, Devon, England; part-time translator; freelance writer, 1990—.

Awards, Honors

Books for the Teen Age selection, New York Public Library, 1995, for *Midget;* Carnegie Medal, British Library Association, 1997, and Angus Book Award, 1999, both for *River Boy;* Angus Book Award, and Children's Book of the Year Award, Lancashire County Library, both 2000, both for *Shadows;* South Lanarkshire Book Award, 2002, for *Storm Catchers;* Hull Book Award, Highland Book Award, Redbridge Book Award, all 2007, South Lanarkshire Children's Book Award, 2008, all for *Frozen Fire;* Somerset Teenage Fiction Award, 2009, for *Playing Dead.*

Writings

FOR CHILDREN

Midget, Oxford University Press (Oxford, England), 1994, Margaret K. McElderry (New York, NY), 1995, published with *Dragon's Rock,* Oxford University Press (New York, NY), 2007.

Dragon's Rock, Oxford University Press (Oxford, England), 1995, published with *Midget,* Oxford University Press (New York, NY), 2007.

River Boy, Oxford University Press (Oxford, England), 1997, Margaret K. McElderry (New York, NY), 2002.

Shadows, Oxford University Press (Oxford, England), 1999, Oxford University Press (New York, NY), 2007.

Storm Catchers, Oxford University Press (Oxford, England), 2001, Margaret K. McElderry (New York, NY), 2003.

Starseeker, Oxford University Press (Oxford, England), 2002, published as *Firmament,* Margaret K. McElderry (New York, NY), 2004.

Apocalypse, Oxford University Press (Oxford, England), 2004, Margaret K. McElderry Books (New York, NY), 2005.

Blood on Snow, illustrated by Jason Cockcroft, Hodder Children's (London, England), 2004.

Walking with the Dead, illustrated by Jason Cockcroft, Hodder Children's (London, England), 2005.

Frozen Fire, Oxford University Press (Oxford, England), 2006, Philomel (New York, NY), 2008.

Bloodchild, Oxford (Oxford University Press), 2008.

Contributor of short fiction to anthologies *Straight from the Heart* and *Family Tree,* both published by Egmont.

"BLADE" NOVEL SERIES

Playing Dead, Oxford University Press (Oxford, England), 2008, Philomel (New York, NY), 2009.

Closing In, Oxford University Press (Oxford, England), 2008, published as *Out of the Shadows,* Philomel (New York, NY), 2010.

Breaking Free, Oxford University Press (Oxford, England), 2009.

Running Scared, Oxford University Press (Oxford, England), 2009.

Fighting Back, Oxford University Press (Oxford, England), 2009.

Mixing It, Oxford University Press (Oxford, England), 2010.

Cutting Loose, Oxford University Press (Oxford, England), 2010.

Risking All, Oxford University Press (Oxford, England), 2010.

Adaptations

Film rights for *Midget, River Boy,* and *Storm Catchers* have been sold. *Starseeker* was adapted as a play for younger readers by Phil Porter, produced in Northampton, England, and published by Oberon (London, England), 2007.

Sidelights

Tim Bowler started writing at the age of five, but it did not become his career for many years. He worked in forestry and then as a language teacher for nearly twenty years, doing his writing between 3 a.m. and 7 a.m. before he left for work. He started what would become his award-winning first novel, *Midget,* when he was twenty-five years old and continued writing in this fashion for over fifteen years. The novel was finally pub-

Cover of British writer Tim Bowler's Storm Catchers, *featuring artwork by Cliff Nielsen.* (Illustration copyright © 2003 by Cliff Nielsen. Reproduced by permission.)

lished in the mid-1990s. With this success, Bowler was able to make writing his full-time job, and his focus on teen readers has continued in a series of novels that have been compared to the works of David Almond due to their complex and haunting themes and intense, gripping storylines.

Midget is a psychological thriller that "might have been a *Twilight Zone* episode," according to a *Publishers Weekly* contributor. The titular character in the novel is a tiny fifteen-year-old boy who is physically and emotionally warped by the abuse he suffers at the hands of his outwardly devoted older brother, Seb. The story is set in Bowler's native Leigh-on-Sea, a fishing village in southeastern England, and the ocean features prominently in the tale. Midget's one escape is the marina, where he takes great pleasure in watching Old Joseph restore a vintage wooden sailboat. Midget wants to sail this boat, a fact that is apparently known to Old Joseph because he leaves the boat to Midget in his will. At the same time, the short-of-stature teen discovers his ability to influence events with his mind, and he uses this skill to do minor harm to his therapist and also to win a sailboat race against his brother. Furious at his defeat, Seb

attempts to make good on his oft-repeated threat to kill Midget, a decision that results in tragedy. In *Horn Book* Nancy Vasilakis praised *Midget,* writing that Bowler's "tightly scripted plot with its steadily building tension will keep readers spellbound to the end."

Winner of the prestigious Carnegie Medal, Bowler's novel *River Boy* is a story about "the embodiment of hope, the circle of life, and an artist's spiritual quest," in the words of *School Library Journal* critic Alison Follos. In the story, Jess's grandfather is dying. The man convinces Jess's parents to take him back to his rural boyhood home, along the banks of a river, so that he can finish his painting, "River Boy," before he dies. While the man works on his painting, fifteen-year-old Jess, a competitive swimmer, explores the river. There she meets the "river boy," a mysterious, otherworldly character. When he asks her to join him in swimming the length of the river all the way to the sea, she learns that he has a mysterious connection to her grandfather. "There's poetry in the simple, elemental words and the space between them," Hazel Rochman commented in a review of *River Boy* for *Booklist,* and Follos also praised Bowler's "lyrical metaphors and fluid writing style." The author "succeeds in conveying the strong bond between Jess and her grandfather," noted a *Publishers Weekly* contributor, highlighting the multigenerational element in the award-winning novel.

In *Shadows* Bowler tells the story of a young man named Jamie who is pushed by his obsessive and abusive father to become a champion squash player. His relationship with his father begins to change when Jamie meets a pregnant teen named Abby, who is hiding in his shed after fleeing from a very bad situation. "The story zips along," commented London *Observer* reviewer Caroline Boucher, the critic adding that *Shadows* is "much tighter, grittier, and, I think, better," than *River Boy.* In *School Librarian,* Michael Lockwood wrote that *Shadows,* with its faced-paced narrative and dramatic tension, is "very different from *River Boy* in style, but just as successful in its own terms."

Like *Shadows, Storm Catchers* also features a flawed father and a young woman in danger. Ella, the thirteen-year-old middle child, is kidnapped from her family's seaside home one stormy night while her parents are out. While fifteen-year-old brother Fin feels responsible for Ella's fate, three-year-old Sam begins seeing the ghost of another girl. The point of view in *Storm Catchers* alternates between Fin, Ella, and Sam, as they slowly learn about their family's dark secret and the motive of the young kidnapper. "It's the fast, realistic action and dialogue and the stormy coastal setting that drive this story," wrote Rochman, while Connie Tyrrell Burns noted in *School Library Journal* that "complex themes of guilt and betrayal enhance the suspense" in *Storm Catchers.*

In *Frozen Fire* Dusty is also haunted by a missing sibling. The fifteen-year-old girl, who lives in rural Cumbria, has found her world to be surreal since her brother

Josh disappeared two years ago. Now, when a mysterious telephone caller mentions Josh's name, Dusty believes that the caller holds the key to setting things to rights, and knows she must find him. Trekking through the winter snow, she searches for the caller, only to find that he is a teen on the run from the police for the crime of rape. By aiding this illusive boy in the hopes that he will provide information about Josh's whereabouts, Dusty soon finds herself the target of a citizen mob fueled by the fear and anger caused by the boy's crime. Driven to confront the boy's menace, she also gains an odd closure, making *Frozen Fire* "an engrossing, tantalising psychological and supernatural thriller" that leads "a fine heroine" to "a quite unexpected denouement," according to London *Guardian* contributor Mal Peet. "Bowler's writing chills," asserted *Booklist* critic Ilene Cooper, and in *Horn Book* Claire E. Gross described the novel's setting as "brittle and otherworldly," adding that the "creepy, supernaturally tinted" story that plays out in *Frozen Fire* will leave readers as captivated as Dusty over its "lingering mystery."

Published in England as *Starseeker, Firmament* focuses on another teen in trouble. Luke is headed down a rough path in life, and when readers meet him he is busy

Cover of Bowler's novel Frozen Fire, *a haunting story about a sister's grief and a brother who may or may not have returned from the lost.*
(Philomel Books, 2008. Jacket images © by Shutterstock. Reproduced by permission of Philomel Books, a division of Penguin Putnam Books for Young Readers.)

breaking into the house of an elderly woman, goaded on by a gang of toughs. Although the sounds of a child's sobbing deter him at first, peer pressure sends Luke back, and this time his is caught by the home's owner. The woman agrees not to call the authorities if Luke, a talented pianist, agrees to play music to sooth her grandchild, a girl who is both blind and mentally impaired. Although Luke enjoys making the girl happy because it takes his mind off his troubles at school and home—where his widowed mom is now dating a new boyfriend—he gradually realizes that the house is not the child's real home, and the woman is not her real grandmother. In a story that features "poetic language and the supernatural," according to *Kliatt* critic Paula Rohrlick, Bowler treats readers to "an unusual and poignant coming-of-age tale." *Firmament* is enriched by "lyrical writing [that] will enthrall readers," according to *School Library Journal* critic Susan Riley, and a *Publishers Weekly* critic concluded that the "English village setting . . . and the quirky characters . . . lend the novel a fairytale quality."

In *Apocalypse* Bowler again takes readers to the harsh coasts of England, in this instance the island of Skaer. Remote and unmapped, Skaer is where Kit and his parents land their sailboat during an unanticipated storm, only to find themselves at the mercy of a bizarre religious sect. After his parents disappear, the fourteen year old is befriended by an outcast named Ula, who tells him that, because of the large birthmark on his face, Kit is feared by the Skaerlanders as a devil. Woven with what Gross described as "Messianic imagery," Kit's efforts to save his parents and survive the island ordeal make *Apocalypse* a novel of "good and evil, love and hope, faith and remembrance." Although Jennifer Mattson maintained in *Booklist* that the author's use of "religious symbolism overwhelms rather than extends Kit's personal story," *School Library Journal* reviewer Sharon Rawlings described the novel as "beautifully written" and "intriguing," adding that Bowler's "creepy, allegorical thriller . . . grabs readers from the very first page."

Called "an appealingly complex take on the supernatural" by London *Guardian* reviewer S.F. Said, Bowler's chillingly titled *Bloodchild* takes readers inside the mind of Will, a troubled teen who experiences vivid hallucinations. After an accident that nearly kills him, Will has a vision that is particularly vivid: in it he senses a threat to his home town of Havenmouth. Although his efforts to warn his neighbors are dismissed by the adults around him, the teen determines to understand and fight the evil that he has been warned of, resulting in a story that "offers a resonant metaphor for [the] teenage experience" of being an outsider, according to Said.

Bowler channels his complex and evocative storytelling into a longer saga, creating the eight-volume "Blade" series for young adults. In *Playing Dead* readers meet the fourteen-year-old title character, a runaway who survives a life on the streets due to his intelligence, per-

ception, and excellent knife-fighting skills. Blade has no qualms about killing, so when he is jumped by a girl gang and bested in a fight, he takes it as an omen. As he tells his story to the anonymous "Bigeyes," his luck goes from bad to worse as he finds himself shadowed by a threatening figure. Pulled into solving the predicament of troubled gang member Becky and Becky's daughter Jaz, Blade has his compassion for her plight rewarded by even more violence. Reviewing *Playing Dead* for *Horn Book,* Jonathan Hunt noted that Bowler's "addictive blend of paranoia and suspense" proves an excellent vehicle for the "Blade" series, and a *Publishers Weekly* critic asserted that "readers who like their thrillers brutally realistic will find much to enjoy" in *Playing Dead.*

Blade's story continues in *Closing In,* (published in the United States as *Out of the Shadows*) as well as *Breaking Free, Running Scared, Fighting Back, Mixing It, Cutting Loose,* and *Risking All. Closing In* finds Blade, Becky, and Jaz attempting to elude the same pursuers that haunted Blade in *Playing Dead.* Adding another layer of threat, Becky's gang is also out to do the trio as a way to avenge the death of the gang's leader. In *Breaking Free* the teen is wounded and his pursuers are almost upon him. As he fights for survival, Blade also realizes that he needs to escape his gritty urban reality in order to make it out of his teens. Commenting on Bowler's use of cliff-hanger endings in each installment of the "Blade" novels, John Peters predicted in *Booklist* that "reluctant readers . . . will be pleased by the fast pace and the action's immediacy."

"The level of violence isn't something you choose as a writer," Bowler noted on his home page. "At least I don't. When I'm writing a story, the characters and scenes and places start to form pictures, and then the momentum builds up and it's as though you find the direction the story wants to go. . . . It's the writing itself for me that unlocks the story. Writing *Midget* scared the pants off me when the violent stuff started coming out. I started to wonder what was wrong with me and it took ten drafts to work the thing out."

"Some people think there must be a set of rules for writing," Bowler added, "but the truth is there aren't any. It's more like tickling trout, holding your hand out and trying to coax the ideas to swim into your grasp; or being a potter, throwing the rough clay of your thoughts down and letting the story twist out under the palms of your hands; or being a sorcerer, stirring the cauldron of your imagination and watching the vapour of the story rise. Writing is all these things and many more. It's something you never bottom, never crack, never stop learning about. And that's why I love it."

Bowler is a writer who craves seclusion in which to work. "I used to write in a converted bedroom overlooking the churchyard," he told *SATA.* "It was a lovely peaceful place but since 2002 I have been working in an even quieter spot: an old stone outhouse in a remote part of the village. Family and friends call it Tim's Bolthole. It's perfect for solitude and reflection. There's a meadow nearby and hills rolling into the distance. I write my books to the sound of birdsong."

Biographical and Critical Sources

PERIODICALS

Booklist, May 1, 2000, Hazel Rochman, review of *River Boy,* p. 1660; September 1, 2003, Hazel Rochman, review of *Storm Catchers,* p. 112; September 15, 2005, Jennifer Mattson, review of *Apocalypse,* p. 55; May 15, 2008, Ilene Cooper, review of *Frozen Fire,* p. 55; May 1, 2009, John Peters, review of *Playing Dead,* p. 82.

Book Report, November-December, 1995, Jo Rae Peiffer, review of *Midget,* p. 31.

Books for Keeps, November, 1995, Val Randall, review of *Dragon's Rock,* p. 13; July, 2000, Lesley de Meza, review of *Shadows,* p. 6.

Daily Telegraph (London, England), November 27, 2004, Jake Kerridge, review of *Apocalypse.*

Guardian (London, England), October 28, 2006, Mal Peet, review of *Frozen Fire,* p. 20; November 22, 2008, S.F. Said, review of *Bloodchild,* p. 13.

Horn Book, March-April, 1996, Nancy Vasilakis, review of *Midget,* pp. 203-204; November-December, 2005, Claire E. Gross, review of *Apocalypse,* p. 713; July-August, 2008, Claire E. Gross, review of *Frozen Fire,* p. 440; May-June, 2009, Jonathan Hunt, review of *Playing Dead,* p. 291.

Independent (London, England), July 16, 1998, Anne Treneman, "You Can Cry Me a River," p. S10.

Junior Bookshelf, August, 1995, review of *Dragon's Rock,* p. 142.

Kirkus Reviews, September 15, 1999, review of *Midget,* p. 1347; May 15, 2003, review of *Storm Catchers,* p. 746.

Kliatt, March, 2004, Paula Rohrlick, review of *Firmament,* p. 8.

Magpies, March, 2002, Rayma Turton, review of *Storm Catchers,* p. 41.

Observer (London, England), February 14, 1999, Caroline Boucher, review of *Shadows,* p. 15; October 27, 2002, Nicci Gerrard, review of *Starseeker,* p. 18.

Publishers Weekly, September 25, 1995, review of *Midget,* p. 57; July 10, 2000, review of *River Boy,* p. 64; June 2, 2003, review of *Storm Catchers,* p. 53; April 26, 2004, review of *Firmament,* p. 67; April 27, 2009, review of *Playing Dead,* p. 133.

School Librarian, summer, 1999, Michael Lockwood, review of *Shadows,* p. 98.

School Library Journal, October, 1995, Kelly Diller, review of *Midget,* p. 152; October, 1999, Brian E. Wilson, review of *River Boy,* p. 88; August, 2000, Alison Follos, review of *River Boy,* p. 177; May, 2003, Connie Tyrrell Burns, review of *Storm Catchers,* p. 144; April, 2004, Susan Ripley, review of *Firmament,* p.

148; October, 2005, Sharon Rawlins, review of *Apocalypse,* p. 154; July, 2008, Heather M. Campbell, review of *Frozen Fire,* p. 94.

Spectator, July 18, 1998, Jane Gardam, review of *River Boy,* pp. 36-37.

Sunday Times (London, England), October 3, 2004, Nicolette Jones, review of *Apocalypse,* p. 54.

Times Educational Supplement, September 23, 1994, Geoff Fox, review of *Midget,* p. A19; May 12, 1995, David Buckley, review of *Dragon's Rock,* p. 16; July 17, 1998, Geraldine Brennan, "Journey Man," p. A12; February 12, 1999, Geraldine Brennan, review of *Shadows,* p. 27; September 27, 2002, Linda Newbery, review of *Starseeker,* p. 12.

ONLINE

Oxford University Press Web site, http://www.oup.co.uk/ (November 6, 2001), "Oxford Children's Authors: Tim Bowler."

Tim Bowler Home Page, http://www.timbowler.co.uk (December 15, 2009).

*   *   *

BRITTNEY, L.

Personal

Born in England. *Education:* Attended college.

Addresses

Home—Axminster, Devon, England.

Career

Author and educator. University of Kent, Kent, England, former teacher of creative writing; former teacher of drama.

Awards, Honors

Waterstone Prize shortlist, 2007, for *Nathan Fox: Dangerous Times.*

Writings

"NATHAN FOX" MYSTERY SERIES

Nathan Fox: Dangerous Times, Macmillan Children's (London, England), 2007, published as *Dangerous Times: The First Nathan Fox Misson,* Feiwel & Friends (New York, NY), 2008.

Traitor's Gold, Macmillan Children's (London, England), 2008.

Books translated into German and Spanish.

Sidelights

A former teacher of creative writing and drama, L. Brittney combines her two passions in a series of young-adult novels that take place in the Elizabethan era. In series opener, *Dangerous Times: The First Nathan Fox Mission,* she introduces a thirteen-year-old orphan who acts in the company that stages William Shakespeare's plays. Fox's acrobatic skills, his quick thinking, and his facility with language make him valuable on stage, and it is there that the teen attracts the attention of Sir Francis Walsingham, spymaster general to England's Queen Elizabeth I. While also keeping his connections to the theatre, Nathan is recruited and trained by ace spy and bon vivant John Pearce, learning the skills that will make him an affective agent. As readers follow his career, they join the teen on his first mission: a trip to Venice to assure General Othello's support in England's looming war against Spain. Nathan's experiences are eventually known to Shakespeare, who ultimately weaves them into a new play: *Othello.* Nathan's adventures continue in *Traitor's Gold,* as the teen tracks a consignment of gold that will be used to fund the Spanish Armada and ultimately helps friend Will Shakespeare set the stage for *Measure to Measure.*

Cover of **Dangerous Times,** *a historical thriller in L. Brittney's "Nathan Fox" series featuring artwork by Adam Willis.* (Feiwel & Friends, 2008. Illustration copyright © 2007 by Adam Willis. Reproduced by permission.)

Noting that the novel's setting, "a largely undocumented period in Shakespeare's life," permits Brittney to take full creative license with her real-life characters, Wendy Scalfaro added in *School Library Journal* that *Dangerous Times* treats readers to a "rich" story. According to Scalfaro, Brittney "masterfully . . . sustains a mood of suspense and intrigue" in her fiction debut, and praised her "use of action and dialogue." In *Kliatt*, Claire Rosser praised the novel as "cleverly written," and featuring captivating "descriptions of . . . sea travel and warfare" as well as Nathan's "training with daggers, swords and secret codes." In *Booklist* Ian Chipman described *Dangerous Times* as a "unique" work of historical fiction that "slyly stitch[es] . . . lines from the play" *Othello* into a "proto-swashbuckling, Elizabethan espionage tale."

Biographical and Critical Sources

PERIODICALS

Booklist, November 1, 2008, Ian Chipman, review of *Dangerous Times: The First Nathan Fox Mission,* p. 38.
Kirkus Reviews, September 15, 2008, review of *Dangerous Times.*
Kliatt, September, 2008, Claire Rosser, review of *Dangerous Times,* p. 8.
School Library Journal, November, 2008, Wendy Scalfaro, review of *Dangerous Times,* p. 116.

ONLINE

Nathan Fox Web site, http://www.natahnfox-dangerous times.co.uk (December 20, 2009).*

*   *   *

BRODA, Ron 1954-

Personal

Born May 26, 1954, in New Hamburg, Ontario, Canada; married; wife's name Joanne; children: three. *Education:* Attended Conestoga College.

Addresses

Home—Sarnia, Ontario, Canada. *Agent*—David and Lynn Bennett, Transatlantic Literary Agency, 72 Glengowan Rd., Toronto, Ontario M4N 1G4, Canada. *E-mail*—brodabunch@sympatico.ca.

Career

Paper sculptor and children's book illustrator. Director of Discovery House Museum, Sarnia, Ontario, Canada.

Member

Writers' Union of Canada, Canadian Society of Children's Authors, Illustrators, and Performers.

Awards, Honors

Illustration & Design Award of Excellence, 1983, 1984, 1985, 1986; bronze medal in children's book inside page category, 3-Dimensional Art Directors and Illustrators Awards Show, 1995, bronze medal in children's book complete book category, 3-Dimensional Art Directors and Illustrators Awards Show, 1996, Amelia Frances Howard-Gibbon Illustrator's Award shortlist, 1997, all for *Have You Seen Bugs?;* bronze medal in children's book category, 3-Dimensional Art Directors and Illustrators Awards Show, 1999, for *Dinosaur: Digging up a Giant;* Canadian Toy Testing Council recommended book, 2004, for *Why Animals Show Off;* Blue Spruce nominee, Ontario Library Association, 2008, for *In My Backyard.*

Writings

SELF-ILLUSTRATED

(With Joanne Webb) *3-D Paper Crafts,* photographs by Wally Randall, Scholastic Canada (Markham, Ontario, Canada), 1997.

ILLUSTRATOR

Michael Cutting, *The Little Crooked Christmas Tree,* Scholastic, Inc. (New York, NY), 1990, reprinted, Scholastic Canada (Toronto, Ontario, Canada), 2007.
Toni Eugene, *Caterpillar Magic,* National Geographic (Washington, DC), 1990.
Bonnie S. Laurence, *Blue Jay Babies,* National Geographic (Washington, DC), 1991.
Edith Newlin Chase, *Waters,* Scholastic Canada (Richmond Hill, Ontario, Canada), 1993.
Joanna Cole, *Spider's Lunch: All about Garden Spiders,* Grosset & Dunlap (New York, NY), 1995.
Joanne Oppenheim, *Have You Seen Bugs?,* Scholastic, Inc. (New York, NY), 1996.
Chris McGowan, *Dinosaur: Digging up a Giant,* Scholastic Canada (Markham, Ontario, Canada), 1999.
Emily Neye, *Butterflies,* Grosset & Dunlap (New York, NY), 2000.
Peter Cook and Laura Suzuki, *Why Animals Show Off,* Scholastic Canada (Markham, Ontario, Canada), 2003.
Ray Leonie, *I Am Big,* Scholastic Canada (Markham, Ontario, Canada), 2005.
Margriet Ruurs, *In My Backyard,* Tundra Books (Toronto, Ontario, Canada), 2007.

Adaptations

The Little Crooked Christmas Tree was adapted for television.

Sidelights

Canadian Ron Broda is an award-winning children's book illustrator and paper sculpture artist. Born and raised in New Hamburg, Ontario, Broda attended Con-

estoga College, where he received his formal art training. He then spent more than twenty years in advertising, art directing, and commercial illustration, preparing advertising campaigns and art pieces for such clients as Coca Cola, National Geographic, and Xerox. Broda illustrated his first work for young readers in 1990. According to a contributor on the *Canadian Society of Children's Authors, Illustrators, and Performers* Web site, the artist's "three-dimensional pieces are enhanced with water colour and other 'trade secrets' to produce finished works of art that have beauty and depth. Meticulous attention to detail enhances the life-like quality of every piece."

One of Broda's favorite illustration projects, *The Little Crooked Christmas Tree* by Michael Cutting, addresses ecological themes. After a small tree allows a dove to build its nest in its branches, it develops an imperfection in its trunk, making it unacceptable to the patrons who visit Farmer Brown's tree farm. Cutting's narrative is "accompanied by delightful photographs of the bright cut-paper illustrations by Broda," noted Patricia L.M. Butler in the *Canadian Review of Materials. The Little Crooked Christmas Tree* has since been adapted as a popular television program that is considered a holiday classic.

Edith Newlin Chase describes how water travels from its source in the mountains to the raging sea in *Waters,* a work told in verse. "Visually the book is breath-taking," Theo Hersh wrote in the *Canadian Review of Materials.* Hersh added that the artist's "luminescent paper sculpture illustrations take the reader on a nature tour of Canada." Joanne Oppenheim's *Have You Seen Bugs?,* another rhyming work, introduces a host of insects, including moon moths and lacewing dragonflies. The book contains "incredible, three-dimensional paper sculptures of bugs," Naomi Gerrard remarked in the *Canadian Review of Materials,* and a contributor in *Publishers Weekly* stated that Broda's "exquisite painted paper sculptures . . . give the pages depth, texture and a brilliantly surreal flavor."

In *Dinosaur: Digging up a Giant,* Chris McGowan, a curator at the Royal Ontario Museum's Department of Paleobiology, explains the process of unearthing, marking, photographing, preserving, and reconstructing a dinosaur skeleton. Reviewing the work in the *Canadian Review of Materials,* Gail Hamilton stated that "Broda's fabulous illustrations enhance the text and almost steal the show. Made with paper sculpture and watercolour, they have been carefully lit and photographed to produce a realistic, three-dimensional quality."

Why Animals Show Off, a work by Peter Cook and Laura Suzuki, explores how color and pattern enable animals to survive in the wild. "Using his amazing paper sculpture art," wrote *Quill & Quire* reviewer Pamela Hickman, "Broda has created brilliant scenes and fantastic creatures that nearly leap off the page." "The tiger amid long grass, the salmon run, and the incredibly life-like bird species are superb examples of the effectiveness" of Broda's three-dimensional illustrations, remarked *Canadian Review of Materials* contributor Gillian Richardson.

Margriet Ruurs explores familiar creatures such as ladybugs, wasps, sanils, wrens, and hummingbirds in her picture book, *In My Backyard.* In this work "Broda's detailed paper-sculpture artwork adds enormously to the text," observed Gregory Bryan in the *Canadian Review of Materials.* "With liberal splashes of colour, Broda's paper-sculptures create vivid and surprisingly realistic images." The illustrator's "remarkable paper sculptures are hyper-real, delicate, and enchanting," Carlyn Zwarenstein noted in *Quill & Quire,* while *Resource Links,* critic Wendy Hogan stated that "Broda's colour palette is stunning."

Sharing his skill with others, Broda and coauthor Joanne Webb present step-by-step instructions for ten paper sculpture projects in *3-D Paper Crafts.* "All of the projects are beautifully executed by Broda," commented Lorraine Douglas in the *Canadian Review of Materials.* Sheila McGraw, reviewing the work in *Quill & Quire,* similarly noted that "the 3-D paper crafts in this book are flawlessly executed by Ron Broda's experienced hand."

Biographical and Critical Sources

PERIODICALS

Booklist, April, 1998, Carolyn Phelan, review of *Have You Seen Bugs?,* p. 1326; February 15, 2001, Carolyn Phelan, review of *Butterflies,* p. 1143.

Canadian Review of Materials, November, 1990, Patricia L.M. Butler, review of *The Little Crooked Christmas Tree;* September, 1993, Theo Hersh, review of *Waters;* November 28, 1997, Lorraine Douglas, review of *3-D Paper Crafts;* February 4, 2000, Gail Hamilton, review of *Dinosaur: Digging up a Giant;* June 6, 2003, Gillian Richardson, review of *Why Animals Show Off;* January 4, 2007, Gregory Bryan, review of *In My Backyard.*

Publishers Weekly, May 4, 1998, review of *Have You Seen Bugs?,* p. 213.

Quill & Quire, October, 1996, Bridget Donald, review of *Have You Seen Bugs?,* p. 47; May, 1997, Sheila McGraw, review of *3-D Paper Crafts,* p. 41; June 2003, Pamela Hickman, review of *Why Animals Show Off;* April, 2007, Carlyn Zwarenstein, review of *In My Backyard.*

Resource Links, June, 2003, Carolyn Cutt, review of *Why Animals Show Off,* p. 20; April, 2007, Wendy Hogan, review of *In My Backyard,* p. 9.

School Library Journal, March, 2007, Kathy Piehl, review of *In My Backyard,* p. 200.

ONLINE

Canadian Society of Children's Authors, Illustrators, and Performers Web site, http://www.canscaip.org/ (February 10, 2010), "Ron Broda."

Transatlantic Literary Agency, http://www.tla1.com/ (February 10, 2010), "Ron Broda."*

* * *

BROOKS, Laurie

Personal

Born in IL; children: three daughters. *Education:* Hofstra University, B.A.; New York University, M.A.

Addresses

Home—Phoenix, AZ. *E-mail*—brooksplays@aol.com.

Career

Playwright and novelist. New York University, professor and playwright-in-residence, 1997-2006. Alley Theatre HYPE Institute, Houston, TX, playwright-in-residence; guest lecturer at University of Missouri—Kansas City, 2005, and University of Texas—Austin, 2006; Arizona State University, artist-in-residence, 2007-08. National Endowment for the Arts, site reporter and panelist, 2001-06.

Member

Theatre for Young Audiences/USA (member of board), Dramatists Guild.

Awards, Honors

Distinguished Play Award, American Alliance for Theatre and Education (AATE), 1998, for *Selkie,* 2001, for *The Wrestling Season,* 2008, for *Brave No World: Community, Identity, Stand-up Comedy;* AT&T Firststage Award, Theatre Communications Group (TCG), 2002, for *The Tangled Web;* Charlotte B. Chorpenning Playwright Award, AATE, 2003; theatre residency, TCG/National Endowment for the Arts, 2004-05; Irish Arts Council Commissioning grant.

Writings

STAGE PLAYS; "LIES AND DECEPTIONS QUARTET"

Deadly Weapons (commissioned by Graffiti Theatre Company, Cork, Ireland, 1998), Dramatic Publishing (Woodstock, IL), 2002.
The Wrestling Season (commissioned by Cotierie Theatre, Kansas City, MO, 1999), Dramatic Publishing (Woodstock, IL), 2000.
The Tangled Web (commissioned by Grafitti Theatre Company, Cork, Ireland, 2000), Dramatic Publishing (Woodstock, IL), 2006.
Everyday Heroes (commissioned by Kennedy Center Imagination Celebration, Salt Lake City, UT, 2002), Dramatic Publishing (Woodstock, IL), 2006.

PLAYS

Selkie (commissioned by New York University, 1995), revised as *Between Land and Sea: A Selkie Myth,,* 2006.
The Match Girl's Gift: A Christmas Story (commissioned by Nashville Children's Theatre, Nashville, TN, 1998), Dramatic Publishing (Woodstock, IL), 2008.
Franklin's Apprentice (comissioned by Louisville Children's Theatre, Louisville, KY, 2000), Dramatists Play Service (New York, NY), 2005.
Devon's Hurt, Dramatic Publishing (Woodstock, IL), 2001.
A Laura Ingalls Wilder Christmas (commissioned by Cotierie Theatre, Kansas City, MO, 2002), Dramatic Publishing (Woodstock, IL), 2005.
The Lost Ones, commissioned by Graffiti Theatre Company, Cork, Ireland, 2005.
Brave No World: Community, Identity, Stand-up Comedy (commissioned by Kennedy Center Family Theater, 2006), Dramatic Publishing (Woodstock, IL), 2007.
Triangle (commissioned by Arizona State University, 2008), Dramatic Publishing, Woodstock, IL), 2010.
Atypical Boy (commissioned by Coterie Theatre, Kansas City, MO, 2009), Dramatic Publishing (Woodstock, IL), 2010.

Cover of Laurie Brooks' young-adult novel Selkie Girl, *featuring artwork by Ella Tjader.* (Illustration copyright © 2008 by Ella Tjader. Used by permission of Alfred A. Knopf, an imprint of Random House Children's Books, a division of Random House, Inc.)

OTHER

Selkie Girl (young-adult novel; adapted from her play of the same title), Knopf (New York, NY), 2008.

Contributor of articles to *American Theatre.*

Sidelights

An award-winning playwright, Laurie Brooks has also written a novel for young adults that was inspired by one of her works for the stage. Based on her play *Between Land and Sea: A Selkie Myth, Selkie Girl* features a traditional Celtic story about a shape-shifting seal that is forced to take human form after a fisherman steals its pelt. As readers meet sixteen-year-old Elin Jean, the girl has been ostracized by the other residents of her Orkney Island village, in part because of her webbed fingers and her strong affinity for the sea. Elin Jean now forms a close relationship with another outcast, a Gypsy boy named Tam whom the villagers also shun. Confused about where she belongs within her oceanside community, Elin Jean discovers her mother's seal skin and realizes that the woman was in fact a selkie held captive by Elin Jean's human father. Regaining possession of her true outer skin, the girl's mother ultimately returns to the sea, followed by her daughter. Ultimately, as a half-human Elin Jean is now marked by her human fingers and she now feels like an outcast within the pinniped community. When she learns that a mixed-breed creature will rescue the selkies, who are now under attack by the girl's father, Elin Jean must discover whether she is the one who is destined to protect her mother's people.

Reviewing *Selkie Girl, Journal of Adolescent and Adult Literacy* critic Michael Jung wrote that the book "simultaneously reads like a timeless myth and a contemporary coming-of-age novel." Writing in *School Library Journal,* Renee Steinberg described Brooks's work as "an extraordinary, beautifully written tale" in which the author's "rich prose reverberates with vivid, cinematic images." A *Kirkus Reviews* critic also found Brooks to be successful in reinventing the age-old folktale, writing that the author excels at producing "compelling, compassionate characters and creatively detailed descriptions" about life both in and out of the sea.

"I have always been dedicated to writing for young adults in both my plays and novels," Brooks told *SATA.* "A friend once suggested that I must have died as a teenager in a past life and now I can't grow up. Maybe so. All I know is that I care deeply about writing material that is authentic to the lives of young people, that is challenging on both a thinking and feeling level, and most of all, that tells a great, page-turning story. I love to hear from my readers and I write back!"

Biographical and Critical Sources

PERIODICALS

Booklist, November 15, 2008, Chris Sherman, review of *Selkie Girl,* p. 54.

Journal of Adolescent and Adult Literacy, May, 2009, Michael Jung, review of *Selkie Girl,* p. 725.
Kirkus Reviews, September 15, 2008, review of *Selkie Girl.*
School Library Journal, December, 2008, Renee Steinberg, review of *Selkie Girl,* p. 120.

ONLINE

Laurie Brooks Home Page, http://www.lauriebrooks.com (December 16, 2009).

* * *

BULION, Leslie 1958-

Personal

Born 1958, in New York, NY; children: two daughters. *Education:* Cornell University, B.A.; University of Rhode Island, M.S. (biological oceanography); Southern Connecticut State University, M.S.W. *Hobbies and other interests:* Hiking, bicycling, cross-country skiing, SCUBA diving, knitting, reading.

Addresses

Home—CT. *E-mail*—leslie@lesliebulion.com.

Career

Children's book writer and editor.

Member

Society of Children's Book Writers and Illustrators, Authors Guild, Authors League of America, Young Audiences of Connecticut.

Awards, Honors

Tassy Walden New Voices in Children's Literature Award for Young-Adult Novel, 2001; Children's Africana Book Award, African Studies Association, 2003, for *Fatuma's New Cloth;* Best Books for Children designation, Association of Booksellers for Children, 2006, Capitol Choices Noteworthy Books for Children honor, and Outstanding Children's Book Award finalist, Animal Behavior Society, both 2007, and Young Hoosier Book Award nomination, 2010, all for *Hey There, Stink Bug!;* Best Book designation, Bank Street College of Education, 2007, and Mark Twain Award nomination, 2008, both for *Uncharted Waters.*

Writings

Fatuma's New Cloth, illustrated by Nicole Tadgell, Moon Mountain Publishing (North Kingstown, RI), 2002.

Leslie Bulion (Reproduced by permission.)

Missing Pieces (reader), illustrated by Janet Wilson, Steck-Vaughn (Austin, TX), 2003.

One Piece at a Time (reader; prequel to *Missing Pieces*), Steck-Vaughn (Austin, TX), 2004.

Tall Ships Fun (activity book), illustrated by Wayne Marcus, Moon Mountain Publishing (North Kingstown, RI), 2004.

Hey There, Stink Bug!, illustrated by Leslie Evans, Charlesbridge (Watertown, MA), 2006.

Uncharted Waters, Peachtree (Atlanta, GA), 2006.

The Trouble with Rules, Peachtree (Atlanta, GA), 2008.

At the Sea Floor Café, Peachtree (Atlanta, GA), 2010.

Contributor to periodicals, including *Parents, Child,* and *Cicada.* Contributing writer to EducationWorld. com, 2000-02; author and editor of readers for educational publishers.

Sidelights

Journalist and writer Leslie Bulion was inspired by her family's travels in East Africa to pen the picture book *Fatuma's New Cloth*, thus beginning her career as a children's author. In addition to her science verse, which includes the poetry collection *Hey There, Sink Bug!*, Bulion also writes middle-grade novels, among them *Uncharted Waters* and *The Trouble with Rules.*

Illustrated by Nicola Tadgell, *Fatuma's New Cloth* follows a young East African girl as she accompanies her mother to the local market one day. Her mother promises Fatuma that, after the family shopping is done, the girl will be allowed to purchase a kanga cloth for a new dress before they return home for a treat: a cup of chai. While at the market many shop merchants try to impress their opinions upon young Fatuma regarding what constitutes the perfect chai. However, it is when Fatuma

selects a brightly colored kanga cloth that the answer is revealed. Printed within the brightly patterned cloth is the saying: "Don't be fooled by the color. The good flavor of chai comes from the sugar." In other words, there is much more to a person than just what meets the eye.

Reviewing Bulion's debut book in *School Library Journal,* Anna DeWind Walls wrote that the overall message of *Fatuma's New Cloth* is "sweet" and "the story drifts along at a dreamy pace." Also praising the text, a *Publishers Weekly* critic added that "Tadgell's artwork highlights the glorious colors of the area's fabrics and landscapes, and demonstrates the warmth of a closely knit community in which tradition is paramount."

Bulion sets insect behavior to verse in the pages of *Hey There, Stink Bug!*, a picture book illustrated by Leslie Evans. From stink bugs to lightning bugs to wolf spiders, Bulion reveals the unique traits to be found within the insect world in poems that "flit and buzz effortlessly from page to page," according to *School Library Journal* contributor Jill Heritage Maza. Scientific terms are defined in a glossary, and each poem is accompanied by bug facts that will fuel the interest of budding entymologists. Noting that "gory, visceral facts . . . pull children" into Bulion's rhyming verse, Gillian Engberg added in *Booklist* that *Hey There, Stink Bug!* "will gen-

Leslie Bulion's picture book Fatuma's New Cloth *is brought to life in Nicole Tadgell's colorful watercolor-and-ink art.* (Moon Mountain Publishing, 2002. Illustration copyright © 2002 by Nicole Tadgell. Reproduced by permission.)

erate lively enthusiasm" due to its mix of humor and "gross-out drama." Another collection of nature-based poetry, Bulion's *At the Sea Floor Café,* shifts readers' focus to the briny deep in the same mix of rhyme and facts.

Bulion's novels *Uncharted Waters* and *The Trouble with Rules* both focus on young people dealing with the changes that accompany maturation. For Jonah, the main character in *Uncharted Waters,* a month spent with Uncle Nate at Nate's seaside cabin allows the seventh grader to reflect on the secret he has kept from his parents and the fear that has prompted his action. One secret leads to another, Jonah soon discovers, but the teen's bravery in rescuing a new friend during an ocean storm helps him confront his underlying fears in a novel that features "realistic details about marine biology" and "a climactic rescue," according to *School Library Journal* critic Vicki Reutter. *Uncharted Waters* is enriched by Bulion's own studies in oceanography, and its focus on boat engines, school problems, and adventure make it a good choice for boys who only reluctantly pick up a book.

In *The Trouble with Rules* fourth-grade neighbors Nick and Nadie are also long-time best friends. Things change in fourth grade, however, where peer pressure and the actions of a new student combine to force the two to part company, at least in public. Although Summer befriends Nadie when she arrives at Nadie's school, her relentless teasing of classmate Owen and her need to attract negative attention make Nadie equally guilty by association. Ultimately, Nadie must make the decision whether to follow the "rules" of fourth grade that dictate that girls no longer socialize with boys or break with tradition to save her long-standing friendship with Nick. Writing that readers will identify with Bulion's heroine "as she struggles with peer relationships," *School Library Journal* critic Jennifer Cogan added that the girl is aided by positive adult role models. Recommending the novel to upper elementary-grade readers, a *Kirkus Reviews* writer predicted that "Nadie's thought-provoking predicaments and her personal responses" will serve as useful guides for others facing a similar problem.

Biographical and Critical Sources

BOOKS

Bulion, Leslie, *Fatuma's New Cloth,* Moon Mountain (North Kingstown, RI), 2002.

PERIODICALS

Booklist, July 1, 2006, Gillian Engberg, review of *Hey There, Stink Bug!,* p. 53.
Kirkus Reviews, March 15, 2008, review of *The Trouble with Rules.*

Cover of Bulion's middle-grade novel The Trouble with Rules, *featuring artwork by Loraine M. Joyner.* (Peachtree Publishers, 2008. All rights reserved. Reproduced by permission.)

Publishers Weekly, May 20, 2002, review of *Fatuma's New Cloth,* p. 65.
School Library Journal, December, 2002, Anna DeWind Walls, review of *Fatuma's New Cloth,* p. 85; June, 2006, Vicki Reutter, review of *Uncharted Waters,* p. 148; July, 2006, Jill Heritage Maza, review of *Hey There, Stink Bug!,* p. 90; September, 2008, Jennifer Cogan, review of *The Trouble with Rules,* p. 140.

ONLINE

Leslie Bulion Home Page, http://www.lesliebulion.com (December 10, 2009).
Moon Mountain Publishing Web site, http://www. moonmountainpub.com/ (December 10, 2009).

* * *

BUSBY, John 1942-

Personal

Born 1942; married; wife's name Polly (a registered nurse); children: Cylin (daughter), two sons. *Education:* Earned degree from Cape Cod Community College.

Addresses

Home—Bar Harbor, ME.

Career

Author. Formerly worked as a police officer in Cape Cod, MA. *Military service:* Served in U.S. Air Force.

Writings

(With daughter, Cylin Busby) *The Year We Disappeared: A Father-Daughter Memoir,* Bloomsbury (New York, NY), 2008.

Sidelights

Nearly thirty years after surviving an assassination attempt, John Busby and his daughter Cylin Busby put their family's experiences into print in *The Year We Disappeared: A Father-Daughter Memoir.* A police officer on Massachusetts's Cape Cod, John took a shotgun blast in the face while on route to work one evening, an attack that was credited to a local arsonist but never proven in a court of law. Fearing for his family's safety following the incident, John moved his wife and children around the United States, changing addresses every few years to prevent anyone associated with the New England crime from locating them. Losing much of his lower jaw as well as twelve teeth and part of his tongue, the former police officer also underwent numerous reconstructive surgeries in an attempt to rebuild his face and regain enough function in his mouth to appear in public without drawing unwanted attention.

In sharing their experiences recovering from the crime in *The Year We Disappeared,* father and daughter offer two perspectives, with John concentrating on his suspicions about the true perpetrator of the crime and Cylin explaining how the incident shattered the previously idyllic life she shared with her parents and siblings. Nine years of age at the time of the shooting, Cylin lost contact with many of her childhood friends as the family moved, making her early adolescence a struggle. Ultimately, observed *School Library Journal* reviewer Joyce Adams Burner, *The Year We Disappeared* "is a story of survival and triumph." Writing in *Publishers Weekly,* a critic suggested that "no one with even a marginal interest in true crime writing should miss this page-turner," while *Booklist* contributor Lynn Rutan predicted that the Busbys' "riveting story will stay with readers."

Biographical and Critical Sources

PERIODICALS

Booklist, September 1, 2008, Lynn Rutan, review of *The Year We Disappeared: A Father-Daughter Memoir,* p. 86.
Horn Book, November-December, 2008, Christine M. Heppermann, review of *The Year We Disappeared,* p. 721.
Publishers Weekly, September 1, 2008, review of *The Year We Disappeared,* p. 55.
School Library Journal, October, 2008, Joyce Adams Burner, review of *The Year We Disappeared,* p. 165.*

C

CARRILLO, Patricia S.
See CARRILLO, P.S.

* * *

CARRILLO, P.S.
(Patricia S. Carrillo)

Personal

Born in CA; mother an elementary school teacher. *Education:* California State University, Fresno, B.A.; J.D. *Hobbies and other interests:* Reading, films, playing piano, opera, traveling.

Addresses

Home—Fresno, CA.

Career

Attorney and author. In private practice of law, Fresno, CA.

Awards, Honors

OneBookAZ Project nomination, 2009, for *Desert Passage.*

Writings

Desert Passage, Piñata Books (Houston, TX), 2009.

Biographical and Critical Sources

PERIODICALS

Booklist, October, 2008, Hazel Rochman, review of *Desert Passage.*

Kirkus Reviews, September 15, 2008, review of *Desert Passage.*
Multicultural Review, summer, 2009, review of *Desert Passage.*

ONLINE

P.S. Carrillo Home Page, http://www.roadtosomewhere books.com (December 15, 2009).*

* * *

CARTER, Anne Laurel 1953-

Personal

Born September 22, 1953, in Toronto, Ontario, Canada; daughter of Norm and Ruth Ovenden; married Craig Carter (a lawyer), 1986; children: David, Geordie, James, Kaitlyn. *Education:* University of Toronto, B.Ed., 1978, M.Ed., 1984. *Hobbies and other interests:* Classical piano.

Addresses

Home—Toronto, Ontario, Canada. *Agent*—Leona Trainer, Transatlantic Literary Agency, Inc., 72 Glengowan Rd., Toronto, Ontario MAN 164, Canada. *E-mail*—anne @annecarter.com.

Career

Teacher of English as a second language and of French.

Member

International Board on Books for Youth, Canadian Society of Children's Authors, Illustrators and Performers, Canadian Children's Book Centre, Writers Union of Canada.

Awards, Honors

Toronto Star Short-Story Competition Second Prize, 1997, for "No Missing Parts"; Vicky Metcalf Award, 1999, for "Leaving the Iron Lung"; Pick of the List se-

lection, American Booksellers Association, 1999, for *Tall in the Saddle;* Thistledown Young-Adult Short-Story Competition winner, 2001, for "The Piano Lesson"; Ontario Silver Birch Award nomination, 2002, for *In the Clear;* Canadian Children's Book Centre Our Choice selection, 2003, for *My Home Bay;* Mr. Christie's Book Award for Best Book for Readers Aged Seven and Younger, 2003, for *Under a Prairie Sky;* Red Maple Award nomination, Jane Addams Book Award Honor Book designation, Notable Book for a Global Society designation, International Reading Association, U.S. Board on Books for Young People Outstanding International Book designation, and Canadian Library Association (CLA) Book of the Year Award for Children short-list, all 2009, all for *The Shepherd's Granddaughter;* Amelia Frances Hoard-Gibbon Award finalist, CLA, 2009, for *Out of the Deeps;* (with Susan Whelehan) Golden Oak Award, Ontario Library Association, 2009, for *My Wedding Dress.*

Writings

PICTURE BOOKS

Tall in the Saddle, illustrated by David McPhail, Orca Books (Custer, WA), 1999.
From Poppa, illustrated by Kasia Charko, Lobster Press (Montreal, Quebec, Canada), 1999.
Under a Prairie Sky, illustrated by Alan and Lea Daniel, Orca Books (Custer, WA), 2002.
Circus Play, illustrated by Joanne Fitzgerald, Orca Books (Custer, WA), 2002.
My Home Bay, illustrated by Alan and Lea Daniel, Red Deer Press (Calgary, Ontario, Canada), 2003.
The F Team, illustrated by Rose Cowles, Orca Books (Custer, WA), 2003.
Out of the Deeps, illustrated by Nicholas Debon, Orca Book Publishers (Victoria, British Columbia, Canada), 2008.

"YOUNG-ADULT NOVELS

The Girl on Evangeline Beach, Stoddart (Don Mills, Ontario, Canada), 2000.
In the Clear, Orca Books (Custer, WA), 2001.
Last Chance Bay, Penguin Canada (Toronto, Ontario, Canada), 2004.
The Shepherd's Granddaughter, Groundwood Books (Toronto, Ontario, Canada), 2008.

"OUR CANADIAN GIRL" SERIES

Elizabeth: Bless This House, Penguin Canada (Toronto, Ontario, Canada), 2002.
Elizabeth: To Pirate Island, Penguin Canada (Toronto, Ontario, Canada), 2004.
Elizabeth: A Hornbook Christmas, Penguin Canada (Toronto, Ontario, Canada), 2005.

Elizabeth Wide as Wings, Penguin Canada (Toronto, Ontario, Canada), 2006.

OTHER

No Missing Parts, and Other Stories about Real Princesses, Red Deer Press (Calgary, Ontario, Canada), 2002.
(Editor with Susan Whelehan; and contributor) *My Wedding Dress: True-life Tales of Lace, Laughter, Tears, and Tulle,* Vintage Canada (Toronto, Ontario, Canada), 2007.

Contributor of stories to periodicals.

Sidelights

Anne Laurel Carter often looks to both contemporary life and Canadian history for the inspiration that fuels her creation of picture books, stories, and novels. She began her writing career producing award-winning short stories such as "No Missing Parts," and then moved to picture books with *Tall in the Saddle, From Poppa,* and *Under a Prairie Sky.* Carter's novels for teen readers include the highly praised *Girl on Evangeline Beach* and *The Shepherd's Daughter,* while her contributions to the popular "Our Canadian Girl" series are crafted with an eye to preteens who identify with Canadian history and culture. Carter's recognition of the importance of role models inspired her anthology *No Missing Parts, and Other Stories about Real Princesses,* which introduces readers to independent-minded young women throughout history who have acted in an exemplary manner. Praising the protagonists in these stories as "characters of depth, shadows, and edge," *Quill & Quire* critic Sherie Posesorski concluded that *No Missing Parts, and Other Stories about Real Princesses* introduces readers to "achingly real heroines to identify with and learn from."

In *Tall in the Saddle,* which *Quill & Quire* reviewer Arlene Perly Rae called "a rollicking cowboy fantasy," a father and son play cowboy together. Rae commented that "both drawings and text reflect the overwhelming love" the two share, and in *Resource Links* a reviewer described Carter's book as "a gentle affirmative story," dubbing it a "winning picture book." *From Poppa* also deals with a special relationship, this time between a grandfather who has to leave his home to winter in a warmer climate and his granddaughter, who will feel the man's absence. A reviewer for *Resource Links* dubbed the picture book "charming and true to life," and a *Quill & Quire* writer commented that the "great strength" of *From Poppa* lies in Carter's portrayal of a multigenerational relationship that contains "all the nuanced detail of real life."

Carter collaborates with illustrators Alan and Lea Daniel in two picture books that bring to life a unique Canadian landscape. In *Under a Prairie Sky* her story takes readers to Canada's vast interior grasslands as a thun-

derstorm threatens and an older brother mounts his horse and goes in search of his young sibling, who has wandered away from home and safety. The author's "brief, lyrical text brings the sights and sounds of the Prairie Provinces to life," wrote *Booklist* critic Kay Weisman, the critic also citing the book's "attractive" water-color art. In *My Home Bay* Gwyn deals with a move across the whole of Canada to costal Nova Scotia when her family relocates from its comfortable home in Vancouver, British Columbia. Although spunky and up-beat older sister Linden enjoys exploring the salt marshes that are a feature of Mahone Bay, Gwyn is more cautious. Ultimately, the gift of a new fiddle, a new tree house, and an aquarium to care for finally make her feel at home. In "simple words" the author captures Gwyn's "sense of dislocation," wrote Hazel Rochman in her *Booklist* appraisal of *My Home Bay,* and *School Library Journal* critic Liza Grayhill maintained that "the story is enriched by a sweet and trusting interaction between the sisters." "Carter's reflective text . . . evokes a child's anticipation, fear, and wavering acceptance," wrote *Resource Links* contributor Denise Parrott, the critic adding that the Daniels' "pastel yet earthy watercolor illustrations" pair with the story to reflect things unique to the coastal locale.

Carter's first young-adult novel, *Girl on Evangeline Beach,* reflects her interest in Canadian history. A time-slip fantasy, the novel revolves around the efforts of a teenaged boy, Michael, to rescue an Acadian girl from 1755, whom he had previously met as a ghost in the twentieth century and whom he meets again in the past. According to a *Resource Links* critic, with this novel "Carter weaves historical events with modern day circumstances to bring a story gripping with adventure, excitement and romance." Another novel that intersects Canadian history with a fictional young character is *Last Chance Bay.* Here young Meg is inspired to take to the skies when she meets British aviatrix Beryl Markham. Markham has just crash-landed her plane near Meg's home in Cape Breton, Nova Scotia, while attempting the first transatlantic flight from England to New York City. Calling Carter "an excellent scene builder," *Quill & Quire* critic Kenneth Oppel added that Meg's "peppy first-person narration" contributes to the "appealing frankness, and oral verve" of Carter's tale.

Amani has always wanted to become a shepherd like her grandfather, and in *The Shepherd's Granddaughter* readers follower her life in modern Palestine, as the Muslim teen worries about the encroachment of Israeli settlements that now threatens her family's traditions and livelihood. When Grandfather Seedo passes the responsibility for his large herd to his granddaughter, it is an unusual move, but Amani proves that she can handle it, caretaking the sheep and even tapping into advances in the field of animal husbandry to keep the family business profitable. However, the young woman's task is soon made more challenging: the lands her family's sheep have grazed for generations are diminishing as Jews from Israel move into the area, and their presence soon sparks resent and scattered outbreaks of violence. Calling *The Shepherd's Granddaughter* "a well-intentioned, very earnest narrative," Laurie McNeill added in *Quill & Quire* that "Amani is a likably plucky character with whom readers will empathize." The story "is written simply and clearly," concluded *School Library Journal* contributor Joyce Adams Burner, making *The Shepherd's Granddaughter* "a skillful depiction of a sensitive situation," and a *Kirkus Reviews* writer dubbed the book a "moving narrative" that is "information-packed but never didactic."

Carter once told *SATA:* "Although I didn't notice history as a child, I certainly do now. My first three novels are all historical: a time-travel back to Acadia in *Girl on Evangeline Beach*; a girl's struggle with polio in the 1950s in *In the Clear*; and the settling of Nova Scotia by New England 'Planters' after the deportation of the Acadians in my "Elizabeth" novels. I find history speaks to me. Our world is constantly changing, yet some part of human experience always stays the same. In my collection of short stories, I look at the pivotal experiences a teenaged girl can have: love, loss, adventure, peer pressure. Each girl is given a different setting and time period, yet she could be any girl anywhere. A refugee

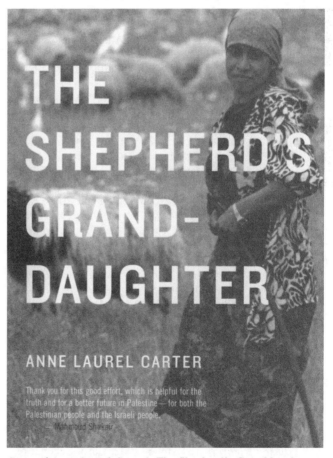

Cover of Anne Laurel Carter's The Shepherd's Granddaughter, *a story about a Muslim teen who inherits her family's business despite the disapproval of many in her traditional village.* (Groundwood Books, 2008. Photograph © by Sophie Elbaz/Sygma/Corbis. Design by Michael Solomon. Reproduced by permission of Groundwood Books Limited.)

in 1756 probably felt many of the same things a refugee feels now, and I find stories a wonderful way to try to understand and capture the essence of our experiences."

Biographical and Critical Sources

PERIODICALS

Booklist, November 15, 2001, Gillian Engberg, review of *In the Clear,* p. 570; May 15, 2002, Kay Weisman, review of *Under a Prairie Sky,* p. 1600; December 1, 2002, Diane Foote, review of *Circus Play,* p. 672; May 1, 2003, Debbie Carton, review of *No Missing Parts, and Other Stories about Real Princesses,* p. 1388; February 1, 2004, Hazel Rochman, review of *My Home Bay,* p. 979.

Books in Canada, February, 2000, review of *Tall in the Saddle,* p. 34; July, 2001, review of *In the Clear,* pp. 31-32.

Canadian Children's Literature, summer, 2000, review of *From Poppa,* p. 109; spring, 2001, review of *Girl on Evangeline Beach,* pp. 180-181.

Globe and Mail (Toronto, Ontario, Canada), September 21, 2002, Susan Perren, review of *Circus Play,* p. 1; September 25, 2004, Susan Perren, review of *Last Chance Bay,* p. D26.

Kirkus Reviews, June, 2002, Veronica Allan, review of *Under a Prairie Sky,* p. 1; September 15, 2002, review of *Circus Play,* p. 1386; March 15, 2003, review of *No Missing Parts, and Other Stories of Real Princesses,* p. 461; August 15, 2008, review of *The Shepherd's Granddaughter.*

Quill & Quire, July, 1999, Arlene Perly Rae, review of *Tall in the Saddle,* p. 51; November, 1999, review of *From Poppa,* p. 45; February, 2002, Jessica Kelley, review of *Under a Prairie Sky;* September, 2002, Sherie Posesorki, review of *No Missing Parts, and Other Stories about Real Princesses;* September, 2004, Kenneth Oppel, review of *Last Chance Bay;* December, 2008, Laurie McNeill review of *The Shepherd's Granddaughter.*

Resource Links, December, 1999, review of *Tall in the Saddle,* p. 4; February, 2000, review of *From Poppa,* p. 2; February, 2001, review of *Girl on Evangeline Beach,* p. 29; June, 2001, Rosemary Anderson, review of *In the Clear,* p. 8; June, 2002, Gillian Richardson, review of *Elizabeth: Bless This House,* p. 10; December, 2002, Sandra Tee, review of *Circus Play,* p. 3; December, 2003, Denise Parrott, review of *My Home Bay,* and Nancy Ryan, review of *The F Team,* both p. 3; June, 2004, Laura Reilly, review of *Elizabeth: To Pirate Island,* p. 5; April, 2006, David Ward, review of *Elizabeth: A Hornbook Christmas,* p. 14.

School Library Journal, January, 2002, Sue Sherif, review of *In the Clear,* p. 131; June, 2002, Carol Schene, review of *Under a Prairie Sky,* p. 90; October, 2002, Gail Lennon, review of *No Missing Parts, and Other Stories about Real Princesses,* p. 33; May, 2003, Kimberly Monaghan, review of *No Missing Parts, and*

Other Stories about Real Princesses, p. 148; December, 2003, Blair Christolon, review of *The F Team,* p. 111; August, 2004, Liza Graybill, review of *My Home Bay,* p. 84; October, 2004, K.V. Johansen, review of *Last Chance Bay,* p. 28; December, 2008, Joyce Adams Burner, review of *The Shepherd's Granddaughter,* p. 120; January, 2009, Madeline Walton-Hadlock, review of *Out of the Deeps,* p. 73.

Toronto Star, March 17, 2002, Deirdre Baker, "Uncertain History."

ONLINE

Anne Laurel Carter Home Page, http://www.annecarter. com (December 15, 2009).*

*   *   *

CASE, Chris 1976-

Personal

Born 1976; married. *Education:* University of Arizona, Tucson, B.F.A., M.F.A. 2005.

Addresses

Agent—c/o Ronnie Anne Herman, Herman Agency, 350 Central Park W., New York, NY 10025. *E-mail*—chris@ christophercase.com.

Chris Case (Reproduced by permission.)

Case pairs his humorous story with his original cartoon art in the picture book **Sophie and the Next-Door Monsters.** (Walker & Company, 2008. Copyright © 2008 by Chris Case. All rights reserved. Reproduced by permission.)

Career

Illustrator.

Writings

SELF-ILLUSTRATED

Sophie and the Next-Door Monsters, Walker (New York, NY), 2008.

Author and illustrator of comics, including "Marmalade" and "Pukey Bear." Contributor to *Highlights High Five* and *Arizona Daily Wildcat.*

Sidelights

Since earning his M.F.A. in illustration from the University of Arizona in Tucson, Chris Case has moved into picture books with his self-illustrated *Sophie and the Next-Door Monsters.* In the book, Sophie's mother invites her new neighbors over for dinner. During the meal, she insists that Sophie be polite, in spite of the fact that the neighbors are tentacled monsters. During dinner, Sophie realizes that the monsters are not so bad, and soon little monster Charlie becomes her good friend due to his similar interests in silliness and fun, enhanced by magic. Case uses water color, ink, and gouache (opaque water color) to create the visual art for his story.

Kathleen Kelly MacMillan, reviewing *Sophie and the Next-Door Monsters* for *School Library Journal,* predicted that readers will "enjoy Charlie's outrageous behavior and the energetic . . . cartoons." Hazel Rochman, writing in *Booklist,* described Case's illustrations as filled with detail, but added that some of the book's "scenes may be a little crowded for young preschoolers." Also reviewing *Sophie and the Next-Door Monsters,* a critic for *Kirkus Reviews* called Case's text "a spot-on complement to the often laugh-out-loud images, telling just enough of the story to allow the pictures to go wild."

Biographical and Critical Sources

PERIODICALS

Booklist, October 15, 2008, Hazel Rochman, review of *Sophie and the Next-Door Monsters,* p. 48.
Kirkus Reviews, September 15, 2008, review of *Sophie and the Next-Door Monsters.*
School Library Journal, November, 2008, Kathleen Kelly MacMillan, review of *Sophie and the Next-Door Monsters,* p. 85.

ONLINE

Chris Case Home Page, http://www.christophercase.com (December 14, 2009).
Herman Agency Web site, http://www.hermanagencyinc.com/ (December 14, 2009), "Chris Case."

* * *

CATT, Louis
See FRENCH, Vivian

* * *

CHICHESTER CLARK, Emma 1955-

Personal

Born October 15, 1955, in London, England; daughter of Robin Chichester Clark (a company director) and Jane Helen Goddard (present surname Falloon); married Lucas van Praag (a management consultant). *Education:* Chelsea School of Art, B.A. (with honors), 1978; Royal College of Art, M.A. (with honors), 1983.

Addresses

Home—London, England. *Agent*—Laura Cecil, 17 Alwyne Villas, London N1, England.

Career

Author, illustrator, and editor of children's books, 1983—. Worked in a design studio and as a freelance illustrator of newspapers, periodicals, and book jackets.

Visiting lecturer at Middlesex Polytechnic and City and Guilds School of Art, 1984-86. *Exhibitions:* Work exhibited at Thumb Gallery, England, 1984, 1987.

Member

Chelsea Arts Club.

Awards, Honors

Mother Goose Award, 1988, for *Listen to This;* Golden Duck Award, 1999, for *Noah and the Space Ark;* Kate Greenaway Medal shortlist, 1999, for *I Love You, Blue Kangaroo!;* Kurt Maschler Award shortlist, 1999, for *Elf Hill;* Blue Peter Book Award shortlist for the Most Fun Story with Pictures, 2007, for *Melrose and Croc: Together at Christmas.*

Writings

SELF-ILLUSTRATED PICTURE BOOKS

Catch That Hat!, Bodley Head (London, England), 1988, Little, Brown (Boston, MA), 1990.
The Story of Horrible Hilda and Henry, Little, Brown (Boston, MA), 1988.
Myrtle, Tertle, and Gertle, Bodley Head (London, England), 1989.
The Bouncing Dinosaur, Farrar, Straus (New York, NY), 1990.
Tea with Aunt Augusta, Methuen (London, England), 1991, published as *Lunch with Aunt Augusta,* Dial (New York), 1992.
Miss Bilberry's New House, Methuen (London, England), 1993, published as *Across the Blue Mountains,* Harcourt (San Diego, CA), 1993.
Little Miss Muffet Counts to Ten, Andersen (London, England), 1997, published as *Little Miss Muffet's Count-Along Surprise,* Bantam (New York, NY), 1997.
More!, Andersen (London, England), 1998, Bantam (New York, NY), 1999.
I Love You, Blue Kangaroo!, Bantam (New York, NY), 1999.
Follow My Leader, Andersen (London, England), 1999.
Where Are You, Blue Kangaroo?, Andersen (London, England), 2000, Random House (New York, NY), 2001.
It Was You, Blue Kangaroo!, Andersen (London, England), 2001, Random House (New York, NY), 2002.
No More Kissing!, Doubleday (New York, NY), 2002.
What Shall We Do, Blue Kangaroo?, Random House (New York, NY), 2003.
Mimi's Book of Opposites, Charlesbridge (Watertown, MA), 2003.
Mimi's Book of Counting, Charlesbridge (Watertown, MA), 2003.
Follow the Leader!, Margaret K. McElderry Books (New York, NY), 2003.
Up in Heaven, Andersen (London, England), 2003, Random House (New York, NY), 2004.

Just for You, Blue Kangaroo, Andersen (London, England), 2004, published as *Merry Christmas, Blue Kangaroo!,* HarperCollins Children's (London, England), 2006, published as *Merry Christmas to You, Blue Kangaroo!,* Random House (New York, NY), 2004.

No More Teasing, Andersen (London, England), 2004.

Piper, Andersen Press (London, England), 2005, Eerdmans Books for Young Readers (Grand Rapids, MI), 2007.

Melrose and Croc: Together at Christmas, HarperCollins Children's (London, England), 2005, published as *Melrose and Croc: A Christmas to Remember,* Walker & Co. (New York, NY), 2006.

Will and Squill, Andersen (London, England), 2005, Carolrhoda Books (Minneapolis, MN), 2006.

Melrose and Croc: Friends for Life, HarperCollins Children's (London, England), 2006.

Melrose and Croc: Find a Smile, HarperCollins Children's (London, England), 2006.

Happy Birthday to You, Blue Kangaroo!, Andersen (London, England), 2006.

Amazing Mr Zooty!, Andersen (London, England), 2007.

Eliza and the Moonchild, Andersen (London, England), 2007.

Melrose and Croc Go to Town, HarperCollins Children's (London, England), 2007.

Melrose and Croc beside the Sea, HarperCollins Children's (London, England), 2007.

Melrose and Croc: An Adventure to Remember, Walker & Co. (New York, NY), 2008.

Minty and Tink, Andersen (London, England), 2008.

Melrose and Croc: A Hero's Birthday, HarperCollins Children's (London, England), 2008.

Author's books have been translated into Spanish and Welsh.

ILLUSTRATOR

Laura Cecil, compiler, *Listen to This,* Greenwillow (New York, NY), 1987.

Janet Lunn, *Shadow in Hawthorn Bay,* Walker (London, England), 1988.

Laura Cecil, compiler, *Stuff and Nonsense,* Greenwillow (New York, NY), 1989.

Primrose Lockwood, *Cissy Lavender,* Little, Brown (Boston, MA), 1989.

James Reeves, *Ragged Robin: Poems from A to Z,* Little, Brown (Boston, MA), 1990.

Margaret Ryan, *Fat Witch Rides Again,* Methuen (London, England), 1990.

Laura Cecil, compiler, *Boo! Stories to Make You Jump,* Greenwillow (New York, NY), 1990.

Roald Dahl, *James and the Giant Peach,* Unwin Hyman (London, England), 1990.

(And compiler) *I Never Saw a Purple Cow and Other Nonsense Rhymes* (anthology), Little, Brown (Boston, MA), 1990.

Pat Thomson, *Beware of the Aunts!,* Margaret K. McElderry Books (New York), 1991.

Margaret Mahy, *The Queen's Goat,* Dial (New York, NY), 1991.

Diana Wynne Jones, *Wild Robert,* Mammoth (London, England), 1991, Chivers North America, 1992.

Diana Wynne Jones, *Castle in the Air,* Mammoth (London, England), 1991.

Jenny Nimmo, *Delilah and the Dogspell,* Methuen (London, England), 1991, included in *Deliah: Three Books in One,* Egmont (London, England), 2007.

Laura Cecil, compiler, *A Thousand Yards of the Sea,* Methuen (London, England), 1992, published as *A Thousand Yards of Sea,* Greenwillow (New York, NY), 1993.

D.J. Enright, *The Way of the Cat,* HarperCollins (New York, NY), 1992.

Anne Fine, *The Haunting of Pip Parker,* Walker (London, England), 1992.

Ben Frankel, *Tertius and Plinty,* Harcourt (San Diego, CA), 1992.

Geraldine McCaughrean, reteller, *The Orchard Book of Greek Myths,* Orchard (London, England), 1992, published as *Greek Myths,* Margaret K. McElderry Books (New York, NY), 1993.

Peter Dickinson, *Time and the Clockmice, et cetera,* Doubleday (London, England), 1993, Delacorte (New York, NY), 1994.

Rosemary Sutcliff, *The Princess and the Dragon Pup,* Walker (London, England), 1993, Candlewick (Cambridge, MA), 1996.

Ann Turnbull, *Too Tired,* Hamish Hamilton (London, England), 1993, Harcourt (San Diego, CA), 1994.

Laura Cecil, *The Frog Princess,* Jonathan Cape (London, England), 1994, Greenwillow (New York, NY), 1995.

Laura Cecil, compiler, *Preposterous Pets,* Hamish Hamilton (London, England), 1994, Greenwillow (New York, NY), 1995.

Charles Ashton, *Ruth and the Blue Horse,* Walker (London, England), 1994.

Kate McMullan, *Good Night, Stella,* Candlewick (Cambridge, MA), 1994.

William S. Gilbert and Arthur Sullivan, *I Have a Song to Sing, O!: An Introduction to the Songs of Gilbert and Sullivan,* selected and edited by John Langstaff, Margaret K. McElderry Books (New York, NY), 1994.

Laura Cecil, *Piper,* Jonathan Cape (London, England), 1995.

Something Rich and Strange: A Treasury of Shakespeare's Verse, compiled by Gina Pollinger, Larousse Kingfisher Chambers (New York, NY), 1995, published as *A Treasury of Shakespeare's Verse,* Kingfisher (New York, NY), 2000.

Allan Ahlberg, *Mrs. Vole the Vet,* Puffin (London, England), 1996.

(And editor with Catherine Asholt and Quentin Blake) *The Candlewick Book of First Rhymes* (anthology), Candlewick (Cambridge, MA), 1996.

Henrietta Branford, *Dimanche Diller at Sea,* Collins (London, England), 1996.

Ian Whybrow, *Miss Wire and the Three Kind Mice,* Kingfisher (London, England), 1996.

Sam McBratney, editor, *Little Red Riding Hood,* 1996.

Emma Alcock, *Sinan,* Hood Books (London, England), 1996.

Laura Mare, *Mehmet the Conqueror,* 1997.

Laura Cecil, *Noah and the Space Ark,* Hamish Hamilton (London, England), 1997, Lerner (New York, NY), 1998.

Geraldine McCaughrean, reteller, *The Orchard Book of Greek Gods and Goddesses,* Orchard (London, England), 1997.

Jane Falloon, reteller, *Thumbelina,* Pavilion (London, England), 1997.

The Little Book of Shakespeare, compiled by Gina Pollinger, Kingfisher (London, England), 1997, published as *Shakespeare's Verse,* Kingfisher (Boston, MA), 2005.

John Yeoman, *The Glove Puppet Man,* Collins (London, England), 1997.

Adrian Mitchell, reteller, *The Adventures of Robin Hood and Marian,* Orchard (London, England), 1998.

Mathew Price, *Where's Alfie?,* Orchard (London, England), 1999.

Mathew Price, *Don't Worry, Alfie,* Orchard (London, England), 1999.

Naomi Lewis, *Elf Hill: Tales from Hans Christian Andersen,* Star Bright Books, 1999, revised edition, Frances Lincoln (London, England), 2005.

Mathew Price, *Patch and the Rabbits,* Orchard (London, England), 1999, Orchard (New York, NY), 2000.

Mathew Price, *Patch Finds a Friend,* Orchard (New York, NY), 2000.

Laura Cecil, compiler, *The Kingfisher Book of Toy Stories,* Kingfisher (New York, NY), 2000.

Geraldine McCaughrean, reteller, *Roman Myths,* Margaret K. McElderry Books (New York, NY), 2001.

Michael Morpurgo, *The McElderry Book of Aesop's Fables,* Margaret K. McElderry Books (New York, NY), 2005.

Saviour Pirotta, reteller, *The McElderry Book of Grimms' Fairy Tales,* Margaret K. McElderry Books (New York, NY), 2006.

Ian Whybrow, *Miss Wire's Christmas Surprise,* Kingfisher (Boston, MA), 2007.

Michael Morpurgo, reteller, *Hansel and Gretel,* Candlewick Press (Cambridge, MA), 2008.

Michael Morpurgo, reteller, *Goldilocks and the Three Bears,* Candlewick Press (Somerville, MA), 2010.

Contributor of illustrations to *Tom's Pirate Ship and Other Stories* and *Mostly Animal Poetry,* both Heinemann (London, England), 1997, and *Alphabet Gallery,* Mammoth (London, England), 1999. Illustrations have also appeared in newspapers and periodicals, including London *Sunday Times, Cosmopolitan,* and *New Scientist.*

Sidelights

A popular and prolific author, illustrator, and anthologist, Emma Chichester Clark is considered one of England's most distinguished picture-book creators. Cited alongside noted illustrators Beatrix Potter, Edward Ardizzone, Tony Ross, and Quentin Blake—her former teacher—Clark has written and illustrated original picture books that include *Amazing Mr Zooty!, I Love You, Blue Kangaroo!, Eliza and the Moonchild,* and her popular "Melrose and Croc" series. Her stories feature child, adult, and animal characters in situations that, although often humorous and fantastic, nonetheless provide realistic portrayals of human feelings and foibles. Gwyneth Evans noted in an essay for the *St. James Guide to Children's Writers* that Chichester Clark's texts "are reassuring, but have an underlying toughness." Their protagonists—boys and girls, older women, and anthropomorphized animals ranging from donkeys to lemurs—are not perfect: they fight, tease, overeat, and are greedy and absent minded. However, they ultimately make positive choices and, at the end of their adventures, return home, satisfied with their situation.

As an artist, Chichester Clark is praised for her distinctive, easily recognizable style, as well as for her use of color and her ability to evoke action and emotion. She often works in watercolor and pen, and her pictures range from bucolic scenes in gentle pastels to luminous, vivid paintings teeming with activity. "While her illustrations often suggest the serenity and charm of a timeless world," stated Evans, "her work has a vitality and a multicultural perspective which also makes it contemporary." Chichester Clark's illustrations can be found in picture books, anthologies, and retellings containing en-

Emma Chichester Clark brings to life a bygone time in **Elf Hill,** *Naomi Lewis's adaptation of a story by Hans Christian Andersen.* (Frances Lincoln Limited, 2001. Illustration © 1999 by Emma Chichester Clark. Reproduced by permission.)

tertaining texts by writers that include Roald Dahl, Anne Fine, Peter Dickinson, Allan Ahlberg, Rosemary Sutcliff, Sam McBratney, Diana Wynne Jones, John Yeoman, Jenny Nimmo, Geraldine McCaughrean, and Michael Morpurgo.

Born in London, England, Chichester Clark was brought to Ireland at the age of three and grew up in an old, white farmhouse surrounded by fields. Her family kept many pets, including dogs, roosters, mice, rabbits, and, as the artist wrote in *Ladybug,* "a very old pony who was pretty vicious." Because she lived a long way from any other children, Chichester Clark and her siblings "had to entertain ourselves, which was easy there. I used to draw a lot, houses with windows jammed into the four corners and people with no necks." She also made her own small books, "with proper spines that my mother sewed up for me." "All the way through school," she added, "it didn't ever occur to me that I would do anything other than illustrate books when I was 'grown up.'"

In 1975, Chichester Clark left Ireland to attend the Chelsea School of Art in London. After graduating with honors, she began to submit original picture books to publishers. When two of them were rejected, she suspended her quest to work in a design studio. Here she designed book jackets and also submitted illustrations to newspapers and magazines. A few years later, she enrolled at the Royal College of Art, where she was taught by Quentin Blake and prominent author/illustrator Michael Foreman. After receiving her master's degree, again with honors, Chichester Clark received a phone call from an editor at London publisher Bodley Head, who had found copies of the drawings she had submitted several years previously. She was asked to illustrate the story anthology *Listen to This,* which began her fruitful collaboration with the book's editor, Laura Cecil.

Listen to This contains thirteen stories, including works by Rudyard Kipling, Philippa Pearce, Virginia Hamilton, Margaret Mahy, and the Brothers Grimm. Writing in the *Times Educational Supplement,* Jenny Marshall noted that Chichester Clark's colorful illustrations for the work "have verve and wit," while Lesley Chamberlain concluded in the *Times Literary Supplement* that the artist "has brought an energetic and unsentimental streak to very varied material." In response to her work the illustrator received the Mother Goose Award in 1988, acknowledging her position as the most exciting newcomer to British children's book illustration.

Chichester Clark and Cecil have continued their collaboration, producing several other well-received compilations as well as original stories. In *Noah and the Space Ark,* a picture book by Cecil that features an environmental theme, Biblical character find themselves in a future in which Earth is so polluted that people and animals are in danger of extinction. Noah builds a rocket ship and takes the small animals—the larger

ones have already died out—up into space to find a new home. After they find a planet that resembles Earth, they disembark and vow to take better care of their planetary home than the stewards of Earth had done.

While she has illustrated many works by others, Chichester Clark also creates original self-illustrated stories that have earned her a wide following, both in her native England and in the United States. Her first story was published in 1988 as *Catch That Hat!* In this picture book, which features a rhyming text, Rose loses her pink hat to the wind as she chases a cat. As she retrieves and then loses her hat again, Rose is aided in her chase by a cow, a rabbit, and a kangaroo, as well as by a boy. The hat finally lands in a monkey puzzle tree that no one can climb. A cockatoo lands on the hat and makes a nest, which pleases Rose even as she sheds a tear for her lost chapeau. At the end of the story, Rose's friends give her a new hat, complete with a ribbon to tie under her chin. In *Booklist* Barbara Elleman predicted that children "will enjoy the whimsy of this airy, light-as-a-breeze tale."

An early book by Chichester Clark, *The Story of Horrible Hilda and Henry* is a cautionary tale in picture-book form about a brother and sister who like to misbehave. They trash their house, squirt their parents with a hose, have food fights, and tease each other unmercifully. Finally, the children's parents send them to the zoo. After annoying the animals, Hilda and Henry are placed in a cage with Brian, a bad-tempered lion who frightens the siblings so much that they become model children. Their parents take Brian home along with Hilda and Henry, hoping that the lion will act as insurance; however, Clark's last picture shows the children reverting back to their former disobedient ways. Writing in *Booklist,* Ilene Cooper noted that Chichester Clarks's use of "comic-book strips, full-page pictures, and two-page spreads" all work to relay her humorous story "to good effect," while a *Kirkus Reviews* critic claimed that young readers will enjoy the "gleefully exaggerated pranks here, which [Chichester] Clark illustrates with her usual zest."

Tea with Aunt Augusta—published in the United States as *Lunch with Aunt Augusta*—is one of Chichester Clark's most popular works. The story outlines what happens when Jemima, a ring-tailed lemur who is the youngest in her family, goes with her two older brothers to visit their beloved Aunt Augusta. After Jemima gorges herself on the lavish variety of mixed fruits provided by Aunt Augusta, the little lemur cannot keep up with her older brothers on their way home. Lost in the dark, she is rescued by a group of friendly fruit bats, who carry her home in a leaf sling. Jemima is lectured by her parents on overeating, but they welcome her with hugs and kisses. Her brothers, on the other hand, are sent to bed without supper for abandoning their sister in the jungle. Calling Chichester Clark's illustrations "delightfully vivid, witty, and tender," *Times Educational Supplement* reviewer Andrew Davies concluded,

"I've never given ring-tailed lemurs much thought before. Now I wish I owned one. In fact I wish I was one." A *Publisher Weekly* reviewer noted the book's "unique and captivating cast" and "playful artwork," while in *Booklist* Rochman concluded that, "with all its nonsense . . . this satisfying story combines the small child's fear of being lost with the dream of adventure."

With *Little Miss Muffet Counts to Ten*—published in the United States as *Little Miss Muffet's Count-Along Surprise*—Chichester Clark extends the traditional nursery rhyme in a concept book that teaches basic mathematics. Instead of frightening Miss Muffet away, the spider asks her politely to stay. The arachnid is pleased when her animal friends—including bears with chairs and puffins with muffins—arrive to give her a surprise birthday party. When two crocodiles with greedy smiles show up, things get tense; however, they are just bringing the cake. Writing in *School Librarian*, Sarah Reed termed the book a "successful combination of a counting book, traditional rhyme, repetition, a chain story, all beautifully illustrated," while *FamilyFun* reviewer Sandy MacDonald wrote that "the rhymes are tightly sprung, the imagery deliciously imaginative." A critic for *Kirkus Reviews* concluded by calling *Little Miss Muffet's Count-Along Surprise* "a wonderful variation on the nursery rhyme that for once will frighten no one away."

In *More!* little Billy stalls, demanding one more story, one more ice cream, one more game to avoid the dreaded bedtime. When his mother refuses, Billy stomps off to his room, gathers his stuffed toys and the life-size lion that lives behind the curtain, and goes off to the center of the Earth, where he gets more rides, more spins, and more lollipops than he could ever want. Billy becomes over-saturated and finally realizes that all he wants to do is to go home to bed, which he does. *School Librarian* critic Jane Doonan raved that, with *More!*, Chichester Clark "succeeds in picturing the indescribable."

Called "bibliotherapy at its best" by *School Library Journal* reviewer Rosalyn Pierini, *Up in Heaven* tackles a subject that almost every child has to face at some point: the death of a beloved pet. Arthur spends much of his play time with the family dog, Daisy, but eventually the elderly pup starts to sit out the most rambunctious games on the sidelines. When Daisy finally passes away, she looks down from Doggy Heaven and sees how sad Arthur is, she sends the young boy a dream to let him know that she is happy and that it is okay to give his affection to a new puppy. Martha V. Parravano praised the story in *Horn Book* as "comforting and uplifting but not in the least saccharine," while in *Booklist* Hazel Rochman noted that in her "joyful fantasy" Chichester Clark presents a forthright way to view the loss of a loved one; because *Up in Heaven* "never denies the child's sorrow and loss, the hopeful, loving scenes will help preschoolers move on," Rochman added.

Shortlisted for the coveted Kate Greenaway Medal for illustration, *I Love You, Blue Kangaroo!* begins a series that includes some of Chichester Clark's most popular books. Lily loves her stuffed blue kangaroo more than any of her other toys, but when she receives new stuffed animals, Blue Kangaroo is pushed to the side. The toy eventually makes his way to the crib of Lily's baby brother, where he is welcomed joyfully. Not surprisingly, when Lily sees Blue Kangaroo in her brother's arms, she realizes that she still loves him and wants him back. Ultimately, Lily comes up with a mutually beneficial plan: she trades all of her new stuffed toys to her baby brother in exchange for her beloved Blue Kangaroo. Writing in the *Times Educational Supplement,* William Feaver stated that Chichester Clark "has perfect pitch as an author/illustrator" and hailed *I Love You, Blue Kangaroo* as "a winner." Stephanie Zvirin, writing in *Booklist,* praised the book's illustrations, noting that they "can open the way to parent-child discussions of selfishness and generosity." A reviewer for *School Library Journal* called *I Love You, Blue Kangaroo!* a "heartwarming story" that is "wholly satisfactory."

Other books featuring Blue Kangaroo include *Where Are You, Blue Kangaroo?*, *It Was You, Blue Kangaroo!*, and *What Shall We Do, Blue Kangaroo?*, the last which finds Lily and her favorite toy thinking of ways to pass some free time and ultimately hosting a garden tea party to which all the household toys are invited. Noting that Chichester Clark's technique of depicting the kangaroo's face close up "pulls [readers] . . . into his perspective" and presents a toy's-eye view of childhood, *Horn Book* contributor Christine M. Heppermann praised the author/illustrator's use of an "appealingly repetitive text and joyful spring-like colors" throughout the "Blue Kangaroo" series. Citing the "can-do message" of *What Shall We Do, Blue Kangaroo?*, Lisa Dennis added in her *School Library Journal* review that the illustrations "show a cozy, idealized domestic setting. . .—the perfect place for a preschooler to develop a bit of independence."

A pair of young monkeys is the focus of several books by Chichester Clark. In *No More Kissing!* Momo ducks the kisses of relatives, and decides that, even among his own affectionate family, there is too much smooching going on. Realizing that not only monkeys, but also lion, snake, and even crocodile families engage in this off-putting practice, Momo goes to the extreme of wearing a sign pronouncing "No More Kissing" when he walks through the jungle, as a way to make his point. However, his attitude starts to change when a new baby brother arrives, causing *School Library Journal* contributor Linda M. Kenton to note that *No More Kissing!* provides parents with "a fresh approach to introducing a new baby in a family." In the board books *Mimi's Book of Opposites* and *Mimi's Book of Counting* Momo's older cousin is introduced, presenting basic concept to toddlers with the help of several family members.

Momo returns to share center stage with his cousin in the picture-book *No More Teasing!*, as Mimi becomes exasperated by Momo's constant joking and just plain pestering. Fortunately, Grandma comes to the rescue and together the two hatch a plot that the impish Momo will not forget. Although their solution involves a cape and a scary mask, Chichester Clark's art "with its happy colors and exotic locale, is not so terrifying as to curdle young readers' blood," concluded a *Kirkus Reviews* contributor.

Described by a *Kirkus Reviews* writer as "a fanciful tale about color and friendship," *Eliza and the Moonchild* finds Chichester Clark in a fanciful mood. In the story, the moonchild is tired of the cool white that is every-where on the moon. Longing for color, he travels down to earth and finds Eliza, a young artist who shows a tal-ent for color. As the moon disappears and the sun rises, Eliza uses her paints to capture the colors of the earth's flowers, animals, and bright blue sky. She then gives the moonchild her pictures as well as her paint box so that he can bring color to his own world. In *School Li-brary Journal* Kim T. Ha found the story's theme "in-spiring" and called *Eliza and the Moonchild* "a sooth-ing bedtime read," while in the London *Guardian* Julia Eccleshare praised Chichester Clark's "delicate and pre-cise use of colour" in a picture book that encourages children to ponder "the impact different colors have."

Baby meets squirrel in *Will and Squill*, a picture book by Chichester Clark that finds a toddler named Will be-friending a young squirrel named Squill. Although the two spend time playing together in Will's yard every time the child is allowed to spend time outside, when the boy is given a kitten by his parents Squill feels hurt and jealous. Over time, Will realizes that while the kit-ten is cute, it is not Squill, and the friendship is soon repaired in a book that Carolyn Phelan recommended should be placed on "the story hour list of picture books celebrating friendship." Chichester Clark's "tongue-twisting text further animates" her story of "an unlikely friendship," asserted a *Kirkus Reviews* writer in a favor-able review of *Will and Squill*.

Chichester Clark's popular "Melrose and Croc" series begins with *Melrose and Croc: A Christmas to Remem-ber* (also published as *Melrose and Croc: Together at Christmas*) and also includes *Melrose and Croc: Friends for Life*, *Melrose and Croc: Beside the Sea*, and *Mel-rose and Croc: An Adventure to Remember*. Croc, a lithe green crocodile, hurries to town to meet Santa Claus, but he arrives too late and Santa has already taken to the sky. However, when he meets a lonely dog named Melrose at a skating rink Croc makes a friend for life and enjoys a festive holiday in *A Christmas to Remember*. Melrose and Croc enjoy reflecting on the many things that make their friendship strong, even while they also enjoy each other's company because of their differences in *Friends for Ever*, while *An Adven-ture to Remember* finds Melrose planning Croc's birth-day celebration at the seaside until his efforts to catch a

fish for lunch require the assistance of his fast-swimming friend. In *Publishers Weekly* a critic wrote that *Melrose and Croc: A Christmas to Remember* pairs a "sweet" story with Chichester Clark's "gently humor-ous, heart-tugging paintings," while *School Library Journal* writer Eva Mitnick predicted that the gentle holiday-themed story "will strike a chord with chil-dren." Catherine Threadgill wrote in the same periodi-cal that *Melrose and Croc: An Adventure to Remember* pairs an "affectionate message" with "expressive" art to produce a "reassuring" tale suitable for toddler reading, and *Horn Book* critic Robin L. Smith praised the book's "quiet, old-timey quality."

Biographical and Critical Sources

BOOKS

St. James Guide to Children's Writers, edited by Sara and Tom Pendergast, St. James Press (Detroit, MI), 1999, pp. 230-232.

PERIODICALS

Booklist, April 15, 1989, Ilene Cooper, review of *The Story of Horrible Hilda and Henry,* p. 1464; May 15, 1990, Barbara Elleman, review of *Catch That Hat!,* pp. 1797-1798; May 1, 1992, Hazel Rochman, review of *Lunch with Aunt Augusta,* p. 1606; January 1, 1999, Stephanie Zvirin, review of *I Love You, Blue Kanga-roo!,* p. 886; November 1, 2002, Hazel Rochman, re-view of *It Was You, Blue Kangaroo!,* p. 504; May 15, 2003, Gillian Engberg, review of *What Shall We Do, Blue Kangaroo?,* p. 1669; February 1, 2004, Hazel Rochman, review of *Up in Heaven,* p. 979; May 1, 2005, Hazel Rochman, review of *The McElderry Book of Aesop's Fables,* p. 1588; March 1, 2006, Carolyn Phelan, review of *Will and Squill,* p. 99; January 1, 2007, Ilene Cooper, review of *Piper,* p. 112.

FamilyFun, November, 1997, Sandy MacDonald, review of *Little Miss Muffet's Count-Along Surprise.*

Guardian (London, England), October 29, 2005, Julia Eccleshare, review of *Alfie, Where Are You?,* p. 20; November 19, 2005, Julia Eccleshare, review of *Mel-rose and Croc,* p. 20; December 17, 2005, Joanna Carey, interview with Chichester Clark, p. 20; May 5, 2007, Julia Eccleshare, review of *Eliza and the Moon-child,* p. 20.

Horn Book, March-April, 2002, Martha V. Parravano, re-view of *No More Kissing!,* p. 201; March-April, 2004, Martha V. Parravano, review of *Up in Heaven,* p. 169; September-October, 2003, Christine M. Heppermann, review of *What Shall We Do, Blue Kangaroo?,* p. 492; July-August, 2008, Robin L. Smith, review of *Mel-rose and Croc: An Adventure to Remember,* p. 432.

Independent (London, England), May 14, 1998. Sally Wil-liams, review of *More!*

Kirkus Reviews, April 15, 1989, review of *The Story of Horrible Hilda and Henry,* p. 622; April 15, 1991, re-view of *I Never Saw a Purple Cow and Other Non-*

sense Rhymes; September 15, 1997, review of *Little Miss Muffet's Count-Along Surprise,* p. 1454; December 15, 2001, review of *No More Kissing!,* p. 1755; February 14, 2004, review of *Up in Heaven,* p. 175; January 1, 2005, review of *No More Teasing!,* p. 50; June 1, 2002, review of *It Was You, Blue Kangaroo!,* p. 802; January 1, 2006, review of *Will and Squill,* p. 38; October 1, 2006, review of *The McElderry Book of Grimms' Fairy Tales,* p. 1022; November 1, 2006, review of *Melrose and Croc: A Christmas to Remember,* p. 1127; June 15, 2008, review of *Eliza and the Moonchild;* September 1, 2008, review of *Hansel and Gretel.*

Ladybug, March, 1997, "Meet the Artist: Emma Chichester Clark," p. 39.

Publishers Weekly, January 6, 1992, review of *Lunch with Aunt Augusta,* p. 65; January 20, 2003, review of *Follow the Leader!,* p. 80; September 25, 2006, review of *Melrose and Croc: A Christmas to Remember,* p. 70.

San Francisco Chronicle, November 26, 2006, Regan McMahon, review of *Melrose and Croc: A Christmas to Remember,* p. M3.

School Librarian, August, 1987, Sarah Reed, review of *Little Miss Muffet Counts to Ten,* p. 130; May, 1991, Joan Nellist, review of *I Never Saw a Purple Cow and Other Nonsense Rhymes,* pp. 681-682; autumn, 1998, Jane Doonan, review of *More!,* p. 129.

School Library Journal, April, 1999, review of *I Love You, Blue Kangaroo!;* January, 2002, Linda M. Kenton, review of *No More Kissing!,* p. 96; May, 2003, Rosalyn Pierini, review of *Follow the Leader!,* p. 110; July, 2003, Lisa Dennis, review of *What Shall We Do, Blue Kangaroo?,* p. 88; November, 2003, Olga R. Kuharets, review of *Mimi's Book of Counting,* p. 90; March, 2004, Rosalyn Pierini, review of *Up in Heaven,* p. 155; June, 2005, Margaret Bush, review of *The McElderry Book of Aesop's Fables,* p. 140; October, 2006, Eva Mitnick, review of *Melrose and Croc: A Christmas to Remember,* p. 95; November, 2006, Robin L. Gibson, review of *The McElderry Book of Grimms' Fairy Tales,* p. 123; May, 2007, Jessica Lamarre, review of *Piper,* p. 90; June, 2008, Kim T. Ha, review of *Eliza and the Moonchild,* p. 98; August, 2008, Catherine Threadgill, review of *Melrose and Croc: An Adventure to Remember,* p. 84; January, 2009, Susan Scheps, review of *Hansel and Gretel,* p. 93.

Sunday Times (London, England), April 13, 2008, Nicolette Jones, review of *Minty and Tink,* p. 48.

Times Educational Supplement, November 6, 1987, Jenny Marshall, "Storybook Worlds," p. 27; February 14, 1992, Andrew Davies, "Having a Good Time," p. 27; December 11, 1998, William Feaver, "Leap of Imagination," p. 37.

Times Literary Supplement, December 4, 1989, Lesley Chamberlain, "Igniting the Imagination," p. 1361.

ONLINE

Andersen Press Web site, http://www.andersenpress.co.uk/ (December 2, 2004).

British Council Contemporary Writers Web site, http://www.contemporarywriters.com/ (December 15, 2009), "Emma Chichester Clark."*

CLAYTON, Elaine 1961-

Personal

Born September 17, 1961, in TX; daughter of Robert (a doctor) and Bonnie (a homemaker) Clayton; married Simon Boughton (a publisher), September 14, 1996. *Education:* Atlanta College of Art, B.F.A., 1984; attended Georgia State University, 1986, School of Visual Arts, New York City, M.F.A., 1996. *Hobbies and other interests:* "Riding horses, western and English style, in-line skating, playing with my dog Ah Wing, traveling, learning to speak Italian."

Addresses

Home and office—65 Sussex St., Jersey City, NJ 07302. *Agent*—William Reiss, John Hawkins and Associates, Inc., 71 W. 23rd St., Ste. 1600, New York, NY 10010.

Career

Illustrator, fine-art painter, and author. Cesar Chavez Migrant Camp, Mobile, AL, head start teacher, 1980; High Museum of Art, Atlanta, GA, gallery instructor, 1980-85; St. Anthony's Summer Camp, Atlanta, art instructor, 1983; Woodruff Memorial Arts Center Gallery, Atlanta, gallery manager, 1984; Paideia School, Atlanta, assistant teacher and artist-in-residence, 1985-89; Mary Lin Elementary School, Atlanta, artist-in-residence, 1985; Atrium School, Watertown, MA, elementary teacher, 1990-94. Volunteer with Glen Mary Missionary; presenter at schools. *Exhibitions:* Work included in exhibitions at Woodruff Memorial Arts Center, Atlanta, GA; Visual Club, New York, NY; Art Directors Club, New York, NY; New York Women's Foundation, New York, NY; and Arsenal Center for the Arts, Watertown, MA.

Writings

SELF-ILLUSTRATED

Pup in School, Crown (New York, NY), 1993.
Ella's Trip to the Museum, Crown (New York, NY), 1996.
The Yeoman's Daring Daughter and the Princes in the Tower, Crown (New York, NY), 1999.
A Blue Ribbon for Sugar, Roaring Brook Press (New Milford, CT), 2006.

ILLUSTRATOR

Al Carusone, *The Boy with Dinosaur Hands,* Clarion (New York, NY), 1998.
Stephanie Greene, *Show and Tell,* Clarion (New York, NY), 1998.
April Halprin Wayland, *Girl Coming in for a Landing,* Knopf (New York, NY), 2002.
Tracie Vaughn Zimmer, *42 Miles,* Clarion Books (New York, NY), 2008.

Elaine Clayton (Reproduced by permission.)

ILLUSTRATOR; "HAMLET CHRONICLES" SERIES

Gregory Maguire, *Six Haunted Hairdos,* Clarion (New York, NY), 1997.

Gregory Maguire, *Five Alien Elves,* Clarion (New York, NY), 1998.

Gregory Maguire, *Four Stupid Cupids,* Clarion (New York, NY), 2000.

Gregory Maguire, *Three Rotten Eggs,* Clarion (New York, NY), 2002.

Gregory Maguire, *A Couple of April Fools,* Clarion (New York, NY), 2004.

Gregory Maguire, *One Final Firecracker,* Clarion (New York, NY), 2005.

OTHER

Editor, "Puzzle Gallery Books," Crown, 1997. Contributor of reviews and illustrations to magazines and newspapers, including *Drawing, Raygun, Curio, Drawing Instructor, Southline,* and *New York Times.*

Sidelights

Ellen Clayton is an author and illustrator whose projects for children include creating the artwork for Gregory Maguire's "Hamlet Chronicles" chapter-book series. However, Clayton is also the author of several self-illustrated books for younger readers, including *Pup in School, Ella's Trip to the Museum, The Yeoman's Daring Daughter and the Princes in the Tower,* and *A Blue Ribbon for Sugar.*

Clayton's first self-authored book, *Pup in School,* tells a simple story about a puppy that finds the courage to stand up to class bully Rodney-dog after watching a film about a brave cow-dog. In *Ella's Trip to the Museum* Clayton switches to a human protagonist. When Ella and her class go to an art museum, the young girl is carried away by the exhibits. In her imagination, she dances with painted ballerinas and a sculpted Roman goddess, much to the displeasure of the docent and a security guard, but by the end of the book, even Ella's more well-behaved classmates have joined in the fun. The students' "blissed-out expressions show without a doubt that fine art should transport its viewers," concluded a *Publishers Weekly* reviewer.

The Yeoman's Daring Daughter and the Princes in the Tower was inspired by an actual, historical mystery: what happened to the English princes Edward and Richard? In 1483 the boys' uncle, Richard, duke of Gloucester, had them imprisoned in the Tower of London so that he himself could be crowned king, and the two were never seen nor heard from again. Historians generally assume that Richard III had the princes murdered, but Clayton imagines another possible outcome. In her telling of the story, a young commoner named Jane, the daughter of one of the Tower's guards, works for the palace as a seamstress. One of Jane's duties is making robes for royal coronations, and she begins to worry about the fate of princes Edward and Richard when she overhears the duke of Gloucester plotting against them and realizes that the coronation robes have been ordered in an adult's rather than child's size. When the young woman attempts to communicate with the boys, Clayton's tale is spun through the letters passed between Jane and the young captives. "The epistolary conceit works well," commented a *Publishers Weekly* reviewer, "hinting at daily activity in the Tower as well as palace intrigue." Clayton's paintings for the book were also praised by *Booklist* contributor GraceAnne A. DeCandido, who noted that "the view of the Tower and surroundings" in *The Yeoman's Daring Daughter and the Princes in the Tower* "is properly looming and impressive."

In *A Blue Ribbon for Sugar* Clayton introduces a young girl named Bonnie, who dreams of being a cowgirl and plays out her fantasy on her wooden hobbyhorse, Sugar. With so much riding, Sugar eventually breaks, leaving Bonnie brokenhearted. Fortunately, the girl's father is there to help her achieve her dream, and soon she is sitting atop a real pony and learning basic cowgirl skills. By including basic equestrian skills in her simple story, Clayton attracts horse-loving readers, who will "find the story to be a sweet treat," according to *Booklist* critic Julie Cummins. In *School Library Journal,* Carol Schene praised the "pleasant watercolor illustrations" that Clayton creates to bring to life *A Blue Ribbon for Sugar,* the critic adding that they "accurately portray" equestrian equipment and methods.

Geared for middle-grade readers, Maguire's popular "Hamlet Chronicles" books follow a fifth-grade class as they deal with the usual school-age travails of friend-

Clayton's illustration projects include **42 Miles,** *a picture book by Tracie Vaughn Zimmer.* (Illustration copyright © 2008 by Elaine Clayton. Reprinted by permission of Clarion Books, an imprint of Houghton Mifflin Harcourt Publishing Company. All rights reserved.)

ship and family issues, as well as less-common problems such as four newly released cupids run amok and genetically engineered chicks. In addition to illustrating this saga, Clayton also provides illustrations for books by other writers, such as April Halprin Wayland's novel-in-poems, *Girl Coming in for a Landing.* The poems, written in the first person, follow the life of an early-teenage girl as she navigates such adolescent challenges as shaving her legs for the first time, crushes on boys, and her first kiss. Clayton's "eclectic collage artwork," as Christine M. Heppermann described it in *Horn Book,* "add[s] to the volume's personalized feel," and *School Library Journal* contributor Lauralyn Persson wrote that readers will "find the book's . . . sophisticated mixed-media illustrations on most pages appealing." In a review of *42 Miles,* a verse novel by Tracie Vaughn Zimmer that also features Clayton's artwork, *School Library Journal* critic Lee Bock concluded that the book's "mixed-media collage illustrations . . . reinforce the complicated and changing moods of the story."

Clayton once told *SATA:* "I grew up in a big family and learned the importance of lively conversation and storytelling. As I grew up, my private world was one involving characters I drew, whole families of people with stories I made up. Before and while studying art in college, I worked with children—never doing art without being at times surrounded by children to even out the intensity of painting and drawing, and never working with children without bringing my creative process (and theirs) to the forefront.

"Eventually, children asked that I put my stories on paper, not disposable marker boards or chalk boards where they disappear when story time is over. I had to do as they asked since, as a teacher, I expected stories from them on paper! This is when I began pursuing publication of my work, and I have loved the entire process. I make stories involving the same types of characters I made up as a child, always meeting new ones in real life along the way. I want more than anything to encourage children to delight in their view of the world and, through art and stories, change the world by showing us what they see."

Biographical and Critical Sources

PERIODICALS

Booklist, April 1, 1999, GraceAnne A. DeCandido, review of *The Yeoman's Daring Daughter and the Princes in the Tower,* p. 1429; April 1, 2002, Kay Weisman, review of *Three Rotten Eggs,* p. 1328; October 15, 2002, Gillian Engberg, review of *Girl Coming in for a Landing,* p. 400; June 1, 2006, Julie Cummins, review of *A Blue Ribbon for Sugar,* p. 80; April 1, 2008, Hazel Rochman, review of *42 Miles,* p. 43.

Horn Book, September-October, 2002, Christine M. Heppermann, review of *Girl Coming in for a Landing,* p. 584; April 1, 2004, review of *A Couple of April Fools,* p. 333.

Kirkus Reviews, March 1, 2002, review of *Three Rotten Eggs,* p. 339; June 15, 2002, review of *Girl Coming in for a Landing,* p. 889; April 1, 2008, review of *42 Miles.*

New York Times Book Review, May 19, 1996, review of *Ella's Trip to the Museum,* p. 28.

Publishers Weekly, June 28, 1993, review of *Pup in School,* p. 75; June 3, 1996, review of *Ella's Trip to the Museum,* p. 82; March 22, 1999, review of *The Yeoman's Daring Daughter and the Princes in the Tower,* p. 92; July 8, 2002, review of *Girl Coming in for a Landing,* p. 50.

School Library Journal, October, 1993, Kay McPherson, review of *Pup in School,* p. 97; June, 1996, p. 99; October, 2000, Eva Mitnick, review of *Four Stupid Cupids,* p. 164; August, 2002, Lauralyn Persson, review of *Girl Coming in for a Landing,* p. 220; May, 2006, Carol Schene, review of *A Blue Ribbon for Sugar,* p. 84; April, 2008, Lee Bock, review of *42 Miles,* p. 154.

ONLINE

Elaine Clayton Home Page, http://www.elaineclayton.com (December 15, 2009).*

D

DAVIS, Eleanor 1983(?)-

Personal

Born c. 1983, in Tucson, AZ; daughter of Edward Ellison Davis, Jr.; married Drew Weing (a cartoonist), April, 2009. *Education:* Savannah College of Art and Design, degree.

Addresses

Office—Little House Comics, P.O. Box 1926, Athens, GA 30603. *Agent*—Denis Kitchen, Kitchen, Lind & Associates, P.O. Box 2250, Amherst, MA 01004. *E-mail*—eleanor@doing-fine.com.

Career

Writer, illustrator, and cartoonist. Little House Comics, cofounder and publisher with Drew Weing.

Awards, Honors

Russ Manning Promising Newcomer Award, Eisner Awards, Bank Street College of Education Best Children's Book designation, and Theodor Seuss Geisel Award Honor Book designation, all 2009, all for *Stinky*.

Writings

SELF-ILLUSTRATED

Stinky, RAW Junior (New York, NY), 2008.
The Secret Science Alliance and the Copycat Crook (graphic novel), inked by Drew Weing, Bloomsbury (New York, NY), 2009.

Contributor to periodicals, including *Hoax, Little Moments, Scheherazade, Fluke* and *Print.* Creator of comics, including "The Beast Mother" and (with Drew Weing) "Bugbear."

Sidelights

An illustrator and cartoonist based in Athens, Georgia, Eleanor Davis grew up reading comics. Unlike many children, her habit was encouraged by her parents, both of whom loved comics as well, and she began producing original comics at age fourteen. Although she was unsure what direction her artistic talent would ultimately take her when she enrolled at the Savannah College of Art, Davis was given an opportunity that quickly decided her career path. In addition to creating comics for magazines and anthologies, she has also produced several award-winning children's books.

Davis was still in art school when she was approached by François Mouly, the publisher of Toon Books and editor, with cartoonist husband Art Speigelman, of the Little Lit Library. Mouly requested that Davis work with Toon Books, which publishes comics geared for beginning readers that combine innovative art with stories that are vetted by early-childhood educators. Davis met the request with *Stinky,* which was named a The-

Eleanor Davis pairs a simple story with animated cartoon art in her graphic-styled picturebook Stinky, *part of the Little Lit Library.* (Copyright © 2008 by RAW Junior, LLC/Toon Books. Reproduced by permission.)

odor Seuss Geisel Award honor book. Horned and spiky-haired Stinky is a purple, pickle-loving monster who lives in the swamp so he can avoid the creature he fears most: squeaky-clean human children. When a little boy enters the swamp and sets about building a tree-house, the monster first intends to scare the boy away, but while he watches he learns that he and the boy share many interests, including toads, slugs, mud, and other stinky stuff. In *School Library Journal*, Mari Ponhkhamsing wrote that Davis's "charming cartoon artwork" is "full of humorous details," and the monster "is endearing rather than scary." The author/illustrator pairs her comic drawings with a simple, repetitive text designed to appeal to beginning readers, added the critic. A *Kirkus Reviews* writer had praise for both story and art, writing that Davis's "agreeably distinct, faintly retro" cartoons pairs with a "winning story [that] carries itself on spunk."

Davis often collaborates with her husband, cartoonist Drew Weing. Her year-long work on her first graphic novel, *The Secret Science Alliance and the Copycat Crook,* was aided by Weing, who inked all Davis's drawings; the images were colored by Joey Weister and Michele Chidester. In *The Secret Science Alliance and the Copycat Crook* readers meet eleven-year-old nerd Julian Calendar, who finds two kindred spirits when he moves to a new middle school. Ben and Greta love science as much as Julian does, and the trio starts a club with a super-secret club house where they work on all their super-secret inventions, like the Stinkometer, glue-bombs, the Distract-a-Dad, and nightsneak goggles. When the three preteens learn of a plan to rob a local museum, they must put their inventions to the ultimate test in a graphic novel that "is packed full of detail" and moves "at a quick pace," according to *School Library Journal* contributor Carrie Rogers-Whitehead. "Davis's creativity is evident," added Rogers-Whitehead, citing the trio's imaginative inventions, while in *Booklist* Jesse Karp praised *The Secret Science Alliance and the Copycat Crook* for "celebrat[ing] . . . smarts and . . . delivering lessons as to what's really valuable in life." Karp anticipated further adventures of the SSA, praising Davis's ability to capture "the gee-whiz wonderment of Johnny Quest cartoons." Citing the "bounty of factlets slipped in for learning on the sly," a *Kirkus Reviews* writer dubbed *The Secret Science Alliance and the Copycat Crook* "a sure kid and teacher pleaser," and in *Publishers Weekly* a critic predicted that Davis's "very original story" combines with her "stunning" art to "enthrall young readers with its sense of discovery."

Biographical and Critical Sources

PERIODICALS

Booklist, September 1, 2008, Kat Kan, review of *Stinky,* p. 108; July 1, 2009, Jesse Karp, review of *The Secret Science Alliance and the Copycat Crook,* p. 63.
Kirkus Reviews, July 1, 2008, review of *Stinky;* July 15, 2009, review of *The Secret Science Alliance and the Copycat Crook.*

Publishers Weekly, May 5, 2008, Heidi MacDonald, "Comics Class of '08," p. 34; September 7, 2009, review of *The Secret Science Alliance and the Copycat Crook,* p. 35.
School Library Journal, September, 2008, Mari Pongkhamsing, review of *Stinky,* p. 214; September, 2009, Carrie Rogers-Whitehead, review of *The Secret Science Alliance and the Copycat Crook,* p. 187.

ONLINE

Eleanor Davis Home Page, http://www.doing-fine.com (December 15, 2009).
Eleanor Davis Web log, http://squinkyelo.livejournal.com (December 15, 2009).
Secret Science Alliance Web site, http://secretscience alliance.ding-fine.com/ (December 15, 2009).*

* * *

DELACRE, Lulu 1957-

Personal

Born December 20, 1957, in Hato Rey, PR; daughter of Georges (a philosophy professor) and Marta (a French professor) Delacre; married Arturo E. Betancourt (a physician), August 2, 1980; children: Alicia (deceased). *Education:* Attended University of Puerto Rico, 1976-77; École Supérieure d'Arts Graphiques, degree (first in class), 1980.

Addresses

Home and office—14721 Silverstone Dr., Silver Springs, MD 20105. *E-mail*—luludela@verizon.net.

Career

Children's book author and illustrator, 1980—. Juror for Society of Illustrators Original Art Show, 1997, and National Book Award, 2003. *Exhibitions:* Artwork exhibited at Muséo de Arte de Puerto Rico, San Juan; University of Puerto Rico Art Museum, Memorial Art Gallery, Rochester, NY; Keene State College Children's Literature Gallery; Museo de Arte de Ponce, Puerto Rico; University of Findlay Mazza Museum; Kerlan Collection, University of Minnesota; and elsewhere.

Member

Authors Guild, Children's Book Guild of Washington, DC, Society of Children's Book Writers and Illustrators.

Awards, Honors

American Bookseller Pick of the Lists designation, 1991, for *Peter Cottontail's Easter Book,* 1993, for *Vejigantes Masquerader,* and 1994 for *The Bossy Gallito; Américas* Book Award, and National Council of Teachers of English Notable Children's Book in Language Arts designation, both 1993, both for *Vejigantes Mas-*

querader; Notable Trade Book in the Field of Social Studies designation, Aesop Accolade listee, and New York Public Library Best Book for Reading and Sharing designation, all 1994, and Pura Belpré Honor designation, American Library Association (ALA), 1996, all for *The Bossy Gallito; Américas* Commended Title, 1996, for *Golden Tales: Myths, Legends, and Folktales from Latin America,* and 2000, for *Salsa Stories;* named Maryland Woman in the Arts, 1998; named Write from Maryland Author, 1999; Notable Book for a Global Society designation, and Outstanding International Books listee, both International Reading Association, and Notable Social Studies Trade Book for Young People designation, Children's Book Council, all 2000, and *Criticas* Best Books for 2002 listee, all for *Salsa Stories;* Pura Belpré Honor designation, 2006, for *Arrorró, mi niño; Bloomsbury Review* Editor Favorites designation, 2008, and Best Children's Books of the Year designation, Bank Street College of Education, 2009, both for *Alicia Afterimage;* Pura Belpré Honor designation, ALA Notable Book designation, Jane Addams Award Honor Book designation, *Américas* Honor Book designation, and Latino Book Awards Honorable Mention designation, all 2009, all for *The Storyteller's Candle* by Lucía González.

Writings

SELF-ILLUSTRATED

A.B.C. Rhymes, Little Simon (New York, NY), 1984.

Counting Rhymes, Little Simon (New York, NY), 1984.

Kitten Rhymes, Little Simon (New York, NY), 1984.

Lullabies, Little Simon (New York, NY), 1984.

Nathan and Nicholas Alexander, Scholastic, Inc. (New York, NY), 1986.

Nathan's Fishing Trip, Scholastic, Inc. (New York, NY), 1988.

Good Time with Baby, Grosset & Dunlap (New York, NY), 1989.

Time for School, Nathan!, Scholastic, Inc. (New York, NY), 1989.

Arroz con leche: Popular Songs and Rhymes from Latin America, translation by Elena Paz, Scholastic, Inc. (New York, NY), 1989.

Las navidades: Popular Christmas Songs from Latin America, translation by Elena Paz, Scholastic, (New York, NY), 1990.

Peter Cottontail's Easter Book, Scholastic, Inc. (New York, NY), 1991.

Nathan's Balloon Adventure, Scholastic, Inc. (New York, NY), 1991.

Vejigantes Masquerader, Scholastic, Inc. (New York, NY), 1993.

Golden Tales: Myths, Legends, and Folktales from Latin America, Scholastic, Inc. (New York, NY), 1996.

Salsa Stories, Scholastic, Inc. (New York, NY), 2000.

Rafi and Rosi, HarperCollins (New York, NY), 2003.

(Selector) *Arrorró mi niño: Latino Lullabies and Gentle Games,* musical arrangements by Cecilia Esquivel and Diana Sáez, Lee & Low (New York, NY), 2004.

Rafi and Rosi: Carnival!, HarperCollins (New York, NY), 2006.

ILLUSTRATOR

Hannah Kimball, *Maria and Mr. Feathers,* Follett (Chicago, IL), 1982.

Oretta Leigh, *Aloysius Sebastian Mozart Mouse,* Simon & Schuster (New York, NY), 1984.

Beatrix Potter, *The Tale of Peter Rabbit, and Other Stories,* J. Messner (New York, NY), 1985.

Kenneth Grahame, *The Wind in the Willows: The Open Road,* Little Simon (New York, NY), 1985.

Lucía González, reteller, *The Bossy Gallito,* Scholastic, Inc. (New York, NY), 1994.

Lucía González, reteller, *Señor Cat's Romance, and Other Favorite Stories from Latin America,* Scholastic, Inc. (New York, NY), 1997.

Carmen T. Bernier-Grand, *Shake It, Morena!, and Other Folklore from Puerto Rico,* Millbrook Press (Brookfield, CT), 2002.

Georgina Lázaro, *El flamboyán amarillo,* Lectorum Publications (New York, NY), 2004.

Lucía González, *The Storyteller's Candle/La velita de los cuentos,* Children's Book Press (New York, NY), 2008.

Contributor to periodicals, including *Sesame Street, World, Your Big Backyard, Nuestra Gente,* and *Scholastic Storyworks,* as well as to textbooks for Macmillan, Houghton Mifflin, Follett Publishing Co., Scott Foresman, Addison Wesley, and Rigby Elsevier.

OTHER

Alicia Afterimage (novel), Lee & Low (New York, NY), 2008.

Sidelights

Lulu Delacre began her career as an illustrator in 1980, shortly after graduating from art school, and quickly moved into writing original picture-book texts for young children with her 1986 work *Nathan and Nicholas Alexander.* While continuing to create artwork for authors such as Georgina Lázaro, Carmen T. Bernier-Grand, and Lucía González, Delacre has also explored her own Latina heritage in works such as *Golden Tales: Myths, Legends, and Folktales from Latin America, Arrorró mi niño: Latino Lullabies and Gentle Games,* and *Rafi and Rosi,* the last a picture book that depicts the day-to-day goings-on in the lives of two tree frogs in Delacre's text and characteristic pastel-toned pencil-and-watercolor images. "I delight in creating books that portray my own culture with authenticity in both words and pictures," Delacre noted on her home page. "And if painting the people and the places of Latin America true to their own beauty fosters respect; or if sharing some of their golden tales builds bridges, I want to keep on doing it."

Of Argentinian ancestry, Delacre was born in Puerto Rico, and had an idyllic childhood exploring the nearby beaches with her older sister Cecilia. The two sisters

Lulu Delacre's warm-toned pictures are featured in Lucia Gonzalez's picture book **The Storyteller's Candle.** (Children's Book Press, 2008. Illustration copyright © 2008 by Lulu Delacre. All rights reserved. Reproduced by permission.)

often were put in the care of their grandmother, and Delacre once recalled to *SATA* that the woman "set a space aside where each one of us had a big pile of drawings that we did while at her home. I liked to colour a lot and always rejoiced at the sight of the growing pile." Encouraging the girls' efforts, Delacre's grandmother never threw away any of their artwork, and when Delacre—who described herself as "a skinny, small, big-eared girl"—turned ten years old, her equally supportive parents enrolled her in drawing lessons.

By the time she was in high school, Delacre was certain that she wanted to become a commercial artist. After graduation she moved to Paris, France, where she studied photography, typography, design, and illustration at the École Supérieure d'Arts Graphiques and graduated at the top of her class. As she recalled to *SATA:* "One day, during my second year of studies in Paris, I went to see an exhibit at a small gallery near the school. It was an exhibit on the work of Maurice Sendak. When I

left the gallery, very much impressed, I suddenly realized that I wanted to become a good children's book illustrator; something I am still working at."

Golden Tales collects stories that Delacre recalls from her childhood in Puerto Rico. Some of these stories are drawn from native cultures while others concern the Spanish conquistadores or have even more-recent origins. Delacre also includes a map showing the areas referred to in the stories, as well as a guide to the pronunciation of Spanish and native-Indian terms for detail-oriented readers. Containing what *Booklist* reviewer Hazel Rochman described as "bright beautiful oil-wash illustrations," Delacre's *Arrorró mi niño* similarly collects fifteen lullabies, singing games, and other cradle songs that "reflect the diversity of the Latino experience." Praising *Golden Tales* as "impressively presented," *Booklist* contributor Annie Ayers commended Delacre for assembling an anthology sure to be "welcomed by all who have . . . sought in vain for such an introductory treasury."

Delacre's self-illustrated beginning readers *Rafi and Rosi* and *Rafi and Rosi: Carnival!* focus on brother and sister *coquíes* (tree frogs) who live in Ponce, Puerto Rico, where their adventures help introduce readers to the wildlife and culture of the region. Among the short vignettes Delacre illustrates with her colorful cartoon art are Rafi's efforts to trick little sister Rosi with a simple magic trick and the frog children's search for a missing pet *cobrito* or hermit crab. The three chapters of *Rafi and Rosi: Carnival!* follow Rosi as she hopes to be crowned Carnival Queen during a parade to celebrate the holiday. When Rafi makes a scary mask for the occasion, he frightens his little frog sister, and must then seek her out and reassure her. A *Kirkus Reviews* writer praised *Rafi and Rosi* as a collection of "sweet tales, with an unusual setting," and in *School Library Journal* Marilyn Taniguchi had special praise for the author/illustrator's "brightly colored cartoon illustration," which "add detail and a light touch" to her book. In *Booklist* Ilene Cooper praised Delacre for including Spanish terms within her text and cited the "chance to learn about a new celebration" as one of the "draws" of *Rafi and Rosi: Carnival!* A *Kirkus Reviews* writer noted of the same book that "Delacre affectionately depicts the . . . love" between brother and sister in her text and her "appealing watercolor illustrations."

Delacre's contributions to illustrated children's literature continue to be significant. As Maeve Visser Knoth noted in a *Horn Book* review of her work illustrating González' *Señor Cat's Romance, and Other Favorite Stories from Latin America*, Delacre's "vivid, sprightly paintings" contain the "many regional details" that strengthen the book's multicultural appeal. Another collaboration with González, *The Storyteller's Candle*, marked Delacre's third Pura Belpré honor. The book, which tells the story of Pura Belpré herself, describes how the woman won young children to reading through her colorful storytelling and dedicated efforts as New York City's first Puerto Rican librarian. In her illustrations, Delacre creates multimedia images that include layers of thin oil paint in sepia tones, studded with torn pieces of the *New York Times* that provide "hits of the larger world" in their decipherable text, according to *School Library Journal* contributor Mary Jean Smith. The book's "glowing oil-and-collage artwork" captures the move from past to present by transitioning from nostalgic sepia tones to clear, brilliant color, effectively "blend[ing] . . . the two cultures in a way that enriches both," observed Rochman.

Delacre's first novel, *Alicia Afterimage*, was inspired by a personal tragedy: the death of her sixteen-year-old daughter Alicia in an automobile accident. Written while Delacre was attempting to come to terms with this unbearable loss, the book collects the thoughts and words of her daughter's friends and family, who in third-person narratives recall their memories of the girl while also expressing their anger, sadness, and bewilderment at life. The girl's friends "express their grief realistically and without platitudes," noted a *Publishers Weekly*

critic, and in *School Library Journal* Suzanne Gordon remarked on Delacre's "faint line sketches," which "appear like shadows beneath the text." In *Booklist* Rochman noted the value of Delacre's novel to others who are dealing with loss, writing that "its messages about healing" make *Alicia Afterimage* "an excellent title for grief counseling." "I believe that if this book helps bring some solace to others who must endure grief," Delacre commented, "it will have achieved its goal."

Now living in the United States, Delacre has visited schools across the country and has also toured overseas. "I believe childhood should be a wonderful stage in a person's life," she once told *SATA,* "and if my drawings add a little happiness in a child's day, I consider my life fulfilled." Delacre continues to create books for children, "out of love and the conviction that they are sorely needed," she more recently added. "I've measured their successes in the proud smiles of Latino children and the heartfelt letters I've received from many teens."

Biographical and Critical Sources

PERIODICALS

Booklist, May 15, 1994, Ilene Cooper, review of *The Bossy Gallito*, p. 1680; December 15, 1996, Annie Ayers, review of *Golden Tales: Myths, Legends, and Folktales from Latin America*, p. 722; February 1, 1997, Karen Morgan, review of *Señor Cat's Romance, and Other Favorite Stories from Latin America*, p. 943; May 1, 2000, Gillian Engberg, review of *Salsa Stories*, p. 1665; July, 2004, Hazel Rochman, review of *Arrorró mi niño: Latino Lullabies and Gentle Games*, p. 1846; March 1, 2006, Ilene Cooper, review of *Rafi and Rosi: Carnival!*, p. 99; March 15, 2008, Hazel Rochman, review of *The Storyteller's Candle/La velita de los cuentos*, p. 57; December 15, 2008, Hazel Rochman, review of *Alicia Afterimage*, p. 38.

Horn Book, September-October, 1994, Maeve Visser Knoth, review of *The Bossy Gallito: A Traditional Cuban Folk Tale*, p. 602; March-April, 1997, Maeve Visser Knoth, review of *Señor Cat's Romance, and Other Favorite Stories from Latin America*, p. 207; July-August, 2004, Tim Wadham, review of *Arrorró mi niño*, p. 463.

Kirkus Reviews, March 15, 2002, review of *Shake It, Morena!, and Other Folklore from Puerto Rico*, p. 406; January 1, 2004, review of *Rafi and Rosi*, p. 35; February 15, 2006, review of *Rafi and Rosi: Carnival!*, p. 181; April 1, 2008, review of *The Storyteller's Candle;* August 1, 2008, review of *Alicia Afterimage*.

Publishers Weekly, January 11, 1993, review of *Vejigantes Masquerader*, p. 63; January 6, 1997, review of *Señor Cat's Romance, and Other Favorite Stories from Latin America*, p. 73; March 20, 2000, review of *Salsa Stories*, p. 94; April 7, 2008, review of *The Storyteller's Candle*, p. 59; September 29, 2008, review of *Alicia Afterimage*, p. 83.

School Library Journal, March, 2000, Ann Welton, review of *Salsa Stories,* p. 237; March, 2004, Marilyn Taniguchi, review of *Rafi and Rosi,* p. 156; April, 2004, Ann Welton, review of *Arrorró, mi niño,* p. 146; December, 2004, Ginny Gustin, review of *Arroz con leche: Popular Songs and Rhymes from Latin America,* p. 59; April, 2006, Elaine Lesh Morgan, review of *Rafi and Rosi: Carnival!,* p. 99; April, 2008, Mary Jean Smith, review of *The Storyteller's Candle,* p. 108; November, 2008, Suzanne Gordon, review of *Alicia Afterimage,* p. 118.

ONLINE

Lulu Delacre Home Page, http://www.luludelacre.com (December 15, 2009).

*   *   *

DONOFRIO, Beverly 1950-

Personal

Born 1950; father a police officer, mother a factory worker; married (divorced); children: Jason. *Education:* Wesleyan University, B.A., 1978; Columbia University, M.A., 1983. *Religion:* Roman Catholic.

Addresses

Home—Crestone, CO. *E-mail*—bevdono@yahoo.com.

Career

Writer and memoirist. Wilkes University, instructor in low-residency M.F.A. program; San Miguel Workshops, San Miguel de Allende, Mexico, founder; commentator on National Public Radio; coproducer of film adaptation of *Riding in Cars with Boys,* 2001.

Writings

FOR CHILDREN

Mary and the Mouse, the Mouse and Mary, illustrated by Barbara McClintock, Schwartz & Wade (New York, NY), 2007.
Thank You, Lucky Stars, Schwartz & Wade (New York, NY), 2008.

FOR YOUNG ADULTS

Riding in Cars with Boys: Confessions of a Bad Girl Who Makes Good (memoir), Morrow (New York, NY), 1990.

OTHER

(With Rosalie Bonanno) *Mafia Marriage: My Story,* Morrow (New York, NY), 1990.

Looking for Mary; or, The Blessed Mother and Me (memoir), Viking Compass (New York, NY), 2000.

Contributor to periodicals, including *Village Voice, New York Times, Washington Post, Los Angeles Times, Allure, Cosmopolitan, Marie Claire, Mademoiselle, Spirituality and Health,* and *O* magazine. Also contributor of essays to *National Public Radio.*

Author's work has been translated into seventeen languages.

Adaptations

Riding in Cars with Boys was adapted as an audiobook by Recorded Books (Prince Frederick, MD). It was also adapted by Morgan Ward as a 2001 film directed by Penny Marshall and starring Drew Barrymore, Steve Zahn, and Britanny Murphy. *Looking for Mary* was adapted as an audiobook by Recorded Books.

Sidelights

While Beverly Donofrio has written in a range of genres, she is perhaps best known as the author of *Riding in Cars with Boys: Confessions of a Bad Girl Who Makes Good,* a memoir that was also adapted as a film starring Drew Barrymore. Turning to younger readers, Donofrio has also produced several picture books, among them *Looking for Mary; or, The Blessed Mother and Me* and the elementary-grade novel *Thank You, Lucky Stars.*

Raised in Wallingford, Connecticut, Donofrio was the daughter of a police officer and her mother worked in a factory. She was an imaginative child who dreamed of becoming an actress or a princess when she grew up. In reality, however, Donofrio had a wild streak, and by the time she reached high school she had earned a reputation as a bad girl. Pregnant at age seventeen, she married the child's father, a high-school dropout who soon developed a drug habit. The family moved into the housing project nearby her parents' home, but within two years Donofrio was divorced and trying to support her son on her own, relying on welfare to survive. Her situation went from bad to worse when she was arrested along with several friends who were dealing drugs out of her home. Depressed and suicidal, she sought help instead, determined to pull herself out of this negative cycle. Ultimately, Donofrio turned her life around: she graduated from Wesleyan University in 1978, and completing her master's degree at Columbia University. Her transition from wild child to self-sufficient and educated woman is the subject of *Riding in Cars with Boys,* which *People* critic Leah Rozen called an "affecting, direct memoir."

Looking for Mary is a very different type of memoir and draws on Donofrio's hobby of collecting statues and other images of the Virgin Mary at yard sales and secondhand stores. Over the years, her collection grew and eventually Donofrio's home was filled with this

quirky collection. One piece in particular, a picture of Mary that hung in her bathroom, caused the writer to view her collection in a new light. This print image of Mary was reflected in the mirror when Donofrio stood at the sink. One day, when she was washing her hands, she glanced up at her reflection and Mary's smiling, kind visage appeared just next to her own. This juxtaposition profoundly affected Donofrio, a lapsed Catholic, and inspired her to reinvestigate her religion and, ultimately, to forge a strong religious connection to Mary and everything she represented. The writer began attending mass every Sunday and also traveling to places around the world in order to investigate sightings and visions of the Virgin Mary.

Donofrio's investigations allowed her to meet a wide range of people, and she transformed her adventures into a documentary performed on National Public Radio. The documentary led to *Looking for Mary,* a book that recounts a journey that was both physical and spiritual. John-Leonard Berg, in a review for *Library Journal,* described Donofrio's memoir as "deeply personal and wonderfully written," adding that it "invites the reader to confront skeptical attitudes about religion."

Cover of Beverly Donofrio's young-adult novel Thank You, Lucky Stars, *featuring artwork by Rachael Cole.* (Illustration © 2008 by Rachael Cole. Reproduced by permission of Schwartz & Wade Books, an imprint of Random House Children's Books.)

Kathy O'Connell, in a review of *Looking for Mary* for *America,* commented of the author "that she is often heart-wrenchingly open to what can happen when she makes her pilgrimage," and *Booklist* critic Margaret Flanagan wrote that Donofrio "paints a full-bodied portrait of her inner struggle to achieve grace."

With *Mary and the Mouse, the Mouse and Mary,* her first book for younger children, Donofrio tackles a very different type of writing. Illustrated by Barbara McClintock, the book introduces readers to a little girl who likes to wear skirts that bounce when she walks. Mary lives with her parents and siblings in an old house, and in the house's walls lives a little mouse who also has parents and siblings. Mary's parents warn their daughter to be wary of the mice, and the little mouse is warned to beware of humans. Despite these warnings, Mary and the mouseling become secret friends, and this friendship ultimately reaches into subsequent generations of both girl and mouse. A reviewer for *Publishers Weekly* remarked that "Donofrio and McClintock give exquisite attention to the girl's and mouse's parallel lives, emphasizing cross-generational connections and shared secrets."

Called a "conventional yet compellingly realistic story," *Thank You, Lucky Stars* captures the ups and down of life as a fifth grader. In Donofrio's novel, Ally and Betsy have always been friends, but in fifth grade they go their separate ways. Ally finds a new friend in Tina, a transfer student who has an upbeat but sometimes strange personality that attracts the teasing of her classmates. Betsy proves to be a pragmatist; when her clique requires someone with dancing ability to help with their act for the upcoming talent show, she attempts to rekindle her friendship with Ally. Torn between her new friend and her old friend, Ally must resolve a dilemma that is common to many girls her age. Calling the free-spirited Tina an "engaging" character, Susan Dove Lempke added in *Horn Book* that "Ally's friendship drama rings true" in *Thank You, Lucky Stars,* while a *Publishers Weekly* contributor wrote that in Ally Donofrio creates a believable "classreject personality" in which the girl's "manner and style . . . come across as immature."

Biographical and Critical Sources

BOOKS

Donofrio, Beverly, *Riding in Cars with Boys: Confessions of a Bad Girl Who Makes Good* (memoir), Morrow (New York, NY), 1990.

Donofrio, Beverly, *Looking for Mary: or, The Blessed Mother and Me* (memoir), Viking Compass (New York, NY), 2000.

PERIODICALS

America, December 16, 2000, Kathy O'Connell, review of *Looking for Mary,* p. 16.

Booklist, April 15, 1992, review of *Riding in Cars with Boys,* p. 1518; August 1, 2000, Margaret Flanagan, review of *Looking for Mary,* p. 2079; August 1, 2007, Carolyn Phelan, review of *Mary and the Mouse, the Mouse and Mary,* p. 84; January 1, 2008, Kathleen Isaacs, review of *Thank You, Lucky Stars,* p. 84.

Bulletin of the Center for Children's Books, January 1, 2008, Deborah Stevenson, review of *Thank You, Lucky Stars,* p. 207.

Entertainment Weekly, August 17, 2001, review of *Looking for Mary,* p. 65.

Glamour, August 1, 1990, Laura Mathews, review of *Riding in Cars with Boys,* p. 160.

Horn Book, May 1, 2008, Susan Dove Lempke, review of *Thank You, Lucky Stars,* p. 310.

Kirkus Reviews, July 15, 2007, review of *Mary and the Mouse, the Mouse and Mary;* December 15, 2007, review of *Thank You, Lucky Stars.*

Library Journal, July 1, 1990, Rosellen Brewer, review of *Riding in Cars with Boys,* p. 104; December 1, 1990, Gregor A. Peston, review of *Mafia Marriage: My Story,* p. 140; September 1, 2000, John-Leonard Berg, review of *Looking for Mary,* p. 215.

Los Angeles Times, October 19, 2001, interview with Donofrio, p. 16.

Mademoiselle, August 1, 1990, Anne Lamott, review of *Riding in Cars with Boys,* p. 108.

National Catholic Reporter, June 15, 2001, Teresa Malcolm, review of *Looking for Mary,* p. 16.

New York Times Book Review, August 13, 2000, review of *Looking for Mary,* p. 9.

O, April 1, 2004, "A Roof of One's Own," p. 189.

People, October 15, 1990, Leah Rozen, review of *Riding in Cars with Boys,* p. 24.

Publishers Weekly, June 22, 1990, Genevieve Stuttaford, review of *Riding in Cars with Boys,* p. 40; December 20, 1991, review of *Riding in Cars with Boys,* p. 76; July 24, 2000, review of *Looking for Mary,* p. 90; July 30, 2007, review of *Mary and the Mouse, the Mouse and Mary,* p. 81; January 28, 2008, review of *Thank You, Lucky Stars,* p. 68.

School Library Journal, September 1, 2007, Catherine Threadgill, review of *Mary and the Mouse, the Mouse and Mary,* p. 162; May, 2008, Laura Lutz, review of *Thank You, Lucky Stars,* p. 122.

Spectator, December 8, 2001, Mark Steyn, review of *Riding in Cars with Boys,* p. 64.

Tribune Books (Chicago, IL), August 5, 1990, review of *Riding in Cars with Boys,* p. 5; January 5, 1992, review of *Riding in Cars with Boys,* p. 2; October 6, 2007, Mary Harris Russell, review of *Mary and the Mouse, the Mouse and Mary,* p. 10.

U.S. Catholic, November 1, 2004, review of *Looking for Mary,* p. 6.

Wall Street Journal, October 19, 2001, review of *Riding in Cars with Boys,* p. 11.

ONLINE

Beverly Donofrio Home Page, http://www.beverlydono frio.com (December 15, 2009).

Curled Up with a Good Kid's Book Web site, http://www. curledupkids.com/ (August 13, 2008), review of *Thank You, Lucky Stars.*

*　　*　　*

DRUMMOND, Allan 1957-

Personal

Born 1957, in England; immigrated to United States. *Education:* London College of Printing, B.A.; Royal College of Art, M.A.

Addresses

Home—Savannah, GA. *Office*—Savannah College of Art and Design, P.O. Box 3146, Savannah, GA 31402-3146. *E-mail*—mail@allandrummond.com.

Career

Writer and illustrator. Savannah College of Art and Design, Savannah, GA, chair of illustration department. Former journalist for *East Anglian Daily Times.*

Awards, Honors

American Booksellers Association Pick of the Lists citation, 1992, for *The Willow Pattern Story.*

Writings

SELF-ILLUSTRATED

The Willow Pattern Story, North-South (New York, NY), 1992.
(Adapter) Herman Melville, *Moby Dick,* Farrar, Straus & Giroux (New York, NY), 1997.
Casey Jones, Frances Foster (New York, NY), 2001.
Liberty, Frances Foster (New York, NY), 2002.
The Flyers, Farrar, Straus & Giroux (New York, NY), 2003.
Tin Lizzie, Farrar, Straus & Giroux (New York, NY), 2008.

ILLUSTRATOR

Poems of Friendship: A Treasury of Verse, Running Press (Philadelphia, PA), 1993.
David Borgenicht, compiler, *A Treasury of Children's Poetry,* Running Press (Philadelphia, PA), 1994.
Edward Le Joly and Jaya Chaliha, *Stories Told by Mother Teresa,* Element, 2000.
Louise Borden, *The Journey That Saved Curious George: The True Wartime Escape of Margaret and H.A. Rey,* Houghton Mifflin (Boston, MA), 2005.

Contributor to periodicals, including *New Yorker, Time,* and London *Observer.*

Sidelights

Illustrator and writer Allan Drummond began his career as a journalist before attending the London College of Printing, where he earned his B.A., and then went on to earn his M.A. at the Royal College of Art. Drummond's training in both writing and illustrating led to his first book for children, *The Willow Pattern Story,* which has remained in publication since its original publication in 1992.

Based on a story Drummond heard while growing up in Essex, England, *The Willow Pattern Story* tells the legend behind the popular blue-and-white pattern found on chinaware. Although the pattern was developed in England, the story behind it, according to Drummond's tale, is based on two Chinese lovers and their transformation into doves. In an interview, Drummond noted that the image is "so well-known that people don't even bother to look at it. But children do—children will always ask, What's going on in this picture? As an adult you just say, 'Well, it's the willow pattern.'"

Drummond was convinced by his editor to add color to the illustrations, rather than using the traditional blue and white of the china pattern. A reviewer for the *New York Times* praised the author/illustrator's "handsome, stylized illustrations" and a *Publishers Weekly* contributor wrote of *The Willow Pattern Story* that Drummond's "ingenious use of uncommon source material may inspire readers to watch for hidden stories in everyday objects."

Based on an American folk story, Drummond's self-illustrated *Casey Jones* retells the traditional story of the heroic railroad engineer and weaves into the tale in-

Allan Drummond pairs his entertaining picture-book art with a lighthearted story in **Tin Lizzie.** (Illustration © 2008 by Allan Drummond. All rights reserved. Reproduced by permission of Frances Foster Books, a division of Farrar, Straus & Giroux.)

formation regarding the development of the U.S. railroad system during the 1800s. "Soft watercolor illustrations capture the feeling of movement and adventure that railroad travel inspired," wrote Marta Segal in her *Booklist* review of the book, and a *Publishers Weekly* contributor noted that Drummond's "pen-and-ink images washed with invigorating swathes of color echo the rhythms of the narrative." Commenting on the book's prose, Sheilah Kosco noted in *School Library Journal* that it "reads like a ballad."

Drummond mixes truth and legend in his story about the arrival of the Statue of Liberty in New York Harbor in *Liberty!* The story is told from the perspective of a young boy who has the job of letting the sculptor know when to remove the statue's veil. "Drummond takes a kernel of history—a boy chosen to signal the sculptor—and turns it into both a thoughtful lesson and a visual pageant," wrote GraceAnne A. DeCandido in *Booklist*, and Grace Oliff noted in *School Library Journal* that the author/illustrator "is meticulous regarding historical details." Praising the art in *Liberty!*, a *Publishers Weekly* contributor wrote that Drummond's "pen-and-wash illustrations [are] so lively [that] they seem to dance on the page."

The Wright brothers are the subject of another self-illustrated book, *The Flyers*. Told from the perspective of a neighborhood boy, Drummond's story features not only the work of the famous aviators, but also the dreams that the neighborhood children have of flying. Noting the many books written about the Wright brothers, Carolyn Phelan commented in *Booklist* that "few offer such a child-centered perspective of the men and their work." Maintaining that Drummond captures the excitement of his young characters in both his text and illustrations, a *Publishers Weekly* reviewer concluded that *The Flyers* "stands out for its ability to harness the imagination of youngest readers and make it soar."

Tin Lizzie celebrates the hundredth anniversary of the invention of Henry Ford's Model T. Young Eliza and her siblings love the wheels they own, from rollerblades to bicycles and skateboards, but they get a special treat when their grandfather takes them out in his hundred-year-old Model T. In addition to presenting a simple story about children riding with their grandfather, *Tin Lizzie* includes a discussion among the narrator and her siblings regarding the automobile's involvement in the problems facing the world, such as oil shortages, that "makes the current crisis understandable to young children and provides a jumping-off point for many important discussions," according to *Horn Book* critic Robin L. Smith. Gay Lynn Van Vleck commented in *School Library Journal* that "Drummond's spirited illustrations neatly depict vehicles both old and new," and Carolyn

Phelan wrote in *Booklist* that the book's "color-washed ink drawings are charming, . . . and the text is thought-provoking."

Along with his self-illustrated titles, Drummond has also provided artwork for books by other authors. His illustrations for *The Journey That Saved Curious George: The True Wartime Escape of Margaret and H.A. Rey* were called "spirited" and "brimming with action and details" by Phelan, and a *Kirkus Reviews* critic wrote that "Drummond's movement-filled watercolors evok[e] . . . but never imitat[e] . . . the work of his subjects." A contributor to *Publishers Weekly* similarly commented that the author/illustrator's work "display[s] a whimsy and energy appealingly reminiscent of the Reys' art, while still uniquely his own."

Biographical and Critical Sources

PERIODICALS

Booklist, March 15, 2000, Shelley Townsend-Hudson, review of *Stories Told by Mother Teresa,* p. 1384; February 15, 2001, Marta Segal, review of *Casey Jones,* p. 1140; March 15, 2002, GraceAnne A. DeCandido, review of *Liberty!,* p. 1256; October 1, 2003, Carolyn Phelan, review of *The Flyers,* p. 326; October 15, 2005, Carolyn Phelan, review of *The Journey That Saved Curious George: The True Wartime Escape of Margaret and H.A. Rey,* p. 45.
Horn Book, September-October, 2003, Betty Carter, review of *The Flyers,* p. 594.
Kirkus Reviews, April 1, 2002, review of *Liberty!,* p. 490; August 1, 2003, review of *The Flyers,* p. 1015.
New York Times Book Review, September 20, 1992, review of *The Willow Pattern Story*; May 19, 2002, Alexander Stille, review of *Liberty!,* p. 20.
Publishers Weekly, August 17, 1992, review of *The Willow Pattern Story,* p. 498; August 31, 1992, Amanda Smith, interview with Drummond, p. 40; January 31, 2000, review of *Stories Told by Mother Teresa,* p. 103; December 18, 2000, review of *Casey Jones,* p. 78; January 7, 2002, review of *Liberty!,* p. 64; August 25, 2003, review of *The Flyers,* p. 63.
School Library Journal, April, 2001, Sheilah Kosco, review of *Casey Jones,* p. 106; May, 2002, Grace Oliff, review of *Liberty!,* p. 111; August, 2003, Kathleen Kelly MacMillan, review of *Liberty!,* p. 64; October, 2003, Harriett Fargnoli, review of *The Flyers,* p. 118.

ONLINE

Allan Drummond Home Page, http://www.allandrummond.com (December 17, 2009).
Savannah College of Art and Design Web site, http://www.scad.edu/ (December 17, 2009), "Alan Drummond."*

E-F

ELLISON, Elizabeth Stow 1970-

Personal

Born 1970, in Oakland, CA. *Education:* University of California, Santa Cruz, B.A., 1993; California State University Fullerton, M.A., 2002. *Hobbies and other interests:* Collecting antique toasters, traveling, reading.

Addresses

E-mail—mailbox@elizabethstowellison.com.

Career

Teacher and writer. Teacher of eighth grade.

Awards, Honors

Best Books designation, Bank Street College of Education, 2009, for *Flight*.

Writings

Flight, Holiday House (New York, NY), 2008.

Elizabeth Stow Ellison (Cantrell Photography, Fullerton, CA. Reproduced by permission.)

Sidelights

In addition to teaching eighth grade, Elizabeth Stow Ellison is also the author of the middle-grade novel *Flight.* *Flight* is told from the perspective of Samantha, the twelve-year-old, youngest child of three. Samantha's oldest brother, Andy, is a star athlete who is currently in the running for being crowned his schools' Homecoming King, while middle child Evan is struggling with school. Evan excels at art, however, and he wishes to be free like the three owls he and Samantha see one night. Although the children's mother refuses to have Evan tested for learning disabilities, it eventually emerges that the boy cannot read, and neither can his mother. The final revelation of the truth behind the façade causes the family to confront the learning disabilities of both mother and son. As Ellison told *SATA,* "The message that I hope readers of all ages take away from reading my novel is that we all can take flight in our lives to accomplish the goals we set for ourselves."

Ellen Fader, reviewing Ellison's novel in *School Library Journal,* predicted that *Flight* will treat readers to "a sensitively told story about the toll that hidden illiteracy has on one family." A critic for *Kirkus Reviews* also praised the book, commenting that Ellison's "plot gradually builds and pulls readers into Sam and Evan's dilemma."

Cover of Ellison's elementary-grade novel **Flight**, *featuring artwork by* **Alan Garns.** (Holiday House, 2008. Illustration copyright © 2008 by Alan Garns. Reproduced by permission of the illustrator.)

Biographical and Critical Sources

PERIODICALS

Kirkus Reviews, September 15, 2008, review of *Flight.*
School Library Journal, November, 2008, Ellen Fader, review of *Flight,* p. 118.

ONLINE

Elizabeth Stow Ellison Home Page, http://www.elizabeth stowellison.com (December 16, 2009).

*   *   *

EMERSON, Kevin

Personal

Married. *Education:* Colby College, degree.

Addresses

Home—Seattle, WA.

Career

Writer, songwriter, and musician. Worked variously at a bank and as a camp counselor. Former elementary school teacher in Dorchester, MA.

Writings

Carlos Is Gonna Get It, Arthur A. Levine (New York, NY), 2008.

"OLIVER NOCTURNE" SERIES

The Vampire's Photograph, Scholastic, Inc. (New York, NY), 2008.
The Sunlight Slayings, Scholastic, Inc. (New York, NY), 2008.
Blood Ties, Scholastic, Inc. (New York, NY), 2008.
The Demon Hunter, Scholastic, Inc. (New York, NY), 2009.
The Eternal Tomb, Scholastic, Inc. (New York, NY), 2009.

Sidelights

A former elementary-school science teacher, Kevin Emerson got the idea for his "Oliver Nocturne" series by contemplating how vampires would actually live in

Cover of Kevin Emerson's middle-grade novel **Oliver Nocturne: The Demon Hunter,** *featuring artwork by Michael Frost.* (Scholastic, Inc., 2009. Cover photographs © by Michael Frost. Reproduced by permission of Scholastic, Inc.)

modern society. Imagining an unhappy middle-school vampire whose photograph is taken by a human girl, the author produced the tale of Oliver Nocturne, which begins in *The Vampire's Photograph* and continue in *The Sunlight Slayings, The Demon Hunter,* and *The Eternal Tomb.* Reviewing *The Vampire's Photograph* in *School Library Journal,* Elaine E. Knight wrote that the book's "details help to fully realize the idea of parallel human and undead worlds, and the cliff-hanger ending promises more excitement."

Emerson is also the author of the stand-alone novel *Carlos Is Gonna Get It,* a story based on some of the interactions Emerson witnessed among his students when he took them on a hiking trip. Told from the perspective of African-American seventh-grader Trina, the novel follows Trina's growing friendship with outcast Carlos, who is mocked by his classmates. When a prank on Carlos gets out of control, Trina must decide whether to be silent or come to the aid of her friend. Emerson "perfectly captures the classroom power struggles," wrote Hazel Rochman in her *Booklist* review of *Carlos Is Gonna Get It,* while a *Kirkus Reviews* contributor complimented Emerson for his "ability to write realistic dialogue." In *Publishers Weekly,* a critic called Trina's narration "authentic" and the dialogue in Emerson's novel effectively "lifelike."

Biographical and Critical Sources

PERIODICALS

Booklist, October 1, 2008, Hazel Rochman, review of *Carlos Is Gonna Get It,* p. 42.
Kirkus Reviews, September 15, 2008, review of *Carlos Is Gonna Get It.*
Kliatt, September, 2008, Paula Rohrlick, review of *Carlos Is Gonna Get It,* p. 10.
Publishers Weekly, October 20, 2008, review of *Carlos Is Gonna Get It,* p. 50.
School Library Journal, September, 2008, Elaine E. Knight, review of *The Vampire's Photograph,* p. 178; December, 2008, review of *Carlos Is Gonna Get It,* p. 122.

ONLINE

Kevin Emerson Home Page, http://www.kevinemerson.net (December 17, 2009).
Oliver Nocturne Web site, http://www.olivernocturne.com/ (December 17, 2009).*

* * *

FARR, Richard 1960-

Personal

Born 1960; married; two children. *Education:* Durham University, B.A.; Reading University, M.A.; Cornell University, Ph.D., c. 1984.

Richard Farr (Photograph by Kerry Fitz-Gerald. Reproduced by permission.)

Addresses

Home—Seattle, WA. *E-mail*—richard@richardfarr.net.

Career

Author and educator. Taught philosophy at Colgate University and University of Hawai'i; has worked as a speechwriter, journalist, copywriter, corporate trainer, voiceover artist, stay-at-home Dad, farm hand, and gas-station attendant.

Awards, Honors

Outstanding Science Trade Books for Students selection, National Science Teachers Association, and Washington State Book Award in young-adult category, both 2009, both for *Emperors of the Ice.*

Writings

Emperors of the Ice: A True Story of Disaster and Survival in the Antarctic, 1910-13, Farrar, Straus & Giroux (New York, NY), 2008.

Sidelights

Deliberately combining historical research with novelistic techniques, Richard Farr unearths a little-known exploit within a famous adventure in *Emperors of the Ice: A True Story of Disaster and Survival in the Antarctic, 1910-13.* "Fiction? Nonfiction? Historical fiction? Readers and reviewers seem unsure," Farr noted to *SATA.*

While explorer Robert Falcon Scott waited for the ideal time to make his ill-fated journey to the South Pole, three of Scott's men took the opportunity to harvest some eggs from an Emperor penguin colony. One of

the trio, young Oxford University graduate Apsley Cherry-Garrard, ultimately survived, and his experiences while on this trek have become familiar to readers interested in Arctic exploration. In *Emperors of the Ice* Farr describes how Cherry-Garrard and his companions struggled to endure the brutal conditions during both their egg-hunting trek and the larger voyage to the earth's southern-most point.

Emperors of the Ice is as much about the science that drove the expedition as it is about the expedition itself. *Horn Book* critic Martha V. Parravano called Farr's book "an enthralling tale" that is "told with marked immediacy, verve, and force of personality." In *School Library Journal* reviewer Kelly McGorray similarly found the work to be "engrossing" and "harrowing," going on to recommend the saga "to readers looking for an adventure story." Suggesting that *Emperors of the Ice* provides an "authoritative replacement" to more-dated books covering Scott's final expedition, *Booklist* contributor John Peters concluded that Farr's "deceptively light-toned account makes compelling reading."

Emperors of the Ice won the 2009 Washington State Book Award in the young-adult category. While welcoming the award, Farr noted to *SATA* that he has trouble with the "Young Adult" label. "Condescension is the carbon monoxide of children's publishing," he asserted. "Especially in nonfiction, if writing for young adults is really any good then adults should find it compelling too. If adults don't, then it probably isn't any good for young adults either." He described the appropriate age-range for *Emperors of the Ice* as "12 to 112."

Biographical and Critical Sources

PERIODICALS

Booklist, September 1, 2008, John Peters, review of *Emperors of the Ice: A True Story of Disaster and Survival in the Antarctic, 1910-13,* p. 89.

Horn Book, November-December, 2008, Martha V. Parravano, review of *Emperors of the Ice,* p. 701.

Kirkus Reviews, September 15, 2008, review of *Emperors of the Ice.*

Kliatt, September, 2008, Janis Flint-Ferguson, review of *Emperors of the Ice,* p. 10.

School Library Journal, December, 2008, Kelly McGorray, review of *Emperors of the Ice,* p. 147.

ONLINE

Richard Farr Home Page, http://www.richardfarr.net (December 11, 2009).

*   *   *

FONTENOT, Mary Alice 1910-2003

OBITUARY NOTICE—

See index for *SATA* sketch: Born April 16, 1910, in Eunice, LA; died of Parkinson's disease and related illnesses, May 12, 2003, in Carencro, LA. Author, reporter, journalist, and radio show host. Fontenot was known in the children's literary community for her "Clovis Crawfish" series. The books, published in both English and French, incorporated Cajun terminology into stories about animals from the Louisiana bayou. In addition to teaching moral lessons, the "Clovis Crawfish" books educated children about the scientific traits of animals, encouraging an understanding and appreciation of nature. The inspiration for Fontenot's writings was often attributed to her childhood experiences at her grandfather's farm in Bayou Tigre. She was a mostly self-educated woman, who later took classes at the University of Southwestern Louisiana in an effort to improve her French. In addition, she taught kindergarten classes at Louisiana's St. Edmund Elementary School. Ultimately, the curiosity of her students inspired Fontenot to focus on writing specifically for children. Fontenot's work contributed to the preservation of Louisiana history and culture, placing a special recognition on Cajun heritage and pride in French-Acadian culture. As her writings became more well known, she was frequently invited to speak to organizations and in schools and libraries. A member of the League of American Pen Women, Fontenot received numerous awards for her writing including a first prize award from National Press Women, a Louisiana Literary award from the Louisiana Library Association, and the Acadiana Arts Council Lifetime Achievement Award. In 2003, she was named a Louisiana Legend by Louisiana Public Broadcasting. Fontenot's writings include the children's books *Clovis Crawfish and His Friends* (1962), *Clovis Crawfish and Michelle Mantis* (1976), and *Clovis Crawfish and the Orphan Zozo* (1983). Her books for adults include *Acadia Parish: A History to 1900* (1976), the cookbook *Cajun Accent* (1979), and *The Louisiana Experience: An Introduction to the Culture of the Bayou State* (1983).

OBITUARIES AND OTHER SOURCES:

PERIODICALS

Acadia Profile, October, 2003, Julie Fontenot Landry, "The Enchanted World of Mary Alice Fontenot," pp. 6-18.

Lafayette Daily Advertiser, May 13, 2003.

ONLINE

Acadian Museum Web site, http://www.acadianmuseum.com/ (January 22, 2010), "Mary Alice Fontenot."

Life in Legacy Web site, http://www.lifeinlegacy.com/ (May 17, 2003).

Pelican Publishing Company Web site, http://pelicanpub.com/ (January 22, 2010), "Mary Alice Fontenot."

FRENCH, Vivian
   ## (Louis Catt)

Personal

Born in England; daughter of a headmaster; married (marriage ended) married; second husband's name Derek (divorced, 1982) married; third husband's name Davy; children: (first marriage) Alice; (second marriage) Jessica, Jemima; (third marriage) Nancy. *Education:* University degree (English). *Hobbies and other interests:* Live music, traveling.

Addresses

Home—Edinburgh, Scotland. *Agent*—Lindsey Fraser, Fraser Ross, 6 Wellington Place, Leithbridge EH6 7EQ, England.

Career

Writer and storyteller. National Book Trust, London, England, member of staff in information centre; worked in theater as an actor and writer, beginning c. 1960s; former counselor. Visiting lecturer, University of the West of England; writer-in-residence at schools and festivals; teacher at Edinburgh College of Art. *Guardian* (newspaper), London, England, former reviewer. Scottish Book Trust Rediscovery Book Bus project, participant, c. late 1990s.

Awards, Honors

Emil/Kurt Maschler Award shortlist, 1993, for *Caterpillar, Caterpillar;* Nestlé Smarties' Book Prize shortlist, 1995, for *A Song for Little Toad;* Sheffield Children's Book Award; numerous Parents' Honor awards; Stockton Children's Book of the Year designation, 2008, and BRAW/Royal Mail Award shortlist, both for *The Robe of Skulls.*

Writings

Tottie Pig's Noisy Christmas, illustrated by Clive Scruton, Walker (London, England), 1990.
Tottie Pig's Special Birthday, illustrated by Clive Scruton, Walker (London, England), 1990.
Doctor Elsie, illustrated by Rowan Barnes-Murphy, Walker (London, England), 1991.
Baker Ben, illustrated by Rowan Barnes-Murphy, Walker (London, England), 1991.
One Ballerina Two, illustrated by Jan Ormerod, Walker (London, England), 1991.
It's a Go to the Park Day, illustrated by Clive Scruton, Walker (London, England), 1991, Simon & Schuster (New York, NY), 1992.
Christmas Mouse, illustrated by Chris Fisher, Walker (London, England), 1992, Candlewick (Cambridge, MA), 1995.

(Abridger) Charles Dickens, *A Christmas Carol,* illustrated by Patrick Benson, Walker (London, England), 1992, Candlewick (Cambridge, MA), 1993.
Tillie McGillie's Fantastical Chair, illustrated by Sue Heap, Walker (London, England), 1992.
Caterpillar, Caterpillar, illustrated by Charlotte Voake, Walker (London, England), 1993, Candlewick (Cambridge, MA), 1995.
Under the Moon, illustrated by Chris Fisher, Walker (London, England), 1993, Candlewick (Cambridge, MA), 1994.
Kim and the Sooper Glooper Torch, illustrated by Chris Fisher, Young Lions (London, England), 1993.
Kevin and the Invisible Safety Pin, illustrated by Chris Fisher, Young Lions (London, England), 1993.
Mary Poggs and the Sunshine, illustrated by Colin West, Walker (London, England), 1993.
Mandy and the Purple Spotted Hanky, illustrated by Chris Fisher, Young Lions (London, England), 1993.
Hedgehogs Don't Eat Hamburgers, illustrated by Chris Fisher, Puffin (London, England), 1993.
Why the Sea Is Salt, illustrated by Patrice Aggs, Candlewick (Cambridge, MA), 1993.
Ian and the Stripy Bath Plug, illustrated by Chris Fisher, Young Lions (London, England), 1993.
Jackson's Juniors, illustrated by Thelma Lambert, Walker (London, England), 1993.
Once upon a Time, illustrated by John Prater, Candlewick (Cambridge, MA), 1993.
Little Tiger Goes Shopping, illustrated by Andy Cooke, Candlewick (Cambridge, MA), 1994.
Little Ghost, illustrated by John Prater, Candlewick (Cambridge, MA), 1994.
Spider Watching, illustrated by Alison Wisenfeld, Walker (London, England), 1994, Candlewick (Cambridge, MA), 1995.
The Little Red Hen and the Sly Fox, illustrated by Sally Hobson, ABC (London, England), 1994, published as *Red Hen and Sly Fox,* Simon & Schuster (New York, NY), 1995.
Robbie and the Amazing Presents, illustrated by Selina Young, Orchard (London, England), 1994.
Princess Primrose, illustrated by Chris Fisher, Walker (London, England), 1994.
Mervyn and the Hopping Hat, illustrated by Chris Fisher, Young Lions (London, England), 1994.
The Hedgehogs and the Big Bag, illustrated by Chris Fisher, Puffin (London, England), 1994.
Fat Ginger and the Awful Aliens, illustrated by Chris Fisher, Young Lions (London, England), 1994.
Warren and the Flying Football, illustrated by Chris Fisher, Young Lions (London, England), 1994.
Buster and the Bike Burglar, illustrated by Chris Fisher, Young Lions (London, England), 1994.
Please, Princess Primrose, illustrated by Chris Fisher, Walker (London, England), 1994.
The Apple Trees, illustrated by Terry Milne, Walker (London, England), 1994.
(Reteller) *Lazy Jack,* illustrated by Russell Ayto, Walker (London, England), 1995.
Jolly Roger and the Underwater Treasure, illustrated by Chris Fisher, Hodder (London, England), 1995.

First Mate Mutt and the Wind Machine Mutiny, illustrated by Chris Fisher, Hodder (London, England), 1995.

Captain Jennifer Jellyfish Jones, illustrated by Chris Fisher, Hodder (London, England), 1995.

Morris in the Apple Tree, illustrated by Guy Parker-Rees, Collins (London, England), 1995.

Morris the Mouse Hunter, illustrated by Guy Parker-Rees, Collins (London, England), 1995.

Oliver's Vegetables, illustrated by Alison Bartlett, Orchard (New York, NY), 1995.

Sea Dog Williams and the Frozen North, illustrated by Chris Fisher, Hodder (London, England), 1995.

A Walker Treasury: Magical Stories, Walker (London, England), 1995, published as *The Walker Book of Magical Stories,* Walker (London, England), 2000.

The Thistle Princess and Other Stories (also see below), illustrated by Chris Fisher, Walker (London, England), 1995.

A Song for Little Toad, illustrated by Barbara Firth, Candlewick (Cambridge, MA), 1995.

Painter Bear, illustrated by Chris Fisher, Candlewick (Cambridge, MA), 1995.

Molly in the Middle, illustrated by Venice Shone, Candlewick (Cambridge, MA), 1996.

Little Tiger Finds a Friend, illustrated by Andy Cooke, Candlewick (Cambridge, MA), 1996.

Bob the Dog, illustrated by Alison Bartlett, Hodder (London, England), 1996.

Squeaky Cleaners in a Tip!, illustrated by Anna Currey, Hodder (London, England), 1996.

Squeaky Cleaners in a Stew!, illustrated by Anna Currey, Hodder (London, England), 1996.

Squeaky Cleaners in a Muddle!, illustrated by Anna Currey, Hodder (London, England), 1996.

Once upon a Picnic, illustrated by John Prater, Candlewick (Cambridge, MA), 1996.

Squeaky Cleaners in a Hole!, illustrated by Anna Currey, Hodder (London, England), 1996.

Morris and the Cat Flap, illustrated by Olivia Villet, Collins (London, England), 1996.

The Christmas Kitten, illustrated by Chris Fisher, Candlewick (Cambridge, MA), 1996.

(Reteller) *Aesop's Funky Fables,* illustrated by Korky Paul, Hamilton (London, England), 1997, Viking (New York, NY), 1998.

Guinea Pigs on the Go, illustrated by Clive Scruton, Collins (London, England), 1997.

Kelly and the Crime Club, illustrated by Lesley Harker, Hodder (London, England), 1997.

Zenobia and Mouse, illustrated by Duncan Smith, Walker (London, England), 1997.

Peter and the Ghost, illustrated by Lesley Harker, Hodder (London, England), 1997.

Oh No Anna!, illustrated by Alex Ayliffe, Peachtree (Atlanta, GA), 1997.

A Christmas Star Called Hannah, illustrated by Anne Yvonne Gilbert, Candlewick (Cambridge, MA), 1997.

The Thistle Princess, illustrated by Elizabeth Harbour, Candlewick (Cambridge, MA), 1998.

Kick Back, illustrated by Jake Abrams, Barrington Stoke (Edinburgh, Scotland), 1998.

Oliver's Fruit Salad, illustrated by Alison Bartlett, Orchard (New York, NY), 1998.

The Boy Who Walked on Water, and Other Stories, Walker (London, England), 1998.

I Spy ABC, illustrated by Sally Holmes, Walker (London, England), 1998.

(With Ross Collins) *Write around the World: The Story of How and Why We Learnt to Write,* Zero to Ten (New York, NY), 1998 published as *Write around the World,* Zero to Ten (Slough, England), 1999.

Whale Journey, illustrated by Lisa Flather, Zero to Ten (New York, NY), 1998.

Not Again, Anna!, illustrated by Alex Ayliffe, Levinson (London, England), 1998.

Lullaby Lion, Candlewick (Cambridge, MA), 1998.

The Story of Christmas, illustrated by Jane Chapman, Candlewick (Cambridge, MA), 1999.

Mrs Hippo's Pizza Parlour, illustrated by Clive Scruton, Kingfisher (London, England), 1999, published as *Mrs. Hippo's Pizza Parlor,* Kingfisher (Boston, MA), 2004.

The Snow Dragon, illustrated by Chris Fisher, Doubleday (London, England), 1999.

(With Rebecca Elgar) *Tiger and the New Baby,* Kingfisher (New York, NY), 1999.

Rainbow House, illustrated by Biz Hull, Tamarind (Camberley, England), 1999.

(With Jan Lewis) *Big Fat Hen and the Hairy Goat,* David & Charles (London, England), 1999.

(With Jan Lewis) *Big Fat Hen and the Red Rooster,* David & Charles (London, England), 1999.

(With Rebecca Elgar) *Tiger and the Temper Tantrum,* Kingfisher (New York, NY), 1999.

(Adapter) Michael Rosen, *We're Going on a Bear Hunt* (play), Walker (London, England), 2000.

Growing Frogs, illustrated by Alison Bartlett, Candlewick (Cambridge, MA), 2000.

The Gingerbread Boy, illustrated by John Prater, Walker (London, England), 2000.

(Reteller) *Funky Tales,* illustrated by Korky Paul, Hamish Hamilton (London, England), 2000.

(Reteller) *The Three Billy Goats Gruff* (play), illustrated by Arthur Robins, Walker (London, England), 2000.

(Adapter) Martin Waddell, *Farmer Duck* (play), Walker (London, England), 2000.

Falling Awake, illustrated by Roy Petrie, Barrington Stoke (Edinburgh, Scotland), 2000.

(Adapter) Sarah Hayes, *This Is the Bear* (play), Walker (London, England), 2000.

(Reteller) *Noah's Ark, and Other Bible Stories,* illustrated by Jane Chapman, Early Learning Centre (Swindon, England), 2000.

(Reteller) Michael Rosen, *Little Rabbit Foo Foo,* illustrated by Arthur Robins, Walker (London, England), 2000.

Let's Go, Anna!, illustrated by Alex Ayliffe, David & Charles (London, England), 2000.

Swallow Journey, illustrated by Karin Littlewood, Zero to Ten (Slough, England), 2000.

(Reteller) *The Kingfisher Book of Fairy Tales,* illustrated by Peter Malone, Kingfisher (New York, NY), 2000.

From Zero to Ten: The Story of Numbers, Oxford University Press (New York, NY), 2000.

Ladybird, Ladybird, illustrated by Selina Young, Orion (London, England), 2001.

Oliver's Milk Shake, illustrated by Alison Bartlett, Orchard (New York, NY), 2001.

(Reteller) *The Tiger and the Jackal: A Traditional Indian Tale,* illustrated by Alison Bartlett, Walker (London, England), 2001.

Big Bad Bug, illustrated by Emily Bolam, Walker (London, England), 2001.

Mean Green Machine, illustrated by Ana Martín Larrañíaga, Walker (London, England), 2001.

Singing to the Sun, and Other Magical Tales, illustrated by Chris Fisher, Walker (London, England), 2001, portions published as *Singing to the Sun: A Fairy Tale,* illustrated by Jackie Morris, Kane/Miller (La Jolla, CA), 2008.

Guinea Pigs Go to Sea, illustrated by Clive Scruton, Collins (London, England), 2001.

(Reteller) *Jack and the Beanstalk* (play), illustrated by Harry Horse, Walker (London, England), 2001.

(Reteller) *The Three Little Pigs* (play), illustrated by Liz Million, Walker (London, England), 2001.

Five Little Ducks, illustrated by Paul Dowling, Walker (London, England), 2001.

One Fat Cat (play), illustrated by Liz Million, Walker (London, England), 2001.

To Mum, with Love, illustrated by Dana Kubick, Walker (London, England), 2002.

(Editor) *Survivor, and Other Stories,* Walker (London, England), 2002.

(Editor) *Paying for It, and Other Stories,* Walker (London, England), 2002.

Baby Baby (also see below), Barrington Stoke (Edinburgh, Scotland), 2002.

A Present for Mom, illustrated by Dana Kubick, Candlewick (Cambridge, MA), 2002.

Wicked Chickens, illustrated by John Bradley, Macmillan (London, England), 2003.

(Reteller) *The Kingfisher Book of Nursery Tales,* illustrated by Stephen Lambert, Kingfisher (Boston, MA), 2003.

Morris the Mouse Hunter, illustrated by Olivia Villet, Collins (London, England), 2003.

T. Rex, illustrated by Alison Bartlett, Candlewick (Cambridge, MA), 2004.

I Love You, Grandpa, illustrated by Dana Kubick, Candlewick (Cambridge, MA), 2004.

Bert and the Burglar, illustrated by Ed Boxall, Walker (London, England), 2004.

Bill Bird's New Boots, illustrated by Alison Bartlett, Egmont Books (London, England), 2004.

Detective Dan, illustrated by Alison Bartlett, A. & C. Black (London, England), 2004.

I Wish I Was an Alien, illustrated by Lisa Williams, Evans (London, England), 2005, published as *I Wish I Were an Alien,* Gingham Dog (Columbus, OH), 2005.

Brian the Giant, illustrated by Sue Heap, Walker (London, England), 2005.

Buck and His Truck, illustrated by Julie Lacome, Walker (London, England), 2005.

The Cat in the Coat, illustrated by Alison Bartlett, Evans (London, England) 2005.

Pig in Love, illustrated by Tim Archbold, Gingham Dog (Columbus, OH), 2005.

Meet the Mammoth!, illustrated by Lisa Williams, Gingham Dog (Columbus, OH), 2005.

A Cat in a Coat, illustrated by Alison Bartlett, Gingham Dog (Columbus, OH), 2005.

Sharp Sheep, illustrated by John Bradley, Macmillan (London, England), 2005.

The Magic Bedtime Storybook, illustrated by Emily Bolam, Orion (London, England), 2005.

The Three-legged Mummy, illustrated by Dave Sutton, Barrington Stoke (Edinburgh, Scotland), 2006.

Henny Penny, illustrated by Sophie Windham, Bloomsbury (New York, NY), 2006.

Ellie and Elvis, illustrated by Michael Terry, Bloomsbury (London, England), 2006.

Little Dog, illustrated by Chris Fisher, Oxford University Press (Oxford, England), 2006.

Growl!, illustrated by Tim Archbold, Evans (London, England), 2007.

Chocolate: The Bean That Conquered the World, illustrated by Paul Howard, Walker (London, England), 2007.

The Magic Bedtime Storybook, illustrated by Emily Bolam, Orion Children's (London, England), 2007.

A Mouse in the House, Evans (London, England), 2007.

The Daddy Goose Collection, Chicken House (Frome, England), 2007.

Mrs Floss and Mrs Fleece: A Highland Tale, illustrated by Natalie Russell, Happy Cat Books (London, England), 2008.

Caterpillar Butterfly, illustrated by Charlotte Voake, Walker (London, England), 2008.

Sparkle Street: Barnaby Baker's Cake Shop, illustrated by Joanne Partis, Macmillan Children's Books (London, England), 2009.

Sparkle Street: Lizzie Ribbon's Hat Shop, illustrated by Joanne Partis, Macmillan Children's Books (London, England), 2009.

Yucky Worms, illustrated by Jessica Ahlberg, Candlewick Press (Somerville, MA), 2010.

Author of plays adapted from her books, including *Baby Baby,* produced in Scotland, 2009.

French's books have been translated into more than thirty languages.

"IGGY PIG" SERIES

Iggy Pig's Skippy Day, illustrated by David Melling, Hodder (London, England), 1998.

Iggy Pig's Party, illustrated by David Melling, Hodder (London, England), 1998.

Iggy Pig's Big Bad Wolf Trouble, illustrated by David Melling, Scholastic (New York, NY), 1998.

Iggy Pig at the Seaside, illustrated by David Melling, Hodder (London, England), 1999.

Iggy Pig's Dark Night, illustrated by David Melling, Hodder (London, England), 1999.

Iggy Pig's Shopping Day, illustrated by David Melling, Hodder (London, England), 1999.

Iggy Pig's Snow Day, illustrated by David Melling, Hodder (London, England), 1999.

"SLEEPOVER CLUB" SERIES; UNDER NAME LOUIS CATT

Sleepover on Friday the Thirteenth (also see below), Collins (London, England), 1998.
Sleepover Girls Go Detective, Collins (London, England), 1999.
(With Fiona Cummings) *Sleepover on Friday the Thirteenth; Sleepover Girls Go Camping; Sleepover Girls at Camp* ("Mega Sleepover Club" omnibus volume), Collins (London, England), 2002.

"SPACE DOG" SERIES

Space Dog Finds Treasure, illustrated by Sue Heap, Hodder (London, England), 1999.
Space Dog Meets Space Cat, illustrated by Sue Heap, Hodder (London, England), 1999.
Space Dog to the Rescue, illustrated by Sue Heap, Hodder (London, England), 1999.
Space Dog Visits Planet Earth, illustrated by Sue Heap, Hodder (London, England), 1999.
Space Dog, illustrated by Sue Heap, Hodder (London, England), 2000.
Space Dog Goes to Planet Purrgo, illustrated by Sue Heap, Hodder (London, England), 2000.
Space Dog and the Space Egg, illustrated by Sue Heap, Hodder (London, England), 2000.

"TIARA CLUB" SERIES

Princess Charlotte and the Birthday Ball, illustrated by Sarah Gibb, Orchard (London, England), 2005, HarperColllins (New York, NY), 2007.
Princess Katie and the Silver Pony, illustrated by Sarah Gibb, Orchard (London, England) 2005, HarperCollins (New York, NY), 2007.
Princess Daisy and the Dazzling Dragon, illustrated by Sarah Gibb, Orchard (London, England), 2005, HarperCollins (New York, NY), 2007.
Princess Alice and the Magical Mirror, illustrated by Sarah Gibb, Orchard (London, England), 2005, HarperCollins (New York, NY), 2007.
Princess Sophia and the Sparkling Surprise, illustrated by Sarah Gibb, Orchard (London, England) 2005, HarperCollins (New York, NY), 2007.
Princess Emily and the Beautiful Fairy, illustrated by Sarah Gibb, Orchard (London, England), 2005, HarperCollins (New York, NY), 2007.
Christmas Wonderland, illustrated by Sarah Gibb, Orchard (London, England), 2006.
Princess Charlotte and the Enchanted Rose, illustrated by Sarah Gibb, Orchard (London England), 2006.
Princess Katie and the Dancing Broom, illustrated by Sarah Gibb, Orchard (London, England), 2006.
Princess Alice and the Crystal Slipper, illustrated by Sarah Gibb, Orchard (London, England), 2006, published as *Princess Alice and the Glass Slipper,* HarperCollins (New York, NY), 2007.

Princess Daisy and the Magical Merry-go-round, illustrated by Sarah Gibb, Orchard (London, England), 2006, Katherine Tegen Books (New York, NY), 2007.
Princess Emily and the Wishing Star, illustrated by Sarah Gibb, Orchard (London, England), 2006, HarperTrophy (New York, NY), 2007.
Princess Sophia and the Prince's Party, illustrated by Sarah Gibb, Orchard (London, England), 2006, HarperTrophy (New York, NY), 2007.
Princess Katie and the Mixed-up Potion, illustrated by Sarah Gibb, Katherine Tegen Books (New York, NY), 2007.
Princess Emily and the Substitute Fairy, illustrated by Sarah Gibb, Katherine Tegen Books (New York, NY), 2007.
Princess Amy and the Golden Coach, illustrated by Sarah Gibbs, Orchard (London, England), 2007, published as *Princess Amy and the Forgetting Dust,* illustrated by Sarah Gibb, Katherine Teegan Books (New York, NY), 2008.
Princess Georgia and the Shimmering Pearl, illustrated by Sarah Gibb, Orchard (London, England), 2007, HarperTrophy (New York, NY), 2008.
Princess Jessica and the Best-friend Bracelet, illustrated by Sarah Gibb, Orchard (London, England), 2007, Katherine Tegen Books (New York, NY), 2008.
Princess Lauren and the Diamond Necklace, illustrated by Sarah Gibb, Orchard (London, England), 2007, HarperTrophy (New York, NY), 2008.
Princess Parade, illustrated by Sarah Gibb, Orchard (London, England), 2007.
Princess Olivia and the Velvet Cloak, illustrated by Sarah Gibb, Orchard (London, England), 2007, published as *Princess Olivia and the Velvet Cape,* Harper Trophy (New York, NY), 2008.
Princess Chloe and the Primrose Petticoats, illustrated by Sarah Gibb, Orchard (London, England), 2007.
Butterfly Ball, illustrated by Sarah Gibb, Orchard (London, England), 2007.
Princess Ellie and the Enchanted Fawn, illustrated by Sarah Gibb, Orchard (London, England), 2007, Katherine Tegen, HarperTrophy (New York, NY), 2009.
Princess Grace and the Golden Nightingale, illustrated by Sarah Gibb, Orchard (London, England), 2007, Katherine Tegen, HarperTrophy (New York, NY), 2009.
Princess Hannah and the Little Black Kitten, illustrated by Sarah Gibb, Orchard (London, England), 2007, Katherine Tegan, HarperTrophy (New York, NY), 2009.
Princess Isabella and the Snow-white Unicorn, illustrated by Sarah Gibb, Katherine Tegen, Orchard (London, England), 2007, HarperTrophy (New York, NY), 2009.
Princess Lucy and the Precious Puppy, illustrated by Sarah Gibb, Orchard (London, England), 2007, published as *Princess Lucy and the Runaway Puppy,* Katherine Tegen, HarperTrophy (New York, NY), 2009.
Princess Sarah and the Silver Swan, illustrated by Sarah Gibb, Orchard (London, England), 2007, Katherine Tegen, HarperTrophy (New York, NY), 2009.

Princess Ruby and the Enchanted Whale, illustrated by Sarah Gibb, Orchard (London, England), 2008.

Princess Leah and the Golden Seahorse, illustrated by Sarah Gibb, Orchard (London, England), 2008.

Princess Amelia and the Silver Seal, illustrated by Sarah Gibb, Orchard (London, England), 2008.

Princess Millie and the Magical Mermaid, illustrated by Sarah Gibb, Orchard (London, England), 2008.

Princess Rachel and the Dancing Dolphin, illustrated by Sarah Gibb, Orchard (London, England), 2008.

Princess Zoe and the Wishing Well, illustrated by Sarah Gibb, Orchard (London, England), 2008.

"DRAGLINS" SERIES

Draglins Lost!, illustrated by Chris Fisher, Orchard (London, England), 2007.

Alison Bartlett's folk-style art for Vivian French's **Growing Frogs** *enhances the story of a budding naturalist.* (Candlewick Press, 2000. Reproduced by permission of the publisher Candlewick Press, Inc., on behalf of Walker Books, London.)

Draglins in Danger, illustrated by Chris Fisher, Orchard (London, England), 2007.

Draglins Find a Hero, illustrated by Chris Fisher, Orchard (London, England), 2007.

Draglins Escape!, illustrated by Chris Fisher, Orchard (London, England), 2007.

Draglins and the Flood, illustrated by Chris Fisher, Orchard (London, England), 2007.

Draglins and the Bully!, illustrated by Chris Fisher, Orchard (London, England), 2007.

Draglins and the Fire!, illustrated by Chris Fisher, Orchard (London, England), 2007.

"TALES FROM THE FIVE KINGDOMS" SERIES

The Robe of Skulls, illustrated by Ross Collins, Walker (London, England), 2007, Candlewick Press (Cambridge, MA), 2008.

The Bag of Bones, illustrated by Ross Collins, Walker (London, England), 2008, Candlewick Press (Somerville, MA), 2009.

The Heart of Glass, illustrated by Ross Collins, Walker (London, England), 2009, Candlewick Press (Somerville, MA), 2010.

Adaptations

The Daddy Goose Treasury was adapted for audiobook, read by Daniel Hill, Chivers Audio, 2009.

Sidelights

Vivian French is a professional storyteller and the prolific author of picture books, plays, and novels for children and young adults. In addition to her popular "Tiara Club" and "Draglins" books, French has created such memorable characters as Iggy Pig, Space Dog, the Staple Street Gang, the Squeaky Cleaners, and Tottie Pig. Her retellings of folk and fairy tales have been published in her native England in story collections as well as in plays for young performers. Her "Tales from the Five Kingdoms" series, which are geared for middle-grade readers, serve up a fantastical mixture of fairy-tale fun complete with evil crones, ill-tempered stepsisters, and spells galore. As Louis Catt—a pen name inspired by the author's cat, Louis—French has also contributed novels to Rose Impey's "Sleepover Club" series, based on a popular British television series. Describing French in the *Scotsman,* interviewer Lee Randall described her as "that rare adult who shows excitement by yelping 'Yay!', without sounding annoying or childish. Her enthusiasm for life is infectious, and the same warmth pervades her books—even her villains reveal their humanity, while her good guys are not so angelic as to induce nausea."

French has been interested in stories since childhood, when she read all the fairy tales she could find. "I especially remember a copy of *Grimm's Fairy Tales* belonging to my grandfather," she told a Jubilee Books Web site interviewer. "It had really crude woodcut pictures, and it gave me nightmares—but I kept going back and reading it again and again." Although she eventually established a career in the theatre, juggling acting performances with raising her four daughters, French was eventually inspired to channel her storytelling skills into writing by friend and poet Diana Hendry. In her interview with Randall, French explained another motivation for writing: "I think I write for the child I would have liked to have been, a confident child who has lots of friends and is quite practical. If anything happened, I just stood and flapped my arms. It was a long time before anyone realised I was very short-sighted, and I did live in a kind of a mist."

Publishing her first three children's books in 1990, French then went on to produce dozens of other titles, most of them picture books for young readers. In *Little Tiger Goes Shopping* she focuses on teamwork, as Little Tiger and Big Tiger want to bake a cake but find that they have no eggs. They head out to the store, only to discover that many other animals are also headed that way to pick up various ingredients. When the animals arrive at the store, however, it is closed, so they decide to pool their resources and make a cake that all can enjoy. "Kids (and cooks) will identify with this all-too-frequent culinary predicament," wrote Deborah Abbott in her review of *Little Tiger Goes Shopping* for *Booklist.* Little Tiger returns in several more stories, such as *Little Tiger Finds a Friend,* while a different young tiger stars in *Tiger and the New Baby* and *Tiger and the Temper Tantrum,* the latter which *Booklist* reviewer Ilene Cooper deemed "on target for the audience."

French's "Oliver" stories introduce a young protagonist who likes prepared foods such as French fries but absolutely detests fresh vegetables. In *Oliver's Vegetables,* the boy's grandfather convinces Oliver that certain vegetables might be worth trying. Julie Corsaro wrote in *Booklist* that "this breezy story" is suitable "as the centerpiece in a preschool story time . . . or just for plain old fun." While noting that some adults may question French's assertion that a child would find beet salad to be "very, very, very good," in the opinion of a *Publishers Weekly* reviewer "agreeable readers will accept her try-it-you'll-like-it approach."

Oliver's second adventure with food takes place in *Oliver's Fruit Salad.* When the boy is hesitant to eat canned fruit, his mother thinks the remedy is a trip to the grocery store. Fortunately, memories of his grandfather's garden help Oliver enjoy the fresh fruit his mother soon sets before him. Stephanie Zvirin considered the title "great for lap sharing or use with small groups." Food is central to another incident from Oliver's life, as the boy and his cousin take a trip to the dairy farm in *Oliver's Milk Shake.* As DeAnn Tabuchi noted in a review of the series for *School Library Journal,* "Oliver is a charmer."

Stanley, the youngest of his siblings, cannot figure out what he should get his mother for Mother's Day in *A Present for Mom.* When he tries to copy older family

members the gift does not seem right; finally, his older sister helps Stanley figure out just the right present for mom. French's "simple tale rings true for little ones," according to a *Kirkus Reviews* critic. "Children will identify with Stanley, his quest, and his ultimate triumph," assured Heather E. Miller in her *School Library Journal* review. A *Publishers Weekly* reviewer felt that "French's use of detail gives her story its individuality," and *Booklist* contributor Hazel Rochman suspected that readers "will enjoy [Stanley's] . . . bumbling, messy failures as much as the final triumphant encircling embrace."

Stanley returns in *I Love You, Grandpa,* as both Stanley and Grandpa realize they cannot keep up with the activities of Stanley's energetic older siblings. However, after a nap and a song, the boy and older man discover an activity they both enjoy: swinging at the playground. Ilene Cooper, in a *Booklist* review of *I Love You, Grandpa,* noted that "the special bond between young and old plays out sweetly in this happy picture book," while a *Kirkus Reviews* contributor recommended *I Love You, Grandpa* as a "wonderful selection for the littlest one in any family and for the grandpa that is special in his or her life." Andrea Tarr, writing in *School Library Journal,* considered French's title "a delightful choice for reading aloud or for family sharing."

Some of French's picture books focus on nature-related topics. For example, in *Spider Watching* three cousins study the spiders living in a nearby garden shed. While two of the children are enthusiastic, the third is initially afraid of the spiders, but she eventually gets over her fear as she watches the fascinating creatures. *Whale Journey* follows a pod of whales on their migration from Baja California to the Arctic. "French's text keeps the story moving, offering information and action to capture children's attention," Carolyn Phelan wrote of the title in her *Booklist* review. *Growing Frogs* describes the life-cycle of a frog from tadpole to adult, showing readers that many types of frogs are endangered. Jody McCoy, writing in *School Library Journal,* considered the book, illustrated by Alison Bartlett, to be "a hopping good collaboration," while a *Horn Book* reviewer pointed out that "French provides enough step-by-step guidance so that readers can gather and observe their own frog spawn."

Like *Whale Journey,* both *Caribou Journey* and *Swallow Journey* focus on animal migration. In both books "French writes in the present tense with a quiet immediacy," according to *Booklist* reviewer Hazel Rochman. While *Whale Journey* and *Caribou Journey* both focus on a mother animal and her new baby, *Swallow Journey* shows the journey of a whole flock on its voyage from England, through Spain and France, as it crosses the Sahara and finally ends its trip in southern Africa.

Dinosaurs, particularly the tyrannosaurus rex, are the focus of *T. Rex.* Focusing on dino-facts and discussing how paleontologists piece together information about the prehistoric creatures, French's story is told from the perspective of a grandfather and a young boy who are touring a science museum together. "This brief tale simply and succinctly sums up how much is still unknowable in the scientific world, while also acknowledging how much can be proven through study," commented a *Publishers Weekly* critic. Karin Snelson, writing for *Booklist,* considered *T. Rex* to be "a sprightly picture book that's as much about the mysteries of science as it is about dinosaurs." Noting that French suggests that young readers may be the ones to grow up and discover more about dinosaurs, a *Kirkus Reviews* contributor commented that such suggestions serve as "an energizing idea for young dinosaur fans." Marge Loch-Wouters commented in *School Library Journal* that "young dinosaur lovers will enjoy the story and return to the book often."

French's retellings of folk tales are perhaps her most popular titles. In *Red Hen and Sly Fox* the traditional story of the gullible hen that outsmarts a wily fox "is given new life by French's fresh text," according to *Booklist* critic Lauren Peterson. "This energetic book is as fresh as it is classic," a *Publishers Weekly* contributor commented, while Mary M. Burns, in her review for *Horn Book,* praised French's use of language, noting: "The dialogue is pithy and concrete—attuned to the sensibilities of young audiences."

Lazy Jack is a retelling of the traditional story about a lackadaisical boy who keeps losing the pay he receives from his various jobs. French "nicely tweaks the traditional ending to show redemption on Jack's part without losing the comedic tone," a *Publishers Weekly* contributor noted. Hazel Rochman, writing in *Booklist,* commented that "any child who's messed up with the best intentions will love the disaster tale and will relish Jack's sweet revenge."

Not all of French's folk tales are traditional; the story in *The Thistle Princess* is a fairy tale of French's own creation. A king and queen want a daughter, and a thistle tells the royal couple how they can have a child. Soon, a little thistle girl appears, and the parents are at first over protective, but when they allow the princess to play outside, she truly thrives. "Readers with a strong taste for . . . nostalgic and happily-ever-after endings will take to this one from the start," predicted a reviewer for *Publishers Weekly.*

Princesses are the focus of French's "Tiara Club" series, which is set in a land where every girl is a princess. Geared for elementary-grade girls and featuring artwork by Sarah Gibb, the popular series focuses on the girls attending the Royal Palace Academy for the Preparation of Perfect Princesses, as they attend masquerades and balls, cultivate a glamorous wardrobe and royal demeanor, and live a life that mixes magic with typical teen enthusiasms in collectible novels that include *Princess Charlotte and the Enchanted Rose, Princess Kate and the Dancing Broom, Princess Daisy and*

the Dazzling Dragon, Princess Isabella and the Snow-White Unicorn, and *Princess Rachel and the Dancing Dolphin.* French does not discount boy readers from the fantasy fun, however: her eight "Draglins" books follow the Draglin family—Dennis, Dora, Daffodil, and Danny—as they are forced to leave their secure home in the attic of a city tenement and make their way in a modern world that does not tolerate traditional fire-breathing-dragon behavior. Reviewing *Princess Daisy and the Dazzling Dragon* in *School Library Journal,* Alison Grant noted the familiarity of French's light-hearted text and predicted that the series will "appeal to girly girls who like royalty, fantasy, and adventure."

Chronicled in the novels *The Robe of Skulls, The Bag of Bones,* and *The Heart of Glass,* French's "Tales from the Five Kingdoms" series focuses on an entertaining cast of quirky characters that includes a spunky orphan named Grace Gillypot, the twin princes of Gorebreath, brave Gubble the troll, a group of grandmotherly witches, Looby the half-elf, and the chatty bats Marlon and Alf. In *The Robe of Skulls* French carries readers with her to the village of Fracture, a mountain community located in the Five Kingdoms that is ruled by King Frank. Over Fracture looms the crumbling castle of Lady Lamorna, an evil sorceress. When Lady Lamorna covets a costly new velvet gown, she will stop at nothing to acquire it, even turning the local royalty into frogs to obtain their money, until Gracie and her assorted friends save the day. Truda Hangnail is the evil-doer in *The Bag of Bones,* and she has been banned from the Five Kingdoms because of her use of deep magic. After turning the kingdom's good witches to the dark side, Truda sets her sights on ousting King Frank, but when her evil-doing is spotted by Loobly, the quasi-elf calls on Gracie and Prince Marcus for help. Romance is at the core of *The Heart of Glass,* as Prince Marcus captures the heart of a princess of Dreghorn just as a pair of determined trolls decides that the prince is well suited to be their own leader.

Reviewing *The Robe of Skulls,* Francisca Goldsmith wrote in *Booklist* that French treats fans to "a charmingly witty adventure" that will be enjoyed by "devotees of fractured fairy tales," and in *Horn Book* Betty Carter deemed the book "a romp filled with language play and just plain nonsense." Noting the "tall-tale" aspects of *The Bag of Bones,* Goldsmith also cited the "spidery" pen-and-ink drawings by series illustrator Ross Collins, writing that they "amplify . . . [the] inner traits" of the novel's quirky cast.

French assembles seven of her favorite fairy tales in *The Kingfisher Book of Fairy Tales.* In retelling and shortening such stories as "Cinderella," "Jack and the Beanstalk," and "Rumplestiltskin" for a younger audience, she does not shy away from the darker aspects of some of these tales. She also works to retain the traditional "fairy" elements, as she notes in her introduction to the collection. *School Library Journal* reviewer Barbara Buckley considered *The Kingfisher Book of Fairy Tales* to be "a well-executed anthology." Continuing to re-explore the stories of childhood, French has also produced *The Kingfisher Book of Nursery Tales,* a related anthology of retellings that "playfully retells eight . . . best-known fairy tales," according to a *Publishers Weekly* critic. In *School Library Journal,* Carolyn Janssen dubbed French's work on this second anthology "well done."

The prolific French has also created story collections composed of folk-tale retellings as well as original stories, producing *Under the Moon, The Daddy Goose Collection,* and *The Magic Bedtime Storybook,* among others. In *Under the Moon,* she presents three stories: one a folktale from Eastern Europe and the others original stories. "All the stories exhibit a folkloric style, with a timelessness that should make for broad appeal," wrote Kay Weisman in *Booklist.* French takes a new approach to an old favorite in *Aesop's Funky Fables,* using plenty of sound-words to encourage acting-out storytelling. The author's "impressive range of voice reveals a keen ear for dialogue and description," noted a critic for *Publishers Weekly.*

French's thrilling fantasy novel The Robe of Skulls *features artwork by Ross Collins.* (Illustration copyright © 2007 by Ross Collins. Reproduced by permission of Candlewick Press, Inc., on behalf of Walker Books, London.)

In her online interview for the Jubilee Books Web site, French recommended the following advice to young writers: "Talk a lot, read a lot, listen, watch people and be around people. . . . Don't EVER let the fact that you can't spell or write neatly put you off writing stories—use a tape recorder, tell the story to a friend, draw it out in pictures—it's the story that matters, not the packaging."

Biographical and Critical Sources

PERIODICALS

Booklist, February 1, 1994, Deborah Abbott, review of *Little Tiger Goes Shopping,* p. 1009; March 15, 1994, Kay Weisman, review of *Under the Moon,* p. 1365; March 1, 1995, Carolyn Phelan, review of *Spider Watching,* p. 1247; May 1, 1995, Lauren Peterson, review of *Red Hen and Sly Fox,* p. 1579; September 1, 1995, Hazel Rochman, review of *Lazy Jack,* p. 73; September 15, 1995, Julie Corsaro, review of *Oliver's Vegetables,* p. 175; November 1, 1997, Ilene Cooper, review of *A Christmas Star Called Hannah,* p. 480; October 15, 1998, Stephanie Zvirin, review of *Oliver's Fruit Salad,* p. 426; January 1, 1999, Carolyn Phelan, review of *Whale Journey,* p. 887; January 1, 1999, Kathleen Squires, review of *Not Again, Anna!,* p. 887; May 1, 1999, Ilene Cooper, reviews of *Tiger and the New Baby* and *Tiger and the Temper Tantrum,* both p. 1598; May 1, 2000, Susan Dove Lempke, review of *Growing Frogs,* p. 1672; August, 2001, Shelley Townsend-Hudson, review of *Oliver's Milk Shake,* p. 2129; January 1, 2002, Hazel Rochman, review of *Swallow Journey,* p. 861; May 1, 2002, Hazel Rochman, review of *A Present for Mom,* p. 1532; November 1, 2004, Ilene Cooper, review of *I Love You, Grandpa,* p. 488; December 1, 2004, Karin Snelson, review of *T. Rex,* p. 672; December 15, 2004, Hazel Rochman, review of *Mrs. Hippo's Pizza Parlor,* p. 746; August 1, 2006, GraceAnne A. DeCandido, review of *Henny Penny,* p. 86; September, 2006, Kirsten Cutler, review of *The Daddy Goose Treasury,* p. 171; July, 2007, Alison Grant, review of *Princess Daisy and the Dazzling Dragon,* p. 76; September 1, 2008, Francisca Goldsmith, review of *The Robe of Skulls,* p. 100; December, 2008, Madeline Walton-Hadlock, review of *Singing to the Sun: A Fairy Tale,* p. 90; May 1, 2009, Francisca Goldsmith, review of *The Bag of Bones,* p. 78.

Five Owls, March, 1995, review of *Spider Watching,* p. 87.

Horn Book, July-August, 1995, Mary M. Burns, review of *Red Hen and Sly Fox,* p. 469; May, 2000, review of *Growing Frogs,* p. 332; November-December, 2004, Danielle J. Ford, review of *T. Rex,* p. 726; July-August, 2008, Betty Carter, review of *The Robe of Skulls,* p. 443.

Kirkus Reviews, March 1, 2002, review of *A Present for Mom,* p. 334; September 1, 2004, review of *I Love You, Grandpa,* p. 864; October 15, 2004, review of *T. Rex,* p. 1005; November 1, 2005, review of *Morris in the Apple Tree,* p. 1183.

Publishers Weekly, May 8, 1995, review of *Red Hen and Sly Fox,* p. 295; July 10, 1995, review of *Lazy Jack,* p. 57; July 31, 1995, review of *A Song for Little Toad,* p. 80; October 9, 1995, review of *Oliver's Vegetables,* p. 84; October 6, 1997, review of *A Christmas Star Called Hannah,* p. 55; February 9, 1998, review of *Aesop's Funky Fables,* p. 95; October 19, 1998, review of *The Thistle Princess,* p. 80; May 22, 2000, "Many Happy Returns," p. 95; March 11, 2002, review of *A Present for Mom,* p. 71; November 24, 2003, "Enduring Favorites," p. 66; November 29, 2004, review of *T. Rex,* p. 39; July 7, 2008, review of *The Robe of Skulls,* p. 85.

Scotsman, January 10, 2009, Lee Randall, interview with French.

School Library Journal, June, 1994, Susan Helper, review of *Under the Moon,* p. 98; May, 2000, Jody McCoy, review of *Growing Frogs,* p. 161; January, 2001, Barbara Buckley, review of *The Kingfisher Book of Fairy Tales,* p. 116; March, 2001, Martha Link, review of *Let's Go, Anna!,* p. 208; June, 2001, DeAnn Tabuchi, review of *Oliver's Milk Shake,* p. 114; December, 2001, Sally Bates Goodroe, review of *Caribou Journey,* p. 158; May, 2002, Heather E. Miller, review of *A Present for Mom,* p. 114; January, 2004, Carolyn Janssen, review of *The Kingfisher Book of Nursery Tales,* p. 114; October, 2004, Andrea Tarr, review of *I Love You, Grandpa,* p. 113; December, 2004, Marge Loch-Wouters, review of *T. Rex,* p. 108; July, 2006, Kirsten Cutler, review of *Henny Penny,* p. 77.

ONLINE

Jubilee Books Web site, http://www.jubileebooks.co.uk/ (October 31, 2005), interview with French.

Vivian French Home Page, http://www.vivianfrench.com (December 20, 2009).

Walker Books Web site, http://www.walkerbooks.co.uk/ (December 20, 2009), "Vivian French."*

*   *   *

FUNKE, Cornelia 1958- (Cornelia Caroline Funke)

Personal

Born December 10, 1958, in Dorsten, Westphalia, Germany; married, 1980; married Rolfe Funke (a printer), 1981 (died, 2006); children: Anna, Ben. *Education:* University of Hamburg, degree (education theory); Hamburg State College of Design (book illustration).

Addresses

Home—Los Angeles, CA. *Agent*—Oliver Latsch Literary Agency and Translations, 631 N. Fuller Ave., Los Angeles, CA 99036.

Career

Children's book author and illustrator. Social worker for three years; freelance illustrator and board game designer; writer, beginning 1994. Has worked for German state television channel ZDF.

Cornelia Funke (Photograph courtesy of Ulrich Perrey/Landov. Reproduced by permission.)

Member

Amnesty International.

Awards, Honors

Kalbacher Klapperschlange, 2000, for *Drachenreiter*; Wildweibchenpreis, 2000, for collected works; Vache qui Lit (Venice), and Kalbacher Klapperschlange, both 2001, Preis der Jury der Jungen Leser, 2002, and Corine award, and Evangelischer Buchpreis, both 2003, all for *Herr der Diebe*; Mildred L. Batchelder Award for best translated children's book, and Torchlight Prize, Askews Library Services, both 2003, both for *The Thief Lord*; Nordstemmer Zuckerrübe, 2004, for *Kleiner Werwolf*; Preis der Jury der Jungen Leser, Phantastik-Preis der Stadt Wetzlar, and Kalbacher Klapperschlange, all 2004, all for *Tintenherz*; Booksense Award, and Children's Literature Book of the Year award, American Booksellers Association, 2004, for *Inkheart*; Booksense Book of the Year Award, 2006, for *Inkspell*; Roswitha Prize, 2008.

Writings

CHILDREN'S FICTION

(Self-illustrated) *Monstergeschichten,* Loewe Verlag (Bindlach, Germany), 1993.

(Self-illustrated) *Rittergeschichten,* Loewe Verlag (Bindlach, Germany), 1994.

(Self-illustrated) *Zwei wilde kleine Hexen,* Cecilie Dressler Verlag (Hamburg, Germany), 1994.

(Self-illustrated) *Kein Keks für Kobolde,* Fischer Verlag (Frankfurt, Germany), 1994.

(Self-illustrated) *Hinter verzauberten Fenstern: eine geheimnisvolle Adventsgeschichte,* Fischer Verlag (Frankfurt, Germany), 1995.

(Self-illustrated) *Greta und Eule, Hundesitter,* Cecilie Dressler Verlag (Hamburg, Germany), 1995.

(Self-illustrated) *Der Mondscheindrache,* Loewe Verlag (Bindlach, Germany), 1996.

(Self-illustrated) *Hände weg von Mississippi,* Cecilie Dressler Verlag (Hamburg, Germany), 1997.

Prinzessin Isabella, illustrated by Kerstin Meyer, Friedrich Oetinger (Hamburg, Germany), 1997, translated by Chantal Wright as *Princess Pigsty,* Chicken House (New York, NY), 2007.

(Self-illustrated) *Das verzauberte Klassenzimmer,* Loewe Verlag (Bindlach, Germany), 1997.

(Self-illustrated) *Tiergeschichten,* Loewe Verlag (Bindlach, Germany), 1997.

(Self-illustrated) *Drachenreiter,* Cecelie Dressler Verlag (Hamburg, Germany), 1997, translated by Anthea Bell as *Dragon Rider,* Scholastic (New York, NY), 2004.

Dachbodengeschichten, illustrated by Wilfried Gebhard, Loewe Verlag (Bindlach, Germany), 1998.

(Self-illustrated) *Igraine Ohnefurcht,* Cecilie Dressler Verlag (Hamburg, Germany), 1998, translated by Anthea Bell as *Igraine the Brave,* Chicken House (New York, NY), 2007.

Dicke Freundinnen, illustrated by Daniela Kulot, Friedrich Oetinger (Hamburg, Germany), 1998, translated by Oliver G. Latsch as *Best Girl Friends,* 2003.

Kleiner Werwolf, Fischer Verlag (Frankfurt, Germany), 1999.

Das Piratenschwein, illustrated by Kerstin Meyer, Cecelie Dressler Verlag (Hamburg, Germany), 1999.

Strandgeschichten, illustrated by Karin Schliehe and Bernhard Mark, Loewe Verlag (Bindlach, Germany), 1999.

(Self-illustrated) *Herr der Diebe,* Cecelie Dressler Verlag (Hamburg, Germany), 2000, translated by Oliver G. Latsch as *The Thief Lord,* Chicken House/Scholastic (New York, NY), 2002.

Der verlorene Wackelzahn, illustrated by Julia Kaergel, Friedrich Oetinger (Hamburg, Germany), 2000.

(Self-illustrated) *Mick und Mo im Wilden Westen,* Friedrich Oetinger (Hamburg, Germany), 2000, translated by Oliver G. Lasche as *Mick and Mo in the Wild West,* 2002.

Der geheimnisvolle Ritter Namenlos, illustrated by Kerstin Meyer, Fischer Verlag (Frankfurt, Germany), 2001, translated as *Princess Knight,* Chicken House/Scholastic (New York, NY), 2004.

Dicke Freundinnen und der Pferdedieb, illustrated by Daniela Kulot, Friedrich Oetinger (Hamburg, Germany), 2001, translated by Oliver G. Latsch as *Best Girl Friends and the Horse Thief,* 2005.

Als der Weihnachtsmann vom Himmel fiel, illustrated by Regina Kehn, Cecilie Dressler Verlag (Hamburg, Germany), 2001, translated by Oliver G. Latsch as *When Santa Fell to Earth,* illustrated by Paul Howard, Chicken House (New York, NY), 2006.

Emma und der Blaue Dschinn, illustrated by Kerstin Meyer, Cecelie Dressler Verlag (Hamburg, Germany), 2002.

(Self-illustrated) *Die schönsten Erstlesegeschichten,* Fischer Verlag (Frankfurt, Germany), 2002.

Die Glücksfee, illustrated by Sybille Hein, Fischer Verlag (Frankfurt, Germany), 2003.

Kápten Knitterbart und seine Bande, illustrated by Kerstin Meyer, Friedrich Oetinger (Hamburg, Germany), 2003, translated as *Pirate Girl,* Scholastic (New York, NY), 2005.

(Self-illustrated) *Kribbel Krabbel Käferwetter,* Fischer Verlag (Frankfurt, Germany), 2003.

(Self-illustrated) *Vorlesegeschichten von Anna,* Heinrich Ellermann (München, Germany), 2003.

(Self-illustrated) *Lilli und Flosse,* Cecilie Dressler Verlag (Hamburg, Germany), 2004.

(Self-illustrated) *Potilla,* Cecilie Dressler Verlag (Hamburg, Germany), 2004.

Mick und Mo im Weltraum, illustrated by Tina Schulte, Friedrich Oetinger (Hamburg, Germany), 2004.

Der wildeste Bruder der Welt, illustrated by Kerstin Meyer, Friedrich Oetinger (Hamburg, Germany), 2004, translated by Chantal Wright as *The Wildest Brother,* Scholastic (New York, NY), 2006.

Rosannas großer Bruder, illustrated by Jacky Gleich, Friedrich Oetinger (Hamburg, Germany), 2005.

(Self-illustrated) *Zottelkralle,* Cecilie Dressler Verlag (Hamburg, Germany), 2005.

Kápten Knitterbart auf der Schatzinsel, Friedrich Oetinger (Hamburg, Germany), 2006.

Author's books have been translated into dozens of languages.

"WILDEN HÜHNER" SERIES; SELF-ILLUSTRATED FICTION

Die wilden Hühner, Cecilie Dressler Verlag (Hamburg, Germany), 1993.

Die wilden Hühner auf Klassenfahrt, Cecilie Dressler Verlag (Hamburg, Germany), 1996.

Die wilden Hühner: Fuchsalarm, Cecilie Dressler Verlag (Hamburg, Germany), 1998.

Die wilden Hühner un das Glück der Erde, Cecilie Dressler Verlag (Hamburg, Germany), 2000.

Die wilden Hühner: das Bandenbuch zum Mitmachen, Cecilie Dressler Verlag (Hamburg, Germany), 2001.

Die wilden Hühner und die Liebe, Cecilie Dressler Verlag (Hamburg, Germany), 2003.

"GHOSTHUNTERS" SERIES; SELF-ILLUSTRATED FICTION

Gespernsterjäger auf eisiger spur, Loewe Verlag (Bindlach, Germany), 2001, translated by Helena Ragg as *Ghosthuters and the Incredibly Revolting Ghost,* Scholastic (New York, NY), 2006.

Gespernsterjäger im Feuerspuk, Loewe Verlag (Bindlach, Germany), 2001, translated by Helena Ragg as *Ghosthuters and the Gruesome, Invincible Lightning Ghost,* Scholastic (New York, NY), 2006.

Gespernsterjäger in der Gruselburg, Loewe Verlag (Bindlach, Germany), 2001, translated by Helena Ragg as *Ghosthunters and the Totally Mouldy Baroness!,* Scholastic (New York, NY), 2007, published as *Ghosthuters and the Bloodthirsty Baroness!,* Chicken House (London, England), 2007.

Gespernsterjäger in großer Gefahr, Loewe Verlag (Bindlach, Germany), 2001, translated by Helena Ragg as *Ghosthunters and the Muddy Monster of Doom!,* Scholastic (New York, NY), 2007, published as *Ghosthuters and the Mud-dripping Monster!,* Chicken House (London, England), 2007.

"INKWORLD TRILOGY"; SELF-ILLUSTRATED FICTION

Tintenherz, Cecelie Dressler Verlag (Hamburg, Germany), 2003, translated by Anthea Bell as *Inkheart,* Chicken House/Scholastic (New York, NY), 2003.

Tintenblut, Cecelie Dressler Verlag (Hamburg, Germany), 2005, translated by Anthea Bell as *Inkspell,* Chicken House/Scholastic (New York, NY), 2006.

Tintentod, Cecelie Dressler Verlag (Hamburg, Germany), 2007, translated by Anthea Bell as *Inkdeath,* Chicken House/Scholastic (New York, NY), 2008.

Adaptations

The Thief Lord was adapted for audio, read by Simon Jones, Listening Library, 2002, and was adapted and directed by Richard Claus as a feature film, Warner Bros., 2006. *Tintenherz* was adapted as a musical play produced in Bonn, Germany, 2006; *Tintenblut* was adapted as a play produced in Hannover, Germany, 2006. The "Wilden Hüner in Liebe" series was adapted as a German-language film, directed by Vivian Naefe, 2006, and for audiobook. *Inkheart* was adapted as a film starring Brendan Fraser, Helen Mirren, and Jim Broadbent, and produced by New Line Cinema, 2008. *Inkheart* and *Inkspell* were adapted as audiobooks read by Fraser, Listening Library, 2005. *Dragon Rider* was adapted as an audiobook, read by Fraser, and was optioned for film. Several books have been based the films adapted from Funke's books.

Sidelights

English-speaking readers would never have discovered the fantasy fiction of Cornelia Funke if it had not been for one particularly devoted reader. A young fan in Funke's native Germany was prompted to write to British publisher Chicken House when she discovered that she could not read her favorite books in English as well as in German. This letter inspired curiosity in the publisher, and a little research revealed Funke to be one of the most popular children's book writers in all of Germany. Funke's books, which include novels as well as chapter books, and picture books such as *Dragon Rider, The Wildest Brother,* and *The Princess Knight,* are now published in twenty-eight countries. Appraising her work in *Time,* Clive Barker wrote that, refreshingly free of "mawkishness or attendant melodrama," Funke's books gain added depth due to "her moody, unpredictable characters and the distinctive feel of her plots."

Although Funke was educated as a social worker, after graduating from the University of Hamburg she put herself through a program in book illustration while working with underprivileged children during the day. She began an illustration career designing board games and book art, but at first had no plans to become a children's author. Exposed to the books being written for children while working as an illustrator, Funke grew frustrated with the lack of imaginative storytelling, and in the mid-1990s she saw her first book published in

her native Germany. Funke's books—which are based on meticulous research and feature children stepping into magical worlds brought to life in her engaging pen-and-ink illustrations—quickly became popular.

After translating Funke's illustrated novel *Herr der Diebe* into English—a task undertaken by the author's cousin—Chicken House had a bestseller on its hands when the book was published in 2002. *The Thief Lord* is about orphan brothers Prosper, aged twelve, and five-year-old Boniface (Bo), who run away when their childless aunt and uncle decide that they only want Bo to live with them in their house in Hamburg. Before she died, the boys' mother had told the siblings about the wonders of Venice, Italy, and that is where the fugitives now flee. Unfortunately, the boys' relatives are angered at Bo's departure and hire relentless private investigator Victor Getz to follow the brothers' trail. Hiding in an abandoned movie theater, Prosper and Bo live among other street urchins, such as twelve-year-old Scipio—the Thief Lord of the title—who steals from the rich to support this band of pickpockets and petty thieves. Other friends include a girl named Hornet, who *New York Times Book Review* contributor Rebecca Pepper Sinkler described as "a Wendy for the twenty-first century" because "she rides herd on the lost boys but

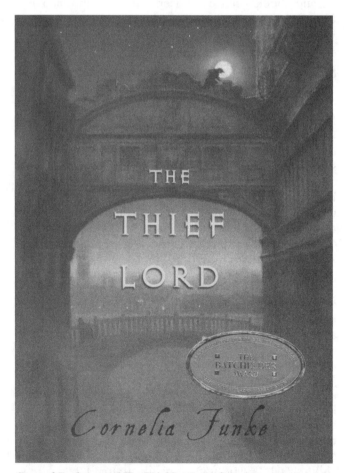

Cover of Funke's novel **The Thief Lord,** *the first of the author's works to be published in English.* (Illustration © 2002 by Christian Birmingham. Reproduced by permission of Scholastic, Inc.)

doesn't do their laundry." When Scipio accepts a job to steal a broken wooden wing from a carved lion, the gang is drawn into a fantastic adventure: the lion is found to be part of a magic carousel that has the power to change children into adults and adults into children.

Praising *The Thief Lord* as a "spellbinding story," a *Kirkus Reviews* contributor wrote that "the magical city of Venice, with its moonlit waters, maze of canals, and magnificent palaces, is an excellent setting." Anita L. Burkam wrote in *Horn Book* that *The Thief Lord* has a "sweet and comforting conclusion that will satisfy readers whose hearts have been touched" by Funke's characters. *School Library Journal* critic John Peters called the book "a compelling tale, rich in ingenious twists, with a setting and cast that will linger in readers' memories," while Sinkler maintained that "what lifts this radiant novel beyond run-of-the-mill fantasy is its palpable respect for both the struggle to grow up and the mixed blessings of growing old."

The Thief Lord won Funke even more English-language fans when it was released in the United States by Scholastic. In the years since, more of her books have been released in translation, and her popularity among English-language readers has been further enhanced by film adaptations of her books *The Thief Lord* and *Inkheart.*

Inkheart, Funke's 2002 novel, is part of a series that also includes *Inkspell* and *Inkdeath.* *Inkheart* revolves around twelve-year-old Meggie, whose bookbinder father, Mo, has a special gift that has almost become a curse. Whenever Mo reads aloud, the characters from the book he is reading are pulled into the real world, while real-world people are pulled into the characters' fictional world. Almost a decade earlier problems arose when Mo read Fenoglio's *Inkheart;* the characters that were released included the evil Capricorn, while Meggie's mother disappeared into the book. Now, nine years have past and a much-older Meggie learns Mo's secret, which explains why her father never read to her while she was growing up. Mo's secret also explains the complexity of the chain of events that begin to unwind after Meggie meets a scarred stranger named Dustfinger. Dustfinger warns Mo that Capricorn's evil henchmen are on his trail: They hope to force Mo to read a monster out of the troublemaking book and then direct the creature to kill Capricorn's enemies. Together with Dustfinger, Meggie, Mo, and Meggie's great-aunt Elinor set off to find Fenoglio, hoping that he can write a new ending to the story that now threatens their lives.

Reviewing *Inkheart* in *School Library Journal,* Sharon Rawlins predicted that Funke's "'story within a story' will delight not just fantasy fans, but all readers who like an exciting plot with larger-than-life characters," while in *Kirkus Reviews* a contributor praised the novel as "a true feast for anyone who has ever been lost in a book."

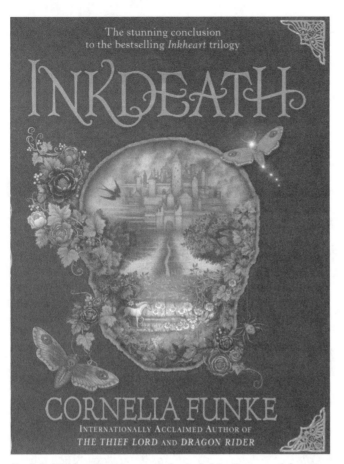

Funke's "Inkheart" series concludes in **Inkdeath,** *a novel featuring cover art by Carol Lawson.* (Illustration © 2008 by Carol Lawson. Reproduced by permission of Scholastic, Inc.)

As *Inkspell* opens, Meggie is serving as Dustfinger's apprentice, joined in that capacity by a boy named Farid. With the aid of a stranger named Orpheus, the three are allowed to travel into the Inkworld, home of Fenoglio and the only place where the evil caused by Capricorn can be written out of *Inkheart*. Orpheus possesses the same talent as Meggie's father, and when he reads several other characters back into the book he allows Meggie and Mo to rejoin Meggie's long-lost mother. As events continue to unfold, wars, intrigues, and other threats mask Funke's underlying question: "what might happen if authors try to change the world they have created," as Beth L. Meister explained in her *School Library Journal* review of the novel. Also noting Funke's complex premise, *Horn Book* critic Claire E. Gross dubbed *Inkspell* a "bibliophilic fantasy" that "pits the power of words against the power of death." Noting the long list of "clearly drawn" characters that people the epic fantasy, Meister praised *Inkheart*'s sequel as an "involving" novel, and in *Booklist* Carolyn Phelan described it as "a stronger book than its predecessor."

In *Inkdeath* Fenoglio can no longer sustain Inkworld with his writing and the land and its people now suffer under the story of Orpheus and the oppressive rule of the evil and moldering Adderhead. Mo fights back by becoming an outlaw on the order of Robin Hood, and with the help of Meggie and the reincarnated Dustfinger he seeks a way to use his ability to transforms stories into reality and overthrow the work's immortal ruler. As Mo and Adderhead inexorably approach a final battle that pits good against evil and posits questions about the value of means versus ends, "Funke successfully explores ideas of fate, [and] free will. . . . in a multi-layered tale with many dramatic moments," according to *School Library Journal* critic Steven Engelfried. Calling the series finale "grueling, blood-spattered, [and] mortality-obsessed," a *Kirkus Reviews* writer maintained that the sophisticated themes in *Inkdeath* make it appropriate for a more-mature readership than *Inkheart.*

Another translated fantasy novel by Funke, *Dragon Rider,* transports readers to the wilds of Scotland, where Earth's last silver dragons live. When their secluded home is finally threatened by humans, a young dragon named Firedrake and a taciturn brownie named Sorrel set out to locate the ancient home of the silver dragons, a place located in the Himalayan mountains. On their journey to the Rim of Heaven, Firedrake and Sorrel are joined by an orphaned boy named Ben and Twigleg, a golem-like creature that is under the sway of the silver dragon's arch enemy, Nettlebrand. The companions' journey, overshadowed by Nettlebrand's sinister machinations, involves encounters with a host of mythic creatures, including djinni, elves, basilisks, roc, sea serpents, and dwarves, and reveals the laws that underlie dragon magic. "Readers will delight in the creatures that turn up in this extended quest," wrote a *Publishers Weekly* contributor in a review of *Dragon Rider,* the critic going on to praise Funke's "lively" protagonists "and their often hilarious banter." Noting the book's extreme popularity among the author's German fans, *Booklist* writer Jennifer Mattson compared *Dragon Rider* to the novels of Lloyd Alexander and praised its "good, old-fashioned ensemble-cast quest." While a *Kirkus Reviews* writer praised the story's "breakneck pace," Mattson maintained that, in relation to *The Thief Lord,* its "gentler, lighter, and more straightforward" plot will make *Dragon Rider* a "winner" among middle-grade readers.

In *Igraine the Brave* Funke introduces readers to another in her series of spunky young heroines. Twelve-year-old Igraine comes from a long line of magicians who make their home at Castle Pimpernel and are the custodians of three very magical books. For Igraine, a life of magic does not hold the adventure she craves; she would rather be a dashing knight in shining armor. Her skill with spell-casting reflects her lack of interest in the magic arts, and one day Igraine accidentally transforms her parents into swine. With the help of her younger brother, Albert, the preteen consults the books and goes in search of the hair of a giant, an ingredient required in order to set her parents to rights. On the way, she also learns of the plans of the baroness of Darkrock, who plans to steal the magic books, and soon the girl has the chance to test her knightly sword-

wielding abilities. In *Kliatt* Janis Flint-Ferguson called *Igraine the Brave* "a delightful, lighthearted romp" that features "the kind of dark, suspenseful occurrences" frequently enjoyed by the book's intended middle-grade readership. Funke's "engaging" novel "is 'joust' the ticket for all young fans of non-gender-specific knightly valor," quipped a *Kirkus Reviews* writer, and in *Publishers Weekly* a critic wrote that the author's "inventive re-imagining of the knight-in-shining-armor story benefits from its playful details" and "an abundance of action and humor."

In addition to epic fantasies, Funke has authored a number of picture books for younger readers, some featuring her own artwork while others are collaborations with German illustrator Kerstin Meyer. In *Pirate Girl* Funke and Meyer pair up to tell the story of an imaginative little girl named Molly, who is sailing to the home of her grandmother. Forced to engage in such horrid activities as peeling potatoes and swabbing decks after being abducted by Captain Firebeard and his band of bloodthirsty pirates, Molly attempts to escape but gets caught. A walk on the plank is only avoided by the arrival of one of the most feared pirates of all—a swashbuckler who coincidently looks a great deal like Molly's real mom! Meyer's "bright, droll mixed-media pen-and-ink" illustrations add to the humor of *Pirate Girl*, according to a *Kirkus Reviews* writer, and Funke's story of "personal cleverness and parental heroism" is one with "universal appeal," in the opinion of *Booklist* contributor Mattson.

Another collaboration between Funke and Meyer, *The Wildest Brother*, introduces Ben, a loving younger brother whose vivid imagination transforms the playful torments he visits on annoyed older sister Anna into battles against a terrible monster. Meyer's "color-soaked cartoons" in *The Wildest Brother* "are bursting with a zany energy," according to *School Library Journal* contributor Susan Weitz, and a *Publishers Weekly* critic wrote that Funke's "exploration of the relationship between a real-world sister and brother" yields "riproaring results."

Funke's self-illustrated "Ghosthunters" series is geared for middle-grade and younger boys who are not keen on reading. In the chapter books *Ghosthunters and the Incredibly Revolting Ghost, Ghosthunters and the Gruesome, Invincible Lightning Ghost, Ghosthunters and the Totally Mouldy Baroness!*, and *Ghosthunters and the Muddy Monster of Doom!* Funke focuses on Hetty Hyssop and friend Tom, who team up with a ghost named Hugo to get to the root of a series of unfortunate hauntings. In *Ghosthunters and the Gruesome, Invincible Lightning Ghost*, for example, the children get slimed at a seaside hotel in a story that *Booklist* critic Francisca Goldsmith described as "more silly than scary." A testy spirit from the seventeenth century causes problems in *Ghosthunters and the Totally Mouldy Baroness!*, while *Ghosthunters and the Muddy Monster of Doom!* finds Hetty and Tom in the village of Bogpool, hoping to

complete a ghost-catching assignment that will help Tom graduate as an official ghosthunter. Funke's "Ghosthunter" books "are more humorous than horrific, and their plots gallop along, accompanied by fun pen-and-ink cartoons," concluded Walter Minkel in his review of the series for *School Library Journal*.

Biographical and Critical Sources

PERIODICALS

Booklist, October 15, 2002, GraceAnne A. DeCandido, review of *The Thief Lord,* p. 401; September 1, 2003, Carolyn Phelan, review of *Inkheart,* p. 114; August, 2004, Jennifer Mattson, review of *Dragon Rider,* p. 1924; June 1, 2005, Jennifer Mattson, review of *Pirate Girl,* p. 1821; October 1, 2005, Carolyn Phelan, review of *Inkspell,* p. 52; December 15, 2006, Francisca Goldsmith, review of *Ghosthunters and the Gruesome Invincible Lightning Ghost!,* p. 48.

Bookseller, June 20, 2003, review of *Inkheart,* p. 32.

Horn Book, November-December, 2002, Anita L. Burkam, review of *The Thief Lord,* pp. 754-755; September-October, 2004, Anita L. Burkam, review of *Dragon Rider,* p. 583; July-August, 2005, Kitty Flynn, review of *Pirate Girl,* p. 449; January-February, 2006, Claire E. Gross, review of *Inkspell,* p. 78.

Journal of Adolescent and Adult Literacy, September, 2003, Jean Boreen, review of *The Thief Lord,* pp. 91-93.

Kirkus Reviews, August 1, 2002, review of *The Thief Lord,* pp. 1128-1129; September 15, 2003, review of *Inkheart,* p. 1174; July 15, 2004, review of *Dragon Rider,* p. 685; June 1, 2005, review of *Pirate Girl,* p. 636; September 1, 2005, review of *Inkspell,* p. 973; April 15, 2006, review of *The Wildest Brother,* p. 406; September 15, 2006, review of *Ghosthunters and the Gruesome Invincible Lightning Ghost!,* p. 953; November 1, 2006, review of *When Santa Fell to Earth,* p. 1129; September 1, 2007, review of *Igraine the Brave;* September 1, 2008, review of *Inkdeath.*

Kliatt, November, 2007, Janis Flint-Ferguson, review of *Igraine the Brave,* p. 10.

Language Arts, January, 2003, Junko Yokota, review of *The Thief Lord,* p. 236.

New York Times Book Review, November 17, 2002, Rebecca Pepper Sinkler, review of *The Thief Lord,* p. 1.

Publishers Weekly, June 24, 2002, review of *The Thief Lord,* pp. 57-58; July 21, 2003, review of *Inkheart,* p. 196; July 19, 2004, review of *Dragon Rider,* p. 162; May 1, 2006, review of *The Wildest Brother,* p. 63; July 24, 2006, review of *Ghosthunters and the Incredibly Revolting Ghost!,* p. 58; February 19, 2007, review of *Princess Pigsty,* p. 168; September 10, 2007, review of *Igraine the Brave,* p. 61; September 22, 2008, review of *Inkdeath,* p. 59.

School Library Journal, October, 2002, John Peters, review of *The Thief Lord,* pp. 163-164; October, 2003, Sharon Rawlins, review of *Inkheart,* p. 164; October,

2004, Beth Wright, review of _Dragon Rider,_ p. 164; August, 2005, Grace Oliff, review of _Pirate Girl,_ p. 94; October, 2005, Beth L. Meister, review of _Inkspell,_ p. 161; June, 2006, Susan Weitz, review of _The Wildest Brother,_ p. 112; October, 2006, Mara Alpert, review of _When Santa Fell to Earth,_ p. 96; November, 2006, Elaine E. Knight, review of _Ghosthunters and the Gruesome Invincible Lightning Ghost!,_ p. 94; April, 2007, Catherine Callegari, review of _Princess Pigsty,_ p. 105; September, 2007, Walter Minkel, review of _Ghosthunters and the Muddy Monsters of Doom!,_ p. 164; December, 2008, Steven Engelfried, review of _Inkdeath,_ p. 124.

Time, April 18, 2005, Clive Barker, "The Next J.K. Rowling?," p. 120.

ONLINE

Cornelia Funke Home Page, http://www.corneliafunke.de (December 20, 2009).

Guardian Unlimited, http://www.guardian.co.uk/ (June 22, 2002), Jan Mark, review of _The Thief Lord;_ (November 22, 2003) Diana Wynne Jones, review of _Inkheart._

Scholastic Web site, http://www.scholastic.com/ (December 20, 2009), "Cornelia Funke."*

*   *   *

FUNKE, Cornelia Caroline
See FUNKE, Cornelia

G

GIFALDI, David 1950-

Personal

Born February 24, 1950, in Brockport, NY; son of Americo and Angie Gifaldi; married Marita Keys, November 25, 1989. *Education:* Duquesne University, B.A., 1972; Western Washington University, elementary and secondary teaching credentials. *Hobbies and other interests:* Reading, swimming, backpacking, gardening, baseball.

Addresses

Home—Portland, OR. *E-mail*—dg@davidgifaldi.com.

Career

Educator and author. Bellingham School District, Bellingham, WA, and Vancouver School District, Vancouver, WA, substitute teacher, 1980-83; Vancouver School District, teacher, beginning 1985. Vermont College, member of faculty in M.F.A. program in writing for children and young adults.

Member

Society of Children's Book Writers and Illustrators, National Educational Association.

Awards, Honors

Best Book for Reluctant Young-Adult Readers designation, American Library Association, 1990, and Michigan Library Association Young-Adult Forum Award nominee, both for *Yours till Forever;* Notable Book for a Global Society designation, and Cooperative Children's Book Center Best-of-the-Year listee, both 2008, both for *Listening for Crickets.*

Writings

MIDDLE-GRADE NOVELS

One Thing for Sure, Clarion (New York, NY), 1986.

Yours till Forever, Lippincott/HarperCollins (New York, NY), 1989.

Gregory, Maw, and the Mean One, Clarion (New York, NY), 1992.

Toby Scudder, Ultimate Warrior, Clarion (New York, NY), 1993, published as *Toby Scudder, King of the School,* Clarion (New York, NY), 2005.

Ben, King of the River, illustrated by Layne Johnson, Albert Whitman (Morton Grove, IL), 2001.

Listening for Crickets, Henry Holt (New York, NY), 2008.

OTHER

The Boy Who Spoke Colors (picture book), illustrated by C. Shana Greger, Houghton Mifflin (Boston, MA), 1993.

Rearranging, and Other Stories, Atheneum Books for Young Readers (New York, NY), 1998.

Contributor to periodicals, including *Cricket, Teen, Highlights for Children, Alive! for Young Teens, Children's Digest,* and *Jack and Jill.*

Sidelights

A fifth-grade teacher from Portland, Oregon, David Gifaldi is also the author of the picture book *The Boy Who Spoke Colors,* as well as of middle-grade novels such as *Toby Scudder, King of the School* and *Listening for Crickets* and the anthology *Rearranging, and Other Stories.* In addition to teaching and writing, Gifaldi lectures at schools and conferences and also serves on the faculty of Vermont College's M.F.A. program in writing for children and young adults. Praising *Rearranging, and Other Stories* in *Booklist,* John Peters described Gifaldi's nine stories as "smoothy crafted" tales geared "for readers teetering on the brink of adolescence."

Gifaldi grew up in Holley, New York, a small town near Lake Ontario. "Summers in Holley were filled with baseball, band concerts, carnivals, and playing Tarzan off the rope swings at various swimming holes," he

once told *SATA*. "Winters were for ice skating and sledding. The town had an outdoor rink, really just a scooped out pond that the firemen would fill when the cold came down from Canada. There was a little shed for changing and taking a breather after playing hockey or trying out some of the figure skating moves we kids saw on TV. The best was skating at night with the floodlights on and stars shivering in the dark overhead . . . the cold sucking your breath. I recall the sound of skate blades on ice, the cries of children and adults at play, and the warm feeling inside knowing that Christmas was just a week away." It was during his childhood that the magic of books such as *Tom Sawyer* came alive for Gifaldi.

Although Gifaldi began writing poetry and keeping a journal following college, he did not become serious about writing until he met young-adult novelist Richard Peck at a summer workshop and Peck encouraged him to write. While completing his teacher-certification program at Western Washington University, Gifaldi also took a correspondence writing course. His persistence in writing stories for children led to his first sale of a short story printed in *Children's Digest*. He continued to write while supporting himself as a substitute teacher.

In his first middle-grade novel, *One Thing for Sure,* Gifaldi focuses on twelve-year old Dylan, who is shocked and disillusioned when his father is arrested. Since he lives in a small town, Dylan must cope with being labeled a thief himself, while also feeling that he must defend his father while in reality he resents him. A *Publishers Weekly* critic noted of the novel that "Gifaldi has great flair for figurative language" and uses it to demonstrate the preteen's perception of the world.

In *Yours till Forever* Rick, a high-school senior, notices that his two friends were born the same day his parents were killed in a car accident. When the friends fall in love with each other, Rick suspects that they are the reincarnation of his parents and therefore destined for the same tragic fate. Portrayed through a lens melding Eastern religion and American high-school culture, "the concept of forever takes on special meaning . . . in a competently sketched tale," noted Margaret A. Bush in her *Horn Book* review of *Yours till Forever.* In *Locus* Carolyn Cushman described the novel as "an involving and intelligent tale of teenagers just starting out in life" that also presents an informative exploration of the topic of reincarnation.

Gifaldi mimics the style of folk stories and tall tales in *Gregory, Maw, and the Mean One.* In this original tall tale, a seven-foot-tall, grizzly outlaw known as the Mean One terrorizes the citizens of Sharpesville. Fortunately, with the help of Gregory and his Maw, the Mean One is helped to change his mood from dark to upbeat after a trip back into the past to reclaim his lost heart. As a reviewer stated in *Publishers Weekly,* Gifaldi's "clever writing bears a subtle though worthwhile message about the potential good in everyone." A book for

David Gifaldi tells a story about the close relationship between two brothers in Ben, King of the River, *featuring artwork by Layne Johnson.* (Albert Whitman & Company, 2001. Illustration copyright © 2001 by Layne Johnson. Reproduced by permission.)

even younger children, *The Boy Who Spoke Colors* has more of a folk-tale feel. Here Gifaldi focuses on a young couple whose infant son learns to speak in magical puffs of color after being swaddled in a colorful patchwork blanket that was lovingly crafted by his mother.

Originally published as *Toby Scudder, Ultimate Warrior, Toby Scudder, King of the School* focuses on an overweight soon-to-be sixth grader. Upset by the situation at home, twelve-year-old Toby has used his intimidating size and crude personality to bully his classmates throughout fifth grade. Although his final year of elementary school holds great promise, Toby finds his view of progress changing when he is assigned to mentor a younger student by his new sixth-grade science teacher. In her review of *Toby Scudder, Ultimate Warrior, Booklist* critic Janice Del Negro described Gifaldi's young protagonist as "a well-developed character" who "evolves realistically" from a bully to a confident teen, while a *Publishers Weekly* critic cited the "gritty reality" that "informs [the story's] dialogue."

Featuring artwork by Layne Johnson, *Ben, King of the River* focuses on a boy's relationship with his developmentally disabled little brother. Although Chad is excited about the camping trip his family has planned, he also worries about five-year-old Ben. Still in diapers, Ben dislikes changes in his normal routine and the

younger boy's preferences seem to dictate much of the activity in the family. Praising Johnson's contribution of "expressive watercolors," *Booklist* contributor Lauren Peterson added that *Ben, King of the River* will be useful for adults hoping to "increase awareness and sensitivity" to the disabled. Margaret C. Howell also noted Gifaldi's inclusion of "useful tips" for children "living with a mentally disabled sibling,"

In *Listening for Crickets* Jake is ten years old and worried. His teacher has labeled him a below-par learner, his mom and dad are fighting, and his little sister has asthma. The boy's curiosity and desire to be friendly and helpful allow him to deal with these worries, however, and even try to make things better in his own way. Gifaldi tells the story in Jake's voice, bringing to life a "capable and resilient" young boy who sees the people in his life "compassionately." The author "strikes just the right chord, never preaching" or becoming "maudlin," according to a *Kirkus Reviews* writer, and in *Booklist* Hazel Rochman described Jake's first-person narration as "touching" and realistic.

Gifaldi enjoys both teaching and writing because the two go together: Both the teaching experiences and the students give him numerous ideas to write about. "I like writing for young people because I enjoy looking at the

world through the eyes of a ten or twelve or sixteen year old," he once explained. "Things always seem fresher that way. Growing up is hard. But it's also a time of wonder and discovery. Writing keeps me on my toes, wondering and discovering."

Biographical and Critical Sources

PERIODICALS

Booklist, May 1, 1993, Annie Ayers, review of *The Boy Who Spoke Colors,* p. 1603; October 15, 1993, Janice Del Negro, review of *Toby Scudder, Ultimate Warrior,* p. 442; April 15, 1998, John Peters, review of *Rearranging, and Other Stories,* p. 1435; March 1, 2001, Lauren Peterson, review of *Ben, King of the River,* p. 1286; May 15, 2008, Hazel Rochman, review of *Listening for Crickets,* p. 43.
Horn Book, September-October, 1989, Margaret A. Bush, review of *Yours till Forever,* p. 627; September-October, 2008, Susan Dove Lempke, review of *Listening for Crickets,* p. 583.
Junior Literary Guild, October, 1986, review of *One Thing for Sure.*
Kirkus Reviews, April 15, 2008, review of *Listening for Crickets.*
Locus, July, 1989, Carolyn Cushman, review of *Yours till Forever,* p. 50.
Publishers Weekly, August 22, 1986, review of *One Thing for Sure,* p. 99; August 3, 1992, review of *Gregory, Maw, and the Mean One,* p. 72; May 10, 1993, review of *Publishers Weekly,* p. 72; August 16, 1993, review of *Toby Scudder, Ultimate Warrior,* p. 104; May 25, 1998, review of *Rearranging, and Other Stories,* p. 91.
School Library Journal, June, 1993, Nancy A. Gifford, review of *The Boy Who Spoke Colors,* p. 74; October, 1993, Jacqueline Rose, review of *Toby Scudder, Ultimate Warrior,* p. 124; June, 1998, Dona J. Helmer, review of *Rearranging, and Other Stories,* p. 145; June, 2001, Margaret C. Howell, review of *Ben, King of the River,* p. 114.

ONLINE

Cynsations Web log, http://www.cynthialeitichsmith. blogspot.com/ (July 2, 2008), Cynthia Leitich Smith, interview with Gifaldi.
David Gifaldi Home Page, http://www.davidgifaldi.com (December 12, 2009).*

Cover of Gifaldi's middle-grade novel Listening for Crickets, **featuring artwork by Steve Adams.** (Illustration © 2008 by Steve Adams. Reprinted by permission of Henry Holt & Company, LLC.)

*   *   *

GILMORE, Rachna 1953-
(Rachna Mara)

Personal

Born October 11, 1953, in India; married Ian Gilmore; children: two. *Education:* King's College London, B.Sc.

(biology); University of Prince Edward Island, B.Ed. *Hobbies and other interests:* Walking, reading, gardening, traveling.

Addresses

Home—Ottawa, Ontario, Canada. *E-mail*—rachnagil more@hotmail.com.

Career

Author. Briefly worked as a paralegal; formerly operated a pottery studio.

Member

PEN, Writer's Union of Canada, Society of Children's Book Writers and Illustrators, Canadian Society of Authors, Illustrators, and Performers, Ottawa Children's Literature Roundtable, Arts Ottawa East.

Awards, Honors

Canadian Children's Book Centre (CCBC) Choice designation, 1994, for *Lights for Gita,* 1995, for *A Friend like Zilla,* 1996, for *Roses for Gita,* 1999, for *A Gift for Gita* and *Fangs and Me,* 2000, for *A Screaming Kind of Day,* 2001, for *Mina's Spring of Colors,* 2006, for *The Sower of Tales,* 2007, for *Grandpa's Clock* and *When-I-was-a-little-girl;* International Reading Association Children's Book Award shortlist, Mr, Christie Book Award shortlist, and Silver Birch Award shortlist, all 1996, all for *A Friend like Zilla;* Governor Genera's Literary Award for Children's Literature, 1999, for *A Screaming Kind of Day;* Silver Birch Award shortlist, 2001, for *Mina's Spring of Colors;* Gloucester (Ontario) Arts Award for outstanding artistic achievement, 2000; New York Public Library Books for the Teen Age selection, Books of the Year selection, Bank Street College of Education, Jane Addams Children's Book Award Honor Book designation, and Cooperative Children's Book Center Choices designation, all 2002, all for *A Group of One;* Red Maple Book Award nomination, and IODE Violet Downey Book Award, both 2006, and Manitoba Young Readers' Choice Award nomination, 2007, all for *The Sower of Tales;* Blue Spruce Award nomination, 2009, for *Making Grizzle Grow;* CCBC Best Books designation, 2009, for *Making Grizzle Grow.*

Writings

JUVENILE

My Mother Is Weird, illustrated by Brenda Jones, Ragweed Press (Charlottetown, Prince Edward Island, Canada), 1988.

Wheniwasalittlegirl, illustrated by Sally J.K. Davies, Second Story Press (Toronto, Ontario, Canada), 1989, published as *When-I-Was-a-Little-Girl,* illustrated by Renné Benoit, Second Story Press (Toronto, Ontario, Canada), 2006.

Jane's Loud Mouth, illustrated by Kimberly Hart, Ragweed Press (Charlottetown, Prince Edward Island, Canada), 1990.

Aunt Fred Is a Witch, illustrated by Chum McLeod, Second Story Press (Toronto, Ontario, Canada), 1991.

Lights for Gita, illustrated by Alice Priestly, Tilbury House (Gardiner, ME), 1994.

A Friend like Zilla, illustrated by Alice Priestly, Second Story Press (Toronto, Ontario, Canada), 1995.

Roses for Gita, illustrated by Alice Priestly, Second Story Press (Toronto, Ontario, Canada), 1996, Tilbury House (Gardiner, ME), 2001.

Wild Rilla, illustrated by Yvonne Cathcart, Second Story Press (Toronto, Ontario, Canada), 1997.

A Gift for Gita, illustrated by Alice Priestly, Second Story Press (Toronto, Ontario, Canada), 1998, Tilbury House (Gardiner, ME), 2002.

A Screaming Kind of Day, illustrated by Gordon Suave, Fitzhenry & Whiteside (Markham, Ontario, Canada), 1999.

Fangs and Me, illustrated by Gordon Suave, Fitzhenry & Whiteside (Toronto, Ontario, Canada), 1999.

Ellen's Terrible TV Troubles, illustrated by John Mardon, Fitzhenry & Whiteside (Toronto, Ontario, Canada), 1999.

Mina's Spring of Colors, Fitzhenry & Whiteside (Markham, Ontario, Canada), 2000.

A Group of One, Holt (New York, NY), 2001.

The Sower of Tales, Fitzhenry & Whiteside (Markham, Ontario, Canada), 2005.

Grandpa's Clock, illustrated by Amy Meissner, Orca Book Publishers (Custer, WA), 2006.

Making Grizzle Grow, illustrated by Leslie Elizabeth Watts, Fitzhenry & Whiteside (Markham, Ontario, Canada), 2007.

The Trouble with Dilly, HarperCollins Canada (Toronto, Ontario, Canada), 2009.

Gilmore's books have been translated into Belgian, Catalan, French, German, Danish, Korean, and Spanish.

OTHER

(As Rachna Mara) *Of Customs and Excise* (adult fiction), Second Story Press (Toronto, Ontario, Canada), 1991.

Sidelights

Canadian children's author Rachna Gilmore draws on her experiences as an immigrant and as a child of diverse cultures in writing her books for children. In addition to producing picture books such as *A Screaming Kind of Day, When-I-Was-a-Little-Girl,* and *Grandpa's Clock,* she is also the author of the young-adult novel *A Group of One,* the middle-grade fantasy *The Sower of Tales,* and a series of elementary-grade novel featuring an engaging young girl named Gita.

Gilmore was born in India and moved to England when she was fourteen years old. After earning her university degree in London, Gilmore moved across the Atlantic

Rachna Gilmore's energetic picture book **A Screaming Kind of Day** *features artwork by Gordon Suave.* (Fitzhenry & Whiteside, 1999. Illustration © 1999 by Gordon Sauve. Reproduced by permission.)

to Prince Edward Island, Canada. While living in this eastern Canadian province, she earned another university degree, married, and had two daughters. After working for attorneys and even establishing her own pottery studio, Gilmore decided that she should no longer put off her dream of being a writer. As she noted on her home page, "I realized that I kept putting it off because I was afraid I wouldn't succeed. But I didn't want to wake up one morning and find that I was eighty years old, and wished I had tried."

Gilmore published her first children's book, *My Mother Is Weird,* in 1988. *Aunt Fred Is a Witch,* another early work, "challenges our sometimes narrow way of looking at things," according to *Canadian Children's Literature* reviewer Jennifer Charles. Believing that other members of her family consider eccentric Aunt Fred to be an oddity, Lelia fears the worst when she is sent away to the elderly woman's home for the weekend. As she and Aunt Fred participate in a series of exciting activities, the girl cannot enjoy them due to worries that Fred may cast a spell on her. However, by the end of her trip, Lelia comes to realize that her family ostracizes the independent woman not because Fred is a witch, but because she insists on doing things her own way and rejects limits placed on her because of her age. *Canadian Literature* critic Lynn Wytenbroek predicted that *Aunt Fred Is a Witch* "should be very engaging for young readers."

First published in 1989 with illustrations by Sally J.K. Davies, *When-I-Was-a-Little-Girl* has been more-recently re-illustrated by Renné Benoit. In the book, a young girl named Lisabeth wants to be good, but her

mother always finds her lacking when she compares Lisabeth's behavior to her memories of her own, perfect, childhood. Fortunately, Grandma sets the record straight when she comes for a visit, and she assures Lisabeth that the girl's mother—and Grandma's own little girl—was actually not as perfect as Mom asserted and Lisbeth has imagined in conjuring up visions of "When-I-Was-a-Little-Girl." Calling Gilmore's story "simple," *Quill & Quire* critic Gwyneth Evans added that "its sweetly humorous message will amuse parents as well as children."

Another multigenerational story, *Grandpa's Clock* features artwork by Amy Meissner. Called a "richly textured tale of family relationships" by Evans, the book follows Cayley, a girl who loves her grandfather. When Cayley was little and frightened by nightmares, Grandpa made her a ticking clock to help coax her into a calm sleep. Now that she is older, the elderly clockmaker is working on a new clock, but when the man suffers a heart attack and can no longer work to finish the promised timepiece, the girl is willing to give up her clock so that it can comfort the infirm man. Both Cayley and young readers learn "the value of intergenerational relationships," asserted Carol L. MacKay in her *School Library Journal* review of *Grandpa's Clock,* and Evans observed that the author also "uses the craft of clockmaking to show how creating a beautiful and useful object has a value beyond the material."

Another picture book by Gilmore, *Making Grizzle Grow,* features illustrations by Leslie Elizabeth Watts. In the story, a little girl named Emily is frustrated that her father cannot take time to play with her in the snow. She constructs a dinosaur out of snow, names it Grizzle, and uses her imagination to make the icy creature grow into a voraciously hungry beast that represents her childishly self-centered frustration. "Written with humor and creativity," the picture book "dramatizes the tenderness of a parent-child relationship," according to a *Kirkus Reviews* writer, observing that the little girl's "love [ultimately] outweighs her anger" toward her father. Gilmore's "personification" of Emily's "anger . . . is effective, funny, and just a little bit scary," asserted Janice Del Negro in a *School Library Journal* review of *Making Grizzle Grow,* and in *Resource Links* Linda Berezowski recommended the story as "an excellent opening for discussions about family relationships and roles." Berezowski also praised Watts's illustrations, which she described as "bright and bold" and perfect for "group presentation."

In 1994 Gilmore published the first of several books that focus on a young immigrant girl named Gita. *Lights for Gita* finds the young Canadian desperately missing the friends and extended family she remembers from her former home in New Delhi. When the Hindu festival of Divali arrives, Gita looks forward to celebrating the festival of lights with her immediate family and new acquaintances. However, an ice storm interrupts the intended celebration, preventing some guests from

arriving and keeping Gita's father from lighting the traditional fireworks. After the electricity goes out, the girl thinks all is lost. However, when she and her new best friend place a lit mustard-oil lamp in front of each window, Gita sees that her new home is unique and its light from within represents the true spirit of the festival. "Gilmore's smooth prose and thoughtful imagery invite readers into Gita's not so foreign world," noted a *Publishers Weekly* reviewer, while in *Booklist* Hazel Rochman wrote that the book's "words and pictures weave the particular holiday traditions into a universal story of disappointment and hope."

Gita returns in *Roses for Gita* and *A Gift for Gita*. In *Roses for Gita* the girl desperately wishes for a garden like the one her grandmother tended back home in India. While her mother works to complete a university degree, Gita longingly looks at the cultivated backyard of her neighbor, Mr. Flinch. Although she fears her neighbor, who has warned the girl to stay off his property, she eventually decides to put aside her fears and build a friendship with the old man. The seemingly curmudgeonly Mr. Flinch obliges, and their friendship fills some of the emptiness in Gita's heart. Reviewers cited Gilmore's ability to express the young girl's emotions in the story, *Books in Canada* contributor Gillian Chan writing that the author "concentrates on Gita's emotions, rather than the events that caused them." This

Gilmore's award-winning picture book Making Grizzle Grow *features the story of an unusual pet and is brought to life in artwork by Leslie Elizabeth Watts.* (Fitzhenry & Whiteside, 2007. Illustration copyright © 2007 by Leslie Elizabeth Watts. All rights reserved. Reproduced by permission.)

technique lets "the reader empathize with her situation" and involves them in the girl's story, the critic added. Writing in *Quill & Quire,* Janet McNaughton noted that Gilmore "is remarkably adept at presenting subtle emotions," calling *Roses for Gita* a book "about the importance of beauty in life, and the ability of kindness to overcome fear."

In *A Gift for Gita,* the girl has finally adjusted to life in her new country. Now she grows upset when her father announces that he has received an offer for a job that would return the family to India. With an enjoyable life and good friends in Canada, she is not sure that she wants to leave her new home. After discussing the potential move with her grandmother, Gita learns that change is hard for adults as well. Although her parents decide to stay in Canada, the young girl treasures the new knowledge she gained from her grandmother: that the memories she carries inside her are ultimately more important that what is occurring in the world around her. Calling *A Gift for Gita* a fitting installment in the series, *Canadian Children's Literature* contributor Judith Carson added that "the intergenerational aspects of the Gita stories are very instructional to children who do not have older adults in their lives."

In *The Sower of Tales* Gilmore moves to fantasy, telling a story about Calantha. Like many others in her village, the girl eagerly anticipates the upcoming Talemeet, an event where story pods are collected and their ripened stories told before the hushed gathering of attentive residents. Calantha expects to be apprenticed to the town's Gatherer, so when the story pod plants mysteriously disappear she is given the task of locating the sower of tales so that another crop of story pods can be harvested to entertain her village. Although Gilmore's story contains well-known fantasy elements, such as an evil sorcerer and the threat of war by a neighboring kingdom, *The Sower of Tales* "is suspensefully rooted in well-drawn characters and is emotionally affecting," according to *Quill & Quire* critic Robert Wiersema. In *Booklist* Krista Hutley characterized Gilmore's novel as "a classic hero's journey" that features "a likeably stubborn heroine," while in *School Library Journal* Sue Giffard wrote that in *The Sower of Tales* "the power of story to heal and give courage takes center stage."

Geared for older readers, *A Group of One* follows the story of fifteen-year-old Tara Mehta. Born in Canada to Indian parents, Tara struggles between identifying with the ethnic heritage of her family and the culture of her birth country. At school, the teenager insists that she is just as Canadian as everyone else, despite her teacher's attempts to hold her up as an outsider. When Tara's alienated grandmother decides to visit her family in Canada for an extended vacation, the visit raises new questions for the teen. Assuming herself to be an ordinary Canadian, Tara is surprised to learn about her grandmother's participation in India's movement for independence and the suffering endured by the family as a result of the woman's involvement. At first shocked

and disappointed that her children do not know their family's history, Tara's grandmother eventually plays an important role in educating Tara and giving her a better sense of who she is. *A Group of One* "asks a number of important questions within the framework of a good story," wrote Bruce Anne Shook in a *School Library Journal* review. In *Horn Book* Jennifer M. Brabander maintained that the novel's power "lies in its refusal to simplify things" and predicted that Tara's "fight for the right to choose her own identity will resonate with young people."

In an interview with Noreen Kruzich Violetta on the Society of Children's Book Writers and Illustrators—Canada Web site, Gilmore offered the following advice to aspiring authors. "I think the most important thing to remember is that you can take courses on writing, think about writing, dream about writing, and read about writing—but there is only one way to learn, and that is to actually WRITE. . .," she noted. "If you keep an open mind and learn from each of the dead ends that you encounter, then you will succeed."

Biographical and Critical Sources

PERIODICALS

Booklist, June 1, 1995, Hazel Rochman, review of *Lights for Gita,* p. 1785; September 15, 2002, Ilene Cooper, review of *A Gift for Gita,* p. 240; December 15, 2005, Krista Hutley, review of *The Sower of Tales,* p. 39; January 1, 2008, Janice Del Negro, review of *Making Grizzle Grow,* p. 95.

Books in Canada, May, 1992, Phil Hall, "Moving Parts," pp. 58-59; May, 1997, Gillian Chan, review of *Roses for Gita,* p. 34.

Canadian Children's Literature, Volume 137, number 67, Jennifer Charles, "Witches without Broomsticks and Beds That Go 'Creak' in the Night," pp. 84-85; winter, 1999, Judith Carson, "The Immigrant and a Sense of Belonging," pp. 92-94.

Canadian Literature, autumn, 1992, Lynn Wytenbroek, review of *Aunt Fred Is a Witch,* pp. 164-166.

Globe & Mail (Toronto, Ontario, Canada), November 24, 2007, Susan Perren, review of *Making Grizzle Grow,* p. D16.

Horn Book, September, 2001, Jennifer M. Brabander, review of *A Group of One,* p. 583.

Kirkus Reviews, December 15, 2007, review of *Making Grizzle Grow.*

Publishers Weekly, June 26, 1995, review of *Lights for Gita,* p. 107; July 9, 2001, review of *A Group of One,* p. 69.

Quill & Quire, November, 1996, Janet McNaughton, review of *Roses for Gita,* p. 45; November, 2005, Robert Wiersema, review of *The Sower of Tales;* March, 2006, Gwyneth Evans, review of *Grandpa's Clock;* November, 2006, Gwyneth Evans, review of *When-I-Was-a-Little-Girl;* November, 2007, review of *Making Grizzle Grow.*

Resource Links, October, 2001, Gail Lennon, review of *A Group of One,* p. 13; December, 2005, K.V. Johansen, review of *The Sower of Tales,* p. 28; April, 2006, Adriane Pettit, review of *Grandpa's Clock,* p. 5; December, 2006, Kathryn McNaughton, review of *When-I-Was-a-Little-Girl,* p. 2; December, 2007, Linda Berezowski, review of *Making Grizzle Grow,* p. 3.

School Librarian, autumn, 1999, David Lewis, review of *A Gift for Gita,* p. 136.

School Library Journal, July, 2001, Bruce Anne Shook, review of *A Group of One,* p. 108; January, 2006, Sue Giffard, review of *The Sower of Tales,* p. 132; June, 2006, Carol L. MacKay, review of *Grandpa's Clock,* p. 113; March, 2008, Kathleen Kelly MacMillan, review of *Making Grizzle Grow,* p. 162.

ONLINE

Rachna Gilmore Home Page, http://www.rachnagilmore.ca (December 15, 2009).

Society of Children's Book Writers and Illustrators—Canada Web site, http://wwwscbwicanada.org/ (November 6, 2001), interview with Gilmore.

*   *   *

GONSALVES, Rob 1959-

Personal

Born 1959, in Toronto, Ontario, Canada. *Education:* Attended college. *Hobbies and other interests:* Playing guitar.

Addresses

Home—Mallorytown, Ontario, Canada.

Career

Architect and illustrator. Designer of theatre backdrops; muralist. Full-time painter, beginning 1990. *Exhibitions:* Work exhibited at Toronto Outdoor Art Exhibition. Art Expo New York, Art Expo Los Angeles, Decor Atlanta, Fine Art Forum, Discovery Galleries, Hudson River Art Gallery, Saper Galleries, and Kaleidoscope Gallery, and included in private collections.

Member

Fellowship of the Gourd and the Arrow (founder).

Awards, Honors

Governor General's Award for Illustration, 2005, for *Imagine a Day* by Sarah L. Thomson.

Illustrator

Sarah L. Thomson, *Imagine a Night,* Atheneum Books for Young Readers (New York, NY), 2003.

Sarah L. Thomson, *Imagine a Day,* Atheneum Books for Young Readers (New York, NY), 2005.

Sarah L. Thomson, *Imagine a Place,* Atheneum Books for Young Readers (New York, NY), 2008.

Biographical and Critical Sources

PERIODICALS

Booklist, January 1, 2005, Carolyn Phelan, review of *Imagine a Day,* p. 862.

Kirkus Reviews, May 15, 2003, review of *Imagine a Night,* p. 758; January 1, 2005, review of *Imagine a Day,* p. 58.

New York Times Book Review, November 1, 2003, Susan Perren, review of *Imagine a Night,* p. D22.

Publishers Weekly, June 9, 2003, review of *Imagine a Night,* p. 50.

Quill & Quire, July, 2003, Ingrid Masak Mida, review of *Imagine a Night;* February, 2005, Philippa Sheppard, review of *Imagine a Day.*

School Arts, October, 2005, Ken Marantz, review of *Imagine a Day,* p. 67.

School Library Journal, April, 2005, Catherine Threadgill, review of *Imagine a Day,* p. 114; December, 2008, Kathy Krasniewicz, review of *Imagine a Place,* p. 104.*

*   *   *

GUAY, Rebecca
(Rebecca Guay-Mitchell)

Personal

Married; children: one daughter. *Education:* Pratt Institute, B.F.A. (fine art), 1992.

Addresses

Home—Amherst, MA. *E-mail*—rebeccaguay@yahoo.com.

Career

Painter and illustrator. Creator of art for video games and role-playing games, including *Magic: The Gathering.* Guest lecturer at Savannah School of Art and Design, 1994, University of Massachusetts, 1999, 2002, Rhode Island School of Design, 2007, and Eric Carle Museum of Picture-Book Art, 2007, 2008. *Exhibitions:* Work exhibited at Society of Illustrators Best of Contemporary Fantastic Art show, 2006, 2009; Eric Carle Museum of Picture Book Art, 2007; and R. Michelson Gallery, Northampton, MA, 2003-09. Work included in private collections.

Awards, Honors

Eisner Award nomination for Best New Artist, 1994; Gen Con Art Show Judges Choice award, 1999, Best in Show award, 2004; *Inquest* magazine Best Artist award, 2005; Chesley Award for Outstanding Achievement in Fantasy Art nomination, 2008; Chesley Award for Best Monochrome Image nomination, 2009.

Illustrator

Terry LaBan, *Green Lantern: 1,001 Emerald Nights* (graphic novel), DC Comics (New York, NY), 2001

Stephen Krensky, *Nellie Bly: A Name to Be Reckoned With,* Aladdin (New York, NY), 2003.

Burleigh Mutten, *Goddesses: A World of Myth and Magic,* Barefoot Books (Cambridge, MA), 2003.

Jane Yolen and Heidi E.Y. Stemple, *The Barefoot Book of Ballet Stories,* Barefoot Books (Cambridge, MA), 2004.

(As Rebecca Guy-Mitchell) Louise Hawes, *Muti's Necklace: The Oldest Story in the World,* Houghton Mifflin (Boston, MA), 2006.

Louise Hawes, *Black Pearls: A Faerie Strand,* Houghton Mifflin (Boston, MA), 2008.

Contributor of illustrations to role-playing games published by White Wolf and Wizards of the Coast, beginning 1995. Contributor to periodicals, including *Dragon* and *Game Trade* magazine.

Biographical and Critical Sources

PERIODICALS

Booklist, November 1, 2004, Ilene Cooper, review of *The Barefoot Book of Ballet Stories,* p. 498.

Publishers Weekly, September 20, 2004, review of *The Barefoot Book of Ballet Stories,* p. 65.

School Library Journal, September, 2003, Laura Scott, review of *Nellie Bly: A Name to Be Reckoned With,* p. 224; July, 2004, Miriam Lang Budin, review of *Goddesses: A World of Myth and Magic,* p. 126; December, 2004, Carol Schene, review of *The Barefoot Book of Ballet Stories,* p. 172.

ONLINE

Pen and Paper Role-Playing Game Database, http://www.pen-paper.net/ (December 15, 2009), "Rebecca Guay."

Rebecca Guay Home Page, http://www.rebeccaguay.com (December 15, 2009).*

*   *   *

GUAY-MITCHELL, Rebecca
See GUAY, Rebecca

H

HEARN, Diane Dawson 1952-

Personal
Born April 24, 1952, in Galveston, TX; daughter of Wilfred Thomas (a vice president of CBS Radio) and Nita (a librarian) Dawson; married Walter Lee Hearn (a graphic designer), May 19, 1984; children: Leana Beth, Melanie June. *Education:* Attended Stephens College, 1970-71, and Rhode Island School of Design 1971-73; School of Visual Arts, B.F.A. (illustration), 1975. *Hobbies and other interests:* Reading, gardening, tai chi, movies, playing board games.

Addresses
Home—Blacksburg, VA. *Agent*—Liza Voges, Kirchoff-Wohlberg, 866 United Nations Plaza, Ste. 525, New York, NY 10017. *E-mail*—ddh@dianedawsonhearn.com.

Career
Author and illustrator, beginning 1975. Character designer for *The Tale of the Bunny Picnic* (television special), produced by Jim Henson.

Member
Society of Children's Book Writers and Illustrators.

Awards, Honors
Children's Choice award, 1993, for *Dad's Dinosaur Day.*

Writings

SELF-ILLUSTRATED

Who Lives in the Field? (board book), Silver Moon Press (New York, NY), 1992.

Who Lives in the Forest? (board book), Silver Moon Press (New York, NY), 1992.
Who Lives in the Garden? (board book), Silver Moon Press (New York, NY), 1992.
Who Lives in the Lake? (board book), Silver Moon Press (New York, NY), 1992.
Dad's Dinosaur Day, Macmillan (New York, NY), 1993.
Anna in the Garden, Silver Moon Press (New York, NY), 1994.
Bad Luck Boswell, Simon & Schuster Books for Young Readers (New York, NY), 1995.

ILLUSTRATOR

Lillian Moore, *See My Lovely Poison Ivy; and Other Verses about Witches, Ghosts, and Things,* Atheneum (New York, NY), 1975.
Kathryn Osebold Galbraith, *Spots Are Special!,* Atheneum (New York, NY), 1976.
Maria Robbins, reteller, *My Very First Teeny Tiny Strawberry Paperback Library: Six Delightful and Charming Tales,* One Strawberry, 1976.
Andrew Greely, *Nora Maeve and Sebi,* Paulist Press, 1976.
Judi Barrett, *The Wind Thief,* Atheneum (New York, NY), 1977.
Larry, National Association for the Visually Handicapped, 1978.
Maria Robbins, reteller, *My Favorite Teeny Tiny Strawberry Animal Story Library: Six Delightful and Charming Tales,* One Strawberry, 1978.
Donna Hill, *Ms. Glee Was Waiting,* Atheneum (New York, NY), 1978.
Maria Polushkin, *Mother, Mother, I Want Another,* Crown (New York, NY), 1978.
Ann Tompert, *Three Foolish Tales,* Crown (New York, NY), 1979.
Sue Beth Pfeffer, *Awful Evelina,* Albert Whitman (Morton Grove, IL), 1979.
Norma Q. Hare, *Wish upon a Birthday,* Garrard, 1979.
Lillie Patterson, *Jenny, the Halloween Spy,* Garrard, 1979.
Marjorie and Mitchell Sharmat, *I Am Not a Pest,* Dutton (New York, NY), 1979.

Marjorie and Mitchell Sharmat, *The Day I Was Born,* Dutton (New York, NY), 1980.

Joan Lowery Nixon, *Gloria Chipmunk, Star!,* Houghton/Clarion (Boston, MA), 1980.

Charlotte Herman, *On the Way to the Movies,* Dutton (New York, NY), 1980.

Leonard Kessler, *Mixed-up Mother Goose,* Garrard, 1980.

Nancy Evans Cooney, *The Blanket That Had to Go,* Putnam (New York, NY), 1981.

Edith Kundhart, *The Mouse Family's New Home,* Western Publishing, 1981.

Marcia Keyser, *Roger on His Own,* Crown (New York, NY), 1982.

Sally Freedman, *Monster Birthday Party,* Albert Whitman (Morton Grove, IL), 1983.

Carol North, *The Christmas Tree Book,* Western Publishing, 1983.

Margaret Madigan, *Good Night, Aunt Lily,* Western Publishing, 1983.

Vivian Vande Velde, *Once upon a Test: Three Light Tales of Love,* Albert Whitman (Morton Grove, IL), 1984.

Michaela Muntean, *The Doozer Disaster,* Holt (New York, NY), 1984.

Elizabeth Winthrop, *Happy Easter, Mother Duck,* Western Publishing, 1985.

Tish Sommers, *Bert and the Broken Teapot,* Western Publishing, 1985.

Michaela Muntean, *Fraggle Countdown,* Holt (New York, NY), 1985.

Joseph Killorin Brennan, *Gobo and the River,* Holt (New York, NY), 1985.

Mary Blount Christian, *April Fool,* Macmillan (New York, NY), 1986.

Mercer Mayer, *Whinnie, the Lovesick Dragon,* Macmillan (New York, NY), 1986.

Louise Gikow, *Jim Henson Presents: The Tale of the Bunny Picnic,* Scholastic (New York, NY), 1987.

(With others) Kathryn B. Jackson, Carol North, M. Hover, and Clement C. Moore, *Two-Minute Christmas Stories,* Western Publishing, 1989.

Eric Christian Haugaard, *Princess Horrid,* Macmillan (New York, NY), 1990.

Alison Jackson, *My Brother the Star,* Dutton (New York, NY), 1990.

Alison Jackson, *Crane's Rebound,* Dutton (New York, NY), 1991.

Diane Dawson Hearn's illustration projects include her work for Nancy Smiler Levinson's Southwestern-themed **Death Valley: A Day in the Desert.**

Teddy Slater, *Shopping with Samantha,* Silver Moon Press (New York, NY), 1991.

Kevin Roth, editor, *Unbearable Bears,* Random House (New York, NY), 1991.

Teddy Slater, *Dining with Prunella,* Silver Moon Press (New York, NY), 1991.

C.L.G. Martin, *Down Dairy Farm Road,* Macmillan (New York, NY), 1994.

Mallory Loehr, *The Little Pirate Ship,* Random House (New York, NY), 1997.

Marion Dane Bauer, *Turtle Dreams,* Holiday House (New York, NY), 1997.

Marion Dane Bauer, *Bear's Hiccups,* Holiday House (New York, NY), 1998.

Marion Dane Bauer, *Christmas in the Forest,* Holiday House (New York, NY), 1998.

Nancy Smiler Levinson, *Death Valley: A Day in the Desert,* Holiday House (New York, NY), 2001.

Marion Dane Bauer, *Frog's Best Friend,* Holiday House (New York, NY), 2002.

Nancy Smiler Levinson, *North Pole, South Pole,* Holiday House (New York, NY), 2002.

Maryann Dobeck, reteller, *Three Fables,* Scholastic, Inc. (New York, NY), 2002.

Stephen Krensky, *George Washington's First Victory,* Aladdin Paperbacks (New York, NY), 2005.

Nancy Smiler Levinson, *Rain Forests,* Holiday House (New York, NY), 2008.

Also illustrator of *Muppet Babies Mother Goose,* Random House. Contributor to periodicals, including *Reader's Digest, Games, Sesame Street* magazine, and *Highlights for Children.*

Sidelights

In addition to writing several self-illustrated books for children, Diane Dawson Hearn has contributed pen-and-ink and watercolor artwork to picture-book texts by authors such as Joan Lowry Nixon, Nancy Smiler Levinson, Stephen Krensky, and Marion Dane Bauer. Praising her illustrations for Bauer's holiday-themed picture book *Christmas in the Forest,* Shelley Townsend-Hudson wrote that the "action and feeling" of the story's animal characters "are well connected by the appealing pictures and . . . engaging text." Hearn's "full-color artwork [also] captures the laidback feeling of the . . . 1950s setting" in *Down Dairy Farm Road,* a story by C.L.G. Martin that a *Publishers Weekly* critic praised for its "winsome, cartoonlike watercolors." Another book by Bauer, *Frog's Best Friend,* features what a *Kirkus Reviews* contributor described as "appealing animal character [that] add considerable charm" to the story.

Hearn's original children's books include *Dad's Dinosaur Day, Anna in the Garden,* and *Bad Luck Boswell,* as well as a series of board books for toddlers. In *Dad's Dinosaur Day* a grouchy dad is described as a dinosaur in a humorous and imaginative exchange between a little boy and his mother. Hearn brings her engaging

Hearn's detailed artwork provides an excellent visual aid for readers of Nancy Smiler Levinson's nonfiction picture book Rain Forests.

story to life in what a *Publishers Weekly* critic described as "cheerful and cartoony" images that are "never threatening" while also noting the story's "whimsical" ending.

"Ever since I could hold a pencil I was drawing and eventually writing stories that I would illustrate," Hearn once explained to *SATA.* "My first book was called 'The Funny Bird.' I wrote it when I was eight and it was 103 pages long, mostly sketchy cartoons with about two or three lines per page. I still tend to make my stories too long, which is probably why I've had more success as an illustrator, though I love to write.

"My first published story, *Dad's Dinosaur Day,* is, miraculously, very short. It is appropriate that a dinosaur is the subject of my first published book since, as a child, dinosaurs and monsters were my very favorite things. Many of my early stories were about dinosaurs and monsters and I still enjoy drawing them, though my creatures are more humorous than horrific. Given a choice, I would illustrate books having to do with strange creatures, humorous fantasy, or just plain silli-

ness. Oddly, many editors tend to offer me more down-to-earth stories. However, most stories have something in them that I can find interesting or challenging or just plain fun. I try to match my artwork to the story as I feel strongly that the pictures should serve the story and not distract from it.

"Writing and illustrating children's books was a childhood dream that I am lucky to have had fulfilled. Within my limitations, I strive to do my best to contribute to this important art form. I'm keenly aware that my best may fall short of greatness, but I keep trying in the hopes that one day I will create a book worthy enough for children to call their own. For, in the end, the only really great children's books are the ones children love."

Biographical and Critical Sources

PERIODICALS

Booklist, February 1, 1998, Hazel Rochman, review of *Turtle Dreams,* p. 925; May 1, 1998, Lauren Peterson, review of *Bear's Hiccups,* p. 1524; December 1, 1998, Shelley Townsend-Hudson, review of *Christmas in the Forest,* p. 665; April 15, 2001, Ilene Cooper, review of *Death Valley: A Day in the Desert,* p. 1568; May 1, 2002, Ilene Cooper, review of *Frog's Best Friend,* p. 1530; June 1, 2004, Kay Weisman, review of *Down Dairy Farm Road,* p. 1841; May 1, 2008, Carolyn Phelan, review of *Rain Forests,* p. 92.

Kirkus Reviews, February 15, 2002, review of *Frog's Best Friend,* p. 250; November 15, 2002, review of *North Pole, South Pole,* p. 1696; March 1, 2008, review of *Rain Forests.*

Publishers Weekly, July 26, 1993, review of *Dad's Dinosaur Day,* p. 72; January 24, 1994, review of *Down Dairy Farm Road,* p. 55.

School Library Journal, April, 2001, John Sigwald, review of *Death Valley,* p. 132; June, 2002, Sandra Weizenbach, review of *Frog's Best Friend,* p. 87; December, 2002, Blair Christolon, review of *North Pole, South Pole,* p. 126; May, 2008, Kathy Piehl, review of *Rain Forests,* p. 116.

ONLINE

Diane Dawson Hearn Home Page, http://www.dianedaw sonhearn.com (December 7, 2009).*

*   *   *

HEGAMIN, Tonya C. 1975-

Personal

Born 1975. *Education:* Attended University of Pittsburgh; New School University, M.F.A., 2004.

Addresses

Home—Philadelphia, PA. *E-mail*—tonyacheriehegamin @gmail.com.

Career

Author. Former educator for nonprofit organizations, including Women Against Rape and Planned Parenthood; worked variously as a vintage-clothing vendor and a caterer specializing in vegan soul food.

Writings

M+O 4evr, Houghton Mifflin (Boston, MA), 2008.
(With Marilyn Nelson) *Pemba's Song: A Ghost Story,* Scholastic (New York, NY), 2008.
Most Loved in All the World, illustrated by Cozbi A. Cabrera, Houghton Mifflin (Boston, MA), 2009.

Sidelights

After earning a master's degree in writing for children at New York City's New School University, author Tonya C. Hegamin published two novels for children in 2008. Her debut work, *M+O 4evr,* follows the friendship of Marianne and Opal, two girls of African-American heritage who live in a rural town in Pennsylvania. As the girls reach high school, each takes a

Tonya C. Hegamin collaborated with poet Marilyn Nelson in writing the haunting young-adult novel **Pemba's Song.** (Jacket photograph © Anne-Marie Weber/Taxi/Getty Images. Reproduced by permission of Scholastic, Inc.)

different path: Opal becomes more studious and Marianne becomes more interested in having fun. Marianne's choices eventually take a tragic turn near a local ravine that was rumored to be haunted by a runaway slave. Learning of Marianne's death following an overdose of drugs, Opal mourns the loss of her best friend and, ultimately, her first love interest. "Girls will soak up the sad story with its focus on friendship," concluded *Booklist* reviewer Cindy Dobrez, while in *School Library Journal* Janet Hilbun called *M+O 4evr* a "richly imaginative" work "that packs a big wallop."

Cowritten with award-winning poet and author Marilyn Nelson, *Pemba's Song: A Ghost Story* focuses on a young teenager who resents her family's recent move from Brooklyn to a small town in Connecticut. In addition to missing her boyfriend and her closest companions, Pemba suspects that she is now being haunted by a ghost in the old house she and her mother now live in. This suspicion is confirmed by Abraham, an older local historian who provides the teen with knowledge about the town's past. After experiencing a series of fainting spells, the fourteen year old becomes convinced that Phyllys, a slave girl who lived in the house two centuries earlier, needs her help and she enlists Abraham's aid in discovering the mystery behind this spirit. According to *Booklist* critic Gillian Engberg, the passages of poetry attributed to Pemba "powerfully translate her deepening sense of African American history and her own strength." In the opinion of *School Library Journal* contributor Ginny Collier, *Pemba's Song* will likely appeal to a variety of audiences, from "reluctant readers" to "fans of ghost stories as well as historical fiction."

Most Loved in All the World offers younger readers a story about the enduring bonds between a mother and her child. Illustrated by Cozbi A. Cabrera, the book finds a slave mother who is weary from brutal working conditions and mistreatment making a special quilt for her young daughter. Designing the blanket with a little girl in the center, the mother fills her work with affection, knowing that one day the two might be separated. When a chance comes to send her daughter to freedom via the Underground Railroad, the woman gives the girl the homespun quilt to carry with her in the hope that she will understand the depth of her mother's love. Writing in *School Library Journal*, Angela J. Reynolds deemed *Most Loved in All the World* "a straightforward, heartfelt story" about the difficult choices that parents sometime must make, while a *Publishers Weekly* reviewer wrote that Hegamin's "poignant book" captures the "difficult concepts of slavery, courage and sacrifice."

Biographical and Critical Sources

PERIODICALS

Booklist, July 1, 2008, Cindy Dobrez, review of *M+O 4evr,* p. 55; November 1, 2008, Gillian Engberg, review of *Pemba's Song: A Ghost Story,* p. 34.

Kirkus Reviews, May 15, 2008, review of *M+O 4evr;* November 15, 2008, review of *Most Loved in All the World.*

Publishers Weekly, December 1, 2008, review of *Most Loved in All the World,* p. 45.

School Library Journal, November, 2008, Janet Hilbun, review of *M+O 4evr,* p. 122; December, 2008, Ginny Collier, review of *Pemba's Song,* p. 124; January, 2009, Angela J. Reynolds, review of *Most Loved in All the World,* p. 104.

ONLINE

Tonya C. Hegamin Home Page, http://www.tonyacheriehegamin.com (December 11, 2009).*

* * *

HERRICK, Steven 1958-

Personal

Born December 31, 1958, in Brisbane, Queensland, Australia; son of William (a factory worker) and May (a homemaker) Herrick; married Catherine Gorman (a bank officer); children: Jack Gorman, Joe Gorman. *Education:* University of Queensland, B.A., 1982. *Hobbies and other interests:* Playing soccer, bicycling, traveling.

Addresses

Home—Katoomba, New South Wales, Australia. *Office*—P.O. Box 640, Katoomba, New South Wales 2780, Australia. *Agent*—Glen Leitch Management, 332 Victoria St., Darlinghurst, New South Wales 2010, Australia. *E-mail*—stevenherrick@gmail.com.

Career

Poet, 1988—. Presenter and readers at schools throughout Australia.

Member

Australian Society of Authors.

Awards, Honors

Australian Children's Book of the Year for Older Readers shortlist, Children' Book Council of Australia (CBCA), and New South Wales Premier's Literary Award shortlist, both 1997, both for *Love, Ghosts, & Nose Hair;* Victorian Premier's Literary Award commendation, 1998, and CBCA book of the Year shortlist, and New South Wales Premier's Literary Award shortlist, both 1999, all for *A Place like This;* New South Wales Premier's Literary Award, 2000, for *The Spangled Drongo,* 2005, for *By the River;* KOALA/YABBA Book of the Year Award shortlist, 2000, for *My Life, My Love, My Lasagna;* CBC Book of the Year shortlist, and New South Wales Premier's Literary Award shortlist, both

Steven Herrick (Photograph by Mark Gio. Reproduced by permission.)

2001, both for *The Simple Gift;* CBCA Book of the Year shortlist, 2003, for *Tom Jones Saves the World,* and 2004, for *Do-wrong Ron;* Children's Literature Peace Prize highly commended designation, for *The Simple Gift* and *Tom Jones Saves the World;* Honor Book citation, CBCA, and Australia Speech Pathologist Book of the Year designation, both 2005, both for *By the River.*

Writings

POETRY AND NOVELS; FOR CHILDREN AND YOUNG ADULTS

Caboolture, Five Islands, 1990.

Water Bombs: A Book of Poems for Teenagers, Jam Roll Press (Nundah, Queensland, Australia), 1992.

My Life, My Love, My Lasagna, illustrated by Annmarie Scott, University of Queensland Press (St. Lucia, Queensland, Australia), 1997.

Poetry to the Rescue, illustrated by Catherine Gorman, University of Queensland Press (St. Lucia, Queensland, Australia), 1998.

Love Poems and Leg Spinners: A Month in the Life of Class 5B, illustrated by Joe Gorman, University of Queensland Press (St. Lucia, Queensland, Australia), 2001.

Do-wrong Ron, illustrated by Caroline Magerl, Allen & Unwin (Crows Nest, New South Wales, Australia), 2003.

Naked Bunyip Dancing, illustrated by Beth Norling, Allen & Unwin (Crows Nest, New South Wales, Australia), 2005, Front Street (Asheville, NC), 2008.

Rhyming Boy, University of Queensland Press (St. Lucia, Queensland, Australia), 2008.

Untangled Spaghetti: Selected Poems, University of Queensland Press (St. Lucia, Queensland, Australia), 2009.

PICTURE BOOKS

The Place Where the Planes Take Off, illustrated by Annmarie Scott, University of Queensland Press (St. Lucia, Queensland, Australia), 1995.

YOUNG-ADULT NOVELS

Love, Ghosts, and Nose Hair (verse novel), University of Queensland Press (St. Lucia, Queensland, Australia), 1996, published as *Love, Ghosts, and Facial Hair,* Simon Pulse (New York, NY), 2004.

A Place like This (verse novel), University of Queensland Press (St. Lucia, Queensland, Australia), 1998, Simon Pulse (New York, NY), 2004.

The Spangled Drongo, University of Queensland Press (St. Lucia, Queensland, Australia), 1999.

The Simple Gift, University of Queensland Press (St. Lucia, Queensland, Australia), 2001, Simon & Schuster (New York, NY), 2004.

Tom Jones Saves the World (verse novel), University of Queensland Press (St. Lucia, Queensland, Australia), 2002.

By the River (verse novel), Allen & Unwin (Crows Nest, New South Wales, Australia), 2004, Front Street (Asheville, NC), 2006.

Lonesome Howl (verse novel), Allen & Unwin (Crows Nest, New South Wales, Australia), 2006, published as *The Wolf,* Front Street (Asheville, NC), 2007.

Cold Skin (verse novel), Allen & Unwin (Crows Nest, New South Wales, Australia), 2007, Front Street (Honesdale, PA), 2009.

POETRY; FOR ADULTS

The Esoteric Herrick: Poems and Things, illustrated by Roger Norris, Red Hill, 1982.

The Sound of Chopping, Five Islands, 1994.

Adaptations

The Simple Gift was adapted for the stage by Bootlace Productions, Coffs Harbour, Australia), c. 2009.

Sidelights

Steven Herrick is an Australian poet who is dedicated to spreading the word about the magic of language to young people. Through his popular verse novels, which carry such compelling titles as *Love, Ghosts, and Nose Hair, Naked Bunyip Dancing, Tom Jones Saves the*

World, and *Cold Skin,* Herrick has captivated young readers in his native country as well as in Great Britain and North America, where his books have also been published. "I love the power of poetry and the potential of poetry," Herrick once explained to *SATA.* "I've always believed that poetry can talk to an audience or reader in the most concise, direct, and thought-provoking way." In 2008 Herrick also expanded his range into prose by publishing the young-adult novel *Rhyming Boy.*

With his 1992 poetry collection *Water Bombs: A Book of Poems for Teenagers* Herrick uses his frank style to mark the milestones of two lives through a group of stand-alone poems that collectively reveal the cyclical nature of life. The reader glimpses verbal snapshots of Joe and Debbie's lives, from their separate childhood dreams to their united hopes for their children. In "almost everyday speech," observed Felicity Norman in a *Magpies* review, *Water Bombs* "speaks easily to its audience and will be very popular."

Herrick's verse-novel *Love, Ghosts, and Nose Hair,* which was published in the United States as *Love, Ghosts, and Facial Hair,* exemplifies his preferred writ-

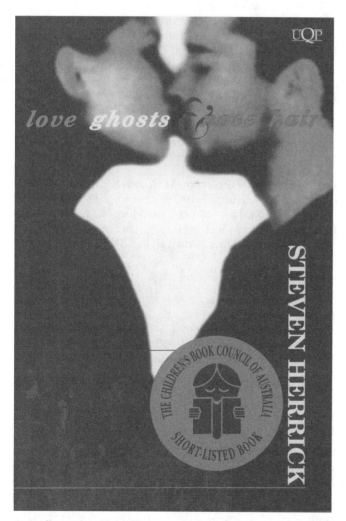

Australian writer Herrick's verse novels include the quirkily titled **Love, Ghosts, and Nose Hair.** (University of Queensland Press, 1996. Reproduced by permission.)

ing format. Comprised of a series of first-person poems, the novel looks at how a family copes with the death of a loved one. Each voice examines the loss from its own perspective, like one of several cameras set to catch the same action from its own unique angle. While the predominant perspective belongs to Jack, a sixteen-year-old writer who is preoccupied with his girlfriend, Annabel, sports, and the death of his mother to cancer seven years ago, the reader sees Jack through the eyes of his sister and now-widowed father. In the companion novel, *A Place like This,* Jack and Annabel decide to take a year off before college and, despite their plans for taking of a motor tour around Australia, wind up working long hours as apple pickers for a family with troubles of its own. *Magpies* critic Anne Hanzl commented that *Love, Ghosts, and Nose Hair* is a "sad, funny, moving, and thoughtful" book. In *Booklist,* Jennifer Mattson praised Herrick's "rich, layered verse" and noted that the two novels "speak with sincerity and sensitivity" to the trauma of family upheavals. *A Place like This,* according to Mattson, includes "a Kerouacian fantasy that will resonate with many teens."

Other verse novels by Herrick include *Tom Jones Saves the World,* about a boy frustrated by his stuffy parents who escapes from his gated community and has a series of adventures that connect him to his family's past and make him appreciate his advantages in life. Another boy escapes from his family in *The Simple Gift,* although this time his family life is a bit more daunting. Sixteen-year-old Billy makes a new home for himself in an abandoned railway freight car, and meets a new community of friends that sustain him in a novel that *Booklist* contributor Jennifer Mattson called "tender [and] uplifting," adding that the book is characteristic Herrick: "crowd-pleasing" and "swift-reading." *The Simple Gift* is "a dramatic and compelling story that will appeal even to reluctant readers," predicted Susan Oliver in her *School Library Journal* review of the novel.

The first-person narrative in *By the River* takes readers back to the 1950s and 1960s and focuses on a teen's experiences living with his widowed father and younger brother in small-town Australia. Harry Hodby's reflections on his past include the telling details of his childhood, from an exhilarating ride on his homemade go-cart down a steep hill to a school friend's caring gift of homemade orange cake. Poignant moments, such as the death of his mother and the drowning of a classmate, as well as the interesting people that Harry encounters in his small town, enrich what a *Publishers Weekly* critic described as an "atmospheric tale" in which Herrick's young narrator is obsessed by death and loss and "wrestles with searching questions." Citing the "wistful nostalgia" evoked in *By the River, Booklist* reviewer Gillian Engberg went on to praise the "terse, shimmering lines" in Herrick's coming-of-age tale. In the book, Engberg continued, the author "creates a luminous sense of place and character" through his story, and Renee Steinberg asserted in *School Library Journal* that *By*

the River treats readers to "a beautiful and sensitively written novel featuring a caring, intelligent protagonist." In *Kliatt* Claire Rosser also recommended the novel as "unforgettable" and "accessible to all ages," adding that "any YA serious about poetry will recognize Herrick's fine gift."

Described by *School Library Journal* contributor Laura Amos as "a multilayered and affecting read," *Cold Skin* introduces another young boy coming of age following World War II. Unlike the narrator of *By the River*, life for Eddie Holder is far more difficult. While his older brother Larry wants to escape from life in small-town Burruga, Australia, Eddie longs to quit school and go to work in the local mill. When the teen's bitter father, a war veteran, forbids Eddie to abandon his education, the disappointment is somewhat ameliorated by a budding romance with his longtime friend Sally. Then another classmate, Colleen, is murdered, and the changes that this tragedy create in the lives of Eddie, as well as his friends, father, and older brother, play out in the hidden thoughts captured in Herrick's finely crafted overlapping narratives. In its "fast free verse," *Cold Skin* "build[s] suspense about Colleen's killer," wrote *Booklist* critic Hazel Rochman, the critic recommending the verse novel as "a great title for readers' theatre." In *Kirkus Reviews* a contributor deemed the novel "a taut and tender tale of courage and revenge" in which the "adroit" interweaving of various characters' hidden thoughts gradually reveals the source of the novel's mystery.

Subjected to physical abuse at the hands of her alcoholic father, sixteen-year-old Lucy Harding gains a sense of her own strength during a hiking mishap in *The Wolf*. Called an "emotionally taut survival story" by *School Library Journal* critic Ellen Fader, Herrick's dramatic verse novel finds Lucy joining friend and neighbor Jake in Jake's search for the predator that has been killing his family's sheep. Lucy is convinced that the animal is not a wolf but the dog that her father had abused before it escaped into the mountains nearby. She accompanies Jake in his search so that she can protect the animal from further violence. When Jake is injured, the teens take refuge in a cave, their location unknown to their respective families. Noting the "universal" themes of self-actualization that are central to Herrick's story, a *Kirkus Reviews* writer added that "the exotic Australian countryside adds . . . interest" to the novel. In *Publishers Weekly* a critic praised *The Wolf* as a "touching, well-written story," and *Horn Book* contributor Martha V. Parravano deemed it a "poignant coming-of-age . . . novel." In his *Journal of Adolescence and Adult Literacy* review, James Blasingame noted the powerful metaphors that run through Herrick's story and added that the author's "enchanting" verse text contains "just enough Australian colloquialism to give it a nice flavor."

In addition to his writing, Herrick visits hundreds of schools each year in his capacity as a self-appointed ambassador of verse. He has also traveled to Canada,

Herrick's Aussie-themed middle-grade novel **Naked Bunyip Dancing** *features artwork by Beth Norling.* (Front Street, 2008. Illustration copyright © 2005 by Beth Norling. Reproduced by permission.)

the United Kingdom, the United States, Spain, Croatia, the Czech Republic, the Netherlands, Vietnam, and Singapore, performing his work in schools. "I have a touch of the evangelist in me when it comes to poetry," the author once admitted—"I want the public to recognize poetry as an enjoyable, entertaining medium. That's why I not only write poetry, but I also read it in front of an audience. I believe writers need to see (and hear) how an audience reacts to their writing. Performing my poetry allows me that luxury." "One of the great joys I feel in visiting so many schools is talking to children and young adults," Herrick added. "I listen to what they say and how they say it. I hope my books reflect some of what I've heard over the years. I hope they get more people of all ages reading poetry and believing that poetry, as a medium, can tell a story as well as prose."

An entertaining performer—Herrick has been a frequent guest on live radio shows and has appeared on various Australian television programs—Herrick's writing and performance styles are similar, reported *Sydney Morning Herald* critic Shelli-Anne Couch. They are "extraordinarily simple on the surface but spliced with subtle bites and small twists." The straightforward quality

common to Herrick's spoken and written word, was also noted by Norman, who wrote in *Magpies* that the poet's writings reflect the "directness and immediate impact" required of performance poetry.

Explaining his reason for writing verse-novels in addition to "straight" poetry, Herrick noted that a free-verse text "allows me into the personality of each character—his or her thoughts, emotions, insecurities, and ambitions. The verse-novel form lets me tell the story from a number of perspectives, and, hopefully, with an economy of words. In short, it allows each character to tell the story in his or her own language, from his or her own angle."

Biographical and Critical Sources

PERIODICALS

Booklist, March 15, 2004, Jennifer Mattson, reviews of *Love, Ghosts, and Facial Hair* and *A Place like This*, both p. 1299; August, 2004, Jennifer Mattson, review of *The Simple Gift*, p. 1919; August 1, 2006, Gillian Engberg, review of *By the River*, p. 66; April 15, 2009, Hazel Rochman, review of *Cold Skin*, p. 49.

Horn Book, May-June, 2007, Martha V. Parravano, review of *The Wolf*, p. 283; May-June, 2008, Deirdre F. Baker, review of *Naked Bunyip Dancing*, p. 313.

Kirkus Reviews, February 15, 2007, review of *The Wolf*; March 15, 2008, review of *Naked Bunyip Dancing*; March 1, 2009, review of *Cold Skin*.

Journal of Adolescent and Adult Literacy, December, 2007, James Blasingame, review of *The Wolf*, p. 364.

Kliatt, May, 2004, Nancy Zachary, review of *The Simple Gift*, p. 18; July, 2004, Heather Lisowski, review of *Love, Ghosts, and Facial Hair*, p. 18; May, 2006, Claire Rosser, review of *By the River*, p. 10.

Magpies, September, 1992, Felicity Norman, review of *Water Bombs: A Book of Poems for Teenagers*, p. 24; July, 1996, Anne Hanzl, review of *Love, Ghosts, and Nose Hair*, p. 33.

Publishers Weekly, February 9, 2004, reviews of *Love, Ghosts, and Facial Hair* and *A Place like This*, both p. 82; July 10, 2006, review of *By the River*, p. 83; April 9, 2007, review of *The Wolf*, p. 55.

School Library Journal, March, 2004, Sharon Korbeck, review of *Love, Ghosts, and Facial Hair*, p. 213; September, 2004, Susan Oliver, review of *The Simple Gift*, p. 208; July, 2006, Renee Steinberg, review of *By the River*, p. 104; April, 2007, Ellen Fader, review of *The Wolf*, p. 136; April, 2008, Connie Tyrell Burns, review of *Naked Bunyip Dancing*, p. 142; May, 2009, Laura Amos, review of *Cold Skin*, p. 108.

Sydney Morning Herald, April 26, 1994, Shelli-Anne Couch, "When There's Pure Poetry in the Making," p. 23.

Sunday Times (London, England), June 17, 2007, Nicolette Jones, review of *Naked Bunyip Dancing*, p. 48.

ONLINE

Steven Herrick Home Page, http://www.stevenherrick.com.au (December 20, 2009).

*   *   *

HINES, Anna Grossnickle 1946-

Personal

Born July 13, 1946, in Cincinnati, OH; daughter of Earl S. (a mathematical analyst) and Ruth (a personnel service representative) Grossnickle; married Steve Carlson, August 12, 1965 (divorced, 1973); married Gary Roger Hines (a forest ranger, writer, and musician), June 19, 1976; children: (first marriage) Bethany, Sarah; (second marriage) Lassen. *Education:* Attended San Fernando State College (now California State University, Northridge), 1965-67; Pacific Oaks College, B.A., 1974, M.A., 1979. *Hobbies and other interests:* Needlework, quilting, knitting, gardening, grandparenting.

Addresses

Home—Gualala, CA. *E-mail*—anna@aghines.com.

Career

Los Angeles City Children's Centers, Los Angeles, CA, preschool teacher, 1967-68, 1968-70; Columbia Elementary School, Columbia, CA, third grade teacher, 1975-78; full-time writer and illustrator, 1978—. Member, Gualala Art Center and Pacific Piecemakers Quilt Guild. *Exhibitions:* Work included in Society of Illustrator's Original Art Show, 2001, Allentown Art Museum, 2001, American Textile History Museum, 2002, Road to California Quilt Show, 2006, Quilter's Gathering, 2007, and Trutter Museum, Lincoln Land Community College, 2009.

Member

Society of Children's Book Writers and Illustrators.

Awards, Honors

Children's Book of the Year list, Child Study Association of America, 1985, for *All by Myself;* Children's Choice Award, International Reading Association/ Children's Book Council (IRA/CBC), 1987, for *Daddy Makes the Best Spaghetti*, 1990, for *Grandma Gets Grumpy;* Outstanding Science Book for Children designation, National Science Teachers Association, 1991, for *Remember the Butterflies;* Children's Books of the Year listee, Bank Street College of Education, 1991, for *Tell Me Your Best Thing;* Notable Children's Trade Book designation, National Council for the Social Studies, 1993, for *Flying Firefighters;* Carolyn W. Field Award Honor Book designation, Pennsylvania Library Association, 1995, for *What Joe Saw;* National Parent-

Anna Grossnickle Hines. (Photograph by Nathan Snippen Stephens. Reproduced by permission.)

ing Publications Award for Poetry and Folklore, and Lee Bennett Hopkins Award for Children's Poetry, both 2001, National Council of Teachers of English Notable Children's Books designation, 2002, and Beverly Cleary Children's Choice Award nomination, 2004, all for *Pieces;* Best Books designation, Bank Street College of Education, 2005, for *Winter Lights.*

Writings

SELF-ILLUSTRATED

Taste the Raindrops, Greenwillow (New York, NY), 1983.
Come to the Meadow, Clarion (New York, NY), 1984.
Maybe a Band-Aid Will Help, Dutton (New York, NY), 1984.
All by Myself, Clarion (New York, NY), 1985.
Bethany for Real, Greenwillow (New York, NY), 1985.
Daddy Makes the Best Spaghetti, Clarion (New York, NY), 1986.
Don't Worry, I'll Find You, Dutton (New York, NY), 1986.
I'll Tell You What They Say, Greenwillow (New York, NY), 1987.
It's Just Me, Emily, Clarion (New York, NY), 1987.
Keep Your Old Hat, Dutton (New York, NY), 1987.
Grandma Gets Grumpy, Dutton (New York, NY), 1988.
Sky All Around, Clarion (New York, NY), 1989.
Big like Me, Greenwillow (New York, NY), 1989.

They Really Like Me, Greenwillow (New York, NY), 1989.
The Secret Keeper, Greenwillow (New York, NY), 1990.
Mean Old Uncle Jack, Clarion (New York, NY), 1990.
The Greatest Picnic in the World, Clarion (New York, NY), 1991.
Remember the Butterflies, Dutton (New York, NY), 1991.
Jackie's Lunch Box, Greenwillow (New York, NY), 1991.
Moon's Wish, Clarion (New York, NY), 1992.
Rumble Thumble Boom!, Greenwillow (New York, NY), 1992.
Moompa, Toby, and Bomp, Clarion (New York, NY), 1993.
Gramma's Walk, Greenwillow (New York, NY), 1993.
Even If I Spill My Milk?, Clarion (New York, NY), 1994.
What Joe Saw, Greenwillow (New York, NY), 1994.
Big Help!, Clarion (New York, NY), 1995.
When the Goblins Came Knocking, Greenwillow (New York, NY), 1995.
When We Married Gary, Greenwillow (New York, NY), 1996.
Miss Emma's Wild Garden, Greenwillow (New York, NY), 1997.
Not Without Bear, Orchard Books (New York, NY), 2000.
William's Turn, Children's Press (New York, NY), 2001.
Got You!, Children's Press (New York, NY), 2001.
Pieces: A Year in Poems and Quilts, Greenwillow (New York, NY), 2001.
Winter Lights: A Season in Poems and Quilts, Greenwillow Books (New York, NY), 2005.
1, 2, Buckle My Shoe, Harcourt (Orlando, FL), 2008.
I Am a Backhoe, Tricycle Press (Berkeley, CA), 2010.
Peaceful Pieces: Poems and Quilts about Peace, Henry Holt (New York, NY), 2011.

FOR CHILDREN

Cassie Bowen Takes Witch Lessons (juvenile novel), illustrated by Gail Owens, Dutton (New York, NY), 1985.
Boys Are Yucko! (sequel to *Cassie Bowen Takes Witch Lessons*), illustrated by Pat Henderson Lincoln, Dutton (New York, NY), 1989.
Tell Me Your Best Thing (juvenile novel), illustrated by Karen Ritz, Dutton (New York, NY), 1991.
My Own Big Bed, illustrated by Mary Watson, Greenwillow (New York, NY), 1998.
What Can You Do in the Rain?, illustrated by Thea Kliros, Greenwillow (New York, NY), 1998.
What Can You Do in the Wind?, illustrated by Thea Kliros, Greenwillow (New York, NY), 1999.
What Can You Do in the Snow?, illustrated by Thea Kliros, Greenwillow (New York, NY), 1999.
What Can You Do in the Sunshine?, illustrated by Thea Kliros, Greenwillow (New York, NY), 1999.
Whose Shoes?, illustrated by LeUyen Pham, Harcourt (San Diego, CA), 2001.
Which Hat Is That? illustrated by LeUyen Pham, Harcourt (San Diego, CA), 2002.
My Grandma Is Coming to Town, illustrated by Melissa Sweet, Candlewick Press (Cambridge, MA), 2003.

ILLUSTRATOR

Gary Hines, *A Ride in the Crummy,* Greenwillow (New York, NY), 1991.

Gary Hines, *Flying Firefighters,* Clarion (New York, NY), 1993.

Gary Hines, *The Day of the High Climber,* Greenwillow (New York, NY), 1994.

Sarah Hines-Stephens, *Bean,* Harcourt (San Diego, CA), 1998.

Sarah Hines-Stephens, *Bean's Games,* Harcourt (San Diego, CA), 1998.

Sarah Hines-Stephens, *Bean's Night,* Harcourt (San Diego, CA), 1998.

Jackie French Koller, *Bouncing on the Bed,* Orchard Books (New York, NY), 1998.

Sarah Hines-Stephens, *Bean Soup,* Harcourt (San Diego, CA), 2000.

Sarah Hines-Stephens, *Soup Too?,* Harcourt (San Diego, CA), 2000.

Sarah Hines-Stephens, *Soup's Oops!,* Harcourt (San Diego, CA), 2000.

Elizabeth Partridge, *Whistling: Story,* Greenwillow Books (New York, NY), 2003.

Contributor to magazines, including *Society of Children's Book Writers Bulletin.*

ILLUSTRATOR; "CURIOUS GEORGE" PICTURE-BOOK SERIES; BASED ON CHARACTERS CREATED BY MARGRET AND H.A. REY

Curious George and the Firefighters, Houghton Mifflin (Boston, MA), 2004.

Curious George Learns to Count from 1 to 100, Houghton Mifflin (Boston, MA), 2005.

Curious George's First Day of School, Houghton Mifflin (Boston, MA), 2005.

Cathy Hapka, *Curious George's Dinosaur Discovery,* Houghton Mifflin (Boston, MA), 2006.

Laura Driscoll, *Curious George at the Baseball Game,* Houghton Mifflin (Boston, MA), 2006.

(With Greg Paprocki) Monica Perez, *Curious George and Me!,* Houghton Mifflin (Boston, MA), 2007.

R.P. Anderson, *Curious George at the Aquarium,* Houghton Mifflin (Boston, MA), 2007.

Monica Perez, *Curious George Plants a Tree,* Houghton Mifflin Harcourt (Boston, MA), 2009.

Emily Flaschner Meyer and Julie M. Bartynski, *Curious George Says Thank You,* Houghton Mifflin Harcourt (Boston, MA), 2011.

Illustrations included in *Curious George's Dictionary,* Houghton Mifflin Harcourt (Boston, MA), 2008.

Adaptations

Daddy Makes the Best Spaghetti and *It's Just Me, Emily* have been adapted for audio cassette.

Sidelights

Praised for her sensitive depiction of family relationships, as well as for her skill as an artist, Anna Grossnickle Hines has written and illustrated picture books and chapter books for primary graders and has illustrated texts for both her author husband, Gary Hines, and her daughter, Sarah Hines-Stephens. Hines blends her accomplished art with stories about family and sibling relations, first friendships, and the delights of nature, among other subjects. "My stories come mostly from my experiences and feelings as a child and with my own children," she once told *SATA.* "The stories are mostly about the discovery, imagination, playfulness, and wonder in young children's everyday lives, so often missed by busy adults." In 2004 Hines was selected to illustrate a series of picture books based on the beloved monkey character Curious George, the star of several picture books written by Margret and H.A. Rey and published in the 1940s. Adopting the style of H.A. Rey's original illustrations, her work for *Curious George Learns to Count from 1 to 100* was praised by *Booklist* critic Carolyn Phelan for "captur[ing] . . . the spirit of the original character."

Born in Ohio as the oldest of seven children, Hines moved to California as a child and grew up in Los Angeles, studying art at what was then San Fernando Valley State College. "In early college I was discouraged from pursuing my interest in picture books," she once told *SATA.* "I was told it was not a worthy interest because a picture book was not truly 'fine art' on the one hand or 'commercial' on the other. To me, the art of the picture book, which can be held in the hands, carried about, taken to bed, is much more personal and intimate than the art which hangs in galleries or museums."

Hines married in 1965 and had two daughters, teaching preschool as well. After her first marriage ended in divorce in 1973, she finished her college education and married Gary Hines, a forest ranger, writer, and musician. Moving to California's Gold Country in the Sierra Nevadas, she taught third grade in a small elementary school. Hines also read many books, both to her own children and to the children she taught, and gradually learned what made a good book. Although she first planned to create illustrations for others, she soon realized that she had her own stories to tell. By the time her third child was born, Hines had collected over a hundred rejection slips. With a new baby in the house, she stopped teaching and became a stay-at-home mom. She took this opportunity to make "writing and illustrating a priority," as she recalled in *SATA.* "I decided I should either pursue my goal of doing children's books more seriously or give it up." To this end, Hines began writing every day, even if only for a matter of minutes. The rest of the family pitched in, helping with chores and child-rearing, and after about twenty months, her renewed efforts paid off when she sold her first picture book, *Taste the Raindrops.*

Hines's second picture book, *Come to the Meadow,* started with an idea for a story about a child playing and discovering things in a meadow. The idea developed into the tale of little Mattie, who desperately wants to go to the meadow. Unfortunately, everyone in the

family is too busy, except for Granny, who proposes a picnic and convinces everyone to take some time off from their projects. A *Publishers Weekly* critic called *Come to the Meadow* a "poetic, unpretentious story" featuring pictures in "clear green and yellow offset with pristine-white spaces."

The importance of extended family, especially grandparents, is a theme that echoes in Hines' other books. In *Grandma Gets Grumpy,* for example, five cousins spend the night with their doting grandmother, but quickly learn that she has rules too. "This slice of real life is depicted with such humor and affection that kids are sure to enjoy recognizing themselves and their elders," noted a critic for *Kirkus Reviews,* the reviewer adding that Hines' "soft, realistic pictures make each character an individual." Writing in *Horn Book,* Ellen Fader noted

that the book's "familiar, gentle, colored-pencil illustrations . . . bring this pleasant story to life," adding that Hines has the "envious ability to focus on the most ordinary situation, mix in a bit of gentle humor, and create, as the result, a charming and intimate glimpse into a preschooler's world." Another multigenerational tale, *Gramma's Walk,* depicts young Donnie and wheelchair-bound Gramma as they join in an imagined walk to the seashore. The bond between a boy and his grandfather is explored in *Moompa, Toby, and Bomp,* "a charming tale of simple pleasures," according to Anna DeWind in *School Library Journal.*

Another favorite subject for Hines is child development. In *All by Myself,* she writes about a child's first steps toward independence by giving up night diapers and going unassisted to the bathroom in the middle of

In **My Grandma Is Coming to Town** *Hines collaborates with artist Melissa Sweet to produce a story of anticipation and affection.* (Illustration copyright © 2003 by Melissa Sweet. Reproduced by permission of the publisher, Candlewick Press, Inc., Somerville, MA.)

the night. Noting that *All by Myself* "holds a unique position in the . . . genre of self-help books for young children," *School Library Journal* reviewer B.P. Goldstone concluded that Hines' book is "a welcome addition to library collections that will help children . . . develop] a growing sense of worth." In *Even If I Spill My Milk?* Hines deals with children's fear of separation. In the story, Jamie does not want his parents to go to a party and leave him with a babysitter, and so he delays their departure with a litany of questions.

The common childhood fear of thunder is the focus of *Rumble Thumble Boom!*, which finds a boy and his dog fearful of such loud noises. Andrew W. Hunter commented in his *School Library Journal* review of *Rumble Thumble Boom!* that Hines' "colorful effects enhance the book's use for storytelling with either a group or with a single child," and *Booklist* critic Hazel Rochman predicted that it "will evoke smiles of wry recognition in adults without condescending to kids." The job of introducing a new sibling into the home is explored in *Big like Me,* as a boy tells his baby sister of all the things he will show her when she gets bigger. Denise Wilms noted in *Booklist* that "Hines has an eye for pint-size anatomy," and that the book is an "affectionate and refreshingly positive celebration of a new infant." In *Horn Book* Fader remarked of *Big like Me* that the "watercolor and pencil illustrations have a gentle, cozy, and contented feeling which reinforces the mood of this distinctly useful book."

My Own Big Bed focuses on a little girl who has outgrown her crib and is preparing to sleep in a big bed for the first time. This experience is "both exciting and scary" for the narrator, noted a reviewer for *Publishers Weekly.* Now she can get in and out of bed all on her own, but she also has fears about falling out of the bed. Thus, the resourceful young girl props her stuffed animals around the edge of the bed, so that if she does fall out, her landing will be a soft, padded one. "This rite of passage is astutely and economically observed," noted the *Publishers Weekly* critic, while in *Booklist* Karen Simonetti described *My Own Big Bed* as "ideal for bedtime and lapsits." Karen James, writing in *School Library Journal,* predicted that Hines' "warm and reassuring" book will "strike a chord" with youngsters graduating from babyhood.

Hines also focuses a child's development in board books such as *What Can You Do in the Rain?,* a work that prompted Jennifer M. Brown to note in *Publishers Weekly* that Hines "invites kids to revel in the weather" by suggesting that they wave a flag on a windy day, watch their shadow in the sun, or gaze at the clouds on a rainy day. In *Miss Emma's Wild Garden* young Chloe explores her neighbor's garden with the help of the gardener, who gladly points out all the animals and wild plants to the young girl. In *Booklist* Ilene Cooper called *Miss Emma's Wild Garden* an "intergenerational story and a mini-nature lesson in one attractive package." Another energetic young girl stars in *1, 2, Buckle My*

Shoe, as Hines brings to life the child's exploration of counting in textile collage art. Reviewing the work in *Booklist,* Phelan wrote that the author/illustrator's "decorative use of rickrack and stitching make the playful art visually pleasing," while a *Kirkus Reviews* writer dubbed *1, 2, Buckle My Shoe* an "incandescent concept book" by "a gifted quilt artist."

In *Pieces: A Year in Poems and Quilts* Hines again showcases her quilting talents, combining free-verse poems about the seasons with intricately crafted textile art. "Some of my earliest writings were poems, a few of which are in this book," the author explained on her home page. "Over the years most of my efforts have gone into stories, but every now and then I'd write another poem or two, most of them about nature." In 1993 she discovered that she had almost enough poems about the seasons to comprise a collection, so she wrote a few more verses to fill in the gaps. Her decision to use quilts to illustrate her poems came about while she was working on a quilt as a present for her mother. Looking for advice from her mother, a more-experienced quilter, she fibbed and said that the quilt was going to accompany her book of poems. Soon, she realized that this would in fact be an excellent idea. Over the next several years, she crafted half a dozen quilts to illustrate her poems, winning the enthusiastic support of her editor. Ultimately thirteen more quilts were crafted and scanned for illustrations, and a two-page explanation of the quilting process is included at the end of the book.

Hines' blending of verse and needlework in *Pieces* earned the praise of many critics, a *Publishers Weekly* contributor characterizing it as a "deceptively simple, unique collection of poems" that pairs with "quilted designs worthy of an exhibition." Cooper commended the "lovely book" for mixing "the intricacies of quilting with the wonders of the changing seasons," while a contributor for *Bulletin of the Center for Children's Books* maintained that the "visual appeal and detail of the quilt work will engage young viewers." A *Kirkus Reviews* writer commented that Hines "raises the bar considerably for illustrators working in fabric," and praised *Pieces* as a "tour de force."

A companion volume, *Winter Lights: A Season in Poems and Quilts,* contains sixteen poems that describe the warmth that can be found even in the cold of winter in candlelight, the sparkle of sun on ice, brightly lit holiday decorations, or the warm glow of embers from an evening fire. In *Horn Book* Lolly Robinson cited the combination of "simple language" and "ambitious art," while Cooper wrote that "Hines celebrates the season in thoughtful poems and . . . gorgeous quilts full of bright, beautiful colors." The author/illustrator's "astonishingly beautiful" textile art captures the traditions of the winter season, wrote a *Kirkus Reviews* writer, making *Winter Lights* "a sparkling read-aloud for the holiday-time of the year," and a *Publishers Weekly* critic asserted of the work that, "if ever there were a perfect book to curl up with on a cold night, this is it."

Whose Shoes? also started life as a poem. "What little child hasn't tried on big people's shoes?" Hines asked on her home page. "I don't remember exactly when I first wrote it, or if there was a particular event that inspired it, but *Whose Shoes?* started out as a poem." Later on, sharing the poem with her writing group, Hines was informed that what she had was really a picture book, and after working on the concept for a time, she came up with the idea of using it in a lift-the-flap puzzle-adventure tale. It was decided, also, that Hines would not illustrate the book. Instead she worked with illustrator LeUyen Pham, whose "mouse character is so full of energy and charm!," Hines wrote on her home page. In the story, the little mouse is trying on the shoes of family members on each successive page and readers need to lift the flap to discover whose shoes they are. Anne Parker, reviewing *Whose Shoes?* in *School Library Journal,* called it "well-written," with rhyming sounds that will "entertain youngsters and have them chiming right along." A critic for *Kirkus Reviews* also praised the "exuberant rhymes" as well as the "clever illustrations" in this book. This collaborative effort was so successful that Hines and Pham also teamed up for *Which Hat Is That?,* employing the same guessing-game motif and blend of strong mouse illustrations and rhyming, sing-song text.

Hines turns her attention to older children in her juvenile novels. *Cassie Bowen Takes Witch Lessons* tells the story of a fourth grader who learns about not only herself, but also about the real meaning of friendship when she is paired with an unpopular girl to do a class assignment. Phyllis Ingram noted in *School Library Journal* that "readers will suffer along with Cassie as she strives to make the right decisions about friendship and loyalty," while a *Booklist* critic praised Hines for "injecting her story with realistic characterizations and dialogue and a solid understanding of the problems of growing up." A sequel, *Boys Are Yucko!,* finds Cassie planning her tenth birthday party and hoping that her divorced father will come, while also dealing with her boy-crazy friend Stacy and Stacy's insistence that members of the opposite sex be invited to the event. Another novel, *Tell Me Your Best Thing,* focuses on a young girl's decision to stand up to a class bully. *Publishers Weekly* commented of this book that "the story's quick pace and believable portrayal of third grade angst will appeal to the chapter book set."

Although she writes about a variety of childhood experiences, Hines is frequently inspired by her own family. Her daughter, Sarah, provided the ideas for a trio of books about a young girl and her doll, Abigail. In *Maybe a Band-Aid Will Help,* the doll's leg comes off, but Mother is too busy to help Sarah fix it right away. Sarah and Abigail get lost in a shopping mall in *Don't Worry, I'll Find You,* and *Keep Your Old Hat* finds Sarah disagreeing with friend Mandy over who gets to play Mother. Hines' remarriage inspired *When We Married Gary.* Here young Sarah does not remember her father, but older sister Beth does, so when a new man en-

ters their mother's life, adjustments must be made. "Hines has done a superb job of tackling a realistic subject . . . without oversimplifying it," noted Lisa Marie Gangemi in a *School Library Journal* review of *When We Married Gary,* and Phelan commented that, "once again, Hines gets the child's perspective and the emotional tone of the story just right."

Hines' older daughter Bethany also inspired *Bethany for Real,* and husband Gary is cast as the nurturing father in *Daddy Makes the Best Spaghetti.* "Spaghetti is one of my husband's favorite things to cook, second only to popcorn," the author once explained. "His spaghetti is very good, but it got to be a kind of family joke that if he were cooking, it would be spaghetti for dinner . . . again." The resulting book, according to Mary M. Burns in *Horn Book,* is "a natural for picture-book programs. . . . Precise, fine lines combined with clear colors on snowy white backgrounds capture the circumscribed world of the preschooler while celebrating the joys to be found in daily events."

In addition to casting Gary in her stories, Hines teams up with her writer husband on several books that deal with his expertise: the outdoors and forestry work. In *A Ride in the Crummy* two boys have an exciting ride in the caboose of a large train, while the companion volume, *The Day of the High Climber,* finds the two brothers spending the summer at their father's logging camp and marveling at the work of the high climber who must chop top branches off a tall tree. Donna L. Scanlon, writing in *School Library Journal,* noted that *The Day of the High Climber* possesses a "coziness that is nostalgic but not cloying." Another family collaboration finds Hines working with Sarah on board books such as *Bean, Bean's Games, Bean's Night,* and *Soup's Oops!* Bean is a black cat and Soup is a white-and-black puppy, and the two love to play together.

Hines' childhood dream of becoming an author and illustrator for children has come true in manifold ways and in *Something about the Author Autobiography Series,* she explained her joys and expectations in writing. Acknowledging that in her stories she is the child protagonist and not the adult author, she went on to note that she "creat[ed] . . . the world the way I wanted it to be when I was young. I hope young children, and their parents, will find comfort in my books, maybe even a model of positive family relationships. But mostly I hope they'll enjoy them, and that I'll get to go on creating them for a long, long time." "One of the great joys of my career is that I've been around long enough that, every now and then, I get a request for one of my early books that is remembered as a favorite by a now-grown child," Hines also admitted. "It doesn't get better than that!"

Biographical and Critical Sources

BOOKS

McElmeel, Sharron L., *Children's Authors and Illustrators Too Good to Miss,* Libraries Unlimited, 2004.

Something about the Author Autobiography Series, Gale (Detroit, MI), 1995, pp. 209-228.

PERIODICALS

Booklist, February 1, 1986, review of *Cassie Bowen Takes Witch Lessons,* p. 810; October 1, 1989, Denise Wilms, review of *Big like Me,* p. 350; September 15, 1992, Hazel Rochman, review of *Rumble Thumble Boom!,* pp. 154-155; March 1, 1996, Carolyn Phelan, review of *When We Married Gary,* p. 1188; March 1, 1997, Ilene Cooper, review of *Miss Emma's Wild Garden,* p. 1172; October 15, 1998, Karen Simonetti, review of *My Own Big Bed,* p. 427; June 1, 1999, Hazel Rochman, review of *What Can You Do in the Rain?,* p. 1842; January 1, 2001, Ilene Cooper, review of *Pieces: A Year in Poems and Quilts,* p. 951; August, 2003, Carolyn Phelan, review of *Whistling,* p. 1190; September 15, 2005, Carolyn Phelan, review of *Curious George Learns to Count from 1 to 100,* p. 71, and Ilene Cooper, review of *Winter Lights: A Season in Poems and Quilts,* p. 124; May 15, 2008, Carolyn Phelan, review of *1, 2, Buckle My Shoe,* p. 44; February 15, 2009, Carolyn Phelan, review of *Curious George Plants a Tree,* p. 93.

Bulletin of the Center for Children's Books, February, 2001, review of *Pieces,* p. 223.

California Kids!, November, 2004, Patricia Newman, profile of Hines.

Horn Book, September-October, 1986, Mary M. Burns, review of *Daddy Makes the Best Spaghetti,* pp. 580-581; July-August, 1988, Ellen Fader, review of *Grandma Gets Grumpy,* pp. 479-480; September-October, 1989, Ellen Fader, review of *Big like Me,* pp. 611-612; November-December, 2005, Lolly Robinson, review of *Winter Lights,* p. 694.

Kirkus Reviews, February 15, 1986, review of *Daddy Makes the Best Spaghetti,* p. 303; April 1, 1988, review of *Grandma Gets Grumpy,* p. 539; December 15, 2000, review of *Pieces;* August 1, 2001, review of *Whose Shoes?,* p. 1124; March 1, 2003, review of *Whistling,* p. 394; November 1, 2005, review of *Winter Lights,* p. 1193; April 15, 2008, review of *1, 2, Buckle My Shoe.*

Publishers Weekly, March 30, 1984, review of *Come to the Meadow,* p. 56; August 2, 1991, review of *Tell Me Your Best Thing,* pp. 72-73; November 9, 1998, review of *My Own Big Bed,* p. 76; April 12, 1999, Jennifer M. Brown, review of *What Can You Do in the Rain?,* p. 78; January 8, 2001, review of *Pieces,* p. 67; September 26, 2005, review of *Winter Lights,* p. 89.

School Library Journal, May, 1985, B.P. Goldstone, review of *All by Myself,* p. 76; January, 1986, Phyllis Ingram, review of *Cassie Bowen Takes Witch Lessons,* p. 68; February, 1993, Andrew W. Hunter, review of *Rumble Thumble Boom!,* p. 72; September, 1993, Anna DeWind, review of *Moompa, Toby and Bomp,* p. 208; June, 1994, Donna L. Scanlon, review of *The Day of the High Climber,* p. 101; May, 1996, Lisa Marie Gangemi, review of *When We Married Gary,* p. 92; May, 1997, Marianne Saccardi, review of *Miss*

Emma's Wild Garden, p. 100; April, 1999, Karen James, review of *My Own Big Bed,* p. 97; June, 1999, Dawn Amsberry, review of *What Can You Do in the Rain?,* p. 97; March, 2001, Nina Lindsay, review of *Pieces,* p. 236; August, 2001, Anne Parker, review of *Whose Shoes?,* p. 153; August, 2003, Laurie Edwards, review of *Whistling,* p. 134; October, 2005, Tracy Bell, review of *Curious George Learns to Count from 1 to 100,* p. 110; May, 2008, Martha Simpson, review of *1, 2, Buckle My Shoe,* p. 114.

ONLINE

Anna Grossnickle Hines Home Page, http://www.aghines. com (December 10, 2009).

*   *   *

HOPPE, Paul

Personal

Born in Poland. *Education:* University of Applied Sciences (Pforzheim, Germany), degree; School of Visual Arts, M.F.A.

Addresses

Home—Brooklyn, NY. *E-mail*—info@paulhoppe.com.

Career

Author, illustrator, and graphic designer. Clients include Adidas, IBM, and OgilvyOne World Wide. *Rabid Rabbit* magazine, art director; School of Visual Arts, instructor.

Awards, Honors

Joseph Morgan Henninger Best of Show Award, Los Angeles Society of Illustrators.

Writings

SELF-ILLUSTRATED

Das Muster, Fake Press (Ruhrgebeit, Germany), 1999.
Die Schlange, Zwerchfell Verlag (Stuttgart, Germany), 2008.
Hat, Bloomsbury (New York, NY), 2009.

ILLUSTRATOR

Aaron Reynolds, *Metal Man,* Charlesbridge (Watertown, MA), 2008.

Contributor of illustrations to periodicals, including *Wall Street Journal, Village Voice, New Yorker, Washington Post,* and *New York Times.*

Sidelights

After attending the School of Visual Arts in New York City, Polish-born artist Paul Hoppe decided to remain in the United States and embark on a career as a graphic artist. In addition to his corporate work and his work for periodicals such as the *Wall Street Journal,* Hoppe has expanded his role as an artist by venturing into children's books. In his first illustrative effort, he teamed with author Aaron Reynolds to create *Metal Man,* the story of Mitch Levin, an artist who fashions sculptures from leftover materials found on city streets, and Mitch's young protégé, Devon. Uninterested in the conventional school he attends, Devon prefers to spend time with Mitch, learning how to use the tools in the artist's workshop to express his inner emotions in a creative way.

Describing *Metal Man* as an "unusual picture book," *School Library Journal* contributor Heidi Estrin applauded Hoppe's ability to "depict the metal man as tall, strong, gentle, and wise, a larger-than-life hero." A *Kirkus Reviews* contributor also wrote that the illustrations enliven Reynolds' story, claiming that Hoppe's "kinetic mixed-media illustrations have a raw grittiness that well represents the metal man's work."

Hoppe's self-illustrated *Hat* treats readers to a story about an imaginative little boy named Henry who finds a bright red hat while visiting the park. Letting his imagination soar, Henry thinks of all the ways he could play with this broad-brimmed hat, from creating magic tricks to sailing the ocean inside it. However, when the boy's mother reminds him that the chapeau belongs to someone else, this thought conjures up different pictures in Henry's mind, from an explorer without a tool to fight off crocodiles to a lifeguard at the beach without protection from the sun. In the end, the boy leaves the red hat on a bench, hoping that it will be found by its rightful owner. In both art and story, "Hoppe stays true to the child's viewpoint," according to *Booklist* critic Hazel Rochman, and a *Publishers Weekly* reviewer maintained that *Hat* contains "an indomitable, ebullient innocence reminiscent of kids' books from the early 1960s." Finding the narrative "simple but imaginative," *School Library Journal* contributor Laura Stanfield concluded her review by predicting that both "Henry and *Hat* are sure to be a hit."

Biographical and Critical Sources

PERIODICALS

Booklist, March 1, 2009, Hazel Rochman, review of *Hat,* p. 50.
Kirkus Reviews, June 15, 2008, review of *Metal Man.*

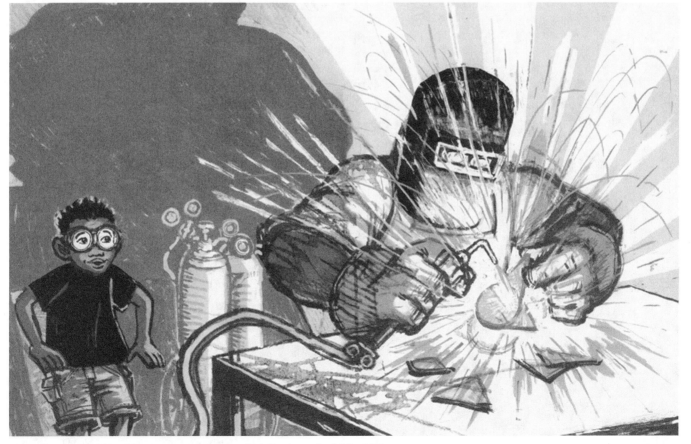

Paul Hoppe creates the art for Aaron Reynolds' boy-friendly picture book **Metal Man.** (Illustration copyright © 2008 by Paul Hoppe. Used with permission of Charlesbridge Publishing, Inc. All rights reserved.)

Publishers Weekly, March 9, 2009, review of *Hat,* p. 46.
School Library Journal, July, 2008, Heidi Estrin, review of *Metal Man,* p. 80; April, 2009, Laura Stanfield, review of *Hat,* p. 106.

ONLINE

Paul Hoppe Home Page, http://www.paulhoppe.de (December 14, 2009).
Paul Hoppe Web log, http://paulhoppeblog.blogspot.com/ (December 14, 2009).

*   *   *

HUBBARD, Crystal

Personal

Married; children: three daughters, one son. *Hobbies and other interests:* Spending time with her children, skateboarding, biking, watching sports.

Addresses

Home—St. Louis, MO.

Career

Author. Formerly worked as a journalist and sports editor.

Member

Society of Children's Book Writers and Illustrators, Romance Writers of America, Interracial/Multicultural Romanc Readers, Boston Author's Club.

Awards, Honors

Storytelling World Honor Award, Children's Book of the Year designation, Bank Street College of Education, and Amelia Bloomer Project inclusion, American Library Association, all 2006, all for *Catching the Moon.*

Crystal Hubbard profiles the life and career of a noted African-American jockey in **The Last Black King of the Kentucky Derby,** *featuring artwork by Robert McGuire.* (Illustration copyright © 2008 by Robert McGuire. Reproduced by permission of Lee & Low Books, Inc.)

Writings

FOR CHILDREN

Catching the Moon: The Story of a Young Girl's Baseball Dream, illustrated by Randy DuBurke, Lee & Low Books (New York, NY), 2005.

The Last Black King of the Kentucky Derby: The Story of Jimmy Winkfield, illustrated by Robert McGuire, Lee & Low Books (New York, NY), 2008.

OTHER

Suddenly You, Genesis Press (Columbus, MS), 2005.

Only You, Genesis Press (Columbus, MS), 2006.

Always You, Genesis Press (Columbus, MS), 2007.

Crush, Genesis Press (Columbus, MS), 2007.

Blame It on Paradise, Genesis Press (Columbus, MS), 2008.

Mr. Fix-It, Genesis Press (Columbus, MS), 2008.

Tempting Faith, Genesis Press (Columbus, MS), 2009.

Sidelights

Crystal Hubbard worked as a journalist before starting her career as a writer. While most of her published work consists of adult novels, Hubbard also turns to younger readers in the picture books *Catching the Moon: The Story of a Young Girl's Baseball Dream* and *The Last Black King of the Kentucky Derby: The Story of Jimmy Winkfield.* "I began writing when I was ten years old," she explained on her home page, "but I didn't fall in love with it until I was in the sixth grade. My teacher . . . introduced me to the work of Mark Twain, Washington Irving, Lois Lowry, Ursula LeGuin, and many other authors who inspired me to tell stories of my own."

In *Catching the Moon,* which is illustrated by Randy DuBurke, Hubbard takes readers back to the early 1930s. Young Marcenia Lyle Alberga can play baseball as well as any boy in her St. Louis neighborhood, and she is determined to do more with her life than fit into the limited opportunities available to young black girls of her generation. Although her parents disapprove of her passion for the game, Marcenia looks forward to trying out for the St. Louis Cardinals baseball camp, realizing the opportunity it will afford her. When camp manager Gabby Street makes it clear that girls are not allowed at camp, the girl sets her mind to confronting the challenge of changing the status quo. Based on a true story about Alberga, who as Toni Stone became the first professional female baseball player, *Catching the Moon* features a text that is "rich in dialogue and detail" and effectively "conveys the thrilling feel" of athletic competition, according to *Booklist* critic Gillian Engberg. "Hubbard's lively text does a fine job of capturing" the young athlete's "unquenchable spirit," wrote Marilyn Taniguchi, the *School Library Journal* critic also describing *Catching the Moon* as a "heartwarming picture book." In *Kirkus Reviews* a critic also praised DuBurke's acrylic paintings, which "beautifully enhance the text," according to the reviewer.

"The prevalence and success of African American jockeys in the late nineteenth and early twentieth centuries are what first caught my attention when I began researching" *The Last Black King of the Kentucky Derby,* Hubbard explained on the Lee & Low Web site. "I hadn't been aware of the fact that horse racing, America's first professional sport, featured predominantly black jockeys. What surprised me most were the successes of African American jockeys." In her nonfiction picture book, which is illustrated by Robert McGuire, Hubbard relates the story of Jimmy Winkfield, a sharecropper's son who grew up to become one of the country's best jockeys as well as the last African Americans to ride to victory in the Kentucky Derby. Born in 1882, Winkfield—or Wink, as he was known—spent a lot of time around horses, and he was racing competitively by his late teens. He raced his first Derby in 1900 and won, repeating the fête the following year. Ironically, Winkfield became a victim of his own success; like other African Americans he was shut out of racing within a few years as white jockeys recognized the opportunities for fame to be found in horse racing. In *School Library Journal* Carole Schene praised *The Last Black King of the Kentucky Derby* as "a personal story of determination and dedication" that is brought to life in McGuire's "vibrant oil paintings." Engberg dubbed the book "a solid introduction to a fascinating subject" and noted Hubbard's "richly informative" text, while in *Kirkus Reviews* a critic praised the book as "a dramatic picture-book biography."

Biographical and Critical Sources

PERIODICALS

Booklist, September 1, 2005, Gillian Engberg, review of *Catching the Moon: The Story of a Young Girl's Baseball Dream,* p. 119; September 1, 2009, Gillian Engberg, review of *The Last Black King of the Kentucky Derby: The Story of Jimmy Winkfield,* p. 112.

Kirkus Reviews, September 1, 2005, review of *Catching the Moon,* p. 974; August 1, 2008, review of *The Last Black King of the Kentucky Derby.*

School Library Journal, November, 2005, Marilyn Taniguchi, review of *Catching the Moon,* p. 116; November, 2008, Carol Schene, review of *The Last Black King of the Kentucky Derby,* p. 108.

ONLINE

Crystal Hubbard Home Page, http://www.hubbiekids.com (December 15, 2009).

Lee & Low Web site, http://www.leeandlow.com/ (December 15, 2009), interview with Hubbard.*

K

KIMMEL, Elizabeth Cody
(Elizabeth Kimmel Willard)

Personal

Born in New York, NY; married; children: Emma. *Education:* Kenyon College, degree. *Hobbies and other interests:* Reading, hiking, singing, rock climbing.

Addresses

Home—Hudson River Valley, NY. *E-mail*—codykimmel@earthlink.net.

Career

Children's book writer.

Writings

FICTION

In the Stone Circle, Scholastic (New York, NY), 1998.

Balto and the Great Race, illustrated by Nora Koerber, Random House (New York, NY), 1999.

Visiting Miss Caples, Dial (New York, NY), 2000.

To the Frontier ("Adventures of Young Buffalo Bill" series), illustrated by Scott Snow, HarperCollins (New York, NY), 2001.

One Sky above Us ("Adventures of Young Buffalo Bill" series), illustrated by Scott Snow, HarperCollins (New York, NY), 2002.

My Wagon Will Take Me Anywhere, illustrated by Tom Newsom, Dutton (New York, NY), 2002.

In the Eye of the Storm ("Adventures of Young Buffalo Bill" series), illustrated by Scott Snow, HarperCollins (New York, NY), 2003.

West on the Wagon Train ("Adventures of Young Buffalo Bill" series), illustrated by Scott Snow, HarperCollins (New York, NY), 2003.

Lily B. on the Brink of Cool, HarperCollins (New York, NY), 2003.

What Do You Dream?, illustrated by Joung un Kim, Candlewick Press (Cambridge, MA), 2003.

My Penguin Osbert, illustrated by H.B. Lewis, Candlewick Press (Cambridge, MA), 2004.

Lily B. on the Brink of Love, HarperCollins (New York, NY), 2005.

Lily B. on the Brink of Paris, HarperCollins (New York, NY), 2006.

The Top Job, illustrated by Robert Neubecker, Dutton Children's Books (New York, NY), 2007.

Glamsters, illustrated by Jackie Urbanovic, Hyperion Books for Children (New York, NY), 2008.

(Under name Elizabeth Kimmel Willard) *Mary Ingalls on Her Own,* HarperCollins (New York, NY), 2008.

School Spirit ("Suddenly Supernatural" series), Little, Brown (Boston, MA), 2008.

Spin the Bottle, Dial Books for Young Readers (New York, NY), 2008.

My Penguin Osbert in Love, illustrated by H.B. Lewis, Candlewick Press (Cambridge, MA), 2009.

Scaredy Kat ("Suddenly Supernatural" series), Little, Brown (New York, NY), 2009.

Unhappy Medium ("Suddenly Supernatural" series), Little Brown (New York, NY), 2009.

Author of one-act play *Hudson Adrift,* produced in 2009.

Kimmel's "Lily B." books have been translated into several languages.

NONFICTION

Ice Story: Shackleton's Lost Expedition, Clarion (New York, NY), 1999.

Before Columbus: The Leif Eriksson Expedition, Random House (New York, NY), 2003.

As Far as the Eye Can Reach: Lewis and Clark's Westward Quest, Random House (New York, NY), 2003.

The Look-It-up Book of Explorers, Random House (New York, NY), 2004.

Ladies First: Forty Daring American Women Who Were Second to None, National Geographic (Washington, DC), 2005.

Dinosaur Bone War: Cope and Marsh's Fossil Feud, Random House (New York, NY), 2006.

Boy on the Lion Throne: The Childhood of the 14th Dalai Lama, foreword by His Holiness the Dalai Lama, Roaring Book Press (New York, NY), 2009.

Sidelights

Elizabeth Cody Kimmel grew up in both New York and Brussels, Belgium. As a writer of fiction and nonfiction for children and young adults, she focuses on subjects she finds interesting—from Antarctica to ghost stories to medieval history to the life of the Dalai Lama—in her books. Several of Kimmel's nonfiction titles, such as *Ice Story: Shackleton's Lost Expedition* and *As Far as the Eye Can Reach: Lewis and Clark's Westward Quest,* focus on explorers, while her young-adult novels deal with themes such as multi-generational friendships and being true to yourself while also introducing readers to an engaging and upbeat characters.

Cover of Elizabeth Cody Kimmel's middle-grade novel Spin the Bottle, *featuring artwork by Natalie C. Sousa.* (Jacket art © 2008 and design by Natalie C. Sousa. Reproduced by permission of Dial Books for Young Readers, a division of Penguin Putnam Books for Young Readers.)

The Lewis and Clark Expedition is the subject of *As Far as the Eye Can Reach,* which follows the explorers' efforts to locate a northern route to the Pacific Ocean. The book was described as "a well written, lively account for young readers" by a contributor to *Kirkus Reviews,* and *Booklist* critic Carolyn Phelan wrote that Kimmel's "clearly written summary provides a useful overview for students." As Renee Steinberg commented in her review of *As Far as the Eye Can Reach* for *School Library Journal,* "a book such as this can excite young readers to delve further into U.S. history."

Another nonfiction title by Kimmel, *Before Columbus: The Leif Eriksson Expedition,* introduces readers to the Viking exploration of the Americas. A *Kirkus Reviews* contributor characterized this book as "more a quick once-over than a systematic study," but added that *Before Columbus* is "well designed to stimulate an early interest" in its subject. Ginny Gustin, writing in *School Library Journal,* noted that the nonfiction title reads more like an historical novel, and acknowledged that "Kimmel's book will captivate and entertain young readers." More clearly designed as a reference resource, *The Look-It-up Book of Explorers* covers the expeditions of world explorers through the ages. Carol Wichman, writing in *School Library Journal,* deemed the work "a concise and useful guide to virtually all of the explorers usually studied in public schools."

In *Dinosaur Bone War: Cope and Marsh's Fossil Feud* Kimmel focuses on a different kind of exploration. In a text that Ilene Cooper characterized in *Booklist* as "lively," she introduces readers to the facts surrounding a feud that existed between two scientists during the 1870s and 1880s. Edward Cope and Othniel "Charlie" Marsh were initially colleagues and friends, but their work excavating for prehistoric bones in the American West destroyed that friendship after trust was violated and supremacy was measured in the number of bones unearthed and species discovered. While discussing the many scientific discoveries that came about during these "Bone Wars"—March discovered eighty new species, while Marsh found fifty-six—Kimmel also steps back and allows readers to see the huge advances that occurred in the field of paleontology as a result of the competition between Cope and Marsh. A *Kirkus Reviews* writer characterized *Dinosaur Bone War* as "a straightforward chronological account" of two pioneering scientists, adding that "the drama of the . . . escalating quarrel . . . carries the reader along."

Boy on the Lion Throne: The Childhood of the 14th Dalai Lama, In 1937 monks on a secret mission identify Lhamo Thondup as the fourteenth reincarnation of Tibet's most revered lama. From his simple life in a mountain village to the thousand-room Potala Palace where he is worshipped as a god-king, as well as his perilous escape into exile, this dramatic narrative follows the remarkable childhood of the Dalai Lama, one of the most loved and honored spiritual leaders in the

world. The 160-page text is generously illustrated with historic black-and-white photos. The book features a foreword by His Holiness the Dalai Lama, and some of the profits from the sale of *Boy on the Lion Throne* benefit Tibet Aid.

Turning to fiction, Kimmel entertains teens with her first novel-length work, *Visiting Miss Caples*. The book tells the story of thirteen-year-old Jenna, whose father abandons her family. To make things worse, the girl's best friend no longer speaks to her. Jenna assumes that a class project to visit Mrs. Caples, an elderly shut-in, will be just one more bad aspect of the year. However, she soon realizes that Mrs. Caples, despite her difference in age, understands a lot of what Jenna is going through. "Kimmel ably articulates a young person's experience," wrote Gillian Engberg in a *Booklist* review of the multigenerational novel.

Kimmel entertains 'tween readers with her "Lily B." and "Suddenly Supernatural" series, both of which find a spunky teen heroine coping with various misadventures. In *Lily B. on the Brink of Cool* Lily is convinced that her family is anything but cool. When she meets distant cousin Karma and Karma's family, Lily is determined to fit in, becoming more sophisticated by proximity. However, it soon appears that Karma's family has more in mind than befriending Lily, and the teen ultimately learns that sometimes first impressions are deceiving. "Lily is a likable teen who wants more than she has, only to discover that what she has is pretty darn good," wrote Linda Binder in *School Library Journal*. A *Kirkus Reviews* contributor found Lily to be "a delightful heroine, sweeter than [other teen heroines] and hilarious," while Louise Bruggemann noted in her *Booklist* review that *Lily B. on the Brink of Cool* is a "funny, fast-moving . . . novel." A *Publishers Weekly* critic described Lily as, "by turns chirpy, sardonic, glib, and melodramatic—and always likable."

Lily B. on the Brink of Love finds Lily serving as her middle school's newspaper advice columnist. As she soon learns, dealing with her own love life is more difficult than sorting out the romantic foibles of her classmates. In *Lily B. on the Brink of Paris*, the thirteen year old joins seven friends on a trip to gay Paree, where the highlights include her efforts to begin writing a novel and the real-life drama of getting lost. "Lily's journal entries and advice columns . . . deliver laughs and substance," wrote Wendi Hoffenberg in a *School Library Journal* review of *Lily B. on the Brink of Love*, and a *Kirkus Reviews* contributor called the book "heartwarming and funny." In *School Library Journal* Cheryl Ashton described Kimmel's third "Lily B." installment as "light, fun fiction" featuring the "detail-disoriented Lily," and a *Kirkus Reviews* writer concluded that, "as always, Lily's offbeat adventures are good for a laugh."

In the "Suddenly Supernatural" series readers meet Kat, a preteen who learns to cope with an unwanted new talent in *School Spirit, Scaredy Kat,* and *Unhappy Me-*

dium. When readers meet her in *School Spirit,* the seventh grader realizes that by turning thirteen she has inherited her mother's ability to communicate with the deceased. She worries that this talent for talking to the dead will ruin her reputation in middle school, where being different is also deadly. Through her friendship with Jac, a cello-playing teen with a similarly strange family situation, Kat gradually comes to terms with her talent, and begins to embrace her gift as a bridge to the dearly departed. A trip to an old house is the focus of *Scaredy Kat,* the second installment in the "Suddenly Supernatural" series, while in *Unhappy Medium* Kat and Jac travel to the haunted Whispering Pines Mountain House. Confident in her ability to talk with the dead, Kat attempts to persuade a ghost to pass along to the next realm, but her discussions are soon disrupted by something far more evil. Praising Kat as "a smart and witty narrator with a wry sense of humor," Kitty Flynn added in *Horn Book* that *School Spirit* is an "inviting" story that includes telling insights into "middle-school [life] and mother-daughter dynamics." In another review of *School Spirit,* a *Kirkus Reviews* writer deemed the book "a satisfying start to a new series," while in her *School Library Journal* review of *Scaredy Kat* Elaine E. Knight called the story's teen heroines "an engaging team" whose "dialogue generally rings true."

Along with nonfiction and novels, Kimmel has also crafted picture books, including *My Penguin Osbert* and its sequel, *My Penguin Osbert in Love,* both of which feature artwork by H.B. Lewis. *My Penguin Osbert* tells the story of a Christmas wish gone wrong: Joe wanted a live penguin, but when Osbert is delivered by Santa, the boy realizes that having a pet penguin is not quite what he imagined. When Joe finally brings Osbert to a new home in the zoo, both boy and penguin end up happy. "Kimmel sneaks some sly humor into the well-told, nicely paced tale," wrote Cooper in a *Booklist* review of *My Penguin Osbert,* and a *Kirkus Reviews* contributor recommended the story as "salutary reading for all children campaigning for a pet." In *Horn Book* Lauren E. Raece deemed the picture book a "satisfying tale," and a *Publishers Weekly* critic predicted that readers would "find much to enjoy in this lighthearted fantasy with realistic holiday roots."

Joe and his penguin return in *My Penguin Osbert in Love.* Escaping from the zoo, Osbert and his gang of penguin friends ask the boy for help in getting to Antarctica in time to witness the southern lights. Traveling in a overcrowded helicopter, the group makes its way to the South Pole where it meets Aurora Australis. Osbert is immediately smitten with this southern belle, leaving Joe to manage amid a sea of penguins in a story that features Lewis's "colorful and softly muted . . . watercolor, pastel, and digital" artwork, according to *School Library Journal* critic Kirsten Cutler. Also citing Lewis's art, Phelan praised Kimmel's ability to give Joe a "wonderfully evocative" narrative voice vand concluded that *My Penguin Osbert in Love* is "a winner for winter storytimes."

Featuring artwork by Jackie Urbanovic, *Glamsters* is another storyhour treat by Kimmel. Harriet Hamster worries that she is being overlooked while all the other hamsters awaiting adoption at Hamster World quickly find homes. Harriet finds a unique answer to her dilemma in a magazine: a rodent makeover that involves whisker extensions, fur volumizer, and claw polish. Harriet's efforts yield surprising results in a story that Mary Hazelton recommended in *School Library Journal* as "a starting point for discussions about popularity and love." "Kimmel makes the most of her [story's] silly premise," asserted a *Kirkus Reviews* writer, the critic calling *Glamsters* "a hoot and a half."

Biographical and Critical Sources

PERIODICALS

Booklist, May 15, 2000, Gillian Engberg, review of *Visiting Miss Caples,* p. 1739; January 1, 2003, Carolyn Phelan, "Lewis & Clark on the Road Again," p. 885; July, 2003, Roger Leslie, review of *Before Columbus: The Leif Eriksson Expedition* p. 1882; October 1, 2003, Lauren Peterson, review of *What Do You Dream?,* p. 328; December 1, 2003, Louise Brueggemann, review of *Lily B. on the Brink of Cool,* p. 666; December 1, 2004, Ilene Cooper, review of *My Penguin Osbert,* p. 659; October 1, 2005, Anne O'Malley, review of *Lily B. on the Brink of Love,* p. 58; December 1, 2006, Ilene Cooper, review of *Dinosaur Bone War: Cope and Marsh's Fossil Feud,* p. 57; January 1, 2007, Ilene Cooper, review of *Lily B on the Brink of Paris,* p. 81; July 1, 2007, Debbie Carton, review of *The Top Job,* p. 61; May 1, 2008, Hazel Rochman, review of *Spin the Bottle,* p. 90; February 1, 2009, Carolyn Phelan, review of *My Penguin Osbert in Love,* p. 47.

Bulletin of the Center for Children's Books, April, 2000, review of *Visiting Miss Caples,* p. 285; February, 2004, review of *Lily B. on the Brink of Cool,* p. 237.

Horn Book, November-December, 2004, Lauren E. Raece, review of *My Penguin Osbert,* p. 662; July-August, 2008, Kitty Flynn, review of *School Spirit,* p. 451.

Kirkus Reviews, December 15, 2002, review of *As Far as the Eye Can Reach,* p. 1851; July 15, 2003, review of *Before Columbus,* p. 965; October 15, 2003, review of *Lily B. on the Brink of Cool,* p. 1272; November 1, 2004, review of *My Penguin Osbert,* p. 1051; August 1, 2005, review of *Lily B. on the Brink of Love,* p. 851; December 1, 2006, reviews of *Lily B. on the Brink of Paris* and *Dinosaur Bone War,* both p. 1222; March 15, 2008, review of *Spin the Bottle;* May 15, 2008, review of *School Spirit;* October 1, 2008, review of *Glamsters;* November 15, 2008, review of *My Penguin Osbert in Love.*

Kliatt, July, 2004, Sherri Ginsberg, review of *Lily B. on the Brink of Cool,* p. 53; September, 2005, Heidi Hauser Green, review of *Lily B. on the Brink of Cool,* p. 20.

Publishers Weekly, December 10, 2001, review of *Visiting Miss Caples,* p. 73; June 9, 2003, review of "Adventures of Young Buffalo Bill" series, p. 54; December 8, 2003, review of *Lily B. on the Brink of Cool,* p. 62; November 22, 2004, review of *My Penguin Osbert,* p. 60; July 23, 2007, review of *The Top Job,* p. 67.

School Librarian, autumn, 2004, Chris Brown, review of *Lily B. on the Brink of Cool,* p. 156.

School Library Journal, July, 2002, Anne Knickerbocker, review of *My Wagon Will Take Me Anywhere,* p. 94; March, 2003, Renee Steinberg, review of *As Far as the Eye Can Reach,* pp. 172, 253; October, 2003, Ginny Gustin, review of *Before Columbus,* p. 152, and Linda Binder, review of *Lily B. on the Brink of Cool,* p. 169; February 2004, Sanda Kitain, review of *What Do You Dream?,* p. 116; January, 2005, Wendi Hoffengberg, review of *Lily B. on the Brink of Love,* p. 104, and Carol Wichman, review of *The Look-It-up Book of Explorers,* p. 149; July, 2005, Wendi Hoffenberg, review of *Lily B. on the Brink of Love,* p. 104; January, 2007, Cheryl Ashton, review of *Lily B. on the Brink of Paris,* p. 130; September, 2008, Danielle Serra, review of *School Spirit,* p. 188; November, 2008, Mary Hazelton, review of *Glamsters,* p. 90; March, 2009, Elaine E. Knight, review of *Scaredy Kat,* p. 146; May, 2009, Kirsten Cutler, review of *My Penguin Osbert in Love,* p. 82.

Voice of Youth Advocates, August, 2000, review of *Ice Story,* p. 165; October, 2003, review of *Lily B. on the Brink of Cool,* p. 312.

ONLINE

Elizabeth Cody Kimmel Home Page, http://www.codykimmel.com (December 15, 2009).

Kids Reads Web site, http://www.kidsreads.com/ (April 27, 2006), profile of Kimmel.

*   *   *

KINGFISHER, Rupert

Personal

Born in England. *Education:* Attended Bristol University and University of London Central School of Speech and Drama.

Addresses

Home—Brentford, England.

Career

Author and playwright.

Writings

Madame Pamplemousse and Her Incredible Edibles, illustrated by Sue Hellard, Bloomsbury (New York, NY), 2008.

Madame Pamplemousse and the Time Travelling Café, illustrated by Sue Hellard, Bloomsbury (London, England), 2009.

Author of plays produced in Edinburgh, Scotland, Dublin, Ireland, and London, England, and broadcast on BBC Radio 4.

Sidelights

In addition to his work as a playwright, British author Rupert Kingfisher has also penned the middle-grade novels *Madame Pamplemousse and Her Incredible Edibles* and its sequel, *Madame Pamplemousse and the Time Travelling Café.* Set in the labyrinthine streets of Paris, *Madame Pamplemousse and Her Incredible Edibles* features a diminutive heroine named Madeline who lives with her uncle, Monsieur Lard, owner of the Squealing Pig restaurant. A greedy man, Monsieur Lard sends Madeline out for paté one day, an in her search the young girl discovers a delicatessen that sells the most delightful food. Wishing to learn the secrets of its owner, Monsieur Lard apprentices his niece to Madame Pamplemousse and presses Madeline to steal the wom-

an's recipes. A truly talented cook, Madeline develops an important bond with Madame Pamplemousse and begins to solve the true mystery behind preparing delicious meals.

A *Kirkus Reviews* critic called Kingfisher's debut work "a sensory delight," echoing the "well-paced prose and the playful language of Roald Dahl and Lemony Snicket." London *Times* book reviewer Amanda Craig deemed *Madame Pamplemousse and Her Incredible Edibles* a humorous commentary on the phoniness of many figures in the world of gastronomy, particularly celebrity chefs and restaurant critics. Craig further described Kingfisher's novel as "witty, warm-hearted and as delectable as one of the dishes it describes" before going on to suggest that *Madame Pamplemousse and Her Incredible Edibles* works as "as much a hymn to the culinary arts as to the magic of kindness."

Madeline's adventures continue in *Madame Pamplemousse and the Time Travelling Café,* as she joins Madame Pamplemousse and close friend and scientist Monsieur Moutarde on a trip in his time-travel machine. Together the trio sets out to collect exotic specimens from history in a race to save Paris from blandness.

Biographical and Critical Sources

PERIODICALS

Financial Times (London, England), August 30, 2008, Neville Hawcock, review of *Madame Pamplemousse and Her Incredible Edibles,* p. 15.
Kirkus Reviews, October 1, 2008, review of *Madame Pamplemousse and Her Incredible Edibles.*
New York Times Book Review, April 12, 2009, review of *Madame Pamplemousse and Her Incredible Edibles,* p. 15.
School Library Journal, March, 2009, Debbie S. Hoskins, review of *Madame Pamplemousse and Her Incredible Edibles,* p. 118.
Times (London, England), September 20, 2008, Amanda Craig, review of *Madame Pamplemousse and Her Incredible Edibles,* p. 15.*

* * *

KISSEL, Richard

Personal

Son of a coal miner. *Education:* Bowling Green State University, B.S. (geology), 1997; Texas Tech University, M.S. (geosciences), 1999; University of Toronto, Ph.D. (ecology and evolutionary biology), 2009.

Addresses

Office—Paleontolotical Research Institution/Museum of the Earth, 1259 Trumansburg Rd., Ithaca, NY 14850. *E-mail*—kissel@museumoftheearth.org.

Sue Hellard contributes cartoon art to Rupert Kingfisher's humorous story in Madame Pamplemousse and Her Incredible Edibles. (Bloomsbury Children's Books, 2008. Illustration copyright © 2008 by Sue Hellard. Reproduced by permission.)

Career

Paleontologist and writer. Carnegie Museum of Natural History, curatorial assistant, vertebrate fossils, 1994-97; Field Museum, Chicago, IL, paleontologist and science program developer, 2003-08, and founder and teacher at Mastodon Camp! (two-week camp), summer, 2007; Paleontological Research Institution, Ithaca, NY, director of teacher programs, 2008—. Featured scientist on *ScienceNOW* (television program); presenter at conventions and panels.

Writings

(With Erica Kelly) *Evolving Planet: Four Billion Years of Life on Earth,* Harry N. Abrams (New York, NY), 2008.

Contributor to periodicals, including *Natural History, Canadian Journal of Earth Sciences, Bulletin of Carnegie Museum of Natural History, Annals of Carnegie Museum,* and *Journal of Paleontology.* Author of column "The Nature of Science" for *American Paleontologist.*

Biographical and Critical Sources

PERIODICALS

Booklist, September 15, 2008, Hazel Rochman, review of *Evolving Planet: Four Billion Years of Life on Earth,* p. 54.
Horn Book, January-February, 2009, Danielle J. Ford, review of *Evolving Planet,* p. 118.
School Library Journal, February, 2009, Patricia Manning, review of *Evolving Planet,* p. 121.
Science Books and Film, January-February, 2009, Kevin Koepnick, review of *Evolving Planet,* p. 34.

ONLINE

Agency for Instructional Technology Web site, http://www.ait/net/technos/e-zine/ (December 10, 2009), interview with Kissel.
NOVA Web site, http://www.pbs.org/ (April, 2005), Richard Kissel, "Ask the Expert."
Paleontological Research Institution Web site, http://www.museumoftheearth.org/ (December 10, 2009), "Richard Kissel."*

*   *   *

KNUDSON, Mike 1965-

Personal

Born October 30, 1965, in Salt Lake City, UT; married; wife's name Annette; children: three sons, two daughters. *Hobbies and other interests:* Playing the banjo.

Addresses

Home—UT. *E-mail*—mike knudson@yahoo.com.

Career

Author and editor.

Writings

(With Steve Wilkinson) *Raymond and Graham Rule the School,* illustrated by Stacy Curtis, Viking Children's Books (New York, NY), 2008.
Raymond and Graham, Dancing Dudes, illustrated by Stacy Curtis, Viking (New York, NY), 2008.
Raymond and Graham: Bases Loaded, illustrated by Stacy Curtis, Viking (New York, NY), 2010.
Raymond and Graham: Cool Campers, illustrated by Stacy Curtis, Viking (New York, NY), 2010.

Biographical and Critical Sources

PERIODICALS

Kirkus Reviews, June 15, 2008, review of *Raymond and Graham Rule the School.*
School Library Journal, November, 2008, Terrie Dorio, review of *Dancing Dudes,* p. 92; September, 2009, Andrea Tarr, review of *Raymond and Graham Rule the School,* p. 152.

ONLINE

Mike Knudson Home Page, http://www.mikeknudson.com (December 13, 2009).*

*   *   *

KOERTGE, Ron 1940-

Personal

Surname is pronounced "*kur*-chee"; born April 22, 1940, in Olney, IL; son of William Henry (an owner of an ice-cream store and school janitor) and Bulis Olive (a homemaker) Koertge; married Cheryl Vasconcellos (marriage ended); married Bianca Richards (a counselor), November 4, 1992. *Education:* University of Illinois, B.A., 1962; University of Arizona, M.A., 1965.

Addresses

Home—South Pasadena, CA. *Agent*—William Reiss, John Hawkins & Associates, 71 W. 23rd St., No. 1600, New York, NY 10010. *E-mail*—ronkoe@earthlink.net.

Career

Writer, 1962—. Pasadena City College, Pasadena, CA, professor of English, 1965-2002.

Ron Koertge (Photograph by Judy Heinrichs. Reproduced by permission.)

Awards, Honors

American Library Association (ALA) Best Book citation and ALA Book for Reluctant Readers designation, both for *Where the Kissing Never Stops;* ALA Best Book citation, *Booklist* Books of the Decade designation, and Young Adult School Library Association (YASLA) 100 Best of the Best designation, all for *The Arizona Kid;* National Endowment for the Arts fellowship, 1990; ALA Best Book citation, and Friends of American Writers award, both 1991, both for *The Boy in the Moon;* California Arts Council grant, 1993, ALA Best Book and Notable Book citations, and New York Public Library Books for the Teen Age designation, all for *The Harmony Arms;* ALA Best Book citation, New York Public Library 100 Best Children's Books listee, *Bulletin of the Center for Children's Books* Blue Ribbon Book selection, Bank Street Child Study Children's Book Committee Book-of-the-Year choice, Judy Lopez Memorial Award Honor Book designation, and ALA/YASLA Best Books for Young Adults listee, all 1994, all for *Tiger, Tiger, Burning Bright; School Library Journal* Best Books citation, 1996, for *Confess-o-Rama;* YASLA Best Book citation and Quick Pick citation, and New York Public Library Books for the Teen Age selection, all 2001, all for *The Brimstone Journals;* YALSA Best Book for Young Adults designation, and Quick Pick for Reluctant Young-Adult Readers citation, Michigan Thumbs Up! Award Honor Book designation, New York Public Library Books for the Teen Age selection, and PEN Center USA West Literary Award for Best Children's Book, all 2003, all for *Stoner and Spaz;*

YALSA Best Book for Young Adults designation, and New York Public Library Books for the Teen Age selection, both 2005, both for *Margaux with an X;* New York Public Library Books for the Teen Age selection, 2004, for *Shakespeare Bats Cleanup;* PEN Center/USA West Literary Award for Best Children's Book, 2007, for *Strays.*

Writings

FOR YOUNG ADULTS

Where the Kissing Never Stops, Atlantic Monthly Press (Boston, MA), 1986, reprinted, Candlewick Press (Cambridge, MA), 2005.
The Arizona Kid, Joy Street Books (Boston, MA), 1988, reprinted, Candlewick Press (Cambridge, MA), 2005.
The Boy in the Moon, Joy Street Books (Boston, MA), 1990.
Mariposa Blues, Joy Street Books (Boston, MA), 1991.
The Harmony Arms, Joy Street Books (Boston, MA), 1992.
Tiger, Tiger Burning Bright, Orchard Books (New York, NY), 1994.
Confess-o-Rama, Orchard Books (New York, NY), 1996.
The Heart of the City, Orchard Books (New York, NY), 1998.
The Brimstone Journals (verse novel), Candlewick Press (Cambridge, MA), 2001.
Stoner and Spaz, Candlewick Press (Cambridge, MA), 2002.
Shakespeare Bats Cleanup (verse novel), Candlewick Press (Cambridge, MA), 2003.
Margaux with an X, Candlewick Press (Cambridge, MA), 2004.
Boy Girl Boy, Harcourt Children's Books (Orlando, FL), 2005.
Strays, Candlewick Press (Cambridge, MA), 2007.
Deadville, Candlewick Press (Cambridge, MA), 2008.
Shakespeare Makes the Playoffs, Candlewick Press (Cambridge, MA), 2010.

POETRY; FOR ADULTS

The Father-Poems, Sumac Press, 1973.
Meat: Cheryl's Market-Diary, MAG Press, 1973.
The Hired Nose, MAG Press, 1974.
My Summer Vacation, Venice Poetry, 1975.
Sex Object, Country Press, 1975, revised edition, Little Caesar, 1979.
(With Charles Stetler and Gerald Locklin) *Tarzan and Shane Meet the Toad,* Haas, 1975.
Cheap Thrills, Wormwood Review, 1976.
Men under Fire, Duck Down, 1976.
Twelve Photographs of Yellowstone, Red Hill, 1976.
How to Live on Five Dollars a Week, Etc., Venice Poetry, 1977.
The Jockey Poems, Maelstrom, 1980.
Diary Cows, Little Caesar, 1981.
Fresh Meat, Kenmore, 1981.

Life on the Edge of the Continent: Selected Poems, University of Arkansas Press (Fayetteville, AR), 1982.

High School Dirty Poems, Red Wind (Los Angeles, CA), 1991.

Making Love to Roget's Wife: Poems New and Selected, University of Arkansas Press (Fayetteville, AR), 1997.

Geography of the Forehead, University of Arkansas Press (Fayetteville, AR), 2000.

Fever, Red Hen Press (Los Angeles, CA), 2006.

Indigo, Red Hen Press (Los Angeles, CA), 2009.

Contributor to *The Maverick Poets: An Anthology,* edited by Steve Kowit, Gorilla Press, 1988.

OTHER

The Boogeyman (adult novel), Norton (New York, NY), 1980.

One Hundred Things to Write About (college textbook), Holt (New York, NY), 1990.

Contributor to periodicals, including the *Los Angeles Times Book Review.*

Sidelights

Despite his long career as a college English professor, Ron Koertge has not forgotten what it was like to ride the emotional roller-coaster through adolescence into adulthood. The protagonists in Koertge's young-adult novels suffer the universal anxieties suffered by teen boys over acne pimples, and bemoan the fact that they are shorter than their classmates. They ponder their futures and quarrel with eccentric or domineering parents. In Koertge's novels particularly, these boys learn to deal with the sexual longings that become tangled up with romantic impulses when they become seriously involved with girls they care about. While Koertge often uses humor in his stories, he never downplays the seriousness of adolescent concerns. In an essay for the *Dictionary of Literary Biography,* Jane Hoogestraat maintained that Koertge's books are "remarkable for the realism with which they present tough and not-so-tough teenage characters coming of age in a world of AIDS and widespread divorce, but often in a world in which tenderness and love are not absent." Michael Cart, writing in *School Library Journal* called Koertge "a brilliant writer" who has positioned himself among "America's finest authors for young adults."

Koertge was born in 1940, in Olney, Illinois, where his parents worked at a large dairy farm. While Koertge was still young, the family left farm country and moved to Collinsville, Illinois, to open an ice-cream business. The store flourished until the town's first supermarket opened, forcing it and several other specialty stores out of business. Koertge's father became a janitor in the public school system while his mother stayed at home to raise Ron. They were comfortable financially and, as Koertge recalled, "fairly happy."

An only child, Koertge enjoyed sports and school, and as a teen he discovered that he had a knack for writing. "I discovered I was more glib than most of my friends,"

he once noted, "but I also somehow sensed that my gift wouldn't be really valuable until I was older. Very early on, words seemed to have lives of their own. Still today, the way the words fit together and the way they lie on the music they generate is more interesting to me than the so-called arc of the story." He also discovered that he had a flair for drama and enjoyed saying and doing outrageous things. "I would say out loud things that other kids seemed reluctant to say," he once admitted. "I liked to shock people—to leave them lurching, not laughing." Koertge's sense of life's quirks was heightened when he suffered a serious bout of rheumatic fever as a young teen. The illness—which might have left him with a weakened heart for the rest of his life, or even killed him—instilled in the fortunate young man a "sense of the insubstantiality of my body and made me alternately tentative and foolishly bold," as he recalled.

Koertge began writing in high school, "something I was drawn to, partly because it was something I could do," he remembered. He pursued this interest at the University of Illinois, where he earned his bachelor's degree in 1962, and then at the University of Arizona, where

Cover of Koertge's middle-grade novel **The Harmony Arms,** *featuring artwork by Amy L. Wasserman.* (Little, Brown & Company, 1992. Reproduced by permission.)

he received a master's degree in 1965 and began writing poetry. After graduation, Koertge took a position as a professor of English at Pasadena City College, where he continued to teach until 2002. He began publishing poems in magazines as early as 1970, and a few years after that released the first of many chapbooks of verse. In 1980 he published his only novel for adults, *The Boogeyman.* "The two novels after that were pitiful. Embarrassing," Koertge later admitted. "Then a friend suggested that I try young adults since I'm a chronic smart ass. I went to the library, read a couple, and figured I could do at least that well. Sure enough: the two failed grown-up novels became *Where the Kissing Never Stops* and *The Arizona Kid.*"

Published in 1986 and 1988 respectively, Koertge's first two young-adult novels, although humorous and touching coming-of-age stories, ignited controversy due to their frank and realistic depiction of sexual encounters and alternative lifestyles. "It might have been naive of me to think that straight talk about sex would be universally welcomed in the secret garden of children's books or that a gay character in a YA would be treated like any other character," Koertge admitted in the *Los Angeles Times Book Review.* "But I was simply looking for something interesting to write." *Where the Kissing Never Stops* finds seventeen-year-old Walker plagued with problems. His craving for junk food is running unchecked, his girlfriend has left town, and worst of all, his mother has taken a job as a stripper in a nearby burlesque parlor. At his lowest ebb, Walker meets Rachel, a mall-loving, cosmopolitan teen. Different as they are, Walker and Rachel begin a romance and ultimately learn to trust one another. *School Library Journal* contributor Marjorie Lewis noted that "Walker's attempts to keep his mother's occupation a secret and make his romance with Rachel a rich, fulfilling one are believable and engrossing."

In *The Arizona Kid* sixteen-year-old Billy faces a summer of change and discovery as he experiences firsthand the colorful world of horse racing, falling in love, losing his virginity, and learning about the gay lifestyle of his Uncle Wes, with whom he is spending the summer in Tucson. "Billy's relationship with his feisty, understanding girlfriend Cara Mae boosts his shaky self-confidence," explained an essayist in *St. James Guide to Young-Adult Writers,* while "warm, witty, and generous Uncle Wes fosters Billy's growing sense of independence" despite an initial period of discomfort between the two men.

These first two novels set the standard for much of Koertge's more recent books for teens, humorous tales featuring young men coming of age amid sometimes frustrating, sometimes humorous circumstances. In *The Harmony Arms,* for example, Gabriel McKay moves temporarily with his divorced and eccentric father to Los Angeles. Living at the Harmony Arms apartment complex, the boy becomes acquainted with a host of individuals with equally eccentric personalities—including his new friend Tess, an aspiring young film maker who carries a camcorder with her everywhere in order to document her life. "Koertge's brash, outrageous characters give new meaning to the word *diversity,*" noted *Horn Book* critic Nancy Vasilakis, adding that the author "offers a lively defense of the West Coast's let-it-all-hang-out spirit in his funniest novel to date." *Voice of Youth Advocates* contributor John Lord maintained that the "strength" of *The Harmony Arms* "lies in its . . . well-drawn and believable" characters.

In *Tiger, Tiger, Burning Bright* Koertge introduces readers to life in rural central California, where Jesse's grandfather Pappy, a retired cowboy with long hair and a love of the Western desert, now lives. As Pappy becomes more forgetful and begins to get lost during walks in the nearby hill country, Jesse tries to conceal these lapses of memory to keep his mother from taking Pappy away from the place he loves and putting him in a nursing home. A reviewer for *Publishers Weekly* appreciated Koertge's "imaginative characterizations, wacky humor and crackling, authentically adolescent dialogue," while *Booklist* contributor Hazel Rochman maintained that "what carries the story . . . is the perfect pitch of Jesse's voice, somewhere between farce and melancholy parody and grief."

Confess-o-Rama follows fifteen-year-old Tony as he gains an unusual circle of friends after he and his mother move to a new town after his fourth stepfather dies. Stressed by the constant moves, worried about his widowed mom, and suffering from typical teen angst, Tony resorts to a confessional hotline: just say your problem out loud and then hang up. Finding out that fellow classmate and potential crush Jordan is on the other end of the hotline comes as a surprise to the unsuspecting Tony and creates a novel in which the "narrative, characterization, setting, and pacing are realistic, humorous, and insightful," according to *Booklist* critic Karen Simonetti. Deborah Stevenson noted in her review of *Confess-o-Rama* for the *Bulletin of the Center for Children's Books* that Koertge "blend[s] humor and genuine emotion in a way many YA authors essay but fail: Tony's quips and the outrageousness of the plot are genuinely funny but never superficial."

The perspectives of fifteen modern teens are the focus of *The Brimstone Journals.* Branston High School suffers the same acts of violence as many urban schools in the United States, and the anger and frustration of several of its students have given the school the nickname "Brimstone" High. Within the school walls are individual high school seniors dealing with a variety of issues: Kitty has an eating disorder, Sheila is confronting the fact of her homosexuality, Tran is pressured by his Vietnamese father toward a way of life he does not wish to share, and Boyd is fueled by his racist heritage and his father's alcoholism into planning a school shooting. Koertge expresses the thoughts of each of his fifteen students through verses that read like diary entries. *School Library Journal* contributor Sharon Korbeck

noted that the book's "sometimes raw voices provide poignant, honest, and fresh insights into today's teens." While Hazel Rochman maintained in *Booklist* that the end of *The Brimstone Journals* sees too many problems solved, she nonetheless noted that Koertge "avoids simplistic therapy, and the dramatic monologues are spare, poetic, and immediate," as well as providing effective ways to open "group discussion."

An unlikely romance between a drug addict and a disabled boy is the focus of *Stoner and Spaz,* a novel inspired by the work of Koertge's wife, a counselor for children with disabilities. While sixteen-year-old Benjamin is intelligent and sensitive, he also suffers from cerebral palsy. When he meets classmate Colleen, a streetwise teen with a reputation for using drugs, their shared passion for films and black humor forges a friendship that gradually turns to love, much to the dismay of Benjamin's grandmother. Calling *Stoner and Spaz* "vintage Koertge," *Booklist* critic Frances Bradburn praise the story as a "hopeful yet realistic view of things as they are and as they could be."

A beautiful, popular L.A. teen with all the trappings of status is the focus of *Margaux with an X,* but as Koertge's novel shows, the girl's appearance hides a darker truth. Margaux's family is dysfunctional in the extreme: her reckless dad is a professional gambler and her mom hides her anger and sadness by spending hours watching the television. Margaux keeps her own sadness hidden, until a friendship with the dorky and old-fashioned Danny allows her to exhibit her own intelligence and gives her the freedom to express her feelings. Along the way, Danny faces his own secrets in a novel containing what Gillian Engberg described in *Booklist* as the "dramatic situations" that "will intrigue teens." By featuring two characters that tap into common teen stereotypes, Koertge "destroys all assumptions," concluded *School Library Journal* contributor Leigh Ann Morlock, "giving readers a glimpse into the complexities of . . . [teens'] hidden emotional struggles."

Described by *Booklist* contributor Daniel Kraus as "perceptive and understated," Koertge's novel *Deadville* also focuses on a popular high schooler. For Charlotte, however, there is no new friendship: she has been injured in an accident and is hospitalized, in a coma. When Ryan, a sophomore slacker who travels in a very different social sphere, discovers her there, he begins to visit Charlotte every day. There, the forced quiet of her bedside, as well as the chance interaction with Charlotte's visiting friends, allows Ryan to reflect on the things that have driven him to smoking pot. According to Kraus, Koertge's evocative writing "captures the randomness of high-school life" that has so strongly affected both teens, although *Kliatt* critic Janis Flint-Ferguson added that *Deadville* also has moments of humor and is enlivened by Ryan's "witty, sarcastic, [and] irreverent" narrative. In characteristic fashion, according to *School Library Journal* contributor Sue

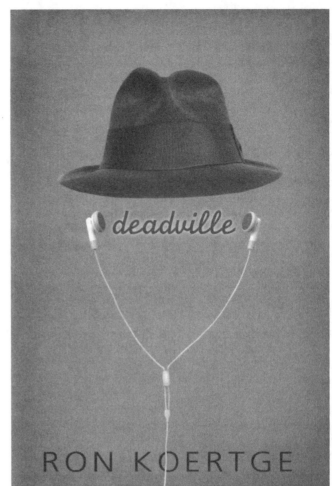

Cover of Koertge's young-adult novel Deadville, *which finds a depressed teen searching for a way to reconnect with life.* (Jacket photographs: © 2008 by iStockphoto (fedora); © 2008 Jasmin Awad/iStockphoto (earphones); © 2008 by Maxim Filipchuk/iStockphoto (background). Reproduced by permission of Candlewick Press, Inc., Somerville, MA.)

Lloyd, the author of *Deadville* "masterfully maintains reader interest with rich, right-on dialogue and details about teen life, attitudes, and relationships."

For sixteen-year-old Ted O'Connor, the central character in *Strays,* animals are much more loyal companions than humans. The teen feels like a stray himself: both his parents died in an automobile accident, and his foster-child status makes him feel like a misfit at his new school. Plus, he misses working at his parents' pet store. Now, at his new foster home, Ted feels an affinity for his two foster siblings, Astin, and C.W., and as he starts a new school he feels a sense of belonging that brings with it a growing self-confidence. Ted's conversations with animals reflect his loneliness and also contain "outsider's observations of human nature [that] are . . . insightful, [and] devastatingly funny," as Krista Hutley observed in her *Booklist* review of *Strays.* Koertge's "light magical touch," as well as his focus on an unreliable narrator, "adds a clever flavor to this appealing coming-of-age story," wrote a *Kirkus Reviews* contributor. For *School Library Journal* reviewer Johanna Lewis, *Strays* skillfully depicts Ted's "slow trans-

formation from introverted destitution to tentative but authentic affirmation," making the "smoothly plotted, perfectly pitched novel . . . among the author's best work."

In the verse novels *Shakespeare Bats Cleanup* and *Shakespeare Makes the Playoffs* readers meet fourteen-year-old Kevin Boland. Sidelined from his baseball team by a case of mononucleosis in *Shakespeare Bats Cleanup,* Kevin begins writing poems, first to pass the time but eventually to express his feelings regarding the death of his mom, his love of baseball, and his attraction for various girls. A "funny and poignant novel," *Shakespeare Bats Cleanup* "celebrates the power of writing to help young people make sense of their lives and . . . confront their problems," wrote *School Library Journal* critic Edward Sullivan, while in *Booklist* Todd Morning praised Kevin's "funny, touching, and . . . energetic" verses as capturing the teen's "growing love for poetry."

About writing for young adults, Koertge once explained to *SATA:* "I never think of myself as writing for children; I never think I know anything special about young people. I don't have children and am not much interested in them as such. But I like to write. And writing YA's is obviously what I'm up to at the moment. I'm as surprised as anyone else at the success I've had. Maybe more." For teen readers, Koertge's continued success and enjoyment of writing is good news. "As readers navigate the perilous realms of their own adolescence," noted the *St. James Guide to Young-Adult Writers* contributor, "they will surely want Koertge's books along to help ease their way."

Biographical and Critical Sources

BOOKS

Dictionary of Literary Biography, Volume 105: *American Poets since World War II,* Gale (Detroit, MI), 1992.
Gallo, Donald R., editor, *Speaking for Ourselves, Too,* National Council of Teachers of English (Urbana, IL), 1993.
St. James Guide to Young-Adult Writers, St. James Press (Detroit, MI), 1999.

PERIODICALS

Booklist, October 15, 1992, Stephanie Zvirin, review of *The Harmony Arms,* p. 418; February 15, 1994, Hazel Rochman, review of *Tiger, Tiger, Burning Bright,* p. 1075; October 1, 1996, Karen Simonetti, review of *Confess-o-Rama,* p. 342; April, 1998, Linda Perkins, review of *The Heart of the City,* p. 1320; April 15, 2001, Hazel Rochman, review of *The Brimstone Journals,* p. 1548; May 1, 2007, Krista Hutley, review of *Strays,* p. 86; November 15, 2008, Daniel Kraus, review of *Deadville,* p. 37.

Book Report, September-October, 1994, Lynne Hofflund, review of *Tiger, Tiger, Burning Bright,* p. 40; March-April, 1997, Rosie Peasley, review of *Confess-o-Rama,* p. 37.

Buffalo News (Buffalo, NY), July 21, 1998, review of *The Heart of the City,* p. N7.

Bulletin of the Center for Children's Books, November, 1996, Deborah Stevenson, review of *Confess-o-Rama,* p. 102.

English Journal, December, 1993, Alleen Pace Nilsen, review of *The Harmony Arms,* p. 73.

Horn Book, November-December, 1992, Nancy Vasilakis, review of *The Harmony Arms,* p. 727; September-October, 1994, Nancy Vasilakis, review of *Tiger, Tiger, Burning Bright,* p. 600; July-August, 2002, Kitty Flynn, review of *Stoner and Spaz,* p. 464; November-December, 2004, Jennifer M. Brabander, review of *Margaux with an X,* p. 711; September-October, 2005, Christine M. Heppermann, review of *Boy Girl Boy,* p. 582.

Journal of Adolescent and Adult Literacy, December, 2002, S. Graber, review of *Stoner and Spaz,* p. 367; November, 2003, Rachel Seftel, review of *Shakespeare Bats Cleanup,* p. 273; March, 2005, James Blasingame, review of *Margaux with an X,* p. 522, and interview with Koertge, p. 526; April, 2006, David M. Pegram, review of *Boy Girl Boy,* p. 633.

Kirkus Reviews, February 15, 2003, review of *Shakespeare Bats Cleanup,* p. 309; August 15, 2005, review of *Boy Girl Boy,* p. 917; June 1, 2007, review of *Strays.*

Kliatt, May, 2002, Paula Rohrlick, review of *Stoner and Spaz,* p. 11; March, 2003, Claire Rosser, review of *Shakespeare Bats Cleanup,* p. 12; September, 2004, Paula Rohrlick, review of *Margaux with an X,* p. 12; November, 2008, Janis Flint-Ferguson, review of *Deadville,* p. 13.

New York Times Book Review, May 20, 2001, Robin Tzannes, "Arms and the Boy."

Los Angeles Times Book Review, March 21, 1993, Ron Koertge, "Sex and the Single Kid."

Publishers Weekly, April 13, 1990, review of *The Boy in the Moon,* p. 67; May 10, 1991, review of *Mariposa Blues,* p. 284; September 14, 1992, review of *The Harmony Arms,* p. 126; April 18, 1994, review of *Tiger, Tiger, Burning Bright,* p. 63; April 20, 1998, review of *The Heart of the City,* p. 67; February 12, 2001, review of *The Brimstone Journals,* p. 213; April 22, 2002, review of *Stoner and Spaz,* p. 71; September 20, 2004, review of *Margaux with an X,* p. 64; September 19, 2005, review of *Boy Girl Boy,* p. 67.

School Library Journal, December, 1986, Marjorie Lewis, review of *Where the Kissing Never Stops,* p. 119; March, 1994, Michael Cart, review of *Tiger, Tiger, Burning Bright,* p. 236; September, 1996, Susan R. Farber, review of *Confess-o-Rama,* p. 227; March, 1998, Kathleen Isaacs, review of *The Heart of the City,* p. 214; March, 2001, Sharon Korbeck, review of *The Brimstone Journals,* p. 270; May, 2003, Edward Sullivan, review of *Shakespeare Bats Cleanup,* p. 156; September, 2004, Leigh Ann Morlock, review of *Margaux with an X,* p. 209; July, 2007, Johanna Lewis,

review of *Strays,* p. 105; November, 2008, Sue Lloyd, review of *Deadville,* p. 126.

Voice of Youth Advocates, October, 1992, John Lord, review of *The Harmony Arms,* pp. 224-225.

Wilson Library Bulletin, March, 1993, Frances Bradburn, review of *The Harmony Arms,* p. 84.

ONLINE

Booksource.com, http://www.booksource.com/ (December 20, 2009), Sarah Erwin, interview with Koertge.

Teenreads Web site, http://www.teenreads.com/ (December 20, 2009), interview with Koertge.

*   *   *

KOZJAN, Drazen

Personal

Born in Karlovac, Croatia; immigrated to Canada; married; wife's name Alison. *Hobbies and other interests:* Bike riding, going to the movies.

Addresses

Home—Etobicoke, Ontario, Canada. *Agent*—Pippin Properties, Inc., 155 E. 38th St., Ste. 2H, New York, NY 10016. *E-mail*—drazenart@rogers.com.

Career

Illustrator. Created artwork for videos and television commercials; designer and storyboard artist on animated films, including *The Neverending Story, Rupert the Bear,* and *George Shrinks. Exhibitions:* Works included in group shows.

Illustrator

Esmé Raji Codel, *Diary of a Fairy Godmother,* Hyperion Books for Children (New York, NY), 2005

Alison McGhee, *Julia Gillian (and the Art of Knowing),* Scholastic (New York, NY), 2008

Alison McGhee, *Julia Gillian (and the Quest for Joy),* Scholastic (New York, NY), 2009

Alison McGhee, *Julia Gillian (and the Dream of the Dog),* Scholastic (New York, NY), 2009

Janet Reed Ahearn, *Don't Call Me Pruneface!,* Hyperion (New York, NY), 2009.

Robert Kinerk, *Oh, How Sylvester Can Pester!,* Simon & Schuster (New York, NY), 2009.

Creator of "The Happy Undertaker" (comic strip), published online and in *Carousel.* Contributor to periodicals.

Sidelights

The illustrations of Canadian artist Drazan Kozjan are familiar to middle-grade fans of Esmé Raji Codel's *Diary of a Fairy Godmother* and Alison McGhee's "Julia Gillian" novels series. Codel's book, about a teen witch who wants to transition from the dark side, features what *Booklist* contributor Jennifer Mattson described as "sly, stylish" pen-and-ink drawings by Kozjan that "contribute added appeal" to the quirky novel. Bina Williams noted in the same periodical that *Julia Gillian (and the Art of Knowing)* features "plentiful sketches" by Kozjan that capture the "appealing, if quirky, personality" of McGhee's nine-year-old character, while a *Kirkus Reviews* critic wrote that Kozjan's "loose art . . . exudes personality" while bringing to life series installment *Julia Gillian (and the Quest for Joy).*

Born in Karlovac, Croatia, Kozjan has fond memories of the stories told him by his mother and grandmother. Immigrating to eastern Canada as a child, he was inspired by the illustrations of artists such as N.C. Wyeth and Harry Clarke, as well as by books written by Dr. Seuss and the comics of Jack Kirby. His talent for art was publicly acknowledged in middle school, when Kozjan was entrusted with the task of designing posters for his classroom. As a professional illustrator, his artwork appeared on posters and album covers, and he has also worked in commercial design and storyboarding for animated films. Kozjan's work was introduced to young audiences in 2005, when he created the illustrations for *Diary of A Fairy Godmother.* in addition to middle-grade novels, he has also created art for picture

Drazen Kozjan's illustration projects have included creating art for Alison McGhee's **Julia Gillian (and the Art of Knowing).** (Illustration copyright © 2008 by Drazen Kozjan. Reproduced by permission of Scholastic, Inc.)

books such as Janet Reed Ahearn's *Don't Call Me Pruneface!* and Robert Kinerk's *Oh How Sylvester Can Pester!*

In addition to his work in book publishing, Kozjan is also the creator of the "Happy Undertaker," a weekly online comic. "The pages are drawn traditionally with pencil, pen and ink on Strathmore bristol, then scanned and colored in Photoshop," the artist explained on Jewcy.com. "I love the old Sunday newspaper strips like Winsor McCay's *Little Nemo in Slumberland,* Lyonel Feininger's *The Kinder Kids* and Charles Forbell's *Naughty Pete,* where every page feels like a surprise."

Biographical and Critical Sources

PERIODICALS

Booklist, August, 2005, Jennifer Mattson, review of *Diary of a Fairy Godmother,* p. 2020; August 1, 2008, Bina Williams, review of *Julia Gillian (and the Art of Knowing),* p. 70.
Horn Book, July-August, 2008, Christine M. Heppermann, review of *Julia Gillian (and the Art of Knowing),* p. 453; May-June, 2009, Christine M. Heppermann, review of *Julia Gillian (and the Quest for Joy),* p. 302.
Kirkus Reviews, May 15, 2008, review of *Julia Gillian (and the Art of Knowing).*
Publishers Weekly, June 23, 2008, review of *Julia Gillian (and the Art of Knowing),* p. 54; April 13, 2009, review of *Julia Gillian (and the Quest for Joy),* p. 50.
School Library Journal, July, 2008, Lillian Hecker, review of *Julia Gillian (and the Art of Knowing),* p. 77.

ONLINE

Drazen Kozjan Home Page, http://www.drazenkozjan.com (December 15, 2009).
Drazen Kozjan Web log, http://hypnotikeye.blogspot.com/ (December 15, 2009).
Jewcy.com, http://www.jewcy.com/ (June 11, 2007), "Drazen Jozjan."*

L

LARKSPUR, Penelope
See WYATT, Valerie

*   *   *

LESSAC, Frané 1954-

Personal

Given name is pronounced "Fra-*nay*"; born June 18, 1954, in Jersey City, NJ; daughter of Arthur J. (a comedian) and Estelle (a travel agency owner) Lessac; married Mark Greenwood (an author), April 19, 1986; children: Luke, Cody. *Education:* Attended New School for Social Research (now New School University), 1973, University of Southern California, 1974, and University of California—Los Angeles, 1975-76.

Addresses

Home and office—P.O. Box 1110, Fremantle, Western Australia 6160, Australia. *Agent*—Marcia Wernick, Sheldon Fogelman Agency, 10 E. 40th St., Ste. 3205, New York, NY 10016; marcia.wernicksheldonfogelmanagency.com. *E-mail*—frane@franelessac.com.

Career

Filmmaker, artist, and illustrator, 1983—. *Exhibitions:* Work exhibited at numerous galleries and museums, including Fowler Mills Gallery, Los Angeles, CA; Courtyard Gallery, Montserrat; Exhibition de Intercaribe de Peniture, Guadeloupe; Gallerie Antoinette, Paris, France; Centre des Arts et de la Culture, Guadeloupe; Bankside Gallery, London, England; Libertys Gallery, London; Sugar Mill, Montserrat; Barbican Center, London; Brixton Art Gallery, London; Chelsea Manor Street Gallery, London; Rona Gallery, London; Craft and Folk Art Museum, Los Angeles; Metropolitan Museum of

Frané Lessac (Reproduced by permission.)

Art, New York, NY; Riverside Studios, London; Commonwealth Institute, London; Yellow Poui Art Gallery, Grenada, Spain; Vanessa Devereux Gallery, London; Harmony Hall, Antigua; Broughton House Gallery,

Cambridge, England; Centrespace Gallery, London; Society of Illustrators, New York, NY; Perth Galleries, Perth, New South Wales, Australia; Australian Naive Gallery, Sydney, New South Wales, Australia; Every Picture Tells a Story, Los Angeles; Santa Monica Heritage Museum, Los Angeles; Barry Stern Gallery, Sydney; Children's Literature Centre, Fremantle, Australia; Kimberly Kreations, Broome, Australia; A-Shed Gallery, Fremantle; Perth Mint, Perth; Catanach's Gallery, Broome; Moore's Building, Fremantle; Fremantle Arts Centre; and Australian National Maritime Museum, Sydney. Work represented in private collections worldwide.

Member

Society of Children's Book Writers and Illustrators (illustrator liaison, West Australia), Australian Society of Authors (member of executive committee).

Awards, Honors

Children's Book of the Year, Island of St. Martin's, 1984, and Books for Children selection, Library of Congress, 1985, both for *The Little Island;* Notable Trade Book in Social Studies, National Council for the Social Studies/Children's Book Council (NCSS/CBC), 1989, and Book Show Award, American Institute of Graphic Arts, 1990, both for *Caribbean Canvas;* Editor's Choice citation, American Library Association (ALA), Parent's Choice Gold Award, and Notable Trade Book in Social Studies, NCSS/CBC, 1989, all for *The Chalk Doll* by Charlotte Pomerantz; Reading Magic Award, *Parenting* magazine, and Notable Trade Book in Social Studies designation, NCSS/CBC, 1990, both for *The Bird Who Was an Elephant* by Aleph Kamal; 100 Best Books selection, New York Public Library, Children's Books of the Year citation, Bank Street College, and Notable Trade Book in Social Studies designation, NCSS/CBC, 1993, all for *Caribbean Carnival: Songs of the West Indies* by Irving Burgle; Notable Trade Book in Social Studies designation, NCSS/CBC, 1994, for *Caribbean Alphabet;* Notable Children's Book citation, Language Arts/National Council of Teachers, and Américas Children's and Young Adult Literature commendation, both 1994, both for *Not a Copper Penny in Me House* by Monica Gunning; Children's Book of Distinction finalist, Emphasis on Reading List inclusion, State of Alabama, and Notable Trade Book in Social Studies designation, NCSS/CBC, Notable Books for Children, ALA, and Notable Book for a Global Society Award, all 1996, all for *The Distant Talking Drum* by Isaac Olaleye; Book of the Year, Bank Street College, 1996, and Notable Trade Book in Social Studies designation, NCSS/CBC, 1997, both for *O Christmas Tree* by Vashanti Rahaman; Sydney Taylor Award for Younger Readers, for *Queen Esther Saves Her People* by Rita Golden Gelman; Top Ten Science Books citation, *Booklist,* and Notable Trade Book in Social Studies designation, NCSS/CBC, both 2000, both for *On the Same Day in March* by Marilyn Singer; West Australia Premier's Book Award, 2002, for *The Legend of Moondyne Joe* by Mark Greenwood; English Association in the English Award for Best Children's Illustrated Book, 2008, and USBBY Outstanding International Book designation, 2009, both for *We Are All Born Free;* Notable Trade Book in Social Studies designation, NCSS/CBC, and CBC Honor Book designation, both 2008, and USBBY Outstanding International Books designation, 2009, all for *The Donkey of Gallipoli.*

Writings

SELF-ILLUSTRATED

My Little Island, Lippincott (Philadelphia, PA), 1984, published as *The Little Island,* Macmillan Caribbean (London, England), 1984.
Caribbean Canvas, Macmillan Caribbean (London, England), 1987, Lippincott (Philadelphia, PA), 1989.
(Compiler and illustrator) *Camp Granada: Sing-Along Camp Songs,* Holt (New York, NY), 2003.
Island Counting 1 2 3, Candlewick Press (Cambridge, MA), 2005.

ILLUSTRATOR

Jan Jackson, *The Dragon of Redonda,* Macmillan (London, England), 1986.
Charlotte Pomerantz, *The Chalk Doll,* Lippincott (Philadelphia, PA), 1989.
Mark Greenwood, *Caribbean Alphabet* Macmillan Caribbean (London, England), 1989, Tambourine Books (New York, NY), 1994.
Aleph Kamal, *The Bird Who Was an Elephant,* Cambridge University Press (Cambridge, England), 1989, Lippincott (Philadelphia, PA), 1990.
Barbara Ker Wilson, *The Turtle and the Island: A Folktale from Papua New Guinea,* Lippincott (Philadelphia, PA), 1990.
Marilyn Singer, *Nine o'Clock Lullaby,* HarperCollins (New York, NY), 1991.
Irving Burgle, lyricist, *Caribbean Carnival: Songs of the West Indies,* Tambourine Books (New York, NY), 1992.
Monica Gunning, *Not a Copper Penny in Me House: Poems from the Caribbean,* Wordsong (Honesdale, PA), 1993.
Eric Maddern, *The Fire Children: A West African Creation Tale,* Dial (New York, NY), 1993.
Jan Wahl, *Little Gray One,* Tambourine Books (New York, NY), 1993.
Patricia Zelver, *The Wonderful Towers of Watts,* Tambourine Books (New York, NY), 1994.
Mark Greenwood, *Magic Boomerang,* Artbeat Publishers (Freemantle, Western Australia, Australia), 1994.
Mark Greenwood, *Outback Adventure,* Plantagenet Press (Fremantle, West Australia, Australia), 1994.
Isaac Olaleye, *The Distant Talking Drum: Poems from Nigeria,* Wordsong (Honesdale, PA), 1994.

Lee Bennett Hopkins, *Good Rhymes, Good Times: Original Poems,* HarperCollins (New York, NY), 1995.

Mark Greenwood, *Our Big Island,* Plantagenet Press (Fremantle, West Australia, Australia), 1995.

Vashanti Rahaman, *O Christmas Tree,* Boyds Mills Press (Honesdale, PA), 1996.

Rita Golden Gelman, *Queen Esther Saves Her People,* Scholastic (New York, NY), 1998.

Marilyn Singer, *On the Same Day in March: A Tour of the World's Weather,* HarperCollins (New York, NY), 2000.

Mark Greenwood, *The Legend of Moondyne Joe,* Cygnet Books (Crawley, WA), 2002.

Mark Greenwood, *The Magic Boomerang,* Artbeat Publishers (Fremantle, West Australia, Australia), 2002.

Laura Krauss Melmed, *Capital! Washington, DC, from A to Z,* HarperCollins (New York, NY), 2003.

Barbara Ker Wilson, *Maui and the Big Fish,* Frances Lincoln (London, England), 2003.

Marilyn Singer, *Monday on the Mississippi,* Henry Holt (New York, NY), 2005.

Barbara Ker Wilson, *The Day of the Elephant,* HarperCollins (New York, NY), 2005.

Laura Krauss Melmed, *New York, New York!: The Big Apple from A to Z,* HarperCollins (New York, NY), 2005.

Anne Rockwell, *Clouds,* HarperCollins (New York, NY), 2008.

Mark Greenwood, *Simpson and His Donkey,* Walker Books Australia (Newtown, New South Wales, Australia), 2008, published as *The Donkey of Gallipoli: A True Story of Courage in World War I,* Candlewick Press (Cambridge, MA), 2008.

We Are All Born Free, Frances Lincoln/Amnesty International (London, England), 2008.

Laura Krauss Melmed, *Heart of Texas: A Lone Star ABC,* HarperCollins (New York, NY), 2009.

Mark Greenwood, *Ned Kelly and the Green Sash,* Walker Books Australia (Newtown, New South Wales, Australia), 2009.

Sidelights

A children's book author, illustrator, and internationally respected artist, Frané Lessac has lived around the world with her family, and the places she has called home are often reflected in her works. Born in the United States, the author/illustrator has also called home the island of Montserrat and the continent of Australia, and in her painting she captures the subtle nuances of a variety of cultures. In addition to producing original picture books, Lessac has collaborated with her husband, writer Mark Greenwood, on award-winning books such as *Caribbean Alphabet, The Legend of Moondyne Joe,* and *The Donkey of Gallipoli: A True Story of Courage in World War I.* She has also created art that illuminates the stories of Marilyn Singer, Jan Wahl, Rita Goldman Gelman, and Anne Rockwell, among others. "My aim is to produce multi-cultural, non-sexist books for children, to break down racial barriers, and educate at the same time," the artist once told *SATA.* "I also want children to be aware of our precious environment."

In *Caribbean Alphabet,* Lessac creates gouache paintings in her characteristic naïve style that illustrate the sights, sounds, and activities of island life. Each letter represents some aspect of Caribbean culture, and unfamiliar terms such as "agouti," "Junkanoo," and "dasheen" are explained in a pictorial glossary. "Each picture has its own little narrative on this celebratory island tour—fun, fluid, and imaginative," remarked a *Publishers Weekly* reviewer. Lessac's color selections and style allow all the hues of the island to "glow from the inside," wrote Mary Harris Veeder in Chicago's *Tribune Books.* A similar book, *Island Counting 1 2 3,* pairs Lessac's simple phrases with paintings that features what *School Library Journal* contributor Sheilah Kosco described as "vibrant island colors that will catch readers' interest."

Lessac has also compiled and illustrated *Camp Granada: Sing-Along Camp Songs.* The book gathers the lyrics to more than thirty well-known songs performed over the years in summer camps and get-togethers. Well-known songs such as "If You're Happy," "Hello Muddah, Hello Faddah (Camp Granada)," and "Kum Ba Yah" are included, as well as lesser-known tunes such as "Found a Peanut" and "Ship Titanic." The book even includes the lyrics to "Taps," the sombre tune played as days in camp draw to a close. Marge Loch-Wouters, writing in *School Library Journal,* remarked on Lessac's "folksy, lush gouaches," while a *Publishers Weekly* reviewer commented that the pictures in *Camp Granada* "add to the homey humor" of the song collection. Todd Morning, in a *Booklist* review, noted that the book "offer[s] an amusing glimpse of the community and landscape that make up camp life."

In addition to creating original self-illustrated books, Lessac has created artwork for many books by other writers. *Nine o'Clock Lullaby,* written by Marilyn Singer, answers a curious child's question. While children are getting ready to go to bed in Brooklyn, New York, what are kids in other parts of the world doing? Lessac's pictures for the book depict young children dancing in Puerto Rico, drawing water at dawn in India, and getting an early-morning snack in London, among other things. *Nine o'Clock Lullaby* serves as a "primer on time and the time zones, as an introduction to foreign cultures, and as a rhythmic, pleasing lullaby," commented a *Publishers Weekly* reviewer.

Another illustration project, Eric Maddern's *The Fire Children: A West African Creation Tale,* is a porquoi story that describes how the spirit people Kwaku Ananse (a male) and Aso Yaa (a female) end up on Earth and create the earthbound people of the world. One day, as sky god Nyame looks down on the world from a trapdoor in the moon, Kwaku Ananse and Aso Yaa crawl out of Nyame's mouth to have a look, and they ultimately both tumble down to Earth's surface. Loneliness prompts the spirit people to make clay figures in their image, and when these statues are hidden in the fire

Lessac's illustration projects includes her artwork for Monica Gunning's **Not a Copper Penny in Me House.** (Illustration copyright © 1993 by Frané Lessac. Published by Wordsong, Boyds Mills Press, Inc. Reprinted by permission.)

during a visit from the jealous Nyame, they gain various patinas of color, from pale to dark brown. Ultimately, the spirit people breathe life into their clay creations, creating the diverse human races that now populate the planet. A *Publishers Weekly* critic described *The Fire Children* as "elegantly told" and "gorgeously illustrated," while *School Library Journal* reviewer Lyn Miller-Lachmann observed that "Lessac's gouache illustrations . . . combine West African designs with her own characteristic style, [and] work well with the text." Ellen Fader, writing in *Horn Book,* commented that the book's "ocher, brown, and blue-toned gouache paintings in a naïve style enhance and expand upon the story's folkloric quality."

The true story of Simon Rodia, an artist and sculptor, is recounted in Patricia Zelver's *The Wonderful Towers of Watts.* Rodia, an Italian immigrant, lived in the impoverished Los Angeles neighborhood of Watts. Over the course of more than thirty-three years, he collected discarded materials, such as broken tiles from the factory where he worked and things other people were throwing away, and used these items to construct three multicolored towers that still stand as a testament to his creativity. Rodia's life's work "bear[s] witness to one man's

dream of beauty," wrote a *Publishers Weekly* reviewer in a review of *The Wonderful Towers of Watts,* and Lessac's illustrations capture "the gaudy beauty of his achievement." Corrine Camarata, writing in *School Library Journal,* remarked of Zelver's picture book that "Lessac's familiar gouache paintings fill the pages with soft, rich colors."

Set largely in a Nigerian farming village, Isasc Olaleye's *The Distant Talking Drum: Poems from Nigeria* collects fifteen free-verse poems that tell simple but evocative stories of daily village life, including the making of a spicy but delicious soup, the effects of a sudden rainstorm, farming activities, doing laundry by the stream, and going to the marketplace. Lessac's illustrations for the book "provide a perfect complement to the appealing poetry," remarked Dot Minzer in *School Library Journal.* Sheilamae O'Hara, writing in *Booklist,* also praised the paintings, which she described as "colorful and exuberant," while in *Horn Book* Maeve Visser Knoth commented that Lessac's use of "brilliant colors" and her "flat, folk-art style" combine "to complete the picture of a vital, lively village."

Queen Esther Saves Her People, a picture book by Rita Golden Gelman, examines the background of the Jewish holiday Purim, which is celebrated each spring. Gel-

man retells the biblical story of Esther, who was taken into the court of the Persian king Ahasuerus. When Esther finds out about the prime minister's plot to kill all the Jews in the land, she risks her own life to warn the king and save her people, and Purim celebrates Esther's courage. In *Booklist* Ilene Cooper cited Lessac's intricate illustrations, particularly the cover painting of Esther "holding a tiny, almost unnoticeable white bird in her hand." A *Publishers Weekly* reviewer commented that the book's illustrations "are steeped in details," such as realistic Persian clothing, luxurious courtyard scenes, and fruit trees, imbuing Gelman's story with "a distinct sense of time and place."

Other collaborations with Singer include *On the Same Day in March: A Tour of the World's Weather* and *Monday on the Mississippi. On the Same Day in March* examines the many types of weather occurring in different parts of the world on the same March day. From tornadoes in the Texas panhandle to bitter snowstorms in Antarctica, rains in Africa, and sunshine in Barbados, children are introduced to concepts of meteorology and climatology and shown how volatile the earth's weather patterns can be. *Monday on the Mississippi* takes on a less-changeable topic: it follows the vast waterway known as the "Big Muddy" as it flows south from the great lakes to the Gulf of Mexico. Jody McCoy, writing in *School Library Journal*, remarked on the "carefully crafted, childlike illustrations" Lessac creates for *On the Same Day in March*, and Michael Cart commented in *Booklist* that her paintings "colorfully show us the way the weather and the world look." In her detailed artwork for *Monday on the Mississippi* the artist "captures both the changing environment and the water's chameleon-like shifts in color," wrote *Booklist* critic Jennifer Mattson, while in *School Library Journal* Judith Constantinides praised Lessac's contributions of "primitive gouache" artwork to a book that is "beautifully executed in text and illustrations."

In *Capital! Washington, DC, from A to Z, New York, New York!: The Big Apple from A to Z*, and *Heart of Texas: A Lone Star ABC*, Lessac teams up with writer Laura Krauss Melmed to offer readers a tour of several U.S. points of interest. Arranged alphabetically, *Capital!* focuses on the National Zoo, Smithsonian Institution, Lincoln Memorial, Capitol Building, and Holocaust Museum, among other places of interest in the U.S. capital city, while *New York, New York!* takes readers on a tour of the Bronx Zoo, Times Square, and the Metropolitan Museum of Art. In *Heart of Texas* Lessac's paintings depict the Alamo, the Quarter-Horse Museum, and Ziller Park as they roll through an alphabetical highlight of the vast southern state. Lessac's illustrations for each book are accompanied by a brief paragraph by Melmed that provides additional description and elaboration on the subject pictured. A *Kirkus Reviews* critic noted that Lessac's "cheery folk-arty illustrations" for *Capital!* "present thumbnail details with as much energy as broad landscapes," and in *Booklist* Kathleen Odean dubbed the work an "attractive offer-

ing." Patricia Austin noted in the same periodical that in *Heart of Texas* the artist "perfectly conveys the multicultural panorama" of Texas in her "detailed and colorful folk art," while a *Kirkus Reviews* writer dubbed Lessac's work for *New York, New York!* "bright and colorful."

Taking an important page from Australia history, *The Donkey of Gallipoli* has also been published as *Simpson and His Donkey*. In Greenwood's story, readers follow Jack Simpson, an English-born stretcher bearer who, while serving with Australian forces during World War I, heroically rescued many wounded comrades from the front lines of battle with the help of a stalwart donkey before meeting his own end on the battlefield. In her artwork for a wartime saga that is little-known to U.S. readers, Lessac "downplays" the brutal aspects of war by scattering wild flowers and bushes amid the vague, uniform-clad figures in her "stylized, richly hued" battlefield images, according to a *Kirkus Reviews* writer. Although a *School Library Journal* contributor questioned whether the drama of Greenwood's simplified wartime drama would be understood by younger children, *Booklist* contributor Hazel Rochman concluded that in *The Donkey of Gallipoli* the author's "stirring" story is brought to life by his wife's "folk-art . . . paintings" resonate "in shades that reflect the heat of a sandy [Turkish] landscape."

"When I was at school, the art teachers considered me unteachable," Lessac recalled to *SATA*. "Because my lines were never straight and my paintings didn't have dimension, the art teachers told me that they were wrong. My school wasn't progressive enough to recognize my work as a legitimate art form. Sometimes I even climbed in through the classroom window after school to change my grade in the professors' book.

"At the age of eighteen, I headed for film school in California. My aim was to make films about 'primitive' tribes before they were swamped by Western culture. Initially, I borrowed camera equipment and, given film, took off on the long road in the American Southwest, documenting a rodeo team, a long-distance trucker, and even the birth of a baby.

"Then in 1978, I moved from California to the small Caribbean island of Montserrat, and, stunned by its visual beauty, I concentrated on painting the old-style West Indian architecture and its peoples. The locals would say to me, 'You live in de cement house, no worry de hurricanes,' and my feelings were torn as the houses were torn down. I wish there was a house museum. The beautiful images of Montserrat were the inspiration for my book of paintings, *The Little Island*.

"In 1987, I published *Caribbean Canvas*, a collection of works, painted on my . . . travels to Barbados, Grenada, Antigua, Palm Island, and St. Kitts. This is aimed at a more extensive audience and also includes poetry by Caribbean writers."

"*The Bird Who Was an Elephant* is my favorite book," Lessac added, in discussing her work for young children. "How could a bird become an elephant? Children will understand this, of course. But grown-ups, who always need explanations, may need to know that in India it is believed that we have many lives and that when we die, we can become another human being—or an animal. So this is the story of the bird."

Biographical and Critical Sources

PERIODICALS

Belles Lettres, spring, 1995, Bettina Berch, review of *Caribbean Canvas*, p. 60.

Booklist, October 1, 1992, Julie Corsaro, review of *Caribbean Carnival: Songs of the West Indies*, p. 331; July, 1993, Janice Del Negro, review of *The Fire Children: A West African Creation Tale*, p. 1971; September 15, 1993, Julie Corsaro, review of *Little Gray One*, p. 162, and Quarash Ali, review of *Not a Copper Penny in Me House: Poems from the Caribbean*, pp. 153-154; May 1, 1994, Carolyn Phelan, review of *The Wonderful Towers of Watts*, p. 1605; June 1, 1994, Hazel Rochman, review of *Caribbean Alphabet*, p. 1827; January 1, 1995, Sheilamae O'Hara, review of *The Distant Talking Drum: Poems from Nigeria*, p. 824; July, 1995, Hazel Rochman, review of *Good Rhymes, Good Times: Original Poems*, p. 188; September 1, 1996, Susan Dove Lempke, review of *O Christmas Tree*, p. 137; March 1, 1998, Ilene Cooper, review of *Queen Esther Saves Her People*, p. 1138; February 15, 2000, Michael Cart, review of *On the Same Day in March: A Tour of the World's Weather*, p. 1116; February 1, 2003, Kathleen Odean, review of *Capital! Washington, DC, from A to Z*, pp. 998-999; March 1, 2003, Todd Morning, review of *Camp Granada: Sing-along Camp Songs*, p. 1195; April 1, 2005, Jennifer Mattson, review of *Monday on the Mississippi*, p. 1370; May 15, 2005, Carolyn Phelan, review of *Island Counting 1 2 3*, p. 1665; May 1, 2008, Hazel Rochman, review of *The Donkey of Gallipoli: A True Story of Courage in World War I*, p. 82; December 15, 2008, Randall Enos, review of *Clouds*, p. 48; May 1, 2009, Patricia Austin, review of *Heart of Texas: A Lone Star ABC*, p. 76.

Entertainment Weekly, Leonard S. Marcus, review of *Not a Copper Penny in Me House*, p. 73.

Horn Book, September-October, 1993, Ellen Fader, review of *The Fire Children*, pp. 610-611; March-April, 1995, Maeve Visser Knoth, review of *The Distant Talking Drum*, p. 211.

Kirkus Reviews, November 15, 2002, review of *Capital!*, p. 1698; March 15, 2005, review of *Monday on the Mississippi*, p. 358; June 1, 2005, review of *New York, New York!: The Big Apple from A to Z*, p. 640; April 15, 2008, review of *The Donkey of Gallipoli*; October 15, 2008, review of *Clouds*.

New York Times Book Review, June 5, 1994, review of *The Wonderful Towers of Watts*, p. 30; January, 2003, review of *Capital!*, p. 16; August 10, 2003, review of *Camp Granada*, p. 18; April 1, 2009, review of *Heart of Texas;* February 15, 2009, Julie Just, review of *Clouds*, p. 15

People, November 28, 1994, review of *The Wonderful Towers of Watts*, pp. 35-36.

Publishers Weekly, March 30, 1990, review of *The Bird Who Was an Elephant*, p. 62; March 1, 1991, review of *Nine o'Clock Lullaby*, pp. 72-73; October 5, 1992, review of *Caribbean Carnival*, p. 72; June 7, 1993, review of *The Fire Children*, p. 69; July 5, 1993, review of *Not a Copper Penny in Me House*, p. 73; August 9, 1993, review of *Little Gray One*, p. 476; May 9, 1994, review of *The Wonderful Towers of Watts*, p. 72, and review of *Caribbean Alphabet*, p. 72; December 19, 1994, review of *The Distant Talking Drum*, p. 54; July 3, 1995, review of *Good Rhymes, Good Times*, pp. 60-61; September 30, 1996, review of *O Christmas Tree*, p. 90; December 22, 1997, review of *Queen Esther Saves Her People*, p. 54; January 25, 1999, review of *Not a Copper Penny in Me House*, p. 98; January 24, 2000, review of *On the Same Day in March*, p. 311; June 16, 2003, review of *Camp Granada*, p. 73.

Reading Teacher, October, 1995, review of *Caribbean Canvas*, p. 156.

School Library Journal, August, 1990, Marilyn Iarusso, review of *The Bird Who Was an Elephant*, pp. 130-131; January, 1991, Patricia Dooley, review of *The Turtle and the Island: A Folktale from Papua New Guinea*, p. 87; July, 1991, Patricia Dooley, review of *Nine o'Clock Lullaby*, p. 64; November, 1992, Lyn Miller-Lachmann, review of *Caribbean Carnival*, pp. 83-84; August, 1993, Lyn Miller-Lachmann, review of *The Fire Children*, p. 160; December, 1993, Ellen D. Warwick, review of *Not a Copper Penny in Me House*, p. 105; March, 1994, Liza Bliss, review of *Little Gray One*, p. 210; July, 1994, Lyn Miller-Lachmann, review of *Caribbean Alphabet*, p. 96; September, 1994, Corinne Camarata, review of *The Wonderful Towers of Watts*, p. 212; February, 1995, Dot Minzer, review of *The Distant Talking Drum*, p. 92; August, 1995, Sally R. Dow, review of *Good Rhymes, Good Times*, p. 135; October, 1996, Jane Marino, review of *O Christmas Tree*, p. 39; April, 2000, Jody McCoy, review of *On the Same Day in March*, p. 126; June, 2003, Marge Loch-Wouters, review of *Camp Granada*, p. 130; June, 2005, Judith Constantinides, review of *Monday on the Mississippi*, p. 128, and Elizabeth Bird, review of *New York, New York!*, p. 140; July, 2005, Sheilah Kosco, review of *Island Counting 1 2 3*, p. 78; July, 2008, Heidi Estrin, review of *The Donkey of Gallipoli*, p. 88; December, 2008, Sandra Welzenbach, review of *Clouds*, p. 115; April, 2009, Mary Elam, review of *Heart of Texas*, p. 124.

Tribune Books (Chicago, IL), June 12, 1994, Mary Harris Veeder, review of *Caribbean Alphabet*, p. 9.

ONLINE

Frané Lessac Home Page, http://www.franelessac.com (December 20, 2009).

LEWIS, Richard 1956-

Personal

Born 1956, in Bali, Indonesia; son of missionaries; married; children: one son. *Education:* Attended college in the United States. *Hobbies and other interests:* Surfing.

Addresses

Home—Bali, Indonesia. *Agent*—Scott Miller, Trident Media Group, 41 Madison Ave., 36th Fl., New York, NY 10010. *E-mail*—richard@richardlewisauthor.com.

Career

Author.

Writings

The Flame Tree, Simon & Schuster (New York, NY), 2004.
The Killing Sea, Simon & Schuster (New York, NY), 2006.
The Demon Queen, Simon & Schuster (New York, NY), 2008.
Monster's Proof, Simon & Schuster (New York, NY), 2009.

Author of short story *Shallow Water Blackout,* published by Amazon.com.

Adaptations

The Killing Sea was optioned for film by Fox 2000 and Scott Free Productions.

Sidelights

The son of missionaries, young-adult novelist Richard Lewis was born and raised in Indonesia, a place he continues to call home as he pursues his career as a full-time writer. This setting appears in his first novel, *The Flame Tree,* a story about a twelve-year-old boy named Isaac Williams who lives on the island of Java with his parents. Prior to the terrorist attacks on New York City's World Trade Center in September of 2001, Isaac lived an idyllic life in the archipelago nation, going to school and enjoying his status as the son of missionary physicians who work in an American hospital. After September 11, however, the young boy's world changes as local rebels take him hostage and force him to live as a Muslim. As a captive, Isaac begins to compare the teachings of his Christian religion with those taught to him by the local imam, noting the similarities between each belief system. Eventually released, Isaac emerges with a greater understanding of the followers of fundamentalist Muslim teachings and the motivations behind their actions.

The Flame Tree offers "a remarkable reading experience for students willing to enmesh themselves in a different world," declared *School Library Journal* reviewer Kathleen Isaacs, while a *Publishers Weekly* contributor called the book "a riveting read," explaining "how religious ideas and ideals can breed atrocities against humanity."

In *The Killing Sea* Lewis uses the deadly 2004 tsunami that devastated Southeast Asia as the backdrop for his story about two teenagers who are struggling to find help for their families. On vacation in Indonesia, well-off American tourist Sarah and her little brother Peter become separated from their parents by the deadly wall of water. Trying to find medical assistance for the injured Peter, Sarah befriends a local Indonesian teen named Ruslan who fears the worst about his own father. Together the trio tries not only to keep themselves alive amid the destruction but also locate missing family members and make contact with rescuers. Lewis develops "a vivid picture of the many horrors and challenges faced in the immediate aftermath of a large-scale natural disaster," wrote *School Library Journal* contributor Jayne Damron. This opinion was echoed by *Booklist* critic John Peters, who described *The Killing Sea* as "a powerful fictional tale of survival and cooperation."

Cover of Richard Lewis's novel **The Demon Queen,** *which finds a teen with a hidden past hoping to live a quiet life with his new foster family.*
(Jacket photograph copyright © by Jonathan Dorfman. Reproduced by permission of Simon & Schuster Books for Young Readers.)

In *The Demon Queen* Lewis offers a supernatural tale featuring a youth in foster care who tries to live a nondescript existence after becoming an unexplained target of the U.S. Homeland Security Agency. Found abandoned on a boat as a child, Jesse narrowly escapes deportation to Cambodia after officials learn that his birth certificate is a fake. However, strange events surrounding a new girl at school force Jesse to take action against what he believes might be a demon in disguise. Now enrolled at Jesse's school, Honor Clarke recently arrived in the United States. According to school gossip, her father died under suspicious circumstances, and Honor stands out from the other students, wearing insects as accessories. When dangerous events begin to overtake his classmates, Jesse fingers Honor as a suspect. Compelled to learn more about his own hidden past, he must also discover a way to combat the Balinese Demon Queen that Honor intends to resurrect.

Writing in *Kliatt,* Cara Chancellor suggested *The Demon Queen* for teens who are "ready for more grown-up thrills." In *Booklist* Todd Morning appreciated the drawn-out pacing of Lewis's novel, applauding the "slow unfolding of the dark forces against the backdrop of normal high-school life" that leads to a "full-blown, earthshaking ending." In her *School Library Journal* review, Amy J. Chow also predicted that *The Demon Queen* will prove popular with mystery fans, who "will soak up the over-the-top, gloomy atmosphere and bloodsmattered, monster-filled action."

Biographical and Critical Sources

PERIODICALS

Booklist, December 15, 2006, John Peters, review of *The Killing Sea,* p. 43; May 15, 2008, Todd Morning, review of *The Demon Queen,* p. 51.

Kirkus Reviews, July 15, 2004, review of *The Flame Tree,* p. 689; May 1, 2008, review of *The Demon Queen.*

Kliatt, November, 2006, Samantha Musher, review of *The Killing Sea,* p. 17; July, 2008, Cara Chancellor, review of *The Demon Queen,* p. 17.

Publishers Weekly, September 6, 2004, review of *The Flame Tree,* p. 63; July 13, 2009, review of *Monster's Proof,* p. 59.

School Library Journal, October, 2004, Kathleen Isaacs, review of *The Flame Tree,* p. 171; February, 2007, Jayne Damron, review of *The Killing Sea,* p. 122; September, 2008, Amy J. Chow, review of *The Demon Queen,* p. 190.

ONLINE

Richard Lewis Home Page, http://www.richardlewisauthor. com (December 15, 2009).

Richard Lewis Web log, http://www.novelistinparadise.com (December 15, 2009).

LEWIS, Rose
(Rose A. Lewis)

Personal

Children: Ming (daughter). *Education:* University of Rochester, B.S. (psychology); Northwestern University, M.A. (journalism).

Addresses

Home—Needham, MA.

Career

Author, journalist, television producer, and marketing executive. WCVB-TV, Boston, MA, news producer and writer, for eighteen years; Lahey Clinic Medical Center, Burlington, MA, manager of media relations, 2002-08; Beth Israel Deaconess Hospital-Needham, Needham, MA, director of marketing and communications, 2008—.

Awards, Honors

Best Books of the Year selection, *Child* magazine, 2000, Book Sense Book of the Year Award finalist, 2001, and Children's Crown Gallery Award, all for *I Love You like Crazy Cakes.*

Writings

I Love You like Crazy Cakes, illustrated by Jane Dyer, Little, Brown (Boston, MA), 2000.

Every Year on Your Birthday, illustrated by Jane Dyer, Little, Brown (Boston, MA), 2007.

Sidelights

Rose Lewis is the author of *I Love You like Crazy Cakes* and *Every Year on Your Birthday,* a pair of works based on her experiences with her adopted Chinese daughter, Ming. Adopting Ming is "the best thing I ever did," Lewis told *Business Week Online* contributor Cathy Arnst. "She is extraordinary. She makes my life infinitely more interesting."

In *I Love You like Crazy Cakes,* Lewis describes an adoptive mother's journey to China and her first meeting with her infant daughter. Lewis "taps into a well of genuine emotion," noted a reviewer in *Publishers Weekly.* "That the narrator speaks in the first person and addresses the daughter directly brings readers young and old into the characters' intimate circle," remarked *New York Times* critic Heather Davis. "For adopted children," the critic added, "the book may prove especially useful, providing insight into the feelings of their own adoptive parents." Anita D. McClellan, writing in the *Women's Review of Books,* recommended *I Love You like Crazy Cakes* as "an ideal way to introduce a child to any story of transracial, international adoption."

In *Every Year on Your Birthday,* a mother recounts prized memories of her adopted daughter, who was born in China. "The text reads almost like a diary, the entries teeming with emotional and thoughtful observations," a *Publishers Weekly* contributor observed. Lewis "carefully integrates her daughter's birth culture and customs," remarked a critic in *Kirkus Reviews,* and *Booklist* reviewer Julie Cummins noted that *Every Year on Your Birthday* "will be welcomed by families of all kinds adopting an Asian child."

Biographical and Critical Sources

PERIODICALS

Book, May, 2001, Kathleen Odean, review of *I Love You like Crazy Cakes,* p. 80.
Booklist, September 1, 2001, Connie Fletcher, review of *I Love You like Crazy Cakes,* p. 124; June 1, 2007, Julie Cummins, review of *Every Year on Your Birthday,* p. 70.
Kirkus Reviews, April 15, 2007, review of *Every Year on Your Birthday.*
New York Times, October 19, 2000, Heather Davis, "How I Found You," review of *I Love You like Crazy Cakes.*
Publishers Weekly, July 31, 2000, review of *I Love You like Crazy Cakes,* p. 94; April 9, 2007, review of *Every Year on Your Birthday,* p. 52.
School Library Journal, October, 2000, Gay Lynn Van Vleck, review of *I Love You like Crazy Cakes,* p. 129; June, 2007, June Wolfe, review of *Every Year on Your Birthday,* p. 112.
Women's Review of Books, January, 2002, Anita D. McClellan, "Bridging the Ocean," review of *I Love You like Crazy Cakes,* p. 7.

ONLINE

Business Week Online, http://www.businessweek.com/careers/workingparents/blog/ (May 14, 2007), Cathy Lewis, "Meet Rose Lewis, Single, Working Mother—And Author."*

*   *   *

LEWIS, Rose A.
See LEWIS, Rose

*   *   *

LUDWIG, Trudy 1959-

Personal

Born June 29, 1959, in New Bedford, MA; daughter of Herbert (a construction consultant) and Ethyle (a marriage and family therapist) Ludwig; married Brad Long

Trudy Ludwig (Photograph by Allie Long. Reproduced by permission.)

(a senior footwear innovator) October 27, 1991; children: Allison, Bennett. *Education:* Attended University of New Hampshire, 1977-79; University of California, Santa Barbara, B.A. (communications and Spanish), 1981.

Addresses

Office—Ludwig Creative, Inc., P.O. Box 25505, Portland, OR 97298-0505. *E-mail*—trudy@trudyludwig.com.

Career

Children's author and lecturer. Bilingual immigration consultant, 1982-85; Carnegie Mellon University, Pittsburgh, PA, projects manager and editor of *Accent on Research,* 1985-88; senior advertising/marketing copywriter in Lynwood, WA, 1988-92; freelance copywriter and editor, 1992-2002. Collaborator with organizations, including Ophelia Project, Hands & Words Are Not for Hurting Project, and Putting Family First. Has appeared on television programs, including *Good Morning America* and *Keeping Kids Healthy.*

Member

International Bullying Prevention Association, International Reading Association, Council for the Social Studies, Society of Children's Book Writers and Illustrators, Willamette Writers, Phi Beta Kappa.

Awards, Honors

Silver CASE National Award, Council for the Advancement and Support of Education, and Women in Communications Matrix Award honorable mention, both 1988, both for *Accent on Research;* CUNA Diamond Award of Merit, 2002; Mom's Choice Gold Award, Na-

tional Council for the Social Studies/Children's Book Council Notable Social Studies Books for Young People designation, and Cooperative Children's Book Center Best of the Year selection, all 2009, all for *Trouble Talk;* Moonbeam Gold Award, and Oppenheim Toy Portfolio Best Book Award Gold Seal, both 2009, both for *Too Perfect.*

Writings

My Secret Bully, illustrated by Abigail Marble, RiverWood Books (Ashland, OR), 2003.
Just Kidding, illustrated by Adam Gustavson, Tricycle Press (Berkeley, CA), 2005.
Sorry!, illustrated by Maurie Manning, Tricycle Press (Berkeley, CA), 2006.
Trouble Talk, illustrated by Mikela Prevost, foreword by Charisse Nixon, Tricycle Press (Berkeley, CA), 2008.
Too Perfect, illustrated by Lisa Fields, Tricycle Press (Berkeley, CA), 2009.
Confessions of a Former Bully, illustrated by Beth Adams, Tricycle Press (Berkeley, CA), 2010.

Author's work has been translated into Spanish.

Sidelights

Trudy Ludwig creates children's books that focus on the social interactions that are an important part of elementary-school life. Her first book, *My Secret Bully,* was inspired by Ludwig's efforts to deal with children who bullied her own daughter. Although she was already working as a freelance writer when she started the manuscript for her first children's book, Ludwig enjoyed working on the book project so much that she ended her freelance writing career in favor of penning other books with an educational focus. In addition to her work as a writer, Ludwig also speaks at schools and conferences and has appeared on radio and television, where she shares her insights regarding bullying and other hurtful interrelational behaviors.

Both *My Secret Bully* and *Just Kidding* deal with the hurtful one-on-one interactions that are common among elementary-aged children. In *My Secret Bully* Katie controls her relationship with Monica by making belittling comments, withholding attention, and excluding Monica from group activities she enjoys with other friends. D.J. takes the brunt of classmate Vince's biting sarcasm in *Just Kidding.* Noting that *Just Kidding* includes a helpful guide for children who are subjected to teasing behavior, *Booklist* critic Carolyn Phelan added that Ludwig's book features a positive outcome and includes "sensitive portrayals of children in realistic settings." In *School Library Journal* Carol L. MacKay also praised the illustrations by Adam Gustavson that bring to life D.J.'s plight, writing that the artist's "realistic acrylic paintings beautifully capture the . . . mood and action" in *Just Kidding.*

In *Sorry!* Ludwig focuses on the way that a fake apology can help children avoid taking responsibility for hurting others. In the story, Charlie says he is sorry every time he is called to account for his bad behavior. Friend Jack witnesses Charlie's many apologies, but also knows that his self-centered friend does not really mean what he says. Praising Ludwig's effort "to tackle serious subjects" in *Sorry!,* Catherine Callegari added that illustrator Maurie J. Manning contributes watercolor and pastel images to the story that "effectively capture the . . . myriad emotions" generated by Charlie's manipulative insincerity.

Gossip is the focus of *Trouble Talk,* in which new-girl-at-school Bailey always has something interesting to say about everyone. While Maya enjoys Bailey's talkative, entertaining nature at first, she quickly learns that most of the talk is negative and designed to diminish other people that she knows and likes. Perfectionism, like gossip, is also common in school-aged girls, and Ludwig addresses the need to discount one's own good qualities in favor of the standards set by others in *Too Perfect.* Noting the value of *Trouble Talk* to parents and counselors in addition to children, Martha Topol wrote in *School Library Journal* that "young readers will readily identify with Maya's dilemma and appreciate the straightforward text" by Ludwig. A *Kirkus Reviews* writer cited the book's "potential as a discussion starter" and commended the author for "avoid[ing] . . . a dry, preachy tone despite the seriousness of the subject." In another *Kirkus Reviews* appraisal, a critic judged *Too Perfect* to be "well-intentioned but highly didactic," yet added that Ludwig's book "is one of few on a very timely social problem."

In *Confessions of a Former Bully* nine-year-old Katie gets caught bullying on the school playground and faces consequences for her behavior. One of her key consequences is restitution. To help make up for the hurt she has caused others, Katie decides to take all that she has learned from caring adults about bullying and friendship and turn her personal journal into a book that helps other kids. Included in this story are tips, tools, and resources to help empower children in their social world.

Ludwig once told *SATA:* "Throughout my earlier career as an advertising/marketing copywriter, I never quite felt passionate about my craft. I knew I loved to write. I just didn't love what I was writing.

"My creative life turned around when my daughter, who was seven at the time, became the target of bullying friends. It was one of those experiences that had a profound impact on the both of us. I didn't want to fight my daughter's battles; I wanted to give her the social skills and tools she would need to fight her own battles in life.

"In my search for age-appropriate books to address the very real and rampant problem of social cruelty among peers, I came up empty-handed. Frustrated with this re-

Ludwig focuses on the ups and downs of elementary-grade relationships in **Trouble Talk,** *featuring artwork by Mikela Prevost.* (Illustration copyright © 2008 by Mikela Prevost. Used by permission of Tricycle Press, an imprint of Crown Publishing Group, a division of Random House, Inc.)

source gap, I wrote *My Secret Bully,* my first children's book, to help empower my daughter and many children like her to make healthier friendship choices. It was such a rewarding and energizing experience for me that I quit my freelance copywriting career to focus on making a difference in kids' lives, one book at a time.

"Because the social world of today's children is very complex and difficult to navigate, I try to incorporate into my stories the wisdom and insights of young readers, so that my books resonate with the authenticity of real life experiences and views. I also have the added pleasure of tapping into my own inner child—letting her laugh, cry, and simply breathe. I've finally reached the point where I not only love to write, I truly love what I'm writing."

Biographical and Critical Sources

PERIODICALS

Booklist, April 15, 2006, Carolyn Phelan, review of *Just Kidding,* p. 52.

Kirkus Reviews, April 15, 2008, review of *Trouble Talk;* April 1, 2009, review of *Too Perfect.*

School Library Journal, January, 2004, Rosalyn Pierini, review of *My Secret Bully,* p. 100; June, 2006, Carol L. MacKay, review of *Just Kidding,* p. 121; December, 2006, Catherine Callegari, review of *Sorry!,* p. 107; June, 2008, Martha Topol, review of *Trouble Talk,* p. 110.

ONLINE

Books to Grow With Newsletter Online, http://www.lutrapress.com/ (April, 2005).

Embracing the Child Web site, http://www.embracingthechild.com/ (March 24, 2004), interview with Ludwig.

My Secret Bully Web site, http://www.mysecretbully.com/ (November 6, 2005).

Random House Web site, http://www.randomhouse.com/ (January 10, 2010), "Trudy Ludwig."

Trudy Ludwig Web site, http://www.trudyludwig.com (December 15, 2009).

LYNCH, Chris 1962-

Personal

Born July 2, 1962, in Boston, MA; son of Edward (a bus driver) and Dorothy (a receptionist) Lynch; married Tina Coviello (a technical support manager), August 5, 1989; children: Sophia, Walker. *Education:* Suffolk University, B.A. (journalism), 1983; Emerson University, M.A. (professional writing and publishing), 1991. *Hobbies and other interests:* Running.

Addresses

Home—Ayrshire, Scotland. *Agent*—Fran Lebowitz, Writers House, 21 W. 26th St., New York, NY 10010.

Career

Writer. Teacher of writing at Emerson University, 1995, and Vermont College, 1997—. Proofreader of financial reports, 1985-89. Conducted a writing workshop at Boston Public Library, summer, 1994.

Member

Authors Guild, Author's League of America.

Awards, Honors

American Library Association (ALA) Best Books for Young Adults and Quick Picks for Reluctant Young-Adult Readers citations, 1993, for *Shadow Boxer*, 1994, for *Iceman* and *Gypsy Davey*, and 1996, for *Slot Machine;* Best Books of the Year designation, *School Library Journal*, 1993, for *Shadow Boxer;* Blue Ribbon Award, *Bulletin of the Center for Children's Books*, 1994, for *Iceman* and *Gypsy Davey;* Editors' Choice award, *Booklist*, 1994, for *Gypsy Davey;* Dorothy Canfield Fisher Award finalist, Book of the Year award, *Hungry Mind Review*, and Young Adults' Choice citation, International Reading Association, 1997, all for *Slot Machine;* Michael L. Printz Honor Book designation, and ALA Best Book for Young Adults designation, both 2002, both for *Freewill;* National Book Award nomination, 2005, for *Inexcusable*.

Writings

Shadow Boxer, HarperCollins (New York, NY), 1993.
Iceman, HarperCollins (New York, NY), 1994.
Gypsy Davey, HarperCollins (New York, NY), 1994.
Slot Machine, HarperCollins (New York, NY), 1995.
Political Timber, HarperCollins (New York, NY), 1996.
Extreme Elvin, HarperCollins (New York, NY), 1999.
Whitechurch, HarperCollins (New York, NY), 1999.
Gold Dust, HarperCollins (New York, NY), 2000.
Freewill, HarperCollins (New York, NY), 2001.
All the Old Haunts (stories), HarperCollins (New York, NY), 2001.

Chris Lynch (Photograph by Jeff Thiebauth. Reproduced by permission.)

Who the Man, HarperCollins (New York, NY), 2002.
The Gravedigger's Cottage HarperCollins (New York, NY), 2004.
Inexcusable, Atheneum Books for Young Readers (New York, NY), 2005.
Me, Dead Dad, and Alcatraz, HarperCollins (New York, NY), 2005.
Sins of the Fathers, HarperTempest (New York, NY), 2006.
Cyberia, Scholastic Press (New York, NY), 2008.
The Big Game of Everything, HarperTeen (New York, NY), 2008.
Monkey See, Monkey Don't, Scholastic Press (New York, NY), 2009.

Contributor of short stories to anthologies, including *Ultimate Sports*, edited by Donald Gallo, Delacorte, 1995, *Night Terrors*, edited by Lois Duncan, Simon & Schuster, 1996, and *No Such Thing as the Real World*, HarperCollins, 2009. Contributor of stories and articles to periodicals, including *Signal, School Library Journal*, and *Boston* magazine.

Lynch's books have been translated into Taiwanese and Italian.

"BLUE-EYED SON" SERIES

Mick, HarperCollins (New York, NY), 1996.
Blood Relations, HarperCollins (New York, NY), 1996.
Dog Eat Dog, HarperCollins (New York, NY), 1996.

"HE-MAN WOMAN-HATERS CLUB" SERIES; FOR YOUNG READERS

Johnny Chesthair, HarperCollins (New York, NY), 1997.
Babes in the Woods, HarperCollins (New York, NY), 1997.
Scratch and the Sniffs, HarperTrophy (New York, NY), 1997.
Ladies' Choice, HarperTrophy (New York, NY), 1997.
The Wolf Gang, HarperCollins (New York, NY), 1998.

Sidelights

An American author of teen fiction who now makes his home in Scotland, Chris Lynch "is less concerned with constructing plot-driven narratives than in creating impressionist portraits of confused and misunderstood teenagers," wrote a *Horn Book* contributor in a review of Lynch's story collection, *All the Old Haunts.* Indeed, creating realistic and compelling portraits of confused and misunderstood teens has become Lynch's stock in trade; these youths populate the pages of his groundbreaking novels *Shadow Boxer* and *Iceman,* as well as his "Blue-Eyed Son" series. Episodic and fast paced, Lynch's fiction questions the male stereotypes of macho identity and inarticulate violence. His youthful outsider characters are often athletes, wannabe athletes, or kids who have been churned up and spit out by the system. Their stories reveal what it means to be young and urban and male in America, warts and all.

"Growing up I listened way too much to the rules as they were handed down," Lynch recalled in an interview for *Authors and Artists for Young Adults* (*AAYA*). Although he was raised in Boston, the fifth of seven children in a stable family, his Jamaica Plains neighborhood was transitioning from an Irish stronghold to Hispanic during his childhood. After Lynch's father died when the future author was five years old, his mother was left to raise her children alone and finances became somewhat strained. "She did a good job of covering it up, but things were pretty lean back then," Lynch remembered. "We were definitely a free cheese family, though I never felt deprived as a kid."

A somewhat reclusive child, Lynch attended primary and secondary levels Catholic schools, and while grammar school was enjoyable, high school was a different matter. "I hated high school—every minute. It was rigid, kind of a factory. An all-boys' football factory. Nothing like the arts was encouraged in any way." Although Lynch played street hockey, football, and baseball as a child, during high school he stopped playing as a way of rebelling against the pro-sports culture. "I'm not against all athletics," he explained in his *AAYA* interview, because "sports has a tremendous potential for channeling energy. But . . . it mostly encourages the macho ethos and schools let athletes run wild."

Although Lynch dropped out of high school in his junior year, he eventually enrolled at Boston University, where he studied political science. A journalism course

sparked his interest in writing, and after transferring to Suffolk University, he majored in the subject. After graduation, Lynch spent six years working at odd jobs such as painting houses, driving a moving van, and proofreading financial reports. While pursuing a master's program in professional writing and publishing at Boston's Emerson University, he took a children's writing class from Y.A. author Jack Gantos, and it was here that Lynch began what became his first published novel, *Shadow Boxer.* "We were supposed to write five pages on a childhood incident," the author recalled in *AAYA.* "I had a vague idea of writing about some things my brother and I had done in our youth, but as soon as I sat down with it, I was off to the races. The stuff just poured out."

Shadow Boxer is a story of two brothers learning to deal with life after the death of their father, a journeyman boxer. Fourteen-year-old George becomes the man of the house after his father dies, a casualty of years of battering he endured in the boxing ring. George's mother is bitter and hates the sport that cost her husband his life, but George's younger brother, Monty, wants to follow in his father's footsteps. Monty begins to train at the local gym with his uncle, and when George tries to discourage him from this path it exacer-

Cover of Chris Lynch's young-adult novel **The Big Game of Everything,** *which finds a teen learning to appreciate his quirky relatives while working in the family business.* (Jacket photography by Maurice Harmon/Graphistock Photography/Veer. Used by permission of HarperCollins Children's Books, a division of HarperCollins Publishers.)

bates the boys' sibling rivalry. Told in brief, episodic vignettes with urban slang, the novel reaches its climax when Monty is shown a video of one of the brutal beatings his father took in the ring.

Reviewing *Shadow Boxer* in *Horn Book,* Peter D. Sieruta wrote that Lynch captures, "with unflinching honesty," the novel's working-class Boston setting. While the book's episodic style, with short, terse paragraphs, weakens the plot, according to Sieruta, several chapters of the novel "read like polished short stories and are stunning in their impact." Tom S. Hurlburt, writing in *School Library Journal,* dubbed *Shadow Boxer* "a gritty, streetwise novel that is much more than a sports story," and several critics recommended that Lynch's style—creating a series of brief, hard-hitting vignettes that reveal character—makes the novel accessible to reluctant readers.

In *Iceman* Lynch tells the story of a troubled youth for whom violence on the ice is a much-needed release. Fourteen-year-old Eric is a hockey player with a reputation as a fine shooter and a strong defensive player with a penchant for hitting. Known as the "Iceman" due to his antics on the ice, Eric actually seems to enjoy hurting people. His only friends are his older brother Duane, whose act of trading his skates for a guitar impresses Eric, and the local embalmer, McLaughlin, who also impresses Eric with his devotion to his work. The source of Eric's rage comes from his dysfunctional family: his mother, a former nun, continually spouts verses from the Bible while his father only seems interested in Eric when the boy is doing damage on the ice. As his actions on the ice become increasingly violent, Eric is soon shunned by even his own teammates. McLaughlin gives the teen some comfort in his world of death, and Eric considers a future in mortuary science until a shocking observation prompts the teen to face his current problems.

Randy Brough, reviewing *Iceman* for *Voice of Youth Advocates,* noted that Lynch's "novel of disaffected adolescence" is "as satisfying as a hard, clean hip check." Jack Forman, while noting the book's appeal to hockey enthusiasts in his *School Library Journal* review, also pointed out that *Iceman* "is no advertisement for the sport." Stephanie Zvirin, summed up the effect of the novel in *Booklist,* wrote that Lynch's "totally unpredictable novel . . . is an unsettling, complicated portrayal of growing up in a dysfunctional family" as well as "a thought-provoking book guaranteed to compel and touch a teenage audience."

In *Gypsy Davey,* Lynch tells the story of a brain-damaged youth and an uncaring family, as well as of the tenement neighborhood surrounding the boy: cheap bars and drug dealers. Living in this bleak atmosphere, young Davey tries to break the cycle of neglect initiated by his parents and seemingly perpetuated by his older sister, Jo. Jo's unhappy marriage forms the centerpiece of Lynch's novel, and it is Davey's attempts to bring love to Jo's son, his own nephew, that is one of the bright spots in *Gypsy Davey.* W. Keith McCoy, writing in *Voice of Youth Advocates,* noted that, in spite of his story's dreary atmosphere, "Lynch provokes empathy for this family and its situation, and perhaps that is the only positive outcome in the book." Also focusing on the bleakness in *Gypsy Davey,* Elizabeth Bush concluded in the *Bulletin of the Center for Children's Books* that "young adults will appreciate its honesty and fast pace" and that Lynch "paints characters who . . . ring true every time."

A reviewer for *Publishers Weekly* called Lynch's novel *Whitechurch* an "unsettling, coolly polished" story that again demonstrates the author's "profound understanding of society's casualties, misfits and losers." In the novel, teens Pauly, Oakley, and Lilly must learn to navigate the treacherous shoals that exist in their dilapidated New England town in a series of interconnecting short stories. Seemingly trapped in the dead-end environment of Whitechurch, each teen finds his or her own way to break out of the stagnant environment. A reviewer for *Horn Book* wrote of *Whitechurch* that the "sharply evoked characters and their complex relationship are the novel's greatest strengths."

Praised by *School Library Journal* critic Michael McCullough for containing "some of the best sports writing readers will ever find in a YA novel," *Gold Dust* is set in Boston during the 1975 school-busing integration controversy. In Lynch's story, seventh-grade baseball fan Richard Moncrief dreams of transforming the new transfer student from Dominica into a first-rate baseball player. The two plan to team up and become the adolescent equivalents of Boston Red Sox players Fred Lynn and Jim Rice, dubbed the "Gold Dust Twins" during the 1975 season. However, Richard soon realizes that his new teammate, Napoleon "Charlie" Ellis, is a difficult friend to have, because Charlie's actions force the white boy to address the racial tensions in his Boston neighborhood. Lauren Adams, writing in *Horn Book,* noted that "Lynch's provocative novel tells a piece of the city's history and the more intimate story of a transforming friendship." *Gold Dust* "is a wonderful baseball book," declared *Booklist* contributor Debbie Carton, and a *Publishers Weekly* critic dubbed the story's denouement "as honest as it is heartbreaking."

Lynch's award-winning novel *Freewill* is considered something of a departure from the author's usual style: it is written in the form of a mystery and utilizes second-person narration. Having lost his father and stepmother in a strange accident, Will is sent to a special school where a sudden rash of suicides forces the reader to wonder if Will is not responsible. One of Will's wood carvings is found at the scene of each of these suicides, making the police suspicious of the boy and also attracting the attention of a weird group of hangers-on. Finally, Will's grandfather helps the boy unravel the mystery and find out what is really going on. Described by Adams as an "unsettling narrative," *Freewill* is a "dark, rich young-adult novel that offers something to think about as well as an intriguing story," according to *Booklist* contributor Susan Dove Lempke.

Lynch's protagonist in *Who the Man* is deeply misunderstood. Because thirteen-year-old Earl is physically mature for his age, he is assumed to be older and more mature than his years. Because of his size, Earl is constantly teased by his classmates, and his frustration results in fist fights and, ultimately, his suspension from school. Readers soon realize that Earl's problems do not end at school; at home the teen silently watches the disintegration of his parent's marriage and witnesses his father contemplate an extramarital affair. In *Booklist* Ed Sullivan wrote that "Lynch challenges readers to consider gender stereotypes . . . as he follows a young man's painful journey toward self-discovery." Similarly, a *Publishers Weekly* reviewer acknowledged Lynch for his "hypnotic voice," and called *Who the Man* is a "striking chronicle of a painful transition from boyhood to manhood."

The McLuckie family is the focal point of *Gravedigger's Cottage,* a novel that centers on a family's losses and attempt to recuperate. Described by *School Library Journal* reviewer Francesca Goldsmith as a "dark and clever fable," Lynch's novel is narrated by Sylvia and recounts the teen's story of her father and her half-brother Walter. After the deaths of two mothers and several pets, the McLuckies attempt to change their fate by moving to a seaside cabin. In their rustic new home, Sylvia and Walter witness a mysterious change in their dad's behavior as the man becomes obsessed with sealing the cabin from unseen and imagined dangers. While *Kliatt* contributor Michele Winship characterized *Gravedigger's Cottage* as a "dark" tale that "at times leaves the reader wondering what is real and what is not," *Horn Book* writer Laurence Adams dubbed it "a sweet, offbeat picture of three people looking after one another, making ready to give life another chance."

Booklist reviewer Gillian Engberg called *Inexcusable* a "bone-chilling" and "daring story [that] is told in the defensive voice of the accused rapist." In the novel, which was nominated for a National Book award, high-school senior Keir Sarafian is a popular football player who is accused of rape. Lynch's readers initially enter the story believing Keir's narration of events, but he proves to be an unreliable source when he begins to realize certain things about himself. Paula Rohrlick remarked in *Kliatt* that "Keir is a good example of an unreliable narrator, whose version of reality and sense of himself . . . are dangerously off base." In a *Publishers Weekly* review of *Inexcusable,* "Lynch makes it nearly impossible for readers to see the world in black-and-white terms" in a novel that is "guaranteed to prompt heated discussion."

Three thirteen year olds living in a working-class Boston neighborhood are captivated by the energy of their charismatic new parish priest in Lynch's novel *Sins of the Fathers.* Drew, the narrator, as well as Skitz and Hector have been friends forever, and they all serve at altar boys at Blessed Sacrament. When Father Mullarkey joins the church, he is a welcome counterpoint to the two staid, older priests that the boys nickname Fa-

thers Blarney and Shenanigan because the younger man shares the same love of rock music that the boys do. While the pragmatic Drew credits Father Mullarkey with helping him to see the world in a new way, he also realizes that Hector's increasingly strange behavior may be the consequence of an inappropriate relationship with one of the three parish priests. While noting that the theme of sexual abuse is treated by Lynch with subtlety, Paula Rohrlick added in *Kliatt* that *Sins of the Father* is a story "related with rare wit and candor." Grounded in the boys' strong friendship, the novel "conveys . . . the damage that young people can be subjected to when adult influence goes unchecked," according to *School Library Journal* critic Carolyn Lehman.

In his "Blue-eyed Son" novel trilogy, Lynch returns to the grittier mean streets of Boston to explore latent and sometimes overt racism. In *Mick* a fifteen year old sees his predominately Irish neighborhood becoming racially mixed as African Americans, Hispanics, and Asians move in. Although Mick disagree with his friends and older brother Terry's plans to disrupt the upcoming St. Patrick's Day parade by harassing gay and Cambodian marchers, he participates in their activities, and when he throws an egg at a Cambodian marcher, Mick's action is caught on television. Now hailed as a hero in the local bar, Mick also becomes a pariah at school. Soon only the mysterious Toy remains his friend, and Mick begins to sever ties with his close-knit Irish neighborhood and hang out with a group of Latinos instead. Ultimately, Mick's behavior has consequences that are meted out by an angry Terry.

In *Blood Relations* Mick struggles to find himself, forming a brief liaison with beautiful Evelyn and finally ending up in the bed of Toy's mother, while in *Dog Eat Dog* he and Terry face off for a final showdown while Mick's friend Toy comes out of the closet as a homosexual. "With realistic street language and an in-your-face writing style . . . Lynch immerses readers in Mick's world," Kelly Diller wrote in a review of *Mick* for *School Library Journal.* According to Diller, Lynch has created a "noble anti-hero" in his series opener. Reviewing *Blood Relations* for *School Library Journal,* Kellie Flynn commented that "this story moves quickly, Mick's seriocomic edginess is endearing, and the racism theme is compelling." Flynn's comment that the series concept makes the ending of *Blood Relations* something of a let-down was echoed by Elizabeth Bush, who wrote in *Bulletin of the Center for Children's Books* that, "when the finish finally arrives, the unrelenting brutalities of the earlier volumes will leave the audience virtually unshockable."

In addition to his hard-hitting novels for older teens, Lynch also addresses younger readers in several works of fiction. *Slot Machine* is a boys-at-summer-camp comedy about an overweight youth who resists all attempts to turn him into a jock. Thirteen-year-old Elvin Bishop is attending a Christian Brothers summer camp, with its heavy emphasis on sports as preparation for high

school—the coaches literally 'slot' young athletes for specific sports. Friends with Mike, who seems to fit in anywhere, and Frank, who sells his soul to fit in, Elvin endures torment but steers a middle course and finally finds a niche for himself with the help of an arts instructor. According to Stephanie Zvirin, writing in *Booklist, Slot Machine* is a "funny, poignant coming-of-age story." While noting Lynch's ability to write broad, physical comedy as well as dark humor, Zvirin concluded that "this wry, thoughtful book speaks with wisdom and heart to the victim and outsider in us all." Maeve Visser Knoth, writing in *Horn Book,* also noted the use of humor and sarcasm in this "biting, sometimes hilarious novel," as well as the serious purpose in back of it all. "Lynch writes a damning commentary on the costs of conformity and the power gained by standing up for oneself," the critic concluded.

Lynch reprises Elvin in the novels *Extreme Elvin* and *Me, Dead Dad, and Alcatraz.* In *Extreme Elvin* the teen is starting his first year at a Catholic all-boys high school. As a *Publishers Weekly* critic noted, Lynch's "wisecracking, irrepressible" character is "just as funny—and perhaps even more likable" in this new installment as the "pudgy hero has one scatological misadventure after the next." In the book, the newly girl-crazy Elvin gains a terrible reputation for his eternal hemorrhoids before being tricked into believing he has caught a sexually transmitted disease from holding hands. In the end, the young teen goes against his buddies' advice, opting to date the plump girl he really likes instead of a pretty but standoffish thinner girl. The *Publishers Weekly* critic deemed *Extreme Elvis* "witty and knowing."

Elvin is fourteen years old in *Me, Dead Dad, and Alcatraz,* and now he meets his uncle Alex, who he had been told was dead. As the teen learns, his mother lied about the relative's demise in order to hide the truth: that Alex has been serving a prison term for theft. Comedic stories unfold as Elvin's uncle attempts to become a father figure for the boy, with disastrous results. *School Library Journal* critic Miranda Doyle predicted that readers "will identify with Elvin's outsider status and enjoy his hilarious missteps on the path to adulthood," while *Booklist* critic Michael Cart called Elvin "the quintessential adolescent male—worried about sex, personal identity, and just about everything." Paula Rohrlick, writing in *Kliatt,* called *Me, Dead Dad, and Alcatraz* a "funny and poignant novel" that will appeal to "Elvin's fans."

Described by *Horn Book* contributor Claire E. Gross as an "oddball futuristic conspiracy-adventure story," Lynch's middle-grade novel *Cyberia* finds Zane in possession of a technologically advanced communications device. A payoff from his father to keep Zane entertained during the many hours the boy is left home alone, the device allows the boy to communicate with his dog, Hugo. The pup recounts stories of animal abuse that inspire Zane to become an animal rights advocate. Although family veterinary Dr. Gristle seems to be at the

source of the mistreatment of a local group of greyhound race dogs, Zane must find a way to get around the monitoring system—including a microchip implanted in his ankle—that keeps him under constant surveillance in the novel's uncomfortably familiar future world. Gross cited, in particular, "the tenderness" that characterizes Zane's relationship with Hugo as well as the "hefty dose of dry situational comedy" that Lynch includes in *Cyberia.* Lynch's "very funny book occasionally strikes notes of unexpected poignancy," wrote *Booklist* contributor Daniel Kraus, and a *Publishers Weekly* observed that the author also explores a serious theme: "the double edge of technology that offers shortcuts but erodes independence."

Union Jack, the middle-grade hero in *The Big Game of Everything,* reacts to the name his hippy parents gave him by renaming himself Onion Jock. Although Jock is looking forward to a summer spent outside, working at his grandfather's golf course, he dreads having to deal with his mischievous brother Egon, his boy-crazy sister Meredith, and his totally laid-back parents. At sibling tensions begin to escalate, Grampus becomes openly curmudgeonly and expresses discontent with the family as well as with his seemingly comfortable life. It soon becomes clear to Jock that the materialistic retirees who daily play their way through Grampus's golf course may be exacerbating the older man's unhappiness and pushing him toward senility. Reviewing the novel for *Horn Book,* Adams wrote that the "motley group of eccentric characters" Lynch allows to roam, club in hand, "on a giant [golf-course] playground" provides readers with "a welcome [fictional] getaway." For Rohrlick, *The Big Game of Everything* is "an affirmation of the value of family" in which Lynch's "dialogue is often a delight," and in *School Library Journal* Jeffrey Hastings dubbed the novel a "funny and thoughtful" exploration of what is most important in life as seen "through the eyes of a teenage boy."

Written for even-younger readers, Lynch's "He-Man Woman-Haters Club" novels employ the same broad humor as the "Elvin" books to poke fun at the stereotypes of younger adolescent boys. Lincoln—also known as Johnny Chesthair—decides to start a club in his uncle's garage, including in membership wimpy Jerome, wheelchair-bound Wolfgang, and huge Ling-Ling. Later members include a guitarist named Scratch and Cecil, who is "gentle and synaptically challenged," according to *Booklist* contributor Randy Meyer in a review of *Scratch and the Sniffs.* Each of the original members takes a turn narrating a book in the five-volume series, each title involving the humorous undoing of these would-be heroes. Reviewing *The Wolf Gang,* Shelle Rosenfeld concluded in *Booklist* that "Lynch's presentation of the boys' seesawing view of girls as enemies or attractions is dead-on, as is his portrayal of the ties of friendship that bind—and survive even the toughest tests in the end."

In his story collection *All the Old Haunts* Lynch creates a mix of ten tales describing family ties, man-woman relationships, and friendship, among other themes. A re-

viewer for *Publishers Weekly* noted that the author "once again excels in describing family bonds," and concluded that "there's something here for everyone." Angela J. Reynolds, writing in *School Library Journal*, also praised the "fresh twist" Lynch puts on old themes, concluding that "teens who enjoy deftly crafted tales with more than a hint of the dark side will appreciate this sophisticated prose." A contributor for *Kirkus Reviews* also commented positively on Lynch's short fiction, stating that "fans of [Lynch's] edgy novels will find [*All the Old Haunts*] lit with the same wry, raw view of adolescence."

As a writer, Lynch avoids studying a story's "why's too closely," as he told an interview for *Teenreads.com*. "I want to tell realistic stories, which I think come with their own messages built into them without my having to preach. Specifically, the issue of substance abuse—like violence, or racism—is a fact of our lives, and the only way I can contribute anything is merely to chronicle the facts of lives as I see them."

Biographical and Critical Sources

BOOKS

Authors and Artists for Young Adults, Gale (Detroit, MI), Volume 19, 1996, Volume 44, 2002.
Children's Literature Review, Volume 58, Gale (Detroit, MI), 2000.
St. James Guide to Young-Adult Writers, 2nd edition, St. James Press (Detroit, MI), 1999.

PERIODICALS

Booklist, December 15, 1993, Gary Young, review of *Shadow Boxer,* p. 747; February 1, 1994, Stephanie Zvirin, review of *Iceman,* p. 1001; September 1, 1995, Stephanie Zvirin, review of *Slot Machine,* p. 74; October 15, 1996, Anne O'Malley, review of *Political Timber,* p. 414l; April 15, 1997, Randy Meyer, review of *Scratch and the Sniffs,* pp. 1429-1430; August, 1998, Shelle Rosenfeld, review of *The Wolf Gang,* pp. 2006-2007; September 1, 2000, Debbie Carton, review of *Gold Dust,* p. 116; May 15, 2001, Susan Dove Lempke, review of *Freewill,* p. 1745; November 15, 2002, Ed Sullivan, review of *Who the Man,* p. 588; September 1, 2005, Michael Cart, review of *Me, Dead Dad, and Alcatraz,* p. 111; September 15, 2005, Gillian Engberg, review of *Inexcusable,* p. 55; September 1, 2008, Ian Chapman, review of *The Big Game of Everything,* p. 110; September 15, 2008, Daniel Kraus, review of *Cyberia,* p. 50.
Bulletin of the Center for Children's Books, November, 1994, Elizabeth Bush, review of *Gypsy Davey,* p. 93; April, 1996, Elizabeth Bush, reviews of *Mick, Blood Relations,* and *Dog Eat Dog,* p. 270.
Horn Book, May-June, 1994, Patty Campbell, "The Sand in the Oyster," pp. 358-362; November-December, 1995, Maeve Visser Knoth, review of *Slot Machine,* pp. 746-747; November-December, 1995, Peter D. Sieruta, review of *Shadow Boxer,* pp. 745-746; March-April, 1997, Elizabeth S. Watson, review of *Political Timber,* p. 201; July-August, 1999, review of *Whitechurch,* p. 469; November-December, 2000, Lauren Adams, review of *Gold Dust,* p. 758; July-August, 2001, Lauren Adams, review of *Freewill,* p. 457; September-October, 2001, review of *All the Old Haunts,* p. 588; July-August, 2004, Laurence Adams, review of *The Gravedigger's Cottage,* p. 456; January-February, 2006, Betty Carter, review of *Inexcusable,* p. 83, and Christine M. Hepperman, review of *Me, Dead Dad, and Alcatraz,* p. 84: September-October, Lauren Adams, review of *The Big Game of Everything,* p. 592; January-February, 2009, Claire E. Gross, review of *Cyberia,* p. 96.
Kirkus Reviews, October 15, 2001, review of *All the Old Haunts,* p. 1488; August 15, 2005, review of *Me, Dead Dad, and Alcatraz,* p. 918.
Kliatt, May, 2004, Michele Winship, review of *The Gravedigger's Cottage,* p. 10; September, 2005, Paula Rohrlick, review of *Me, Dead Dad, and Alcatraz,* p. 10; November, 2005, Paula Rohrlick, review of *Inexcusable,* p. 8; September 8, 2008, Paula Rohrlick, reviews of *Sins of the Fathers,* p. 14, and *Sins of the Fathers,* p. 15.
Publishers Weekly, October 21, 1996, review of *Political Timber,* p. 84; January 11, 1999, review of *Extremely Elvin,* p. 73; May 10, 1999, review of *Whitechurch,* p. 69; August 21, 2000, review of *Gold Dust,* p. 74; October 29, 2001, review of *All the Old Haunts,* p. 65; November 11, 2002, review of *Who the Man,* p. 65; October 17, 2005, review of *Inexcusable,* p. 69; October 23, 2006, review of *Sins of the Father,* p. 53; September 8, 2008, review of *Cyberia,* p. 51.
School Library Journal, September, 1993, Tom S. Hurlburt, review of *Shadow Boxer,* p. 252; March, 1994, Jack Forman, review of *Iceman,* p. 239; March, 1996, Kelly Diller, review of *Mick,* pp. 220-221; March, 1996, Kellie Flynn, review of *Blood Relations,* p. 221; October, 2000, Michael McCullough, review of *Gold Dust,* p. 164; November, 2001, Angela J. Reynolds, review of *All the Old Haunts,* p. 160; September, 2005, Miranda Doyle, review of *Me, Dead Dad, and Alcatraz,* p. 207; September, 2006, Carolyn Lehman, review of *Sins of the Fathers,* p. 211; October, 2008, Jeffrey Hastings, review of *The Big Game of Everything,* p. 152.
Voice of Youth Advocates, December, 1993, John R. Lord, review of *Shadow Boxer,* p. 295; April, 1994, Randy Brough, review of *Iceman,* p. 28; December, 1994, Keith W. McCoy, review of *Gypsy Davey,* p. 277.

ONLINE

HarperCollins Web site, http://www.harperchildren.com/ (December 10, 2009), "Chris Lynch."
National Book Award Web site, http://www.nationalbook.org/ (December 20, 2009), "Chris Lynch."
Teenreads.com, http://www.teenreads.com/ (December 20, 2009), interviews with Lynch.*

M

MARA, Rachna
See GILMORE, Rachna

* * *

McCALL, Bruce 1935-

Personal

Born May 10, 1935, in Simcoe, Ontario, Canada; son of Thomas Cameron and Helen Margaret McCall; married, 1976; children: one daughter.

Addresses

Home—New York, NY.

Career

Illustrator and humorist. Formerly worked in advertising; Ford Motor Company, Detroit, MI, illustrator, c. 1950s; Ogilvy & Mather (advertising agency), New York, NY, former copywriter; freelance cartoonist and writer, beginning c. 1970s. *Exhibitions:* Work included in numerous exhibits in New York, NY.

Writings

Zany Afternoons; and Other Glimpses of the Golden Age of Play, Knopf (New York, NY), 1982.
(Author of text) *Sit! The Dog Portraits of Thierry Poncelet,* Workman Publishing (New York, NY), 1993.
Thin Ice: Coming of Age in Canada, Random House (New York, NY), 1997.
(With Lee Eisenberg) *Viagra Nation,* Harper Perennial (New York, NY), 1998.
The Last Dream-o-Rama: The Cars Detroit Forgot to Build, Crown (New York, NY), 2001.
All Meat Looks like South America: The World of Bruce McCall (cartoon collection), Crown (New York, NY), 2003.

Marveltown, Farrar, Straus & Giroux (New York, NY), 2008.
Fifty Things to Do with a Book: (Now That Reading Is Dead), Collins (New York, NY), 2009.

Contributor to *Velvet Eden: The Richard Merkin Collection of Erotic Photography,* Methuen (New York, NY), 1979. Contributor of art and essays to periodicals, including *National Lampoon, Vanity Fair, Military History, Car and Driver, Esquire, Playboy,* and *New Yorker.* Author of sketches for *Saturday Night Live* (television program).

Sidelights

Bruce McCall is a Canadian-born cartoonist, illustrator, and humorist whose work has appeared in the prestigious *New Yorker* magazine for over three decades. Before turning to illustration and cartooning, he worked in advertising and graphic design in New York City, his adopted home. Known for his ironic, and sometimes cynical take on modern life, McCall's detailed artwork, which he has characterized as both "faux nostalgia" and "retrofuturism," draws on the stylized images of the 1930s and 1940s while satirizing the belief that the modern world will be improved by technology. In addition to *New Yorker* essays and covers, humor collections, and the memoir *Thin Ice: Coming of Age in Canada,* McCall has also produced the children's book *Marveltown.*

Born in 1935, McCall was raised in rural Ontario, and he recalls collecting the trash tossed from cars with U.S. license plates that sped through his hometown of Simcoe. As a teen artist, he invented a fantastical universe complete with futuristic modes of transport inspired by postwar advances in technology and dreams of the future. McCall's less-than-idyllic childhood, together with his fascination with everything American, eventually propelled him south; after a stint illustrating promotional literature for the Ford Motor Company in Detroit, he moved east to New York City and a career in advertising.

During the 1970s McCall decided to take his cartoon work freelance. A contract with *National Lampoon* led to other illustration opportunities, and in time his work could be found in *Esquire* and *Playboy*. It also fount its way into the *New Yorker,* which, McCall explained on the Macmillan Books Web site, he considered to be "the Everest of the magazine world, cold and distant and resistant to uneducated clods like myself, despite a lifetime of readership and persistent daydreams of glory in its vaunted pages." In fact, it was the *New Yorker* and its roster of stellar cartoonists that had originally fueled McCall's pen-and-ink ambitions as a youngster in Simcoe.

While living and working in New York City, McCall became keenly aware of the differences in the way he and his colleagues perceived the world as a result of his rural Canadian upbringing. He began to write a memoir about growing up Canadian, and the result was 1997's *Thin Ice*. In the book, McCall avoids the characteristic humorous jabs at Canadian dialogue and provincialism; instead, he recounts his bleak and somewhat impoverished small-town childhood as one of six children and ends his story with his decision to drop out of high school and use his talent for art to fuel his flight to Detroit and then Manhattan.

As readers learn in *Thin Ice,* McCall inherited his wanderlust from his parents, who had once dreamed of escaping their small-town life. However, the McCall's became stuck in Simcoe due to the economic depression of the 1930s and by their growing brood, and the elder McCall was notable for his temper while his wife escaped from her unhappiness through books and alcohol. The McCall family finally moved to Toronto after World War II. Now a lonely teenager, Bruce spent his time drawing cartoons and accompanying texts, eventually creating the cultural pastiche that comprised the imaginary country of Punerania. Reviewing *Thin Ice* for *Maclean's,* Joe Chidley described the memoir as "an eloquent, often bitter" autobiography that, while tinged with a "lingering expat resentment," is also "moving."

The fantasy world of Punerania provided the inspiration for the images that McCall collects in *Zany Afternoons, and Other Glimpses of the Golden Age of Play,* a book published in 1982. An assemblage of the artist's drawings that were culled from periodicals such as the *National Lampoon* and *Esquire, Zany Afternoons, and Other Glimpses of the Golden Age of Play* treats readers to glimpses of a mid-twentieth-century world that never quite was—but perhaps should have been. In one image, for example, McCall creates a pastoral Central Europe setting in which rifle-toting men in full hunting regalia take aim at giant airborne zeppelins cruising across the sky. He accompanies his art with a series of essays that describe the cultural underpinnings of each fantastic vision. Reviewing the book for the *New York Times Book Review,* Christopher Lehmann-Haupt described *Zany Afternoons* as a "coolly elegant lampoon of the excesses of American commerce."

McCall returns to Punerania in his children's book *Marveltown,* a story that gives free rein to the artist's wry mix of nostalgia and pragmatism. In the book, he takes readers to a community that values ingenuity and creativity. Floating skyways, rocket-jumpers, a mechanical zoo, skis that fly, holograms, robot helpers to do all the hard work: Marveltown is the culmination of the futuristic fantasy shared by many during the Atomic era of the 1950s. Every Saturday, the children of Marveltown flock to the Invent-o-Drome, where they can access the materials, robot helpers, and hand tools needed to tinker to their heart's content. Then a mouse bites a wire at Robot Central Command, and the resulting short circuit makes the Invent-o-Drome robots uncontrollable, destructive, and a threat to Marveltown. With the grown ups now in hiding, it is up to the town's inventive children to channel their smarts and some nifty new technology to save their town.

Featuring McCall's characteristic detailed paintings, done in gouache on paper and evoking in the glossy, mid-century style that made such an impact on McCall

Bruce McCall shares his love of mid-twentieth-century marvels in his self-illustrated picture book **Marveltown.** (Copyright © 2008 by Bruce McCall. All rights reserved. Reproduced by permission of Farrar, Straus & Giroux.)

as a youth, *Marveltown* was described by *Booklist* contributor Ian Chipman as "a lighthearted romp through the possibilities of the unbounded imagination." Praising the book's "nifty illustrations," a *Publishers Weekly* critic cited McCall's use of "superprecise brush strokes and streamlined shapes," noting that the artwork "suggest[s] a mid-20th-century architect's rendering." In *School Library Journal* Catherine Callegari wrote that McCall's "nostalgic-looking" paintings exude "vitality, and humor," and his energetic story "will get kids thinking of their own inventions," while a *Kirkus Reviews* writer characterized McCall's creative vision as "*Star Wars* meets *The Jetsons,* a place where if you can imagine it, you can make it happen."

Biographical and Critical Sources

BOOKS

McCall, Bruce, *Thin Ice: Coming of Age in Canada,* Random House (New York, NY), 1997.

PERIODICALS

Booklist, January 1, 1998, review of *Thin Ice: Coming of Age in Canada,* p. 732; November 1, 2008, Ian Chipman, review of *Marveltown,* p. 48.
Books in Canada, September, 1997, Phil Surguy, review of *Thin Ice* and interview with McCall, pp. 12-14.
Globe & Mail (Toronto, Ontario, Canada), June 5, 1997, Pamela Cuthbert, "Reborn in the U.S.A.: Identity Crisis," pp. C1-C2; June 14, 1997, review of *Thin Ice,* p. D16; December 4, 2003, Jessica Johnson, "The Cartoonist of Woe," p. R3.
Kirkus Reviews, September 1, 2008, review of *Marveltown.*
Library Journal, January 1, 1983, interview of *Zany Afternoons, and Other Glimpses of the Golden Age of Play,* p. 52; May 1, 1997, review of *Thin Ice,* p. 114.
Maclean's, June 23, 1997, Joe Chidley, review of *Thin Ice,* p. 61.
New Yorker, September 22, 1997, review of *Thin Ice,* p. 139.
New York Times, June 12, 1997, review of *Thin Ice;* August 4, 1997, William Grimes, interview with McCall, pp. B1, C11.
New York Times Book Review, December 19, 1982, Christopher Lehman-Haupt, review of *Zany Afternoons, and Other Glimpses of the Golden Age of Play,* p. 8; December 15, 2001, Ihsan Taylor, review of *The Last Dream-o-Rama: The Cars Detroit Forgot to Build,* p. 19.
Publishers Weekly, September 24, 1982, interview of *Zany Afternoons, and Other Glimpses of the Golden Age of Play,* p. 70; April 21, 1997, interview with McCall and review of *Thin Ice,* p. 52; July 7, 2003, review of *All Meat Looks like South America: The World of Bruce McCall,* p. 66; August 18, 2008, review of *Marveltown,* p. 61.
School Library Journal, October, 1997, Francisca Goldsmith, review of *Thin Ice,* p. 162; September, 2008, Catherine Callegari, review of *Marveltown,* p. 154.
Tribune Books (Chicago, IL), July 27, 1997, review of *Thin Ice,* p. 6.

ONLINE

Macmillan Web site, http://us.macmillan.com/ (December 20, 2009), "Bruce McCall,"
TED Web site, http://www.ted.com/talks/ (May, 2008), "Bruce McCall's Faux Nostalgia" (video).

OTHER

Thin Ice (documentary film), directed by Laurence Green, 2000.

*   *   *

McCAULEY, Adam 1965-

Personal

Born December 23, 1965, in Berkeley, CA; son of Gardiner (a painter, professor, and foundation director) and Nancy (an art-history slide librarian, installation artist, and teacher) McCauley; married Cynthia Wigginton (a designer and musician). *Education:* Parsons School of Design, B.F.A., 1987. *Hobbies and other interests:* Playing music (drums, guitar, bass), singing.

Addresses

Home—San Francisco, CA. *Agent*—Dutch Uncle, 1-5 Clerkenwell Rd., 1st Fl. E., London EC1M 5PA, England. *E-mail*—info@adammccauley.com.

Career

Freelance illustrator. Performer in bands, includin Bermuda Triangle Service. Member, Picture Mechanics. *Exhibitions:* Work included in Society of Illustrators member shows, New York, NY, beginning 1996, and at shows in Osaka, Japan, 1997, San Francisco, CA, 1998, and Tokyo, Japan, 1999.

Awards, Honors

Awards from Society of Illustrators, *American Illustration,* and *Print;* Gold Medal, Society of Illustrators, 2009.

Writings

SELF-ILLUSTRATED

My Friend Chicken, Chronicle Books (San Francisco, CA), 1998.

Adam McCauley (Photograph by Joanne Wigginton. Reproduced by permission.)

ILLUSTRATOR

Dan Yaccarino, *The Lima Bean Monster,* Walker Books (New York, NY), 2001.

Charles Ghinga, *Halloween Night: Twenty-one Spooktacular Poems,* Running Press Kids (Philadelphia, PA), 2003.

Lisa Broadie Cook, *Martin MacGregor's Snowman,* Walker (New York, NY), 2003.

Louis Sachar, *Sideways Stories from Wayside School,* revised edition, HarperTrophy (New York, NY), 2005.

Louis Sachar, *Wayside School Is Falling Down*, revised edition, HarperTrophy (New York, NY), 2005.

Louis Sachar, *Wayside School Gets a Little Stranger*, revised edition, HarperTrophy (New York, NY), 2005.

Mark Shulman, *Mom and Dad Are Palindromes: A Dilemma for Words—Backwards,* Chronicle Books (San Francisco, CA), 2006.

Richard Michelson, *Oh No, Not Ghosts!,* Harcourt (Orlando, FL), 2006.

Bobbi Katz, *The Monsterologist: A Memoir in Rhyme,* Sterling Publishing (New York, NY), 2009.

Vivian Walsh, *June and August,* Harry Abrams (New York, NY), 2009.

Contributor of illustrations to periodicals.

ILLUSTRATOR; "TIME WARP TRIO" SERIES

Jon Scieszka, *See You Later, Gladiator,* Viking (New York, NY), 2000.

Jon Scieszka, *Hey Kid, Want to Buy a Bridge?,* Viking (New York, NY), 2001.

Jon Scieszka, *Sam Samurai,* Viking (New York, NY), 2001.

Jon Scieszka, *Viking It and Liking It,* Viking (New York, NY), 2002.

Jon Scieszka, *Me Oh Maya!,* Viking (New York, NY), 2003.

Jon Scieszka, *Da Wild, Da Crazy, Da Vinci,* Viking (New York, NY), 2004.

Jon Scieszka, *Oh Say, I Can't See,* Viking (New York, NY), 2005.

Jon Scieszka, *Marco? Polo!,* Viking (New York, NY), 2006.

ILLUSTRATOR; "GYM SHORTS" CHAPTER-BOOK SERIES

Betty Hicks, *Basketball Bats,* Roaring Brook Press (New York, NY), 2008.

Betty Hicks, *Goof-off Goalie,* Roaring Brook Press (New York, NY), 2008.

Betty Hicks, *Swimming with Sharks,* Roaring Brook Press (New York, NY), 2008.

Vivian Walsh, *June and August,* Abrams Books for Young Readers (New York, NY), 2009.

Betty Hicks, *Scaredy-cat Catcher,* Roaring Brook Press (New York, NY), 2009.

Sidelights

Working from his studio in San Francisco, Adam McCauley creates illustrations for magazines, advertising, and children's books that features stories that benefit from his whimsical humor. McCauley's stylized images feature heavy black accents and have a distinctly retro and slightly unsettling feel; as a *Kirkus Reviews* writer noted in reviewing his work for Lisa Broadie Cook's *Martin MacGregor's Snowman,* McCauley's "mixed-media" illustrations "add to the absurdity, with cartoon-style drawings stressing Martin's fiendish and somewhat devilish mood," while a *Publishers Weekly* critic hailed the artist's "tempestuous watercolors, which feature sinuous curves, explosive diagonals and dark, choppy outlines reminiscent of linocuts." McCauley's other book illustration projects include *Oh No, Not Ghosts!,* a collaboration with author Richard Michelson, and Mark Shulman's *Mom and Dad Are Palindromes: A Dilemma for Words—and Backwards,* an imaginative, high-energy picture book that was designed by McCauley's wife, Cynthia Wigginton.

McCauley's art was first introduced to children in his original picture book *My Friend Chicken,* which was published in 1998. His unique style has also proved to be a perfect match for John Scieszka's irreverent "Time Warp Trio" novels, about three middle-schoolers whose adventures through time play out in books such as *See You Later, Gladiator, Viking It and Liking It, Me Oh*

Maya!, and *Da Wild, Da Crazy, Da Vinci.* McCauley's pen-and-ink spot art for *Da Wild, Da Crazy, Da Vinci* is effective in "enticing a transitional-reader audience," stated *School Library Journal* critic Debbie Whitbeck, and in *Booklist* Kay Weisman dubbed his illustrations for *Me Oh Maya!* "appropriately goofy."

McCauley's artwork also adds to the popularity of Betty Hicks's "Gym Shorts" series of easy-readers geared for sports-minded children. In the first installment in the series, *Basketball Bats,* Henry and his five friends must change their strategy when they confront a dishonest team on the basketball court. A *Kirkus Reviews* writer cited "McCauley's expressive spot illustrations" as an effective counterpoint to the book's "breezily simple text," while in *Horn Book* Robin L. Smith concluded that the artist's "pencil sketches . . . add . . . meaning and interest to the entertaining" tale. Reviewing *Swimming with Sharks* in *Booklist,* Gillian Engberg also praised McCauley, commenting that his "lighthearted, stylized sketches" "reinforce . . . all the action and emotion" in Hicks's story.

McCauley once told *SATA:* "Having been raised by two artists, my inclinations toward the visual arts have al-ways been number one. My mother encouraged me to read Dr. Seuss, Beatrix Potter, and Richard Scarry, while my dad pushed Maurice Sendak, J.R.R. Tolkien, and perhaps my favorite, the 'Oz' books. I consider myself a far more developed illustrator than writer, so I look at writing as my big challenge. I've had the extraordinary honor now of illustrating books by Dan Yaccarino and Jon Scieszka, whose skills with words make drawing easy. In the future I hope to make books that will encourage kids to use their imaginations and learn to appreciate the world around them."

Biographical and Critical Sources

PERIODICALS

Booklist, January 1, 2001, Gillian Engberg, review of *See You Later, Gladiator,* p. 961; November 1, 2001, Gillian Engberg, review of *Sam Samurai,* p. 475; December 1, 2002, Karin Snelson, review of *Viking It and Liking It,* p. 668; September 1, 2003, Gillian Engberg, review of *Halloween Night: Twenty-one Spooktacular*

McCauley's cartoon art appears in a range of books that include Betty Hicks's beginning reader Scaredy-Cat Catcher. (Illustration copyright © 2008 by Adam McCauley. Reprinted by permission of Henry Holt & Company, LLC.)

Poems, p. 134; September 15, 2003, Kay Weisman, review of *Me Oh Maya,* p. 241; September 15, 2008, Gillian Engberg, review of *Swimming with Sharks,* p. 58.

Horn Book, July-August, 2008, Robin L. Smith, review of *Basketball Bats,* p. 448.

Kirkus Reviews, September 15, 2003, review of *Halloween Night,* p. 1174; October 1, 2003, review of *Martin MacGregor's Snowman,* p. 1221; June 1, 2006, review of *Mom and Dad Are Palindromes,* p. 580; August 1, 2006, review of *Oh, No, Not Ghosts!,* p. 792; May 1, 2008, review of *Baseball Bats.*

Print (annual), 1999, "Culture Shock."

Publishers Weekly, April 26, 1999, review of *My Friend Chicken,* p. 80; July 30, 2001, review of *The Lima Bean Monster,* p. 84; November 24, 2003, review of *Martin MacGregor's Snowman,* p. 64; July 10, 2006, review of *Mom and Dad Are Palindromes: A Dilemma for Words—and Backwards,* p. 81.

School Library Journal, September, 2001, Sally R. Dow, review of *The Lima Bean Monster,* p. 209; December, 2003, Pat Leach, review of *Me Oh Maya,* p. 125; December, 2004, Debbie Whitbeck, review of *Da Wild, Da Crazy, Da Vinci,* p. 122; August, 2006, Linda Ludke, review of *Oh, No, Not Ghosts!,* p. 93.

ONLINE

Adam McCauley Home Page, http://www.adammccauley. com (December 15, 2009).

Picture Mechanics Web site, http://www.picturemechanics. com/ (December 15, 2009), "Adam McCauley."

Seven Impossible Things before Breakfast Web site, http:// blaine.org/sevenimpossiblethings/ (October 20, 2009), "Adam McCauley."

*   *   *

McLAUGHLIN, Lauren

Personal

Married Andrew Woffinden; children: Adelina. *Education:* Holy Cross College, B.A., 1989; attended New York University. *Hobbies and other interests:* Running, dancing, baking, and composing music.

Addresses

Home and office—Brooklyn, NY.

Career

Writer, producer, and screenwriter. Work in the film industry includes production assistant, beginning 1991.

Writings

Cycler, Random House (New York, NY), 2008.
(Re)Cycler, Random House (New York, NY), 2009.

Adaptations

Cycler was optioned by Angryfilms.

Sidelights

While working in the film industry, Lauren McLaughlin wrote what would become her first novel, *Cycler.* Although she intended it for film, the screenplay version of *Cycler* was never picked up. Eventually transitioning from screenplays to fiction, McLaughlin wrote two other novels before returning to the manuscript and turning the screenplay into a novel.

Unlike other adolescent girls, Jill McTeague does not menstruate normally each month. During the four days prior to each cycle, Jill becomes Jack, and her body fully transforms into a teenage boy. This is the premise of *Cycler,* and the action picks up when Jack decides that he no longer wants to be locked away as a hidden part of Jill. In addition to the problems faced by its central character, McLaughlin's story also questions gender identity and sexuality as both the Jill and Jack personas pursue their romantic interests. Calling Jill's trials "truly terrible PMS," a *Kirkus Reviews* critic added that the novel is "touched with intrigue, humor and fascinating

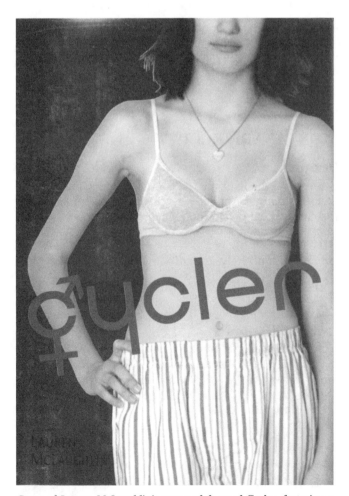

Cover of Lauren McLaughlin's young-adult novel Cycler, *featuring a photograph by Andrew Woffinden.* (Jacket photograph copyright © 2008 by Andrew Woffinden. Reproduced by permission of Random House, an imprint of Random House Children's Books.)

questions." *Cycler* "is humorous, the friendships believable, the dialogue entertaining," Myrna Marler concluded in *Kliatt,* while Jennifer Schultz wrote in *School Library Journal* that McLaughlin's "writing is witty without being overly precious or self-conscious."

The premise of *Cycler* continues to play out in the sequel, *(Re)Cycler,* as Jill and Jack move to Brooklyn. A *Kirkus Reviews* contributor described the second installment in McLaughlin's continuing "journey of self-discovery" as "funny, heartwarming and just a little bit smutty."

Biographical and Critical Sources

PERIODICALS

Kirkus Reviews, July 1, 2008, review of *Cycler;* July 1, 2009, review of *(Re)Cycler.*
Kliatt, July, 2008, Myrna Marler, review of *Cycler,* p. 18.
New York Times Book Review, September 14, 2008, review of *Cycler,* p. 17.
Publishers Weekly, June 9, 2008, review of *Cycler,* p. 51.
School Library Journal, August, 2008, Jennifer Schultz, review of *Cycler,* p. 128.

ONLINE

Lauren McLaughlin Home Page, http://www.laurenmclaughlin.net (December 17, 2009).*

*   *   *

MONTANARI, Eva 1977-

Personal

Born 1977, in Rimini, Italy. *Education:* Graduate of State Institute of Applied Arts (Riccione, Italy), and European Institute of Design (Milan, Italy).

Addresses

Home—Rimini, Italy. *E-mail*—info@evamontanari.com.

Career

Artist.

Awards, Honors

Bologna Children's Book Fair selections, 2000, 2001, 2002, 2003; Alpi Apuane award, 2002, for *The Crocodile's True Colors;* Illustration Prize of Cento, 2003; *Tiff, Taff, and Lulu* selected for Society of Illustrators original art show, 2004.

Writings

SELF-ILLUSTRATED

The Crocodile's True Colors, Watson-Guptill (New York, NY), 2002.
Dino Bikes, North-South Books (New York, NY), 2004.

Tiff, Taff, and Lulu, Houghton Mifflin (Boston, MA), 2004.
Go Cart Number One, Gareth Stevens (Milwaukee, WI), 2005.
A Very Full Morning, Houghton Mifflin (Boston, MA), 2006.
Carlo Castlecrusher, Purple Bear (New York, NY), 2006.
My First—, Houghton Mifflin (Boston, MA), 2007.

ILLUSTRATOR

Josephine Nobisso, *Show, Don't Tell!: Secrets of Writing,* Gingerbread House (Westhampton Beach, NY), 2004.

Sidelights

Eva Montanari is an artist whose work has been exhibited throughout her native Italy. She also has created a number of picture books for children, including *The Crocodile's True Colors, Tiff, Taff, and Lulu,* and *A Very Full Morning.*

In Montanari's *The Crocodile's True Colors,* a school full of African animals is asked by their teacher to draw a picture of the crocodile they can see in a nearby river. Each animal draws the crocodile in a different style that serves as an example of a modern art movement. Dada, expressionism, cubism, futurism, and abstractionism are among those movements illustrated by the young artists. When one frustrated student throws his paints into the river, the crocodile becomes covered in many colors. Angry, the reptile comes out of the water to draw his own pictures: of the students. Montanari "does a fine job of explaining difficult art concepts to the very young," wrote Gillian Engberg in her *Booklist* review of *The Crocodile's True Colors.*

Three monster sisters cannot get along in Montanari's *Tiff, Taff, and Lulu.* Each sister sees herself as getting less attention from Mother than the others do. When their mother is injured in a motor accident, however, the three sisters must put aside their bickering and help her get well. "The narrative is enhanced by dreamy illustrations," wrote Linda L. Walkins in the *School Library Journal* review of *Tiff, Taff, and Lulu.* In her picture book, "Montanari invents a family with whom many youngsters can identify," according to a *Publishers Weekly* critic.

In *A Very Full Morning* Montanari tells of a nerve-wracking first day of school. A rabbit named Little Tooth is very nervous about going to school. She cannot sleep the night before, she is scared as she follows the other rabbits into the school building, and she is nervous as she takes her seat in class. It is only then that the reader discovers that Little Tooth is actually a new teacher who is worried about meeting her first students. Linda Staskus, writing in *School Library Journal,* called *A Very Full Morning* "a clever twist on first-day jitters," and a *Publishers Weekly* critic predicted that "youngsters will relish this story full of fun while appreciating its comforting message."

Biographical and Critical Sources

PERIODICALS

Booklist, December 1, 2002, Gillian Engberg, review of *The Crocodile's True Colors,* p. 675.

Children's Bookwatch, September, 2004, review of *Show, Don't Tell!: Secrets of Writing,* p. 1.

Horn Book, September-October, 2004, Lauren Adams, review of *Tiff, Taff, and Lulu,* p. 573.

Kirkus Reviews, July 15, 2004, review of *Tiff, Taff, and Lulu,* p. 691; October 15, 2007, review of *My First—.*

Library Media Connection, January, 2003, review of *The Crocodile's True Colors,* p. 80.

Publishers Weekly, July 26, 2004, review of *Tiff, Taff, and Lulu,* p. 53; August 7, 2006, review of *A Very Full Morning,* p. 58.

School Library Journal, November, 2002, Kathleen Simonetta, review of *The Crocodile's True Colors,* p. 132; September, 2004, Kathleen Kelly MacMillan, review of *Dino Bikes,* p. 175, and Linda L. Walkins, review of *Tiff, Taff, and Lulu,* p. 175; October, 2004, Gloria Koster, review of *Show, Don't Tell!,* p. 146; August, 2006, Amy Lilien-Harper, review of *Carlo Castlecrusher,* p. 94; October, 2006, Linda Staskus, review of *A Very Full Morning,* p. 120.

ONLINE

Cynsations Web site, http://cynthialeitichsmith.blogspot.com/ (November 14, 2005), Cynthia Leitich Smith, "Interview with Josephine Nobisso on *Show, Don't Tell!.*"

Eva Montanari Home Page, http://www.evamontanari.com (April 15, 2008).

Gingerbread House Web site, http://gingerbreadbooks.com/ (April 15, 2008), "Eva Montanari."*

N-O

NAYLOR, Phyllis Reynolds 1933-
(P.R. Tedesco)

Personal

Born January 4, 1933, in Anderson, IN; daughter of Eugene S. (a salesperson) and Lura (a teacher) Reynolds; married (marriage ended); married Rex V. Naylor (a speech pathologist), May 26, 1960; children: (second marriage) Jeffrey Alan, Michael Scott. *Education:* Joliet Junior College, diploma, 1953; American University, B.A. (clinical psychology), 1963. *Religion:* Unitarian Universalist. *Hobbies and other interests:* Playing piano, hiking, baking bread, drama, swimming, spending time with family.

Addresses

Home—Bethesda, MD. *Agent*—John Hawkins & Associates, Inc., 71 W. 23rd St., Ste. 1600, New York, NY 10010.

Career

Educator and author. Elementary school teacher in Hazel Crest, IL, 1956; Montgomery County Education Association, Rockville, MD, assistant executive secretary, 1958-59; National Education Association, Washington, DC, editorial assistant for *NEA Journal,* 1959-60; full-time writer, beginning 1960. Active in civil rights and peace organizations.

Member

Society of Children's Book Writers and Illustrators, Authors Guild, Authors League of America, Children's Book Guild (president, 1974-75, 1983-84).

Awards, Honors

Children's Book of the Year designation, Child Study Association of America, 1971, for *Wrestle the Mountain;* Golden Kite Award for nonfiction, Society of Chil-

Phyllis Reynolds Naylor (Photograph by Lee M. Friedman. Reproduced by permission.)

dren's Book Authors, 1978, and International Reading Association (IRA) Children's Choice citation, 1979, both for *How I Came to Be a Writer;* Children's Book of the Year designation, Child Study Association of America, 1979, and IRA Children's Choice citation, 1980, for *How Lazy Can You Get?;* American Library Association (ALA) Young Adult Services Division (YASD) Best Book for Young Adults citation, and Notable Children's Book in the Field of Social Studies citation, National Council for Social Studies, both 1982, and South Carolina Young-Adult Book Award, 1985-86,

all for *A String of Chances;* Child Study Award, Bank Street College, 1983, for *The Solomon System;* ALA Notable Book citation, 1985, and IRA Children's Choice citation, 1986, both for *The Agony of Alice;* Edgar Allan Poe Award, Mystery Writers of America, 1985, for *Night Cry,* 2003, for *Bernie Magruder and the Bats in the Belfry;* Notable Children's Book in the Field of Social Studies citation, 1985, for *The Dark of the Tunnel;* YASD Best Book for Young Adults citation, 1986, for *The Keeper* and *Unexpected Pleasures;* creative writing fellowship grant, National Endowment for the Arts, 1987; YASD Best Book for Young Adults citation, 1987, and Best Young Adult Book of the Year, Michigan Library Association, 1988, both for *Year of the Gopher;* Society of School Librarians International Book Award, 1988, for *Maudie in the Middle;* Christopher Award, 1989, for *Keeping a Christmas Secret;* ALA Notable Book for Young Adults citation, 1989, for *Send No Blessings,* and 1998, for *Outrageously Alice;* Hedda Seisler Mason Award, Enoch Pratt Free Library, 1991, for *Alice in Rapture, Sort Of;* Newbery Medal, 1992, for *Shiloh;* Dorothy Canfield Fisher Award, 1993; Kerlan Award, University of Minnesota Kerlan Collection, 1995, for body of work; Appalachian Medallion for distinguished writing, University of Charleston, 1997; Heartland Award, 2003, for *Jade Green;* numerous state and child-selected awards (twenty-six for *Shiloh* alone).

Writings

PICTURE BOOKS

Jennifer Jean, the Cross-eyed Queen, illustrated by Harold K. Lamson, Lerner, 1967.

The New Schoolmaster, illustrated by Mamoru Funai, Silver Burdett, 1967.

A New Year's Surprise, by Jack Endewelt, Silver Burdett, 1967.

Meet Murdock, illustrated by Gioia Fiammenghi, Follett (New York, NY), 1969.

The Boy with the Helium Head, illustrated by Kay Chorao, Atheneum (New York, NY), 1982.

Old Sadie and the Christmas Bear, illustrated by Patricia Montgomery, Atheneum (New York, NY), 1984.

The Baby, the Bed, and the Rose, illustrated by Mary Stilagyi, Atheneum (New York, NY), 1987.

Keeping a Christmas Secret, illustrated by Lena Shiffman, Atheneum (New York, NY), 1989.

King of the Playground, illustrated by Nola Langner Malone, Atheneum (New York, NY), 1991.

Ducks Disappearing, illustrated by Tony Maddox, Atheneum (New York, NY), 1996.

I Can't Take You Anywhere, illustrated by Jef Kaminsky, Atheneum (New York, NY), 1997.

Sweet Strawberries, illustrated by Rosalind Charney Kaye, Atheneum (New York, NY), 1999.

Please Do Feed the Bears, illustrated by Ana Lopez Escriva, Atheneum (New York, NY), 2002.

JUVENILE FICTION

What the Gulls Were Singing, illustrated by Jack Smith, Follett (New York, NY), 1967.

To Shake a Shadow, Abingdon (Nashville, TN), 1967.

When Rivers Meet, Friendship, 1968.

To Make a Wee Moon, Follett (New York, NY), 1969.

Making It Happen, Follett (New York, NY), 1970.

Wrestle the Mountain, Follett (New York, NY), 1971.

No Easy Circle, Follett (New York, NY), 1972.

To Walk the Sky Path, Follett (New York, NY), 1973.

Walking through the Dark, Atheneum (New York, NY), 1976.

How Lazy Can You Get?, illustrated by Alan Daniel, Atheneum (New York, NY), 1979.

Eddie, Incorporated, illustrated by Blanche Sims, Atheneum (New York, NY), 1980.

All Because I'm Older, illustrated by Leslie Morrill, Atheneum (New York, NY), 1981.

A String of Chances, Atheneum (New York, NY), 1982.

The Solomon System, Atheneum (New York, NY), 1983.

Night Cry, Atheneum (New York, NY), 1984.

The Dark of the Tunnel, Atheneum (New York, NY), 1985.

The Keeper, Atheneum (New York, NY), 1986.

The Year of the Gopher, Atheneum (New York, NY), 1987.

Beetles, Lightly Toasted, Atheneum (New York, NY), 1987.

(With mother, Lura Schield Reynolds) *Maudie in the Middle,* illustrated by Judith Gwyn Brown, Atheneum (New York, NY), 1988.

One of the Third Grade Thonkers, illustrated by Walter Gaffney-Kessell, Atheneum (New York, NY), 1988.

Send No Blessings, Atheneum (New York, NY), 1990.

Josie's Troubles, illustrated by Shelley Matheis, Atheneum (New York, NY), 1992.

The Fear Place, Atheneum (New York, NY), 1994.

Being Danny's Dog, Atheneum (New York, NY), 1995.

Ice, Atheneum (New York, NY), 1996.

Danny's Desert Rats (sequel to *Being Danny's Dog*), Atheneum (New York, NY), 1998.

Sang Spell, Atheneum (New York, NY), 1998.

Walker's Crossing, Atheneum (New York, NY), 1999.

Jade Green: A Ghost Story, Atheneum (New York, NY), 2000.

The Great Chicken Debacle, Marshall Cavendish (New York, NY), 2001.

Blizzard's Wake, Atheneum (New York, NY), 2002.

Roxie and the Hooligans, illustrated by Alexandra Boiger, Atheneum Books for Young Readers (New York, NY), 2006.

Cricket Man, Atheneum Books for Young Readers (New York, NY), 2008.

Faith, Hope, and Ivy June, Delacorte Press (New York, NY), 2009.

Emily's Fortune, Delacorte Press (New York, NY), 2010.

"WITCH" SERIES

Witch's Sister, illustrated by Gail Owens, Atheneum (New York, NY), 1975.

Witch Water, illustrated by Gail Owens, Atheneum (New York, NY), 1977.

The Witch Herself, illustrated by Gale Owens, Atheneum (New York, NY), 1978.

The Witch's Eye, illustrated by Joe Burleson, Delacorte (New York, NY), 1990.

Witch Weed, illustrated by Joe Burleson, Delacorte (New York, NY), 1991.

The Witch Returns, illustrated by Joe Burleson, Delacorte (New York, NY), 1992.

"YORK" TRILOGY

Shadows on the Wall, Atheneum (New York, NY), 1980.

Faces in the Water, Atheneum (New York, NY), 1981.

Footprints at the Window, Atheneum (New York, NY), 1981.

"BESSLEDORF"/"BERNIE MAGRUDER" SERIES

The Mad Gasser of Bessledorf Street, Atheneum (New York, NY), 1983, published as *Bernie Magruder and the Big Stink,* Aladdin (New York, NY), 2001.

The Bodies in the Bessledorf Hotel, Atheneum (New York, NY), 1986, published as *Bernie Magruder and the Disappearing Bodies,* Aladdin (New York, NY), 2001.

Bernie and the Bessledorf Ghost, Atheneum (New York, NY), 1990, published as *Bernie Magruder and the Haunted Hotel,* Aladdin (New York, NY), 2000.

The Face in the Bessledorf Funeral Parlor, Atheneum (New York, NY), 1993, published as *Bernie Magruder and the Drive-Thru Funeral Parlor,* Aladdin (New York, NY), 2000.

The Bomb in the Bessledorf Bus Depot, Atheneum (New York, NY), 1996, published as *Bernie Magruder and the Bus Station Blow-up,* Aladdin (New York, NY), 2001.

The Treasure of Bessledorf Hill, Atheneum (New York, NY), 1997, published as *Bernie Magruder and the Pirate's Treasure,* Aladdin (New York, NY), 2001.

Peril in the Besseldorf Parachute Factory, Atheneum (New York, NY), 1999, published as *Bernie Magruder and the Parachute Peril,* Aladdin (New York, NY), 2001.

Bernie Magruder and the Bats in the Belfry, Atheneum (New York, NY), 2003.

"ALICE" NOVEL SERIES

The Agony of Alice (also see below), Atheneum (New York, NY), 1985.

Alice in Rapture, Sort Of (also see below), Atheneum (New York, NY), 1989.

Reluctantly Alice (also see below), Atheneum (New York, NY), 1991.

All but Alice (also see below), Atheneum (New York, NY), 1992.

Alice in April, Atheneum (New York, NY), 1993.

Alice In-Between, Atheneum (New York, NY), 1994.

Alice the Brave, Atheneum (New York, NY), 1995.

Alice in Lace, Atheneum (New York, NY), 1996.

Outrageously Alice, Atheneum (New York, NY), 1997.

Achingly Alice, Atheneum (New York, NY), 1998.

Alice on the Outside, Atheneum (New York, NY), 1999.

The Grooming of Alice, Atheneum (New York, NY), 2000.

Alice Alone, Atheneum (New York, NY), 2001.

Starting with Alice, Atheneum (New York, NY), 2002.

Simply Alice, Atheneum (New York, NY), 2002.

Patiently Alice, Atheneum (New York, NY), 2003.

Alice in Blunderland, Atheneum (New York, NY), 2003.

Including Alice, Atheneum (New York, NY), 2004.

Lovingly Alice, Atheneum (New York, NY), 2004.

Alice on Her Way, Atheneum Books for Young Readers (New York, NY), 2005.

Alice in the Know, Atheneum Books for Young Readers (New York, NY), 2006.

Dangerously Alice, Atheneum Books for Young Readers (New York, NY), 2007.

Almost Alice, Atheneum Books for Young Readers (New York, NY), 2008.

Intensely Alice, Atheneum Books for Young Readers (New York, NY), 2009.

The Agony of Alice, Alice in Rapture, Sort Of, Reluctantly Alice, and *All but Alice* were released in a boxed set as *The World of Alice.*

"SHILOH" NOVEL TRILOGY

Shiloh (also see below), Atheneum (New York, NY), 1991.

Shiloh Season (also see below), Atheneum (New York, NY), 1996.

Saving Shiloh (also see below), Atheneum (New York, NY), 1997.

The Shiloh Collection (contains *Shiloh, Shiloh Season,* and *Saving Shiloh*), Atheneum (New York, NY), 2004.

"CAT PACK" CHAPTER-BOOK SERIES

The Grand Escape, illustrated by Alan Daniel, Atheneum (New York, NY), 1993.

The Healing of Texas Jake (sequel to *The Grand Escape*), illustrated by Alan Daniel, Atheneum (New York, NY), 1997.

Carlotta's Kittens and the Club of Mysteries, Atheneum (New York, NY), 2000.

Polo's Mother, Atheneum (New York, NY), 2005.

"BOYS VERSUS GIRLS" MIDDLE-GRADE NOVEL SERIES

The Boys Start the War, Delacorte (New York, NY), 1993.

The Girls Get Even, Delacorte (New York, NY), 1993.

Boys against Girls, Delacorte (New York, NY), 1994.

The Girls' Revenge, Delacorte (New York, NY), 1998.

A Traitor among the Boys, Delacorte (New York, NY), 1999.

A Spy among the Girls, Delacorte (New York, NY), 2000.

The Boys Return, Delacorte (New York, NY), 2001.

The Girls Take Over, Delacorte (New York, NY), 2002.

Boys in Control, Delacorte (New York, NY), 2003.

Girls Rule!, Delacorte (New York, NY), 2004.

Boys Rock!, Delacorte (New York, NY), 2005.

Who Won the War?, Delacorte (New York, NY), 2006.

"SIMPLY SARAH" CHAPTER-BOOK SERIES

Anyone Can Eat Squid!, illustrated by Marcy Ramsey, Marshall Cavendish (New York, NY), 2005.

Cuckoo Feathers, illustrated by Marcy Ramsey, Marshall Cavendish (Tarrytown, NY), 2006.

Patches and Scratches, illustrated by Marcy Ramsey, Marshall Cavendish (New York, NY), 2007.

Eating Enchiladas, illustrated by Marcy Ramsey, Marshall Cavendish (New York, NY), 2008.

SHORT FICTION

The Galloping Goat, and Other Stories, illustrated by Robert L. Jefferson, Abingdon (Nashville, TN), 1965.

Grasshoppers in the Soup: Short Stories for Teen-agers, Fortress Press (Minneapolis, MN), 1965.

Knee-Deep in Ice Cream, and Other Stories, Fortress Press (Minneapolis, MN), 1967.

The Dark Side of the Moon, Fortress Press (Minneapolis, MN), 1969.

The Private I and Other Stories, Fortress Press (Minneapolis, MN), 1969.

Ships in the Night, Fortress Press (Minneapolis, MN), 1970.

A Change in the Wind, Augsburg Press (Minneapolis, MN), 1980.

Never Born a Hero, Augsburg Press (Minneapolis, MN), 1982.

A Triangle Has Four Sides, Augsburg Press (Minneapolis, MN), 1984.

JUVENILE NONFICTION

How to Find Your Wonderful Someone, How to Keep Him/ Her if You Do, How to Survive if You Don't, Fortress Press (Minneapolis, MN), 1972.

An Amish Family, illustrated by George Armstrong, J. Philip O'Hara, 1974.

Getting Along in Your Family, illustrated by Rick Cooley, Abingdon (Nashville, TN), 1976.

How I Came to Be a Writer, Atheneum (New York, NY), 1978, revised edition, Aladdin Books (New York, NY), 1987.

Getting Along with Your Friends, illustrated by Rick Cooley, Abingdon (Nashville, TN), 1980.

Getting Along with Your Teachers, illustrated by Rick Cooley, Abingdon (Nashville, TN), 1981.

OTHER

Crazy Love: An Autobiographical Account of Marriage and Madness (nonfiction), Morrow (New York, NY), 1977.

In Small Doses (essays), Atheneum (New York, NY), 1979.

Revelations (adult novel), St. Martin's (New York, NY), 1979.

Unexpected Pleasures (adult novel), Putnam (New York, NY), 1986.

The Craft of Writing the Novel (nonfiction), The Writer, 1989.

After (adult novel), Soho (New York, NY), 2003.

Under pseudonym P.R. Tedesco, author of humorous essay column for church magazines for twenty-five years. Contributor to numerous newspapers and magazines.

Naylor's papers are housed at the de Grummond Collection, University of Southern Mississippi, and the Kerlan Collection, University of Minnesota.

Adaptations

The Keeper was adapted as the ABC Afterschool Special *My Dad Can't Be Crazy, Can He? Shiloh* was adapted as a feature film, 1997; *Shiloh Season* was adapted as a feature film, 1999. Audio recordings of *Shiloh, Shiloh Season,* and *Saving Shiloh* were released by Bantam Doubleday Dell Audio Publishing, 1992, 1997, and 1999, respectively; unabridged sound recordings of *Alice the Brave* and *The Fear Place* were released by Recorded Books, 1996. Audio recordings of *Sang Spell* and *Walker's Crossing* were released by Bantam Doubleday Dell Audio Publishing, 1999 and 2000, respectively. Sound recordings by American Audio Prose Library were made of Naylor reading from her own works: excerpts from *The Agony of Alice* and *The Keeper* were recorded in 1987; excerpts from *Unexpected Pleasures* were recorded, 1987. *The Agony of Alice* was adapted for film as *Alice Upside Down,* Anchor Bay, 2008.

Sidelights

A prolific author who is often celebrated both for her versatility and for the diversity of her works, Phyllis Reynolds Naylor writes award-winning books for children, teens, and adult readers that span genres and styles. She is the creator of novels, short stories, picture books, and nonfiction for children as well as of fiction and nonfiction for adults. As a writer for young people, Naylor has earned fans ranging from preschool through high school, captivating then through fiction in popular genres such as historical fiction, the gothic novel, mysteries, time-travel fantasy, and problem novels. Her works for older readers sensitively treat serious issues while her picture books and chapter books capture the humorous, lighthearted aspects of life. Naylor is perhaps best known as the author of *Shiloh,* a Newbery Award-winning novel for middle graders about a West Virginia boy and an abused dog that sparked several sequels. Another popular series, her "Alice" books, span the middle-grade and YA categories as they follow the life of a girl growing to adulthood in contemporary times.

Naylor's fiction usually features young people facing adversity and their own fears on their way to self-actualization and maturity. Addressing moral, religious, psychological, and family issues, she writes about such

subjects as mental and physical illness, loss of faith, crib death, war, and sex. Consequently, some of Naylor's books have been regarded as controversial, and a few have even been banned by school libraries. Although she often writes about the difficulties of living, Naylor presents young readers with a positive, optimistic view of life and a philosophy that stresses the acceptance of both one's self and others. Interestingly, she often includes autobiographical elements in her works. Writing in *Horn Book,* her husband Rex Naylor commented: "Life-affirming and positive, Phyllis has nevertheless used writing to work through all manner of vexing concerns about herself, her work, family, and friends."

Praised for her acute observations of human nature as well as for her sympathetic understanding of the young, Naylor is noted for her appealing characterizations and evocations of place. Although initially her prose was often considered crisp but pedestrian, she has developed into a well-regarded, craftsmanlike writer with a distinctive voice. In *Twentieth-Century Children's Writers,* John D. Stahl commented that, "from comedy to tragedy, from books for younger children to books for older young adults, in novels with rural settings or urban landscapes, from fantasy to realism, she reveals a fine

Cover of Naylor's novel **Faith, Hope, and Ivy June,** *featuring artwork by Ericka O'Rourke.* (Cover art © 2009 by Ericka O'Rourke. Reproduced by permission of Delacorte Press, an imprint of Random House Children's Books.)

sense of the unexpected difficulties and rewards of life." "Symptomatic of Naylor's vision," Stahl continued, "is her willingness to present religious, ethical, and psychological issues without a hidden . . . agenda, but simply with honesty and sensitivity." Deborah Stevenson, commenting in the *Bulletin of the Center for Children's Books,* deemed Naylor "one of our best writers of everyday junior-high life."

Born in Anderson, Indiana, Naylor grew up in a home that treasured the arts. Her parents, a traveling salesman and a primary school teacher, had met at Anderson College, where they were both involved in dramatic productions. As she and her siblings grew up during the Great Depression of the 1930s, they did not have much, but they did have books: a family collection that included two volumes of Grimm's fairy tales, Egermeier's *Bible Story Book, Child-Rhymes* by James Whitcomb Riley, *Missionary Stories for Little Folks,* a set of Sherlock Holmes detective stories, the complete works of Mark Twain, a set of Collier's encyclopedias, and a book about righteous living. "My mother, and sometimes my father, read to us each night till we were well into our teens, though I would never have admitted it to anyone," Naylor once recalled.

In school, Naylor became known for her writing talent. In fifth grade, for example, she was called upon to write a poem in twenty minutes that would be read aloud at a school assembly in honor of her principal's birthday. However, as the author later observed in *How I Came to Be a Writer,* "I never considered myself 'bookish.'" An active child, she preferred arts and crafts and playing with her friends. She also began going to religious revival meetings at around age nine and later would explore her views on faith in several of her books.

At age sixteen, Naylor published her first story, a tale about baseball that was printed in a church-school paper edited by one of her former Sunday school teachers. "Send me more, my teacher-turned-editor said," the author later recalled, and Naylor obliged, turning out holiday poems, adventure stories, and morality tales. Deciding to expand her market, she sent her writings to youth magazines such as *Highlights for Children, Seventeen,* and *Jack and Jill;* after two years of rejection letters, she developed what she called "a new respect for the business of writing." However, a weekly column she wrote for a church paper—humor for teenagers written from the viewpoint of a fifteen-year-old boy—continued for twenty-five years and appeared in church magazines throughout the United States. In her senior year, Naylor was selected as class poet; writing in an essay for *Something about the Author Autobiographical Series (SAAS),* she commented, "[I] am convinced that I won because no one else wanted the job."

Although Naylor loved writing, she considered it merely a hobby and pondered full-time careers in teaching and clinical psychology. At the age of eighteen, she married a young man from her hometown who was eight years

her senior. After graduating from junior college, she moved to Chicago with her husband, who was working on his Ph.D. While he was in school, Naylor worked as a clinical secretary in a university hospital and then as a third-grade teacher. She also began reading the plays of Shakespeare and books by such authors as Dickens, Tolstoy, Chaucer, Dostoevski, Steinbeck, Faulkner, and Freud. "But always," the author noted in *How I Came to Be a Writer,* "when I wasn't working and wasn't reading, I wrote."

When Naylor was twenty-three, her husband began showing signs of severe mental illness. For the next three years, Naylor noted, "while we moved from state to state, hospital to hospital, I wrote in earnest and in panic to support us. . . . Not all of the ideas were workable, of course, but I was able to use enough of them to pay the rent and buy our food." In retrospect, she realized that this period "is still very sad to me, but it also made me think, you know, I'm really stronger than I thought. . . . And sometimes when I'm facing something difficult I have to say to myself 'Hey, I went through that, I can go through this.' And so, there is something to be said for weathering storms and becoming stronger." After hospitalizing her husband at a sanitarium in Maryland, it became clear to Naylor that his paranoid schizophrenia was incurable. After their divorce became final, Naylor went back to college with the intention of becoming a clinical psychologist. In 1977, she published *Crazy Love: An Autobiographical Account of Marriage and Madness* as a chronicle of her experience.

In 1960, Naylor married Dr. Rex Naylor, a speech pathologist, and the couple has raised two children, Jeffrey and Michael. In 1965, Naylor published her first book, *The Galloping Goat, and Other Stories,* a collection of tales originally published in magazines. Since then she has published over a hundred books and thousands of stories and articles. While a select few authors for children may have written more than Naylor, few have been as warmly and consistently praised for their work. It is this consistency that makes the quantity of Naylor's published work all the more remarkable.

Naylor's first novel for children, *What the Gulls Were Singing,* was published in 1967 and describes how a ten-year-old middle child learns about the love of her family and community during a beach holiday. After its publication, Naylor began to write an average of two books per year. Settling with her husband in Bethesda, Maryland, she was not far from Marbury, Maryland, an area familiar to her from childhood visits to her paternal grandparents. She uses Marbury as the setting for one of her most popular—and controversial—books: *A String of Chances.*

Published in 1982, *A String of Chances* features sixteen-year-old Evie Hutchins, the daughter of a small-town fundamentalist preacher. Evie begins to question her faith, and her doubts are intensified when her cousin's baby dies of SIDS; eventually, Evie comes to grips with his death and embarks upon what *Booklist* critic Sally Estes described as "a search for a God in whom she can believe." Estes concluded that the story's scenes and themes "all smoothly converge and interlock to give [it] vivid dimension . . . and . . . delineate the individuals within it. The effect is totally involving and moving." Writing in *School Library Journal,* Roger Sutton called Naylor's style "sensible and warm, but not florid," and added that her "handling of a large cast of characters is skillful, and her depiction of contemporary small-town life is exact and evocative, without sentimentality." Naylor used her grandparents as the models for the parents in *A String of Chances.*

Another of Naylor's distinguished early books, *Night Cry,* is a mystery that won her the first of her two Edgar Allan Poe awards from the Mystery Writers of America. In this 1985 novel, thirteen-year-old Ellen Stump, a motherless girl living on a backwoods farm in Mississippi, faces her fears to rescue a small boy from a husband-and-wife team of kidnappers. Writing in *Booklist,* Carolyn Phelan noted that, "so skillful is Naylor's portrayal of Ellen that aspects of the background and plot are convincing, seen through the girl's eyes." Charlotte W. Draper, commenting in *Horn Book,* observed that the "sense of place integral to the author's fiction provides the backdrop for Ellen's suspenseful struggle" in *Night Cry.*

The Keeper, a young-adult novel published two years after *Night Cry,* is also considered one of Naylor's best works. Based loosely on the author's adult nonfiction book *Crazy Love, The Keeper* depicts the struggles of teenager Nick Karpinski as he watches his father's descent into mental illness. Mr. Karpinski refuses to get help, while Mrs. Karpinski refuses to acknowledge her husband's symptoms. Although Nick feels helpless and is filled with anguish, he recognizes his father's problem and, despite his difficulties at home, makes friends and even goes on a successful first date. At the end of the novel, Mr. Karpinski's condition deteriorates to a point where hospitalization is the only alternative. Writing in *Booklist,* Denise M. Wilms commented that *The Keeper* "is a sensitively wrought novel with no happy ending but certainly with an affirmation of individual strength and emotional survival in the face of adversity." A reviewer in the *Bulletin of the Center for Children's Books* noted that Naylor's "focus on the problem is unrelenting, but the story is grippingly detailed, with characters emerging full-dimensional rather than being cast into roles of typical reactions." Ann A. Flowers, writing in *Horn Book,* noted that the author is "extremely adept at showing us the destruction of comfort and happiness and the horror and misery of having someone we know and love turn into a frightening, suspicious stranger." Flowers deemed *The Keeper* a book "of considerable power."

Throughout her career, Naylor has written several well-regarded fiction series for both middle-grade and older readers. The "Bessledorf" stories, also called the

"Bernie Magruder" series, are humorous mysteries that center on the adventures of young Bernie Magruder, whose father is the manager of the Bessledorf Hotel in Middleburg, Indiana. The "Witch" gothic fiction series features Lynn Morley, a brave young girl who, with her best friend Marjorie (nicknamed Mouse), battles the evil Mrs. Tuggle, a witch who threatens their peaceful Indiana neighborhood. The "York" trilogy offers supernatural fantasies for young adults in which fifteen-year-old Dan Roberts becomes involved with several generations of gypsies he meets in York, England, who may know if he and his father have the genes for Huntington's disease.

Naylor's most popular series focuses on Alice McKinley, a motherless girl whom Naylor depicts at various ages and stages of development, from grade school on through the awkward middle-school years and into high school and beyond. In the "Alice" books, the protagonist longs for a female role model, learns about relationships with boys, tries to establish her popularity as a young teen, conquers her fear of swimming, learns about her changing body, deals with the suicide of a classmate, and grows into a thoughtful and mature

Cover of Naylor's young-adult novel **Achingly Alice,** *featuring artwork by Kam Mak.* (Atheneum Books, 1998. Illustration © 1998 by Kam Mak. Reproduced by permission of the illustrator.)

young woman. Reviewers have appreciated both the humor and poignancy of the series, acknowledging Alice as an especially charming character and favorably comparing Naylor to Betsy Byars for the freshness and authenticity of her series, which is noted for growing in sophistication as its heroine progresses.

Naylor produces at least one book about Alice each year, sometimes more, drawing inspiration from memories of her own youth as well as from talking to teenaged girls and listening to their interactions. She also pays close attention to topical issues affecting young women, from eating disorders to self-esteem and teen pregnancy, and her candid exploration of these and sexual topics sometimes arouses controversy. In several cases, certain "Alice" books have been removed from school libraries for their frank discussion of puberty and its physical and psychological changes. Naylor relies on e-mails sent to her Web site and the letters she receives from readers—male and female—who have learned about adolescence from Alice's trials and triumphs. "I believe in honesty and telling kids what they need to know (about) what they ask," she told an interviewer for Missouri's *Springfield News-Leader.* "I'm going to keep on doing that."

Most reviewers find Alice to be an engaging, realistic, and heartfelt character with whom girls can identify and from whom boys can learn about the opposite sex. In *Booklist,* Hazel Rochman remarked of *Alice in the Know,* the twenty-first book in the series, that the author "avoids heavy messages, even as she dramatizes hard, contemporary issues with pitch perfect dialogue." In *School Library Journal* Catherine Threadgill called Alice "a favorite young adult heroine," and in her *Bulletin of the Center for Children's Books* review of *Alice the Brave,* Deborah Stevenson stated that "There's nobody quite like Alice, yet she's like everybody." Stevenson concluded her review of *Achingly Alice* by commenting: "Alice fans will be grateful that, aching or not, Alice is everlastingly Alice."

Naylor's Newbery Award-winning novel *Shiloh* and its two sequels, *Shiloh Season* and *Saving Shiloh,* feature young Marty Preston and his beagle Shiloh, who live in modern rural West Virginia. In the "Shiloh" stories, Marty rescues the runaway dog and hides it from its abusive owner, Judd Travers. Marty blackmails Judd and makes a deal with him to keep the dog, faces the consequences of his bargain, makes peace with Judd after an accident, and ends up defending the man against accusations of murder and robbery. At the conclusion of *Saving Shiloh,* a novel published in 1997, Judd saves Shiloh—the dog he formerly abused—from drowning. In assessing the first novel in the series, reviewers noted the ethical questions that Naylor explores in the book, such as the nature of the truth, and praised her suspenseful plot and rounded characterizations. In her review of *Shiloh* in *Horn Book,* Elizabeth S. Watson commented that the adventures of a boy and his dog almost always make an appealing story, but "when the boy

Cover of Naylor's award-winning middle-grade novel Shiloh, *which finds a young boy risking much to keep an abused puppy from harm.* (Yearling Books, 1992. Used by permission of Dell Publishing, a division of Random House, Inc.)

faces a very difficult decision and takes a giant step toward maturity, the story acquires depth and importance." The critic ended her review by quoting Marty: "I saved Shiloh and opened my eyes some. Now that ain't bad for eleven."

A critic in *Kirkus Reviews* called *Shiloh* a "gripping account" and declared that "young readers will rejoice that Shiloh and Marty end up together," while Betsy Hearne commented in the *Bulletin of the Center for Children's Books* that young readers will be "absorbed by the suspenseful plot, which will leave them with some memorable characterizations as well as several intriguing questions." Writing for *Booklist,* Ellen Mandel noted that "Naylor offers a moving and powerful look at the best and the worst of human nature as well as the shades of gray that color most of life's dilemmas."

Writing in *Horn Book* about *Shiloh Season,* Elizabeth S. Watson noted that Marty's voice "is consistently strong and true" and that fans of *Shiloh* "will be well served by the sequel." A reviewer in *Publishers Weekly* concluded that Naylor's "sympathy for her characters . . . communicates itself almost invisibly to the reader, who

may well come away hoping for a full-fledged Shiloh series." Although the story's focus blurs and the dialogue "sounds right out of made-for-TV movies," a critic in *Kirkus Reviews* concluded that readers "will find Marty's anxiety, and his love for Shiloh, engrossingly genuine." Writing in *Booklist,* Mandel called the third volume of the series, *Saving Shiloh,* a "masterfully written conclusion to a sterling trilogy." In his *Horn Book* review, Roger Sutton wrote that the book's strongest virtue is "its sure evocation, without quaintness or sentimentality, of contemporary rural life."

Naylor has gained a loyal following among middle-grade and younger readers through her "Shiloh" books as well as more lighthearted series, such as her "Boys versus Girls" series and her "Simply Sarah" chapter books. With tongue planted firmly in cheek, she chronicles the ongoing neighborhood feud between the three Malloy girls and the four Hatford boys of Buckman, West Virginia in her "Boys versus Girls" novels. These conniving grade-schoolers go to great lengths to get the best of each other, one gender triumphing in one novel, the other in the next—and both enjoying the thrill of the competition in each outing. In *The Girls Take Over,* for instance, the Malloy and Hatford siblings team up to see who can float a message bottle farther down river from their home. Needless to say, the plot hinges on the various acts of sabotage they try to enact on each others' bottles, and the ways in which these attempts go awry. *Boys Rock!* finds the two factions warring over words: the rival newspapers each group of siblings decides to start over one summer vacation. *Booklist* contributor Todd Morning called "Boys and Girls" a "sweet-natured series," and Shelle Rosenfeld agreed in the same periodical, dubbing *Boys Rock!* another installment in "the ongoing ultimately good natured feud."

Naylor's "Simply Sarah" chapter-book series focuses on an urban animal lover and her attempts to be helpful. Matching friends who desire pets with animals that are in need of a good home is the dilemma in *Patches and Scratches,* for example, as Peter longs for a dog, but the apartment where he and his family live prohibits large pets. Noting the lighthearted nature of Nolan's "Simply Sarah" books, *Booklist* critic Hazel Rochman cited the "fast and easy" dialogue and "fun" adult characters in *Patches and Scratches.* The "kindhearted compassion" of Sarah, as well as the girl's "dogged determination to resolve dilemmas," will attract young readers, predicted a *Kirkus Reviews* contributor, appraising the same book.

With so many series running simultaneously, it is all the more phenomenal that Naylor also writes well-received stand-alone novels. In *Sang Spell,* Josh Vardy loses his way deep in Appalachia and winds up in a community of Melungeons, a people who seem forgotten by time. Orphaned himself, Josh must decide whether he wants to stay in this warm community or return to the outside world. *Walker's Crossing* is set on a ranch in Wyoming

Naylor weaves fantasy with a little-known facet of American history in her novel **Sang Spell**, *which features artwork by Jana Duda.* (Atheneum, 1998. Illustration © by Jana Duda. Reproduced by permission of the illustrator.)

and explores the troubling moral issues facing Ryan Walker when his older brother joins a racist militia movement and deals with the murderous consequences. Fifteen-year-old Kate Sterling must overcome the hatred and bitterness she feels toward the man who killed her mother in a drunken driving accident as the events unfold in *Blizzard's Wake*. A *Publishers Weekly* critic stated that *Blizzard's Wake* "pulses with drama" as its protagonist makes her "slow movement toward forgiveness."

A horror movie inspired Naylor to write *Jade Green: A Ghost Story,* a Gothic tale of murder and ghostly revenge. Taken in by her eccentric uncle in South Carolina, Judith Sparrow wonders why she is not allowed to bring anything green into the man's huge home. Only after she disobeys her uncle's command does she realize that she has awakened the spirit of another young girl who was brutally killed in the home. In the *Journal of Adolescent and Adult Literacy,* James Blasingame noted of *Jade Green* that "readers who enjoy a good ghost story will love this one, especially if they require a truly horrific supernatural being."

Cricket Man, another novel for young teens, finds eighth-grader Kenny Sykes aspiring to super-hero sta-

tus. Although his life does not present many opportunities to rescue others, Kenny imagines that he is Cricket Man, and he occupies himself with rescuing crickets from a watery death in the family swimming pool. When his help is required from a true-to-life damsel in distress (wealthy next-door neighbor and high-schooler Jodie Poindexter), who seeks his confidence, Kenny finds that he may not be up to the challenge in what Phelan described as "an involving novel by a fine story-teller." Also focusing on middle schoolers, *Faith, Hope, and Ivy June* follows two Kentucky teens—poor, rural-born Ivy June Mosley and affluent city girl Catherine Combs—as they exchange lives for two weeks during a school exchange program. "Readers will connect to these engaging girls and celebrate as they learn they are 'more alike than different,'" concluded Lynn Rutan in her *Booklist* review of the novel, while a *Publishers Weekly* critic hailed *Faith, Hope, and Ivy June* as a "reflective, resonant novel" crafted from the girls' "thoughtful, articulate journal entries."

As an author of nonfiction, Naylor writes instructional books about such subjects as relationships and writing as a profession. In *How I Came to Be a Writer* she demonstrates the development of a literary work from inception to publication while including personal examples and career advice. Writing in *Horn Book,* Karen M. Klockner noted that the book "presents an interesting personal account of what it is like to be a professional writer." Another instructional book, *The Craft of Writing the Novel,* is an informational book for adults. Throughout her career, Naylor has commented on the satisfaction she has received from her profession, once telling *SATA:* "Writing, for me, is the best occupation I can think of, and there is nothing in the world I would rather do."

In *How I Came to Be a Writer* Naylor also describes her work habits. "I already know what my next five books will be, and this is probably the way it will be for the rest of my life," she explains. "On my deathbed, I am sure, I will gasp, 'But I still have five more books to write!' . . . I am happy and miserable and excited and devastated and encouraged and depressed all at the same time. But accepted or rejected, I will go on writing, because an idea in the head is like a rock in the shoe; I just can't wait to get it out."

Biographical and Critical Sources

BOOKS

Children's Literature Review, Volume 17, Gale (Detroit, MI), 1989.

Naylor, Phyllis Reynolds, *How I Came to Be a Writer,* Atheneum (New York, NY), 1978, revised edition, Aladdin Books (New York, NY), 1987.

Silvey, Anita, editor, *Children's Books and Their Creators,* Houghton Mifflin (Boston, MA), 1995.

Something about the Author Autobiography Series, Volume 10, Gale (Detroit, MI), 1990.

Stover, Lois Thomas, *Presenting Phyllis Reynolds Naylor,* Twayne (New York, NY), 1997.

Twentieth-Century Young-Adult Writers, St. James (Detroit, MI), 1994.

PERIODICALS

Booklist, August, 1982, Sally Estes, review of *A String of Chances,* p. 1518; July, 1984, Carolyn Phelan, review of *Night Cry,* p. 1550; April 1, 1986, Denise M. Wilms, review of *The Keeper,* p. 1144; December 1, 1991, Ellen Mandel, review of *Shiloh,* p. 696; May 1, 1994, Hazel Rochman, review of *Alice In Between,* p. 1601; September 1, 1997, Ellen Mandel, review of *Saving Shiloh,* p. 118; June 1, 2000, Hazel Rochman, review of *The Grooming of Alice,* p. 1880; December 15, 2001, Todd Morning, review of *The Boys Return,* p. 732; June 1, 2002, Hazel Rochman, review of *Simply Alice,* p. 1708; October 15, 2002, Ed Sullivan, review of *Blizzard's Wake,* p. 401; November 1, 2004, Hazel Rochman, review of *Lovingly Alice,* p. 486; December 1, 2004, Hazel Rochman, review of *Girls Rule!,* p. 653; June 1, 2005, Julie Cummins, review of *Polo's Mother,* p. 1814; October 1, 2005, Shelle Rosenfeld, review of *Boys Rock!,* p. 59; May 1, 2006, Hazel Rochman, review of *Alice in the Know,* p. 81; November 1, 2006, Carolyn Phelan, review of *Who Won the War?,* p. 50; March 1, 2007, Hazel Rochman, review of *Patches and Scratches,* p. 83; April 1, 2007, Hazel Rochman, review of *Dangerously Alice,* p. 41; August 1, 2008, Carolyn Phelan, review of *Cricket Man,* p. 59; May 1, 2009, Hazel Rochman, review of *Intensely Alice,* p. 78; May 15, 2009, Lynn Rutan, review of *Faith, Hope, and Ivy June,* p. 42.

Bulletin of the Center for Children's Books, May, 1986, review of *The Keeper,* pp. 175-176; April, 1995, Deborah Stevenson, review of *Alice the Brave,* p. 283; April, 1996, Deborah Stevenson, review of *Alice in Lace,* pp. 273-274; April, 1998, Deborah Stevenson, review of *Achingly Alice,* pp. 290-291.

Horn Book, August, 1978, Karen M. Klockner, review of *How I Came to Be a Writer,* pp. 410-411; June, 1984, Charlotte W. Draper, review of *Night Cry,* p. 331; September-October, 1986, Ann A. Flowers, review of *The Keeper,* pp. 598-599; January-February, 1992, Elizabeth S. Watson, review of *Shiloh,* pp. 78-79; July-August, 1992, Rex Naylor, "Phyllis Reynolds Naylor," pp. 412-415; December, 1996, Elizabeth S. Watson, review of *Shiloh Season,* pp. 737-738; September-October, 1997, Roger Sutton, review of *Saving Shiloh,* p. 576; July, 2000, review of *The Grooming of Alice,* p. 463; July-August, 2004, Kitty Flynn, review of *Including Alice,* p. 458; November-December, 2004, Kitty Flynn, review of *Lovingly Alice,* p. 714; March-April, 2006, Vicky Smith, review of *Roxie and the Hooligans,* p. 193; July-August, 2007, Kitty Flynn, review of *Dangerously Alice,* p. 400; July-August, 2008, Kitty Flynn, review of *Almost Alice,* p. 454.

Journal of Adolescent and Adult Literacy, March, 2003, James Blasingame, "An Interview with Phyllis Reynolds Naylor," p. 525; review of *Jade Green,* p. 529.

Kirkus Reviews, September 1, 1991, review of *Shiloh,* p. 1163; July 15, 1995, review of *Shiloh Season,* p. 1053; May 15, 2005, review of *Alice on Her Way,* p. 593; March 1, 2007, review of *Patches and Scratches,* p. 229; August 15, 2008, review of *Cricket Man.*

Kliatt, January, 2004, Claire Rosser, review of *Achingly Alice,* p. 18; May, 2004, Paula Rohrlick, review of *Including Alice,* p. 12; May, 2006, Claire Rosser, review of *Alice in the Know,* p. 12; May, 2007, Claire Rosser, review of *Dangerously Alice,* p. 17.

New York Times Book Review, May 10, 1992, Jane Langton, review of *Shiloh,* p. 21.

Publishers Weekly, July 1, 1996, review of *Shiloh Season,* p. 60; February 14, 2000, "An Impressive Output by Phyllis Reynolds Naylor," p. 116; October 28, 2002, review of *Blizzard's Wake,* p. 73; August 25, 2003, review of *Alice in Blunderland,* p. 64; February 20, 2006, review of *Roxie and the Hooligans,* p. 156; June 15, 2009, review of *Faith, Hope, and Ivy June,* p. 49.

School Library Journal, September, 1982, Roger Sutton, review of *A String of Chances,* p. 142; February, 2000, Patricia J. Fontes, "Good Conversation!: A Talk with Phyllis Reynolds Naylor," p. 60; May, 2000, Dina Sherman, review of *The Grooming of Alice,* p. 175; December, 2002, Susan Cooley, review of *Blizzard's Wake,* p. 146; September, 2003, Catherine Threadgill, review of *Alice in Blunderland,* p. 218; May, 2004, Angela M. Boccuzzi, review of *Including Alice,* p. 156; September, 2004, Tina Zubak, review of *Lovingly Alice,* p. 213; May, 2005, Debbie Whitbeck, review of *Polo's Mother,* and Tina Zubak, review of *Alice on Her Way,* both p. 134; January, 2006, Tina Zubak, review of *Boys Rock!,* p. 139; August, 2006, Catherine Ensley, review of *Alice in the Know,* p. 126; September, 2006, Rebecca Sheridan, review of *Who Won the War?,* p. 214; August, 2007, Joyce Adams Burner, review of *Dangerously Alice,* p. 122; May, 2008, Jessie Spalding, review of *Almost Alice,* p. 134; October, 2008, Catherine Ensley, review of *Cricket Man,* p. 156

Springfield News-Leader (Springfield, MO), September 15, 2002, Angela Wilson, "Banned Books Week Hits Close to Home," p. B1.

ONLINE

Alice Web site, http://www.simonsays.com/alice/ (December 20, 2009).

Children's Book Guild Web site, http://www.childrens bookguild.org/ (June 19, 2004), "Phyllis Reynolds Naylor."

Houghton Mifflin Web site, http://www.eduplace.com/kids/ (December 20, 2009), "Phyllis Reynolds Naylor."

Simon & Schuster Web site, http://www.simonandscuster. biz/ (December 20, 2009), "Phyllis Reynolds Naylor."

OTHER

Phyllis Reynolds Naylor (sound recording; interview with Kay Bonetti), American Audio Prose Library, 1987.*

NICHOLLS, Sally 1983-

Personal

Born June 22, 1983, in Stockton-on-Tees, England. *Education:* University of Warwick, B.A. (philosophy), Bath Spa University, M.F.A. (writing for young people). *Hobbies and other interests:* Travel.

Addresses

Home—London, England. *Agent*—Rosemary Canter, United Agents, 130 Shaftesbury Ave., London W1D 5EU, England.

Career

Author.

Awards, Honors

Orange New Voices Children's Prize, 2006, for short story; Waterstone's Children's Book Prize, Glen Dimplex New Writer of the Year Award, and (with Birgitt Kollmann) Luchs des Jahres, *Die Ziet* (German newspaper), all 2008, and Bolton Book Award, North East Book Award, Catherdale Book of the Year designation, Branford Boase Award shortlist, Deutscher Jugendliteraturpreis shortlist, Lancashire Book of the Year award shortlist, UKLA Award shortlist, and Redbridge Book Award shortlist, all 2009, all for *Ways to Live Forever.*

Writings

Ways to Live Forever, Arthur A. Levine Books (New York, NY), 2008.
Season of Secrets, Scholastic UK (London, England), 2009.

Adaptations

Ways to Live Forever was adapted as an audiobook, read by Charlotte Parry, Recorded Books, 2008, and a feature film, directed by Gustavo Ron, 2010.

Sidelights

Sally Nicholls' first novel, *Ways to Live Forever,* gained her the notice of both readers and critics alike when the novel won several major awards in both her native United Kingdom and Germany, and was adapted for a feature film. Nicholls, then a recent M.F.A. graduate, had written the novel at age twenty-three; its success has allowed her to pursue a dream that is shared by many but rarely achieved: the opportunity to devote her full time to her writing.

"I've always loved reading," Nicholls noted on her home page, "and I spent most of my childhood trying to make real life as much like a book as possible. . . . I was a real tomboy—I liked riding my bike, climbing trees and building dens in our garden. And I liked making up stories. I used to wander round my school playground at break, making up stories in my head." After secondary school, Nicholls took some time out to travel around Australia and New Zealand, then worked at a Red Cross hospital in Japan for several months before returning to England and beginning her college education. A bachelor's degree in philosophy at the University of Warwick was followed by a master's degree in writing for children, and an award for being the student writer with the most potential earned Nicholls an agent. Her student manuscript, *Ways to Live Forever,* became her first published book.

In *Ways to Live Forever* eleven-year-old Sam has leukemia. Death is a fact of life for Sam, and his natural curiosity makes him wonder about all manner of things in the world that he will never experience, from traveling in space to running up a down escalator. Nicholls' novel, written in the first person and framed as Sam's scrapbook diary, chronicles the last two months of the boy's life. The book is scattered with sketches, tickets and other ephemera, and lists of Sam's many questions as well as lists of the facts that defined his tenuous life. Through the boy's diary, readers also experience the

Cover of Sally Nicholls' novel Ways to Live Forever, *featuring artwork by Jutte Klee.* (Jacket photo © by Jutta Klee/Corbis. Reproduced by permission of Scholastic, Inc.)

emotions of Sam's mother, father, and nine-year-old sister Ella, all of whom deal with the imminence of the boy's death in different ways.

Comparing *Ways to Live Forever* with Katherine Patterson's classic novel *Bridge to Terabithia*, Wendy Smith-D'Arezzo called Nicholls' fiction debut "well-researched and beautifully written," and Sarah Ellis wrote in *Horn Book* that "the energy and joy of this novel is a remarkable feat." A *Kirkus Reviews* contributor praised the author for skillfully avoid[ing] . . . bathos at every turn," predicting that "readers will be glad they've met [Sam] and sorry to bid farewell." Noting that "Nicholls has been either courageous or reckless" in choosing to write about the death of an engaging child character, London *Guardian* reviewer Mal Peet added that her gamble pays off for the reader. "Sam's is the voice of an unexceptional boy transformed by the enormity of what awaits him, and getting it to ring true is a hugely impressive achievement," Peet wrote, calling *Ways to Live Forever* "an elegant, intelligent, moving and sometimes even funny book."

In *Season of Secrets* Nicholls injects a thread of fantasy into her story by evoking the ancient British myth of the Green Man, a symbol of the season of re-growth. On her home page, the author explained that she wanted to retell the story of the Green Man in a modern context to make it relevant to contemporary children. "I decided to use his cycle of death and rebirth to represent the grief-story of a child whose mother has just died," Nicholls explained. "Like winter, grief isn't something that happens once and then goes away forever. But I wanted to show that hope does come back. And after writing *Ways to Live Forever,* I wanted this book to end happily."

In *Seasons of Secrets* Molly Brooke and her sister Hannah live in Northumberland, England, with their grandparents now that their mother has suddenly died. The girls' depressed father is absent much of the time, and his loss haunts Molly even more than her mother's death does. With her love of reading, Molly looks for answers in her beloved books, such as *Peter Pan* and the stories of beloved British children's writers such as Enid Blyton and Jacqueline Wilson. At dusk one evening, the girl sees a man running, avoiding the men and dogs who pursue him. Later, she discovers the man hiding in a nearby barn, and because the man seems to be invisible to everyone but her, the imaginative and grief-stricken girl links the fugitive to the ancient deity she has heard about from stories. In his review for the London *Financial Times*, James Lovegrove noted Nicholls' focus on underlying themes such as "the power of myth" and "resurrection" in her "character-driven plot." In the *Guardian*, Kathryn Hughes called *Season of Secrets* a "standout story" in which Nicholls successfully "graft[s] a story of modern childhood on to one of myth and natural magic." Through the character of Molly, the author creates "a heroine whose love of books is deep

and true," Hughes added, and her depiction of Molly's emotional growth is both "exciting" and "profound."

"I . . . try and write the sort of books that I would have liked as a child," Nicholls explained on her home page. "The things that I liked then—families, love, damaged people, bits that make me laugh—still interest me today. I always knew that I wanted to be a writer and when I was a child I had very definite ideas about what sort of books I would write. I wanted them to be real. Often, when I'm writing, I'll hear that ten-year-old voice saying, 'But that wouldn't happen!' or 'Put that in, that's real.'"

Biographical and Critical Sources

PERIODICALS

Booklist, November 15, 2008, Thom Barthelmess, review of *Ways to Live Forever*, p. 60.

Bookseller, February 15, 2008, Joel Rickett, interview with Nicholls, p. 10.

Financial Times (London, England), April 25, 2009, James Lovegrove, review of *Season of Secrets*, p. 15.

Guardian (London, England), January 26, 2008, Mal Peet, review of *Ways to Live Forever*, p. 20; April 25, 2009, Kathryn Hughes, review of *Season of Secrets*, p. 11.

Horn Book, January-February, 2009, Sarah Ellis, review of *Ways to Live Forever*, p. 99.

Kirkus Reviews, September 1, 2008, review of *Ways to Live Forever*.

Publishers Weekly, September 15, 2008, review of *Ways to Live Forever*, p. 67.

School Library Journal, November, 2008, Wendy Smith-D'Arezzo, review of *Ways to Live Forever*, p. 134.

Times (London, England), February 22, 2008, Amanda Craig, review of "Grim-lit for Kids."

ONLINE

Sally Nicholls Home Page, http://www.sallynicholls.com (December 20, 2009).*

*   *   *

ODONE, Jamison 1980-

Personal

Born 1980, in RI. *Education:* Art Institute of Boston, B.F.A., 2002; Western Connecticut State University, M.F.A., 2010.

Addresses

Home—Ridgefield, CT. *E-mail*—jamisonodone@gmail.com.

Career

Illustrator and author of books for children. Silvermine Art School, New Caanan, CT, instructor, beginning 2009; teacher at workshops; presenter at schools and libraries; lecturer. *Exhibitions:* Works exhibited at galleries, including Connecticut Commission on Culture and Tourism Gallery, Hartford, and University of Connecticut Stamford Art Gallery.

Awards, Honors

Connecticut Commission on Culture and Tourism Art state artist fellowship and grant, 2008-09.

Writings

SELF-ILLUSTRATED

Honey Badgers, Front Street (Asheville, NC), 2007.
Alice's Adventures in Wonderland ("Stickfiguratively Speaking" series; based on the story by Lewis Carroll), PublishingWorks Inc., 2010.

ILLUSTRATOR

Joy Cowley, *The Bedtime Train,* Front Street (Asheville, NC), 2008.

Sidelights

"My career as an illustrator began in Boston shortly after college in 2002," Jamison Odone told *SATA.* "Truthfully though, I was lucky enough to get a few illustration commissions while still in school. My work soon became directed towards the narrative, telling stories with pictures. In 2004, I moved to Ridgefield, Connecticut, where I met and became friends with Maurice Sendak. His advice, guidance, and friendship cemented the craft of picture books and story telling for me. I knew that it was what I wanted to be doing. Being an author and illustrator is something that I truly could not do without.

"I like to write stories that have been described as 'absurd' in theme. I enjoy the search for odd subject matter, for something that may make people scratch their heads and laugh at the same time. When writing or illustrating any kind of story, I always make it my goal to extract something from the text that the viewer may not be reading or feeling, and show it to them in my pictures. To successfully add something to the story that nobody knew needed to be there is one of the greatest honors an illustrator can pay to a good story."

Biographical and Critical Sources

PERIODICALS

Kirkus Reviews, March 1, 2007, review of *Honey Badgers,* p. 229; September 15, 2008, review of *The Bedtime Train.*

Publishers Weekly, February 19, 2007, review of *Honey Badgers,* p. 168; September 22, 2008, review of *The Bedtime Train,* p. 58.
School Library Journal, April, 2007, Lynne Mattern, review of *Honey Badgers,* p. 113; October, 2008, Julie Roach, review of *The Bedtime Train,* p. 104.

ONLINE

Jamison Odone Home Page, http://jamisonodone.word press.com (December 15, 2009).

*   *   *

O'DONNELL, Liam 1970-

Personal

Born 1970, in Northern Ireland. *Education:* Attended Ryerson University.

Addresses

Home and office—Toronto, Ontario, Canada.

Career

Writer and elementary school teacher, in Toronto, Ontario, Canada. Previously worked in film industry.

Writings

System Shock (graphic novel), illustrated by Janek Matysiak, A. & C. Black (London, England), 2000, Stone Arch (Minneapolis, MN), 2007.
A United Force, Scholastic Canada (Toronto, Ontario, Canada), 2006.
Max Finder Mystery: Collected Casebooks, three volumes, illustrated by Michael Cho, Owlkids (Toronto, Ontario, Canada), 2006–2007.
Blackbeard's Sword: The Pirate King of the Carolinas, illustrated by Mike Spoor, Stone Arch Books(Minneapolis, MN), 2007.
Democracy ("Cartoon Nation" series), illustrated by Patricia Storms, Capstone Press (Mankato, MN), 2008.
Amazing Animal Journeys, DK Publishing (New York, NY), 2008.
U.S. Immigration ("Cartoon Nation" series), illustrated by Charles Barnett III, Capstone Press (Mankato, MN), 2009.

Also author of graphic novels *Moville Mysteries* and *My Dad the Rock Star.* Developer of radio plays; adapter of television scripts; contributor to periodicals.

"PET TALES" PICTURE-BOOK SERIES

Pepper, a Snowy Search, illustrated by Cathy Diefendorf, Soundprints (Norwalk, CT), 2004.

Baxter Needs a Home, illustrated by Robert Hynes, Soundprints (Norwalk, CT), 2004.

Tracker: On the Job, illustrated by Robert Hynes, Soundprints (Norwalk, CT), 2004.

Ginger Leads the Way, illustrated by Cathy Diefendorf, Soundprints (Norwalk, CT), 2004.

Lucy and the Busy Boat, illustrated by Robert Hynes, Soundprints (Norwalk, CT), 2004.

Duncan: A Brave Rescue, illustrated by Robert Hynes, Soundprints (Norwalk, CT), 2004.

Daisy on the Farm, illustrated by Dan Hatala, Soundprints (Norwalk, CT), 2005.

Winston in the City, illustrated by Dan Hatala, Soundprints (Norwalk, CT), 2005.

Scout Hits the Trail, illustrated by Catherine Huerta, Soundprints (Norwalk, CT), 2007.

"REAL WORLD OF PIRATES" SERIES

The Pirate Code: Life of a Pirate, Capstone Press (Mankato, MN), 2007.

Pirate Gear: Cannons, Swords, and the Jolly Roger, Capstone Press (Mankato, MN), 2007.

Pirate Ships: Sailing the High Seas, Capstone Press (Mankato, MN), 2007.

Pirate Treasure: Stolen Riches, Capstone Press (Mankato, MN), 2007.

NONFICTION GRAPHIC NOVELS; "MAX AXIOM, SUPER SCIENTIST" SERIES

The Shocking World of Electricity, illustrated by Richard Dominguez and Charles Bennett III, Capstone Press (Mankato, MN), 2007.

Understanding Photosynthesis, illustrated by Richard Dominguez and Charles Barnett III, Capstone Press (Mankato, MN), 2007.

The World of Food Chains, illustrated by Cynthia Martin and Bill Anderson, Capstone Press (Mankato, MN), 2007.

"GRAPHIC GUIDE ADVENTURES" SERIES

Wild Ride, illustrated by Michael Deas, Orca (Vancouver, British Columbia, Canada), 2007.

Ramp Rats, illustrated by Michael Deas, Orca (Vancouver, British Columbia, Canada), 2008.

Soccer Sabotage, illustrated by Michael Deas, Orca (Vancouver, British Columbia, Canada), 2009.

Media Meltdown, illustrated by Michael Deas, Orca (Vancouver, British Columbia, Canada), 2009.

Sidelights

Liam O'Donnell is the author of several graphic-novel series for young readers. Since leaving the film industry in 2000 when his first graphic novel, *System Shock,* was published in his native United Kingdom, O'Donnell has authored mysteries, nonfiction titles, and adventure stories, all in the graphic-novel format.

O'Donnell has penned several chapter books about pirates for the "Real World of Pirates" series. In *Blackbeard's Sword: The Pirate King of the Carolinas* readers learn about the infamous pirate through the story of Jacob, a boy who saves Blackbeard's life only to later regret his action. In addition to the main story, O'Donnell provides an historical essay providing insight into the life of the real Blackbeard. In *School Library Journal* Kathleen Meulen recommended *Blackbeard's Sword* as "a popular choice for pirate lovers and reluctant readers alike."

O'Donnell's "Max Finder Mystery" series began as a comic strip for *Owl* magazine. Published in three volumes, each containing ten four-to six-page mysteries, the series introduces seventh grader Max Finder and his friend Allison Santos, who solve crimes in their neighborhood. Each script features a one-page puzzle, and readers are urged to solve the mysteries along with Max and Allison. The solutions are not given in the text, but readers can check the back of the book to find the correct answer. In *Resource Links* Gail de Vos noted that both heroes and villains "are regular neighbourhood kids and readers should have no problems identifying with the characters." As Sadie Mattox wrote in *School Library Journal,* the solutions to O'Donnell's mysteries are "not so easy that younger readers won't enjoy a challenge."

O'Donnell's "Graphic Guide Adventure" series combines adventure stories with tips on how to survive a crisis in the real world. In *Wild Ride* three children who are battling a corrupt logging company survive a plane crash in the Canadian wilderness. Fortunately, the children have excellent survival skills and are able to set a broken bone, start a fire, and complete other tasks. The book features diagrams that supplement their actions to show readers how their many problems are solved. Kevin King, reviewing *Wild Ride* for *Booklist,* wrote that O'Donnell's "easy-to-follow survival adventure will engage reluctant readers, especially ones curious about survival skills."

Ramp Rats continues the "Graphic Guide Adventure" series, this time offering tips for skateboarding fans. The children in this book take on corrupt small-town officials. Although finding the plot predictable, a *Kirkus Reviews* contributor commented of *Ramp Rats* that "the graphic format and step-by-step instructions on skating technique may draw in reluctant readers or young novice skaters." Writing in *Booklist,* Kat Kan recommended O'Donnell's tale for its "action-packed story, great characters, and colorful artwork."

The three young survivalists from *White Ride* return in *Soccer Sabotage,* and this time, they must solve a sports mystery. Tips on how to play soccer are included, and the story features "a solid mystery" according to Kan. The "Graphic Guide Adventure" series made a huge impact when Orca decided to release it online for free,

and O'Donnell's installment titled *Media Meltdown* was launched as a free PDF download the same day the print version was released.

Biographical and Critical Sources

PERIODICALS

Booklist, January 1, 2008, Kevin King, review of *Wild Ride,* p. 86; September 15, 2008, Kat Kan, review of *Ramp Rats,* p. 51; March 1, 2009, Kat Kan, review of *Soccer Sabotage,* p. 66.
Kirkus Reviews, September 1, 2008, review of *Ramp Rats.*
Resource Links, February, 2008, Karen Loch, review of *Wild Ride,* p. 11; October, 2008, Gail de Vos, review of "Max Finder Mystery" series, p. 8.
School Library Journal, August, 2007, Kathleen Meulen, review of *Blackbeard's Sword: The Pirate King of the Carolinas,* p. 88; April, 2008, Ann Elders, review of *The Shocking World of Electricity,* p. 83; July, 2008, Lauren Anduri, review of *Wild Ride,* p. 121; March, 2009, Lauren Anduri, review of *Ramp Rats,* p. 173; May, 2009, Sadie Mattox, review of "Max Finder Mystery" series, p. 135.

ONLINE

Liam O'Donnell Home Page, http://liamodonnell.com (December 17, 2009).
PW Comics Week Online, http://www.publishersweekly.com/ (October 19, 2009), Calvin Reid, "Orca Book Publishers' Graphic Adventure Line."*

*　　　*　　　*

ORLEAN, Susan 1955-

Personal

Born October 31, 1955, in Cleveland, OH; daughter of Arthur (a real estate developer) and Edith (a bank officer) Orlean; married John Gillespie (an investment banker), September 15, 2001; children: one son. *Education:* University of Michigan, B.A. (English literature; with honors), 1976.

Addresses

Home—Columbia County, NY; New York, NY; Los Angeles, CA. *Office*—The New Yorker, 4 Times Sq., New York, NY 10036. *Agent*—Richard S. Pine, Arthur Pine Associates, Inc., 250 W. 57th St., New York, NY 10019. *E-mail*—webmail@susanorlean.com.

Career

Journalist and writer. *Wilamette Week,* Portland, OR, reporter, c. late 1970s; *Boston Phoenix,* Boston, MA, staff writer, 1983-86; *Boston Globe,* Boston, MA, columnist,

Susan Orlean (Vince Bucci/Getty Images. Reproduced by permission.)

1986-87; *Rolling Stone,* New York, NY, contributing editor, 1987—; *New Yorker,* New York, NY, staff writer, 1987—. Freelance writer, 1987—.

Member

Authors Guild, Author's League of America, PEN.

Awards, Honors

PEN/New England Discovery Award, PEN American Center, 1984; *New York Times* Notable Book, for *Saturday Night,* 1990; six Sigma Delta Chi distinguished service awards for reporting, Society of Professional Journalists; Book of the Year designation, New York Public Library, and Book of the Year selection, American Library Association, both 1998, both for *The Orchid Thief.*

Writings

Red Sox and Bluefish: Meditations of What Makes New England New England, Faber & Faber (Winchester, MA), 1987.
Saturday Night, Knopf (New York, NY), 1990.
The Orchid Thief: A True Story of Beauty and Obsession, Random House (New York, NY), 1998.

The Bullfighter Checks Her Makeup: My Encounters with Extraordinary People, Random House (New York, NY), 2000.

My Kind of Place: Travel Stories from a Woman Who's Been Everywhere, Random House (New York, NY), 2004.

(Editor) *The Best American Essays, 2005,* Houghton Mifflin (Boston, MA), 2005.

(Editor and author of introduction) *The Best American Travel Writing 2007,* Houghton Mifflin (Boston, MA), 2007.

Throw Me a Bone: Fifty Healthy, Canine Taste-tested Recipes for Snacks, Meals, and Treats, recipes by Sally Sampson, Simon & Schuster (New York, NY), 2007.

Lazy Little Loafers (for children), illustrated by G. Brian Karas, Abrams Books for Young Readers (New York, NY), 2008.

Contributor of articles to periodicals, including the *New Yorker, Rolling Stone, Vogue, Writer,* and *Esquire.*

Adaptations

Orlean's magazine article "Surf Girls of Maui" was adapted for film by Lizzy Weiss and directed by John Stockwell as *Blue Crush,* Universal Pictures, 2002. *The Orchid Thief* was adapted for film by Charlie Kaufman and directed by Spike Jonze as *Adaptation,* Columbia Pictures, 2002.

Sidelights

A journalist, editor, and writer based in New York City, Susan Orlean credits her innate curiosity with fuelling her career. Her inclination to translate her feature articles for magazines such as the *New Yorker* and *Rolling Stone,* into book-length ruminations on contemporary life has produced *The Orchid Thief: A True Story of Beauty and Obsession, The Bullfighter Checks Her Makeup: My Encounters with Extraordinary People,* and *My Kind of Place: Travel Stories from a Woman Who's Been Everywhere,* among others. Ted Conover, writing in the *New York Times Book Review,* characterized Orleans' writing as "stylishly written, whimsical yet sophisticated, quirkily detailed and full of empathy for a person you might not have thought about empathetically before."

Born in Cleveland, Ohio, Orlean attended the University of Michigan, where she studied English literature but had no real idea of how to translate that degree into a life as a writer. After a move to Portland, Oregon, she linked up with a community newspaper and gained publishing experience, working as a feature writer and music reviewer. On the strength of her work there, she was able to sell articles to the *Rolling Stone* and *Village Voice,* establishing her career in journalism. During the early 1980s Orlean moved to Boston and wrote both for the *Boston Globe* and the city's alternative newspaper, the *Boston Phoenix.* Four years later, with two published books to her credit, she moved to New York City, got married, and earned a coveted staff position on the prestigious *New Yorker.*

Orlean's first book-length work, the essay collection *Red Sox and Bluefish: Meditations of What Makes New England New England,* details some of the unique characteristics of life in New England, including the region's distinctive language, driving habits, and cuisine. Praised for its effective combination of wit and wisdom, the work initially appeared as a series of essays Orlean wrote for the *Boston Globe.*

Moving its focus away from New England, *Saturday Night* tracks the author's travels throughout the United States—including stops in Portland, Oregon, New York City, Miami Beach, Florida, and Elkhart, Indiana—as she seeks to discover the range of activities pursued by typical Americans on a typical Saturday night. In the book, Orlean describes practices that run the gamut from cruising, bowling, and watching television to dating, dining, and drinking, as well as gambling, thieving, and murdering. While the author blends her observations with information obtained from academic authorities on human behavior, she also speculates on why many people cannot stay home on a Saturday night and why many then practice ordinary activities with more intensity. David Finkle, reviewing in the *Chicago Tribune,* described *Saturday Night* as "convivial, amusing and informative," while Scott Simon concluded in the *New York Times Book Review* that Orlean makes "mostly splendid use of the conglomeration of those moments that can steer people through the sameness of a week."

In 1994 Orlean's curiosity was captured by a newspaper article that planted the seeds of the article that grew into her book *The Orchid Thief.* The article described the theft of 200 rare orchid plants from the swamps of south Florida's Fakahatchee Strand State Preserve. The flowers were taken by amateur botanist John Laroche and several Seminole Indians to supply Laroche's nursery. When Laroche was arrested and tried for stealing the orchids, Orlean interviewed him, followed the trial, and published her impressions as the *New Yorker* article "Orchid Fever." Fascinated by the orchid-collector subculture, where a rare plant will sometimes sell for a thousand dollars, she returned to Florida and continued her research, expanding the article into *The Orchid Thief,* a book that was eventually adapted as the film *Adaptation,* starring Meryl Streep playing the part of Orlean.

In *The Orchid Thief* Laroche emerges as a disturbed personality who monomaniacally pursues one passion after another—photography, turtles, fossils, orchids, designing Web sites—and is convinced that he is smarter than anyone else. In the course of her narrative, Orlean discusses the passion for orchid collecting that swept through Victorian England, the fanaticism of contemporary orchid aficionados, the Seminoles' ongoing battle with the U.S. Government for control of their tribal lands in the Fakahatchee preserve, and the destruction of Florida's swamps by land developers. Brian Lym, writing in *Library Journal,* observed that Orlean's "nar-

rative forays underscore a central theme—the costs and consequences of the single-minded pursuit of an ideal or passion." Donna Seaman concluded in *Booklist* that, "in prose as lush and full of surprises as the Fakahatchee itself, Orlean connects orchid-related excesses of the past with exploits of the present so dramatically an orchid will never be just an orchid again."

Compiled mostly from a series of profiles Orlean originally wrote for the *New Yorker, The Bullfighter Checks Her Makeup* illuminates for readers the author's belief that extraordinary people are not always famous ones. Among the twenty individuals profiled, are designer Bill Blass, figure skater Tanya Harding, a New York cab driver who is also the king of Ghana's Ashanti tribe, Hawaiian surfer girls, a ten-year-old boy from New Jersey, and Orlean's own hairdresser. A writer in *Kirkus Reviews* commented that, while "some essays work better than others," the collection is "well-paced and good-humored; a page turner." "Orlean's curiosity, faith in improvisation, fundamental respect and fondness for humankind, and a ready sense of humor inform each of these well-crafted pieces," Seaman concluded.

Orlean's travels inspired *My Kind of Place,* in which readers follow the intrepid author to such diverse locations as a grocery store in New York's Queens neighborhood, a windy hill in Iceland, a fertility ceremony in Bhutan, the Maidenform Bra museum, a taxidermy convention, the town of Midland, Texas, and a store in

The frustrations of an older sibling are given full voice in Orlean's **Lazy Little Loafers,** *a picture book illustrated by G. Brian Karas.* (Abrams Books for Young Readers, 2008. Illustration copyright © 2008 by G. Brian Karas. Reproduced by permission.)

Paris that specializes in African music. Observing that, for Orleans, travel is as much an exploration of culture as place, a *Publishers Weekly* reviewer commended the author's essays as "rich in color, metaphor, and crafty language," while in *Booklist* Seaman wrote that *My Kind of Place* reveals Orlean to be "an adventurous journalist with a great instinct for offbeat stories, a playful sense of humor, and a dynamic prose style." The author's "sly humor perfumes her writing with a wonderful quiet crackle," wrote a *Kirkus Reviews* writer, "like pine needles on fire."

Like her books for adult readers, Orlean's first book for children, *Lazy Little Loafers,* had its roots in an article for the *New Yorker* column "Shouts and Murmers." Titled "Shiftless Little Loafers," the article features the comments of a testy child who bemoans the fact that cute infants can do no wrong while children live under the sharp eye of vigilant parents. In its picture-book adaptation, Orlean's story is paired with quirky and colorful cartoon art by G. Brian Karas and features the narrative of a young Manhattanite who has felt increasingly put-upon since the arrival of her new baby brother. The young narrator's "irresistibly ironic tirade is effectively reflected in Karas's jaunty collage illustrations," wrote Thom Barthelmess in *Booklist,* and a *Publishers Weekly* critic dubbed *Lazy Little Loafers* "one of the wittiest new-baby-in-the-family books of recent years." Also praising Orlean's tongue-in-cheek narrative, *School Library Journal* contributor Lisa Glasscock recommended *Lazy Little Loafers* "for any youngster who has wondered why the baby doesn't have to go to school."

Biographical and Critical Sources

PERIODICALS

Booklist, December 1, 1998, Donna Seaman, review of *The Orchid Thief: A True Story of Beauty and Obsession,* p. 634; October 1, 2000, Donna Seaman, review of *The Bullfighter Checks Her Makeup: My Encounters with Extraordinary People,* p. 387; September 15, 2004, Donna Seaman, review of *My Kind of Place: Travel Stories from a Woman Who's Been Everywhere,* p. 178; September 1, 2008, Thom Barthelmess, review of *Lazy Little Loafers,* p. 105.

Chicago Tribune, May 28, 1990, review of *Saturday Night.*

Economist (US), March 27, 1999, "Lifting Orchids," p. 87.

Kirkus Reviews, November 1, 2000, review of *The Bullfighter Checks Her Makeup,* p. 1533; August 1, 2004, review of *My Kind of Place;* September 1, 2008, review of *Lazy Little Loafers.*

Library Journal, January, 1999, Brian Lym, review of *The Orchid Thief,* p. 126.

New York Times, April 26, 1990, review of *Saturday Night*; January 4, 1999, Christopher Lehmann-Haupt, "Seeing with New Eyes in a World of Exotic Obsession."

New York Times Book Review, May 6, 1990, review of *Saturday Night,* p. 9; January 3, 1999, Ted Conover, "Flower Power"; November 9, 2008, Jessica Bruder, review of *Lazy Little Loafers,* p. 39.

Publishers Weekly, November 23, 1998, review of *The Orchid Thief,* p. 51; November 13, 2000, review of *The Bullfighter Checks Her Makeup,* p. 92; August 15, 2004, review of *My Kind of Place,* p. 49; July 21, 2008, review of *Lazy Little Loafers,* p. 159.

School Library Journal, October, 2008, Lisa Glasscock, review of *Lazy Little Loafers,* p. 118.

Time, January 25, 1999, John Skow, review of *The Orchid Thief,* p. 80.

ONLINE

Powell's Books Web site, http://www.powels.com/authors/ (January 6, 2001), Dave Weich, interview with Orlean.

Susan Orlean Home Page, http://www.susanorlean.com (December 20, 2009).*

P

PAUL, Ann Whitford 1941-

Personal

Born February, 1, 1941, in Evanston, IL; daughter of George (a business executive) and Genevieve (a homemaker and poet) Whitford; married Ronald S. Paul (a surgeon), July 21, 1968; children: Henya Ann, Jonathon David, Alan Douglas, Sarah Elizabeth. *Education:* University of Wisconsin—Madison, B.A. (sociology), 1963; Columbia University School of Social Work, M.S.W. (with honors), 1965. *Hobbies and other interests:* Quilting, knitting, cooking, reading, walking.

Addresses

Home and office—2531 N. Catalina St., Los Angeles, CA 90027. *E-mail*—ann@annwhitfordpaul.net.

Career

Writer; worked as a social worker in medical hospitals and adoption agencies, 1965-70.

Member

Society of Children's Book Writers and Illustrators, Southern California Council on Literature for Children and Young People.

Awards, Honors

New York Times Notable Children's Book citation, and Notable Social Studies Book citation, both 1991, both for *Eight Hands Round;* Outstanding Science Trade Book citation, 1992, for *Shadows Are About;* Carl Sandburg Award for Children's Literature, and *New York Times* Best Illustrated Books selection, both 1996, both for *The Seasons Sewn;* Best Under-Fives selection, Bank Street College of Education, 2003, for *Little Monkey Says Good Night;* Best Children's Books of the Year selection, Bank Street College of Education, 2005, and state reader award nominations, all for *Mañana, Iguana.*

Ann Whitford Paul (Photograph by Donna Zweig. Reproduced by permission.)

Writings

FOR CHILDREN

Owl at Night, Putnam (New York, NY), 1985.

Eight Hands Round: A Patchwork Alphabet, HarperCollins (New York, NY), 1991.

Shadows Are About, Scholastic (New York, NY), 1992.

The Seasons Sewn: A Year in Patchwork, illustrated by Michael McCurdy, Browndeer Press/Harcourt Brace (San Diego, CA), 1996.

Hello Toes! Hello Feet!, DK Ink (New York, NY), 1998.

Silly Sadie, Silly Samuel, illustrated by Sylvie Wickstrom, Simon & Schuster Books for Young Readers (New York, NY), 1998.

All by Herself: 14 Girls Who Made a Difference: Poems, illustrated by Michael Steirnagle, Browndeer Press/ Harcourt Brace (San Diego, CA), 1999.

Everything to Spend the Night: From A to Z, DK Publishing (New York, NY), 1999.

Little Monkey Says Good Night, illustrated by David Walker, Melanie Kroupa Books (New York, NY), 2003.

Mañana, Iguana, illustrated by Ethan Long, Holiday House (New York, NY), 2004.

Hop! Hop! Hop!, illustrated by Jan Gerardi, Random House (New York, NY), 2005.

Fiesta Fiasco, illustrated by Ethan Long, Holiday House (New York, NY), 2007.

Snail's Good Night, illustrated by Rosanne Litzinger, Holiday House (New York, NY), 2007.

Count on Culebra: Go from 1 to 10 in Spanish, illustrated by Ethan Long, Holiday House (New York, NY), 2008.

If Animals Kissed Good Night, illustrated by David Walker, Farrar, Straus & Giroux (New York, NY), 2008.

Tortuga in Trouble, illustrated by Ethan Long, Holiday House (New York, NY), 2009.

Word Builder, illustrated by Kurt Cyrus, Simon & Schuster Books for Young Readers (New York, NY), 2009.

Contributor to *Poems for Grandmothers* and *Dog Poems,* both edited by Myra Cohn Livingston; *Snuffles and Snouts,* edited by Laura Robb; *Hannukkah Lights; Oh, No! Where Are My Pants?;* and *Hoofbeats, Claws & Rippled Fins, Wonderful Words, My America, America at War,* and *Home to Me,* all edited by Lee Bennett Hopkins. Contributor to periodicals, including *Cricket* and *Spider.*

OTHER

Writing Picture Books: A Hands-on Guide from Story Creation to Publication, Writer's Digest Books (Cincinnati, OH), 2009.

Sidelights

A popular writer for young children, Ann Whitford Paul creates picture books and early readers that feature engaging animal characters, rhyming texts, and colorful illustrations by a variety of talented artists. In a number of her picture books, such as *Fiesta Fiasco* and *Tortuga in Trouble,* Paul crafts entertaining texts from a rich-sounding mix of two languages, introducing English-speaking children to common Spanish words while treating children of both languages to her Southwestern adaptations of traditional folk tales.

Paul published her first book, *Owl at Night,* in 1985. The simple story focuses on two children and their family as they settle down to sleep just as an owl begins its activities in the night. Susan Hepler, in her review for

School Library Journal, called *Owl at Night* "a cozy catalog of nighttime activity that would make a good addition to the bedtime story collection." A *Publishers Weekly* reviewer wrote that Paul's writing in the book contains "a gentle touch and a lyrical voice."

Paul's second book, *Eight Hands Round: A Patchwork Alphabet,* is designed for children between ages eight and twelve. The book combines the alphabet-book format with twenty-six patchwork-quilt patterns, from A for anvil to Z for zigzag. Paul also presents the historical background, customs, and events that inspired each of the designs. Through it all, "a fine history lesson emerges," noted Denise Wilms in her review of the work for *Booklist,* while a *Kirkus Reviews* critic praised *Eight Hands Round* as "a novel way to introduce patchwork's economic, social, and artistic role while relating it to history."

Like *Eight Hands Round, The Seasons Sewn: A Year in Patchwork* also features quilt patterns among the book's illustrations. Paul selects six quilt patterns for each of the four seasons and includes a fanciful explanation as to how each pattern got its name. For the pattern called Rising Star, for example, she tells of two slaves who escape to freedom by navigating their way by the North Star. Each story is illustrated by Michael McCurdy with the appropriate pattern as well as a picture from the story told. Noel Perrin, writing in the *New York Times Book Review,* noted that Paul's book is "so beautiful and so filled with real archetypal patterns that it could

Paul's picture book Everything to Spend the Night *features endearing illustrations by Maggie Smith.* (Illustration copyright © 1999 by Maggie Smith. Reproduced by permission of DK Publishing, Inc.)

easily make quilt lovers, if not quilt makers, of us all," and *Booklist* critic Carolyn Phelan called *The Seasons Sewn* "an attractive combination of craft and history."

Another book for younger children, *Shadows Are About*, features a rhyming chronicle of the shadow explorations of a brother and sister. The book was praised for its "simple, lyrical text," by Stephanie Loer in the *Boston Globe*, while Deborah Abbott, in her *Booklist* review, concluded that "shadows, which are about light and movement and new perspectives, take on a life of their own in this beautifully crafted picture book."

For her collection *All by Herself: 14 Girls Who Made a Difference: Poems*, Paul presents verses about real-life American girls who have done something heroic for others. Ida Lewis, for example, saved a crew whose boat was sinking, while Kate Shelley rescued two men injured in a train wreck. "Paul keeps the flow lively," according to a *Publishers Weekly* contributor, "by employing a range of poetic styles." Phelan described the poems as "plain, forthright, and sometimes dramatic," while a *Kirkus Reviews* critic concluded that *All by Herself* "honors both quiet and noisy acts of heroism."

In *Little Monkey Says Good Night*, an impish circus monkey delays bedtime by telling its father that it first has to say good night to everyone. Jumping and swinging all around the big top, with its father chasing him, the monkey says good night to all the circus performers. It even jumps into its mother's arms while Mother Monkey is swinging on a trapeze. Finally, the curtain comes down on the little monkey's bedtime hijinks: Mother gracefully drops it into Father's arms to be put to bed, and the audience applauds. "The only drawback is that when listeners reach the end they'll ask to start again," noted a critic for *Kirkus Reviews*, and in *Publishers Weekly* a critic concluded: "As lively as Barnum and Bailey, Little Monkey's circus adventure is just plain fun."

Like *Little Monkey Says Good Night*, *If Animals Kissed Good Night* features engaging watercolor illustrations by David Walker. In the book, Paul focuses her rhyme on a diverse selection of animal parents and children as they prepare for sleep, from walruses to sloths, and penguins to elephants. The book's "charming, fanciful" vignettes are paired with "a rhyme that seems crafted for reading aloud," noted *Booklist* contributor Abby Nolan, while Walker's "rounded, stuffed toy-like" animals "radiate unconditional love," according to a *Publishers Weekly* writer.

Animals take center stage in many of Paul's stories. *Hop! Hop! Hop!* finds Little Rabbit struggling to keep up with Big Rabbit, while in *Snail's Good Night* a slow-moving snail's desire to wish each of his friends good night turns into an early good-morning. Lisa S. Schindler noted in *School Library Journal* that Paul's gentle story in *Hop! Hop! Hop!* will encourage "fledgling read-

ers," while its "positive message about believing in one's self and succeeding on one's own terms will be appreciated."

Paul's picture-book collaborations with artist Ethan Long include *Mañana, Iguana, Fiesta Fiasco, Count on Culebra: Go from 1 to 10 in Spanish*, and *Tortuga in Trouble*. In *Mañana, Iguana* an iguana plans a party for friends, but when she asks for help in preparing the meal, Culebra (a snake), Conejo (a rabbit), and Tortuga (a turtle) avoid doing work. Iguana makes the invitations, cooks the food, and prepares a piñata, all by herself. On the day of the party, when they are not invited, her three lazy friends realize their mistake; while Iguana is napping at party's end, they clean up the mess and thereby repair the friendship. Mary Elam, writing in *School Library Journal*, noted the "appeal" of *Mañana, Iguana*, while a *Kirkus Reviews* critic judged the book to be "a clever dual-language update of *The Little Red Hen*."

Iguana and friends return in *Fiesta Fiasco*, as well as in the concept book *Count on Culebra*. In *Fiesta Fiasco* the fast rabbit Conejo finds a way to get his friends to buy presents for Culebra that would be much more suited to . . . a fast rabbit! Noting Long's incorporation of "witty details" in his "vibrant" pencil and gouache cartoons for *Fiesta Fiasco*, *Booklist* critic Shelle Rosenfeld called Paul's bilingual picture book "a fun story with a message," while in *School Library Journal* Jane Marino wrote that the book treats readers to "an ending that is sure to elicit giggles." A play on the story of Little Red Riding Hood, *Tortuga in Trouble* finds Tortuga carrying a meal of tamales to his aunt, followed by hungry friends Culebra, Iguana, and Conejo. When hungry Coyote makes an appearance, the three friends find a way to save their slow-moving friend. In *Horn Book*, Joanna Rudge Long praised Long's "endearingly expressive" cartoons as "a fine complement to a tale that's sure to enliven storytimes," and Catherine Callegari recommended *Tortuga in Trouble* as a "fresh look on an old classic [that] is sure to be a hit with children."

Featuring artwork by Kurt Cyrus, *Word Builder* finds an industrious young boy busy creating a book by crafting letters, words, sentences, and paragraphs, all by using traditional construction tools. In *Publishers Weekly* a critic cited the "ginormous-scaled, blocky images" Cyrus renders "with loving detail" to bring to life Paul's free-verse story in *Word Builder*. The "direct language and terrific artwork" combines to "show children how literal and figurative construction works," added *Booklist* critic Ilene Cooper, and a *Kirkus Reviews* writer dubbed *Word Builder* a "visually dazzling effort" that will engage "abstract thinkers."

Paul once told *SATA:* "As the oldest of five children, I lived a normal, happy and uneventful life in the Midwest. Although I once entertained the idea of being a writer, it was quickly repressed in the seventh grade when a neighbor girl stole my diary and read all the

Paul's gentle bedtime story is brought to life in artwork by Rosanne Litzinger in **Snail's Good Night.** (Illustration copyright © 2007 by Rosanne Litzinger. Reproduced by permission of Holiday House, Inc.)

nasty things I'd written about *her!* It put a big damper on our friendship and watching the hurt and angry expression on my first reader's face discouraged my writing ambition. In addition, no matter how hard I tried in school, I never got above a B on any creative writing assignment—final proof that I was not cut out to write. I turned my sights to a more attainable goal and graduated from the University of Wisconsin with a degree in sociology and then attended Columbia University School of Social Work, where I received an M.S.W.

"It was not until I was thirty-five years old and had just given birth to the third of my four children that I began to think about writing books. The inspiration came from my children. As you can imagine, life was chaotic in our crowded house—someone always needed a diaper changed, or a drink of apple juice, or a tear to be dried—except for that time when darkness wrapped around our house. Then I would sit with each child in a rocking chair, or in bed under the covers. Without noise and distractions, we read a book together.

"I loved the peace and closeness of those bedtime readings so much, I decided I would try to write books that other adults and children could share together.

"I prefer writing picture books because of their brevity (which doesn't necessarily make them easier to write!) and their musical, poetic language. Inspiration comes from my children and things they did when they were young. Now that my children are grown and out of the house, I'm fortunate enough to be able to write every day—weekends included. If I don't write, watch out! I get cranky and anxious.

"It took me five years of submitting eighteen different stories a total of 180 times before I made my first sale. That number isn't meant to be discouraging, but encouraging. Persistence is the name of the game. Those who give up will never succeed. Those who keep trying will either succeed, or at the very least, have a wonderful journey along the way.

"My advice to people who are thinking about writing for children is to first of all, get to know yourself and what interests you. Secondly, read lots and lots of picture books, especially those published in the last ten years. Picture books have a form. It behooves you to learn that form before you experiment with ways to break it. And third—write, write, write and write some more. Fourth, don't be shy about seeking knowledge from others. And last and most important of all, enjoy the process!"

Biographical and Critical Sources

PERIODICALS

Booklist, April 1, 1996, Carolyn Phelan, review of *The Seasons Sewn: A Year in Patchwork,* p. 1358; November 17, 1999, Carolyn Phelan, review of *All by Herself: 14 Girls Who Made a Difference: Poems;* March 15, 2003, Shelle Rosenfeld, review of *Little Monkey Says Good Night,* p. 1333; November 1, 2004, Connie Fletcher, review of *Mañana, Iguana,* p. 493; May 15, 2007, Shelle Rosenfeld, review of *Fiesta Fiasco,* p. 51; February 15, 2008, Linda Perkins, review of *Count on Culebra: Go from 1 to 10 in Spanish,* p. 84; March 1, 2008, Carolyn Phelan, review of *Snail's Good Night,* p. 74; June 1, 2008, Abby Nolan, review of *If Animals Kissed Good Night,* p. 88; January 1, 2009, Ilene Cooper, review of *Word Builder,* p. 96; May 1, 2009, Ilene Cooper, review of *Tortuga in Trouble,* p. 88.

Bulletin of the Center for Children's Books, May 1, 2003, review of *Little Monkey Says Good Night.*

Horn Book, March-April, 2009, Joanna Rudge-Long, review of *Tortuga in Trouble,* p. 184.

Kirkus Reviews, November 1, 1999, review of *All by Herself;* February 19, 2003, review of *Little Monkey Says Good Night;* September 15, 2004, review of *Mañana, Iguana,* p. 917; April 1, 2007, review of *Fiesta Fiasco;* January 1, 2008, review of *Snail's Good Night;* February 15, 2008, review of *Count on Culebra;* April 1, 2008, review of *If Animals Kissed Good Night;* January 15, 2009, review of *Word Builder.*

New York Times Book Review, November 10, 1996, Noel Perrin, review of *The Seasons Sewn.*

Publishers Weekly, April 22, 1996, review of *The Seasons Sewn,* p. 71; December 13, 1999, review of *All by Herself,* p. 82; February 7, 2000, review of *The Seasons Sewn,* p. 87; March 24, 2003, review of *Little Monkey Says Good Night,* p. 74; August 30, 2004, review of *Mañana, Iguana,* p. 54; March 17, 2008, review of *Count on Culebra,* p. 69; March 24, 2008, review of *If Animals Kissed Good Night,* p. 69; January 26, 2009, review of *Word Builder,* p. 118.

School Library Journal, January, 2000, Margaret Bush, review of *All by Herself,* p. 152; March, 2000, Diane Janoff, review of *Silly Sadie, Silly Samuel,* p. 211; July, 2003, Marianne Saccardi, review of *Little Monkey Says Good Night,* p. 104; September, 2004, Mary Elam, review of *Mañana, Iguana,* p. 176; August, 2005, Lisa S. Schindler, review of *Hop! Hop! Hop!,* p. 104; May, 2007, Linda M. Kenton, review of *Fiesta Fiasco,* p. 106; February, 2008, Kelly Roth, review of *Snail's Good Night,* p. 94; June, 2008, Jane Marino, review of *If Animals Kissed Good Night,* p. 113; July, 2008, Marian Drabkin, review of *Count on Culebra,* p. 79; February, 2009, Catherine Callegari, review of *Tortuga in Trouble,* p. 82.

ONLINE

Ann Whitford Paul Home Page, http://www.annwhitford-paul.net (December 20, 2009).

Childrenslit.com, http://www.childrenslit.com/ (December 20, 2009), "Ann Whitford Paul."

* * *

PRELLER, James 1961-

Personal

Born February 1, 1961, in Wantagh, NY; son of Alan Jay (in insurance) and Ann Theresa (a homemaker) Preller; married Maria Buhl (a writer and editor), September 3, 1988; children: Nicholas Neal, two other children. *Education:* State University of New York College at Oneonta, B.A., 1983. *Politics:* Democrat. *Hobbies and other interests:* Music, basketball, racquetball, running, hanging out.

Addresses

Home—Delmar, NY. *Agent*—Sue Cohen, Writers House, 21 W. 26th St., New York, NY 10010. *E-mail*—jamespreller@aol.com.

Career

Author and editor. Scholastic, Inc., New York, NY, copywriter and promotion manager, 1985-90; freelance writer and editor, 1990—. Formerly worked as a waiter.

Awards, Honors

Children's Books of the Year designation, Bank Street College of Education, 1994, for *Wake Me in Spring.*

Writings

FOR CHILDREN

Wake Me in Spring, illustrated by Jeffrey Scherer, Scholastic, Inc. (New York, NY), 1994.

Hiccups for Elephant, illustrated by Hans Wilhelm, Scholastic, Inc. (New York, NY), 1995.

Kratts' Creatures: In Search of the Real Tasmanian Devil, Scholastic (New York, NY), 1996.

Kratts' Creatures: Off to Elephant School, Scholastic, Inc. (New York, NY), 1996.

Space Jam (adapted from the movie screenplay), Scholastic, Inc. (New York, NY), 1996.

Kratts' Creatures: Amazing Insects, Scholastic, Inc. (New York, NY), 1997.

(With Joe Layden) *NBA Game Day: An Inside Look at the NBA,* Scholastic, Inc. (New York, NY), 1997.

(With others) *The Lost World, Jurassic Park: The Complete Dinosaur Scrapbook,* Scholastic, Inc. (New York, NY), 1997.

Cardinal and Sunflower, illustrated by Huy Voun Lee, HarperCollins (New York, NY), 1998.

(Adapter) *Godzilla* (based on the screenplay by Dean Devlin and Roland Emmerich), Scholastic, Inc. (New York, NY), 1998.

McGwire and Sosa: A Season to Remember, Aladdin (New York, NY), 1998.

(With Joe Layden) *Inside the WNBA: A behind-the-Scenes Photo Scrapbook,* Scholastic, Inc. (New York, NY), 1999.

(Adaptor, with others) *The Mummy: Movie Scrapbook,* Scholastic, Inc. (New York, NY), 1999.

Rain, Rain, Go Away!, illustrated by Duendes Del Sur, Scholastic Inc. (New York, NY), 2000.

Rock Solid, Scholastic, Inc. (New York, NY), 2000.

The NBA Book of Opposites, Scholastic, Inc. (New York, NY), 2000.

3 in 1 Table-top Sports, illustrated by Billy Davis, Tangerine Press (New York, NY), 2003.

The Major League Baseball Guide to Card Collecting, Scholastic, Inc. (New York, NY), 2003.

National Football League Megastars, Scholastic, Inc. (New York, NY), 2004.

World Series Scrapbook, Scholastic, Inc. (New York, NY), 2005.

Ghost Cat and Other Spooky Tales, Scholastic, Inc. (New York, NY), 2006.

Along Came Spider, Scholastic, Inc. (New York, NY), 2008.

Mighty Casey, illustrated by Matthew Cordell, Feiwel & Friends (New York, NY), 2008.

Six Innings: A Game in the Life, Feiwel & Friends (New York, NY), 2008.

Bystander, Feiwel & Friends (New York, NY), 2009.

"JIGSAW JONES" SERIES; FOR CHILDREN

The Case of the Runaway Dog, illustrated by John Speirs, Scholastic, Inc. (New York, NY), 1999.

The Case of the Spooky Sleepover, illustrated by John Speirs, Scholastic, Inc. (New York, NY), 1999.

The Case of the Class Clown, illustrated by Jamie Smith, Scholastic, Inc. (New York, NY), 2000.

The Case of the Ghostwriter, illustrated by Jamie Smith, Scholastic, Inc. (New York, NY), 2000

The Case of the Stinky Science Project, illustrated by John Speirs, Scholastic, Inc. (New York, NY), 2000.

The Case of the Detective in Disguise, illustrated by Jamie Smith, Scholastic, Inc. (New York, NY), 2001.

The Case of the Haunted Scarecrow, illustrated by Jamie Smith, Scholastic, Inc. (New York, NY), 2001.

The Case of the Sneaker Sneak, illustrated by Jamie Smith, Scholastic, Inc. (New York, NY), 2001.

The Case of the Bear Scare, illustrated by Jamie Smith, Scholastic, Inc. (New York, NY), 2002.

The Case of the Buried Treasure, illustrated by Jamie Smith, Scholastic, Inc. (New York, NY), 2002.

The Case of the Disappearing Dinosaur, illustrated by Jamie Smith, Scholastic, Inc. (New York, NY), 2002.

The Case of the Golden Key, illustrated by Jamie Smith, Scholastic, Inc. (New York, NY), 2002.

The Case of the Million-Dollar Mystery, illustrated by Jamie Smith, Scholastic, Inc. (New York, NY), 2002.

The Case of the Race against Time, illustrated by Jamie Smith, Scholastic, Inc. (New York, NY), 2003.

The Case of the Rainy Day Mystery, illustrated by Jamie Smith, Scholastic, Inc. (New York, NY), 2003.

The Case of the Glow-in-the-Dark Ghost, illustrated by Jamie Smith, Scholastic, Inc. (New York, NY), 2004.

The Case of the Perfect Prank, illustrated by Jamie Smith, Scholastic, Inc. (New York, NY), 2004.

The Case of the Double Trouble Detectives, illustrated by Jamie Smith, Scholastic, Inc. (New York, NY), 2005.

The Case of the Food Fight, illustrated by Jamie Smith, Scholastic, Inc. (New York, NY), 2005.

The Case of the Frog-jumping Contest, Scholastic, Inc. (New York, NY), 2005.

The Case of the Groaning Ghost, illustrated by Jamie Smith, Scholastic, Inc. (New York, NY), 2006.

The Case of the Santa Claus Mystery, illustrated by Jamie Smith, Scholastic, Inc. (New York, NY), 2006.

The Case of the Snowboarding Superstar, illustrated by Jamie Smith, Scholastic, Inc. (New York, NY), 2006.

The Case of the Kidnapped Candy, illustrated by Jamie Smith, Scholastic, Inc. (New York, NY), 2007.

The Case of the Spoiled Rotten Spy, illustrated by Jamie Smith, Scholastic, Inc. (New York, NY), 2007.

(With Maria S. Barbo) *The Case of the Four-leaf Clover,* illustrated by Jamie Smith, Scholastic, Inc. (New York, NY), 2008.

OTHER

(With Deborah Kovacs) *Meet the Authors and Illustrators,* two volumes, Scholastic, Inc. (New York, NY), 1991–1993.

Sidelights

Although his early dream was to play baseball as a member of the New York Mets, James Preller found his ultimate career in writing. A job at New York City pub-

lisher Scholastic, Inc., introduced him to children's books as well as to the people who wrote them, and he was quickly inspired to try his luck in the field. Within a decade, Preller had dozens of books to his credit, among them the "Jigsaw Jones" mystery series, picture books such as *Cardinal and Sunflower* and the middle-grade novels *Along Came Spider* and *Six Innings: A Game in the Life,* as well as nonfiction titles that focus on professional sports. Reviewing *NBA Game Day: An Inside Look at the NBA, Booklist* critic Helen Rosenberg praised Preller's text as a celebration of both the sport of basketball and "the photographers. . . . who capture the essence of the game."

Featuring cut-paper collage artwork by Huy Voun Lee, *Cardinal and Sunflower* tells a simple story about a family of cardinals and their activities during the passage of a single year. Another picture book by Preller, *Mighty Casey,* adapts Ernest Thayer's well-known early-twentieth-century poem "Casey at the Bat" to the Little League and a pivotal game involving the last-placed Delmar Dogs. In *Booklist* Carolyn Phelan praised *Cardinal and Sunflower* as "effective for reading aloud," while a *Publishers Weekly* critic dubbed *Mighty Casey* "a spirited celebration of a team with the right attitude, if not skills." The humor in Preller's humorous version of Thayer's poem comes from the typically childlike antics that occurred on and off the field. The quirky drama builds to its exciting culmination in Matthew Cordell's "simply drawn cartoons of geeky, distracted children," according to a *Kirkus Reviews* writer, and Ernie Cox concluded in *Booklist* that *Mighty Casey* "is assured a place in (Little League) baseball lore."

In addition to being best friends, Trey and Spider are also neighbors when readers first meet them in Preller's juvenile novel *Along Came Spider.* As the boys move up from grade to grade, however, their differences prove to be more obvious than their similarities. Trey is autistic and his compulsive tendencies and difficulty in focusing are making many of the fifth-grade classmates who found him funny in third grade starts to avoid him. Spider now confronts a quandary shared by many children on the cusp of adolescence: should he try to conform to the social norm and win acceptance from his peers by shunning his long-time friend or remain loyal to Trey and risk becoming an outcast. Preller's "perceptive" novel allows readers to view personal differences and handicaps with compassion, wrote John Peters in a *Booklist* review of *Along Came Spider.* Comparing the novel to boy-friendly stories by Jack Gantos and Jerry Spinelli, a *Kirkus Reviews* critic also praised the character of Trey as "realistic as sympathetic" and predicted that the novel "will resonate with middle-grade readers."

In *Six Innings* Preller recounts the events that transpire on the day of an important Little League game. Sam is a member of the team, but while he used to play he now awakes and anticipates the fun of announcing the game. From Sam, Preller's text moves to other players

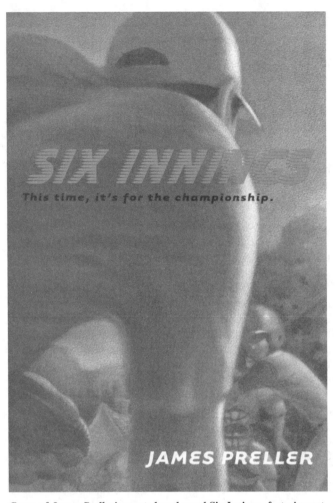

Cover of James Preller's sports-based novel Six Innings, *featuring artwork by Chris Sheban.* (Feiwel & Friends, 2008. Cover art copyright © 2008 by Chris Sheban. Reproduced by permission.)

on the team, and the fears, excitement, and personal challenges of each player are gradually revealed, whether dramatic—Sam has been stricken with bone cancer—or more commonplace. This technique "builds suspense and brings the reader right into the action," maintained a *Kirkus Reviews* writer, calling the novel a window into "the special world of baseball and the people who love it." Praising *Six Innings* as a "fast read," Sara Rofofsky added in *School Library Journal* that the book "will grasp any reader who enjoys sports," and in *Booklist* Peters cited Preller's book as "a rare example of a character-driven tale that is also suspenseful and exciting."

"I stumbled into my career in children's books fresh out of college," Preller once told *SATA,* "and after an unforgettable ten-month stint as a waiter . . . I took a job with a children's publisher, Scholastic, Inc., as a junior copywriter. I worked on the SeeSaw Book Club for children in kindergarten through first grade, writing the little promotional blurbs about each book, in addition to other writing assignments (ads, brochures, author bios, and such).

"While working at Scholastic, I came into contact with some of the most wonderful books in the world . . . [and] I began to develop strong interests, likes, and dislikes. I grew to love many, many books and authors (Arnold Lobel, James Marshall, Bernard Waber, Margaret Wise Brown, and more). I also grew to dislike the depressing number of books that didn't seem to be for children at all. . . . Many of them have weak stories—or stories that don't seem intended for children at all—but feature elaborate illustrations completed by today's coolest technicians. I knew then, as I do now, that I wanted to write books that children will genuinely enjoy. I'm not worried about earning the approval of adults (frightening creatures, many of 'em); I want kids to like my stories. And, of course, I've got to like them too.

"During this apprenticeship of sorts, I had the opportunity to interview and profile almost one hundred leading children's authors and illustrators. I've liked just about all of them—and learned from every one. In short: work on more than one story at a time, don't dwell on rejection, write from the heart, and always remember, it's a bunny-eat-bunny world out there."

Biographical and Critical Sources

PERIODICALS

Booklist, January 1, 1998, Helen Rosenberg, review of *NBA Game Day: An Inside Look at the NBA,* p. 807; July 1, 1998, Carolyn Phelan, review of *Cardinal and Sunflower,* p. 1781; January 1, 1999, Ilene Cooper, review of *McGwire and Sosa: A Season to Remember,* p. 870; April 1, 2008, review of *Six Innings: A Game in the Life,* p. 49; December 1, 2008, John Peters, review of *Along Came Spider,* p. 47; April 1, 2009, Ernie Cox, review of *Mighty Casey,* p. 43.

Kirkus Reviews, March 1, 2008, review of *Six Innings;* August 1, 2008, review of *Along Came Spider;* January 15, 2009, review of *Mighty Casey.*

New York Times Book Review, June 1, 2008, Lisa Von Drasek, review of *Six Innings,* p. 26.

Publishers Weekly, March 24, 2008, review of *Six Innings,* p. 71; March 2, 2009, review of *Mighty Casey,* p. 61.

School Library Journal, April, 2008, Sara Rofofsky, review of *Six Innings,* p. 147; December, 2008, Elizabeth Swistock, review of *Along Came Spider,* p. 100; March, 2009, Ieva Bates, review of *Mighty Casey,* p. 126.

ONLINE

James Preller Home Page, http://www.jamespreller.com (December 10, 2009).

Scholastic Web site, http://www2.scholastic.com/ (December 10, 2009), "James Preller."*

PREUS, Margi

Personal

Female. *Education:* State University of New York at Binghamton, B.A. *Hobbies and other interests:* Hiking, skiing, paddling, the outdoors.

Addresses

Home—Duluth, MN. *Agent*—Jennifer De Chiara Literary Agency, 31 E. 32nd St., Ste. 300, New York, NY 10016. *E-mail*—margipreus@mac.com.

Career

Educator and author of books for children. College of St. Scholastica, Duluth, MN, adjunct instructor in educational media and technology and teacher of children's literature; University of Minnesota—Duluth, teacher. Artistic director of a comedy theatre. Presenter at schools.

Awards, Honors

Great Lakes Book Award finalist, and Notable Social Studies Trade Book for Young People designation, both 1999, both for *The Legend of the Ladyslipper;* Cooperative Children's Book Center Choices designation, and Kansas State Reading Circle recommendation, both 2009, both for *The Peace Bell.*

Margi Preus (Photograph by Shirleen Hieb. Reproduced by permission.)

Writings

(With Lise Lunge-Larson) *The Legend of the Lady Slipper: An Ojibwe Tale,* illustrated by Andrea Arroyo, Houghton Mifflin (Boston, MA), 1999.

(Editor, with Ann Treacy) *Sacred Words: A Collection of Prayers from around the World,* Sourcebooks (Naperville, IL), 2002.

(Editor, with Ann Treacy) *A Book of Grace: Words to Bring You Peace,* Sourcebooks (Naperville, IL), 2002.

The Peace Bell, illustrated by Hideko Takahashi, Henry Holt (New York, NY), 2008.

Celebritrees: Historic and Famous Trees of the World, illustrated by Rebecca Gibbon, Henry Holt (New York, NY), 2010.

Heart of a Samurai (historical fiction), Harry Abrams (New York, NY), 2010.

Author of plays produced in MN, including (with Jean Sramek) *Pirates of the Carrot Bean, Phantom of the Norshor, Les Uncomfortables,* and *The Idiot and the Oddity.* Contributor to periodicals, including *Ladybug.*

Sidelights

Based in Minnesota, Margi Preus is a children's author who also writes plays and comic operas. The author of the picture books *The Legend of the Lady Slipper: An Ojibwe Tale* and *The Peace Bell,* Preus has also edited a prayer anthology and contributed short fiction for adults and children to periodicals and anthologies. In her day job, she serves as an adjunct instructor at the College of St. Scholastica and also teaches, on occasion, at the University of Minnesota-Duluth.

A collaboration between Preus and fellow author Lise Lunge-Larsen, *The Legend of the Lady Slipper* shares a Native-American legend about one of North America's most unique wild flowers. Brought to life in illustrations by Andrea Arroyo, the story takes place many years in the past, as a young girl attempts to save her people from a terrible sickness. Going out into the wilderness, she collects the herbs that will help her craft a cure. Although she becomes lost in the deep drifts of snow, she returns home by listening and watching the nature that surrounds her. During her trek, the girl loses one of her moccasins, and in honor of her work the delicate plant known to many as the lady slipper now grows wild in the region's woodlands and blooms each spring. Noting that the coauthors base their story on authentic Ojibwa sources, GraceAnne A. DeCandido added in *Booklist* that *The Legend of the Lady Slipper* retells "the sweet legend in a powerful way." In *Publishers Weekly* a critic had special praise for Arroyo's "stylized watercolors," concluding that the "unusual

girls are entertained by the stories of Yuko's grand-mother. The aged woman remembers her childhood, and the beautiful temple bell that would ring in the New Year. When war broke out, the bell was taken down and its metal contributed to Japan's war effort. While it was lost to the woman's town, the bell was never actually melted down. Instead, it was discovered, discarded, in a shipyard by an American sailor who brought it home as a souvenir. Years later, it was returned to Japan as a symbol of the renewal of friendship between the two great counties. Preus's "simple plot is clearly developed with descriptive language," wrote Margaret R. Tassia in her *School Library Journal* review of *The Peace Bell*. For Tassia, the book also benefits from the "cultural details [that] are woven into both text and pictures," while a *Kirkus Reviews* critic maintained that illustrator Hideko Takahashi's "lovely acrylics are as sweet and precise as the text."

Biographical and Critical Sources

PERIODICALS

Booklist, April 15, 1999, GraceAnne A. DeCandido, review of *The Legend of the Lady Slipper: An Ojibwe Tale*, p. 1533.
Kirkus Reviews, September 15, 2008, review of *The Peace Bell*.
Publishers Weekly, April 12, 1999, review of *The Legend of the Lady Slipper*, p. 74.
School Library Journal, May, 1999, Kate McClelland, review of *The Legend of the Lady Slipper*, p. 109; December, 2008, Margaret R. Tassia, review of *The Peace Bell*, p. 100.

ONLINE

Children's Literature Network Web site, http://www.childrensliteraturnetwork.org/ (December 15, 2009), "Margi Preus."
Margi Preus Home Page, http://www.margipreus.com (December 15, 2009).*

Preus tells an unusual wartime story in **The Peace Bell,** *a picture book illustrated by Hideko Takahashi.* (Illustration copyright © 2008 by Hideko Takahashi. Reprinted by permission of Henry Holt & Company, LLC.)

simplicity and fluidity" of "both text and art" make *The Legend of the Lady Slipper* an "ideal choice for a springtime readaloud."

In *The Peace Bell* Preus uses a fictional story to share the history of the American-Japanese Friendship Bell that once hung in the city of Duluth. When Yuko welcomes American friend Katie to her home in Japan, the

R

ROLSTON, Steve 1978-

Personal

Born 1978, in Vancouver, British Columbia, Canada. *Education:* Capilano College, degree (animation).

Addresses

Office—Box 93570, Nelson Park RPO, Vancouver, British Columbia V6E 4L7, Canada. *E-mail*—steve@steverolston.com.

Career

Illustrator, animator, and comic artist. A.k.a. Cartoon, storyboard artist; Barking Bullfrog Cartoon Company, storyboard artist; freelance comic artist. Vancouver Institute of Media Arts, instructor in comic-book art.

Awards, Honors

Ispies Award for Best New Talent, 2002; (with others) Eisner Award for Best New Series, and nominations for Eisner awards for Best Serialized Story and Best Continuing Series, all 2002, all for "Queen and Country"; Russ Manning Award nomination for Most Promising Newcomer, 2002; Cybils Award for Best Young-Adult Graphic Novel (with Mariko Tamaki), Joe Shuster Comics for Kids Award nomination (with Tamaki), and Joe Shuster Award for Outstanding Artist nomination, all 2008, all for *Emiko Superstar;* Harvey Award for Best Graphic Album of Previously Published Work (with others), 2009, for *Queen and Country.*

Writings

SELF-ILLUSTRATED

One Bad Day (graphic novel), Oni Press (Portland, OR), 2003.

Creator of Web comics, including "Jack Spade and Tony Two-Fist"; creator of minicomics, including "Lost Souls in Love," 2004, and "Little Ghost," 2006.

ILLUSTRATOR

(With Mike Norton) Greg Rucka, *Queen and Country: Operation Broken Ground* (originally published in comic-book form), Oni Press (Portland, OR), 2002.

Brian Wood, *Pounded* (graphic novel; originally published in comic-book form), Oni Press (Portland, OR), 2002.

Warren Ellis, *Mek* (originally published in comic-book form), WildStorm (La Jolla, CA), 2004.

(With Mike Norton) Greg Rucka, *Queen and Country: Operation Saddlebags* (graphic novel; originally published in comic-book form), Oni Press (Portland, OR), 2005.

(With Jason Shawn Alexander) Brian K. Vaughan, *The Escapists* (originally published in comic-book form), Dark Horse (Milwaukie, OR), 2007.

J. Torres, *Degrassi the Next Generation: Safety Dance* (graphic novel; originally published in comic-book form), Pocket Books (New York, NY), 2008.

Mariko Tamaki, *Emiko Superstar* (graphic novel), Minx (New York, NY), 2008.

Cora Lee, *The Great Motion Mission: A Surprising Story of Physics in Everyday Life,* Annick Press (Toronto, Ontario, Canada), 2009.

Illustrator of comic-book series, including "Queen and Country," by Greg Rucka, Oni Press; "Jingle Belle Jubilee," by Paul Dini; "Mek," by Warren Ellis, DC/Wildstorm; "Tales of the TMNT," by Murphy; "Degrassi the Next Generation: Safety Dance," by J. Torres, Fenn, 2007; and "Ghost Projekt," by Joe Harris, Oni Press. Contributor of illustrations to anthologies, including *9-11: Artists Respond,* Volume 1, Dark Horse, 2002; *A United Front,* Cartoon Militia, 2004; and *Four-Letter Worlds,* Image Comics, 2005; and *You Ain't No Dancer,* Volume 3, New Reliable Press, 2008.

Sidelights

Trained as an animator, Canadian artist Steve Rolston has dedicated most of his career to creating, illustrating,

and teaching comic books. An award-winning illustrator whose work includes contributions to series such as "Queen and Country," "Ghost Projekt," and "The Escapists," Rolston has also sidestepped into children's book illustration through his work on Cora Lee's nonfiction picture book *The Great Motion Mission: A Surprising Story of Physics in Everyday Life.* Comparing Rolston's work to that of European cartoonists, a *Publishers Weekly* critic noted in a review of his work for *Queen and Country: Operation Broken Ground* that the artist "combines bold outlines, expressive body language and clean, cartoonish lines for his characters, with detailed, realistic backgrounds."

A native of Vancouver, British Columbia, Rolston studied animation techniques at Capilano College, then worked as a storyboard artist for cartoon series that include *Ed, Edd 'n' Eddy, PB&J Otter, Rescue Heroes,* and *Sabrina.* Turning to comics in the late 1990s, he created the original Web comic "Jack Spade and Tony Two-Fist," which landed Rolston a job illustrating four

issues of Greg Rucka's Eisner Award-winning comic-book series "Queen and Country." For his work on "Queen and Country," which was eventually anthologized in *Queen and Country: Operation Broken Ground,* Rolston earned a nomination for the Russ Manning award for most promising newcomer in the comic-book field.

In 2003 Rolston produced his first original graphic novel, *One Bad Day,* an achievement that led him to a gig with publisher Dark Horse Comics to co-illustrate *The Escapists* with writer Brian K. Vaughan. He returned to graphic novels in 2008, illustrating Mariko Tamaki's text for *Emiko Superstar* for DC Comics' Minx Books imprint. An award-winning work that earned Rolston a nomination for the prestigious Joe Shuster Award for Outstanding Artist, *Emiko Superstar* was described by a *Publishers Weekly* critic as a "light but charming fantasy for awkward girls everywhere." The story's teen heroine, who is half-Japanese and half-Canadian, prepares for a boring summer of babysitting until she discovers an underground theatre group that gives Emiko the opportunity to explore her acting talents and ultimately shine on stage. Rolston's talent for capturing the myriad emotions of the teen actress in his "playful, vibrant" drawings earned special praise from the *Publishers Weekly* contributor, and in *Booklist* Snow Wildsmith cited the artist's "strong, realistic" graphic style.

Biographical and Critical Sources

PERIODICALS

Booklist, December 1, 2008, Snow Wildsmith, review of *Emiko Superstar,* p. 44.
Kirkus Reviews, September 1, 2008, review of *Emiko Superstar.*
Publishers Weekly, June 3, 2002, review of *Queen and Country: Operation Broken Ground,* p. 66; October 27, 2008, review of *Emiko Superstar,* p. 39.
School Library Journal, November, 2008, Barbara M. Moon, review of *Emiko Superstar,* p. 153.

ONLINE

Steve Rolston Home Page, http://www.steverolston.com (December 20, 2009).
Steve Rolston Web log, http://steverolston.livejournal.com (December 20, 2009).

* * *

ROSOFF, Meg 1956-

Personal

Born 1956, in Boston, MA; daughter of Chester (a surgeon) and Lois (a psychiatric social worker) Rosoff; married Paul Hamlyn (a painter and illustrator); chil-

Canadian comic-book artist Steve Rolston teams up with writer Mariko Tamaki to create the graphic novel **Emiko Superstar.**

dren: Gloria. *Education:* Harvard University, B.A. (English and fine arts), 1979; attended St. Martin's College of Art (London, England). *Religion:* Jewish.

Addresses

Home—Highbury, North London, England. *Agent*—Catherine Clarke, Felicity Bryan Literary Agency, 2a N. Parade Ave., Oxford OX2 6LX, England.

Career

Writer. Copy editor for advertising agencies, New York, NY, 1980-89; worked in publishing in London, England, 1990-2003; freelance writer.

Awards, Honors

London *Guardian* Children's Fiction Prize, and Whitbread Children's Book Award shortlist, both 2004, and Julia Ward Howe Award for Young Readers, Boston Authors Club, Branford Boase Award, and Michael L. Printz Award, all 2005, all for *How I Live Now;* Carnegie Medal, 2007, for *Just in Case.*

Writings

(With Caren Acker) *London Guide,* Open Road (New York, NY), 1995, second edition, 1998.
How I Live Now, Wendy Lamb (New York, NY), 2004.
Meet Wild Boars, illustrated by Sophie Blackall, Henry Holt (New York, NY), 2005.
Just in Case, Wendy Lamb Books (New York, NY), 2006.
What I Was, Penguin (New York, NY), 2007.
Jumpy Jack and Googily, illustrated by Sophie Blackall, Henry Holt (New York, NY), 2008.
Wild Boars Cook, illustrated by Sophie Blackall, Henry Holt (New York, NY), 2008.
The Bride's Farewell, Viking (New York, NY), 2009.

Also author of screenplay adaptation of *How I Live Now.*

Adaptations

Rosoff's novels have been adapted as audiobooks by Penguin Audio.

Sidelights

When Meg Rosoff's youngest sister died of breast cancer, Rosoff decided that life was too short not to make an attempt to follow her own dream of being a writer. She left her job in advertising and began writing a novel, and the result was *How I Live Now.* The winner of several awards, *How I Live Now* was the first of several acclaimed books that Rosoff has produced: others include *What I Was, The Bride's Farewell,* and the Carnegie Medal-winning *Just in Case.* In addition to her

novels for teens, Rosoff also entertains younger children with several amusing picture books that feature engaging cartoon art by Sophie Blackall.

Rosoff grew up in a suburb of Boston, Massachusetts, in an affluent family where she could give her love of reading full rein. Deciding to make her living as a writer shortly after entering elementary school, she eventually enrolled at Harvard University, where she planned to major in English literature. During her junior year, Rosoff traveled to England and studied at St. Martin's College of Art and Design. Although she returned to Cambridge, Massachusetts, to complete her degree, she knew that she wanted to eventually make London, England, her home. In 1980, after graduating, she first did what many east-coast English majors do and scouted up a job in a New York City advertising agency. As Rosoff later told *School Library Journal* interviewer Meg McCaffrey, "It was soul destroying. I always felt like a train slightly derailed."

Finally, in 1989, after working for several of Manhattan's major ad agencies, Rosoff decided to apply for a work visa, figuring that she would find a temporary job at a London advertising agency and return to the United

Cover of Meg Rosoff's novel **How I Live Now,** *featuring artwork by Istvan Banyai.* (Illustration copyright © 2004 by Istvan Banyai. Used by permission of Random House Children's Books, a division of Random House, Inc.)

States when her three-month visa expired. However, her plans changed: Rosoff stayed in London, met and married painter and illustrator Paul Hamlyn, and started a family. She also continued to work in the advertising field until she was inspired to make a life change by the tragedy of her sister's death.

In *How I Live Now,* a work of speculative fiction, Rosoff tells the story of fifteen-year-old Daisy, who is spending the summer with her aunt and uncles in rural England. The teen is relieved to get away from her father and her "wicked" stepmother, and she falls in love with her relatives' farm as well as with her first cousin, Edward. When her aunt leaves home to attend a conference, Daisy and Edward enjoy unsupervised freedom, but then World War II erupts and everything falls apart. Soon soldiers seize the farm and place Daisy with her much-younger female cousin while the boys are marched away to an unknown location. While searching for Edward, Daisy and her cousin witness the violent effects of the war.

Deirdre F. Baker, reviewing Rosoff's debut for *Horn Book,* called *How I Live Now* "a winning combination of acerbic commentary, innocence, and sober vision," and in *Bookseller* Benedicte Page cited Daisy's "funny, spiky, and vulnerable" voice as one of the strengths of the book. Claire Rosser also praised Rosoff's "unforgettable heroine," calling Daisy "fiercely loving and tough as well." A critic for *Kirkus Reviews* wrote that the novel is "told in honest, raw first-person and filled with humor, love, pathos, and carnage," and a *Publishers Weekly* critic predicted that, "like the heroine, readers will emerge from the rubble much shaken, a little wiser, and with perhaps a greater sense of humanity."

Critically acclaimed, *How I Live Now* was also shortlisted for the Whitbread Children's Book Award and earned Rosoff the London *Guardian* Children's Fiction Prize. Ironically, at the time her first novel was published Rosoff herself had been diagnosed with breast cancer. "I was in the hospital for my first operation when the book was released and all these flowers started arriving," the author recalled to a *Publishers Weekly* interviewer. "Half of the cards said 'Congratulations,' the other half said, 'We're so sorry.'"

Described by *Horn Book* contributor Christine M. Hepperman as "an intelligent, uniquely embellished view of teen angst gone too far," Rosoff's second novel *Just in Case* focuses on fifteen-year-old David Case. After he stops his toddler brother from climbing out of an open window in the house, David begins to obsess over the myriad dangers that loom during the course of an average day, as well as over newsworthy threats such as deadly floods and serial killers. He soon personifies Fate, and decides to avoid imminent death by changing his name and eventually even abandoning his home. As Justin, David changes his wardrobe, manufactures a nonexistent pet dog, and starts a relationship with an older teen photographer named Agnes who looks upon

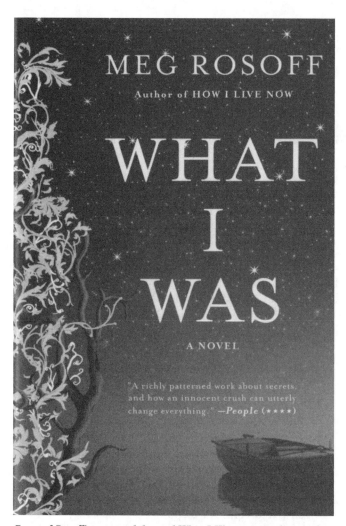

Cover of Rosoff's young-adult novel **What I Was,** *a story about a close friendship between two boys living in 1960s England.* (Cover photograph © by Sophie Molins/Millenium Images, UK. All rights reserved. Used by permission of Penguin Group (USA), Inc.)

Justin more as a creative project than as a friend. Against David/Justin's story, Rosoff weaves the comments of Fate, and readers realize that the teen is fighting a true threat rather than experiencing delusions. Although "readers may feel distanced" by the complex philosophical issues Rosoff explores through her teen characters, *Just in Case* also encourages teens to "ponder the provocative questions that wrap around their own hopes and terrors," concluded *Booklist* critic Gillian Engberg. Calling the novel "more complicated" than Rosoff's debut novel *How I Live Now,* Claire Rosser added in *Kliatt* that "superb" writing and an "inventive" storyline combine with "a touch of British absurdity" in *Just in Case.* In *Kirkus Reviews* a critic dubbed the novel "funny, ironic, magically real; stunning."

In *What I Was* Rosoff transports readers into the future in order to allow them to look back to 1962. That is the year that the one-hundred-year-old narrator turned sixteen and began his education at St. Oswald's School, having been expelled from two other boarding schools.

Using what *School Library Journal* critic Jackie Gropman described as "spellbinding immediacy and evocative language," Rosoff captures the teen narrator's apathetic tone—overlaid with an adult's cynicism—as he remembers the school and his teachers, friends, and family. She also depicts the young man's growing sense of freedom as he meets and becomes fascinated by Finn, an older teen living alone in a remote cabin. As the months pass, Finn shows the narrator how to survive on his own and introduces him to the lore and secrets of the coastline near St. Oswald's. As he is pulled into Finn's archaic way of life, the narrator detaches himself from relationships at school, with ultimately haunting consequences. For Gropman, "love and friendship are a dominant theme" of *What I Was,* while a *Publishers Weekly* critic described the book as an "unconventional coming-of-age tale [that] is elegantly crafted. Recommending the book for older teens and adults, Engberg wrote in *Booklist* that *What I Was* prompts "questions about the nature of time, memory, and the events that become . . . [a life's] defining moments."

Rosoff's first historical novel, *The Bride's Farewell,* begins as heroine Pell Ridley leaves Birdie, her childhood sweetheart, at the altar on what would have been their wedding day. Living in mid-nineteenth-century England and feeling confined by the limited options open to women in Victorian society, Pell is determined not to take up the domestic duties of other women her age. Escaping with her mute brother, Bean, as well as her beloved horse, Jack, she also flees the abuse of her father. The travels of the two siblings take them to Salisbury, where Pell finds work but ultimately loses contact with both Bean and Jack. Now truly on her own, she is helped by a sequence of people until she finally takes up with a wandering poacher called Dogman. Through her travels with Dogman and his dogs she learns how to survive, and also learns to understand the depth of true love as she searches for the missing Bean. In *Publishers Weekly* a critic called *The Bride's Farewell* a "simple but satisfying story," while in *School Library Journal* Karen E. Brooks-Reese maintained that the novel features "simple yet descriptive language" in which Rosoff "paints a clear picture of a world both bleak and beautiful." Also praising *The Bride's Farewell,* Engberg wrote that the author's "richly metaphoric story of a young survivor" also addresses "life's largest questions."

In addition to her novels for teen readers, Rosoff also writes for younger children. In *Meet Wild Boars* and *Wild Boars Cook,* both illustrated by Sophie Blackall, she follows the antics of titular characters Boris, Doris, Horace, and Morris as they demonstrate what NOT to do in all sorts of social—and unsocial—situations, from consuming the toys of others to loudly snorting to making bad smells and bathing in the toilet. Chaos in the kitchen is the focus of *Wild Boars Cook,* as the toothy, stinky foursome attempt to cook up a pudding and then consume it, demonstrating some of the most atrocious table manners depicted in the whole of children's litera-

ture. Reviewing *Meet Wild Boars* in *Publishers Weekly,* a critic predicted that readers will share the horror of witnessing atrocious behavior while also "secretly delighting in the boars' unmitigated chutzpah." "Wild they may be," concluded *Booklist* contributor Ilene Cooper of Rosoff's uncouth characters. "Bores, they are not."

Another book Rosoff has written for younger children, *Jumpy Jack and Googily,* also features artwork by Blackall. Jack is a toothsome but timid garden snail, while Googily is a four-fingered, sharp-toothed blue monster with a kindly personality. As the two friends walk together, Googily repeatedly checks their surroundings at Jumpy Jack's request, because the snail is terrified of monsters. Although Jack's fears come alive during the day, the skittish snail becomes a soothing influence at night, when friend Googily begins to voice his own fears of the dark in a story that "highlights . . . the power of a trusted friend to allay" life's difficult moments, according to *School Library Journal* contributor Rachel Vilmar. Blackall's artwork is "filled with whimsical detail," Vilmar added, and a *Kirkus Reviews* writer recommended *Jumpy Jack and Googily* as "a humorous tamer of monsters" for imaginative young children.

Discussing her work as a writer with a *Bookbrowse.com* interviewer, Rosoff noted: "I like writing for and about teens because it's a very extreme time of life, and that makes for intense transformations, intense possibilities for growth. I think many people find their teens a difficult and disturbing time, but also a time of great excitement and intensity. As a writer, you can't ask for a better set-up than that."

Rosoff teams up with artist Sophie Blackall on the amusing picture book **Meet Wild Boars.** (Illustration copyright © 2005 by Sophie Blackall. Reprinted by permission of Henry Holt & Company, LLC.)

Biographical and Critical Sources

PERIODICALS

Booklist, September 1, 2004, Jennifer Mattson, review of *How I Live Now,* p. 123; March 15, 2005, Ilene Cooper, review of *Meet Wild Boars,* p. 1287, and interview with Rosoff, p. 1289; June 1, 2006, Gillian Engberg, review of *Just in Case,* p. 64; December 1, 2007, Gillian Engberg, review of *What I Was,* p. 23; October 15, 2008, Ilene Cooper, review of *Wild Boars Cook,* p. 46; August 1, 2009, Gillian Engberg, review of *The Bride's Farewell,* p. 26.

Bookseller, June 4, 2004, Benedicte Page, "Living through Wartime," p. 28.

Christian Century, December 14, 2004, review of *How I Live Now,* p. 24.

Horn Book, September-October, 2004, Deirdre F. Baker, review of *How I Live Now,* p. 597; September-October, 2006, Christine M. Hepperman, review of *Just in Case,* p. 597.

Kirkus Reviews, July 15, 2004, review of *How I Live Now,* p. 693; July 15, 2006, review of *Just in Case,* p. 729; April 15, 2008, review of *Jumpy Jack and Goggily;* July 1, 2009, review of *The Bride's Farewell.*

Kliatt, July, 2004, Claire Rosser, review of *How I Live Now,* p. 12; July, 2006, Claire Rosser, review of *Just in Case,* p. 14.

Publishers Weekly, June 30, 2003, p. 12; July 5, 2004, review of *How I Live Now,* p. 56; December 20, 2004, "Flying Starts: Five Acclaimed Fall Children's Book Debuts," p. 30; March 28, 2005, review of *Meet Wild Boars,* p. 78; October 15, 2007, review of *What I Was,* p. 38; July 14, 2008, review of *Wild Boars Cook,* p. 65; June 15, 2009, review of *The Bride's Farewell,* p. 33.

School Library Journal, September, 2004, Douglas P. Davey, review of *How I Live Now,* p. 216; March, 2005, Meg McCaffrey, "Answering the Call" (profile), p. 46; July, 2005, Mary Elam, review of *Meet Wild Boars,* p. 82; May, 2008, Rachael Vilmar, review of *Jumpy Jack and Googily,* p. 107; June, 2008, Jackie Gropman, review of *What I Was,* p. 172; August, 2008, Judith Constantinides, review of *Wild Boars Cook,* p. 101; December, 2009, Karen E. Brooks-Reese, review of *The Bride's Farewell,* p. 146.

ONLINE

Bookbrowse.com, http://wwwbookbrowse.com/ (April 27, 2005), interview with Rosoff.

Meg Rosoff Home Page, http://megrossof.co.uk (December 20, 2009).

*Penguin Web site,*http://www.penguin.co.uk/ (August 27, 2005), interview with Rosoff.*

*   *   *

RUELLE, Karen Gray 1957-

Personal

Born June 17, 1957, in MD; daughter of Edward (an engineer) and Barbara (an artist) Gray; married Lee Gray Ruelle (an artist), September 18, 1988; children: Nina Sophia. *Education:* University of Michigan, B.G.S. (with distinction), 1979, M.L.S., 1980. *Religion:* Jewish.

Addresses

Home—New York, NY. *Agent*—Kirchoff/Wohlberg Inc., 866 United Nations Plaza, No. 525, New York, NY 10017.

Career

Author, editor, and illustrator. *Library Journal,* New York, NY, assistant editor, 1980-83; *Publishers Weekly,* New York, NY, associate editor, 1983-85; English-Speaking Union, New York, NY, librarian, 1985-90.

Awards, Honors

First runner-up, Partners and Crimes (bookstore) writing competition, 1994; Oppenheim Toy Portfolio Gold Book Award, 2002, for *Easy as Apple Pie,* and 2004, for *Just in Time for New Year's!;* Sydney Taylor Book Award Notable Book for Teens designation, Association of Jewish Libraries, 2008, for *Hidden on the Mountain.*

Writings

Seventy-five Fun Things to Make and Do by Yourself, illustrated by Sandy Haight, Sterling Publications (New York, NY), 1993.

The Book of Baths, illustrated by Lizi Boyd, Harcourt Brace (San Diego, CA), 1997.

The Book of Breakfasts, illustrated by Lizi Boyd, Harcourt Brace (San Diego, CA), 1997.

The Book of Bedtimes, illustrated by Lizi Boyd, Harcourt Brace (San Diego, CA), 1997.

(With Deborah Durland DeSaix) *Hidden on the Mountain: Stories of Children Sheltered from the Nazis in Le Chambon,* Holiday House (New York, NY), 2007.

(Self-illustrated) *Bark Park,* Peachtree Publishers (Atlanta, GA), 2007.

Contributor of book reviews to *Library Journal, Publishers Weekly,* and *Kirkus Reviews,* and of articles to the *Stamford Advocate/Greenwich Times.*

"HARRY AND EMILY" SERIES; SELF-ILLUSTRATED

The Monster in Harry's Backyard, Holiday House (New York, NY), 1999.

The Thanksgiving Beast Feast, Holiday House (New York, NY), 1999.

Snow Valentines, Holiday House (New York, NY), 2000.

Spookier than a Ghost, Holiday House (New York, NY), 2001.

April Fool!, Holiday House (New York, NY), 2002.

Easy as Apple Pie, Holiday House (New York, NY), 2002.

The Crunchy, Munchy Christmas Tree, Holiday House (New York, NY), 2003.

Mother's Day Mess, Holiday House (New York, NY), 2003.

Just in Time for New Year's!, Holiday House (New York, NY), 2004.

Easter Egg Disaster, Holiday House (New York, NY), 2004.

Great Groundhogs!, Holiday House (New York, NY), 2006.

Dear Tooth Fairy, Holiday House (New York, NY), 2006.

Sidelights

Karen Gray Ruelle is the author and illustrator of the popular "Harry and Emily" series of chapter books featuring a pair of energetic, entertaining feline siblings. She is also the author of several works of nonfiction, most notably *Hidden on the Mountain: Stories of Children Sheltered from the Nazis in Le Chambon,* which she wrote with Deborah Durland DeSaix. Ruelle once told *SATA:* "When I was growing up, I wanted to be a writer and I also wanted to be an artist. Since it never occurred to me that I could be both as an adult, I was in a state of constant conflict about what I would be when I grew up. Then a dear friend suggested that I write and illustrate children's books. A great fog lifted, and I've been pursuing that dream ever since!"

Born in Maryland, Ruelle spent much of her childhood in London, England. "From a very young age, I started making up my own little books," she once recalled to *SATA.* "The first was about penguins and how to dress them up for various special occasions—I think I was six years old at the time! I keep coming back to making up books. It's the only place where I do feel completely at home—with my writing and drawing and painting, making up little stories that develop often from a single image or phrase or sound."

After graduating from the University of Michigan, Ruelle moved to New York City and worked as an editor, a reviewer, and a librarian. "I've always been an avid reader, a flashlight-under-the-covers-at-night kind of person," she remarked. "In fact, for a while I was a librarian, just so that I could be surrounded by books. (I thought of myself as not only a Keeper of the Books, but also as a kind of Private Investigator of Information, answering all sorts of odd and fascinating reference questions.)" Ruelle made her literary debut in 1993. "My first book, *Seventy-five Fun Things to Make and Do by Yourself,* evolved quite naturally," she told *SATA.* "I must have the sensibilities of a ten-year-old because it was easy for me to think from that viewpoint. Brainstorming to come up with projects for the book was an extremely creative time for me, and soon my apartment was filled with a jumble of materials, half-finished projects, junk everywhere. From the midst of this constructive chaos, the book emerged. I like to think that my book is not only a useful resource of activities and projects, but that it also motivates independent and creative thinking in its readers. In addition, I hope the informal, anecdotal tone reads like a storybook, almost a documentation of the development of the creative process."

In 1999 Ruelle introduced her popular kitten characters Harry and Emily. In *The Monster in Harry's Backyard,* Harry receives a tent for his birthday and happily plays with it indoors for a week before his mother suggests he try his new tent out of doors. As soon as Harry beds down for the night in the backyard, however, strange noises from what appears to be a masked monster send him skittering back indoors to hide under his bed. Early morning investigations reveal the source of the noises to be a raccoon. Although *School Library Journal* reviewer Jackie Hechtkopf observed that Ruelle's illustrations make a confusing distinction between animals that act like people and animals that act like animals, she also noted the appropriateness of the author's "easy, repetitive language." A contributor to *Kirkus Reviews* also reviewed *The Monster in Harry's Backyard* and concluded that "the suspense of the story and Ruelle's friendly watercolors make this . . . ideal for beginners."

Harry and Emily reappear in *The Thanksgiving Beast Feast,* another short chapter book for early readers. In this story, Harry and Emily learn about the Thanksgiving holiday from their mother and decide to make a small feast for the animals that live in their backyard. They distribute peanuts to the squirrels, peanut-butter-smeared pinecones to the birds, and cranberries to the chipmunks. Since Emily cannot bear the thought of pumpkin pie, they make pumpkin-shaped cookies instead and share those too. "Ruelle's minimalist watercolors give this beginning reader an unusually fresh look," remarked a reviewer for *Horn Book,* the critic also praising the author's text for its gentle humor and theme of helping others.

In *Snow Valentines* Harry and Emily join forces to surprise their parents with the perfect gift on Valentine's Day. After the kittens's efforts to write a special song, create a new dance, and bake a delicious dessert draw the attention of their mother and father, Harry and Emily head outdoors, drawing fresh inspiration from a sudden snowstorm. "Colorful cartoons portray the loving family," observed *School Library Journal* contributor Lisa Smith, and Carolyn Phelan, writing in *Booklist,* described Ruelle's narrative and pictures as "simple, clear, and engaging."

Harry and Emily ready themselves for Halloween in the easy reader *Spookier than a Ghost,* another installment in Ruelle's self-illustrated series. Though Harry's homemade dinosaur costume is a big success, Emily's grand costume plans fail to materialize, leaving her with a tangled mess. Fortunately, Harry knows just how to soothe his little sister's bruised ego. "Children whose best efforts haven't produced exactly the imagined result will sympathize with Emily," noted a critic in *Kirkus Reviews.*

The two kittens celebrate more holiday fun in *April Fool!* After Harry, a notorious practical joker, declares that no one can top his April Fool's Day pranks, Emily quietly proves herself worthy of the challenge. Ruelle's "pen-and-watercolor illustrations are jaunty," wrote Ilene Cooper in a *Booklist* review of the book, and a *Kirkus Reviews* contributor described the pictures in *April Fool!* as "charmingly direct and humorous." In *The Crunchy, Munchy Christmas Tree,* a snowstorm prevents Harry and Emily from spending the holiday with their grandparents. To make the best of the situation, the kittens decorates a live tree with popcorn and cranberries for the local wildlife to eat. "The chief delight is in the characters' natural dialogue," Susan Patron remarked in a *School Library Journal* review of *The Crunchy, Munchy Christmas Tree.*

In *Mother's Day Mess,* the kittens decide to shower their mother with homemade presents on her special day. During the festive presentation, however, the marigolds and peanut-butter-and-marshmallow pancakes end up all over Mom's bed. "The simple, stylized line drawings, washed with gentle colors, are spontaneous and expressive," Phelan noted, and a *Kirkus Reviews* contributor stated that "the earnest endeavors of the charming kittens are . . . engaging." Harry and Emily attempt to stay up past midnight in *Just in Time for New Year's!* Here, according to *School Library Journal* reviewer Susan Lissim, Ruelle's "enjoyable book deals with a subject with which many youngsters can identify."

The feline siblings break a number of raw eggs, mix a batch of muddy-colored dye, and hide chocolates in several unusual spots around the house in *Easter Egg Disaster.* Ruelle's pictures for this series installment "have a childlike quality and complement the narrative," Melinda Piehler wrote in *School Library Journal.* In *Dear Tooth Fairy,* as Emily anxiously waits for her first baby tooth to fall out, Harry offers a wealth of information about the magical creature's visiting habits. In *Booklist,* Jennifer Mattson described the work as "a small drama that realistically reflects childhood curiosity and resourcefulness," and *School Library Journal* critic Laura Scott remarked that "Ruelle's colorful cartoons depict a cast of appealing feline characters."

Taking a break from her "Harry and Emily" stories, Ruelle collaborated with DeSaix to produce *Hidden on the Mountain,* a highly regarded nonfiction title. The work details how the residents of Chambon-sur-Lignon, a Protestant community in southern France, helped more than 3,000 Jewish children escape the horrors of the Holocaust during World War II. Ruelle and DeSaix first developed the idea for their book during a visit to an historical museum in France. "We were awed and moved," the authors wrote on their *Hidden on the Mountain* Web site. "We tried to imagine what the refugees must have gone through, and what their lives must have been like. We wanted to learn more. And we decided that we had to tell this story to others." While re-

searching the work, Ruelle and DeSaix traveled to New York, Florida, Virginia, Switzerland, and France to interview surviving refugees and rescuers. "The risks that were taken by the people of Le Chambon, the generosity and bravery in the face of such extreme danger, were astounding," the authors stated. "Yet they did it unassumingly because they felt it was the right thing to do to protect these refugees."

Hidden on the Mountain was named a Sydney Taylor Book Award notable book and garnered strong reviews. Rachel Kamin, writing in *School Library Journal,* commented that "the book is an invaluable resource for Holocaust educators, and many of the children's narratives would read beautifully out loud." "Many readers will focus on the dramatic overviews and commentaries, but the personal details . . . are unforgettable," noted *Booklist* critic Hazel Rochman, and a contributor in *Kirkus Reviews* stated that "the authors have brought the inspiring deeds of the Chambonese to life."

"I've never had a problem coming up with ideas," Ruelle once remarked to *SATA.* "My life is filled with little stories, made-up and real. I'm the kind of person who sees the humorous and ironic side of everything, and I'm forever imagining shapes and personalities in everything I see. A fire hydrant is a strange creature breaking through the concrete sidewalk; trees express powerful emotions with their branched arms; birds actually talk; houses listen. And I love the music of language. So it makes sense that I like to put these things down, as pictures and stories.

"I strive to make my work both entertaining and moving. My goal is to combine sweetness and humor without making my work too sentimental or goofy."

Biographical and Critical Sources

PERIODICALS

Booklist, July, 2000, Carolyn Phelan, review of *Snow Valentines,* p. 2045; September 15, 2001, Carolyn Phelan, review of *Spookier than a Ghost,* p. 236; February 1, 2002, Ilene Cooper, review of *April Fool!,* p. 949; August, 2002, Carolyn Phelan, review of *Easy as Apple Pie,* p. 1976; March 1, 2003, Carolyn Phelan, review of *Mother's Day Mess,* p. 1294; September 1, 2003, Carolyn Phelan, review of *The Crunchy, Munchy Christmas Tree,* p. 136; March 15, 2004, Carolyn Phelan, review of *Easter Egg Disaster,* p. 1310; February 15, 2006, Jennifer Mattson, review of *Dear Tooth Fairy,* p. 104; March 15, 2007, Hazel Rochman, review of *Hidden on the Mountain: Stories of Children Sheltered from the Nazis in Le Chambon,* p. 42.

Horn Book, September, 1999, review of *The Thanksgiving Beast Feast,* p. 617.

Kirkus Reviews, February 1, 1999, review of *The Monster in Harry's Backyard,* p. 228; September 15, 2001, review of *Spookier than a Ghost,* p. 1367; February 1,

2002, review of *April Fool!,* p. 188; August 1, 2002, review of *Easy as Apple Pie,* p. 1141; February 15, 2003, review of *Mother's Day Mess,* p. 316; March 1, 2003, review of *Hidden on the Mountain.*

Publishers Weekly, September 27, 1999, review of *The Thanksgiving Beast Feast,* p. 51; May 14, 2007, review of *Hidden on the Mountain,* p. 56.

School Library Journal, April, 1999, Jackie Hechtkopf, review of *The Monster in Harry's Backyard,* p. 108; September, 2000, Lisa Smith, review of *Snow Valentines,* p. 207; September, 2001, Shara Alpern, review of *Spookier than a Ghost,* p. 204; June, 2002, Sandra Welzenbach, review of *Frog's Best Friend,* p. 87; October, 2002, Elaine Lesh Morgan, review of *Easy as Apple Pie,* p. 121; March, 2003, Marilyn Taniguchi, review of *Mother's Day Mess,* p. 206; October, 2003, Susan Patron, review of *The Crunchy, Munchy Christmas Tree,* p. 67; April, 2004, Melinda Piehler, review of *Easter Egg Disaster,* p. 122; October, 2004, Susan Lissim, review of *Just in Time for New Year's!,* p. 128; September, 2005, Jane Barrer, review of *Great Groundhogs!,* p. 185; May, 2006, Laura Scott, review of *Dear Tooth Fairy,* p. 103; May, 2007, Rachel Kamin, review of *Hidden on the Mountain,* p. 152.

ONLINE

Hidden on the Mountain Web site, http://www.hiddenon themountain.com/ (April 1, 2008).*

S

SANCHEZ, Anita 1956-

Personal
Born 1956, in Boston, MA; married George Steele; children: Alex, Timothy. *Education:* Vassar College, B.A. (ecology/conservation), 1977.

Addresses
Home—Amsterdam, NY. *E-mail*—anasanchezh@aol. com.

Career
Environmental educator and author. New York State Department of Environmental Conservation, member of nature-center staff, then senior environmental educator at Five Rivers Evironmental Education Center, Albany, beginning 1984. Presenter at schools and other groups.

Writings

The Teeth of the Lion: The Story of the Beloved and Despised Dandelion, illustrated by Joan Jobson, McDonald & Woodward (Blacksburg, VA), 2006.
The Invasion of Sandy Bay, Calkins Creek (Honesdale, PA), 2008.
Mr. Lincoln's Chair: The Shakers and Their Quest for Peace, illustrated by Joan Jobson, McDonald & Woodward (Granville, OH), 2009.

Biographical and Critical Sources

PERIODICALS

Booklist, October 1, 2008, Carolyn Phelan, review of *The Invasion of Sandy Bay,* p. 46.

Childhood Education, summer, 2009, Gina Hoagland, review of *The Invasion of Sandy Bay,* p. 265.
Kirkus Reviews, September 1, 2009, review of *The Invasion of Sandy Bay.*

ONLINE

Anita Sanchez Home Page, http://www.anitasanchez.webs. com (December 20, 2009).
McDonald & Woodward Web site, http://www.mwpubco. com/ (December 20, 2009), "Anita Sanchez."*

* * *

SMITH, Andrew 1959-
(Andrew Anselmo Smith)

Personal
Born 1959; married; children: one son, one daughter.

Addresses
Home—CA. *Agent*—Laura Rennert, Andrea Brown Literary Agency, 1076 Eagle Dr., Salinas, CA 93905. *E-mail*—andrew@ghostmedicine.com.

Career
Author and educator. High school teacher and rugby coach.

Writings

Ghost Medicine, Feiwel & Friends (New York, NY), 2008.
In the Path of Falling Objects, Feiwel & Friends (New York, NY), 2009.

Sidelights
A high-school teacher and rugby coach, Andrew Smith published his first work, *Ghost Medicine,* for young adults in 2008 and followed it with *In the Path of Fall-*

Andrew Smith (Reproduced by permission.)

ing Objects. Described by a *Publishers Weekly* critic as "a deceptively simple coming-of-age story," *Ghost Medicine* features Troy Stotts, a sixteen year old who is mourning the recent loss of his mother to cancer. Detaching himself from his emotionally distant father, Troy decides to spend his summer vacation working on a ranch owned by the Benavidez family. Best friends with Gabe Benavidez and in love with Gabe's sister Luz, the troubled teen attempts to sort out his future while living on the desolate terrain, using the wide open space to fill the absence left by his mother. When the brutish son of the local sheriff attempts to assault Luz, however, Troy's life takes an unexpected path.

In his debut work, Smith "reveals his deep understanding of young people and horses," according to *Kliatt* reviewer Claire Rosser, and in *School Library Journal* Terri Clark predicted that *Ghost Medicine* will "inspire readers to prod the boundaries of their own courage." Although several critics wrote that Smith's story proceeds at a leisurely pace, a *Kirkus Reviews* critic decided that "the slowly building narrative gathers the heart-wrenching moments together to create a fully engrossing tale."

In the Path of Falling Objects, a thriller for teens, finds brothers Jonas and Simon abandoned by their mother. Homeless, the boys decide to hitchhike to Arizona in the hope that they can rejoin their father, who has been released from prison, and their older brother, who became mentally ill while fighting in the jungles of Vietnam. During their trek through several states, Jonas and Simon accept a ride from Mitch and his pregnant girlfriend, Lilly. Unknown to the brothers, Mitch is a sociopath who murders strangers for pleasure. Slowly recognizing the seriousness of the situation, sixteen-year-old Jonas searches for a way to escape without meeting the same fate as Mitch's other victims. In her *School*

Library Journal review of *In the Path of Falling Objects*, Maggie Knapp wrote that the novel's "intensity" "will suit serious readers who don't mind a little blood and gore," and a *Kirkus Reviews* critic suggested that "older teens will be riveted" to the "brutal but mesmerizing road trip that steers an unswerving course toward tragedy." In addition to applauding the well-developed relationship between the brothers, *Booklist* contributor Ian Chipman called Smith's second novel "a relentless, bleak thriller that nails the claustrophobic sense of being totally out of control."

Biographical and Critical Sources

PERIODICALS

Booklist, November 1, 2009, Ian Chipman, review of *In the Path of Falling Objects,* p. 32.

Kirkus Reviews, August 1, 2008, review of *Ghost Medicine;* September 1, 2009, review of *In the Path of Falling Objects.*

Kliatt, September, 2008, Claire Rosser, review of *Ghost Medicine,* p. 21.

Cover of Smith's novel **Ghost Medicine,** *featuring artwork by Matt Mahurin.* (Feiwel & Friends, 2008. Illustration © 2008 by Matt Mahurin. Reproduced by permission.)

Publishers Weekly, September 22, 2008, review of *Ghost Medicine,* p. 59; October 12, 2009, review of *In the Path of Falling Objects,* p. 50.

School Library Journal, September, 2008, Terri Clark, review of *Ghost Medicine,* p. 193; November, 2009, Maggie Knapp, review of *In the Path of Falling Objects,* p. 120.

ONLINE

Andrew Smith Home Page, http://www.ghostmedicine.com (December 17, 2009).

Andrew Smith Web log, http://ghostmedicine.blogspot.com (December 17, 2009).*

* * *

SMITH, Andrew Anselmo
See SMITH, Andrew

* * *

SMUCKER, Anna Egan 1948-

Personal

Born May 9, 1948, in Steubenville, OH; daughter of John and Sarah Egan; married: husband's name Kim; children: Ben, Mary. *Education:* Carlow College (now Carlow University), B.A.; Michigan State University, M.A.

Addresses

Home and office—Bridgeport, WV. *E-mail*—wvsmucker @aol.com.

Career

Writer, speaker, and workshop presenter. Worked variously as a children's librarian, public-school teacher, college instructor, consultant, and writer-in-residence.

Awards, Honors

Notable Children's Trade Book in the Field of Social Studies designation, and American Library Association Notable Book citation, both 1989, and International Reading Association Children's Book Award, 1990, all for *No Star Nights*; West Virginia Arts Commission artist fellowship in children's literature, 2005; Literary Merit Award, Historical Society of Michigan, 2006, for *To Keep the South Manitou Light.*

Writings

No Star Nights, illustrated by Steve Johnson, Knopf (New York, NY), 1989.

Outside the Window, illustrated by Stacey Schuett, Knopf (New York, NY), 1994.

A History of West Virginia, West Virginia Humanities Council (Charleston, WV), 1997.

To Keep the South Manitou Light, Wayne State University Press (Detroit, MI), 2005.

The Life of Saint Brigid, Appletree (Belfast, Northern Ireland), 2007.

Golden Delicious: A Cinderella Apple Story, illustrated by Kathleen Kemly, Albert Whitman (Morton Grove, IL), 2008.

Contributor of poems to anthologies *The Best of West Virginia Writers, A Gathering at the Forks, Wild Sweet Notes,* and *Seeking the Swan.* Author of educational materials in the areas of reading and social studies, Macmillan/McGraw-Hill School Division.

Sidelights

In addition to her work as a writer, Anna Egan Smucker has been a college instructor, a public-school teacher, and a writer-in-residence. Among her many projects, Smucker particularly enjoys writing children's literature, and her books include *No Star Nights* and *Outside the Window.* On the Reading Tub Web site, Smucker maintained that a good book for children should be exciting and interesting for adult readers as well.

Smucker's award-winning picture book *No Star Nights* describes the author's 1950s childhood in a West Virginia steel-mill town, "where all night long the sky glowed red." *To Keep the South Manitou Light,* another of her books, is an historical novel inspired by her visit to a lighthouse in Michigan. A group of baby birds gets tucked into bed with a story told by their mother in *Outside the Window,* a story by Smucker that is geared for younger readers. Hazel Rochman, reviewing *Outside the Window* for *Booklist,* wrote that "children will enjoy seeing themselves from a bird's-eye view" in Smucker's gentle story.

Horticulture, business, and sheer good luck make up the tale of *Golden Delicious: A Cinderella Apple Story,* Smucker's account of how the first golden delicious apples were discovered, cultivated, and brought to market. Lee Bock, a writer for *School Library Journal,* noted of the book that "the narrative is simple and direct, with an occasional flair." A critic for *Kirkus Reviews* also praised Smucker's nonfiction story, calling *Golden Delicious* "a standout amidst the proliferation of apple books found in elementary classrooms."

Smucker firmly believes that we all have stories to tell, and in her school programs she hopes to inspire children to want to read and write. Discussing the experiences that made her a writer, Smucker told *SATA:* "I learned to write by reading. I don't think you can be a writer unless you're a reader, and I trace my love of reading to having been read aloud to as a young child. My favorite aunt lived right across the street from a

Anna Egan Smucker presents an unusual adaptation of the Cinderella story in **Golden Delicious,** *a picture book featuring artwork by Kathleen Kemly.* (Albert Whitman & Company, 2008. Illustration copyright © 2008 by Kathleen Kemly. Reproduced by permission.)

little library on the bottom floor of an old apartment building. I remember going to that library with her and coming back home loaded down with books that she would then proceed to read to me, reading my favorites over and over again. It was that experience of hearing wonderful stories read aloud that made me want to write my own stories.

"Often students will ask me how old I was when I wrote my first book. I tell them I think I was around four years old. Using an old piano stool as my desk, I would get little pieces of paper and staple them together to make a book. I didn't know how to write the alphabet, so my writing was 'zig-zags,' but I knew what each page said. Those little books were the presents I would give to my parents and relatives. So I guess you could say I've been writing for a long time."

Biographical and Critical Sources

BOOKS

Smucker, Anna Egan, *No Star Nights,* Knopf (New York, NY), 1989.

PERIODICALS

Booklist, August, 1994, Hazel Rochman, review of *Outside the Window,* p. 2056; August 1, 2008, Hazel

Rochman, review of *Golden Delicious: A Cinderella Apple Story,* p. 78.
Bulletin of the Center for Children's Books, June, 1994, review of *Outside the Window,* p. 335.
Horn Book, March-April, 1990, Hanna B. Zeiger, review of *No Star Nights,* p. 195.
Kirkus Reviews, October 1, 1989, review of *No Star Nights;* September 1, 2008, review of *Golden Delicious.*
New York Times Book Review, November 12, 1989, Steve Tesich, review of *No Star Nights,* p. 51.
School Library Journal, September, 1994, Karen James, review of *Outside the Window,* pp. 199-200; October, 2008, Lee Bock, review of *Golden Delicious,* p 137.

ONLINE

Anna Egan Smucker Home Page, http://www.annasmucker.com (December 17, 2009).
Reading Tub Web site, http://www.thereadingtub.com/ (December 17, 2009), profile of Smucker.

*   *   *

SNYDER, Laurel 1974-

Personal

Born 1974, in Baltimore, MD; married; children: Mose, Lewis. *Education:* University of Tennessee at Chattanooga, degree; attended Iowa Writers' Workshop.

Addresses

Home and office—1986 McAfee Rd., Decatur, GA 30032. *E-mail*—laurelsnyder@hotmail.com.

Career

Writer. Worked variously as a waitress and college instructor; commentator for National Public Radio program *All Things Considered;* HILLEL: Foundation for Jewish Campus Life, former program director.

Awards, Honors

Michener-Engle fellow; Truman Capote scholar; *Smithsonian* magazine Notable Book designation, 2008, for *Up and Down the Scratchy Mountains.*

Writings

Daphne and Jim: A Choose-Your-Own-Adventure Biography in Verse (for adults), Burnside Review, 2005.
(Editor) *Half/Life: Jew-ish Tales from Interfaith Homes,* Soft Skull (Brooklyn, NY), 2006.
The Myth of the Simple Machines (poetry; for adults), No Tell, 2007.
Inside the Slidy Diner, illustrated by Jaime Zollars, Tricycle Press (Berkeley, CA), 2008.

Up and Down the Scratchy Mountains; or, The Search for a Proper Princess, illustrated by Greg Call, Random House (New York, NY), 2008.

Any Which Wall, illustrated by LeUyean Pham, Random House (New York, NY), 2009.

Baxter, the Pig Who Wanted to Be Kosher, illustrated by David Goldin, Tricycle Press (Berkeley, CA), 2010.

(Author of introduction) E. Nesbit, *Five Children and It,* new edition, Random House (New York, NY), 2010.

Penny Dreadful, illustrated by Abigail Halpin, Random House (New York, NY), 2010.

Nosh, Schlep, Schluff, illustrated by Tiphanie Beeke, Random House (New York, NY), 2011.

Contributor to periodicals, including *Utne Reader, Chicago Sun-Times, Revealer, Salon.com, Iowa Review,* and *American Letters and Commentary.*

Sidelights

In 2005, after several years spent traveling, working as a waitress and teaching college, Laurel Snyder published a collection of poetry for adults titled *Daphne and Jim: A Choose-Your-Own-Adventure Biography in Verse.* After several more books for general readers, Snyder turned to younger readers with *Inside the Slidy Diner* a picture book that takes place in a diner that disobeys the health code in every possible way. Young Edie has to stay in the diner, giving tours to visitors (in-

Laurel Snyder's debut children's story, **Up and Down the Scratchy Mountains,** *is brought to life in Greg Call's detailed art.* (Illustration copyright © 2008 by Greg Call. Reproduced by permission of Random House, an imprint of Random House Children's Books.)

cluding the readers), because she stole a lemon drop. Performing her punishment, she guides the readers through, offering tales both gross and gleeful of her time there. "Here's a diner well worth repeated visits," wrote a critic for *Kirkus Reviews,* while a *Publishers Weekly* contributor predicted of *Inside the Slidy Diner* that "the gross-out crowd will eat this up."

Snyder's first novel, *Up and Down the Scratchy Mountains; or, The Search for a Proper Princess,* is the tale of Lucy the milkmaid and her friend, Prince Wynston, who team up to go in search of Lucy's missing mother. Wynston follows Lucy on her quest, despite being assigned to learn the rules of courtship, so that he can find a proper princess to marry. Together, the friends encounter the rules-fanatic town of Torrent, where they not only discover information vabout Lucy's past, but also learn the value of not always following the rules. "Snyder's breezy text incorporates droll humor," commented *Horn Book* critic Elissa Gershowitz, while in *Booklist* Carolyn Phelan complimented the "likable characters within a simply written, well-paced story." Mari Pongkhamsing, reviewing *Up and Down the Scratchy Mountains* for *School Library Journal,* noted the combination of "appealing characters who grow and develop; clear, accessible language; lively dialogue; and a light humorous tone."

Any Which Wall, Snyder's second novel for young readers, features four children on summer vacation in Iowa. Siblings Emma and Henry, in first and fifth grade respectively, along with their neighbors Roy and Susan, in fifth and seventh grade, are bored until they find a strange wall standing in the middle of a cornfield. When they realize that the wall can transport them anywhere, real or imaginary, the children start their adventures, helped by advice from the wizard Merlin, who explains the wall's rules. Their adventures in New York City, Camelot, a frontier town of the Old West, and a pirate ship bring the friends closer together and teach them not only about each other, but also about themselves. Elissa Gershowitz, writing for *Horn Book,* noted the inspiration of the stories of Edith Nesbit and Edward Eager for giving Snyder's "contemporary-set story . . . [an] old-fashioned sensibility." Eva Mitnick also noted these literary influences, writing in *School Library Journal* of the "fresh, down-to-earth voice" in *Any Which Wall.* Courtney Jones concluded in her review of the novel for *Booklist* that Snyder's "breezy and fun tale is just the right sort of book for a rainy summer afternoon indoors."

"I do feel astoundingly, amazing, incredibly lucky to be writing books for children," Snyder wrote on her home page. She continued by thanking her readers, noting that, without them, "I wouldn't be enjoying myself half so much as I am at this very minute."

"When I began to work on *Up and Down the Scratchy Mountains* (by accident!), I had no idea I was embarking on an exciting new career," Snyder admitted to

SATA. "But children's literature has absolutely become my passion and my focus. To me, children's books are more inventive and more fun than most of the books being written for adults, and I wonder sometimes if this isn't because children are simply better readers than grownups. Children are open minded and thoughtful, and they want to suspend disbelief. They want to like a book! As both a reader and a writer, I feel very lucky to be writing for kids, and I only hope I can grow alongside my readers, and learn as I go."

Biographical and Critical Sources

PERIODICALS

Booklist, September 15, 2008, Carolyn Phelan, review of *Up and Down the Scratchy Mountains; or, The Search for a Proper Princess,* p. 51; May 15, 2009, Courtney Jones, review of *Any Which Wall,* p. 54.

Horn Book, January-February, 2009, Elissa Gershowitz, review of *Up and Down the Scratchy Mountains,* p. 102; May-June, 2009, Elissa Gershowitz, review of *Any Which Wall,* p. 308.

Kirkus Reviews, July 15, 2008, review of *Up and Down the Scratchy Mountains;* September 1, 2008, review of *Inside the Slidy Diner.*

Publishers Weekly, January 30, 2006, review of *Half/Life: Jew-ish Tales from Interfaith Homes,* p. 64; October 13, 2008, review of *Inside the Slidy Diner,* p. 54.

School Library Journal, September, 2008, Mari Pongkhamsing, review of *Up and Down the Scratchy Mountains,* p. 194; November, 2008, Beth Cuddy, review of *Inside the Slidy Diner,* p. 101; June, 2009, Eva Mitnick, review of *Any Which Wall,* p. 138.

Tikkun, May-June, 2006, Julia Bloch, review of *Half-Life,* p. 74.

ONLINE

Laurel Snyder Home Page, http://laurelsnyder.com (December 17, 2009).

*   *   *

STAAKE, Bob 1957-

Personal

Born September 26, 1957, in Los Angeles, CA; married Paulette Fehlig; children: Ryan, Kevin. *Education:* University of Southern California, B.S. (journalism), 1977. *Hobbies and other interests:* Traveling, house renovation, painting, foreign movies, collecting mid-century modern furnishings, engineering stone walls.

Addresses

Office—Chatham, MA. *E-mail*—bob@bobstaake.com.

Career

Illustrator, cartoonist, graphic artist, and writer. Freelance artist and designer for corporate and private clients; designer of greeting cards, multimedia, and internet sites.

Awards, Honors

Reuben Award nominations for Best Newspaper Illustrator and Best Greeting Card Cartoonist, both 1997; Book of the Year nomination, Children's Choice Book Awards, 2009, for *The Donut Chef.*

Writings

FOR CHILDREN; SELF-ILLUSTRATED

My Little 1 2 3 Book, Little Simon (New York, NY), 1998.
My Little A B C Book, Little Simon (New York, NY), 1998.
My Little Color Book, Little Simon (New York, NY), 2001.
My Little Opposites Book, Little Simon (New York, NY), 2001.
Hello, Robots, Viking (New York, NY), 2004.
The Red Lemon, Golden Books (New York, NY), 2006.
This Is Not a Pumpkin, Little Simon (New York, NY), 2007.
Pets Go Pop!, Little, Brown (New York, NY), 2008.
The Donut Chef, Golden Books (New York, NY), 2008.

FOR ADULTS; SELF-ILLUSTRATED

Humor and Cartoon Market (annual), Writer's Digest Books (Cincinnati, OH), 1990, 1991, 1993.
The Complete Book of Caricature, North Light Books (Cincinnati, OH), 1991.
The Complete Book of Humorous Art, North Light Books (Cincinnati, OH), 1996.
The Orb of Chatham, Commonwealth Editions (Beverly, MA), 2005.
(Adaptor) Heinrich Hoffmann, *Struwwelpeter and Other Disturbing Tales for Human Beings,* Fantagraphics (Seattle, WA), 2006.

ILLUSTRATOR; FOR CHILDREN

Boing!: A Hands-free Guide to Tricks, Gizmos, and Natural Blunders, Simon & Schuster/Nickelodeon (New York, NY), 1996.
Splish!: A Hands-free Guide to the Sea Monkeys' Greatest Show, Simon & Schuster/Nickelodeon (New York, NY), 1996.
Susan Pohlmann and Priscilla Turner, *The Boy's Guide to Life,* Addison Wesley Longman (Boston, MA), 1998.
Susan Pohlmann and Priscilla Turner, *The Girl's Guide to Life,* Addison Wesley Longman (Boston, MA), 1998.
Sindy McKay, *June's Tune,* Treasure Bay (South San Francisco, CA), 2000.

Jess Brallier, *Bouncing Science,* Planet Dexter (New York, NY), 2000.

Jess Brallier, *Hairy Science,* Planet Dexter (New York, NY), 2000.

Jess Brallier, *Shadowy Science: All You Need Is a Shadow!,* Planet Dexter (New York, NY), 2000.

Jess Brallier, *Thumbs up Science,* Planet Dexter (New York, NY), 2000.

Jana Carson, *The Mighty Little Lion Hunter,* Treasure Bay, 2000.

Little Golden Picture Dictionary, Golden Books (New York, NY), 2002.

Charles Ghigna, *One Hundred Shoes: A Math Reader,* Random House (New York, NY), 2002.

Melanie Davis Jones, *Pigs Rock!,* Viking (New York, NY), 2003.

Dennis Shealy, *I'm a Truck,* Random House (New York, NY), 2006.

Jack Lechner, *Mary Had a Little Lamp,* Bloomsbury Children's Books (New York, NY), 2008.

Babs Bell, *Sputter, Sputter, Sput!,* HarperCollins (New York, NY), 2008.

Diane Muldrow, *We Planted a Tree,* Golden Books (New York, NY), 2010.

ILLUSTRATOR; OTHER

Jay Leno, *Headlines: The Tonight Show, Book I,* Warner Books (New York, NY), 1989.

Dr. Lendon H. Smith, M.D., *Happiness Is a Healthy Life,* Keats Publishing (New Canaan, CT), 1992.

True and Tacky II: More Weird Stories from the World's Newswires, Topper Books (New York, NY), 1992.

Gene Weingarten, *The Hypochondriac's Guide to Life and Death,* Simon & Schuster (New York, NY), 1998.

Contributor to periodicals, including *Chicago Tribune, Parents, Forbes, Los Angeles Times, Los Angeles Weekly, New Yorker, New York Times, Nickelodeon, Mad, Playboy, San Francisco Weekly, Soap Opera Digest, Time, USA Today, Wall Street Journal, Washington Business Review,* and *Washington Post.* Author of newsletter *The Sporadic Bob.*

Sidelights

A popular illustrator and cartoonist whose abstract artwork has been featured on the cover of the *New Yorker,* Bob Staake has never taken an art class. His colorful il-

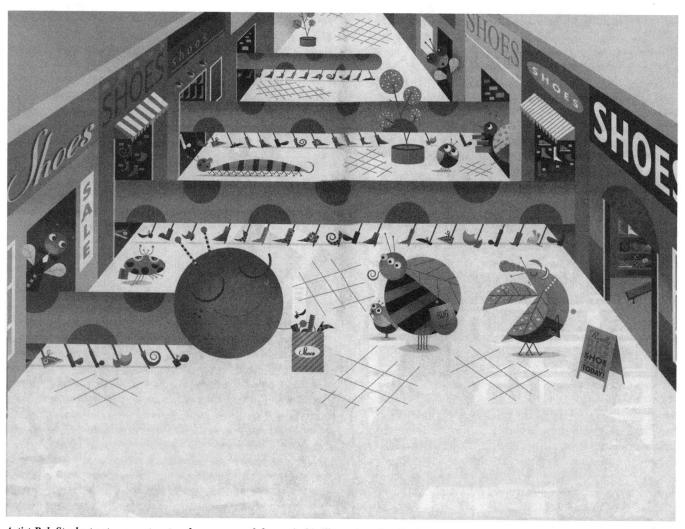

Artist Bob Staake treats youngsters to a humorous math lesson in his illustrations for Charles Ghigna's **One Hundred Shoes.** (Random House, 2002. Reproduced by permission of Random House, an imprint of Random House Children's Books, a division of Random House, Inc.)

lustrations, which feature flat, geometric shapes and a layered, Colorforms effect, have appeared in advertisements, editorial cartoons, animated cartoons, and books since the late 1980s. In 1991, while transitioning to digital art, Staake added "writer" to his list of accomplishments, producing *The Complete Book of Caricature* and *The Complete Book of Humorous Art* and then move into children's books. In addition to illustrating books by other writers, Staake has created board books, original picture books such as *The Red Lemon* and *The Donut Chef,* and has produced a modern retelling of nineteenth-century writer Heinrich Hoffman's *Struwwelpeter and Other Disturbing Tales for Human Beings,* the last which contains ten stories that are designed specifically to give young children bad dreams. Praising his artwork for *Pigs Rock!,* a picture book by Melanie Davis Jones, a *Kirkus Reviews* writer characterized Staake's "evocative graphic art" as utilizing a "flat, but varied, color scale" and a "dazzling array of shapes."

Staake's career began at West Torrance, California, High School, where he drew editorial cartoons for the school newspaper. When one of his cartoons won a contest and was featured in *People* magazine, it gained the young illustrator national attention, and Staake began to receive job offers. "When I began working for my school newspaper, I realized that there was power in my drawings," he recalled to Renee Stovsky in an interview for the *St. Louis Post-Dispatch.* "I no longer viewed them from an aesthetic standpoint. The drawings became subservient to the expression of my ideas."

Not long after the *People* article was published, *Los Angeles Times* cartoonist Paul Conrad became Staake's mentor. Conrad even helped the young man gain admission to the University of Southern California on a full scholarship, and there Staake wrote editorial cartoons for the campus newspaper, the *Daily Trojan,* while majoring in journalism. After graduating from college, he worked for a while before making the decision to become a full-time freelance illustrator.

Staake's first self-illustrated children's books are the toddler-friendly concept books *My Little 1 2 3 Book, My Little A B C Book, My Little Color Book,* and *My Little Opposites Book.* Although these colorful books exhibit "a certain sophistication," as Staake commented in the *St. Louis Journalism Review,* they remain "very accessible to kids." "They just don't insult children," the author added. "There's not a bunch of little ducklings running around. The books have a certain digital aesthetic with lots of graphics." "Although many board books introduce concepts, Staake's are notable for the sophistication of their graphic design," observed Carolyn Phelan in a *Booklist* review of the four-book series.

Hello, Robots, Staake's first large-format picture book, taps into boys' love of robots. In its story, four robots run a human household, each one specializing in a specific task. In another picture book, *The Red Lemon* a conventional farmer who believes that all lemons should

Staake was inspired to create his quirky picture book **The Donut Chef** *by contemplating his favorite breakfast food.* (Copyright © 2008 by Bob Staake. All rights reserved. Reproduced by permission of A Golden Book, an imprint of Random House Children's Books, a division of Random House, Inc.)

be exactly the same tosses out a mutant fruit in disgust when it appears in his tidy lemon grove. The red lemon stands the test of time, however, and after several generations it has supplanted its yellow cousin in popularity due to its superior flavor. *Hello, Robots* will captivate children with its futuristic story as well as the "fascinating computer-enhanced artwork that features crisp geometric shapes and Technicolor hues," according to *Booklist* critic Ilene Cooper. Kathleen Kelly MacMillan praised the same work in *School Library Journal,* noting its "clean graphic style, . . . staccato rhyming text, and a surefire kid-pleaser of a subject." Comparing *The Red Lemon* to books by Dr. Seuss, Susan Myers Harold wrote in the same periodical that the book's "effortlessly rhyming text" is balanced by its "polished, graphic-arts feel." "Filled with visual and verbal humor," according to a *Kirkus Reviews* writer, Staake's *The Red Lemon* treats readers to a picture book that is both "vividly cartoonish and exuberant, yet deceptively simple."

Staake was inspired to write *The Donut Chef* while mulling over the fact that bagels, while starting out simple and unadorned, have gradually evolved into something more and more complicated and donut-like. In the book, two bakers operate donut shops in close proximity, and their efforts to win more customers prompt them to create ever-more-bizarre donut variet-

ies. The bakers are finally reminded of their original calling—to create the perfect classic donut—when a little girl rejects the stores' bakery cases, overflowing with complex pastries, in favor of a simple glazed donut. The "lively rhythmic text and colorful artwork" will make *The Donut Chef* "a good pick for storytime," predicted Jane Marino in a *School Library Journal* review of Staake's picture book. "Everywhere readers look, there are delectable surprises," asserted a *Publishers Weekly* critic, the reviewer adding that the author/illustrator salutes "simple pleasures" in his "jubilant" rhyming text.

Reflecting on the task of contemporary children's books, Staake noted on the Random House Web site: "In an age when writers, illustrators, publishers, and booksellers are faced with the challenges of a world where video game explosions, blasts, and over-the-top sound effects seem so effortlessly capable of capturing the attention of kids, competing with that sort of baroqueness is an uphill battle. But by accepting and building upon the more quiet and poetic aspects of a children's picture book, it's my greatest hope that these simple words and images really do more to inspire, nurture, and encourage a child's imagination."

Biographical and Critical Sources

PERIODICALS

Booklist, July, 2001, Carolyn Phelan, review of *My Little Opposites Book,* p. 2021; December 1, 2004, Ilene Cooper, review of *Hello, Robots,* p. 662.

Kirkus Reviews, March 1, 2003, review of *Pigs Rock!,* pp. 388-389; August 1, 2004, review of *Hello, Robots,* p. 749; August 1, 2006, review of *The Red Lemon,* p. 796; March 15, 2008, review of *Mary Had a Little Lamp;* September 1, 2008, review of *The Donut Chef.*

New York Times Book Review, November 12, 2006, Rebecca Zerkin, review of *The Red Lemon,* p. 47; October 14, 2007, Julie Just, review of *This Is Not a Pumpkin,* p. 19.

Publishers Weekly, January 6, 2003, review of *Pigs Rock!,* p. 58; October 9, 2006, review of *The Red Lemon,* p. 55; October 27, 2008, review of *The Donut Chef,* p. 53.

St. Louis Journalism Review, May, 1998, Don Corrigan, "Bob Staake: Future of Newspapers Belongs to Visual Artists," pp. 1-2; August, 2007, Joe Pollack, "Bob Staake: Computer Savvy, Still Likes to Paint Bathrooms," p. 26.

St. Louis Post-Dispatch, April 8, 1998, Renee Stovsky, interview with Staake.

School Arts, September, 1998, Kent Anderson, review of *The Complete Book of Humorous Art,* pp. 56-57.

School Library Journal, March, 2003, Rosalyn Pierini, review of *Pigs Rock,* p. 196; December, 2004, Kathleen Kelly MacMillan, review of *Hello, Robots,* p. 122; September, 2006, Suzanne Myers Harold, review of *The Red Lemon,* p. 184; March, 2008, Linda L. Walkins, review of *Mary Had a Little Lamp,* p. 170; October, 2008, Jane Marino, review of *The Donut Chef,* p. 125.

ONLINE

Bob Staake Home Page, http://www.bobstaake.com (December 15, 2009).

Bob Staake Web log, http://www.drawger.com/bobstaake (December 15, 2009).

Random House Web site, http://www.randomhouse.com/ (December 15, 2009), "Bob Staake."*

*   *   *

STAMPLER, Ann Redisch

Personal

Married; children. *Education:* Pomona College, B.A.; University of California at Berkeley, J.D.; University of California Los Angeles, Ph.D. (psychology). *Religion:* Jewish.

Addresses

Home—Los Angeles, CA. *E-mail*—ann@annstampler. com.

Career

Author of books for children. Former attorney and psychotherapist; freelance writer, beginning 1993; presenter at schools.

Member

Society of Children's Book Writers and Illustrators, Children's Book Council of Southern California.

Awards, Honors

Sydney Taylor Award Notable Book designation, Association of Jewish Libraries, Best Book of the Year designation, Bank Street College School of Education, and Aesop Accolade honor, American Folklore Society, all 2003, all for *Something for Nothing;* Sydney Taylor Award Honor Book designation, National Jewish Book Award finalist for best illustrated children's book, Jewish Book Council, and P.J. Library selection, Harold Grinspoon Foundation, all 2006, all for *Shlemazel and the Remarkable Spoon of Pohost;* CYBILS Award nomination for Fiction Picture Book, 2008, for *Go Home, Mrs. Beekman.*

Writings

Something for Nothing, illustrated by Jacqueline M. Cohen, Clarion Books (New York, NY), 2003.

Shlemazel and the Remarkable Spoon of Pohost, illustrated by Jacqueline M. Cohen, Clarion Books (New York, NY), 2006.

Go Home, Mrs. Beekman!, illustrated by Marsha Gray Carrington, Dutton Children's Books (New York, NY), 2008.

The Rooster Prince of Breslov, illustrated by Eugene Yelchin, Clarion Books (New York, NY), 2010.

Sidelights

Although she enjoyed writing as a child, Ann Redisch Stampler went on to work as a practicing lawyer while also earning her doctorate in psychology. Her career trajectory took an unplanned turn, however, when a serious illness prompted Stampler to step back and reassess her priorities. Tapping her creative talents, she decided to return to writing, and the Yiddish stories from her family's past provided the inspiration for her first picture book, _Something for Nothing._

A story about a city dog that moves to the county only to confront a trio of mean cats bent on causing trouble, _Something for Nothing_ was published in 2003 with watercolor illustrations by Jacqueline M. Cohen. A "clever story," according to a _Publishers Weekly_ reviewer, Stampler's picture-book debut features a "cache of onomatopoeic words [that] makes for a diverting read-aloud." In _School Library Journal,_ Genevieve Gallagher cited the cats' clever but noisy comeuppance and recommended _Something for Nothing_ as "an appealing story that would make a fine read-aloud with lots of sound effects."

Stampler's grandparents emigrated from Eastern Europe during the 1920s, and her parents "were born here but spoke Yiddish in their homes," as she recalled on her home page. "When I was born in the 1950s, they had just failed in their struggle to get past the I.N.S. anti-immigration regulations to save their extended families from the Holocaust. No one made it to America; no one was saved. The culture they had come from was utterly destroyed, and though _Yiddishkeit_ and folklore were greatly respected, there was a real push to raise the grandchildren as all American.

"Jewish folklore took on an exotic, almost mysterious quality for me growing up, tied as it was to an aspect of my family's history that no one was willing to discuss. It served as a vital link for me between my life as an all-American blonde girl giggling through the Eisenhower years, and the dark, rich foreign roots that so shaped my deeper values and world view."

In _Shlemazel and the Remarkable Spoon of Pohost,_ Stampler mines another story from her Easter European heritage. Also featuring Cohen's art, the book is set in the city of Pohost, where the author's grandmother was born, and tells a story of hope that reassures readers that true fulfillment comes from working to help others. Shlemazel is a shiftless young man who claims he is so unlucky that the only way he can stay out of trouble is to do absolutely nothing. When the village tinker gives Shlemazel a spoon that he claims will bring its owner luck, he tricks the lazy man into using the spoon to search for luck by digging up a field to make it ready for planting, helping the miller bag mountains of flour, and stirring up the baker's batter, ultimately learning to prepare tasty challah bread and pastries for the village and also winning the pretty baker as his kind and beau-

tiful wife. The story ends with Shlemazel's realization that it was hard work and not luck that brought him to this happy outcome.

"Stampler's sweet tale of success will resonate with children," predicted a _Kirkus Reviews_ writer in reviewing _Shlemazel and the Remarkable Spoon of Pohost,_ while in _School Library Journal_ Teri Markson called the author's retelling "a storyteller's delight" due to her use of "humor, hyperbole, and delicious adjectives." In _Booklist,_ Hazel Rochman also had praise for the story, citing Cohen's "swirling, folk-art watercolors" for contributing to Stampler's "wry twist on the trickster tradition."

Discussing her second folk-tale retelling, _The Rooster Prince of Breslov,_ Stampler described the work to _SATA_ as "a beloved and hilarious Yiddish folk tale in which a young prince suddenly tears off his clothes and insists that he's a rooster! After failing miserably in their attempts to find someone to return the prince to human demeanor, the king and queen finally find a gnarled, old teacher who has quite a peculiar plan to cure him. My family's version, which I share in _The Rooster Prince of Breslov,_ has an American immigrant spin and is a coming-of-age story in which the prince learns the empathy and compassion he needs to be a man."

Stampler contributes to the genre of children's picture books designed to overcome first-day-of-school worries with _Go Home, Mrs. Beekman!,_ a picture book illustrated by Marsha Gray Carrington. In this story, Emily demands that her mother accompany her to school and stay with her constantly, and Mrs. Beekman agrees to remain. Unfortunately, after Emily makes friends, forms a relationship with her supportive teacher, and feels perfectly safe on her own, Mrs. Beekman refuses to leave, disguising herself as a coat rack, a purple hat, a green, dog, and a yellow bird dangling from a helicopter over the schoolyard. Ultimately, Emily finds the solution, communicating her desire and readiness to be on her own to a mother who is ready to listen and hug her daughter good-bye at the school gate. In _School Library Journal_ Catherine Callegari praised the colorful artwork in _Go Home, Mrs. Beekman!,_ noting that Carrington's illustrations capture the loving parent-child relationship depicted in Stampler's story, as well as Emily's "first steps toward independence." According to _Booklist_ contributor Hazel Rochman, Stampler's story of separation "nicely captures a young child's dramatic, first-school-day feelings."

Biographical and Critical Sources

PERIODICALS

Booklist, May 15, 2003, Karin Snelson, review of _Something for Nothing,_ p. 1668; June 1, 2006, Hazel Rochman, review of _Shlemazel and the Remarkable Spoon of Pohost,_ p. 78.

Kirkus Reviews, February 1, 2003, review of *Something for Nothing;* June 15, 2006, review of *Shlemazel and the Remarkable Spoon of Pohost;* June 15, 2008, review of *Go Home, Mrs. Beekman!*

Publishers Weekly, February 17, 2003, review of *Something for Nothing,* p. 75.

School Library Journal, April, 2003, Genevieve Gallagher, review of *Something for Nothing,* p. 156; July, 2006, Teri Markson, review of *Shlemazel and the Remarkable Spoon of Pohost,* p. 95; July, 2008, Catherine Callegari, review of *Go Home, Mrs. Beekman,* p. 82.

ONLINE

Ann Redisch Stampler Home Page, http://www.ann redischstampler.com (December 15, 2009).

Jewish Journal Online, http://www.jewishjournal.com/ (December 11, 2003), Beverly Gray, "Awaken Your Inner J.K. Rowling."

* * *

STEVENS, Helen

Personal

Born in Trieste, Italy; married Gordon Stevens; children: two. *Education:* Attended University of Maryland, Philadelphia Museum College of Fine Art, Pasadena City College, and San Francisco State University. *Hobbies and other interests:* Italian and Asian cooking, baking, gardening, travel.

Addresses

Home—Gardiner, ME. *E-mail*—gordon@helenstevens gallery.com.

Career

Illustrator, poet, and cartoonist. Member, Maine Arts Commission; chairperson, Gardiner, ME, Library board of trustees.

Member

Society of Children's Book Writers and Illustrators, Graphic Artist Guild, Maine Poets Society, Rotary International.

Awards, Honors

First Place Award for Writing (Editorial Cartoon; Daily), Maine Press Association.

Illustrator

Elizabeth Patten, *Healthy Foods from Healthy Soils: A Hands-on Resource for Educators,* Tilbury House Publishers (Gardner, ME), 2003.

Susan Williams Beckhorn, *Moose Eggs; or, Why Moose Has Flat Antlers,* Down East Books (Camden, ME), 2007.

Diane Keyes, *Spirit of the Snowpeople,* Down East Books (Camden, ME), 2008.

Biographical and Critical Sources

PERIODICALS

Kirkus Reviews, August 15, 2008, review of *Spirit of the Snowpeople.*

School Library Journal, January, 2009, Martha Simpson, review of *Spirit of the Snowpeople,* p. 78.

ONLINE

Helen Stevens Home Page, http://www.helenstevens gallery.com (December 20, 2009).

* * *

STEWART, Melissa 1968-

Personal

Born December 9, 1968, in Hartford, CT; daughter of Bruce (a mechanical engineer) and Dorothy (a laboratory supervisor) Stewart. *Education:* Union College, Schenectady, NY, B.S. (cum laude), 1990; New York University, M.A., 1991.

Addresses

Home and office—Honeybee Productions, 24 Kinsley Rd., Acton, MA 01720. *E-mail*—mas@melissa-stewart. com.

Career

Healthmark Medical Education Media, New York, NY, associate editor, 1991; Foca Co., New York, NY, project editor, 1992-93, managing editor, 1993-95; Grolier Publishing Co., Danbury, CT, science editor, 1995-97, senior science editor, 1997-2000; freelance writer, 1991—. Member, American Institute of Physics Children's Science Writing Award committee.

Member

American Association for the Advancement of Science, National Association of Science Writers, Foundation for Children's Books, Society of Children's Book Writer and Illustrators (director of New England conference, 2006), Massachusetts Environmental Education Society, Sigma Xi.

Awards, Honors

New York Public Library Books for the Teen Age citation, and Best Books for Children designation, *Science Books and Film,* 1998, for *Life without Light;* Best

Melissa Stewart (Photograph by Sarah Brannen. Reproduced by permission.)

Books for Children designation, *Science Books and Film,* 2001, for *Amphibians, Birds, Fish, Insects, Mammals,* and *Reptiles,* 2002, for *Antelopes, Elephants, Hippopotamuses, Rhinoceroses,* and *Zebras;* Notable Social Studies Trade Book for Young People designation, National Council for Social Studies/Children's Book Council, 2003, for *Maggots, Grubs, and More;* Recommended designation, National Science Teachers Association (NSTA), 2002, for *Life in a Lake,* 2003, for *Life in a Wetland;* NSTA Recommended designation, and Best Books for Children designation, *Science Books and Film,* both 2004, both for "Investigate Science" series; Society of School Librarians International Honor Book designation, 2005, for *Sloths;* Bank Street College Best Children's Book of the Year designation, Green Earth Book Award, Izaak Walton League of America Conservation Book of the Year designation, *Science Books and Film* Best Books for Children designation, Society of School Librarians International Best Science Book designation, and Young Hoosier Book Award nomination, all 2006, all for *A Place for Butterflies;* Keystone to Reading Book Award nomination, and *Science Books and Film* Best Books for Children designation, both 2008, both for *When Rain Falls;* NSTA Recommended designation, 2009, for "Rainbow Animals" series; Cornerstone of Science Book Award nomination, and Pacific Northwest Booksellers Book Award nomination, both 2009, both for *Under the Snow;* Society of Children's Book Writers and Illustrators nonfiction research grant.

Writings

NONFICTION

Life without Light: A Journey to Earth's Dark Ecosystems, F. Watts (Danbury, CT), 1998.

Science in Ancient India, F. Watts (Danbury, CT), 1999.
Rachel Carson: Writer and Biologist, Ferguson (Chicago, IL), 2001.
Tim Berners-Less: Inventor of the World Wide Web, Ferguson (Chicago, IL), 2001.
Seals, Sea Lions, and Walruses, F. Watts (New York, NY), 2001.
Uranus, F. Watts (New York, NY), 2002.
Life in a Lake, Lerner (Minneapolis, MN), 2003.
Small Birds, Benchmark Books (New York, NY), 2003.
Life in a Wetland, photographs by Stephen K. Maka, Lerner (Minneapolis, MN), 2003.
Maggots, Grubs, and More: The Secret Lives of Young Insects, Millbrook (Brookfield, CT), 2003.
How Animals Breathe, Newbridge Publishing (New York, NY), 2003.
Robotic Scorpions, Silver Dolphin Press (San Diego, CA), 2004.
Claws and Jaws!, Becker & Mayer, 2004.
Meet the Beetles, Newbridge, 2005.
Get a Grip: How Your Hand Really Works, Becker & Mayer, 2005.
Treating Earth's Trouble Spots, Newbridge, 2005.
The Hand Book, Tangerine Press (New York, NY), 2005.
Sloths, Carolrhoda (Minneapolis, MN), 2005.
Eye See You: A Poster Book, Storey Publishing, 2006.
Extreme Nature, HarperCollins (New York, NY), 2006.
A Place for Butterflies, illustrated by Higgins Bond, Peachtree (Atlanta, GA), 2006.
Energy in Motion, Children's Press (New York, NY), 2006.
Will It Float or Sink?, Children's Press (Danbury, CT), 2006.
Baboons, Lerner Publications (Minneapolis, MN), 2007.
Butterflies, NorthWord (Minnetonka, MN), 2007.
Extreme Rocks and Minerals!, HarperCollins (New York, NY), 2007.
Extreme Coral Reef!, HarperCollins (New York, NY), 2007.
Dinosaurs, Publications International (Lincolnwood, IL), 2007.
Giraffe Graphs, Children's Press (New York, NY), 2007.
Cell Biology, Twenty-first Century Books (Minneapolis, MN), 2008.
Classification of Life, Twenty-first Century Books (Minneapolis, MN), 2008.
Earthquakes and Volcanoes, Smithsonian (Washington, DC), 2008.
My Bug Book, Collins (New York, NY), 2008.
My Butterfly Book, Collins (New York, NY), 2008.
New World Monkeys, Lerner (Minneapolis, MN), 2008.
Rabbits ("Animals Animals" series), Marshall Cavendish Benchmark (New York, NY), 2008.
Swans ("Animals Animals" series), Marshall Cavendish Benchmark (New York, NY), 2008.
When Rain Falls, illustrated by Constance R. Bergum, Peachtree (Atlanta, GA), 2008.
Snakes!, National Geographic (Washington, DC), 2009.
Under the Snow, illustrated by Constance R. Bergum, Peachtree Publishers (Atlanta, GA), 2009.
A Place for Birds, Peachtree (Atlanta, GA), 2009.
How Does Sand become Glass?, Heineman/Raintree (Chicago, IL), 2009.
How Does a Bone become a Fossil?, Heineman/Raintree (Chicago, IL), 2009.

A Daddy Longlegs Isn't a Spider, Winward Books (Lakeville, MN), 2009.

Contributor to books, including *Blueprint for Life, Secrets of the Inner Mind,* Time-Life (Alexandria, VA); *Biology: Visualizing Life,* Holt (New York, NY); and *Biology,* Addison-Wesley (Reading, MA). Contributor of articles and columns to magazines and newspapers, including *American Forests, American Heritage of Invention and Technology, Ask, Book Links, ChemMatters, Click, Family Planning Perspectives, Highlights for Children, Instructor, Math, National Geographic World, Natural New England, New York Daily News, New York Doctor, Northern Woodlands, North Maine Woods Bulletin, Odyssey, Parent and Child, Ranger Rick, Reading Today, Science World, Spider, Today's Science, Washington Square News, Wildlife Conservation, Wild Outdoor World, Writer,* and *ZooGoer.*

"TRUE BOOKS" SERIES

Mammals, Children's Press (Danbury, CT), 2001.
Amphibians, Children's Press (Danbury, CT), 2001.
Birds, Children's Press (Danbury, CT), 2001.
Fishes, Children's Press (Danbury, CT), 2001.
Reptiles, Children's Press (Danbury, CT), 2001.
Insects, Children's Press (Danbury, CT), 2001.
Hippopotamuses, Children's Press (Danbury, CT), 2002.
Elephants, Children's Press (Danbury, CT), 2002.
Antelope, Children's Press (Danbury, CT), 2002.
Zebras, Children's Press (Danbury, CT), 2002.
Rhinoceroses, Children's Press (Danbury, CT), 2002.

"ROCKS AND MINERALS" SERIES

Minerals, Heinemann Library (Chicago, IL), 2002.
Metamorphic Rocks, Heinemann Library (Chicago, IL), 2002.
Igneous Rocks, Heinemann Library (Chicago, IL), 2002.
Fossils, Heinemann Library (Chicago, IL), 2002.
Crystals, Heinemann Library (Chicago, IL), 2002.
Soil, Heinemann Library (Chicago, IL), 2002.
Sedimentary Rocks, Heinemann Library (Chicago, IL), 2002.

"SIMPLY SCIENCE" SERIES

Atoms, Compass Point (Minneapolis, MN), 2003.
Fossils, Compass Point (Minneapolis, MN), 2003.
Motion, Compass Point (Minneapolis, MN), 2003.
Plants, Compass Point (Minneapolis, MN), 2003.

"RANGER RICK SCIENCE PROGRAM" SERIES

Cells to Systems, Newbridge, 2003.
The Producers, Newbridge, 2003.
Shorebirds, Newbridge, 2003.

"INVESTIGATE SCIENCE" SERIES

Animals All Around, Compass Point (Minneapolis, MN), 2004.
Down to Earth, illustrated by Jeffrey Scherer, Compass Point (Minneapolis, MN), 2004.
A Parade of Plants, illustrated by Jeffrey Scherer, Compass Point (Minneapolis, MN), 2004.
Fun with the Sun, Compass Point (Minneapolis, MN), 2004.
Use Your Senses, Compass Point (Minneapolis, MN), 2005.
What's the Weather, Compass Point (Minneapolis, MN), 2005.
Air Is Everywhere, Compass Point (Minneapolis, MN), 2005.
The Wonders of Water, Compass Point (Minneapolis, MN), 2005.

"TELL ME WHY, TELL ME HOW" SERIES

How Do Birds Fly?, Marshall Cavendish Benchmark (New York, NY), 2006.
How Do Fish Breathe Underwater?, Marshall Cavendish Benchmark (New York, NY), 2006.
Why Do the Seasons Change?, Marshall Cavendish Benchmark (New York, NY), 2006.
How Do Plants Grow?, Marshall Cavendish Benchmark (New York, NY), 2006.
How Do Bats Fly in the Dark?, Marshall Cavendish Benchmark (New York, NY). 2008.
How Does Sand Become Glass?, Raintree (Chicago, IL), 2008.
Why Do We See Rainbows?, Raintree (Chicago, IL), 2008.
Why Does the Moon Change Shape?, Raintree (Chicago, IL), 2008.
How Does a Bone Become a Fossil?, Raintree (Chicago, IL). 2008.
How Do Bees Make Honey?, Marshall Cavendish Benchmark (New York, NY), 2009.
How Do Chameleons Change Color?, Marshall Cavendish Benchmark (New York, NY), 2009.
How Do Spiders Make Webs?, Marshall Cavendish Benchmark (New York, NY), 2009.

"RAINBOW OF ANIMALS" SERIES

Why Are Animals Blue?, Enslow Publishers (Berkeley Heights, NJ), 2009.
Why Are Animals Green?, Enslow Publishers (Berkeley Heights, NJ), 2009.
Why Are Animals Orange?, Enslow Publishers (Berkeley Heights, NJ), 2009.
Why Are Animals Purple?, Enslow Publishers (Berkeley Heights, NJ), 2009.
Why Are Animals Red?, Enslow Publishers (Berkeley Heights, NJ), 2009.
Why Are Animals Yellow?, Enslow Publishers (Berkeley Heights, NJ), 2009.

"GROSS AND GOOFY BODY" SERIES

Blasts of Gas: The Secrets of Breathing, Burping, and Passing Gas, Marshall Cavendish Benchmark (New York, NY), 2009.

It's Spit-acular!: The Secrets of Saliva, Marshall Cavendish Benchmark (New York, NY), 2009.

Now Hear This!: The Secrets of Ears and Hearing, Marshall Cavendish Benchmark (New York, NY), 2009.

Pump It Up!: The Secrets of the Heart and Blood, Marshall Cavendish Benchmark (New York, NY), 2009.

The Eyes Have It: The Secrets of Eyes and Seeing, Marshall Cavendish Benchmark (New York, NY), 2009.

Up Your Nose!: The Secrets of Schnozes and Snouts, Marshall Cavendish Benchmark (New York, NY), 2009.

Dolphins, National Geographic (Washington, DC), 2010.

Germ Wars!: The Secrets of Keeping Healthy, Marshall Cavendish Benchmark (New York, NY), 2010.

Give Me a Hand: The Secrets of Hands, Feet, Arms, and Legs, Marshall Cavendish Benchmark (New York, NY), 2010.

Here We Grow: The Secrets of Hair and Nails, Marshall Cavendish Benchmark (New York, NY), 2010.

Moving and Grooving: The Secrets of Muscles and Bones, Marshall Cavendish Benchmark (New York, NY), 2010.

The Skin You're In: The Secrets of Skin, Marshall Cavendish Benchmark (New York, NY), 2010.

You've Got Nerve!: The Secrets of the Brain and Nerves, Marshall Cavendish Benchmark (New York, NY) 2010.

Sidelights

Melissa Stewart is the author of more than one hundred books for children that focus on science and the natural world. After serving as science editor of Grolier Publishing Company during the 1990s, Stewart turned to a new career in writing. Inspired by her curiosity, books such as *A Place for Birds, Extreme Rocks and Minerals!,* and *Seals, Sea Lions, and Walruses* contain a wealth of nature facts, all highlighted by intriguing in-

Stewart's award-winning nature book **A Place for Butterflies** *features detailed artwork by Higgins Bond.* (Illustration © 2006 by Higgins Bond. Reproduced courtesy of Peachtree Publishers.)

Stewart collaborates with artist Constance R. Bergum on the nature-themed picture book **When Rain Falls.** (Peachtree Publishers, 2008. Illustration © by Constance R. Bergum. Reproduced by permission.)

sights gained from the author's on-site research: among other places, Stewart has traveled to the Costa Rican rain forest, the African savannah, and the rocky Galapagos Islands while gathering information for her many

books. Her many nonfiction books include contribution to several series, such as "Investigate Science," "Rainbow of Animals," and "Tell Me Why, Tell Me How." Standalone volumes that also feature nature topics in-

clude *When Rain Falls,* a picture-book introduction to the ways diverse creatures keep dry during a rainstorm. Reviewing the book, which features watercolor illustrations by Constance R. Bergum, Kathy Piehl wrote in *School Library Journal* that Stewart's text "would be a good choice for rainy-day sharing."

Stewart was born in Hartford, Connecticut, and grew up in an area where forests, farmland, mountains, rivers, lakes, and oceans were all close at hand and changed dramatically during the four seasons. In *Life without Light: A Journey to Earth's Dark Ecosystems,* her first book, she recalled walking in the New England woods with her father as a child. Asked if she noticed anything different about the trees in that particular part of the woods, the future author observed that the trees were smaller. Stewart's father explained that a fire had raged there approximately twenty-five years earlier, and that all the trees were they now stood were new growth. "I was hooked," Stewart wrote in her book. "Ever since that moment, I have wanted to know everything about the natural world."

Geared for teen readers, *Life without Light* describes the creatures that exist near the hydrothermal vents located far below the surface of the ocean. Carolyn Phelan commented in her review of the work in *Booklist* that "the quality of the writing" is superior and the text "well-researched." Stewart's exploration of another hidden world, *Maggots, Grubs, and More: The Secret Lives of Young Insects,* also pairs fascinating photographs with an informational text that follows various insects as they grow from eggs through insect adolescence to full maturity. Karey Wehner, writing in *School Library Journal,* considered this book to be a "lucid, well-organized introduction" to insect development. More insects are featured in *Butterflies,* which pairs what Wehner described as "a crisp text" with large-scale color photographs and selected diagrams.

Moving from insects to mammals, *Animals All Around* introduces readers to the techniques scientists use in making observations about different animal species. In *School Library Journal,* Kathryn Kosiorek complimented the "clear, precise sentences and carefully chosen questions" that lead readers in Stewart's exploration. Other books featuring larger creatures include *A Place for Birds,* in which the author describes the changes humans have has wrought in birds' traditional habitats. Structured "as a set of conservation lessons," the book goes beyond bird-based facts, according to *School Library Journal* critic Margaret Bush, who recommended *A Place for Birds* as a means of "sparking classroom discussion."

Like *Animals All Around, Air Is Everywhere* involves readers in the process of scientific investigation by posing questions. From there, Stewart "asks students to make predictions, and suggests simple experiments and observations that will enhance their understanding of basic science concepts," according to Sandra Welzen-bach, a *School Library Journal* contributor reviewing *Air Is Everywhere.* More questions are posed in *Extreme Rocks and Minerals!,* as Stewart compares the different forms of rock and contrasts their characteristics, uses, and where on earth they are found. "It's hard to beat this title for a clear, accurate, and appealing survey," wrote Ellen Heath in describing *Extreme Rocks and Minerals!* for *School Library Journal.*

Stewart's biographies *Tim Berners-Lee: Inventor of the World Wide Web* and *Rachel Carson: Biologist and Writer* focus on scientists who have impacted advances in technology and environmentalism. For the book on Berners-Lee, Stewart combines a limited biography of the inventor—a very private person—with advice on how to become involved in the computer-science field. "This interesting combination of biography and career guide should have strong appeal for students," wrote Sandra L. Doggett in her *School Library Journal* review. When Stewart discovered the writings of Rachel Carson, an early-twentieth-century environmentalist and the author of *Silent Spring,* she "felt a deep affinity toward her life and work," as she recalled to Sue Reichard in a *Suite 101* online interview. For some time Carson wrestled with the choice between being a scientist and a writer. Then came an epiphany: she realized that she could do both. "That's exactly how I felt when one of my college biology professors suggested that I become a writer," Stewart told Reichard. "It was a great aha moment for me, as it was for Ms. Carson."

Stewart writes articles for adults as well as producing nonfiction books for children. Discussing what she considers when writing for multiple audiences, the author told Reichard: "I like the variety of writing for many different audiences and the challenges associated with each group. Writing for young children is fun because they are so naturally curious, and I know they will listen intently as a loving adult reads the story to them or pay close attention as they struggle to read it themselves. Middle graders and high school students can understand more sophisticated language and more complex concerns, and they have a broader view of the world. When I write for adults, I can really stretch as a writer, using my vocabulary reserves and including allusions that kids just won't get. I like doing that once in awhile." Commenting on her prolific career as a writer, Stewart wrote on her home page: "Now I get paid to learn all about the natural world and share it with other people. What could be better?"

Biographical and Critical Sources

BOOKS

Stewart, Melissa, *Life without Light: A Journey to Earth's Dark Ecosystems,* F. Watts (Danbury, CT), 1999.

PERIODICALS

Booklist, July, 1999, Carolyn Phelan, review of *Life without Light,* p. 1945; March 15, 2006, Carolyn Phelan, review of *A Place for Butterflies,* p. 52; October 15, 2006, Kay Weisman, review of *How Do Fish Breathe Underwater?,* p. 80; March 15, 2009, Carolyn Phelan, review of *A Place for Birds,* p. 63; April 1, 2009, Hazel Rochman, review of *Why Are Animals Orange?,* p. 64.

Kirkus Reviews, March 1, 2006, review of *A Place for Butterflies,* p. 241; February 15, 2008, review of *When Rain Falls;* February 15, 2009, review of *A Place for Birds.*

School Librarian, spring, 2003, review of *Sedimentary Rocks,* p. 52.

School Library Journal, August, 1999, Lynn W. Zimmerman, review of *Life without Light,* p. 180; October, 2001, Sandra L. Doggett, review of *Tim Berners-Lee: Inventor of the World Wide Web,* p. 192; November, 2001, Kathleen Isaacs, review of *Rachel Carson: Biologist and Writer,* p. 186; July, 2003, Kathryn Kosioreki, review of *Fossils,* p. 119; January, 2004, Karey Wehner, review of *Maggots, Grubs, and More: The Secret Lives of Young Insects,* p. 160; March, 2005, Sandra Welzenbach, review of *Air Is Everywhere,* p. 202; June, 2006, Patricia Manning, review of *A Place for Butterflies,* p. 141; December, 2006, Lynda Ritterman, review of *How Do Birds Fly?,* p. 126; July, 2007, Karey Wehner, review of *Butterflies,* p. 121; November, 2007, Nancy Call, review of *Rabbits,* p. 110; April, 2008, Kathy Piehl, review of *When Rain Falls,* p. 123, and Ellen Heath, review of *Extreme Rocks and Minerals!,* p. 138; January, 2009, Maren Ostergard, review of *How Do Bees Make Honey?, How Do Spiders Make Webs?,* and *Why Does the Moon Change Shape?,* all p. 96; May, 2009, Margaret Bush, review of *A Place for Birds,* p. 99.

School Science Review, Terry Jennings, review of *Life in a Lake,* pp. 133-134.

Science Books and Films, March, 2003, review of *Crystals,* p. 71; July, 2003, review of *Life in a Wetland,* p. 167; July-August, 2004, Mary Jane Davis, review of *Animals All Around,* p. 180.

ONLINE

Melissa Stewart Home Page, http://www.melissa-stewart.com (December 15, 2009).

Suite 101 Web site, http://www.suite101.com/ (November 1, 2005), Sue Reichard, interview with Stewart.

*   *   *

STRICKLAND, Shadra

Personal

Born in GA. *Education:* Syracuse University, B.F.A. (design, illustration, and writing), 1999; School of Visual Arts, M.F.A. (illustration as visual essay), 2005.

Shadra Strickland (Photograph by Christopher Myers. Reproduced by permission.)

Addresses

Home—Brooklyn, NY. *Agent*—Lori Nowicki, 310 W. 97th St., Ste. 24, New York, NY 10025; loripainted-words.com.

Career

Illustrator and graphic designer. Atlanta Public Schools, Atlanta, GA, art teacher and artist mentor of Atlanta Bureau of Cultural Affairs, 1995-2000; freelance illustrator and book designer, beginning 2000.

Member

Society of Children's Book Writers and Illustrators.

Awards, Honors

Paterson Prize for Books for Young People, Ezra Jack Keats Book Award, Bank Street College Best Children's Book of the Year designation, American Library Association Notable Children's Book designation, and John Steptoe Award for New Talent, all 2009, all for *Bird* by Zetta Elliott.

Illustrator

Zetta Elliot, *Bird,* Lee & Low (New York, NY), 2008.

Renee Watson, *A Place Where Hurricanes Happen,* Random House (New York, NY), 2010.

Contributor to anthology *Our Children Can Soar: A Celebration of Rosa, Barack, and the Pioneers of Change,* Bloomsbury (New York, NY), 2009.

Sidelights

Illustrator and graphic designer Shadra Strickland earned the John Steptoe Award for New Talent for her work in *Bird,* a picture book with a text by New York City poet and playwright Zetta Elliott. In Elliott's story, called "a promising debut" by a *Publishers Weekly*

Illustration by Shadra Strickland, from **Bird,** *a picture book by Zetta Elliot.* (Illustration courtesy of Shadra Strickland.)

critic, Mehkai is broken hearted following the death of his older brother. Marcus, a talented graffiti artist, has finally lost his long battle against drug addiction, and following Marcus's funeral death soon overtakes the brothers' grief-stricken grandfather as well. Fortunately, Mehkai—nicknamed Bird—has a talent for drawing, and with the wise counsel of an older friend, he learns that his art can provide him with a place to hide and a constructive way to work through his emotions while trying to find his purpose and path in the world.

Writing in *Booklist,* Hazel Rochman called *Bird* a "beautiful picture book for older readers," citing Elliott's "spare free verse" and Strickland's "clear mixed-media pictures." The *Publishers Weekly* critic was impressed by the artist's "complicated weaving" of multimedia images throughout Elliott's story, writing that they enhance "the metaphors and action of the poetic text." In *School Library Journal* Kate McClelland wrote that the artwork in *Bird* is "rendered with a delicate touch in watercolor, gouache, charcoal, and pen, emphasiz[ing] . . . the textual theme of resilience in adversity." Also appraising Elliott and Strickland's award-winning picture-book collaboration, a *Kirkus Reviews* writer cited the artist's ability to capture the instability of a drug addict through the use of "shifting perspectives and colors" as well as "off-kilter lines [that] exude . . . random energy."

Biographical and Critical Sources

PERIODICALS

Booklist, November 1, 2008, Hazel Rochman, review of *Bird,* p. 54.
Kirkus Reviews, September 1, 2008, review of *Bird.*
Publishers Weekly, October 20, 2008, review of *Bird,* p. 50.
School Library Journal, October, 2008, Kate McClelland, review of *Bird,* p. 106.

ONLINE

Lee & Low Web site, http://www.leeandlow.com/ (December 15, 2009), "Shadra Strickland."
Shadra Strickland Home Page, http://www.shadrastrickland.com (December 15, 2009).

*   *   *

STUCHNER, Joan Betty

Personal

Born in Leeds, England; immigrated to Canada, 1965. *Education:* Attended Langara College; University of British Columbia, B.A. (English), 1977, teaching diploma, 1979. *Hobbies and other interests:* Ballet, galleries, museums.

Addresses

Home—Vancouver, British Columbia, Canada. *E-mail*—hayabat@shaw.ca.

Career

Author, storyteller, librarian, and educator. Part-time teacher; University of British Columbia, Vancouver, British Columbia, Canada, member of library staff. Actor in community theatre and on television; professional storyteller.

Member

Children's Writers and Illustrators of British Columbia.

Awards, Honors

Canadian Center for Books for Children Our Choice selection, 2007, and Shining Willow Award, 2008, both for *Sadie the Ballerina;* Pacific Northwest Bookseller's Association Award nomination, Sydney Taylor Book Award Notable Book designation, Association of Jewish Libraries, and Chocolate Lily Award, all 2009, and Red Cedar Award nomination, 2010, all for *Honey Cake;* Amelia Bloomer Award nomination, 2009, for *Josephine's Dream.*

Writings

A Peanut Butter Waltz, illustrated by Diana Durrand, Annick Press (Toronto, Ontario, Canada), 1990.

Shira's Hanukkah Gift, illustrated by Richard Row, Scholastic Canada (Toronto, Ontario, Canada), 1998, published as *The Kugel Valley Klezmer Band,* North Winds Press (Richmond Hill, Ontario, Canada), 1998, Crocodile Books (New York, NY), 2001.

Sadie the Ballerina, illustrated by Bruno St. Aubin, Scholastic Canada (Toronto, Ontario, Canada), 2006.

Honey Cake, illustrated by Cynthia Nugent, Tradewinds Books (Vancouver, British Columbia, Canada), 2007, Random House (New York, NY), 2008.

Josephine's Dream, illustrated by Chantelle Walther, Silverleaf, 2008.

Author's work has been translated into French.

Sidelights

Living in Vancouver, British Columbia, Canada, Joan Betty Stuchner has managed to integrate her love of books and her interests in storytelling into her multifaceted career. A part-time teacher and a librarian at the University of British Columbia, Stuchner also works as a storyteller and an actor in civic theater. Although she published her first book, *A Peanut Butter Waltz,* in 1990, she did not pursue a career writing for children until later in the decade. Stuchner's other books for children include the picture books *Shira's Hanukkah Gift, Sadie the Ballerina,* and *Josephine's Dream,* as well as the award-winning chapter book *Honey Cake.*

Several of Stuchner's books are based in Jewish history and culture. First published as *Shira's Hanukkah Gift, The Kugel Valley Klezmer Band* pairs Richard Row's illustrations with Stuchner's story about a ten-year-old girl whose dream is to play the fiddle in her father's klezmer band. Her friend Isaac, the band's violinist, gives Shira a toy violin and encourages her to practice. Ultimately, the girl is able to return the favor when she becomes proficient enough to substitute for Isaac when he is too ill to perform with his bandmates. Praising the "lively narrative oil paintings" Row contributes to *The Kugel Valley Klezmer Band* for capturing life in a transplanted "Eastern European shtetl community," Annette Goldsmith added in *Quill & Quire* that Stuchner's story has "panache." In *Resource Links* "Joanne de Groot cited the book's "easy-to-read style" and called Shira "a girl that children will admire for her courage and her determination."

Other picture books by Stuchner include *Sadie the Ballerina,* a story about a young girl's dream of becoming a graceful dancer. The author also focuses on the world

Joan Stuchner recounts a true story of World War II in her picture book Honey Cake, *featuring artwork by Cynthia Nugent.* (Illustration copyright © 2007 by Cynthia Nugent. Used in the U.S. by permission of Random House Children's Books, a division of Random House, Inc. In U.K. and Canada by permission of Tradewind Books.)

of the arts in the picture-book biography *Josephine's Dream*. Stuchner's story is based on the life of twentieth-century vocalist Josephine Baker and features what Joan Kindig described in *School Library Journal* as "stylized color illustrations" by Chantelle Walther. Raised in the slums of St. Louis, Missouri, Baker dreamed of becoming a singer and entertainer, but as she grew older she recognized that this would not be easy because of the barriers against people of color within the United States. A move to France in the 1920s allowed Baker to fulfill her dream, and she supported her adopted country by aiding the French resistance during World War II. Later in her career she returned to the country of her birth, joining the historic March on Washington alongside the Reverend Martin Luther King, Jr. and also using her fame to fight segregation in her audiences as well. In *Library Media Connection*, Stacey Rosenthal dubbed *Josephine's Dream* a "powerful" story in which "Stuchner's words are as commanding as the story itself."

In *Honey Cake* Stuchner takes readers to 1943 Copenhagen, as the Nazis occupy that city during World War II. For a ten-year-old Jewish boy named David Nathan, things in his family have changed since the German soldiers' arrival. Mr. Nathan has difficulty finding the butter and cream needed to keep his bakery running, and both parents seem worried about David's older sister, Rachel, who has joined the Resistance and now comes and goes at odd hours. When David's father suddenly makes a batch of rich pastries, the boy is surprised. Who has the money to order such a lavish treat? The boy soon finds out when he is asked to make an important delivery that binds him closer to his family as well as to the larger community of people resisting the occupying force. In *Quill & Quire* Marnie Parsons called *Honey Cake* a "well-constructed novel with some finely developed images and motifs," and also praised Stuchner's prose as "clear and competent." Victoria Pennell noted the "gentle manner" in which the author tells her war-time tale, adding in *Resource Links* that the story nonetheless conveys "the kind of fear these people were living under" as the Holocaust approached.

Biographical and Critical Sources

PERIODICALS

Booklist, July 1, 2008 Hazel Rochman, review of *Honey Cake*, p. 66.
Canadian Review of Materials, December 8, 2006, Karen Kiddey, review of *Sadie the Ballerina*.
Kirkus Reviews, July 15, 2008, review of *Honey Cake*.
Library Media Connection, April-May, 2008, Stacy Rosenthal, review of *Josephine's Dream*.
Publishers Weekly, January 28, 2002, review of *The Kugel Valley Klezmer Band*, p. 289.
Quill & Quire, November, 1998, Annette Goldsmith, review of *The Kugel Valley Klezmer Band;* July, 2007, Marnie Parsons, review of *Honey Cake*.

Resource Links, June 2002, Joanne de Groot, review of *Shira's Hanukkah Gift*, p. 7; April, 2007, John Dryden, review of *Sadie the Ballerina*, p. 10; October, 2007, Victoria Pennell, review of *Honey Cakes*, p. 22.
School Library Journal, June, 2002, Amy Lilien-Harper, review of *The Kugel Valley Klezmer Band*, p. 112; August, 2008, Joan Kindig, review of *Josephine's Dream*, p. 103.

ONLINE

Children's Writers and Illustrators of British Columbia Web site, http://www.cwill.bc.ca/ (December 15, 2009), "Joan Betty Stuchner."
Joan Betty Stuchner Web log, http://joanbettystuchner. blogspot.com (December 15, 2009).*

*   *   *

SUE, Majella Lue

Personal

Born in Trinidad and Tobago. *Education:* Art Center College of Design (Pasadena, CA), B.F.A. (illustration; with honors), 2005.

Addresses

Home—Pasadena, CA. *E-mail*—majellals@majellaluesue.com.

Career

Illustrator and graphic designer.

Illustrator

Rebecca O'Connell, *Penina Levine Is a Hard-boiled Egg*, Roaring Brook Press (New Milford, CT), 2007.
Rebecca O'Connell, *Penina Levine Is a Potato Pancake*, Roaring Brook Press (New York, NY), 2008.

Sidelights

Majella Lue Sue grew up in Trinidad and Tobago, but moved to California to attend the prestigious Art Center College of Design. Remaining in Pasadena following her graduation, with honors, from the school's illustration program, Sue now works as a graphic designer in addition to beginning her career in book illustration.

In a review of Sue's first illustration project, creating artwork for Rebecca O'Connell's middle-grade novel *Penina Levine Is a Hard-boiled Egg, School Library Journal* contributor Kim Dare cited the way Sue "complement[s] the dynamic humor" of O'Connell's entertaining story. In the book, Penina Levine is a sixth grader who deals with a pesky sister and annoying parents until a bad grade on a school writing assignment casts an even darker pall on her life. Penina's Jewish

Majella Lue Sue's illustration projects include creating the artwork for Rebecca O'Connell's elementary-grade novel Penina Levine Is a Hard-boiled Egg. (Illustration copyright © 2007 by Majella Lue Sue. Reprinted by permission of Henry Holt & Company, LLC.)

traditions are a central focus of the novel, and they also reappear in a sequel, *Penina Levine Is a Potato Pancake,* which finds the preteen celebrating Hanukkah despite a series of disappointments and disruptions. O'Connell's "sweet and funny holiday tale" is enlivened by Sue's "quirky cartoons," which "add interest" to the second "Penina Levine" novel, according to *School Library Journal* critic Kathleen Meulen.

Biographical and Critical Sources

PERIODICALS

Booklist, March 15, 2007, Kay Weisman, review of *Penina Levine Is a Hard-boiled Egg,* p. 49.

Kirkus Reviews, Septmeber 1, 2008, review of *Penina Levine Is a Potato Pancake.*

School Library Journal, March, 2007, Kim Dare, review of *Penina Levine Is a Hard-boiled Egg,* p. 216; December, 2008, Kathleen Meulen, review of *Penina Levine Is a Potato Pancake,* p. 134.

ONLINE

Majella Lue Sue Home Page, http://www.majellaluesue.com (December 15, 2009).*

*   *   *

SWANSON, Susan Marie 1955-

Personal

Born May 19, 1955, in Hinsdale, IL; daughter of David W. (a physician) and Lois (a teacher and musician) Swanson; married; children: two sons. *Education:* St. Olaf College, B.A. (English and poetry), 1977; University of Massachusetts Amherst, M.F.A. (English), 1981; Augsburg College, teaching credential, 1988.

Addresses

Home—St. Paul, MN.

Career

Writer. University of Massachusetts at Amherst, instructor in rhetoric, 1979-80; COMPAS Writers and Artists in the School program, visiting author and teacher, beginning 1983; St. Paul Academy, early childhood arts instructor in summer arts program, 1988-2007; Metropolitan State University, member of community faculty, 2005-07; instructor at Friends School of Minnesota, 2008. Children's book review editor, *Hungry Mind Review,* 1991-93.

Member

Phi Beta Kappa.

Awards, Honors

Bush Foundation poetry fellowship; McKnight Foundation poetry fellowship; Minnesota State Arts Board fellowship in poetry; McKnight Foundation fellowship in children's literature; *Booklinks* Lasting Connection selection, 1998, for *Letter to the Lake;* Charlotte Zolotow Honor Book designation, and Picture-Book Honor designation, Cooperative Children's Book Center, both 2002, both for *The First Thing My Mama Told Me;* Minnesota Book Award, Titles for Reading and Sharing designation, New York Public Library, and AARP Book for Grandparents designation, all 2009, all for *The House in the Night; The House in the Night* was awarded the Caldecot Medal in 2009, for illustrations by Beth Krommes.

Writings

FOR CHILDREN

Getting Used to the Dark: Twenty-six Night Poems, illustrated by Peter Catalanotto, DK Ink (New York, NY), 1997.
Letter to the Lake, illustrated by Peter Catalanotto, DK Ink, 1998.
The First Thing My Mama Told Me, illustrated by Christine Davenier, Harcourt (New York, NY), 2002.
The House in the Night, illustrated by Beth Krommes, Houghton Mifflin (Boston, MA), 2008.
To Be like the Sun, illustrated by Margaret Chodos-Irvine, Harcourt (Orlando, FL), 2008.

OTHER

(Editor, under name Susan M. Swanson) *The Large Sky Reaches Down* (anthology of student writing), COMPAS, 1986.
(Editor) *Northern Lights* (anthology of student writing), COMPAS, 1986.

Work included in anthology *This Place I Know: Poems of Comfort,* edited by Georgia Heard, Candlewick Press, 2002. Contributor of poems, essays, and reviews to periodicals, including *American Poetry Review, Five Owls, Horn Book, How(ever), Hungry Mind Review, Ironwood, Minnesota Writes: Poetry, New York Times Book Review, Primavera, Riverbank Review,* and *Ruminator Review.* Member of editorial committee, *Riverbank Review,* 1999-2003.

Adaptations

"Trouble, Fly" (poem) was set to music for children's choir by Patricia McKernon, and published by Boosey & Hawkes.

Sidelights

A writer based in St. Paul, Minnesota, Susan Marie Swanson has dedicated a large part of her career to children's poetry and literature. In addition to editing the children's book supplement of the *Hungry Mind Review,* Swanson is a published poet and author of award-winning picture books such as *To Be like the Sun* and *The House in the Night.*

Swanson grew up in a small town near Chicago, Illinois, and this setting was influential in sparking her love of writing and literature. "My town had a wonderful public library and a cozy bookstore, and I loved to visit those places by myself when I was young," she recalled to interviewer Cynthia Leitich Smith for *Cynsations* online. Swanson's first published work, a poem about snowflakes, appeared in her local newspaper when she was ten years old, and her writing habit was firmly in place by her teen years, when she and her family relocated to Minnesota. Although she left Minnesota while earning her M.F.A. in poetry at the University of Massachusetts Amherst, Swanson returned to that state upon completion of her degree and has lived in St. Paul since 1983.

Swanson's first picture book, *Letter to the Lake,* is brought to life in colorful paintings by illustrator Peter Catalanotto. The book introduces a young girl named Rosie who, along with her mother, is having a difficult winter day: there are worries over money and difficulties getting the car started in the cold. Rosie copes by remembering her summer days by the lake and by composing an imaginary letter to the lake that gave her such joy. She has a treasured rock from the lake area that she keeps with her, and she gives this talisman to her mother in the hope that it will help the woman think of better times as well. While a *Kirkus Reviews* critic speculated that young readers might find the realistic worries in *Letter to the Lake* somewhat "unsettling," the reviewer added that "if all love letters are made poignant by the sorrows of separation, this one rings true." Tana Elias, evaluating Swanson's story in *School Library Journal,* applauded *Letter to the Lake* as an "excellent" choice "for reading to one or more children who will . . . identify with the yearning for the uncomplicated times of summer."

As its title suggests, *Getting Used to the Dark: Twenty-six Night Poems* explores the many feelings children have as nightfall approach. In the poem "Karla's Worries" a little girl fears that she will not remember her father's new phone number. Nick, the protagonist of another poem, is staying with his grandmother because his mother is away on a business trip. A *Kirkus Reviews* contributor thought highly of *Getting Used to the Dark*, hailing it as a "consistently high-quality gathering of unrhymed observations and meditations." Sharon Korbeck noted in her *School Library Journal* review of the book that Swanson's verses "are quite down to earth, and are, for the most part, understandable to a young audience."

Paired with colorful block-print art by Margaret Chodos-Irvine, *To Be like the Sun* focuses on a happy childhood moment, as a young girl plants a sunflower seed in her family's garden and watches it grow to a colorful flower over the summer. The young child's "contagious curiosity . . . and the sun-soaked images of summer gardens will easily engage young" readers, predicted Gillian Engberg in her *Booklist* review of *To Be like the Sun.* In Swanson's "lyrical free verse" readers are carried through the cycle of growth and the changing of the seasons, observed *School Library Journal* contributor Heidi Estrin. A *Kirkus Reviews* writer noted that "the poetic lines are exquisite, philosophical yet concrete," and pair with Chodos-Irvine's "wonderfully patterned" pictures to create a "spare, elegant" book that is "perfect for sharing."

Honored with the 2009 Randolph Caldecott Medal for the scratchboard illustrations by New England artist Beth Krommes, *The House in the Night* features a lyrical text that takes readers on a nighttime ride. Beginning in a quiet house, Swanson's rhyming text carries readers through the starlit sky and up to the home of the sun and moon before turning back again. In black-and-white scratchboard images highlighted with a warm, marigold yellow, Krommes "make[s] the world of the poem an enchanted place," wrote *School Library Journal* critic Jayne Damron, the critic predicting that *The House in the Night* "will be loved for generations to come." Ilene Cooper wrote in *Booklist* that Krommes and Swanson's collaboration results in "a beautiful piece of bookmaking that will delight both parents and children," and in *Publishers Weekly* a critic cited the poet's talent for capturing her story in "only a few graceful words per page."

Susan Marie Swanson's engaging story in* Letter to the Lake *is captured in Peter Catalanotto's light-filled art. (DK Publishing, Inc., 1998. Illustration copyright © 1998 by Peter Catalanotto. Reproduced by permission of the illustrator.)

***Beth Krommes won a Caldecott Medal for her illustrations for Swanson's story in* The House in the Night.** (Illustration copyright © 2008 by Beth Krommes. Reprinted by permission of Houghton Mifflin Harcourt Publishing Company. All rights reserved.)

Biographical and Critical Sources

PERIODICALS

Booklist, July, 2002, Lauren Peterson, review of *The First Thing My Mama Told Me,* p. 1861; April 15, 2008, Ilene Cooper, review of *The House in the Night,* p. 46, and Gillian Engberg, review of *To Be like the Sun,* p. 51.

Kirkus Reviews, October 15, 1997, review of *Getting Used to the Dark: Twenty-six Night Poems,* p. 1589; January 15, 1998, review of *Letter to the Lake,* pp. 118-119; April 15, 2002, review of *The First Thing My Mama Told Me,* p. 580; March 15, 2008, review of *To Be like the Sun;* April 1, 2008, review of *The House in the Night.*

New York Times Book Review, October 20, 2002, Abby McGanney Nolan, review of *The First Thing My Mama Told Me,* p. 23; February 15, 2009, Julie Just, review of *The House in the Night,* p. 15.

Publishers Weekly, April 20, 1998, review of *Letter to the Lake,* p. 65; April 22, 2002, review of *The First Thing My Mama Told Me,* p. 68; May 12, 2008, review of *The House in the Night,* p. 53.

School Library Journal, January, 1998, Sharon Korbeck, review of *Getting Used to the Dark,* pp. 105-106; May, 1998, Tana Elias, review of *Letter to the Lake,* pp. 126-127; August, 2002, Martha Link, review of *The First Thing My Mama Told Me,* p. 170; April, 2008, Jayne Damron, review of *The House in the Night,* and Heidi Estrin, review of *To Be like the Sun,* both p. 123.

ONLINE

Children's Literature Network Web site, http://www.childrensliteraturenetwork.org/ (December 15, 2009), "Susan Marie Swanson."

Cynsations Web log, http://www.cynthialetichsmith.blogspot.com/ (April 30, 2008), Cynthia Leitich Smith, interview with Swanson.

Minnesota Public Radio Web site, http://minnesota.publicradio.org/ (January 26, 2009), "Susan Marie Swanson."

T-W

TAKAHASHI, Hideko

Personal

Born in Osaka, Japan; immigrated to United States. *Education:* Doshisha University (Kyoto, Japan), degree; Otis College of Art and Design, B.F.A., 1994.

Addresses

Home—Seattle, WA. *Agent*—Lindgren & Smith Artists Representatives, 676A 9th Ave., New York, NY 10036. *E-mail*—info@hidekotakahashi.com.

Career

Illustrator.

Illustrator

Diana Stoneberg, *French Lessons,* Snapping Turtle Press (Hollywood, CA), 1995.

Marsha Hayles, *Beach Play,* Henry Holt (New York, NY), 1998.

Susan Hayboer O'Keefe, *Good Night, God Bless,* Henry Holt (New York, NY), 1999.

Stephen Krensky, *My Loose Tooth,* Random House (New York, NY), 1999.

Carol H. Behrman, *The Ding Dong Clock,* Holt (New York, NY), 1999.

Caroline Hatton, *Where Is My Puppy?* (board book), Lee & Low (New York, NY), 2000.

Eileen Spinelli, *In My New Yellow Shirt,* Henry Holt (New York, NY), 2001.

Lynn Plourde, *Snow Day,* Simon & Schuster Books for Young Readers (New York, NY), 2001.

Heidi Roemer, *Come to My Party, and Other Shape Poems,* Henry Holt (New York, NY), 2004.

Annie Auerbach, *Hello, New Baby!: A Touch and Feel Book,* Piggy Toes Press (Inglewood, CA), 2004.

Karen T. Taha, *Hotdog on TV,* Dial Books for Young Readers (New York, NY), 2005.

Katherine Ayres, *Matthew's Truck,* Candlewick Press (Cambridge, MA), 2005.

Ellen Leroe, *Princess Fun: Count 10 to 1* (board book), Simon & Schuster (New York, NY), 2005.

Dianne Ochiltree, *Lull-a-bye, Little One,* G.P. Putnam's Sons (New York, NY), 2006.

Shelly Becker, *Mine! Mine! Mine!,* Sterling Pub. (New York, NY), 2006.

Kathryn Heling, *Midnight Fright,* Scholastic, Inc. (New York, NY), 2008.

Margi Preus, *The Peace Bell,* Henry Holt (New York, NY), 2008.

"MOVE THE PIECES AND LEARN!" SERIES

Rachele Keith, *Animals,* Running Press (Philadelphia, PA), 2003.

Rachele Keith, *Beach Fun,* Running Press (Philadelphia, PA), 2003.

Rachele Keith, *Bugs,* Running Press Book Publishers (Philadelphia, PA), 2003.

Rachele Keith, *Silly Hats,* Running Press (Philadelphia, PA), 2003.

"TRANSITION TIME" SERIES

Lawrence E. Shapiro, *It's Time to Give up Your Pacifier,* Instant Help Books (Oakland, CA), 2008.

Lawrence E. Shapiro, *It's Time to Sit Still in Your Own Chair,* Instant Help Books (Oakland, CA), 2008.

Lawrence E. Shapiro, *It's Time to Sleep in Your Own Bed,* Instant Help Books (Oakland, CA), 2008.

Lawrence E. Shapiro, *It's Time to Start Using Your Words,* Instant Help Books (Oakland, CA), 2008.

Also illustrator of educational material.

Sidelights

Hideko Takahashi was born in Osaka, Japan, and began her art training at Kyoto's Doshisha University. A move to the United States led to further fine-arts studies at Otis College of Art and Design, in Los Angeles, California, and thence to a career as a children's book illus-

trator. Now making her home in Seattle, Washington, Takahashi has contributed to several picture books, including Stephen Krensky's *My Loose Tooth,* Karen T. Taha's *Hotdog on TV,* and Margi Preus's *The Peace Bell,* as well as to the "Move the Pieces and Learn!" and "Transition Time" concept-book series.

Takahashi enjoys creating illustrations that feature "cute little people, dogs, and bugs," according to the Lindgren and Smith Web site, and she portrays these characters in her brightly colored, round-edged digital art. Her debut work, 1998's *Beach Play,* pairs a rhyming story by Marsha Hayles with what a *Publishers Weekly* contributor characterized as "energetic acrylic" paintings featuring "gently prankish humor and skewed perspectives." A more recent illustration project, Preus's *The Peace Bell,* allowed Takahashi to draw from her own Japanese culture: the story describes a woman's recollections of a bell that rang in each village the New Year in her native Japan, its disappearance during World War II, and its eventual return to the small Japanese town. "In her "realistic illustrations," the artist incorporates "cultural details" that "accurately portray" the story's Japanese setting, according to *School Library Journal* contributor Margaret R. Tassia, while a *Kirkus Reviews* critic concluded of *The Peace Bell* that "Takahashi's lovely acrylics are as sweet and precise as the text."

Calling the "simple, richly hued outdoor scenes" in Heidi Roemer's *Come to My Party, and Other Shape Poems* "Takahashi's most inventive work yet," a *Kirkus*

Reviews writer added that the artist finds inventive ways to incorporate Roemer's concrete poems into her colorful images. "Far from intrusive, these illustrations . . . help youngsters to better understand the poem shapes," added *Horn Book* critic Betty Carter. Takahashi's "cleverly conceived format" for Katherine Ayres' *Matthew's Truck* "merits extra attention," in the opinion of *Booklist* contributor Jennifer Mattson, and Bina Williams wrote in *School Library Journal* that the artist's "winsome acrylics" incorporate "charming details" that bring to life Ayres' story about a boy and his favorite toy.

Biographical and Critical Sources

PERIODICALS

Booklist, March 15, 1999, Ilene Cooper, review of *My Loose Tooth,* p. 1337; October 1, 1999, Ilene Cooper, review of *Good Night, God Bless,* p. 374; June 1, 2001, Shelley Townsend-Hudson, review of *In My New Shirt,* p. 1896; June 1, 2004, Gillian Engberg, review of *Come to My Party, and Other Shape Poems,* p. 1736; March 1, 2005, Jennifer Mattson, review of *Matthew's Truck,* p. 1201; June 1, 2005, Ilene Cooper, review of *Hotdog on TV,* p. 1824.
Horn Book, May-June, 2004, Betty Carter, review of *Come to My Party, and Other Shape Poems,* p. 340.

Hideko Takahashi's artwork is a calming feature of Kathryn Heling and Deborah Hembrook's picture book Midnight Fright. (Illustration copyright © 2008 by Scholastic, Inc. Reproduced by permission.)

Kirkus Reviews, October 1, 2001, review of *Snow Day,* p. 1431; March 1, 2004, review of *Come to My Party, and Other Shape Poems*; September 1, 2008, review of *The Peace Bell.*

Publishers Weekly, May 4, 1998, review of *Beach Play,* p. 211; December 3, 2001, review of *Snow Day,* p. 59; June 25, 2001, review of *In My New Yellow Shirt,* p. 71.

School Library Journal, August, 2001, Marianne Saccardi, review of *In My New Yellow Shirt,* p. 162; January, 2002, Maryann H. Owen, review of *Snow Day,* p. 108; May, 2004, Jane Marino, review of *Come to My Party, and Other Shape Poems,* p. 136; July, 2005, Bina Williams, review of *Matthew's Truck,* p. 64, and Linda L. Walkins, review of *Hotdog on TV,* p. 83; June, 2006, Julie Roach, review of *Lull-a-Bye, Little One,* p. 124; October, 2006, Sally R. Dow, review of *Mine! Mine! Mine!,* p. 102; December, 2008, Margaret R. Tassia, review of *The Peace Bell,* p. 100; January, 2009, Amy Lilien-Harper, review of "Transition Time" series, p. 86.

ONLINE

Hideko Takahashi Home Page, http://www.hidekotakahashi.com (December 20, 2009).

Lindgren & Smith Web site, http://www.lindgrensmith. com/ (December 20, 2009), "Hideko Takahashi."

Otis College of Art and Design Web site, http://www.otis. edu/alumni/ (December 20, 2009), "Hideko Takahashi."*

*   *   *

TEDESCO, P.R.
See NAYLOR, Phyllis Reynolds

*   *   *

TUBB, Kristin O'Donnell 1971-

Personal

Born February 7, 1971. *Education:* Auburn University, B.A., M.A. (communications). *Hobbies and other interests:* Writing, illustrating, knitting poorly, doing anything outdoors.

Addresses

Home—Franklin, TN. *E-mail*—ktubb@comcast.net.

Career

Author of books for children. Presenter at schools.

Writings

The Bill of Rights: Freedom from Cruel and Unusual Punishment, Greenhaven Press (Detroit, MI), 2005.

Sunny Days, illustrated by Kellee Riley, Simon Scribbles (New York, NY), 2006.

Craft Corner Art Studio, illustrated by Kellee Riley, Simon Scribbles (New York, NY), 2007.

Autumn Winifred Oliver Does Things Different, Delacorte Press (New York, NY), 2008.

Selling Hope; or, Gaining Glorious Asylum from Mr. Halley's Fiery Beast, Feiwel & Friends (New York, NY), 2010.

Sidelights

Beginning her writing career producing nonfiction and a series of craft books for younger children, Tennessee author Kristin O'Donnell Tubb published her first middle-grade novel in 2008. The year is 1934 when eleven-year-old Autumn Winifred Oliver, the heroine of Tubb's *Autumn Winifred Oliver Does Things Different,* begins her campaign to save her beloved Smoky Mountain logging community from a U.S. government plan to annex the region to the national park system. Autumn lives in Cades Cove, Tennessee, and although she is excited about the chance to move to Knoxville, with its movie theatre and other modern conveniences, she treasures her small town and does not want to see it de-

Cover of Kristin O'Donnell Tubb's middle-grade novel Autumn Winifred Oliver Does Things Differently, *featuring artwork by Merrillee Liddiard.* (Jacket art © 2008 by Merrillee Liddiard. Used by permission of Delacorte Press, an imprint of Random House Children's Books, a division of Random House, Inc.)

stroyed. Meanwhile, Autumn's grandfather is aiding the government efforts in the belief that it will bring tourist dollars to the region. To advance her own side of the controversial issue, the preteen decides to engage in a letter-writing campaign to the park project's funder, John D. Rockefeller himself. Autumn's act of civil disobedience—siccing her family's bloodhound on a group of Civilian Conservation Corps workers—also helps to inspire the involvement of other Cades Cove residents, many of whom share the girl's worries.

Praising Autumn as an "inventive heroine," *Booklist* contributor Jennifer Hubert also cited Tubb for treating readers to a "homespun tale" that combines "folksy humor and . . . historical fact." In *School Library Journal,* Kathleen Isaacs noted the inclusion of "bits of Appalachian folklore," while a *Kirkus Reviews* writer described Autumn's narrative voice as "peppered . . . with Appalachian superstitions and homey, colorful phrases."

"My elementary school librarian, Ms. Shelia Rollins, was a major influence on my becoming a writer," Tubb told *SATA.* "She arranged a telephone interview for me and a handful of other students with Madeleine L'Engle—yes, THAT Madeleine L'Engle! I was in sixth grade, and I told Ms. L'Engle that I wanted to be a writer. 'Good for you!,' she replied. 'Keep reading and you can do it!'

"That phone call changed the course of my life. That's why I love visiting schools: the hope that maybe I'll have the opportunity to fan a spark of interest into a flame, just like Ms. L'Engle did for me."

Biographical and Critical Sources

PERIODICALS

Booklist, November 15, 2008, Jennifer Hubert, review of *Autumn Winifred Oliver Does Things Different,* p. 43.
Kirkus Reviews, September 1, 2008, review of *Autumn Winifred Oliver Does Things Different.*
School Library Journal, January, 2009, Kathleen Isaacs, review of *Autumn Winifred Oliver Does Things Different,* p. 120.

ONLINE

Kristin O'Donnell Tubb Home Page, http://www.kristin tubb.com (December 15, 2009).

*   *   *

WEBER, Jill 1950-

Personal

Born September 26, 1950, in Norwalk, CT; daughter of Lew (a cartoonist) and Barbara (in sales) Schwartz; married Frank Weber (in hotel management), December 31, 1974; children: Remy. *Education:* Attended Rhode Island School of Design. *Religion:* Jewish.

Addresses

Home and office—P.O. Box 13, Mont Vernon, NH 03057. *E-mail*—jill@frajilfarms.com.

Career

Illustrator and designer of children's and adult books. Worked in animation studio in New York, NY; T.Y. Crowell (publisher), New York, NY, worked in art department; Simon & Schuster, New York, NY, former assistant to art director. New Hampshire Institute of Art, instructor in children's book illustration, 2010.

Illustrator

Meredith Brokaw and Annie Gilbar, *The Penny Whistle Halloween Book,* Weidenfeld & Nicolson (New York, NY), 1989.
Meredith Brokaw and Annie Gilbar, *The Penny Whistle Lunch Box Book,* Simon & Schuster (New York, NY), 1991.
Meredith Brokaw and Annie Gilbar, *The Penny Whistle Christmas Party Book: Including Hanukkah, New Year's and Twelfth Night Family Parties,* Simon & Schuster (New York, NY), 1991.
Meredith Brokaw and Annie Gilbar, *The Penny Whistle Party Planner,* Simon & Schuster (New York, NY), 1991.
Meredith Brokaw and Annie Gilbar, *The Penny Whistle Birthday Party Book,* Simon & Schuster (New York, NY), 1992.
Meredith Brokaw and Annie Gilbar, *The Penny Whistle Sick-in-Bed Book: What to Do with Kids When They're Home for a Day, a Week, a Month, or More,* Simon & Schuster (New York, NY), 1993.
Franklyn Mansfield Branley, *Keeping Time,* Houghton Mifflin (Boston, MA), 1993.
Meredith Brokaw and Annie Gilbar, *The Penny Whistle Traveling with Kids Book: Whether by Boat, Train, Car, or Plane—How to Take the Best Trip Ever with Kids of All Ages,* Simon & Schuster (New York, NY), 1995.
Meredith Brokaw and Annie Gilbar, *The Penny Whistle Any Day Is a Holiday Party Book,* Simon & Schuster (New York, NY), 1996.
Terry Lee Bilsky, *Expectations: Best Kept Secrets Every New Mother Should Know,* Andrews McMeel (Kansas City, KS), 1996.
Terry Lee Bilsky, *Newborn Expectations: My First Journal,* Andrews McMeel (Kansas City, KS), 1996.
Terry Lee Bilsky, *Teenage Expectations: The Real Parents' Guide to the Terrible Teens,* Andrews McMeel (Kansas City, KS), 1996.
Julie Salamon, *The Christmas Tree,* Random House (New York, NY), 1996.
Benecia Aronwald, *Things You Can Give When You Open Your Heart,* Random House (New York, NY), 1997.

Benecia Aronwald, *Things You Can Save When You Lose Someone Close to Your Heart,* Random House (New York, NY), 1997.

Benecia Aronwald, *Things You Can Be When You Believe in Yourself,* Random House (New York, NY), 1998.

Teresa Bateman, *Harp o' Gold,* Holiday House (New York, NY), 2001.

W. Nikola-Lisa, *To Hear the Angels Sing: A Christmas Poem,* Holiday House (New York, NY), 2002.

Laura Driscoll, *George Washington Carver: The Peanut Wizard,* Grosset & Dunlap (New York, NY), 2003.

Row, Row, Row Your Boat, AOL Time Warner (New York, NY), 2003.

Yankee Doodle, AOL Time Warner (New York, NY), 2003.

Yona Zeldis McDonough, *Who Was John F. Kennedy?,* Grosset & Dunlap (New York, NY), 2005.

Ann Purmell, *Christmas Tree Farm,* Holiday House (New York, NY), 2006.

Ann Purmell, *Maple Syrup Season,* Holiday House (New York, NY), 2008.

Jenny Meyerhoff, *Third Grade Baby,* Farrar, Straus & Giroux (New York, NY), 2008.

Eric A. Kimmel, adaptor, *Even Higher!: A Rosh Hashanah Story by I.L. Peretz,* Holiday House (New York, NY), 2009.

"ANGEL" SERIES BY JUDY DELTON; ILLUSTRATOR

Angel's Mother's Boyfriend, Houghton Mifflin (Boston, MA), 1999.

Angel Spreads Her Wings, Houghton Mifflin (Boston, MA), 1999.

Backyard Angel, Houghton Mifflin (Boston, MA), 1999.

Angel in Charge, Houghton Mifflin (Boston, MA), 1999.

Angel Bites the Bullet, Houghton Mifflin (Boston, MA), 2000.

Angel's Mother's Wedding, Houghton Mifflin (Boston, MA), 2001.

Angel's Mother's Baby, Houghton Mifflin (Boston, MA), 2003.

Jill Weber's illustration projects include her work for Teresa Bateman's folk-tale-type story in **Harp o' Gold.** (Holiday House, 2001. Illustration copyright © 2000 by Jill Weber. Reproduced by permission of Holiday House, Inc.)

Sidelights

Illustrator Jill Weber creates vibrantly colored paintings as well as pen-and-ink drawings to pair with text in books for both adults and children. Praising her images in W. Nikola-Lisa's *To Hear the Angels Sing: A Christmas Poem,* Eva Mitnick wrote in *School Library Journal* that Weber's "ebullient and colorful" paintings "are full of child appeal," while a *Kirkus Reviews* writer maintained that her "appealing" art "add[s] to the joyful atmosphere" of Nikola-Lisa's version of the Nativity story. Turning to a Jewish legend, Weber's "delicate, simple watercolor, crayon and ink drawings" for Eric A. Kimmel's *Even Higher!: A Rosh Hashanah Story by I.L. Peretz* "add a guileless charm to the Old World . . . scenes," according to another *Kirkus Reviews* critic, and in *Publishers Weekly* a contributor cited the energy in the book's "colorful, openhearted drawings."

Weber's art has brought to life text by other writers, such as Julie Salamon, Teresa Bateman, Ann Purmell, and Judy Denton. In Salamon's *The Christmas Tree,* the head gardener of New York's Rockefeller Center takes up his annual task of finding a suitable Christmas tree to decorate the large plaza. Locating the perfect tree on property owned by a New Jersey convent, he must convince Sister Anthony to allow him to cut down the majestic Norway spruce, a tree with which the sister has a particularly deep attachment. Eventually Sister Anthony decides to share her favorite tree with the people of New York, giving them her own special Christmas present. A holiday tree is also the focus of Purmell's *Christmas Tree Farm,* in which a boy describes the year-long efforts of a family that makes its livelihood from a local tree farm. Inspired by a visit to a real-life family farm similar to the one described in Purmell's story, Weber contributes illustrations that a *Kirkus Reviews* writer cited for their "appealing, primitive style." "The barrage of green" in these paintings, "mostly set against white snow, gives the book an irresistible freshness," concluded *Booklist* contributor Ilene Cooper.

Harp o' Gold, an original story by Bateman, tells the story of a talented harpist named Tom who trades his tarnished but treasured instrument with a leprechaun who offers him a shiny golden one in return. Disappointed with the poor sound of the new harp, Tom is surprised when audiences seem to enjoy the music he plays on the new golden harp. Tom soon becomes famous and wealthy, but despite his newfound success, he misses the sound of his old harp. In *Booklist* Cooper wrote that Weber's "acrylic and pastel pictures . . . show a lush, green countryside and present a varied cast of high-and low-class characters." A *Publishers Weekly* reviewer compared the artist's illustrations for *Harp o' Gold* to the works of Petra Mathers and Giselle Potter, describing her images as "playful in tone, [and] starring plucky animal figures and rubbery-limbed characters with expressive facial features."

Jenny Meyerhoff's lighthearted chapter book *Third Grade Baby* features Weber's black-and-white illustrations throughout. In the story, Polly finds herself in a

Weber teams up with author Jenny Meyerhoff to create the engaging beginning reader **Third Grade Baby.** *(Illustration copyright © 2008 by Jill Weber. Used by permission of Farrar, Straus & Giroux, LLC.)*

minority of one when her third-grade teacher tallies the total number of baby teeth lost by her class members. Unlike her classmates, Polly has not lost any, and a class tease dubs her "Babyteeth." Although the girl first feels bad, as the days go by she gets to know her tormentor and realizes that he is as insecure as she is. "Weber's fresh pencil illustrations add credibility to" Meyerhoff's story, wrote a *Kirkus Reviews* writer, and in *Booklist* Hazel Rochman called the artwork in *Third Grade Baby* "cheerful."

Weber has also provided the illustrations for Judy Delton's "Angel" series, which featuring the adventures of a slightly older girl. *Angel Spreads Her Wings,* the first book in the series, follows sixth-grade Angel as she and her family travel to Greece to meet her stepfather's relatives. After dreaming up a series of potential disasters that might occur on the way, the preteen worrywart realizes that her worst fears are never realized and that it is better to enjoy oneself than to fret about imagined catastrophes. In *Horn Book* Elizabeth S. Watson wrote that Weber's illustrations for *Angel Spreads Her Wings* give Angel "a fresh, sprightly look," and *School*

Library Journal contributor Kate McLean called *Angel Bites the Bullet* a "delightful" work in which Weber's "realistic" cartoons highlight each chapter.

Weber once told *SATA:* "Illustrating books is my first love. There is really nothing quite like transforming someone's words into pictures and being able to decide what the scenery, the costumes, and the characters all look like. But then I really do love to design books, and there is great satisfaction in accomplishing a design in the designated number of pages in the allotted amount of time. It helps offset the agony of never knowing when that painting is quite finished. So, in my career of now thirty years, I straddle the fence of children's and trade books, enjoying most those projects where I get to wear both hats as designer and illustrator.

"My favorite books are the ones where I am able to collaborate with the authors. The "Penny Whistle" series of eight books spanned almost ten years of a marvelous exchange with Annie Gilbar and Meredith Brokaw. . . . The 'Expectations' books are really picture books for adults where Terry Lee Bilsky and I were able to draw on our 'other job' as mothers. I love their warmth and humor. *The Christmas Tree* was an exciting project where I was actually painting while the story was being written, so [author] Julie Salamon and I worked very closely together discovering the joys of e-mail. The fruits of our labors hit the *New York Times* bestseller list that Christmas."

Weber continued to *SATA,* "I work in a small studio in my house on Frajil Farms in New Hampshire. When I am not drawing, I am gardening, picking, pickling, and cooking, hoping that my [art] projects will grow light over the summer months when the gardens are most demanding and that they will be plentiful in the winter when we are snowed in."

Biographical and Critical Sources

PERIODICALS

Booklist, March 1, 2001, Ilene Cooper, review of *Harp o' Gold,* p. 1285; September 1, 2006, Ilene Cooper, review of *Christmas Tree Farm,* p. 140; March 15, 2008, Jennifer Mattson, review of *Maple Syrup Season,* p. 56; December 1, 2008, Hazel Rochman, review of *Third Grade Baby,* p. 52.

Horn Book, July, 1999, Elizabeth S. Watson, review of *Angel Spreads Her Wings,* p. 463.

Kirkus Reviews, November 1, 2002, review of *To Hear the Angels Sing: A Christmas Poem,* p. 1623; November 1, 2006, review of *Christmas Tree Farm;* August 15, 2008, review of *Third Grade Baby;* February 15, 2008, review of *Maple Syrup Season;* August 15, 2009, review of *Even Higher!: A Rosh Hashanah Story by I.L. Peretz.*

Library Journal, February 15, 1995, Caroline Mitchell, review of *The Penny Whistle Traveling with Kids Book: Whether by Boat, Train, Car, or Plane—How to Take the Best Trip Ever with Kids of All Ages,* pp. 173-174.

Publishers Weekly, August 5, 1996, review of *The Christmas Tree,* p. 428; March 5, 2001, review of *Harp o' Gold,* p. 78; August 24, 2009, review of *Even Higher!,* p. 61.

School Library Journal, April, 1999, Susan Hepler, review of *Angel Spreads Her Wings,* p. 133; October, 2000, Kate McLean, review of *Angel Bites the Bullet,* p. 156; October, 2002, Eva Mitnick, review of *To Hear the Angels Sing,* p. 62; October, 2006, Susan Patron, review of *Christmas Tree Farm,* p. 100; March, 2008, Mary Hazelton, review of *Maple Syrup Season,* p. 174; November, 2008, Debbie S. Hoskins, review of *Third Grade Baby,* p. 96; May, 2009, Helen Foster James, review of *Harp o' Gold,* p. 109; September, 2009, Heidi Estrin, review of *Even Higher!,* p. 126.

ONLINE

Jill Weber Home Page, http://www.frajilfarms.com (December 15, 2009).

*   *   *

WESTON, Robert Paul

Personal

Born in Canada. *Education:* University of British Columbia, M.F.A. (creative writing).

Addresses

Home—Toronto, Ontario, Canada. *E-mail*—rpweston@zorgamazoo.com.

Career

Writer. Presenter at schools.

Member

Writers' Union of Canada.

Awards, Honors

Journey Prize nomination, 2005; Fountain Award for Speculative Literature nomination, 2005.

Writings

Zorgamazoo, illustrated by Victor Rivas, Razorbill (New York, NY), 2008.

Author of television scripts for *Powerpuff Girls Z* (animated series), produced by Cartoon Network, 2006-07. Contributor to periodicals, including *Crimewave, Postcripts, New Orleans Review,* and *On Spec.*

Sidelights

Canadian writer Robert Paul Weston attracted critical attention with his first book-length work, the whimsically titled children's novel *Zorgamazoo.* A graduate of

the University of British Columbia's master's-level program in creative writing, Weston won award nominations for several short stories for adults, and in *Booklist* Ian Chipman cited his first book as "a natural descendant" of the works of Dr. Seuss and Roald Dahl, two writers well known for their eccentric approach to writing for children.

Illustrated by Spanish artist Victor Rivas, *Zorgamazoo* follows an imaginative girl's amazing adventures as she escapes her home and explores tunnels that run below through the surface of the earth, meets the inhabitants of a secret city, and ultimately travels to the moon. A classic picture-book heroine, Katrina Katrell is bereft of parents, and she is currently in the care of a detestable relative. Joining Katrina is Morty the zorgle, a shy creature that is searching for his missing brother. Soon the two companions find themselves taking sides in the battle between the magical and the mundane when they discover a plan to extricate all whimsy from the world. In *Booklist* Chipman cited Weston's use of "bouncing, fanciful rhymes" in telling his "atmospheric" tale and *Quill & Quire* contributor Ciabh McEvenue noted the

book's "Seussian language and at-times challenging wordplay." *Zorgamazoo* is "written in a form virtually unseen since the days of epic poetry," according to *Horn Book* critic Shoshana Flax, and Weston's playful story is "well-constructed" and with "fully realized characters and plenty of humor." Recommending the illustrated novel to children who "enjoy a little nonsense," Laurie Slagenwhite added in *School Library Journal* that *Zorgamazoo* is also salted with "suspense and dashes of humor."

Biographical and Critical Sources

PERIODICALS

Booklist, September 1, 2008, Ian Chipman, review of *Zorgamazoo,* p. 98.
Canadian Review of Materials, September 12, 2008, Myra Junyk, review of *Zorgamazoo.*
Horn Book, November-December, 2008, Shoshana Flax, review of *Zorgamazoo,* p. 717.
Kirkus Reviews, September 1, 2008, review of *Zorgamazoo.*
Quill & Quire, October, 2008, Ciabh McEvenue, review of *Zorgamazoo.*
School Library Journal, January, 2009, Laurie Slagenwhite, review of *Zorgamazoo,* p. 122.

ONLINE

Robert Paul Weston Home Page, http://www.zorgamazoo. com (December 15, 2009).
Robert Paul Weston Web Log, http://wayofthewest. wordpress.com/ (December 15, 2009).*

* * *

WIDENER, Terry 1950-

Personal

Born December 15, 1950, in Tulsa, OK; son of Floyd Widener and Jean Hutchinson Edwards; married Leslie Stall (an art director), October 1, 1977; children: Kate, Kellee, Mitchell. *Education:* University of Tulsa, B.F.A. (graphic design), 1974. *Hobbies and other interests:* Golf, soccer (coaching), travel.

Addresses

Home—McKinney, TX. *Agent*—Michèle Manasse, 20 Aquetong Rd., New Hope, PA 18938; mmanassenewwork.com.

Career

Illustrator. Phillips Knight Walsh, Inc., Tulsa, OK, designer, 1975-79; Richards, Sullivan, Brock & Associates, Dallas, TX, designer, 1980-81; Terry Widener Stu-

Robert Paul Weston's fascinating alphabet book Zorgamazoo *features illustrations by Victor Rivas.* (Illustration copyright © 2008 by Victor Rivas. Reproduced by permission of Razorbill, a division of Penguin Putnam Books for Young Readers.)

Terry Widener (Reproduced by permission.)

dio, McKinney, TX, illustrator, 1981—. Texas A & M University at Commerce, adjunct professor. Judge in Marion Vannett Ridgway Memorial Award, 2001-05; presenter at schools. *Exhibitions:* Work has been exhibited at Galerie St. Michel, Lambertville, NJ, and in Society of Illustrators Original Art Show and traveling exhibitions to Japan. Work included in permanent collections.

Member
Society of Children's Book Writers and Illustrators.

Awards, Honors
Honor Book designation, *Boston Globe/Horn Book* Award, National Parenting Publications Gold Award, Marion Vannett Ridgway Memorial Award Honor Book designation, Golden Kite Award finalist, Notable Book designation, American Library Association (ALA), and New York Public Library 100 Titles for Reading and Sharing inclusion, all 1997, and Red Clover Award nomination, and Texas Bluebonnet Award nomination, both 1998, all for *Lou Gehrig* by Adler; *Smithsonian* magazine Best Children's Book designation, American Booksellers (ABA) Pick of the List inclusion, both 1999, Oppenheim Toy Portfolio Gold Award, 2000, Kentucky Bluegrass Award, 2001, and California Young Reader Medal, 2002, all for *The Babe and I* by Adler; Oppenheim Toy Portfolio Platinum Award, and Orbis Pictus Award Honor Book designation, 2001, both for *America's Champion Swimmer* by Adler; Aesop Award, and New York Public Library 100 Titles for Reading and Sharing, both 2005, both for *Roy Makes a Car* by Mary E. Lyons; Notable Social Studies Trade Book for Young People designation, National Council for the Social Studies/Children's Book Council, 2006, for *Joe*

Louis, by Adler; awards for design and illustration from Society of illustrators, Society of Publication Designers, *Communication Arts, Print, Art Directors,* and Art Directors Club of New Jersey.

Illustrator

FOR CHILDREN

David A. Adler, *Lou Gehrig: The Luckiest Man,* Harcourt (New York, NY), 1997.

David A. Adler, *The Babe and I,* Harcourt (New York, NY), 1997.

Joy Jones, *Tambourine Moon,* Simon & Schuster (New York, NY), 1999.

Kenneth Oppel, *Peg and the Whale,* Simon & Schuster (New York, NY), 2000.

David A. Adler, *America's Champion Swimmer: Gertrude Ederle,* Harcourt (San Diego, CA), 2000.

Nikki Grimes, *Shoe Magic,* Orchard Books (New York, NY), 2000.

Odds Bodkin, *The Christmas Cobwebs,* Harcourt (New York, NY), 2001.

Gary Soto, *If the Shoe Fits,* G.P. Putnam's Sons (New York, NY), 2002.

Robert D. San Souci, *The Twins and the Bird of Darkness: A Hero Tale from the Caribbean,* Simon & Schuster Books for Young Readers (New York, NY), 2002.

Deborah Hopkinson, *Girl Wonder: A Baseball Story in Nine Innings,* Atheneum Books for Young Readers (New York, NY), 2003.

Jonathan London, *When the Fireflies Come,* Dutton Children's Books (New York, NY), 2003.

Charles R. Smith, Jr., *Let's Play Basketball!,* Candlewick Press (Cambridge, MA), 2004.

Rita Gray, *Nonna's Porch,* Hyperion Books for Children (New York, NY), 2004.

Maribeth Boelts, *The Firefighters' Thanksgiving,* Putnam's (New York, NY), 2004.

David A. Adler, *Joe Louis: America's Fighter,* Harcourt (Orlando, FL), 2005.

Jennifer Guess McKerley, *Man o' War: Best Racehorse Ever,* Random House (New York, NY), 2005.

Mary E. Lyons, adaptor, *Roy Makes a Car,* based on a story collected by Zora Neale Hurston, Atheneum Books for Young Readers (New York, NY), 2005.

David A. Adler, *Satchel Paige: Don't Look Back,* Harcourt (Orlando, FL), 2007.

Jonah Winter, *Steel Town,* Atheneum Books for Young Readers (New York, NY), 2008.

Roni Schotter, *The House of Joyful Living,* Farrar, Straus & Giroux (New York, NY), 2008.

OTHER

Virginia Mattingly, editor, *Mothers: A Celebration of Love,* Running Press (Philadelphia, PA), 1995.

The Peter Yarrow Songbook: Sleepytime Songs, Sterling Pub. (New York, NY), 2008.

The Peter Yarrow Songbook: Favorite Folk Songs, Sterling Pub. (New York, NY), 2008.

The Peter Yarrow Songbook: Nursery Songs, Sterling (New York, NY), 2010.

Sidelights

Trained as a graphic designer, Terry Widener spent several years in that field before moving to book illustration. He received critical accolades for his very first illustration project, creating the artwork for David A. Adler's *Lou Gehrig: The Luckiest Man*, and his highly praised work also includes several more award-winning collaborations with Adler. In addition to juvenile nonfiction, Widener has proved himself to be equally adept at capturing the emotional elements of fiction through his stylized images and imaginative use of perspective in his work for picture books such as Nikki Grimes' *Shoe Magic*, Jonathan London's *When the Fireflies Come*, and Roni Schotter's *The House of Joyful Living*. Praising *Shoe Magic*, Gillian Engberg wrote in *Booklist* that Widener's "bright . . . artwork, brimming with fanciful, stylized shapes," enhance the "exuberance and energy" in Grimes' engaging story, and *School Library Journal* critic Kathleen Whalin wrote that the artist's "exuberant acrylic paintings capture the joys and hopes expressed" in each of the book's poems. The illustrator's "stylized paintings adopt a variety of perspectives . . . to convey the multi-layered harmony" of Schotter's family-centered story, according to a *Publishers Weekly* critic; Widener's urban-themed images for *The House of Joyful Living* are "rendered as affectionately as the text," the critic added.

With a text by Adler, *Lou Gehrig* recalls Gehrig's childhood and successful career in baseball. Portrayed as a genuine hero on and off the field, the talented athlete left college early to help his family financially by playing ball for the New York Yankees. Gehrig brought to the game of baseball the disciplined behavior from his early school days: playing 2,130 consecutive games, he maintained a perfect attendance record for fourteen seasons. A *Publishers Weekly* contributor dubbed Widener's acrylic paintings for the book "memorable" images that "vividly recreate the look and feel" of the game during the early decades of the twentieth century, and in *School Library Journal* Tom S. Hurlburt wrote that the illustrations "sweep across the pages, melding comfortably with Adler's spare writing style." Ilene Cooper, writing in *Booklist,* praised Widener's "impressive" artwork and noted that the book's final image "provides a silent but powerful ending to Gehrig's story."

Other sports-themed biographies generated by the creative collaborations between Widener and Adler include *Satchel Paige: Don't Look Back, The Babe and I, America's Champion Swimmer: Gertrude Ederle,* and *Joe Lewis: America's Fighter.* One of the first pitchers to break the color barrier during the early twentieth century is the focus of *Satchel Paige,* a book in which the athlete's "innate dignity shines" through in Widener's "acrylic illustrations," according to a *Publishers Weekly* critic. Another social barrier is broken in *America's Champion Swimmer,* which follows Gertrude Ederle from her childhood as a competitive swimmer in New York state to her triumphant crossing of the English Channel in August of 1926, at age nineteen. "Widener's . . . strongly physical deep-hued artwork displays the right muscle" for Adler's inspiring story, wrote Cooper in a review of the book.

Described by a *Kirkus Reviews* writer as "another perfect marriage of words and pictures from an award-winning team," *Joe Lewis* follows the inspiring life of the grandson of slaves who, raised in rural Alabama and spending his teen years in Detroit, worked up through the ranks of the amateur boxing circuit and fought German boxer Max Schmeling to win the world

Widener's illustration projects include creating the stylized art for Maribeth Boelts' **The Firefighters' Thanksgiving.** (Illustration copyright © 2004 by Terry Widener. Used by permission of G.P. Putnam's Sons, a division of Penguin Young Readers Group, a member of Penguin Group (USA), Inc., 345 Hudson St., New York, NY 10014. All rights reserved.)

championship and also strike a symbolic blow against Nazi Germany on the eve of World War II. Praising the book's "signature muscular figures," *School Library Journal* critic Barbara Auerbach added that Widener's "action-packed acrylics capture the [book's] setting and emotions."

Working with author Deborah Hopkinson, Widener also creates the illustrations for *Girl Wonder: A Baseball Story in Nine Innings,* a picture book that is based on the life of one of the first female U.S. semi-pro baseball players. After a strenuous training regimen, Alta Weiss gained the skills that qualified her to pitch for Ohio's Vermilion Independents. However, extraordinary skills of persuasion were needed to convince the team to sign on a woman to their 1907 roster, as Hopkinson shows in her picture-book text. In *Horn Book* Martha V. Parravano wrote that *Girl Wonder* features Widener's characteristic "broad, somewhat exaggerated" forms "conveying much emotion and narrative content," and a *Publishers Weekly* reviewer called *Girl Wonder* a "graphically rich, rewarding tale [that] will inspire readers."

While Widener's work on picture-book biographies has comprised a substantial part of his oeuvre, imaginative stories have also been enriched by his art, among them Kenneth Oppel's *Peg and the Whale,* Nikki Grimes' *Shoe Magic,* and Maribeth Boelts' *The Firefighter's Thanksgiving.* For *Peg and the Whale,* a story based on the biblical story of Jonah and the whale is enhanced by Widener's "vibrant acrylics," which "showcase . . . the witty exaggerations" in Oppel's retelling, according to *Booklist* critic Connie Fletcher. Boelts' rhyming tale follows Firefighter Lou as he prepares a special turkey dinner for his fellow firefighters despite the many disruptions that occur at the busy station during the holiday. Widener's "bold, expressive" images "pay silent tribute to these everyday heroes," concluded Gillian Engberg in her *Booklist* review of the book. *If the Shoe Fits,* a story by Gary Soto, pairs what *Horn Book* critic Nell D. Beram described as a "subtle story about . . . kindness, and dignity" with Widener's "inviting and unpretentious" paintings. Dubbed "a bedtime story like no other" by *Horn Book* contributor Betty Carter, Jonah Winter's *Steel Town* features acrylic paintings by Widener that depict "man and machine" in a manner that is "reminiscent of the paintings of [twentieth-century muralist] Thomas Hart Benton."

"Early in my career I almost always included illustration in my graphic design work," Widener once told *SATA,* "so my decision to become an illustrator was easy." "When I illustrate," he added, "my hope is to create a beautiful book, . . . to make the author's words come alive visually. My aim is to show the emotions and events that authors write about in their stories. Artists N.C. Wyeth and Paul Davis have been my most important influences. Over all, my primary goal is to provide fun and exciting entertainment for children. The best advice I can give to young illustrators is to be patient. It's very hard to wait, but I have found that if you work towards your goal, things seem to happen."

Biographical and Critical Sources

PERIODICALS

Booklist, May 15, 1997, Ilene Cooper, review of *Lou Gehrig: The Luckiest Man,* p. 1575; March 15, 1999, Kathleen Squires, review of *The Babe and I,* p. 1327; March 15, 2000, Ilene Cooper, review of *America's Champion Swimmer: Gertrude Ederle,* p. 1374; September 15, 2000, Gillian Engberg, review of *Shoe Magic,* p. 234; November 15, 2000, Connie Fletcher, review of *Peg and the Whale,* p. 639; September 1, 2001, Gillian Engberg, review of *The Christmas Cobwebs,* p. 234; January 1, 2003, GraceAnne A. DeCandido, review of *Girl Wonder: A Baseball Story in Nine Innings,* p. 880; August, 2004, Gillian Engberg, review of *The Firefighter's Thanksgiving,* p. 1940; November 1, 2005, Hazel Rochman, review of *Man o' War: Best Racehorse Ever,* p. 50; April 1, 2008, Thom Barthelmess, review of *Steel Town,* p. 59; November 15, 2008, Hazel Rochman, review of *The House of Joyful Living,* p. 50.

Horn Book, July-August, 1997, review of *Lou Gehrig,* pp. 471-472; March, 1999, Mary M. Burns, review of *The Babe and I,* p. 182; May, 2000, review of *America's Champion Swimmer,* p. 328; July-August, 2002, Nell D. Beram, review of *If the Shoe Fits,* p. 451; March-April, 2003, Martha V. Parravano, review of *Girl Wonder: A Baseball Story,* p. 204; March-April, 2005, Barbara Bader, review of *Roy Makes a Car,* p. 211; January-February, 2006, Betty Carter, review of *Joe Lewis: America's Fighter,* p. 95; July-August, 2008, Betty Carter, review of *Steel Town,* p. 436.

Kirkus Reviews, February 1, 1997, review of *Lou Gehrig;* September 15, 2001, review of *The Christmas Cobwebs,* p. 1354; February 1, 2002, review of *If the Shoe Fits,* p. 189; May 1, 2003, review of *When the Fireflies Come,* p. 679; July 1, 2004, review of *The Firefighters' Thanksgiving,* p. 625; October 15, 2005, review of *Joe Lewis,* p. 1133; May 1, 2007, review of *Satchel Paige: Don't Look Back.*

New York Times Book Review, November 19, 2000, Jen Nessel, review of *Shoe Magic,* p. 32; November 30, 2000, Christopher Lehmann-Haupt, review of *America's Champion Swimmer,* p. E7; May 18, 2003, review of *The Twins and the Bird of Darkness: A Hero Tale from the Caribbean,* p. 17.

Publishers Weekly, February 24, 1997, review of *Lou Gehrig,* p. 91; December 23, 2002, review of *Girl Wonder,* p. 71; April 28, 2003, review of *When the Fireflies Come,* p. 69; November 29, 2004, review of *Nonna's Porch,* p. 39; January 24, 2005, review of *Roy Makes a Car,* p. 243; December 11, 2006, review of *Satchel Paige,* p. 68; November 10, 2008, review of *The House of Joyful Living,* p. 50.

School Library Journal, May, 1997, Tom S. Hurlburt, review of *Lou Gehrig,* p. 118; October, 2000, Kathleen Whalin, review of *Shoe Magic,* p. 148; November,

2000, Kathleen Kelly, review of *Peg and the Whale*, p. 129; September, 2002, Barbara Buckley, review of *The Twins and the Bird of Darkness*, p. 218; November, 2004, Kathy Piehl, review of *Nonna's Porch*, p. 104; December, 2005, Barbara Auerbach, review of *Joe Louis*, p. 122.

ONLINE

Michèle Mannase Web page, http://www.new-work.com/ (December 17, 2009), "Terry Widener."*

* * *

WILLARD, Elizabeth Kimmel
See KIMMEL, Elizabeth Cody

* * *

WILLIAMS, Alex 1969-

Personal

Born 1969, in London, England. *Hobbies and other interests:* Movies, painting, model-building.

Addresses

Home—England. *Agent*—David Higham Associates, 508 Lower John St., Golden Square, London W1F 9HA, England.

Career

Scriptwriter and author of books for children.

Awards, Honors

Fuji Scholarship Award for film, 1991; British Association of Film and Television Actors Award for Best Children's Writer, 2003, for *Sir Gadabout* television series.

Writings

The Talent Thief: An Extraordinary Tale of an Ordinary Boy, illustrated by David Roberts, Macmillan Children's (London, England), 2006, Philomel Books (New York, NY), 2010.
The Deep Freeze of Bartholomew Tullock, Philomel Books (New York, NY), 2008, published as *The Storm Maker: A Hair-raising Adventure for All Weathers,* Macmillan Children's (London, England), 2008.

Author of scripts for children's television series, including *Sir Gadabout* and *Bookaboo!*

Adaptations

The Talent Thief was optioned for film by Universal Pictures.

Sidelights

Alex Williams began his writing career as a scriptwriter, and his award-winning work for children's television included the script for the television series *Sir Galahad.* Published in 2006, Williams' first novel, *The Talent Thief: An Extraordinary Tale of an Ordinary Boy,* was inspired by a dream the author had and focuses on orphans Adam and Cressida Bloom. Despite his family's wealth and social standing, Adam feels destined to be overlooked in life, especially when compared to his glamorous sister with her talent for singing. When Cressida is invited to join other talented young people at an Arctic retreat for the Festival of Youthful Genius, tagalong Adam suddenly comes into his own, however: when the talents of those assembled suddenly start to disappear, he is the one who recognizes that a sinister thief is at work. Praising *The Talent Thief* as an "excellent first novel," London *Independent* critic Christina Hardyment added that the story treats readers to a "fast-paced adventure in the best Fleming tradition."

In *The Deep Freeze of Bartholomew Tullock*—first published in England as *The Storm Maker: A Hair-raising*

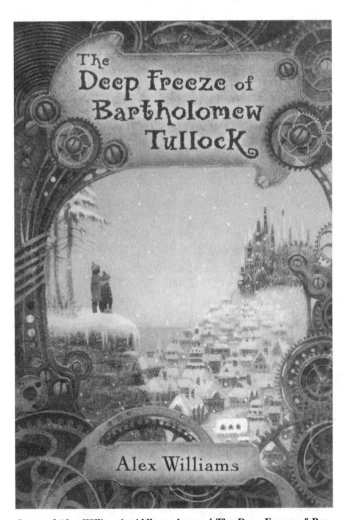

Cover of Alex Williams' middle-grade novel The Deep Freeze of Bartholomew Tullock, *featuring artwork by Kristin Smith.* (Jacket art © 2008 by Igor Oleynikov. Reproduced by permission of Philomel Books, a division of Penguin Putnam Books for Young Readers, a member of Penguin Group (USA), Inc., 345 Hudson St., New York, NY 10014. All rights reserved.)

Adventure for All Weathers, Williams spins another quirky fantasy. Like *The Talent Thief,* Rufus and Madeline Breeze find themselves in icy weather, but in this case it is the result of a bizarre and inexplicable climate disorder that seems to hover over the small, turnip-growing town of Pinrut. The children's parents are in the fan-making business, and when the warmth disappears they lose all their customers. While most Pinrutians suffer, greedy landlord Bartholomew Tullock seems to thrive, and thirteen-year-old Rufus intends to find out why. Brought to life in pen-and-ink illustrations by David Roberts that recall the macabre work of the late Edward Gorey, *The Deep Freeze of Bartholomew Tullock* was described by a *Kirkus Reviews* writer as a "can-you-top-this page-turner" full of "bone-chilling suspense." While citing the author's "overly descriptive style," *Booklist* critic Ian Chipman lauded Williams' novel as a book that "welds invention and adventure together with charming results."

Biographical and Critical Sources

PERIODICALS

Booklist, October 1, 2008, Ian Chipman, review of *The Deep Freeze of Bartholomew Tullock,* p. 44.
Independent (London, England), December 8, 2006, Christina Hardyment, review of *The Talent Thief: An Extraordinary Tale of an Ordinary Boy.*
Kirkus Reviews, September 1, 2008, review of *The Deep Freeze of Bartholomew Tullock.*
School Library Journal, January, 2009, Eva Mitnick, review of *The Deep Freeze of Bartholomew Tullock,* p. 123.

ONLINE

Alex Williams Home Page, http://www.alexwilliamsbooks.co.uk (December 20, 2009).*

* * *

WINTERS, Katharine
See WINTERS, Kay

* * *

WINTERS, Kay 1936-
(Katharine Winters)

Personal

Born October 5, 1936, in Trenton, NJ; daughter of Robert (an aerospace engineer) and Luella (a homemaker) Lanning; married Earl D. Winters (a physical chemist and consultant), August 27, 1960; children: Linda. *Edu-*

Kay Winters (Photograph by Earl Winters. Reproduced by permission.)

cation: Beaver College (now Arcadia University), B.S. (education); attended Boston University; Wheelock College, M.S. (education); graduate study at Lehigh University; attended New School of Social Research (now New School University). *Politics:* Democrat. *Religion:* Protestant. *Hobbies and other interests:* Reading, biking, walking, gardening, traveling.

Addresses

Home and office—P.O. Box 339, Richlandtown, PA 18955. *E-mail*—AuthorK@aol.com.

Career

Children's book author. Newton, MA, Public Schools, elementary education teacher, 1960-63; Palisades School District, Kintnersville, PA, elementary education teacher and supervisor, 1968-92. American International Schools, education consultant, 1970-80. Presenter at schools and conferences.

Member

Society of Children's Book Writers and Illustrators, Authors Guild, Inkweavers, Bucks County Authors of Books for Children.

Awards, Honors

Pick of the List selection, American Booksellers Association, 1997, and Best Books of the Year citation, Bank Street College of Education, both for *Wolf Watch;* Best One Hundred Books of the Year selection, International Reading Association, 2000, for *Tiger Trail;* Golden

Disc Award for Distinguished Achievement in Her Chosen Profession, Arcadia University Alumni Association, 2001; Best Books of the Year citation, Bank Street College of Education, and Best Book citation, Chicago Public Library, Chapman Award for Best Classroom Read Aloud, and Best Books designation, Center for Children's Books, all 2003, all for *Abe Lincoln;* Best Book citation, Chicago Public Library, and Notable Social Studies Book designation, American Library Association (ALA)/Children's Book Council, both 2003, both for *Voices of Ancient Egypt;* County Friend of Education Award, Northampton County Coordinating Council of Education Associations, 2005; Teacher's Choice selection, ALA, and Carol Otis Hurst Book Prize, both 2009, both for *Colonial Voices.*

Writings

FOR CHILDREN

Did You See What I Saw?: Poems about School, illustrated by Martha Weston, Viking (New York, NY), 1996.

(Reteller) *Talk! Talk! Talk! A Haitian Fable,* illustrated by JoAnn Kitchel, Celebration Press (Glenview, IL), 1996.

The Teeny Tiny Ghost, illustrated by Lynn Munsinger, HarperCollins (New York, NY), 1997.

Wolf Watch, illustrated by Laura Regan, Simon & Schuster (New York, NY), 1997.

Where Are the Bears?, illustrated by Brian Lies, Bantam Doubleday Dell (New York, NY), 1998.

How Will the Easter Bunny Know?, illustrated by Martha Weston, Yearling (New York, NY), 1999.

Whooo's Haunting the Teeny Tiny Ghost?, illustrated by Lynn Munsinger, HarperCollins (New York, NY), 1999.

Tiger Trail, illustrated by Laura Regan, Simon & Schuster (New York, NY), 2000.

But Mom, Everybody Else Does, illustrated by Doug Cushman, Dutton Children's Books (New York, NY), 2002.

Abe Lincoln: The Boy Who Loved Books, illustrated by Nancy Carpenter, Simon & Schuster (New York, NY), 2003.

Voices of Ancient Egypt, illustrated by Barry Moser, National Geographic Society (Washington, DC), 2003.

My Teacher for President, illustrated by Denise Brunkus, Dutton Children's Books (New York, NY), 2004.

The Teeny Tiny Ghost and the Monster, illustrated by Lynn Munsinger, HarperCollins (New York, NY), 2004.

Colonial Voices: Hear Them Speak, illustrated by Larry Day, Dutton Children's Books (New York, NY), 2008.

Whooo's That?: A Lift-the-Flap Pumpkin Fun Book, illustrated by Jeannie Winston, Harcourt (Orlando, FL), 2009.

This School Year Will Be the Best, illustrated by Renee Andriani, Dutton Children's Books (New York, NY), 2010.

Who's Coming for Christmas? A Holly Jolly Lift-the-Flap Book, illustrated by Jeannie Winston, Harcourt (Orlando, FL), 2010.

OTHER

(With Marta Felber) *The Teacher's Copebook: How to End the Year Better than You Started,* Fearon, 1980.

Author of reading textbooks for Scott Foresman and Houghton Mifflin.

Sidelights

Kay Winters worked as a teacher for many years before shifting her attention to writing books for children. "Stories have always been magical to me," Winters noted on her home page in describing her career transition. In addition to fictional stories such as *The Teeny Tiny Ghost* and verse collections *Did You See What I Saw?: Poems about School,* she has also created the picture-book biography *Abe Lincoln: The Boy Who Loved Books.*

"From the time I was seven years old, I was a writer," Winters once told *SATA.* Writing in diaries and journals, she also contributed to newspapers during both high school and college. After graduating from Beaver Col-

Winters' entertaining holiday story in **How Will the Easter Bunny Know?** *is brought to life in Martha Weston's cartoon art.* (Illustration © 1999 by Martha Weston. All rights reserved. Used by permission of Yearling, an imprint of Random House Children's Books, a division of Random House, Inc.)

lege (now Arcadia University) with a B.S. in elementary education, she continued the study of writing and submitted poems, essays, articles, and stories to educational periodicals. "Now and then they were published," she added, "but making a living by writing books did not seem like a viable possibility at that time. My husband and I were just out of graduate school, and we had a big educational debt to pay to Massachusetts Institute of Technology (MIT), as well as a new baby."

Instead of writing, Winters established a successful career as an educator, working as a public-school teacher and a reading specialist and educational consultant, and even teaching on the college level. However, she recalled, "at every conference I attended, I always went to hear the authors instead of the latest theory on the wonder of phonics." Winters continued to dabble with writing in her spare time until 1980, when she collaborated with Marta Felber on *The Teachers Copebook: How to End the Year Better than You Started.* "In order to finish that project, I had to get up every morning at 4 a.m., sneak downstairs to my frosty office and, garbed in a fur robe, woolen gloves, and fleece-lined boots, typed until it was time to teach," the writer remembered.

Offered early retirement in 1992, Winters took it, and now had the time to write full time. She also attended writing classes at New York City's New School and elsewhere, and availed herself of other resources. Two years later her book *The Teeny Tiny Ghost* was accepted. "From there," she recalled, "my writing career began to take off."

In *The Teeny Tiny Ghost* Winters addresses the importance of mastering one's fears. In this take on a well-known tale, a diminutive specter is afraid of even his own "Boo"'s and nighttime howls. On Halloween night, a rap on the door sends shivers through the teeny tiny ghost and his teeny tiny kittens. Summoning up all his courage, however, he swears to protect his feline companions and opens the door. Surprise! He is greeted by his ghostly pals, who have come to take the teeny tiny ghost trick-or-treating. Janice M. Del Negro, writing in the *Bulletin of the Center for Children's Books,* wrote that, "tucked into this humorously written and illustrated tale is the kernel of stout-heartedness that makes young children love the hero." Winters' "tale of banishing fear has just the right blend of wit and supernatural suspense," commented a reviewer in a *Publishers Weekly* appraisal of *The Teeny Tiny Ghost.*

The Teeny Tiny Ghost returns in *Whooo's Haunting the Teeny Tiny Ghost?* and *The Teeny Tiny Ghost and the Monster,* both of which feature illustrations by Lynn Munsinger. Returning home to his teeny tiny school one day, the pint-sized phantom finds an invisible creature stomping around his teeny tiny house. The teeny tiny ghost and his two teeny tiny kittens are scared, but once again, the small spirit finds the courage to save the day. New challenges face our teeny tiny hero at school in the third book in the series, as the ghost stands up to

two bullies and is helped by his two teeny tiny kittens in crafting a scary monster for a school contest. *Whooo's Haunting the Teeny Tiny Ghost?* "convey[s] a feeling of spookiness without being overtly scary," Lauren Peterson noted in *Booklist,* the critic adding that Winters' upbeat story is suitable "for younger, more sensitive children." Describing the work as "an all out charmer," a *Publishers Weekly* went on to proclaim *Whooo's Haunting the Teeny Tiny Ghost?* "the treat of the Halloween season."

In the award-winning *Wolf Watch,* Winters tells the story of four wolf pups from their birth until their first foray outside their den. The habits of a wolf pack are introduced in her rhyming text, from howling to hunting and fending for one's young. Danger is present in the form of a golden eagle that lurks nearby, waiting for the chance to pounce upon one of the defenseless pups. In *School Library Journal* Susan Scheps called *Wolf Watch* "a treasure of a book," noting that "there is a lot of information to be gleaned from this sparsely written visual masterpiece." A critic for *Kirkus Reviews* hailed *Wolf Watch* as "a splendid complement to titles with a more fact-based approach to wolf life."

Another fictional story by Winters, *But Mom, Everybody Else Does!* captures the childhood tendency to exaggerate. In the story a young girl tries to "convince her mother that her acts and desires are not only legitimate but also universal," according to a *Kirkus Reviews* contributor. ALL children have messy rooms, they ALL failed the test at school, and they ALL get bigger allowances, the girl asserts. Cushman's illustrations stretch the heroine's "statements to the point of absurdity," Kathy Piehl noted in *School Library Journal,* citing the humor of Winters' story. In *Booklist* Hazel Rochman called *But Mom, Everybody Else Does!* a child-friendly "farce [that] reinforces every kid's frustration about bossy grown-ups."

In her picture-book biography *Abe Lincoln,* Winters uses what a *Kirkus Reviews* writer described as "strong, economical language" to tell the story of America's sixteenth president. Written in free verse, the book recounts several vignettes from Lincoln's life to explain how the poor frontier boy's love of books and learning led him to the White House. Winters has "an eye for details of particular interest to a young audience," noted a *Publishers Weekly* reviewer, while in *Booklist* Kay Weisman wrote that the author's "simple language" and "engaging narrative" make *Abe Lincoln* "a good choice for reading aloud." A reviewer for *Kirkus Reviews* called *Abe Lincoln* "a moving tribute to the power of books and words."

In *Voices of Ancient Egypt* Winters uses "evocative words and an arresting design to bring a long-gone civilization to life," as Ilene Cooper explained in *Booklist.* In the book, Winters profiles a variety of prototypical Egyptians, from the scribes and pyramid-builders to the often overlooked weavers, bird-catchers, clothes-washers, and other laborers living in that ancient cul-

Winters brings to life the culture of an ancient people in her book Voices of Ancient Egypt, *featuring artwork by Barry Moser.* (National Geographical Society, 2003. Illustration copyright © 2003 by Barry Moser. Reproduced by permission.)

ture. On a double-page spread, each character explains his or her duties via free-verse poems written in the first person. Calling *Voices of Ancient Egypt* "a lovely browsing title," *School Library Journal* critic Eve Ortega also recommended the book to young history scholars, writing that it "contain[s] valuable information for students."

Colonial Voices features the same format as *Voice of Ancient Egypt,* but this time Winters takes readers to the city of Boston on December 16, 1773, as the spirit of revolution spreads among the colonists. Through the travels of a young errand boy distributing patriotic pamphlets, readers can listen in on the talk of local shopkeepers, a teacher, a tavern keeper, a Native American basketmaker, and others as they voice the growing political tensions that will ultimately erupt in the historic Boston Tea Party. Praising the free-verse narratives as "layered and textured," Ilene Cooper added in *Booklist* that Winters' "strong, moving text is supported . . . by rich paintings [by Larry Day that] capture the individuals and their circumstances." In *School Library Journal* Lucinda Snyder Whitehead noted the author's inclusion of a glossary to help children with archaic colonial-era terminology, and praised the "historical notes [that] go into more detail" about the men, women, and children

Winters selects to represent the ordinary citizens living during this pivotal era. Dubbing *Colonial Voices* "savory historical fare," a *Kirkus Reviews* writer commended the book for "convey[ing] . . . the diversity and defiance of the times."

Winters once explained to *SATA,* "I write because that's how I know what I think. When I see what I say, ideas that were fuzzy come clear to me. And sometimes I am surprised at what I find out about myself. . . .

"I write because I love to learn. Writers have the chance to play many parts, hear many voices, and dream many dreams. One of the exciting fringe benefits of being a writer is the ability to pursue what you care about. I am interested in so many things: nature, people, history, humor. Writing gives me a powerful motivation for learning.

"I loved finding out about wolves, presenting their warm family life, and dispelling the 'big bad wolf' myth in *Wolf Watch.* It's important to examine how to face fears and cope, as I explored in *The Teeny Tiny Ghost,* or how to observe and share experiences and memories, as in *Did You See What I Saw?* I liked putting myself in the place of a six year old . . . in *How Will the Easter Bunny Know?,* or imagining twin bear cubs, Sassy and Lum, meeting campers for the first time in *Where Are the Bears?* As I worked on the book about Abraham Lincoln, I lost myself in the wilderness, suffered on his hundred-mile trek to Indiana, and sympathized with Abe as he searched for books and learned to use words to lift himself out of grinding poverty. In *Tiger Trail,* I love putting myself in the place of the mother tigress and feeling her fear, her concern, and her triumph as she taught her cubs survival skills. When I was writing my book on ancient Egypt, the pharaohs seemed to come alive and walk right off the pages in their royal sandals. I hope that as readers meet the characters in my stories, they will realize that whatever their own circumstances may be, they can choose—to be brave, to forge ahead, to take positive risks, to be kind, to overcome severe obstacles, to appreciate the moment."

"My work habits are similar to those I used when I was teaching," Winters also explained. "I work every day. I am always on the watch for a story, even when we are on vacation riding elephants in Thailand or sailing on a tall ship in Tahiti. . . . And even though I frequently try to use other genres, poetic prose seems to speak up the most often. I am more interested in character development than plot. The story comes from the characters, and they frequently have a mind of their own. Still, writing the book is only the beginning. I also visit schools, attend book signings, speak at colleges, conferences, and bookstores.

"My advice for aspiring writers is to work, revise, and persist. Treat writing like a job. Make contacts. Go to conferences. Read current children's books. Join a writer's group. I am lucky to have a husband who is an excellent editor. Don't send your manuscript right off

when you finish it. Let it breathe. Look at it again. And be grateful that you have chosen a career that makes every day matter. Whatever is going on in your life today will fit somewhere, sometime, in a story."

Biographical and Critical Sources

PERIODICALS

Booklist, August, 1996, Hazel Rochman, review of *Did You See What I Saw?: Poems about School*, p. 1903; September 1, 1997, Lauren Peterson, review of *The Teeny Tiny Ghost*, p. 141; November 1, 1997, Julie Corsaro, review of *Wolf Watch*, p. 485; March 15, 1999, Carolyn Phelan, review of *How Will the Easter Bunny Know?*, p. 1339; September 1, 1999, Lauren Peterson, review of *Whooo's Haunting the Teeny Tiny Ghost?*, p. 151; October 15, 2000, Lauren Peterson, review of *Tiger Trail*, p. 448; December 15, 2002, Hazel Rochman, review of *But Mom, Everybody Else Does*, p. 770; January 1, 2003, Kay Weisman, review of *Abe Lincoln: The Boy Who Loved Books*, p. 901; September 15, 2003, Ilene Cooper, review of *Voices of Ancient Egypt*, p. 239; May 15, 2008, Ilene Cooper, review of *Colonial Voices: Hear Them Speak*, p. 44.

Bulletin of the Center for Children's Books, November, 1997, Janice M. Del Negro, review of *The Teeny Tiny Ghost*, p. 107.

Kirkus Reviews, October 1, 1997, review of *Wolf Watch*, p. 1539; August 15, 2002, review of *But Mom, Everybody Else Does*, p. 1239; November 15, 2002, review of *Abe Lincoln*, p. 1703; April 1, 2008, review of *Colonial Voices*.

New York Times Book Review, November 16, 1997, J.D. Biersdorfer, review of *Wolf Watch*, p. 58.

Publishers Weekly, October 6, 1997, review of *The Teeny Tiny Ghost*, p. 48; October 27, 1997, review of *Wolf Watch*, p. 75; September 27, 1999, review of *Whooo's*

A teacher decides to trade the classroom for the oval office in Winters' **My Teacher for President,** *a picture book featuring artwork by Denise Brunkus.* (Illustration copyright © Denise Brunkus, 2004. Reproduced by permission of Puffin Books, a division of Penguin Putnam Books for Young Readers.)

Haunting the Teeny Tiny Ghost?, p. 47; November 25, 2002, review of *Abe Lincoln*, p. 67.

School Library Journal, October, 1996, Marilyn Taniguchi, review of *Did You See What I Saw?*, p. 119; November, 1997, Meg Stackpole, review of *The Teeny Tiny Ghost*, pp. 103-104, and Susan Scheps, review of *Wolf Watch*, p. 104; April, 1999, Gale W. Sherman, review of *How Will the Easter Bunny Know?*, p. 110; September, 1999, Martha Link, review of *Whooo's Haunting the Teeny Tiny Ghost?*, p. 210; September, 2002, Kathy Piehl, review of *But Mom, Everybody Else Does*, p. 208; November 25, 2002, review of *Abe Lincoln*, p. 67; September, 2003, Eve Ortega, review of *Voices of Ancient Egypt*, p. 239; August, 2005, Blair Christolon, review of *Abe Lincoln*, p. 49; June, 2008, Lucinda Snyder Whitehurst, review of *Colonial Voices*, p. 169.

ONLINE

Kay Winters Home Page, http://www.kaywinters.com (December 15, 2009).

*   *   *

WYATT, Valerie
(Penelope Larkspur)

Personal

Born in Winnipeg, Manitoba, Canada; married. *Education:* University of Manitoba, B.A. (English); Queen's University (Kingston, Ontario, Canada), M.A. (English literature).

Addresses

Home—Victoria, British Columbia, Canada. *Office*—Kids Can Press Ltd., 29 Birch Ave., Toronto, Ontario M4V 1E2, Canada.

Career

Writer and editor. *Owl* magazine, member of editorial staff, beginning 1978; Kids Can Press, Toronto, Ontario, Canada, editor of books for children, beginning 1984.

Awards, Honors

American Bookseller Pick of the Lists designation, 1997, for *The Science Book for Girls and Other Intelligent Beings;* Parents' Guide to Children's Media award, and Parents' Choice Recommended designation, both 2000, both for *The Math Book for Girls and Other Beings Who Count;* Parents' Choice Recommended designation, and Society of School Librarians International Honor Book designation, both 2000, both for *Weather;* Tom Fairley Award for Editorial Excellence, 2004.

Writings

NONFICTION

Inventions: An Amazing Investigation, illustrated by Jerzy Kolacz, Grey de Pencier Books (Toronto, Ontario, Canada), 1987, Prentice Hall (New York, NY), 1988.

Pets, illustrated by Eric Parker, Simon & Schuster Books for Young Readers (New York, NY), 1988.

(With Paulette Bourgeouis) *The Amazing Dirt Book,* illustrated by Craig Terlson, Addison-Wesley (Reading, MA), 1990.

Weather Watch, illustrated by Pat Cupples, Addison-Wesley (Reading, MA), 1990.

The Science Book for Girls and Other Intelligent Beings, illustrated by Pat Cupples, Kids Can Press (Toronto, Ontario, Canada), 1993, reprinted, 2009.

Earthlings Inside and Out: A Space Alien Studies the Human Body, illustrated by Dušan Petričić, Kids Can Press (Toronto, Ontario, Canada), 1999.

(As Penelope Larkspur) *The Secret Life of Fairies,* illustrated by Leslie Watts, Kids Can Press (Toronto, Ontario, Canada), 1999.

Wacky Plant Cycles, illustrated by Lilith Jones, Mondo (New York, NY), 2000.

The Math Book for Girls and Other Beings Who Count, illustrated by Pat Cupples, Kids Can Press (Toronto, Ontario, Canada), 2000.

Weather: Frequently Asked Questions, illustrated by Brian Share, Kids Can Press (Tonawanda, NY), 2000.

The Kids Book of Canadian Firsts, illustrated by John Mantha, Kids Can Press (Tonawanda, NY), 2001.

Space: Frequently Asked Questions, illustrated by Matthew Fernandes, Kids Can Press (Toronto, Ontario, Canada), 2002.

Inventions: Frequently Asked Questions, illustrated by Matthew Fernandes, Kids Can Press (Toronto, Ontario, Canada), 2003.

Who Discovered America?, illustrated by Howie Woo, Kids Can Press (Tonawanda, NY), 2008.

How to Build Your Own Country, illustrated by Karen Fredericks, Kids Can Press (Toronto, Ontario, Canada), 2009.

Sidelights

Canadian writer Valerie Wyatt shares her curiosity about the natural world with younger readers in her work as an editor at Toronto's Kids Can Press as well as through her authorship of many science-based books beginning in the late 1980s. Praising *Earthlings Inside and Out: A Space Alien Studies the Human Body,* Wyatt's book about human anatomy, a *Resource Links* critic praised the author's "interesting, informative and humorous style" as well as her injection of a "sense of humor" that does not talk down to young readers. Balancing her interest in science, Wyatt also enjoys tapping into the imaginative world of fantasy, and her book *The Secret Life of Fairies*—published under the pen name Penelope Larkspur—is designed as a reference book in which the author studies the lives of fairies from an anthropological point of view.

Wyatt was born in Winnipeg, Manitoba, Canada, and she started her career in children's publishing in the late 1970s, after earning a master's degree in English literature at Queen's University. Her job as an editor for *Owl* magazine included answering readers' questions about science and nature. This interaction with young children tapped into Wyatt's own curiosity and interest in nature and inspired her to begin writing.

Valerie Wyatt's fact-filled picture book Who Discovered America? *features engaging cartoon art by Canadian illustrator Howie Woo.* (Kids Can Press, 2008. Illustrations © 2008 Kids Can Press. Used by permission of Kids Can Press Ltd., Toronto.)

Wyatt's first book for children, *Inventions: An Amazing for Investigation,* was published in 1987. Even though she was working as a children's book editor by this time, writing her own original texts served as a welcome complement to her day job. In the years since, she has continued to write and research on topics that interest her, producing books such as *The Kids Book of Canadian Firsts, Who Discovered America?,* and *How to Build Your Own Country,* as well as several science-based titles in the "Frequently Asked Questions" series. "I got hooked on children's books because they are like a puzzle," Wyatt explained. "You've got the words and you've got the pictures and the challenge is to get them to fit together like a jigsaw puzzle. You have to learn to think visually. I like the challenge of going beyond the words."

While encouraging children of all ages to see the wonders in the world around them, Wyatt focuses several of her books specifically on girls, who often turn away from math and science during the elementary and middle-school years. *The Science Book for Girls and Other Intelligent Beings* and *The Math Book for Girls and Other Beings Who Count* are designed to address this trend and use an engaging, fairy-godmother-type narrator to draw girls into technical topics and inspire them with stories about real-life women who have found

success in math and science-based fields. Reviewing *The Math Book for Girls and Other Beings Who Count* for *Booklist,* Ilene Cooper praised Wyatt's use of "lively, conversational prose" and "abundant humor" as a constructive way to "close the gender learning gap."

"When I was 12 years old, I read a book about a marine biologist named Eugenie Clark who swam with sharks," Wyatt recalled on the Kids Can Press Web site. "It was fabulous! Her adventures thrilled me, and for a long time, I wanted to be a marine biologist like her. I guess that's why I write and edit children's books. I know the power they can have."

Biographical and Critical Sources

PERIODICALS

Booklist, November 1, 1999, Ilene Cooper, review of *The Secret Life of Fairies,* p. 520; February 15, 2001, Shelle Rosenfeld, review of *The Math Book for Girls and Other Beings Who Count,* p. 1136; October 1, 2008, Carolyn Phelan, review of *Who Discovered America?,* p. 40.
Canadian Review of Materials, April 28, 2000, review of *The Secret Life of Fairies.*
Kirkus Reviews, February, 2009, review of *Who Discovered America?*
Publishers Weekly, December 6, 1999, review of *The Secret Life of Fairies,* p. 79.
Quill & Quire, April, 1999, Arlene Perly Rae, review of *Earthlings Inside and Out: A Space Alien Studies the Human Body;* March, 2003, Sherie Posesorski, review of *Inventions: Frequently Asked Questions.*
Resource Links, October, 1996, review of *Weather Watch,* p. 39; October, 1999, review of *Earthlings Inside and Out,* p. 51; February, 2000, review of *The Secret Life of Fairies,* pp. 10-11; June, 2000, review of *Weather: Frequently Asked Questions,* p. 16; December, 2000, review of *The Math Book for Girls and Other Beings Who Count,* p. 23; December, 2001, Victoria Pennell, review of *The Kid's Book of Canadian Firsts,* p. 35; February, 2003, Linda Irvine, review of *Space: Frequently Asked Questions,* p. 45; April, 2003, Grace Sheppard, review of *Inventions,* p. 29.
School Library Journal, August, 2000, Patricia Manning, review of *FAQ: Weather,* p. 210; November, 2000, Nancy A. Gifford, review of *The Math Book for Girls and Other Beings Who Count,* p. 149; July, 2003, Sandra Welzenbach, review of *Inventions,* p. 120; February, 2009, Anne Chapman Callaghan, review of *Who Discovered America?,* p. 128.
Teaching Pre K-8, February, 2001, Becky Rodia, "Valerie Wyatt: Self-Taught Artist."

ONLINE

Kids Can Press Web site, http://www.kidscanpress.com/ (December 20, 2009), "Valerie Wyatt."*

Illustrations Index

(In the following index, the number of the *volume* in which an illustrator's work appears is given *before* the colon, and the *page number* on which it appears is given *after* the colon. For example, a drawing by Adams, Adrienne appears in Volume 2 on page 6, another drawing by her appears in Volume 3 on page 80, another drawing in Volume 8 on page 1, and so on and so on. . . .)

YABC

Index references to *YABC* refer to listings appearing in the two-volume *Yesterday's Authors of Books for Children*, also published by Gale, Cengage Learning. *YABC* covers prominent authors and illustrators who died prior to 1960.

A

Aas, Ulf *5:* 174
Abbe, S. van
  See van Abbe, S.
Abel, Raymond *6:* 122; *7:* 195; *12:* 3; *21:* 86; *25:* 119
Abelliera, Aldo *71:* 120
Abolafia, Yossi *60:* 2; *93:* 163; *152:* 202
Abrahams, Hilary *26:* 205; *29:* 24, 25; *53:* 61
Abrams, Kathie *36:* 170
Abrams, Lester *49:* 26
Abulafia, Yossi *154:* 67; *177:* 3
Accardo, Anthony *191:* 3, 8
Accornero, Franco *184:* 8
Accorsi, William *11:* 198
Acs, Laszlo *14:* 156; *42:* 22
Acuna, Ed *198:* 79
Adams, Adrienne *2:* 6; *3:* 80; *8:* 1; *15:* 107; *16:* 180; *20:* 65; *22:* 134, 135; *33:* 75; *36:* 103, 112; *39:* 74; *86:* 54; *90:* 2, 3
Adams, Connie J. *129:* 68
Adams, John Wolcott *17:* 162
Adams, Lynn *96:* 44
Adams, Norman *55:* 82
Adams, Pam *112:* 1, 2
Adams, Sarah *98:* 126; *164:* 180
Adams, Steve *209:* 64
Adamson, George *30:* 23, 24; *69:* 64
Addams, Charles *55:* 5
Addison, Kenneth *192:* 173
Addy, Sean *180:* 8
Ade, Rene *76:* 198; *195:* 162
Adinolfi, JoAnn *115:* 42; *176:* 2
Adkins, Alta *22:* 250
Adkins, Jan *8:* 3; *69:* 4; *144:* 2, 3, 4
Adler, Kelynn *195:* 47
Adler, Peggy *22:* 6; *29:* 31
Adler, Ruth *29:* 29
Adlerman, Daniel *163:* 2
Adragna, Robert *47:* 145
Agard, Nadema *18:* 1
Agee, Jon *116:* 8, 9, 10; *157:* 4; *196:* 3, 4, 5, 6, 7, 8
Agre, Patricia *47:* 195
Aguirre, Alfredo *152:* 218
Ahjar, Brian *207:* 126
Ahl, Anna Maria *32:* 24
Ahlberg, Allan *68:* 6, 7, 9; *165:* 5
Ahlberg, Janet *68:* 6, 7, 9

Aicher-Scholl, Inge *63:* 127
Aichinger, Helga *4:* 5, 45
Aitken, Amy *31:* 34
Akaba, Suekichi *46:* 23; *53:* 127
Akasaka, Miyoshi *YABC 2:* 261
Akib, Jamel *181:* 13; *182:* 99
Akino, Fuku *6:* 144
Alain *40:* 41
Alajalov *2:* 226
Albert, Chris *200:* 64
Alborough, Jez *86:* 1, 2, 3; *149:* 3
Albrecht, Jan *37:* 176
Albright, Donn *1:* 91
Alcala, Alfredo *91:* 128
Alcantará, Felipe Ugalde *171:* 186
Alcorn, John *3:* 159; *7:* 165; *31:* 22; *44:* 127; *46:* 23, 170
Alcorn, Stephen *110:* 4; *125:* 106; *128:* 172; *150:* 97; *160:* 188; *165:* 48; *201:* 113; *203:* 39; *207:* 3
Alcott, May *100:* 3
Alda, Arlene *44:* 24; *158:* 2
Alden, Albert *11:* 103
Aldridge, Andy *27:* 131
Aldridge, George *105:* 125
Aldridge, Sheila *192:* 4
Alejandro, Cliff *176:* 75
Alex, Ben *45:* 25, 26
Alexander, Ellen *91:* 3
Alexander, Lloyd *49:* 34
Alexander, Martha *3:* 206; *11:* 103; *13:* 109; *25:* 100; *36:* 131; *70:* 6, 7; *136:* 3, 4, 5; *169:* 120
Alexander, Paul *85:* 57; *90:* 9
Alexeieff, Alexander *14:* 6; *26:* 199
Alfano, Wayne *80:* 69
Aliki
  See Brandenberg, Aliki
Allamand, Pascale *12:* 9
Allan, Judith *38:* 166
Alland, Alexandra *16:* 255
Allen, Gertrude *9:* 6
Allen, Graham *31:* 145
Allen, Jonathan *131:* 3, 4; *177:* 8, 9, 10
Allen, Joy *168:* 185
Allen, Pamela *50:* 25, 26, 27, 28; *81:* 9, 10; *123:* 4, 5
Allen, Raul *207:* 94
Allen, Rowena *47:* 75
Allen, Thomas B. *81:* 101; *82:* 248; *89:* 37; *104:* 9

Allen, Tom *85:* 176
Allender, David *73:* 223
Alley, R.W. *80:* 183; *95:* 187; *156:* 100, 153; *169:* 4, 5; *179:* 17
Allison, Linda *43:* 27
Allon, Jeffrey *119:* 174
Allport, Mike *71:* 55
Almquist, Don *11:* 8; *12:* 128; *17:* 46; *22:* 110
Aloise, Frank *5:* 38; *10:* 133; *30:* 92
Alsenas, Linas *186:* 2
Alter, Ann *206:* 4, 5
Althea
  See Braithwaite, Althea
Altschuler, Franz *11:* 185; *23:* 141; *40:* 48; *45:* 29; *57:* 181
Alvin, John *117:* 5
Ambrus, Victor G. *1:* 6, 7, 194; *3:* 69; *5:* 15; *6:* 44; *7:* 36; *8:* 210; *12:* 227; *14:* 213; *15:* 213; *22:* 209; *24:* 36; *28:* 179; *30:* 178; *32:* 44, 46; *38:* 143; *41:* 25, 26, 27, 28, 29, 30, 31, 32; *42:* 87; *44:* 190; *55:* 172; *62:* 30, 144, 145, 148; *86:* 99, 100, 101; *87:* 66, 137; *89:* 162; *134:* 160
Ames, Lee J. *3:* 12; *9:* 130; *10:* 69; *17:* 214; *22:* 124; *151:* 13
Amon, Aline *9:* 9
Amoss, Berthe *5:* 5
Amstutz, Andre *152:* 102
Amundsen, Dick *7:* 77
Amundsen, Richard E. *5:* 10; *24:* 122
Ancona, George *12:* 11; *55:* 144; *145:* 7; *208:* 13
Anderson, Alasdair *18:* 122
Andersen, Bethanne *116:* 167; *162:* 189; *175:* 17; *191:* 4, 5
Anderson, Bob *139:* 16
Anderson, Brad *33:* 28
Anderson, C.W. *11:* 10
Anderson, Carl *7:* 4
Anderson, Catherine Corley *72:* 2
Anderson, Cecil *127:* 152
Anderson, David Lee *118:* 176
Anderson, Derek *169:* 9; *174:* 180
Anderson, Doug *40:* 111
Anderson, Erica *23:* 65
Anderson, Laurie *12:* 153, 155
Anderson, Lena *99:* 26
Anderson, Peggy Perry *179:* 2
Anderson, Sara *173:* 3
Anderson, Scoular *138:* 13; *201:* 6
Anderson, Susan *90:* 12

Anderson, Tara *188:* 132
Anderson, Wayne *23:* 119; *41:* 239; *56:* 7; *62:* 26; *147:* 6; *202:* 4, 5
Andreasen, Daniel *86:* 157; *87:* 104; *103:* 201, 202; *159:* 75; *167:* 106, 107; *168:* 184; *180:* 247; *186:* 9
Andrew, Ian *111:* 37; *116:* 12; *166:* 2
Andrew, John *22:* 4
Andrews, Benny *14:* 251; *31:* 24; *57:* 6, 7; *183:* 8
Andrews, Vaughn *166:* 28
Anelay, Henry *57:* 173
Angel, Marie *47:* 22
Angelo, Valenti *14:* 8; *18:* 100; *20:* 232; *32:* 70
Anglund, Joan Walsh *2:* 7, 250, 251; *37:* 198, 199, 200
Anholt, Catherine *74:* 8; *131:* 7; *141:* 5
Anholt, Laurence *141:* 4
Anno, Mitsumasa *5:* 7; *38:* 25, 26, 27, 28, 29, 30, 31, 32; *77:* 3, 4; *157:* 10, 11
Antal, Andrew *1:* 124; *30:* 145
Antram, David *152:* 133
Apostolou, Christy Hale
    See Hale, Christy
Apple, Margot *33:* 25; *35:* 206; *46:* 81; *53:* 8; *61:* 109; *64:* 21, 22, 24, 25, 27; *71:* 176; *77:* 53; *82:* 245; *92:* 39; *94:* 180; *96:* 107; *152:* 4, 5; *162:* 192, 194; *173:* 44
Appleyard, Dev *2:* 192
Aragones, Sergio *48:* 23, 24, 25, 26, 27
Araneus *40:* 29
Arbo, Cris *103:* 4
Archambault, Matt *85:* 173; *138:* 19, 20; *143:* 33; *145:* 144; *179:* 103; *187:* 7
Archer, Janet *16:* 69; *178:* 156
Ardizzone, Edward *1:* 11, 12; *2:* 105; *3:* 258; *4:* 78; *7:* 79; *10:* 100; *15:* 232; *20:* 69,178; *23:* 223; *24:* 125; *28:* 25, 26, 27, 28, 29, 30, 31,33, 34, 35, 36, 37; *31:* 192, 193; *34:* 215, 217; *60:* 173; *64:* 145; *87:* 176; *YABC 2:* 25
Arena, Jill *176:* 49
Arenella, Roy *14:* 9
Argemi, David *197:* 2
Argent, Kerry *103:* 56; *138:* 17; *158:* 134
Arihara, Shino *201:* 98
Arisman, Marshall *162:* 50
Armer, Austin *13:* 3
Armer, Laura Adams *13:* 3
Armer, Sidney *13:* 3
Armitage, David *47:* 23; *99:* 5; *155:* 4
Armitage, Eileen *4:* 16
Armstrong, George *10:* 6; *21:* 72
Armstrong, Shelagh *102:* 114
Armstrong-Ellis, Carey *185:* 196
Arno, Enrico *1:* 217; *2:* 22, 210; *4:* 9; *5:* 43; *6:* 52; *29:* 217, 219; *33:* 152; *35:* 99; *43:* 31, 32, 33; *45:* 212, 213, 214; *72:* 72; *74:* 166; *100:* 169
Arnold, Alli *187:* 40, 41
Arnold, Caroline *174:* 5
Arnold, Emily *76:* 7, 9, 10
Arnold, Katya *115:* 11; *168:* 2, 3
Arnold, Tedd *116:* 14; *133:* 152; *160:* 5; *208:* 24, 25, 26, 176
Arnosky, Jim *22:* 20; *70:* 9, 10, 11; *118:* 3, 5; *160:* 8, 10; *189:* 5, 7, 8, 9, 10
Arnsteen, Katy Keck *105:* 97; *116:* 145
Arsenault, Isabelle *207:* 7
Arting, Fred J. *41:* 63
Artzybasheff, Boris *13:* 143; *14:* 15; *40:* 152, 155
Aruego, Ariane *6:* 4
Aruego, José *4:* 140; *6:* 4; *7:* 64; *33:* 195; *35:* 208; *68:* 16, 17; *75:* 46; *93:* 91, 92; *94:* 197; *109:* 65, 67; *125:* 2, 3, 4, 5; *127:* 188; *143:* 25; *178:* 17, 19, 74; *188:* 166; *202:* 164
Arzoumanian, Alik *177:* 12; *194:* 115
Asare, Meshack *86:* 9; *139:* 19

Ascensios, Natalie *105:* 139
Asch, Frank *5:* 9; *66:* 2, 4, 6, 7, 9, 10; *102:* 18, 19,21; *154:* 12
Ashby, Gail *11:* 135
Ashby, Gil *146:* 4
Ashby, Gwynneth *44:* 26
Ashley, C.W. *19:* 197
Ashmead, Hal *8:* 70
Aska, Warabe *56:* 10
Assel, Steven *44:* 153; *77:* 22, 97
Astrop, John *32:* 56
Atene, Ann *12:* 18
Atherton, Lisa *38:* 198
Atkinson, Allen *60:* 5
Atkinson, J. Priestman *17:* 275
Atkinson, Janet *86:* 147; *103:* 138
Atkinson, Mike *127:* 74
Atkinson, Wayne *40:* 46
Attard, Karl *196:* 22, 23
Attebery, Charles *38:* 170
Atwell, Debby *150:* 6
Atwood, Ann *7:* 9
Aubrey, Meg Kelleher *77:* 159
Auch, Herm *173:* 7, 8
Auch, Mary Jane *173:* 7
Augarde, Steve *25:* 22; *159:* 7
Austerman, Miriam *23:* 107
Austin, Margot *11:* 16
Austin, Robert *3:* 44
Austin, Virginia *81:* 205; *127:* 221
Auth, Tony *51:* 5; *192:* 18
Avendano, Dolores *158:* 74
Avedon, Richard *57:* 140
Averill, Esther *1:* 17; *28:* 39, 40, 41
Axeman, Lois *2:* 32; *11:* 84; *13:* 165; *22:* 8; *23:* 49; *61:* 116; *101:* 124
Axtel, David *155:* 110
Ayer, Jacqueline *13:* 7
Ayer, Margaret *15:* 12; *50:* 120
Ayers, Alan *91:* 58; *107:* 169
Ayliffe, Alex *95:* 164
Ayto, Russell *111:* 5; *112:* 54; *206:* 7, 8
Azarian, Mary *112:* 9, 10; *114:* 129; *117:* 171; *137:* 163; *171:* 4, 5; *181:* 161; *188:* 128

B

B.T.B.
    See Blackwell, Basil T.
Babbitt, Bradford *33:* 158
Babbitt, Natalie *6:* 6; *8:* 220; *68:* 20; *70:* 242, 243; *194:* 8, 9
Baca, Maria *104:* 5
Bacchus, Andy *94:* 87
Bacha, Andy *109:* 169
Bachelet, Gilles *196:* 18
Bachem, Paul *48:* 180; *67:* 65; *144:* 206
Back, Adam *63:* 125
Back, George *31:* 161
Backes, Nick *190:* 72
Backhouse, Colin *78:* 142
Bacon, Bruce *4:* 74
Bacon, Paul *7:* 155; *8:* 121; *31:* 55; *50:* 42; *56:* 175; *62:* 82, 84
Bacon, Peggy *2:* 11, 228; *46:* 44
Baek, Matthew J. *169:* 95; *202:* 8
Baer, Julie *161:* 2
Baicker-McKee, Carol *177:* 15; *180:* 215
Bailey, Peter *58:* 174; *87:* 221; *194:* 12
Bailey, Sheila *155:* 11
Baker, Alan *22:* 22; *61:* 134; *93:* 11, 12; *146:* 6, 7, 10
Baker, Charlotte *2:* 12
Baker, Garin *89:* 65
Baker, Jeannie *23:* 4; *88:* 18, 19, 20
Baker, Jim *22:* 24
Baker, Joe *82:* 188; *111:* 55; *124:* 70; *197:* 73
Baker, Keith *179:* 6, 7

Baker, Leslie *112:* 214; *132:* 103, 246; *180:* 74, 246
Baldacci, Rudy *184:* 9
Baldridge, Cyrus LeRoy *19:* 69; *44:* 50
Baldus, Zachary *152:* 231; *187:* 60
Balet, Jan *11:* 22
Balian, Lorna *9:* 16; *91:* 16
Balit, Christina *102:* 24; *159:* 9; *162:* 118, 119
Ballantyne, R.M. *24:* 34
Ballis, George *14:* 199
Balouch, Kristen *176:* 11
Baltzer, Hans *40:* 30
Banbery, Fred *58:* 15
Banfill, A. Scott *98:* 7; *112:* 59
Bang, Molly Garrett *24:* 37, 38; *69:* 8, 9, 10; *111:* 7,9, 10, 11; *140:* 11; *158:* 37, 38, 39; *195:* 3
Banik, Yvette Santiago *21:* 136
Banner, Angela
    See Maddison, Angela Mary
Bannerman, Helen *19:* 13, 14
Banning, Greg *202:* 98
Bannon, Laura *6:* 10; *23:* 8
Bantock, Nick *74:* 229; *95:* 6
Banyai, Istvan *185:* 209; *193:* 14, 16; *209:* 155
Baptist, Michael *37:* 208
Baracca, Sal *135:* 206
Baranaski, Marcin *182:* 113
Barasch, Lynne *126:* 16; *186:* 15
Barbarin, Lucien C., Jr. *89:* 88
Barbour, Karen *96:* 5; *74:* 209; *170:* 16
Bare, Arnold Edwin *16:* 31
Bare, Colleen Stanley *32:* 33
Barger, Jan *147:* 11
Bargery, Geoffrey *14:* 258
Barkat, Jonathan *149:* 177; *164:* 254; *181:* 106; *184:* 186; *196:* 11; *198:* 148
Barker, Carol *31:* 27
Barker, Cicely Mary *49:* 50, 51
Barkley, James *4:* 13; *6:* 11; *13:* 112
Barks, Carl *37:* 27, 28, 29, 30, 31, 32, 33, 34
Barling, Joy *62:* 148
Barling, Tom *9:* 23
Barlow, Gillian *62:* 20
Barlow, Perry *35:* 28
Barlowe, Dot *30:* 223
Barlowe, Wayne *37:* 72; *84:* 43; *105:* 5
Barnard, Bryn *88:* 53; *13:* 55; *169:* 13; *193:* 194
Barneda, David *206:* 11
Barner, Bob *29:* 37; *128:* 33; *136:* 19, 20; *177:* 27
Barnes, Hiram P. *20:* 28
Barnes, Tim *137:* 28
Barnes-Murphy, Rowan *88:* 22
Barnett, Charles II *175:* 150
Barnett, Ivan *70:* 14
Barnett, Moneta *16:* 89; *19:* 142; *31:* 102; *33:* 30, 31, 32; *41:* 153; *61:* 94, 97
Barney, Maginel Wright *39:* 32, 33, 34; *YABC 2:* 306
Barnum, Jay Hyde *11:* 224; *20:* 5; *37:* 189, 190
Baron, Alan *80:* 3; *89:* 123
Barr, George *60:* 74; *69:* 64
Barragan, Paula S. *134:* 116; *186:* 158
Barrall, Tim *115:* 152
Barraud, Martin *189:* 38
Barrauds *33:* 114
Barrer-Russell, Gertrude *9:* 65; *27:* 31
Barret, Robert *85:* 134
Barrett, Angela *40:* 136, 137; *62:* 74; *75:* 10; *76:* 142; *144:* 137; *145:* 14
Barrett, Jennifer *58:* 149
Barrett, John E. *43:* 119
Barrett, Moneta *74:* 10
Barrett, Peter *55:* 169; *86:* 111
Barrett, Robert *62:* 145; *77:* 146; *82:* 35
Barrett, Ron *14:* 24; *26:* 35
Barron, John N. *3:* 261; *5:* 101; *14:* 220
Barrow, Ann *136:* 27

Barrows, Walter *14:* 268
Barry, Ethelred B. *37:* 79; *YABC 1:* 229
Barry, James *14:* 25
Barry, Katharina *2:* 159; *4:* 22
Barry, Robert E. *6:* 12
Barry, Scott *32:* 35
Barshaw, Ruth McNally *203:* 9
Bartenbach, Jean *40:* 31
Barth, Ernest Kurt *2:* 172; *3:* 160; *8:* 26; *10:* 31
Bartholomew, Caty *208:* 153
Bartholomew, Marie *200:* 66
Bartlett, Alison *101:* 88; *165:* 93; *209:* 51
Barton, Byron *8:* 207; *9:* 18; *23:* 66; *80:* 181; *90:* 18, 19, 20, 21; *126:* 29, 30
Barton, Harriett *30:* 71
Barton, Jill *129:* 108; *135:* 120; *145:* 185, 189; *184:* 177
Bartram, Robert *10:* 42
Bartsch, Jochen *8:* 105; *39:* 38
Bascove, Barbara *45:* 73
Base, Graeme *101:* 15, 16, 17, 18; *162:* 8, 10, 12
Baseman, Gary *174:* 12
Bash, Barbara *132:* 9
Baskin, Leonard *30:* 42, 43, 46, 47; *49:* 125, 126, 128, 129,133; *173:* 120
Bass, Saul *49:* 192
Bassett, Jeni *40:* 99; *64:* 30
Basso, Bill *99:* 139; *189:* 134
Batchelor, Joy *29:* 41, 47, 48
Bate, Norman *5:* 16
Bates, Amy June *188:* 170; *189:* 27, 28
Bates, Leo *24:* 35
Batet, Carmen *39:* 134
Batherman, Muriel *31:* 79; *45:* 185
Battaglia, Aurelius *50:* 44
Batten, John D. *25:* 161, 162
Batten, Mary *162:* 14, 15
Battles, Asa *32:* 94, 95
Bauer, Carla *193:* 6
Bauer, Jutta *150:* 32
Bauernschmidt, Marjorie *15:* 15
Baum, Allyn *20:* 10
Baum, Willi *4:* 24, 25; *7:* 173
Bauman, Leslie *61:* 121
Baumann, Jill *34:* 170
Baumhauer, Hans *11:* 218; *15:* 163, 165, 167
Baxter, Glen *57:* 100
Baxter, Leon *59:* 102
Baxter, Robert *87:* 129
Bayer, Herbert *181:* 16
Bayley, Dorothy *37:* 195
Bayley, Nicola *40:* 104; *41:* 34, 35; *69:* 15; *129:* 33, 34, 35
Baylin, Mark *158:* 233
Baynes, Pauline *2:* 244; *3:* 149; *13:* 133, 135,137, 141; *19:* 18, 19, 20; *32:* 208, 213, 214; *36:* 105, 108; *59:* 12, 13, 14, 16, 17, 18, 20; *100:* 158, 159, 243; *133:* 3, 4
Beach, Lou *150:* 150; *207:* 117, 118
Beame, Rona *12:* 40
Bean, Jonathan *196:* 102
Bear's Heart *73:* 215
Beard, Dan *22:* 31, 32
Beard, J.H. *YABC 1:* 158
Bearden, Romare *9:* 7; *22:* 35
Beardshaw, Rosalind *169:* 22; *190:* 22
Beardsley, Aubrey *17:* 14; *23:* 181; *59:* 130, 131
Bearman, Jane *29:* 38
Beaton, Cecil *24:* 208
Beaton, Clare *125:* 28; *208:* 67
Beauce, J.A. *18:* 103
Beaujard, Sophie *81:* 54
Beccia, Carlyn *189:* 29
Bechtold, Lisze *208:* 29
Beck, Charles *11:* 169; *51:* 173
Beck, Ian *138:* 27; *182:* 150; *190:* 25
Beck, Melinda *203:* 112
Beck, Ruth *13:* 11

Becker, Harriet *12:* 211
Beckerman, Jonathan *208:* 194
Beckett, Sheilah *25:* 5; *33:* 37, 38
Beckhoff, Harry *1:* 78; *5:* 163
Beckhorn, Susan Williams *189:* 32
Beckman, Kaj *45:* 38, 39, 40, 41
Beckman, Per *45:* 42, 43
Beddows, Eric *72:* 70
Bedford, F.D. *20:* 118, 122; *33:* 170; *41:* 220, 221,230, 233
Bee, Joyce *19:* 62
Bee, William *188:* 6
Beeby, Betty *25:* 36
Beech, Carol *9:* 149
Beech, Mark *192:* 122
Beek *25:* 51, 55, 59
Beeke, Tiphanie *177:* 127; *204:* 140
Beekman, Doug *125:* 146, 148
Beerbohm, Max *24:* 208
Beeson, Bob *108:* 57
Begin, Mary Jane *82:* 13; *206:* 13
Beha, Philippe *172:* 85
Behr, Joyce *15:* 15; *21:* 132; *23:* 161
Behrens, Hans *5:* 97
Beier, Ellen *135:* 170; *139:* 47; *183:* 164
Beinicke, Steve *69:* 18
Beisner, Monika *46:* 128, 131; *112:* 127
Belden, Charles J. *12:* 182
Belina, Renate *39:* 132
Bell, Corydon *3:* 20
Bell, Graham *54:* 48
Bell, Julia *151:* 214
Bell, Julie *159:* 172; *165:* 18
Bell, Thomas P. *76:* 182
Bellamy, Glen *127:* 15
Beltran, Alberto *43:* 37
Bemelmans, Ludwig *15:* 19, 21; *100:* 27
Ben-Ami, Doron *75:* 96; *84:* 107; *108:* 132; *110:* 63; *159:* 157; *197:* 142
Bendall-Brunello, John *150:* 4; *157:* 163; *185:* 3, 4; *203:* 5
Benda, Wladyslaw T. *15:* 256; *30:* 76, 77; *44:* 182
Bender, Robert *77:* 162; *79:* 13; *160:* 23
Bendick, Jeanne *2:* 24; *68:* 27, 28
Benioff, Carol *121:* 42; *175:* 23
Benner, Cheryl *80:* 11
Bennett, Charles H. *64:* 6
Bennett, Erin Susanne *165:* 216
Bennett, F.I. *YABC 1:* 134
Bennett, James *146:* 240
Bennett, Jill *26:* 61; *41:* 38, 39; *45:* 54
Bennett, Rainey *15:* 26; *23:* 53
Bennett, Richard *15:* 45; *21:* 11, 12, 13; *25:* 175
Bennett, Susan *5:* 55
Benny, Mike *142:* 78; *203:* 13, 14; *207:* 85
Benoit, Elise *77:* 74
Benson, Linda *60:* 130; *62:* 91; *75:* 101; *79:* 156; *134:* 129
Benson, Patrick *68:* 162; *147:* 17, 18, 19, 20
Bentley, Carolyn *46:* 153
Bentley, James *149:* 30
Bentley, Roy *30:* 162
Benton, Jim *172:* 22
Benton, Thomas Hart *2:* 99
Berelson, Howard *5:* 20; *16:* 58; *31:* 50
Berenstain, Jan *12:* 47; *64:* 33, 34, 36, 37, 38, 40, 42, 44; *135:* 25, 28, 31, 35
Berenstain, Stan *12:* 47; *64:* 33, 34, 36, 37, 38, 40, 42, 44; *135:* 25, 28, 31, 35
Berenzy, Alix *65:* 13; *73:* 6; *78:* 115
Berg, Joan *1:* 115; *3:* 156; *6:* 26, 58
Berg, Ron *36:* 48, 49; *48:* 37, 38; *67:* 72
Bergen, David *115:* 44; *207:* 34
Berger, Barbara *77:* 14
Berger, Carin *185:* 6
Berger, William M. *14:* 143; *YABC 1:* 204
Bergherr, Mary *74:* 170; *151:* 123
Bergin, Mark *114:* 8, 9; *143:* 95; *160:* 26, 27
Bergstreser, Douglas *69:* 76

Bergum, Constance R. *121:* 14, 15; *208:* 31, 32, 33; *209:* 176
Bering, Claus *13:* 14
Berkeley, Jon *139:* 218
Berkowitz, Jeanette *3:* 249
Berman, Paul *66:* 14
Bernal, Richard *154:* 176
Bernadette
  See Watts, Bernadette
Bernardin, James *112:* 24; *167:* 94
Bernasconi, Pablo *183:* 10, 11
Bernath, Stefen *32:* 76
Bernhard, Durga *80:* 13
Bernstein, Michel J. *51:* 71
Bernstein, Ted *38:* 183; *50:* 131
Bernstein, Zena *23:* 46
Berridge, Celia *86:* 63
Berrill, Jacquelyn *12:* 50
Berry, Erick
  See Best, Allena
Berry, Holly *205:* 116
Berry, William D. *14:* 29; *19:* 48
Berry, William A. *6:* 219
Berson, Harold *2:* 17, 18; *4:* 28, 29, 220; *9:* 10; *12:* 19; *17:* 45; *18:* 193; *22:* 85; *34:* 172; *44:* 120; *46:* 42; *80:* 240
Bertholf, Bret *187:* 9; *189:* 32, 33
Berton, Patsy *99:* 16
Bertschmann, Harry *16:* 1
Besco, Don *70:* 99
Beskow, Elsa *20:* 13, 14, 15
Bess, Clayton *63:* 94
Best, Allena *2:* 26; *34:* 76
Betera, Carol *74:* 68
Bethell, Thomas N. *61:* 169
Bethers, Ray *6:* 22
Bettina
  See Ehrlich, Bettina
Betts, Ethel Franklin *17:* 161, 164, 165; *YABC 2:* 47
Betz, Rudolf *59:* 161
Bewick, Thomas *16:* 40, 41, 43, 44, 45, 47; *54:* 150; *YABC 1:* 107
Beyer, Paul J. III *74:* 24
Bezencon, Jacqueline *48:* 40
Biamonte, Daniel *40:* 90
Bianchi, John *91:* 19
Bianco, Pamela *15:* 31; *28:* 44, 45, 46
Bible, Charles *13:* 15
Bice, Clare *22:* 40
Biedrzycki, David *186:* 170
Bierman, Don *57:* 184
Biggers, John *2:* 123
Biggs, Brian *192:* 38; *196:* 15; *207:* 170
Bikadoroff, Roxanna *201:* 74
Bileck, Marvin *3:* 102; *40:* 36, 37
Bilibin, Ivan *61:* 8, 9, 12, 13, 14, 15, 151, 152, 154, 162
Billington, Patrick *98:* 71
Billout, Guy *144:* 38, 39
Bimen, Levent *5:* 179
Binch, Caroline *81:* 18; *140:* 15, 16; *144:* 115
Binder, Hannes *169:* 163
Bing, Christopher *126:* 34
Binger, Bill *121:* 46
Binks, Robert *25:* 150
Binzen, Bill *24:* 47
Birch, Reginald *15:* 150; *19:* 33, 34, 35, 36; *37:* 196,197; *44:* 182; *46:* 176; *YABC 1:* 84; *2:* 34, 39
Birchall, Mark *123:* 188
Bird, Esther Brock *1:* 36; *25:* 66
Birdsong, Keith *167:* 85
Birkett, Georgie *204:* 121
Birkett, Rachel *78:* 206
Birling, Paul *109:* 30
Birmingham, Christian *132:* 243; *143:* 114; *209:* 58
Birmingham, Lloyd P. *12:* 51; *83:* 13
Biro, Val *1:* 26; *41:* 42; *60:* 178; *67:* 23, 24; *84:* 242, 243

Bischoff, Ilse *44:* 51
Bishop, Don *199:* 133
Bishop, Gavin *97:* 17, 18; *144:* 42, 44
Bishop, Kathleen Wong *115:* 67
Bishop, Rich *56:* 43
Bite, I. *60:* 14
Bittinger, Ned *93:* 117; *205:* 115
Bjorklund, Lorence *3:* 188, 252; *7:* 100; *9:* 113; *10:* 66; *19:* 178; *33:* 122, 123; *35:* 36, 37, 38, 39,41, 42, 43; *36:* 185; *38:* 93; *47:* 106; *66:* 194; *YABC 1:* 242
Bjorkman, Steve *91:* 199; *160:* 110; *198:* 18
Black Sheep *164:* 100
Blackburn, Loren H. *63:* 10
Blackall, Sophie *194:* 140; *209:* 157
Blackford, John *137:* 105; *180:* 36
Blackwell, Basil T. *YABC 1:* 68, 69
Blackwood, Freya *199:* 9
Blackwood, Gary L. *118:* 17
Blades, Ann *16:* 52; *37:* 213; *50:* 41; *69:* 21; *99:* 215
Blair, Jay *45:* 46; *46:* 155
Blaisdell, Elinore *1:* 121; *3:* 134; *35:* 63
Blake, Anne Catharine *189:* 71
Blake, Francis *198:* 4
Blake, Quentin *3:* 170; *10:* 48; *13:* 38; *21:* 180; *26:* 60; *28:* 228; *30:* 29, 31; *40:* 108; *45:* 219; *46:* 165, 168; *48:* 196; *52:* 10, 11, 12,13, 14, 15, 16, 17; *73:* 41, 43; *78:* 84, 86; *80:* 250, 251; *84:* 210, 211, 212; *87:* 177; *96:* 24, 26, 28; *124:* 79; *125:* 32, 34; *181:* 139
Blake, Robert J. *37:* 90; *53:* 67; *54:* 23; *160:* 28, 29
Blake, William *30:* 54, 56, 57, 58, 59, 60
Blanchard, N. Taylor *82:* 140
Blass, Jacqueline *8:* 215
Blazek, Scott R. *91:* 71
Bleck, Cathie *118:* 116
Bleck, Linda *204:* 124
Blegvad, Erik *2:* 59; *3:* 98; *5:* 117; *7:* 131; *11:* 149; *14:* 34, 35; *18:* 237; *32:* 219; *60:* 106; *66:* 16, 17, 18, 19; *70:* 233; *76:* 18; *82:* 106; *87:* 45; *100:* 188; *129:* 125; *132:* 17, 18, 19, 20; *176:* 14; *200:* 100; *YABC 1:* 201
Blessen, Karen *93:* 126
Bliss, Corinne Demas *37:* 38
Bliss, Harry *196:* 27, 28, 29
Blitt, Barry *179:* 199; *187:* 13
Bloch, Lucienne *10:* 12
Blondon, Herve *129:* 48; *183:* 22
Bloom, Lloyd *35:* 180; *36:* 149; *47:* 99; *62:* 117; *68:* 231; *72:* 136; *75:* 185; *83:* 99; *108:* 19
Bloom, Suzanne *172:* 23, 24
Blossom, Dave *34:* 29
Blumenschein, E.L. *YABC 1:* 113, 115
Blumer, Patt *29:* 214
Blundell, Kim *29:* 36
Bluthenthal, Diana Cain *93:* 32; *104:* 106; *177:* 26
Blythe, Benjamin *128:* 7
Blythe, Gary *112:* 52; *181:* 166; *182:* 64; *185:* 7; *186:* 116, 117
Boake, Kathy *176:* 185
Board, Perry *171:* 99
Boardman, Gwenn *12:* 60
Bober, Richard *125:* 145; *132:* 40
Bobri *30:* 138; *47:* 27
Bock, Vera *1:* 187; *21:* 41
Bock, William Sauts *8:* 7; *14:* 37; *16:* 120; *21:* 141; *36:* 177; *62:* 203
Bodecker, N(iels) M(ogens) *8:* 13; *14:* 2; *17:* 55, 56, 57; *73:* 22, 23, 24
Boehm, Linda *40:* 31
Bogacki, Tomek *138:* 31, 32; *144:* 123; *202:* 13
Bogan, Paulette *197:* 152; *201:* 17
Bogdan, Florentina *107:* 43
Bohdal, Susi *22:* 44; *101:* 20
Bohlen, Nina *58:* 13

Boies, Alex *96:* 53
Bok, Chip *205:* 16
Bolam, Emily *101:* 216; *159:* 12; *205:* 59
Bolian, Polly *3:* 270; *4:* 30; *13:* 77; *29:* 197
Bolle, Frank *87:* 100; *208:* 101
Bollen, Roger *79:* 186; *83:* 16
Bolling, Vickey *114:* 44
Bollinger, Peter *101:* 7; *128:* 198; *172:* 26
Bolognese, Don *2:* 147, 231; *4:* 176; *7:* 146; *17:* 43; *23:* 192; *24:* 50; *34:* 108; *36:* 133; *71:* 24, 25; *103:* 131; *129:* 39, 40
Bolster, Rob *186:* 169
Bolton, A.T. *57:* 158
Bond, Arnold *18:* 116
Bond, Barbara Higgins *21:* 102
Bond, Bruce *52:* 97
Bond, Felicia *38:* 197; *49:* 55, 56; *89:* 170; *90:* 171; *126:* 37
Bond, Higgins *177:* 22, 23; *209:* 175
Bonn, Pat *43:* 40
Bonner, Hannah *197:* 13, 14
Bonners, Susan *41:* 40; *85:* 36; *94:* 99, 100; *151:* 105, 106
Bono, Mary *184:* 73
Bonsall, Crosby *23:* 6
Boon, Debbie *103:* 6; *144:* 188
Boon, Emilie *86:* 23, 24
Boone, Debbie *165:* 77
Boore, Sara *60:* 73
Bootman, Colin *155:* 13; *159:* 35; *174:* 192
Booth, Franklin *YABC 2:* 76
Booth, George *191:* 13
Booth, Graham *32:* 193; *37:* 41, 42
Borda, Juliette *102:* 188
Bordier, Georgette *16:* 54
Boren, Tinka *27:* 128
Borges, Jose Francisco *119:* 62
Borja, Robert *22:* 48
Born, Adolf *49:* 63
Bornstein, Ruth *14:* 44; *88:* 45, 46; *107:* 30
Borten, Helen *3:* 54; *5:* 24
Bosin, Blackbear *69:* 104
Bossom, Naomi *35:* 48
Bostock, Mike *83:* 221; *114:* 14; *188:* 205
Boston, Peter *19:* 42
Bosustow, Stephen *34:* 202
Boszko, Ron *75:* 47
Bottner, Barbara *14:* 46
Boucher, Joelle *41:* 138
Boulat, Pierre *44:* 40
Boulet, Susan Seddon *50:* 47
Bouma, Paddy *118:* 25; *128:* 16
Bour, Daniele *66:* 145
Bourke-White, Margaret *15:* 286, 287; *57:* 102
Boutavant, Marc *200:* 136
Boutet de Monvel, M. *30:* 61, 62, 63, 65
Bowen, Betsy *105:* 222
Bowen, Richard *42:* 134
Bowen, Ruth *31:* 188
Bower, Ron *29:* 33
Bowers, David *95:* 38; *115:* 20; *127:* 169, 170; *165:* 57; *207:* 11
Bowers, Tim *185:* 35; *201:* 41
Bowman, Claire *174:* 177
Bowman, Eric *151:* 23
Bowman, Leslie *85:* 203; *105:* 108; *116:* 76; *128:* 234; *182:* 24, 25
Bowman, Peter *146:* 214, 215; *150:* 115
Bowser, Carolyn Ewing *22:* 253
Boxall, Ed *178:* 28
Boyd, Aaron *158:* 242
Boyd, Patti *45:* 31
Boyle, Eleanor Vere *28:* 50, 51
Boynton, Sandra *57:* 13, 14, 15; *107:* 36, 37; *152:* 12, 13, 14
Bozzo, Frank *4:* 154
Brabbs, Derry *55:* 170
Brace, Eric *132:* 193, 194; *152:* 71; *184:* 195; *197:* 94; *201:* 54
Brackers de Hugo, Pierre *115:* 21
Bradford, June *158:* 138

Bradford, Ron *7:* 157
Bradley, David P. *69:* 105
Bradley, Richard D. *26:* 182
Bradley, William *5:* 164
Brady, Irene *4:* 31; *42:* 37; *68:* 191
Bragg, Michael *32:* 78; *46:* 31
Bragg, Ruth Gembicki *77:* 18
Brainerd, John W. *65:* 19
Braithwaite, Althea *23:* 12, 13; *119:* 16
Brak, Syd *146:* 187
Bralds, Braldt *90:* 28; *91:* 151
Bram, Elizabeth *30:* 67
Bramley, Peter *4:* 3
Brandenberg, Aliki *2:* 36, 37; *24:* 222; *35:* 49, 50, 51,52, 53, 54, 56, 57; *75:* 15, 17; *92:* 205; *113:* 18, 19, 20; *157:* 28; *156:* 111
Brandenburg, Alexa *75:* 19
Brandenburg, Jim *47:* 58; *150:* 212
Brandi, Lillian *31:* 158
Brandon, Brumsic, Jr. *9:* 25
Brannen, Sarah S. *202:* 15
Bransom, Paul *17:* 121; *43:* 44
Braren, Loretta Trezzo *87:* 193
Brassard, France *186:* 22
Braun, Wendy *80:* 17, 18
Brautigam, Don *115:* 175, 176
Brazell, Derek *75:* 105; *79:* 9
Breathed, Berkeley *86:* 27, 28, 29; *161:* 13, 14
Breckenreid, Julia *192:* 209
Breen, Steve *186:* 23
Brennan, Steve *83:* 230; *101:* 184
Brenner, Fred *22:* 85; *36:* 34; *42:* 34
Brett, Bernard *22:* 54
Brett, Harold M. *26:* 98, 99, 100
Brett, Jan *30:* 135; *42:* 39; *71:* 31, 32; *130:* 23, 24, 25, 26, 27; *171:* 15, 16
Brewer, Paul *106:* 115; *145:* 202
Brewer, Sally King *33:* 44
Brewster, Patience *40:* 68; *45:* 22, 183; *51:* 20; *66:* 144; *89:* 4; *97:* 30, 31
Brick, John *10:* 15
Brickman, Robin D. *131:* 88; *142:* 150; *155:* 18; *178:* 109; *184:* 32
Bridge, David R. *45:* 28
Bridgman, L.J. *37:* 77
Bridwell, Norman *4:* 37; *138:* 36, 37, 40
Brierley, Louise *91:* 22; *96:* 165; *183:* 51
Briggs, Harry *172:* 187
Briggs, Raymond *10:* 168; *23:* 20, 21; *66:* 29, 31, 32; *131:* 28, 29; *184:* 15, 16
Brigham, Grace A. *37:* 148
Bright, Robert *24:* 55
Brighton, Catherine *107:* 39; *206:* 23
Brinckloe, Julie *13:* 18; *24:* 79, 115; *29:* 35; *63:* 140; *81:* 131
Brion *47:* 116
Brisley, Joyce L. *22:* 57
Brisson, James F. *110:* 60
Brittingham, Geoffrey *88:* 37
Brix-Henker, Silke *81:* 194
Broadway, Hannah *208:* 104
Brock, Charles E. *15:* 97; *19:* 247, 249; *23:* 224, 225; *36:* 88; *42:* 41, 42, 43, 44, 45; *100:* 189; *YABC 1:* 194, 196, 203
Brock, Emma *7:* 21
Brock, Henry Matthew *15:* 81; *16:* 141; *19:* 71; *34:* 115; *40:* 164; *42:* 47, 48, 49; *49:* 66
Brocksopp, Arthur *57:* 157
Broda, Ron *136:* 180; *174:* 123
Brodkin, Gwen *34:* 135
Brodovitch, Alexi *52:* 22
Bromhall, Winifred *5:* 11; *26:* 38
Bromley, Lizzy *159:* 179
Bronson, Linda *150:* 210; *174:* 133; *203:* 16, 17
Brooke, L. Leslie *16:* 181, 182, 183, 186; *17:* 15, 16, 17; *18:* 194
Brooker, Christopher *15:* 251
Brooker, Kyrsten *111:* 94; *140:* 28; *162:* 111; *175:* 108; *186:* 42, 225; *199:* 12; *201:* 30
Brooks, Erik *166:* 52; *182:* 30

Brooks, Karen Stormer *186:* 110
Brooks, Maya Itzna *92:* 153
Brooks, Ron *94:* 15; *197:* 188
Brooks, S.G. *178:* 127
Broomfield, Maurice *40:* 141
Brotman, Adolph E. *5:* 21
Brown, Buck *45:* 48
Brown, Calef *179:* 18
Brown, Christopher *62:* 124, 125, 127, 128
Brown, Craig McFarland *73:* 28; *84:* 65
Brown, Dan *61:* 167; *115:* 183, 184; *116:* 28, 29; *193:* 190; *200:* 21, 23
Brown, David *7:* 47; *48:* 52
Brown, Denise *11:* 213
Brown, Don *172:* 29
Brown, Elbrite *195:* 39; *198:* 5
Brown, Ford Madox *48:* 74
Brown, Hunter *191:* 111, 112
Brown, Judith Gwyn *1:* 45; *7:* 5; *8:* 167; *9:* 182, 190; *20:* 16, 17, 18; *23:* 142; *29:* 117; *33:* 97; *36:* 23, 26; *43:* 184; *48:* 201, 223; *49:* 69; *86:* 227; *110:* 188; *153:* 7
Brown, Kathryn *98:* 26
Brown, Lisa *187:* 175
Brown, Laurie Krasny *99:* 30
Brown, Marc (Tolon) *10:* 17, 197; *14:* 263; *51:* 18; *53:* 11, 12, 13, 15, 16, 17; *75:* 58; *80:* 24, 25, 26; *82:* 261; *99:* 29; *145:* 22, 23, 25, 27; *162:* 198
Brown, Marcia *7:* 30; *25:* 203; *47:* 31, 32, 33, 34, 35,36, 37, 38, 39, 40, 42, 43, 44; *YABC 1:* 27
Brown, Margery W. *5:* 32, 33; *10:* 3
Brown, Martin *101:* 43
Brown, Mary Barrett *97:* 74
Brown, Palmer *36:* 40
Brown, Paul *25:* 26; *26:* 107
Brown, Richard *61:* 18; *67:* 30
Brown, Rick *78:* 71; *150:* 154
Brown, Robert S. *85:* 33
Brown, Rod *157:* 142
Brown, Ruth *55:* 165; *86:* 112, 113; *105:* 16, 17, 18; *171:* 178
Brown, Trevor *99:* 160; *139:* 247; *189:* 206
Browne, Anthony *45:* 50, 51, 52; *61:* 21, 22, 23, 24, 25; *105:* 21, 22, 23, 25
Browne, Dik *8:* 212; *67:* 32, 33, 35, 37, 39
Browne, Gordon *16:* 97; *64:* 114, 116, 117, 119, 121
Browne, Hablot K. *15:* 65, 80; *21:* 14, 15, 16, 17, 18, 19,20; *24:* 25
Browne, Jane *165:* 222
Browning, Coleen *4:* 132
Browning, Mary Eleanor *24:* 84
Bruce, Robert *23:* 23
Brude, Dick *48:* 215
Bruel, Nick *166:* 41; *205:* 17, 18
Brule, Al *3:* 135
Brumbeau, Jeff *157:* 29
Bruna, Dick *43:* 48, 49, 50; *76:* 27, 28
Brundage, Frances *19:* 244
Brunhoff, Jean de *24:* 57, 58
Brunhoff, Laurent de *24:* 60; *71:* 35, 36, 37
Brunkus, Denise *84:* 50; *123:* 117; *178:* 209; *193:* 99; *204:* 10, 11, 12; *209:* 202
Brunson, Bob *43:* 135
Bryan, Ashley *31:* 44; *72:* 27, 28, 29; *107:* 92; *116:* 192; *132:* 24; *178:* 33, 34, 35; *208:* 83
Bryant, Laura J. *176:* 36; *183:* 168
Bryant, Michael *93:* 74
Brychta, Alex *21:* 21
Bryer, Diana *107:* 121
Bryson, Bernarda *3:* 88, 146; *39:* 26; *44:* 185; *131:* 40
Buba, Joy *12:* 83; *30:* 226; *44:* 56
Buchanan, George *166:* 198
Buchanan, Lilian *13:* 16
Buchanan, Rachel *171:* 71
Bucholtz-Ross, Linda *44:* 137
Buchs, Thomas *40:* 38
Buck, Margaret Waring *3:* 30

Buckhardt, Marc *172:* 59
Buckley, Mike *166:* 180
Budwine, Greg *175:* 172
Buehner, Mark *104:* 12, 15; *105:* 160; *119:* 98; *157:* 188; *159:* 39, 40, 43; *192:* 111
Buehr, Walter *3:* 31
Buff, Conrad *19:* 52, 53, 54
Buff, Mary *19:* 52, 53
Bull, Charles Livingston *18:* 207; *88:* 175, 176
Bullen, Anne *3:* 166, 167
Buller, Jon *205:* 21
Bullock, Kathleen *77:* 24
Bumgarner-Kirby, Claudia *77:* 194
Burbank, Addison *37:* 43
Burchard, Peter Duncan *3:* 197; *5:* 35; *6:* 158, 218; *143:* 17
Burckhardt, Marc *94:* 48; *110:* 89; *196:* 41; *199:* 116
Burger, Carl *3:* 33; *45:* 160, 162
Burgeson, Marjorie *19:* 31
Burgess, Anne *76:* 252
Burgess, Gelett *32:* 39, 42
Burgess, Mark *157:* 31
Burke, Jim *179:* 19; *185:* 63
Burke, Phillip *95:* 117
Burkert, Nancy Ekholm *18:* 186; *22:* 140; *24:* 62, 63,64, 65; *26:* 53; *29:* 60, 61; *46:* 171; *YABC 1:* 46
Burkhardt, Bruce *142:* 86
Burkhardt, Melissa A. *142:* 86
Burleson, Joe *104:* 35; *172:* 139
Burn, Doris *6:* 172
Burn, Jeffrey *89:* 125; *152:* 132
Burn, Ted
  See Burn, Thomas E.
Burn, Thomas E. *151:* 41
Burnard, Damon *115:* 23
Burnett, Virgil *44:* 42
Burningham, John *9:* 68; *16:* 60, 61; *59:* 28, 29, 30,31, 32, 33, 35; *111:* 18, 19, 21; *160:* 37
Burns, Howard M. *12:* 173
Burns, Jim *47:* 70; *86:* 32; *91:* 197; *123:* 16
Burns, M.F. *26:* 69
Burns, Raymond *9:* 29
Burns, Robert *24:* 106
Burr, Dan *65:* 28; *108:* 134; *164:* 203; *182:* 68
Burr, Dane *12:* 2
Burra, Edward *YABC 2:* 68
Burrell, Galen *56:* 76
Burri, Rene *41:* 143; *54:* 166
Burridge, Marge Opitz *14:* 42
Burris, Burmah *4:* 81
Burroughs, John Coleman *41:* 64
Burroughs, Studley O. *41:* 65
Burton, Marilee Robin *46:* 33
Burton, Virginia Lee *2:* 43; *44:* 49, 51; *100:* 46, 47; *YABC 1:* 24; *147:* 56
Busoni, Rafaello *1:* 186; *3:* 224; *6:* 126; *14:* 5; *16:* 62, 63
Butchkes, Sidney *50:* 58
Butler, Geoff *94:* 20
Butler, Ralph *116:* 212
Butterfield, Ned *1:* 153; *27:* 128; *79:* 63
Butterworth, Ian *184:* 48, 49
Butterworth, Nick *106:* 43, 44; *149:* 34
Buxton, John *123:* 12
Buzelli, Christopher *105:* 149
Buzonas, Gail *29:* 88
Buzzell, Russ W. *12:* 177
Byard, Carole *39:* 44; *57:* 18, 19, 20; *60:* 60; *61:* 93, 96; *69:* 210; *78:* 246; *79:* 227
Byars, Betsy *46:* 35
Byfield, Barbara Ninde *8:* 18
Byfield, Graham *32:* 29
Bynum, Janie *176:* 50
Byrd, Robert *13:* 218; *33:* 46; *158:* 70
Byrd, Samuel *123:* 104

C

Cabat, Erni *74:* 38
Cabban, Vanessa *138:* 73; *176:* 39; *185:* 65
Cabrera, Jane *103:* 24; *152:* 27; *182:* 33, 34
Caceres, Ana Palmero *198:* 106
Caddy, Alice *6:* 41
Cady, Harrison *17:* 21, 23; *19:* 57, 58
Caffrey, Aileen *72:* 223; *141:* 154
Cairns, Julia *177:* 37
Caldecott, Randolph *16:* 98, 103; *17:* 32, 33, 36, 38, 39; *26:* 90; *100:* 49, 50; *YABC 2:* 172
Calder, Alexander *18:* 168
Calderón, Gloria *179:* 5
Calderon, W. Frank *25:* 160
Caldwell, Ben *105:* 75; *149:* 60; *195:* 61
Caldwell, Clyde *98:* 100; *116:* 39; *208:* 145
Caldwell, Doreen *23:* 77; *71:* 41
Caldwell, John *46:* 225
Call, Greg *126:* 135; *165:* 49; *182:* 105, 163; *197:* 18, 19; *200:* 159; *209:* 166
Callahan, Kevin *22:* 42
Callahan, Philip S. *25:* 77
Callan, Jamie *59:* 37
Calvin, James *61:* 92
Camburn-Bracalente, Carol A. *118:* 22
Cameron, Chad *190:* 144
Cameron, Julia Margaret *19:* 203
Cameron, Scott *99:* 18
Camm, Martin *140:* 208, 209, 210
Campbell, Ann *11:* 43; *123:* 182; *183:* 68
Campbell, Bill *89:* 39
Campbell, Ken *126:* 143; *205:* 162
Campbell, Robert *55:* 120
Campbell, Rod *51:* 27; *98:* 34
Campbell, Walter M. *YABC 2:* 158
Camps, Luis *28:* 120, 121; *66:* 35
Canga, C.B. *187:* 165
Caniglia, Jeremy *201:* 89
Cann, Helen *124:* 50; *141:* 78; *170:* 138; *179:* 22, 23
Cannell, Jon *196:* 43
Cannon, Janell *78:* 25; *128:* 40
Canright, David *36:* 162
Cantone, AnnaLaura *182:* 146; *196:* 80
Canty, Thomas *85:* 161; *92:* 47; *113:* 192; *134:* 60; *185:* 117
Canyon, Christopher *150:* 44; *151:* 112
Caparo, Antonio Javier *204:* 128
Caporale, Wende *70:* 42
Capp, Al *61:* 28, 30, 31, 40, 41, 43, 44
Cappon, Manuela *154:* 64
Caras, Peter *36:* 64
Caraway, Caren *57:* 22
Caraway, James *3:* 200, 201
Carbe, Nino *29:* 183
Cares, Linda *67:* 176
Carigiet, Alois *24:* 67
Carle, Eric *4:* 42; *11:* 121; *12:* 29; *65:* 32,33, 34, 36; *73:* 63, 65; *163:* 55, 56
Carling, Amelia Lau *164:* 46
Carlino, Angela *168:* 43; *188:* 20
Carlson, Nancy L. *41:* 116; *56:* 25; *90:* 45; *144:* 48, 50
Carlluccio, Maria *175:* 129
Carmi, Giora *79:* 35; *149:* 40; *208:* 126
Carpenter, Nancy *76:* 128; *86:* 173; *89:* 171; *131:* 186; *134:* 8; *138:* 215; *153:* 204; *159:* 93; *165:* 232
Carr, Archie *37:* 225
Carrick, Donald *5:* 194; *39:* 97; *49:* 70; *53:* 156; *63:* 15, 16, 17, 18, 19, 21; *80:* 131; *86:* 151; *118:* 24
Carrick, Malcolm *28:* 59, 60
Carrick, Paul *118:* 26; *194:* 28
Carrick, Valery *21:* 47
Carrier, Lark *71:* 43
Carroll, Jim *88:* 211; *140:* 177; *153:* 99; *195:* 75

Carroll, Lewis
See Dodgson, Charles L.
Carroll, Michael 72: 5
Carroll, Pamela 84: 68; 128: 214; 199: 130
Carroll, Ruth 7: 41; 10: 68
Carter, Abby 81: 32; 97: 121; 102: 61; 163:
139; 164: 125; 184: 22, 23; 191: 85
Carter, Barbara 47: 167, 169
Carter, David A. 114: 24, 25; 170: 42, 43
Carter, Don 124: 54; 184: 100; 192: 43, 44, 45
Carter, Harry 22: 179
Carter, Helene 15: 38; 22: 202, 203; YABC 2:
220, 221
Carter, Penny 173: 91
Cartlidge, Michelle 49: 65; 96: 50, 51
Cartwright, Reg 63: 61, 62; 78: 26; 143: 4
Cartwright, Shannon 176: 81
Carty, Leo 4: 196; 7: 163; 58: 131
Cary 4: 133; 9: 32; 20: 2; 21: 143
Cary, Page 12: 41
Casale, Paul 71: 63; 109: 122; 136: 28
Case, Chris 209: 23
Case, Sandra E. 16: 2
Caseley, Judith 87: 36; 159: 47, 48, 49
Casilla, Robert 78: 7; 167: 124
Casino, Steve 85: 193
Cassel, Lili
See Wronker, Lili Cassel
Cassel-Wronker, Lili
See Wronker, Lili Cassel
Cassels, Jean 8: 50; 150: 119; 173: 37; 186:
182
Cassen, Melody 140: 51
Cassity, Don 104: 24
Cassler, Carl 75: 137, 138; 82: 162
Casson, Hugh 65: 38, 40, 42, 43
Castellon, Federico 48: 45, 46, 47, 48
Castle, Jane 4: 80
Castro, Antonio 84: 71
Casu, Danny "casroc" 201: 10
Catalano, Dominic 94: 79; 163: 60, 61; 162:
54
Catalanotto, Peter 63: 170; 70: 23; 71: 182;
72: 96; 74: 114; 76: 194, 195; 77: 7; 79:
157; 80: 28, 67; 83: 157; 85: 27; 108: 11;
113: 30, 31, 33, 34, 36; 114: 27, 28, 29; 117:
53; 124: 168; 159: 54, 55; 195: 19, 20, 21,
22, 24, 174; 200: 156; 207: 103; 209: 184
Catania, Tom 68: 82
Cather, Carolyn 3: 83; 15: 203; 34: 216
Catrow, David 117: 179; 152: 31, 33; 173: 24;
206: 29
Cauley, Lorinda Bryan 44: 135; 46: 49
Cayard, Bruce 38: 67
Cazet, Denys 52: 27; 99: 39, 40; 163: 65, 66;
191: 25, 27, 28
Ceccoli, Nicoletta 181: 39; 188: 99; 199: 118;
209: 6
Cecil, Randy 127: 132, 133; 187: 16, 17; 191:
168; 209: 5
Cellini, Joseph 2: 73; 3: 35; 16: 116; 47: 103
Cepeda, Joe 90: 62; 109: 91; 134: 172; 159:
57, 58, 164; 197: 157; 203: 69, 95
Chabrian, Debbi 45: 55
Chabrian, Deborah 51: 182; 53: 124; 63: 107;
75: 84; 79: 85; 82: 247; 89: 93; 101: 197
Chagnon, Mary 37: 158
Chalmers, Mary 3: 145; 13: 148; 33: 125; 66:
214
Chamberlain, Christopher 45: 57
Chamberlain, Margaret 46: 51; 106: 89; 188:
193
Chamberlain, Nigel 78: 140
Chambers, C.E. 17: 230
Chambers, Dave 12: 151
Chambers, Jill 134: 110
Chambers, Mary 4: 188
Chambliss, Maxie 42: 186; 56: 159; 93: 163,
164; 103: 178; 186: 33, 34; 196: 39
Champlin, Dale 136: 124

Chan, Harvey 96: 236; 99: 153; 143: 218;
179: 144
Chan, Peter 207: 21
Chandler, David P. 28: 62
Chaney, Howard 139: 27
Chang, Warren 101: 209
Chapel, Jody 68: 20
Chapman, C.H. 13: 83, 85, 87
Chapman, Frederick T. 6: 27; 44: 28
Chapman, Gaye 203: 133
Chapman, Gaynor 32: 52, 53
Chapman, Jane 145: 186; 150: 56; 166: 220;
174: 202; 176: 43, 44; 179: 131; 202: 189
Chapman, Lynne 175: 31; 197: 25; 208: 44
Chappell, Warren 3: 172; 21: 56; 27: 125
Charles, Donald 30: 154, 155
Charlip, Remy 4: 48; 34: 138; 68: 53, 54; 119:
29, 30
Charlot, Jean 1: 137, 138; 8: 23; 14: 31; 48:
151; 56: 21
Charlot, Martin 64: 72
Charlton, Michael 34: 50; 37: 39
Charmatz, Bill 7: 45
Chartier, Normand 9: 36; 52: 49; 66: 40; 74:
220; 145: 169; 168: 91; 177: 108
Chase, Lynwood M. 14: 4
Chast, Roz 97: 39, 40
Chastain, Madye Lee 4: 50
Chateron, Ann 152: 19
Chatterton, Martin 68: 102; 152: 19
Chau, Tungwai 140: 35
Chauncy, Francis 24: 158
Chayka, Doug 145: 97; 177: 150; 196: 46
Chee, Cheng-Khee 79: 42; 81: 224; 180: 245
Chen, Chih-sien 90: 226
Chen, Tony 6: 45; 19: 131; 29: 126; 34: 160
Chen, Yong 183: 34
Cheney, T.A. 11: 47
Cheng, Andrea 205: 28
Cheng, Judith 36: 45; 51: 16
Chermayeff, Ivan 47: 53
Cherry, David 93: 40
Cherry, Lynne 34: 52; 65: 184; 87: 111; 99:
46, 47
Chesak, Lina 135: 118
Chess, Victoria 12: 6; 33: 42, 48, 49; 40: 194;
41: 145; 69: 80; 72: 100; 92: 33, 34; 104:
167
Chessare, Michele 41: 50; 56: 48; 69: 145
Chesterton, G.K. 27: 43, 44, 45, 47
Chestnutt, David 47: 217
Chesworth, Michael 75: 24, 152; 88: 136; 94:
25; 98: 155; 160: 42; 207: 23, 24, 25
Chetham, Celia 134: 34
Chetwin, Grace 86: 40
Cheung, Irving 158: 96
Chevalier, Christa 35: 66
Chew, Ruth 7: 46; 132: 147
Chewning, Randy 92: 206
Chichester Clark, Emma 72: 121; 77: 212; 78:
209; 87: 143; 117: 37, 39, 40; 144: 138;
156: 24, 25; 209: 26
Chifflart 47: 113, 127
Child, Lauren 119: 32; 183: 30, 31
Chin, Alex 28: 54
Chitwood, Susan Tanner 163: 16
Cho, Shinta 8: 126
Chodos-Irvine, Margaret 52: 102, 103, 107;
152: 44
Choi, Yangsook 171: 134; 173: 135; 178: 38,
39, 40
Chollat, Emilie 170: 203
Chollick, Jay 25: 175
Choma, Christina 99: 169
Chomey, Steve 188: 53
Chorao, Kay 7: 200, 201; 8: 25; 11: 234; 33:
187; 35: 239; 69: 35; 70: 235; 123: 174;
193: 179
Chow, Frances J. Soo Ping 206: 36
Chowdhury, Subrata 62: 130; 162: 22, 23

Christelow, Eileen 38: 44; 83: 198, 199; 90:
57, 58; 184: 26
Christensen, Bonnie 93: 100; 153: 67
Christensen, Gardell Dano 1: 57
Christensen, James C. 140: 226
Christiana, David 90: 64; 135: 13; 171: 7;
195: 26, 27
Christiansen, Per 40: 24
Christie, R. Gregory 116: 107; 127: 20, 21;
162: 179; 164: 114; 165: 137; 174: 157;
179: 172; 185: 17, 18, 19; 200: 2; 204: 85
Christy, Howard Chandler 17: 163, 164, 165,
168, 169; 19: 186, 187; 21: 22, 23, 24, 25
Christy, Jana 194: 21
Chronister, Robert 23: 138; 63: 27; 69: 167
Church, Caroline Jayne 179: 27
Church, Frederick YABC 1: 155
Chute, Marchette 1: 59
Chwast, Jacqueline 1: 63; 2: 275; 6: 46, 47;
11: 125; 12: 202; 14: 235
Chwast, Seymour 3: 128, 129; 18: 43; 27:
152; 92: 79; 96: 56, 57, 58; 146: 32, 33;
197: 99
Cieslawksi, Steve 101: 142; 127: 116; 158:
169, 171; 190: 174
Cinelli, Lisa 146: 253
Cirlin, Edgard 2: 168
Clairin, Georges 53: 109
Clapp, John 105: 66; 109: 58; 126: 7; 129:
148; 130: 165; 195: 48
Clark, Brenda 119: 85; 153: 55
Clark, David 77: 164; 134: 144, 145
Clark, Emma Chichester
See Chichester Clark, Emma
Clark, Victoria 35: 159
Clarke, Greg 169: 134
Clarke, Gus 72: 226; 134: 31
Clarke, Harry 23: 172, 173
Clarke, Peter 75: 102
Claverie, Jean 38: 46; 88: 29
Clavis, Philippe Goossens 182: 167
Clay, Wil 203: 29
Clayton, Elaine 159: 60; 209: 32
Clayton, Robert 9: 181
Cleary, Brian P. 186: 37
Cleaver, Elizabeth 8: 204; 23: 36
Cleland, T.M. 26: 92
Clemens, Peter 61: 125
Clement, Charles 20: 38
Clement, Gary 186: 79; 191: 32
Clement, Janet 182: 50
Clement, Nathan 200: 30
Clement, Rod 97: 42
Clement, Stephen 88: 3
Clementson, John 84: 213
Clemesha, David 192: 49, 50
Clevin, Jorgen 7: 50
Clifford, Judy 34: 163; 45: 198
Clokey, Art 59: 44
Clouse, Dennis 187: 158
Clouse, James 84: 15
Clouse, Nancy L. 78: 31; 114: 90
Clover, Peter 152: 45
Cneut, Carll 156: 166; 165: 67; 197: 26
Coalson, Glo 9: 72, 85; 25: 155; 26: 42; 35:
212; 53: 31; 56: 154; 94: 37, 38, 193
Cober, Alan E. 17: 158; 32: 77; 49: 127
Cober-Gentry, Leslie 92: 111
Cocca-Leffler, Maryann 80: 46; 136: 60; 139:
193; 194: 31, 33, 34
Cochran, Bobbye 11: 52
CoConis, Ted 4: 41; 46: 41; 51: 104
Cocozza, Chris 87: 18; 110: 173; 111: 149
Cockroft, Jason 152: 20
Coerr, Eleanor 1: 64; 67: 52
Coes, Peter 35: 172
Cogancherry, Helen 52: 143; 69: 131; 77: 93;
78: 220; 109: 204; 110: 129; 203: 92
Coggins, Jack 2: 69
Cohen, Alix 7: 53
Cohen, Miriam 155: 23, 24

Cohen, Nancy R. *165:* 35
Cohen, Santiago *164:* 26
Cohen, Sheldon *105:* 33, 34; *166:* 46, 47
Cohen, Vincent O. *19:* 243
Cohen, Vivien *11:* 112
Coker, Paul *51:* 172
Colbert, Anthony *15:* 41; *20:* 193
Colby, C.B. *3:* 47
Cole, Babette *58:* 172; *96:* 63, 64; *155:* 29
Cole, Brock *68:* 223; *72:* 36, 37, 38, 192; *127:* 23; *136:* 64, 65; *197:*
Cole, Gwen *87:* 185
Cole, Henry *178:* 120; *181:* 42, 43; *189:* 60
Cole, Herbert *28:* 104
Cole, Michael *59:* 46
Cole, Olivia H.H. *1:* 134; *3:* 223; *9:* 111; *38:* 104
Cole, Rachael *209:* 39
Colin, Paul *102:* 59; *123:* 118; *126:* 152; *192:* 129
Colley, Jacqui *202:* 20
Collicott, Sharleen *98:* 39; *143:* 29, 30
Collier, Bryan *126:* 54; *151:* 166; *174:* 16, 17, 18; *204:* 18, 19; *208:* 84
Collier, David *13:* 127
Collier, John *27:* 179; *208:* 154
Collier, Steven *50:* 52
Collier-Morales, Roberta *168:* 61
Collins, Heather *66:* 84; *67:* 68; *81:* 40; *98:* 192, 193; *129:* 95, 96, 98
Collins, Matt *167:* 90
Collins, Ross *140:* 23, 24; *200:* 36, 37; *209:* 54
Colman, Audrey *146:* 161
Colón, Raul *108:* 112; *113:* 5; *117:* 167; *134:* 112; *146:* 23; *159:* 92; *166:* 73; *180:* 107; *186:* 156; *190:* 6; *193:* 24, 205; *202:* 21, 22, 23
Colonna, Bernard *21:* 50; *28:* 103; *34:* 140; *43:* 180; *78:* 150
Comport, Sally Wern *117:* 169; *169:* 104; *190:* 42; *207:* 50
Conde, J.M. *100:* 120
Condon, Grattan *54:* 85 Condon, Ken *161:* 44; *195:* 28, 29
Cone, Ferne Geller *39:* 49
Cone, J. Morton *39:* 49
Conklin, Paul *43:* 62
Connelly, James *198:* 12
Connolly, Howard *67:* 88
Connolly, Jerome P. *4:* 128; *28:* 52
Connolly, Peter *47:* 60
Conoly, Walle *110:* 224
Conover, Chris *31:* 52; *40:* 184; *41:* 51; *44:* 79
Constantin, Pascale *207:* 159
Contreras, Gerry *72:* 9
Converse, James *38:* 70
Conway *62:* 62
Conway, Michael *69:* 12; *81:* 3; *92:* 108
Cook, Ande *188:* 135
Cook, G.R. *29:* 165
Cook, Joel *108:* 160
Cookburn, W.V. *29:* 204
Cooke, Donald E. *2:* 77
Cooke, Tom *52:* 118
Coomaraswamy, A.K. *50:* 100
Coombs, Charles *43:* 65
Coombs, Deborah *139:* 175
Coombs, Patricia *2:* 82; *3:* 52; *22:* 119; *51:* 32, 33, 34, 35, 36, 37, 38, 39, 40, 42, 43
Cooney, Barbara *6:* 16, 17, 50; *12:* 42; *13:* 92; *15:* 145; *16:* 74, 111; *18:* 189; *23:* 38, 89, 93; *32:* 138; *38:* 105; *59:* 48, 49, 51, 52, 53; *74:* 222; *81:* 100; *91:* 25; *96:* 71, 72, 74; *100:* 149; *YABC2:* 10
Cooper, Elisha *157:* 38, 39
Cooper, Floyd *79:* 95; *81:* 45; *84:* 82; *85:* 74; *91:* 118; *96:* 77, 78; *103:* 149; *144:* 54; *145:* 151; *159:* 198; *176:* 133, 134; *187:* 26, 27, 28, 29; *188:* 22; *199:* 175
Cooper, Heather *50:* 39

Cooper, Helen *102:* 42, 43, 44
Cooper, Mario *24:* 107
Cooper, Marjorie *7:* 112
Cope, Jane *61:* 201; *108* 52
Copeland, Mark *180:* 6
Copelman, Evelyn *8:* 61; *18:* 25
Copley, Heather *30:* 86; *45:* 57
Corace, Jen *208:* 48
Corbett, Grahame *30:* 114; *43:* 67
Corbino, John *19:* 248
Corcos, Lucille *2:* 223; *10:* 27; *34:* 66
Corey, Robert *9:* 34
Corlass, Heather *10:* 7
Cornell, James *27:* 60
Cornell, Jeff *11:* 58
Cornell, Laura *94:* 179; *95:* 25
Corr, Christopher *204:* 98
Corrigan, Barbara *8:* 37
Corrigan, Patrick *145:* 149
Corwin, Judith Hoffman *10:* 28
Corwin, Oliver *191:* 119
Cory, Fanny Y. *20:* 113; *48:* 29
Cosentino, Ralph *169:* 32
Cosgrove, Margaret *3:* 100; *47:* 63; *82:* 133
Costabel, Eva Deutsch *45:* 66, 67
Costanza, John *58:* 7, 8, 9
Costello, Chris *86:* 78
Costello, David F. *23:* 55
Côté, Geneviéve *184:* 37, 39
Cote, Nancy *126:* 139; *156:* 101; *174:* 101; *182:* 53, 54, 55
Cottenden, Jeff *190:* 45
Couch, Greg *94:* 124; *110:* 13; *162:* 31; *168:* 149; *199:* 22
Councell, Ruth Tietjen *79:* 29
Courtney, Cathy *58:* 69, 144; *59:* 15; *61:* 20, 87
Courtney, R. *35:* 110
Counihan, Claire *133:* 106
Cousineau, Normand *89:* 180; *112:* 76
Cousins, Lucy *172:* 53, 54; *205:* 34, 35
Couture, Christin *41:* 209
Covarrubias, Miguel *35:* 118, 119, 123, 124, 125
Coville, Katherine *32:* 57; *36:* 167; *92:* 38
Covington, Neverne *113:* 87
Cowdrey, Richard *169:* 170; *178:* 205; *204:* 22, 23
Cowell, Cressida *140:* 39
Cowell, Lucinda *77:* 54
Cowles, Rose *203:* 164, 167
Cox *43:* 93
Cox, Charles *8:* 20
Cox, David *56:* 37; *90:* 63; *119:* 38
Cox, Palmer *24:* 76, 77
Cox, Steve *140:* 96
Coxe, Molly *69:* 44
Coxon, Michele *158:* 80
Crabb, Gordon *70:* 39
Crabtree, Judith *98:* 42
Craft, Kinuko *22:* 182; *36:* 220; *53:* 122, 123, 148,149; *74:* 12; *81:* 129; *86:* 31; *89:* 139; *127:* 27, 28, 29; *132:* 142; *139:* 38
Craig, Daniel *177:* 67; *180:* 11; *185:* 203
Craig, David *136:* 198; *205:* 37
Craig, Helen *49:* 76; *62:* 70, 71, 72; *69:* 141; *94:* 42, 43, 44; *112:* 53; *135:* 101, 102
Crane, Alan H. *1:* 217
Crane, H.M. *13:* 111
Crane, Jack *43:* 183
Crane, Jordan *174:* 21
Crane, Walter *18:* 46, 47, 48, 49, 53, 54, 56, 57, 59, 60, 61; *22:* 128; *24:* 210, 217; *100:* 70, 71
Cravath, Lynne W. *98:* 45; *182:* 58, 59
Crawford, Denise *137:* 213
Crawford, Will *43:* 77
Credle, Ellis *1:* 69
Czernecki, Stefan *154:* 104; *178:* 68, 69
Crespi, Francesca *87:* 90

Cressy, Michael *124:* 55; *203:* 132
Crews, Donald *32:* 59, 60; *76:* 42, 43, 44
Crews, Nina *97:* 49
Crichlow, Ernest *74:* 88; *83:* 203
Croft, James *150:* 57
Crofut, Bob *80:* 87; *81:* 47
Crofut, Susan *23:* 61
Croll, Carolyn *80:* 137; *102:* 52
Cross, Peter *56:* 78; *63:* 60, 65
Crowe, Elizabeth *88:* 144
Crowell, Pers *3:* 125
Cruikshank, George *15:* 76, 83; *22:* 74, 75, 76, 77, 78, 79,80, 81, 82, 84, 137; *24:* 22, 23
Crump, Fred H. *11:* 62
Cruz, Ray *6:* 55; *70:* 234; *123:* 173; *172:* 192
Csatari, Joe *44:* 82; *55:* 152; *63:* 25, 28; *102:* 58
Cuetara, Mittie *158:* 85
Cuffari, Richard *4:* 75; *5:* 98; *6:* 56; *7:* 13,84, 153; *8:* 148, 155; *9:* 89; *11:* 19; *12:* 55, 96,114; *15:* 51, 202; *18:* 5; *20:* 139; *21:* 197; *22:* 14, 192; *23:* 15, 106; *25:* 97; *27:* 133; *28:* 196; *29:* 54; *30:* 85; *31:* 35; *36:* 101; *38:* 171; *42:* 97; *44:* 92, 192; *45:* 212, 213; *46:* 36, 198; *50:* 164; *54:* 80, 136, 137, 145; *56:* 17; *60:* 63; *66:* 49, 50; *70:* 41; *71:* 132; *77:* 157; *78:* 58, 149; *79:* 120; *85:* 2, 152
Cugat, Xavier *19:* 120
Cumings, Art *35:* 160
Cummings, Chris *29:* 167
Cummings, Michael *159:* 142
Cummings, Pat *42:* 61; *61:* 99; *69:* 205; *71:* 57,58; *78:* 24, 25; *93:* 75; *107:* 49, 50; *164:* 259; *203:* 45, 46
Cummings, Richard *24:* 119
Cunette, Lou *20:* 93; *22:* 125
Cunningham, Aline *25:* 180
Cunningham, David *11:* 13
Cunningham, Imogene *16:* 122, 127
Cunningham, Kelley *176:* 159
Cupples, Pat *107:* 12; *126:* 109; *182:* 13; *198:* 68
Curlee, Lynn *98:* 48; *141:* 39; *190:* 48
Currey, Anna *190:* 145; *202:* 130, 132
Curry, John Steuart *2:* 5; *19:* 84; *34:* 36; *144:* 126
Curry, Tom *127:* 131; *185:* 25, 26
Curtis, Bruce *23:* 96; *30:* 88; *36:* 22
Curtis, Neil *167:* 30
Curtis, Stacy *205:* 38
Cusack, Margaret *58:* 49, 50, 51
Cushman, Doug *65:* 57; *101:* 39, 40; *133:* 179; *157:* 45; *186:* 157
Cutting, Ann *196:* 194
Cyrus, Kurt *132:* 39; *179:* 36, 37
Czechowski, Alicia *95:* 21; *171:* 37
Czernecki, Stefan *117:* 173

D

Dabcovich, Lydia *25:* 105; *40:* 114; *99:* 75, 76
Dacey, Bob *82:* 175; *152:* 65
d'Achille, Gino *127:* 175, 176
Dailey, Don *78:* 197
Dain, Martin J. *35:* 75
Dale, Penny *127:* 224; *151:* 57; *160:* 89; *197:* 75
Dale, Rae *72:* 197
Daley, Joann *50:* 22
Dalton, Anne *40:* 62; *63:* 119
Daly, Deborah M. *74:* 213
Daly, Jim *103:* 60; *150:* 48
Daly, Jude *138:* 118, 119
Daly, Nicholas *37:* 53; *76:* 48, 49
Daly, Niki *107:* 15; *114:* 38, 39, 40; *164:* 86; *192:* 53; *198:* 26, 27
Daly, Paul *97:* 205
Dalziel, Brothers *33:* 113
D'Amato, Alex *9:* 48; *20:* 25

D'Amato, Janet *9:* 48; *20:* 25; *26:* 118
D'Amico, Steve *170:* 52
Danalis, Johnny *167:* 27
D'Andrea, Domenick *183:* 108
Daniel, Alan *23:* 59; *29:* 110; *76:* 50, 53, 55, 56; *153:* 76 *115:* 74; *134:* 70
Daniel, Lea *76:* 53, 55; *153:* 76
Daniel, Lewis C. *20:* 216
Daniels, Beau *73:* 4
Daniels, Steve *22:* 16
Daniels, Stewart *56:* 12
Dann, Bonnie *31:* 83
Dann, Penny *82:* 128
Danska, Herbert *24:* 219
Danyell, Alice *20:* 27
Dardik, Helen *208:* 200
Darley, F.O.C. *16:* 145; *19:* 79, 86, 88, 185; *21:* 28,36; *35:* 76, 77, 78, 79, 80, 81; *YABC 2:* 175
Darling, Lois *3:* 59; *23:* 30, 31
Darling, Louis *1:* 40, 41; *2:* 63; *3:* 59; *23:* 30,31; *43:* 54, 57, 59; *121:* 53
Darrow, David R. *84:* 101
Darrow, Whitney, Jr. *13:* 25; *38:* 220, 221
Darwin, Beatrice *43:* 54
Darwin, Len *24:* 82
Dastolfo, Frank *33:* 179
Dauber, Liz *1:* 22; *3:* 266; *30:* 49
Daugherty, James *3:* 66; *8:* 178; *13:* 27, 28, 161; *18:* 101; *19:* 72; *29:* 108; *32:* 156; *42:* 84; *YABC 1:* 256; *2:* 174
d'Aulaire, Edgar Parin *5:* 51; *66:* 53
d'Aulaire, Ingri Parin *5:* 51; *66:* 53
Davalos, Felipe *99:* 197; *159:* 66; *174:* 163
Davenier, Christine *125:* 88; *127:* 32; *128:* 152; *179:* 39, 40
Davick, Linda *151:* 124; *208:* 187
David, Jacques-Louis *193:* 22
David, Jonathan *19:* 37
Davidson, Kevin *28:* 154
Davidson, Raymond *32:* 61
Davie, Helen K. *77:* 48, 49
Davies, Andy Robert *205:* 169
Davis, Allen *20:* 11; *22:* 45; *27:* 222; *29:* 157; *41:* 99; *47:* 99; *50:* 84; *52:* 105
Davis, Bette J. *15:* 53; *23:* 95
Davis, Dimitris *45:* 95
Davis, Eleanor *209:* 33
Davis, Hendon *151:* 122
Davis, Jack E. *145:* 139; *175:* 84, 85; *208:* 102
Davis, Jim *32:* 63, 64
Davis, Katie *152:* 52, 53, 54; *208:* 52
Davis, Lambert *110:* 23, 24; *176:* 58
Davis, Marguerite *31:* 38; *34:* 69, 70; *100:* 34; *YABC 1:* 126, 230
Davis, Nelle *69:* 191
Davis, Paul *78:* 214
Davis, Rich *206:* 38
Davis, Yvonne LeBrun *94:* 144
Davisson, Virginia H. *44:* 178
DaVolls, Andy *85:* 53
Dawson, Diane *24:* 127; *42:* 126; *52:* 130; *68:* 104
Dawson, Willow *208:* 54
Day, Alexandra *67:* 59; *97:* 54; *166:* 65; *169:* 40; *197:* 50, 51, 52, 54
Day, Larry *169:* 88; *185:* 59
Day, Rob *94:* 110; *127:* 24; *197:* 32
Dean, Bob *19:* 211
Dean, David *192:* 55
de Angeli, Marguerite *1:* 77; *27:* 62, 65, 66, 67, 69, 70, 72; *100:* 75, 76; *YABC 1:* 166
DeArmond, Dale *70:* 47
Deas, Michael *27:* 219, 221; *30:* 156; *67:* 134; *72:* 24; *75:* 155; *84:* 206; *88:* 124
Deas, Rich *191:* 87; *193:* 10
deBarros, Jim *196:* 60
Debon, Nicolas *151:* 60; *177:* 46
de Bosschere, Jean *19:* 252; *21:* 4; *186:* 44, 45
De Bruyn, M(onica) G. *13:* 30, 31

Decker, C.B. *172:* 120
De Cuir, John F. *1:* 28, 29
Deeter, Catherine *74:* 110; *103:* 150; *137:* 50
Degen, Bruce *40:* 227, 229; *57:* 28, 29; *56:* 156; *75:* 229; *76:* 19; *81:* 36, 37; *92:* 26; *93:* 199; *97:* 56, 58, 59; *124:* 40; *147:* 39, 40, 41; *168:* 23; *205:* 45, 46
De Grazia *14:* 59; *39:* 56, 57
DeGrazio, George *88:* 40
deGroat, Diane *9:* 39; *18:* 7; *23:* 123; *28:* 200, 201; *31:* 58, 59; *34:* 151; *41:* 152; *43:* 88; *46:* 40, 200; *49:* 163; *50:* 89; *52:* 30, 34; *54:* 43; *63:* 5; *70:* 136; *71:* 99; *73:* 117,156; *77:* 34; *85:* 48; *86:* 201; *87:* 142; *90:* 72, 73, 143; *95:* 182; *111:* 123; *118:* 160; *126:* 8; *130:* 130; *138:* 93, 94; *169:* 46, 47
de Groot, Lee *6:* 21
Deines, Brian *110:* 139
DeJohn, Marie *89:* 78
Dekhteryov, B. *61:* 158
de Kiefte, Kees *94:* 107
Delacre, Lulu *36:* 66; *156:* 35; *202:* 10, 53; *209:* 36
Delaney, A. *21:* 78
Delaney, Michael *180:* 16
Delaney, Molly *80:* 43
Delaney, Ned *28:* 68; *56:* 80; *102:* 11
DeLange, Alex Pardo *179:* 128
DeLapine, Jim *79:* 21
De La Roche Saint Andre, Anne *75:* 37
de Larrea, Victoria *6:* 119, 204; *29:* 103; *72:* 203; *87:* 199
Delessert, Étienne *7:* 140; *46:* 61, 62, 63, 65, 67, 68; *130:* 38, 39, 40, 41, 42; *179:* 46, 47, 48, 49; *YABC 2:* 209
Delezenne, Christine *186:* 126
Del Negro, Janice *196:* 161
DeLorenzo, Christopher *154:* 149
Delulio, John *15:* 54
DeLuna, Tony *88:* 95
Demarest, Chris L. *45:* 68, 69, 70; *73:* 172, 173, 176; *78:* 106; *82:* 48, 49; *89:* 212; *92:* 86; *128:* 57, 58; *175:* 46, 48
De Mejo, Oscar *40:* 67
De Muth, Roger *205:* 184
Demi *11:* 135; *15:* 245; *66:* 129, 130; *89:* 216; *102:* 66, 67, 68
Denetsosie, Hoke *13:* 126; *82:* 34
Denise, Christopher *147:* 43, 44; *176:* 101; *193:* 35, 36, 37; *201:* 37
Dennis, Morgan *18:* 68, 69; *64:* 89
Dennis, Wesley *2:* 87; *3:* 111; *11:* 132; *18:* 71, 72, 73, 74; *22:* 9; *24:* 196, 200; *46:* 178; *69:* 94, 96; *129:* 62
Denos, Julia *202:* 26
Denslow, W.W. *16:* 84, 85, 86, 87; *18:* 19, 20, 24; *29:* 211; *100:* 21
Denton, Kady MacDonald *110:* 82; *130:* 70; *181:* 54, 55, 56; *192:* 75
Denton, Terry *72:* 163; *174:* 26; *186:* 52; *196:* 83, 84
DePalma, Mary Newell *132:* 114; *139:* 75; *185:* 30, 31; *186:* 121
dePaola, Tomie *8:* 95; *9:* 93; *11:* 69; 25; *103:* 28: 157; *29:* 80; *39:* 52, 53; *40:* 226; *46:* 187; *59:* 61, 62, 63, 64, 65, 66, 67, 68, 69, 71, 72, 74; *62:* 19; *108:* 63, 67, 68, 70; *155:* 62, 64, 66; *180:* 105; *200:* 47, 48, 49, 50
Deraney, Michael J. *77:* 35; *78:* 148
deRosa, Dee *70:* 48; *71:* 210; *91:* 78
Dervaux, Isabelle *111:* 117
DeSaix, Deborah Durland *180:* 15; *188:* 24
De Saulles, Tony *119:* 39
de Seve, Peter *146:* 261; *207:* 78
Deshaprabhu, Meera Dayal *86:* 192
Desimini, Lisa *86:* 68; *94:* 47; *96:* 7; *104:* 107; *125:* 194; *131:* 180; *172:* 56
de St. Menin, Charles *70:* 17
Detmold, Edward J. *22:* 104, 105, 106, 107; *35:* 120; *64:* 5; *YABC 2:* 203
Detrich, Susan *20:* 133

Deutermann, Diana *77:* 175
DeVelasco, Joseph E. *21:* 51
de Veyrac, Robert *YABC 2:* 19
DeVille, Edward A. *4:* 235
de Visser, John *55:* 119
Devito, Bert *12:* 164
Devlin, Harry *11:* 74; *74:* 63, 65; *136:* 77, 78
Dewan, Ted *108:* 73; *157:* 55; *165:* 129
Dewar, Nick *133:* 122
Dewdney, Anna *184:* 43, 44
Dewey, Ariane *7:* 64; *33:* 195; *35:* 208; *68:* 16,17; *75:* 46; *93:* 91; *94:* 197; *109:* 65, 66, 67; *125:* 2, 3, 4, 5; *127:* 188; *143:* 25; *178:* 17, 19, 74; *188:* 166; *202:* 164
Dewey, Jennifer (Owings) *58:* 54; *64:* 214; *65:* 207; *88:* 169; *103:* 45
Dewey, Kenneth *39:* 62; *51:* 23; *56:* 163
de Zanger, Arie *30:* 40
Diakité, Baba Wagué *174:* 28
Diamond, Donna *21:* 200; *23:* 63; *26:* 142; *35:* 83, 84, 85, 86, 87, 88, 89; *38:* 78; *40:* 147; *44:* 152; *50:* 144; *53:* 126; *69:* 46, 47, 48, 201; *71:* 133; *123:* 19
Dias, Ron *71:* 67
Diaz, David *80:* 213; *96:* 83, 84; *108:* 228; *110:* 29; *149:* 106; *150:* 63; *179:* 160; *184:* 95, 97; *189:* 51, 52, 53
Dibley, Glin *138:* 83; *141:* 128
DiCesare, Joe *70:* 38; *71:* 63, 106; *79:* 214; *93:* 147; *116:* 217; *143:* 111; *166:* 57
Dick, John Henry *8:* 181
Dickens, Frank *34:* 131
Dickey, Robert L. *15:* 279
Dickson, Mora *84:* 21
Didier, Sam *166:* 114
Dietz, James *128:* 223; *193:* 136
di Fate, Vincent *37:* 70; *90:* 11; *93:* 60; *109:* 219, 220
Di Fiori, Lawrence *10:* 51; *12:* 190; *27:* 97; *40:* 219; *93:* 57; *130:* 45
Digby, Desmond *97:* 180
Dignan, James *196:* 143
Di Grazia, Thomas *32:* 66; *35:* 241
Dillard, Annie *10:* 32
Dillard, Sarah *136:* 186
Dillon, Corinne B. *1:* 139
Dillon, Diane *4:* 104, 167; *6:* 23; *13:* 29; *15:* 99; *26:* 148; *27:* 136, 201; *51:* 29, 48, 51, 52, 53, 54,55, 56, 57, 58, 59, 60, 61, 62; *54:* 155; *56:* 69; *58:* 127,128; *61:* 95; *62:* 27; *64:* 46; *68:* 3; *69:* 209; *74:* 89; *79:* 92; *86:* 89; *92:* 28, 177; *93:* 7, 210; *94:* 239, 240; *97:* 167; *106:* 58, 59,61, 64; *107:* 3; *139:* 246; *167:* 77; *189:* 202; *191:* 191; *194:* 45, 46, 48, 49
Dillon, Leo *4:* 104, 167; *6:* 23; *13:* 29; *15:* 99; *26:* 148; *27:* 136, 201; *51:* 29, 48, 51, 52, 53, 54,55, 56, 57, 58, 59, 60, 61, 62; *54:* 155; *56:* 69; *58:* 127,128; *61:* 95; *62:* 27; *64:* 46; *68:* 3; *69:* 209; *74:* 89; *79:* 92; *86:* 89; *92:* 28, 177; *93:* 7, 210; *94:* 239, 240; *97:* 167; *106:* 58, 59,61, 64; *107:* 3; *139:* 246; *167:* 77; *189:* 202; *191:* 191; *194:* 45, 46, 48, 49
Dillon, Sharon Saseen *59:* 179, 188
DiMaccio, Gerald *121:* 80
DiMaggio, Joe *36:* 22
DiMassi, Gina *169:* 17
Dinan, Carol *25:* 169; *59:* 75
Dines, Glen *7:* 66, 67
Dinesen, Thomas *44:* 37
Dinh, Pham Viet *167:* 184
Dinnerstein, Harvey *42:* 63, 64, 65, 66, 67, 68; *50:* 146
Dinsdale, Mary *10:* 65; *11:* 171
Dinyer, Eric *86:* 148; *109:* 163; *110:* 239; *124:* 11; *150:* 69; *170:* 4; *171:* 30
Dion, Nathalie *170:* 124
DiRocco, Carl *181:* 23
DiSalvo-Ryan, DyAnne *59:* 77; *62:* 185; *117:* 46; *144:* 64; *150:* 153; *186:* 162

Disney, Walt *28:* 71, 72, 73, 76, 77, 78, 79, 80, 81, 87, 88, 89,90, 91, 94
DiTerlizzi, Tony *105:* 7; *147:* 22; *154:* 31, 32, 33
Divito, Anna *83:* 159
Dixon, Don *74:* 17; *109:* 196
Dixon, Larry *127:* 125
Dixon, Maynard *20:* 165
Doares, Robert G. *20:* 39
Dob, Bob *205:* 14
Dobias, Frank *22:* 162
Dobrin, Arnold *4:* 68
Dobson, Steven Gaston *102:* 103
Dockray, Tracy *139:* 77
Docktor, Irv *43:* 70
Dodd, Ed *4:* 69
Dodd, Emma *203:* 57
Dodd, Julie *74:* 73
Dodd, Lynley *35:* 92; *86:* 71; *132:* 45, 46, 47
Dodge, Bill *96:* 36; *118:* 7, 8, 9; *133:* 135
Dodgson, Charles L. *20:* 148; *33:* 146; *YABC 2:* 98
Dodson, Bert *9:* 138; *14:* 195; *42:* 55; *54:* 8; *60:* 49; *101:* 125
Dodson, Liz Brenner *105:* 117; *111:* 15
Dohanos, Stevan *16:* 10
Dolce, J. Ellen *74:* 147; *75:* 41
Dolch, Marguerite P. *50:* 64
Dolesch, Susanne *34:* 49
Dollar, Diane *57:* 32
Dolobowsky, Mena *81:* 54
Dolson, Hildegarde *5:* 57
Domanska, Janina *6:* 66, 67; *YABC 1:* 166
Domi *134:* 113
Dominguez, El *53:* 94
Domjan, Joseph *25:* 93
Domm, Jeffrey C. *84:* 69; *135:* 70
Donahey, William *68:* 209
Donahue, Dorothy *76:* 170
Donahue, Vic *2:* 93; *3:* 190; *9:* 44
Donald, Elizabeth *4:* 18
Donalty, Alison *149:* 195, 196, 197
Donato *85:* 59; *149:* 204; *191:* 19
Donato, Michael A. *200:* 143
Doner, Kim *208:* 57
Doney, Todd L.W. *87:* 12; *93:* 112; *98:* 135; *101:* 57; *104:* 40; *118:* 163; *135:* 162, 163; *151:* 18
Donna, Natalie *9:* 52
Donohue, Dorothy *95:* 2; *132:* 30; *176:* 54, 55; *178:* 77, 78, 79
Dooling, Michael *82:* 19; *105:* 55; *106:* 224; *125:* 135; *171:* 46; *172:* 12; *176:* 120; *197:* 89
Doran, Ben-Ami *128:* 189
Dore, Gustave *18:* 169, 172, 175; *19:* 93, 94, 95, 96, 97, 98,99, 100, 101, 102, 103, 104, 105; *23:* 188; *25:* 197, 199
Doremus, Robert *6:* 62; *13:* 90; *30:* 95, 96, 97; *38:* 97
Dorfman, Ronald *11:* 128
Doriau *86:* 59; *91:* 152
Dorman, Brandon *197:* 35; *204:* 6
Dormer, Frank W. *200:* 55
Dorros, Arthur *78:* 42, 43; *91:* 28
Doruyter, Karel *165:* 105
dos Santos, Joyce Audy *57:* 187, 189
Doty, Roy *28:* 98; *31:* 32; *32:* 224; *46:* 157; *82:* 71; *142:* 7
Doucet, Bob *132:* 238; *169:* 159
Dougherty, Charles *16:* 204; *18:* 74
Doughty, Rebecca *177:* 174
Doughty, Thomas *118:* 31; *140:* 60
Douglas, Aaron *31:* 103
Douglas, Carole Nelson *73:* 48
Douglas, Goray *13:* 151
Dow, Brian *150:* 92
Dowd, Jason *132:* 51, 52; *164:* 244
Dowd, Vic *3:* 244; *10:* 97
Dowden, Anne Ophelia *7:* 70, 71; *13:* 120
Dowdy, Mrs. Regera *29:* 100

Downard, Barry *202:* 32
Downes, Belinda *180:* 29
Downing, Julie *60:* 140; *81:* 50; *86:* 200; *99:* 129
Doyle, Janet *56:* 31
Doyle, Richard *21:* 31, 32, 33; *23:* 231; *24:* 177; *31:* 87
Draper, Angie *43:* 84
Drath, Bill *26:* 34
Drawson, Blair *17:* 53; *126:* 65
Dray, Matt *177:* 47
Drescher, Henrik *105:* 60, 62, 63; *172:* 72
Drescher, Joan *30:* 100, 101; *35:* 245; *52:* 168; *137:* 52
Dressell, Peggy *186:* 41
Drew, Janet *201:* 177
Drew, Patricia *15:* 100
Dronzek, Laura *199:* 28, 29; *207:* 69
Drummond, Allan *209:* 41
Drummond, V.H. *6:* 70
Drury, Christian Potter *105:* 97; *186:* 224
Dubanevich, Arlene *56:* 44
Dubin, Jill *205:* 56
Dubois, Claude K. *196:* 2
Dubois, Gerard *182:* 9
DuBurke, Randy *187:* 89
Ducak, Danilo *99:* 130; *108:* 214
Duchesne, Janet *6:* 162; *79:* 8
Duda, Jana *102:* 155; *209:* 134
Dudash, Michael *32:* 122; *77:* 134; *82:* 149
Duer, Douglas *34:* 177
Duewell, Kristina *195:* 76
Duffy, Daniel Mark *76:* 37; *101:* 196; *108:* 147, 148
Duffy, Joseph *38:* 203
Duffy, Pat *28:* 153
Dugan, Karen *181:* 26; *202:* 35
Dugin, Andrej *77:* 60
Dugina, Olga *77:* 60
Duke, Chris *8:* 195; *139:* 164
Duke, Kate *87:* 186; *90:* 78, 79, 80, 81; *192:* 21, 59, 60, 61, 63
Duke, Marion *165:* 87
Dulac, Edmund *19:* 108, 109, 110, 111, 112, 113, 114, 115, 117; *23:* 187; *25:* 152; *YABC 1:* 37; *2:* 147
Dulac, Jean *13:* 64
Dumas, Philippe *52:* 36, 37, 38, 39, 40, 41, 42, 43, 45; *119:* 40, 41, 42
Dunaway, Nancy *108:* 161
Dunbar, James *76:* 63
Dunbar, Polly *181:* 60, 61
Duncan, Beverly *72:* 92
Duncan, John *116:* 94
Dunn, H.T. *62:* 196
Dunn, Harvey *34:* 78, 79, 80, 81
Dunn, Iris *5:* 175
Dunn, Phoebe *5:* 175
Dunne, Jeanette *72:* 57, 173, 222
Dunnick, Regan *176:* 51; *178:* 83, 84
Dunnington, Tom *3:* 36; *18:* 281; *25:* 61; *31:* 159; *35:* 168; *48:* 195; *79:* 144; *82:* 230
Dunn-Ramsey, Marcy *117:* 131
Dunrea, Olivier *59:* 81; *118:* 53, 54; *124:* 43
Duntze, Dorothee *88:* 28; *160:* 76
Dupasquier, Philippe *86:* 75; *104:* 76; *151:* 63
duPont, Lindsay Harper *207:* 39
DuQuette, Keith *90:* 83; *155:* 73, 74
Durand, Delphine *200:* 56
Durham, Sarah *192:* 248
Durney, Ryan *208:* 122
Duroussy, Nathalie *146:* 150
Durrell, Julie *82:* 62; *94:* 62
Dutz *6:* 59
Duvoisin, Roger *2:* 95; *6:* 76, 77; *7:* 197; *28:* 125; *30:* 101, 102, 103, 104, 105, 107; *47:* 205; *84:* 254
Dyer, Dale *141:* 71
Dyer, Jane *75:* 219; *129:* 28; *147:* 49, 50, 51; *168:* 121; *190:* 4; *191:* 57, 59, 60; *203:* 4
Dypold, Pat *15:* 37

E

E.V.B.
   See Boyle, Eleanor Vere (Gordon)
Eachus, Jennifer *29:* 74; *82:* 201; *164:* 153
Eadie, Bob *63:* 36
Eagle, Bruce *95:* 119
Eagle, Ellen *82:* 121; *89:* 3
Eagle, Jeremy *141:* 71
Eagle, Michael *11:* 86; *20:* 9; *23:* 18; *27:* 122; *28:* 57; *34:* 201; *44:* 189; *73:* 9; *78:* 235; *85:* 43
Earl-Bridges, Michele *159:* 128
Earle, Edwin *56:* 27
Earle, Olive L. *7:* 75
Earle, Vana *27:* 99
Earley, Lori *132:* 2; *186:* 4; *195:* 8
Early, Margaret *72:* 59
East, Stella *131:* 223
Eastman, P.D. *33:* 57
Easton, Reginald *29:* 181
Eaton, Tom *4:* 62; *6:* 64; *22:* 99; *24:* 124
Ebbeler, Jeffrey *193:* 62; *206:* 45
Ebel, Alex *11:* 89
Eberbach, Andrea *192:* 115
Ebert, Len *9:* 191; *44:* 47
Echevarria, Abe *37:* 69
Echo Hawk, Bunky *187:* 192
Eckersley, Maureen *48:* 62
Eckert, Horst *72:* 62
Ede, Janina *33:* 59
Edens, Cooper *49:* 81, 82, 83, 84, 85; *112:* 58
Edens, John *109:* 115
Edgar, Sarah E. *41:* 97
Edgerton, Perky *195:* 144
Edliq, Emily S. *131:* 107
Edrien *11:* 53
Edwards, Freya *45:* 102
Edwards, George Wharton *31:* 155
Edwards, Gunvor *2:* 71; *25:* 47; *32:* 71; *54:* 106
Edwards, Jeanne *29:* 257
Edwards, Linda Strauss *21:* 134; *39:* 123; *49:* 88, 89
Edwards, Michelle *152:* 62, 63
Edwards, Wallace *170:* 55
Egan, Tim *155:* 76, 77, 78
Egge, David *102:* 71
Eggenhofer, Nicholas *2:* 81
Eggleton, Bob *74:* 40; *81:* 190, 191; *105:* 6; *121:* 183; *149:* 203; *166:* 215
Egielski, Richard *11:* 90; *16:* 208; *33:* 236; *38:* 35; *49:* 91, 92, 93, 95, 212, 213, 214, 216; *79:* 122; *106:* 67, 68, 69; *134:* 135; *144:* 244; *163:* 82, 84; *207:* 125
Ehlert, Lois *35:* 97; *69:* 51; *112:* 7; *113:* 208; *128:* 63, 64, 65; *172:* 77, 79, 80
Ehrlich, Bettina *1:* 83
Eitan, Ora *160:* 165
Eichenberg, Fritz *1:* 79; *9:* 54; *19:* 248; *23:* 170; *24:* 200; *26:* 208; *50:* 67, 68, 69, 70, 71, 72, 73,74, 75, 77, 79, 80, 81; *60:* 165; *100:* 137; *YABC 1:* 104, 105; *2:* 213
Einsel, Naiad *10:* 35; *29:* 136
Einsel, Walter *10:* 37
Einzig, Susan *3:* 77; *43:* 78; *67:* 155; *129:* 154
Eisner, Will *165:* 82, 83
Eitzen, Allan *9:* 56; *12:* 212; *14:* 226; *21:* 194; *38:* 162; *76:* 218
Eldridge, H. *54:* 109
Eldridge, Harold *43:* 83
Elgaard, Greta *19:* 241
Elgin, Kathleen *9:* 188; *39:* 69
Ellacott, S.E. *19:* 118
Elliot, David *192:* 26; *208:* 62, 63
Elliott, Mark *93:* 69; *105:* 108; *107:* 123; *140:* 53; *165:* 189; *173:* 67; *195:* 95; *203:* 67
Elliott, Sarah M. *14:* 58
Ellis, Dianne *130:* 208
Ellis, Jan Davey *88:* 50; *115:* 80

Ellis, Richard *130:* 47, 48
Ellison, Chris *196:* 66; *199:* 131; *207:* 193
Ellison, Pauline *55:* 21
Elmer, Richard *78:* 5
Elmore, Larry *90:* 8
Elschner, Géraldine *183:* 38
Elwell, Peter *195:* 150
Elwell, Tristan *110:* 39; *121:* 182; *127:* 46; *137:* 144; *141:* 173; *151:* 236; *158:* 264; *167:* 119, 120, 121; *169:* 20; *190:* 12; *202:* 16
Elzbieta *88:* 80, 81
Emberley, Ed *8:* 53; *70:* 53, 54; *146:* 65, 69, 70
Emberley, Michael *34:* 83; *80:* 72; *119:* 47, 48; *147:* 100; *158:* 115; *189:* 62, 64; *203:* 87, 89
Emerling, Dorothy *104:* 27
Emery, Leslie *49:* 187
Emmett, Bruce *49:* 147; *80:* 175; *101:* 206
Emry-Perrott, Jennifer *61:* 57
Emshwiller, Ed *174:* 45
Endle, Kate *191:* 167; *207:* 41
Engel, Diana *70:* 57
Engle, Mort *38:* 64
Englebert, Victor *8:* 54
English, Mark *101:* 207
Enik, Ted *142:* 39
Enos, Randall *20:* 183
Enright, Maginel Wright *19:* 240, 243; *39:* 31, 35, 36
Enrique, Romeo *34:* 135
Ensor, Barbara *180:* 30
Epstein, Stephen *50:* 142, 148
Erdogan, Buket *174:* 179
Erdrich, Louise *141:* 62
Erhard, Walter *1:* 152
Erickson, Jim *196:* 190
Erickson, Phoebe *11:* 83; *59:* 85
Erikson, Mel *31:* 69
Eriksson, Eva *63:* 88, 90, 92, 93; *203:* 99; *207:* 44
Ering, Timothy Basil *131:* 100; *176:* 63, 64; *202:* 29; *204:* 8
Erlbruch, Wolf *181:* 66
Ernst, Lisa Campbell *47:* 147; *95:* 47; *154:* 46, 47, 48; *164:* 88
Esco, Jo *61:* 103
Escourido, Joseph *4:* 81
Escrivá, Viví *119:* 51; *181:* 36
Essakalli, Julie Klear *200:* 58
Este, Kirk *33:* 111
Estep, David *73:* 57
Estes, Eleanor *91:* 66
Estoril, Jean *32:* 27
Estrada, Pau *74:* 76
Estrada, Ric *5:* 52, 146; *13:* 174
Etchemendy, Teje *38:* 68
Etheredges, the *73:* 12
Etienne, Kirk-Albert *145:* 184
Ets, Marie Hall *2:* 102
Ettlinger, Doris *171:* 98; *186:* 106; *197:* 126
Eulalie *YABC 2:* 315
Evans, Greg *73:* 54, 55, 56; *143:* 40, 41
Evans, Katherine *5:* 64
Evans, Leslie *144:* 227; *207:* 57
Evans, Shane W. *159:* 142; *160:* 190; *168:* 39; *188:* 88; *189:* 66, 67, 68
Everitt, Betsy *151:* 110
Ewart, Claire *76:* 69; *145:* 59, 60
Ewing, Carolyn *66:* 143; *79:* 52
Ewing, Juliana Horatia *16:* 92
Eyolfson, Norman *98:* 154

F

Fabian, Limbert *136:* 114
Facklam, Paul *132:* 62
Falconer, Ian *125:* 66; *179:* 59

Falconer, Pearl *34:* 23
Falkenstern, Lisa *70:* 34; *76:* 133; *78:* 171; *127:* 16; *191:* 151
Falls, C.B. *1:* 19; *38:* 71, 72, 73, 74
Falter, John *40:* 169, 170
Falwell, Cathryn *118:* 77; *137:* 185; *196:* 71, 72
Fancher, Lou *138:* 219; *141:* 64; *144:* 199; *177:* 51
Fanelli, Sara *89:* 63; *126:* 69
Faria, Rosana *150:* 143
Faricy, Patrick *185:* 182
Farooqi, Musharraf Ali *207:* 46
Farmer, Andrew *49:* 102
Farmer, Peter *24:* 108; *38:* 75
Farnsworth, Bill *93:* 189; *116:* 147; *124:* 8; *135:* 52; *146:* 242, 243, 244; *182:* 176; *186:* 31, 83, 84, 85; *191:* 197
Farquharson, Alexander *46:* 75
Farrell, David *40:* 135
Farrell, Russell *196:* 38
Farris, David *74:* 42
Fasolino, Teresa *118:* 145
Fatigati, Evelyn *24:* 112
Fatus, Sophie *182:* 74; *190:* 218
Faul-Jansen, Regina *22:* 117
Faulkner, Jack *6:* 169
Faulkner, Matt *161:* 174; *167:* 75
Fava, Rita *2:* 29
Fax, Elton C. *1:* 101; *4:* 2; *12:* 77; *25:* 107
Fay *43:* 93
Fearnley, Jan *153:* 82, 83; *205:* 63, 64, 65
Fearrington, Ann *146:* 80
Federspiel, Marian *33:* 51
Fedorov, Nickolai Ivanovich *110:* 102
Feelings, Tom *5:* 22; *8:* 56; *12:* 153; *16:* 105; *30:* 196; *49:* 37; *61:* 101; *69:* 56, 57; *93:* 74; *105:* 88
Fehr, Terrence *21:* 87
Feiffer, Jules *3:* 91; *8:* 58; *61:* 66, 67, 70, 74, 76,77, 78; *111:* 47, 48, 49, 50; *132:* 122; *157:* 62; *201:* 48, 49, 50
Feigeles, Neil *41:* 242
Feldman, Elyse *86:* 7
Feller, Gene *33:* 130
Fellows, Muriel H. *10:* 42
Felstead, Cathie *116:* 85
Felts, Shirley *33:* 71; *48:* 59
Fennell, Tracy *171:* 69
Fennelli, Maureen *38:* 181
Fenton, Carroll Lane *5:* 66; *21:* 39
Fenton, Mildred Adams *5:* 66; *21:* 39
Ferguson, Peter *177:* 30, 31; *181:* 154; *197:* 4; *199:* 40
Ferguson, Walter W. *34:* 86
Fernandes, Eugenie *77:* 67; *205:* 68
Fernandes, Stanislaw *70:* 28
Fernandez, Fernando *77:* 57
Fernandez, Laura *77:* 153; *101:* 117; *131:* 222; *170:* 119; *175:* 182
Ferrari, Alex *188:* 121
Ferrington, Susan *172:* 22
Fetz, Ingrid *11:* 67; *12:* 52; *16:* 205; *17:* 59; *29:* 105; *30:* 108, 109; *32:* 149; *43:* 142; *56:* 29; *60:* 34; *85:* 48; *87:* 146
Fiammenghi, Gioia *9:* 66; *11:* 44; *12:* 206; *13:* 57, 59; *52:* 126, 129; *66:* 64; *85:* 83; *91:* 161; *166:* 169
Fiedler, Joseph Daniel *96:* 42; *113:* 173; *129:* 164; *146:* 17; *159:* 68; *162:* 104
Field, Rachel *15:* 113
Fielding, David *70:* 124
Fieser, Stephen *152:* 36
Fine, Howard *145:* 159; *159:* 64; *165:* 134; *174:* 129; *181:* 68
Fine, Peter K. *43:* 210
Finger, Helen *42:* 81
Fink, Sam *18:* 119
Finlay, Winifred *23:* 72
Finney, Pat *79:* 215

Fiore, Peter *99:* 196; *125:* 139; *144:* 225; *160:* 169; *180:* 72
Fiorentino, Al *3:* 240
Firehammer, Karla *174:* 202
Firmin, Charlotte *29:* 75; *48:* 70
Firmin, Peter *58:* 63, 64, 65, 67, 68, 70, 71
Firth, Barbara *81:* 208; *127:* 218; *179:* 62
Fischel, Lillian *40:* 204
Fischer, Hans *25:* 202
Fischer, Scott *207:* 37
Fischer-Nagel, Andreas *56:* 50
Fischer-Nagel, Heiderose *56:* 50
Fisher, Carolyn *154:* 50
Fisher, Chris *79:* 62; *158:* 248; *188:* 195
Fisher, Cynthia *117:* 45; *137:* 118; *195:* 40
Fisher, Jeffrey *142:* 80
Fisher, Leonard Everett *3:* 6; *4:* 72, 86; *6:* 197; *9:* 59; *16:* 151, 153; *23:* 44; *27:* 134; *29:* 26; *34:* 87, 89, 90, 91, 93, 94, 95, 96; *40:* 206; *50:* 150; *60:* 158; *73:* 68, 70, 71, 72, 73; *176:* 71, 72, 73; *208:* 131; *YABC 2:* 169
Fisher, Lois *20:* 62; *21:* 7
Fisher, Valorie *177:* 55
Fisk, Nicholas *25:* 112
Fitschen, Marilyn *2:* 20, 21; *20:* 48
Fitz-Maurice, Jeff *175:* 2
Fitzgerald, F.A. *15:* 116; *25:* 86, 87
Fitzgerald, Joanne *157:* 153, 154; *198:* 34, 35
Fitzgerald, Royce *205:* 5
Fitzhugh, Louise *1:* 94; *9:* 163; *45:* 75, 78
Fitzhugh, Susie *11:* 117
Fitzpatrick, Jim *109:* 130
Fitzpatrick, Marie-Louise *125:* 69, 70, *189:* 72, 73
Fitzsimmons, Arthur *14:* 128
Fix, Philippe *26:* 102
Flack, Marjorie *21:* 67; *100:* 93; *YABC 2:* 122
Flagg, James Montgomery *17:* 227
Flavin, Teresa *132:* 115; *186:* 119
Flax, Zeona *2:* 245
Fleetwood, Tony *171:* 51
Fleishman, Seymour *14:* 232; *24:* 87
Fleming, Denise *71:* 179; *81:* 58; *126:* 71, 72, 73; *173:* 52, 53
Fleming, Guy *18:* 41
Flesher, Vivienne *85:* 55
Fletcher, Claire *80:* 106; *157:* 159
Flint, Russ *74:* 80
Floate, Helen *111:* 163
Floca, Brian *155:* 88, 89; *190:* 10, 66, 67
Floethe, Richard *3:* 131; *4:* 90
Floherty, John J., Jr. *5:* 68
Flook, Helen *160:* 81
Flora, James *1:* 96; *30:* 111, 112
Florczak, Robert *166:* 51
Florian, Douglas *19:* 122; *83:* 64, 65; *125:* 71, 72, 74, 76; *128:* 130; *177:* 58, 60
Flory, Jane *22:* 111
Flower, Renee *125:* 109
Floyd, Gareth *1:* 74; *17:* 245; *48:* 63; *62:* 35,36, 37, 39, 40, 41; *74:* 245; *79:* 56
Fluchere, Henri A. *40:* 79
Flynn, Alice *183:* 2
Flynn, Barbara *7:* 31; *9:* 70
Fogarty, Thomas *15:* 89
Foley, Greg *190:* 69
Folger, Joseph *9:* 100
Folkard, Charles *22:* 132; *29:* 128, 257, 258
Foott, Jeff *42:* 202
Forberg, Ati *12:* 71, 205; *14:* 1; *22:* 113; *26:* 22; *48:* 64, 65
Ford, George *24:* 120; *31:* 70, 177; *58:* 126; *81:* 103; *107:* 91; *136:* 100; *194:* 47; *208:* 81
Ford, Gilbert *199:* 10
Ford, H.J. *16:* 185, 186
Ford, Jason *174:* 119
Ford, Pamela Baldwin *27:* 104
Fordham, John *168:* 160, 161

Foreman, Michael *2:* 110, 111; *67:* 99; *73:* 78, 79, 80,81, 82; *93:* 146; *135:* 55, 56, 57; *184:* 58, 59
Forrester, Victoria *40:* 83
Forsey, Chris *140:* 210
Fortnum, Peggy *6:* 29; *20:* 179; *24:* 211; *26:* 76, 77, 78; *39:* 78; *58:* 19, 21, 23, 27; *YABC 1:* 148
Fortune, Eric *191:* 52
Foster, Brad W. *34:* 99
Foster, Genevieve *2:* 112
Foster, Gerald L. *7:* 78; *198:* 40
Foster, Jon *146:* 18; *198:* 7
Foster, Laura Louise *6:* 79
Foster, Marian Curtis *23:* 74; *40:* 42
Foster, Sally *58:* 73, 74
Foucher, Adele *47:* 118
Foust, Mitch *168:* 50
Fowler, Jim *184:* 190
Fowler, Mel *36:* 127
Fowler, Richard *87:* 219
Fowles, Shelley *165:* 127; *205:* 72
Fox, Charles Phillip *12:* 84
Fox, Christyan *188:* 36
Fox, Jim *6:* 187
Fox, Nathan *208:* 64
Fox-Davies, Sarah *76:* 150; *182:* 63; *199:* 42, 43
Frace, Charles *15:* 118
Frailey, Joy *72:* 108
Frame, Paul *2:* 45, 145; *9:* 153; *10:* 124; *21:* 71; *23:* 62; *24:* 123; *27:* 106; *31:* 48; *32:* 159; *34:* 195; *38:* 136; *42:* 55; *44:* 139; *60:* 39, 40, 41, 42, 43, 44, 46; *73:* 183
Frampton, David *85:* 72; *102:* 33; *139:* 182; *152:* 37; *189:* 171
Francis, Guy *198:* 164
Francois, Andre *25:* 117
Francoise
   See Seignobosc, Francoise
Frank, Lola Edick *2:* 199
Frank, Mary *4:* 54; *34:* 100
Franke, Phil *45:* 91
Frankel, Alona *66:* 70
Frankel, Julie *40:* 84, 85, 202
Frankenberg, Robert *22:* 116; *30:* 50; *38:* 92, 94, 95; *68:* 111
Frankfeldt, Gwen *84:* 223; *110:* 92
Frankland, David *169:* 137; *182:* 164; *201:* 159
Franklin, Ashton *165:* 144
Franklin, John *24:* 22
Franson, Leanne R. *111:* 57, 58; *151:* 7
Frascino, Edward *9:* 133; *29:* 229; *33:* 190; *48:* 80, 81, 82, 83, 84, 85, 86
Frasconi, Antonio *6:* 80; *27:* 208; *53:* 41, 43, 45, 47,48; *68:* 145; *73:* 226; *131:* 68
Fraser, Betty *2:* 212; *6:* 185; *8:* 103; *31:* 72,73; *43:* 136; *111:* 76
Fraser, Eric *38:* 78; *41:* 149, 151
Fraser, F.A. *22:* 234
Fraser, James *171:* 68
Fraser, Mary Ann *137:* 63
Frasier, Debra *69:* 60; *112:* 67; *182:* 81, 82, 83
Fraustino, Lisa Rowe *146:* 87
Frazee, Marla *72:* 98; *105:* 79, 80; *151:* 67, 68; *164:* 165; *171:* 190, 191; *187:* 53, 54,55, 56, 143
Frazetta, Frank *41:* 72; *58:* 77, 78, 79, 80, 81, 82, 83
Frazier, Craig *177:* 63
Freas, John *25:* 207
Fredrickson, Mark *103:* 33
Freeland, Michael J. *118:* 115
Freeman, Don *2:* 15; *13:* 249; *17:* 62, 63, 65, 67, 68; *18:* 243; *20:* 195; *23:* 213, 217; *32:* 155; *55:* 129
Freeman, Irving *67:* 150
Freeman, Laura *144:* 111; *200:* 62, 63
Freeman, Pietri *140:* 223
Freeman, Tom *167:* 118

Freeman, Tor *164:* 93
Fregosi, Claudia *24:* 117
Fremaux, Charlotte Murray *138:* 29; *141:* 95
French, Fiona *6:* 82, 83; *75:* 61; *109:* 170; *132:* 79, 80, 81, 82
French, Martin *163:* 4
Frendak, Rodney *126:* 97, 98
Freschet, Gina *175:* 73
Freynet, Gilbert *72:* 221
Fried, Janice *202:* 121
Friedman, Judith *43:* 197; *131:* 221
Friedman, Marvin *19:* 59; *42:* 86
Frinta, Dagmar *36:* 42
Frith, Michael K. *15:* 138; *18:* 120
Fritz, Ronald *46:* 73; *82:* 124
Fromm, Lilo *29:* 85; *40:* 197
Frost, A.B. *17:* 6, 7; *19:* 123, 124, 125, 126, 127, 128, 129,130; *100:* 119; *YABC 1:* 156, 157, 160; *2:* 107
Frost, Helen *183:* 51
Frost, Kristi *118:* 113
Frost, Michael *151:* 209; *209:* 44
Froud, Brian *150:* 82, 83
Froud, Wendy *151:* 237
Fry, Guy *2:* 224
Fry, Rosalie *3:* 72; *YABC 2:* 180, 181
Fry, Rosalind *21:* 153, 168
Fryer, Elmer *34:* 115
Fuchs, Bernie *110:* 10; *162:* 46
Fuchs, Erich *6:* 84
Fuchshuber, Annegert *43:* 96
Fufuka, Mahiri *32:* 146
Fuge, Charles *144:* 91, 93
Fujikawa, Gyo *39:* 75, 76; *76:* 72, 73, 74
Fulford, Deborah *23:* 159
Fuller, Margaret *25:* 189
Fulweiler, John *93:* 99
Funai, Mamoru *38:* 105
Funfhausen, Christian *196:* 30
Funk, Tom *7:* 17, 99
Furchgott, Terry *29:* 86
Furness, William Henry, Jr. *94:* 18
Furukawa, Mel *25:* 42
Fusari, Erika *164:* 227

G

Gaadt, David *78:* 212; *121:* 166; *201:* 171
Gaadt, George *71:* 9
Gaber, Susan *99:* 33; *115:* 57, 58; *164:* 195; *169:* 61, 62, 63; *185:* 50, 51; *188:* 124
Gaberell, J. *19:* 236
Gable, Brian *195:* 68, 69
Gabler, Mirko *99:* 71; *195:* 32
Gackenbach, Dick *19:* 168; *41:* 81; *48:* 89, 90, 91, 92,93, 94; *54:* 105; *79:* 75, 76, 77
Gad, Victor *87:* 161
Gaetano, Nicholas *23:* 209
Gaffney-Kessell, Walter *94:* 219; *174:* 188
Gag, Flavia *17:* 49, 52
Gag, Wanda *100:* 101, 102; *YABC 1:* 135, 137, 138, 141, 143
Gagnon, Cecile *11:* 77; *58:* 87
Gaillard, Jason *200:* 69; *204:* 74
Gal, Laszlo *14:* 127; *52:* 54, 55, 56; *65:* 142; *68:* 150; *81:* 185; *96:* 104, 105
Galazinski, Tom *55:* 13
Galbraith, Ben *200:* 70
Galdone, Paul *1:* 156, 181, 206; *2:* 40, 241; *3:* 42,144; *4:* 141; *10:* 109, 158; *11:* 21; *12:* 118, 210; *14:* 12; *16:* 36, 37; *17:* 70, 71, 72, 73, 74; *18:* 111, 230; *19:* 183; *21:* 154; *22:* 150, 245; *33:* 126; *39:* 136, 137; *42:* 57; *51:* 169; *55:* 110; *66:* 80, 82, 139; *72:* 73; *100:* 84
Gale, Cathy *140:* 22; *143:* 52
Gall, Chris *176:* 79, 80
Gallagher, Jack *187:* 100
Gallagher, S. Saelig *105:* 154; *198:* 91

Gallagher, Sears *20:* 112Gallagher-Cole, Mernie *206:* 56
Galloway, Ewing *51:* 154
Galouchka, Annouchka Gravel *95:* 55; *182:* 40
Galster, Robert *1:* 66
Galsworthy, Gay John *35:* 232
Galvez, Daniel *125:* 182
Gamble, Kim *112:* 64, 65; *124:* 77; *183:* 40, 42, 43, 56, 57; *187:* 170
Gammell, Stephen *7:* 48; *13:* 149; *29:* 82; *33:* 209; *41:* 88; *50:* 185, 186, 187; *53:* 51, 52, 53, 54, 55, 56,57, 58; *54:* 24, 25; *56:* 147, 148, 150; *57:* 27, 66; *81:* 62, 63; *87:* 88; *89:* 10; *106:* 223; *126:* 2; *128:* 71, 73, 74, 77; *154:* 34
Gamper, Ruth *84:* 198
Gampert, John *58:* 94
Ganly, Helen *56:* 56
Gannett, Ruth Chrisman *3:* 74; *18:* 254; *33:* 77, 78
Gannon, Ned *205:* 6
Gantschev, Ivan *45:* 32
Garafano, Marie *73:* 33
Garbot, Dave *131:* 106
Garbutt, Bernard *23:* 68
Garcia *37:* 71
Garcia, Manuel *74:* 145
Garcia-Franco, Rebecca *173:* 46
Gardiner, Lindsey *178:* 128; *186:* 137
Gardner, Earle *45:* 167
Gardner, Joan *40:* 87
Gardner, Joel *40:* 87, 92
Gardner, John *40:* 87
Gardner, Lucy *40:* 87
Gardner, Richard
   See Cummings, Richard
Gardner, Sally *171:* 177; *177:* 66, 68
Gargiulo, Frank *84:* 158
Garland, Michael *36:* 29; *38:* 83; *44:* 168; *48:* 78, 221, 222; *49:* 161; *60:* 139; *71:* 6, 11; *72:* 229; *74:* 142; *89:* 187; *93:* 183; *104:* 110; *131:* 55; *139:* 209; *168:* 56; *208:* 72, 73, 75
Garland, Peggy *60:* 139
Garland, Sarah *62:* 45; *135:* 67, 68; *171:* 118
Garn, Aimee *75:* 47
Garner, Joan *128:* 170
Garneray, Ambroise Louis *59:* 140
Garnett, Eve *3:* 75
Garnett, Gary *39:* 184
Garns, Allen *80:* 125; *84:* 39; *165:* 231; *209:* 44
Garófoli, Viviana *186:* 123
Garraty, Gail *4:* 142; *52:* 106
Garrett, Agnes *46:* 110; *47:* 157
Garrett, Edmund H. *20:* 29
Garrett, Tom *107:* 194
Garrick, Jacqueline *67:* 42, 43; *77:* 94
Garrison, Barbara *19:* 133; *104:* 146; *109:* 87
Garro, Mark *108:* 131; *128:* 210
Garvey, Robert *98:* 222
Garza, Carmen Lomas *80:* 211; *182:* 86
Garza, Xavier *184:* 64
Gates, Frieda *26:* 80
Gaughan, Jack *26:* 79; *43:* 185
Gaver, Becky *20:* 61
Gawing, Toby *72:* 52
Gay, Marie-Louise *68:* 76, 77, 78; *102:* 136; *126:* 76, 78, 81, 83; *127:* 55, 56; *179:* 70, 72, 73, 74
Gay, Zhenya *19:* 135, 136
Gaydos, Tim *62:* 201
Gazsi, Ed *80:* 48
Gazso, Gabriel *73:* 85
Geary, Clifford N. *1:* 122; *9:* 104; *51:* 74
Geary, Rick *142:* 44, 46
Gee, Frank *33:* 26
Geehan, Wayne *157:* 181
Geer, Charles *1:* 91; *3:* 179; *4:* 201; *6:* 168; *7:* 96; *9:* 58; *10:* 72; *12:* 127; *39:* 156,157, 158, 159, 160; *42:* 88, 89, 90, 91; *55:* 111, 116

Geerinck, Manuel *173:* 128
Gehm, Charlie *36:* 65; *57:* 117; *62:* 60, 138
Geis, Alissa Imre *189:* 77
Geisel, Theodor Seuss *1:* 104, 105, 106; *28:* 108, 109, 110,111, 112, 113; *75:* 67, 68, 69, 70, 71; *89:* 127, 128; *100:* 106, 107, 108
Geisert, Arthur *92:* 67, 68; *133:* 72, 73, 74; *165:* 97, 98; *171:* 64, 65
Geldart, William *15:* 121; *21:* 202
Genia *4:* 84
Gentry, Cyrille R. *12:* 66
Genzo, John Paul *136:* 74
George, Jean *2:* 113
George, Lindsay Barrett *95:* 57; *155:* 97, 98
Geraghty, Paul *130:* 60, 61
Gerard, Jean Ignace *45:* 80
Gerard, Rolf *27:* 147, 150
Gerber, Mark *61:* 105
Gerber, Mary Jane *112:* 124; *171:* 56
Gerber, Stephanie *71:* 195
Gerdstein, Mordecai *169:* 105
Gergely, Tibor *54:* 15, 16
Geritz, Franz *17:* 135
Gerlach, Geff *42:* 58
Gerrard, Roy *47:* 78; *90:* 96, 97, 98, 99
Gerritsen, Paula *177:* 69
Gershinowitz, George *36:* 27
Gerstein, Mordicai *31:* 117; *47:* 80, 81, 82, 83, 84, 85, 86; *51:* 173; *69:* 134; *107:* 122; *142:* 49, 52; *165:* 209; *176:* 119; *178:* 95, 97, 99
Gervase *12:* 27
Geter, Tyrone *146:* 249; *150:* 86
Getz, Arthur *32:* 148
Gévry, Claudine *188:* 47
Gewirtz, Bina *61:* 81
Giancola, Donato *95:* 146; *164:* 226
Gibala-Broxholm, Scott *205:* 76
Gibbons, Gail *23:* 78; *72:* 77, 78, 79; *82:* 182; *104:* 65; *160:* 99, 100; *201:* 59, 60, 62
Gibbs, Tony *40:* 95
Gibran, Kahlil *32:* 116
Gibson, Barbara Leonard *205:* 77
Gider, Iskender *81:* 193
Giebfried, Rosemary *170:* 135
Giesen, Rosemary *34:* 192, 193
Giffard, Hannah *83:* 70
Giguere, George *20:* 111
Gilbert, John *19:* 184; *54:* 115; *YABC 2:* 287
Gilbert, W.S. *36:* 83, 85, 96
Gilbert, Yvonne *116:* 70; *128:* 84; *149:* 119; *185:* 69; *192:* 25; *195:* 81
Gilchrist, Jan Spivey *72:* 82, 83, 84, 85, 87; *77:* 90; *105:* 89, 91; *130:* 63, 64; *155:* 105, 107; *182:* 67
Giles, Will *41:* 218
Gili, Phillida *70:* 73
Gill, Margery *4:* 57; *7:* 7; *22:* 122; *25:* 166; *26:* 146, 147
Gillen, Denver *28:* 216
Gillette, Henry J. *23:* 237
Gilliam, Stan *39:* 64, 81
Gillies, Chuck *62:* 31
Gilliland, Jillian *87:* 58
Gillman, Alec *98:* 105
Gilman, Esther *15:* 124
Gilman, Phoebe *104:* 70, 71
Ginsberg, Sari *111:* 184
Ginsburg, Max *62:* 59; *68:* 194 *Girard, Roge* *161:* 30
Girouard, Patrick *155:* 100
Giovanopoulos, Paul *7:* 104; *60:* 36
Giovine, Sergio *79:* 12; *93:* 118; *139:* 118; *205:* 114
Gist, E.M. *206:* 60
Githens, Elizabeth M. *5:* 47
Gladden, Scott *99:* 108; *103:* 160; *193:* 46, 47
Gladstone, Gary *12:* 89; *13:* 190
Gladstone, Lise *15:* 273
Glanzman, Louis S. *2:* 177; *3:* 182; *36:* 97, 98; *38:* 120, 122; *52:* 141, 144; *71:* 191; *91:* 54, 56

Glaser, Byron *154:* 59, 60
Glaser, Milton *3:* 5; *5:* 156; *11:* 107; *30:* 26; *36:* 112; *54:* 141; *151:* 70
Glass, Andrew *36:* 38; *44:* 133; *48:* 205; *65:* 3; *68:* 43, 45; *90:* 104, 105; *150:* 89
Glass, Marvin *9:* 174
Glasser, Judy *41:* 156; *56:* 140; *69:* 79; *72:* 101
Glattauer, Ned *5:* 84; *13:* 224; *14:* 26
Glauber, Uta *17:* 76
Gleeson, J.M. *YABC 2:* 207
Glegg, Creina *36:* 100
Glienke, Amelie *63:* 150
Gliewe, Unada *3:* 78, 79; *21:* 73; *30:* 220
Gliori, Debi *72:* 91; *138:* 82; *162:* 37; *189:* 79, 81, 82
Glovach, Linda *7:* 105
Gobbato, Imero *3:* 180, 181; *6:* 213; *7:* 58; *9:* 150; *18:* 39; *21:* 167; *39:* 82, 83; *41:* 137, 251; *59:* 177
Goble, Paul *25:* 121; *26:* 86; *33:* 65; *69:* 68, 69; *131:* 79, 80
Goble, Warwick *46:* 78, 79; *194:* 143
Godal, Eric *36:* 93
Godkin, Celia *145:* 84, 86
Godfrey, Michael *17:* 279
Godon, Ingrid *166:* 163; *186:* 99
Goede, Irene *208:* 87
Goembel, Ponder *42:* 124
Goffe, Toni *61:* 83, 84, 85; *89:* 11; *90:* 124; *178:* 118
Goffstein, M.B. *8:* 71; *70:* 75, 76, 77
Golbin, Andre *15:* 125
Gold, Robert *166:* 151, 152
Goldfeder, Cheryl *11:* 191
Goldfinger, Jennifer P. *185:* 71
Goldsborough, June *5:* 154, 155; *8:* 92, 14: 226; *19:* 139; *54:* 165
Goldsmith, Robert *110:* 77
Goldstein, Barry *198:* 147
Goldstein, Leslie *5:* 8; *6:* 60; *10:* 106
Goldstein, Nathan *1:* 175; *2:* 79; *11:* 41, 232; *16:* 55
Goldstrom, Robert *98:* 36; *145:* 51, 52
Golembe, Carla *79:* 80, 81; *136:* 91; *144:* 113; *193:* 53
Golin, Carlo *74:* 112
Gomez, Elena *188:* 122; *191:* 72
Gomez, Elizabeth *127:* 70; *133:* 76
Gomi, Taro *64:* 102; *103:* 74, 76
Gon, Adriano *101:* 112
Gonsalve, Ron *178:* 213
Gonzalez, Maya Christina *104:* 3; *136:* 92
Goodall, John S. *4:* 92, 93; *10:* 132; *66:* 92, 93; *YABC 1:* 198
Goode, Diane *15:* 126; *50:* 183; *52:* 114, 115; *76:* 195; *84:* 94; *99:* 141; *114:* 76, 77, 78; *170:* 99, 101
Goodelman, Aaron *40:* 203
Goodenow, Earle *40:* 97
Goodfellow, Peter *62:* 95; *94:* 202
Goodman, Joan Elizabeth *50:* 86
Goodman, Vivienne *82:* 251; *146:* 181, 182
Goodnow, Patti *117:* 33
Goodwin, Harold *13:* 74
Goodwin, Philip R. *18:* 206
Goor, Nancy *39:* 85, 86
Goor, Ron *39:* 85, 86
Goossens, Philippe *195:* 71
Gorbachev, Valeri *89:* 96; *112:* 97; *143:* 63, 64; *184:* 66, 67, 68, 101
Gordon, Gwen *12:* 151
Gordon, Margaret *4:* 147; *5:* 48, 49; *9:* 79
Gordon, Mike *101:* 62, 63, 64
Gordon, Russell *136:* 204; *137:* 214
Gordon, Walter *138:* 9
Gore, Leonid *89:* 51; *94:* 74; *136:* 8; *158:* 117; *166:* 136; *168:* 36; *170:* 107; *181:* 94; *185:* 73
Gorecka-Egan, Erica *18:* 35

Gorey, Edward *1:* 60, 61; *13:* 169; *18:* 192; *20:* 201; *29:* 90, 91, 92, 93, 94, 95, 96, 97, 98, 99, 100; *30:* 129; *32:* 90; *34:* 200, *65:* 48; *68:* 24, 25; *69:* 79; *70:* 80, 82, 83, 84; *85:* 136; *127:* 62
Gorsline, Douglas *1:* 98; *6:* 13; *11:* 113; *13:* 104; *15:* 14; *28:* 117, 118; *YABC 1:* 15
Gorton, Julia *108:* 94; *178:* 81, 82
Gosfield, Josh *118:* 165, 166; *149:* 67
Gosner, Kenneth *5:* 135
Gosney, Joy *167:* 142
Gotlieb, Jules *6:* 127
Goto, Scott *115:* 86; *136:* 69; *203:* 77, 78
Gott, Barry *197:* 95
Gottlieb, Dale *67:* 162; *107:* 16; *149:* 6
Goudey, Ray *97:* 86
Gough, Alan *91:* 57
Gough, Philip *23:* 47; *45:* 90
Gould, Chester *49:* 112, 113, 114, 116, 117, 118
Gould, Jason *151:* 232
Gourbault, Martine *177:* 159
Govern, Elaine R. *26:* 94
Gower, Teri *102:* 184
Gowing, Toby *60:* 25; *63:* 33; *78:* 70, 252; *83:* 228; *86:* 187; *93:* 145; *108:* 133; *110:* 217; *184:* 125
Grabianski *20:* 144
Grabianski, Janusz *39:* 92, 93, 94, 95
Graboff, Abner *35:* 103, 104
Graef, Renée *61:* 188; *72:* 207; *204:* 45
Grafe, Max *156:* 173; *178:* 237; *192:* 240; *198:* 51
Graham, A.B. *11:* 61
Graham, Bob *101:* 66, 67, 68; *151:* 74, 75; *187:* 65, 67, 68, 70
Graham, Georgia *188:* 3; *190:* 75
Graham, L. *7:* 108
Graham, Margaret Bloy *11:* 120; *18:* 305, 307
Graham, Mark *88:* 208; *159:* 153; *182:* 3
Grahame-Johnstone, Janet *13:* 61
Grahame-Johnstone, Anne *13:* 61
Grainger, Sam *42:* 95
Gralley, Jean *166:* 86
Gramatky, Hardie *1:* 107; *30:* 116, 119, 120, 122, 123
Gran, Julie *168:* 118
Granahan, Julie *84:* 84
GrandPré, Mary *84:* 131; *109:* 199; *118:* 76; *180:* 65; *184:* 70, 71, 180; *192:* 87
Grandström, Brita *176:* 139
Grandville, J.J. *45:* 81, 82, 83, 84, 85, 86, 87, 88; *47:* 125; *64:* 10
Granger, Paul *39:* 153
Granström, Brita *162:* 35; *167:* 46
Grant, (Alice) Leigh *10:* 52; *15:* 131; *20:* 20; *26:* 119; *48:* 202
Grant, Gordon *17:* 230, 234; *25:* 123, 124, 125, 126; *52:* 69; *YABC 1:* 164
Grant, Melvyn *159:* 186, 187; *170:* 48, 49
Grant, Renee *77:* 40
Grant, Shirley *109:* 45
Graves, Elizabeth *45:* 101
Graves, Keith *167:* 89; *191:* 74
Gray, Harold *33:* 87, 88
Gray, Les *82:* 76; *83:* 232
Gray, Reginald *6:* 69
Greco, Tony *184:* 6
Greder, Armin *76:* 235
Green, Ann Canevari *62:* 48
Green, Eileen *6:* 97
Green, Elizabeth Shippen *139:* 109
Green, Jonathan *86:* 135; *105:* 109
Green, Ken *111:* 68
Green, Michael *32:* 216
Green, Robina *87:* 138
Green, Jonathan *157:* 105
Greene, Jeffrey *117:* 93
Greenaway, Kate *17:* 275; *24:* 180; *26:* 107; *41:* 222, 232; *100:* 115, 116; *YABC 1:* 88, 89; *2:* 131, 133, 136,138, 139, 141

Greenberg, Melanie Hope *72:* 93; *80:* 125; *101:* 174; *133:* 180; *186:* 189
Greenseid, Diane *178:* 106, 107
Greenstein, Elaine *150:* 100
Greenwald, Sheila *1:* 34; *3:* 99; *8:* 72
Greger, Carol *76:* 86
Gregorian, Joyce Ballou *30:* 125
Gregory, Emilian *177:* 146; *187:* 10
Gregory, Fran *130:* 4; *140:* 93
Gregory, Frank M. *29:* 107
Greiffenhagen, Maurice *16:* 137; *27:* 57; *YABC 2:* 288
Greiner, Robert *6:* 86
Gretter, J. Clemens *31:* 134
Gretz, Susanna *7:* 114
Gretzer, John *1:* 54; *3:* 26; *4:* 162; *7:* 125; *16:* 247; *18:* 117; *28:* 66; *30:* 85, 211; *33:* 235; *56:* 16
Grey, Mini *166:* 90; *192:* 71
Grey Owl *24:* 41
Gri *25:* 90
Grieder, Walter *9:* 84
Griesbach/Martucci *59:* 3
Grifalconi, Ann *2:* 126; *3:* 248; *11:* 18; *13:* 182; *46:* 38; *50:* 145; *66:* 99, 100, 101, 104, 106; *69:* 38; *70:* 64; *87:* 128; *90:* 53; *93:* 49; *128:* 48; *133:* 79, 81
Griffin, Gillett Good *26:* 96
Griffin, James *30:* 166
Griffin, John Howard *59:* 186
Griffin, Rachel *131:* 23
Griffith, Gershom *94:* 214
Griffiths, Dave *29:* 76
Griffiths, Dean *168:* 180; *169:* 182
Grimly, Gris *186:* 102; *192:* 112; *197:* 86
Grimsdell, Jeremy *83:* 75
Grimwood, Brian *82:* 89
Gringhuis, Dirk *6:* 98; *9:* 196
Gripe, Harald *2:* 127; *74:* 98
Grisha *3:* 71
Grobler, Piet *201:* 100
Grohmann, Susan *84:* 97
Gropper, William *27:* 93; *37:* 193
Gros *60:* 199
Grose, Helen Mason *YABC 1:* 260; *2:* 150
Grossman, Nancy *24:* 130; *29:* 101
Grossman, Robert *11:* 124; *46:* 39
Groth, John *15:* 79; *21:* 53, 54; *83:* 230
Grover, Lorie Ann *168:* 59
Grubb, Lisa *160:* 116
Grue, Lisa *187:* 193
Gruelle, Johnny *35:* 107
Gschwind, William *11:* 72
Guarnaccia, Steven *201:* 170, 173
Guay-Mitchell, Rebecca *110:* 95, 96; *135:* 240; *180:* 76; *181:* 71, 73
Guback, Georgia *88:* 102
Guerguerion, Claudine *105:* 73
Guevara, Susan *97:* 87; *167:* 49; *194:* 54
Guggenheim, Hans *2:* 10; *3:* 37; *8:* 136
Guhathaakurta, Ajanta *183:* 199
Guida, Lisa Chauncy *172:* 188
Guilbeau, Honore *22:* 69
Guillette, Joseph *137:* 37
Guisewite, Cathy *57:* 52, 53, 54, 56, 57
Gukova, Julia *95:* 104; *154:* 103; *168:* 195
Gundersheimer, Karen *35:* 240; *82:* 100
Gunderson, Nick *57:* 120
Gunnella *192:* 144
Gurney, James *76:* 97; *86:* 32
Gurney, John Steven *75:* 39, 82; *110:* 175; *143:* 67, 68; *169:* 172
Gusman, Annie *38:* 62
Gustafson, Scott *34:* 111; *43:* 40
Gustavson, Adam *104:* 10; *171:* 183; *176:* 87; *197:* 94; *204:* 35
Guthridge, Bettina *108:* 79; *186:* 92
Guthrie, R. Dale *64:* 143
Guthrie, Robin *20:* 122
Gutierrez, Akemi *172:* 87; *205:* 135
Gutierrez, Alan *136:* 31, 32

Gutierrez, Rudy *97:* 162; *203:* 79
Gutmann, Bessie Pease *73:* 93, 94
Gwynne, Fred *41:* 94, 95
Gyberg, Bo-Erik *38:* 131

H

Haas, Irene *17:* 77; *87:* 46; *96:* 117
Hack, Konrad *51:* 127
Hader, Berta H. *16:* 126
Hader, Elmer S. *16:* 126
Haeffele, Deborah *76:* 99
Haemer, Alan *62:* 109
Hafner, Marylin *22:* 196, 216; *24:* 44; *30:* 51; *35:* 95; *51:* 25, 160, 164; *86:* 16; *105:* 196; *121:* 93, 94; *149:* 208, 209; *179:* 82, 83, 84, 115; *190:* 200; *201:* 29
Hagerty, Sean *62:* 181
Hague, Michael *32:* 128; *48:* 98, 99, 100, 101, 103, 105,106, 107, 108, 109, 110; *49:* 121; *51:* 105; *64:* 14, 15; *79:* 134; *80:* 91, 92; *83:* 135; *100:* 241; *102:* 29; *129:* 101, 103, 104; *185:* 80, 81, 82
Hair, Jonathan *115:* 135
Halas, John *29:* 41, 47, 48
Haldane, Roger *13:* 76; *14:* 202
Hale, Bruce *203:* 83
Hale, Christy *79:* 124; *84:* 200; *114:* 201; *128:* 2, 3; *146:* 203; *158:* 243; *167:* 99; *179:* 87
Hale, Irina *26:* 97
Hale, James Graham *88:* 207
Hale, Kathleen *17:* 79; *66:* 114, 116, 118
Haley, Amanda *205:* 82, 83
Haley, Gail E. *43:* 102, 103, 104, 105; *78:* 65, 67; *136:* 106, 107
Hall, Amanda *96:* 110
Hall, Chuck *30:* 189
Hall, Douglas *15:* 184; *43:* 106, 107; *86:* 100; *87:* 82; *129:* 72
Hall, H. Tom *1:* 227; *30:* 210
Hall, Melanie *116:* 48, 49; *169:* 77, 78
Hall, Sydney P. *31:* 89
Hall, Tim *164:* 196; *202:* 41
Hall, Vicki *20:* 24
Hallinan, P.K. *39:* 98
Hallman, Tom *98:* 166
Hally, Greg *101:* 200; *151:* 224
Halperin, Wendy Anderson *96:* 151; *125:* 96, 97, 98, 99; *139:* 22; *140:* 84; *200:* 77, 78
Halpern, Joan *10:* 25
Halpern, Shari *174:* 172
Halsey, Megan *96:* 172; *114:* 185; *180:* 8; *185:* 85
Halstead, Virginia *125:* 105
Halverson, Janet *49:* 38, 42, 44
Hallensleben, Georg *134:* 5, 6; *172:* 17
Hamanaka, Sheila *71:* 100
Hamann, Brad *78:* 151
Hamann, Sigune *104:* 115
Hamberger, John *6:* 8; *8:* 32; *14:* 79; *34:* 136; *88:* 78
Hamil, Tom *14:* 80; *43:* 163
Hamilton, Bill and Associates *26:* 215
Hamilton, Helen S. *2:* 238
Hamilton, J. *19:* 83, 85, 87
Hamilton, Laurie *116:* 210
Hamilton, Todd Cameron *84:* 15
Hamlin, Janet *97:* 136; *124:* 90; *137:* 157; *182:* 117
Hamlin, Louise *71:* 135
Hammill, Matt *206:* 65
Hammond, Chris *21:* 37
Hammond, Elizabeth *5:* 36, 203
Hampshire, Michael *5:* 187; *7:* 110, 111; *48:* 150; *51:* 129
Hampson, Denman *10:* 155; *15:* 130
Hampton, Blake *41:* 244
Handford, Martin *64:* 105, 106, 107, 109

Handforth, Thomas *42:* 100, 101, 102, 103, 104, 105, 107
Handville, Robert *1:* 89; *38:* 76; *45:* 108, 109
Hane, Roger *17:* 239; *44:* 54
Haney, Elizabeth Mathieu *34:* 84
Hanke, Ted *71:* 10
Hankinson, Phil *181:* 164
Hanley, Catherine *8:* 161
Hann, Jacquie *19:* 144
Hanna, Cheryl *91:* 133
Hanna, Wayne A. *67:* 145
Hannon, Mark *38:* 37
Hanrahan, Kelly-Anne *203:* 142
Hansen, Gaby *159:* 11; *186:* 25
Hansen, Mia *149:* 76
Hanson, Joan *8:* 76; *11:* 139
Hanson, Peter E. *52:* 47; *54:* 99, 100; *73:* 21; *84:* 79; *116:* 144
Hansson, Gunilla *64:* 111, 112
Hardcastle, Nick *121:* 82; *175:* 185
Hardy, David A. *9:* 96; *119:* 74
Hardy, Paul *YABC 2:* 245 Haring, Keith *145:* 65
Harlan, Jerry *3:* 96
Harlin, Greg *89:* 194; *103:* 82; *118:* 161; *121:* 167; *182:* 76; *201:* 172
Harman, Dominic *206:* 48
Harness, Cheryl *106:* 80; *131:* 87; *178:* 111; *200:* 39
Harnischfeger *18:* 121
Harper, Arthur *YABC 2:* 121
Harper, Betty *126:* 90
Harper, Jamie *174:* 71
Harper, Piers *79:* 27; *105:* 102; *161:* 67
Harrington, Glenn *82:* 18; *94:* 66, 68; *185:* 118
Harrington, Jack *83:* 162
Harrington, Richard *5:* 81
Harris, Andrew N. *191:* 78
Harris, Jim *127:* 130; *183:* 4
Harris, John *83:* 25
Harris, Nick *86:* 177
Harris, Susan Yard *42:* 121
Harrison, Florence *20:* 150, 152
Harrison, Harry *4:* 103
Harrison, Jack *28:* 149
Harrison, Mark *105:* 157; *165:* 190
Harrison, Ted *56:* 73
Harsh, Fred *72:* 107
Harston, Jerry *105:* 143
Hart, Lewis *98:* 115
Hart, Thomas *181:* 165
Hart, William *13:* 72
Hartland, Jessie *171:* 80, 81; *186:* 165
Hartung, Susan Kathleen *150:* 107, 108; *173:* 106; *175:* 106; *192:* 78
Hartelius, Margaret *10:* 24
Hartshorn, Ruth *5:* 115; *11:* 129
Harvey, Amanda *145:* 44
Harvey, Bob *48:* 219
Harvey, Gerry *7:* 180
Harvey, Lisa *97:* 21
Harvey, Paul *88:* 74
Harvey, Roland *71:* 88; *123:* 63; *179:* 94
Haskamp, Steve *195:* 36
Hassall, Joan *43:* 108, 109
Hassell, Hilton *YABC 1:* 187
Hassett, John *162:* 59
Hasselriis, Else *18:* 87; *YABC 1:* 96
Hastings, Glenn *89:* 183
Hastings, Ian *62:* 67
Hauman, Doris *2:* 184; *29:* 58, 59; *32:* 85, 86, 87
Hauman, George *2:* 184; *29:* 58, 59; *32:* 85, 86, 87
Hausherr, Rosmarie *15:* 29
Hawkes, Kevin *78:* 72; *104:* 198; *105:* 197; *112:* 109; *126:* 87; *144:* 88; *149:* 210; *150:* 110, 135; *156:* 94; *164:* 35; *186:* 18; *190:* 197; *198:* 152; *201:* 70, 71, 72
Hawkins, Jacqui *112:* 86; *162:* 64

Hawkinson, John *4:* 109; *7:* 83; *21:* 64
Hawkinson, Lucy *21:* 64
Hawthorne, Mike *140:* 228
Haxton, Elaine *28:* 131
Haydock, Robert *4:* 95
Hayes, Geoffrey *26:* 111; *44:* 133; *91:* 85; *207:* 63
Hayes, Karel *207:* 65
Haynes, Max *72:* 107
Hays, Michael *73:* 207; *83:* 93; *139:* 197; *146:* 202, 250; *202:* 47
Haywood, Carolyn *1:* 112; *29:* 104
Heale, Jonathan *104:* 117
Healy, Daty *12:* 143
Healy, Deborah *58:* 181, 182; *101:* 111
Heap, Sue *102:* 207; *150:* 113, 114; *187:* 84, 85, 87
Hearn, Diane Dawson *79:* 99; *113:* 13; *209:* 71, 72
Hearon, Dorothy *34:* 69
Heaslip, William *57:* 24, 25
Hechtkopf, H. *11:* 110
Heck, Ed *173:* 81
Hector, Julian *205:* 85
Hedderwick, Mairi *30:* 127; *32:* 47; *36:* 104; *77:* 86; *145:* 91, 93, 95
Heffernan, Phil *146:* 197; *195:* 172
Hefter, Richard *28:* 170; *31:* 81, 82; *33:* 183
Hehenberger, Shelly *126:* 91
Heigh, James *22:* 98
Heighway, Richard *25:* 160; *64:* 4
Heighway-Bury, Robin *159:* 89
Heine, Helme *67:* 86; *135:* 91, 92
Heinly, John *45:* 113
Hellard, Susan *81:* 21; *204:* 82; *209:* 92
Hellebrand, Nancy *26:* 57
Heller, Linda *46:* 86
Heller, Ruth M. *66:* 125; *77:* 30, 32
Hellmuth, Jim *38:* 164
Helms, Georgeann *33:* 62
Helquist, Brett *142:* 203; *146:* 133, 134; *156:* 10; *173:* 25; *180:* 106; *187:* 90, 91; *193:* 12
Helweg, Hans *41:* 118; *50:* 93; *58:* 22, 26
Hemphill, Helen *179:* 95
Henba, Bobbie *90:* 195
Henderson, Dave *73:* 76; *75:* 191, 192, 193, 194; *82:* 4
Henderson, Douglas *103:* 68
Henderson, Kathy *55:* 32; *155:* 118
Henderson, Keith *35:* 122
Henderson, Meryl *127:* 58, 60; *169:* 81
Hendrix, John *187:* 133; *208:* 106, 107, 108
Hendry, Linda *80:* 104; *83:* 83; *164:* 216
Hengeveld, Dennis *142:* 86
Henkes, Kevin *43:* 111; *108:* 106, 107, 108
Henneberger, Robert *1:* 42; *2:* 237; *25:* 83
Henriksen, Harold *35:* 26; *48:* 68
Henriquez, Celeste *103:* 137
Henriquez, Elsa *82:* 260
Henriquez, Emile F. *89:* 88
Henry, Everett *29:* 191
Henry, Matthew *117:* 58
Henry, Paul *93:* 121; *194:* 125
Henry, Thomas *5:* 102
Hensel *27:* 119
Henshaw, Jacqui *141:* 127
Henstra, Friso *8:* 80; *36:* 70; *40:* 222; *41:* 250; *73:* 100, 101
Henterly, Jamichael *93:* 4
Heo, Yumi *89:* 85, 86; *94:* 89, 90; *146:* 40, 137, 138; *163:* 227; *201:* 192
Hepple, Norman *28:* 198
Herbert, Helen *57:* 70
Herbert, Jennifer *189:* 47
Herbert, Wally *23:* 101
Herbster, Mary Lee *9:* 33
Herder, Edwin *182:* 104
Herge
    See Remi, Georges
Hermansen, Pal *133:* 113
Hermanson, Dennis *10:* 55

Hermes, Gertrude *54:* 161
Herr, Margo *57:* 191
Herr, Susan *83:* 163
Herriman, George *140:* 74, 75, 76, 77, 78
Herriman, Lisa *87:* 190
Herring, Michael *121:* 76; *182:* 103
Herrington, Roger *3:* 161
Herscovici, C. *165:* 240
Hescox, Richard *85:* 86; *90:* 30; *139:* 35
Heslop, Mike *38:* 60; *40:* 130
Hess, Lydia J. *85:* 17
Hess, Mark *111:* 146; *113:* 207
Hess, Paul *134:* 47; *166:* 133; *193:* 13
Hess, Richard *42:* 31
Hester, Ronnie *37:* 85
Heuser, Olga J. *121:* 116
Heusser, Sibylle *168:* 195
Heustis, Louise L. *20:* 28
Hewgill, Jodi *201:* 90
Hewitson, Jennifer *74:* 119; *124:* 167
Hewitt, Kathryn *80:* 126; *149:* 105; *184:* 93; *196:* 36
Hewitt, Margaret *84:* 112
Heyduck-Huth, Hilde *8:* 82
Heyer, Carol *74:* 122; *130:* 72, 73; *192:* 35; *203:* 78
Heyer, Hermann *20:* 114, 115
Heyer, Marilee *102:* 108
Heyman, Ken *8:* 33; *34:* 113
Heyne, Ulrike *146:* 151
Heywood, Karen *48:* 114
Hickling, P.B. *40:* 165
Hickman, Stephen *85:* 58; *136:* 33; *171:* 128
Hierstein, Judy *56:* 40; *162:* 168
Higashi, Sandra *154:* 59, 60
Higginbottom, J. Winslow *8:* 170; *29:* 105, 106
Higgins, Chester *101:* 79
Higham, David *50:* 104
Hilb, Nora *176:* 8
Hildebrandt, Greg *8:* 191; *55:* 35, 36, 38, 39, 40, 42, 46; *172:* 110
Hildebrandt, Tim *8:* 191; *55:* 44, 45, 46
Hilder, Rowland *19:* 207
Hill, Eric *66:* 127, 128; *133:* 91
Hill, Gregory *35:* 190
Hill, Pat *49:* 120
Hillenbrand, Will *84:* 115; *92:* 76, 80; *93:* 131; *104:* 168; *128:* 137; *145:* 187; *146:* 184; *147:* 105, 106, 107; *152:* 59; *184:* 179; *195:* 34, 180; *196:* 125
Hilliard, Richard *183:* 74
Hillier, Matthew *45:* 205
Hillman, Priscilla *48:* 115
Hills, Tad *113:* 4; *137:* 147; *173:* 83; *208:* 199
Himler, Ronald *6:* 114; *7:* 162; *8:* 17, 84, 125; *14:* 76; *19:* 145; *26:* 160; *31:* 43; *38:* 116; *41:* 44, 79; *43:* 52; *45:* 120; *46:* 43; *54:* 44, 83; *58:* 180; *59:* 38; *68:* 146; *69:* 231; *70:* 98; *71:* 177, 178; *77:* 219; *79:* 212; *83:* 62; *89:* 5; *91:* 160; *92:* 91, 92, 93; *94:* 93; *95:* 69, 174, 194; *99:* 99, 112; *113:* 92; *118:* 114; *137:* 73, 74, 77, 167; *163:* 99; *165:* 138; *178:* 9, 220; *183:* 77, 79, 80, 81; *184:* 80, 83
Himmelman, John *47:* 109; *65:* 87; *94:* 96, 97; *159:* 85
Hinds, Bill *37:* 127, 130
Hines, Anna Grossnickle *51:* 90; *74:* 124; *95:* 78, 79, 80, 81
Hines, Bob *135:* 149, 150
Hirao, Amiko *203:* 98
Hiroko *99:* 61
Hiroshige *25:* 71
Hirsh, Marilyn *7:* 126
Hiscock, Bruce *137:* 80, 81; *204:* 51, 53
Hissey, Jane *103:* 90; *130:* 81
Hitch, Jeff *99:* 206; *128:* 86
Hitz, Demi *11:* 135; *15:* 245; *66:* 129, 130; *152:* 94, 95
Hnizdovsky, Jacques *32:* 96; *76:* 187
Ho, Kwoncjan *15:* 132

Hoban, Lillian *1:* 114; *22:* 157; *26:* 72; *29:* 53; *40:* 105, 107, 195; *41:* 80; *69:* 107, 108; *71:* 98; *77:* 168; *106:* 50; *113:* 86; *136:* 118
Hoban, Tana *22:* 159; *104:* 82, 83, 85
Hobbie, Jocelyn *190:* 78; *196:* 92
Hobbie, Nathaniel *196:* 92
Hobbs, Leigh *166:* 95
Hoberman, Norman *5:* 82
Hobson, Sally *77:* 185
Hockerman, Dennis *39:* 22; *56:* 23
Hodgell, P.C. *42:* 114
Hodges, C. Walter *2:* 139; *11:* 15; *12:* 25; *23:* 34; *25:* 96; *38:* 165; *44:* 197; *45:* 95; *100:* 57; *YABC 2:* 62, 63
Hodges, David *9:* 98
Hodgetts, Victoria *43:* 132
Hofbauer, Imre *2:* 162
Hoff, Syd *9:* 107; *10:* 128; *33:* 94; *72:* 115,116, 117, 118; *138:* 114, 115
Hoffman, Rosekrans *15:* 133; *50:* 219; *63:* 97
Hoffman, Sanford *38:* 208; *76:* 174; *88:* 160, 161; *151:* 156
Hoffmann, Felix *9:* 109
Hoffnung, Gerard *66:* 76, 77
Hofsinde, Robert *21:* 70
Hogan, Inez *2:* 141
Hogan, Jamie *192:* 94; *198:* 177
Hogarth, Burne *41:* 58; *63:* 46, 48, 49, 50, 52, 53, 54, 55,56
Hogarth, Paul *41:* 102, 103, 104; *YABC 1:* 16
Hogarth, William *42:* 33
Hogenbyl, Jan *1:* 35
Hogner, Nils *4:* 122; *25:* 144
Hogrogian, Nonny *3:* 221; *4:* 106, 107; *5:* 166; *7:* 129; *15:* 2; *16:* 176; *20:* 154; *22:* 146; *25:* 217; *27:* 206; *74:* 127, 128, 129, 149, 152; *127:* 99; *YABC 2:* 84, 94
Hokanson, Lars *93:* 111; *172:* 137
Hokusai *25:* 71
Hol, Colby *126:* 96
Holberg, Richard *2:* 51
Holbrook, Kathy *107:* 114
Holdcroft, Tina *38:* 109
Holden, Caroline *55:* 159
Holder, Heidi *36:* 99; *64:* 9
Holder, Jim *204:* 163
Holder, Jimmy *151:* 224
Hole, Stian *204:* 55
Holiday, Henry *YABC 2:* 107
Holl, F. *36:* 91
Holland, Brad *45:* 59, 159
Holland, Gay W. *128:* 105
Holland, Janice *18:* 118
Holland, Marion *6:* 116
Holldobler, Turid *26:* 120
Holliday, Keaf *144:* 236
Holling, Holling C. *15:* 136, 137
Hollinger, Deanne *12:* 116
Holm, Sharon Lane *114:* 84; *115:* 52
Holmes, B. *3:* 82
Holmes, Bea *7:* 74; *24:* 156; *31:* 93
Holmes, Dave *54:* 22
Holmes, Lesley *135:* 96
Holmgren, George Ellen *45:* 112
Holmlund, Heather D. *150:* 140
Holt, Norma *44:* 106
Holt, Pater *151:* 188
Holtan, Gene *32:* 192
Holub, Joan *149:* 72
Holyfield, John *149:* 231
Holz, Loretta *17:* 81
Hom, Nancy *79:* 195
Homar, Lorenzo *6:* 2
Homer, Winslow *128:* 8; *YABC 2:* 87
Honey, Elizabeth *112:* 95, 96; *137:* 93, 94
Honeywood, Varnette P. *110:* 68, 70
Hong, Lily Toy *76:* 104
Honigman, Marian *3:* 2
Honore, Paul *42:* 77, 79, 81, 82
Hood, Alun *69:* 145, 218; *72:* 41; *80:* 226; *87:* 4; *95:* 139

Hood, Susan *12:* 43
Hook, Christian *104:* 103
Hook, Frances *26:* 188; *27:* 127
Hook, Jeff *14:* 137; *103:* 105
Hook, Richard *26:* 188
Hooks *63:* 30
Hooper, Hadley *177:* 145
Hoover, Carol A. *21:* 77
Hoover, Russell *12:* 95; *17:* 2; *34:* 156
Hope, James *141:* 116
Hopkins, Chris *99:* 127
Hopkinson, Leigh *202:* 70
Hopman, Philip *178:* 184
Hoppe, Paul *209:* 85
Hoppin, Augustus *34:* 66
Horacek, Petr *163:* 117
Horder, Margaret *2:* 108; *73:* 75
Horen, Michael *45:* 121
Horne, Daniel *73:* 106; *91:* 153; *109:* 127;
 110: 232; *164:* 176
Horne, Richard *111:* 80
Horowitz, Dave *204:* 58
Horse, Harry *128:* 195; *169:* 86
Horvat, Laurel *12:* 201
Horvath, David *192:* 95
Horvath, Ferdinand Kusati *24:* 176
Horvath, Maria *57:* 171
Horwitz, Richard *57:* 174
Hotchkiss, De Wolfe *20:* 49
Hough, Charlotte *9:* 112; *13:* 98; *17:* 83; *24:*
 195
Houlihan, Ray *11:* 214
House, Caroline *183:* 121
Housman, Laurence *25:* 146, 147
Houston, James *13:* 107; *74:* 132, 134, 135
Hovland, Gary *88:* 172; *171:* 148
Hoyt, Eleanor *158:* 231
How, W.E. *20:* 47
Howard, Alan *16:* 80; *34:* 58; *45:* 114
Howard, Arthur *165:* 111, 112; *190:* 5
Howard, J.N. *15:* 234
Howard, John *33:* 179
Howard, Kim *116:* 71
Howard, Paul *142:* 126, 129; *144:* 187
Howard, Rob *40:* 161
Howarth, Daniel *170:* 34
Howe, John *79:* 101; *80:* 150; *115:* 47; *176:*
 106; *207:* 32, 35
Howe, Phillip *79:* 117; *175:* 115
Howe, Stephen *1:* 232
Howell, Karen *119:* 123
Howell, Pat *15:* 159
Howell, Troy *23:* 24; *31:* 61; *36:* 158; *37:*
 184; *41:* 76, 235; *48:* 112; *56:* 13; *57:* 3; *59:*
 174; *63:* 5; *74:* 46; *89:* 188; *90:* 231; *95:* 97;
 98: 130; *99:* 189; *153:* 156, 157, 158; *176:*
 104; *199:* 96, 98
Howes, Charles *22:* 17
Hoyt, Ard *145:* 141; *190:* 82; *207:* 148
Hranilovich, Barbara *127:* 51
Hu, Ying-Hwa *116:* 107; *152:* 236; *173:* 171
Huang, Benrei *137:* 55
Huang, Zhong-Yang *117:* 30, 32
Hubbard, Woodleigh Marx *98:* 67; *115:* 79;
 160: 138
Hubley, Faith *48:* 120, 121, 125, 130, 131,
 132, 134
Hubley, John *48:* 125, 130, 131, 132, 134
Hudak, Michal *143:* 74
Hudnut, Robin *14:* 62
Huerta, Catherine *76:* 178; *77:* 44, 45; *90:* 182
Huffaker, Sandy *10:* 56
Huffman, Joan *13:* 33
Huffman, Tom *13:* 180; *17:* 212; *21:* 116; *24:*
 132; *33:* 154; *38:* 59; *42:* 147
Hughes, Arthur *20:* 148, 149, 150; *33:* 114,
 148, 149
Hughes, Darren *95:* 44
Hughes, David *36:* 197

Hughes, Shirley *1:* 20, 21; *7:* 3; *12:* 217; *16:*
 163; *29:* 154; *63:* 118; *70:* 102, 103, 104;
 73: 169; *88:* 70; *110:* 118, 119; *159:* 103
Hugo, Victor *47:* 112
Huliska-Beith, Laura *204:* 108
Hull, Cathy *78:* 29
Hull, Richard *95:* 120; *123:* 175; *172:* 195
Hulsmann, Eva *16:* 166
Hume, Lachie *189:* 93
Hummel, Berta *43:* 137, 138, 139
Hummel, Lisl *29:* 109; *YABC 2:* 333, 334
Humphrey, Henry *16:* 167
Humphreys, Graham *25:* 168
Humphries, Tudor *76:* 66; *80:* 4; *124:* 4, 5
Huneck, Stephen *183:* 88, 89
Hunt, James *2:* 143
Hunt, Jonathan *84:* 120
Hunt, Paul *119:* 104; *129:* 135; *139:* 160; *173:*
 112
Hunt, Robert *110:* 206, 235; *147:* 136, 137;
 170: 3
Hunt, Scott *190:* 143
Hunter, Anne *133:* 190; *178:* 150
Huntington, Amy *180:* 99
Hurd, Clement *2:* 148, 149; *64:* 127, 128, 129,
 131, 133, 134,135, 136; *100:* 37, 38
Hurd, Peter *24:* 30, 31,; *YABC 2:* 56
Hurd, Thacher *46:* 88, 89; *94:* 114, 115, 116;
 123: 81, 82, 84
Hurlimann, Ruth *32:* 99
Hurst, Carol Otis *185:* 92
Hurst, Philip *196:* 79
Hurst, Tracey *192:* 238
Hussar, Michael *114:* 113; *117:* 159
Hustler, Tom *6:* 105
Hutchins, Laurence *55:* 22
Hutchins, Pat *15:* 142; *70:* 106, 107, 108; *178:*
 131, 132
Hutchinson, Sascha *95:* 211
Hutchinson, William M. *6:* 3, 138; *46:* 70
Hutchison, Paula *23:* 10
Hutton, Clarke *YABC 2:* 335
Hutton, Kathryn *35:* 155; *89:* 91
Hutton, Warwick *20:* 91
Huyette, Marcia *29:* 188
Hyatt, John *54:* 7
Hyatt, Mitch *178:* 162
Hyde, Maureen *82:* 17; *121:* 145, 146
Hyman, David *117:* 64
Hyman, Trina Schart *1:* 204; *2:* 194; *5:* 153;
 6: 106; *7:* 138, 145; *8:* 22; *10:* 196; *13:* 96;
 14: 114; *15:* 204; *16:* 234; *20:* 82; *22:* 133;
 24: 151; *25:* 79, 82; *26:* 82; *29:* 83; *31:* 37,
 39; *34:* 104; *38:* 84, 100, 128; *41:* 49; *43:*
 146; *46:* 91, 92, 93, 95, 96, 97, 98, 99, 100,
 101, 102, 103, 104, 105,108, 109, 111, 197;
 48: 60, 61; *52:* 32; *60:* 168; *66:* 38; *67:* 214;
 72: 74; *75:* 92; *79:* 57; *82:* 95, 238; *89:* 46;
 95: 91, 92, 93; *100:* 33, 199; *132:* 12; *147:*
 33, 35, 36; *167:* 58, 60; *177:* 189, 190

I

Ibarra, Rosa *147:* 91
Ibatoulline, Bagram *156:* 48; *174:* 33, 82; *202:*
 30
Ichikawa, Satomi *29:* 152; *41:* 52; *47:* 133,
 134,135, 136; *78:* 93, 94; *80:* 81; *146:* 143,
 145, 146; *208:* 117, 118, 119
Ide, Jacqueline *YABC 1:* 39
Ilsley, Velma *3:* 1; *7:* 55; *12:* 109; *37:* 62; *38:*
 184
Imai, Ayano *190:* 85, 86
in den Bosch, Nicole *150:* 204
Inga *1:* 142
Ingman, Bruce *134:* 50; *182:* 91, 92
Ingpen, Robert *109:* 103, 104; *132:* 138; *137:*
 177; *166:* 103; *181:* 140
Ingraham, Erick *21:* 177; *84:* 256; *103:* 66

Inkpen, Mick *99:* 104, 105; *106:* 44
Innerst, Stacy *149:* 104
Innocenti, Roberto *21:* 123; *96:* 122; *159:* 111,
 197; *199:* 176
Inoue, Yosuke *24:* 118
Iofin, Michael *97:* 157
Iosa, Ann *63:* 189
Ipcar, Dahlov *1:* 124, 125; *49:* 137, 138, 139,
 140, 141, 142,143, 144, 145; *147:* 122, 124,
 126
Irvin, Fred *13:* 166; *15:* 143, 144; *27:* 175
Irving, Jay *45:* 72
Irving, Laurence *27:* 50
Isaac, Joanne *21:* 76
Isaacs, Gary *170:* 188
Isadora, Rachel *43:* 159, 160; *54:* 31; *79:* 106,
 107,108; *121:* 100, 102; *165:* 116, 117; *204:*
 61, 63, 64
Ishmael, Woodi *24:* 111; *31:* 99
Ives, Ruth *15:* 257
Iwai, Melissa *149:* 233; *183:* 92; *199:* 115

J

Jabar, Cynthia *101:* 201
Jackness, Andrew *94:* 237
Jackson, Julian *91:* 104, 106
Jackson, Michael *43:* 42
Jackson, Shelley *79:* 71; *99:* 109; *187:* 82
Jacob, Murv *89:* 30
Jacobi, Kathy *62:* 118
Jacobs, Barbara *9:* 136
Jacobs, Lou, Jr. *9:* 136; *15:* 128
Jacobsen, Laura *176:* 98; *177:* 85, 86
Jacobson, Rick *131:* 222; *170:* 119
Jacobus, Tim *79:* 140; *109:* 126; *129:* 180
Jacques, Robin *1:* 70; *2:* 1; *8:* 46; *9:* 20; *15:*
 187; *19:* 253; *32:* 102, 103, 104; *43:* 184;
 73: 135; *YABC 1:* 42
Jaeggi, Yoshiko *186:* 184
Jaffee, Al *66:* 131, 132
Jagr, Miloslav *13:* 197
Jahn-Clough, Lisa *88:* 114; *152:* 104; *193:* 70,
 71
Jahnke, Robert *84:* 24
Jainschigg, Nicholas *80:* 64; *91:* 138; *95:* 63;
 99: 25; *108:* 50; *171:* 41
Jakesavic, Nenad *85:* 102
Jakobsen, Kathy *116:* 83
Jakubowski, Charles *14:* 192
Jambor, Louis *YABC 1:* 11
James, Ann *73:* 50; *82:* 113; *158:* 61; *183:* 44
James, Brian *140:* 91
James, Curtis E. *182:* 93
James, Derek *35:* 187; *44:* 91; *61:* 133; *74:* 2;
 80: 57; *86:* 88; *130:* 30; *179:* 29
James, Gilbert *YABC 1:* 43
James, Gordon C. *195:* 89
James, Harold *2:* 151; *3:* 62; *8:* 79; *29:* 113;
 51: 195; *74:* 90
James, Kennon *126:* 211
James, Robin *50:* 106; *53:* 32, 34, 35
James, Simon *202:* 73, 74
James, Will *19:* 150, 152, 153, 155, 163
Janosch
 See Eckert, Horst
Janovitch, Marilyn *68:* 168
Janovitz, Marilyn *87:* 187; *130:* 198; *194:* 91
Jansons, Inese *48:* 117
Jansson, Tove *3:* 90; *41:* 106, 108, 109, 110,
 111, 113, 114
Jaques, Faith *7:* 11, 132, 133; *21:* 83, 84; *69:*
 114,116; *73:* 170
Jaques, Frances Lee *29:* 224
Jarrett, Clare *201:* 77
Jauss, Anne Marie *1:* 139; *3:* 34; *10:* 57, 119;
 11: 205; *23:* 194
Jay, Alison *158:* 97, 98; *183:* 126, 127; *196:*
 95, 96, 97, 98; *200:* 72, 73, 74

Jeffers, Oliver *175:* 111
Jeffers, Susan *17:* 86, 87; *25:* 164, 165; *26:*
    112; *50:* 132, 134, 135; *70:* 111, 112, 113;
    137: 107, 108, 109, 110, 111; *202:* 77, 78
Jefferson, Louise E. *4:* 160
Jenkin-Pearce, Susie *78:* 16
Jenkins, Debra Reid *85:* 202; *114:* 89; *173:*
    134
Jenkins, Jean *98:* 79, 102
Jenkins, Leonard *157:* 169; *167:* 128; *189:* 96,
    97; *190:* 89
Jenkins, Patrick *72:* 126
Jenkins, Steve *124:* 177; *154:* 90, 91, 92, 93;
    185: 194; *188:* 81, 82, 83, 84, 85, 86
Jenks, Aleta *73:* 117; *124:* 225
Jenkyns, Chris *51:* 97
Jensen, Bruce *95:* 39
Jensinius, Kirsten *56:* 58
Jeram, Anita *89:* 135; *102:* 122, 123; *129:*
    112; *154:* 96, 97, 98; *164:* 154; *203:* 123,
    124
Jernigan, E. Wesley *85:* 92
Jerome, Karen A. *72:* 194
Jeruchim, Simon *6:* 173; *15:* 250
Jeschke, Susan *20:* 89; *39:* 161; *41:* 84; *42:*
    120
Jessel, Camilla *29:* 115
Jessell, Tim *159:* 3; *177:* 87; *181:* 95; *205:* 4
Jeyaveeran, Ruth *182:* 100
Jiang, Cheng An *109:* 108
Jiang, Wei *109:* 108
Jimenez, Maria *77:* 158; *93:* 127
Jobling, Curtis *138:* 74
Jocelyn, Marthe *118:* 83; *137:* 219; *163:* 119,
    120; *198:* 62
Joerns, Consuelo *38:* 36; *44:* 94
John, Diana *12:* 209
John, Helen *1:* 215; *28:* 204
Johns, Elizabeth *127:* 33
Johns, Jasper *61:* 172
Johns, Jeanne *24:* 114
Johnson, Adrian *143:* 50
Johnson, Bruce *9:* 47
Johnson, Cathy *92:* 136
Johnson, Crockett
    See Leisk, David
Johnson, D. William *23:* 104
Johnson, D.B. *183:* 98, 139
Johnson, David *175:* 18; *191:* 91
Johnson, Gillian *119:* 175; *164:* 217
Johnson, Harper *1:* 27; *2:* 33; *18:* 302; *19:* 61;
    31: 181; *44:* 46, 50, 95
Johnson, Ingrid *37:* 118
Johnson, James Ralph *1:* 23, 127
Johnson, James David *12:* 195
Johnson, Jane *48:* 136
Johnson, Joel Peter *98:* 18; *128:* 111; *201:* 13
Johnson, John E. *34:* 133
Johnson, Kevin *72:* 44
Johnson, Kevin Eugene *109:* 215
Johnson, Larry *47:* 56; *123:* 107; *159:* 203
Johnson, Layne *187:* 94; *209:* 63
Johnson, Margaret S. *35:* 131
Johnson, Meredith Merrell *71:* 181; *83:* 158;
    89: 103; *104:* 88
Johnson, Milton *1:* 67; *2:* 71; *26:* 45; *31:* 107;
    60: 112; *68:* 96
Johnson, Pamela *16:* 174; *52:* 145; *62:* 140;
    73: 116; *85:* 64
Johnson, Paul Brett *83:* 95; *132:* 119
Johnson, Stephen T. *80:* 15; *131:* 35; *141:* 96;
    145: 40; *164:* 187; *175:* 32; *189:* 99, 100;
    208: 43
Johnson, Steve *138:* 219; *141:* 64; *144:* 199;
    177: 51
Johnson, William R. *38:* 91
Johnson-Petrov, Arden *115:* 206
Johnston, David McCall *50:* 131, 133
Johnston, Lynne *118:* 85, 87, 89
Johnstone, Anne *8:* 120; *36:* 89
Johnstone, Janet Grahame *8:* 120; *36:* 89

Jonas, Ann *50:* 107, 108, 109; *135:* 113
Jones, Bob *71:* 5; *77:* 199
Jones, Carol *5:* 131; *72:* 185, 186; *153:* 111,
    112
Jones, Chuck *53:* 70, 71
Jones, Davy *89:* 176
Jones, Douglas B. *185:* 192; *202:* 82
Jones, Elizabeth Orton *18:* 124, 126, 128, 129
Jones, Harold *14:* 88; *52:* 50
Jones, Holly *127:* 3
Jones, Jeff *41:* 64
Jones, Laurian *25:* 24, 27
Jones, Margaret *74:* 57
Jones, Noah Z. *182:* 37; *203:* 159
Jones, Randy *131:* 104
Jones, Richard *127:* 222
Jones, Robert *25:* 67
Jones, Wilfred *35:* 115; *YABC 1:* 163
Jordan, Charles *89:* 58
Jordan, Jess *158:* 136; *203:* 111
Jordan, Martin George *84:* 127
Jordan, Richard *84:* 36
Jorgenson, Andrea *91:* 111
Jorisch, Stéphane *153:* 56, 193; *177:* 29; *178:*
    138, 139; *187:* 23
Joseph, James *53:* 88
Joudrey, Ken *64:* 145; *78:* 6
Joyce, William *72:* 131, 132, 133, 134; *73:*
    227; *145:* 37
Joyner, Jerry *34:* 138
Joyner, Loraine M. *209:* 17
Juan, Ana *175:* 38; *179:* 111, 112
Jucker, Sita *5:* 93
Judge, Lita *192:* 99
Judkis, Jim *37:* 38
Juhasz, Victor *31:* 67
Jullian, Philippe *24:* 206; *25:* 203
Jung, Tom *91:* 217
Junge, Alexandra *183:* 37
Junge, Walter *67:* 150
Jupo, Frank *7:* 148, 149
Jurisch, Stephane *154:* 105
Justice, Martin *34:* 72

K

Kabatova-Taborska, Zdenka *107:* 153
Kachik, John *165:* 230
Kaczman, James *156:* 98
Kadair, Deborah Ousley *184:* 45, 89
Kahl, David *74:* 95; *97:* 35; *109:* 174; *110:*
    213; *198:* 15
Kahl, M.P. *37:* 83
Kahl, Virginia *48:* 138
Kahn, Katherine Janus *90:* 135
Kakimoo, Kozo *11:* 148
Kalett, Jim *48:* 159, 160, 161
Kalin, Victor *39:* 186
Kalis, Jennifer *207:* 82
Kalman, Maira *96:* 131, 132; *137:* 115
Kalmenoff, Matthew *22:* 191
Kalow, Gisela *32:* 105
Kamen, Gloria *1:* 41; *9:* 119; *10:* 178; *35:*
    157; *78:* 236; *98:* 82
Kaminsky, Jef *102:* 153
Kandell, Alice *35:* 133
Kane, Henry B. *14:* 90; *18:* 219, 220
Kane, Robert *18:* 131
Kanfer, Larry *66:* 141
Kangas, Juli *200:* 88
Kappes, Alfred *28:* 104
Karalus, Bob *41:* 157
Karas, G. Brian *80:* 60; *99:* 179; *115:* 41; *118:*
    50; *136:* 168; *145:* 166; *149:* 245; *159:* 65;
    171: 192; *178:* 142, 143; *202:* 38; *209:* 142
Karasz, Ilonka *128:* 163
Karlin, Eugene *10:* 63; *20:* 131
Karlin, Nurit *63:* 78; *103:* 110
Karpinski, Tony *134:* 160

Kasamatsu, Shiro *139:* 155
Kasparavicius, Kestutis *139:* 210
Kassian, Olena *64:* 94
Kastner, Jill *79:* 135; *117:* 84, 85
Kasuya, Masahiro *41:* 206, 207; *51:* 100
Kasza, Keiko *191:* 99, 100, 101, 102, 103
Katona, Robert *21:* 85; *24:* 126
Katz, Avi *199:* 55
Katz, Karen *158:* 123
Kauffer, E. McKnight *33:* 103; *35:* 127; *63:* 67
Kaufman, Angelika *15:* 156
Kaufman, Joe *33:* 119
Kaufman, John *13:* 158
Kaufman, Stuart *62:* 64; *68:* 226; *137:* 44
Kaufmann, John *1:* 174; *4:* 159; *8:* 43, 1; *10:*
    102; *18:* 133, 134; *22:* 251
Kaye, Graham *1:* 9; *67:* 7, 8
Kaye, M.M. *62:* 95
Kazalovski, Nata *40:* 205
Keane, Bil *4:* 135
Kearney, David *72:* 47; *121:* 83
Keating, Pamel T. *77:* 37
Keats, Ezra Jack *3:* 18, 105, 257; *14:* 101,
    102; *33:* 129; *57:* 79, 80, 82, 83, 84, 87
Keegan, Charles *166:* 211
Keegan, Marcia *9:* 122; *32:* 93
Keeler, Patricia A. *81:* 56; *183:* 102, 103
Keely, Jack *119:* 95
Keely, John *26:* 104; *48:* 214
Keen, Eliot *25:* 213
Keep, Richard C. *170:* 122
Keeping, Charles *9:* 124, 185; *15:* 28, 134; *18:*
    115; *44:* 194, 196; *47:* 25; *52:* 3; *54:* 156;
    69: 123, 124; *74:* 56; *155:* 9
Keeter, Susan *168:* 46; *183:* 192
Keith, Eros *4:* 98; *5:* 138; *31:* 29; *43:* 220; *52:*
    91, 92, 93, 94; *56:* 64, 66; *60:* 37; *79:* 93
Keleinikov, Andrei *65:* 101, 102
Kelen, Emery *13:* 115
Keller, A.J. *62:* 198
Keller, Arthur I. *26:* 106
Keller, Dick *36:* 123, 125
Keller, Holly *45:* 79; *76:* 118, 119, 120, 121;
    108: 137, 138, 140; *157:* 117, 118, 119
Keller, Katie *79:* 222; *93:* 108
Keller, Laurie *196:* 105, 106
Keller, Ronald *45:* 208
Kelley, Gary *183:* 105
Kelley, True *41:* 114, 115; *42:* 137; *75:* 35;
    92: 104, 105; *124:* 62; *130:* 100, 101; *179:*
    120, 121, 122; *192:* 251
Kellogg, Steven *8:* 96; *11:* 207; *14:* 130; *20:* ;
    201: 38 58; *29:* 140, 141; *30:* 35; *41:* 141;
    57: 89, 90, 92,93, 94, 96; *59:* 182; *73:* 141;
    77: 129; *130:* 105, 106; *177:* 94, 95, 96, 97;
    199: 57; *YABC 1:* 65, 73
Kelly, Billy *158:* 143
Kelly, Geoff *97:* 196; *112:* 25
Kelly, Irene *147:* 134
Kelly, John *194:* 186
Kelly, Joseph *174:* 94
Kelly, Kathleen M. *71:* 109
Kelly, Laura *89:* 217
Kelly, True *163:* 87
Kelly, Walt *18:* 136, 137, 138, 139, 140, 141,
    144, 145, 146, 148, 149
Kemble, E.W. *34:* 75; *44:* 178; *YABC 2:* 54,
    59
Kemly, Kathleen *209:* 165
Kemp-Welsh, Lucy *24:* 197; *100:* 214
Kendall, Jane *150:* 105; *186:* 109
Kendall, Peter *152:* 85
Kendrick, Dennis *79:* 213
Kennaway, Adrienne *60:* 55, 56; *171:* 88, 89
Kennedy, Doug *189:* 104
Kennedy, Paul Edward *6:* 190; *8:* 132; *33:* 120
Kennedy, Richard *3:* 93; *12:* 179; *44:* 193;
    100: 15; *YABC 1:* 57
Kent, Jack *24:* 136; *37:* 37; *40:* 81; *84:* 89;
    86: 150; *88:* 77

Kent, Rockwell *5:* 166; *6:* 129; *20:* 225, 226, 227,229; *59:* 144
Kenyon, Tony *81:* 201; *127:* 74
Kepes, Juliet *13:* 119
Kerins, Anthony *76:* 84
Kerr, Judity *24:* 137
Kerr, Phyllis Forbes *72:* 141
Kessler, Leonard *1:* 108; *7:* 139; *14:* 107, 227; *22:* 101; *44:* 96; *67:* 79; *82:* 123
Kest, Kristin *168:* 99; *173:* 23
Kesteven, Peter *35:* 189
Ketcham, Hank *28:* 140, 141, 142
Kettelkamp, Larry *2:* 164
Key, Alexander *8:* 99
Khalsa, Dayal Kaur *62:* 99
Kiakshuk *8:* 59
Kid, Tom *207:* 54
Kidd, Chip *94:* 23
Kidd, Richard *152:* 110
Kidd, Tom *64:* 199; *81:* 189; *185:* 173
Kiddell-Monroe, Joan *19:* 201; *55:* 59, 60; *87:* 174; *121:* 112
Kidder, Harvey *9:* 105; *80:* 41
Kidwell, Carl *43:* 145
Kieffer, Christa *41:* 89
Kiesler, Kate *110:* 105; *136:* 142
Kiff, Ken *40:* 45
Kilbride, Robert *37:* 100
Kilby, Don *141:* 144
Kim, David *201:* 79; *202:* 97
Kim, Glenn *99:* 82
Kimball, Anton *78:* 114; *119:* 105
Kimball, Yeffe *23:* 116; *37:* 88
Kimber, Murray *171:* 91
Kimmel, Warren *176:* 112
Kincade, Orin *34:* 116
Kindersley, Barnabas *96:* 110
Kindred, Wendy *7:* 151
King, Colin *53:* 3
King, Robin *10:* 164, 165
King, Stephen Michael *141:* 31; *197:* 191
King, Tara Calahan *139:* 172
King, Tony *39:* 121
Kingman, Dong *16:* 287; *44:* 100, 102, 104
Kingsley, Charles *YABC 2:* 182
Kingston, Julie *147:* 14
Kingston, Maxine Hong *53:* 92
Kinney, Jeff *187:* 97
Kipling, John Lockwood *YABC 2:* 198
Kipling, Rudyard *YABC 2:* 196
Kipniss, Robert *29:* 59
Kirchherr, Astrid *55:* 23
Kirchhoff, Art *28:* 136
Kirk, Daniel *153:* 115, 116, 117; *173:* 101; *196:* 113, 114, 115, 116
Kirk, David *117:* 88, 89; *161:* 97, 98
Kirk, Ruth *5:* 96
Kirk, Steve *170:* 37
Kirk, Tim *32:* 209, 211; *72:* 89; *83:* 49
Kirmse, Marguerite *15:* 283; *18:* 153
Kirsch, Vincent X. *124:* 207
Kirschner, Ruth *22:* 154
Kirwan, Wednesday *198:* 73
Kish, Ely *73:* 119; *79:* 2
Kitamura, Satoshi *62:* 102; *98:* 91; *101:* 147; *138:* 2; *143:* 83, 85, 86; *201:* 83
Kiss, Andrew *168:* 115
Kitchel, JoAnn E. *133:* 32
Kitchen, Bert *70:* 126; *193:* 49
Kittelsen, Theodor *62:* 14
Kiuchi, Tatsuro *114:* 71
Kiwak, Barbara *172:* 135
Klahr, Susan *176:* 196
Klapholz, Mel *13:* 35
Klee, Jutte *209:* 136
Klein, Bill *89:* 105
Klein, Robert *55:* 77
Klein, Suzanna *63:* 104
Kleinman, Zalman *28:* 143
Kleven, Elisa *173:* 96, 97
Kliban, B. *35:* 137, 138

Kline, Michael *127:* 66
Klise, M. Sarah *180:* 117, 118; *181:* 97
Knabel, Lonnie *73:* 103; *75:* 187, 228; *194:* 216
Kneen, Maggie *140:* 139
Knight, Ann *34:* 143
Knight, Christopher *13:* 125
Knight, Hilary *1:* 233; *3:* 21; *15:* 92, 158, 159; *16:* 258, 259, 260; *18:* 235; *19:* 169; *35:* 242; *46:* 167; *52:* 116; *69:* 126, 127; *132:* 129; *YABC 1:* 168, 169, 172
Knorr, Laura *200:* 91
Knorr, Peter *126:* 92, 93
Knotts, Howard *20:* 4; *25:* 170; *36:* 163
Knutson, Barbara *112:* 134; *202:* 108
Knutson, Kimberley *115:* 90
Kobayashi, Ann *39:* 58
Kochalka, James *196:* 120, 121, 122
Kocsis, J.C.
    See Paul, James
Kodman, Stanislawa *201:* 85
Koehler, Hanne Lore *176:* 203
Koehn, Ilse *34:* 198; *79:* 123
Koelsch, Michael *99:* 182; *107:* 164; *109:* 239; *138:* 142; *150:* 94; *176:* 105; *187:* 63; *198:* 63
Koering, Ursula *3:* 28; *4:* 14; *44:* 5; *64:* 140,141; *85:* 46
Koerner, Henry
    See Koerner, W.H.D.
Koerner, W.H.D. *14:* 216; *21:* 88, 89, 90, 91; *23:* 211
Koetsch, Mike *166:* 68
Koffler, Camilla *36:* 113
Kogan, Deborah Ray *161:* 101, 102
Koide, Yasuko *50:* 114
Kolado, Karen *102:* 228
Komoda, Kiyo *9:* 128; *13:* 214
Kompaneyets, Marc *169:* 92
Konashevich, Vladimir *61:* 160
Konashevicha, V. *YABC 1:* 26
Konigsburg, E.L. *4:* 138; *48:* 141, 142, 144, 145; *94:* 129, 130; *126:* 129, 130, 131; *194:* 95, 98
Kono, Erin Eitter *177:* 99
Kooiker, Leonie *48:* 148
Koonook, Simon *65:* 157
Koontz, Robin Michal *136:* 155
Koopmans, Loek *101:* 121
Kopelke, Lisa *154:* 107
Kopper, Lisa *72:* 152, 153; *105:* 135, 136
Korach, Mimi *1:* 128, 129; *2:* 52; *4:* 39; *5:* 159; *9:* 129; *10:* 21; *24:* 69
Koren, Edward *5:* 100; *65:* 65, 67
Kosaka, Fumi *164:* 130
Koscielniak, Bruce *99:* 122; *153:* 120, 121, 122
Koshkin, Alexander *92:* 180
Kossin, Sandy *10:* 71; *23:* 105
Kostin, Andrej *26:* 204
Kosturko, Bob *164:* 56
Kotzky, Brian *68:* 184
Kovacevic, Zivojin *13:* 247
Kovalski, Maryann *58:* 120; *84:* 88; *97:* 124, 125, 126; *158:* 3; *186:* 80
Kozjan, Drazen *209:* 99
Krahn, Fernando *2:* 257; *34:* 206; *49:* 152
Kramer, Anthony *33:* 81
Kramer, David *96:* 162; *109:* 132; *150:* 220
Kramer, Frank *6:* 121
Krantz, Kathy *35:* 83
Kratter, Paul *139:* 65
Kraus, Robert *13:* 217; *65:* 113; *93:* 93, 94
Krause, Jon *176:* 62
Krauss, Trisha *174:* 10
Kredel, Fritz *6:* 35; *17:* 93, 94, 95, 96; *22:* 147; *24:* 175; *29:* 130; *35:* 77; *YABC 2:* 166, 300
Kreloff, Eliot *189:* 107, 108; *205:* 182
Krementz, Jill *17:* 98; *49:* 41
Krenina, Katya *117:* 106; *125:* 133; *176:* 117

Kresin, Robert *23:* 19
Krieger, Salem *54:* 164
Kriegler, Lyn *73:* 29
Krinitz, Esther Nisenthal *193:* 196
Krommes, Beth *128:* 141; *149:* 136; *181:* 100, 101; *184:* 105; *188:* 125; *208:* 135; *209:* 185
Krone, Mike *101:* 71
Kronheimer, Ann *135:* 119
Krosoczka, Jarrett J. *155:* 142; *200:* 93, 94
Kruck, Gerald *88:* 181
Krudop, Walter Lyon *199:* 19
Krupinski, Loretta *67:* 104; *102:* 131; *161:* 105, 106
Krupp, Robin Rector *53:* 96, 98
Krush, Beth *1:* 51, 85; *2:* 233; *4:* 115; *9:* 61; *10:* 191; *11:* 196; *18:* 164, 165; *32:* 72; *37:* 203; *43:* 57; *60:* 102, 103, 107, 108, 109
Krush, Joe *2:* 233; *4:* 115; *9:* 61; *10:* 191; *11:* 196; *18:* 164, 165; *32:* 72, 91; *37:* 203; *43:* 57; *60:* 102, 103, 107, 108, 109
Krych, Duane *91:* 43
Krykorka, Vladyana *96:* 147; *143:* 90, 91; *168:* 14
Kubick, Dana *165:* 91
Kubinyi, Laszlo *4:* 116; *6:* 113; *16:* 118; *17:* 100; *28:* 227; *30:* 172; *49:* 24, 28; *54:* 23; *167:* 149
Kubricht, Mary *73:* 118
Kucharik, Elena *139:* 31
Kuchera, Kathleen *84:* 5
Kuhn, Bob *17:* 91; *35:* 235
Kulikov, Boris *163:* 185; *185:* 23; *205:* 99, 100
Kulka, Joe *188:* 110
Kukalis, Romas *90:* 27; *139:* 37
Kuklin, Susan *63:* 82, 83, 84
Kunhardt, Dorothy *53:* 101
Kunhardt, Edith *67:* 105, 106
Kunstler, Mort *10:* 73; *32:* 143
Kurchevsky, V. *34:* 61
Kurczok, Belinda *121:* 118
Kurelek, William *8:* 107
Kuriloff, Ron *13:* 19
Kurisu, Jane *160:* 120
Kuskin, Karla *2:* 170; *68:* 115, 116; *111:* 116
Kutzer, Ernst *19:* 249
Kuzma, Steve *57:* 8; *62:* 93
Kuznetsova, Berta *74:* 45
Kvasnosky, Laura McGee *93:* 103; *142:* 83; *182:* 108
Kwas, Susan Estelle *179:* 116
Kyong, Yunmee *165:* 139

L

LaBlanc, Andre *24:* 146
Laboccetta, Mario *27:* 120
LaBrose, Darcie *157:* 134
Labrosse, Darcia *58:* 88; *108:* 77; *178:* 89
LaCava, Vince *95:* 118
Laceky, Adam *32:* 121
Lacis, Astra *85:* 117
Lacome, Julie *174:* 96, 97
La Croix *YABC 2:* 4
Ladd, London *206:* 50
Ladwig, Tim *98:* 212; *117:* 76
La Farge, Margaret *47:* 141
LaFave, Kim *64:* 177; *72:* 39; *97:* 146; *99:* 172; *106:* 123; *149:* 126; *196:* 128, 129
Lafontaine, Roger *167:* 158
Lafrance, Marie *197:* 109
Lagarrigue, Jerome *136:* 102; *187:* 81
Laimgruber, Monika *11:* 153
Laite, Gordon *1:* 130, 131; *8:* 209; *31:* 113; *40:* 63; *46:* 117
Laliberté, Louise-Andrée *169:* 98
LaMarche, Jim *46:* 204; *61:* 56; *94:* 69; *114:* 22; *129:* 163; *162:* 78, 80
Lamb, Jim *10:* 117

Lambase, Barbara *101:* 185; *150:* 221; *166:* 234
Lambert, J.K. *38:* 129; *39:* 24
Lambert, Sally Anne *133:* 191
Lambert, Saul *23:* 112; *33:* 107; *54:* 136
Lambert, Stephen *109:* 33; *174:* 99
Lambo, Don *6:* 156; *35:* 115; *36:* 146
Lamontagne, Jacques *166:* 227
Lamut, Sonja *57:* 193
Lamut, Sonya *85:* 102
Landa, Peter *11:* 95; *13:* 177; *53:* 119
Landau, Jacob *38:* 111
Landis, Joan *104:* 23; *203:* 32
Landon, Lucinda *79:* 31
Landshoff, Ursula *13:* 124
Landström, Lena *146:* 165, 166
Landström, Olof *146:* 166, 168; *170:* 22
Lane, Daniel *112:* 60
Lane, John R. *8:* 145
Lane, John *15:* 176, 177; *30:* 146
Lane, Nancy *166:* 74
Lang, G.D. *48:* 56
Lang, Gary *73:* 75
Lang, Jerry *18:* 295
Langdo, Bryan *186:* 187; *191:* 113, 114, 115
Lange, Dorothea *50:* 141
Langley, Jonathan *162:* 128
Langner, Nola *8:* 110; *42:* 36
Lanino, Deborah *105:* 148
Lantz, Paul *1:* 82, 102; *27:* 88; *34:* 102; *45:* 123
Larkin, Bob *84:* 225
Laroche, Giles *126:* 140; *146:* 81
LaRochelle, David *171:* 97
Larrecq, John *44:* 108; *68:* 56
Larsen, Suzanne *1:* 13
Larson, Gary *57:* 121, 122, 123, 124, 125, 126, 127
Larsson, Carl *35:* 144, 145, 146, 147, 148, 149, 150, 152, 153, 154
Larsson, Karl *19:* 177
Lartitegui, Ana G. *105:* 167
LaRue, Jenna *167:* 20
La Rue, Michael D. *13:* 215
Lasker, Joe *7:* 186, 187; *14:* 55; *38:* 115; *39:* 47; *83:* 113, 114, 115
Latham, Barbara *16:* 188, 189; *43:* 71
Lathrop, Dorothy *14:* 117, 118, 119; *15:* 109; *16:* 78, 79, 81; *32:* 201, 203; *33:* 112; *YABC 2:* 301
Lattimore, Eleanor Frances *7:* 156
Lauden, Claire *16:* 173
Lauden, George, Jr. *16:* 173
Laune, Paul *2:* 235; *34:* 31
Laure, Jason *49:* 53; *50:* 122
Lauter, Richard *63:* 29; *67:* 111; *77:* 198
Lavallee, Barbara *74:* 157; *92:* 154; *96:* 126; *145:* 193; *166:* 125, 126; *186:* 155; *192:* 172
Lave, Fitz Hugh *59:* 139
Lavis, Stephen *43:* 143; *87:* 137, 164, 165
Layton, Neal *152:* 120, 121; *182:* 65; *187:* 103, 105, 106
Law, Jenny *201:* 31
Lawrason, June *168:* 30
Lawrence, John *25:* 131; *30:* 141; *44:* 198, 200
Lawrence, Stephen *20:* 195
Lawson, Carol *6:* 38; *42:* 93, 131; *174:* 56; *189:* 89; *209:* 59
Lawson, George *17:* 280
Lawson, Robert *5:* 26; *6:* 94; *13:* 39; *16:* 11; *20:* 100, 102, 103; *54:* 3; *66:* 12; *100:* 144, 145; *YABC 2:* 222, 224, 225, 227, 228, 229, 230, 231, 232, 233, 234, 235, 237, 238, 239, 240, 241
Layfield, Kathie *60:* 194
Lazare, Jerry *44:* 109; *74:* 28
Lazarevich, Mila *17:* 118
Lazarus, Claire *103:* 30
Lazarus, Keo Felker *21:* 94
Lazzaro, Victor *11:* 126

Lea, Bob *166:* 208; *203:* 108
Lea, Tom *43:* 72, 74
Leacroft, Richard *6:* 140
Leaf, Munro *20:* 99
Leake, Donald *70:* 41
Leander, Patricia *23:* 27
Lear, Edward *18:* 183, 184, 185
Lear, Rebecca *149:* 46
Lebenson, Richard *6:* 209; *7:* 76; *23:* 145; *44:* 191; *87:* 153
Le Cain, Errol *6:* 141; *9:* 3; *22:* 142; *25:* 198; *28:* 173; *68:* 128, 129; *86:* 49
Lechon, Daniel *113:* 211
Leder, Dora *129:* 172
Ledger, Bill *181:* 58
Leduc, Bernard *102:* 36
Lee, Alan *62:* 25, 28
Lee, Bryce *99:* 60; *101:* 195; *196:* 53
Lee, Chinlun *181:* 138; *182:* 112
Lee, Declan *191:* 20
Lee, Dom *83:* 118, 120; *93:* 123; *121:* 121, 126; *146:* 174, 175, 206, 207; *174:* 204
Lee, Doris *13:* 246; *32:* 183; *44:* 111
Lee, Hector Viveros *115:* 96
Lee, Ho Baek *200:* 160
Lee, Jeanne M. *158:* 56
Lee, Jared *93:* 200; *157:* 229
Lee, Jody *81:* 121; *82:* 225; *91:* 155; *100:* 182
Lee, Jody A. *127:* 124, 126, 127
See also Lee, Jody
Lee, Manning de V. *2:* 200; *17:* 12; *27:* 87; *37:* 102, 103, 104; *YABC 2:* 304
Lee, Marie G. *138:* 157
Lee, Paul *97:* 100; *105:* 72, 209; *109:* 177; *128:* 113; *202:* 45
Lee, Robert J. *3:* 97; *67:* 124
Lee, Victor *96:* 228; *105:* 182; *140:* 196; *208:* 191
Lee, Virginia *208:* 139, 140
Leech, Dorothy *98:* 76
Leech, John *15:* 59
Leedy, Loreen *84:* 142; *128:* 144, 145, 146; *175:* 125, 126, 127
Leeman, Michael *44:* 157
Leeming, Catherine *87:* 39
Lees, Harry *6:* 112
LeFever, Bill *88:* 220, 221
Legenisel *47:* 111
Legrand, Edy *8:* 89, 93
Lehman, Barbara *73:* 123; *170:* 130
Lehrman, Rosalie *2:* 180
Leichman, Seymour *5:* 107
Leick, Bonnie *205:* 104
Leighton, Clare *25:* 130; *33:* 168; *37:* 105, 106, 108,109
Leisk, David *1:* 140, 141; *11:* 54; *30:* 137, 142, 143,144
Leister, Brian *89:* 45; *106:* 37; *114:* 67; *149:* 236
Leloir, Maurice *18:* 77, 80, 83, 99
Lemaître, Pascal *144:* 175; *176:* 130; *189:* 135
Lemieux, Michele *100:* 148; *139:* 153
Lemke, Horst *14:* 98; *38:* 117, 118, 119
Lemke, R.W. *42:* 162
Lemon, David Gwynne *9:* 1
LeMoult, Adolph *82:* 116
Lenn, Michael *136:* 89
Lennon, John *114:* 100
Lennox, Elsie *95:* 163; *143:* 160
Lenski, Lois *1:* 144; *26:* 135, 137, 139, 141; *100:* 153, 154
Lent, Blair *1:* 116, 117; *2:* 174; *3:* 206, 207; *7:* 168, 169; *34:* 62; *68:* 217; *133:* 101; *183:* 60
Leonard, Richard *91:* 128
Leonard, Tom *207:* 95
Leone, Leonard *49:* 190
Lerner, Carol *86:* 140, 141, 142
Lerner, Judith *116:* 138
Lerner, Sharon *11:* 157; *22:* 56
Leroux-Hugon, Helene *132:* 139

Leslie, Cecil *19:* 244
Lessac, Frané *80:* 182, 207; *96:* 182; *202:* 58; *209:* 104
Lessing, Erich *167:* 52; *173:* 60
Lester, Alison *50:* 124; *90:* 147, 148; *129:* 130
Lester, Mike *208:* 50
Lethcoe, Jason *191:* 116, 117
Le Tord, Bijou *49:* 156; *95:* 112
Leutz, Emanuel *165:* 27
Levai, Blaise *39:* 130
Levin, Ted *12:* 148
Levine, David *43:* 147, 149, 150, 151, 152; *64:* 11
Levine, Joe *71:* 88
Levine, Marge *81:* 127
Levinson, David *178:* 232
Levit, Herschel *24:* 223
Levstek, Ljuba *131:* 192; *134:* 216; *149:* 65; *168:* 180
Levy, Jessica Ann *19:* 225; *39:* 191
Levy, Lina *117:* 126
Lewin, Betsy *32:* 114; *48:* 177; *90:* 151; *91:* 125; *92:* 85; *115:* 105; *169:* 110, 111; *178:* 47; *186:* 188; *194:* 201
Lewin, Ted *4:* 77; *8:* 168; *20:* 110; *21:* 99,100; *27:* 110; *28:* 96, 97; *31:* 49; *45:* 55; *48:* 223; *60:* 20, 119, 120; *62:* 139; *66:* 108; *71:* 12; *72:* 21; *74:* 226; *76:* 139, 140; *77:* 82; *79:* 87; *85:* 49, 177; *86:* 55; *88:* 182; *93:* 28, 29; *94:* 34, 182, 194; *99:* 156; *104:* 8; *115:* 123; *118:* 74; *119:* 114, 116; *131:* 54; *145:* 99; *165:* 151; *177:* 75; *178:* 42; *190:* 30; *192:* 86; *195:* 101, 102; *203:* 52
Lewis, Allen *15:* 112
Lewis, E.B. *88:* 143; *93:* 109; *119:* 79; *124:* 113; *128:* 49; *151:* 167; *168:* 110; *173:* 121; *174:* 66; *176:* 7; *184:* 150; *185:* 191
Lewis, H.B. *170:* 124
Lewis, J. Patrick *162:* 83
Lewis, Jan *81:* 22
Lewis, Kim *136:* 165
Lewis, Richard W. *52:* 25
Lewis, Robin Baird *98:* 193
Leydon, Rita Floden *21:* 101
Li, Xiojun *187:* 172
Liao, Jimmy *202:* 100
Lichtenheld, Tom *152:* 125, 126
Lieblich, Irene *22:* 173; *27:* 209, 214
Lieder, Rick *108:* 197; *199:* 58, 59, 60
Lies, Brian *92:* 40; *141:* 101; *150:* 138; *190:* 97, 98, 99,
Liese, Charles *4:* 222
Life, Kay *79:* 49
Lifton, Robert Jay *66:* 154
Lightburn, Ron *86:* 153; *91:* 122
Lightfoot, Norman R. *45:* 47
Lignell, Lois *37:* 114
Lill, Debra *121:* 70
Lilly, Charles *8:* 73; *20:* 127; *48:* 53; *72:* 9,16; *77:* 98; *102:* 94
Lilly, Ken *37:* 224
Lim, John *43:* 153
Limona, Mercedes *51:* 183
Lin, Grace *143:* 217; *162:* 86, 87; *174:* 185
Lincoln, Patricia Henderson *27:* 27; *78:* 127
Lindahn, Ron *84:* 17
Lindahn, Val *84:* 17
Lindberg, Howard *10:* 123; *16:* 190
Lindberg, Jeffrey *64:* 77; *77:* 71; *79:* 54; *80:* 149; *174:* 109; *179:* 52
Linden, Seymour *18:* 200, 201; *43:* 140
Lindenbaum, Pija *144:* 143; *183:* 113
Linder, Richard *27:* 119
Lindman, Maj *43:* 154
Lindsay, Norman *67:* 114
Lindsay, Vachel *40:* 118
Lindstrom, Jack *145:* 118
Line, Les *27:* 143
Linell
See Smith, Linell
Lionni, Leo *8:* 115; *72:* 159, 160, 161

Lipinsky, Lino 2: 156; 22: 175
Lippincott, Gary A. 70: 35; 119: 118
Lippman, Peter 8: 31; 31: 119, 120, 160
Lisi, Victoria 89: 145
Lisker, Emily 169: 114
Lisker, Sonia O. 16: 274; 31: 31; 44: 113, 114
Lisowski, Gabriel 47: 144; 49: 157
Lissim, Simon 17: 138
Little, Ed 89: 145; 151: 53
Little, Harold 16: 72
Little, Mary E. 28: 146
Littlewood, Karen 165: 126
Litty, Julie 111: 63
Litzinger, Rosanne 151: 101; 176: 118; 196: 133, 134, 135; 208: 129; 209: 147
Liu, Lesley 143: 72
Lively, Lorna 19: 216
Livingston, Susan 95: 22
Liwska, Renata 164: 113; 199: 25, 69
Ljungkvist, Laura 180: 120
Llerena, Carlos Antonio 19: 181
Lloyd, Errol 11: 39; 22: 178
Lloyd, Megan 77: 118; 80: 113; 97: 75; 117: 94, 95; 189: 121, 122; 208: 128
Lloyd, Sam 183: 116, 117
Lo, Beth 165: 154
Lo, Koon-chiu 7: 134
Loates, Glen 63: 76
Lobel, Anita 6: 87; 9: 141; 18: 248; 55: 85,86, 87, 88, 93, 104; 60: 67; 78: 263; 82: 110; 96: 157, 159; 101: 84; 132: 35; 162: 93, 94
Lobel, Arnold 1: 188, 189; 5: 12; 6: 147; 7: 167, 209; 18: 190, 191; 25: 39, 43; 27: 40; 29: 174; 52: 127; 55: 89, 91, 94, 95, 97, 98, 99, 100, 101, 102,103, 105, 106; 60: 18, 31; 66: 181, 183; 75: 57; 82: 246; 136: 146
Lobel, Gillian 190: 21
Locker, Thomas 109: 134
Lodge, Bernard 107: 125, 126; 153: 93
Loeb, Jeph 153: 177
Lodge, Jo 112: 119
Loefgren, Ulf 3: 108
Loescher, Ann 20: 108
Loescher, Gil 20: 108
Loew, David 93: 184; 171: 120
Lofting, Hugh 15: 182, 183; 100: 161, 162
Lofts, Pamela 60: 188
Loh, George 38: 88
Lomberg, Jon 58: 160
Lonette, Reisie 11: 211; 12: 168; 13: 56; 36: 122; 43: 155
Long, Ethan 168: 146; 178: 12; 182: 120, 121; 196: 124
Long, Laurel 162: 135; 190: 11; 203: 113, 114
Long, Loren 99: 176; 172: 65; 182: 78; 188: 114, 115
Long, Melinda 152: 128
Long, Miles 115: 174
Long, Sally 42: 184
Long, Sylvia 74: 168; 132: 63; 179: 134
Longoni, Eduardo 73: 85
Longtemps, Ken 17: 123; 29: 221; 69: 82
Looser, Heinz YABC 2: 208
Lopez, Loretta 190: 100
López, Rafael 197: 160; 198: 85
Lopshire, Robert 6: 149; 21: 117; 34: 166; 73: 13
Lord, John Vernon 21: 104; 23: 25; 51: 22
Lorenz, Albert 40: 146; 115: 127
Loretta, Sister Mary 33: 73
Lorraine, Walter H. 3: 110; 4: 123; 16: 192; 103: 119
Los, Marek 146: 22; 193: 23
Loss, Joan 11: 163
Louderback, Walt YABC 1: 164
Lousada, Sandra 40: 138
Louth, Jack 149: 252; 151: 191, 192
Love, Judy 173: 43; 196: 40
Low, Joseph 14: 124, 125; 18: 68; 19: 194; 31: 166; 80: 239

Low, William 62: 175; 80: 147; 112: 194; 150: 202; 169: 175; 177: 110; 192: 27
Lowe, Vicky 177: 130
Lowenheim, Alfred 13: 65, 66
Lowenstein, Sallie 116: 90, 91
Lowitz, Anson 17: 124; 18: 215
Lowrey, Jo 8: 133
Lubach, Vanessa 142: 152
Lubell, Winifred 1: 207; 3: 15; 6: 151
Lubin, Leonard B. 19: 224; 36: 79, 80; 45: 128, 129,131, 132, 133, 134, 135, 136, 137, 139, 140, 141; 70: 95; YABC2: 96
Lucas, David 208: 148
Lucht, Irmgard 82: 145
Ludwig, Helen 33: 144, 145
Lufkin, Raymond 38: 138; 44: 48
Luhrs, Henry 7: 123; 11: 120
Lujan, Tonita 82: 33
Lupo, Dom 4: 204
Lustig, Loretta 30: 186; 46: 134, 135, 136, 137
Luthardt, Kevin 172: 125, 126
Luxbacher, Irene 153: 145
Luzak, Dennis 52: 121; 99: 142
Lydbury, Jane 82: 98
Lydecker, Laura 21: 113; 42: 53
Lynch, Charles 16: 33
Lynch, Marietta 29: 137; 30: 171
Lynch, P.J. 126: 228; 129: 110; 132: 247; 183: 64; 207: 184
Lyne, Alison Davis 188: 118, 198
Lyon, Carol 102: 26
Lyon, Elinor 6: 154
Lyon, Fred 14: 16
Lyon, Tammie 175: 170
Lyons, Oren 8: 193
Lyster, Michael 26: 41

M

Maas, Dorothy 6: 175
Maas, Julie 47: 61
Macaulay, David 46: 139, 140, 141, 142, 143, 144, 145, 147, 149, 150; 72: 167, 168, 169; 137: 129, 130, 131, 132
MacCarthy, Patricia 69: 141
Macdonald, Alister 21: 55
Macdonald, Roberta 19: 237; 52: 164
MacDonald, Norman 13: 99
MacDonald, Ross 201: 103
MacDonald, Suse 54: 41; 109 138; 130: 156; 193: 106, 107, 109, 110
Mace, Varian 49: 159
MacEachern, Stephen 206: 2
Macguire, Robert Reid 18: 67
Machetanz, Fredrick 34: 147, 148
MacInnes, Ian 35: 59
MacIntyre, Elisabeth 17: 127, 128
Mack, Jeff 161: 128; 194: 119, 120
Mack, Stan 17: 129; 96: 33
Mackay, Donald 17: 60
MacKaye, Arvia 32: 119
Mackenzie, Robert 204: 78
Mackenzie, Stuart 73: 213
MacKenzie, Garry 33: 159
Mackie, Clare 87: 134
Mackinlay, Miguel 27: 22
MacKinstry, Elizabeth 15: 110; 42: 139, 140, 141, 142, 143,144, 145
MacLeod, Lee 91: 167
Maclise, Daniel YABC 2: 257
Macnaughton, Tina 182: 145
MacRae, Tom 181: 112
Madden, Don 3: 112, 113; 4: 33, 108, 155; 7: 193; 78: 12; YABC 2: 211
Maddison, Angela Mary 10: 83
Madsen, Jim 146: 259; 152: 237; 184: 106; 197: 21; 202: 103, 104

Maestro, Giulio 8: 124; 12: 17; 13: 108; 25: 182; 54: 147; 59: 114, 115, 116, 117, 118, 121, 123, 124, 125,126, 127; 68: 37, 38; 106: 129, 130, 131, 136, 137, 138
Maffia, Daniel 60: 200
Maggio, Viqui 58: 136, 181; 74: 150; 75: 90; 85: 159; 90: 158; 109: 184; 193: 113
Magnus, Erica 77: 123
Magnuson, Diana 28: 102; 34: 190; 41: 175
Magoon, Scott 181: 104
Magovern, Peg 103: 123
Maguire, Sheila 41: 100
Magurn, Susan 91: 30
Mahony, Will 37: 120
Mahony, Will 85: 116
Mahood, Kenneth 24: 141
Mahurin, Matt 164: 225; 175: 95; 189: 37; 196: 14; 209: 163
Maik, Henri 9: 102
Maione, Heather 106: 5; 178: 8; 189: 126, 127; 193: 58
Maisto, Carol 29: 87
Maitland, Antony 1: 100, 176; 8: 41; 17: 246; 24: 46; 25: 177, 178; 32: 74; 60: 65, 195; 67: 156; 87: 131; 101: 110
Majewski, Dawn W. 169: 95
Mak, Kam 72: 25; 75: 43; 87: 186; 97: 24; 102: 154; 149: 195; 186: 28; 209: 132
Makie, Pam 37: 117
Maktima, Joe 116: 191
Maland, Nick 99: 77
Male, Alan 132: 64
Malone, James Hiram 84: 161
Malone, Nola Langner 82: 239
Malone, Peter 191: 121, 122, 123
Malsberg, Edward 51: 175
Malvern, Corinne 2: 13; 34: 148, 149
Manchess, Gregory 165: 241; 203: 119
Mancusi, Stephen 63: 198, 199
Mandelbaum, Ira 31: 115
Manders, John 138: 152, 155; 188: 171; 190: 92; 199: 5
Manet, Edouard 23: 170
Mangiat, Jeff 173: 127
Mangurian, David 14: 133
Manham, Allan 42: 109; 77: 180; 80: 227
Manley, Matt 103: 167; 117: 98; 172: 49
Manna, Giovanni 178: 44
Manniche, Lise 31: 121
Manning, Jane 96: 203
Manning, Jo 63: 154
Manning, Lawrence 191: 153
Manning, Mick 176: 139
Manning, Samuel F. 5: 75
Mantel, Richard 57: 73; 63: 106; 82: 255
Mantha, John 205: 164
Maraja 15: 86; YABC 1: 28; 2: 115
Marcellino, Fred 20: 125; 34: 222; 53: 125; 58: 205; 61: 64, 121, 122; 68: 154, 156, 157, 158, 159; 72: 25; 86: 184; 98: 181; 118: 129, 130, 131; 149: 218; 194: 7
Marchesi, Stephen 34: 140; 46: 72; 50: 147; 66: 239; 70: 33; 73: 18, 114, 163; 77: 47, 76,147; 78: 79; 80: 30; 81: 6; 89: 66; 93: 21,130; 94: 94; 97: 66; 98: 96; 114: 115, 116
Marchiori, Carlos 14: 60
Marciano, John Bemelmans 118: 133; 167: 110, 111, 112
Marcus, Barry David 139: 248; 145: 18
Maren, Julie 199: 73
Margules, Gabriele 21: 120
Mariana
    See Foster, Marian Curtis
Mariano, Michael 52: 108
Marino, Dorothy 6: 37; 14: 135
Mario, Heide Stetson 101: 202
Maris, Ron 71: 123
Maritz, Nicolaas 85: 123
Mark, Mona 65: 105; 68: 205; 116: 213
Markham, R.L. 17: 240

Marks, Alan *104:* 104; *109:* 182; *164:* 92; *185:* 134; *187:* 120, 121, 122
Marks, Cara *54:* 9
Marks, Colin *203:* 129
Marokvia, Artur *31:* 122
Marquez, Susan *108:* 121
Marrella, Maria Pia *62:* 116
Marriott, Pat *30:* 30; *34:* 39; *35:* 164, 165, 166; *44:* 170; *48:* 186, 187, 188, 189, 191, 192, 193; *91:* 92
Mars, W.T. *1:* 161; *3:* 115; *4:* 208, 225; *5:* 92, 105, 186; *8:* 214; *9:* 12; *13:* 121; *27:* 151; *31:* 180; *38:* 102; *48:* 66; *62:* 164, 165; *64:* 62; *68:* 229; *79:* 55
Marschall, Ken *85:* 29
Marsh, Christine *3:* 164
Marsh, James *73:* 137
Marsh, Reginald *17:* 5; *19:* 89; *22:* 90, 96
Marshall, Anthony D. *18:* 216
Marshall, Felicia *170:* 190
Marshall, James *6:* 160; *40:* 221; *42:* 24, 25, 29; *51:* 111, 112, 113, 114, 115, 116, 117, 118, 119, 120, 121; *64:* 13; *75:* 126, 127, 128, 129; *102:* 10, 12
Marshall, Janet *97:* 154
Marstall, Bob *55:* 145; *84:* 153, 170; *104:* 145; *154:* 166, 167, 168
Martchenko, Michael *50:* 129, 153, 155, 156, 157; *83:* 144,145; *154:* 137, 138, 139
Marten, Ruth *129:* 52
Martin, Brad *199:* 186
Martin, Charles E. *70:* 144
Martin, David Stone *24:* 232; *62:* 4
Martin, Fletcher *18:* 213; *23:* 151
Martin, Rene *7:* 144; *42:* 148, 149, 150
Martin, Richard E. *51:* 157; *131:* 203
Martin, Ron *32:* 81
Martin, Stefan *8:* 68; *32:* 124, 126; *56:* 33
Martin, Whitney *166:* 137
Martinez, Ed *58:* 192; *72:* 231; *77:* 33; *80:* 214; *167:* 123
Martinez, John *6:* 113; *118:* 13; *139:* 143
Martinez, Sergio *158:* 190
Martini, Angela *183:* 161
Martiniere, Stephan *171:* 130
Marton, Jirina *95:* 127, 128; *144:* 145
Martorell, Antonio *84:* 6; *97:* 161
Martucci, Griesbach *52:* 106
Marvin, Frederic *83:* 86
Marx, Robert F. *24:* 143
Marzollo, Jean *190:* 127
Masefield, Judith *19:* 208, 209
Masheris, Robert *78:* 51
Masiello, Ralph *186:* 171
Mason, George F. *14:* 139
Mason, Robert *84:* 96
Masse, Josée *208:* 45
Massey, Barbara *68:* 142
Massie, Diane Redfield *16:* 194
Massie, Kim *31:* 43
Mataya, David *121:* 66
Mathers, Petra *119:* 135; *163:* 104; *176:* 143, 144; *187:* 142; *196:* 101
Mathewuse, James *51:* 143
Mathieu, Joseph *14:* 33; *39:* 206; *43:* 167; *56:* 180; *79:* 126; *94:* 147; *185:* 140
Matje, Martin *169:* 177, 178; *172:* 180
Matsubara, Naoko *12:* 121
Matsuda, Shizu *13:* 167
Matsuoka, Mei *192:* 135
Matte, L'Enc *22:* 183
Mattelson, Marvin *36:* 50, 51
Mattheson, Jenny *180:* 132
Matthews, Elizabeth *194:* 128
Matthews, F. Leslie *4:* 216
Matthews, Tina *190:* 130
Mattingly, David *71:* 76, 77; *82:* 64; *91:* 216, 217; *109:* 25
Matulay, Laszlo *5:* 18; *43:* 168
Matus, Greta *12:* 142
Maughan, William *181:* 31

Mauldin, Bill *27:* 23
Mauterer, Erin Marie *119:* 5
Mawicke, Tran *9:* 137; *15:* 191; *47:* 100
Mawson, Matt *74:* 115
Max, Peter *45:* 146, 147, 148, 149, 150
Maxie, Betty *40:* 135
Maxwell, John Alan *1:* 148
May, Steve *204:* 30
Mayan, Earl *7:* 193
Mayer, Bill *200:* 138
Mayer, Danuta *117:* 103
Mayer, Marianna *32:* 132
Mayer, Mercer *11:* 192; *16:* 195, 196; *20:* 55, 57; *32:* 129, 130, 132, 133, 134; *41:* 144, 248, 252; *58:* 186; *73:* 140, 142, 143; *137:* 137, 138
Mayforth, Hal *166:* 77
Mayhew, James *85:* 121; *138:* 187; *149:* 140; *204:* 81
Mayhew, Richard *3:* 106
Mayo, Gretchen Will *38:* 81; *84:* 166
Mays, Victor *5:* 127; *8:* 45, 153; *14:* 245; *23:* 50; *34:* 155; *40:* 79; *45:* 158; *54:* 91; *66:* 240
Mazal, Chanan *49:* 104
Maze, Deborah *71:* 83
Mazellan, Ron *75:* 97, 98
Mazetti, Alan *112:* 72
Mazille, Capucine *96:* 168
Mazza, Adriana Saviozzi *19:* 215
Mazzella, Mary Jo *82:* 165
Mazzetti, Alan *45:* 210
McAfee, Steve *135:* 146; *167:* 176; *191:* 84
McAlinden, Paul *112:* 128
McBride, Angus *28:* 49; *103:* 40
McBride, Will *30:* 110
McCaffery, Janet *38:* 145
McCall, Bruce *209:* 119
McCallum, Graham *78:* 78
McCallum, Stephen *141:* 143; *156:* 5; *166:* 228
McCann, Gerald *3:* 50; *4:* 94; *7:* 54; *41:* 121
McCarthy, Dan *174:* 74
McCarthy, Linda *177:* 128
McCarthy, Meghan *168:* 134; *199:* 74
McCauley, Adam *157:* 36; *184:* 199; *193:* 100; *209:* 122
McCay, Winsor *41:* 124, 126, 128, 129, 130, 131; *134:* 77, 79
McClary, Nelson *1:* 111
McClements, George *196:* 146
McClintock, Barbara *57:* 135; *95:* 130; *146:* 190
McClintock, Theodore *14:* 141
McCloskey, Robert *1:* 184, 185; *2:* 186, 187; *17:* 209; *39:* 139, 140, 141, 142, 143, 146, 147, 148; *85:* 150, 151; *100:* 172, 173, 174
McClung, Robert *2:* 189; *68:* 166, 167
McClure, Gillian *31:* 132; *150:* 53
McConnel, Jerry *31:* 75, 187
McConnell, Mary *102:* 49
McCord, Kathleen Garry *78:* 236
McCormack, John *66:* 193
McCormick, A.D. *35:* 119
McCormick, Dell J. *19:* 216
McCrady, Lady *16:* 198; *39:* 127
McCrea, James *3:* 122; *33:* 216
McCrea, Ruth *3:* 122; *27:* 102; *33:* 216
McCue, Lisa *65:* 148, 149; *77:* 54; *80:* 132; *175:* 33; *177:* 133, 135
McCully, Emily Arnold *2:* 89; *4:* 120, 121, 146, 197; *5:* 2, 129; *7:* 191; *11:* 122; *15:* 210; *33:* 23; *35:* 244; *37:* 122; *39:* 88; *40:* 103; *50:* 30,31, 32, 33, 34, 35, 36, 37; *52:* 89, 90; *57:* 6; *62:* 3; *70:* 195; *86:* 82; *96:* 192; *97:* 93; *110:* 143,144; *117:* 47; *167:* 96
McCurdy, Michael *13:* 153; *24:* 85; *81:* 160; *82:* 157, 158; *86:* 125; *97:* 92; *117:* 178; *132:* 6; *147:* 159, 160
McCusker, Paul *99:* 19
McDaniel, Jerry *132:* 135

McDaniel, Preston *160:* 206; *170:* 139
McDermott, Beverly Brodsky *11:* 180
McDermott, Gerald *16:* 201; *74:* 174, 175; *163:* 150, 151
McDermott, Mike *96:* 187
McDonald, Jill *13:* 155; *26:* 128
McDonald, Mercedes *169:* 118
McDonald, Ralph J. *5:* 123, 195
McDonnell, Flora *146:* 199, 200
McDonnell, Patrick *179:* 153, 154
McDonough, Don *10:* 163
McElligott, Matt *196:* 147
McElmurry, Jill *137:* 148; *163:* 141; *202:* 186
McElrath-Eslick, Lori *129:* 145; *142:* 21; *173:* 123; *202:* 194; *204:* 88, 89
McEntee, Dorothy *37:* 124
McEwan, Keith *88:* 116; *165:* 122, 123
McEwen, Katharine *169:* 34
McFall, Christie *12:* 144
McFeely, Daniel *160:* 213
McGaw, Laurie *109:* 243; *143:* 216
McGee, Barbara *6:* 165
McGee, Marni *163:* 153
McGillvray, Kim *158:* 171; *165:* 213; *186:* 183; *190:* 175
McGinley-Nally, Sharon *131:* 19
McGinnis, Robert *110:* 113; *177:* 80
McGovern, Tara *98:* 171
McGraw, Sheila *83:* 146
McGregor, Barbara *200:* 155
McGregor, Malcolm *23:* 27
McGrory, Anik *193:* 120
McGuire, Robert *204:* 57; *209:* 86
McGuirk, Leslie *152:* 159
McHale, John *138:* 190
McHenry, E.B. *193:* 122
McHugh, Tom *23:* 64
McIntosh, Jon *42:* 56
McKay, Donald *2:* 118; *32:* 157; *45:* 151, 152
McKean, Dave *150:* 71; *174:* 156; *197:* 83, 118
McKeating, Eileen *44:* 58
McKee, David *10:* 48; *21:* 9; *70:* 154, 155; *107:* 139, 140, 141; *134:* 218; *158:* 148, 149, 150, 151
McKee, Diana *109:* 185
McKelvey, Patrick *164:* 141
McKendry, Joe *170:* 136
McKeveny, Tom *164:* 60; *173:* 79
McKie, Roy *7:* 44
McKie, Todd *205:* 181
McKillip, Kathy *30:* 153
McKinney, Ena *26:* 39
McKinnon, James *136:* 75
McKowen, Scott *172:* 63; *202:* 49
McLachlan, Edward *5:* 89
McLaren, Chesley *133:* 53
McLaren, Kirsty *123:* 99; *124:* 226
Mclean, Andrew *113:* 117, 118, 120, 121; *172:* 130, 131
Mclean, Janet *172:* 130
McLean, Meg *94:* 196
McLean, Sammis *32:* 197
McLean, Wilson *90:* 29; *113:* 195
McLoughlin, John C. *47:* 149
McLoughlin, Wayne *102:* 230; *134:* 178
McMahon, Robert *36:* 155; *69:* 169
McManus, Shawn *85:* 71
McMenemy, Sarah *156:* 139
McMillan, Bruce *22:* 184
McMullan, James *40:* 33; *67:* 172; *87:* 142; *99:* 63, 64; *189:* 133; *196:* 51
McMullen, Nigel *146:* 177
McNeely, Tom *162:* 55
McNaught, Harry *12:* 80; *32:* 136
McNaughton, Colin *39:* 149; *40:* 108; *92:* 144, 145, 146; *134:* 104, 106
McNicholas, Maureen *38:* 148
McNicholas, Shelagh *173:* 61; *191:* 125, 126

McPhail, David *14:* 105; *23:* 135; *37:* 217, 218, 220,221; *47:* 151, 152, 153, 154, 155, 156, 158, 159, 160, 162, 163, 164; *71:* 211; *81:* 139, 140, 142; *86:* 123; *132:* 150; *140:* 129, 131, 132; *183:* 134, 135, 137; *189:* 132
McPhee, Richard B. *41:* 133
McPheeters, Neal *78:* 132; *86:* 90; *99:* 162; *111:* 141; *142:* 162
McQuade, Jacqueline *124:* 223
McQueen, Lucinda *28:* 149; *41:* 249; *46:* 206; *53:* 103
McQuillan, Mary *153:* 97; *200:* 140
McVay, Tracy *11:* 68
McVicker, Charles *39:* 150
Mead, Ben Carlton *43:* 75
Meade, Holly *90:* 102; *94:* 101; *149:* 8; *151:* 107
Mecray, John *33:* 62
Meddaugh, Susan *20:* 42; *29:* 143; *41:* 241; *77:* 50; *84:* 173, 174, 175, 176, 177, 178; *125:* 160, 161, 162; *176:* 148, 149, 150, 151
Meehan, Dennis B. *56:* 144
Meents, Len W. *73:* 147, 150
Meers, Tony *99:* 113
Meisel, Paul *98:* 137; *124:* 18; *162:* 180; *179:* 16; *181:* 62; *194:* 154
Melanson, Luc *149:* 229; *198:* 97, 98
Melendez, Francisco *72:* 180
Melling, David *202:* 199
Melnychuk, Monika *153:* 65
Melo, Esperança *196:* 90
Melo, John *16:* 285; *58:* 203
Meloni, Maria Teresa *98:* 62
Meltzer, Ericka
    See O'Rourke, Ericka
Menasco, Milton *43:* 85
Menchin, Scott *188:* 129
Mendelson, Steven T. *86:* 154
Mendelssohn, Felix *19:* 170
Mendola, Christopher *88:* 223
Meng, Heinz *13:* 158
Merian, Maria Sibylla *140:* 88
Mero, Lee *34:* 68
Merrell, David *205:* 3
Merrill, Frank T. *16:* 147; *19:* 71; *YABC 1:* 226, 229,273
Merriman, Rachel *98:* 108; *114:* 122; *149:* 142
Merveille, David *200:* 142
Meryman, Hope *27:* 41
Meryweather, Jack *10:* 179
Meseldzija, Petar *168:* 97
Meserve, Jess *184:* 137
Messick, Dale *64:* 150, 151, 152
Meth, Harold *24:* 203
Meyer, Herbert *19:* 189
Meyer, Renate *6:* 170
Meyers, Bob *11:* 136
Meyers, Nancy *172:* 124
Meynell, Louis *37:* 76
Micale, Albert *2:* 65; *22:* 185
Miccuci, Charles *82:* 163; *144:* 150
Micich, Paul *164:* 163
Middleton, Jeffrey *177:* 173
Middleton, Joshua *208:* 146
Middleton-Sandford, Betty *2:* 125
Mieke, Anne *45:* 74
Mighell, Patricia *43:* 134
Miglio, Paige *101:* 203; *151:* 223; *201:* 118, 119; *204:* 162
Mikec, Larry *204:* 125
Mikolaycak, Charles *9:* 144; *12:* 101; *13:* 212; *21:* 121; *22:* 168; *30:* 187; *34:* 103, 150; *37:* 183; *43:* 179; *44:* 90; *46:* 115, 118, 119; *49:* 25; *78:* 121, 122, 205, 207; *81:* 4
Milelli, Pascal *129:* 66; *135:* 153; *187:* 45
Miles, Elizabeth *117:* 77
Miles, Jennifer *17:* 278
Milgrim, David *158:* 157; *187:* 125, 126, 128
Milhous, Katherine *15:* 193; *17:* 51
Millais, John E. *22:* 230, 231
Millar, H.R. *YABC 1:* 194, 195, 203

Millard, C.E. *28:* 186
Millard, Kerry *105:* 124; *204:* 93, 94
Miller, Don *15:* 195; *16:* 71; *20:* 106; *31:* 178
Miller, Edna *29:* 148
Miller, Edward *115:* 64; *183:* 140, 141
Miller, Frank J. *25:* 94
Miller, Grambs *18:* 38; *23:* 16
Miller, Ian *99:* 128
Miller, Jane *15:* 196
Miller, Marcia *13:* 233
Miller, Marilyn *1:* 87; *31:* 69; *33:* 157
Miller, Mitchell *28:* 183; *34:* 207
Miller, Phil *175:* 150
Miller, Shane *5:* 140
Miller, Virginia *81:* 206
Millman, Isaac *172:* 18
Mills, Elaine *72:* 181
Mills, Judith Christine *130:* 168, 169
Mills, Lauren *92:* 170
Mills, Yaroslava Surmach *35:* 169, 170; *46:* 114
Millsap, Darrel *51:* 102
Milone, Karen *89:* 169
Milord, Susan *147:* 163, 164; *200:* 144
Milton, Debbie *162:* 161
Mims, Ashley *170:* 51
Miner, Julia *98:* 69
Minor, Wendell *39:* 188; *52:* 87; *56:* 171; *58:* 116; *62:* 56; *66:* 109; *74:* 93; *78:* 129; *94:* 67; *117:* 12, 13; *124:* 84, 86; *136:* 121; *164:* 168, 169; *170:* 71; *199:* 79, 80, 81, 82
Minter, Daniel *176:* 154; *179:* 177
Mirocha, Paul *81:* 133; *192:* 148; *194:* 36
Misako Rocks! *192:* 149, 150
Mitchell, Judith *109:* 117
Mitchell, Mark *91:* 208
Mitchell, Tracy *190:* 15
Mitgutsch, Ali *76:* 161
Mitsuhashi, Yoko *45:* 153
Miyake, Yoshi *38:* 141
Mizumura, Kazue *10:* 143; *18:* 223; *36:* 159
Mochi, Ugo *8:* 122; *38:* 150
Mock, Paul *55:* 83; *123:* 32
Modarressi, Mitra *90:* 236; *126:* 168; *173:* 165, 166; *200:* 147, 148
Modell, Frank *39:* 152
Mogenson, Jan *74:* 183
Mohn, Susan *89:* 224
Mohr, Mark *133:* 201
Mohr, Nicholasa *8:* 139; *113:* 127
Molan, Christine *60:* 177; *84:* 183
Moldon, Peter L. *49:* 168
Molk, Laurel *92:* 150
Mollica, Gene *197:* 11
Momaday, N. Scott *48:* 159
Mombourquette, Paul *112:* 91; *126:* 142
Monk, Julie *165:* 231; *191:* 96
Monks, Lydia *189:* 136, 137
Monroy, Manuel *199:* 192
Montgomery, Lucy *150:* 126
Montgomery, Michael G. *208:* 159
Montgomery-Higham, Amanda *169:* 131
Monteiel, David *201:* 95
Montiel, David *69:* 106; *84:* 145
Montijo, Rhode *193:* 164
Montresor, Beni *2:* 91; *3:* 138; *38:* 152, 153, 154,155, 156, 157, 158, 159, 160; *68:* 63
Montserrat, Pep *128:* 135; *181:* 119; *184:* 53
Moon, Carl *25:* 183, 184, 185
Moon, Eliza *14:* 40
Moon, Ivan *22:* 39; *38:* 140
Moore, Adrienne *67:* 147
Moore, Agnes Kay Randall *43:* 187
Moore, Cyd *117:* 107, 108; *159:* 137, 138; *186:* 148, 149, 151; *203:* 15
Moore, Gustav *127:* 181, 182; *170:* 162, 163
Moore, Jackie *128:* 79
Moore, Janet *63:* 153
Moore, Margie *176:* 156
Moore, Mary *29:* 160
Moore, Patrick *184:* 121

Moore, Yvette *101:* 11, 12; *154:* 141
Mora, Giovanni *179:* 127; *184:* 11
Mora, Raul Mina *20:* 41
Moraes, Odilon *102:* 144
Morales, Yuyi *154:* 144
Moran, Rosslyn *111:* 26
Moran, Tom *60:* 100
Mordan, C.B. *193:* 115
Mordvinoff, Nicolas *15:* 179
Moreno, René King *169:* 59; *190:* 133, 209
Morgan, Barbara *169:* 116
Morgan, Jacqui *58:* 57
Morgan, Mary *114:* 133, 134, 135; *123:* 11
Morgan, Tom *42:* 157
Morgan, Pierr *173:* 148
Morgenstern, Michael *158:* 7, 57; *171:* 103; *174:* 60
Morice, Dave *93:* 142
Morin, Paul *73:* 132; *79:* 130; *88:* 140; *137:* 143
Moriuchi, Mique *177:* 203
Morning, Tuesday *205:* 25
Morozumi, Atsuko *110:* 155
Morrill, Leslie *18:* 218; *29:* 177; *33:* 84; *38:* 147; *42:* 127; *44:* 93; *48:* 164, 165, 167, 168, 169, 170,171; *49:* 162; *63:* 136, 180; *70:* 72; *71:* 70, 91,92; *72:* 228; *80:* 163, 164, 165; *90:* 121; *121:* 88; *178:* 117
Morrill, Rowena A. *84:* 16; *98:* 163
Morris *47:* 91
Morris, Frank *55:* 133; *60:* 28; *76:* 2
Morris, Harry O. *119:* 138
Morris, Jackie *128:* 194; *144:* 119; *151:* 146; *202:* 126, 127; *204:* 83
Morris, Jennifer E. *179:* 157
Morris, Oradel Nolen *128:* 180
Morris, Tony *62:* 146; *70:* 97
Morrison, Bill *42:* 116; *66:* 170; *69:* 40
Morrison, Gordon *87:* 150; *113:* 93; *128:* 181, 182; *183:* 144, 145, 146
Morrison, Frank *169:* 162; *205:* 156
Morrison, Taylor *159:* 144, 145; *187:* 131
Morrow, Gray *2:* 64; *5:* 200; *10:* 103, 114; *14:* 175
Morse, Scott *200:* 149, 150
Morton, Lee Jack *32:* 140
Morton, Marian *3:* 185
Mosberg, Hilary *117:* 195; *118:* 164; *149:* 55
Moser, Barry *56:* 68, 117, 118, 119, 120, 121, 122, 123, 124; *59:* 141; *60:* 160; *79:* 91, 147, 149, 151, 152; *82:* 81; *90:* 118; *91:* 35; *95:* 210; *97:* 91, 93; *102:* 152; *126:* 4; *128:* 175; *133:* 141; *138:* 167, 171, 174; *153:* 205; *174:* 130; *185:* 152, 154; *195:* 163; *204:* 115; *209:* 201
Moser, Cara *90:* 118; *138:* 167
Moses, Grandma *18:* 228
Moses, Will *178:* 170, 171
Moskof, Martin Stephen *27:* 152
Mosley, Francis *57:* 144
Moss, Donald *11:* 184
Moss, Geoffrey *32:* 198
Moss, Marissa *71:* 130; *104:* 127; *163:* 156
Most, Bernard *48:* 173; *91:* 142, 143; *134:* 120
Mowll, Joshua *188:* 133
Mowry, Carmen *50:* 62
Moxley, Sheila *96:* 174; *169:* 26; *206:* 16
Moyers, William *21:* 65
Moyler, Alan *36:* 142
Mozley, Charles *9:* 87; *20:* 176, 192, 193; *22:* 228; *25:* 205; *33:* 150; *43:* 170, 171, 172, 173, 174; *YABC2:* 89
Mueller, Hans Alexander *26:* 64; *27:* 52, 53
Mugnaini, Joseph *11:* 35; *27:* 52, 53; *35:* 62
Mujica, Rick *72:* 67; *88:* 95; *111:* 53; *180:* 185; *197:* 70
Mullen, Douglas *180:* 178
Muller, Robin *86:* 161
Muller, Steven *32:* 167
Muller, Jorg *35:* 215; *67:* 138, 139
Mulock, Julie *163:* 112

Mullins, Edward S. *10:* 101
Mullins, Patricia *51:* 68
Multer, Scott *80:* 108
Munari, Bruno *15:* 200
Munch, Edvard *140:* 143
Munowitz, Ken *14:* 148; *72:* 178, 179
Muñoz, Claudio *208:* 161
Munoz, William *42:* 160
Munro, Roxie *58:* 134; *136:* 177; *137:* 218; *184:* 133, 134
Munsinger, Lynn *33:* 161; *46:* 126; *71:* 92; *82:* 80; *89:* 218; *92:* 125; *94:* 157, 158, 159, 160; *98:* 196; *103:* 198; *142:* 143; *145:* 133, 134, 136; *153:* 203; *176:* 162; *177:* 140, 141, 142; *189:* 113, 114, 116, 117; *201:* 42
Munson, Russell *13:* 9
Munster, Sebastian *166:* 107
Munzar, Barbara *149:* 75
Murdocca, Salvatore *73:* 212; *98:* 132; *111:* 168; *157:* 228; *164:* 257
Murphy, Bill *5:* 138; *130:* 170
Murphy, Jill *37:* 142; *70:* 166; *142:* 132, 134
Murphy, Kelly *130:* 212; *143:* 119; *176:* 158; *190:* 135
Murphy, Mary *196:* 158
Murphy, Tom *192:* 40
Murr, Karl *20:* 62
Murray, Joe *175:* 37
Murray, Ossie *43:* 176
Mussino, Attilio *29:* 131; *100:* 164
Mutchler, Dwight *1:* 25
Myers, Bernice *9:* 147; *36:* 75; *81:* 146, 147, 148
Muth, Jon J. *165:* 169; *167:* 109; *190:* 227; *193:* 59
Myers, Christopher *183:* 150; *193:* 139
Myers, Duane O. *99:* 145
Myers, Tim *147:* 168
Myers, V.G. *142:* 41
Myers, Lou *11:* 2

N

Nachreiner, Tom *29:* 182
Nacht, Merle *65:* 49
Nadler, Ellis *88:* 91
Nagle, Shane *180:* 223
Nagy, Ian *195:* 64
Najaka, Marlies *62:* 101
Nakai, Michael *30:* 217; *54:* 29
Nakata, Hiroe *157:* 156; *162:* 30; *205:* 124, 125
Nakatani, Chiyoko *12:* 124
Narahashi, Keiko *77:* 188; *82:* 213; *115:* 142, 143, 144
Nascimbene, Yan *133:* 128; *173:* 132, 133
Nash, Lesa *87:* 135
Nash, Linell *46:* 175
Nash, Scott *130:* 36; *188:* 196
Naso, John *33:* 183
Nason, Thomas W. *14:* 68
Nasser, Muriel *48:* 74
Nast, Thomas *21:* 29; *28:* 23; *51:* 132, 133, 134, 135,136, 137, 138, 139, 141
Nasta, Vincent *78:* 185
Natale, Vincent *76:* 3; *78:* 125; *112:* 47; *166:* 81; *174:* 189; *185:* 212; *197:* 59
Natchev, Alexi *96:* 177
Nathan, Charlott *125:* 151
Nathan, Cheryl *150:* 104; *186:* 112
Natti, Susanna *20:* 146; *32:* 141, 142; *35:* 178; *37:* 143; *71:* 49; *93:* 98; *125:* 166, 168; *126:* 228; *151:* 6; *178:* 8; *188:* 106
Navarra, Celeste Scala *8:* 142
Naylor, Penelope *10:* 104
Nazz, James *72:* 8
Nebel, M. *45:* 154
Neebe, William *7:* 93
Needham, Dave *196:* 85

Needler, Jerry *12:* 93
Neel, Alice *31:* 23
Neely, Beth *119:* 184
Neely, Keith R. *46:* 124
Neff, Leland *78:* 74
Negri, Rocco *3:* 213; *5:* 67; *6:* 91, 108; *12:* 159
Negrin, Fabian *174:* 125; *175:* 15
Neidigh, Sherry *128:* 53; *204:* 101, 102, 103
Neilan, Eujin Kim *180:* 241; *200:* 151, 152
Neill, John R. *18:* 8, 10, 11, 21, 30; *100:* 22
Neilsen, Cliff *158:* 131; *177:* 112, 121; *209:* 8
Neilsen, Terese *116:* 74
Nelson, Craig *62:* 151; *153:* *183:* 86
Nelson, Gail White *68:* 140
Nelson, Jennifer *129:* 152; *199:* 132
Nelson, Kadir *151:* 185; *154:* 146, 147; *157:* 189, 222; *181:* 122, 124; *197:* 155
Nelson, Mary *36:* 138, 147
Nelson, S.D. *131:* 34; *181:* 126, 127
Ness, Evaline *1:* 164, 165; *2:* 39; *3:* 8; *10:* 147; *12:* 53; *26:* 150, 151, 152, 153; *49:* 30, 31, 32; *56:* 30; *60:* 113
Neubecker, Robert *170:* 143
Neville, Vera *2:* 182
Nevins, Daniel *191:* 173
Nevwirth, Allan *79:* 168
Newberry, Clare Turlay *1:* 170
Newbold, Greg *108:* 125; *145:* 199; *151:* 23; *193:* 178; *197:* 10; *199:* 92, 93
Newfeld, Frank *14:* 121; *26:* 154
Newman, Andy *149:* 61; *195:* 63
Newman, Ann *43:* 90
Newman, Barbara Johansen *191:* 137, 138
Newsham, Ian *143:* 162
Newsom, Carol *40:* 159; *44:* 60; *47:* 189; *65:* 29; *70:* 192; *80:* 36; *85:* 137, 138; *92:* 167; *191:* 82
Newsom, Tom *49:* 149; *71:* 13, 62; *75:* 156; *91:* 113
Newton, Jill *83:* 105; *200:* 154
Ng, Michael *29:* 171
Ng, Simon *167:* 7
Nguyen, Vincent *189:* 49
Nicholson, William *15:* 33, 34; *16:* 48
Nickens, Bessie *104:* 153
Nicklaus, Carol *45:* 194; *62:* 132, 133
Nickle, John *181:* 128
Nickless, Will *16:* 139
Nicholas, Corasue *154:* 20
Nicolas *17:* 130, 132, 133; *YABC 2:* 215
Niebrugge, Jane *6:* 118
Nielsen, Cliff *95:* 207, 208; *105:* 58; *114:* 112; *124:* 12; *125:* 91, 92; *132:* 224; *135:* 187; *136:* 40; *137:* 168; *145:* 54; *149:* 28; *158:* 129; *165:* 64, 158; *168:* 169; *170:* 6; *175:* 114, 116; *187:* 75, 76; *194:* 107; *197:* 172; *201:* 14; *208:* 192
Nielsen, Jon *6:* 100; *24:* 202
Nielsen, Kay *15:* 7; *16:* 211, 212, 213, 215, 217; *22:* 143; *YABC 1:* 32, 33
Niemann, Christoph *191:* 141
Nikola-Lisa, W. *180:* 180
Niland, Deborah *25:* 191; *27:* 156; *135:* 50; *172:* 143
Niland, Kilmeny *25:* 191; *75:* 143
Nino, Alex *59:* 145
Ninon *1:* 5; *38:* 101, 103, 108
Nissen, Rie *44:* 35
Nithael, Mark *158:* 237
Nivola, Claire A. *78:* 126; *140:* 147; *208:* 164
Nixon, K. *14:* 152
Nobati, Eugenia *194:* 118
Noble, Louise *61:* 170
Noble, Marty *97:* 168; *125:* 171
Noble, Trinka Hakes *39:* 162; *84:* 157
Noda, Takayo *168:* 143
Noguchi, Yoshie *30:* 99
Nolan, Dennis *42:* 163; *67:* 163; *78:* 189; *82:* 225; *83:* 26; *92:* 169, 170; *103:* 166; *111:* 35; *112:* 213; *127:* 171; *166:* 161; *194:* 218
Noll, Sally *82:* 171

Nolte, Larry *121:* 63, 65
Nones, Eric Jon *61:* 111; *76:* 38; *77:* 177
Noonan, Daniel *100:* 224
Noonan, Julia *4:* 163; *7:* 207; *25:* 151; *91:* 29; *95:* 149
Norcia, Ernie *108:* 155; *140:* 47
Nordenskjold, Birgitta *2:* 208
Noreika, Robert *173:* 20
Norling, Beth *149:* 153, 154; *209:* 77
Norman, Elaine *77:* 72, 176; *94:* 35; *136:* 63; *178:* 42
Norman, Mary *36:* 138, 147
Norman, Michael *12:* 117; *27:* 168
Northway, Jennifer *85:* 96
Nostlinger, Christiana *162:* 131
Novak, Linda *166:* 205
Novak, Matt *104:* 132, 133; *165:* 173, 174; *204:* 104, 106
Novelli, Luca *61:* 137
Nugent, Cynthia *106:* 189; *205:* 126, 127; *209:* 180
Numeroff, Laura Joffe *28:* 161; *30:* 177
Nurse, Chris *164:* 91
Nussbaumer, Paul *16:* 219; *39:* 117
Nutt, Ken *72:* 69; *97:* 170
Nyce, Helene *19:* 219
Nygren, Tord *30:* 148; *127:* 164

O

Oakley, Graham *8:* 112; *30:* 164, 165; *84:* 188,189, 190, 191, 192
Oakley, Thornton *YABC 2:* 189
Oberheide, Heide *118:* 37
Obligado, Lilian *2:* 28, 66, 67; *6:* 30; *14:* 179; *15:* 103; *25:* 84; *61:* 138, 139, 140, 141, 143
Oblinski, Rafael *190:* 139
Obrant, Susan *11:* 186
O'Brien, Anne Sibley *53:* 116, 117; *155:* 115
O'Brien, John *41:* 253; *72:* 12; *89:* 59, 60; *98:* 16; *161:* 185; *169:* 16; *180:* 196
O'Brien, Patrick *193:* 142, 143, 144
O'Brien, Teresa *87:* 89
O'Brien, Tim *93:* 25; *136:* 94; *164:* 57; *169:* 57; *173:* 55; *175:* 86; *184:* 192; *191:* 134; *193:* 137
O'Clair, Dennis *127:* 25
O'Connor, George *183:* 153
Odell, Carole *35:* 47
Odem, Mel *99:* 164; *167:* 84, 87
O'Donohue, Thomas *40:* 89
Oechsli, Kelly *5:* 144, 145; *7:* 115; *8:* 83, 183; *13:* 117; *20:* 94; *81:* 199
Ofer, Avi *208:* 143
Offen, Hilda *42:* 207
Ogden, Bill *42:* 59; *47:* 55
Ogg, Oscar *33:* 34
Ogle, Nancy Gray *163:* 144
Ohi, Ruth *90:* 175, 177; *131:* 63; *135:* 106; *175:* 107; *179:* 55
Ohlsson, Ib *4:* 152; *7:* 57; *10:* 20; *11:* 90; *19:* 217; *41:* 246; *82:* 106; *92:* 213
Ohtomo, Yasuo *37:* 146; *39:* 212, 213
O'Keefe, Jennifer *136:* 184
O'Kelley, Mattie Lou *36:* 150
Olbinski, Rafal *149:* 27; *158:* 77; *203:* 36
O'Leary, Chris *208:* 166
Oleynikov, Igor *202:* 134
Oliver, Isaac *171:* 182
Oliver, Jenni *23:* 121; *35:* 112
Oliver, Narelle *152:* 192; *197:* 129, 130
Oller, Erika *128:* 186; *134:* 126
Olschewski, Alfred *7:* 172
Olsen, Ib Spang *6:* 178, 179; *81:* 164
Olson, Alan *77:* 229
Olson-Brown, Ellen *183:* 154
Olugebefola, Ademola *15:* 205
O'Malley, Kevin *94:* 180; *106:* 8; *113:* 108; *136:* 70; *157:* 193; *191:* 146; *203:* 78

O'Neil, Dan IV 7: 176
O'Neill, Catharine 72: 113; 84: 78; 134: 153
O'Neill, Jean 22: 146
O'Neill, Martin 187: 39; 203: 118
O'Neill, Michael J. 54: 172
O'Neill, Rose 48: 30, 31
O'Neill, Steve 21: 118
Ono, Chiyo 7: 97
Orbaan, Albert 2: 31; 5: 65, 171; 9: 8; 14: 241; 20: 109
Orbach, Ruth 21: 112
Orback, Craig 197: 132
Orfe, Joan 20: 81
Org, Ed 119: 93
Ormai, Stella 72: 129
Ormerod, Jan 55: 124; 70: 170, 171; 90: 39; 132: 172, 173, 174; 147: 98
Ormsby, Virginia H. 11: 187
O'Rourke, Ericka 108: 216; 117: 194; 111: 142; 119: 194; 137: 152; 150: 134; 167: 64; 172: 164; 188: 163; 191: 172; 201: 15; 203: 75; 209: 130
O'Rourke, Ericka Meltzer
    See O'Rourke, Ericka
Orozco, Jose Clemente 9: 177
Orr, Forrest W. 23: 9
Orr, N. 19: 70
Ortiz, Vilma 88: 158
Osborn, Kathy 152: 232; 199: 101, 102; 206: 67
Osborn, Robert 65: 49
Osborne, Billie Jean 35: 209
Osmond, Edward 10: 111
O'Sullivan, Tom 3: 176; 4: 55; 78: 195
Otani, June 124: 42; 156: 53
Otis, Rebecca 185: 92
Ottley, Matt 147: 221; 171: 133
Otto, Svend 22: 130, 141; 67: 188, 189
Oudry, J.B. 18: 167
Oughton, Taylor 5: 23; 104: 136
Overeng, Johannes 44: 36
Overlie, George 11: 156
Owens, Carl 2: 35; 23: 521
Owens, Gail 10: 170; 12: 157; 19: 16; 22: 70; 25: 81; 28: 203, 205; 32: 221, 222; 36: 132; 46: 40; 47: 57; 54: 66, 67, 68, 69, 70, 71, 72, 73; 71: 100; 73: 64; 77: 157; 80: 32; 82: 3; 99: 226
Owens, Mary Beth 113: 202, 203; 191: 148, 149
Owens, Nubia 84: 74
Oxenbury, Helen 3: 150, 151; 24: 81; 68: 174, 175,176; 81: 209; 84: 213, 245; 129: 56; 149: 159; 184: 181
Oz, Robin 88: 167; 185: 181

P

Padgett, Jim 12: 165
Page, Gail 205: 128
Page, Homer 14: 145
Page, Mark 162: 70
Paget, Sidney 24: 90, 91, 93, 95, 97
Paget, Walter 64: 122
Paillot, Jim 173: 89
Pajouhesh, Noushin 160: 121
Pak 12: 76
Pak, Yu Cha 86: 174
Paladino, Lance 134: 30
Palazzo, Tony 3: 152, 153
Palecek, Josef 56: 136; 89: 158
Palen, Debbie 135: 88; 195: 148, 149
Palencar, John Jude 84: 12, 45; 85: 87; 92: 187; 99: 128; 110: 204; 150: 122; 171: 86; 207: 36
Palin, Nicki 81: 201; 89: 161
Palladini, David 4: 113; 40: 176, 177, 178, 179, 181,224, 225; 50: 138; 78: 186
Pallarito, Don 43: 36

Palmer, Carol 158: 230; 195: 187
Palmer, Heidi 15: 207; 29: 102
Palmer, Jan 42: 153; 82: 161
Palmer, Judd 153: 160, 161
Palmer, Juliette 6: 89; 15: 208
Palmer, Kate Salley 104: 143; 154: 169
Palmer, Lemuel 17: 25, 29
Palmisciano, Diane 110: 62; 162: 26; 202: 138, 139
Palmquist, Eric 38: 133
Panesis, Nicholas 3: 127
Panter, Gary 182: 191
Panton, Doug 52: 99
Paparone, Pamela 129: 174
Papas, William 11: 223; 50: 160
Papin, Joseph 26: 113
Papish, Robin Lloyd 10: 80
Papp, Robert 198: 41; 205: 130
Paradis, Susan 40: 216
Paraquin, Charles H. 18: 166
Paris, Peter 31: 127
Parisi, Elizabeth B. 141: 82; 164: 57
Park, Nick 113: 143
Park, Seho 39: 110
Park, W.B. 22: 189
Parker, Ant 82: 87, 88; 104: 121
Parker, Lewis 2: 179
Parker, Nancy Winslow 10: 113; 22: 164; 28: 47, 144; 52: 7; 69: 153; 91: 171, 174; 132: 175
Parker, Robert 4: 161; 5: 74; 9: 136; 29: 39
Parker, Robert Andrew 11: 81; 29: 186; 39: 165; 40: 25; 41: 78; 42: 123; 43: 144; 48: 182; 54: 140; 74: 141; 91: 24; 111: 115; 151: 201; 154: 156; 200: 163, 164
Parker-Rees, Guy 149: 145; 193: 149, 150
Parkin, Trevor 140: 151
Parkins, David 114: 123; 146: 176; 176: 168; 192: 107
Parkinson, Kathy 71: 143; 144: 234
Parkinson, Keith 70: 66
Parks, Gordon, Jr. 33: 228
Parnall, Peter 5: 137; 16: 221; 24: 70; 40: 78; 51: 130; 69: 17, 155; 136: 22, 23, 24
Parnall, Virginia 40: 78
Parow, Lorraine 158: 127
Parr, Todd 134: 139, 140; 179: 163, 164, 165
Parrish, Anne 27: 159, 160
Parrish, Dillwyn 27: 159
Parrish, Maxfield 14: 160, 161, 164, 165; 16: 109; 18: 12, 13; YABC 1: 149, 152, 267; 2: 146, 149
Parry, David 26: 156
Parry, Marian 13: 176; 19: 179
Parsons, Garry 197: 135
Partch, Virgil 45: 163, 165
Pascal, David 14: 174
Paschkis, Julie 177: 153, 154
Pasquier, J.A. 16: 91
Pastel, Elyse 201: 123
Pasternak, Robert 119: 53
Paterson, Diane 13: 116; 39: 163; 59: 164, 165, 166,167; 72: 51, 53; 129: 175; 177: 156, 157
Paterson, Helen 16: 93
Patkau, Karen 112: 123
Paton, Jane 15: 271; 35: 176
Patricelli, Leslie 207: 129
Patrick, John 139: 190
Patrick, Pamela 90: 160; 93: 211; 105: 12
Patrick, Tom 190: 103
Patterson, Geoffrey 54: 75
Patterson, Robert 25: 118
Patti, Joyce 187: 145, 146
Patz, Nancy 111: 40; 154: 161
Paul, James 4: 130; 23: 161
Paul, Korky 102: 85
Paull, Grace 24: 157; 87: 127
Paulsen, Ruth Wright 79: 160, 164; 189: 146
Pavlov, Elena 80: 49
Payne, Adam S. 135: 166

Payne, C.F. 145: 138, 140; 179: 168
Payne, Joan Balfour 1: 118
Payne, Tom 170: 27
Payson, Dale 7: 34; 9: 151; 20: 140; 37: 22
Payzant, Charles 21: 147
Peacock, Ralph 64: 118
Peake, Mervyn 22: 136, 149; 23: 162, 163, 164; YABC2: 307
Pearson, Larry 38: 225
Pearson, Tracey Campbell 64: 163, 164, 167, 168, 169; 118: 51; 156: 169, 171, 172; 163: 140
Peat, Fern B. 16: 115
Peck, Anne Merriman 18: 241; 24: 155
Peck, Beth 66: 242; 79: 166; 80: 136; 91: 34; 95: 9; 101: 77; 164: 197; 190: 170
Peddicord, Jane Ann 199: 106
Pedersen, Janet 193: 152
Pedersen, Judy 66: 217; 121: 36; 172: 67
Pedersen, Vilhelm YABC 1: 40
Pederson, Sharleen 12: 92
Pedlar, Elaine 161: 45
Peek, Merle 39: 168
Peet, Bill 2: 203; 41: 159, 160, 161, 162, 163; 78: 158, 159, 160, 161
Peguero, Adrian 116: 133
Peguero, Gerard 116: 133
Pels, Winslow Pinney 55: 126
Peltier, Leslie C. 13: 178
Peltzer, Marc 202: 92
Penberthy, Mark 171: 78
Pendle, Alexy 7: 159; 13: 34; 29: 161; 33: 215; 86: 62
Pendola, Joanne 76: 203; 81: 125; 105: 181; 178: 152, 153
Pene du Bois, William 4: 70; 10: 122; 26: 61; 27: 145, 211; 35: 243; 41: 216; 68: 180, 181; 73: 45
Penfound, David 102: 185
Pennington, Eunice 27: 162
Peppe, Mark 28: 142
Peppe, Rodney 4: 164, 165; 74: 187, 188, 189
Pepper, Hubert 64: 143
Percy, Graham 63: 2
Pericoli, Matteo 178: 177
Perini, Ben 173: 77
Perkins, David 60: 68
Perkins, Lucy Fitch 72: 199
Perkins, Lynne Rae 172: 146
Perl, Susan 2: 98; 4: 231; 5: 44, 45, 118; 6: 199; 8: 137; 12: 88; 22: 193; 34: 54, 55; 52: 128; YABC 1: 176
Perrone, Donna 78: 166
Perry, Marie Fritz 165: 180
Perry, Patricia 29: 137; 30: 171
Perry, Roger 27: 163
Perske, Martha 46: 83; 51: 108, 147
Persson, Stina 175: 166
Pesek, Ludek 15: 237
Petach, Heidi 149: 166; 200: 207
Peters, David 72: 205; 182: 116
Petersen, Jeff 181: 95
Petersham, Maud 17: 108, 147, 148, 149, 150, 151, 152, 153
Petersham, Miska 17: 108, 147, 148, 149, 150, 151, 152, 153
Peterson, Eric 109: 125
Peterson, Nisse 99: 27
Peterson, R.F. 7: 101
Peterson, Russell 7: 130
Petie, Haris 2: 3; 10: 41, 118; 11: 227; 12: 70
Petricic, Dusan 153: 75, 76, 77; 170: 12; 172: 13; 176: 170; 179: 56
Petrides, Heidrun 19: 223
Petrone, Valeria 159: 160; 171: 92; 186: 173; 204: 49
Petrosino, Tamara 177: 40; 193: 154, 155
Petruccio, Steven James 67: 159; 127: 5
Pettingill, Ondre 64: 181; 70: 64
Peyo 40: 56, 57
Peyton, K.M. 15: 212

Pfeifer, Herman *15:* 262
Pfister, Marcus *83:* 165, 166, 167; *146:* 152; *150:* 160; *207:* 132, 134, 135, 136
Pfloog, Jan *124:* 60
Pham, LeUyen *160:* 48; *175:* 154, 156; *179:* 149; *201:* 124, 125, 126, 127; *204:* 28; *208:* 206
Phelan, Matt *182:* 160; *184:* 222
Phillips, Craig *70:* 151; *207:* 74
Phillips, Douglas *1:* 19
Phillips, F.D. *6:* 202
Phillips, Louise *133:* 67
Phillips, Matt *184:* 173
Phillips, Thomas *30:* 55
Philpot, Glyn *54:* 46
Phiz
    See Browne, Hablot K.
Piatti, Celestino *16:* 223
Pica, Steve *115:* 181
Picarella, Joseph *13:* 147
Picart, Gabriel *121:* 165; *201:* 169
Pichon, Liz *174:* 139
Pickard, Charles *12:* 38; *18:* 203; *36:* 152
Picken, George A. *23:* 150
Pickens, David *22:* 156
Pickering, Jimmy *195:* 152; *197:* 163
Pienkowski, Jan *6:* 183; *30:* 32; *58:* 140, 141, 142,143, 146, 147; *73:* 3; *87:* 156, 157; *131:* 189
Pieper, Christiane *200:* 168
Pignataro, Anna *163:* 220 Pileggi, Steve *145:* 122
Pilkey, Dav *68:* 186; *115:* 164, 166; *166:* 173, 174, 175
Pimlott, John *10:* 205
Pincus, Harriet *4:* 186; *8:* 179; *22:* 148; *27:* 164, 165; *66:* 202
Pini, Wendy *89:* 166
Pinkett, Neil *60:* 8
Pinkney, Brian *81:* 184, 185; *94:* 107; *113:* 146, 147; *117:* 121, 166; *132:* 145; *158:* 108, 191; *160:* 189; *200:* 8
Pinkney, Jerry *8:* 218; *10:* 40; *15:* 276; *20:* 66; *24:* 121; *33:* 109; *36:* 222; *38:* 200; *41:* 165, 166, 167, 168, 169, 170, 171, 173, 174; *44:* 198; *48:* 51; *53:* 20; *56:* 61, 68; *58:* 184; *60:* 59; *61:* 91; *71:* 146, 148, 149; *72:* 17; *73:* 149; *74:* 159,192; *75:* 45; *80:* 206; *81:* 44; *85:* 144; *95:* 50; *107:* 158, 159, 160; *108:* 164; *112:* 114, 115; *133:* 58; *195:* 140
Pinkwater, Daniel Manus *46:* 180, 181, 182, 185, 188, 189, 190; *151:* 161 76: 178, 179, 180
Pinkwater, Manus *8:* 156; *46:* 180
    See also Pinkwater, Daniel Manus
Pinkwater, Jill *114:* 160, 161; *158:* 179; *188:* 143, 145, 146
Pinto, Ralph *10:* 131; *45:* 93
Pinto, Sara *200:* 165
Pinon, Mark *74:* 22
Piven, Hanoch *173:* 142
Pistolesi *73:* 211
Pitcairn, Ansel *188:* 10
Pitz, Henry C. *4:* 168; *19:* 165; *35:* 128; *42:* 80; *YABC 2:* 95, 176
Pitzenberger, Lawrence J. *26:* 94
Pitzer, Susanna *181:* 131
Player, Stephen *82:* 190
Plecas, Jennifer *84:* 201; *106:* 124; *149:* 168; *205:* 180
Ploog, Mike *180:* 19
Plowden, David *52:* 135, 136
Plume, Ilse *170:* 149
Plummer, William *32:* 31
Podevin, Jean François *184:* 185
Podwal, Mark *56:* 170, 173; *101:* 154, 155, 157; *149:* 176; *160:* 194
Pogany, Willy *15:* 46, 49; *19:* 222, 256; *25:* 214; *44:* 142, 143, 144, 145, 146, 147, 148

Pohrt, Tom *67:* 116; *104:* 80; *152:* 199; *195:* 154; *199:* 85
Poirson, V.A. *26:* 89
Polacco, Patricia *74:* 195, 196, 197, 198; *123:* 121, 122, 123; *180:* 189, 190, 191, 193, 194
Polgreen, John *21:* 44
Politi, Leo *1:* 178; *4:* 53; *21:* 48; *47:* 173,174, 176, 178, 179, 180, 181
Pollema-Cahill, Phyllis *123:* 126
Pollen, Samson *64:* 80
Polonsky, Arthur *34:* 168
Polseno, Jo *1:* 53; *3:* 117; *5:* 114; *17:* 154; *20:* 87; *32:* 49; *41:* 245
Pomaska, Anna *117:* 148
Pons, Bernadette *184:* 100
Ponter, James *5:* 204
Poole, Colin *111:* 27
Poortvliet, Rien *6:* 212; *65:* 165, 166, 167
Pope, Kevin *183:* 158
Popp, Wendy *72:* 122; *158:* 68
Poppel, Hans *71:* 154, 155
Porfirio, Guy *76:* 134
Portal, Colette *6:* 186; *11:* 203
Porter, George *7:* 181
Porter, Janice Lee *136:* 175; *164:* 37
Porter, John *113:* 47
Porter, Pat Grant *84:* 112; *125:* 101
Porter, Sue *146:* 246, 247
Porter, Walter *124:* 175
Posada, Mia *187:* 151
Posen, Michael *175:* 82
Posthuma, Sieb *150:* 163
Postier, Jim *202:* 140; *204:* 25
Postma, Lidia *79:* 17
Potter, Beatrix *100:* 194, 195; *132:* 179, 180, 181, 182; *YABC 1:* 208, 209, 210, 212, 213
Potter, Giselle *117:* 123; *143:* 44; *144:* 170, 197; *149:* 7; *150:* 165; *187:* 152, 153; *190:* 198; *196:* 152; *200:* 12
Potter, Katherine *104:* 147; *171:* 135; *173:* 136
Potter, Miriam Clark *3:* 162
Poulin, Stephane *98:* 140, 141
Poullis, Nick *146:* 210
Powell, Constance Buffington *174:* 141
Powell, Gary *151:* 208
Powell, Ivan *67:* 219
Power, Margaret *105:* 122
Powers, Daniel *161:* 173
Powers, Richard M. *1:* 230; *3:* 218; *7:* 194; *26:* 186
Powledge, Fred *37:* 154
Powzyk, Joyce *74:* 214
Poydar, Nancy *96:* 149; *190:* 180, 181, 182
Pracher, Richard *91:* 166
Prachaticka, Marketa *126:* 126
Prange, Beckie *181:* 169
Prap, Lila *177:* 165
Prater, John *103:* 142, 143, 144; *149:* 172
Pratt, Charles *23:* 29
Pratt, George *116:* 208
Pratt, Pierre *150:* 73; *166:* 183; *168:* 172; *201:* 27; *208:* 171, 172, 173
Prebenna, David *73:* 174
Preiss-Glasser, Robin *123:* 176; *152* 40; *172:* 194
Press, Jenny *116:* 95
Preston, Mark *152:* 162
Pretro, Korinna *91:* 126
Prevost, Mikela *209:* 111
Price, Christine *2:* 247; *3:* 163, 253; *8:* 166
Price, Cynthia *118:* 156
Price, Edward *33:* 34
Price, Garrett *1:* 76; *2:* 42
Price, Hattie Longstreet *17:* 13
Price, Norman *YABC 1:* 129
Price, Willard *48:* 184
Priceman, Marjorie *81:* 171; *136:* 169; *156:* 200; *168:* 153, 154; *188:* 45
Priestley, Alice *168:* 33
Priestley, Chris *198:* 144

Primavera, Elise *26:* 95; *58:* 151; *73:* 37; *80:* 79; *86:* 156; *105:* 161
Primrose, Jean *36:* 109
Prince, Alison *86:* 188, 189
Prince, Leonora E. *7:* 170
Pritchett, Shelley *116:* 148
Prittie, Edwin J. *YABC 1:* 120
Proimos, James *176:* 4
Proimos, John *173:* 144
Prosmitsky, Jenya *132:* 33
Provensen, Alice *37:* 204, 215, 222; *70:* 176, 177, 178, 180; *71:* 213; *147:* 184; *191:* 190
Provensen, Martin *37:* 204, 215, 222; *70:* 176, 177, 178, 180; *71:* 213; *191:* 190
Pucci, Albert John *44:* 154
Pudlo *8:* 59
Puggaard, Ulla *196:* 25
Pulver, Harry, Jr. *129:* 159
Pulver, Robin *160:* 4
Punchatz, Don *99:* 57
Purdy, Susan *8:* 162
Pursell, Weimer *55:* 18
Purtscher, Alfons *97:* 6
Puskas, James *5:* 141
Pyk, Jan *7:* 26; *38:* 123
Pyle, Chuck *99:* 149; *191:* 83
Pyle, Howard *16:* 225, 226, 227, 228, 230, 231, 232, 235; *24:* 27; *34:* 124, 125, 127, 128; *59:* 132; *100:* 198

Q

Quackenbush, Robert *4:* 190; *6:* 166; *7:* 175, 178; *9:* 86; *11:* 65, 221; *41:* 154; *43:* 157; *70:* 185, 186; *71:* 137; *85:* 47; *92:* 148; *133:* 154, 164, 169
Qualls, Sean *177:* 167, 168; *193:* 43
Quennell, Marjorie (Courtney) *29:* 163, 164
Quidor, John *19:* 82
Quirk, John *62:* 170
Quirk, Thomas *12:* 81

R

Rackham, Arthur *15:* 32, 78, 214-227; *17:* 105, 115; *18:* 233; *19:* 254; *20:* 151; *22:* 129, 131, 132, 133; *23:* 175; *24:* 161, 181; *26:* 91; *32:* 118; *64:* 18; *100:* 9, 16, 203, 204; *YABC 1:* 25, 45, 55, 147; *2:* 103, 142, 173, 210
Racz, Michael *56:* 134
Raczka, Bob *191:* 155, 156
Radcliffe, Andrew *82:* 215
Rader, Laura *101:* 219; *197:* 147; *203:* 53
Radunsky, Vladimir *177:* 170; *192:* 30
Rafilson, Sidney *11:* 172
Raglin, Tim *125:* 24
Raible, Alton *1:* 202, 203; *28:* 193; *35:* 181; *110:* 207
Raine, Patricia *82:* 74; *88:* 154
Ramá, Sue *173:* 45; *185:* 186; *190:* 184
Ramhorst, John *117:* 11
Ramirez, Gladys *177:* 19
Ramirez, Jose *207:* 27
Ramsey, James *16:* 41
Ramsey, Marcy Dunn *82:* 11; *180:* 186
Ramus, Michael *51:* 171
Rand, Paul *6:* 188
Rand, Ted *67:* 9, 10, 121, 123; *74:* 190; *84:* 170; *103:* 170; *112:* 6; *114:* 73; *139:* 168; *143:* 194; *156:* 154; *161:* 9, 10; *200:* 38; *204:* 7
Randazzo, Tony *81:* 98
Randell, William *55:* 54
Rane, Walter *93:* 144; *143:* 109; *184:* 126
Rankin, Joan *163:* 40

Rankin, Laura *176:* 173, 174; *179:* 150
Ransome, Arthur *22:* 201
Ransome, James E. *74:* 137; *75:* 80; *84:* 181; *94:* 108; *117:* 115; *123:* 128, 129, 130; *158:* 101, 102; *159:* 205; *178:* 188, 189, 190
Rantz, Don *119:* 184
Rao, Anthony *28:* 126
Raphael, Elaine *23:* 192; *71:* 24, 25
Rappaport, Eva *6:* 190
Raschka, Chris *80:* 187, 189, 190; *97:* 211; *115:* 210; *117:* 151, 152, 153, 154; *143:* 195; *145:* 153; *166:* 190, 191; *170:* 114; *207:* 140, 143, 144, 145; *208:* 82
Rash, Andy *158:* 178; *162:* 172
Raskin, Ellen *2:* 208, 209; *4:* 142; *13:* 183; *22:* 68; *29:* 139; *36:* 134; *38:* 173, 174, 175, 176, 177, 178,179, 180, 181; *60:* 163; *86:* 81
Rathmann, Peggy *93:* 32; *94:* 168; *157:* 212, 214
Ratkus, Tony *77:* 133
Ratzkin, Lawrence *40:* 143
Rau, Margaret *9:* 157
Raverat, Gwen *YABC 1:* 152
Ravid, Joyce *61:* 73
Ravielli, Anthony *1:* 198; *3:* 168; *11:* 143
Ravilious, Robin *77:* 169
Rawlins, Donna *72:* 198; *73:* 15, 129
Rawlins, Janet *76:* 79
Rawlings, Steve *143:* 139; *151:* 54; *208:* 150
Rawlinson, Debbie *75:* 132
Ray, Deborah Kogan *8:* 164; *29:* 238; *50:* 112, 113; *62:* 119; *78:* 191; *203:* 149, 150, 151
Ray, Jane *96:* 166; *97:* 104; *152:* 208; *190:* 221; *196:* 165
Ray, Ralph *2:* 239; *5:* 73
Rayann, Omar *162:* 205; *186:* 29, 30
Rayevsky, Robert *64:* 17; *70:* 173; *80:* 204; *117:* 79; *190:* 187, 188
Raymond, Larry *31:* 108; *97:* 109
Rayner, Hugh *151:* 170
Rayner, Mary *22:* 207; *47:* 140; *72:* 191; *87:* 171, 172; *192:* 104
Rayner, Shoo
  See Rayner, Hugh
Raynes, John *71:* 19
Raynor, Dorka *28:* 168
Raynor, Paul *24:* 73
Rayyan, Omar *110:* 222; *112:* 17; *125:* 131
Razzi, James *10:* 127
Read, Alexander D. *20:* 45
Reader, Dennis *71:* 157
Reasoner, Charles *53:* 33, 36, 37
Rebenschied, Shane *203:* 76
Reczuch, Karen *115:* 132; *145:* 131
Redlich, Ben *163:* 221; *198:* 193
Reddy, Mike *203:* 67
Reed, Joseph *116:* 139
Reed, Lynn Rowe *115:* 173; *171:* 146; *208:* 177
Reed, Tom *34:* 171
Reeder, Colin *74:* 202; *77:* 113
Rees, Mary *134:* 219
Reese, Bob *60:* 135
Reeve, Philip *171:* 50
Reeves, Eira B. *130:* 173, 174; *141:* 151
Reeves, Rick *181:* 179
Reeves, Rosie *202:* 200
Regan, Dana *117:* 116
Regan, Laura *103:* 198; *153:* 206
Reichert, Renée *169:* 127
Reid, Barbara *82:* 178; *92:* 17; *93:* 169, 170
Reid, Stephen *19:* 213; *22:* 89
Reim, Melanie *104:* 156; *150:* 98
Reinert, Kirk *89:* 138; *195:* 129
Reinertson, Barbara *44:* 150; *62:* 103
Reiniger, Lotte *40:* 185
Reisberg, Mira *119:* 2
Reisch, Jesse *158:* 130
Reiser, Lynn *81:* 175; *138:* 184; *180:* 200
Reiss, John J. *23:* 193
Relf, Douglas *3:* 63

Relyea, C.M. *16:* 29; *31:* 153
Remi, Georges *13:* 184
Remington, Frederic *19:* 188; *41:* 178, 179, 180, 181, 183,184, 185, 186, 187, 188; *62:* 197
Remkiewicz, Frank *67:* 102; *77:* 171; *80:* 130; *113:* 107; *152:* 116; *152:* 211, 212; *157:* 148
Rendon, Maria *116:* 141; *192:* *134:* 152
Renier, Aaron *202:* 141; *207:* 119
Renlie, Frank *11:* 200
Reschofsky, Jean *7:* 118
Rethi *60:* 181
Rethi, Lili *2:* 153; *36:* 156
Reusswig, William *3:* 267
Revell, Cindy *195:* 93
Rex, Adam *156:* 172; *169:* 91; *186:* 178, 179
Rex, Michael *157:* 147; *191:* 159, 160
Rey, H.A. *1:* 182; *26:* 163, 164, 166, 167, 169; *69:* 172, 173, 174, 175; *86:* 195, 196, 197; *100:* 211; *YABC 2:* 17
Rey, Luis V. *201:* 162
Reynolds, Adrian *192:* 159, 160
Reynolds, Doris *5:* 71; *31:* 77
Reynolds, Peter H. *142:* 12; *179:* 175, 176; *202:* 113, 114
Rhead, Louis *31:* 91; *100:* 228
Rhodes, Andrew *38:* 204; *50:* 163; *54:* 76; *61:* 123, 124; *87:* 200
Ribbons, Ian *3:* 10; *37:* 161; *40:* 76
Ricci, Regolo *93:* 22; *164:* 148
Rice, Elizabeth *2:* 53, 214
Rice, Eve *34:* 174, 175; *91:* 172
Rice, James *22:* 210; *93:* 173
Rich, Martha *195:* 16
Richards, Chuck *170:* 154
Richards, George *40:* 116, 119, 121; *44:* 179
Richards, Henry *YABC 1:* 228, 231
Richardson, Ernest *2:* 144
Richardson, Frederick *18:* 27, 31
Richardson, John *110:* 88
Richman, Hilda *26:* 132
Richmond, George *24:* 179
Riddell, Chris *114:* 170, 195; *166:* 179; *199:* 164, 166, 167
Riddle, Tohby *74:* 204; *151:* 179
Riding, Peter *63:* 195
Rienietz, Judy King *14:* 28
Riger, Bob *2:* 166
Riggio, Anita *73:* 191; *85:* 63; *137:* 184; *172:* 165
Riley, Jon *74:* 70
Riley, Kenneth *22:* 230
Riley, Terry *203:* 100
Riley-Webb, Charlotte *153:* 143
Rinaldi, Angelo *165:* 60, 69
Ringgold, Faith *71:* 162; *114:* 173, 174, 176; *187:* 160, 161, 163
Ringi, Kjell *12:* 171
Rios, Tere
  See Versace, Marie
Ripper, Charles L. *3:* 175
Ripplinger, Henry *117:* 31
Ritchie, William *74:* 183
Ritter, John *175:* 14
Ritz, Karen *41:* 117; *72:* 239; *87:* 125; *102:* 7; *106:* 6
Rivas, Victor *209:* 193
Rivers, Ruth *178:* 193
Rivkin, Jay *15:* 230
Rivoche, Paul *45:* 125
Roach, Marilynne *9:* 158
Robbin, Jodi *44:* 156, 159
Robbins, Frank *42:* 167
Robbins, Ken *147:* 191, 192
Robbins, Ruth *52:* 102
Roberts, Cliff *4:* 126
Roberts, David *154:* 4, 6; *191:* 162; *196:* 184; *197:* 105
Roberts, Doreen *4:* 230; *28:* 105
Roberts, Jim *22:* 166; *23:* 69; *31:* 110

Roberts, Tony *109:* 195, 214
Roberts, W. *22:* 2, 3
Robertson, M.P. *197:* 153
Robins, Arthur *137:* 172; *151:* 225; *204:* 161
Robinson, Aminah Brenda Lynn *86:* 205; *103:* 55; *159:* 175
Robinson, Charles [1870-1937] *17:* 157, 171, 172, 173, 175, 176; *24:* 207; *25:* 204; *YABC 2:* 308, 309, 310, 331
Robinson, Charles *3:* 53; *5:* 14; *6:* 193; *7:* 150; *7:* 183; *8:* 38; *9:* 81; *13:* 188; *14:* 248, 249; *23:* 149; *26:* 115; *27:* 48; *28:* 191; *32:* 28; *35:* 210; *36:* 37; *48:* 96; *52:* 33; *53:* 157; *56:* 15; *62:* 142; *77:* 41; *111:* 148
Robinson, Jerry *3:* 262
Robinson, Joan G. *7:* 184
Robinson, Lolly *90:* 227
Robinson, T.H. *17:* 179, 181, 182, 183; *29:* 254
Robinson, W. Heath *17:* 185, 187, 189, 191, 193, 195, 197, 199, 202; *23:* 167; *25:* 194; *29:* 150; *YABC 1:* 44; *2:* 183
Rocco, John *187:* 4; *188:* 151; *208:* 180, 181, 182
Roche, Denis *99:* 184; *180:* 32; *196:* 168
Roche, Christine *41:* 98
Roche, P.K. *57:* 151, 152
Rocker, Fermin *7:* 34; *13:* 21; *31:* 40; *40:* 190,191
Rocklen, Margot *101:* 181
Rockwell, Anne *5:* 147; *33:* 171, 173; *71:* 166, 167,168; *114:* 183, 184; *194:* 152, 155
Rockwell, Gail *7:* 186
Rockwell, Harlow *33:* 171, 173, 175
Rockwell, Lizzy *114:* 182; *162:* 182; *185:* 189
Rockwell, Norman *23:* 39, 196, 197, 199, 200, 203, 204, 207; *41:* 140, 143; *123:* 47; *YABC 2:* 60
Rockwood, Richard *119:* 75
Rodanas, Kristina *156:* 183, 184
Rodegast, Roland *43:* 100
Rodgers, Frank *69:* 177
Rodriguez, Albert G. *182:* 50
Rodriguez, Christina *184:* 12
Rodriguez, Edel *204:* 86
Rodriguez, Joel *16:* 65
Rodriguez, Robert *145:* 145
Rodriguez-Howard, Pauline *177:* 18
Roeckelein, Katrina *134:* 223
Roennfeldt, Robert *66:* 243
Roever, J.M. *4:* 119; *26:* 170
Roffey, Maureen *33:* 142, 176, 177
Rogasky, Barbara *46:* 90
Rogé *173:* 160
Rogers, Carol *2:* 262; *6:* 164; *26:* 129
Rogers, Chris M. *150:* 59; *196:* 61
Rogers, Forest *87:* 160; *101:* 76
Rogers, Frances *10:* 130
Rogers, Gregory *104:* 76; *126:* 57; *171:* 26
Rogers, Jacqueline *78:* 249; *80:* 34; *86:* 54 *103:* 70; *115:* 72; *129:* 173; *131:* 57, 225; *143:* 211; *153:* 100; *193:* 186; *203:* 51
Rogers, Sherry *191:* 66
Rogers, Walter S. *31:* 135, 138; *67:* 65, 168; *100:* 81
Rogers, William A. *15:* 151, 153, 154; *33:* 35
Rogoff, Barbara *95:* 20
Rohmann, Eric *103:* 152; *198:* 151
Rojankovsky, Feodor *6:* 134, 136; *10:* 183; *21:* 128,129, 130; *25:* 110; *28:* 42; *68:* 120
Rolfsen, Alf *62:* 15
Rolston, Steve *209:* 154
Romain, Trevor *134:* 157
Roman, Barbara J. *103:* 171
Romas *114:* 111; *165:* 63
Romano, Robert *64:* 68
Romero, Alejandro *187:* 185
Roos, Maryn *168:* 198
Root, Barry *80:* 212; *90:* 196; *146:* 78; *156:* 165; *159:* 161; *182:* 18, 172

Root, Kimberly Bulcken *86:* 72; *98:* 21; *108:* 111; *127:* 114; *159:* 162; *176:* 134; *192:* 163
Roper, Bob *65:* 153
Roraback, Robin *111:* 156
Rorer, Abigail *43:* 222; *85:* 155
Rosales, Melodye *80:* 35
Rosamilia, Patricia *36:* 120
Rose, Carl *5:* 62
Rose, David S. *29:* 109; *70:* 120
Rose, Gerald *68:* 200, 201; *86:* 48
Rose, Ted *93:* 178
Rosen, Elizabeth *205:* 137
Rosenbaum, Jonathan *50:* 46
Rosenberg, Amye *74:* 207, 208
Rosenberry, Vera *87:* 22, 26; *144:* 212, 213; *158:* 120
Rosenblum, Richard *11:* 202; *18:* 18
Rosenstiehl, Agnès *203:* 153
Rosier, Lydia *16:* 236; *20:* 104; *21:* 109; *22:* 125; *30:* 151, 158; *42:* 128; *45:* 214; *77:* 227, 228
Rosing, Jens *85:* 142
Ross
   See Thomson, Ross
Ross, Christine *83:* 172, 173
Ross, Clare Romano *3:* 123; *21:* 45; *48:* 199
Ross, Dave *32:* 152; *57:* 108
Ross, Graham *199:* 4
Ross, Herbert *37:* 78
Ross, John *3:* 123; *21:* 45
Ross, Johnny *32:* 190
Ross, Larry *47:* 168; *60:* 62
Ross, Ruth *109:* 233
Ross, Tony *17:* 204; *56:* 132; *65:* 176, 177, 179; *90:* 123; *123:* 186, 187, 190; *130:* 188, 190, 191, 192; *132:* 242; *174:* 159; *176:* 181, 182, 183; *202:* 198
Rossetti, Dante Gabriel *20:* 151, 153
Rostant, Larry *180:* 221; *194:* 108; *195:* 96; *197:* 12; *207:* 53
Roth, Arnold *4:* 238; *21:* 133
Roth, Julie Jersild *180:* 206
Roth, Marci *135:* 223
Roth, R.G. *184:* 50
Roth, Rob *105:* 98; *146:* 41
Roth, Robert *176:* 159
Roth, Roger *61:* 128; *190:* 192
Roth, Stephanie *136:* 171, 172
Roth, Susan L. *80:* 38; *93:* 78; *134:* 165, 166; *181:* 145, 146
Rothenberg, Joani Keller *162:* 190, 191
Rothman, Michael *139:* 62; *184:* 34 Rotman, Jeffrey L. *145:* 30
Rotondo, Pat *32:* 158
Roughsey, Dick *35:* 186
Rouille, M. *11:* 96
Rounds, Glen *8:* 173; *9:* 171; *12:* 56; *32:* 194; *40:* 230; *51:* 161, 162, 166; *56:* 149; *70:* 198, 199; *YABC 1:* 1, 2, 3; *112:* 163
Roundtree, Katherine *114:* 88; *168:* 102
Rovetch, Lissa *201:* 164
Rowan, Evadne *52:* 51
Rowe, Eric *111:* 161
Rowe, Gavin *27:* 144; *72:* 47; *88:* 201
Rowe, John *132:* 70, 71; *180:* 126
Rowell, Kenneth *40:* 72
Rowen, Amy *52:* 143
Rowena *116:* 101
Rowland, Andrew *164:* 136
Rowland, Jada *83:* 73
Rowles, Daphne *58:* 24
Roy, Jeroo *27:* 229; *36:* 110
Royo *118:* 32; *144:* 105, 106, 108; *165:* 19; *166:* 166
Rubel, Nicole *18:* 255; *20:* 59; *81:* 66, 67; *95:* 169, 170; *119:* 60; *135:* 177, 179, 180; *169:* 68; *181:* 150
Rubel, Reina *33:* 217
Rud, Borghild *6:* 15
Ruddell, Gary *110:* 238; *116:* 207
Rudolph, Norman Guthrie *17:* 13

Rue, Leonard Lee III *37:* 164
Rueda, Claudia *183:* 170, 171
Ruelle, Karen Gray *126:* 193
Ruff, Donna *50:* 173; *72:* 203; *78:* 49; *80:* 120,121; *93:* 162; *164:* 121
Ruffins, Reynold *10:* 134, 135; *41:* 191, 192, 193, 194, 195, 196; *125:* 187, 188, 189; *162:* 197
Ruhlin, Roger *34:* 44
Ruiz, Art *95:* 154; *110:* 91
Rumford, James *193:* 167
Runnerstroem, Bengt Arne *75:* 161
Ruse, Margaret *24:* 155
Rush, Ken *98:* 74
Rush, Peter *42:* 75
Russell, Charles M. *167:* 171
Russell, E.B. *18:* 177, 182
Russell, Jim *53:* 134
Russell, P. Craig *80:* 196; *146:* 102; *162:* 186
Russo, Marisabina *84:* 51; *106:* 164; *151:* 183; *188:* 153, 154, 155, 156
Russo, Susan *30:* 182; *36:* 144
Russon, Mary *87:* 145
Ruth, Greg *183:* 125
Ruth, Rod *9:* 161
Rutherford, Alexa *110:* 108
Rutherford, Jenny *78:* 5
Rutherford, Meg *25:* 174; *34:* 178, 179; *69:* 73; *72:* 31
Rutland, Jonathan *31:* 126
Ruurs, Margriet *147:* 195
Ruzzier, Sergio *159:* 176, 177; *163:* 184
Ryan, Amy *188:* 50
Ryan, Will *86:* 134
Ryden, Hope *8:* 176
Rylant, Cynthia *112:* 170, 172
Rymer, Alta M. *34:* 181
Ryniak, Christopher *178:* 11
Rystedt, Rex *49:* 80

S

Saaf, Chuck *49:* 179
Saaf, Donald *101:* 220; *124:* 180
Sabaka, Donna R. *21:* 172
Sabin, Robert *45:* 35; *60:* 30; *99:* 161
Sabuda, Robert *170:* 166, 167, 168
Sacker, Amy *16:* 100
Saelig, S.M. *129:* 73; *173:* 59
Saffioti, Lino *36:* 176; *48:* 60
Saflund, Birgitta *94:* 2
Sagsoorian, Paul *12:* 183; *22:* 154; *33:* 106; *87:* 152
Sahara, Tony *168:* 106; *177:* 181; *178:* 228; *186:* 132; *207:* 89
Sahlberg, Myron *57:* 165
Saidens, Amy *145:* 162; *191:* 131
Saint Exupery, Antoine de *20:* 157
Saint James, Synthia *152:* 220; *188:* 90; *200:* 7
Saldutti, Denise *39:* 186; *57:* 178
Sale, Morton *YABC 2:* 31
Sale, Tim *153:* 177
Salerno, Steven *150:* 79; *176:* 188; *202:* 39
Salter, George *72:* 128, 130
Saltzberg, Barney *135:* 184, 185; *194:* 160
Saltzman, David *86:* 209
Salwowski, Mark *71:* 54
Salzman, Yuri *86:* 12
Sambourne, Linley *YABC 2:* 181
Sampson, Katherine *9:* 197
Samson, Anne S. *2:* 216
San Souci, Daniel *40:* 200; *96:* 199, 200; *113:* 171; *157:* 149; *170:* 69; *192:* 167, 168
Sancha, Sheila *38:* 185
Sanchez, Enrique O. *155:* 84
Sand, George X. *45:* 182
Sandberg, Lasse *15:* 239, 241
Sanders, Beryl *39:* 173

Sanderson, Ruth *21:* 126; *24:* 53; *28:* 63; *33:* 67; *41:* 48, 198, 199, 200, 201, 202, 203; *43:* 79; *46:* 36,44; *47:* 102; *49:* 58; *62:* 121, 122; *85:* 3; *109:* 207, 208, 209, 210; *172:* 157, 158
Sandia *119:* 74
Sandin, Joan *4:* 36; *6:* 194; *7:* 177; *12:* 145,185; *20:* 43; *21:* 74; *26:* 144; *27:* 142; *28:* 224, 225; *38:* 86; *41:* 46; *42:* 35; *59:* 6; *80:* 136; *94:* 188; *140:* 116; *153:* 179, 180; *197:* 168
Sandland, Reg *39:* 215
Sandoz, Edouard *26:* 45, 47
Sanford, John *66:* 96, 97
Sanger, Amy Wilson *205:* 140
Sankey, Tom *72:* 103
Sano, Kazuhiko *153:* 208; *195:* 171; *203:* 21
Santat, Dan *188:* 160
Santore, Charles *54:* 139; *200:* 171, 172
Santoro, Christopher *74:* 215
Santos, Jesse J. *99:* 24
Sapieha, Christine *1:* 180
Saport, Linda *123:* 137, 138
Sara
   See De La Roche Saint Andre, Anne
Sardinha, Rick *175:* 151
Sarg, Tony *YABC 2:* 236
Sargent, Claudia *64:* 181
Sargent, Robert *2:* 217
Saris *1:* 33
Sarony *YABC 2:* 170
Saroff, Phyllis V. *202:* 160
Sasaki, Goro *170:* 46
Sasek, Miroslav *16:* 239, 240, 241, 242
Sassman, David *9:* 79
Satty *29:* 203, 205
Sauber, Robert *40:* 183; *76:* 256; *78:* 154; *87:* 92
Saunders, Dave *85:* 163, 164, 165
Savadier, Elivia *84:* 50; *145:* 45; *164:* 206
Savage, Naomi *56:* 172
Savage, Steele *10:* 203; *20:* 77; *35:* 28
Savage, Stephen *174:* 182
Savio *76:* 4
Savitt, Sam *8:* 66, 182; *15:* 278; *20:* 96; *24:* 192; *28:* 98
Sawyer, Kem Knapp *84:* 228, 229
Say, Allen *28:* 178; *69:* 182, 183, 232; *110:* 194, 195,196; *161:* 154, 155
Sayles, Elizabeth *82:* 93; *105:* 155; *109:* 116; *180:* 64
Scabrini, Janet *13:* 191; *44:* 128
Scanlan, Peter *83:* 27; *153:* 165; *187:* 149
Scanlon, Paul *83:* 87
Scannell, Reece *105:* 105
Scarry, Huck *35:* 204, 205
Scarry, Richard *2:* 220, 221; *18:* 20; *35:* 193, 194, 195,196, 197, 198, 199, 200, 201, 202; *75:* 165, 167, 168
Schachner, Judith Byron *88:* 180; *92:* 163; *93:* 102; *142:* 82; *178:* 199, 200; *190:* 140
Schade, Susan *205:* 21
Schaeffer, Mead *18:* 81, 94; *21:* 137, 138, 139; *47:* 128
Schaffer, Amanda *90:* 206
Schanzer, Rosalyn *138:* 192, 193
Scharl, Josef *20:* 132; *22:* 128
Scheel, Lita *11:* 230
Scheffler, Axel *180:* 23, 24
Scheib, Ida *29:* 28
Schermer, Judith *30:* 184
Schick, Eleanor *82:* 210, 211; *144:* 222
Schick, Joel *16:* 160; *17:* 167; *22:* 12; *27:* 176; *31:* 147, 148; *36:* 23; *38:* 64; *45:* 116, 117; *52:* 5, 85; *104:* 159
Schields, Gretchen *75:* 171, 203
Schindelman, Joseph *1:* 74; *4:* 101; *12:* 49; *26:* 51; *40:* 146; *56:* 158; *73:* 40
Schindler, Edith *7:* 22

Schindler, S.D. *38:* 107; *46:* 196; *74:* 162; *75:* 172, 173; *99:* 133; *112:* 177; *118:* 185, 186; *121:* 71; *136:* 159; *143:* 45; *149:* 120; *156:* 30; *169:* 135; *171:* 161, 162, 163; *172:* 9; *186:* 163; *194:* 109; *195:* 35; *198:* 170, 171, 172
Schlesinger, Bret *7:* 77
Schmid, Eleanore *12:* 188; *126:* 196, 197
Schmiderer, Dorothy *19:* 224
Schmidt, Bill *73:* 34; *76:* 220, 222, 224
Schmidt, Elizabeth *13:* 242
Schmidt, George Paul *132:* 122
Schmidt, Karen Lee *54:* 12; *71:* 174; *92:* 56; *94:* 190, 191; *127:* 103
Schmidt, Lynette *76:* 205
Schmitz, Tamara *207:* 147
Schneider, Christine M. *171:* 165
Schneider, Howie *181:* 159
Schneider, Rex *29:* 64; *44:* 171
Schnurr, Edward *170:* 62
Schoberle, Cecile *80:* 200; *92:* 134
Schoenherr, Ian *32:* 83; *173:* 41
Schoenherr, John *1:* 146, 147, 173; *3:* 39, 139; *17:* 75; *29:* 72; *32:* 83; *37:* 168, 169, 170; *43:* 164, 165; *45:* 160, 162; *51:* 127; *66:* 196, 197, 198; *68:* 83; *72:* 240; *75:* 225; *88:* 176
Scholder, Fritz *69:* 103
Schomburg, Alex *13:* 23
Schongut, Emanuel *4:* 102; *15:* 186; *47:* 218, 219; *52:* 147, 148, 149, 150; *185:* 27
Schoonover, Frank *17:* 107; *19:* 81, 190, 233; *22:* 88,129; *24:* 189; *31:* 88; *41:* 69; *YABC 2:* 282, 316
Schories, Pat *164:* 210
Schottland, Miriam *22:* 172
Schramm, Ulrik *2:* 16; *14:* 112
Schreiber, Elizabeth Anne *13:* 193
Schreiber, Ralph W. *13:* 193
Schreiter, Rick *14:* 97; *23:* 171; *41:* 247; *49:* 131
Schroeder, Binette *56:* 128, 129
Schroeder, E. Peter *12:* 112
Schroeder, Ted *11:* 160; *15:* 189; *30:* 91; *34:* 43
Schrotter, Gustav *22:* 212; *30:* 225
Schubert, Dieter *101:* 167, 168
Schubert-Gabrys, Ingrid *101:* 167, 168
Schucker, James *31:* 163
Schuett, Stacey *72:* 137; *208:* 204
Schulder, Lili *146:* 29
Schulke, Debra *57:* 167
Schulke, Flip *57:* 167
Schulz, Barbara *167:* 24
Schulz, Charles M. *10:* 137, 138, 139, 140, 141, 142; *118:* 192, 193, 194, 196, 199
Schutzer, Dena *109:* 32
Schwark, Mary Beth *51:* 155; *72:* 175
Schwartz, Amy *47:* 191; *82:* 100; *83:* 178, 179, 180,181; *129:* 107; *131:* 197, 198; *189:* 166, 168
Schwartz, Carol *124:* 41; *130:* 199
Schwartz, Charles *8:* 184
Schwartz, Daniel *46:* 37
Schwartz, Joanie *124:* 170
Schwartzberg, Joan *3:* 208
Schwarz, Viviane *204:* 132
Schweitzer, Iris *2:* 137; *6:* 207
Schweninger, Ann *29:* 172; *82:* 246; *159:* 202; *168:* 166
Schwinger, Laurence *84:* 44; *91:* 61
Scofield, Penrod *61:* 107; *62:* 160
Scott, Anita Walker *7:* 38
Scott, Art *39:* 41
Scott, Frances Gruse *38:* 43
Scott, Julian *34:* 126
Scott, Roszel *33:* 238
Scott, Sally *87:* 27
Scott, Steve *166:* 230, 231; *171:* 93
Scott, Trudy *27:* 172
Scrace, Carolyn *143:* 95, 96

Scrambly, Crab *198:* 196
Scribner, Joanne *14:* 236; *29:* 78; *33:* 185; *34:* 208; *78:* 75; *164:* 237; *203:* 73
Scrofani, Joseph *31:* 65; *74:* 225
Scroggs, Kirk *187:* 169
Seaman, Mary Lott *34:* 64
Searle, Ronald *24:* 98; *42:* 172, 173, 174, 176, 177, 179; *66:* 73, 74; *70:* 205, 206, 207
Searle, Townley *36:* 85
Sebree, Charles *18:* 65
Sedacca, Joseph M. *11:* 25; *22:* 36
Seder, Jason *108:* 102
Seeger, Laura Vaccaro *172:* 162
Seegmiller, Don *174:* 57
Seely, David *164:* 173
Seeley, Laura L. *97:* 105
Segal, John *178:* 202
Segar, E.C. *61:* 179, 181
Segur, Adrienne *27:* 121
Seibold, J. Otto *83:* 188, 190, 191; *149:* 212, 214, 215, 216; *196:* 177, 179
Seignobosc, Francoise *21:* 145, 146
Sejima, Yoshimasa *8:* 187
Selig, Sylvie *13:* 199
Seltzer, Isadore *6:* 18; *133:* 59
Seltzer, Meyer *17:* 214
Selven, Maniam *144:* 133
Selway, Martina *169:* 157
Selznick, Brian *79:* 192; *104:* 25; *117:* 175; *126:* 156; *134:* 171; *158:* 76, 78; *169:* 70; *171:* 172, 173; *191:* 106; *192:* 130; *197:* 158; *203:* 35; *205:* 92
Sempe, Jean-Jacques *47:* 92; *YABC 2:* 109
Sendak, Maurice *1:* 135, 190; *3:* 204; *7:* 142; *15:* 199; *17:* 210; *27:* 181, 182, 183, 185, 186, 187, 189,190, 191, 192, 193, 194, 195, 197, 198, 199, 203; *28:* 181, 182; *32:* 108; *33:* 148, 149; *35:* 238; *44:* 180, 181; *45:* 97, 99; *46:* 174; *73:* 225; *91:* 10, 11 *YABC1:* 167; *113:* 163, 165, 167, 168; *118:* 153; *127:* 161
Senders, Marci *180:* 79
Sengler, Johanna *18:* 256
Senn, Steve *60:* 145
Seredy, Kate *1:* 192; *14:* 20, 21; *17:* 210
Sergeant, John *6:* 74
Servello, Joe *10:* 144; *24:* 139; *40:* 91; *70:* 130, 131; *146:* 159
Seton, Ernest Thompson *18:* 260-269, 271
Seuss, Dr.
    See Geisel, Theodor
Severin, John Powers *7:* 62
Sewall, Marcia *15:* 8; *22:* 170; *37:* 171, 172, 173; *39:* 73; *45:* 209; *62:* 117; *69:* 185, 186; *71:* 212; *90:* 232; *96:* 127; *102:* 101; *107:* 129; *119:* 176, 177, 178, 180
Seward, James *70:* 35
Seward, Prudence *16:* 243
Sewell, Helen *3:* 186; *15:* 308; *33:* 102; *38:* 189, 190, 191, 192
Seymour, Stephen *54:* 21
Sfar, Joann *182:* 183
Shachat, Andrew *82:* 179
Shadbolt, Robert *203:* 68
Shahn, Ben *39:* 178; *46:* 193
Shalansky, Len *38:* 167
Shanks, Anne Zane *10:* 149
Shannon, David *57:* 137; *107:* 184; *112:* 216; *135:* 12; *152:* 223, 224, 225; *158:* 192
Sharp, Paul *52:* 60
Sharp, William *6:* 131; *19:* 241; *20:* 112; *25:* 141
Sharratt, Nick *102:* 207, 208; *104:* 163; *153:* 198; *175:* 176; *192:* 208; *199:* 141, 142, 143, 184, 187, 188
Shaw, Barclay *74:* 14, 16; *118:* 138
Shaw, Charles *21:* 135; *38:* 187; *47:* 124; *126:* 219
Shaw, Charles G. *13:* 200
Shaw-Smith, Emma *144:* 117
Shea, Edmund *56:* 19

Shearer, Ted *43:* 193, 194, 195, 196
Sheban, Chris *182:* 185; *190:* 102, 104; *202:* 28; *204:* 112, 114; *209:* 150
Shecter, Ben *16:* 244; *25:* 109; *33:* 188, 191; *41:* 77
Shed, Greg *74:* 94; *84:* 204; *129:* 149, *167:* 91; *179:* 192
Sheeban, Chris *144:* 190; *158:* 163
Shefcik, James *48:* 221, 222; *60:* 141
Shefelman, Karl *58:* 168
Shefelman, Tom *204:* 137
Shefts, Joelle *48:* 210
Shein, Bob *139:* 189
Sheinkin, Stephen *204:* 139
Shekerjian, Haig *16:* 245
Shekerjian, Regina *16:* 245; *25:* 73
Sheldon, David *184:* 174; *185:* 204
Shelley, John *186:* 223
Shemie, Bonnie *96:* 207
Shenton, Edward *45:* 187, 188, 189; *YABC 1:* 218, 219, 221
Shepard, Ernest H. *3:* 193; *4:* 74; *16:* 101; *17:* 109; *25:* 148; *33:* 152, 199, 200, 201, 202, 203, 204, 205, 206,207; *46:* 194; *98:* 114; *100:* 111, 178, 179, 217, 219, 220,221; *YABC 1:* 148, 153, 174, 176, 180, 181
Shepard, Mary *4:* 210; *22:* 205; *30:* 132, 133; *54:* 150, 152, 153, 157, 158; *59:* 108, 109, 111; *100:* 246
Shepherd, Amanda *198:* 14
Shepherd, Irana *171:* 112
Sheppard, Kate *195:* 176
Shepperson, Rob *96:* 153; *177:* 163; *178:* 204; *197:* 34; *205:* 108
Sheridan, Brian *196:* 193
Sherman, Theresa *27:* 167
Sherwan, Earl *3:* 196
Shields, Charles *10:* 150; *36:* 63
Shields, Leonard *13:* 83, 85, 87
Shiffman, Lena *139:* 167; *168:* 136
Shigley, Neil K. *66:* 219
Shillabeer, Mary *35:* 74
Shilston, Arthur *49:* 61; *62:* 58
Shimin, Symeon *1:* 93; *2:* 128, 129; *3:* 202; *7:* 85; *11:* 177; *12:* 139; *13:* 202, 203; *27:* 138; *28:* 65; *35:* 129; *36:* 130; *48:* 151; *49:* 59; *56:* 63, 65, 153
Shine, Andrea *104:* 165; *128:* 34
Shinn, Everett *16:* 148; *18:* 229; *21:* 149, 150, 151; *24:* 218
Shinn, Florence Scovel *63:* 133, 135
Shore, Robert *27:* 54; *39:* 192, 193; *YABC 2:* 200
Shortall, Leonard *4:* 144; *8:* 196; *10:* 166; *19:* 227, 228, 229, 230; *25:* 78; *28:* 66, 167; *33:* 127; *52:* 125; *73:* 12, 212
Shortt, T.M. *27:* 36
Shpitalnik, Vladimir *83:* 194
Shropshire, Sandy *170:* 191
Shtainments, Leon *32:* 161
Shulevitz, Uri *3:* 198, 199; *17:* 85; *22:* 204; *27:* 212; *28:* 184; *50:* 190, 191, 192, 193, 194, 195, 196,197, 198, 199, 201; *106:* 181, 182, 183; *165:* 203, 205; *166:* 138
Shulman, Dee *180:* 140
Shupe, Bobbi *139:* 80, 81
Shute, A.B. *67:* 196
Shute, Linda *46:* 59; *74:* 118
Siberell, Anne *29:* 193
Sibley, Don *1:* 39; *12:* 196; *31:* 47
Sibthorp, Fletcher *94:* 111, 112
Sidjakov, Nicolas *18:* 274
Siebel, Fritz *3:* 120; *17:* 145
Siebold, J. Otto *158:* 227
Siegel, Hal *74:* 246
Sieger, Ted *189:* 172
Siegl, Helen *12:* 166; *23:* 216; *34:* 185, 186
Silin-Palmer, Pamela *184:* 102
Sill, John *140:* 194; *141:* 157
Sills, Joyce *5:* 199
Silva, Simon *108:* 122

Silver, Maggie 85: 210
Silveria, Gordon 96: 44
Silverstein, Alvin 8: 189
Silverstein, Shel 33: 211; 92: 209, 210
Silverstein, Virginia 8: 189
Silvey, Joe 135: 203
Simard, Remy 95: 156
Simmons, Elly 110: 2; 127: 69; 134: 181
Simon, Eric M. 7: 82
Simon, Hilda 28: 189
Simon, Howard 2: 175; 5: 132; 19: 199; 32: 163, 164, 165
Simont, Marc 2: 119; 4: 213; 9: 168; 13: 238,240; 14: 262; 16: 179; 18: 221; 26: 210; 33: 189, 194; 44: 132; 58: 122; 68: 117; 73: 204, 205, 206; 74: 221; 126: 199, 200; 133: 195; 164: 128
Sims, Agnes 54: 152
Sims, Blanche 44: 116; 57: 129; 75: 179, 180; 77: 92; 104: 192; 152: 117; 156: 160; 160: 70; 168: 174, 175; 198: 17
Singer, Edith G. 2: 30
Singer, Gloria 34: 56; 36: 43
Singer, Julia 28: 190
Singh, Jen 178: 146
Siomades, Lorianne 134: 45; 204: 48
Simont, Marc 163: 40
Siracusa, Catherine 68: 135; 82: 218
Sís, Peter 67: 179, 181, 183, 184, 185; 96: 96, 98; 106: 193, 194, 195; 149: 224, 226; 180: 177; 192: 180, 182
Sivard, Robert 26: 124
Sivertson, Liz 116: 84
Skardinski, Stanley 23: 144; 32: 84; 66: 122; 84: 108
Slack, Michael 185: 108; 189: 173, 174
Slackman, Charles B. 12: 201
Slade, Christian 193: 187; 204: 134
Slade, Paul 61: 170
Slark, Albert 99: 212; 205: 161
Slater, Rod 25: 167
Slavin, Bill 182: 14, 15; 196: 90; 199: 148, 149, 150
Sloan, Joseph 16: 68
Sloane, Eric 21: 3; 52: 153, 154, 155, 156, 157, 158, 160
Sloat, Teri 164: 231
Slobodkin, Louis 1: 200; 3: 232; 5: 168; 13: 251; 15: 13, 88; 26: 173, 174, 175, 176, 178, 179; 60: 180
Slobodkina, Esphyr 1: 201
Slonim, David 166: 167, 168
Small, David 50: 204, 205; 79: 44; 95: 189, 190, 191; 126: 203, 204; 136: 119; 143: 201, 202, 203; 144: 246; 150: 5; 161: 176; 183: 181, 182, 183, 184; 200: 211
Small, W. 33: 113
Smalley, Janet 1: 154
Smath, Jerry 198: 179, 180
Smedley, William T. 34: 129
Smee, David 14: 78; 62: 30
Smee, Nicola 167: 156
Smith, A.G., Jr. 35: 182
Smith, Ali 204: 68
Smith, Alvin 1: 31, 229; 13: 187; 27: 216; 28: 226; 48: 149; 49: 60
Smith, Andy 188: 20; 207: 151
Smith, Anne 194: 147
Smith, Anne Warren 41: 212
Smith, Barry 75: 183
Smith, Brian 200: 183
Smith, Carl 36: 41
Smith, Cat Bowman 146: 39; 164: 219; 201: 55, 184
Smith, Craig 97: 197; 172: 175; 206: 40
Smith, Donald A. 178: 7
Smith, Doris Susan 41: 139
Smith, Douglas 189: 159
Smith, Duane 171: 152; 208: 97
Smith, E. Boyd 19: 70; 22: 89; 26: 63; YABC 1: 4, 5, 240, 248, 249

Smith, Edward J. 4: 224
Smith, Elwood H. 157: 231; 181: 79; 203: 160, 161, 162
Smith, Eunice Young 5: 170
Smith, Gary 113: 216
Smith, George 102: 169
Smith, Howard 19: 196
Smith, J. Gerard 95: 42
Smith, Jacqueline Bardner 27: 108; 39: 197
Smith, Jay J. 61: 119
Smith, Jeff 93: 191
Smith, Jessie Willcox 15: 91; 16: 95; 18: 231; 19: 57, 242; 21: 29, 156, 157, 158, 159, 160, 161; 34: 65; 100: 223; YABC 1: 6; 2: 180, 185, 191, 311, 325
Smith, Jos. A. 52: 131; 72: 120; 74: 151; 84: 147, 148; 85: 146; 87: 96; 94: 219; 96: 97; 104: 33; 108: 126, 127, 128; 111: 140; 136: 145; 181: 173; 200: 213; 201: 94
Smith, Kenneth R. 47: 182
Smith, Kevin Warren 89: 112
Smith, Kristin 209: 197
Smith, L.H. 35: 174
Smith, Lane 76: 211, 213; 88: 115; 105: 202, 203,204, 205; 131: 207; 160: 217, 221; 179: 183, 184, 185, 186; 199: 122, 123, 124, 126
Smith, Lee 29: 32
Smith, Linell Nash 2: 195
Smith, Maggie Kaufman 13: 205; 35: 191; 110: 158; 178: 226; 190: 204; 209: 145
Smith, Mavis 101: 219
Smith, Moishe 33: 155
Smith, Philip 44: 134; 46: 203
Smith, Ralph Crosby 2: 267; 49: 203
Smith, Robert D. 5: 63
Smith, Sally J. 84: 55
Smith, Susan Carlton 12: 208
Smith, Terry 12: 106; 33: 158
Smith, Virginia 3: 157; 33: 72
Smith, William A. 1: 36; 10: 154; 25: 65
Smith-Moore, J.J. 98: 147
Smolinski, Dick 84: 217
Smoljan, Joe 112: 201
Smollin, Mike 39: 203
Smyth, Iain 105: 207
Smyth, M. Jane 12: 15
Smythe, Fiona 151: 213
Smythe, Theresa 141: 37
Snair, Andy 176: 4
Sneed, Brad 125: 25; 191: 175, 176
Snyder, Andrew A. 30: 212
Snyder, Jerome 13: 207; 30: 173
Snyder, Joel 28: 163
So, Meilo 162: 201; 208: 188
Soentpiet, Chris K. 97: 208; 110: 33; 159: 184; 161: 10; 163: 130
Sofia 1: 62; 5: 90; 32: 166; 86: 43
Sofilas, Mark 93: 157
Sogabe, Aki 207: 153
Sohn, Jiho 182: 78
Sokol, Bill 37: 178; 49: 23
Sokolov, Kirill 34: 188
Solbert, Ronni 1: 159; 2: 232; 5: 121; 6: 34; 17: 249
Solomon, Michael 174: 115
Solonevich, George 15: 246; 17: 47
Soma, Liana 81: 118
Soman, David 90: 122; 102: 126; 140: 120; 93; 188: 43, 89; 200: 180, 181
Sommer, Robert 12: 211
Song, Jae 203: 27
Soo, Kean 201: 185
Sorel, Edward 4: 61; 36: 82; 65: 191, 193; 126: 214
Sorensen, Henri 196: 58
Sorensen, Henrik 62: 16
Sorensen, Svend Otto 22: 130, 141; 67: 188, 189
Sorra, Kristin 155: 80
Sosa, Hernan 198: 66
Sostre, Maria 187: 36

Sotomayor, Antonio 11: 215
Souhami, Jessica 112: 128; 176: 193
Sousa, Natalie C. 209: 89
Souza, Diana 71: 139
Sovak, Jan 115: 190
Soyer, Moses 20: 177
Spaenkuch, August 16: 28
Spafford, Suzy 160: 228
Spain, Valerie 105: 76
Spain, Sunday Sahara 133: 204
Spalenka, Greg 149: 69; 151: 228; 184: 195; 191: 21; 196: 12; 198: 181, 182, 201; 208: 92
Spanfeller, James 1: 72, 149; 2: 183; 19: 230, 231,232; 22: 66; 36: 160, 161; 40: 75; 52: 166; 76: 37
Sparks, Mary Walker 15: 247
Spears, Rick 182: 187
Speidel, Sandra 78: 233; 94: 178; 134: 180
Speirs, John 67: 178
Spence, Geraldine 21: 163; 47: 196
Spence, Jim 38: 89; 50: 102
Spencer, Laurie 113: 12
Spencer, Mark 57: 170
Spengler, Kenneth J. 146: 256
Sperling, Andrea 133: 182
Spiegel, Beth 184: 203
Spiegel, Doris 29: 111
Spiegelman, Art 109: 227
Spier, Jo 10: 30
Spier, Peter 3: 155; 4: 200; 7: 61; 11: 78; 38: 106; 54: 120, 121, 122, 123, 124, 125, 126, 127, 128, 129, 130,131, 132, 133, 134
Spilka, Arnold 5: 120; 6: 204; 8: 131
Spirin, Gennady 95: 196, 197; 113: 172; 128: 9; 129: 49; 134: 210; 153: 9; 204: 143, 144, 145
Spiro, Ruth 208: 197
Spivak, I. Howard 8: 10; 13: 172
Spohn, David 72: 233
Spohn, Kate 87: 195; 147: 201, 202
Spollen, Christopher J. 12: 214
Spooner, Malcolm 40: 142
Spowart, Robin 82: 228; 92: 149; 133: 131; 176: 163; 177: 183, 184
Sprague, Kevin 150: 60; 196: 62
Spranger, Nina 201: 199
Sprattler, Rob 12: 176
Spring, Bob 5: 60
Spring, Ira 5: 60
Springer, Harriet 31: 92
Spudvilas, Anne 110: 74; 197: 192; 199: 154
Spurll, Barbara 78: 199; 88: 141, 142; 99: 215
Spurrier, Steven 28: 198
Spuvilas, Anne 85: 114
Spy
    See Ward, Leslie
Squires, Stuart 127: 74
St. Aubin, Bruno 179: 54
St. John, J. Allen 41: 62
Staake, Bob 209: 168, 169
Stabin, Victor 101: 131; 164: 158
Stadler, John 62: 33; 204: 149
Staffan, Alvin E. 11: 56; 12: 187
Stahl, Ben 5: 181; 12: 91; 49: 122; 71: 128; 87: 206; 112: 107
Stair, Gobin 35: 214
Stallwood, Karen 73: 126
Stamaty, Mark Alan 12: 215
Stammen, JoEllen McAllister 113: 14
Stampnick, Ken 51: 142
Stanbridge, Joanne 150: 91
Stanley, Diane 3: 45; 37: 180; 80: 217, 219
Stanley, Sanna 145: 228
Starcke, Helmut 86: 217
Stark, Ken 197: 102
Starr, Branka 73: 25
Stasiak, Krystyna 49: 181; 64: 194
Staub, Leslie 103: 54
Staunton, Ted 112: 192
Stawicki, Matt 164: 250

Stead, L. *55:* 51, 56
Steadman, Broeck *97:* 185, 186; *99:* 56; *121:* 48; *208:* 190
Steadman, Ralph *32:* 180; *123:* 143, 145
Stearn, Nick *183:* 26
Steckler, June *90:* 178
Steele, Robert Gantt *169:* 174
Steichen, Edward *30:* 79
Steig, William *18:* 275, 276; *70:* 215, 216, 217, 218; *111:* 173, 174, 175, 176, 177
Stein, Harve *1:* 109
Steinberg, Saul *47:* 193
Steinel, William *23:* 146
Steiner, Charlotte *45:* 196
Steiner, Joan *110:* 219; *199:* 160, 161
Steirnagel, Michael *80:* 56
Stemp, Eric *60:* 184
Stephens, Alice Barber *66:* 208, 209
Stephens, Charles H. *YABC 2:* 279
Stephens, Pam *198:* 69
Stephens, Pat *126:* 110; *128:* 101
Stephens, William M. *21:* 165
Steptoe, Javaka *151:* 203, 204; *190:* 169
Steptoe, John *8:* 197; *57:* 9; *63:* 158, 159, 160, 161,163, 164, 165, 166, 167; *96:* 4; *105:* 87
Stern, Simon *15:* 249, 250; *17:* 58; *34:* 192, 193
Sterret, Jane *53:* 27
Stetsios, Debbie *165:* 108, 109
Steven, Kat *158:* 237
Stevens, David *62:* 44
Stevens, Helen *189:* 31; *207:* 83
Stevens, Janet *40:* 126; *57:* 10, 11; *80:* 112; *90:* 221, 222; *109:* 156; *130:* 34; *166:* 202; *176:* 53, 116; *193:* 199, 200, 202; *208:* 127
Stevens, Mary *11:* 193; *13:* 129; *43:* 95
Stevenson, Harvey *66:* 143; *80:* 201, 221; *153:* 60; *191:* 166
Stevenson, James *42:* 182, 183; *51:* 163; *66:* 184; *71:* 185, 187, 188; *78:* 262; *87:* 97; *113:* 182, 183,184, 185; *161:* 182, 183
Stevenson, Sucie *92:* 27; *104:* 194, 195; *112:* 168; *160:* 202; *194:* 172, 173; *195:* 166
Stewart, April Blair *75:* 210
Stewart, Arvis *33:* 98; *36:* 69; *60:* 118; *75:* 91; *127:* 4
Stewart, Charles *2:* 205
Stewart, Joel *151:* 205
Stieg, William *172:* 58
Stiles, Fran *26:* 85; *78:* 56; *82:* 150
Stillman, Susan *44:* 130; *76:* 83
Stimpson, Tom *49:* 171
Stimson, James *208:* 46
Stinemetz, Morgan *40:* 151
Stinson, Paul *110:* 86
Stirnweis, Shannon *10:* 164
Stites, Joe *86:* 96
Stobbs, William *1:* 48, 49; *3:* 68; *6:* 20; *17:* 117, 217; *24:* 150; *29:* 250; *60:* 179; *87:* 204, 205,206
Stock, Catherine *37:* 55; *65:* 198; *72:* 7; *99:* 225; *114:* 197, 198, 199; *126:* 3; *145:* 161; *161:* 82; *173:* 149; *208:* 210
Stockman, Jack *113:* 24
Stoeke, Janet Morgan *90:* 225; *136:* 196; *202:* 182, 183
Stoerrle, Tom *55:* 147
Stolp, Jaap *49:* 98
Stolp, Todd *89:* 195
Stone, David L. *87:* 154
Stone, David *9:* 173
Stone, David K. *4:* 38; *6:* 124; *9:* 180; *43:* 182; *60:* 70
Stone, Helen V. *6:* 209
Stone, Helen *44:* 121, 122, 126
Stone, Kazuko G. *134:* 43
Stone, Kyle M. *202:* 185
Stone, Phoebe *86:* 212; *134:* 213; *162:* 188; *205:* 145
Stone, Steve *166:* 213; *208:* 185
Stone, Tony *150:* 34, 35

Storrings, Michael *191:* 108
Stoud, Virginia A. *89:* 31
Stover, Jill *82:* 234
Strachan, Bruce *205:* 146
Stratton, Helen *33:* 151
Stratton-Porter, Gene *15:* 254, 259, 263, 264, 268, 269
Straub, Matt *192:* 176
Straub, Phillip *197:* 22
Streano, Vince *20:* 173
Street, Janet Travell *84:* 235
Streeter, Clive *121:* 2
Strickland, Shadra *209:* 179
Stringer, Lauren *129:* 187; *154:* 172, 173; *161:* 127; *183:* 187, 188
Strodl, Daniel *47:* 95
Strogart, Alexander *63:* 139
Stromoski, Rick *111:* 179; *124:* 161, 190
Strong, Joseph D., Jr. *YABC 2:* 330
Stroyer, Poul *13:* 221
Strugnell, Ann *27:* 38
Struzan, Drew *117:* 6
Stubbs, William *73:* 196
Stubis, Talivaldis *5:* 182, 183; *10:* 45; *11:* 9; *18:* 304; *20:* 127
Stubley, Trevor *14:* 43; *22:* 219; *23:* 37; *28:* 61; *87:* 26
Stuck, Marion *104:* 44
Stuecklen, Karl W. *8:* 34, 65; *23:* 103
Stull, Betty *11:* 46
Stutzman, Mark *119:* 99
Stutzmann, Laura *73:* 185
Suarez, Maribel *162:* 208; *200:* 202
Suave, Gordon *209:* 66
Suba, Susanne *4:* 202, 203; *14:* 261; *23:* 134; *29:* 222; *32:* 30
Sue, Majella Lue *209:* 182
Sueling, Barbara *98:* 185
Sueling, Gwenn *98:* 186
Sugarman, Tracy *3:* 76; *8:* 199; *37:* 181, 182
Sugimoto, Yugo *170:* 144
Sugita, Yutaka *36:* 180, 181
Suh, John *80:* 157
Sullivan, Dorothy *89:* 113
Sullivan, Edmund J. *31:* 86
Sullivan, James F. *19:* 280; *20:* 192
Sully, Tom *104:* 199, 200; *182:* 77
Sumichrast, Jozef *14:* 253; *29:* 168, 213
Sumiko *46:* 57
Summers, Leo *1:* 177; *2:* 273; *13:* 22
Summers, Mark *118:* 144
Summers, Mike *190:* 176
Sutton, Judith *94:* 164
Svarez, Juan *56:* 113
Svendsen, Mark *181:* 176
Svolinsky, Karel *17:* 104
Swain, Carol *172:* 182
Swain, Su Zan Noguchi *21:* 170
Swan, Susan *22:* 220, 221; *37:* 66; *60:* 146; *145:* 205; *181:* 168
Swann, Susan *86:* 55
Swanson, Karl *79:* 65; *89:* 186
Swarner, Kristina *203:* 62
Swayne, Sam *53:* 143, 145
Swayne, Zoa *53:* 143, 145
Swearingen, Greg *152:* 56; *165:* 135; *173:* 2
Sweat, Lynn *25:* 206; *57:* 176; *73:* 184; *168:* 178
Sweet, Darrell K. *60:* 9; *69:* 86; *74:* 15; *75:* 215; *76:* 130, 131; *81:* 96, 122; *82:* 253; *83:* 11; *84:* 14; *85:* 37; *89:* 140; *90:* 6; *91:* 137,139; *95:* 160, 161; *126:* 25; *185:* 175; *195:* 132
Sweet, Darrell K. *1:* 163; *4:* 136; *164:* 175
Sweet, Melissa *71:* 94; *72:* 172; *111:* 82; *139:* 53, 58; *141:* 88; *142:* 231; *155:* 121; *159:* 121, 122; *172:* 185; *188:* 127; *209:* 81
Sweet, Ozzie *31:* 149, 151, 152
Sweetland, Robert *12:* 194
Swiatkowska, Gabi *132:* 43; *175:* 139; *180:* 218; *183:* 176

Swope, Martha *43:* 160; *56:* 86, 87, 89
Sylvada, Peter *154:* 174
Sylvester, Natalie G. *22:* 222
Szafran, Gene *24:* 144
Szasz, Susanne *13:* 55, 226; *14:* 48
Szekeres, Cyndy *2:* 218; *5:* 185; *8:* 85; *11:* 166; *14:* 19; *16:* 57, 159; *26:* 49, 214; *34:* 205; *60:* 150, 151, 152, 153, 154; *73:* 224; *74:* 218; *131:* 213, 215
Szpura, Beata *81:* 68; *119:* 65; *168:* 201

T

Taback, Simms *40:* 207; *52:* 120; *57:* 34; *80:* 241; *104:* 202, 203; *170:* 176, 177; *205:* 183
Taber, Patricia *75:* 124
Tabor, Nancy Maria Grande *89:* 210; *161:* 188
Taddei, Richard *112:* 13, 14
Tadgell, Nicole *150:* 77; *161:* 20; *177:* 186; *209:* 16
Tadiello, Ed *133:* 200
Tafuri, Nancy *39:* 210; *75:* 199, 200; *92:* 75; *130:* 215, 216, 217
Tailfeathers, Gerald *86:* 85
Tait, Douglas *12:* 220; *74:* 105, 106
Takabayashi, Mari *113:* 112; *130:* 22; *156:* 169
Takahashi, Hideko *136:* 160; *187:* 6; *209:* 152, 187
Takakjian, Portia *15:* 274
Takashima, Shizuye *13:* 228
Talarczyk, June *4:* 173
Talbott, Hudson *84:* 240; *163:* 100
Tallarico, Tony *116:* 197
Tallon, Robert *2:* 228; *43:* 200, 201, 202, 203, 204, 205,206, 207, 209
Tamaki, Jillian *201:* 188
Tamas, Szecsko *29:* 135
Tamburine, Jean *12:* 222
Tandy, H.R. *13:* 69
Tandy, Russell H. *65:* 9; *100:* 30, 131
Tang, Charles *81:* 202; *90:* 192
Tang, Susan *80:* 174; *108:* 158
Tang, You-shan *63:* 100
Tankersley, Paul *69:* 206; *133:* 219
Tannenbaum, Robert *48:* 181
Tanner, Jane *87:* 13; *97:* 37
Tanner, Tim *72:* 192; *84:* 35
Tanobe, Miyuki *23:* 221
Tarabay, Sharif *110:* 149; *113:* 123; *169:* 83
Tarkington, Booth *17:* 224, 225
Tarlow, Phyllis *61:* 198
Tate, Don *159:* 141, 191; *183:* 69; *186:* 120
Tauss, Herbert *95:* 179
Tauss, Marc *117:* 160; *126:* 155; *178:* 221; *197:* 7
Tavares, Matt *159:* 192, 193; *198:* 188, 189, 190; *199:* 86
Taylor, Ann *41:* 226
Taylor, Dahl *129:* 157
Taylor, Geoff *93:* 156; *197:* 173, 175; *204:* 151, 152
Taylor, Isaac *41:* 228
Taylor, Mike *143:* 99, 100
Teague, Mark *83:* 6; *139:* 241; *170:* 180, 181; *205:* 150, 151
Teale, Edwin Way *7:* 196
Teason, James *1:* 14
Teckentrup, Britta *200:* 191, 192
Teeple, Lyn *33:* 147
Tee-Van, Helen Damrosch *10:* 176; *11:* 182
Teicher, Dick *50:* 211
Teichman, Mary *77:* 220; *124:* 208; *127:* 22; *197:* 33
Temertey, Ludmilla *96:* 232; *104:* 43, 45; *109:* 244
Tempest, Margaret *3:* 237, 238; *88:* 200
Temple, Frances *85:* 185, 186, 187
Temple, Herbert *45:* 201
Templeton, Owen *11:* 77

ten Cate, Marijke *183:* 193
Tenggren, Gustaf *18:* 277, 278, 279; *19:* 15; *28:* 86; *YABC2:* 145
Tennent, Julie *81:* 105
Tenneson, Joyce *153:* 166
Tenney, Gordon *24:* 204
Tenniel, John *74:* 234, 235; *100:* 89; *YABC 2:* 99; *153:* 63
Tepper, Matt *116:* 80
Terkel, Ari *103:* 162
Terry, Michael *180:* 209
Terry, Will *131:* 73; *205:* 155
Teskey, Donald *71:* 51
Tessler, Manya *200:* 193
Thacher, Mary M. *30:* 72
Thackeray, William Makepeace *23:* 224, 228
Thamer, Katie *42:* 187
Tharlet, Eve *146:* 149
Thelwell, Norman *14:* 201
Theobalds, Prue *40:* 23
Theurer, Marilyn Churchill *39:* 195
Thiesing, Lisa *89:* 134; *95:* 202; *156:* 190; *159:* 195
Thiewes, Sam *133:* 114
Thistlethwaite, Miles *12:* 224
Thollander, Earl *11:* 47; *18:* 112; *22:* 224
Thomas, Allan *22:* 13
Thomas, Art *48:* 217
Thomas, Eric *28:* 49
Thomas, Harold *20:* 98
Thomas, Jacqui *125:* 95
Thomas, Jan *197:* 190
Thomas, Mark *42:* 136
Thomas, Martin *14:* 255
Thomas, Middy *177:* 114
Thompson, Arthur *34:* 107
Thompson, Carol *85:* 189; *95:* 75; *102:* 86; *147:* 166; *189:* 179, 180, 181; *190:* 84; *207:* 18
Thompson, Colin *95:* 204
Thompson, Ellen *51:* 88, 151; *60:* 33; *67:* 42; *77:* 148; *78:* 75, 219; *79:* 122, 170; *84:* 219; *85:* 97; *87:* 37; *88:* 192, 194; *89:* 80; *93:* 37; *98:* 59; *132:* 14
Thompson, George W. *22:* 18; *28:* 150; *33:* 135
Thompson, John *58:* 201; *102:* 226; *124:* 154; *128:* 228; *129:* 157; *150:* 49; *185:* 160; *191:* 192
Thompson, Julie *44:* 158
Thompson, Katherine *132:* 146
Thompson, K. Dyble *84:* 6
Thompson, Miles *152:* 77
Thompson, Sharon *74:* 113; *158:* 60; *165:* 87
Thomson, Arline K. *3:* 264
Thomson, Bill *186:* 160
Thomson, Hugh *26:* 88
Thomson, Ross *36:* 179
Thorkelson, Gregg *95:* 183, 184; *98:* 58; *165:* 30, 31
Thorn, Lori *189:* 119
Thornberg, Dan *104:* 125
Thornburgh, Rebecca McKillip *143:* 37
Thorne, Diana *25:* 212
Thornhill, Jan *77:* 213
Thorpe, Peter *58:* 109
Thorvall, Kerstin *13:* 235
Threadgall, Colin *77:* 215
Thurber, James *13:* 239, 242, 243, 245, 248, 249
Thurman, Mark *63:* 173; *168:* 116
Tibbles, Jean-Paul *115:* 200
Tibbles, Paul *45:* 23
Tibo, Gilles *67:* 207; *107:* 199, 201
Tichenor, Tom *14:* 207
Tichnor, Richard *90:* 218
Tiegreen, Alan *36:* 143; *43:* 55, 56, 58; *77:* 200; *94:* 216, 217; *121:* 54, 59
Tierney, Tom *113:* 198, 200, 201
Tilley, Debbie *102:* 134; *133:* 226; *137:* 101; *159:* 96; *190:* 211, 212

Tilney, F.C. *22:* 231
Timbs, Gloria *36:* 90
Timmins, Harry *2:* 171
Timmons, Bonnie *194:* 189
Tinkelman, Murray *12:* 225; *35:* 44
Titherington, Jeanne *39:* 90; *58:* 138; *75:* 79; *135:* 161
Tjader, Ella *209:* 14
Tobin, Nancy *145:* 197
Toddy, Irving *172:* 144
Tokunbo, Dimitrea *181:* 183; *187:* 182, 183
Tolbert, Jeff *128:* 69
Toledo, Francisco *197:* 182; *198:* 199
Toledo, Natalia *197:* 182
Tolford, Joshua *1:* 221
Tolkien, J.R.R. *2:* 243; *32:* 215
Tolman, Marije *195:* 43
Tolmie, Ken *15:* 292
Tomei, Lorna *47:* 168, 171
Tomes, Jacqueline *2:* 117; *12:* 139
Tomes, Margot *1:* 224; *2:* 120, 121; *16:* 207; *18:* 250; *20:* 7; *25:* 62; *27:* 78, 79; *29:* 81, 199; *33:* 82; *36:* 186, 187, 188, 189, 190; *46:* 129; *56:* 71; *58:* 183; *70:* 228; *75:* 73, 75; *80:* 80; *83:* 97; *90:* 205
Tommaso, Rich *200:* 198
Toner, Raymond John *10:* 179
Tong, Gary *66:* 215
Tongier, Stephen *82:* 32
Tooke, Susan *173:* 162
Toothill, Harry *6:* 54; *7:* 49; *25:* 219; *42:* 192
Toothill, Ilse *6:* 58
Topolski, Feliks *44:* 48
Torbert, Floyd James *22:* 226
Torgersen, Don *55:* 157
Torline, Kevin *169:* 171
Tormey, Bertram M. *75:* 3, 4
Torrecilla, Pablo *176:* 207
Torres, Leyla *156:* 199, 201
Torrey, Helen *87:* 41
Torrey, Marjorie *34:* 105
Torrey, Richard *189:* 182; *205:* 24
Toschik, Larry *6:* 102
Totten, Bob *13:* 93
Toy, Julie *128:* 112
Trachok, Cathy *131:* 16
Tracy, Libba *82:* 24
Trago, Keith *158:* 253
Trail, Lee *55:* 157
Trang, To Ngoc *167:* 180
Trang, Winson *89:* 151
Trapani, Iza *116:* 202
Travers, Bob *49:* 100; *63:* 145
Treatner, Meryl *95:* 180
Tremain, Ruthven *17:* 238
Tresilian, Stuart *25:* 53; *40:* 212
Trez, Alain *17:* 236
Trezzo, Loretta *86:* 45
Trier, Walter *14:* 96
Trimby, Elisa *47:* 199
Trinkle, Sally *53:* 27
Triplett, Gina *182:* 193; *188:* 100; *198:* 38
Tripp, F.J. *24:* 167
Tripp, Wallace *2:* 48; *7:* 28; *8:* 94; *10:* 54,76; *11:* 92; *31:* 170, 171; *34:* 203; *42:* 57; *60:* 157; *73:* 182
Trivas, Irene *53:* 4; *54:* 168; *82:* 46, 101
Trnka, Jiri *22:* 151; *43:* 212, 213, 214, 215; *YABC 1:* 30, 31
Trondheim, Lewis *182:* 183
Troughton, Joanna *37:* 186; *48:* 72
Troyer, Johannes *3:* 16; *7:* 18
Trudeau, G.B. *35:* 220, 221, 222; *48:* 119, 123, 126, 127,128, 129, 133; *168:* 189
Trueman, Matthew *165:* 208; *183:* 191
Truesdell, Sue *55:* 142; *108:* 219, 220
Tryon, Leslie *84:* 7; *139:* 214; *143:* 10; *181:* 10
Tseng, Jean *72:* 195; *94:* 102; *119:* 126; *151:* 106; *173:* 138, 139; *200:* 158

Tseng, Mou-sien *72:* 195; *94:* 102; *119:* 126; *151:* 106; *173:* 138, 139; *200:* 158
Tsinajinie, Andy *2:* 62
Tsinganos, Jim *180:* 142
Tsugami, Kyuzo *18:* 198, 199
Tucker, Ezra *156:* 31
Tuckwell, Jennifer *17:* 205
Tudor, Bethany *7:* 103
Tudor, Tasha *18:* 227; *20:* 185, 186, 187; *36:* 111; *69:* 196, 198; *100:* 44; *YABC 2:* 46, 314; *160:* 234
Tuerk, Hanne *71:* 201
Tugeau, Jeremy *199:* 170; *203:* 96
Tulloch, Maurice *24:* 79
Tunis, Edwin *1:* 218, 219; *28:* 209, 210, 211, 212
Tunnicliffe, C.F. *62:* 176; 177; 178, 179; 181
Turkle, Brinton *1:* 211, 213; *2:* 249; *3:* 226; *11:* 3; *16:* 209; *20:* 22; *50:* 23; *67:* 50; *68:* 65; *79:* 205, 206, 207; *128:* 47; *YABC 1:* 79
Turnbull, Christopher J. *143:* 99, 100
Turner, Gwenda *59:* 195
Turner, Helen *203:* 154
Turska, Krystyna *12:* 103; *31:* 173, 174, 175; *56:* 32,34; *100:* 66
Tusa, Tricia *72:* 242; *111:* 180, 181; *157:* 165; *164:* 186; *189:* 40; *201:* 9; *207:* 163, 164
Tusan, Stan *6:* 58; *22:* 236, 237
Tworkov, Jack *47:* 207
Tyers, Jenny *89:* 220
Tylden-Wright, Jenny *114:* 119
Tyrol, Adelaide Murphy *103:* 27
Tyrrell, Frances *107:* 204
Tzimoulis, Paul *12:* 104

U

Uchida, Yoshiko *1:* 220
Uderzo *47:* 88
Udovic, David *189:* 185; *195:* 201
Ueno, Noriko *59:* 155
Ugliano, Natascia *196:* 186
Ulm, Robert *17:* 238
Ulrich, George *73:* 15; *75:* 136, 139; *99:* 150
Ulriksen, Mark *101:* 58; *182:* 43
Unada *84:* 67
See Gliewe, Unada
Underhill, Liz *53:* 159
Underwood, Beck *192:* 36
Underwood, Clarence *40:* 166
Unger, Jim *67:* 208
Ungerer, Tomi *5:* 188; *9:* 40; *18:* 188; *29:* 175; *33:* 221, 222, 223, 225; *71:* 48; *106:* 209, 210, 211, 212
Unwin, Nora S. *3:* 65, 234, 235; *4:* 237; *44:* 173, 174; *YABC 1:* 59; *2:* 301
Upitis, Alvis *145:* 179
Urban, Helle *149:* 243
Urbanovic, Jackie *86:* 86; *189:* 186, 187
Uris, Jill *49:* 188, 197
Ursell, Martin *50:* 51
Utpatel, Frank *18:* 114
Utz, Lois *5:* 190

V

Vagin, Vladimir *66:* 10; *142:* 215
Vaillancourt, Francois *107:* 199
Vainio, Pirkko *123:* 157, 158
Valério, Geraldo *180:* 225; *194:* 116
Vallejo, Boris *62:* 130; *72:* 212; *91:* 38; *93:* 61
Van Abbe, S. *16:* 142; *18:* 282; *31:* 90; *YABC 2:* 157, 161
Van Allsburg, Chris *37:* 205, 206; *53:* 161, 162, 163, 165,166, 167, 168, 169, 170, 171; *105:* 215, 216, 217, 218; *156:* 176, 177, 178

Vance, James *65:* 28
Van Der Linde, Henry *99:* 17
van der Meer, Ron *98:* 204, 205
van der Meer, Atie *98:* 204, 205
Vandivert, William *21:* 175
Van Dongen, H.R. *81:* 97
Van Dusen, Chris W. *173:* 169
Van Everen, Jay *13:* 160; *YABC 1:* 121
Van Fleet, John *165:* 12, 13
Van Frankenhuyzen, Gijsbert *145:* 230; *149:* 164; *184:* 151
van Genechten, Guido *165:* 226
van Haeringen, Annemarie *193:* 206
Van Horn, William *43:* 218
van Hout, Mies *195:* 191; *207:* 58
van Kampen, Vlasta *194:* 217
van Lawick, Hugo *62:* 76, 79
Van Lieshout, Maria *201:* 196
Van Loon, Hendrik Willem *18:* 285, 289, 291
Van Munching, Paul *83:* 85
van Ommen, Sylvia *186:* 192
Van Patter, Bruce *183:* 195
Van Rynbach, Iris *102:* 192
Van Sciver, Ruth *37:* 162
VanSeveren, Joe *63:* 182
Van Stockum, Hilda *5:* 193
Van Wassenhove, Sue *202:* 193
Van Wely, Babs *16:* 50; *79:* 16
Van Wright, Cornelius *72:* 18; *102:* 208; *116:* 107; *152:* 236; *173:* 170, 171; *199:* 185
Van Zyle, Jon *103:* 125; *160:* 181, 182; *176:* 199, 200
Vardzigulyants, Ruben *90:* 54
Varga, Judy *29:* 196
Vargo, Kurt *79:* 224
Varley, Susan *61:* 199; *63:* 176, 177; *101:* 148; *134:* 220
Varon, Sara *195:* 208
Vasconcellos, Daniel *80:* 42
Vasiliu, Mircea *2:* 166, 253; *9:* 166; *13:* 58; *68:* 42
Vaughn, Frank *34:* 157
Vavra, Robert *8:* 206
Vawter, Will *17:* 163
Vayas, Diana *71:* 61
Vazquez, Carlos *125:* 184
Veeder, Larry *18:* 4
Velasquez, Eric *45:* 217; *61:* 45; *63:* 110, 111; *88:* 162; *90:* 34, 144; *94:* 213; *107:* 147; *132:* 192; *138:* 213; *159:* 126; *181:* 184; *184:* 96; *191:* 16; *192:* 234; *208:* 37
Velasquez, Jose A. *63:* 73
Velez, Walter *71:* 75; *91:* 154; *121:* 181; *168:* 49; *207:* 52
Velthuijs, Max *110:* 228, 229
Vendrell, Carme Sole *42:* 205
Venezia, Mike *54:* 17
Venti, Anthony Bacon *124:* 103; *126:* 26
Venturo, Piero *61:* 194, 195
Ver Beck, Frank *18:* 16, 17
Verkaaik, Ben *110:* 209
Verling, John *71:* 27
Verney, John *14:* 225; *75:* 8
Vernon, Ursula *204:* 157
Verrier, Suzanne *5:* 20; *23:* 212
Versace, Marie *2:* 255
Verstraete, Randy *108:* 193
Vestal, H.B. *9:* 134; *11:* 101; *27:* 25; *34:* 158
Vestergaard, Hope *190:* 203
Vicatan *59:* 146
Vickrey, Robert *45:* 59, 64
Victor, Joan Berg *30:* 193
Viereck, Ellen *3:* 242; *14:* 229
Vigna, Judith *15:* 293; *102:* 194, 195, 196, 197
Vila, Laura *207:* 172
Vilato, Gaspar E. *5:* 41
Villiard, Paul *51:* 178
Vimnera, A. *23:* 154
Vincent, Eric *34:* 98
Vincent, Felix *41:* 237
Vincent, Gabrielle *121:* 175

Vip *45:* 164
Viskupic, Gary *83:* 48
Vitale, Stefano *109:* 71, 107; *114:* 219, 220; *123:* 106; *138:* 232; *180:* 228, 229
Vivas, Julie *51:* 67, 69; *96:* 225; *197:* 190; *199:* 71
Voake, Charlotte *114:* 221, 222; *180:* 232
Vo-Dinh, Mai *16:* 272; *60:* 191
Vogel, Ilse-Margret *14:* 230
Voigt, Erna *35:* 228
Vojnar, Kamil *95:* 31; *114:* 4; *115:* 62; *121:* 90; *124:* 72; *130:* 31; *141:* 81; *146:* 196; *150:* 123; *158:* 5, 6; *158:* 154; *171:* 119, 188; *179:* 15; *180:* 112; *203:* 74
Vojtech, Anna *42:* 190; *108:* 222, 223; *150:* 203; *174:* 173
von Buhler, Cynthia *149:* 237; *162:* 177; *177:* 205; *180:* 77; *185:* 214, 215, 216
von Roehl, Angela *126:* 191
von Schmidt, Eric *8:* 62; *50:* 209, 210
von Schmidt, Harold *30:* 80
Vosburgh, Leonard *1:* 161; *7:* 32; *15:* 295, 296; *23:* 110; *30:* 214; *43:* 181
Voss, Tom *127:* 104
Voter, Thomas W. *19:* 3, 9
Vroman, Tom *10:* 29
Vulliamy, Clara *72:* 65

W

Waber, Bernard *47:* 209, 210, 211, 212, 213, 214; *95:* 215, 216, 217; *156:* 203, 205, 206, 207
Wachenje, Benjamin *194:* 170
Wack, Jeff *95:* 140; *110:* 90
Wagner, John *8:* 200; *52:* 104
Wagner, Ken *2:* 59
Waide, Jan *29:* 225; *36:* 139
Wainwright, Jerry *14:* 85
Waites, Joan C. *171:* 2
Wakeen, Sandra *47:* 97
Wakiyama, Hanako *171:* 96; *192:* 236; *200:* 16
Waldherr, Kris *81:* 186
Waldman, Bruce *15:* 297; *43:* 178
Waldman, Neil *35:* 141; *50:* 163; *51:* 180; *54:* 78; *77:* 112; *79:* 162; *82:* 174; *84:* 5, 56, 106; *94:* 232, 233, 234; *96:* 41; *111:* 139; *113:* 9; *118:* 30; *142:* 220, 223; *203:* 173, 174
Waldrep, Richard *111:* 147; *198:* 202
Walker, Brian *144:* 128
Walker, Charles *1:* 46; *4:* 59; *5:* 177; *11:* 115; *19:* 45; *34:* 74; *62:* 168; *72:* 218
Walker, Dugald Stewart *15:* 47; *32:* 202; *33:* 112
Walker, Gil *8:* 49; *23:* 132; *34:* 42
Walker, Jeff *55:* 154; *123:* 116
Walker, Jim *10:* 94
Walker, Mort *8:* 213
Walker, Norman *41:* 37; *45:* 58
Walker, Stephen *12:* 229; *21:* 174
Wallace, Beverly Dobrin *19:* 259
Wallace, Cly *87:* 93
Wallace, Ian *53:* 176, 177; *56:* 165, 166; *58:* 4; *98:* 4; *101:* 191; *112:* 124; *141:* 197, 198, 199, 200; *151:* 212
Wallace, John *105:* 228
Wallace, Nancy Elizabeth *141:* 204; *186:* 195, 197, 199
Wallenta, Adam *123:* 180
Waller, S.E. *24:* 36
Wallner, Alexandra *15:* 120; *156:* 183
Wallner, John C. *9:* 77; *10:* 188; *11:* 28; *14:* 209; *31:* 56, 118; *37:* 64; *51:* 186, 187, 188, 189, 190, 191,192, 193, 194, 195; *52:* 96; *53:* 23, 26; *71:* 99; *73:* 158; *89:* 215; *141:* 9
Wallner, John *162:* 17
Wallower, Lucille *11:* 226
Walotsky, Ron *93:* 87

Walsh, Ellen Stoll *99:* 209; *147:* 219; *194:* 194, 195, 196
Walsh, Rebecca *158:* 193
Walsh, Vivian *149:* 215; *158:* 227
Walters, Anita *205:* 163
Walters, Audrey *18:* 294
Walther, Tom *31:* 179
Walton, Garry *69:* 149
Walton, Tony *11:* 164; *24:* 209; *153:* 8; *177:* 73
Waltrip, Lela *9:* 195
Waltrip, Mildred *3:* 209; *37:* 211
Waltrip, Rufus *9:* 195
Wan *12:* 76
Wang, Suling *191:* 183
Warburton, Sarah *154:* 187
Wappers, G. *121:* 40
Ward, Fred *52:* 19
Ward, Helen *72:* 244; *144:* 240, 242
Ward, John *42:* 191; *96:* 54; *97:* 110; *123:* 105; *124:* 71; *173:* 66
Ward, Keith *107:* 110; *132:* 69
Ward, Leslie *34:* 126; *36:* 87
Ward, Lynd *1:* 99, 132, 133, 150; *2:* 108, 158, 196, 259; *18:* 86; *27:* 56; *29:* 79, 187, 253, 255; *36:* 199,200, 201, 202, 203, 204, 205, 206, 207, 209; *43:* 34; *56:* 28; *60:* 116; *100:* 65
Ward, Peter *37:* 116
Waring, Geoff *172:* 84
Warhola, James *92:* 5; *115:* 85, 87; *118:* 174, 175, 177; *176:* 84; *187:* 189, 190
Warner, Ben *159:* 171
Warner, Peter *14:* 87
Warnes, Tim *175:* 159; *202:* 188
Warnick, Elsa *113:* 223
Warren, Betsy *2:* 101
Warren, Jim *85:* 81
Warren, Marion Cray *14:* 215
Warshaw, Jerry *30:* 197, 198; *42:* 165
Wasden, Kevin *102:* 162
Washington, Nevin *20:* 123
Washington, Phyllis *20:* 123
Wasserman, Amy L. *92:* 110; *209:* 95
Waterman, Stan *11:* 76
Watkins-Pitchford, D.J. *6:* 215, 217
Watling, James *67:* 210; *78:* 112; *101:* 81; *117:* 189, 190; *127:* 119, 120
Watson, Aldren A. *2:* 267; *5:* 94; *13:* 71; *19:* 253; *32:* 220; *42:* 193, 194, 195, 196, 197, 198, 199, 200, 201; *YABC 2:* 202
Watson, G. *83:* 162
Watson, Gary *19:* 147; *36:* 68; *41:* 122; *47:* 139
Watson, J.D. *22:* 86
Watson, Jesse Joshua *197:* 124; *199:* 181; *202:* 136
Watson, Karen *11:* 26
Watson, Mary *117:* 193
Watson, Richard Jesse *62:* 188, 189
Watson, Wendy *5:* 197; *13:* 101; *33:* 116; *46:* 163; *64:* 12; *74:* 242, 243; *91:* 21; *142:* 228
Watt, Mélanie *136:* 206; *193:* 211
Wattenberg, Jane *174:* 200; *185:* 46; *187:* 108
Watterson, Bill *66:* 223, 225, 226
Watts, Bernadette *4:* 227; *103:* 182, 183
Watts, James *59:* 197; *74:* 145; *86:* 124
Watts, John *37:* 149
Watts, Leslie Elizabeth *150:* 207; *165:* 106; *209:* 67
Watts, Stan *116:* 205
Weatherby, Mark Alan *77:* 141
Webb, Jennifer *110:* 79
Webb, Lanny *142:* 175
Webb, Sophie *135:* 214
Webber, Helen *3:* 141
Webber, Irma E. *14:* 238
Weber, Erik *56:* 19, 20
Weber, Florence *40:* 153
Weber, Jill *127:* 227, 228; *189:* 163; *208:* 157; *209:* 190, 191

Weber, Roland *61:* 204
Weber, Sam *190:* 227
Weber, William J. *14:* 239
Webster, Jean *17:* 241
Weeks, Sarah *162:* 39
Wegman, William *78:* 243
Wegner, Fritz *14:* 250; *20:* 189; *44:* 165; *86:* 62
Weidenear, Reynold H. *21:* 122
Weigel, Jeff *170:* 193
Weihs, Erika *4:* 21; *15:* 299; *72:* 201; *107:* 207, 208
Weil, Lisl *7:* 203; *10:* 58; *21:* 95; *22:* 188,217; *33:* 193
Weiman, Jon *50:* 162, 165; *52:* 103; *54:* 78, 79, 81; *78:* 80; *82:* 107; *93:* 82; *97:* 69; *105:* 179; *193:* 65
Weiner, Sandra *14:* 240
Weiner, Scott *55:* 27
Weinhaus, Karen Ann *53:* 90; *71:* 50; *86:* 124
Weinman, Brad *197:* 20
Weinstock, Robert *204:* 165, 166
Weisgard, Leonard *1:* 65; *2:* 191, 197, 204, 264, 265; *5:* 108; *21:* 42; *30:* 200, 201, 203, 204; *41:* 47; *44:* 125; *53:* 25; *85:* 196, 198, 200, 201; *100:* 139,207; *YABC 2:* 13
Weisman, David *173:* 47
Weiss, Ellen *44:* 202
Weiss, Emil *1:* 168; *7:* 60
Weiss, Harvey *1:* 145, 223; *27:* 224, 227; *68:* 214; *76:* 245, 246, 247
Weiss, Nicki *33:* 229
Weissman, Bari *49:* 72; *90:* 125; *139:* 142
Weitzman, David L. *172:* 199
Welch, Sheila Kelly *130:* 221
Welkes, Allen *68:* 218
Wellington, Monica *99:* 223; *157:* 259, 260, 261
Welliver, Norma *76:* 94
Wellner, Fred *127:* 53
Wells, Frances *1:* 183
Wells, H.G. *20:* 194, 200
Wells, Haru *53:* 120, 121
Wells, Robert E. *184:* 208
Wells, Rosemary *6:* 49; *18:* 297; *60:* 32; *66:* 203; *69:* 215, 216; *114:* 227; *118:* 149, 150; *156:* 188, 189, 190, 191; *207:* 180, 181, 182, 183
Wells, Rufus III *56:* 111, 113
Wells, Susan *22:* 43
Wendelin, Rudolph *23:* 234
Wengenroth, Stow *37:* 47
Weninger, Brigitte *189:* 192, 194
Werenskiold, Erik *15:* 6; *62:* 17
Werner, Honi *24:* 110; *33:* 41; *88:* 122
Werth, Kurt *7:* 122; *14:* 157; *20:* 214; *39:* 128
Wesson,
West, Harry A. *124:* 38
Westcott, Nadine Bernard *68:* 46; *84:* 49; *86:* 133; *106:* 199; *111:* 78; *113:* 111; *130:* 224; *139:* 54; *158:* 256; *194:* 199
Westerberg, Christine *29:* 226
Westerduin, Anne *105:* 229
Westerman, Johanna *162:* 206
Weston, Martha *29:* 116; *30:* 213; *33:* 85, 100; *53:* 181, 182, 183, 184; *77:* 95; *80:* 152; *119:* 196,197, 198, 199; *127:* 189; *133:* 196; *209:* 199
Wetherbee, Margaret *5:* 3
Wexler, Jerome *49:* 73; *150:* 129
Whalley, Peter *50:* 49
Whatley, Bruce *186:* 93, 95; *207:* 127
Wheatley, Arabelle *11:* 231; *16:* 276
Wheeler, Cindy *49:* 205
Wheeler, Dora *44:* 179
Wheelright, Rowland *15:* 81; *YABC 2:* 286
Whelan, Michael *56:* 108; *70:* 27, 29, 67, 68, 148; *74:* 18; *84:* 14; *91:* 195, 196; *95:* 147; *98:* 150, 151; *106:* 157; *113:* 218, 220; *116:* 99, 100
Whelan, Patrick *135:* 145

Whistler, Rex *16:* 75; *30:* 207, 208
White, Craig *110:* 130; *119:* 193; *130:* 33; *179:* 31
White, David Omar *5:* 56; *18:* 6
White, Joan *83:* 225
White, Martin *51:* 197; *85:* 127
Whitear *32:* 26
Whitehead, Beck *86:* 171
Whitehead, S.B. *154:* 132
Whithorne, H.S. *7:* 49
Whitman, Candace *208:* 208
Whitney, George Gillett *3:* 24
Whitney, Jean *99:* 53
Whitson, Paul *102:* 161
Whittam, Geoffrey *30:* 191
Whyte, Mary *96:* 127
Wiberg, Harald *38:* 127; *93:* 215
Wick, Walter *77:* 128
Wickstrom, Sylvie *106:* 87; *169:* 180
Wickstrom, Thor *200:* 205
Widener, Terry *105:* 230; *106:* 7; *163:* 23; *200:* 17; *209:* 195
Wiese, Kurt *3:* 255; *4:* 206; *14:* 17; *17:* 18, 19; *19:* 47; *24:* 152; *25:* 212; *32:* 184; *36:* 211,213, 214, 215, 216, 217, 218; *45:* 161; *100:* 92
Wiesner, David *33:* 47; *51:* 106; *57:* 67; *58:* 55; *64:* 78, 79, 81; *69:* 233; *72:* 247, 248, 249, 251,252, 253, 254; *83:* 134; *104:* 31; *117:* 197, 199, 200, 202; *139:* 223, 224; *151:* 51; *181:* 189, 190
Wiesner, William *4:* 100; *5:* 200, 201; *14:* 262
Wiggins, George *6:* 133
Wijngaard, Juan *111:* 36; *114:* 124
Wikkelsoe, Otto *45:* 25, 26
Wikland, Ilon *5:* 113; *8:* 150; *38:* 124, 125, 130; *127:* 162
Wikler, Madeline *114:* 233
Wilbur, C. Keith, M.D. *27:* 228
Wilburn, Kathy *53:* 102; *68:* 234
Wilcox, Cathy *105:* 123
Wilcox, J.A.J. *34:* 122
Wilcox, Lydia *207:* 187
Wilcox, R. Turner *36:* 219
Wild, Jocelyn *46:* 220, 221, 222; *80:* 117
Wilde, George *7:* 139
Wildsmith, Brian *16:* 281, 282; *18:* 170, 171; *66:* 25; *69:* 224, 225, 227; *77:* 103; *83:* 218; *124:* 214,217, 219
Wildsmith, Mike *140:* 229
Wilhelm, Hans *58:* 189, 191; *73:* 157; *77:* 127; *135:* 229, 230, 233, 234; *196:* 209
Wilkin, Eloise *36:* 173; *49:* 208, 209, 210
Wilkinson, Barry *50:* 213
Wilkinson, Gerald *3:* 40
Wilkon, Jozef *31:* 183, 184; *71:* 206, 207, 209; *133:* 222
Wilks, Mike *34:* 24; *44:* 203
Willems, Mo *154:* 245, 246, 247; *180:* 236, 237, 239
Willey, Bee *103:* 129; *139:* 159; *173:* 115
Willhoite, Michael A. *71:* 214
William, Maria *168:* 51
Williams, Berkeley, Jr. *64:* 75
Williams, Ferelith Eccles *22:* 238
Williams, Garth *1:* 197; *2:* 49, 270; *4:* 205; *15:* 198, 302, 304, 307; *16:* 34; *18:* 283, 298, 299, 300, 301; *29:* 177, 178, 179, 232, 233, 241, 242, 243, 244, 245, 248; *40:* 106; *66:* 229, 230, 231, 233, 234; *71:* 192; *73:* 218, 219, 220; *78:* 261; *100:* 251, 252, 255; *136:* 117; *YABC 2:* 15, 16, 19
Williams, J. Scott *48:* 28
Williams, Jennifer *102:* 201
Williams, Jenny *60:* 202; *81:* 21; *88:* 71
Williams, Kent *180:* 18
Williams, Kit *44:* 206, 207, 208, 209, 211, 212
Williams, Marcia *97:* 214; *159:* 208, 209
Williams, Maureen *12:* 238
Williams, Patrick *14:* 218

Williams, Richard *44:* 93; *72:* 229; *74:* 133; *78:* 155, 237; *91:* 178; *110:* 212; *136:* 201, 202, 203; *152:* 115
Williams, Sam *124:* 222; *153:* 11; *177:* 201, 202; *180:* 34
Williams, Sophy *135:* 236
Williams, Vera B. *53:* 186, 187, 188, 189; *102:* 201, 202, 203
Williamson, Alex *177:* 180; *205:* 50
Williamson, Mel *60:* 9
Willingham, Fred *104:* 206; *154:* 157
Willis, Adam *181:* 75; *209:* 11
Willmore, J.T. *54:* 113, 114
Wilsdorf, Anne *180:* 122; *189:* 124; *191:* 195
Wilson, Anne *160:* 114
Wilson, Charles Banks *17:* 92; *43:* 73
Wilson, Connie *113:* 179
Wilson, Dagmar *10:* 47
Wilson, Dawn *67:* 161; *81:* 120; *113:* 158
Wilson, Edward A. *6:* 24; *16:* 149; *20:* 220, 221; *22:* 87; *26:* 67; *38:* 212, 214, 215, 216, 217
Wilson, Forrest *27:* 231
Wilson, Gahan *35:* 234; *41:* 136
Wilson, George *76:* 87
Wilson, Helen Miranda *140:* 61
Wilson, Jack *17:* 139
Wilson, Janet *77:* 154; *96:* 114; *99:* 219, 220; *153:* 64 *106:* 122; *130:* 210; *145:* 178; *173:* 64
Wilson, John *22:* 240
Wilson, Maurice *46:* 224
Wilson, Patten *35:* 61
Wilson, Peggy *15:* 4; *84:* 20
Wilson, Phil *181:* 29
Wilson, Rowland B. *30:* 170
Wilson, Sarah *50:* 215
Wilson, Tom *33:* 232
Wilson, W.N. *22:* 26
Wilson-Max, Ken *170:* 196; *180:* 181
Wilton, Nicholas *103:* 52; *183:* 111
Wilwerding, Walter J. *9:* 202
Wimmer, Mike *63:* 6; *70:* 121; *75:* 186; *76:* 21,22, 23; *91:* 114; *97:* 45, 68; *98:* 28; *107:* 130; *146:* 21; *149:* 47; *173:* 126; *193:* 21, 25; *194:* 204, 205
Winborn, Marsha *78:* 34; *99:* 70; *192:* 20
Winch, John *165:* 233
Winchester, Linda *13:* 231
Wind, Betty *28:* 158
Windham, Kathryn Tucker *14:* 260
Windham, Sophie *184:* 212
Winfield, Alison *115:* 78
Winfield, Wayne *72:* 23
Wing, Gary *64:* 147
Wing, Ron *50:* 85
Wingerter, Linda S. *132:* 199; *174:* 181; *200:* 196
Winick, Judd *124:* 227, 228, 229
Winn-Lederer, Ilene *202:* 91
Winslow, Will *21:* 124
Winstead, Rosie *180:* 243
Winsten, Melanie Willa *41:* 41
Winter, Jeanette *151:* 240, 241, 242; *184:* 215, 217, 218, 219
Winter, Milo *15:* 97; *19:* 221; *21:* 181, 203, 204, 205; *64:* 19; *YABC 2:* 144
Winter, Paula *48:* 227
Winter, Susan *163:* 177; *182:* 201
Winters, Greg *70:* 117
Winters, Nina *62:* 194
Wise, Louis *13:* 68
Wiseman, Ann *31:* 187
Wiseman, B. *4:* 233
Wishnefsky, Phillip *3:* 14
Wiskur, Darrell *5:* 72; *10:* 50; *18:* 246
Wisniewski, David *95:* 220, 221
Wisniewski, Robert *95:* 10; *119:* 192
Witschonke, Alan *153:* 149, 150
Witt, Dick *80:* 244
Wittmann, Patrick *162:* 204

Wittman, Sally *30:* 219
Wittner, Dale *99:* 43
Wittwer, Hala *158:* 267; *195:* 80
Woehr, Lois *12:* 5
Wohlberg, Meg *12:* 100; *14:* 197; *41:* 255
Wohnoutka, Mike *137:* 68; *190:* 199; *195:* 218; *205:* 132
Wojtowycz, David *167:* 168
Woldin, Beth Weiner *34:* 211
Wolf, Elizabeth *133:* 151; *208:* 175
Wolf, J. *16:* 91
Wolf, Janet *78:* 254
Wolf, Linda *33:* 163
Wolfe, Corey *72:* 213
Wolfe, Gillian *199:* 193
Wolff, Ashley *50:* 217; *81:* 216; *156:* 216, 217; *170:* 57; *174:* 174; *184:* 72; *203:* 181, 182, 183, 184
Wolff, Glenn *178:* 230
Wolfsgruber, Linda *166:* 61
Wondriska, William *6:* 220
Wong, Janet S. *98:* 225; *152:* 43
Wong, Nicole *174:* 13
Wonsetler, John C. *5:* 168
Wood, Audrey *50:* 221, 222, 223; *81:* 219, 221; *198:* 206
Wood, Don *50:* 220, 225, 226, 228, 229; *81:* 218, 220; *139:* 239, 240
Wood, Grant *19:* 198
Wood, Heather *133:* 108
Wood, Ivor *58:* 17
Wood, Muriel *36:* 119; *77:* 167; *171:* 55; *187:* 46
Wood, Myron *6:* 220
Wood, Owen *18:* 187; *64:* 202, 204, 205, 206, 208, 210
Wood, Rob *193:* 48
Wood, Ruth *8:* 11
Woodbridge, Curtis *133:* 138; *204:* 113
Wooding, Sharon L. *66:* 237
Woodruff, Liza *132:* 239; *182:* 46, 204
Woodruff, Thomas *171:* 73
Woods, John, Jr. *109:* 142
Woodson, Jack *10:* 201
Woodson, Jacqueline *94:* 242
Woodward, Alice *26:* 89; *36:* 81
Wool, David *26:* 27
Woolley, Janet *112:* 75
Woolman, Steven *106:* 47; *163:* 73
Wooten, Vernon *23:* 70; *51:* 170
Worboys, Evelyn *1:* 166, 167
Word, Reagan *103:* 204
Wormell, Christopher *154:* 251; *202:* 206
Worth, Jo *34:* 143
Worth, Wendy *4:* 133
Wosmek, Frances *29:* 251
Wrenn, Charles L. *38:* 96; *YABC 1:* 20, 21
Wright, Barbara Mullarney *98:* 161
Wright, Cliff *168:* 203
Wright, Dare *21:* 206
Wright-Frierson, Virginia *58:* 194; *110:* 246
Wright, George *YABC 1:* 268
Wright, Joseph *30:* 160
Wronker, Lili Cassel *3:* 247; *10:* 204; *21:* 10
Wu, Donald *200:* 18
Wummer, Amy *154:* 181; *168:* 150; *176:* 85; *201:* 202, 203
Wyant, Alexander Helwig *110:* 19
Wyatt, David *97:* 9; *101:* 44; *114:* 194; *140:* 20; *167:* 13; *188:* 48

Wyatt, Stanley *46:* 210
Wyeth, Andrew *13:* 40; *YABC 1:* 133, 134
Wyeth, Jamie *41:* 257
Wyeth, N.C. *13:* 41; *17:* 252, 253, 254, 255, 256, 257, 258, 259, 264, 265, 266, 267, 268; *18:* 181; *19:* 80, 191, 200; *21:* 57, 183; *22:* 91; *23:* 152; *24:* 28, 99; *35:* 61; *41:* 65; *100:* 206; *YABC1:* 133, 223; *2:* 53, 75, 171, 187, 317
Wyman, Cherie R. *91:* 42

X

Xuan, YongSheng *119:* 202, 207, 208; *140:* 36; *187:* 21

Y

Yaccarino, Dan *141:* 208, 209; *147:* 171; *192:* 244, 245; *207:* 168
Yakovetic, Joe *59:* 202; *75:* 85
Yalowitz, Paul *93:* 33
Yamaguchi, Marianne *85:* 118
Yamasaki, James *167:* 93
Yang, Belle *170:* 198
Yang, Jay *1:* 8; *12:* 239
Yap, Weda *6:* 176
Yaroslava
  See Mills, Yaroslava Surmach
Yashima, Taro *14:* 84
Yates, John *74:* 249, 250
Yates, Kelly *208:* 214
Yayo *178:* 88
Yee, Cora *166:* 233
Yee, Wong Herbert *115:* 216, 217; *172:* 204, 205; *194:* 59
Yelchin, Eugene *204:* 4
Yeo, Brad *135:* 121; *192:* 106
Yerxa, Leo *181:* 195
Yezerski, Thomas F. *162:* 29
Ylla
  See Koffler, Camilla
Yohn, F.C. *23:* 128; *YABC 1:* 269
Yoo, Taeeun *191:* 198
Yorinks, Adrienne *144:* 248; *200:* 214
Yorke, David *80:* 178
Yoshida, Toshi *77:* 231
Yoshikawa, Sachiko *168:* 104; *177:* 28; *181:* 196, 197
Youll, Paul *91:* 218
Youll, Stephen *92:* 227; *118:* 136, 137; *164:* 248; *202:* 92
Young, Amy L. *185:* 218; *190:* 46
Young, Cybéle *167:* 9
Young, Ed *7:* 205; *10:* 206; *40:* 124; *63:* 142; *74:* 250, 251, 252, 253; *75:* 227; *81:* 159; *83:* 98; *94:* 154; *115:* 160; *137:* 162; *YABC 2:* 242; *173:* 174, 175, 176; *205:* 29
Young, Mary O'Keefe *77:* 95; *80:* 247; *134:* 214; *140:* 213
Young, Noela *8:* 221; *89:* 231; *97:* 195
Young, Paul *190:* 222
Young, Selina *153:* 12; *201:* 204, 205
Yun, Cheng Mung *60:* 143

Z

Zacharow, Christopher *88:* 98
Zacks, Lewis *10:* 161
Zadig *50:* 58
Zaffo, George *42:* 208
Zagwyn, Deborah Turney *138:* 227
Zahares, Wade *193:* 219
Zaid, Barry *50:* 127; *51:* 201
Zaidenberg, Arthur *34:* 218, 219, 220
Zalben, Jane Breskin *7:* 211; *79:* 230, 231, 233; *170:* 202
Zallinger, Jean *4:* 192; *8:* 8, 129; *14:* 273; *68:* 36; *80:* 254; *115:* 219, 220, 222
Zallinger, Rudolph F. *3:* 245
Zakrajsek, Molly *177:* 146
Zappa, Ahmet *180:* 250
Zebot, George *83:* 214
Zecca, Katherine *207:* 195
Zeck, Gerry *40:* 232
Zeifert, Harriet *154:* 265, 267
Zeiring, Bob *42:* 130
Zeldich, Arieh *49:* 124; *62:* 120
Zeldis, Malcah *86:* 239; *94:* 198; *146:* 265, 266
Zelinsky, Paul O. *14:* 269; *43:* 56; *49:* 218-223; *53:* 111; *68:* 195; *102:* 219, 222, 221, 222; *154:* 255, 256, 257; *171:* 141; *185:* 96
Zelvin, Diana *72:* 190; *76:* 101; *93:* 207
Zemach, Kaethe *149:* 250
Zemach, Margot *3:* 270; *8:* 201; *21:* 210, 211; *27:* 204, 205, 210; *28:* 185; *49:* 22, 183, 224; *53:* 151; *56:* 146; *70:* 245, 246; *92:* 74
Zeman, Ludmila *153* 212
Zemsky, Jessica *10:* 62
Zepelinsky, Paul *35:* 93
Zerbetz, Evon *127:* 34; *158:* 109
Zezejl, Daniel *197:* 74
Zhang, Ange *101:* 190; *172:* 41
Zhang, Son Nang *163:* 113; *170:* 206
Ziegler, Jack *84:* 134
Zimdars, Berta *129:* 155
Zimet, Jay *147:* 94; *152:* 74; *196:* 75
Zimic, Tricia *72:* 95
Zimmer, Dirk *38:* 195; *49:* 71; *56:* 151; *65:* 214; *84:* 159; *89:* 26; *147:* 224
Zimmer, Tracie Vaughn *169:* 183
Zimmerman, Andrea *192:* 49, 50
Zimmermann, H. Werner *101:* 223; *112:* 197
Zimnik, Reiner *36:* 224
Zingone, Robin *180:* 134
Zinkeisen, Anna *13:* 106
Zinn, David *97:* 97
Zoellick, Scott *33:* 231
Zollars, Jaime *190:* 190
Zonia, Dhimitri *20:* 234, 235
Zorn, Peter A., Jr. *142:* 157
Zudeck, Darryl *58:* 129; *63:* 98; *80:* 52
Zug, Mark *88:* 131; *204:* 169
Zulewski, Tim *164:* 95
Zuma *99:* 36
Zvorykin, Boris *61:* 155
Zweifel, Francis *14:* 274; *28:* 187
Zwerger, Lisbeth *54:* 176, 178; *66:* 246, 247, 248; *130:* 230, 231, 232, 233; *181:* 92; *194:* 224, 225, 226
Zwinger, Herman H. *46:* 227
Zwolak, Paul *67:* 69, 71, 73, 74

Author Index

The following index gives the number of the volume in which an author's biographical sketch, Autobiography Feature, Brief Entry, or Obituary appears.

This index includes references to all entries in the following series, which are also published by The Gale Group.

YABC—*Yesterday's Authors of Books for Children: Facts and Pictures about Authors and Illustrators of Books for Young People from Early Times to 1960*
CLR—*Children's Literature Review: Excerpts from Reviews, Criticism, and Commentary on Books for Children*
SAAS—*Something about the Author Autobiography Series*

A

Aardema, Verna 1911-2000 .... *107*
 Obituary *119*
 Earlier sketches in SATA *:4, 68*
 See also CLR *17*
 See also SAAS *8*
Aaron, Chester 1923- *74*
 Earlier sketch in SATA *9*
 See also SAAS *12*
Aaseng, Nate
 See Aaseng, Nathan
Aaseng, Nathan 1953- *172*
 Brief entry *38*
 Earlier sketches in SATA *51, 88*
 See also CLR *54*
 See also SAAS *12*
Abadzis, Nick 1965- *193*
Abalos, Rafael 1956- *197*
Abalos, Rafael 1956-
 See Abalos, Rafael
Abbas, Jailan 1952- *91*
Abbey, Lynn
 See Abbey, Marilyn Lorraine
Abbey, Marilyn Lorraine 1948- *156*
Abbott, Alice
 See Borland, Kathryn Kilby
 and Speicher, Helen Ross S(mith)
Abbott, Jacob 1803-1879 .... *22*
Abbott, Manager Henry
 See Stratemeyer, Edward L.
Abbott, R(obert) Tucker 1919-1995 .... *61*
 Obituary *87*
Abbott, Sarah
 See Zolotow, Charlotte
Abbott, Tony 1952- *205*
 Earlier sketch in SATA *159*
Abdelsayed, Cindy 1962- *123*
Abdul, Raoul 1929- *12*
Abeele, Veronique van den *196*
Abel, Raymond 1911- *12*
Abell, Kathleen 1938- *9*
Abelove, Joan *110*
Abels, Harriette S(heffer) 1926- *50*
Abercrombie, Barbara 1939- *182*
 Earlier sketch in SATA *16*
Abercrombie, Barbara Mattes
 See Abercrombie, Barbara

Abercrombie, Lynn
 See Sorrells, Walter
Abernethy, Robert G(ordon) 1927- *5*
Abisch, Roslyn Kroop 1927- *9*
Abisch, Roz
 See Abisch, Roslyn Kroop
Ablow, Gail 1962- *198*
Abodaher, David J. (Naiph) 1919- *17*
Abolafia, Yossi 1944-
 See Abulafia, Yossi
Abouzeid, Chris *175*
Abrahall, Clare Hoskyns
 See Hoskyns-Abrahall, Clare (Constance Drury)
Abrahams, Hilary (Ruth) 1938- *29*
Abrahams, Peter 1947- *194*
Abrahams, Robert David 1905-1998 .... *4*
Abramovitz, Anita (Zeltner Brooks) 1914- *5*
Abrams, Joy 1941- *16*
Abrams, Lawrence F. *58*
 Brief entry *47*
Abrashkin, Raymond 1911-1960 .... *50*
Abulafia, Yossi 1944- *177*
 Brief entry *46*
 Earlier sketch in SATA *60*
Acampora, Paul *175*
Accardo, Anthony *191*
Acer, David *206*
Achebe, Albert Chinualumogu
 See Achebe, Chinua
Achebe, Chinua 1930- *40*
 Brief entry *38*
 Earlier sketch in SATA *38*
 See also CLR *20*
Ackerman, Diane 1948- *102*
Ackerman, Eugene (Francis) 1888-1974 ...... *10*
Ackerman, Karen 1951- *126*
Ackerman, Susan Yoder 1945- *92*
Ackison, Wendy Wassink 1956- *103*
Ackley, Peggy Jo 1955- *58*
Ackroyd, Peter 1949- *153*
Acorn, John (Harrison) 1958- *79*
Acredolo, Linda (Potter) 1947- *159*
Acs, Laszlo (Bela) 1931- *42*
 Brief entry *32*
Acuff, Selma Boyd 1924- *45*
Ada, Alma Flor 1938- *181*
 Earlier sketches in SATA *43, 84, 143*
 See also CLR *62*

Adair, Gilbert 1944- *98*
Adair, Ian 1942- *53*
Adair, Margaret Weeks (?)-1971 .... *10*
Adam, Cornel
 See Lengyel, Cornel Adam
Adam, Mark
 See Alexander, Marc
Adam, Robert 1948- *93*
Adams, Adrienne 1906- *90*
 Earlier sketch in SATA *8*
 See also CLR *73*
Adams, Andy 1859-1935
 See YABC *1*
Adams, Barbara Johnston 1943- *60*
Adams, Bruin
 See Ellis, Edward S.
Adams, Captain Bruin
 See Ellis, Edward S.
Adams, Captain J. F. C.
 See Ellis, Edward S.
Adams, Dale
 See Quinn, Elisabeth
Adams, Daniel
 See Nicole, Christopher (Robin)
Adams, Debra
 See Speregen, Devra Newberger
Adams, Douglas 1952-2001 .... *116*
 Obituary *128*
Adams, Douglas Noel
 See Adams, Douglas
Adams, Edith
 See Shine, Deborah
Adams, Florence 1932- *61*
Adams, Harriet S(tratemeyer) 1892(?)-1982 .. *1*
 Obituary *29*
Adams, Harrison
 See Rathborne, St. George (Henry)
 and Stratemeyer, Edward L.
Adams, Hazard 1926- *6*
Adams, Hazard Simeon
 See Adams, Hazard
Adams, John Anthony 1944- *67*
Adams, Laurie 1941- *33*
Adams, Lowell
 See Joseph, James (Herz)
Adams, Nicholas
 See Pine, Nicholas
Adams, Nicholas
 See Smith, Sherwood

Adams, Nicholas
  See Doyle, Debra
  and Macdonald, James D.
Adams, Pam 1919- *112*
Adams, Pamela
  See Adams, Pam
Adams, Richard 1920- *69*
  Earlier sketch in SATA *7*
  See also CLR *121*
Adams, Richard George
  See Adams, Richard
Adams, Ruth Joyce *14*
Adams, Tricia
  See Kite, Pat
Adams, William Taylor 1822-1897 .... *28*
Adam Smith, Janet (Buchanan) 1905-1999 .. *63*
Adamson, Gareth 1925-1982(?) *46*
  Obituary *30*
Adamson, George 1906-1989
  Obituary *63*
Adamson, George (Worsley) 1913-2005 ...... *30*
Adamson, Graham
  See Groom, Arthur William
Adamson, Joy(-Friederike Victoria)
  1910-1980 .... *11*
  Obituary *22*
Adamson, Wendy Writson 1942- *22*
Addasi, Maha 1968- *205*
Addison, Kenneth 1949(?)-2005 .... *187*
Addison, Kenneth L.
  See Addison, Kenneth
Addona, Angelo F. 1925- *14*
Addy, Sharon Hart 1943- *192*
  Earlier sketch in SATA *108*
Addy, Ted
  See Winterbotham, R(ussell) R(obert)
Adelberg, Doris
  See Orgel, Doris
Adelson, Leone 1908- *11*
Adinolfi, JoAnn *176*
Adkins, Jan 1944- *144*
  Earlier sketches in SATA *8, 69*
  See also CLR *77*
  See also SAAS *19*
Adler, C(arole) S(chwerdtfeger) 1932- *126*
  Earlier sketches in SATA *26, 63, 102*
  See also CLR *78*
  See also SAAS *15*
Adler, David A. 1947- *178*
  Earlier sketches in SATA *14, 70, 106, 151*
  See also CLR *108*
Adler, Irene
  See Penzler, Otto
  and Storr, Catherine (Cole)
Adler, Irving 1913- *29*
  Autobiography Feature *164*
  Earlier sketch in SATA *1*
  See also CLR *27*
  See also SAAS *15*
Adler, Larry 1939- *36*
Adler, Peggy *22*
Adler, Ruth 1915-1968 .... *1*
Adlerman, Daniel (Ezra) 1963- *163*
  Earlier sketch in SATA *96*
Adlerman, Kim
  See Adlerman, Kimberly M(arie)
Adlerman, Kimberly M(arie) 1964- *163*
  Earlier sketch in SATA *96*
Adoff, Arnold 1935- *96*
  Earlier sketches in SATA *5, 57*
  See also CLR *7*
  See also SAAS *15*
Adoff, Jaime *163*
Adoff, Jaime Levi
  See Adoff, Jaime
Adorjan, Carol (Madden) 1934- *71*
  Earlier sketch in SATA *10*
Adrian, Frances
  See Polland, Madeleine A(ngela Cahill)
Adrian, Mary
  See Jorgensen, Mary Venn

Adshead, Gladys L(ucy) 1896-1985 .... *3*
Aesop 620(?)B.C.-560(?)B.C. *64*
  See also CLR *14*
Aesop, Abraham
  See Newbery, John
Affabee, Eric
  See Stine, R.L.
Agapida, Fray Antonio
  See Irving, Washington
Agard, John 1949- *138*
Agard, Nadema 1948- *18*
Agarwal, Deepa 1947- *141*
Agee, Jon 1960- *196*
  Earlier sketches in SATA *116, 157*
Agell, Charlotte 1959- *150*
  Earlier sketch in SATA *99*
Agent Orange
  See Moseley, James W(illett)
Aghill, Gordon
  See Garrett, Randall
  and Silverberg, Robert
Agle, Nan Hayden 1905- *3*
  See also SAAS *10*
Agnew, Edith J(osephine) 1897-1988 .... *11*
Agonito, Joseph *177*
Agonito, Rosemary 1937- *177*
Ahern, Margaret McCrohan 1921- *10*
Ahl, Anna Maria 1926- *32*
Ahlberg, Allan 1938- *165*
  Brief entry *35*
  Earlier sketches in SATA *68, 120*
  See also CLR *18*
Ahlberg, Janet 1944-1994 .... *120*
  Brief entry *32*
  Obituary *83*
  Earlier sketch in SATA *68*
  See also CLR *18*
Aho, Julia Kay
  See Kay, Julia
Aichinger, Helga 1937- *4*
Aiken, Clarissa (M.) Lorenz 1899-1992 .... *12*
  Obituary *109*
Aiken, Conrad 1889-1973 .... *30*
  Earlier sketch in SATA *3*
Aiken, Conrad Potter
  See Aiken, Conrad
Aiken, Joan (Delano) 1924-2004 .... *73*
  Autobiography Feature *109*
  Obituary *152*
  Earlier sketches in SATA *2, 30*
  See also CLR *90*
  See also SAAS *1*
Aillaud, Cindy Lou 1955- *184*
Ainsley, Alix
  See Steiner, Barbara A(nnette)
Ainsworth, Catherine Harris 1910- *56*
Ainsworth, Norma 1911-1987 .... *9*
Ainsworth, Ruth (Gallard) 1908- *73*
  Earlier sketch in SATA *7*
Ainsworth, William Harrison 1805-1882 ..... *24*
Aistrop, Jack 1916- *14*
Aitken, Amy 1952- *54*
  Brief entry *40*
Aitken, Dorothy 1916- *10*
Aitmatov, Chingiz 1928-2008 .... *56*
Aitmatov, Chingiz Torekulovich
  See Aitmatov, Chingiz
Akaba, Suekichi 1910- *46*
Akers, Floyd
  See Baum, L. Frank
Akib, Jamel *181*
Aks, Patricia 1926-1994 .... *68*
Alagoa, Ebiegberi Joe 1933- *108*
Alain
  See Brustlein, Daniel
Alajalov, Constantin 1900-1987
  Obituary *53*
Alalou, Ali *203*
Alalou, Elizabeth *203*
Alan, David
  See Horsfield, Alan

Alan, Robert
  See Silverstein, Robert Alan
Alarcon, Francisco X. 1954- *104*
Alarcon, Francisco Xavier
  See Alarcon, Francisco X.
Alarcon, Karen Beaumont
  See Beaumont, Karen
Albert, Burton 1936- *22*
Albert, Louise 1928- *157*
Albert, Michael 1966- *202*
Albert, Richard E. 1909-1999 .... *82*
Albert, Susan Wittig 1940- *107*
Alberts, Frances Jacobs 1907-1989 .... *14*
Albertson, Susan
  See Wojciechowski, Susan
Albion, Lee Smith *29*
Alborough, Jez 1959- *149*
  Earlier sketch in SATA *86*
Albrecht, Lillie (Vanderveer H.)
  1894-1985 .... *12*
Albyn, Carole Lisa 1955- *83*
Alchemy, Jack
  See Gershator, David
Alcock, Gudrun 1908- *56*
  Brief entry *33*
Alcock, Vivien (Dolores) 1924-2003 .... *76*
  Brief entry *38*
  Obituary *148*
  Earlier sketch in SATA *45*
  See also CLR *26*
Alcorn, John 1935- *31*
  Brief entry *30*
Alcorn, Stephen 1958- *207*
  Earlier sketch in SATA *110*
Alcott, Louisa May 1832-1888 .... *100*
  See also YABC *1*
  See also CLR *109*
Alda, Arlene 1933- *205*
  Brief entry *36*
  Earlier sketches in SATA *44, 106, 158*
  See also CLR *93*
Alden, Isabella (Macdonald) 1841-1930 ..... *115*
  See also YABC *2*
Alden, Sue
  See Francis, Dorothy
Alderman, Clifford Lindsey 1902-1988 .... *3*
Alderson, Sue Ann 1940- *59*
  Brief entry *48*
Alding, Peter
  See Jeffries, Roderic
Aldis, Dorothy (Keeley) 1896-1966 .... *2*
Aldiss, Brian W. 1925- *34*
Aldiss, Brian Wilson
  See Aldiss, Brian W.
Aldon, Adair
  See Meigs, Cornelia Lynde
Aldous, Allan (Charles) 1911- *27*
Aldrich, Ann
  See Meaker, Marijane
Aldrich, Bess Streeter 1881-1954
  See CLR *70*
Aldrich, Thomas (Bailey) 1836-1907 .... *114*
  Earlier sketch in SATA *17*
Aldridge, (Harold Edward) James 1918- *87*
Aldridge, Josephine Haskell *14*
Aldridge, Sheila 1974- *192*
Aleas, Richard
  See Appelt, Kathi
Alegria, Malin 1974(?)- *190*
Alegria, Ricardo E(nrique) 1921- *6*
Aleksin, Anatolii Georgievich 1924- *36*
Alenov, Lydia 1948- *61*
Alex, Ben (a pseudonym) 1946- *45*
Alex, Marlee (a pseudonym) 1948- *45*
Alexander, Anna B(arbara Cooke) 1913- *1*
Alexander, Anne
  See Alexander, Anna B(arbara Cooke)
Alexander, Ellen 1938- *91*
Alexander, Frances (Laura) 1888-1979 .... *4*
Alexander, Janet 1907-1994 .... *97*
  Earlier sketch in SATA *1*

Alexander, Jocelyn Anne Arundel 1930- *22*
Alexander, Linda 1935- *2*
Alexander, Lloyd 1924-2007 .... *135*
    Obituary *182*
    Earlier sketches in SATA *3, 49, 81, 129*
    See also CLR *48*
    See also SAAS *19*
Alexander, Lloyd Chudley
    See Alexander, Lloyd
Alexander, Marc 1929- *117*
Alexander, Martha 1920- *136*
    Earlier sketches in SATA *11, 70*
Alexander, Rae Pace
    See Alexander, Raymond Pace
Alexander, Raymond Pace 1898-1974 .... *22*
Alexander, Robert *200*
Alexander, Rod
    See Pellowski, Michael (Joseph)
Alexander, Sally Hobart 1943- *84*
Alexander, Sue 1933-2008 .... *136*
    Obituary *195*
    Earlier sketches in SATA *12, 89*
    See also SAAS *15*
Alexander, Vincent Arthur 1925-1980
    Obituary *23*
Alexeieff, Alexandre A. 1901-1979 .... *14*
Alger, Horatio, Jr.
    See Stratemeyer, Edward L.
Alger, Horatio, Jr. 1832-1899 .... *16*
    See also CLR *87*
Alger, Leclaire (Gowans) 1898-1969 .... *15*
Aliki
    See Brandenberg, Aliki
Alkema, Chester Jay 1932- *12*
Al-Khalili, Jim 1962- *124*
Alkiviades, Alkis 1953- *105*
Alkouatli, Claire *186*
Allaby, John Michael
    See Allaby, Michael
Allaby, Michael 1933- *167*
Allamand, Pascale 1942- *12*
Allan, Mabel Esther 1915-1998 .... *75*
    Earlier sketches in SATA *5, 32*
    See also CLR *43*
    See also SAAS *11*
Allan, Nicholas 1956- *123*
    Earlier sketch in SATA *79*
Allan-Meyer, Kathleen 1918- *51*
    Brief entry *46*
Allard, Harry
    See Allard, Harry G(rover), Jr.
Allard, Harry G(rover), Jr. 1928- *102*
    Earlier sketch in SATA *42*
    See also CLR *85*
Allee, Marjorie Hill 1890-1945 .... *17*
Allen, Adam
    See Epstein, Beryl
    and Epstein, Samuel
Allen, Alex B.
    See Heide, Florence Parry
Allen, Allyn
    See Eberle, Irmengarde
Allen, Betsy
    See Harrison, Elizabeth (Allen) Cavanna
Allen, Bob 1961- *76*
Allen, Gertrude E(lizabeth) 1888-1984 .... *9*
Allen, Grace
    See Hogarth, Grace (Weston Allen)
Allen, Jeffrey (Yale) 1948- *42*
Allen, John
    See Perry, Ritchie (John Allen)
Allen, Jonathan 1957- *177*
    Earlier sketch in SATA *131*
Allen, Jonathan Dean
    See Allen, Jonathan
Allen, Judy (Christina) 1941- *124*
    Earlier sketch in SATA *80*
Allen, Kenneth S. 1913-1981 .... *56*
Allen, Leroy 1912- *11*
Allen, Linda 1925- *33*
Allen, Marjorie 1931- *22*

Allen, Maury 1932- *26*
Allen, Merritt Parmelee 1892-1954 .... *22*
Allen, Nancy Kelly 1949- *171*
    Earlier sketch in SATA *127*
Allen, Nina (Stroemgren) 1935- *22*
Allen, Pamela (Kay) 1934- *123*
    Earlier sketches in SATA *50, 81*
    See also CLR *44*
Allen, Raul *205*
Allen, Rodney F. 1938-1999 .... *27*
Allen, Roger MacBride 1957- *105*
Allen, Ruth
    See Peterson, Esther (Allen)
Allen, Samuel W(ashington) 1917- *9*
Allen, T. D.
    See Allen, Terril Diener
Allen, Terril Diener 1908- *35*
Allen, Terry D.
    See Allen, Terril Diener
Allen, Thomas B. 1929- *193*
    Earlier sketches in SATA *45, 140*
Allen, Thomas Benton
    See Allen, Thomas B.
Allen, Tom
    See Allen, Thomas B.
Allende, Isabel 1942- *163*
    See also CLR *99*
Allerton, Mary
    See Govan, (Mary) Christine Noble
Alley, Robert W.
    See Alley, R.W.
Alley, R.W. *169*
Alleyn, Ellen
    See Rossetti, Christina
Allington, Richard L(loyd) 1947- *39*
    Brief entry *35*
Allison, Amy 1956- *138*
Allison, Bob *14*
Allison, Diane Worfolk *78*
Allison, Jennifer *173*
Allison, Linda 1948- *43*
Allison, Margaret
    See Klam, Cheryl
Allman, Barbara 1950- *137*
Allmendinger, David F(rederick), Jr. 1938- . *35*
Allred, Alexandra Powe 1965- *144*
Allred, Gordon T(hatcher) 1930- *10*
Allsop, Kenneth 1920-1973 .... *17*
Allsopp, Sophie *188*
Alma, Ann 1946- *201*
Almedingen, E. M.
    See Almedingen, Martha Edith von
Almedingen, Martha Edith von 1898-1971 .... *3*
Almon, Russell
    See Clevenger, William R.
    and Downing, David A(lmon)
Almond, David 1951- *158*
    Earlier sketch in SATA *114*
    See also CLR *85*
Almond, Linda Stevens 1881(?)-1987
    Obituary *50*
Almquist, Don 1929- *11*
Alonzo, Sandra *199*
Alphin, Elaine Marie 1955- *139*
    Autobiography Feature *139*
    Earlier sketches in SATA *80, 130*
Alsenas, Linas 1979- *186*
Alsop, Mary O'Hara 1885-1980 .... *34*
    Obituary *24*
    Earlier sketch in SATA *2*
Alter, Anna 1974- *206*
    Earlier sketch in SATA *135*
Alter, Judith (MacBain) 1938- *101*
    Earlier sketch in SATA *52*
Alter, Judy
    See Alter, Judith (MacBain)
Alter, Robert Edmond 1925-1965 .... *9*
Alter, Stephen 1956- *187*
Althea
    See Braithwaite, Althea
Altman, Linda Jacobs 1943- *21*

Altman, Suzanne
    See Orgel, Doris
    and Schecter, Ellen
Alton, Steve *169*
Altschuler, Franz 1923- *45*
Altsheler, Joseph A(lexander) 1862-1919
    See YABC *1*
Alvarez, John
    See del Rey, Lester
Alvarez, Joseph A. 1930- *18*
Alvarez, Julia 1950- *129*
al-Windawi, Thura
    See Windawi, Thura al-
Alyer, Philip A.
    See Stratemeyer, Edward L.
Amado, Elisa *193*
Amann, Janet 1951- *79*
Amato, Carol A. 1942- *92*
Amato, Mary 1961- *178*
    Earlier sketch in SATA *140*
Ambrose, Stephen E. 1936-2002 .... *138*
    Earlier sketch in SATA *40*
Ambrose, Stephen Edward
    See Ambrose, Stephen E.
Ambrus, Gyozo Laszlo 1935- *1*
    See also SAAS *4*
Ambrus, Victor G.
    See Ambrus, Gyozo Laszlo
Amend, Bill 1962- *147*
Amerman, Lockhart 1911-1969 .... *3*
Ames, Evelyn 1908-1990 .... *13*
    Obituary *64*
Ames, Gerald 1906-1993 .... *11*
    Obituary *74*
Ames, Lee J(udah) 1921- *151*
    Earlier sketch in SATA *3*
Ames, Mildred 1919-1994 .... *85*
    Earlier sketches in SATA *22, 81*
Amico, Tom 1960(?)- *176*
Amit, Ofra 1966- *205*
Ammon, Richard 1942- *124*
Amon, Aline 1928- *9*
Amoss, Berthe 1925- *112*
    Earlier sketch in SATA *5*
Anastasio, Dina 1941- *94*
    Brief entry *30*
    Earlier sketch in SATA *37*
Anaya, Rudolfo 1937-
    See CLR *129*
Anaya, Rudolfo A.
    See Anaya, Rudolfo
Anaya, Rudolpho Alfonso
    See Anaya, Rudolfo
Anckarsvard, Karin Inez Maria 1915-1969 .... *6*
Ancona, George 1929- *208*
    Autobiography Feature *208*
    Earlier sketches in SATA *12, 85, 145, 192*
    See also SAAS *18*
Anders, C. J.
    See Bennett, Cherie
Anders, Isabel 1946- *101*
Anders, Lou *176*
Andersdatter, Karla M(argaret) 1938- *34*
Andersen, Bethanne 1954- *191*
Andersen, Hans Christian 1805-1875 .... *100*
    See also YABC *1*
    See also CLR *113*
Andersen, Ted
    See Boyd, Waldo T.
Andersen, Yvonne 1932- *27*
Anderson, Bernice G(oudy) 1894-1997 .... *33*
Anderson, Bob 1944- *139*
    Earlier sketch in SATA *136*
Anderson, Brad(ley Jay) 1924- *33*
    Brief entry *31*
Anderson, C. C.
    See Anderson, Catherine Corley
Anderson, C(larence) W(illiam) 1891-1971 . *11*
Anderson, Carolyn Dunn
    See Dunn, Carolyn

Anderson, Catherine C.
See Anderson, Catherine Corley
Anderson, Catherine Corley 1909-2001 72
Anderson, Clifford
See Gardner, Richard (M.)
Anderson, Daryl Shon 1963- 93
Anderson, Dave
See Anderson, David
Anderson, David 1929- 60
Anderson, Derek 1969- 169
Anderson, Eloise Adell 1927- 9
Anderson, George
See Groom, Arthur William
Anderson, Grace Fox 1932- 43
Anderson, J(ohn) R(ichard) L(ane)
1911-1981 15
Obituary 27
Anderson, Jodi Lynn 182
Anderson, John David 1975- 197
Anderson, John L. 1905- 2
Anderson, Joy 1928- 1
Anderson, Kevin J. 1962- 117
Earlier sketch in SATA 74
Anderson, Kevin James
See Anderson, Kevin J.
Anderson, Kirsty 1978- 108
Anderson, K.J.
See Moesta, Rebecca
Anderson, Laurie Halse 1961- 186
Earlier sketches in SATA 95, 132
See also CLR 138
Anderson, LaVere Francis Shoenfelt
1907-1998 27
Anderson, Leone Castell 1923- 53
Brief entry 49
Anderson, Lisa G. 1963- 108
Anderson, Lonzo
See Anderson, John L.
Anderson, Lucia (Lewis) 1922- 10
Anderson, Madelyn Klein 1926-2005 28
Anderson, Margaret J(ean) 1931- 27
See also SAAS 8
Anderson, Marilyn D. 1943- 144
Anderson, Mary 1939- 82
Earlier sketch in SATA 7
See also SAAS 23
Anderson, Matthew Tobin
See Anderson, M.T.
Anderson, Mona 1910-2004 40
Anderson, Mrs. Melvin
See Anderson, Catherine Corley
Anderson, M.T. 1968- 182
Earlier sketches in SATA 97, 146
Anderson, Norman Dean 1928- 22
Anderson, Peggy Perry 1953- 179
Earlier sketch in SATA 84
Anderson, Poul 1926-2001 90
Autobiography Feature 106
Brief entry 39
See also CLR 58
Anderson, Poul William
See Anderson, Poul
Anderson, Rachel 1943- 86
Earlier sketch in SATA 34
See also SAAS 18
Anderson, Rebecca M.
See Moesta, Rebecca
Anderson, Rebecca Moesta
See Moesta, Rebecca
Anderson, Richard
See Anderson, J(ohn) R(ichard) L(ane)
Anderson, Sara 173
Anderson, Scoular 201
Anderson, (Tom) Scoular 138
Anderson, Susan 1952- 90
Anderson, Thomas Scoular
See Anderson, Scoular
Anderson, W. B.
See Schultz, James Willard
Anderson, Wayne 1946- 202
Earlier sketches in SATA 56, 147

Andersson, Kenneth 1970- 200
Andre, Evelyn M(arie) 1924- 27
Andreasen, Dan 186
Andreassen, Karl
See Boyd, Waldo T.
Andreassi, K. Robert
See DeCandido, Keith R.A.
Andree, Louise
See Coury, Louise Andree
Andrew, Ian 1962- 166
Earlier sketch in SATA 116
Andrew, Ian Peter
See Andrew, Ian
Andrew, Prudence (Hastings) 1924- 87
Andrews, Benny 1930-2006 31
Obituary 178
Andrews, Eleanor Lattimore
See Lattimore, Eleanor Frances
Andrews, Elton V.
See Pohl, Frederik
Andrews, F(rank) Emerson 1902-1978 22
Andrews, J(ames) S(ydney) 1934- 4
Andrews, Jan 1942- 167
Brief entry 49
Earlier sketches in SATA 58, 98
Andrews, Julie 1935- 153
Earlier sketch in SATA 7
See also CLR 85
Andrews, Laura
See Coury, Louise Andree
Andrews, Roy Chapman 1884-1960 19
Andrews, Tamra 1959- 129
Andrews, V(irginia) C(leo) 1924(?)-1986
Obituary 50
Andrews, Wendy
See Sharmat, Marjorie Weinman
Andrews, William G(eorge) 1930- 74
Andrezel, Pierre
See Blixen, Karen
Andriani, Renee
See Williams-Andriani, Renee
Andriola, Alfred J. 1912-1983
Obituary 34
Andrist, Ralph K. 1914-2004 45
Andronik, Catherine M. 189
Andryszewski, Tricia 1956- 148
Earlier sketch in SATA 88
Angel, Ann 1952- 192
Angel, Carl 178
Angel, Marie 1923- 47
Angeles, Peter A. 1931- 40
Angeletti, Roberta 1964- 124
Angeli, Marguerite (Lofft) de
See de Angeli, Marguerite (Lofft)
Angell, Judie 1937- 78
Earlier sketch in SATA 22
See also CLR 33
Angell, Madeline 1919- 18
Angelo, Valenti 1897- 14
Angelou, Maya 1928- 136
Earlier sketch in SATA 49
See also CLR 53
Angier, Bradford -1997 12
Angle, Kimberly Greene 203
Angle, Paul M(cClelland) 1900-1975
Obituary 20
Anglund, Joan Walsh 1926- 2
See also CLR 94
Ango, Fan D.
See Longyear, Barry B(rookes)
Angrist, Stanley W(olff) 1933- 4
Anholt, Catherine 1958- 131
Earlier sketch in SATA 74
Anholt, Laurence 1959- 141
Earlier sketch in SATA 74
Anita
See Daniel, Anita
Anmar, Frank
See Nolan, William F.
Annett, Cora
See Scott, Cora Annett (Pipitone)

Annie-Jo
See Blanchard, Patricia
and Suhr, Joanne
Annixter, Jane
See Sturtzel, Jane Levington
Annixter, Paul
See Sturtzel, Howard A(llison)
Anno, Mitsumasa 1926- 157
Earlier sketches in SATA 5, 38, 77
See also CLR 122
Anrooy, Francine Van
See Van Anrooy, Francine
Ansary, Mir Tamim 1948- 140
Anstey, Caroline 1958- 81
Antell, Will D. 1935- 31
Anthony, Barbara
See Barber, Antonia
Anthony, C. L.
See Smith, Dorothy Gladys
Anthony, Edward 1895-1971 21
Anthony, John
See Beckett, Ronald Brymer
and Ciardi, John (Anthony)
and Sabini, John Anthony
Anthony, Joseph Patrick 1964- 103
Anthony, Patricia 1947- 109
Anthony, Piers 1934- 129
Autobiography Feature 129
Earlier sketch in SATA 84
See also CLR 118
See also SAAS 22
Anthony, Susan C(arol) 1953- 87
Anticaglia, Elizabeth 1939- 12
Antilles, Kem
See Moesta, Rebecca
Antle, Nancy 1955- 102
Antolini, Margaret Fishback 1904-1985
Obituary 45
Anton, Michael J(ames) 1940- 12
Antonacci, Robert J(oseph) 1916- 45
Brief entry 37
Anvil, Christopher 1925-2009 102
Anzaldua, Gloria (Evanjelina) 1942-2004
Obituary 154
Aoki, Hisako 1942- 45
Apfel, Necia H(alpern) 1930- 51
Brief entry 41
Aphrodite, J.
See Livingston, Carole
Apikuni
See Schultz, James Willard
Apostolina, M. 184
Apostolina, Michael
See Apostolina, M.
Apostolou, Christine Hale 1955- 179
Earlier sketches in SATA 82, 128
Appel, Allen (R.) 1945- 115
Appel, Benjamin 1907-1977 39
Obituary 21
Appel, Martin 1948- 45
Appel, Martin Eliot
See Appel, Martin
Appel, Marty
See Appel, Martin
Appelbaum, Diana Muir Karter 1953- 132
Appelt, Kathi 1954- 190
Earlier sketches in SATA 83, 129
Apperley, Dawn 1969- 135
Appiah, Peggy 1921-2006 84
Earlier sketch in SATA 15
See also SAAS 19
Apple, Margot 152
Brief entry 42
Earlier sketch in SATA 64
Applebaum, Stan 1922- 45
Applegate, K.A.
See Applegate, Katherine
Applegate, Katherine 1956- 196
Earlier sketches in SATA 109, 162
See also CLR 90

Applegate, Katherine Alice
  See Applegate, Katherine
Appleton, Victor
  See Barrett, Neal, Jr.
  and Doyle, Debra
  and Macdonald, James D.
  and Stratemeyer, Edward L.
  and Vardeman, Robert E(dward)
Appleton, Victor II
  See Goulart, Ron
Apsler, Alfred 1907-1982 10
Aragones, Sergio 1937- 48
  Brief entry 39
Araujo, Frank P. 1937- 86
Arbo, Cris 1950- 103
Arbuckle, Dorothy Fry 1910-1982
  Obituary 33
Arbuthnot, May Hill 1884-1969 2
Archambault, John 163
  Earlier sketches in SATA 67, 112
Archbold, Rick 1950- 97
Archer, Colleen Rutherford 1949- 164
Archer, Frank
  See O'Connor, Richard
Archer, Jules 1915- 85
  Earlier sketch in SATA 4
  See also SAAS 5
Archer, Lily 1981- 193
Archer, Marion Fuller 1917- 11
Archer, Nathan
  See Watt-Evans, Lawrence
Archer, Peggy 1947- 199
Archibald, Joe
  See Archibald, Joseph S(topford)
Archibald, Joseph S(topford) 1898-1986 3
  Obituary 47
Ard, William
  See Jakes, John
Ardagh, Philip 1961- 154
Ardai, Charles 1969- 85
Arden, Barbi
  See Stoutenburg, Adrien (Pearl)
Arden, William
  See Lynds, Dennis
Ardizzone, Edward (Jeffrey Irving)
  1900-1979 28
  Obituary 21
  Earlier sketch in SATA 1
  See also CLR 3
Ardley, Neil (Richard) 1937- 121
  Earlier sketch in SATA 43
Arehart-Treichel, Joan 1942- 22
Arena, Felice 1968- 151
Arenella, Roy 1939- 14
Argent, Kerry 1960- 138
Argueta, Jorge 179
Arihara, Shino 1973- 201
Arkin, Alan 1934- 59
  Brief entry 32
Arkin, Alan Wolf
  See Arkin, Alan
Arksey, Neil 158
Arlen, Leslie
  See Nicole, Christopher (Robin)
Arley, Robert
  See Jackson, Mike
Armer, Alberta (Roller) 1904-1986 9
Armer, Laura Adams 1874-1963 13
Armistead, John 1941- 130
Armitage, David 1943- 155
  Brief entry 38
  Earlier sketch in SATA 99
Armitage, Frank
  See Carpenter, John
Armitage, Ronda (Jacqueline) 1943- 155
  Brief entry 38
  Earlier sketches in SATA 47, 99
Armour, Richard (Willard) 1906-1989 14
  Obituary 61
Armstrong, Alan 1939- 172

Armstrong, Alan W.
  See Armstrong, Alan
Armstrong, George D. 1927- 10
Armstrong, Gerry (Breen) 1929- 10
Armstrong, Jeannette (C.) 1948- 102
Armstrong, Jennifer 1961- 165
  Autobiography Feature 120
  Earlier sketches in SATA 77, 111
  See also CLR 66
  See also SAAS 24
Armstrong, Louise 43
  Brief entry 33
Armstrong, Martin Donisthorpe
  1882-1974 115
Armstrong, Matthew 1975- 188
Armstrong, Matthew S.
  See Armstrong, Matthew
Armstrong, Ralph Richard
  See Armstrong, Richard
Armstrong, Richard 1903-1986 11
Armstrong, William H(oward) 1914-1999 4
  Obituary 111
  See also CLR 117
  See also SAAS 7
Armstrong-Ellis, Carey (Fraser) 1956- 145
Arndt, Ursula (Martha H.) 56
  Brief entry 39
Arneson, D(on) J(on) 1935- 37
Arnett, Caroline
  See Cole, Lois Dwight
Arnett, Jack
  See Goulart, Ron
Arnette, Robert
  See Silverberg, Robert
Arno, Enrico 1913-1981 43
  Obituary 28
Arnold, Ann 1953(?)- 207
Arnold, Caroline 1944- 174
  Brief entry 34
  Earlier sketches in SATA 36, 85, 131
  See also CLR 61
  See also SAAS 23
Arnold, Elizabeth 1944- 164
Arnold, Elliott 1912-1980 5
  Obituary 22
Arnold, Emily 1939- 134
  Autobiography Feature 134
  Earlier sketches in SATA 5, 50, 76, 110
  See also CLR 46
  See also SAAS 7
Arnold, Gillian Clare
  See Cross, Gillian
Arnold, Katya 1947- 168
  Earlier sketches in SATA 82, 115
Arnold, Louise 175
Arnold, Marsha Diane 1948- 147
  Earlier sketch in SATA 93
Arnold, Nick 1961- 113
Arnold, Oren 1900-1980 4
Arnold, Susan (Riser) 1951- 58
Arnold, Tedd 1949- 208
  Earlier sketches in SATA 69, 116, 160
Arnoldy, Julie
  See Bischoff, Julia Bristol
Arnosky, James Edward 1946- 189
  Earlier sketches in SATA 70, 118
  See also CLR 93
Arnosky, Jim
  See Arnosky, James Edward
Arnott, Kathleen 1914- 20
Arnov, Boris, Jr. 1926- 12
Arnow, Harriette (Louisa) Simpson
  1908-1986 42
  Obituary 47
Arnsteen, Katy Keck 1934- 68
Arnstein, Helene S(olomon) 1915- 12
Arntson, Herbert E(dward) 1911-1982 12
Aroner, Miriam 82
Aronin, Ben 1904-1980
  Obituary 25

Aronson, Marc 1950- 189
  Autobiography Feature 189
  Earlier sketches in SATA 126, 175
Aronson, Marc Henry
  See Aronson, Marc
Aronson, Sarah 196
Aronson, Virginia 1954- 122
Arora, Shirley (Lease) 1930- 2
Arrasmith, Patrick 176
Arrick, Fran
  See Angell, Judie
Arrigan, Mary 1943- 142
Arrington, Aileen 183
Arrington, Stephen L. 1948- 97
Arrington, Stephen Lee
  See Arrington, Stephen L.
Arrley, Richmond
  See Delany, Samuel R., Jr.
Arrowood, (McKendrick Lee) Clinton
  1939- 19
Arrowsmith, Pat 1930- 59
Arsenault, Isabelle 1978- 207
Artell, Mike 1948- 183
  Earlier sketches in SATA 89, 134
Arthur, Robert (Andrew) 1909-1969
  See Arthur, Robert, (Jr.)
Arthur, Robert, (Jr.) 1909-1969 118
Arthur, Ruth M(abel) 1905-1979 26
  Earlier sketch in SATA 7
Artis, Vicki Kimmel 1945- 12
Artzybasheff, Boris (Miklailovich)
  1899-1965 14
Aruego, Ariane
  See Dewey, Ariane
Aruego, Jose 1932- 178
  Earlier sketches in SATA 6, 68, 125
  See also CLR 5
Aruego, Jose Espiritu
  See Aruego, Jose
Arundel, Honor (Morfydd) 1919-1973 4
  Obituary 24
  See also CLR 35
Arundel, Jocelyn
  See Alexander, Jocelyn Anne Arundel
Arvey, Michael 1948- 79
Arzoumanian, Alik 177
Asare, Meshack (Yaw) 1945- 139
  Earlier sketch in SATA 86
Asaro, Catherine 1955- 165
  Earlier sketch in SATA 101
Asaro, Catherine Ann 1955-
  See Asaro, Catherine
Asay, Donna Day 1945- 127
Asbjornsen, Peter Christen 1812-1885 15
  See also CLR 104
Asch, Frank 1946- 154
  Earlier sketches in SATA 5, 66, 102
Ash, Jutta 1942- 38
Ashabranner, Brent 1921- 166
  Earlier sketches in SATA 1, 67, 130
  See also CLR 28
  See also SAAS 14
Ashabranner, Brent Kenneth
  See Ashabranner, Brent
Ashbless, William
  See Blaylock, James P.
  and Powers, Tim
Ashby, Gil 1958- 146
Ashby, Gwynneth 1922- 44
Ashby, Ruth 170
Ashby, Yvonne 1955- 121
Ashe, Arthur (Robert, Jr.) 1943-1993 65
  Obituary 87
Ashe, Geoffrey (Thomas) 1923- 17
  Autobiography Feature 125
Ashe, Mary Ann
  See Lewis, Mary
Asher, Bridget
  See Baggott, Julianna
Asher, Sandra Fenichel
  See Asher, Sandy

Asher, Sandy 1942- 71
  Autobiography Feature 158
  Brief entry 34
  Earlier sketch in SATA 36
  See also SAAS 13
Asheron, Sara
  See Moore, Lilian
Ashey, Bella
  See Breinburg, Petronella
Ashford, Daisy
  See Ashford, Margaret Mary
Ashford, Jeffrey
  See Jeffries, Roderic
Ashford, Margaret Mary 1881-1972 10
Ashland, Monk 1972- 207
Ashley, Bernard (John) 1935- 155
  Brief entry 39
  Earlier sketches in SATA 47, 79
  See also CLR 4
Ashley, Elizabeth
  See Salmon, Annie Elizabeth
Ashley, Ray
  See Abrashkin, Raymond
Ashman, Linda 1960- 203
  Earlier sketch in SATA 150
Ashton, Lorayne
  See Gottfried, Theodore Mark
Ashton, Warren T.
  See Adams, William Taylor
Asimov, Isaac 1920-1992 74
  Earlier sketches in SATA 1, 26
  See also CLR 79
Asinof, Eliot 1919-2008 6
Asinof, Eliot Tager
  See Asinof, Eliot
Aska, Warabe
  See Masuda, Takeshi
Asprin, Robert L. 1946-2008 92
Asprin, Robert Lynn
  See Asprin, Robert L.
Asquith, Cynthia Mary Evelyn (Charteris)
  1887-1960 107
Asquith, Ros 153
Astley, Juliet
  See Lofts, Norah (Robinson)
Aston, Dianna Hutts 1964- 176
Aston, James
  See White, T(erence) H(anbury)
Ata, Te 1895-1995 119
Atene, Ann
  See Atene, (Rita) Anna
Atene, (Rita) Anna 1922- 12
Atheling, William, Jr.
  See Blish, James
Atkins, Catherine 160
Atkins, Jeannine 1953- 172
  Earlier sketch in SATA 113
Atkinson, Allen G. 1953(?)-1987 60
  Brief entry 46
  Obituary 55
Atkinson, M. E.
  See Frankau, Mary Evelyn Atkinson
Atkinson, Margaret Fleming 14
Atteberry, Kevan J. 186
Attema, Martha 1949- 156
  Earlier sketch in SATA 94
Atticus
  See Davies, Hunter
  and Fleming, Ian
  and Pawle, Gerald Strachan
  and Wilson, (Thomas) Woodrow
Atwater, Florence (Hasseltine Carroll)
  1896-1979 66
  Earlier sketch in SATA 16
  See also CLR 19
Atwater, Montgomery Meigs 1904-1976 15
Atwater, Richard (Tupper) 1892-1948 66
  Brief entry 27
  Earlier sketch in SATA 54
  See also CLR 19

Atwater-Rhodes, Amelia 1984- 170
  Earlier sketch in SATA 124
Atwell, Debby 1953- 150
  Earlier sketch in SATA 87
Atwood, Ann (Margaret) 1913-1992 7
Atwood, Margaret 1939- 170
  Earlier sketch in SATA 50
Atwood, Margaret Eleanor
  See Atwood, Margaret
Aubrey, Meg Kelleher 1963- 83
Aubry, Claude B. 1914-1984 29
  Obituary 40
Auch, Herm 173
Auch, Mary Jane 173
  Earlier sketch in SATA 138
Auch, M.J.
  See Auch, Mary Jane
Auclair, Joan 1960- 68
Auel, Jean 1936- 91
Auel, Jean M.
  See Auel, Jean
Auel, Jean Marie
  See Auel, Jean
Auer, Martin 1951- 77
Augarde, Steve 1950- 159
  Earlier sketch in SATA 25
Augelli, John P(at) 1921- 46
Augustine, Mildred
  See Benson, Mildred
Ault, Phil
  See Ault, Phillip H(alliday)
Ault, Phillip H(alliday) 1914- 23
Ault, Rosalie Sain 1942- 38
Ault, Roz
  See Ault, Rosalie Sain
Aung, (Maung) Htin 1909- 21
Auntie Deb
  See Coury, Louise Andree
Auntie Louise
  See Coury, Louise Andree
Aunt Weedy
  See Alcott, Louisa May
Auseon, Andrew 1976- 166
Austen, Carrie
  See Bennett, Cherie
Austin, Carrie
  See Seuling, Barbara
Austin, Elizabeth S. 1907-1977 5
Austin, Harry
  See McInerny, Ralph
Austin, Margot 1909(?)-1990 11
  Obituary 66
Austin, Michael 178
Austin, Oliver L(uther), Jr. 1903-1988 7
  Obituary 59
Austin, Patricia 1950- 137
Austin, R. G.
  See Gelman, Rita Golden
  and Lamb, Nancy
Austin, Virginia 1951- 152
  Earlier sketch in SATA 80
Auteur, Hillary
  See Gottfried, Theodore Mark
Auth, Tony
  See Auth, William Anthony, Jr.
Auth, William Anthony, Jr. 1942- 192
Autry, Gloria Diener
  See Allen, Terril Diener
Auvil, Peggy A 1954- 122
Auvil, Peggy Appleby
  See Auvil, Peggy A
Aveni, Anthony F. 1938- 181
Aveni, Anthony Francis
  See Aveni, Anthony F.
Averbeck, Jim 1963- 201
Averill, Esther (Holden) 1902-1992 28
  Obituary 72
  Earlier sketch in SATA 1
Avery, A. A.
  See Montgomery, Rutherford George

Avery, Al
  See Montgomery, Rutherford George
Avery, Gillian (Elise) 1926- 137
  Autobiography Feature 137
  Earlier sketches in SATA 7, 75
  See also SAAS 6
Avery, Kay 1908- 5
Avery, Lorraine
  See Older, Effin
  and Older, Jules
Avery, Lynn
  See Cole, Lois Dwight
Avi 1937- 190
  Earlier sketches in SATA 14, 71, 108, 156
  See also CLR 68
Avishai, Susan 1949- 82
Avril, Francois 1961- 191
Avril, Lynne
  See Cravath, Lynne W.
Awdry, Christopher Vere 1940- 67
Awdry, Wilbert Vere 1911-1997 94
  See also CLR 23
Axelrod, Amy 131
Axelsen, Stephen 1953- 165
Axton, David
  See Koontz, Dean
Ayars, James S(terling) 1898-1986 4
Aye, A. K.
  See Edwards, Hazel (Eileen)
Ayer, Eleanor H. 1947-1998 121
  Earlier sketch in SATA 78
Ayer, Jacqueline 1930- 13
Ayer, Margaret (?)-1981 15
Aylesworth, Jim 1943- 139
  Earlier sketches in SATA 38, 89
  See also CLR 89
Aylesworth, Thomas G(ibbons) 1927-1995 .. 88
  Earlier sketch in SATA 4
  See also CLR 6
  See also SAAS 17
Ayliffe, Alex 190
Aylward, Marcus
  See Alexander, Marc
Aymar, Brandt 1911- 22
Ayme, Marcel (Andre) 1902-1967 91
  See also CLR 25
Ayres, Becky
  See Hickox, Rebecca (Ayres)
Ayres, Katherine 1947- 187
Ayres, Pam 1947- 90
Ayres, Patricia Miller 1923-1985
  Obituary 46
Aytmatov, Chingiz
  See Aitmatov, Chingiz
Ayto, Russell 1960- 206
  Earlier sketches in SATA 111, 166
Azaid
  See Zaidenberg, Arthur
Azar, Penny 1952- 121
Azarian, Mary 1940- 171
  Earlier sketch in SATA 112
Azore, Barbara 1934- 188

B

Baastad, Babbis Friis
  See Friis-Baastad, Babbis Ellinor
Bab
  See Gilbert, W(illiam) S(chwenck)
Babbis, Eleanor
  See Friis-Baastad, Babbis Ellinor
Babbitt, Lucy Cullyford 1960- 85
Babbitt, Natalie 1932- 194
  Earlier sketches in SATA 6, 68, 106
  See also CLR 141
  See also SAAS 5
Babbitt, Natalie Zane Moore
  See Babbitt, Natalie
Babcock, Chris 1963- 83

Babcock, Dennis 1948- 22
Babcock, Dennis Arthur
  See Babcock, Dennis
Baber, Carolyn Stonnell 1936- 96
Baboni, Elena 198
Baca, Ana 1967- 191
Baca, Maria 1951- 104
Bach, Alice (Hendricks) 1942- 93
  Brief entry 27
  Earlier sketch in SATA 30
Bach, Bellamy
  See Windling, Terri
Bach, Mary 1960- 125
Bach, Richard 1936- 13
Bach, Richard David
  See Bach, Richard
Bache, Ellyn 1942- 124
Bachel, Beverly K. 1957- 142
Bachelet, Gilles 1952- 196
Bachman, Fred 1949- 12
Bachman, Richard
  See King, Stephen
Bachrach, Deborah 80
Backus, James Gilmore 1913-1989
  Obituary 63
Backus, Jim
  See Backus, James Gilmore
Bacmeister, Rhoda W(arner) 1893-1991 11
Bacon, Betty
  See Bacon, Elizabeth
Bacon, Elizabeth 1914-2001 3
  Obituary 131
Bacon, Joan Chase
  See Bowden, Joan Chase
Bacon, Josephine Dodge (Daskam)
  1876-1961 48
Bacon, Margaret Frances
  See Bacon, Peggy
Bacon, Margaret Hope 1921- 6
Bacon, Martha Sherman 1917-1981 18
  Obituary 27
  See also CLR 3
Bacon, Melvin 1950- 93
Bacon, Melvin L.
  See Bacon, Melvin
Bacon, Peggy 1895-1987 50
Bacon, R(onald) L(eonard) 1924- 84
  Earlier sketch in SATA 26
Baden, Robert 1936- 70
Baden-Powell, Robert (Stephenson Smyth)
  1857-1941 16
Badt, Karin L(uisa) 1963- 91
Bae, Hyun-Joo 186
Baehr, Kingsley M. 1937- 89
Baehr, Patricia 1952- 65
Baehr, Patricia Goehner
  See Baehr, Patricia
Baek, Matthew J. 1971- 202
Baer, Jill
  See Gilbert, (Agnes) Joan (Sewell)
Baer, Judy 1951- 71
Baer, Julie 1960- 161
Baer-Block, Roxanna 172
Baerg, Harry J(ohn) 1909-1996 12
Baeten, Lieve 1954- 83
Bagert, Brod 1947- 191
  Earlier sketch in SATA 80
Baggette, Susan K. 1942- 126
Baggott, Julianna 1969- 197
Bagnold, Enid 1889-1981 25
  Earlier sketch in SATA 1
Baguley, Elizabeth 1959- 199
Bahlke, Valerie Worth -1994
  See Worth, Valerie
Bahous, Sally 1939- 86
Bahr, Mary (Madelyn) 1946- 95
Bahr, Robert 1940- 38
Bahti, Tom 1926-1972 57
  Brief entry 31
Baicker-McKee, Carol 1958- 177
Bailey, Alice Cooper 1890-1978 12

Bailey, Anne 1958- 71
Bailey, Bernadine (Freeman) 1901-1995 14
Bailey, Carolyn Sherwin 1875-1961 14
Bailey, Debbie 1954- 123
Bailey, Donna (Veronica Anne) 1938- 68
Bailey, Jane H(orton) 1916- 12
Bailey, John (Robert) 1940- 52
Bailey, Len 193
Bailey, Linda 1948- 182
  Earlier sketch in SATA 107
Bailey, Maralyn Collins (Harrison) 1941- 12
Bailey, Matilda
  See Radford, Ruby L(orraine)
Bailey, Maurice Charles 1932- 12
Bailey, Pearl (Mae) 1918-1990 81
Bailey, Peter 1946- 194
Bailey, Ralph Edgar 1893-1982 11
Bailey, Sheila (Lucas) 1960- 155
Baillie, Allan 1943- 151
  Earlier sketch in SATA 87
  See also CLR 49
  See also SAAS 21
Baillie, Allan Stuart
  See Baillie, Allan
Baines, John (David) 1943- 71
Bains, Larry
  See Sabin, Louis
Baird, Alison 1963- 138
Baird, Bil 1904-1987 30
  Obituary 52
Baird, Thomas (P.) 1923-1990 45
  Brief entry 39
  Obituary 64
Baird, William Britton
  See Baird, Bil
Baity, Elizabeth Chesley 1907-1989 1
Baiul, Oksana 1977- 108
Bajoria, Paul 1964- 187
Bakeless, John (Edwin) 1894-1978 9
Bakeless, Katherine Little 1895-1992 9
Baker, Alan 1951- 146
  Earlier sketches in SATA 22, 93
Baker, Augusta 1911-1998 3
Baker, Barbara 1947- 192
Baker, Betty Lou 1928-1987 73
  Obituary 54
  Earlier sketch in SATA 5
Baker, Carin Greenberg 1959- 79
Baker, Charlotte 1910- 2
Baker, Christina
  See Kline, Christina Baker
Baker, Christopher W. 1952- 144
Baker, Deirdre 1955- 195
Baker, E.D. 190
Baker, (Mary) Elizabeth (Gillette) 1923- 7
Baker, Gayle Cunningham 1950- 39
Baker, James W. 1924- 65
  Earlier sketch in SATA 22
Baker, James W. 1926- 122
Baker, Janice E(dla) 1941- 22
Baker, Jeanette 178
Baker, Jeannie 1950- 156
  Earlier sketches in SATA 23, 88
  See also CLR 28
Baker, Jeffrey J(ohn) W(heeler) 1931- 5
Baker, Jim
  See Baker, James W.
Baker, Keith 1953- 179
Baker, Ken 1962- 133
Baker, Laura Nelson 1911- 3
Baker, Margaret 1890-1965 4
Baker, Margaret J(oyce) 1918- 12
  See also SAAS 8
Baker, Mary Gladys Steel 1892-1974 12
Baker, (Robert) Michael (Graham) 1938- 4
Baker, Nina (Brown) 1888-1957 15
Baker, Pamela J. 1947- 66
Baker, Rachel 1904-1978 2
  Obituary 26
Baker, Roberta 206
Baker, Rosalie F. 1945- 166

Baker, Samm Sinclair 1909-1997 12
  Obituary 96
Baker, Sharon Reiss 1962- 207
Baker, Susan (Catherine) 1942-1991 29
Balaam
  See Lamb, G(eoffrey) F(rederick)
Balan, Bruce 1959- 113
Balcavage, Dynise 1965- 137
Balch, Glenn 1902-1989 3
  Obituary 83
  See also SAAS 11
Baldacci, David 1960- 184
Baldacci, David G.
  See Baldacci, David
  and Baldacci, David
Balderose, Nancy Ward 1952- 93
Balderson, Margaret 1935- 151
Baldini, Michelle 205
Baldry, Cherith 1947- 167
  Earlier sketch in SATA 72
Balducci, Carolyn 1946- 5
Balducci, Carolyn Feleppa
  See Balducci, Carolyn
Baldwin, Alex
  See Griffin, W.E.B.
Baldwin, Anne Norris 1938- 5
Baldwin, Clara 11
Baldwin, Gordo
  See Baldwin, Gordon C(ortis)
Baldwin, Gordon C(ortis) 1908-1983 12
Baldwin, James 1841-1925 24
Baldwin, James 1924-1987 9
  Obituary 54
Baldwin, Louis 1919- 110
Baldwin, Margaret
  See Weis, Margaret
Baldwin, Stan(ley C.) 1929- 62
  Brief entry 28
Bales, Carol Ann 1940- 57
  Brief entry 29
Balet, Jan (Bernard) 1913- 11
Balgassi, Haemi 1971- 131
Balian, Lorna 1929- 91
  Earlier sketch in SATA 9
Balit, Christina 1961- 159
  Earlier sketch in SATA 102
Ball, Duncan 1941- 73
Ball, Zachary
  See Janas, Frankie-Lee
  and Masters, Kelly R(ay)
Ballantine, Lesley Frost
  See Frost, Lesley
Ballantyne, R(obert) M(ichael) 1825-1894 ... 24
  See also CLR 137
Ballard, James G.
  See Ballard, J.G.
Ballard, James Graham
  See Ballard, J.G.
Ballard, Jane
  See Gorman, Carol
Ballard, J.G. 1930-2009 93
  Obituary 203
Ballard, Jim G.
  See Ballard, J.G.
Ballard, John 1945- 110
Ballard, Lowell C(lyne) 1904-1986 12
  Obituary 49
Ballard, (Charles) Martin 1929- 1
Ballard, Mignon F. 1934- 64
  Brief entry 49
Ballard, Mignon Franklin
  See Ballard, Mignon F.
Ballard, Robert D(uane) 1942- 85
  See also CLR 60
Ballard, Robin 1965- 126
Balliett, Blue 1955- 156
Ballinger, Bryan 1968- 161
Ballouhey, Pierre 1944- 90
Balogh, Penelope 1916-1975 1
  Obituary 34
Balouch, Kristen 176

Balow, Tom 1931- 12
Baltazzi, Evan S(erge) 1921- 90
Balterman, Marcia Ridlon 1942- 22
Baltimore, J.
    See Catherall, Arthur
Baltzer, Hans (Adolf) 1900- 40
Balzano, Jeanne (Koppel) 1912- 7
Bambara, Toni Cade 1939-1995 112
Bamfylde, Walter
    See Bevan, Tom
Bamman, Henry A. 1918- 12
Banat, D. R.
    See Bradbury, Ray
Bancroft, Griffing 1907-1999 6
Bancroft, Laura
    See Baum, L. Frank
Bandel, Betty 1912- 47
Baner, Skulda Vanadis 1897-1964 10
Banerjee, Anjali 174
Banfill, A. Scott 1956- 98
Bang, Betsy 1912- 48
    Brief entry 37
Bang, Garrett
    See Bang, Molly
Bang, Molly 1943- 158
    Earlier sketches in SATA 24, 69, 111
    See also CLR 8
Bang, Molly Garrett
    See Bang, Molly
Bang-Campbell, Monika 1975(?)- 195
    Earlier sketch in SATA 140
Banjo, The
    See Paterson, A(ndrew) B(arton)
Banke, Cecile de
    See de Banke, Cecile
Banks, Kate 1960- 200
    Earlier sketches in SATA 134, 172
Banks, Laura Stockton Voorhees 1908(?)-1980
    Obituary 23
Banks, Lynne Reid
    See Reid Banks, Lynne
Banks, Merry 197
Banks, Michael A. 1951- 101
Banks, Paul 1952- 174
Banks, Sara (Jeanne Gordon Harrell) 26
    See Harrell, Sara (Jeanne) Gordon
Bannatyne-Cugnet, Elizabeth Jo-Anne
    See Bannatyne-Cugnet, Jo
Bannatyne-Cugnet, Jo 1951- 101
Banner, Angela
    See Maddison, Angela Mary
Bannerman, Helen (Brodie Cowan Watson)
    1862(?)-1946 19
    See also CLR 144
Banning, Evelyn I. 1903-1993 36
Bannon, Laura (?)-1963 6
Bannor, Brett 1959- 143
Banta, Susan 181
Bantock, Nick 1950(?)- 95
Banyai, Istvan 193
Barakat, Ibtisam 1963- 186
Barasch, Lynne 1939- 186
    Earlier sketches in SATA 74, 126
Barbalet, Margaret 1949- 77
Barbary, James
    See Baumann, Amy Beeching
    and Beeching, Jack
Barbash, Shepard 1957- 84
Barbe, Walter Burke 1926- 45
Barber, Antonia 1932- 163
    Earlier sketch in SATA 29
Barber, Atiim Kiambu
    See Barber, Tiki
Barber, Lynda
    See Graham-Barber, Lynda
Barber, Lynda Graham
    See Graham-Barber, Lynda
Barber, Richard (William) 1941- 35
Barber, Ronde 1975- 182
Barber, Tiki 1975- 182

Barbera, Joe 1911-2006 51
    Obituary 179
Barbera, Joseph
    See Barbera, Joe
Barbera, Joseph Roland
    See Barbera, Joe
Barberis, Juan C(arlos) 1920- 61
Barbour, Karen 1956- 170
    Earlier sketches in SATA 63, 121
Barbour, Ralph Henry 1870-1944 16
Barclay, Bill
    See Moorcock, Michael
Barclay, Isabel
    See Dobell, I(sabel) M(arian) B(arclay)
Barclay, William Ewert
    See Moorcock, Michael
Bardhan-Quallen, Sudipta 168
Bardoe, Cheryl 181
Bare, Arnold Edwin 1920- 16
Bare, Colleen Stanley 32
Bar-el, Dan 199
Barenholtz, Bernard 1914-1989
    Obituary 64
Bargar, Gary W. 1947-1985 63
Barger, Jan 1948- 147
Barish, Matthew 1907-2000 12
Barkan, Joanne 127
    Earlier sketch in SATA 77
Barker, Albert W. 1900- 8
Barker, Carol (Minturn) 1938- 31
Barker, Cicely Mary 1895-1973 49
    Brief entry 39
    See also CLR 88
Barker, Melvern 1907-1989 11
Barker, S. Omar 1894-1985 10
Barker, Squire Omar
    See Barker, S. Omar
Barker, Will 1913-1983 8
Barkin, Carol 1944- 52
    Earlier sketch in SATA 42
Barklem, Jill 1951- 96
    See also CLR 31
Barkley, Brad 178
Barkley, James Edward 1941- 6
Barks, Carl 1901-2000 37
Barley, Janet Crane 1934- 95
Barnaby, Ralph S(tanton) 1893-1986 9
Barnard, A. M.
    See Alcott, Louisa May
Barnard, Bryn 1956- 169
    Earlier sketch in SATA 115
Barne, Kitty
    See Barne, Marion Catherine
Barne, Marion Catherine 1883-1957 97
Barneda, David 206
Barner, Bob 1947- 136
    Earlier sketch in SATA 29
Barnes, Dawn 1957- 175
Barnes, Derrick 191
Barnes, Derrick D.
    See Barnes, Derrick
Barnes, (Frank) Eric Wollencott 1907-1962 . 22
Barnes, Joyce Annette 1958- 85
Barnes, Laura T. 1958- 119
Barnes, Loutricia
    See Barnes-Svarney, Patricia L(ou)
Barnes, Malcolm 1909(?)-1984
    Obituary 41
Barnes, Michael 1934- 55
Barnes-Murphy, Frances 1951- 88
Barnes-Murphy, Rowan 1952- 88
Barnes-Svarney, Patricia L(ou) 1953- 67
Barnet, Nancy 1954- 84
Barnett, Ivan 1947- 70
Barnett, Lincoln (Kinnear) 1909-1979 36
Barnett, Moneta 1922-1976 33
Barnett, Naomi 1927- 40
Barney, Maginel Wright 1881(?)-1966 39
    Brief entry 32
Barnhart, Clarence L(ewis) 1900-1993 48
    Obituary 78

Barnouw, Adriaan Jacob 1877-1968
    Obituary 27
Barnouw, Victor 1915-1989 43
    Brief entry 28
Barnstone, Willis 1927- 20
Barnum, Jay Hyde 1888(?)-1962 20
Barnum, P. T., Jr.
    See Stratemeyer, Edward L.
Barnum, Richard 67
    Earlier sketch in SATA 1
Barnum, Theodore
    See Stratemeyer, Edward L.
Barnwell, Ysaye M. 1946- 200
Baron, Kathy 1954- 90
Baron, Virginia Olsen 1931- 46
    Brief entry 28
Barr, Donald 1921-2004 20
    Obituary 152
Barr, George 1907-1992 2
Barr, Jene 1922-1985 16
    Obituary 42
Barr, Nevada 1952- 126
    Earlier sketch in SATA 115
Barrer, Gertrude
    See Barrer-Russell, Gertrude
Barrer-Russell, Gertrude 1921- 27
Barrett, Angela (Jane) 1955- 145
    Earlier sketch in SATA 75
Barrett, Ethel 87
    Brief entry 44
Barrett, Joyce Durham 1943- 138
Barrett, Judi 204
    See Barrett, Judith
Barrett, Judith 1941- 26
    See also CLR 98
    See Barrett, Judi
Barrett, Robert T(heodore) 1949- 92
Barrett, Ron 1937- 14
Barrett, Susan (Mary) 1938- 113
Barrett, Tracy 1955- 207
    Earlier sketches in SATA 84, 115, 156
Barrett, William E(dmund) 1900-1986
    Obituary 49
Barretta, Gene 176
Barretton, Grandall
    See Garrett, Randall
Barrie, Baronet
    See Barrie, J. M.
Barrie, J. M. 1860-1937 100
    See also YABC 1
    See also CLR 124
Barrie, James Matthew
    See Barrie, J. M.
Barringer, William 1940-1996 153
Barrington, Michael
    See Moorcock, Michael
Barris, George 1925- 47
Barrol, Grady
    See Bograd, Larry
Barron, Rex 1951- 84
Barron, T.A. 1952- 192
    Earlier sketches in SATA 83, 126
    See also CLR 86
Barron, Thomas Archibald
    See Barron, T.A.
Barron, Tom
    See Barron, T.A.
Barrow, Lloyd H. 1942- 73
Barrows, Annie 1962- 180
Barry, Dan 1958- 177
Barry, Dana (Marie Malloy) 1949- 139
Barry, James P(otvin) 1918- 14
Barry, Katharina Watjen 1936- 4
Barry, Robert (Everett) 1931- 6
Barry, Scott 1952- 32
Barry, Sheila Anne -2003 91
Barshaw, Ruth McNally 203
Bartell, Susan S. 175
Bartenbach, Jean 1918- 40
Barth, Edna 1914-1980 7
    Obituary 24

Barth, Kelly L. 1964- 152
Barthelme, Donald 1931-1989 7
    Obituary 62
Barth-Grozinger, Inge 1950- 185
Bartholomew, Barbara 1941- 86
    Brief entry 42
Bartholomew, Jean
    See Beatty, Patricia (Robbins)
Bartlett, Alison 153
Bartlett, Philip A. 1
Bartlett, Robert Merrill 1899-1995 12
Bartoletti, Susan Campbell 1958- 173
    Earlier sketches in SATA *88, 129, 135*
Barton, Byron 1930- 126
    Earlier sketches in SATA *9, 90*
Barton, Jill(ian) 1940- 75
Barton, May Hollis 67
    Earlier sketch in SATA *1*
Barton, Pat
    See Arrowsmith, Pat
Bartos-Hoeppner, Barbara 1923- 5
Bartram, Simon 156
Bartsch, Jochen 1906- 39
Baruch, Dorothy W(alter) 1899-1962 21
Barunga, Albert 1912(?)-1977 120
Baryshnikov, Mikhail 1948- 192
Bas, Rutger
    See Rutgers van der Loeff-Basenau, An(na)
    Maria Margaretha
Base, Graeme 1958- 162
    Earlier sketches in SATA *67, 101*
    See also CLR 22
Base, Graeme Rowland
    See Base, Graeme
Baseman, Gary 1960- 174
Bash, Barbara 1948- 132
Bashevis, Isaac
    See Singer, Isaac Bashevis
Bashevis, Yitskhok
    See Singer, Isaac Bashevis
Bashista, Adrienne Ehlert 203
Basile, Gloria Vitanza 1929- 180
Baskin, Leonard 1922-2000 120
    Brief entry 27
    Earlier sketch in SATA *30*
Baskin, Nora Raleigh 1961- 189
    Earlier sketch in SATA *129*
Bason, Lillian 1913- 20
Bass, L. G.
    See Geringer, Laura
Bassett, Jeni 1959- 64
    Brief entry 43
Bassett, John Keith
    See Keating, Lawrence A.
Bassett, Lisa 1958- 61
Bassil, Andrea
    See Nilsen, Anna
Bastyra, Judy 108
Basye, Dale E. 205
Bataille, Marion 1963- 209
Bat-Ami, Miriam 1950- 150
    Autobiography Feature 150
    Earlier sketches in SATA *82, 122*
Bate, Lucy 1939-1993 18
Bate, Norman (Arthur) 1916- 5
Bateman, Colin 1962- 172
Bateman, Donna M. 190
Bateman, Teresa 1957- 168
    Earlier sketch in SATA *112*
Bates, Amy June 189
Bates, Barbara S(nedeker) 1919- 12
Bates, Betty
    See Bates, Elizabeth
Bates, Dianne 1948- 147
Bates, Elizabeth 1921- 19
Bates, Ivan 175
Bates, Katharine Lee 1859-1929 113
Bates, Martine
    See Leavitt, Martine
Bateson, Catherine 1960- 197
    Earlier sketch in SATA *157*

Batey, Tom 1946- 52
    Brief entry 41
Bath, Kevin P.
    See Bath, K.P.
Bath, K.P. 1959- 171
Batherman, Muriel
    See Sheldon, Muriel
Batson, Larry 1930- 35
Batt, Tanya Robyn 1970- 131
Battaglia, Aurelius 1910- 50
    Brief entry 33
Batten, H(arry) Mortimer 1888-1958 25
Batten, Mary 1937- 162
    Earlier sketches in SATA *5, 102*
Batterberry, Ariane Ruskin 1935- 13
Batterberry, Michael Carver 1932- 32
Battle-Lavert, Gwendolyn 1951- 155
    Earlier sketches in SATA *85, 131*
Battles, (Roxy) Edith 1921- 7
Baudouy, Michel-Aime 1909- 7
Bauer, A.C.E. 201
Bauer, Caroline Feller 1935- 98
    Brief entry 46
    Earlier sketch in SATA *52*
    See also SAAS 24
Bauer, Fred 1934- 36
Bauer, Helen 1900-1988 2
Bauer, Joan 1951- 160
    Earlier sketch in SATA *117*
Bauer, Jutta 1955- 150
Bauer, Marion Dane 1938- 192
    Autobiography Feature 144
    Earlier sketches in SATA *20, 69, 113, 144*
    See also SAAS 9
Bauer, Michael Gerard 1955(?)- 167
Bauer, Steven 1948- 125
Bauerschmidt, Marjorie 1926- 15
Baughman, Dorothy 1940- 61
Baum, Allyn Z(elton) 1924-1997 98
    Earlier sketch in SATA *20*
Baum, L. Frank
    See Thompson, Ruth Plumly
Baum, L. Frank 1856-1919 100
    Earlier sketch in SATA *18*
    See also CLR 107
Baum, Louis 1948- 182
    Brief entry 52
    Earlier sketch in SATA *64*
Baum, Louis F.
    See Baum, L. Frank
Baum, Lyman Frank
    See Baum, L. Frank
Baum, Maxie 188
Baum, Willi 1931- 4
Baumann, Amy Beeching 1922- 10
Baumann, Amy Brown Beeching
    See Baumann, Amy Beeching
Baumann, Hans 1914- 2
    See also CLR 35
Baumann, Kurt 1935- 21
Baumgartner, Barbara 1939- 86
Baurys, Flo(rence) 1938- 122
Bausum, Ann 173
Bawden, Nina 1925- 132
    Earlier sketches in SATA *4, 72*
    See also CLR 51
    See also SAAS 16
Bawden, Nina Mary Mabey
    See Bawden, Nina
Baxter, Valerie
    See Meynell, Laurence Walter
Bay, Jeanette Graham 1928- 88
Bayer, Harold
    See Gregg, Andrew K.
Bayer, Jane E. (?)-1985
    Obituary 44
Bayley, Nicola 1949- 129
    Earlier sketches in SATA *41, 69*
Baylor, Byrd 1924- 136
    Earlier sketches in SATA *16, 69*
    See also CLR 3

Baynes, Pauline 1922-2008 133
    Obituary 196
    Earlier sketches in SATA *19, 59*
Baynes, Pauline Diana
    See Baynes, Pauline
Bayoc, Cbabi 186
BB
    See Watkins-Pitchford, Denys James
Beach, Charles
    See Reid, (Thomas) Mayne
Beach, Charles Amory 1
Beach, Edward L. 1918-2002 12
    Obituary 140
Beach, Edward Latimer
    See Beach, Edward L.
Beach, Lisa 1957- 111
Beach, Lynn
    See Lance, Kathryn
Beach, Stewart T(aft) 1899-1979 23
Beachcroft, Nina 1931- 18
Beagle, Peter S. 1939- 130
    Earlier sketch in SATA *60*
Beagle, Peter Soyer
    See Beagle, Peter S.
Beaglehole, Helen 1946- 117
Beake, Lesley 1949- 209
Beale, Fleur 107
Bealer, Alex W(inkler III) 1921-1980 8
    Obituary 22
Beales, Valerie 1915- 74
Beals, Carleton 1893-1979 12
Beals, Frank Lee 1881-1972
    Obituary 26
Beam, Matt 1970- 187
Beame, Rona 1934- 12
Beamer, (George) Charles (Jr.) 1942- 43
Bean, Jonathan 1979- 194
Bean, Normal
    See Burroughs, Edgar Rice
Beaney, Jan
    See Udall, Jan Beaney
Beaney, Jane
    See Udall, Jan Beaney
Bear, Carolyn
    See Rayban, Chloe
Bear, Greg 1951- 105
    Earlier sketch in SATA *65*
Bear, Gregory Dale
    See Bear, Greg
Bearanger, Marie
    See Messier, Claire
Beard, Charles A(ustin) 1874-1948 18
Beard, Dan(iel Carter) 1850-1941 22
Beard, Darleen Bailey 1961- 96
Bearden, Romare (Howard) 1914(?)-1988 ... 22
    Obituary 56
Beardmore, Cedric
    See Beardmore, George
Beardmore, George 1908-1979 20
Beardshaw, Rosalind 1969- 190
Beardsley, Martyn R. 1957- 150
Bearman, Jane (Ruth) 1917- 29
Beaton, Clare 1947- 125
Beatty, Elizabeth
    See Holloway, Teresa (Bragunier)
Beatty, Hetty Burlingame 1907-1971 5
Beatty, Jerome, Jr. 1918- 5
Beatty, John (Louis) 1922-1975 6
    Obituary 25
Beatty, Patricia (Robbins) 1922-1991 73
    Obituary 68
    Earlier sketches in SATA *1, 30*
    See also SAAS 4
Beaty, Andrea 186
Beaty, Mary (T.) 1947- 146
Beaumont, Karen 1954- 204
Beccia, Carlyn 189
Bechard, Margaret 1953- 164
    Earlier sketch in SATA *85*
Bechtel, Louise Seaman 1894-1985 4
    Obituary 43

Bechtold, Lisze 208
Beck, Barbara L. 1927- 12
Beck, Ian 1947- 190
    Earlier sketch in SATA *138*
    See Beck, Ian Archibald
Beck, Peggy 1949- 171
Beck, Scott 197
Becker, Beril 1901-1999 11
Becker, Bonny 184
Becker, Deborah Zimmett 1955- 138
Becker, Helaine 1961- 142
Becker, John (Leonard) 1901- 12
Becker, John E(mil) 1942- 148
Becker, Joyce 1936- 39
Becker, May Lamberton 1873-1958 33
Becker, Neesa 1951- 123
Becker, Shari 174
Beckerman, Chad W. 198
Beckett, Sheilah 1913- 33
Beckhorn, Susan Williams 1953- 189
Beckles Willson, Robina 1930- 27
Beckman, Delores 1914-1994 51
Beckman, Gunnel 1910- 6
    See also CLR 25
    See also SAAS 9
Beckman, Kaj
    See Beckman, Karin
Beckman, Karin 1913- 45
Beckman, Per (Frithiof) 1913- 45
Bedard, Michael 1949- 154
    Earlier sketch in SATA *93*
    See also CLR 35
Beddor, Frank 194
Beddows, Eric
    See Nutt, Ken
Bedford, A. N.
    See Watson, Jane Werner
Bedford, Annie North
    See Watson, Jane Werner
Bedford, David 159
Bedoukian, Kerop 1907-1981 53
Bee, Jay
    See Brainerd, John W(hiting)
Bee, William 188
Beebe, B. F.
    See Johnson, B. F.
Beebe, (Charles) William 1877-1962 19
Beeby, Betty 1923- 25
Beech, Mark 1971- 191
Beech, Webb
    See Griffin, W.E.B.
Beecham, Jahnna 161
Beechcroft, William
    See Hallstead, William F(inn III)
Beeching, Jack 1922- 14
Beeke, Tiphanie 163
Beeler, Janet
    See Shaw, Janet
Beeler, Nelson F(rederick) 1910-1978 13
Beere, Peter 1951- 97
Beers, Dorothy Sands 1917- 9
Beers, Lorna 1897-1989 14
Beers, V(ictor) Gilbert 1928- 130
    Earlier sketch in SATA *9*
Beeton, Max
    See Redding, Robert Hull
Begay, Shonto 1954- 137
Begaye, Lisa Shook
    See Beach, Lisa
Begin, Mary Jane 1963- 82
Begin-Callanan, Mary Jane
    See Begin, Mary Jane
Begley, Kathleen A. 1948- 21
Begley, Kathleen Anne
    See Begley, Kathleen A.
Behan, Leslie
    See Gottfried, Theodore Mark
Behler, Deborah A. 1947- 145
Behler, John L. 1943-2006 145
    Obituary 173

Behler, John Luther
    See Behler, John L.
Behn, Harry 1898-1973 2
    Obituary 34
Behnke, Frances L. 8
Behr, Joyce 1929- 15
Behrens, June York 1925- 19
Behrman, Carol H(elen) 1925- 144
    Earlier sketch in SATA *14*
Beifuss, John, (Jr.) 1959- 92
Beil, Karen Magnuson 1950- 124
Beiler, Edna 1923- 61
Beinicke, Steve 1956- 69
Beirne, Barbara 1933- 71
Beiser, Arthur 1931- 22
Beiser, Germaine 1931- 11
Belair, Richard L. 1934- 45
Belaney, Archibald Stansfeld 1888-1938 24
    See also CLR 32
Belbin, David 1958- 164
    Earlier sketch in SATA *106*
Belden, Wilanne Schneider 1925- 56
Belfrage, Sally 1936-1994 65
    Obituary 79
Belknap, B. H.
    See Ellis, Edward S.
Belknap, Boynton
    See Ellis, Edward S.
Belknap, Boynton M.D.
    See Ellis, Edward S.
Bell, Anthea 1936- 148
    Earlier sketch in SATA *88*
Bell, Cathleen Davitt 1971- 203
Bell, Cece 202
Bell, Clare (Louise) 1952- 99
Bell, Corydon Whitten 1894-1980 3
Bell, David Owen 1949- 99
Bell, Emerson
    See Stratemeyer, Edward L.
Bell, Emily Mary
    See Cason, Mabel Earp
Bell, Frank
    See Benson, Mildred
Bell, Gertrude (Wood) 1911-1987 12
Bell, Gina
    See Balzano, Jeanne (Koppel)
Bell, Hilari 1958- 197
    Earlier sketch in SATA *151*
Bell, Jadrien
    See Golden, Christie
Bell, Janet
    See Clymer, Eleanor
Bell, Janet Cheatham 1937- 127
Bell, Krista 1950- 126
Bell, Krista Anne Blakeney
    See Bell, Krista
Bell, Margaret E(lizabeth) 1898-1990 2
Bell, Mary Reeves 1946- 88
Bell, Norman (Edward) 1899- 11
Bell, Raymond Martin 1907-1999 13
Bell, Siobhan 177
Bell, Thelma Harrington 1896-1985 3
Bell, William 1945- 90
    See also CLR 91
Bellairs, John (Anthony) 1938-1991 160
    Obituary 66
    Earlier sketches in SATA *2, 68*
    See also CLR 37
Beller, Susan Provost 1949- 128
    Earlier sketch in SATA *84*
    See also CLR 106
Bellingham, Brenda 1931- 99
    Brief entry 51
Bello, Rosario de
    See De Bello, Rosario
Belloc, Hilaire 1870-1953 112
    See also YABC *1*
    See also CLR 102
Belloc, Joseph Hilaire Pierre Sebastien Rene
    Swanton
    See Belloc, Hilaire

Belloc, Joseph Peter Rene Hilaire
    See Belloc, Hilaire
Belloc, Joseph Pierre Hilaire
    See Belloc, Hilaire
Belloli, Andrea P. A. 1947- 86
Bell-Rehwoldt, Sheri 1962- 199
Bellville, Cheryl Walsh 1944- 54
    Brief entry 49
Bell-Zano, Gina
    See Balzano, Jeanne (Koppel)
Belpre, Pura 1899-1982 16
    Obituary 30
Belting, Natalia Maree 1915-1997 6
Belton, John Raynor 1931- 22
Belton, Sandra 1939- 186
    Earlier sketches in SATA *85, 134*
Belton, Sandra Yvonne
    See Belton, Sandra
Beltran, Alberto 1923- 43
Beltran-Hernandez, Irene 1945- 74
Belvedere, Lee
    See Grayland, Valerie (Merle Spanner)
Bemelmans, Ludwig 1898-1962 100
    Earlier sketch in SATA *15*
    See also CLR 93
Benander, Carl D. 1941- 74
Benary, Margot
    See Benary-Isbert, Margot
Benary-Isbert, Margot 1889-1979 2
    Obituary 21
    See also CLR 12
Benasutti, Marion 1908-1992 6
Benatar, Raquel 1955- 167
Benchley, Nathaniel (Goddard) 1915-1981 .. 25
    Obituary 28
    Earlier sketch in SATA *3*
Benchley, Peter 1940-2006 164
    Earlier sketches in SATA *3, 89*
Benchley, Peter Bradford
    See Benchley, Peter
Bendall-Brunello, John 185
Bender, Edna 1941- 92
Bender, Esther 1942- 88
Bender, Lucy Ellen 1942- 22
Bender, Robert 1962- 160
    Earlier sketch in SATA *79*
Bendick, Jeanne 1919- 135
    Earlier sketches in SATA *2, 68*
    See also CLR 5
    See also SAAS 4
Bendick, Robert L(ouis) 1917- 11
Benedetto, William R. 1928- 180
Benedetto, William Ralph
    See Benedetto, William R.
Benedict, Andrew
    See Arthur, Robert, (Jr.)
Benedict, Dorothy Potter 1889-1979 11
    Obituary 23
Benedict, Lois Trimble 1902-1967 12
Benedict, Rex 1920-1995 8
Benedict, Stewart H(urd) 1924- 26
Beneduce, Ann Keay 128
Benet, Laura 1884-1979 3
    Obituary 23
Benet, Stephen Vincent 1898-1943
    See YABC *1*
Benet, Sula 1906-1982 21
    Obituary 33
Ben-Ezer, Ehud 1936- 122
Benezra, Barbara (Beardsley) 1921- 10
Benham, Leslie 1922- 48
Benham, Lois (Dakin) 1924- 48
Benham, Mary Lile 1914-1991 55
Benjamin, E. M. J.
    See Bache, Ellyn
Benjamin, Floella 1949- 206
Benjamin, Nora
    See Kubie, Nora Gottheil Benjamin
Benjamin, Saragail Katzman 1953- 86
Benner, Cheryl 1962- 80
Benner, Judith Ann 1942- 94

Bennett, Alice
    See Ziner, Florence
Bennett, Cherie 1960- *158*
    Earlier sketch in SATA 97
Bennett, Dorothea
    See Young, Dorothea Bennett
Bennett, Holly 1957- *181*
Bennett, James (W.) 1942- *153*
    Autobiography Feature *153*
    Earlier sketches in SATA 93, 148
Bennett, Jay 1912- *87*
    Brief entry *27*
    Earlier sketch in SATA 41
    See also SAAS 4
Bennett, Jill (Crawford) 1934- *41*
Bennett, John 1865-1956
    See YABC 1
Bennett, Penelope (Agnes) 1938- *94*
Bennett, Rachel
    See Hill, Margaret (Ohler)
Bennett, Rainey 1907-1998 .... *15*
    Obituary *111*
Bennett, Richard 1899- *21*
Bennett, Russell H(oradley) 1896- *25*
Bennett, Veronica 1953- *178*
Bennett, William (John) 1943- *102*
Benning, Elizabeth
    See Rice, Bebe Faas
Benny, Mike 1964- *203*
Benson, Elizabeth P(olk) 1924- *65*
Benson, Kathleen 1947- *183*
    Earlier sketches in SATA 62, 111
Benson, Linda M(aria) 1959- *84*
Benson, Mildred 1905-2002 .... *100*
    Obituary *135*
    Earlier sketches in SATA 1, 65, 67
Benson, Mildred Augustine Wirt
    See Benson, Mildred
Benson, Mildred Wirt
    See Benson, Mildred
Benson, Millie
    See Benson, Mildred
Benson, Patrick 1956- *147*
Benson, Sally 1900-1972 .... *35*
    Obituary *27*
    Earlier sketch in SATA 1
Bentley, Judith (McBride) 1945- *89*
    Earlier sketch in SATA 40
Bentley, Karen
    See Taschek, Karen
Bentley, Nancy (L.) 1946- *78*
Bentley, Nicolas Clerihew 1907-1978
    Obituary *24*
Bentley, Phyllis Eleanor 1894-1977 .... *6*
    Obituary *25*
Bentley, Roy 1947- *46*
Bentley, William (George) 1916- *84*
Benton, Jim 1963- *172*
ben Uzair, Salem
    See Horne, Richard Henry Hengist
Bercaw, Edna Coe 1961- *124*
Berck, Judith 1960- *75*
Berelson, Howard 1940- *5*
Berends, Polly Berrien 1939- *50*
    Brief entry *38*
Berenstain, Jan 1923- *135*
    Earlier sketches in SATA 12, 64, 129
    See also CLR 150
    See also SAAS 20
Berenstain, Janice
    See Berenstain, Jan
Berenstain, Michael 1951- *45*
Berenstain, Mike
    See Berenstain, Michael
Berenstain, Stan 1923-2005 .... *135*
    Obituary *169*
    Earlier sketches in SATA 12, 64, 129
    See also CLR 150
    See also SAAS 20
Berenstain, Stanley
    See Berenstain, Stan

Berenzy, Alix 1957- *168*
    Earlier sketch in SATA 65
Beresford, Elisabeth 1928- *141*
    Earlier sketches in SATA 25, 86
    See also SAAS 20
Berg, Adriane G(ilda) 1948- *152*
Berg, Dave
    See Berg, David
Berg, David 1920-2002 .... *27*
    Obituary *137*
Berg, Elizabeth 1948- *104*
Berg, Jean Horton 1913-1995 .... *6*
Berg, Joan
    See Victor, Joan Berg
Berg, Ron 1952- *48*
Bergaust, Erik 1925-1978 .... *20*
Bergel, Colin J. 1963- *137*
Bergen, Joyce 1949- *95*
Berger, Barbara (Helen) 1945- *77*
Berger, Carin *185*
Berger, Gilda 1935- *88*
    Brief entry *42*
Berger, Josef 1903-1971 .... *36*
Berger, Melvin H. 1927- *158*
    Autobiography Feature *124*
    Earlier sketches in SATA 5, 88
    See also CLR 32
    See also SAAS 2
Berger, Phil 1942-2001 .... *62*
Berger, Samantha (Allison) 1969- *140*
Berger, Terry 1933- *8*
Bergey, Alyce (Mae) 1934- *45*
Bergin, Mark 1961- *160*
    Earlier sketch in SATA 114
Berglin, Ruth Marie 1970- *181*
Bergman, Donna 1934- *73*
Bergman, Mara 1956- *196*
Bergman, Tamar 1939- *95*
Bergren, Lisa T.
    See Bergren, Lisa Tawn
Bergren, Lisa Tawn *200*
Bergsma, Jody Lynn *163*
Bergum, Constance R. 1952- *208*
    Earlier sketch in SATA 121
Berk, Ari *208*
Berkebile, Fred D(onovan) 1900-1978
    Obituary *26*
Berkeley, Jon 1962- *204*
Berkes, Marianne *173*
Berkey, Barry Robert 1935- *24*
Berkowitz, Freda Pastor 1908-1994 .... *12*
Berkus, Clara Widess 1909- *78*
Berlan, Kathryn Hook 1946- *78*
Berlfein, Judy Reiss 1958- *79*
Berlin, Eric 1968- *195*
Berliner, Don 1930- *33*
Berliner, Franz 1930- *13*
Berlitz, Charles (L. Frambach) 1914-2003 ... *32*
    Obituary *151*
Berman, Linda 1948- *38*
Berman, Paul (Lawrence) 1949- *66*
Berna, Paul 1910-1994 .... *15*
    Obituary *78*
    See also CLR 19
Bernadette
    See Watts, (Anna) Bernadette
Bernard, Bruce 1928-2000 .... *78*
    Obituary *124*
Bernard, George I. 1949- *39*
Bernard, Jacqueline (de Sieyes) 1921-1983 ... *8*
    Obituary *45*
Bernard, Patricia 1942- *181*
    Earlier sketch in SATA 106
Bernard, Trish
    See Bernard, Patricia
Bernardin, James (B.) 1966- *112*
Bernardo, Anilu *184*
Bernards, Neal 1963- *71*
Bernasconi, Pablo 1973- *183*
Bernays, Anne 1930- *32*
Bernhard, Durga T. 1961- *80*

Bernhard, Emery 1950- *80*
Bernheimer, Kate *201*
Bernier-Grand, Carmen T. 1947- *202*
Bernstein, Daryl (Evan) 1976- *81*
Bernstein, Joanne E(ckstein) 1943- *15*
Bernstein, Margery 1933- *114*
Bernstein, Nina 1949- *180*
Bernstein, Theodore M(enline) 1904-1979 ... *12*
    Obituary *27*
Berrien, Edith Heal
    See Heal, Edith
Berrill, Jacquelyn (Batsel) 1905- *12*
Berrington, John
    See Brownjohn, Alan
Berry, B. J.
    See Berry, Barbara J.
Berry, Barbara J. 1937- *7*
Berry, Erick
    See Best, (Evangel) Allena Champlin
Berry, James 1924- *110*
    Earlier sketch in SATA 67
    See also CLR 143
Berry, Jane Cobb 1915(?)-1979
    Obituary *22*
Berry, Joy
    See Berry, Joy Wilt
Berry, Joy Wilt 1944- *58*
    Brief entry *46*
Berry, Lynne *190*
Berry, William D(avid) 1926- *14*
Bersani, Shennen 1961- *164*
Berson, Harold 1926- *4*
Bertagna, Julie 1962- *151*
Bertholf, Bret *189*
Bertin, Charles-Francois
    See Berlitz, Charles (L. Frambach)
Bertolet, Paul
    See McLaughlin, Frank
Berton, Pierre (Francis de Marigny)
    1920-2004 .... *99*
    Obituary *158*
Bertrand, Cecile 1953- *76*
Bertrand, Diane Gonzales 1956- *177*
    Earlier sketch in SATA 106
Bertrand, Lynne 1963- *164*
    Earlier sketch in SATA 81
Beskow, Elsa (Maartman) 1874-1953 .... *20*
    See also CLR 17
Bess, Clayton
    See Locke, Robert
Besson, Luc 1959- *199*
Best, (Evangel) Allena Champlin 1892-1974 . *2*
    Obituary *25*
Best, Cari 1951- *200*
    Earlier sketches in SATA 107, 149
Best, (Oswald) Herbert 1894-1980 .... *2*
Bestall, A(lfred) E(dmeades) 1892-1986 ...... *97*
    Obituary *48*
Betancourt, Jeanne 1941- *148*
    Brief entry *43*
    Earlier sketches in SATA 55, 96
Beth, Mary
    See Miller, Mary Beth
Bethancourt, T. Ernesto
    See Paisley, Tom
Bethel, Dell 1929- *52*
Bethell, Jean (Frankenberry) 1922- *8*
Bethers, Ray 1902-1973 .... *6*
Bethke, Bruce Raymond 1955- *114*
Bethlen, T.D.
    See Silverberg, Robert
Bethune, J. G.
    See Ellis, Edward S.
Bethune, J. H.
    See Ellis, Edward S.
Betteridge, Anne
    See Potter, Margaret
Bettina
    See Ehrlich, Bettina Bauer
Bettmann, Otto Ludwig 1903-1998 .... *46*
Bettoli, Delana *187*

Betts, James
    See Haynes, Betsy
Betz, Eva Kelly 1897-1968 .... *10*
Bevan, Tom 1868-1930(?)
    See YABC 2
Bevis, Mary 1939- *202*
Bewick, Thomas 1753-1828 .... *16*
Beyer, Audrey White 1916- *9*
Beyer, Paul J. III 1950- *74*
Beynon, John
    See Harris, John (Wyndham Parkes Lucas)
    Beynon
Bezencon, Jacqueline (Buxcel) 1924- *48*
Bhatia, Jamunadevi 1919- *48*
Bhatia, June
    See Bhatia, Jamunadevi
Bial, Morrison David 1917- *62*
Bial, Raymond 1948- *165*
    Earlier sketches in SATA *76, 116*
Biala
    See Brustlein, Janice Tworkov
Biale, Rachel 1952- *99*
Bialk, Elisa
    See Krautter, Elisa (Bialk)
Bianchi, John 1947- *91*
Bianchi, Robert S(teven) 1943- *92*
Bianco, Margery
    See Bianco, Margery Williams
Bianco, Margery Williams 1881-1944 .... *15*
    See also CLR *146*
Bianco, Pamela 1906- *28*
Bibby, Violet 1908-1996 .... *24*
Bible, Charles 1937- *13*
Bibo, Bobette
    See Gugliotta, Bobette
Bice, Clare 1909-1976 .... *22*
Bickerstaff, Isaac
    See Swift, Jonathan
Bidner, Jenni 1963- *193*
Biegel, Paul 1925- *79*
    Earlier sketch in SATA *16*
    See also CLR *27*
    See also SAAS *18*
Biemiller, Carl L(udwig), Jr.) 1912-1979 ..... *40*
    Obituary *21*
Bienenfeld, Florence L(ucille) 1929- *39*
Bierhorst, John (William) 1936- *149*
    Autobiography Feature *149*
    Earlier sketches in SATA *6, 91*
    See also SAAS *10*
Biggar, Joan R(awlins) 1936- *120*
Biggle, Lloyd, Jr. 1923-2002 .... *65*
Biggs, Brian 1968- *192*
Bilal, Abdel W(ahab) 1970- *92*
Bilbrough, Norman 1941- *111*
Bildner, Phil *173*
Bileck, Marvin 1920- *40*
Bilibin, Ivan (Iakolevich) 1876-1942 .... *61*
Bill, Alfred Hoyt 1879-1964 .... *44*
Billam, Rosemary 1952- *61*
Billings, Charlene W(interer) 1941- *41*
Billingsley, Franny 1954- *132*
Billington, Elizabeth T(hain) *50*
    Brief entry *43*
Billout, Guy (Rene) 1941- *144*
    Earlier sketch in SATA *10*
    See also CLR *33*
Bilson, Geoffrey 1938-1987 .... *99*
Binch, Caroline (Lesley) 1947- *140*
    Earlier sketch in SATA *81*
Bing, Christopher (H.) *126*
Bingham, Caroline 1962- *158*
Bingham, Jane M. 1941- *163*
Bingham, Jane Marie
    See Bingham, Jane M.
Bingham, Janet 1959- *200*
Bingham, Kelly 1967- *207*
Bingham, Sam(uel A.) 1944- *96*
Bingley, Margaret (Jane Kirby) 1947- *72*
Binkley, Anne
    See Rand, Ann (Binkley)

Binzen, Bill
    See Binzen, William
Binzen, William *24*
Birch, David (W.) 1913-1996 .... *89*
Birch, Reginald B(athurst) 1856-1943 .... *19*
Birchman, David 1949- *72*
Birchmore, Daniel A. 1951- *92*
Bird, Carmel 1940- *124*
Bird, E(lzy) J(ay) 1911- *58*
Birdsall, Jeanne 1952(?)- *170*
Birdseye, Tom 1951- *148*
    Earlier sketches in SATA *66, 98*
Birenbaum, Barbara 1941- *65*
Birmingham, Lloyd P(aul) 1924- *83*
    Earlier sketch in SATA *12*
Birmingham, Ruth
    See Sorrells, Walter
Birney, Betty G. 1947- *169*
    Earlier sketch in SATA *98*
Biro, B.
    See Biro, B. S.
Biro, B. S. 1921- *1*
    See also CLR *28*
    See also SAAS *13*
Biro, Val
    See Biro, B. S.
Bischoff, Julia Bristol 1899-1970 .... *12*
Bishop, Bonnie 1943- *37*
Bishop, Claire Huchet 1899(?)-1993 .... *14*
    Obituary *74*
    See also CLR *80*
Bishop, Courtney
    See Ruemmler, John D(avid)
Bishop, Curtis (Kent) 1912-1967 .... *6*
Bishop, Elizabeth 1911-1979
    Obituary *24*
Bishop, Gavin 1946- *144*
    Earlier sketch in SATA *97*
Bishop, Kathleen Wong 1954- *120*
Bishop, Kathy
    See Bishop, Kathleen Wong
Bishop, Nic 1955- *161*
    Earlier sketch in SATA *107*
Bisset, Donald 1910-1995 .... *86*
    Earlier sketch in SATA *7*
Bisson, Terry 1942- *99*
Bisson, Terry Ballantine
    See Bisson, Terry
Bitter, Gary G(len) 1940- *22*
Bixby, William (Courtney) 1920-1986 .... *6*
    Obituary *47*
Bjoerk, Christina 1938- *99*
    Earlier sketch in SATA *67*
    See also CLR *22*
Bjork, Christina
    See Bjoerk, Christina
Bjorklund, Lorence F. 1913-1978 .... *35*
    Brief entry *32*
Bjorkman, Steve *163*
Black, Algernon David 1900-1993 .... *12*
    Obituary *76*
Black, Holly 1971- *147*
Black, Irma Simonton 1906-1972 .... *2*
    Obituary *25*
Black, Mansell
    See Trevor, Elleston
Black, MaryAnn
    See Easley, MaryAnn
Black, Susan Adams 1953- *40*
Blackall, Bernie 1956- *126*
Blackall, Sophie *182*
Blackburn, Claire
    See Altman, Linda Jacobs
Blackburn, John(ny) Brewton 1952- *15*
Blackburn, Joyce Knight 1920- *29*
Blacker, Terence 1948- *194*
Blacker, Tina
    See Louise, Tina
Blackett, Veronica Heath 1927- *12*
Blackie, Jean Cutler 1943- *79*

Blacklin, Malcolm
    See Chambers, Aidan
Blacklock, Dyan 1951- *112*
Blackman, Malorie 1962- *196*
    Earlier sketches in SATA *83, 128*
Blackton, Peter
    See Wilson, Lionel
Blackwood, Alan 1932- *70*
Blackwood, Freya *199*
Blackwood, Gary L. 1945- *169*
    Earlier sketches in SATA *72, 118*
Blade, Alexander
    See Garrett, Randall
    and Hamilton, Edmond
    and Silverberg, Robert
Blades, Ann (Sager) 1947- *69*
    Earlier sketch in SATA *16*
    See also CLR *15*
Bladow, Suzanne Wilson 1937- *14*
Blaine, Chris
    See Gardner, Craig Shaw
Blaine, John
    See Goodwin, Harold L(eland)
Blaine, Marge
    See Blaine, Margery Kay
Blaine, Margery Kay 1937- *11*
Blair, Alison
    See Lerangis, Peter
Blair, Anne Denton 1914-1993 .... *46*
Blair, David Nelson 1954- *80*
Blair, Eric
    See Orwell, George
Blair, Jay 1953- *45*
Blair, Lucile
    See Yeakley, Marjory Hall
Blair, Margaret Whitman 1951- *124*
Blair, Mary 1911-1978 .... *195*
Blair, Pauline Hunter
    See Clarke, Pauline
Blair, Ruth Van Ness 1912-1999 .... *12*
Blair, Shannon
    See Kaye, Marilyn
Blair, Walter 1900-1992 .... *12*
    Obituary *72*
Blaisdell, Bob
    See Blaisdell, Robert
Blaisdell, Robert 1959- *105*
Blake, Bronwyn 1940- *149*
Blake, Francis *198*
Blake, Jon 1954- *171*
    Earlier sketch in SATA *78*
Blake, Olive
    See Supraner, Robyn
Blake, Quentin (Saxby) 1932- *125*
    Earlier sketches in SATA *9, 52, 96*
    See also CLR *31*
Blake, Robert 1949- *42*
Blake, Robert J. *160*
Blake, Walker E.
    See Griffin, W.E.B.
Blake, William 1757-1827 .... *30*
    See also CLR *52*
Blakely, Gloria 1950- *139*
Blakely, Roger K. 1922- *82*
Blakeney, Jay D.
    See Chester, Deborah
Blakey, Nancy 1955- *94*
Blanc, Esther S. 1913-1997 .... *66*
Blanc, Mel 1908-1989
    Obituary *64*
Blanchard, Patricia *125*
Blanchet, M(uriel) Wylie 1891-1961 .... *106*
Blanco, Richard L(idio) 1926- *63*
Bland, E.
    See Nesbit, E.
Bland, Edith Nesbit
    See Nesbit, E.
Bland, Fabian
    See Nesbit, E.
Blane, Gertrude
    See Blumenthal, Gertrude

Blank, Clarissa Mabel 1915-1965 .... *62*
Blankenship, LeeAnn 1944- *181*
Blassingame, Wyatt Rainey 1909-1985 .... *34*
Obituary *41*
Earlier sketch in SATA *1*
Blatchford, Claire H. 1944- *94*
Blauer, Ettagale 1940- *49*
Bleck, Linda *207*
Bledsoe, Glen L. 1951- *108*
Bledsoe, Glen Leonard
See Bledsoe, Glen L.
Bledsoe, Karen E. 1962- *167*
Earlier sketch in SATA *108*
Bledsoe, Karen Elizabeth
See Bledsoe, Karen E.
Bledsoe, Lucy Jane 1957- *162*
Earlier sketch in SATA *97*
Bleeker, Sonia
See Zim, Sonia Bleeker
Blegen, Daniel M. 1950- *92*
Blegvad, Erik 1923- *132*
Earlier sketches in SATA *14, 66*
Blegvad, Lenore 1926- *176*
Earlier sketches in SATA *14, 66*
Bley, Anette 1967- *188*
Blish, James 1921-1975 .... *66*
Blish, James Benjamin
See Blish, James
Blishen, Edward (William) 1920-1996 .... *66*
Obituary *93*
Earlier sketch in SATA *8*
Bliss, Corinne Demas 1947- *131*
Earlier sketch in SATA *37*
See Demas, Corinne
Bliss, Frederick
See Card, Orson Scott
Bliss, Gillian
See Paton Walsh, Jill
Bliss, Harry 1964- *196*
Earlier sketch in SATA *156*
Bliss, Reginald
See Wells, H. G.
Bliss, Ronald G(ene) 1942- *12*
Blitt, Barry *187*
Bliven, Bruce, Jr. 1916-2002 .... *2*
Blixen, Karen 1885-1962 .... *44*
Blizzard, Gladys S. (?)-1992 .... *79*
Blobaum, Cindy 1966- *123*
Bloch, Lucienne 1909-1999 .... *10*
Bloch, Marie Halun 1910-1998 .... *6*
See also SAAS *9*
Bloch, Robert (Albert) 1917-1994 .... *12*
Obituary *82*
Blochman, Lawrence G(oldtree)
1900-1975 .... *22*
Block, Francesca Lia 1962- *158*
Earlier sketches in SATA *80, 116*
See also CLR *116*
See also SAAS *21*
Block, Irvin 1917- *12*
Blomgren, Jennifer (Alice) 1954- *136*
Blood, Charles Lewis 1929- *28*
Bloom, Barbara Lee 1943- *146*
Bloom, Freddy 1914-2000 .... *37*
Obituary *121*
Bloom, Lloyd 1947- *108*
Brief entry *43*
Bloom, Suzanne 1950- *172*
Bloomfield, Michaela 1966- *70*
Bloor, Edward 1950- *201*
Earlier sketches in SATA *98, 155*
Bloor, Edward William
See Bloor, Edward
Blos, Joan W. 1928- *153*
Autobiography Feature *153*
Brief entry *27*
Earlier sketches in SATA *33, 69, 109*
See also CLR *18*
See also SAAS *11*
Blos, Joan Winsor
See Blos, Joan W.

Blough, Glenn O(rlando) 1907-1995 .... *1*
Blue, Rose 1931- *166*
Autobiography Feature *117*
Earlier sketches in SATA *5, 91, 93*
See also SAAS *24*
Blue, Zachary
See Stine, R.L.
Bluemle, Elizabeth *209*
Bluggage, Oranthy
See Alcott, Louisa May
Blumberg, Leda 1956- *59*
Blumberg, Rhoda 1917- *123*
Earlier sketches in SATA *35, 70*
See also CLR *21*
Blume, Judy 1938- *195*
Earlier sketches in SATA *2, 31, 79, 142*
See also CLR *69*
Blume, Judy Sussman
See Blume, Judy
Blume, Lesley M.M. 1975- *180*
Blumenthal, Deborah *204*
Earlier sketch in SATA *161*
Blumenthal, Gertrude 1907-1971
Obituary *27*
Blumenthal, Shirley 1943- *46*
Blutig, Eduard
See Gorey, Edward (St. John)
Bly, Janet (Chester) 1945- *43*
Bly, Stephen A(rthur) 1944- *116*
Earlier sketch in SATA *43*
Blyler, Allison Lee 1966- *74*
Blythe, Gary 1959- *185*
Blyton, Carey 1932-2002 .... *9*
Obituary *138*
Blyton, Enid 1897-1968 .... *25*
See also CLR *31*
Blyton, Enid Mary
See Blyton, Enid
Bo, Ben
See Richardson, V.A.
Boardman, Fon Wyman, Jr. 1911-2000 .... *6*
Boardman, Gwenn R.
See Petersen, Gwenn Boardman
Boase, Wendy 1944-1999 .... *28*
Obituary *110*
Boatner, Mark Mayo III 1921- *29*
Bobbe, Dorothie de Bear 1905-1975 .... *1*
Obituary *25*
Bober, Natalie S. 1930- *134*
Earlier sketch in SATA *87*
See also SAAS *23*
Bobette, Bibo
See Gugliotta, Bobette
Bobri, Vladimir V. 1898-1986 .... *47*
Brief entry *32*
Bobritsky, Vladimir
See Bobri, Vladimir V.
Bochak, Grayce 1956- *76*
Bock, Hal
See Bock, Harold I.
Bock, Harold I. 1939- *10*
Bock, William Sauts Netamux'we 1939- *14*
Bodanis, David *179*
Bode, Janet 1943-1999 .... *96*
Obituary *118*
Earlier sketch in SATA *60*
Bode, N.E.
See Baggott, Julianna
Bodecker, N(iels) M(ogens) 1922-1988 .... *73*
Obituary *54*
Earlier sketch in SATA *8*
Boden, Hilda
See Bodenham, Hilda Morris
Bodenham, Hilda Morris 1901- *13*
Bodett, Thomas Edward 1955- *70*
Bodett, Tom
See Bodett, Thomas Edward
Bodie, Idella F(allaw) 1925- *89*
Earlier sketch in SATA *12*
Bodker, Cecil
See Bodker, Cecil

Bodker, Cecil 1927- *133*
Earlier sketch in SATA *14*
See also CLR *23*
Bodsworth, (Charles) Fred(erick) 1918- *27*
Boeckman, Charles 1920- *12*
Boegehold, Betty (Doyle) 1913-1985
Obituary *42*
Boelts, Maribeth 1964- *200*
Earlier sketches in SATA *78, 163*
Boerst, William J. 1939- *170*
Earlier sketch in SATA *121*
Boesch, Mark J(oseph) 1917- *12*
Boesen, Victor 1908- *16*
Bogacki, Tomek 1950- *138*
Bogaerts, Gert 1965- *80*
Bogan, Paulette 1960- *201*
Earlier sketch in SATA *129*
Bogart, Jo Ellen 1945- *92*
See also CLR *59*
Boggs, Ralph Steele 1901-1994 .... *7*
Bograd, Larry 1953- *89*
Earlier sketch in SATA *33*
See also SAAS *21*
Bogue, Gary 1938- *195*
Bogue, Gary L.
See Bogue, Gary
Bohdal, Susi 1951- *101*
Earlier sketch in SATA *22*
Bohlen, Nina 1931- *58*
Bohlmeijer, Arno 1956- *94*
Bohner, Charles (Henry) 1927- *62*
Bohnhoff, Maya Kaathryn 1954- *88*
Boiger, Alexandra *178*
Boissard, Janine 1932- *59*
Bojunga, Lygia
See Nunes, Lygia Bojunga
Bojunga-Nunes, Lygia
See Nunes, Lygia Bojunga
Bok, Arthur
See Bok, Chip
Bok, Chip 1952- *205*
Bolam, Emily 1969- *206*
Boland, Janice *98*
Bolden, Tonya 1959- *188*
Earlier sketches in SATA *79, 138*
Bolden, Tonya Wilyce
See Bolden, Tonya
Boles, Paul Darcy 1916-1984 .... *9*
Obituary *38*
Bolian, Polly 1925- *4*
Bollen, Roger 1941(?)- *83*
Brief entry *29*
Bolliger, Max 1929- *7*
Bollinger, Max 1929- *167*
Bollinger, Peter *172*
Bolognese, Don(ald Alan) 1934- *129*
Earlier sketches in SATA *24, 71*
Bolognese, Elaine 1933- *23*
Bolotin, Norman (Phillip) 1951- *93*
Bolton, Carole 1926- *6*
Bolton, Elizabeth
See St. John, Nicole
Bolton, Evelyn
See Bunting, Eve
Bonar, Veronica
See Bailey, Donna (Veronica Anne)
Bond, B. J.
See Heneghan, James
Bond, Bruce 1939- *61*
Bond, Felicia 1954- *126*
Earlier sketch in SATA *49*
Bond, Gladys Baker 1912- *14*
Bond, Higgins 1951- *177*
Earlier sketch in SATA *83*
Bond, J. Harvey
See Winterbotham, R(ussell) R(obert)
Bond, (Thomas) Michael 1926- *157*
Earlier sketches in SATA *6, 58*
See also CLR *95*
See also SAAS *3*

Bond, Nancy 1945- 159
  Autobiography Feature 159
  Earlier sketches in SATA 22, 82
  See also CLR 11
  See also SAAS 13
Bond, Nancy Barbara
  See Bond, Nancy
Bond, Rebecca 1972- 130
Bond, Ruskin 1934- 87
  Earlier sketch in SATA 14
Bondie, J. D.
  See Cunningham, Chet
Bondoux, Anne-Laure 1971- 175
Bone, Ian 1956- 158
  Earlier sketch in SATA 117
Bonehill, Captain Ralph
  See Stratemeyer, Edward L.
Bonestell, Chesley 1888-1986
  Obituary 48
Bonham, Barbara Thomas 1926- 7
Bonham, Frank 1914-1989 49
  Obituary 62
  Earlier sketch in SATA 1
  See also SAAS 3
Boniface, William 1963- 182
  Earlier sketch in SATA 102
Bonino, Louise
  See Williams, Louise Bonino
Bonk, John J. 189
Bonn, Pat
  See Bonn, Patricia Carolyn
Bonn, Patricia Carolyn 1948- 43
Bonner, Hannah 197
Bonner, Mary Graham 1890-1974 19
Bonner, Mike 1951- 121
Bonners, Susan 1947- 85
  Brief entry 48
Bonnett-Rampersaud, Louise 173
Bonning, Tony 1948- 169
Bonsall, Crosby Barbara (Newell)
  1921-1995 23
  Obituary 84
Bonsall, Joseph S. 1948- 119
Bonsignore, Joan 1959- 140
Bontemps, Arna 1902-1973 44
  Obituary 24
  Earlier sketch in SATA 2
  See also CLR 6
Bontemps, Arnaud Wendell
  See Bontemps, Arna
Bonzon, Paul-Jacques 1908-1978 22
Boock, Paula 1964- 134
Booher, Dianna Daniels 1948- 33
Book, Rick 1949- 119
Book, Rita
  See Holub, Joan
Bookman, Charlotte
  See Zolotow, Charlotte
Boon, Debbie 1960- 103
Boon, Emilie (Laetitia) 1958- 86
Boone, Charles Eugene
  See Boone, Pat
Boone, Pat 1934- 7
Boorman, Linda (Kay) 1940- 46
Boorstin, Daniel J(oseph) 1914-2004 52
Boos, Ben 1971- 206
Booth, Coe 187
Booth, Ernest Sheldon 1915-1984 43
Booth, George 1926- 191
Booth, Graham (Charles) 1935- 37
Bootman, Colin 159
Borden, Louise 1949- 190
  Autobiography Feature 141
  Earlier sketches in SATA 68, 104, 141
Bordier, Georgette 1924- 16
Borgman, James
  See Borgman, Jim
Borgman, James Mark
  See Borgman, Jim
Borgman, Jim 1954- 122
Borgo, Lacy Finn 1972- 194

Boring, Mel 1939- 168
  Earlier sketch in SATA 35
Borja, Corinne 1929- 22
Borja, Robert 1923- 22
Borland, Hal
  See Borland, Harold Glen
Borland, Harold Glen 1900-1978 5
  Obituary 24
Borland, Kathryn Kilby 1916- 16
Borlenghi, Patricia 1951- 79
Born, Adolf 1930- 49
Bornstein, Ruth Lercher
  See Bornstein-Lercher, Ruth
Bornstein-Lercher, Ruth 1927- 88
  Autobiography Feature 107
  Earlier sketch in SATA 14
Borski, Lucia Merecka 18
Borten, Helen Jacobson 1930- 5
Bortolotti, Dan 1969- 157
Borton, Elizabeth
  See Trevino, Elizabeth B(orton) de
Borton, Lady 1942- 98
Borton de Trevino, Elizabeth
  See Trevino, Elizabeth B(orton) de
Bortstein, Larry 1942- 16
Bortz, Alfred B(enjamin) 1944- 139
  Earlier sketch in SATA 74
Bortz, Fred
  See Bortz, Alfred B(enjamin)
Bosch, Pseudonymous 199
Bosco, Jack
  See Holliday, Joseph
Boshell, Gordon 1908-1991 15
Boshinski, Blanche 1922- 10
Bosman, Paul 1929- 107
Bosse, Malcolm (Joseph, Jr.) 1926-2002 136
  Earlier sketch in SATA 35
Bosserman, (Charles) Phillip 1931- 84
Bossom, Naomi 1933- 35
Bostock, Mike 1962- 114
Boston, L(ucy) M(aria Wood) 1892-1990 19
  Obituary 64
  See also CLR 3
Bostrom, Kathleen (Susan) Long 1954- 139
Bostrom, Kathy
  See Bostrom, Kathleen (Susan) Long
Boswell, Addie 208
Boswell, Addie Kay
  See Boswell, Addie
Bosworth, J. Allan 1925- 19
Bothwell, Jean (?)-1977 2
Botkin, B(enjamin) A(lbert) 1901-1975 40
Botsford, Ward 1927-2004 66
Botting, Douglas (Scott) 1934- 43
Bottner, Barbara 1943- 170
  Autobiography Feature 121
  Earlier sketches in SATA 14, 93
  See also SAAS 26
Bottone, Frank G., Jr. 1969- 141
Bouchard, David 1952- 117
Boucher, (Clarence) Carter 1954- 129
Boudelang, Bob
  See Pell, Ed(ward)
Boughton, Richard 1954- 75
Boulet, Susan Seddon 1941- 50
Boulle, Pierre (Francois Marie-Louis)
  1912-1994 22
  Obituary 78
Boulton, Jane 1921- 91
Bouma, Paddy 1947- 128
Bour, Daniele 1939- 62
Bourbonniere, Sylvie 1966- 182
Bourdon, David 1934-1998 46
Bourgeois, Paulette 1951- 153
Bourne, Lesley
  See Marshall, Evelyn
Bourne, Miriam Anne 1931-1989 16
  Obituary 63
Boutavant, Marc 1970- 200

Boutet de Monvel, (Louis) M(aurice)
  1850(?)-1913 30
  See also CLR 32
Bouwman, H.M. 209
Bova, Ben 1932- 133
  Earlier sketches in SATA 6, 68
  See also CLR 96
Bova, Benjamin William
  See Bova, Ben
Bovaird, Anne E(lizabeth) 1960- 90
Bow, Patricia 1946- 168
Bowden, Joan Chase 1925- 51
  Brief entry 38
Bowe, Julie 1962- 194
Bowen, Alexandria Russell 97
Bowen, Andy Russell
  See Bowen, Alexandria Russell
Bowen, Anne 1952- 202
  Earlier sketch in SATA 170
Bowen, Betty Morgan
  See West, Betty
Bowen, Catherine (Shober) Drinker
  1897-1973 7
Bowen, David
  See Bowen, Joshua David
Bowen, Fred 1953- 136
Bowen, Joshua David 1930- 22
Bowen, Rhys
  See Quin-Harkin, Janet
Bowen, Robert Sydney 1900-1977 52
  Obituary 21
Bowermaster, Jon 1954- 135
  Earlier sketch in SATA 77
Bowers, Terrell L. 1945- 101
Bowers, Terry
  See Bowers, Terrell L.
Bowers, Tim 185
Bowie, C. W.
  See Old, Wendie C(orbin)
  and Wirths, Claudine (Turner) G(ibson)
Bowie, Jim
  See Norwood, Victor G(eorge) C(harles)
  and Stratemeyer, Edward L.
Bowkett, Stephen 1953- 67
Bowler, Jan Brett
  See Brett, Jan
Bowler, Tim 1953- 209
  Earlier sketch in SATA 149
Bowman, Catherine
  See Smith, Cat Bowman
Bowman, Crystal 1951- 105
Bowman, James Cloyd 1880-1961 23
Bowman, John S(tewart) 1931- 16
Bowman, Kathleen (Gill) 1942- 52
  Brief entry 40
Bowman, Leslie
  See Bowman, Leslie W.
Bowman, Leslie W. 182
Bowsher, Melodie 195
Boxall, Ed 178
Boyce, Frank Cottrell 182
Boyce, George A(rthur) 1898- 19
Boyd, Candy Dawson 1946- 72
  See also CLR 50
Boyd, Pauline
  See Schock, Pauline
Boyd, Selma
  See Acuff, Selma Boyd
Boyd, Waldo T. 1918- 18
Boyden, Linda 1948- 143
Boyer, Allen B. 1963- 153
Boyer, Robert E(rnst) 1929- 22
Boyes, Vivien 1952- 106
Boyes, Vivien Elizabeth
  See Boyes, Vivien
Boyle, Ann (Peters) 1916- 10
Boyle, Eleanor Vere (Gordon) 1825-1916 28
Boyle, Robert H. 1928- 65
Boylston, Helen Dore 1895-1984 23
  Obituary 39
Boyne, John 1971- 181

Boynton, Sandra (Keith) 1953- *152*
  Brief entry *38*
  Earlier sketches in SATA *57, 107*
  See also CLR *105*
Boz
  See Dickens, Charles
Braasch, Gary *201*
Bracken, Charles
  See Pellowski, Michael (Joseph)
Brackers de Hugo, Pierre 1960- *115*
Brackett, Dolli Tingle 1911-1993 .... *137*
Brackett, Virginia 1950- *166*
  Earlier sketch in SATA *121*
Brackett, Virginia Roberts Meredith
  See Brackett, Virginia
Bradbury, Bianca (Ryley) 1908-1982 .... *56*
  Earlier sketch in SATA *3*
Bradbury, Edward P.
  See Moorcock, Michael
Bradbury, Ray 1920- *123*
  Earlier sketches in SATA *11, 64*
Bradbury, Ray Douglas
  See Bradbury, Ray
Bradby, Marie *161*
Bradfield, Carl 1942- *91*
Bradford, Ann (Liddell) 1917- *56*
  Brief entry *38*
Bradford, Barbara Taylor 1933- *66*
Bradford, Karleen 1936- *96*
  Earlier sketch in SATA *48*
Bradford, Lois J(ean) 1936- *36*
Bradford, Richard (Roark) 1932-2002 .... *59*
  Obituary *135*
Bradley, Duane
  See Sanborn, Duane
Bradley, Kimberly Brubaker 1967- *179*
Bradley, Marion Zimmer 1930-1999 .... *139*
  Obituary *116*
  Earlier sketch in SATA *90*
Bradley, Timothy J. *193*
Bradley, Virginia 1912- *23*
Bradley, Will
  See Strickland, Brad
Bradman, Tony 1954- *152*
  Earlier sketch in SATA *81*
Bradshaw, Gillian (Joan) 1949- *118*
Bradshaw, Gillian 1956- *127*
Bradshaw, Gillian Marucha
  See Bradshaw, Gillian
Bradstreet, T. J.
  See Thesman, Jean
Brady, Esther Wood 1905-1987 .... *31*
  Obituary *53*
Brady, Irene 1943- *4*
Brady, Kimberley S. 1953- *101*
Brady, Kimberley Smith
  See Brady, Kimberley S.
Brady, Lillian 1902- *28*
Bragdon, Elspeth MacDuffie 1897-1980 .... *6*
Bragdon, Lillian Jacot *24*
Brager, Bruce L. 1949- *146*
Bragg, Mabel Caroline 1870-1945 .... *24*
Bragg, Michael 1948- *46*
Bragg, Ruth Gembicki 1943- *77*
Brahm, Sumishta 1954- *58*
Brailsford, Frances
  See Wosmek, Frances
Brainerd, John W(hiting) 1918- *65*
Braithwaite, Althea 1940- *23*
  Autobiography Feature *119*
  See also SAAS *24*
Bram, Elizabeth 1948- *30*
Brancato, Robin F(idler) 1936- *97*
  See also CLR *32*
  See also SAAS *9*
Branch, Muriel Miller 1943- *152*
  Earlier sketch in SATA *94*
Brand, Christianna
  See Lewis, Mary
Brand, Rebecca
  See Charnas, Suzy McKee

Brande, Robin *194*
Brandel, Marc 1919- *71*
Brandenberg, Alexa (Demetria) 1966- *97*
Brandenberg, Aliki 1929- *157*
  Earlier sketches in SATA *2, 35, 75, 113*
  See also CLR *71*
Brandenberg, Franz 1932- *75*
  Earlier sketches in SATA *8, 35*
Brandenburg, Jim 1945- *87*
Brandhorst, Carl T(heodore) 1898-1988 .... *23*
Brandis, Marianne 1938- *149*
  Earlier sketches in SATA *59, 96*
Brandon, Brumsic, Jr. 1927- *9*
Brandon, Curt
  See Bishop, Curtis (Kent)
Brandreth, Gyles 1948- *28*
Brandreth, Gyles Daubeney
  See Brandreth, Gyles
Brandt, Catharine 1905-1997 .... *40*
Brandt, Keith
  See Sabin, Louis
Brandt, Sue R(eading) 1916- *59*
Branfield, John (Charles) 1931- *11*
Branford, Henrietta 1946-1999 .... *106*
Branley, Franklyn M(ansfield) 1915-2002 .. *136*
  Earlier sketches in SATA *4, 68*
  See also CLR *13*
  See also SAAS *16*
Brannen, Sarah S. *202*
Branscum, Robbie (Tilley) 1937-1997 .... *72*
  Obituary *96*
  Earlier sketch in SATA *23*
  See also SAAS *17*
Bransom, (John) Paul 1885-1979 .... *43*
Brashares, Ann 1967- *188*
  Earlier sketch in SATA *145*
  See also CLR *113*
Brassard, France 1963- *186*
Braswell, E.J.
  See Lynn, Tracy
Braswell, Elizabeth J.
  See Lynn, Tracy
Braswell, Liz
  See Lynn, Tracy
Bratton, Helen 1899-1986 .... *4*
Bratun, Katy 1950- *160*
  Earlier sketch in SATA *83*
Braude, Michael 1936- *23*
Braun, Lilian Jackson 1916(?)- *109*
Brautigan, Richard 1935-1984 .... *56*
Brautigan, Richard Gary
  See Brautigan, Richard
Bray, Libba *203*
  Earlier sketch in SATA *159*
Bray, Martha E.
  See Bray, Libba
Braymer, Marjorie Elizabeth 1911-1988 .... *6*
Breathed, Berke 1957- *161*
  Earlier sketch in SATA *86*
Breathed, Guy Berkeley
  See Breathed, Berke
Brecht, Edith 1895-1975 .... *6*
  Obituary *25*
Breck, Vivian
  See Breckenfeld, Vivian Gurney
Breckenfeld, Vivian Gurney 1895-1992 .... *1*
Breda, Tjalmar
  See DeJong, David C(ornel)
Bredeson, Carmen 1944- *163*
  Earlier sketch in SATA *98*
Breen, Steve 1970- *186*
Breinburg, Petronella 1927- *11*
  See also CLR *31*
Breisky, William J(ohn) 1928- *22*
Brenaman, Miriam *172*
Brennan, Caitlin
  See Tarr, Judith
Brennan, Gale (Patrick) 1927- *64*
  Brief entry *53*
Brennan, Herbie 1940- *183*
  Earlier sketch in SATA *140*

Brennan, James Herbert
  See Brennan, Herbie
Brennan, Jan
  See Brennan, Herbie
Brennan, J.H.
  See Brennan, Herbie
Brennan, Joseph Lomas 1903-2000 .... *6*
Brennan, Linda Crotta 1952- *130*
Brennan, Tim
  See Conroy, John Wesley
Brennan-Nelson, Denise *203*
Brenner, Anita 1905-1974 .... *56*
Brenner, Barbara (Johnes) 1925- *124*
  Earlier sketches in SATA *4, 42, 76*
  See also SAAS *14*
Brenner, Fred 1920- *36*
  Brief entry *34*
Brent, Hope 1935(?)-1984
  Obituary *39*
Brent, Stuart *14*
Breskin, Jane
  See Zalben, Jane Breskin
Breslin, Theresa *128*
  Autobiography Feature *128*
  Earlier sketch in SATA *70*
Breslow, Maurice 1935- *72*
Breslow, Maurice A
  See Breslow, Maurice
Breslow, Susan 1951- *69*
Brett, Bernard 1925- *22*
Brett, Grace N(eff) 1900-1975 .... *23*
Brett, Jan 1949- *171*
  Earlier sketches in SATA *42, 71, 130*
  See also CLR *27*
Brett, Jan Churchill
  See Brett, Jan
Brett Bowler, Jan
  See Brett, Jan
Brewer, Heather 1973- *196*
Brewer, James D. 1951- *108*
Brewer, Sally King 1947- *33*
Brewster, Benjamin
  See Folsom, Franklin (Brewster)
Brewster, Hugh 1950- *191*
  Earlier sketch in SATA *95*
Brewster, Patience 1952- *97*
Brewton, John E(dmund) 1898-1982 .... *5*
Brian, Janeen (Paulette) 1948- *141*
Briant, Ed *180*
Brick, John 1922-1973 .... *10*
Brickman, Robin D. 1954- *155*
Bride, Nadja
  See Nobisso, Josephine
Bridgers, Sue Ellen 1942- *90*
  Autobiography Feature *109*
  Earlier sketch in SATA *22*
  See also CLR *18*
  See also SAAS *1*
Bridges, Laurie
  See Bruck, Lorraine
Bridges, Ruby (Nell) 1954- *131*
Bridges, William (Andrew) 1901-1984 .... *5*
Bridwell, Norman (Ray) 1928- *138*
  Earlier sketches in SATA *4, 68*
  See also CLR *96*
Brier, Howard M(axwell) 1903-1969 .... *8*
Brierley, (Louise) 1958- *59*
Briggs, Katharine Mary 1898-1980 .... *101*
  Obituary *25*
Briggs, Peter 1921-1975 .... *39*
  Obituary *31*
Briggs, Raymond 1934- *184*
  Earlier sketches in SATA *23, 66, 131*
  See also CLR *10*
Briggs, Raymond Redvers
  See Briggs, Raymond
Bright, Paul 1949- *182*
Bright, Robert Sr.) 1902-1988 .... *63*
  Obituary *60*
  Earlier sketch in SATA *24*

Bright, Robert Douglas
  See Bright, Robert Sr.)
Bright, Sarah
  See Shine, Deborah
Brightfield, Richard 1927- 65
  Brief entry 53
Brightfield, Rick
  See Brightfield, Richard
Brighton, Catherine 1943- 206
  Earlier sketches in SATA 65, 107
Brill, Marlene Targ 1945- 124
  Earlier sketch in SATA 77
Brimberg, Stanlee 1947- 9
Brimner, Larry Dane 1949- 170
  Autobiography Feature 112
  Earlier sketch in SATA 79
Brin, David 1950- 65
Brin, Ruth Firestone 1921- 22
Brinckloe, Julie 1950- 13
Brinckloe, Julie Lorraine
  See Brinckloe, Julie
Brindel, June (Rachuy) 1919- 7
Brindle, Max
  See Fleischman, Sid
Brindze, Ruth 1903-1984 23
Brink, Carol Ryrie 1895-1981 100
  Obituary 27
  Earlier sketches in SATA 1, 31
  See also CLR 149
Brinsmead, H. F(ay)
  See Brinsmead, H(esba) F(ay)
Brinsmead, H. F.
  See Brinsmead, H(esba) F(ay)
Brinsmead, H(esba) F(ay) 1922- 78
  Earlier sketch in SATA 18
  See also CLR 47
  See also SAAS 5
Briquebec, John
  See Rowland-Entwistle, (Arthur) Theodore
  (Henry)
Brisbane, Henry R.
  See Ellis, Edward S.
Brisco, P. A.
  See Matthews, Patricia
Brisco, Patty
  See Matthews, Patricia
  and Matthews, Clayton (Hartley)
Briscoe, Jill (Pauline) 1935- 56
  Brief entry 47
Brisley, Joyce Lankester 1896-1978 22
  Obituary 84
Brissenden, Connie
  See Brissenden, Constance
Brissenden, Constance 1947- 150
Brisson, Pat 1951- 177
  Autobiography Feature 133
  Earlier sketches in SATA 67, 128, 133
Britt, Albert 1874-1969
  Obituary 28
Britt, Dell 1934- 1
Brittain, Bill
  See Brittain, William
Brittain, C. Dale 1948- 82
Brittain, William 1930- 76
  Earlier sketch in SATA 36
  See also SAAS 7
Brittingham, Geoffrey (Hugh) 1959- 76
Brittney, L. 209
Britton, Kate
  See Stegeman, Janet Allais
Britton, Louisa
  See McGuire, Leslie (Sarah)
Britton, Rick 1952- 82
Bro, Marguerite (Harmon) 1894-1977 19
  Obituary 27
Broach, Elise 1963- 173
Broadhead, Helen Cross 1913- 25
Broadway, Hannah 208
Brochmann, Elizabeth 1938- 41
Brock, Betty (Carter) 1923-2003 4
  Obituary 150

Brock, C(harles) E(dmund) 1870-1938 42
  Brief entry 32
Brock, Delia
  See Ephron, Delia
Brock, Emma L(illian) 1886-1974 8
Brock, H(enry) M(atthew) 1875-1960 42
Brockett, Eleanor Hall 1913-1967 10
Brockman, C(hristian) Frank 1902-1985 26
Brockmeier, Kevin 1972- 176
Broda, Ron 1954- 209
Broderick, Dorothy M. 1929- 5
Brodeur, Ruth Wallace
  See Wallace-Brodeur, Ruth
Brodie, Sally
  See Cavin, Ruth (Brodie)
Brodsky, Beverly
  See McDermott, Beverly Brodsky
Brody, Wendy
  See Staub, Wendy Corsi
Broeger, Achim 1944- 31
Broekel, Rainer Lothar 1923- 38
Broekel, Ray
  See Broekel, Rainer Lothar
Broekstra, Lorette 1964- 189
  Earlier sketch in SATA 124
Brogden, Sherryl
  See Jordan, Sherryl
Broger, Achim
  See Broeger, Achim
Broida, Marian 154
Brokamp, Marilyn 1920- 10
Broman, Fred
  See Moseley, James W(illett)
Bromhall, Winifred 26
Brommer, Gerald F(rederick) 1927- 28
Brondfield, Jerome 1913-1998 22
Brondfield, Jerry
  See Brondfield, Jerome
Bronner, Stephen Eric 1949- 101
Bronowski, Jacob 1908-1974 55
Bronson, Alice
  See Watkins, Dawn L.
Bronson, Linda 203
Bronson, Lynn
  See Lampman, Evelyn Sibley
Bronson, Wilfrid Swancourt 1894-1985
  Obituary 43
Brook, Judith (Penelope) 1926- 59
  Brief entry 51
Brook, Judy
  See Brook, Judith (Penelope)
Brooke, L(eonard) Leslie 1862-1940 17
  See also CLR 20
Brooke, William J. 1946- 139
Brooke-Haven, P.
  See Wodehouse, P. G.
Brooker, Kyrsten 199
Brookins, Dana 1931- 28
Brooks, Anita
  See Abramovitz, Anita (Zeltner Brooks)
Brooks, Bill 1939- 59
Brooks, Bruce 1950- 112
  Brief entry 53
  Earlier sketch in SATA 72
  See also CLR 25
Brooks, Caryl 1924- 84
Brooks, Charlotte K(endrick) 1918-1998 24
  Obituary 112
Brooks, Erik 1972- 182
  Earlier sketch in SATA 152
Brooks, George
  See Baum, L. Frank
Brooks, Gwendolyn 1917-2000 6
  Obituary 123
  See also CLR 27
Brooks, Gwendolyn Elizabeth
  See Brooks, Gwendolyn
Brooks, Jerome 1931- 23
Brooks, Kevin 1959- 197
  Earlier sketch in SATA 150

Brooks, Kevin M.
  See Brooks, Kevin
Brooks, Laurie 209
Brooks, Lester 1924- 7
Brooks, Martha 1944- 134
  Autobiography Feature 134
  Earlier sketches in SATA 68, 121
Brooks, Maurice (Graham) 1900- 45
Brooks, Polly Schoyer 1912- 12
Brooks, Ron 1948- 94
  Brief entry 33
Brooks, Ronald George
  See Brooks, Ron
Brooks, Terry 1944- 60
Brooks, Walter R(ollin) 1886-1958 17
Brooks-Hill, Helen (Mason) 1908-1994 59
Broome, Errol 1937- 158
  Earlier sketch in SATA 105
Brophy, Nannette 1963- 73
Brosnan, James Patrick 1929- 14
Brosnan, Jim
  See Brosnan, James Patrick
Brostoff, Anita 1931- 132
Brothers Grimm
  See Grimm, Jacob Ludwig Karl
  and Grimm, Wilhelm Karl
Brothers Hildebrandt, The
  See Hildebrandt, Greg
  and Hildebrandt, Tim
Broun, Emily
  See Sterne, Emma Gelders
Brouwer, S. W.
  See Brouwer, Sigmund (W.)
Brouwer, Sigmund (W.) 1959- 109
Brow, Thea 1934- 60
Brower, Millicent 8
Brower, Pauline 1929- 22
Browin, Frances Williams 1898-1986 5
Brown, Alexis
  See Baumann, Amy Beeching
Brown, Anne Ensign 1937- 61
Brown, Beverly Swerdlow 97
Brown, Bill
  See Brown, William L(ouis)
Brown, Billye Walker
  See Cutchen, Billye Walker
Brown, Bob
  See Brown, Robert Joseph
Brown, Buck 1936- 45
Brown, Calef 1919-1986 179
Brown, Cassie 1919-1986 55
Brown, Charlotte Lewis 181
Brown, Conrad 1922- 31
Brown, Craig McFarland 1947- 73
Brown, David
  See Brown, David A(lan)
  and Myller, Rolf
Brown, Dee 1908-2002 110
  Obituary 141
  Earlier sketch in SATA 5
Brown, Dee Alexander
  See Brown, Dee
Brown, Don 1949- 200
  Earlier sketch in SATA 172
Brown, Drew T. III 1955- 83
Brown, Drollene P. 1939- 53
Brown, Elbrite 198
Brown, Eleanor Frances 1908-1987 3
Brown, Elizabeth Ferguson 1937- 153
Brown, Elizabeth M(yers) 1915- 43
Brown, Fern G. 1918- 34
Brown, (Robert) Fletch 1923- 42
Brown, Fornan 1901-1996 71
  Obituary 88
Brown, George Earl 1883-1964 11
Brown, George Mackay 1921-1996 35
Brown, Irene Bennett 1932- 3
Brown, Irving
  See Adams, William Taylor
Brown, Ivor (John Carnegie) 1891-1974 5
  Obituary 26

Brown, Jane Clark 1930- 81
Brown, Janet Mitsui 87
Brown, Jo 1964- 170
Brown, Joanne 1933- 147
Brown, Joe David 1915-1976 44
Brown, Joseph E(dward) 1929- 59
  Brief entry 51
Brown, Judith Gwyn 1933- 20
Brown, Kathryn 1955- 168
  Earlier sketch in SATA 98
Brown, Kathy
  See Brown, Kathryn
Brown, Ken (James) 129
Brown, Kevin 1960- 101
Brown, Laurene Krasny 1945- 99
  Earlier sketch in SATA 54
Brown, Laurie Krasny
  See Brown, Laurene Krasny
Brown, Lloyd Arnold 1907-1966 36
Brown, Mahlon A.
  See Ellis, Edward S.
Brown, Marc (Tolon) 1946- 145
  Earlier sketches in SATA 10, 53, 80
  See also CLR 29
Brown, Marcia (Joan) 1918- 47
  Earlier sketch in SATA 7
  See also CLR 12
Brown, Margaret Wise 1910-1952 100
  See also YABC 2
  See also CLR 107
Brown, Margery (Wheeler) 78
  Earlier sketch in SATA 5
Brown, Marion Marsh 1908-2001 6
Brown, Myra Berry 1918- 6
Brown, Palmer 1919- 36
Brown, Pamela (Beatrice) 1924-1989 5
  Obituary 61
Brown, Peter 1979- 178
Brown, Rachel W.N. 1947- 203
Brown, Reeve Lindbergh
  See Lindbergh, Reeve
Brown, Richard E. 1946- 61
Brown, Robert Joseph 1907-1989 14
Brown, Roderick (Langmere) Haig-
  See Haig-Brown, Roderick (Langmere)
Brown, Rosalie
  See Moore, Rosalie (Gertrude)
Brown, Roswell
  See Webb, Jean Francis (III)
Brown, Roy (Frederick) 1921-1982 51
  Obituary 39
Brown, Ruth 1941- 170
  Earlier sketch in SATA 105
Brown, Scott 1971- 134
Brown, Sue Ellen 1954- 81
Brown, Tricia 1954- 114
Brown, Vinson 1912-1991 19
Brown, Walter R(eed) 1929- 19
Brown, Will
  See Ainsworth, William Harrison
Brown, William L(ouis) 1910-1964 5
Browne, Anthony 1946- 163
  Brief entry 44
  Earlier sketches in SATA 45, 61, 105
  See also CLR 19
Browne, Anthony Edward Tudor
  See Browne, Anthony
Browne, Dik
  See Browne, Richard Arthur Allen
Browne, Hablot Knight 1815-1882 21
Browne, Matthew
  See Rands, William Brighty
Browne, Nicki M.
  See Browne, N.M.
Browne, Nicky Matthews
  See Browne, N.M.
Browne, N.M. 1960- 167
Browne, Richard Arthur Allen 1917-1989 ... 67
  Brief entry 38
Browne, Vee F(rances) 1956- 90

Browning, Robert 1812-1889
  See YABC 1
  See also CLR 97
Brownjohn, Alan 1931- 6
Brownlee, Walter 1930- 62
Brownlie, Betty 1946- 159
Brownlow, Kevin 1938- 65
Brownlow, Mike 183
Brownridge, William R(oy) 1932- 94
Broyles, Anne 1953- 201
Bruce, Dorita Fairlie 1885-1970
  Obituary 27
Bruce, (William) Harry 1934- 77
Bruce, Mary 1927- 1
Bruchac, Joseph III
  See Bruchac, Joseph
Bruchac, Joseph 1942- 176
  Autobiography Feature 176
  Earlier sketches in SATA 42, 89, 131
  See also CLR 46
Bruchac, Margaret M.
  See Bruchac, Marge
Bruchac, Marge 181
Bruck, Lorraine 1921- 55
  Brief entry 46
Bruel, Nick 205
  Earlier sketch in SATA 166
Bruel, Robert O. 1929-2002 189
Bruemmer, Fred 1929- 47
Brugman, Alyssa (F.) 1974- 152
Brumbeau, Jeff 1955- 157
Bruna, Dick 1927- 76
  Brief entry 30
  Earlier sketch in SATA 43
  See also CLR 7
Brunhoff, Jean de 1899-1937 24
  See also CLR 116
Brunhoff, Laurent de 1925- 150
  Earlier sketches in SATA 24, 71
  See also CLR 116
Brunkus, Denise 204
Brunskill, Elizabeth Ann Flatt
  See Flatt, Lizann
Brush, Karen A(lexandra) 1960- 85
Brussel-Smith, Bernard 1914- 58
Brust, Steven 1955- 121
  Earlier sketch in SATA 86
Brust, Steven K. Zoltan
  See Brust, Steven
Brustlein, Daniel 1904- 40
Brustlein, Janice Tworkov -2000 40
  Obituary 126
Brutschy, Jennifer 1960- 84
Bryan, Ashley 1923- 178
  Earlier sketches in SATA 31, 72, 132
  See also CLR 66
Bryan, Ashley F.
  See Bryan, Ashley
Bryan, Dorothy M. 1896(?)-1984
  Obituary 39
Bryan, Jennifer 190
Bryan, Sean 192
Bryant, Bernice (Morgan) 1908-1976 11
Bryant, Jen 1960- 175
  Earlier sketch in SATA 94
Bryant, Jennifer
  See Bryant, Jen
Bryant, Jennifer Fisher
  See Bryant, Jen
Bryant, Laura J. 176
Brychta, Alex 1956- 21
Brynie, Faith H. 1946- 113
Brynie, Faith Hickman
  See Brynie, Faith H.
Bryson, Bernarda 1903-2004 9
Buba, Joy Flinsch 1904- 44
Buchan, Bryan 1945- 36
Buchan, John 1875-1940
  See YABC 2
Buchan, Stuart 1942-1987
  Obituary 54

Buchanan, Debby 1952- 82
Buchanan, Deborah Leevonne
  See Buchanan, Debby
Buchanan, Jane 1956- 160
Buchanan, Paul 1959- 116
Buchanan, Sue 1939- 139
Buchheimer, Naomi Barnett
  See Barnett, Naomi
Buchignani, Walter 1965- 84
Buchmann, Stephen L. 194
Buchwald, Art 1925-2007 10
Buchwald, Arthur
  See Buchwald, Art
Buchwald, Emilie 1935- 7
Buck, Gisela 1941- 101
Buck, Lewis 1925- 18
Buck, Margaret Waring 1905-1997 3
Buck, Nola
  See Godwin, Laura
Buck, Pearl S. 1892-1973 25
  Earlier sketch in SATA 1
Buck, Pearl Sydenstricker
  See Buck, Pearl S.
Buck, Siegfried 1941- 101
Buckalew, Clare B.
  See Dunkle, Clare B.
Buckeridge, Anthony (Malcolm)
  1912-2004 85
  Earlier sketch in SATA 6
Buckholtz, Eileen (Garber) 1949- 54
  Brief entry 47
Buckler, Ernest 1908-1984 47
Buckless, Andrea K. 1968- 117
Buckley, Helen E(lizabeth) 1918- 90
  Earlier sketch in SATA 2
Buckley, James, Jr. 1963- 166
  Earlier sketch in SATA 114
Buckley, Michael 177
Buckley, Susan 184
Buckley, Susan Washburn
  See Buckley, Susan
Buckley-Archer, Linda 185
Buckmaster, Henrietta
  See Stephens, Henrietta Henkle
Bucks, Brad
  See Holub, Joan
Budd, E. S.
  See Sirimarco, Elizabeth
Budd, Lillian (Peterson) 1897-1989 7
Budhos, Marina 173
Buehler, Stephanie Jona 1956- 83
Buehner, Caralyn (M.) 1963- 159
  Earlier sketch in SATA 104
Buehner, Mark 1959- 159
  Earlier sketch in SATA 104
Buehr, Walter Franklin 1897-1971 3
Buell, Ellen Lewis
  See Cash, Ellen Lewis Buell
Buell, Janet 1952- 185
  Earlier sketch in SATA 106
Buergel, Paul-Hermann H. 1949- 83
Buettner, Dan 1960- 95
Buff, Conrad 1886-1975 19
Buff, Mary (E. Marsh) 1890-1970 19
Buffett, Jimmy 1946- 110
  Earlier sketch in SATA 76
Buffie, Margaret 1945- 161
  Earlier sketches in SATA 71, 107
  See also CLR 39
Bugbee, Emma 1888(?)-1981
  Obituary 29
Bugni, Alice 1951- 122
Buhhos, Marina Tamar
  See Budhos, Marina
Bujold, Lois McMaster 1949- 136
Bulfinch, Thomas 1796-1867 35
Bulion, Leslie 1958- 209
  Earlier sketch in SATA 161
Bull, Angela (Mary) 1936- 45

Bull, Emma 1954- *190*
   Autobiography Feature *103*
   Earlier sketch in SATA *99*
Bull, Norman John 1916- *41*
Bull, Peter (Cecil) 1912-1984
   Obituary *39*
Bull, Schuyler M. 1974- *138*
Bulla, Clyde R. 1914-2007 .... *139*
   Obituary *182*
   Earlier sketches in SATA *2, 41, 91*
   See also SAAS *6*
Bullard, Lisa 1961- *142*
Buller, Jon *205*
Bullock, Kathleen (Mary) 1946- *77*
Bullock, Robert (D.) 1947- *92*
Bulpin, (Barbara) Vicki *92*
Bulwer-Lytton, Edward 1803-1873 .... *23*
Bulwer-Lytton, Edward George Earle Lytton
   See Bulwer-Lytton, Edward
Bumstead, Kathleen Mary 1918-1987 .... *53*
Bundles, A'Lelia Perry 1952- *76*
Bunge, Daniela 1973- *207*
Bunin, Catherine 1967- *30*
Bunin, Sherry 1925- *30*
Bunkers, Suzanne L. 1950- *136*
Bunting, A.E.
   See Bunting, Eve
Bunting, Anne Evelyn
   See Bunting, Eve
Bunting, Eve 1928- *196*
   Earlier sketches in SATA *18, 64, 110, 158*
   See also CLR *82*
Bunting, Glenn (Davison) 1957- *22*
Bunyan, John 1628-1688
   See CLR *124*
Bupp, Walter
   See Garrett, Randall
Burack, Sylvia K. 1916-2003 .... *35*
   Obituary *143*
Burbank, Addison (Buswell) 1895-1961 ...... *37*
Burch, Joann J(ohansen) *75*
Burch, Robert J(oseph) 1925- *74*
   Earlier sketch in SATA *1*
   See also CLR *63*
Burchard, Peter Duncan 1921- *143*
   Earlier sketches in SATA *5, 74*
   See also SAAS *13*
Burchard, S. H.
   See Burchard, Sue
Burchard, Sue 1937- *22*
Burchardt, Nellie 1921- *7*
Burckhardt, Marc 1962- *196*
Burdett, Lois *117*
Burdick, Eugene (Leonard) 1918-1965 .... *22*
Burford, Eleanor
   See Hibbert, Eleanor Alice Burford
Burg, Shana 1968- *204*
Burgan, Michael 1960- *167*
   Earlier sketch in SATA *118*
Burger, Carl 1888-1967 .... *9*
Burgess, Ann Marie
   See Gerson, Noel Bertram
Burgess, Barbara Hood 1926- *69*
Burgess, Em
   See Burgess, Mary Wyche
Burgess, (Frank) Gelett 1866-1951 .... *32*
   Brief entry *30*
Burgess, Mark *157*
Burgess, Mary Wyche 1916- *18*
Burgess, Melvin 1954- *198*
   Earlier sketches in SATA *96, 146*
Burgess, Michael
   See Gerson, Noel Bertram
Burgess, Robert F(orrest) 1927- *4*
Burgess, Starling
   See Tudor, Tasha
Burgess, Thornton Waldo 1874-1965 .... *17*
Burgess, Trevor
   See Trevor, Elleston
Burgwyn, Mebane Holoman 1914-1992 .... *7*
Burke, David 1927- *46*

Burke, Diana G.
   See Gallagher, Diana G.
Burke, Diana Gallagher
   See Gallagher, Diana G.
Burke, Dianne O'Quinn 1940- *89*
Burke, Janine 1952- *139*
Burke, Jim 1973- *179*
Burke, John
   See O'Connor, Richard
Burke, Katie 1953- *168*
Burke, Patrick 1958- *114*
Burke, Ralph
   See Garrett, Randall
   and Silverberg, Robert
Burkert, Nancy Ekholm 1933- *24*
   See also SAAS *14*
Burkett, D. Brent *194*
Burke-Weiner, Kimberly 1962- *95*
Burks, Brian 1955- *95*
Burland, Brian (Berkeley) 1931- *34*
Burland, C. A.
   See Burland, Cottie (Arthur)
Burland, Cottie (Arthur) 1905-1983 .... *5*
Burleigh, Robert 1936- *193*
   Earlier sketches in SATA *55, 98, 146*
Burlingame, (William) Roger 1889-1967 ..... *2*
Burman, Alice Caddy 1896(?)-1977
   Obituary *24*
Burman, Ben Lucien 1896-1984 .... *6*
   Obituary *40*
Burn, Doris 1923- *1*
Burn, Ted
   See Burn, Thomas E.
Burn, Thomas E. 1940- *150*
Burnard, Damon 1963- *115*
Burnett, Constance Buel 1893-1975 .... *36*
Burnett, Frances Eliza Hodgson
   See Burnett, Frances Hodgson
Burnett, Frances Hodgson 1849-1924 .... *100*
   See also YABC *2*
   See also CLR *122*
Burnett Bossi, Lisa *193*
Burney, Anton
   See Hopkins, (Hector) Kenneth
Burnford, Sheila (Philip Cochrane Every)
   1918-1984 .... *3*
   Obituary *38*
   See also CLR *2*
Burnham, Gretchen
   See Sprague, Gretchen
Burnham, Nicole 1970- *161*
Burnham, Niki
   See Burnham, Nicole
Burnham, Sophy 1936- *65*
Burningham, John 1936- *160*
   Earlier sketches in SATA *16, 59, 111*
   See also CLR *9*
Burningham, Robin Yoko
   See Racoma, Robin Yoko
Burns, Diane L. 1950- *81*
   See also SAAS *24*
Burns, Eloise Wilkin
   See Wilkin, Eloise
Burns, Florence M. 1905-1988 .... *61*
Burns, Khephra 1950- *92*
Burns, Loree Griffin *193*
Burns, Marilyn 1941- *96*
   Brief entry *33*
Burns, Olive Ann 1924-1990 .... *65*
Burns, Paul C. *5*
Burns, Ray
   See Burns, Raymond (Howard)
Burns, Raymond (Howard) 1924- *9*
Burns, Theresa 1961- *84*
Burns, William A. 1909-1999 .... *5*
Burr, Dan 1951- *65*
Burr, Lonnie 1943- *47*
Burrell, Roy E(ric) C(harles) 1923- *72*
Burroughs, Edgar Rice 1875-1950 .... *41*
Burroughs, Jean Mitchell 1908- *28*
Burroughs, Polly 1925- *2*

Burroway, Janet (Gay) 1936- *23*
Burstein, Chaya M(alamud) 1923- *64*
Burstein, Fred 1950- *83*
Burstein, John 1949- *54*
   Brief entry *40*
Burstein, Stanley M.
   See Burstein, Stanley Mayer
Burstein, Stanley Mayer 1941- *175*
Bursztynski, Sue 1953- *114*
Burt, Jesse Clifton 1921-1976 .... *46*
   Obituary *20*
Burt, Olive Woolley 1894-1981 .... *4*
Burtinshaw, Julie *185*
Burton, Gennett 1945- *95*
Burton, Hester (Wood-Hill) 1913-2000 .... *74*
   Earlier sketch in SATA *7*
   See also CLR *1*
   See also SAAS *8*
Burton, Leslie
   See McGuire, Leslie (Sarah)
Burton, Marilee Robin 1950- *82*
   Earlier sketch in SATA *46*
Burton, Maurice 1898-1992 .... *23*
Burton, Rebecca 1970- *183*
Burton, Robert (Wellesley) 1941- *22*
Burton, Virginia Lee 1909-1968 .... *100*
   Earlier sketch in SATA *2*
   See also CLR *11*
Burton, William H(enry) 1890-1964 .... *11*
Busby, Ailie *192*
Busby, Cylin 1970- *118*
Busby, Edith (A. Lake) (?)-1964
   Obituary *29*
Busby, John 1942- *209*
Buscaglia, (Felice) Leo(nardo) 1924-1998 ... *65*
Buscaglia, Leo F.
   See Buscaglia, (Felice) Leo(nardo)
Busch, Phyllis S. 1909- *30*
Bush, Anne Kelleher
   See Kelleher, Anne
Bush, Catherine 1961- *128*
Bush, Jenna 1981- *208*
Bush, Laura 1946- *208*
Bushmiller, Ernest Paul 1905-1982 .... *31*
Bushmiller, Ernie
   See Bushmiller, Ernest Paul
Bushnell, Jack 1952- *86*
Busoni, Rafaello 1900-1962 .... *16*
Buss, Helen M.
   See Clarke, Margaret
Busse, Sarah Martin *194*
Busselle, Rebecca 1941- *80*
Bustard, Anne 1951- *173*
Butcher, Kristin 1951- *140*
Butenko, Bohdan 1931- *90*
Butler, Beverly Kathleen 1932- *7*
Butler, Bill
   See Butler, William Vivian
   and Butler, Ernest Alton
   and Butler, William Huxford
Butler, Charles 1963- *175*
   Earlier sketch in SATA *121*
Butler, Charles Cadman
   See Butler, Charles
Butler, Dori Hillestad 1965- *207*
   Earlier sketch in SATA *164*
Butler, Dorothy 1925- *73*
Butler, Geoff 1945- *94*
Butler, M. Christina 1934- *170*
   Earlier sketch in SATA *72*
Butler, Octavia 1947-2006 .... *84*
   See also CLR *65*
Butler, Octavia E.
   See Butler, Octavia
Butler, Octavia Estelle
   See Butler, Octavia
Butler, Vivian
   See Butler, William Vivian
Butler, William
   See Butler, William Vivian
Butler, William Vivian 1927-1987 .... *79*

Butters, Dorothy Gilman
　See Gilman, Dorothy
Butterworth, Emma Macalik 1928- *43*
Butterworth, Nick 1946- *149*
　Earlier sketch in SATA *106*
Butterworth, Oliver 1915-1990 .... *1*
　Obituary *66*
Butterworth, W.E.
　See Griffin, W.E.B.
Butterworth, William E.
　See Griffin, W.E.B.
Butterworth, William Edmund III
　See Griffin, W.E.B.
Butts, Ed 1951- *177*
Butts, Edward P.
　See Butts, Ed
Butts, Ellen R(ubinstein) 1942- *93*
Buxton, Ralph
　See Silverstein, Alvin
　and Silverstein, Virginia B.
Buzzeo, Toni 1951- *135*
Byalick, Marcia 1947- *141*
　Earlier sketch in SATA *97*
Byard, Carole (Marie) 1941- *57*
Byars, Betsy 1928- *163*
　Autobiography Feature *108*
　Earlier sketches in SATA *4, 46, 80*
　See also CLR *72*
　See also SAAS *1*
Byars, Betsy Cromer
　See Byars, Betsy
Byfield, Barbara Ninde 1930- *8*
Byman, Jeremy 1944- *129*
Bynum, Janie *133*
Byrd, Elizabeth 1912-1989 .... *34*
Byrd, Nicole
　See Zach, Cheryl (Byrd)
Byrd, Robert (John) 1942- *158*
　Earlier sketches in SATA *33, 112*
Byrne, Mary Gregg 1951- *162*

C

C. 3. 3.
　See Wilde, Oscar
C. E. M.
　See Mastrangelo, Charles E(lmer)
Cabaniss, J(ames) Allen 1911-1997 .... *5*
Cabat, Erni 1914- *74*
Cabban, Vanessa 1971- *176*
Cable, Mary 1920- *9*
Cabot, Meg 1967- *175*
　Earlier sketch in SATA *127*
　See also CLR *85*
Cabot, Meggin
　See Cabot, Meg
Cabot, Meggin Patricia
　See Cabot, Meg
Cabot, Patricia
　See Cabot, Meg
Cabral, O. M.
　See Cabral, Olga
Cabral, Olga 1909- *46*
Cabrera, Cozbi A. 1963- *177*
Cabrera, Jane 1968- *182*
　Earlier sketches in SATA *103, 152*
Cabrera, Marcela 1966- *90*
Caddy, Alice
　See Burman, Alice Caddy
Cade, Toni
　See Bambara, Toni Cade
Cadmus and Harmonia
　See Buchan, John
Cadnum, Michael 1949- *165*
　Earlier sketches in SATA *87, 121*
　See also CLR *78*
Caduto, Michael J. 1955- *103*
Cadwallader, Sharon 1936- *7*
Cady, (Walter) Harrison 1877(?)-1970 .... *19*

Caffey, Donna (J.) 1954- *110*
Cagle, Malcolm W(infield) 1918- *32*
Cahn, Rhoda 1922- *37*
Cahn, William 1912-1976 .... *37*
Cain, Arthur H(omer) 1913-1981 .... *3*
Cain, Christopher
　See Fleming, Thomas
Cain, Sheridan 1952- *186*
Caine, Geoffrey
　See Walker, Robert W.
Caines, Jeannette (Franklin) 1938- *78*
　Brief entry *43*
　See also CLR *24*
Cairns, Trevor 1922- *14*
Calabro, Marian 1954- *79*
Caldecott, Moyra 1927- *22*
Caldecott, Randolph (J.) 1846-1886 .... *100*
　Earlier sketch in SATA *17*
　See also CLR *110*
Calder, Charlotte 1952- *125*
Calder, David 1932-1997 .... *105*
Calder, Lyn
　See Calmenson, Stephanie
Calder, Marie D(onais) 1948- *96*
Calderone-Stewart, Lisa
　See Calderone-Stewart, Lisa-Marie
Calderone-Stewart, Lisa-Marie 1958- *123*
Caldwell, Doreen (Mary) 1942- *71*
Caldwell, John C(ope) 1913-1984 .... *7*
Caletti, Deb 1963- *171*
Calhoun, B. B. 1961- *98*
Calhoun, Chad
　See Barrett, Neal, Jr.
　and Cunningham, Chet
　and Goulart, Ron
Calhoun, Dia 1959- *183*
　Earlier sketch in SATA *129*
Calhoun, Mary
　See Wilkins, Mary Huiskamp
Calhoun, T.B.
　See Bisson, Terry
Cali, Davide 1972- *190*
Calif, Ruth 1922- *67*
Calkins, Franklin
　See Stratemeyer, Edward L.
Call, Greg *197*
Call, Hughie Florence 1890-1969 .... *1*
Callahan, Dorothy M(onahan) 1934- *39*
　Brief entry *35*
Callahan, Philip Serna 1923- *25*
Callan, Jamie 1954- *59*
Callan, Jim 1951- *181*
Callaway, Bernice (Anne) 1923- *48*
Callaway, Kathy 1943- *36*
Callen, Larry
　See Callen, Lawrence Willard, Jr.
Callen, Lawrence Willard, Jr. 1927- *19*
Calley, Karin 1965- *92*
Calmenson, Stephanie 1952- *139*
　Brief entry *37*
　Earlier sketches in SATA *51, 84*
Calvert, Elinor H.
　See Lasell, Elinor H.
Calvert, John
　See Leaf, (Wilbur) Munro
Calvert, Pam 1966- *205*
Calvert, Patricia 1931- *132*
　Earlier sketches in SATA *45, 69*
　See also SAAS *17*
Camburn, Carol A.
　See Camburn-Bracalente, Carol A.
Camburn-Bracalente, Carol A. 1962- *118*
Cameron, Ann 1943- *129*
　Earlier sketches in SATA *27, 89*
　See also SAAS *20*
Cameron, Edna M. 1905-1999 .... *3*
Cameron, Eleanor (Frances) 1912-1996 .... *25*
　Obituary *93*
　Earlier sketch in SATA *1*
　See also CLR *72*
　See also SAAS *10*

Cameron, Elizabeth
　See Nowell, Elizabeth Cameron
Cameron, Elizabeth Jane 1910-1976 .... *32*
　Obituary *30*
Cameron, Ian
　See Payne, Donald Gordon
Cameron, M(alcolm) G(ordon) Graham
　See Graham-Cameron, M(alcolm) G(ordon)
Cameron, M. Graham
　See Graham-Cameron, M(alcolm) G(ordon)
Cameron, Mike Graham
　See Graham-Cameron, M(alcolm) G(ordon)
Cameron, Polly 1928- *2*
Cameron, Scott 1962- *84*
Camp, Charles L. 1893-1975
　Obituary *31*
Camp, Lindsay 1957- *133*
Camp, Madeleine L'Engle
　See L'Engle, Madeleine
Camp, Walter (Chauncey) 1859-1925
　See YABC *1*
Campbell, (Elizabeth) Andrea 1963- *50*
Campbell, Ann R. 1925- *11*
Campbell, Bill 1960- *89*
Campbell, Bruce
　See Epstein, Samuel
Campbell, Camilla 1905-1992 .... *26*
Campbell, Carole R. 1939- *125*
Campbell, Hope 1925- *20*
Campbell, Hugh 1930- *90*
Campbell, Jane
　See Edwards, Jane Campbell
Campbell, Julie
　See Tatham, Julie Campbell
Campbell, Patricia J(ean) 1930- *45*
Campbell, Patty
　See Campbell, Patricia J(ean)
Campbell, Peter A. 1948- *99*
Campbell, R. W.
　See Campbell, Rosemae Wells
Campbell, Robin
　See Strachan, Ian
Campbell, Rod 1945- *98*
　Brief entry *44*
　Earlier sketch in SATA *51*
Campbell, Rosemae Wells 1909- *1*
Campbell, Sarah C. 1966- *207*
Camper, Cathy 1956- *170*
Campion, Nardi Reeder 1917-2007 .... *22*
Campling, Elizabeth 1948- *53*
Campoy, F. Isabel 1946- *181*
　Earlier sketch in SATA *143*
Camps, Luis 1928- *66*
Canales, Viola 1957- *141*
Candell, Victor 1903-1977
　Obituary *24*
Canfield, Dorothea F.
　See Fisher, Dorothy (Frances) Canfield
Canfield, Dorothea Frances
　See Fisher, Dorothy (Frances) Canfield
Canfield, Dorothy
　See Fisher, Dorothy (Frances) Canfield
Canfield, Jack 1944- *164*
Canfield, Jane White 1897-1984 .... *32*
　Obituary *38*
Canfield, Muriel 1935- *94*
Caniff, Milton 1907-1988
　Obituary *58*
Caniff, Milton Arthur Paul
　See Caniff, Milton
Cann, Helen 1969- *179*
　Earlier sketch in SATA *124*
Cann, Kate 1954- *152*
　Earlier sketch in SATA *103*
Cannan, Joanna
　See Pullein-Thompson, Joanna Maxwell
Cannell, Jon *196*
Cannell, Jonathan C.
　See Cannell, Jon
Cannon, A.E. *202*
　Earlier sketches in SATA *93, 163*

Cannon, Ann Edwards
   See Cannon, A.E.
Cannon, Bettie (Waddell) 1922- 59
Cannon, Curt
   See Hunter, Evan
Cannon, Eileen E(mily) 1948- 119
Cannon, Frank
   See Mayhar, Ardath
Cannon, Janell 1957- 128
   Earlier sketch in SATA 78
   See also CLR 120
Cannon, Marian G. 1923- 85
Cannon, Taffy
   See Cannon, Eileen E(mily)
Cantone, AnnaLaura 182
Canusi, Jose
   See Barker, S. Omar
Canyon, Christopher 1966- 150
   Earlier sketch in SATA 104
Caparo, Antonio
   See Caparo, Antonio Javier
Caparo, Antonio Javier 205
Capek, Michael 1947- 142
   Earlier sketch in SATA 96
Capes, Bernard (Edward Joseph)
   1854-1918 116
Caple, Kathy 193
Caple, Laurie 1958- 201
Caplin, Alfred Gerald 1909-1979 61
   Obituary 21
Caponigro, John Paul 1965- 84
Capote, Truman 1924-1984 91
Capp, Al
   See Caplin, Alfred Gerald
Cappel, Constance 1936- 22
Cappetta, Cynthia 1949- 125
Cappo, Nan Willard 1955- 143
Capps, Benjamin (Franklin) 1922- 9
Cappy Dick
   See Cleveland, George
Captain Kangaroo
   See Keeshan, Robert J.
Captain Wheeler
   See Ellis, Edward S.
Captain Young of Yale
   See Stratemeyer, Edward L.
Capucilli, Alyssa Satin 1957- 203
   Earlier sketches in SATA 115, 163
Capucine
   See Mazille, Capucine
Caraher, Kim(berley Elizabeth) 1961- 105
Caraker, Mary 1929- 74
Caras, Roger A(ndrew) 1928-2001 12
   Obituary 127
Caravantes, Peggy 1935- 140
Caraway, Caren 1939- 57
Carbone, Elisa 1954- 173
   Earlier sketches in SATA 81, 137
Carbone, Elisa Lynn
   See Carbone, Elisa
Carbonnier, Jeanne 1894-1974 3
   Obituary 34
Card, Orson Scott 1951- 127
   Earlier sketch in SATA 83
   See also CLR 116
Care, Felicity
   See Coury, Louise Andree
Carew, Jan 1925- 51
   Brief entry 40
Carew, Jan Rynveld
   See Carew, Jan
Carey, Bonnie
   See Marshall, Bonnie C.
Carey, Charles W., Jr. 1951- 170
Carey, Ernestine Gilbreth 1908-2006 2
   Obituary 177
Carey, Janet Lee 1954(?)- 185
Carey, Lisa 110
Carey, M. V.
   See Carey, Mary V(irginia)

Carey, Mary V(irginia) 1925-1994 44
   Brief entry 39
Carey, Peter 1943- 94
Carey, Peter Philip
   See Carey, Peter
Carey, Valerie Scho 1949- 60
Carheden, Goorel Kristina
   See Naaslund, Goorel Kristina
Carigiet, Alois 1902-1985 24
   Obituary 47
   See also CLR 38
Carini, Edward 1923- 9
Carkeet, David 1946- 75
Carle, Eric 1929- 163
   Earlier sketches in SATA 4, 65, 120
   See also CLR 72
   See also SAAS 6
Carleton, Captain L. C.
   See Ellis, Edward S.
Carleton, Captain Latham C.
   See Ellis, Edward S.
Carleton, Latham C.
   See Ellis, Edward S.
Carley, V(an Ness) Royal 1906-1976
   Obituary 20
Carling, Amelia Lau 1949- 164
   Earlier sketch in SATA 119
Carlisle, Carolyn
   See Hawes, Louise
Carlisle, Clark
   See Holding, James (Clark Carlisle, Jr.)
Carlisle, Olga Andreyev 1930- 35
Carlock, Miriam
   See Eyerly, Jeannette
Carls, Claudia 1978- 198
Carlsen, G(eorge) Robert 1917- 30
Carlsen, Ruth C(hristoffer) 1918- 2
Carlson, Bernice Wells 1910- 8
Carlson, Christopher C. 202
Carlson, Dale (Bick) 1935- 1
Carlson, Daniel (Bick) 1960- 27
Carlson, Kirsten 1968- 192
Carlson, Kirsten M.
   See Carlson, Kirsten
Carlson, Laurie 1952- 173
   Earlier sketch in SATA 101
Carlson, Laurie Winn
   See Carlson, Laurie
Carlson, Melody 1956- 171
   Earlier sketch in SATA 113
Carlson, Nancy L.
   See Carlson, Nancy L(ee)
Carlson, Nancy L(ee) 1953- 144
   Brief entry 45
   Earlier sketches in SATA 56, 90
Carlson, Natalie Savage 1906-1997 68
   Earlier sketch in SATA 2
   See also SAAS 4
Carlson, Susan Johnston 1953- 88
Carlson, Vada F. 1897- 16
Carlstrom, Nancy White 1948- 156
   Brief entry 48
   Earlier sketches in SATA 53, 92
Carlton, Keith
   See Robertson, Keith (Carlton)
Carlton, Susan 1960- 195
Carlyon, Richard 55
Carman, Patrick 1966- 197
   Earlier sketch in SATA 161
Carmer, Carl (Lamson) 1893-1976 37
   Obituary 30
Carmer, Elizabeth Black 1904- 24
Carmi, Giora 1944- 149
   Earlier sketch in SATA 79
Carmichael, Carrie
   See Carmichael, Harriet
Carmichael, Harriet 40
Carmody, Isobelle 1958- 191
   Earlier sketch in SATA 161
Carmody, Isobelle Jane
   See Carmody, Isobelle

Carney, Elizabeth 1981- 199
Carney, Jeff 1962- 196
Carney, Mary Lou 1949- 170
Carol, Bill J.
   See Knott, William C(ecil, Jr.)
Caron, Romi
   See Caron-Kyselkova', Romana
Caron-Kyselkova', Romana 1967- 94
Caroselli, Remus F(rancis) 1916- 36
Carpelan, Bo 1926- 8
Carpelan, Bo Gustaf Bertelsson
   See Carpelan, Bo
Carpenter, (John) Allan 1917- 81
   Earlier sketch in SATA 3
Carpenter, Angelica Shirley 1945- 153
   Earlier sketch in SATA 71
Carpenter, Frances 1890-1972 3
   Obituary 27
Carpenter, John 1948- 58
Carpenter, John Howard
   See Carpenter, John
Carpenter, Johnny
   See Carpenter, John
Carpenter, Patricia (Healy Evans) 1920- 11
Carr, Glyn
   See Styles, (Frank) Showell
Carr, Harriett H(elen) 1899-1977 3
Carr, Jan 1953- 132
   Earlier sketch in SATA 89
Carr, M. J.
   See Carr, Jan
Carr, Mary Jane 1899-1988 2
   Obituary 55
Carr, Philippa
   See Hibbert, Eleanor Alice Burford
Carr, Roger Vaughan 1937- 95
Carrel, Annette Felder 1929- 90
Carrick, Carol (Hatfield) 1935- 118
   Earlier sketches in SATA 7, 63
   See also SAAS 18
Carrick, Donald (F.) 1929-1989 63
   Earlier sketch in SATA 7
Carrick, Malcolm 1945- 28
Carrick, Paul 1972- 194
Carrier, Lark 1947- 71
   Brief entry 50
Carrier, Roch 1937- 166
   Earlier sketch in SATA 105
Carrighar, Sally 1898-1985 24
Carrillo, Patricia S.
   See Carrillo, P.S.
Carrillo, P.S. 209
Carrington, G. A.
   See Cunningham, Chet
Carrington, Marsha Gray 1954- 168
   Earlier sketch in SATA 111
Carris, Joan 1938- 182
   Brief entry 42
   Earlier sketch in SATA 44
Carris, Joan Davenport
   See Carris, Joan
Carroll, Curt
   See Bishop, Curtis (Kent)
Carroll, Elizabeth
   See Barkin, Carol
   and James, Elizabeth
Carroll, Jaye
   See Carroll, Michael
Carroll, Jenny
   See Cabot, Meg
Carroll, (Archer) Latrobe 1894-1996 7
Carroll, Laura
   See Parr, Lucy
Carroll, Lewis 1832-1898 100
   See also YABC 2
   See also CLR 108
Carroll, Michael 1966- 203
Carroll, Raymond 1924- 86
   Brief entry 47
Carruth, Hayden 1921-2008 47
   Obituary 197

Carryl, Charles E. 1841-1920 .... *114*
Carryl, Charles Edward
　See Carryl, Charles E.
Carse, Robert 1902-1971 .... *5*
Carson, J(ohn) Franklin 1920-1981 .... *1*
　Obituary *107*
Carson, Mary Kay 1964- *200*
　Earlier sketch in SATA *150*
Carson, Rachel 1907-1964 .... *23*
Carson, Rachel Louise
　See Carson, Rachel
Carson, Rosalind
　See Chittenden, Margaret
Carson, S. M.
　See Gorsline, (Sally) Marie
Carson, William C. 1928- *154*
Carter, Abby *184*
Carter, Alden R 1947- *137*
　Earlier sketch in SATA *67*
　See also CLR *22*
　See also SAAS *18*
Carter, Alden Richardson
　See Carter, Alden R
Carter, Andy 1948- *134*
Carter, Angela 1940-1992 .... *66*
　Obituary *70*
Carter, Angela Olive
　See Carter, Angela
Carter, Anne Laurel 1953- *209*
　Earlier sketch in SATA *135*
Carter, Asa Earl
　See Carter, Forrest
Carter, Avis Murton
　See Allen, Kenneth S.
Carter, Bruce
　See Hough, Richard (Alexander)
Carter, Carol S(hadis) 1948- *124*
Carter, David A. 1957- *170*
　Earlier sketch in SATA *114*
Carter, Don 1958- *192*
　Earlier sketch in SATA *124*
Carter, Dorothy Sharp 1921- *8*
Carter, Forrest 1927(?)-1979 .... *32*
Carter, Helene 1887-1960 .... *15*
Carter, (William) Hodding, Jr. 1907-1972 ...... *2*
　Obituary *27*
Carter, James Earl, Jr.
　See Carter, Jimmy
Carter, Jimmy 1924- *79*
Carter, Katharine J(ones) 1905-1984 .... *2*
Carter, Lin(wood Vrooman) 1930-1988 .... *91*
Carter, Mike 1936- *138*
Carter, Nick
　See Avallone, Michael (Angelo, Jr.)
　and Ballard, (Willis) Todhunter
　and Crider, Bill
　and Cassiday, Bruce (Bingham)
　and Chastain, Thomas
　and Dey, Frederic (Merrill) Van Rensselaer
　and Garside, Jack
　and Hayes, Ralph E(ugene)
　and Henderson, M(arilyn) R(uth)
　and Lynds, Dennis
　and Lynds, Gayle (Hallenbeck)
　and Randisi, Robert J.
　and Rasof, Henry
　and Stratemeyer, Edward L.
　and Smith, Martin Cruz
　and Swain, Dwight V(reeland)
　and Vardeman, Robert E(dward)
　and Wallmann, Jeffrey M(iner)
　and White, Lionel
Carter, Peter 1929- *57*
Carter, Phyllis Ann
　See Eberle, Irmengarde
Carter, Samuel (Thomson) III 1904-1988 .... *37*
　Obituary *60*
Carter, William E. 1926-1983 .... *1*
　Obituary *35*

Cartlidge, Michelle 1950- *96*
　Brief entry *37*
　Earlier sketch in SATA *49*
Cartner, William Carruthers 1910- *11*
Cartwright, Ann 1940- *78*
Cartwright, Reg(inald Ainsley) 1938- *64*
Cartwright, Sally 1923- *9*
Carusone, Al 1949- *89*
Carvell, Marlene *172*
Carver, John
　See Gardner, Richard (M.)
Carwell, L'Ann
　See McKissack, Patricia C.
Cary
　See Cary, Louis F(avreau)
Cary, Barbara Knapp 1912(?)-1975
　Obituary *31*
Cary, Kate 1967(?)- *174*
Cary, Louis F(avreau) 1915- *9*
Caryl, Jean
　See Kaplan, Jean Caryl Korn
Casanova, Mary 1957- *186*
　Earlier sketches in SATA *94, 136*
Cascone, A.G.
　See Cascone, Annette
　and Cascone, Gina
Cascone, Annette 1960- *103*
Cascone, Gina 1955- *103*
Case, Chris 1976- *209*
Case, Marshal T(aylor) 1941- *9*
Case, Michael
　See Howard, Robert West
Caseley, Judith 1951- *159*
　Brief entry *53*
　Earlier sketch in SATA *87*
Casewit, Curtis W(erner) 1922-2002 .... *4*
Casey, Barbara (Louise) 1944- *147*
　Earlier sketch in SATA *79*
Casey, Brigid 1950- *9*
Casey, Tina 1959- *141*
Cash, Ellen Lewis Buell 1905-1989
　Obituary *64*
Cash, Megan Montague *160*
Cashore, Kristin 1976(?)- *206*
Casilla, Robert 1959- *146*
　Earlier sketch in SATA *75*
Cason, Mabel Earp 1892-1965 .... *10*
Cass, Joan E(velyn) *1*
Cass-Beggs, Barbara 1904- *62*
Cassedy, Patrice (Rinaldo) 1953- *149*
Cassedy, Sylvia 1930-1989 .... *77*
　Obituary *61*
　Earlier sketch in SATA *27*
　See also CLR *26*
Cassel, Lili
　See Wronker, Lili Cassel
Cassels, Jean *173*
Cassidy, Anne 1952- *166*
Cassidy, Cathy 1962- *183*
Casson, Hugh Maxwell 1910-1999 .... *65*
　Obituary *115*
Cassutt, Michael 1954- *78*
Cassutt, Michael Joseph
　See Cassutt, Michael
Castaldi, Elicia *194*
Castaldo, Nancy Fusco 1962- *151*
　Earlier sketch in SATA *93*
Castaneda, Omar S. 1954- *71*
Castell, Megan
　See Williams, Jeanne
Castellanos, Jane Mollie Robinson
　1913-2001 .... *9*
Castellon, Federico 1914-1971 .... *48*
Castellucci, Cecil 1969- *176*
Castillo, Edmund L. 1924-2005 .... *1*
　Obituary *167*
Castillo, Lauren *195*
Castle, Lee
　See Ogan, George F.
　and Ogan, Margaret E. (Nettles)

Castle, Paul
　See Howard, Vernon (Linwood)
Castle, Robert
　See Hamilton, Edmond
Castrovilla, Selene 1966- *186*
Caswell, Brian 1954- *171*
　Earlier sketch in SATA *97*
Caswell, Helen (Rayburn) 1923- *12*
Catalano, Dominic 1956- *163*
　Earlier sketch in SATA *76*
Catalano, Grace (A.) 1961- *99*
Catalanotto, Peter 1959- *195*
　Autobiography Feature *113*
　Earlier sketches in SATA *70, 114, 159*
　See also CLR *68*
　See also SAAS *25*
Catanese, P.W. 1961- *179*
Cate, Annette LeBlanc *196*
Cate, Dick
　See Cate, Richard Edward Nelson
Cate, Richard Edward Nelson 1932- *28*
Cather, Willa 1873-1947 .... *30*
　See also CLR *98*
Catherall, Arthur 1906-1980 .... *74*
　Earlier sketches in SATA *3, 4*
Cathon, Laura E(lizabeth) 1908-1991 .... *27*
Catlett, Elizabeth 1919(?)- *82*
Catlin, Wynelle 1930- *13*
Catlow, Nikalas
　See Catlow, Niki
Catlow, Niki 1975- *193*
Cato, Heather *105*
Cato, Sheila *114*
Catran, Ken 1944- *190*
Catrow, David *206*
　See Catrow, David J. III
Catrow, David J. III *152*
　See Catrow, David
Catt, Louis
　See French, Vivian
Cattell, James 1954- *123*
Catton, (Charles) Bruce 1899-1978 .... *2*
　Obituary *24*
Catz, Max
　See Glaser, Milton
Caudell, Marian 1930- *52*
Caudill, Rebecca 1899-1985 .... *1*
　Obituary *44*
Cauley, Lorinda Bryan 1951- *46*
　Brief entry *43*
Caulfield, Peggy F. 1926-1987
　Obituary *53*
Cauman, Samuel 1910-1971 .... *48*
Causley, Charles (Stanley) 1917-2003 .... *66*
　Obituary *149*
　Earlier sketch in SATA *3*
　See also CLR *30*
Cavallaro, Ann (Abelson) 1918- *62*
Cavallo, Diana 1931- *7*
Cavanagh, Helen (Carol) 1939- *98*
　Brief entry *37*
　Earlier sketch in SATA *48*
Cavanah, Frances 1899-1982 .... *31*
　Earlier sketch in SATA *1*
Cavanna, Betty
　See Harrison, Elizabeth (Allen) Cavanna
Cavanna, Elizabeth
　See Harrison, Elizabeth (Allen) Cavanna
Cave, Kathryn 1948- *123*
　Earlier sketch in SATA *76*
Cavendish, Peter
　See Horler, Sydney
Cavin, Ruth (Brodie) 1918- *38*
Cavoukian, Raffi 1948- *68*
Cawley, Winifred 1915- *13*
Cazeau, Charles J(ay) 1931- *65*
Cazet, Denys 1938- *191*
　Brief entry *41*
　Earlier sketches in SATA *52, 99, 163*
Cazzola, Gus 1934- *73*

Cebulash, Mel 1937- 91
  Earlier sketch in SATA 10
Ceccoli, Nicoletta 181
Cecil, Randy 1968- 187
Cecka, Melanie 199
Ceder, Georgiana Dorcas -1985 10
Celenza, Anna Harwell 133
Celestino, Martha Laing
  See Laing, Martha
Cepeda, Joe 159
Cerf, Bennett (Alfred) 1898-1971 7
Cerf, Christopher (Bennett) 1941- 2
Cermak, Martin
  See Duchacek, Ivo D(uka)
Cerullo, Mary M. 1949- 145
  Earlier sketch in SATA 86
Cervon, Jacqueline
  See Moussard, Jacqueline
Cetin, Frank Stanley 1921- 2
Chabon, Michael 1963- 145
Chaconas, D.J.
  See Chaconas, Dori
Chaconas, Dori 1938- 208
  Earlier sketches in SATA 145, 175
Chaconas, Doris J.
  See Chaconas, Dori
Chadwick, Lester 67
  Earlier sketch in SATA 1
Chaffee, Allen 3
Chaffin, Lillie D(orton) 1925- 4
Chaikin, Miriam 1924- 152
  Earlier sketches in SATA 24, 102
Chall, Marsha Wilson 150
Challand, Helen J(ean) 1921- 64
Challans, Mary
  See Renault, Mary
Chalmers, Mary (Eileen) 1927- 6
  See also SAAS 14
Chamberlain, Barbara A.
  See Azore, Barbara
Chamberlain, Margaret 1954- 46
Chamberlin, Kate 1945- 105
Chamberlin, Mary 1960- 177
Chamberlin, Rich 177
Chamberlin, Richard
  See Chamberlin, Rich
Chambers, Aidan 1934- 171
  Earlier sketches in SATA 1, 69, 108
  See also SAAS 12
Chambers, Bradford 1922-1984
  Obituary 39
Chambers, Catherine E.
  See St. John, Nicole
Chambers, John W. 1933- 57
  Brief entry 46
Chambers, Kate
  See St. John, Nicole
Chambers, Margaret Ada Eastwood 1911- 2
Chambers, Peggy
  See Chambers, Margaret Ada Eastwood
Chambers, Robert W(illiam) 1865-1933 107
Chambliss, Maxie 186
Chan, Gillian 1954- 147
  Earlier sketch in SATA 102
Chan, Peter 1980(?)- 207
Chance, James T.
  See Carpenter, John
Chance, John T.
  See Carpenter, John
Chance, Stephen
  See Turner, Philip (William)
Chandler, Caroline A(ugusta) 1906-1979 22
  Obituary 24
Chandler, David P(orter) 1933- 28
Chandler, Edna Walker 1908-1982 11
  Obituary 31
Chandler, Jennifer
  See Westwood, Jennifer
Chandler, Karen 1959- 122
Chandler, Linda S(mith) 1929- 39
Chandler, Pauline 175

Chandler, Robert 1953- 40
Chandler, Ruth Forbes 1894-1978 2
  Obituary 26
Chandonnet, Ann F. 1943- 92
Chaney, Jill 1932- 87
Chang, Chih-Wei 1966- 111
Chang, Cindy 1968- 90
Chang, Margaret 1941- 71
Chang, Margaret Scrogin
  See Chang, Margaret
Chang, Raymond 1939- 142
  Earlier sketches in SATA 71, 142 PEN
Chanin, Michael 1952- 84
Channel, A. R.
  See Catherall, Arthur
Chapian, Marie 1938- 29
Chapin, Alene Olsen Dalton 1915(?)-1986
  Obituary 47
Chapin, Tom 1945- 83
Chapman, Allen 67
  Earlier sketch in SATA 1
Chapman, Cheryl O(rth) 1948- 80
Chapman, (Constance) Elizabeth (Mann)
  1919- 10
Chapman, Gaye 1970- 200
Chapman, Gaye Coralie
  See Chapman, Gaye
Chapman, Gaynor 1935- 32
Chapman, Gillian 1955- 120
Chapman, Jane 1970- 176
  Earlier sketch in SATA 122
Chapman, Jean 104
  Earlier sketch in SATA 34
  See also CLR 65
Chapman, John Stanton Higham 1891-1972
  Obituary 27
Chapman, Lee
  See Bradley, Marion Zimmer
Chapman, Lynne 1960- 197
Chapman, Lynne F(erguson) 1963- 150
  Earlier sketch in SATA 94
Chapman, Maristan
  See Chapman, John Stanton Higham
Chapman, Vera (Ivy May) 1898-1996 33
Chapman, Walker
  See Silverberg, Robert
Chappell, Audrey 1954- 72
Chappell, Crissa-Jean 198
Chappell, Warren 1904-1991 68
  Obituary 67
  Earlier sketch in SATA 6
  See also SAAS 10
Chapra, Mimi 182
Charbonneau, Eileen 1951- 118
  Earlier sketch in SATA 84
Charbonnet, Gabrielle 1961- 81
Chardiet, Bernice (Kroll) 1927(?)- 27
Charest, Emily MacLachlan 198
Charles, Donald
  See Meighan, Donald Charles
Charles, Louis
  See Stratemeyer, Edward L.
Charles, Nicholas
  See Kuskin, Karla
Charles, Nicholas J.
  See Kuskin, Karla
Charles, Norma 153
Charles, Veronika Martenova 182
Charlip, Remy 1929- 119
  Earlier sketches in SATA 4, 68
  See also CLR 8
Charlot, Jean 1898-1979 8
  Obituary 31
Charlot, Martin (Day) 1944- 64
Charlton, Michael (Alan) 1923- 34
Charlton-Trujillo, e.E. 189
Charmatz, Bill 1925-2005 7
Charnas, Suzy McKee 1939- 110
  Earlier sketch in SATA 61
Charosh, Mannis 1906- 5
Chartier, Normand L. 1945- 66

Chase, Alice
  See McHargue, Georgess
Chase, Alyssa 1965- 92
Chase, Andra 1942- 91
Chase, Emily
  See Aks, Patricia
  and Garwood, Julie
  and Sachs, Judith
  and White, Carol
Chase, Mary (Coyle) 1907-1981 17
  Obituary 29
Chase, Mary Ellen 1887-1973 10
Chase, Richard 1904-1988 64
  Obituary 56
Chase, Samantha
  See Glick, Ruth (Burtnick)
Chast, Roz 1954- 97
Chastain, Madye Lee 1908-1989 4
Chataway, Carol 1955- 140
Chatterjee, Debjani 1952- 83
Chauncy, Nan(cen Beryl Masterman)
  1900-1970 6
  See also CLR 6
Chaundler, Christine 1887-1972 1
  Obituary 25
Chayka, Doug 196
Chbosky, Stephen 1972- 164
Cheaney, Janie B.
  See Cheaney, J.B.
Cheaney, J.B. 1950- 188
Chee, Cheng-Khee 1934- 79
Cheese, Chloe 1952- 118
Chekhonte, Antosha
  See Chekhov, Anton
Chekhov, Anton 1860-1904 90
Chekhov, Anton Pavlovich
  See Chekhov, Anton
Chelushkin, Kirill 1968- 186
Chen, Anthony 1929- 6
Chen, Chih-Yuan 1975- 155
Chen, Ju-Hong 1941- 78
Chen, Pauline 1966- 202
Chen, Sara
  See Odgers, Sally Farrell
Chen, Tony
  See Chen, Anthony
Chen, Yong 1963- 183
Chen, Yuan-tsung 1932- 65
Chenault, Nell
  See Smith, Linell Nash
Chenery, Janet (Dai) 1923- 25
Cheney, Cora 1916-1999 3
  Obituary 110
Cheney, Glenn (Alan) 1951- 99
Cheney, Lynne V. 1941- 152
Cheney, Lynne Vincent
  See Cheney, Lynne V.
Cheney, Ted
  See Cheney, Theodore Albert
Cheney, Theodore A. Rees
  See Cheney, Theodore Albert
Cheney, Theodore Albert 1928- 11
Cheng, Andrea 1957- 205
  Earlier sketches in SATA 128, 172
Cheng, Christopher 1959- 173
  Earlier sketch in SATA 106
Cheng, Judith 1955- 36
Cheng, Shan
  See Jiang, Cheng An
Cheripko, Jan 1951- 155
  Earlier sketch in SATA 83
Chermayeff, Ivan 1932- 47
Chernenko, Dan
  See Chernenko, Dan
Chernoff, Dorothy A.
  See Ernst, (Lyman) John
Chernoff, Goldie Taub 1909- 10
Cherry, Carolyn Janice
  See Cherryh, C.J.
Cherry, Lynne 1952- 99
  Earlier sketch in SATA 34

Cherryh, C.J. 1942- 172
    Earlier sketch in SATA 93
Cherryholmes, Anne
    See Price, Olive
Cheshire, Simon 172
Chesler, Bernice 1932-2002 59
Chess, Victoria (Dickerson) 1939- 92
    Earlier sketch in SATA 33
Chessa, Francesca 191
Chester, Deborah 1957- 85
Chester, Kate
    See Guccione, Leslie Davis
Chesterton, G. K. 1874-1936 27
Chesterton, Gilbert Keith
    See Chesterton, G. K.
Chesworth, Michael 207
    Earlier sketch in SATA 160
Chetin, Helen 1922- 6
Chetwin, Grace 86
    Brief entry 50
Chevalier, Christa 1937- 35
Chevalier, Tracy 1962- 128
Chew, Ruth 1920- 7
Chichester Clark, Emma 1955- 209
    Earlier sketches in SATA 117, 156, 69
Chidsey, Donald Barr 1902-1981 3
    Obituary 27
Chiefari, Janet D. 1942- 58
Chien, Catia 193
Chien-min, Lin
    See Rumford, James
Child, L. Maria
    See Child, Lydia Maria
Child, Lauren 1965- 183
    Earlier sketches in SATA 119, 160
Child, Lincoln 1957- 113
Child, Lincoln B.
    See Child, Lincoln
Child, Lydia Maria 1802-1880 67
Child, Mrs.
    See Child, Lydia Maria
Child, Philip 1898-1978 47
Children's Shepherd, The
    See Westphal, Arnold Carl
Childress, Alice 1920-1994 81
    Earlier sketches in SATA 7, 48
    See also CLR 14
Childs, H(alla) Fay (Cochrane) 1890-1971 1
    Obituary 25
Chilton, Charles (Frederick William)
    1917- 102
Chima, Cinda Williams 192
Chimaera
    See Farjeon, Eleanor
Chin, Richard (M.) 1946- 52
Chinery, Michael 1938- 26
Chin-Lee, Cynthia 1958- 102
Chin-Lee D., Cynthia
    See Chin-Lee, Cynthia
Chippendale, Lisa A. 158
Chipperfield, Joseph Eugene 1912-1980(?) .. 87
    Earlier sketch in SATA 2
Chisholm, P. F.
    See Finney, Patricia
Chislett, Gail (Elaine) 1948- 58
Chittenden, Elizabeth F. 1903-1999 9
Chittenden, Margaret 1935- 28
Chittum, Ida 1918- 7
Chitwood, Suzanne Tanner 1958- 160
Chmielarz, Sharon Lee 1940- 72
Choate, Judith (Newkirk) 1940- 30
Chocolate, Debbi 1954- 96
Chocolate, Deborah M. Newton
    See Chocolate, Debbi
Chodos-Irvine, Margaret 152
Choi, Sook Nyul 1937- 73
    Autobiography Feature 126
    See also CLR 53
Choi, Yangsook 178
Choldenko, Gennifer 1957- 182
    Earlier sketch in SATA 135

Chorao, (Ann Mc)Kay (Sproat) 1936- 162
    Earlier sketches in SATA 8, 69
Choron, Sandra (Zena Samelson) 1950- 146
Choung, Eun-hee 199
Chown, Marcus 1959- 137
Choyce, Lesley 1951- 165
    Earlier sketch in SATA 94
Choyce, Lesley Willis
    See Choyce, Lesley
Chrisman, Arthur Bowie 1889-1953 124
    See also YABC 1
Christelow, Eileen 1943- 184
    Autobiography Feature 120
    Brief entry 35
    Earlier sketches in SATA 38, 90
Christensen, Bonnie 1951- 157
    Earlier sketch in SATA 110
Christensen, Gardell Dano 1907-1991 1
Christensen, Laurie
    See Steding, Laurie
Christesen, Barbara 1940- 40
Christgau, Alice Erickson 1902-1977 13
Christian, Mary Blount 1933- 9
Christiana, David 195
Christie, Agatha 1890-1976 36
Christie, Agatha Mary Clarissa
    See Christie, Agatha
Christie, Ann Philippa
    See Pearce, Philippa
Christie, Gregory
    See Christie, R. Gregory
Christie, Philippa
    See Pearce, Philippa
Christie, R. Gregory 1971- 185
    Earlier sketch in SATA 127
Christopher, John
    See Youd, Samuel
Christopher, Louise
    See Hale, Arlene
Christopher, Matt(hew Frederick)
    1917-1997 80
    Obituary 99
    Earlier sketches in SATA 2, 47
    See also CLR 119
    See also SAAS 9
Christopher, Milbourne 1914(?)-1984 46
Christy, Howard Chandler 1873-1952 21
Chrustowski, Rick 176
Chrystie, Frances N(icholson) 1904-1986 60
Chu, Daniel 1933- 11
Chukovsky, Kornei (Ivanovich) 1882-1969 . 34
    Earlier sketch in SATA 5
Church, Caroline Jayne 179
Church, Richard 1893-1972 3
Churchill, E(lmer) Richard 1937- 11
Churchill, Elizabeth
    See Hough, Richard (Alexander)
Chute, B(eatrice) J(oy) 1913-1987 2
    Obituary 53
Chute, Marchette (Gaylord) 1909-1994 1
Chwast, Jacqueline 1932- 6
Chwast, Seymour 1931- 146
    Earlier sketches in SATA 18, 96
Ciardi, John (Anthony) 1916-1986 65
    Obituary 46
    Earlier sketch in SATA 1
    See also CLR 19
    See also SAAS 26
Ciccone, Madonna Louise Veronica
    See Madonna
Ciment, James D. 1958- 140
Cirrone, Dorian 182
Cisneros, Sandra 1954-
    See CLR 123
Citra, Becky 1954- 137
Citrin, Michael 1965(?)- 183
Claflin, Willy 1944- 208
Clair, Andree 19
Clampett, Bob 1914(?)-1985 44
    Obituary 38

Clampett, Robert
    See Clampett, Bob
Clapp, John 1968- 109
Clapp, Patricia 1912- 74
    Earlier sketch in SATA 4
    See also SAAS 4
Clare, Ellen
    See Sinclair, Olga
Clare, Helen
    See Clarke, Pauline
Claremont, Chris 1950- 87
Claremont, Christopher Simon
    See Claremont, Chris
Clark, Ann Nolan 1896-1995 82
    Obituary 87
    Earlier sketch in SATA 4
    See also CLR 16
    See also SAAS 16
Clark, Champ 1923-2002 47
Clark, Christopher (Anthony) Stuart
    See Stuart-Clark, Christopher (Anthony)
Clark, Clara Gillow 1951- 154
    Earlier sketch in SATA 84
Clark, David
    See Hardcastle, Michael
Clark, David Allen
    See Ernst, (Lyman) John
Clark, Emma Chichester
    See Chichester Clark, Emma
Clark, Frank J(ames) 1922- 18
Clark, Garel
    See Garelick, May
Clark, Halsey
    See Deming, Richard
Clark, Joan
    See Benson, Mildred
Clark, Joan 1934- 182
    Earlier sketches in SATA 59, 96
Clark, Leonard 1905-1981 30
    Obituary 29
Clark, M. R.
    See Clark, Mavis Thorpe
Clark, Margaret (D.) 1943- 126
Clark, Margaret Goff 1913- 82
    Earlier sketch in SATA 8
Clark, Mary Higgins 1929- 46
Clark, Mavis Thorpe 1909-1999 74
    Earlier sketch in SATA 8
    See also CLR 30
    See also SAAS 5
Clark, Merle
    See Gessner, Lynne
Clark, Patricia Denise 1921- 117
Clark, Patricia Finrow 1929- 11
Clark, Ronald Harry 1904-1999 193
Clark, Ronald William 1916-1987 2
    Obituary 52
Clark, Sherryl 1956- 149
Clark, Van D(eusen) 1909-1974 2
Clark, Virginia
    See Gray, Patricia (Clark)
Clark, Walter Van Tilburg 1909-1971 8
Clarke, Arthur
    See Clarke, Arthur C.
Clarke, Arthur C. 1917-2008 115
    Obituary 191
    Earlier sketches in SATA 13, 70
    See also CLR 119
Clarke, Arthur Charles
    See Clarke, Arthur C.
Clarke, Clorinda 1917- 7
Clarke, Gus 1948- 134
Clarke, J.
    See Clarke, Judith
Clarke, James Hall
    See Rowland-Entwistle, (Arthur) Theodore
    (Henry)
Clarke, Joan B. 1921- 42
    Brief entry 27

Clarke, John
    See Laklan, Carli
    and Sontup, Dan(iel)
Clarke, Judith 1943- 164
    Earlier sketches in SATA *75, 110*
    See also CLR *61*
Clarke, Julia 1950- 138
Clarke, Kenneth 1957- 107
Clarke, Lea
    See Rowland-Entwistle, (Arthur) Theodore
    (Henry)
Clarke, Margaret 1941-
    See CLR *99*
Clarke, Mary Stetson 1911-1994 5
Clarke, Michael
    See Newlon, (Frank) Clarke
Clarke, Pauline 1921- 131
    Earlier sketch in SATA *3*
    See also CLR *28*
Clarke-Rich, Elizabeth L. 1934- 103
Clarkson, E(dith) Margaret 1915- 37
Clarkson, Ewan 1929- 9
Claudia, Susan
    See Goulart, Ron
    and Johnston, William
Claverie, Jean 1946- 38
Clay, Patrice 1947- 47
Clay, Wil 203
Clayman, Deborah Paula
    See Da Costa, Deborah
Claypool, Jane
    See Miner, Jane Claypool
Clayton, Elaine 1961- 209
    Earlier sketches in SATA *94, 159*
Clayton, Lawrence (Otto, Jr.) 1945- 75
Clayton, Sandra 1951- 110
Cle, Troy 202
Clea, Super
    See Hantman, Clea
Cleary, Beverly 1916- 121
    Earlier sketches in SATA *2, 43, 79*
    See also CLR *72*
    See also SAAS *20*
Cleary, Beverly Atlee Bunn
    See Cleary, Beverly
Cleary, Brian P. 1959- 186
    Earlier sketches in SATA *93, 132*
Cleaver, Bill
    See Cleaver, William J.
Cleaver, Carole 1934- 6
Cleaver, Elizabeth (Ann Mrazik)
    1939-1985 23
    Obituary 43
    See also CLR *13*
Cleaver, Hylton Reginald 1891-1961 49
Cleaver, Vera 1919-1993 76
    Earlier sketch in SATA *22*
    See also CLR *6*
Cleaver, Vera Allen
    See Cleaver, Vera
Cleaver, William J. 1920-1981 22
    Obituary 27
    See also CLR *6*
Cleishbotham, Jebediah
    See Scott, Sir Walter
Cleland, Mabel
    See Widdemer, Mabel Cleland
Clem, Margaret H(ollingsworth) 1923- 90
Clemens, Samuel
    See Twain, Mark
Clemens, Samuel Langhorne
    See Twain, Mark
Clemens, Virginia Phelps 1941- 35
Clement, Gary 191
Clement, Janet 182
Clement, Nathan 1966- 200
Clement, Priscilla Ferguson 1942- 171
Clement, Rod 97
Clement-Moore, Rosemary 188
Clements, Andrew 1949- 203
    Earlier sketches in SATA *104, 158*

Clements, Bruce 1931- 178
    Earlier sketches in SATA *27, 94*
Clemesha, David 192
Clemons, Elizabeth
    See Nowell, Elizabeth Cameron
Clerk, N. W.
    See Lewis, C. S.
Cleveland, Bob
    See Cleveland, George
Cleveland, George 1903(?)-1985
    Obituary 43
Cleveland-Peck, Patricia 80
Cleven, Cathrine
    See Cleven, Kathryn Seward
Cleven, Kathryn Seward 2
Clevenger, William R. 1954- 84
Clevenger, William Russell
    See Clevenger, William R.
Clevin, Joergen 1920- 7
Clevin, Jorgen
    See Clevin, Joergen
Clewes, Dorothy (Mary) 1907-2003 86
    Obituary 138
    Earlier sketch in SATA *1*
Clifford, David
    See Rosenberg, Eth Clifford
Clifford, Eth
    See Rosenberg, Eth Clifford
Clifford, Harold B(urton) 1893-1988 10
Clifford, Margaret Cort 1929- 1
Clifford, Martin
    See Hamilton, Charles (Harold St. John)
Clifford, Mary Louise Beneway 1926- 23
Clifford, Peggy
    See Clifford, Margaret Cort
Clifford, Rachel Mark
    See Lewis, Brenda Ralph
Clifton, Lucille 1936- 128
    Earlier sketches in SATA *20, 69*
    See also CLR *5*
Clifton, Thelma Lucille
    See Clifton, Lucille
Climo, Shirley 1928- 166
    Autobiography Feature 110
    Brief entry 35
    Earlier sketches in SATA *39, 77*
    See also CLR *69*
Cline-Ransome, Lesa 201
Clinton, Catherine 1952- 203
Clinton, Cathryn 1957- 136
Clinton, Dirk
    See Silverberg, Robert
Clinton, Jon
    See Prince, J(ack) H(arvey)
Clippinger, Carol 193
Clish, (Lee) Marian 1946- 43
Clive, Clifford
    See Hamilton, Charles (Harold St. John)
Clokey, Art 1921- 59
Cloudsley-Thompson, J(ohn) L(eonard)
    1921- 19
Clouse, Nancy L. 1938- 78
Clover, Peter 1952- 152
Clutha, Janet Paterson Frame
    See Frame, Janet
Clymer, Eleanor 1906-2001 85
    Obituary 126
    Earlier sketch in SATA *9*
    See also SAAS *17*
Clyne, Patricia (Edwards) 31
Cneut, Carll 1969- 197
Coalson, Glo 1946- 94
    Earlier sketch in SATA *26*
Coates, Anna 1958- 73
Coates, Belle 1896-1986 2
Coates, Ruth Allison 1915- 11
Coats, Alice M(argaret) 1905-1976 11
Coatsworth, Elizabeth (Jane) 1893-1986 100
    Obituary 49
    Earlier sketches in SATA *2, 56*
    See also CLR *2*

Cobalt, Martin
    See Mayne, William (James Carter)
Cobb, Jane
    See Berry, Jane Cobb
Cobb, Mary 1931- 88
Cobb, Vicki 1938- 136
    Autobiography Feature 136
    Earlier sketches in SATA *8, 69, 131*
    See also CLR *2*
    See also SAAS *6*
Cobbett, Richard
    See Pluckrose, Henry (Arthur)
Cober, Alan E(dwin) 1935-1998 7
    Obituary 101
Cobham, Sir Alan
    See Hamilton, Charles (Harold St. John)
Coburn, Jake 1978- 155
Cocagnac, Augustin Maurice(-Jean) 1924- 7
Cocca-Leffler, Maryann 1958- 194
    Earlier sketches in SATA *80, 136*
Cochran, Bill 187
Cochran, Bobbye A. 1949- 11
Cochran, Thomas 1955- 198
Cockett, Mary 3
Cocks, Peter 204
Cocovini, Abby 202
Coddell, Esme Raji
    See Codell, Esme Raji
Codell, Esme Raji 1968- 160
Cody, C. S.
    See Waller, Leslie
Cody, Jess
    See Cunningham, Chet
Coe, Anne (E.) 1949- 95
Coe, Douglas
    See Epstein, Beryl
    and Epstein, Samuel
Coe, Lloyd 1899(?)-1976
    Obituary 30
Coen, Rena Neumann 1925- 20
Coerr, Eleanor (Beatrice) 1922- 67
    Earlier sketch in SATA *1*
Cofer, Judith Ortiz 1952- 164
    Earlier sketch in SATA *110*
Coffelt, Nancy 1961- 189
Coffey, Brian
    See Koontz, Dean
Coffin, Geoffrey
    See Mason, F(rancis) van Wyck
Coffin, M. T.
    See Stanley, George Edward
Coffman, Ramon Peyton 1896-1989 4
Cogan, Karen 1954- 125
Coggins, Jack (Banham) 1911-2006 2
Cohen, Barbara 1932-1992 77
    Obituary 74
    Earlier sketch in SATA *10*
    See also SAAS *7*
Cohen, Daniel (E.) 1936- 70
    Earlier sketch in SATA *8*
    See also CLR *43*
    See also SAAS *4*
Cohen, Deborah Bodin 1968- 180
Cohen, Jan Barger
    See Barger, Jan
Cohen, Jene Barr
    See Barr, Jene
Cohen, Joan Lebold 1932- 4
Cohen, Judith Love 1933- 78
Cohen, Miriam 1926-1955 155
    Earlier sketches in SATA *29, 106*
    See also SAAS *11*
Cohen, Nora 75
Cohen, Paul S. 1945- 58
Cohen, Peter Zachary 1931- 150
    Earlier sketch in SATA *4*
Cohen, Robert Carl 1930- 8
Cohen, Sholom 1951- 94
Cohn, Angelo 1914-1997 19
Cohn, Diana 194
Cohn, Rachel 1968- 161

Coit, Margaret Louise 1922-2003 2
  Obituary 142
Colato Lainez, Rene 1970- 176
Colbert, Anthony 1934-2007 15
Colbert, Nancy A. 1936- 139
Colby, C(arroll) B(urleigh) 1904-1977 35
  Earlier sketch in SATA 3
Colby, Jean Poindexter 1909-1993 23
Cole, Annette
  See Steiner, Barbara A(nnette)
Cole, Babette 1949- 155
  Earlier sketches in SATA 61, 96
Cole, Betsy 1940- 83
Cole, Brock 1938- 200
  Earlier sketches in SATA 72, 136
  See also CLR 18
Cole, Davis
  See Elting, Mary
Cole, Hannah 1954- 74
Cole, Henry 1955- 181
Cole, Jack -1974
  See Stewart, John
Cole, Jackson
  See Curry, Thomas Albert
  and Germano, Peter B.
  and Heckelmann, Charles N(ewman)
  and Newton, D(wight) B(ennett)
  and Schisgall, Oscar
Cole, Jennifer
  See Zach, Cheryl (Byrd)
Cole, Joanna 1944- 168
  Brief entry 37
  Earlier sketches in SATA 49, 81, 120
  See also CLR 40
Cole, Lois Dwight 1903-1979 10
  Obituary 26
Cole, Michael 1947- 59
Cole, Samantha
  See Cole, Stephen
Cole, Sheila 1939- 171
  Earlier sketches in SATA 24, 95
Cole, Sheila R.
  See Cole, Sheila
Cole, Sheila Rotenberg
  See Cole, Sheila
Cole, Stephen 1971- 161
Cole, William (Rossa) 1919-2000 71
  Earlier sketch in SATA 9
  See also SAAS 9
Coleman, Andrew
  See Pine, Nicholas
Coleman, Clare
  See Bell, Clare (Louise)
  and Easton, M(alcolm) Coleman
Coleman, Janet Wyman 184
Coleman, Loren 1947- 164
Coleman, Loren Elwood, Jr.
  See Coleman, Loren
Coleman, Mary Ann 1928- 83
Coleman, Michael
  See Jones, Allan Frewin
Coleman, Michael 1946- 199
  Autobiography Feature 133
  Earlier sketches in SATA 108, 133
Coleman, Rowan 187
Coleman, William L(eRoy) 1938- 49
  Brief entry 34
Coles, Robert (Martin) 1929- 23
Colfer, Eoin 1965- 197
  Earlier sketch in SATA 148
  See also CLR 112
Colin, Ann
  See Ure, Jean
Collard, Sneed B. III 1959- 184
  Earlier sketches in SATA 84, 139
Colledge, Anne 1939- 142
Colley, Jacqui 1965- 202
Collicott, Sharleen 1937- 143
  Earlier sketch in SATA 98
Collier, Bryan 204
  Earlier sketches in SATA 126, 174

Collier, Christopher 1930- 70
  Earlier sketch in SATA 16
  See also CLR 126
Collier, Ethel 1903-1999 22
Collier, James Lincoln 1928- 166
  Earlier sketches in SATA 8, 70
  See also CLR 126
  See also SAAS 21
Collier, Jane
  See Collier, Zena
Collier, Kristi 182
Collier, Steven 1942- 61
Collier, Zena 1926- 23
Collings, Gillian 1939- 102
Collington, Peter 1948- 99
  Earlier sketch in SATA 59
Collins, Ace 1953- 82
Collins, Andrew J.
  See Collins, Ace
Collins, David R(aymond) 1940-2001 121
  Earlier sketch in SATA 7
Collins, Heather 1946- 81
Collins, Hunt
  See Hunter, Evan
Collins, Michael
  See Lynds, Dennis
Collins, Michael 1930- 58
Collins, Pat(ricia) Lowery 1932- 151
  Earlier sketch in SATA 31
Collins, Paul 1954- 126
Collins, Ross 1972- 200
Collins, Ruth Philpott 1890-1975
  Obituary 30
Collins, Suzanne 180
Collins, Yvonne 194
Collinson, A. S.
  See Collinson, Alan S.
Collinson, Alan S. 1934- 80
Collinson, Roger (Alfred) 1936- 133
Collison, Linda 1953- 185
Collodi, Carlo 1826-1890 100
  Earlier sketch in SATA 29
  See also CLR 120
Colloms, Brenda 1919- 40
Colman, Hila 53
  Earlier sketch in SATA 1
  See also SAAS 14
Colman, Morris 1899(?)-1981
  Obituary 25
Colman, Penny (Morgan) 1944- 160
  Autobiography Feature 160
  Earlier sketches in SATA 77, 114
Colman, Warren (David) 1944- 67
Colombo, John Robert 1936- 50
Colon, Raul 156
Colon, Raul 1952- 202
Colonius, Lillian 1911-1992 3
Colorado, Antonio J.
  See Colorado (Capella), Antonio J(ulio)
Colorado (Capella), Antonio J(ulio)
  1903-1994 23
  Obituary 79
Colquhoun, Glenn 1964- 165
Colston, Fifi E. 1960- 150
Colt, Martin
  See Epstein, Beryl
  and Epstein, Samuel
Colum, Padraic 1881-1972 15
  See also CLR 36
Columbus, Chris 1959- 97
Columbus, Christopher
  See Columbus, Chris
Columella
  See Moore, Clement Clarke
Colver, Anne 1908- 7
Colvin, James
  See Moorcock, Michael
Colwell, Eileen (Hilda) 1904-2002 2
Colwyn, Stewart
  See Pepper, Frank S.

Coman, Carolyn 1951- 197
  Earlier sketch in SATA 127
Combs, Lisa M.
  See McCourt, Lisa
Combs, Robert
  See Murray, John
Comfort, Jane Levington
  See Sturtzel, Jane Levington
Comfort, Mildred Houghton 1886-1976 3
Comins, Ethel M(ae) 11
Comins, Jeremy 1933- 28
Commager, Henry Steele 1902-1998 23
  Obituary 102
Comora, Madeleine 190
Compere, Mickie
  See Davidson, Margaret
Compestine, Ying Chang 1963- 187
  Earlier sketch in SATA 140
Comport, Sally Wern 190
Compton, Patricia A. 1936- 75
Comte, The Great
  See Hawkesworth, Eric
Comus
  See Ballantyne, R(obert) M(ichael)
Comyns, Nance
  See Comyns-Toohey, Nantz
Comyns-Toohey, Nantz 1956- 86
Conan Doyle, Arthur
  See Doyle, Sir Arthur Conan
Condie, Ally 204
Condie, Allyson B.
  See Condie, Ally
Condit, Martha Olson 1913- 28
Condon, Bill 1949- 142
Condon, Judith 83
Condon, Ken 195
Condy, Roy 1942- 96
Cone, Ferne Geller 1921- 39
Cone, Molly (Lamken) 1918- 151
  Autobiography Feature 151
  Earlier sketches in SATA 1, 28, 115
  See also SAAS 11
Cone, Patrick 1954- 89
Coney, Michael G. 1932-2005 61
  Obituary 170
Coney, Michael Greatrex
  See Coney, Michael G.
Coney, Mike
  See Coney, Michael G.
Conford, Ellen 1942- 162
  Earlier sketches in SATA 6, 68, 110
  See also CLR 71
Conger, Lesley
  See Suttles, Shirley (Smith)
Conklin, Gladys Plemon 1903- 2
Conklin, Paul S. 1929(?)-2003 43
  Brief entry 33
  Obituary 147
Conkling, Hilda 1910-1986 23
Conlan, Kathleen Elizabeth 1950- 145
Conlan, Kathy
  See Conlan, Kathleen Elizabeth
Conley, Robyn 1963- 125
Conley-Weaver, Robyn
  See Conley, Robyn
Conlon-McKenna, Marita 1956- 71
Conly, Jane Leslie 1948- 164
  Earlier sketches in SATA 80, 112
Conly, Robert Leslie 1918(?)-1973 23
  See also CLR 2
Connell, Kirk
  See Chapman, John Stanton Higham
Connell, Tom 206
Connelly, Marc(us Cook) 1890-1980
  Obituary 25
Connolly, Jerome P(atrick) 1931- 8
Connolly, Pat 1943- 74
Connolly, Peter 1935- 105
  Earlier sketch in SATA 47
Conover, Chris 1950- 31

Conquest, Owen
  See Hamilton, Charles (Harold St. John)
Conrad, Joseph 1857-1924 27
Conrad, Pam 1947-1996 133
  Brief entry 49
  Obituary 90
  Earlier sketches in SATA *52, 80*
  See also CLR *18*
  See also SAAS *19*
Conroy, Jack
  See Conroy, John Wesley
Conroy, John Wesley 1899-1990 19
  Obituary 65
Conroy, Robert
  See Goldston, Robert (Conroy)
Constable, Kate 1966- 172
Constant, Alberta Wilson 1908-1981 22
  Obituary 28
Constantin, Pascale 185
Conway, Diana C(ohen) 1943- 91
Conway, Gordon
  See Hamilton, Charles (Harold St. John)
Cook, Ande 192
Cook, Bernadine 1924- 11
Cook, Fred J(ames) 1911-2003 2
  Obituary 145
Cook, Glen 1944- 171
  Earlier sketch in SATA *108*
Cook, Glen Charles
  See Cook, Glen
Cook, Hugh 1956- 85
Cook, Hugh, Walter Gilbert
  See Cook, Hugh
Cook, Jean Thor 1930- 94
Cook, Joel 1934- 79
Cook, Joseph Jay 1924- 8
Cook, Lisa Broadie 157
Cook, Lyn
  See Waddell, Evelyn Margaret
Cook, Roy
  See Silverberg, Robert
Cook, Sally 207
Cook, Trish 175
Cooke, Ann
  See Cole, Joanna
Cooke, Arthur
  See Lowndes, Robert A(ugustine) W(ard)
Cooke, Barbara
  See Alexander, Anna B(arbara Cooke)
Cooke, David Coxe 1917- 2
Cooke, Donald Ewin 1916-1985 2
  Obituary 45
Cooke, Frank E. 1920- 87
Cooke, Jean (Isobel Esther) 1929- 74
Cooke, John Estes
  See Baum, L. Frank
Cooke, Trish 1962- 129
Cookson, Catherine (McMullen) 1906-1998 .. 9
  Obituary 116
Cooley, Regina Francoise 1940- 177
Coolidge, Olivia E(nsor) 1908- 26
  Earlier sketch in SATA *1*
Cooling, Wendy 169
  Earlier sketch in SATA *111*
Coombs, Charles I(ra) 1914-1994 43
  Earlier sketch in SATA *3*
  See also SAAS *15*
Coombs, Chick
  See Coombs, Charles I(ra)
Coombs, Jonathan 204
Coombs, Kate 190
Coombs, Patricia 1926- 51
  Earlier sketch in SATA *3*
  See also SAAS *22*
Cooney, Barbara 1917-2000 96
  Obituary 123
  Earlier sketches in SATA *6, 59*
  See also CLR *23*
Cooney, Caroline B. 1947- 179
  Brief entry 41
  Earlier sketches in SATA *48, 80, 113, 130*

Cooney, Doug 181
Cooney, Nancy Evans 1932- 42
Coontz, Otto 1946- 33
Cooper, Ann (Catharine) 1939- 104
Cooper, Dutch
  See Kuyper, Sjoerd
Cooper, Elisha 1971- 157
  Earlier sketch in SATA *99*
Cooper, Elizabeth Keyser -1992 47
Cooper, Floyd 187
  Earlier sketches in SATA *96, 144*
  See also CLR *60*
Cooper, Gordon 1932- 23
Cooper, Helen 1963- 169
  Earlier sketch in SATA *102*
Cooper, Henry S(potswood) F(enimore), Jr.
  1933- 65
Cooper, Ilene 1948- 145
  Earlier sketches in SATA *66, 97*
Cooper, James Fenimore 1789-1851 19
  See also CLR *105*
Cooper, John R. 1
Cooper, Kay 1941- 11
Cooper, Lee Pelham 1926- 5
Cooper, Lester (Irving) 1919-1985 32
  Obituary 43
Cooper, Lettice (Ulpha) 1897-1994 35
  Obituary 82
Cooper, Louise 1952-2009 152
Cooper, M.E.
  See Lerangis, Peter
Cooper, M.E.
  See Davis, Maggie S.
Cooper, Melrose
  See Kroll, Virginia L.
Cooper, Michael L. 1950- 181
  Earlier sketches in SATA *79, 117*
Cooper, Patrick 1949- 134
Cooper, Susan 1935- 151
  Earlier sketches in SATA *4, 64, 104*
  See also CLR *67*
  See also SAAS *6*
Cooper, Susan Mary
  See Cooper, Susan
Cope, Jane U(rsula) 1949- 108
Copeland, Helen 1920- 4
Copeland, Mark 1956- 180
Copeland, Paul W. 23
Coplans, Peta 1951- 84
Copley (Diana) Heather Pickering 1918- 45
Coppard, A(lfred) E(dgar) 1878-1957
  See YABC *1*
Copper, Melinda 1952- 172
Copper, Melinda McConnaughey
  See Copper, Melinda
Corace, Jen 208
Coralie
  See Anderson, Catherine Corley
Corbett, Grahame 43
  Brief entry 36
Corbett, Scott 1913- 42
  Earlier sketch in SATA *2*
  See also CLR *1*
  See also SAAS *2*
Corbett, Sue 174
Corbett, W(illiam) J(esse) 1938- 102
  Brief entry 44
  Earlier sketch in SATA *50*
  See also CLR *19*
Corbin, Sabra Lee
  See Malvern, Gladys
Corbin, William
  See McGraw, William Corbin
Corbman, Marjorie 1987- 179
Corby, Dan
  See Catherall, Arthur
Corcoran, Barbara (Asenath) 1911-2003 77
  Autobiography Feature 125
  Earlier sketch in SATA *3*
  See also CLR *50*
  See also SAAS *20*

Corcos, Lucille 1908-1973 10
Cordell, Alexander
  See Graber, Alexander
Cordell, Matthew 1975- 199
Corder, Zizou
  See Young, Louisa
Corella, Joseph
  See Odgers, Sally Farrell
Coren, Alan 1938-2007 32
  Obituary 187
Corey, Dorothy 23
Corey, Shana 1974- 133
Corfe, Thomas Howell 1928- 27
Corfe, Tom
  See Corfe, Thomas Howell
Corfield, Robin Bell 1952- 74
Corlett, William 1938-2005 46
  Brief entry 39
Cormack, M(argaret) Grant 1913- 11
Cormack, Maribelle B. 1902-1984 39
Cormier, Robert 1925-2000 83
  Obituary 122
  Earlier sketches in SATA *10, 45*
  See also CLR *55*
Cormier, Robert Edmund
  See Cormier, Robert
Cornelius, Carol 1942- 40
Cornelius, Kay 1933- 157
Cornell, J.
  See Cornell, Jeffrey
Cornell, James (Clayton, Jr.) 1938- 27
Cornell, Jean Gay 1920- 23
Cornell, Jeffrey 1945- 11
Cornell, Laura 189
Cornish, D.M. 1972- 185
Cornish, Sam(uel James) 1935- 23
Cornwall, Nellie
  See Sloggett, Nellie
Cornwell, Autumn 195
Corr, Christopher 1955- 189
Correy, Lee
  See Stine, G(eorge) Harry
Corrick, James A. 1945- 76
Corrigan, (Helen) Adeline 1909- 23
Corrigan, Barbara 1922- 8
Corrigan, Eireann 1977- 163
Corrin, Sara 1918- 86
  Brief entry 48
Corrin, Stephen 86
  Brief entry 48
Corsi, Wendy
  See Staub, Wendy Corsi
Cort, M. C.
  See Clifford, Margaret Cort
Cort, Margaret
  See Clifford, Margaret Cort
Corwin, Judith H(offman) 1946- 10
Corwin, Oliver
  See Corwin, Oliver J.
Corwin, Oliver J. 206
Cory, Rowena
  See Lindquist, Rowena Cory
Cosby, Bill 1937- 110
  Earlier sketch in SATA *66*
Cosby, William Henry, Jr.
  See Cosby, Bill
  and Cosby, Bill
Cosentino, Ralph 169
Cosgrave, John O'Hara II 1908-1968
  Obituary 21
Cosgrove, Margaret (Leota) 1926- 47
Cosgrove, Stephen E(dward) 1945- 53
  Brief entry 40
Coskey, Evelyn 1932- 7
Cosner, Shaaron 1940- 43
Cossi, Olga 1921- 102
  Earlier sketch in SATA *67*
Costabel, Eva Deutsch 1924- 45
Costabel-Deutsch, Eva
  See Costabel, Eva Deutsch
Coste, Marion 1938- 183

Costello, David 174
Costello, David F(rancis) 1904-1990 23
Cte, Genevieve 1964- 184
Cote, Nancy 1952- 182
Cott, Jonathan 1942- 23
Cottam, Clarence 1899-1974 25
Cotten, Cynthia 188
Cottle, Joan 1960- 135
Cottler, Joseph 1899-1996 22
Cottonwood, Joe 1947- 92
Cottrell, Leonard 1913-1974 24
Cottringer, Anne 1952- 150
    Earlier sketch in SATA 97
Couch, Greg 199
Coulman, Valerie 1969- 161
Couloumbis, Audrey 173
Counsel, June 1926- 70
Countryman, The
    See Whitlock, Ralph
Courlander, Harold 1908-1996 6
    Obituary 88
Coursen, Valerie 1965(?)- 102
Courtis, Stuart Appleton 1874-1969
    Obituary 29
Courtland, Tyler
    See Stevens, Serita
Courtney, Dayle
    See Goldsmith, Howard
Coury, Louise Andree 1895(?)-1983
    Obituary 34
Cousins, Linda 1946- 90
Cousins, Lucy 1964- 205
    Earlier sketch in SATA 172
Cousins, Margaret 1905-1996 2
    Obituary 92
Cousteau, Jacques-Yves 1910-1997 98
    Earlier sketch in SATA 38
Couture, Christin 1951- 73
Couvillon, Jacques 195
Covert, Ralph 1968- 197
Coville, Bruce 1950- 155
    Autobiography Feature 155
    Earlier sketches in SATA 32, 77, 118
Covington, Dennis 109
Covington, Linda
    See Windsor, Linda
Cowan, Catherine 121
Cowan, Rebecca M.
    See Moesta, Rebecca
Cowan, Rebecca Moesta
    See Moesta, Rebecca
Coward, Fiona 1963- 178
Cowdrey, Richard 1959- 204
Cowell, Cressida 1966- 140
Cowen, Eve
    See Werner, Herma
Cowen, Ida 1898-1993 64
Cowie, Leonard W(allace) 1919- 4
Cowles, Kathleen
    See Krull, Kathleen
Cowley, Cassia Joy
    See Cowley, Joy
Cowley, Joy 1936- 164
Cowley, (Cassia) Joy 1936- 90
    Autobiography Feature 118
    Earlier sketch in SATA 4
    See also CLR 55
    See also SAAS 26
Cowley, Marjorie 1925- 111
Cox, (Christopher) Barry 1931- 62
Cox, Clinton 1934- 108
    Earlier sketch in SATA 74
Cox, David (Dundas) 1933- 56
Cox, Donald William 1921- 23
Cox, Jack
    See Cox, John Roberts
Cox, John Roberts 1915-1981 9
Cox, Judy 1954- 198
    Earlier sketches in SATA 117, 160
Cox, Marion Monroe 1898-1983
    Obituary 34

Cox, Palmer 1840-1924 24
    See also CLR 24
Cox, Vic 1942- 88
Cox, Vicki 1945- 158
Cox, Victoria
    See Garretson, Victoria Diane
Cox, Wallace 1924-1973 25
Cox, Wally
    See Cox, Wallace
Cox, William R(obert) 1901-1988 46
    Brief entry 31
    Obituary 57
Coxe, Molly 1959- 101
    Earlier sketch in SATA 69
Coxon, Michele 1950- 158
    Earlier sketch in SATA 76
Coy, Harold 1902-1986 3
Coy, John 1958- 171
    Earlier sketch in SATA 120
Craats, Rennay 1973- 131
Crabtree, Judith 1928- 98
    Earlier sketch in SATA 63
Cracker, Edward E.B.
    See Odgers, Sally Farrell
Craft, Elizabeth 1971(?)- 204
Craft, K. Y.
    See Craft, Kinuko Y(amabe)
Craft, Kinuko
    See Craft, Kinuko Y(amabe)
Craft, Kinuko Y(amabe) 1940- 127
    Earlier sketch in SATA 65
Craft, Ruth 1935- 87
    Brief entry 31
Craig, A. A.
    See Anderson, Poul
Craig, Alisa
    See MacLeod, Charlotte (Matilda)
Craig, David 205
    See James, Bill
Craig, Helen 1934- 94
    Earlier sketches in SATA 46, 49
Craig, Joe 1979- 198
Craig, Joe Alexander
    See Craig, Joe
Craig, John Eland
    See Chipperfield, Joseph Eugene
Craig, John Ernest 1921- 23
Craig, Kit
    See Reed, Kit
Craig, M. F.
    See Craig, Mary (Francis) Shura
Craig, M. Jean 17
Craig, M. S.
    See Craig, Mary (Francis) Shura
Craig, Margaret (Maze) 1911-1964 9
Craig, Mary
    See Craig, Mary (Francis) Shura
Craig, Mary Shura
    See Craig, Mary (Francis) Shura
Craig, Mary (Francis) Shura 1923-1991 86
    Obituary 65
    Earlier sketch in SATA 6
    See also SAAS 7
Craig, Ruth 1922- 95
Craik, Mrs.
    See Craik, Dinah Maria (Mulock)
Craik, Dinah Maria (Mulock) 1826-1887 34
Crandall, Court 1965- 175
Crandell, Rachel 1943- 152
Crane, Barbara (Joyce) 1934- 31
Crane, Caroline 1930- 11
Crane, Jordan 1973- 174
Crane, M. A.
    See Wartski, Maureen (Ann Crane)
Crane, Royston Campbell 1901-1977
    Obituary 22
Crane, Stephen 1871-1900
    See YABC 2
    See also CLR 132
Crane, Stephen Townley
    See Crane, Stephen

Crane, Walter 1845-1915 100
    Earlier sketch in SATA 18
    See also CLR 56
Crane, William D(wight) 1892-1976 1
Cranfield, Ingrid 1945- 74
Cranshaw, Stanley
    See Fisher, Dorothy (Frances) Canfield
Crary, Elizabeth (Ann) 1942- 99
    Brief entry 43
Crary, Margaret (Coleman) 1906-1986 9
Craste, Marc 201
Cravath, Lynne Avril
    See Cravath, Lynne W.
Cravath, Lynne W. 1951- 182
    Earlier sketches in SATA 98, 148
Craven, Thomas 1889-1969 22
Crawford, Charles P. 1945- 28
Crawford, Deborah 1922- 6
Crawford, John E(dmund) 1904-1971 3
Crawford, K(aren) Michael 1959- 155
Crawford, Mel 1925- 44
    Brief entry 33
Crawford, Phyllis 1899- 3
Crawley, Dave 177
Cray, Roberta
    See Emerson, Ru
Crayder, Dorothy 7
Crayder, Teresa
    See Colman, Hila
Crayon, Geoffrey
    See Irving, Washington
Craz, Albert G. 1926- 24
Crebbin, June 1938- 169
    Earlier sketch in SATA 80
Crecy, Jeanne
    See Williams, Jeanne
Credle, Ellis 1902-1998 1
Creech, Sharon 1945- 172
    Earlier sketches in SATA 94, 139
    See also CLR 89
Creeden, Sharon 1938- 91
Creel, Ann Howard 1953- 187
Creighton, (Mary) Helen 1899-1989
    Obituary 64
Creighton, Jill 1949- 96
Crenson, Victoria 1952- 159
    Earlier sketch in SATA 88
Cresp, Gael 1954- 119
Crespo, George 1962- 82
Cresswell, Helen 1934-2005 79
    Obituary 168
    Earlier sketches in SATA 1, 48
    See also CLR 18
    See also SAAS 20
Cressy, Michael 1955- 124
Cressy, Mike
    See Cressy, Michael
Cretan, Gladys (Yessayan) 1921- 2
Cretzmeyer, Stacy (Megan) 1959- 124
Crew, Gary 1947- 163
    Earlier sketches in SATA 75, 110
    See also CLR 42
Crew, Helen (Cecilia) Coale 1866-1941
    See YABC 2
Crew, Linda (Jean) 1951- 137
    Earlier sketch in SATA 71
Crews, Donald 1938- 76
    Brief entry 30
    Earlier sketch in SATA 32
    See also CLR 7
Crews, Nina 1963- 158
    Earlier sketch in SATA 97
Crichton, John Michael
    See Crichton, Michael
Crichton, Michael 1942-2008 88
    Obituary 199
    Earlier sketch in SATA 9
Crider, Allen Billy
    See Crider, Bill
Crider, Bill 1941- 99

Crilley, Mark 1966- *148*
  Autobiography Feature *148*
  Earlier sketch in SATA *120*
Crimi, Carolyn 1959- *176*
Cripps, Enid Margaret
  See Appiah, Peggy
Crisler, Curtis L. *188*
Crisman, Ruth 1914- *73*
Crisp, Marta Marie 1947- *128*
Crisp, Marty
  See Crisp, Marta Marie
Crispin, A(nn) C(arol) 1950- *86*
Crist, James J. 1961- *168*
Cristall, Barbara *79*
Crist-Evans, Craig 1954- *153*
Crocker, Carter *193*
Crocker, Nancy 1956- *185*
Crofford, Emily (Ardell) 1927- *61*
Crofut, William E. III 1934- *23*
Croggon, Alison 1962- *194*
Croll, Carolyn 1945- *102*
  Brief entry *52*
  Earlier sketch in SATA *56*
Croman, Dorothy Young
  See Rosenberg, Dorothy
Cromie, Alice Hamilton 1914-2000 .... *24*
Cromie, William J(oseph) 1930- *4*
Crompton, Anne Eliot 1930- *73*
  Earlier sketch in SATA *23*
Crompton, Richmal
  See Lamburn, Richmal Crompton
Cronbach, Abraham 1882-1965 .... *11*
Crone, Ruth 1919-2003 .... *4*
Cronin, A(rchibald) J(oseph) 1896-1981 ...... *47*
  Obituary *25*
Cronin, Doreen (A.) *125*
Cronin, Doreen 1966(?)- *178*
  See also CLR *136*
Cronin, Doreen A.
  See Cronin, Doreen
Crook, Beverly Courtney *38*
  Brief entry *35*
Crook, Connie Brummel 1930- *168*
  Earlier sketch in SATA *98*
Crook, Constance
  See Crook, Connie Brummel
Crosby, Alexander L. 1906-1980 .... *2*
  Obituary *23*
Crosby, Harry C.
  See Anvil, Christopher
Crosby, Margaret
  See Rathmann, Peggy
Crosher, G. R. *14*
Cross, Gilbert B. 1939- *60*
  Brief entry *51*
Cross, Gillian 1945- *178*
  Autobiography Feature *178*
  Earlier sketches in SATA *38, 71, 110, 165*
  See also CLR *28*
Cross, Gillian Clare
  See Cross, Gillian
Cross, Helen Reeder
  See Broadhead, Helen Cross
Cross, Peter 1951- *95*
Cross, Shauna 1976(?)- *196*
Cross, Tom 1954- *146*
Cross, Verda 1914- *75*
Cross, Wilbur Lucius III 1918- *2*
Crossland, Caroline 1964- *83*
Crossley-Holland, Kevin 1941- *165*
  Earlier sketches in SATA *5, 74, 120*
  See also CLR *84*
  See also SAAS *20*
Crossley-Holland, Kevin John William
  See Crossley-Holland, Kevin
Crouch, Marcus 1913-1996 .... *4*
Crout, George C(lement) 1917- *11*
Crow, Donna Fletcher 1941- *40*
Crow, Francis Luther
  See Luther, Frank
Crow, Kristyn *208*

Crowe, Andrew *111*
Crowe, Carole 1943- *204*
Crowe, Chris *206*
Crowe, Ellie *203*
Crowe, John
  See Lynds, Dennis
Crowe, (Bettina) Peter Lum 1911- *6*
Crowell, Grace Noll 1877-1969 .... *34*
Crowell, Pers 1910-1990 .... *2*
Crowell, Robert Leland 1909-2001 .... *63*
Crowfield, Christopher
  See Stowe, Harriet Beecher
Crowley, Arthur McBlair 1945- *38*
Crowley, John 1942- *140*
  Earlier sketch in SATA *65*
Crowley, Suzanne 1963- *196*
Crowley, Suzanne Carlisle
  See Crowley, Suzanne
Crownfield, Gertrude 1867-1945
  See YABC *1*
Crowther, James Gerald 1899-1983 .... *14*
Crowther, Robert 1948- *163*
Cruikshank, George 1792-1878 .... *22*
  See also CLR *63*
Cruise, Robin 1951- *179*
Crum, Shutta *192*
  Earlier sketch in SATA *134*
Crummel, Susan Stevens 1949- *176*
  Earlier sketch in SATA *130*
Crump, Fred H., Jr. 1931- *76*
  Earlier sketch in SATA *11*
Crump, J(ames) Irving 1887-1979 .... *57*
  Obituary *21*
Crump, William D(rake) 1949- *138*
Crunden, Reginald
  See Cleaver, Hylton Reginald
Crunk, T.
  See Crunk, Tony
Crunk, Tony 1956- *130*
Crutcher, Chris 1946- *196*
  Earlier sketches in SATA *52, 99, 153*
  See also CLR *28*
Crutcher, Christopher C.
  See Crutcher, Chris
Cruz, Ray(mond) 1933- *6*
Cruz Martinez, Alejandro (?)-1987 .... *74*
Crystal, Billy 1947- *154*
Crystal, William
  See Crystal, Billy
Ctvrtek, Vaclav 1911-1976
  Obituary *27*
Cuetara, Mittie 1957- *158*
  Earlier sketch in SATA *106*
Cuffari, Richard 1925-1978 .... *66*
  Obituary *25*
  Earlier sketch in SATA *6*
Cuffe-Perez, Mary 1946- *199*
Cullen, Countee 1903-1946 .... *18*
Cullen, Lynn *190*
Culliford, Pierre 1928-1992 .... *40*
  Obituary *74*
Cullinan, Bernice E(llinger) 1926- *135*
Culp, Louanna McNary 1901-1965 .... *2*
Culper, Felix
  See McCaughrean, Geraldine
Cumbaa, Stephen 1947- *72*
Cumming, Peter 1951- *168*
Cumming, Primrose Amy 1915- *24*
Cumming, Robert 1945- *65*
Cummings, Betty Sue 1918- *15*
  See also SAAS *9*
Cummings, Mary 1951- *185*
Cummings, Parke 1902-1987 .... *2*
  Obituary *53*
Cummings, Pat 1950- *203*
  Earlier sketches in SATA *42, 71, 107*
  See also CLR *48*
  See also SAAS *13*
Cummings, Phil 1957- *123*
  Earlier sketch in SATA *74*

Cummings, Priscilla 1951- *170*
  Earlier sketch in SATA *129*
Cummings, Richard
  See Gardner, Richard (M.)
Cummins, Julie *200*
Cummins, Maria Susanna 1827-1866
  See YABC *1*
Cumpliano, Ina *207*
Cuneo, Mary Louise -2001 .... *85*
Cunliffe, John Arthur 1933- *86*
  Earlier sketch in SATA *11*
Cunliffe, Marcus (Falkner) 1922-1990 .... *37*
  Obituary *66*
Cunnane, Kelly *175*
Cunningham, Bob
  See May, Julian
Cunningham, Captain Frank
  See Glick, Carl (Cannon)
Cunningham, Cathy
  See Cunningham, Chet
Cunningham, Chet 1928- *23*
Cunningham, Dale S(peers) 1932- *11*
Cunningham, Dru *91*
Cunningham, E. V.
  See Fast, Howard
Cunningham, Julia (Woolfolk) 1916- *132*
  Earlier sketches in SATA *1, 26*
  See also SAAS *2*
Cunningham, Lawrence J. 1943- *125*
Cunningham, Virginia
  See Holmgren, Virginia C(unningham)
Curiae, Amicus
  See Fuller, Edmund (Maybank)
Curie, Eve 1904-2007 .... *1*
  Obituary *188*
Curlee, Lynn 1947- *190*
  Earlier sketches in SATA *98, 141*
Curley, Daniel 1918-1988 .... *23*
  Obituary *61*
Curley, Marianne 1959- *175*
  Earlier sketch in SATA *131*
Currey, Anna *194*
Currie, Robin 1948- *120*
Currie, Stephen 1960- *132*
  Earlier sketch in SATA *82*
Curry, Ann (Gabrielle) 1934- *72*
Curry, Jane L(ouise) 1932- *138*
  Autobiography Feature *138*
  Earlier sketches in SATA *1, 52, 90*
  See also CLR *31*
  See also SAAS *6*
Curry, Peggy Simson 1911-1987 .... *8*
  Obituary *50*
Curry, Tom *185*
Curtis, Bruce (Richard) 1944- *30*
Curtis, Chara M(ahar) 1950- *78*
Curtis, Christopher Paul 1954(?)- *187*
  Earlier sketches in SATA *93, 140*
  See also CLR *68*
Curtis, Gavin 1965- *107*
Curtis, Jamie Lee 1958- *144*
  Earlier sketch in SATA *95*
  See also CLR *88*
Curtis, Jennifer Keats *185*
Curtis, Marci *160*
Curtis, Munzee
  See Caseley, Judith
Curtis, Neil 1950-2006 .... *202*
Curtis, Patricia 1921- *101*
  Earlier sketch in SATA *23*
Curtis, Peter
  See Lofts, Norah (Robinson)
Curtis, Philip (Delacourt) 1920- *62*
Curtis, Richard 1937- *29*
Curtis, Richard Alan
  See Curtis, Richard
Curtis, Richard Hale
  See Deming, Richard
  and Levinson, Leonard
  and Rothweiler, Paul Roger
Curtis, Stacy *205*

Curtis, Wade
  See Pournelle, Jerry (Eugene)
Curtiss, A(rlene) B. 1934- 90
Cusack, Margaret 1945- 58
Cushman, Doug 1953- 157
  Earlier sketches in SATA *65, 101*
Cushman, Jerome 2
Cushman, Karen 1941- 147
  Earlier sketch in SATA *89*
  See also CLR *55*
Cusick, Richie Tankersley 1952- 140
  Earlier sketch in SATA *67*
Cutbill, Andy 1972- 201
Cutchen, Billye Walker 1930- 15
Cutchins, Judy 1947- 59
Cutler, Daniel S(olomon) 1951- 78
Cutler, Ebbitt 1923- 9
Cutler, Ivor 1923-2006 24
  Obituary 174
Cutler, Jane 1936- 162
  Earlier sketches in SATA *75, 118*
Cutler, May Ebbitt
  See Cutler, Ebbitt
Cutler, Samuel
  See Folsom, Franklin (Brewster)
Cutlip, Kimbra L(eigh-Ann) 1964- 128
Cutrate, Joe
  See Spiegelman, Art
Cutt, W(illiam) Towrie 1898-1981 16
  Obituary 85
Cuyler, Margery 1948- 195
  Earlier sketches in SATA *39, 99, 156*
Cuyler, Margery Stuyvesant
  See Cuyler, Margery
Cuyler, Stephen
  See Bates, Barbara S(nedeker)
Cyrus, Kurt 1954- 179
  Earlier sketch in SATA *132*
Czernecki, Stefan 1946- 178

D

Dabba Smith, Frank 174
Dabcovich, Lydia 99
  Brief entry 47
  Earlier sketch in SATA *58*
Dace, Dolores B(oelens) 1929- 89
Da Costa, Deborah 193
Daddo, Andrew 1967- 198
Dadey, Debbie 1959- 136
  Earlier sketch in SATA *73*
Dahl, Borghild (Margarethe) 1890-1984 7
  Obituary 37
Dahl, Roald 1916-1990 73
  Obituary 65
  Earlier sketches in SATA *1, 26*
  See also CLR *111*
Dahlberg, Maurine F. 1951- 171
Dahlstedt, Marden (Stewart) 1921-1983 8
  Obituary 110
Dahme, Joanne 206
Dain, Martin J. 1924-2000 35
Dakos, Kalli 1950- 115
  Earlier sketch in SATA *80*
Dale, Anna 1971- 170
Dale, Gary
  See Reece, Colleen L.
Dale, George E.
  See Asimov, Isaac
Dale, Jack
  See Holliday, Joseph
Dale, Kim 1957- 123
Dale, Margaret J(essy) Miller 1911- 39
Dale, Mitzi
  See Hemstock, Gillian
Dale, Norman
  See Denny, Norman (George)
Dale, Penny 1954- 151
  Earlier sketch in SATA *70*

Daley, Michael J. 170
Dalgliesh, Alice 1893-1979 17
  Obituary 21
  See also CLR *62*
Dalkey, Kara 1953- 132
Dalkey, Kara Mia
  See Dalkey, Kara
Dallas, Ruth 1919- 86
Dalmas, John
  See Jones, John R(obert)
Dalton, Alene
  See Chapin, Alene Olsen Dalton
Dalton, Annie 1948- 140
  Earlier sketch in SATA *40*
Dalton, Kit
  See Cunningham, Chet
Dalton, Pamela
  See Johnson, Pamela
Dalton, Sean
  See Chester, Deborah
Dalton, Sheila 1949- 108
D'Aluisio, Faith 1957- 205
Daly, Jim
  See Stratemeyer, Edward L.
Daly, Jude 1951- 177
Daly, Kathleen N(orah) 124
  Brief entry 37
Daly, Maureen 1921-2006 129
  Obituary 176
  Earlier sketch in SATA *2*
  See also CLR *96*
  See also SAAS *1*
Daly, Nicholas 1946- 164
  Earlier sketches in SATA *37, 76, 114*
  See also CLR *41*
  See also SAAS *21*
  See Daly, Niki
Daly, Niki 198
  See Daly, Nicholas
D'Amato, Alex 1919- 20
D'Amato, Janet (Potter) 1925- 9
Damerow, Gail 1944- 83
Damerow, Gail Jane
  See Damerow, Gail
D'Amico, Carmela 170
D'Amico, Steve 170
Damrell, Liz 1956- 77
Damrosch, Helen
  See Tee-Van, Helen Damrosch
Dana, Barbara 1940- 22
Dana, Richard Henry, Jr. 1815-1882 26
Danachair, Caoimhin O
  See Danaher, Kevin
Danaher, Kevin 1913-2002 22
Danakas, John 1963- 94
Dandi
  See Mackall, Dandi Daley
D'Andrea, Kate
  See Steiner, Barbara A(nnette)
Dangerfield, Balfour
  See McCloskey, (John) Robert
Daniel, Alan 1939- 76
  Brief entry 53
Daniel, Anita 1893(?)-1978 23
  Obituary 24
Daniel, Anne
  See Steiner, Barbara A(nnette)
Daniel, Becky 1947- 56
Daniel, Claire 1949- 164
Daniel, Colin
  See Windsor, Patricia
Daniel, Hawthorne 1890- 8
Daniel, (Donna) Lee 1944- 76
Daniel, Rebecca
  See Daniel, Becky
Daniels, Guy 1919-1989 11
  Obituary 62
Daniels, Lucy
  See Oldfield, Jenny
Daniels, Max
  See Gellis, Roberta

Daniels, Olga
  See Sinclair, Olga
Daniels, Patricia 1955- 93
Daniels, Zoe
  See Laux, Constance
Dank, Gloria Rand 1955- 56
  Brief entry 46
Dank, Leonard D(ewey) 1929- 44
Dank, Milton 1920- 31
Dann, Max 1955- 62
Danneberg, Julie 1958- 173
Dantz, William R.
  See Philbrick, Rodman
Danziger, Paula 1944-2004 149
  Brief entry 30
  Obituary 155
  Earlier sketches in SATA *36, 63, 102*
  See also CLR *20*
Darby, Gene Kegley
  See Darby, Jean (Kegley)
Darby, J. N.
  See Govan, (Mary) Christine Noble
Darby, Jean (Kegley) 1921- 68
Darby, Patricia (Paulsen) 14
Darby, Ray(mond) 1912-1982 7
d'Arcy, Willard
  See Cox, William R(obert)
Dare, Geena
  See McNicoll, Sylvia (Marilyn)
Darian, Shea 1959- 97
Daringer, Helen Fern 1892-1986 1
Darke, Marjorie 1929- 87
  Earlier sketch in SATA *16*
Darley, F(elix) O(ctavius) C(arr)
  1822-1888 35
Darling, David J. 1953- 60
  Brief entry 44
Darling, Kathy
  See Darling, Mary Kathleen
Darling, Lois (MacIntyre) 1917-1989 3
  Obituary 64
Darling, Louis, (Jr.) 1916-1970 3
  Obituary 23
Darling, Mary Kathleen 1943- 124
  Earlier sketches in SATA *9, 79*
Darling, Sandra Louise Woodward
  See Day, Alexandra
Darnell, K(athryn) L(ynne) 1955- 150
Darroll, Sally
  See Odgers, Sally Farrell
Darrow, Sharon 181
Darrow, Whitney, (Jr.) 1909-1999 13
  Obituary 115
Darwin, Len
  See Darwin, Leonard
Darwin, Leonard 1916- 24
Dasent, Sir George Webbe 1817-1896 62
  Brief entry 29
Dash, Joan 1925- 142
Daskam, Josephine Dodge
  See Bacon, Josephine Dodge (Daskam)
D'ath, Justin 1953- 174
  Earlier sketch in SATA *106*
Dauer, Rosamond 1934- 23
Daugherty, Charles Michael 1914- 16
Daugherty, James (Henry) 1889-1974 13
  See also CLR *78*
Daugherty, Richard D(eo) 1922- 35
Daugherty, Sonia Medwedeff (?)-1971
  Obituary 27
d'Aulaire, Edgar Parin 1898-1986 66
  Obituary 47
  Earlier sketch in SATA *5*
  See also CLR *21*
d'Aulaire, Ingri 1904-1980 66
  Obituary 24
  Earlier sketch in SATA *5*
  See also CLR *21*
d'Aulaire, Ingri Mortenson Parin
  See d'Aulaire, Ingri

Dave, Dave
  See Berg, David
Daveluy, Paule Cloutier 1919- 11
Davenier, Christine 1961- 179
  Earlier sketch in SATA 127
Davenport, John 1960- 156
Daves, Michael 1938- 40
David, A. R.
  See David, A(nn) Rosalie
David, A(nn) Rosalie 1946- 103
David, Jonathan
  See Ames, Lee J(udah)
David, Lawrence 1963- 165
  Earlier sketch in SATA 111
David, Peter 1956- 72
David, Peter Allen
  See David, Peter
David, Rosalie
  See David, A(nn) Rosalie
Davidson, Alice Joyce 1932- 54
  Brief entry 45
Davidson, Basil 1914- 13
Davidson, (Marie) Diane 1924- 91
Davidson, Hugh
  See Hamilton, Edmond
Davidson, Jessica 1915-1986 5
Davidson, Judith 1953- 40
Davidson, Lionel 1922-2009 87
Davidson, Margaret 1936- 5
Davidson, Marion
  See Garis, Howard R.
Davidson, Mary R. 1885-1973 9
Davidson, Mary S. 1940- 61
Davidson, Mickie
  See Davidson, Margaret
Davidson, Nicole
  See Jensen, Kathryn
Davidson, R.
  See Davidson, Raymond
Davidson, Raymond 1926- 32
Davidson, Rosalie 1921- 23
Davie, Helen K(ay) 1952- 148
  Earlier sketch in SATA 77
Davies, Andrew (Wynford) 1936- 27
Davies, Andy Robert 200
Davies, Bettilu D(onna) 1942- 33
Davies, Hunter 1936- 55
  Brief entry 45
Davies, Jacqueline 1962- 186
  Earlier sketch in SATA 155
Davies, Joan 1934- 50
  Brief entry 47
Davies, Nicola 1958- 182
  Earlier sketches in SATA 99, 150
Davies, Peter J(oseph) 1937- 52
Davies, Sumiko 1942- 46
Davis, (A.) Aubrey 1949- 153
Davis, Barbara Steincrohn
  See Davis, Maggie S.
Davis, Bette J. 1923- 15
Davis, Burke 1913- 4
Davis, Christopher 1928- 6
Davis, D(elbert) Dwight 1908-1965 33
Davis, Daniel S(heldon) 1936- 12
Davis, David R. 1948- 106
Davis, Donald 1944- 169
  Earlier sketch in SATA 93
Davis, Donald D.
  See Davis, Donald
Davis, Eleanor 1983(?)- 209
Davis, Emma
  See Davis, Maggie S.
Davis, Gibbs 1953- 102
  Brief entry 41
  Earlier sketch in SATA 46
Davis, Grania 1943- 88
  Brief entry 50
Davis, H(arold) L(enoir) 1896-1960 114
Davis, Hubert J(ackson) 1904-1997 31
Davis, Jacky 204
Davis, James Robert 1945- 32

Davis, Jenny 1953- 74
Davis, Jim
  See Davis, James Robert
Davis, Julia 1900(?)-1993 6
  Obituary 75
Davis, Karen (Elizabeth) 1944- 109
Davis, Katie 1959(?)- 208
  Earlier sketch in SATA 152
Davis, Lambert 176
Davis, Leslie
  See Guccione, Leslie Davis
Davis, Louise Littleton 1921- 25
Davis, Maggie S. 1943- 57
Davis, Marguerite 1889- 34
Davis, Mary L(ee) 1935- 9
Davis, Mary Octavia 1901-1976 6
Davis, Nelle 1958- 73
Davis, Ossie 1917-2005 81
  See also CLR 56
Davis, Paxton 1925-1994 16
Davis, Rich 1958- 206
Davis, Robert 1881-1949
  See YABC 1
Davis, Robin W(orks) 1962- 87
Davis, Russell Gerard 1922- 3
Davis, Tim(othy N.) 1957- 94
Davis, Verne Theodore 1889-1973 6
Davis, Yvonne 1927- 115
Davol, Marguerite W. 1928- 146
  Earlier sketch in SATA 82
DaVolls, Andy (P.) 1967- 85
DaVolls, Linda 1966- 85
Davys, Sarah
  See Manning, Rosemary
Dawes, Claiborne 1935- 111
Dawson, Arthur L. 207
Dawson, Elmer A. 67
  Earlier sketch in SATA 1
Dawson, Imogen (Zoe) 1948- 126
  Earlier sketch in SATA 90
Dawson, Janine 1957- 196
Dawson, Mary 1919- 11
Dawson, Willow 1975- 208
Day, A(rthur) Grove 1904-1994 59
Day, Alexandra 1941- 197
  Autobiography Feature 197
  Earlier sketches in SATA 67, 97, 169
  See also CLR 22
  See also SAAS 19
Day, Beth (Feagles) 1924- 33
Day, Donna
  See Asay, Donna Day
Day, Edward C. 1932- 72
Day, Jon 1936(?)- 79
Day, Karen 187
Day, Larry 1956- 181
Day, Nancy 1953- 140
Day, Nancy Raines 1951- 148
  Earlier sketch in SATA 93
Day, Shirley 1962- 94
Day, Thomas 1748-1789
  See YABC 1
Day, Trevor 1955- 124
Dazey, Agnes J(ohnston) 2
Dazey, Frank M. 2
Deacon, Alexis 1978- 139
Deacon, Eileen
  See Geipel, Eileen
Deacon, Richard
  See McCormick, (George) Donald (King)
Deadman, Ronald 1919-1988(?)
  Obituary 56
Deak, Erzsi 1959- 152
Dean, Anabel 1915- 12
Dean, Carolee 1962- 148
Dean, David 1976- 192
Dean, Karen Strickler 1923- 49
Dean, Ruth (Brigham) 1947- 145
Dean, Zoey
  See Bennett, Cherie

de Angeli, Marguerite (Lofft) 1889-1987 ... 100
  Obituary 51
  Earlier sketches in SATA 1, 27
  See also CLR 1
Deans, Karen 195
Deans, Sis Boulos 1955- 136
  Earlier sketch in SATA 78
DeArmand, Frances Ullmann 1904(?)-1984 . 10
  Obituary 38
DeArmond, Dale 1914- 70
DeArmond, Dale Burlison
  See DeArmond, Dale
Deary, Terry 1946- 171
  Brief entry 41
  Earlier sketches in SATA 51, 101
Deaver, Julie Reece 1953- 68
de Banke, Cecile 1889-1965 11
De Bello, Rosario 1923- 89
Debon, Nicolas 186
  Earlier sketch in SATA 151
de Bono, Edward 1933- 66
de Brissac, Malcolm
  See Dickinson, Peter
de Brunhoff, Jean
  See Brunhoff, Jean de
De Brunhoff, Laurent
  See Brunhoff, Laurent de
De Bruyn, Monica G. 1952- 13
De Bruyn, Monica Jean Grembowicz
  See De Bruyn, Monica G.
DeBry, Roger K. 1942- 91
de Camp, Catherine Crook 1907-2000 83
  Earlier sketch in SATA 12
de Camp, L. Sprague 1907-2000 83
  Earlier sketch in SATA 9
de Camp, Lyon Sprague
  See de Camp, L. Sprague
DeCandido, Keith R.A. 112
Dechausay, Sonia E. 94
Decker, C.B. 172
Decker, Cynthia B.
  See Decker, C.B.
Decker, Duane 1910-1964 5
Decker, Timothy 1974- 197
DeClements, Barthe (Faith) 1920- 131
  Earlier sketches in SATA 35, 71
  See also CLR 23
de Clercq Zubli, Rita la Fontaine 1929- 199
de Conte, Sieur Louis
  See Twain, Mark
Dedman, Stephen 108
Dee, Catherine 1964- 138
Dee, Ruby
  See Wallace, Ruby Ann
Deedy, Carmen Agra 1960- 196
Deedy, John 1923- 24
Deegan, Paul Joseph 1937- 48
  Brief entry 38
Deem, James M. 1950- 191
  Autobiography Feature 191
  Earlier sketches in SATA 75, 134
Deem, James Morgan
  See Deem, James M.
Deeter, Catherine 1947- 137
DeFelice, Cynthia 1951- 165
  Earlier sketches in SATA 79, 121
DeFelice, Cynthia C.
  See DeFelice, Cynthia
Defoe, Daniel 1660(?)-1731 22
  See also CLR 61
DeFord, Deborah H. 123
deFrance, Anthony
  See DiFranco, Anthony (Mario)
Degen, Bruce 1945- 205
  Brief entry 47
  Earlier sketches in SATA 57, 97, 147
DeGering, Etta (Belle) Fowler 1898-1996 7
De Goldi, Kate
  See De Goldi, Kathleen Domenica
De Goldi, Kathleen Domenica 1959- 123
de Goursac, Olivier 1959- 184

De Grazia, Ettore 1909-1982 .... *39*
De Grazia, Ted
    See De Grazia, Ettore
deGroat, Diane 1947- *169*
    Earlier sketches in SATA *31, 90*
deGros, J. H.
    See Villiard, Paul
de Grummond, Lena Young *62*
    Earlier sketch in SATA *6*
de Hamel, Joan Littledale 1924- *86*
De Haven, Tom 1949- *72*
de Hugo, Pierre
    See Brackers de Hugo, Pierre
Deiss, Joseph Jay 1915- *12*
de Jenkins, Lyll Becerra 1925-1997 .... *102*
DeJong, David C(ornel) 1905-1967 .... *10*
de Jong, Dola
    See de Jong, Dorothea Rosalie
de Jong, Dorothea Rosalie 1911-2003 .... *7*
    Obituary *149*
DeJong, Meindert 1906-1991 .... *2*
    Obituary *68*
    See also CLR *73*
DeJonge, Joanne E. 1943- *56*
Deka, Connie
    See Laux, Constance
de Kay, Ormonde (Jr.) 1923-1998 .... *7*
    Obituary *106*
de Kiriline, Louise
    See Lawrence, Louise de Kiriline
Dekker, Carl
    See Laffin, John (Alfred Charles)
    and Lynds, Dennis
deKruif, Paul (Henry) 1890-1971 .... *50*
    Earlier sketch in SATA *5*
Delacre, Lulu 1957- *209*
    Earlier sketches in SATA *36, 156*
DeLaCroix, Alice 1940- *195*
    Earlier sketch in SATA *75*
de la Cruz, Melissa 1971- *179*
De la Garza, Phyllis 1942- *169*
De Lage, Ida 1918- *11*
de la Mare, Walter (John) 1873-1956 .... *16*
    See also CLR *148*
Delaney, Harry 1932- *3*
Delaney, Joseph 1945- *172*
Delaney, M.C.
    See Delaney, Michael
Delaney, Michael 1955- *180*
    Earlier sketch in SATA *96*
Delaney, Michael Clark
    See Delaney, Michael
Delaney, Ned
    See Delaney, Thomas Nicholas III
Delaney, Thomas Nicholas III 1951- *28*
Delano, Hugh 1933- *20*
Delany, Samuel R., Jr. 1942- *92*
Delany, Samuel Ray
    See Delany, Samuel R., Jr.
de la Pena, Matt *205*
De La Ramee, Marie Louise 1839-1908 ...... *20*
de la Roche, Mazo 1879-1961 .... *64*
De La Roche Saint Andre, Anne 1950- *75*
Delaune, (Jewel) Lynn (de Grummond) *7*
DeLaurentis, Louise Budde 1920- *12*
del Barco, Lucy Salamanca 1900(?)-1989
    Obituary *64*
Delderfield, Eric R(aymond) 1909-1995 ...... *14*
Delderfield, Ronald Frederick 1912-1972 .... *20*
DeLeeuw, Adele (Louise) 1899-1988 .... *30*
    Obituary *56*
    Earlier sketch in SATA *1*
De Leon, Nephtali 1945- *97*
Delessert, Etienne 1941- *179*
    Brief entry *27*
    Earlier sketches in SATA *46, 130*
    See also CLR *81*
Delgado, James P. 1958- *122*
de Lint, Charles 1951- *207*
    Earlier sketches in SATA *115, 157*

de Lint, Charles Henri Diederick Hofsmit
    See de Lint, Charles
Delmar, Roy
    See Wexler, Jerome (LeRoy)
Del Negro, Janice M. *197*
Deloria, Vine, Jr. 1933-2005 .... *21*
    Obituary *171*
Deloria, Vine Victor, Jr.
    See Deloria, Vine, Jr.
del Rey, Lester 1915-1993 .... *22*
    Obituary *76*
Delrio, Martin
    See Doyle, Debra
    and Macdonald, James D.
Delton, Judy 1931-2001 .... *77*
    Obituary *130*
    Earlier sketch in SATA *14*
    See also SAAS *9*
Delulio, John 1938- *15*
Delving, Michael
    See Williams, Jay
de Marcken, Gail *186*
Demarest, Chris L. 1951- *175*
    Brief entry *44*
    Earlier sketches in SATA *45, 82, 128*
Demarest, Christopher Lynn
    See Demarest, Chris L.
Demarest, Doug
    See Barker, Will
De Mari, Silvana 1953- *193*
Demas, Corinne *203*
    See Bliss, Corinne Demas
Demas, Vida 1927- *9*
Dematons, Charlotte 1957- *203*
DeMatteis, J.M. 1953- *180*
DeMatteis, John Marc
    See DeMatteis, J.M.
De Mejo, Oscar 1911-1992 .... *40*
Demers, Dominique 1956- *177*
de Messieres, Nicole 1930- *39*
Demi
    See Hitz, Demi
Demijohn, Thom
    See Disch, Thomas M.
    and Sladek, John
Deming, Richard 1915-1983 .... *24*
Deming, Sarah *191*
de Monfreid, Dorothee 1973- *189*
Demuth, Patricia Brennan 1948- *84*
    Brief entry *51*
Dendinger, Roger E. 1952- *158*
Denenberg, Barry 1940- *175*
Dengler, Marianna (Herron) 1935- *103*
Dengler, Sandy 1939- *54*
    Brief entry *40*
Denim, Sue
    See Pilkey, Dav
Denise, Christopher 1968- *193*
    Earlier sketch in SATA *147*
Denman, K.L. 1957- *186*
Denmark, Harrison
    See Zelazny, Roger
Dennard, Deborah 1953- *136*
    Earlier sketch in SATA *78*
Denney, Diana 1910-2000 .... *25*
    Obituary *120*
Dennis, Morgan 1891(?)-1960 .... *18*
Dennis, Wesley 1903-1966 .... *18*
Denniston, Elinore 1900-1978
    Obituary *24*
Denny, Norman (George) 1901-1982 .... *43*
Denos, Julia *202*
Denslow, Sharon Phillips 1947- *142*
    Earlier sketch in SATA *68*
Denslow, W(illiam) W(allace) 1856-1915 .... *16*
    See also CLR *15*
Dent, Grace 1973- *187*
Denton, Kady MacDonald *181*
    Earlier sketches in SATA *66, 110*
    See also CLR *71*
Denton, Terry 1950- *186*

Denver, Walt
    See Redding, Robert Hull
    and Sherman, Jory (Tecumseh)
Denzel, Justin F(rancis) 1917-1999 .... *46*
    Brief entry *38*
Denzer, Ann Wiseman
    See Wiseman, Ann (Sayre)
DePalma, Mary Newell 1961- *185*
    Earlier sketch in SATA *139*
De Palma, Toni *199*
dePaola, Thomas Anthony 1934- *155*
    Earlier sketches in SATA *11, 59, 108*
    See also CLR *81*
    See also SAAS *15*
    See dePaola, Tomie
dePaola, Tomie *200*
    See dePaola, Thomas Anthony
deParrie, Paul 1949- *74*
DePauw, Linda Grant 1940- *24*
DeRan, David 1946- *76*
Derby, Ken 1956- *181*
Derby, Kenneth R.
    See Derby, Ken
Derby, Pat 1942- *172*
Derby, Sally 1934- *189*
    Earlier sketches in SATA *89, 132*
de Regniers, Beatrice Schenk (Freedman)
    1914-2000 .... *68*
    Obituary *123*
    Earlier sketch in SATA *2*
    See also SAAS *6*
Dereske, Jo 1947- *72*
Derleth, August (William) 1909-1971 .... *5*
Derman, Martha (Winn) *74*
Derman, Sarah Audrey 1915- *11*
DeRoberts, Lyndon
    See Silverstein, Robert Alan
de Roo, Anne Louise 1931-1997 .... *84*
    Earlier sketch in SATA *25*
    See also CLR *63*
deRosa, Dee *70*
Derrick, Lionel
    See Cunningham, Chet
Derrickson, Jim 1959- *141*
Derry Down Derry
    See Lear, Edward
Dervaux, Isabelle 1961- *106*
Derwent, Lavinia *14*
Desai, Anita 1937- *126*
    Earlier sketch in SATA *63*
DeSaix, Deborah Durland *188*
De Saulles, Tony 1958- *119*
Desbarats, Peter 1933- *39*
de Selincourt, Aubrey 1894-1962 .... *14*
de Seve, Randall *198*
Deshpande, Chris 1950- *69*
Desimini, Lisa 1964- *148*
    Earlier sketch in SATA *86*
Desjarlais, John 1953- *71*
Desjarlais, John J.
    See Desjarlais, John
Desmoinaux, Christel 1967- *149*
    Earlier sketch in SATA *103*
Desmond, Adrian J(ohn) 1947- *51*
Desmond, Alice Curtis 1897-1990 .... *8*
Desnoettes, Caroline *183*
DeSpain, Pleasant 1943- *87*
Desputeaux, Helene 1959- *95*
Dessen, Sarah 1970- *172*
    Earlier sketch in SATA *120*
Detine, Padre
    See Olsen, Ib Spang
de Trevino, Elizabeth B.
    See Trevino, Elizabeth B(orton) de
de Trevino, Elizabeth Borton
    See Trevino, Elizabeth B(orton) de
Detwiler, Susan Dill 1956- *58*
Deuker, Carl 1950- *196*
    Earlier sketches in SATA *82, 150*
Deutsch, Babette 1895-1982 .... *1*
    Obituary *33*

Deutsch, Eva Costabel
See Costabel, Eva Deutsch
Deutsch, Helen 1906-1992 76
Deutsch, Kurt
See Singer, Kurt D.
De Valera, Sinead 1879(?)-1975
Obituary 30
Devaney, John 1926-1994 12
de Varennes, Monique 1947- 168
de Varona, Frank J. 1943- 83
Devereux, Frederick L(eonard), Jr.
1914-1993 9
Devi, Nila
See Woody, Regina Jones
deVinck, Christopher 1951- 85
DeVita, James 195
DeVito, Cara 1956- 80
Devlin, Dorothy Wende
See Devlin, Wende
Devlin, Harry 1918-2001 136
Earlier sketches in SATA 11, 74
Devlin, Wende 1918-2002 74
Earlier sketch in SATA 11
Devon, Paddie 1953- 92
Devons, Sonia 1974- 72
Devorah-Leah 111
de Vos, Gail 1949- 122
DeVries, Douglas 1933- 122
De Waard, E(lliott) John 1935- 7
Dewan, Ted 1961- 157
Earlier sketch in SATA 108
Dewdney, Anna 184
Dewdney, Selwyn (Hanington) 1909-1979 ... 64
DeWeese, Gene
See DeWeese, Thomas Eugene
DeWeese, Jean
See DeWeese, Thomas Eugene
DeWeese, Thomas Eugene 1934- 46
Brief entry 45
Dewey, Ariane 1937- 178
Earlier sketches in SATA 7, 109
Dewey, Jennifer (Owings) 1941- 103
Brief entry 48
Earlier sketch in SATA 58
Dewey, Kenneth Francis 1940- 39
De Wire, Elinor 1953- 180
deWit, Dorothy (May Knowles) 1916-1980 . 39
Obituary 28
Dexter, Alison 1966- 125
Dexter, John
See Bradley, Marion Zimmer
Deyneka, Anita 1943- 24
Deyrup, Astrith Johnson 1923- 24
Dezern, Chad 201
Dhami, Narinder 1958- 152
Dhondy, Farrukh 1944- 152
Earlier sketch in SATA 65
See also CLR 41
Diakite, Baba Wague 1961- 174
Diakite, Penda 1993(?)- 174
Diamond, Arthur 1957- 76
Diamond, Donna 1950- 69
Brief entry 30
Earlier sketch in SATA 35
Diamond, Petra
See Sachs, Judith
Diamond, Rebecca
See Sachs, Judith
Dias, Earl Joseph 1916- 41
Dias, Ron 1937- 71
Diaz, David 1959(?)- 189
Earlier sketches in SATA 96, 150
See also CLR 65
Dibley, Glin 188
DiCamillo, Kate 1964- 202
Earlier sketches in SATA 121, 163
See also CLR 117
Di Certo, J(oseph) J(ohn) 1933- 60
DiCianni, Ron 1952- 107
Dick, Trella Lamson 1889-1974 9

Dickens, Charles 1812-1870 15
See also CLR 95
Dickens, Charles John Huffam
See Dickens, Charles
Dickens, Frank
See Huline-Dickens, Frank William
Dickens, Monica (Enid) 1915-1992 4
Obituary 74
Dickerson, Roy Ernest 1886-1965
Obituary 26
Dickinson, Emily 1830-1886 29
Dickinson, Emily Elizabeth
See Dickinson, Emily
Dickinson, Mary 1949- 48
Brief entry 41
Dickinson, Mary-Anne
See Rodda, Emily
Dickinson, Peter 1927- 150
Earlier sketches in SATA 5, 62, 95
See also CLR 125
Dickinson, Peter Malcolm de Brissac
See Dickinson, Peter
Dickinson, Susan 1931- 8
Dickinson, Terence 1943- 102
Dickinson, W(illiam) Croft 1897-1963 13
Dickson, Gordon R. 1923-2001 77
Dickson, Gordon Rupert
See Dickson, Gordon R.
Dickson, Helen
See Reynolds, Helen Mary Greenwood Campbell
Dickson, Naida 1916- 8
Diehn, Gwen 1943- 80
Dierssen, Andreas 1962- 190
Diesen, Deborah 1967- 200
Dieterich, Michele M. 1962- 78
Dietz, David H(enry) 1897-1984 10
Obituary 41
Dietz, Lew 1907-1997 11
Obituary 95
Diffily, Deborah 159
Di Fiori, Larry
See Di Fiori, Lawrence
Di Fiori, Lawrence 1934- 130
DiFranco, Anthony (Mario) 1945- 42
Digby, Anne 1935- 72
Digges, Jeremiah
See Berger, Josef
Digman, Kristina 1959- 176
D'Ignazio, Fred(erick) 1949- 39
Brief entry 35
Di Grazia, Thomas (?)-1983 32
Dijkstra, Lida 1961- 195
Dikty, Julian May
See May, Julian
Dillard, Annie 1945- 140
Earlier sketch in SATA 10
Dillard, Kristine 1964- 113
Dillard, Polly Hargis 1916- 24
Diller, Harriett 1953- 78
Dillon, Barbara 1927- 44
Brief entry 39
Dillon, Diane 1933- 194
Earlier sketches in SATA 15, 51, 106
See also CLR 44
Dillon, Diane Claire
See Dillon, Diane
Dillon, Eilis 1920-1994 74
Autobiography Feature 105
Obituary 83
Earlier sketch in SATA 2
See also CLR 26
Dillon, Jana (a pseudonym) 1952- 117
Dillon, Leo 1933- 194
Earlier sketches in SATA 15, 51, 106
See also CLR 44
Dillon, Sharon Saseen
See Saseen, Sharon (Dillon)
Dils, Tracey E. 1958- 83
Dilson, Jesse 1914-1988 24

Dinan, Carolyn 59
Brief entry 47
Dines, Carol 1956- 175
Dines, (Harry) Glen 1925-1996 7
Dinesen, Isak
See Blixen, Karen
Dinessi, Alex
See Schembri, Jim
Dinneen, Betty 1929- 61
Dinnerstein, Harvey 1928- 42
Dinsdale, Tim(othy Kay) 1924-1987 11
Diop, Birago (Ismael) 1906-1989
Obituary 64
Diouf, Sylviane A. 168
Diouf, Sylviane Anna
See Diouf, Sylviane A.
DiPucchio, Kelly 204
Earlier sketch in SATA 159
Dirk
See Gringhuis, Richard H.
Dirks, Wilhelmina 1916- 59
Dirks, Willy
See Dirks, Wilhelmina
Dirtmeister
See Tomecek, Steve
DiSalvo, DyAnne 1960- 144
Earlier sketch in SATA 59
DiSalvo-Ryan, DyAnne
See DiSalvo, DyAnne
Disch, Thomas M. 1940-2008 92
Obituary 195
See also CLR 18
See also SAAS 15
Disch, Thomas Michael
See Disch, Thomas M.
Disch, Tom
See Disch, Thomas M.
Disher, Garry 1949- 125
Earlier sketch in SATA 81
Disney, Walt(er Elias) 1901-1966 28
Brief entry 27
Ditchfield, Christin 1973- 189
DiTerlizzi, Tony 1969- 154
Divakaruni, Chitra Banerjee 1956- 160
Di Valentin, Maria (Amelia) Messuri
1911-1985 7
Divine, Arthur Durham 1904-1987
Obituary 52
Divine, David
See Divine, Arthur Durham
Dixon, Ann R. 1954- 127
Earlier sketch in SATA 77
Dixon, Ann Renee
See Dixon, Ann R.
Dixon, Dougal 1947- 190
Earlier sketches in SATA 45, 127
Dixon, Franklin W.
See Barrett, Neal, Jr.
and Goulart, Ron
and Lantz, Francess L(in)
and Lerangis, Peter
and McFarlane, Leslie
and Stanley, George Edward
and Stratemeyer, Edward L.
Dixon, Jeanne 1936- 31
Dixon, Paige
See Corcoran, Barbara (Asenath)
Dixon, Peter L(ee) 1931- 6
Dixon, Rachel 1952- 74
Djoleto, (Solomon Alexander) Amu 1929- ... 80
d'lacey, Chris 1949- 165
Doak, Annie
See Dillard, Annie
Doane, Pelagie 1906-1966 7
Dob, Bob 207
Dobell, I(sabel) M(arian) B(arclay)
1909-1998 11
Dobie, J(ames) Frank 1888-1964 43
Dobkin, Alexander 1908-1975
Obituary 30
Dobler, Lavinia G. 1910- 6

Dobrin, Arnold 1928- *4*
Dobson, Jill 1969- *140*
Dobson, Julia 1941- *48*
Dobson, Mary 1954- *117*
Docherty, James
    See Docherty, Jimmy
Docherty, Jimmy 1976- *204*
Dockery, Wallene T. 1941- *27*
Dockray, Tracy 1962- *139*
Dockrey, Karen 1955- *103*
Doctor, Bernard
    See Doctor, Bernard Aquina
Doctor, Bernard Aquina 1950- *81*
Doctor X
    See Nourse, Alan E(dward)
Dodd, Ed(ward Benton) 1902-1991 .... *4*
    Obituary *68*
Dodd, Emma 1969- *203*
Dodd, Lynley (Stuart) 1941- *132*
    Earlier sketches in SATA *35, 86*
    See also CLR *62*
Dodd, Marty 1921- *142*
Dodd, Quentin 1972- *137*
Dodds, Bill 1952- *78*
Dodds, Dayle Ann 1952- *201*
    Earlier sketches in SATA *75, 150*
Doder, Josh 1968- *187*
Dodge, Bertha S(anford) 1902-1995 .... *8*
Dodge, Fremont
    See Grimes, Lee
Dodge, Gil
    See Hano, Arnold
Dodge, Mary (Elizabeth) Mapes
    1831(?)-1905 .... *100*
    Earlier sketch in SATA *21*
    See also CLR *62*
Dodgson, Charles Lutwidge
    See Carroll, Lewis
Dodson, Kenneth MacKenzie 1907-1999 ..... *11*
Dodson, Susan 1941- *50*
    Brief entry *40*
Dogyear, Drew
    See Gorey, Edward (St. John)
Doherty, Berlie 1943- *111*
    Earlier sketch in SATA *72*
    See also CLR *21*
    See also SAAS *16*
Doherty, Charles Hugh 1913- *6*
Doherty, Craig A. 1951- *169*
    Earlier sketch in SATA *83*
Doherty, Katherine M(ann) 1951- *83*
Doherty, Kieran 1945- *164*
Dokey, Cameron 1956- *97*
Dolan, Edward F(rancis), Jr. 1924- *94*
    Brief entry *31*
    Earlier sketch in SATA *45*
Dolan, Ellen M(eara) 1929-1998 .... *88*
Dolan, Sean J. 1958- *74*
Dolce, J. Ellen 1948- *75*
Dolch, Edward William 1889-1961 .... *50*
Dolch, Marguerite Pierce 1891-1978 .... *50*
Dollar, Diane (Hills) 1933- *57*
Dolson, Hildegarde
    See Lockridge, Hildegarde (Dolson)
Domanska, Janina 1913(?)-1995 .... *68*
    Obituary *84*
    Earlier sketch in SATA *6*
    See also CLR *40*
    See also SAAS *18*
Dominguez, Angel 1953- *76*
Domino, John
    See Averill, Esther (Holden)
Domjan, Joseph (Spiri) 1907-1992 .... *25*
Domm, Jeffrey C. 1958- *84*
Donahue, Dorothy *178*
Donald, Rhonda Lucas 1962- *147*
Donalds, Gordon
    See Shirreffs, Gordon D(onald)
Donaldson, Bryna
    See Stevens, Bryna

Donaldson, Gordon 1913-1993 .... *64*
    Obituary *76*
Donaldson, Joan 1953- *78*
Donaldson, Julia 1948- *180*
    Earlier sketches in SATA *82, 132*
Donaldson, Stephen R. 1947- *121*
Donaldson, Stephen Reeder
    See Donaldson, Stephen R.
Doner, Kim 1955- *208*
    Earlier sketch in SATA *91*
Doney, Todd L. W. 1959- *104*
Dong-Sung, Kim 1970- *195*
Dong-Sung Kim
    See Dong-Sung, Kim
Donkin, Nance (Clare) 1915- *95*
Donna, Natalie 1934-1979 .... *9*
Donnelly, Elfie 1950-
    See CLR *104*
Donnelly, Jennifer 1963- *154*
Donnelly, Matt 1972- *148*
Donnio, Sylviane *188*
Donofrio, Beverly 1950- *209*
Donoghue, Emma 1969- *101*
Donohue, Moira Rose 1954- *201*
Donoughue, Carol 1935- *139*
Donovan, Frank (Robert) 1906-1975
    Obituary *30*
Donovan, John 1928-1992 .... *72*
    Brief entry *29*
    See also CLR *3*
Donovan, Mary Lee 1961- *86*
Donovan, William
    See Berkebile, Fred D(onovan)
Donze, Mary Terese 1911- *89*
Doob, Leonard W(illiam) 1909-2000 .... *8*
Dooley, Norah 1953- *74*
Dooling, Michael 1958- *105*
Dor, Ana
    See Ceder, Georgiana Dorcas
Dore, (Louis Christophe Paul) Gustave
    1832-1883 .... *19*
Doremus, Robert 1913- *30*
Doren, Marion (Walker) 1928- *57*
Dorenkamp, Michelle 1957- *89*
Dorflinger, Carolyn 1953- *91*
Dorfman, Joaquin 1979- *180*
Dorfman, Joaquin Emiliano
    See Dorfman, Joaquin
Dorian, Edith M(cEwen) 1900-1983 .... *5*
Dorian, Harry
    See Hamilton, Charles (Harold St. John)
Dorian, Marguerite *7*
Dorin, Patrick C(arberry) 1939- *59*
    Brief entry *52*
Dorman, Brandon *194*
Dorman, Michael 1932- *7*
Dorman, N. B. 1927- *39*
Dormer, Frank W. *200*
Dorris, Michael 1945-1997 .... *75*
    Obituary *94*
    See also CLR *58*
Dorris, Michael A.
    See Dorris, Michael
Dorris, Michael Anthony
    See Dorris, Michael
Dorritt, Susan
    See Schlein, Miriam
Dorros, Alex 1991- *194*
Dorros, Arthur 1950- *168*
    Earlier sketches in SATA *78, 122*
    See also CLR *42*
    See also SAAS *20*
Dorros, Arthur M.
    See Dorros, Arthur
Dorson, Richard M(ercer) 1916-1981 .... *30*
Doss, Helen (Grigsby) 1918- *20*
Doss, Margot Patterson *6*
dos Santos, Joyce Audy 1949- *57*
    Brief entry *42*
Dothers, Anne
    See Chess, Victoria (Dickerson)

Dotlich, Rebecca Kai 1951- *182*
Dottig
    See Grider, Dorothy
Dotts, Maryann J. 1933- *35*
Doty, Jean Slaughter 1929- *28*
Doty, Roy 1922- *28*
Doubtfire, Dianne (Abrams) 1918- *29*
Doucet, Sharon Arms 1951- *144*
    Autobiography Feature *144*
    Earlier sketch in SATA *125*
Dougherty, Charles 1922- *18*
Dougherty, Terri (L.) 1964- *146*
Doughty, Rebecca 1955- *174*
Douglas, Blaise 1960- *101*
Douglas, Carole Nelson 1944- *73*
Douglas, Garry
    See Kilworth, Garry
Douglas, James McM.
    See Griffin, W.E.B.
Douglas, Kathryn
    See Ewing, Kathryn
Douglas, Leonard
    See Bradbury, Ray
Douglas, Lola
    See Zeises, Lara M.
Douglas, Marjory Stoneman 1890-1998 .... *10*
Douglas, Michael
    See Bright, Robert Sr.)
Douglas, Michael
    See Crichton, Michael
Douglas, Shirley Stewart
    See Tepper, Sheri S.
Douglass, Barbara 1930- *40*
Douglass, Frederick 1817(?)-1895 .... *29*
Douglass, Keith
    See Cunningham, Chet
Douty, Esther M(orris) 1909-1978 .... *8*
    Obituary *23*
Dow, Emily R. 1904-1987 .... *10*
Dow, Vicki
    See McVey, Vicki
Dowd, John David 1945- *78*
Dowd, Siobhan 1960-2007 .... *204*
Dowdell, Dorothy (Florence) Karns 1910- ... *12*
Dowden, Anne Ophelia Todd 1907-2007 .... *7*
    Obituary *180*
    See also SAAS *10*
Dowdey, Landon Gerald 1923- *11*
Dowdy, Mrs. Regera
    See Gorey, Edward (St. John)
Dowell, Frances O'Roark *205*
    Earlier sketch in SATA *157*
Dower, Laura 1967- *185*
Dowling, Terry 1947- *101*
Downard, Barry 1956- *202*
Downer, Ann 1960- *155*
Downer, Marion 1892(?)-1971 .... *25*
Downes, Belinda 1962- *180*
Downey, Fairfax D(avis) 1893-1990 .... *3*
    Obituary *66*
Downey, Lynn 1961- *185*
Downham, Jenny 1964- *192*
Downie, John 1931- *87*
Downie, Mary Alice 1934- *171*
    Earlier sketches in SATA *13, 87*
Downie, Mary Alice Dawe
    See Downie, Mary Alice
Downing, David A(lmon) 1958- *84*
Downing, Johnette *184*
Downing, Julie 1956- *148*
    Earlier sketch in SATA *81*
Downing, Paula E. 1951- *80*
Downing, Warwick 1931- *138*
Downing, Wick
    See Downing, Warwick
Dowswell, Paul 1957- *184*
Doyle, A. Conan
    See Doyle, Sir Arthur Conan
Doyle, Sir Arthur Conan 1859-1930 .... *24*
    See also CLR *106*

Doyle, Brian 1935- 156
  Earlier sketches in SATA 67, 104
  See also CLR 22
  See also SAAS 16
Doyle, Charlotte 1937- 178
  Earlier sketch in SATA 94
Doyle, Charlotte Lackner
  See Doyle, Charlotte
Doyle, Conan
  See Doyle, Sir Arthur Conan
Doyle, Debra 1952- 165
  Earlier sketch in SATA 105
Doyle, Donovan
  See Boegehold, Betty (Doyle)
Doyle, John
  See Graves, Robert
Doyle, Malachy 1954- 165
  Earlier sketch in SATA 120
  See also CLR 83
Doyle, Richard 1824-1883 21
Doyle, Sir A. Conan
  See Doyle, Sir Arthur Conan
Dr. A
  See Asimov, Isaac
  and Silverstein, Alvin
  and Silverstein, Virginia B.
Dr. Alphabet
  See Morice, Dave
Dr. Fred
  See Bortz, Alfred B(enjamin)
Dr. Laura
  See Schlessinger, Laura (Catherine)
Dr. Seuss 1904-1991 100
  Obituary 67
  Earlier sketches in SATA 1, 28, 75
  See also CLR 100
Dr. Zed
  See Penrose, Gordon
Drabble, Margaret 1939- 48
Drackett, Phil(ip Arthur) 1922- 53
Draco, F.
  See Davis, Julia
Dracup, Angela 1943- 74
Dragisic, Patricia 116
Dragonwagon, Crescent 1952- 186
  Autobiography Feature 186
  Earlier sketches in SATA 11, 41, 75, 133
  See also SAAS 14
Drake, David 1945- 85
Drake, David Allen
  See Drake, David
Drake, Frank
  See Hamilton, Charles (Harold St. John)
Drake, Jane 1954- 82
Drakeford, Dale B 1952- 113
Drakeford, Dale Benjamin
  See Drakeford, Dale B
Draper, Hastings
  See Jeffries, Roderic
Draper, Sharon
  See Draper, Sharon M.
Draper, Sharon M. 1948- 195
  Autobiography Feature 146
  Earlier sketches in SATA 98, 146
  See also CLR 57
Draper, Sharon Mills
  See Draper, Sharon M.
Drapier, M. B.
  See Swift, Jonathan
Drawson, Blair 1943- 126
  Earlier sketch in SATA 17
Dray, Matt 1967- 177
Dray, Matthew Frederick
  See Dray, Matt
Dresang, Eliza (Carolyn Timberlake) 1941- . 19
Drescher, Henrik 1955- 172
  Earlier sketches in SATA 67, 105
  See also CLR 20
Drescher, Joan E(lizabeth) 1939- 137
  Earlier sketch in SATA 30
Dressen-McQueen, Stacey 191

Dreves, Veronica R. 1927-1986
  Obituary 50
Drew, Patricia (Mary) 1938- 15
Drewery, Mary 1918- 6
Drewery, Melanie 1970- 165
Drewry, Henry N(athaniel) 1924- 138
Dreyer, Ellen 177
Drial, J. E.
  See Laird, Jean E(louise)
Drimmer, Frederick 1916-2000 60
  Obituary 124
Driskill, J. Lawrence 1920- 90
Driskill, Larry
  See Driskill, J. Lawrence
Driving Hawk, Virginia
  See Sneve, Virginia Driving Hawk
Dron, Laura
  See Matthews, L.S.
Dronzek, Laura 199
Drucker, Malka 1945- 111
  Brief entry 29
  Earlier sketch in SATA 39
Drucker, Olga Levy 1927- 79
Druitt, Tobias
  See Purkiss, Diane
Drummond, Allan 1957- 209
Drummond, V(iolet) H(ilda) 1911-2000 6
Drummond, Walter
  See Silverberg, Robert
Drury, Clare Marie
  See Hoskyns-Abrahall, Clare (Constance
    Drury)
Drury, Roger W(olcott) 1914-1996 15
Druse, Eleanor
  See King, Stephen
Dryden, Pamela
  See St. John, Nicole
D.T., Hughes
  See Hughes, Dean
Duane, Diane (Elizabeth) 1952- 145
  Brief entry 46
  Earlier sketches in SATA 58, 95
Dubanevich, Arlene 1950- 56
Dubelaar, Thea 1947- 60
Dubin, Jill 205
du Blane, Daphne
  See Groom, Arthur William
Duble, Kathleen Benner 1958- 164
Dubois, Claude K. 1960- 196
DuBois, Rochelle Holt 1946- 41
Du Bois, Shirley Graham 1907(?)-1977 24
  See Graham, Shirley
Du Bois, W. E. B. 1868-1963 42
Du Bois, William Edward Burghardt
  See Du Bois, W. E. B.
du Bois, William Pene
  See Pene du Bois, William (Sherman)
Duboise, Novella 1911-1999 88
Dubosarsky, Ursula 1961- 193
  Earlier sketches in SATA 107, 147
DuBose, LaRocque (Russ) 1926- 2
Dubrovin, Vivian 1931- 139
  Earlier sketch in SATA 65
DuBurke, Randy 172
Ducey, Jean Sparks 1915- 93
Duchacek, Ivo D(uka) 1913-1988
  Obituary 55
Du Chaillu, Paul (Belloni) 1835(?)-1903 26
Ducharme, Dede Fox
  See Ducharme, Lilian Fox
Ducharme, Lilian Fox 1950- 122
Ducornet, Erica 1943- 7
Ducornet, Rikki
  See Ducornet, Erica
Duden, Jane 1947- 136
Duder, Tessa 1940- 117
  Earlier sketch in SATA 80
  See also CLR 43
  See also SAAS 23
Dudley, Helen
  See Hope Simpson, Jacynth

Dudley, Martha Ward 1909(?)-1985
  Obituary 45
Dudley, Nancy
  See Cole, Lois Dwight
Dudley, Robert
  See Baldwin, James
Dudley, Ruth H(ubbell) 1905-2001 11
Dudley-Smith, T.
  See Trevor, Elleston
Due, Linnea A. 1948- 64
Dueck, Adele 1955- 97
Dueland, Joy V(ivian) 27
Duerr, Gisela 1968- 89
Duey, Kathleen 1950- 199
  Earlier sketch in SATA 132
Dufault, Joseph Ernest Nephtali
  See James, Will(iam Roderick)
Duff, Annis (James) 1904(?)-1986
  Obituary 49
Duff, Maggie
  See Duff, Margaret K(app)
Duff, Margaret K(app) 1916-2003 37
  Obituary 144
Duffey, Betsy (Byars) 1953- 131
  Earlier sketch in SATA 80
Duffie, Charles 1960- 144
Duffield, Katy S. 1961- 147
Duffy, Carol Ann 1955- 165
  Earlier sketch in SATA 95
Dugan, Jack
  See Griffin, W.E.B.
Dugan, John Kevin
  See Griffin, W.E.B.
Dugan, Karen 202
Dugan, Karen M.
  See Dugan, Karen
Dugan, Michael (Gray) 1947- 15
Duggan, Alfred Leo 1903-1964 25
Duggan, Maurice 1922-1974 40
  Obituary 30
Duggan, Maurice Noel
  See Duggan, Maurice
Duggleby, John 1952- 94
Dugin, Andrej 1955- 77
Dugina, Olga 1964- 77
du Jardin, Rosamond Neal 1902-1963 2
Duka, Ivo
  See Duchacek, Ivo D(uka)
Duke, Kate 1956- 192
  Earlier sketches in SATA 90, 148
  See also CLR 51
Duke, Will
  See Gault, William Campbell
Dulac, Edmund 1882-1953 19
Dumas, Alexandre (pere) 1802-1870 18
  See also CLR 134
Dumas, Jacqueline 1946- 55
Dumas, Philippe 1940- 119
  Earlier sketch in SATA 52
du Maurier, Daphne 1907-1989 27
  Obituary 60
Dumbleton, Mike 1948- 206
  Earlier sketches in SATA 73, 124
Dunbar, Fiona 1961- 167
Dunbar, Joyce 1944- 162
  Earlier sketches in SATA 76, 112
Dunbar, Paul Laurence 1872-1906 34
Dunbar, Polly 1980(?)- 181
Dunbar, Robert E(verett) 1926- 32
Duncan, Alexandra
  See Moore, Ishbel (Lindsay)
Duncan, Alice Faye 1967- 168
  Earlier sketch in SATA 95
Duncan, Gregory
  See McClintock, Marshall
Duncan, Jane
  See Cameron, Elizabeth Jane
Duncan, Julia K.
  See Benson, Mildred

Duncan, Lois 1934- *141*
  Autobiography Feature *141*
  Earlier sketches in SATA *1, 36, 75, 133*
  See also CLR *129*
  See also SAAS *2*
Duncan, Norman 1871-1916
  See YABC *1*
Duncan, Terence
  See Nolan, William F.
Duncombe, Frances (Riker) 1900-1994 .... *25*
  Obituary *82*
Dungy, Anthony
  See Dungy, Tony
Dungy, Tony 1955- *206*
Dunham, Montrew 1919- *162*
Dunham, Montrew Goetz
  See Dunham, Montrew
Dunkle, Clare B. 1964- *155*
Dunlap, Julie 1958- *84*
Dunleavy, Deborah 1951- *133*
Dunlop, Agnes M. R. (?)-1982 .... *87*
Dunlop, Eileen (Rhona) 1938- *76*
  Earlier sketch in SATA *24*
  See also SAAS *12*
Dunmore, Helen 1952- *201*
Dunn, Anne M. 1940- *107*
Dunn, Carolyn 1965- *208*
Dunn, Harvey T(homas) 1884-1952 .... *34*
Dunn, Herb
  See Gutman, Dan
Dunn, John M. (III) 1949- *93*
Dunn, Judy
  See Spangenberg, Judith Dunn
Dunn, Mary Lois 1930- *6*
Dunnahoo, Terry Janson 1927- *7*
Dunne, Jeanette 1952- *72*
Dunne, Kathleen 1933- *126*
Dunne, Marie
  See Clark, Ann Nolan
Dunne, Mary Collins 1914- *11*
Dunne, Mary Jo
  See Dunne, Mary Collins
Dunnett, Kaitlyn
  See Emerson, Kathy Lynn
Dunnett, Margaret (Rosalind) 1909-1977 ..... *42*
Dunnick, Regan *178*
Dunrea, Olivier 1953- *160*
  Brief entry *46*
  Earlier sketches in SATA *59, 118*
Dunrea, Olivier Jean-Paul Dominique
  See Dunrea, Olivier
Dunton, Dorothy 1912- *92*
Dupasquier, Philippe 1955- *151*
  Earlier sketch in SATA *86*
duPont, Lindsay *207*
duPont, Lindsay Harper
  See duPont, Lindsay
DuPrau, Jeanne 1944- *144*
Dupuy, T(revor) N(evitt) 1916-1995 .... *4*
  Obituary *86*
DuQuette, Keith 1960- *155*
  Earlier sketch in SATA *90*
Duran, Gloria 1924- *171*
Duran, Gloria Bradley
  See Duran, Gloria
Duranceau, Suzanne 1952- *162*
Durand, Delphine 1971- *200*
Durango, Julia 1967- *173*
Durant, Alan 1958- *165*
  Earlier sketch in SATA *121*
Durant, John 1902- *27*
Durbin, William 1951- *174*
  Earlier sketch in SATA *143*
Durell, Ann 1930- *66*
Durkee, Sarah *173*
Durney, Ryan *205*
Durrant, Lynda 1954- *148*
  Earlier sketch in SATA *96*
Durrell, Gerald (Malcolm) 1925-1995 .... *8*
  Obituary *84*
Durrell, Julie 1955- *94*

Durrett, Deanne 1940- *144*
  Earlier sketch in SATA *92*
Durst, Sarah Beth 1974- *203*
Du Soe, Robert C. 1892-1958
  See YABC *2*
Dussling, Jennifer 1970- *143*
  Earlier sketch in SATA *96*
DuTemple, Lesley A. 1952- *113*
Dutton, Sandra *191*
Dutz
  See Davis, Mary Octavia
Duval, Katherine
  See James, Elizabeth
Duval, Kathy 1946- *181*
Duvall, Aimee
  See Thurlo, Aimee
  and Thurlo, David
Duvall, Evelyn Millis 1906- *9*
Duvall, Jill D(onovan) 1932- *102*
Duvoisin, Roger (Antoine) 1904-1980 .... *30*
  Obituary *23*
  Earlier sketch in SATA *2*
  See also CLR *23*
Dwiggins, Don(ald J.) 1913-1988 .... *4*
  Obituary *60*
Dwight, Allan
  See Cole, Lois Dwight
Dwyer, Deanna
  See Koontz, Dean
Dwyer, K.R.
  See Koontz, Dean
Dyck, Peter J. 1914- *75*
Dyer, James (Frederick) 1934- *37*
Dyer, Jane *191*
  Earlier sketch in SATA *147*
Dyess, John (Foster) 1939- *76*
Dygard, Thomas J. 1931-1996 .... *97*
  Obituary *92*
  Earlier sketch in SATA *24*
  See also SAAS *15*
Dyke, John 1935- *35*

E

E. V. L.
  See Lucas, E(dward) V(errall)
Eagar, Frances (Elisabeth Stuart)
  1940-1978 .... *11*
  Obituary *55*
Eager, Edward (McMaken) 1911-1964 .... *17*
  See also CLR *43*
Eager, George 1921- *56*
Eager, George B.
  See Eager, George
Eagle, Ellen 1953- *61*
Eagle, Kin
  See Adlerman, Daniel (Ezra)
  and Adlerman, Kimberly M(arie)
Eagle, Mike 1942- *11*
Earle, Olive L(ydia) 1888-1982 .... *7*
Earle, William
  See Johns, W(illiam) E(arle)
Earls, Nick 1963- *156*
  Earlier sketch in SATA *95*
Early, Jack
  See Scoppettone, Sandra
Early, Jon
  See Johns, W(illiam) E(arle)
Early, Margaret 1951- *72*
Earnshaw, Brian 1929- *17*
Earnshaw, Micky
  See Earnshaw, Spencer Wright
Earnshaw, Spencer Wright 1939- *88*
Easley, MaryAnn *94*
Eason, Alethea 1957- *197*
Eastman, Charles A(lexander) 1858-1939
  See YABC *1*
Eastman, P(hilip) D(ey) 1909-1986 .... *33*
  Obituary *46*

Easton, Kelly 1960- *192*
  Earlier sketch in SATA *141*
Eastwick, Ivy (Ethel) O(live) *3*
Eaton, Anne T(haxter) 1881-1971 .... *32*
Eaton, Anthony 1971- *167*
Eaton, George L.
  See Verral, Charles Spain
Eaton, Janet
  See Givens, Janet E(aton)
Eaton, Jeanette 1886-1968 .... *24*
Eaton, Maxwell III 1981- *199*
Eaton, Tom 1940- *22*
Ebbeler, Jeff
  See Ebbeler, Jeffrey
Ebbeler, Jeffrey 1974- *206*
Ebel, Alex 1927- *11*
Eber, Dorothy (Margaret) Harley 1930- *27*
Eberhart, Sheri S.
  See Tepper, Sheri S.
Eberle, Irmengarde 1898-1979 .... *2*
  Obituary *23*
Eble, Diane 1956- *74*
Eboch, Chris *113*
Eccles Williams, Ferelith 1920- *22*
Echlin, Kim 1955- *166*
Eckblad, Edith Berven 1923- *23*
Ecke, Wolfgang 1927-1983
  Obituary *37*
Eckert, Allan W. 1931- *91*
  Brief entry *27*
  Earlier sketch in SATA *29*
  See also SAAS *21*
Eckert, Horst 1931- *72*
  Earlier sketch in SATA *8*
  See also CLR *26*
Ecklar, Julia (Marie) 1964- *112*
Eddings, David 1931-2009 .... *91*
Eddings, David Carroll
  See Eddings, David
Ede, Janina 1937- *33*
Edell, Celeste *12*
Edelman, Lily (Judith) 1915-1981 .... *22*
Edelson, Edward 1932- *51*
Edens, Cooper 1945- *166*
  Earlier sketches in SATA *49, 112*
Edens, (Bishop) David 1926- *39*
Edey, Maitland A(rmstrong) 1910-1992 .... *25*
  Obituary *71*
Edgerton, Perky *196*
Edgeworth, Maria 1768-1849 .... *21*
Edgy, Wardore
  See Gorey, Edward (St. John)
Edison, Theodore
  See Stratemeyer, Edward L.
Edler, Tim(othy) 1948- *56*
Edmiston, Jim 1948- *80*
Edmonds, I(vy) G(ordon) 1917- *8*
Edmonds, Walter D(umaux) 1903-1998 .... *27*
  Obituary *99*
  Earlier sketch in SATA *1*
  See also SAAS *4*
Edmund, Sean
  See Pringle, Laurence
Edsall, Marian (Stickney) 1920- *8*
Edwards, Al
  See Nourse, Alan E(dward)
Edwards, Anne 1927- *35*
Edwards, Audrey 1947- *52*
  Brief entry *31*
Edwards, Becky (Jane) 1966- *125*
Edwards, Bertram
  See Edwards, Herbert Charles
Edwards, Bronwen Elizabeth
  See Rose, Wendy
Edwards, Cecile Pepin 1916- *25*
Edwards, David 1962- *198*
Edwards, Dorothy 1914-1982 .... *88*
  Obituary *31*
  Earlier sketch in SATA *4*
Edwards, F. E.
  See Nolan, William F.

Edwards, Frank B. 1952- *93*
Edwards, Gunvor *32*
Edwards, Harvey 1929- *5*
Edwards, Hazel (Eileen) 1945- *135*
Edwards, Herbert Charles 1912- *12*
Edwards, Jane Campbell 1932- *10*
Edwards, Julia
    See Stratemeyer, Edward L.
Edwards, Julie
    See Andrews, Julie
Edwards, Julie Andrews
    See Andrews, Julie
Edwards, June
    See Bhatia, Jamunadevi
Edwards, Linda Strauss 1948- *49*
    Brief entry *42*
Edwards, Margaret (Alexander) 1902-1988
    Obituary *56*
Edwards, Michelle 1955- *152*
    Earlier sketch in SATA *70*
Edwards, Monica le Doux Newton
    1912-1998 .... *12*
Edwards, Olwen
    See Gater, Dilys
Edwards, Page (Lawrence, Jr.) 1941-1999 ... *59*
Edwards, Pamela Duncan *189*
Edwards, R. T.
    See Goulart, Ron
Edwards, Sally (Cary) 1929- *7*
Edwards, Samuel
    See Gerson, Noel Bertram
Edwards, Wallace 1957(?)- *170*
Eeckhout, Emmanuelle 1976- *208*
Egan, E(dward) W(elstead) 1922- *35*
Egan, Kerry *175*
Egan, Lorraine Hopping 1960- *134*
    Earlier sketch in SATA *91*
Egan, Tim 1957- *191*
    Earlier sketches in SATA *89, 155*
Egermeier, Elsie E(milie) 1890-1986 .... *65*
Eggenberger, David 1918- *6*
Eggleston, Edward 1837-1902 .... *27*
Egielski, Richard 1952- *163*
    Earlier sketches in SATA *11, 49, 106*
Egypt, Ophelia Settle 1903-1984 .... *16*
    Obituary *38*
Ehlert, Lois 1934- *172*
    Earlier sketches in SATA *35, 69, 128*
    See also CLR *28*
Ehlert, Lois Jane
    See Ehlert, Lois
Ehling, Katalin Olah 1941- *93*
Ehrenfreund, Norbert 1921- *86*
Ehrenhaft, Daniel 1970- *185*
Ehrhardt, Karen 1963- *184*
Ehrlich, Amy 1942- *132*
    Earlier sketches in SATA *25, 65, 96*
Ehrlich, Bettina Bauer 1903-1985 .... *1*
Ehrlich, Fred *205*
Ehrlich, Fred M.D.
    See Ehrlich, Fred
Ehrlich, H. M.
    See Ziefert, Harriet
Eichenberg, Fritz 1901-1990 .... *50*
    Earlier sketch in SATA *9*
Eichler, Margrit 1942- *35*
Eichner, James A. 1927- *4*
Eidson, Thomas 1944- *112*
Eifert, Virginia (Louise) S(nider) 1911-1966 . *2*
Eige, (Elizabeth) Lillian 1915- *65*
Eiken, J. Melia 1967- *125*
Einhorn, Edward 1970- *204*
Einsel, Naiad *10*
Einsel, Walter 1926- *10*
Einzig, Susan 1922- *43*
Eiseman, Alberta 1925- *15*
Eisenberg, Azriel (Louis) 1903-1985 .... *12*
Eisenberg, Lisa 1949- *155*
    Brief entry *50*
    Earlier sketch in SATA *57*
Eisenberg, Phyllis Rose 1924- *41*

Eisner, Vivienne
    See Margolis, Vivienne
Eisner, Will 1917-2005 .... *165*
    Earlier sketch in SATA *31*
Eisner, William Erwin
    See Eisner, Will
Eitzen, Allan 1928- *9*
Eitzen, Ruth (Carper) 1924- *9*
Ekwensi, C. O. D.
    See Ekwensi, Cyprian
Ekwensi, Cyprian 1921-2007 .... *66*
Ekwensi, Cyprian Odiatu Duaka
    See Ekwensi, Cyprian
Elam, Richard M(ace, Jr.) 1920- *9*
Elborn, Andrew
    See Clements, Andrew
    and Clements, Andrew
Elboz, Stephen 1956- *152*
Eldin, Peter 1939- *154*
Eldon, Kathy 1946- *107*
Eldridge, Marion *199*
Elfman, Blossom 1925- *8*
Elgin, Kathleen 1923- *39*
Elia
    See Lamb, Charles
Eliot, A. D.
    See Jewett, Sarah Orne
Eliot, Alice
    See Jewett, Sarah Orne
Eliot, Anne
    See Cole, Lois Dwight
Eliot, Dan
    See Silverberg, Robert
Elish, Dan 1960- *204*
    Earlier sketches in SATA *68, 129*
Elisha, Ron 1951- *104*
Elisofon, Eliot 1911-1973
    Obituary *21*
Elkeles, Simone 1970- *187*
Elkin, Benjamin 1911-1995 .... *3*
Elkins, Dov Peretz 1937- *5*
Ellacott, S(amuel) E(rnest) 1911- *19*
Elleman, Barbara 1934- *147*
Ellen, Jaye
    See Nixon, Joan Lowery
Eller, Scott
    See Holinger, William (Jacques)
    and Shepard, Jim
Ellestad, Myrvin
    See Ellestad, Myrvin H.
Ellestad, Myrvin H. 1921- *120*
Elliot, Bruce
    See Field, Edward
Elliot, David 1952- *208*
    Earlier sketch in SATA *122*
Elliott, Bruce
    See Field, Edward
Elliott, David 1947- *201*
    Earlier sketch in SATA *163*
Elliott, Don
    See Silverberg, Robert
Elliott, Elizabeth Shippen Green
    See Green, Elizabeth Shippen
Elliott, Janice 1931-1995 .... *119*
Elliott, Joey
    See Houk, Randy
Elliott, Laura Malone 1957- *197*
Elliott, L.M.
    See Elliott, Laura Malone
Elliott, Louise *111*
Elliott, Odette 1939- *75*
Elliott, Patricia 1946- *176*
Elliott, Sarah M(cCarn) 1930- *14*
Elliott, (Robert) Scott 1970- *153*
Elliott, William
    See Bradbury, Ray
Elliott, Zetta *206*
Ellis, (Mary) Amabel (Nassau Strachey)
    Williams
    See Williams-Ellis, (Mary) Amabel (Nassau
    Strachey)

Ellis, Anyon
    See Rowland-Entwistle, (Arthur) Theodore
    (Henry)
Ellis, Carson 1975- *190*
Ellis, Carson Friedman
    See Ellis, Carson
Ellis, Deborah 1960- *187*
    Earlier sketch in SATA *129*
Ellis, E. S.
    See Ellis, Edward S.
Ellis, Edward S. 1840-1916
    See YABC *1*
Ellis, Edward Sylvester
    See Ellis, Edward S.
Ellis, Ella Thorp 1928- *127*
    Earlier sketch in SATA *7*
    See also SAAS *9*
Ellis, Harry Bearse 1921-2004 .... *9*
Ellis, Herbert
    See Wilson, Lionel
Ellis, Mel(vin Richard) 1912-1984 .... *7*
    Obituary *39*
Ellis, Richard 1938- *130*
Ellis, Sarah 1952- *179*
    Earlier sketches in SATA *68, 131*
    See also CLR *42*
Ellison, Chris *196*
Ellison, Elizabeth Stow 1970- *209*
Ellison, Emily *114*
Ellison, Lucile Watkins 1907(?)-1979 .... *50*
    Obituary *22*
Ellison, Virginia H(owell) 1910- *4*
Ellsberg, Edward 1891-1983 .... *7*
Ellsworth, Loretta 1954- *199*
Ellsworth, Mary Ellen (Tressel) 1940- *146*
Elmer, Robert 1958- *154*
    Earlier sketch in SATA *99*
Elmore, (Carolyn) Patricia 1933- *38*
    Brief entry *35*
El-Moslimany, Ann P(axton) 1937- *90*
Elschner, Geraldine 1954- *183*
Elspeth
    See Bragdon, Elspeth MacDuffie
Elster, Jean Alicia 1953- *150*
Elting, Mary 1906- *88*
    Earlier sketch in SATA *2*
    See also SAAS *20*
Elvgren, Jennifer Riesmeyer *179*
Elwart, Joan Potter 1927- *2*
Elwood, Ann 1931- *55*
    Brief entry *52*
Elwood, Roger 1943-2007 .... *58*
Elya, Susan Middleton 1955- *202*
    Earlier sketches in SATA *106, 159*
Elzbieta *88*
Ember, Kathi *190*
Emberley, Barbara A. 1932- *146*
    Earlier sketches in SATA *8, 70*
    See also CLR *5*
Emberley, Barbara Anne
    See Emberley, Barbara A.
Emberley, Ed 1931- *146*
    Earlier sketches in SATA *8, 70*
    See also CLR *81*
Emberley, Edward Randolph
    See Emberley, Ed
Emberley, Michael 1960- *189*
    Earlier sketches in SATA *34, 80, 119*
Embry, Margaret Jacob 1919-1975 .... *5*
Emecheta, Buchi 1944- *66*
Emecheta, Florence Onye Buchi
    See Emecheta, Buchi
Emerson, Alice B.
    See Benson, Mildred
Emerson, Kathy Lynn 1947- *63*
Emerson, Kevin *209*
Emerson, Ru 1944- *107*
    Earlier sketch in SATA *70*
Emerson, Sally 1952- *111*
Emerson, William K(eith) 1925- *25*
Emert, Phyllis R(aybin) 1947- *93*

Emery, Anne (McGuigan) 1907- *33*
  Earlier sketch in SATA *1*
Emmens, Carol Ann 1944- *39*
Emmett, Jonathan 1965- *188*
  Earlier sketch in SATA *138*
Emmons, Della (Florence) Gould 1890-1983
  Obituary *39*
Emory, Jerry 1957- *96*
Emrich, Duncan (Black Macdonald)
  1908-1970(?) *11*
Emshwiller, Carol 1921- *174*
  Autobiography Feature *174*
Emshwiller, Carol Fries
  See Emshwiller, Carol
Emslie, M. L.
  See Simpson, Myrtle L(illias)
Ende, Michael (Andreas Helmuth)
  1929-1995 .... *130*
  Brief entry *42*
  Obituary *86*
  Earlier sketch in SATA *61*
  See also CLR *138*
Enderle, Dotti 1954- *203*
  Earlier sketch in SATA *145*
Enderle, Judith (Ann) Ross 1941- *89*
  Autobiography Feature *114*
  Earlier sketch in SATA *38*
  See also SAAS *26*
Endle, Kate *207*
Enell, Trinka (Gochenour) 1951- *79*
Enfield, Carrie
  See Smith, Susan Vernon
Engdahl, Sylvia Louise 1933- *4*
  Autobiography Feature *122*
  See also CLR *2*
  See also SAAS *5*
Engel, Diana 1947- *70*
Engelbreit, Mary 1952- *169*
Engelhart, Margaret S. 1924- *59*
Engelmann, Kim (V.) 1959- *87*
England, George Allan 1877-1936 .... *102*
Englart, Mindi Rose 1965- *146*
Engle, Eloise
  See Paananen, Eloise (Katherine)
Engle, Margarita 1951- *193*
Englebert, Victor 1933- *8*
English, James W(ilson) 1915- *37*
English, Karen *202*
Engstrom, Elizabeth 1951- *110*
Enright, D(ennis) J(oseph) 1920-2002 .... *25*
  Obituary *140*
Enright, Dominique *194*
Enright, Elizabeth (Wright) 1909-1968 .... *9*
  See also CLR *4*
Ensor, Barbara *180*
Ensor, Robert (T.) 1922- *93*
Enthoven, Sam 1974- *187*
Entwistle, (Arthur) Theodore (Henry) Rowland
  See Rowland-Entwistle, (Arthur) Theodore
  (Henry)
Enys, Sarah L.
  See Sloggett, Nellie
Epanya, Christian A(rthur Kingue) 1956- *91*
Ephraim, Shelly S(chonebaum) 1952- *97*
Ephron, Delia 1944- *197*
  Brief entry *50*
  Earlier sketch in SATA *65*
Epler, Doris M. 1928- *73*
Epp, Margaret A(gnes) 1913- *20*
Eppenstein, Louise (Kohn) 1892-1987
  Obituary *54*
Epple, Anne Orth 1927- *20*
Epstein, Anne Merrick 1931- *20*
Epstein, Beryl 1910- *31*
  Earlier sketch in SATA *1*
  See also CLR *26*
  See also SAAS *17*
Epstein, Beryl M. Williams
  See Epstein, Beryl
Epstein, Perle S(herry) 1938- *27*
Epstein, Rachel S. 1941- *102*

Epstein, Samuel 1909-2000 .... *31*
  Earlier sketch in SATA *1*
  See also CLR *26*
  See also SAAS *17*
Erdman, Loula Grace 1905(?)-1976 .... *1*
Erdoes, Richard 1912- *33*
  Brief entry *28*
Erdogan, Buket *187*
Erdrich, Karen Louise
  See Erdrich, Louise
Erdrich, Louise 1954- *141*
  Earlier sketch in SATA *94*
Erickson, Betty J. 1923- *97*
Erickson, Betty Jean
  See Erickson, Betty J.
Erickson, John R. 1943- *136*
  Earlier sketch in SATA *70*
Erickson, Jon 1948- *141*
Erickson, Phoebe *59*
Erickson, Russell E(verett) 1932- *27*
Erickson, Sabra Rollins 1912-1995 .... *35*
Erickson, Walter
  See Fast, Howard
Ericson, Walter
  See Fast, Howard
Ericsson, Jennifer A. *170*
Erikson, Mel 1937- *31*
Eriksson, Eva 1949- *207*
Ering, Timothy Basil *176*
Erlanger, Baba
  See Trahey, Jane
Erlbach, Arlene 1948- *160*
  Earlier sketches in SATA *78, 115*
Erlbruch, Wolf 1948- *181*
Erlich, Lillian (Feldman) 1910-1983 .... *10*
Erlings, Fridrik 1962- *196*
Erlingsson, Fri****rik
  See Erlings, Fridrik
Ermatinger, James W. 1959- *170*
Ernest, William
  See Berkebile, Fred D(onovan)
Ernst, (Lyman) John 1940- *39*
Ernst, Kathleen
  See Ernst, Kathleen A.
Ernst, Kathleen A. 1959- *162*
Ernst, Kathryn (Fitzgerald) 1942- *25*
Ernst, Lisa Campbell 1957- *154*
  Brief entry *44*
  Earlier sketches in SATA *55, 95*
Erskine, Kathryn *193*
Ervin, Janet Halliday 1923- *4*
Erwin, Will
  See Eisner, Will
Esbaum, Jill *174*
Esbensen, Barbara J(uster) 1925-1996 .... *97*
  Brief entry *53*
  Earlier sketch in SATA *62*
Eschbacher, Roger *160*
Eschmeyer, R. E. 1898-1989 .... *29*
Escriva, Vivi *182*
Eseki, Bruno
  See Mphahlele, Es'kia
Esekie, Bruno
  See Mphahlele, Es'kia
Eshmeyer, Reinhart Ernst
  See Eschmeyer, R. E.
Eskridge, Ann E. 1949- *84*
Espeland, Pamela (Lee) 1951- *128*
  Brief entry *38*
  Earlier sketch in SATA *52*
Espinosa, Laura *203*
Espinosa, Leo *203*
Espriella, Don Manuel Alvarez
  See Southey, Robert
Espy, Willard R(ichardson) 1910-1999 .... *38*
  Obituary *113*
Essakalli, Julie Klear *200*
Essrig, Harry 1912- *66*
Estep, Irene Compton *5*
Esterl, Arnica 1933- *77*

Estes, Eleanor (Ruth) 1906-1988 .... *91*
  Obituary *56*
  Earlier sketch in SATA *7*
  See also CLR *70*
Estoril, Jean
  See Allan, Mabel Esther
Estrada, Pau 1961- *200*
  Earlier sketch in SATA *74*
Etchemendy, Nancy 1952- *166*
  Earlier sketch in SATA *38*
Etchemendy, Nancy Elise Howell
  See Etchemendy, Nancy
Etchison, Birdie L(ee) 1937- *38*
Etchison, Craig 1945- *133*
Etherington, Frank 1945- *58*
Eton, Robert
  See Meynell, Laurence Walter
Ets, Marie Hall 1893-1984 .... *2*
  See also CLR *33*
Ettlinger, Doris 1950- *173*
Eunson, (John) Dale 1904-2002 .... *5*
  Obituary *132*
Evan, Frances Y. 1951- *167*
Evanoff, Vlad 1916- *59*
Evans, Cambria 1981- *178*
Evans, Douglas 1953- *144*
  Earlier sketch in SATA *93*
Evans, Eva (Knox) 1905-1998 .... *27*
Evans, Freddi Williams 1957- *134*
Evans, Greg 1947- *143*
  Earlier sketch in SATA *73*
Evans, Hubert Reginald 1892-1986 .... *118*
  Obituary *48*
Evans, Katherine (Floyd) 1901-1964 .... *5*
Evans, Larry
  See Evans, Laurence Chubb
Evans, Laurence Chubb 1939- *88*
Evans, Lawrence Watt
  See Watt-Evans, Lawrence
Evans, Lezlie *180*
Evans, Mari 1923- *10*
Evans, Mark *19*
Evans, Nancy 1950- *65*
Evans, Nate *201*
Evans, Patricia Healy
  See Carpenter, Patricia (Healy Evans)
Evans, (Alice) Pearl 1927- *83*
Evans, Shane W. *189*
Evans, Shirlee 1931- *58*
Evans, Tabor
  See Cameron, Lou
  and Knott, William C(ecil, Jr.)
  and Wallmann, Jeffrey M(iner)
  and Whittington, Harry (Benjamin)
Evarts, Esther
  See Benson, Sally
Evarts, Hal G., (Jr.) 1915-1989 .... *6*
Everett, Gail
  See Hale, Arlene
Evernden, Margery 1916- *5*
Eversole, Robyn 1971- *74*
Eversole, Robyn H.
  See Eversole, Robyn
Eversole, Robyn Harbert
  See Eversole, Robyn
Evslin, Bernard 1922-1993 .... *83*
  Brief entry *28*
  Obituary *77*
  Earlier sketch in SATA *45*
Ewart, Claire 1958- *145*
  Earlier sketch in SATA *76*
Ewart, Franzeska G. 1950- *205*
Ewen, David 1907-1985 .... *4*
  Obituary *47*
Ewing, Juliana (Horatia Gatty) 1841-1885 ... *16*
  See also CLR *78*
Ewing, Kathryn 1921- *20*
Eyerly, Jeannette 1908-2008 .... *86*
  Obituary *196*
  Earlier sketch in SATA *4*
  See also SAAS *10*

Eyerly, Jeannette Hyde
   See Eyerly, Jeannette
Eyre, Dorothy
   See McGuire, Leslie (Sarah)
Eyre, Frank 1910-1988
   Obituary 62
Eyre, Katherine Wigmore 1901-1970 26
Ezzell, Marilyn 1937- 42
   Brief entry 38

F

Fabe, Maxene 1943- 15
Faber, Doris (Greenberg) 1924- 78
   Earlier sketch in SATA 3
Faber, Harold 1919-2010 5
Fabre, Jean Henri (Casimir) 1823-1915 22
Fabry, Glenn 1961- 205
Facklam, Margaret
   See Thomas, Peggy
Facklam, Margery (Metz) 1927- 132
   Earlier sketches in SATA 20, 85
Fadden, David Kanietakeron 196
Fadiman, Clifton (Paul) 1904-1999 11
   Obituary 115
Fagan, Cary 1957- 186
Fahs, Sophia Blanche Lyon 1876-1978 102
Failing, Barbara Larmon 182
Fain, Sarah 1971- 204
Fair, David 1952- 96
Fair, Sylvia 1933- 13
Fairfax-Lucy, Brian (Fulke Cameron-Ramsay)
   1898-1974 6
   Obituary 26
Fairfield, Flora
   See Alcott, Louisa May
Fairlie, Gerard 1899-1983
   Obituary 34
Fairman, Joan A(lexandra) 1935- 10
Faithfull, Gail 1936- 8
Falcone, L(ucy) M. 1951- 155
Falconer, Ian 1959- 179
   Earlier sketch in SATA 125
   See also CLR 146
Falconer, James
   See Kirkup, James
Falconer, Lee N.
   See May, Julian
Falkner, Brian 1962- 206
Falkner, Leonard 1900-1977 12
Fall, Andrew
   See Arthur, Robert, (Jr.)
Fall, Thomas
   See Snow, Donald Clifford
Faller, Regis 1968- 187
Falls, C(harles) B(uckles) 1874-1960 38
   Brief entry 27
Falstein, Louis 1909-1995 37
Falwell, Cathryn 1952- 196
Fancher, Lou 1960- 177
Fanelli, Sara 1969- 126
   Earlier sketch in SATA 89
Fanning, Leonard M(ulliken) 1888-1967 5
Faralla, Dana 1909- 9
Faralla, Dorothy W.
   See Faralla, Dana
Farb, Peter 1929-1980 12
   Obituary 22
Farber, Norma 1909-1984 75
   Obituary 38
   Earlier sketch in SATA 25
Fardell, John 1967- 195
Farish, Terry 1947- 146
   Earlier sketch in SATA 82
Farjeon, (Eve) Annabel 1919-2004 11
   Obituary 153
Farjeon, Eleanor 1881-1965 2
   See also CLR 34

Farley, Carol (J.) 1936- 137
   Earlier sketch in SATA 4
Farley, Terri 165
Farley, Walter (Lorimer) 1915-1989 132
   Earlier sketches in SATA 2, 43
Farlow, James O(rville, Jr.) 1951- 75
Farmer, Nancy 1941- 161
   Earlier sketches in SATA 79, 117
Farmer, Patti 1948- 79
Farmer, Penelope (Jane) 1939- 105
   Brief entry 39
   Earlier sketch in SATA 40
   See also CLR 8
   See also SAAS 22
Farmer, Peter 1950- 38
Farmer, Philip Jose
   See Farmer, Philip Jose
Farmer, Philip Jose 1918-2009 93
   Obituary 201
Farmer, Philipe Jos
   See Farmer, Philip Jose
Farnham, Burt
   See Clifford, Harold B(urton)
Farnsworth, Bill 1958- 186
   Earlier sketches in SATA 84, 135
Farooqi, Musharraf Ali 1968- 207
Farquhar, Margaret C(utting) 1905-1988 13
Farquharson, Alexander 1944- 46
Farquharson, Martha
   See Finley, Martha
Farr, Diana 82
   Earlier sketch in SATA 3
Farr, Finis (King) 1904-1982 10
Farr, Richard 1960- 209
Farrar, Jill
   See Morris, Jill
Farrar, Susan Clement 1917- 33
Farrell, Ben
   See Cebulash, Mel
Farrell, John 1951- 204
Farrell, Patrick
   See Odgers, Sally Farrell
Farrell, Sally
   See Odgers, Sally Farrell
Farrer, Vashti 167
Farrington, Benjamin 1891-1974
   Obituary 20
Farrington, S(elwyn) Kip, Jr. 1904-1983 20
Farris, Christine King 1927- 206
Farshtey, Greg(ory T.) 1965- 148
Farthing, Alison 1936- 45
   Brief entry 36
Farthing-Knight, Catherine 1933- 92
Fassler, Joan (Grace) 1931- 11
Fast, Howard 1914-2003 7
   Autobiography Feature 107
Fast, Howard Melvin
   See Fast, Howard
Fasulo, Michael 1963- 83
Fatchen, Max 1920- 84
   Earlier sketch in SATA 20
   See also SAAS 20
Fate, Marilyn
   See Collins, Paul
Father Goose
   See Ghigna, Charles
Fatigati, (Frances) Evelyn 1948- 24
Fatio, Louise 1904-1993 6
Fatus, Sophie 1957- 182
Faulhaber, Martha 1926- 7
Faulkner, Anne Irvin 1906- 23
Faulkner, Frank
   See Ellis, Edward S.
Faulkner, Nancy
   See Faulkner, Anne Irvin
Faulknor, Cliff(ord Vernon) 1913- 86
Favole, Robert J(ames) 1950- 125
Fax, Elton Clay 1909-1993 25
Faxon, Lavinia
   See Russ, Lavinia (Faxon)
Feagles, Anita M(acRae) 1927- 9

Feagles, Elizabeth
   See Day, Beth (Feagles)
Feague, Mildred H. 1915- 14
Fearnley, Jan 1965- 205
   Earlier sketch in SATA 153
Fearrington, Ann (Peyton) 1945- 146
Fecher, Constance
   See Heaven, Constance (Christina)
Feder, Chris Welles 1938- 81
Feder, Harriet K. 1928- 73
Feder, Paula (Kurzband) 1935- 26
Federici, Debbie 1965- 175
Federici, Debbie Tanner
   See Federici, Debbie
Feelings, Muriel 1938- 16
   See also CLR 5
   See also SAAS 8
Feelings, Muriel Lavita Grey
   See Feelings, Muriel
Feelings, Thomas 1933-2003 69
   Obituary 148
   Earlier sketch in SATA 8
   See also CLR 58
   See also SAAS 19
Feelings, Tom
   See Feelings, Thomas
Fehler, Gene 1940- 201
   Earlier sketch in SATA 74
Fehrenbach, T(heodore) R(eed, Jr.) 1925- 33
Feiffer, Jules 1929- 201
   Earlier sketches in SATA 8, 61, 111, 157
Feiffer, Jules Ralph
   See Feiffer, Jules
Feiffer, Kate 1964- 206
   Earlier sketch in SATA 170
Feig, Barbara Krane 1937- 34
Feikema, Feike
   See Manfred, Frederick (Feikema)
Feil, Hila 1942- 12
Feilen, John
   See May, Julian
Feinberg, Barbara Jane 1938- 123
   Earlier sketch in SATA 58
Feinberg, Barbara Silberdick
   See Feinberg, Barbara Jane
Feinstein, John 1956- 195
   Earlier sketch in SATA 163
Feldman, Anne (Rodgers) 1939- 19
Feldman, Elane 79
Feldman, Jody 200
Felin, M. Sindy 194
Felix
   See Vincent, Felix
Fell, Derek 1939- 167
Fell, Derek John
   See Fell, Derek
Fellows, Julian 1950- 198
Fellows, Muriel H. 10
Fellows, Stan 1957- 177
Fellows, Stanley
   See Fellows, Stan
Felsen, Henry Gregor 1916-1995 1
   See also SAAS 2
Felstead, Cathie 1954- 192
Feltenstein, Arlene (H.) 1934- 119
Felton, Harold William 1902-1991 1
Felton, Ronald Oliver 1909- 3
Felts, Shirley 1934- 33
Fenderson, Lewis H., Jr. 1907-1983 47
   Obituary 37
Fenner, Carol (Elizabeth) 1929-2002 89
   Obituary 132
   Earlier sketch in SATA 7
   See also SAAS 24
Fenner, Phyllis R(eid) 1899-1982 1
   Obituary 29
Fensham, Elizabeth 169
Fenten, Barbara D(oris) 1935- 26
Fenten, D(onald) X. 1932- 4
Fenton, Carroll Lane 1900-1969 5

Fenton, Edward 1917-1995 7
    Obituary 89
Fenton, Mildred Adams 1899-1995 21
Fenwick, Patti
    See Grider, Dorothy
Feravolo, Rocco Vincent 1922- 10
Ferber, Brenda A. 1967- 184
Ferber, Edna 1887-1968 7
Fergus, Charles 114
Ferguson, Alane 1957- 182
    Earlier sketch in SATA 85
Ferguson, Bob
    See Ferguson, Robert Bruce
Ferguson, Cecil 1931- 45
Ferguson, Peter 1968- 199
Ferguson, Robert Bruce 1927-2001 13
Ferguson, Sarah 1959- 180
    Earlier sketches in SATA 66, 110
Ferguson, Sarah Margaret
    See Ferguson, Sarah
Ferguson, Walter (W.) 1930- 34
Fergusson, Erna 1888-1964 5
Fermi, Laura 1907-1977 6
    Obituary 28
Fern, Eugene A. 1919-1987 10
    Obituary 54
Fern, Tracey E. 202
Fernandes, Eugenie 1943- 205
    Earlier sketches in SATA 77, 139
Fernandez, Laura 1960- 171
Ferraiolo, Jack D. 208
Ferrari, Maria 123
Ferreiro, Carmen 1958- 158
Ferrell, Nancy Warren 1932- 70
Ferri, Giuliano 1965- 197
Ferrier, Lucy
    See Penzler, Otto
Ferris, Helen Josephine 1890-1969 21
Ferris, James Cody
    See McFarlane, Leslie
Ferris, Jean 1939- 202
    Brief entry 50
    Earlier sketches in SATA 56, 105, 149
Ferris, Jeri Chase 1937- 84
Ferry, Charles 1927- 92
    Earlier sketch in SATA 43
    See also CLR 34
    See also SAAS 20
Fetz, Ingrid 1915- 30
Feydy, Anne Lindbergh
    See Sapieyevski, Anne Lindbergh
Fiammenghi, Gioia 1929- 66
    Earlier sketch in SATA 9
Fiarotta, Noel
    See Ficarotta, Noel
Fiarotta, Phyllis
    See Ficarotta, Phyllis
Ficarotta, Noel 1944- 15
Ficarotta, Phyllis 1942- 15
Fichter, George S. 1922-1993 7
Ficocelli, Elizabeth 189
Fidler, Kathleen (Annie) 1899-1980 87
    Obituary 45
    Earlier sketch in SATA 3
Fiedler, Jean(nette Feldman) 4
Fiedler, Joseph Daniel 159
Fiedler, Lisa 185
Field, Dorothy 1944- 97
Field, Edward 1924- 109
    Earlier sketch in SATA 8
Field, Elinor Whitney 1889-1980
    Obituary 28
Field, Eugene 1850-1895 16
Field, Gans T.
    See Wellman, Manly Wade
Field, James 1959- 113
Field, Peter
    See Drago, Harry Sinclair
    and Dresser, Davis
    and Mann, E(dward) B(everly)

Field, Rachel (Lyman) 1894-1942 15
    See also CLR 21
Fielding, Kate
    See Oldfield, Jenny
Fields, Bryan W. 1958(?)- 188
Fields, Terri 1948- 191
Fields, T.S.
    See Fields, Terri
Fienberg, Anna 1956- 183
    Earlier sketch in SATA 112
Fiery, Ann
    See Barrows, Annie
Fife, Dale (Odile Hollerbach) 1901- 18
Fighter Pilot, A
    See Johnston, H(ugh) A(nthony) S(tephen)
Figler, Jeanie 1949- 123
Figley, Marty Rhodes 1948- 158
    Earlier sketch in SATA 88
Figueredo, D(anilo) H. 1951- 155
Figueroa, Pablo 1938- 9
Fijan, Carol 1918- 12
Filderman, Diane E(lizabeth) 1959- 87
Files, Meg 1946- 107
Fillmore, Parker H(oysted) 1878-1944
    See YABC 1
Filstrup, Chris
    See Filstrup, E(dward) Christian
Filstrup, E(dward) Christian 1942- 43
Filstrup, Janie
    See Merrill, Jane
Finchler, Judy 1943- 93
Finder, Martin
    See Salzmann, Siegmund
Findlay, Jamieson 1958- 169
Findon, Joanne 1957- 161
Fine, Anne 1947- 197
    Earlier sketches in SATA 29, 72, 111, 160
    See also CLR 25
    See also SAAS 15
Fine, Edith Hope 169
Fine, Howard 1961- 181
Fine, Jane
    See Ziefert, Harriet
Finger, Charles J(oseph) 1869(?)-1941 42
Fink, William B(ertrand) 1916- 22
Finke, Blythe Foote 1922- 26
Finkel, George (Irvine) 1909-1975 8
Finkelstein, Norman H. 1941- 137
    Earlier sketch in SATA 73
Finkelstein, Norman Henry
    See Finkelstein, Norman H.
Finlay, Alice Sullivan 1946- 82
Finlay, Winifred Lindsay Crawford
    (McKissack) 1910-1989 23
Finlayson, Ann 1925- 8
Finley, Martha 1828-1909 43
    See also CLR 148
Finley, Mary Peace 1942- 83
Finn, Mary 208
Finney, Jack 1911-1995 109
Finney, Patricia 1958- 163
Finney, Shan 1944- 65
Finney, Walter Braden
    See Finney, Jack
Firer, Ben Zion
    See Firer, Benzion
Firer, Benzion 1914- 64
Fireside, Bryna J. 1932- 73
Firmin, Charlotte 1954- 29
Firmin, Peter 1928- 58
    Earlier sketch in SATA 15
Firth, Barbara 179
Fischbach, Julius 1894-1988 10
Fischer, John
    See Fluke, Joanne
Fischer, R.J.
    See Fluke, Joanne
Fischer, Scott M. 1971- 195
Fischer-Nagel, Andreas 1951- 56
Fischer-Nagel, Heiderose 1956- 56
Fischler, Shirley (Walton) 66

Fischler, Stan(ley I.) 66
    Brief entry 36
Fischtrom, Harvey 1933-1974 3
Fishback, Margaret
    See Antolini, Margaret Fishback
Fishbone, Greg R. 195
Fisher, Aileen (Lucia) 1906-2002 73
    Obituary 143
    Earlier sketches in SATA 1, 25
    See also CLR 49
Fisher, Barbara 1940- 44
    Brief entry 34
Fisher, Carolyn 1968- 154
Fisher, Catherine 1957- 155
Fisher, Chris 1958- 80
Fisher, Clavin C(argill) 1912- 24
Fisher, Cynthia 195
Fisher, Dorothy (Frances) Canfield 1879-1958
    See YABC 1
    See also CLR 71
Fisher, Gary L. 1949- 86
Fisher, John 1909-1996 15
Fisher, John Oswald Hamilton
    See Fisher, John
Fisher, Laura Harrison 1934- 5
Fisher, Leonard Everett 1924- 176
    Autobiography Feature 122
    Earlier sketches in SATA 4, 34, 73, 120
    See also CLR 18
    See also SAAS 1
Fisher, Lois I. 1948- 38
    Brief entry 35
Fisher, Margery (Turner) 1913-1992 20
    Obituary 74
Fisher, Marshall Jon 1963- 113
Fisher, Nikki
    See Strachan, Ian
Fisher, Robert (Tempest) 1943- 47
Fisher, Suzanne
    See Staples, Suzanne Fisher
Fisher, Valorie 177
Fishman, Cathy Goldberg 1951- 106
Fisk, Nicholas
    See Higginbottom, David
Fisk, Pauline 1948- 160
    Earlier sketch in SATA 66
Fiske, Tarleton
    See Bloch, Robert (Albert)
Fisscher, Catharina G. M. 1958- 142
Fisscher, Tiny
    See Fisscher, Catharina G. M.
Fitch, Clarke
    See Sinclair, Upton
Fitch, John IV
    See Cormier, Robert
Fitch, Sheree 1956- 178
    Earlier sketch in SATA 108
Fitschen, Dale 1937- 20
Fitzalan, Roger
    See Trevor, Elleston
Fitzgerald, Captain Hugh
    See Baum, L. Frank
FitzGerald, Cathleen 1932-1987
    Obituary 50
Fitzgerald, Dawn 175
Fitzgerald, Edward Earl 1919-2001 20
Fitzgerald, F(rancis) A(nthony) 1940- 15
Fitzgerald, Joanne 1956- 198
Fitzgerald, John D(ennis) 1907(?)-1988 20
    Obituary 56
    See also CLR 1
Fitzgerald, Merni Ingrassia 1955- 53
Fitzgibbon, Terry 1948- 121
Fitzhardinge, Joan Margaret 1912- 73
    Earlier sketch in SATA 2
    See also CLR 5
    See also SAAS 3
Fitzhugh, Louise (Perkins) 1928-1974 45
    Obituary 24
    Earlier sketch in SATA 1
    See also CLR 72

Fitzhugh, Percy Keese 1876-1950 65
Fitzpatrick, Marie-Louise 1962- 189
  Earlier sketch in SATA 125
FitzRalph, Matthew
  See McInerny, Ralph
Fitz-Randolph, Jane (Currens) 1915- 51
Fitzsimons, Cecilia 1952- 97
Fitzsimons, Cecilia A.L.
  See Fitzsimons, Cecilia
Flack, Marjorie 1897-1958 100
  See also YABC 2
  See also CLR 28
Flack, Naomi John White -1999 40
  Brief entry 35
Flake, Sharon G. 166
Flanagan, John 1944- 180
Flanagan, John Anthony
  See Flanagan, John
Flannery, Kate
  See De Goldi, Kathleen Domenica
Flatt, Lizann 1966- 88
Fleagle, Gail S(hatto) 1940- 117
Fleetwood, Jenni 1947- 80
Fleischer, Jane
  See Oppenheim, Joanne
Fleischhauer-Hardt, Helga 1936- 30
Fleischman, Albert Sidney
  See Fleischman, Sid
Fleischman, John 1948- 145
Fleischman, Paul 1952- 156
  Brief entry 32
  Earlier sketches in SATA 39, 72, 110
  See also CLR 66
  See also SAAS 20
Fleischman, Sid 1920- 185
  Earlier sketches in SATA 8, 59, 96, 148
  See also CLR 15
Fleischner, Jennifer 1956- 188
  Earlier sketch in SATA 93
Fleisher, Paul 1948- 132
  Earlier sketch in SATA 81
Fleisher, Robbin 1951-1977 52
  Brief entry 49
Fleishman, Seymour 1918- 66
  Brief entry 32
Fleming, A. A.
  See Arthur, Robert, (Jr.)
Fleming, Alice Mulcahey 1928- 9
Fleming, Candace 1962- 190
  Earlier sketches in SATA 94, 143
Fleming, Denise 1950- 173
  Earlier sketches in SATA 81, 126
Fleming, Elizabeth P. 1888-1985
  Obituary 48
Fleming, Ian 1908-1964 9
Fleming, Ian Lancaster
  See Fleming, Ian
Fleming, Ronald Lee 1941- 56
Fleming, Sally
  See Walker, Sally M(acArt)
Fleming, Stuart
  See Knight, Damon (Francis)
Fleming, Susan 1932- 32
Fleming, Thomas 1927- 8
Fleming, Thomas James
  See Fleming, Thomas
Fleming, Virginia (Edwards) 1923- 84
Flesch, Y.
  See Flesch, Yolande (Catarina)
Flesch, Yolande (Catarina) 1950- 55
Fletcher, Charlie May Hogue 1897-1977 3
Fletcher, Colin 1922-2007 28
Fletcher, Dirk
  See Cunningham, Chet
Fletcher, George U.
  See Pratt, (Murray) Fletcher
Fletcher, Helen Jill 1910- 13
Fletcher, Ralph 1953- 195
  Earlier sketches in SATA 105, 149
  See also CLR 104

Fletcher, Ralph J.
  See Fletcher, Ralph
Fletcher, Richard E. 1917(?)-1983
  Obituary 34
Fletcher, Rick
  See Fletcher, Richard E.
Fletcher, Susan 1951- 181
  Earlier sketches in SATA 70, 110
Fletcher, Susan Clemens
  See Fletcher, Susan
Fleur, Paul
  See Pohl, Frederik
Flexner, James Thomas 1908-2003 9
Flinn, Alex 1966- 198
  Earlier sketch in SATA 159
Flint, Helen 1952- 102
Flint, Russ 1944- 74
Flitner, David P(erkins), Jr. 1949- 7
Floca, Brian 190
  Earlier sketch in SATA 155
Floethe, Louise Lee 1913-1988 4
Floethe, Richard 1901-1998 4
Floherty, John Joseph 1882-1964 25
Flood, Bo
  See Flood, Nancy Bo
Flood, Nancy Bo 1945- 130
Flood, Pansie Hart 1964- 140
Flood, William 1942- 129
Flooglebuckle, Al
  See Spiegelman, Art
Flora, James (Royer) 1914-1998 30
  Obituary 103
  Earlier sketch in SATA 1
  See also SAAS 6
Flores-Galbis, Enrique 1952- 186
Florian, Douglas 1950- 177
  Earlier sketches in SATA 19, 83, 125
Flory, Jane Trescott 1917- 22
Flournoy, Valerie 1952- 95
Flournoy, Valerie Rose
  See Flournoy, Valerie
Flowerdew, Phyllis -1994 33
Flowers, Pam 1946- 136
Flowers, Sarah 1952- 98
Floyd, Gareth 1940- 62
  Brief entry 31
Fluchere, Henri 1914-1991 40
Fluke, Joanne 1943- 88
Flutsztejn-Gruda, Ilona 1930- 170
Flynn, Barbara 1928- 9
Flynn, Jackson
  See Bensen, Donald R.
  and Shirreffs, Gordon D(onald)
Flynn, Nicholas
  See Odgers, Sally Farrell
Flynn, Rachel 1953- 171
  Earlier sketch in SATA 109
Flynn, Warren (G.) 1950- 154
Fodor, R(onald) V(ictor) 1944- 25
Fogelin, Adrian 1951- 175
  Earlier sketch in SATA 129
Foley, (Anna) Bernice Williams 1902-1987 . 28
Foley, Greg E. 1969- 190
Foley, June 1944- 44
Foley, (Mary) Louise Munro 1933- 106
  Brief entry 40
  Earlier sketch in SATA 54
Foley, Rae
  See Denniston, Elinore
Folke, Will
  See Bloch, Robert (Albert)
Follett, Helen Thomas 1884(?)-1970
  Obituary 27
Folsom, Franklin (Brewster) 1907-1995 5
  Obituary 88
Folsom, Michael (Brewster) 1938-1990 40
  Obituary 88
Fontenot, Mary Alice 1910-2003 91
  Obituary 209
  Earlier sketch in SATA 34
Fontes, Justine 172

Fontes, Ron 1952- 183
Foon, Dennis 1951- 119
Fooner, Michael 22
Foote, Timothy (Gilson) 1926- 52
Forberg, Ati
  See Forberg, Beate Gropius
Forberg, Beate Gropius 1925- 22
Forbes, Anna 1954- 101
Forbes, Bryan 1926- 37
Forbes, Cabot L.
  See Hoyt, Edwin P(almer), Jr.
Forbes, Esther 1891-1967 100
  Earlier sketch in SATA 2
  See also CLR 147
Forbes, Graham B. 1
Forbes, Kathryn
  See McLean, Kathryn (Anderson)
Forbes, Robert
  See Arthur, Robert, (Jr.)
Ford, Albert Lee
  See Stratemeyer, Edward L.
Ford, Barbara 56
  Brief entry 34
Ford, Brian J(ohn) 1939- 49
Ford, Carolyn (Mott) 1938- 98
Ford, Christine 1953- 176
Ford, David
  See Baldacci, David
  and Baldacci, David
Ford, David B.
  See Baldacci, David
Ford, David Baldacci
  See Baldacci, David
Ford, Elbur
  See Hibbert, Eleanor Alice Burford
Ford, Ellen 1949- 89
Ford, George (Jr.) 31
Ford, Hilary
  See Youd, Samuel
Ford, Hildegarde
  See Morrison, Velma Ford
Ford, Jerome W. 1949- 78
Ford, Jerry
  See Ford, Jerome W.
Ford, Juwanda G(ertrude) 1967- 102
Ford, Marcia
  See Radford, Ruby L(orraine)
Ford, Nancy K(effer) 1906-1961
  Obituary 29
Ford, Peter 1936- 59
Ford, S. M.
  See Uhlig, Susan
Forde, Catherine 1961- 170
Foreman, Mark 199
Foreman, Michael 1938- 184
  Earlier sketches in SATA 2, 73, 129, 135
  See also CLR 32
  See also SAAS 21
Foreman, Wilmoth 1939- 153
Forest, Antonia 1915-2003 29
  Obituary 149
Forest, Dial
  See Gault, William Campbell
Forest, Heather 1948- 185
  Earlier sketch in SATA 120
Forester, C. S. 1899-1966 13
Forester, Cecil Scott
  See Forester, C. S.
Forman, Brenda 1936- 4
Forman, James
  See Forman, James D.
Forman, James D. 1932- 70
  Earlier sketch in SATA 8
Forman, James Douglas
  See Forman, James D.
Forman, Ruth 1970- 186
Forrest, Elizabeth
  See Salsitz, Rhondi Vilott
Forrest, Mary
  See Pausacker, Jenny

Forrest, Sybil
　See Markun, Patricia Maloney
Forrestal, Elaine 1941- 165
　Earlier sketch in SATA 117
Forrester, Frank H. 1919(?)-1986
　Obituary 52
Forrester, Helen
　See Bhatia, Jamunadevi
Forrester, Jade
　See Pausacker, Jenny
Forrester, Marian
　See Schachtel, Roger
Forrester, Sandra 1949- 166
　Earlier sketch in SATA 90
Forrester, Victoria 1940- 40
　Brief entry 35
Forsee, (Frances) Aylesa -1986 1
Forsey, Chris 1950- 59
Forshay-Lunsford, Cin 1965- 60
Forster, E. M. 1879-1970 57
Forster, Edward Morgan
　See Forster, E. M.
Forsyth, Kate 1966- 154
Fort, Paul
　See Stockton, Francis Richard
Forte, Maurizio 1961- 110
Fortey, Richard 1946- 109
Fortey, Richard A.
　See Fortey, Richard
Fortey, Richard Alan
　See Fortey, Richard
Forth, Melissa D(eal) 96
Fortnum, Peggy
　See Nuttall-Smith, Margaret Emily Noel
Fortune, Eric 182
Forward, Robert L(ull) 1932-2002 82
Foster, Alan Dean 1946- 70
Foster, Brad W. 1955- 34
Foster, Doris Van Liew 1899-1993 10
Foster, E(lizabeth) C(onnell) 1902- 9
Foster, Elizabeth 1902- 12
Foster, Elizabeth 1905-1963 10
Foster, F. Blanche 1919- 11
Foster, G(eorge) Allen 1907-1969 26
Foster, Genevieve (Stump) 1893-1979 2
　Obituary 23
　See also CLR 7
Foster, Gerald L. 198
Foster, Hal
　See Foster, Harold
Foster, Harold 1892-1982 31
Foster, Jeanne
　See Williams, Jeanne
Foster, John
　See Foster, John L(ouis)
　and Furcolo, Foster
Foster, John (Thomas) 1925- 8
Foster, John L(ouis) 1941- 102
Foster, Juliana 196
Foster, Laura Louise (James) 1918- 6
Foster, Leila Merrell 1929- 73
Foster, Lynne 1937- 74
Foster, Margaret Lesser 1899(?)-1979
　Obituary 21
Foster, Marian Curtis 1909-1978 23
Foster, Mark 1961- 197
Foster, Sally 58
Fotheringham, Edwin 201
Foulds, E. V.
　See Foulds, Elfrida Vipont
Foulds, Elfrida Vipont 1902-1992 52
Fountas, Angela Jane 180
Fourie, Corlia 1944- 91
Fourth Brother, The
　See Aung, (Maung) Htin
Fowke, Edith (Margaret) 1913-1996 14
Fowles, John 1926-2005 22
　Obituary 171
Fowles, John Robert
　See Fowles, John
Fowles, Shelley 1956- 205

Fox, Aileen 1907-2005 58
　Obituary 170
Fox, Aileen Mary
　See Fox, Aileen
Fox, Annie 1950- 175
Fox, Charles Philip 1913-2003 12
　Obituary 150
Fox, Christyan 188
Fox, Diane 188
Fox, Eleanor
　See St. John, Wylly Folk
Fox, Fontaine Talbot, Jr. 1884-1964
　Obituary 23
Fox, Fred 1903(?)-1981
　Obituary 27
Fox, Freeman
　See Hamilton, Charles (Harold St. John)
Fox, Geoffrey 1941- 73
Fox, Grace
　See Anderson, Grace Fox
Fox, Helen 1962- 181
Fox, Larry 30
Fox, Lorraine 1922-1976 27
　Earlier sketch in SATA 11
Fox, Louisa
　See Kroll, Virginia L.
Fox, Mary Virginia 1919- 152
　Brief entry 39
　Earlier sketches in SATA 44, 88
Fox, Mem
　See Fox, Merrion Frances
Fox, Merrion Frances 1946- 155
　Earlier sketches in SATA 51, 103
　See also CLR 80
Fox, Michael W(ilson) 1937- 15
Fox, Norma Diane
　See Mazer, Norma Fox
Fox, Paula 1923- 167
　Earlier sketches in SATA 17, 60, 120
　See also CLR 96
Fox, Robert J. 1927- 33
Fox-Davies, Sarah 1956- 199
Foyt, Victoria .... 187.
Fradin, Dennis
　See Fradin, Dennis Brindell
Fradin, Dennis Brindell 1945- 185
　Earlier sketches in SATA 29, 90, 135
Fradin, Judith Bloom 1945- 185
　Earlier sketches in SATA 90, 152
Frailey, Paige (Menefee) 1965- 82
Frame, Janet 1924-2004 119
Frame, Paul 1913-1994 60
　Brief entry 33
　Obituary 83
Frances, Miss
　See Horwich, Frances R(appaport)
Franchere, Ruth 18
Francis, Charles
　See Holme, Bryan
Francis, Dee
　See Haas, Dorothy F.
Francis, Dorothy 1926- 127
　Earlier sketch in SATA 10
Francis, Dorothy B.
　See Francis, Dorothy
Francis, Dorothy Brenner
　See Francis, Dorothy
Francis, Jaye
　See Pausacker, Jenny
Francis, Pamela (Mary) 1926- 11
Franck, Eddie
　See Cooke, Frank E.
Franco, Betsy 188
　Earlier sketch in SATA 150
Franco, Eloise (Bauder) 1910- 62
Franco, Johan (Henri Gustave) 1908-1988 ... 62
Franco, Marjorie 38
Francois, Andre 1915-2005 25
Francoise
　See Seignobosc, Francoise

Frank, Anne 1929-1945 87
　Brief entry 42
　See also CLR 101
Frank, Annelies Marie
　See Frank, Anne
Frank, Daniel B. 1956- 55
Frank, Emily R.
　See Frank, E.R.
Frank, E.R. 1967- 157
Frank, Helene
　See Vautier, Ghislaine
Frank, Hillary 1976- 148
Frank, John 199
Frank, Josette 1893-1989 10
　Obituary 63
Frank, Lucy 1947- 166
　Earlier sketch in SATA 94
Frank, Mary 1933- 34
Frank, R., Jr.
　See Ross, Frank (Xavier), Jr.
Frankau, Mary Evelyn Atkinson 1899-1974 .. 4
Frankel, Alona 1937- 66
Frankel, Bernice 9
Frankel, Edward 1910- 44
Frankel, Ellen 1951- 78
Frankel, Julie 1947- 40
　Brief entry 34
Frankenberg, Robert 1911- 22
Frankland, David 207
Franklin, Cheryl J. 1955- 70
Franklin, Harold 1926- 13
Franklin, Kristine L. 1958- 124
　Earlier sketch in SATA 80
Franklin, Lance
　See Lantz, Francess L(in)
Franklin, Madeleine
　See L'Engle, Madeleine
Franklin, Madeleine L'Engle
　See L'Engle, Madeleine
Franklin, Madeleine L'Engle Camp
　See L'Engle, Madeleine
Franklin, Max
　See Deming, Richard
Franklin, Steve
　See Stevens, Franklin
Franson, Leanne R. 1963- 111
Franson, Scott E. 1966- 192
Franzen, Nils-Olof 1916- 10
Frascino, Edward 48
　Brief entry 33
　See also SAAS 9
Frasconi, Antonio 1919- 131
　Earlier sketches in SATA 6, 53
　See also SAAS 11
Fraser, Betty
　See Fraser, Elizabeth Marr
Fraser, Elizabeth Marr 1928- 31
Fraser, Eric (George) 1902-1983 38
Fraser, Mary Ann 1959- 137
　Earlier sketch in SATA 76
　See also SAAS 23
Fraser, Wynnette (McFaddin) 1925- 90
Frasier, Debra 1953- 182
　Earlier sketches in SATA 69, 112
Fraustino, Lisa Rowe 1961- 146
　Autobiography Feature 146
　Earlier sketch in SATA 84
Frazee, Marla 1958- 187
　Earlier sketches in SATA 105, 151
Frazetta, Frank 1928- 58
Frazier, Craig 1955- 177
Frazier, Neta (Osborn) Lohnes 1890-1990 7
Frazier, Sundee T. 1968- 198
Frazier, Sundee Tucker
　See Frazier, Sundee T.
Frederic, Mike
　See Cox, William R(obert)
Frederick, Heather Vogel 207
Fredericks, Anthony D. 1947- 113
Freed, Alvyn M. 1913-1993 22
Freedman, Benedict 1919- 27

Freedman, Claire *185*
Freedman, Deborah 1960- *191*
Freedman, Jeff 1953- *90*
Freedman, Nancy 1920- *27*
Freedman, Russell 1929- *175*
  Earlier sketches in SATA *16, 71, 123*
  See also CLR *71*
Freedman, Russell Bruce
  See Freedman, Russell
Freeman, Barbara C. 1906-1999 .... *28*
Freeman, Barbara Constance
  See Freeman, Barbara C.
Freeman, Bill
  See Freeman, William Bradford
Freeman, Don 1908-1978 .... *17*
  See also CLR *90*
Freeman, Ira Maximilian 1905-1987 .... *21*
Freeman, Kimberley
  See Wilkins, Kim
Freeman, Laura *200*
Freeman, Lucy (Greenbaum) 1916-2004 ...... *24*
Freeman, Mae 1907-1985 .... *25*
Freeman, Mae Blacker
  See Freeman, Mae
Freeman, Marcia S. 1937- *102*
Freeman, Martha 1956- *201*
  Earlier sketches in SATA *101, 152*
Freeman, Nancy 1932- *61*
Freeman, Peter J.
  See Calvert, Patricia
Freeman, Sarah (Caroline) 1940- *66*
Freeman, Tor 1977- *164*
Freeman, VicToria
  See Freeman, Tor
Freeman, William Bradford 1938- *58*
  Brief entry *48*
Fregosi, Claudia (Anne Marie) 1946- *24*
Freitas, Donna 1972- *205*
French, Allen 1870-1946
  See YABC *1*
French, Dorothy Kayser 1926- *5*
French, Fiona 1944- *132*
  Earlier sketches in SATA *6, 75*
  See also CLR *37*
  See also SAAS *21*
French, Jackie *186*
  Autobiography Feature *139*
  Earlier sketches in SATA *108, 139*
  See French, Jackie Anne
  and French, Jacqueline Anne
French, Kathryn
  See Mosesson, Gloria R(ubin)
French, Martin *176*
French, Michael 1944- *49*
  Brief entry *38*
French, Paul
  See Asimov, Isaac
French, Simon 1957- *147*
  Earlier sketch in SATA *86*
French, Vivian *209*
  Earlier sketch in SATA *165*
Frenette, Liza *126*
Freschet, Gina 1960- *175*
  Earlier sketch in SATA *139*
Frewer, Glyn (M.) 1931- *11*
Frey, Darcy *98*
Freymann, Saxton 1958(?)- *178*
Freymann-Weyr, (Rhoda) Garret (Michaela)
  1965- *145*
Frick, C. H.
  See Irwin, Constance (H.) Frick
Frick, Constance
  See Irwin, Constance (H.) Frick
Fricke, Aaron 1962- *89*
Fridell, Ron 1943- *124*
Fried, Janice *197*
Friedlander, Joanne K(ohn) 1930- *9*
Friedman, Aimee 1979- *189*
Friedman, D. Dina 1957- *180*
Friedman, Debra 1955- *150*
Friedman, Estelle (Ehrenwald) 1920- *7*

Friedman, Frieda 1905- *43*
Friedman, Ina R(osen) 1926- *136*
  Brief entry *41*
  Earlier sketch in SATA *49*
Friedman, Jerrold David
  See Gerrold, David
Friedman, Judi 1935- *59*
Friedman, Laurie 1964- *179*
  Earlier sketch in SATA *138*
Friedman, Marvin 1930- *42*
  Brief entry *33*
Friedman, Robin 1968- *162*
Friedmann, Stan 1953- *80*
Friedrich, Otto (Alva) 1929-1995 .... *33*
Friedrich, Priscilla 1927- *39*
Friend, Catherine 1957(?)- *194*
Friend, David Michael 1975- *195*
Friend, Natasha 1972- *184*
Friendlich, Dick
  See Friendlich, Richard J.
Friendlich, Richard J. 1909- *11*
Friermood, Elisabeth Hamilton 1903-1992 .... *5*
Friesen, Bernice (Sarah Anne) 1966- *105*
Friesen, Gayle 1960- *200*
  Earlier sketch in SATA *109*
Friesen, Jonathan 1967(?)- *206*
Friesner, Esther 1951- *207*
  Earlier sketches in SATA *71, 168*
Friesner, Esther M.
  See Friesner, Esther
Friis-Baastad, Babbis Ellinor 1921-1970 .... *7*
Frimmer, Steven 1928- *31*
Frischmuth, Barbara 1941- *114*
Friskey, Margaret (Richards) 1901-1995 .... *5*
Fritts, Mary Bahr
  See Bahr, Mary (Madelyn)
Fritz, Jean (Guttery) 1915- *163*
  Autobiography Feature *122*
  Earlier sketches in SATA *1, 29, 72, 119*
  See also CLR *96*
  See also SAAS *2*
Froehlich, Margaret W(alden) 1930- *56*
Frois, Jeanne 1953- *73*
Froissart, Jean 1338(?)-1410(?) *28*
Froman, Elizabeth Hull 1920-1975 .... *10*
Froman, Robert (Winslow) 1917- *8*
Fromm, Lilo 1928- *29*
Frommer, Harvey 1937- *41*
Frost, A(rthur) B(urdett) 1851-1928 .... *19*
Frost, Elizabeth
  See Frost-Knappman, Elizabeth
Frost, Erica
  See Supraner, Robyn
Frost, Helen 1949- *194*
  Autobiography Feature *194*
  Earlier sketches in SATA *157, 183*
Frost, Helen Marie
  See Frost, Helen
Frost, Lesley 1899-1983 .... *14*
  Obituary *34*
Frost, Robert 1874-1963 .... *14*
  See also CLR *67*
Frost, Robert Lee
  See Frost, Robert
Frost, Shelley 1960- *138*
Frost-Knappman, Elizabeth 1943- *179*
Froud, Brian 1947- *150*
Fry, Annette R(iley) *89*
Fry, Christopher 1907-2005 .... *66*
Fry, Edward Bernard 1925- *35*
Fry, Rosalie Kingsmill 1911-1992 .... *3*
  See also SAAS *11*
Fry, Virginia Lynn 1952- *95*
Frye, Sally
  See Moore, Elaine
Fuchs, Bernie 1932- *162*
  Earlier sketch in SATA *95*
Fuchs, Erich 1916- *6*
Fuchshuber, Annegert 1940- *43*
Fuerst, Jeffrey B. 1956- *143*
Fuertes, Gloria 1918-1998 .... *115*

Fuge, Charles 1966- *144*
  Earlier sketch in SATA *74*
Fujikawa, Gyo 1908-1998 .... *76*
  Brief entry *30*
  Obituary *110*
  Earlier sketch in SATA *39*
  See also CLR *25*
  See also SAAS *16*
Fujita, Tamao 1905-1999 .... *7*
Fujiwara, Kim 1957- *81*
Fujiwara, Michiko 1946- *15*
Fuka, Vladimir 1926-1977
  Obituary *27*
Fulcher, Jennifer
  See Westwood, Jennifer
Fuller, Catherine Leuthold 1916- *9*
Fuller, Edmund (Maybank) 1914- *21*
Fuller, Iola
  See McCoy, Iola Fuller
Fuller, John G(rant, Jr.) 1913-1990 .... *65*
Fuller, Kathleen
  See Gottfried, Theodore Mark
Fuller, Lois Hamilton 1915- *11*
Fuller, Margaret 1810-1850 .... *25*
Fuller, Maud
  See Petersham, Maud
Fuller, Roy (Broadbent) 1912-1991 .... *87*
Fuller, Sarah Margaret
  See Fuller, Margaret
Fults, John Lee 1932- *33*
Funk, Thompson 1911- *7*
Funk, Tom
  See Funk, Thompson
Funke, Cornelia 1958- *209*
  Earlier sketches in SATA *154, 174*
  See also CLR *145*
Funke, Cornelia Caroline
  See Funke, Cornelia
Funke, Lewis 1912-1992 .... *11*
Fuqua, Jonathon Scott 1966- *141*
Furbee, Mary R.
  See Furbee, Mary Rodd
Furbee, Mary Rodd 1954- *138*
Furchgott, Terry 1948- *29*
Furlong, Monica (Mavis) 1930-2003 .... *86*
  Obituary *142*
Furman, Gertrude Lerner Kerman 1909- *21*
Furniss, Tim 1948- *49*
Furrow, Robert 1985- *172*
Furukawa, Toshi 1924- *24*
Fusillo, Archimede 1962- *137*
Futcher, Jane P. 1947- *76*
Futehali, Zahida
  See Whitaker, Zai
Fyleman, Rose (Amy) 1877-1957 .... *21*
Fyson, Jenny Grace
  See Fyson, J.G.
Fyson, J.G. 1904-1998 .... *42*

G

Gaan, Margaret 1914- *65*
Gaber, Susan 1956- *169*
  Earlier sketch in SATA *115*
Gaberman, Judie Angell
  See Angell, Judie
Gabhart, Ann
  See Gabhart, Ann H.
Gabhart, Ann H. 1947- *75*
Gable, Brian 1949- *195*
Gabler, Mirko 1951- *77*
Gabriel, Adriana
  See Rojany, Lisa
Gabrys, Ingrid Schubert
  See Schubert-Gabrys, Ingrid
Gackenbach, Dick 1927- *79*
  Brief entry *30*
  Earlier sketch in SATA *48*
Gadd, Jeremy 1949- *116*

Gaddis, Vincent H. 1913-1997 35
Gadler, Steve J. 1905-1985 36
Gaeddert, Lou Ann (Bigge) 1931- 103
  Earlier sketch in SATA 20
Gaeddert, Louann
  See Gaeddert, Lou Ann (Bigge)
Gaer, Joseph 1897-1969 118
Gaer, Yossef
  See Gaer, Joseph
Gaetz, Dayle Campbell 1947- 138
Gaffney, Timothy R. 1951- 170
  Earlier sketch in SATA 69
Gaffron, Norma (Bondeson) 1931- 97
Gag, Flavia 1907-1979
  Obituary 24
Gag, Wanda (Hazel) 1893-1946 100
  See also YABC 1
  See also CLR 150
Gage, Brian 162
Gage, Wilson
  See Steele, Mary Q(uintard Govan)
Gagliano, Eugene M. 1946- 150
Gagliardo, Ruth Garver 1895(?)-1980
  Obituary 22
Gagnon, Cecile 1936- 58
Gaillard, Jason 1965- 200
Gaiman, Neil 1960- 197
  Earlier sketches in SATA 85, 146
  See also CLR 109
Gaiman, Neil Richard
  See Gaiman, Neil
Gainer, Cindy 1962- 74
Gaines, Ernest J. 1933- 86
  See also CLR 62
Gaines, Ernest James
  See Gaines, Ernest J.
Gaither, Gloria 1942- 127
Gal, Laszlo 1933- 96
  Brief entry 32
  Earlier sketch in SATA 52
  See also CLR 61
Galbraith, Ben 1980- 200
Galbraith, Kathryn O(sebold) 1945- 85
Galdone, Paul 1907(?)-1986 66
  Obituary 49
  Earlier sketch in SATA 17
  See also CLR 16
Galindo, Claudia 1979- 203
Galinsky, Ellen 1942- 23
Gall, Chris 1961- 176
Gallagher, Diana G. 1946- 153
Gallagher, Lurlene Nora
  See McDaniel, Lurlene
Gallagher-Cole, Mernie 1958- 206
Gallant, Roy A(rthur) 1924- 110
  Earlier sketches in SATA 4, 68
  See also CLR 30
Gallardo, Evelyn 1948- 78
Gallaz, Christophe 1948- 162
  See also CLR 126
Gallego Garcia, Laura 1977- 173
Gallico, Paul (William) 1897-1976 13
Gallo, Donald R. 1938- 112
  Autobiography Feature 104
Gallo, Donald Robert
  See Gallo, Donald R.
Galloway, Owateka (S.) 1981- 121
Galloway, Priscilla 1930- 112
  Earlier sketch in SATA 66
Gallup, Joan 1957- 128
Galouchko, Annouchka Gravel 1960- 95
Galt, Thomas Franklin, Jr. 1908-1989 5
Galt, Tom
  See Galt, Thomas Franklin, Jr.
Galvin, Matthew R. 1950- 93
Galvin, Matthew Reppert
  See Galvin, Matthew R.
Gamble, Kim 1952- 183
  Earlier sketches in SATA 81, 124
Gambrell, Jamey 82
Gamerman, Martha 1941- 15

Gammell, Stephen 1943- 128
  Earlier sketches in SATA 53, 81
  See also CLR 83
Ganly, Helen (Mary) 1940- 56
Gannett, Ruth Chrisman (Arens)
  1896-1979 33
Gannett, Ruth Stiles 1923- 3
Gannij, Joan 208
Gannij, Joan Levine
  See Gannij, Joan
Gannon, Ned 1974- 205
Gannon, Robert Haines 1931- 8
Gano, Lila 1949- 76
Gans, Roma 1894-1996 45
  Obituary 93
Gant, Matthew
  See Hano, Arnold
Gantner, Susan (Verble) 1939- 63
Gantos, Jack 1951- 169
  Earlier sketches in SATA 20, 81, 119
  See also CLR 85
Gantos, John Bryan, Jr.
  See Gantos, Jack
Ganz, Yaffa 1938- 61
  Brief entry 52
Garafano, Marie 1942- 84
Garant, Andre J. 1968- 123
Garbe, Ruth Moore
  See Moore, Ruth (Ellen)
Garber, Esther
  See Lee, Tanith
Garcia, Cristina 1958- 208
Garcia, Emma 1969- 198
Garcia, Yolanda P. 1952- 113
Garcia, Yolanda Pacheco
  See Garcia, Yolanda P.
Gard, Janice
  See Latham, Jean Lee
Gard, Joyce
  See Reeves, Joyce
Gard, Robert Edward 1910-1992 18
  Obituary 74
Gard, (Sanford) Wayne 1899-1986
  Obituary 49
Gardam, Jane 1928- 130
  Brief entry 28
  Earlier sketches in SATA 39, 76
  See also CLR 12
  See also SAAS 9
Gardam, Jane Mary
  See Gardam, Jane
Gardella, Tricia 1944- 96
Garden, Nancy 1938- 147
  Autobiography Feature 147
  Earlier sketches in SATA 12, 77, 114
  See also CLR 51
  See also SAAS 8
Gardiner, John Reynolds 1944-2006 64
  Obituary 174
Gardiner, Lindsey 1971- 144
Gardner, Craig Shaw 1949- 99
Gardner, Dic
  See Gardner, Richard (M.)
Gardner, Graham 159
Gardner, Hugh 1910-1986
  Obituary 49
Gardner, Jane Mylum 1946- 83
Gardner, Jeanne LeMonnier 1925- 5
Gardner, John, Jr. 1933-1982 40
  Obituary 31
Gardner, John Champlin, Jr.
  See Gardner, John, Jr.
Gardner, John E(dward) 1917- 192
Gardner, Lyn 192
Gardner, Martin 1914- 142
  Earlier sketch in SATA 16
Gardner, Miriam
  See Bradley, Marion Zimmer
Gardner, Richard (M.) 1931- 24
Gardner, Richard A(lan) 1931-2003 13
  Obituary 144

Gardner, Sally 177
Gardner, Sandra 1940- 70
Gardner, Scot 1968- 143
Gardner, Sheldon 1934- 33
Gardner, Ted
  See Gardner, Theodore Roosevelt II
Gardner, Theodore Roosevelt
  See Gardner, Theodore Roosevelt II
Gardner, Theodore Roosevelt II 1934- 84
Garelick, May 1910-1989 19
Garfield, James B. 1881-1984 6
  Obituary 38
Garfield, Leon 1921-1996 76
  Obituary 90
  Earlier sketches in SATA 1, 32
  See also CLR 21
Garfinkle, Debra L.
  See Garfinkle, D.L.
Garfinkle, D.L. 187
Garis, Howard R. 1873-1962 13
Garis, Howard Roger
  See Garis, Howard R.
Garland, Mark 1953- 79
Garland, Mark A.
  See Garland, Mark
Garland, Michael 1952- 208
  Earlier sketch in SATA 168
Garland, Sarah 1944- 135
  Earlier sketch in SATA 62
Garland, Sherry 1948- 145
  Autobiography Feature 145
  Earlier sketches in SATA 73, 114
Garner, Alan 1934- 69
  Autobiography Feature 108
  Earlier sketch in SATA 18
  See also CLR 130
Garner, David 1958- 78
Garner, Eleanor Ramrath 1930- 122
Garner, James Finn 1960(?)- 92
Garnet, A. H.
  See Slote, Alfred
Garnett, Eve C. R. 1900-1991 3
  Obituary 70
Garofoli, Viviana 1970- 186
Garou, Louis P.
  See Bowkett, Stephen
Garraty, John A. 1920-2007 23
  Obituary 189
Garraty, John Arthur
  See Garraty, John A.
Garren, Devorah-Leah
  See Devorah-Leah
Garret, Maxwell R. 1917- 39
Garretson, Victoria Diane 1945- 44
Garrett, Helen 1895- 21
Garrett, Randall 1927-1987 180
Garrett, Richard 1920- 82
Garrigue, Sheila 1931- 21
Garrison, Barbara 1931- 163
  Earlier sketch in SATA 19
Garrison, Frederick
  See Sinclair, Upton
Garrison, Mary 1952- 146
Garrison, Peter
  See Gardner, Craig Shaw
Garrison, Webb B(lack) 1919-2000 25
Garrity, Jennifer Johnson 1961- 124
Garrity, Linda K. 1947- 128
Garsee, Jeannine 199
Garst, Doris Shannon 1894-1981 1
Garst, Shannon
  See Garst, Doris Shannon
Garth, Will
  See Hamilton, Edmond
  and Kuttner, Henry
Garthwaite, Marion H(ook) 1893-1981 7
Garton, Malinda D(ean) (?)-1976
  Obituary 26
Garvie, Maureen 1944- 175
Garvie, Maureen McCallum
  See Garvie, Maureen

Garza, Carmen Lomas 1948- *182*
Garza, Xavier *184*
Gascoigne, Bamber 1935- *62*
Gaskins, Pearl Fuyo 1957- *134*
Gasperini, Jim 1952- *54*
  Brief entry *49*
Gater, Dilys 1944- *41*
Gates, Doris 1901-1987 .... *34*
  Obituary *54*
  Earlier sketch in SATA *1*
  See also SAAS *1*
Gates, Frieda 1933- *26*
Gates, Susan 1950- *153*
Gates, Viola R. 1931- *101*
Gathorne-Hardy, Jonathan G. 1933- *124*
  Earlier sketch in SATA *26*
Gatti, Anne 1952- *103*
Gatty, Juliana Horatia
  See Ewing, Juliana (Horatia Gatty)
Gauch, Patricia Lee 1934- *80*
  Earlier sketch in SATA *26*
  See also CLR *56*
  See also SAAS *21*
Gaudasinska, Elzbieta 1943- *190*
Gaul, Randy 1959- *63*
Gault, Clare 1925- *36*
Gault, Frank 1926-1982 .... *36*
  Brief entry *30*
Gault, William Campbell 1910-1995 .... *8*
Gauthier, Gail 1953- *203*
  Earlier sketches in SATA *118, 160*
Gaver, Becky
  See Gaver, Rebecca
Gaver, Rebecca 1952- *20*
Gavin, Jamila 1941- *125*
  Earlier sketch in SATA *96*
Gay, Amelia
  See Hogarth, Grace (Weston Allen)
Gay, Francis
  See Gee, H(erbert) L(eslie)
Gay, Kathlyn 1930- *144*
  Earlier sketch in SATA *9*
Gay, Marie-Louise 1952- *179*
  Earlier sketches in SATA *68, 126*
  See also CLR *27*
  See also SAAS *21*
Gay, Michel 1947- *162*
Gay, Zhenya 1906-1978 .... *19*
Gaze, Gillian
  See Barklem, Jill
Gear, Kathleen M. O'Neal
  See Gear, Kathleen O'Neal
Gear, Kathleen O'Neal 1954- *166*
  Earlier sketch in SATA *71*
Gear, W. Michael 1955- *166*
  Earlier sketch in SATA *71*
Geary, Rick 1946- *142*
Geason, Susan 1946- *122*
Gedalof, Robin
  See McGrath, Robin
Gedge, Pauline (Alice) 1945- *101*
Gee, H(erbert) L(eslie) 1901-1977
  Obituary *26*
Gee, Maurice 1931- *101*
  Earlier sketch in SATA *46*
  See also CLR *56*
Gee, Maurice Gough
  See Gee, Maurice
Geehan, Wayne (E.) 1947- *107*
Geer, Charles 1922- *42*
  Brief entry *32*
Geeslin, Campbell 1925- *163*
  Earlier sketch in SATA *107*
Gehman, Mary W. 1923- *86*
Gehr, Mary 1910(?)-1997 .... *32*
  Obituary *99*
Geipel, Eileen 1932- *30*
Geis, Alissa Imre 1976- *189*
Geis, Darlene Stern 1918(?)-1999 .... *7*
  Obituary *111*
Geisel, Helen 1898-1967 .... *26*

Geisel, Theodor Seuss
  See Dr. Seuss
Geisert, Arthur 1941- *171*
  Brief entry *52*
  Earlier sketches in SATA *56, 92, 133*
  See also CLR *87*
  See also SAAS *23*
Geisert, Arthur Frederick
  See Geisert, Arthur
Geisert, Bonnie 1942- *165*
  Earlier sketch in SATA *92*
Geist, Ken *191*
Geldart, William 1936- *15*
Gelinas, Paul J. 1904-1996 .... *10*
Gellis, Roberta 1927- *128*
Gellis, Roberta Leah Jacobs
  See Gellis, Roberta
Gellman, Marc *112*
Gelman, Amy 1961- *72*
Gelman, Jan 1963- *58*
Gelman, Rita Golden 1937- *131*
  Brief entry *51*
  Earlier sketch in SATA *84*
Gelman, Steve 1934- *3*
Gemming, Elizabeth 1932- *11*
Gendel, Evelyn W. 1916(?)-1977
  Obituary *27*
Gennaro, Joseph F(rancis), Jr. 1924- *53*
Gentieu, Penny *204*
Gentile, Petrina 1969- *91*
Gentle, Mary 1956- *48*
Gentleman, David (William) 1930- *7*
Geoghegan, Adrienne 1962- *143*
George, Barbara
  See Katz, Bobbi
George, Emily
  See Katz, Bobbi
George, Gail
  See Katz, Bobbi
George, Jean
  See George, Jean Craighead
George, Jean C.
  See George, Jean Craighead
George, Jean Craighead 1919- *170*
  Earlier sketches in SATA *2, 68, 124*
  See also CLR *136*
George, John L(othar) 1916- *2*
George, Kristine O'Connell 1954- *156*
  Earlier sketch in SATA *110*
George, Lindsay Barrett 1952- *206*
  Earlier sketches in SATA *95, 155*
George, S(idney) C(harles) 1898- *11*
George, Sally
  See Orr, Wendy
George, Twig C. 1950- *114*
George, W(illiam) Lloyd 1900(?)-1975
  Obituary *30*
Georgiou, Constantine 1927- *7*
Georgiou, Theo
  See Odgers, Sally Farrell
Geraghty, Paul 1959- *130*
Gerard, Jean Ignace Isidore 1803-1847 .... *45*
Geras, Adele 1944- *180*
  Autobiography Feature *180*
  Earlier sketches in SATA *23, 87, 129, 173*
  See also SAAS *21*
Geras, Adele Daphne Weston
  See Geras, Adele
Gerber, Carole 1947- *207*
Gerber, Merrill Joan 1938- *170*
  Autobiography Feature *170*
  Earlier sketches in SATA *64, 127*
Gerber, Perren 1933- *104*
Gerberg, Mort 1931- *64*
Gergely, Tibor 1900-1978 .... *54*
  Obituary *20*
Geringer, Laura 1948- *164*
  Earlier sketches in SATA *29, 94*
Gerler, William R(obert) 1917-1996 .... *47*
Gerrard, Jean 1933- *51*

Gerrard, Roy 1935-1997 .... *90*
  Brief entry *45*
  Obituary *99*
  Earlier sketch in SATA *47*
  See also CLR *23*
Gerritsen, Paula 1956- *177*
Gerrold, David 1944- *144*
  Earlier sketch in SATA *66*
Gershator, David 1937- *180*
Gershator, Phillis 1942- *188*
  Earlier sketches in SATA *90, 158*
Gershon, Dann 1955- *187*
Gershon, Gina 1962- *187*
Gerson, Corinne 1927- *37*
Gerson, Mary-Joan *136*
  Earlier sketch in SATA *79*
Gerson, Noel Bertram 1914-1988 .... *22*
  Obituary *60*
Gerstein, Mordicai 1935- *178*
  Brief entry *36*
  Earlier sketches in SATA *47, 81, 142*
  See also CLR *102*
Gertridge, Allison 1967- *132*
Gervais, Bernadette 1959- *80*
Gervay, Susanne *183*
Gesner, Clark 1938-2002 .... *40*
  Obituary *143*
Gessner, Lynne 1919- *16*
Geter, Tyrone *150*
Getz, David 1957- *91*
Getzinger, Donna 1968- *128*
Geus, Mireille 1964- *207*
Gevirtz, Eliezer 1950- *49*
Gevry, Claudine *188*
Gewe, Raddory
  See Gorey, Edward (St. John)
Ghan, Linda (R.) 1947- *77*
Ghent, Natale 1962- *148*
Gherman, Beverly 1934- *123*
  Earlier sketch in SATA *68*
Ghigna, Charles 1946- *153*
  Earlier sketch in SATA *108*
Giacobbe, Beppe 1953- *174*
Giambastiani, Kurt R. A. 1958- *141*
Giannini, Enzo 1946- *68*
Gibala-Broxholm, Scott 1959(?)- *205*
Gibbons, Alan 1953- *198*
  Earlier sketch in SATA *124*
Gibbons, Faye 1938- *103*
  Earlier sketch in SATA *65*
Gibbons, Gail 1944- *201*
  Earlier sketches in SATA *23, 72, 104, 160*
  See also CLR *8*
  See also SAAS *12*
Gibbons, Gail Gretchen
  See Gibbons, Gail
Gibbons, Kaye 1960- *117*
Gibbs, Adrea 1960- *126*
Gibbs, Alonzo (Lawrence) 1915-1992 .... *5*
Gibbs, (Cecilia) May 1877-1969
  Obituary *27*
Gibbs, Tony
  See Gibbs, Wolcott, Jr.
Gibbs, Wolcott, Jr. 1935- *40*
Giblin, James Cross 1933- *197*
  Earlier sketches in SATA *33, 75, 122*
  See also CLR *29*
  See also SAAS *12*
Gibson, Andrew (William) 1949- *72*
Gibson, Barbara L. *205*
Gibson, Barbara Leonard
  See Gibson, Barbara L.
Gibson, Betty 1911- *75*
Gibson, Jo
  See Fluke, Joanne
Gibson, Josephine
  See Hine, Sesyle Joslin
  and Hine, Al(fred Blakelee)
Gibson, William 1914-2008 .... *66*
  Obituary *199*

Gibson, William Ford
    See Gibson, William
Gidal, Nachum
    See Gidal, Tim Nachum
Gidal, Sonia (Epstein) 1922- 2
Gidal, Tim Nachum 1909-1996 2
Gidalewitsch, Nachum
    See Gidal, Tim Nachum
Gideon, Melanie 1963- 175
Giegling, John A(llan) 1935- 17
Gifaldi, David 1950- 209
    Earlier sketch in SATA 76
Giff, Patricia Reilly 1935- 203
    Earlier sketches in SATA 33, 70, 121, 160
Giffard, Hannah 1962- 83
Gifford, Clive 1966- 198
Gifford, Griselda 1931- 171
    Earlier sketch in SATA 42
Gifford, Kerri 1961- 91
Gifford, Peggy 1952- 191
Gilbert, Ann
    See Taylor, Ann
Gilbert, Anne Yvonne 1951- 185
Gilbert, Barbara Snow 1954- 97
Gilbert, Catherine
    See Murdock, Catherine Gilbert
Gilbert, Frances
    See Collings, Gillian
Gilbert, Harriett 1948- 30
Gilbert, (Agnes) Joan (Sewell) 1931- 10
Gilbert, John (Raphael) 1926- 36
Gilbert, Nan
    See Gilbertson, Mildred Geiger
Gilbert, Roby Goodale 1966- 90
Gilbert, Ruth Gallard Ainsworth
    See Ainsworth, Ruth (Gallard)
Gilbert, Sara (Dulaney) 1943- 82
    Earlier sketch in SATA 11
Gilbert, Sheri L. 157
Gilbert, Suzie 1956- 97
Gilbert, W(illiam) S(chwenck) 1836-1911 ... 36
Gilbert, Yvonne
    See Gilbert, Anne Yvonne
Gilbertson, Mildred Geiger 1908-1988 2
Gilbreath, Alice 1921- 12
Gilbreth, Frank B., Jr. 1911-2001 2
Gilbreth, Frank Bunker
    See Gilbreth, Frank B., Jr.
Gilchrist, Jan Spivey 1949- 130
    Earlier sketch in SATA 72
Gilden, Mel 1947- 97
Giles, Gail 196
    Earlier sketch in SATA 152
Gilfond, Henry 2
Gilge, Jeanette 1924- 22
Gili, Phillida 1944- 70
Gill, Derek (Lewis Theodore) 1919-1997 9
Gill, Margery Jean 1925- 22
Gill, Shelley 176
Gill, Stephen 1932- 63
Gillespie, Carol Ann 1951- 158
Gillett, Mary (Bledsoe) 7
Gillette, Henry Sampson 1915- 14
Gillette, J(an) Lynett 1946- 103
Gilley, Jeremy 1969- 174
Gillham, Bill
    See Gillham, W(illiam) E(dwin) C(harles)
Gillham, W(illiam) E(dwin) C(harles)
    1936- 42
Gilliam, Stan 1946- 39
    Brief entry 35
Gilliland, Alexis A(rnaldus) 1931- 72
Gilliland, (Cleburne) Hap 1918- 92
Gilliland, Judith Heide 180
Gillmor, Don 1954- 127
Gilman, Dorothy 1923- 5
Gilman, Esther 1925- 15
Gilman, Laura Anne 178
Gilman, Phoebe 1940-2002 104
    Obituary 141
    Earlier sketch in SATA 58

Gilmore, Iris 1900-1982 22
Gilmore, Kate 1931- 87
Gilmore, Mary (Jean Cameron) 1865-1962 . 49
Gilmore, Rachna 1953- 209
Gilmore, Susan 1954- 59
Gilpin, Stephen 177
Gilroy, Beryl (Agatha) 1924- 80
Gilson, Barbara
    See Gilson, Charles James Louis
Gilson, Charles James Louis 1878-1943
    See YABC 2
Gilson, Jamie 1933- 176
    Brief entry 34
    Earlier sketches in SATA 37, 91
Ginsburg, Mirra 1909-2000 92
    Earlier sketch in SATA 6
    See also CLR 45
Giovanni, Nikki 1943- 208
    Earlier sketches in SATA 24, 107
    See also CLR 73
Giovanni, Yolanda Cornelia
    See Giovanni, Nikki
Giovanni, Yolande Cornelia
    See Giovanni, Nikki
Giovanni, Yolande Cornelia, Jr.
    See Giovanni, Nikki
Giovanopoulos, Paul (Arthur) 1939- 7
Gipson, Billie
    See Letts, Billie
Gipson, Fred(erick Benjamin) 1908-1973 2
    Obituary 24
Girard, Linda (Walvoord) 1942- 41
Girion, Barbara 1937- 78
    Earlier sketch in SATA 26
    See also SAAS 14
Girl, Nerdy
    See Castellucci, Cecil
Girouard, Patrick 1957- 155
Girzone, Joseph F. 1930- 76
Girzone, Joseph Francis
    See Girzone, Joseph F.
Gise, Joanne
    See Mattern, Joanne
Gist, E.M. 206
Gittings, Jo (Grenville) Manton 1919- 3
Gittings, Robert (William Victor) 1911-1992 . 6
    Obituary 70
Givens, Janet E(aton) 1932- 60
Givner, Joan 1936- 171
Givner, Joan Mary
    See Givner, Joan
Gladstone, Eve
    See Werner, Herma
Gladstone, Gary 1935- 12
Gladstone, M(yron) J. 1923- 37
Glanville, Brian (Lester) 1931- 42
Glanzman, Louis S. 1922- 36
Glaser, Byron 1954- 154
Glaser, Dianne E(lizabeth) 1937- 50
    Brief entry 31
Glaser, Isabel Joshlin 1929- 94
Glaser, Milton 1929- 151
    Earlier sketch in SATA 11
Glaser, Shirley 151
Glaspell, Susan 1882(?)-1948
    See YABC 2
Glass, Andrew 1949- 150
    Brief entry 46
    Earlier sketch in SATA 90
Glass, Linzi 175
Glass, Linzi Alex
    See Glass, Linzi
Glasscock, Amnesia
    See Steinbeck, John
Glassman, Bruce 1961- 76
Glauber, Uta (Heil) 1936- 17
Glazer, Thomas (Zachariah) 1914-2003 9
Glazer, Tom
    See Glazer, Thomas (Zachariah)
Gleasner, Diana (Cottle) 1936- 29
Gleason, Judith 1929- 24

Gleason, Katherine (A.) 1960- 104
Gleeson, Libby 1950- 142
    Autobiography Feature 142
    Earlier sketches in SATA 82, 118
Gleiter, Jan 1947- 111
Gleitzman, Morris 1953- 156
    Earlier sketch in SATA 88
    See also CLR 88
Glen, Maggie 1944- 88
Glendinning, Richard 1917-1988 24
Glendinning, Sally
    See Glendinning, Sara W(ilson)
Glendinning, Sara W(ilson) 1913-1993 24
Glenn, John W. 195
Glenn, Mel 1943- 93
    Brief entry 45
    Earlier sketch in SATA 51
    See also CLR 51
Glenn, Patricia Brown 1953- 86
Glenn, Sharlee 159
Glenn, Sharlee Mullins
    See Glenn, Sharlee
Glennon, Karen M. 1946- 85
Gles, Margaret Breitmaier 1940- 22
Glick, Carl (Cannon) 1890-1971 14
Glick, Ruth (Burtnick) 1942- 125
Glick, Virginia Kirkus 1893-1980
    Obituary 23
Gliewe, Unada (Grace) 1927- 3
Glimmerveen, Ulco 1958- 85
Glines, Carroll V(ane), Jr. 1920- 19
Gliori, Debi 1959- 189
    Earlier sketches in SATA 72, 138
Globe, Leah Ain 1900- 41
Glori Ann
    See Blakely, Gloria
Glovach, Linda 1947- 105
    Earlier sketch in SATA 7
Glover, Denis (James Matthews) 1912-1980 . 7
Glubok, Shirley (Astor) 146
    Autobiography Feature 146
    Earlier sketches in SATA 6, 68
    See also CLR 1
    See also SAAS 7
Gluck, Felix 1923-1981
    Obituary 25
Glyman, Caroline A. 1967- 103
Glynne-Jones, William 1907-1977 11
Gobbato, Imero 1923- 39
Gobbletree, Richard
    See Quackenbush, Robert M(ead)
Goble, Dorothy 26
Goble, Paul 1933- 131
    Earlier sketches in SATA 25, 69
    See also CLR 21
Goble, Warwick (?)-1943 46
Godden, (Margaret) Rumer 1907-1998 36
    Obituary 109
    Earlier sketch in SATA 3
    See also CLR 20
    See also SAAS 12
Gode, Alexander
    See Gode von Aesch, Alexander (Gottfried
    Friedrich)
Gode von Aesch, Alexander (Gottfried
    Friedrich) 1906-1970 14
Godfrey, Jane
    See Bowden, Joan Chase
Godfrey, Martyn
    See Godfrey, Martyn N.
    and Godfrey, Martyn N.
Godfrey, Martyn N. 1949-2000 95
    See also CLR 57
Godfrey, William
    See Youd, Samuel
Godkin, Celia (Marilyn) 1948- 145
    Earlier sketch in SATA 66
Godon, Ingrid 1958- 186
Godwin, Laura 1956- 179
Godwin, Sam
    See Pirotta, Saviour

Goede, Irene 1966- 208
Goedecke, Christopher (John) 1951- 81
Goekler, Susan
    See Wooley, Susan Frelick
Goembel, Ponder 204
Goertzen, Glenda 172
Goettel, Elinor 1930- 12
Goetz, Delia 1898-1996 22
    Obituary 91
Goffe, Toni 1936- 61
Goffstein, Brooke
    See Goffstein, M(arilyn) B(rooke)
Goffstein, M(arilyn) B(rooke) 1940- 70
    Earlier sketch in SATA 8
    See also CLR 3
Goforth, Ellen
    See Francis, Dorothy
Gogol, Sara 1948-2004 80
Goh, Chan Hon 1969- 145
Going, Kelly L.
    See Going, K.L.
Going, Kelly Louise
    See Going, K.L.
Going, K.L. 199
    Earlier sketch in SATA 156
Golann, Cecil Paige 1921-1995 11
Golbin, Andree 1923- 15
Gold, Alison Leslie 1945- 104
Gold, Bernice 150
Gold, Phyllis
    See Goldberg, Phyllis
Gold, Robert S(tanley) 1924- 63
Gold, Sharlya 9
Gold, Susan
    See Gold, Susan Dudley
Gold, Susan Dudley 1949- 147
Goldberg, Grace 1956- 78
Goldberg, Herbert S. 1926- 25
Goldberg, Jacob 1943- 94
Goldberg, Jake
    See Goldberg, Jacob
Goldberg, Phyllis 1941- 21
Goldberg, Stan J. 1939- 26
Goldberg, Susan 1948- 71
Goldberg, Whoopi 1955- 119
Goldberger, Judith M. 1948- 80
Goldblatt, Stacey 1969(?)- 191
Golden, Christie 1963- 167
    Earlier sketch in SATA 116
Goldentyer, Debra 1960- 84
Goldfeder, Cheryl
    See Pahz, Cheryl Suzanne
Goldfeder, James
    See Pahz, James Alon
Goldfeder, Jim
    See Pahz, James Alon
Goldfinger, Jennifer P. 1963- 185
Goldfrank, Helen Colodny 1912- 6
Goldin, Augusta 1906-1999 13
Goldin, Barbara Diamond 1946- 129
    Autobiography Feature 129
    Earlier sketch in SATA 92
    See also SAAS 26
Goldin, David 1963- 101
Golding, Julia 1969- 188
Golding, Theresa Martin 1960- 150
Golding, William 1911-1993
    See CLR 130
Golding, William Gerald
    See Golding, William
Goldman, Alex J. 1917- 65
Goldman, Arthur Steven
    See Goldman, Steven
Goldman, E(leanor) M(aureen) 1943- 103
Goldman, Elizabeth 1949- 90
Goldman, Steven 1964- 207
Goldring, Ann 1937- 149
Goldsborough, June 1923- 19
Goldschmidt, Judy 202
Goldsmith, Connie 1945- 147

Goldsmith, Howard 1943- 108
    Earlier sketch in SATA 24
Goldsmith, John Herman Thorburn 1903-1987
    Obituary 52
Goldsmith, Oliver 1730(?)-1774 26
Goldsmith, Ruth M. 1919- 62
Goldstein, Nathan 1927- 47
Goldstein, Philip 1910-1997 23
Goldston, Robert (Conroy) 1927- 6
Goldstone, Bruce 183
Goldstone, Lawrence A.
    See Treat, Lawrence
Goldszmit, Henryk 1878-1942 65
Golembe, Carla 1951- 79
Golenbock, Peter 1946- 99
Goll, Reinhold W(eimar) 1897-1993 26
Gollub, Matthew 1960- 134
    Earlier sketch in SATA 83
Gomes, Filomena 1965- 183
Gomez, Elena 191
Gomez, Elizabeth 133
Gomez-Freer, Elizabeth
    See Gomez, Elizabeth
Gomi, Taro 1945- 103
    Earlier sketch in SATA 64
    See also CLR 57
Gondosch, Linda 1944- 58
Gonsalves, Rob 1959- 209
Gonyea, Mark 194
Gonzalez, Catherine Troxell 1917-2000 87
Gonzalez, Christina
    See Gonzalez, Maya Christina
Gonzalez, Gloria 1940- 23
Gonzalez, Julie 1958- 174
Gonzalez, Julie Sehers
    See Gonzalez, Julie
Gonzalez, Lucia M. 1957- 202
Gonzalez, Maya
    See Gonzalez, Maya Christina
Gonzalez, Maya Christina 1964- 175
    Earlier sketch in SATA 115
Gonzalez, Rigoberto 1970- 147
Goobie, Beth 1959- 128
Good, Alice 1950- 73
Good, Clare
    See Romano, Clare
Goodall, Daphne Machin
    See Machin Goodall, Daphne (Edith)
Goodall, Jane 1934- 111
Goodall, John S(trickland) 1908-1996 66
    Obituary 91
    Earlier sketch in SATA 4
    See also CLR 25
Goodbody, Slim
    See Burstein, John
Goode, Diane 1949- 170
    Earlier sketches in SATA 15, 84, 114
Goode, Diane Capuozzo
    See Goode, Diane
Goode, Stephen Ray 1943- 55
    Brief entry 40
Goodenow, Earle 1913- 40
Goodhart, Pippa 1958- 196
    Earlier sketch in SATA 153
Goodhue, Thomas W. 1949- 143
Goodin, Sallie (Brown) 1953- 74
Goodman, Alison 1966- 111
Goodman, Deborah Lerme 1956- 50
    Brief entry 49
Goodman, Elaine 1930- 9
Goodman, Joan Elizabeth 1950- 162
    Earlier sketches in SATA 50, 94
Goodman, Susan E. 1952- 181
Goodman, Walter 1927-2002 9
Goodrich, Samuel Griswold 1793-1860 23
Goodsell, Jane Neuberger 1921(?)-1988
    Obituary 56
GoodWeather, Hartley
    See King, Thomas
Goodweather, Hartley
    See King, Thomas

Goodwin, Hal
    See Goodwin, Harold L(eland)
Goodwin, Harold L(eland) 1914-1990 51
    Obituary 65
    Earlier sketch in SATA 13
Goodwin, William 1943- 117
Goor, Nancy (Ruth Miller) 1944- 39
    Brief entry 34
Goor, Ron(ald Stephen) 1940- 39
    Brief entry 34
Goossen, Agnes
    See Epp, Margaret A(gnes)
Goossens, Philippe 1963- 195
Gootman, Marilyn E. 1944- 179
Gopnik, Adam 1956- 171
Gorbachev, Valeri 1944- 184
    Autobiography Feature 143
    Earlier sketches in SATA 98, 143
Gordion, Mark
    See Turtledove, Harry
Gordon, Ad
    See Hano, Arnold
Gordon, Amy 1949- 197
    Earlier sketches in SATA 115, 156
Gordon, Bernard Ludwig 1931- 27
Gordon, Colonel H. R.
    See Ellis, Edward S.
Gordon, David
    See Garrett, Randall
Gordon, Donald
    See Payne, Donald Gordon
Gordon, Dorothy 1893-1970 20
Gordon, Esther S(aranga) 1935- 10
Gordon, Frederick 1
Gordon, Gaelyn 1939-1997
    See CLR 75
Gordon, Garrett
    See Garrett, Randall
Gordon, Gary
    See Edmonds, I(vy) G(ordon)
Gordon, Hal
    See Goodwin, Harold L(eland)
Gordon, Jeffie Ross
    See Enderle, Judith (Ann) Ross
    and Gordon, Stephanie Jacob
Gordon, John
    See Gesner, Clark
Gordon, John (William) 1925- 84
Gordon, Lew
    See Baldwin, Gordon C(ortis)
Gordon, Margaret (Anna) 1939- 9
Gordon, Mike 1948- 101
Gordon, Mildred 1912-1979
    Obituary 24
Gordon, Selma
    See Lanes, Selma Gordon
Gordon, Sheila 1927- 88
    See also CLR 27
Gordon, Shirley 1921- 48
    Brief entry 41
Gordon, Sol 1923- 11
Gordon, Stephanie Jacob 1940- 89
    Autobiography Feature 114
    Earlier sketch in SATA 64
    See also SAAS 26
Gordon, Stewart
    See Shirreffs, Gordon D(onald)
Gordons, The
    See Gordon, Mildred
    and Gordon, Gordon
Gore, Leonid 185
Gorelick, Molly C(hernow) 1920-2003 9
    Obituary 153
Gorey, Edward (St. John) 1925-2000 70
    Brief entry 27
    Obituary 118
    Earlier sketch in SATA 29
    See also CLR 36
Gorham, Charles Orson 1868-1936 36
Gorham, Michael
    See Folsom, Franklin (Brewster)

Gorman, Carol 187
  Earlier sketch in SATA 150
Gorman, Jacqueline Laks 1955- 148
Gorman, Mike 206
Gormley, Beatrice 1942- 202
  Brief entry 35
  Earlier sketches in SATA 39, 127
Gorog, Judith (Katharine Allen) 1938- 75
  Earlier sketch in SATA 39
Gorrell, Gena K. 1946- 170
Gorsline, Douglas (Warner) 1913-1985 11
  Obituary 43
Gorsline, (Sally) Marie 1928- 28
Gorsline, S. M.
  See Gorsline, (Sally) Marie
Gorton, Kaitlyn
  See Emerson, Kathy Lynn
Gorton, Kathy Lynn
  See Emerson, Kathy Lynn
Goryan, Sirak
  See Saroyan, William
Goschke, Julia 1973- 208
Goscinny, Rene 1926-1977 47
  Brief entry 39
  See also CLR 37
Goss, Clay(ton E.) 1946- 82
Goss, Gary 1947- 124
Goss, Mini 1963- 186
Goto, Scott 203
Gott, Barry 197
Gottesman, S. D.
  See Kornbluth, C(yril) M.
  and Lowndes, Robert A(ugustine) W(ard)
  and Pohl, Frederik
Gottfried, Ted
  See Gottfried, Theodore Mark
Gottfried, Theodore Mark 1928- 150
  Earlier sketch in SATA 85
Gottlieb, Gerald 1923- 7
Gottlieb, William P. 1917-2006 24
Gottlieb, William Paul
  See Gottlieb, William P.
Goudey, Alice E(dwards) 1898-1993 20
Goudge, Eileen 1950- 88
Goudge, Elizabeth (de Beauchamp)
  1900-1984 2
  Obituary 38
  See also CLR 94
Gough, Catherine
  See Mulgan, Catherine
Gough, Philip 1908-1986 45
Gough, Sue 1940- 106
Goulart, Ron 1933- 67
  Earlier sketch in SATA 1
Goulart, Ronald Joseph
  See Goulart, Ron
Gould, Alberta 1945- 96
Gould, Chester 1900-1985 49
  Obituary 43
Gould, Jean R(osalind) 1909-1993 11
  Obituary 77
Gould, Lilian 6
Gould, Marilyn 1928- 76
  Earlier sketch in SATA 15
Gould, Robert 154
Gould, Steven 1955- 95
Gould, Steven Charles
  See Gould, Steven
Gourley, Catherine 1950- 190
  Earlier sketch in SATA 95
Gourse, Leslie 1939-2004 89
Govan, (Mary) Christine Noble 1898-1985 ... 9
Gove, Doris 1944- 72
Govenar, Alan 1952- 189
Govenar, Alan Bruce
  See Govenar, Alan
Govern, Elaine 1939- 26
Gowen, L. Kris 1968- 156
Graaf, Peter
  See Youd, Samuel

Graber, Alexander 1914-1997 98
  Earlier sketch in SATA 7
Graber, George Alexander
  See Graber, Alexander
Graber, Janet 1942- 170
Graber, Richard (Fredrick) 1927- 26
Grabianski, Janusz 1928-1976 39
  Obituary 30
Graboff, Abner 1919-1986 35
Grace, Fran(ces Jane) 45
Grace, N.B.
  See Harper, Suzanne
Grace, Theresa
  See Mattern, Joanne
Gracza, Margaret Young 1928- 56
Graduate of Oxford, A
  See Ruskin, John
Grady, Denise 1952- 189
Graeber, Charlotte Towner 106
  Brief entry 44
  Earlier sketch in SATA 56
Graef, Renee 1956- 204
Graeme, Roderic
  See Jeffries, Roderic
Graf, Michael
  See Graf, Mike
Graf, Mike 1960- 164
Grafe, Max 198
Graff, Lisa 1981- 188
Graff, Polly Anne Colver
  See Colver, Anne
Graff, (S.) Stewart 1908- 9
Graham, Ada 1931- 11
Graham, Alastair 1945- 74
Graham, Arthur Kennon
  See Harrison, David L.
Graham, Bob 1942- 187
  Earlier sketches in SATA 63, 101, 151
  See also CLR 31
Graham, Brenda Knight 1942- 32
Graham, Charlotte
  See Bowden, Joan Chase
Graham, Eleanor 1896-1984 18
  Obituary 38
Graham, Ennis
  See Molesworth, Mary Louisa
Graham, Frank, Jr. 1925- 11
Graham, Georgia 1959- 190
Graham, Ian 1953- 112
Graham, John 1926-2007 11
Graham, Kennon
  See Harrison, David L.
Graham, Larry
  See Graham, Lawrence
Graham, Lawrence 1962- 63
Graham, Lawrence Otis
  See Graham, Lawrence
Graham, Linda
  See Graham-Barber, Lynda
Graham, Lorenz (Bell) 1902-1989 74
  Obituary 63
  Earlier sketch in SATA 2
  See also CLR 10
  See also SAAS 5
Graham, Margaret Bloy 1920- 11
Graham, Robin Lee 1949- 7
Graham, Shirley 1896(?)-1977
  See Du Bois, Shirley Graham
Graham-Barber, Lynda 1944- 159
  Earlier sketch in SATA 42
Graham-Cameron, M.
  See Graham-Cameron, M(alcolm) G(ordon)
Graham-Cameron, M(alcolm) G(ordon)
  1931- 53
  Brief entry 45
Graham-Cameron, Mike
  See Graham-Cameron, M(alcolm) G(ordon)
Grahame, Kenneth 1859-1932 100
  See also YABC 1
  See also CLR 135
Gralley, Jean 166

Gramatky, Hardie 1907-1979 30
  Obituary 23
  Earlier sketch in SATA 1
  See also CLR 22
Grambling, Lois G. 1927- 206
  Earlier sketches in SATA 71, 148
Grambo, Rebecca L(ynn) 1963- 109
Grammer, June Amos 1927- 58
Grand, Samuel 1912-1988 42
Grandits, John 1949- 192
GrandPre, Mary 1954- 184
Grandville, J. J.
  See Gerard, Jean Ignace Isidore
Grandville, Jean Ignace Isidore Gerard
  See Gerard, Jean Ignace Isidore
Granfield, Linda 1950- 160
  Earlier sketch in SATA 96
Grange, Peter
  See Nicole, Christopher (Robin)
Granger, Margaret Jane 1925(?)-1977
  Obituary 27
Granger, Michele 1949- 88
Granger, Peggy
  See Granger, Margaret Jane
Granowsky, Alvin 1936- 101
Granstaff, Bill 1925- 10
Granstrom, Brita 1969- 167
  Earlier sketch in SATA 111
Grant, Bruce 1893-1977 5
  Obituary 25
Grant, Cynthia D. 1950- 147
  Earlier sketches in SATA 33, 77
Grant, Eva 1907-1996 7
Grant, Evva H. 1913-1977
  Obituary 27
Grant, Gordon 1875-1962 25
Grant, Gwen(doline Ellen) 1940- 47
Grant, Katie M.
  See Grant, K.M.
Grant, K.M. 175
Grant, (Alice) Leigh 1947- 10
Grant, Matthew G.
  See May, Julian
Grant, Maxwell
  See Gibson, Walter B(rown)
  and Lynds, Dennis
Grant, Melvyn 183
Grant, Myrna (Lois) 1934- 21
Grant, Neil 1938- 154
  Earlier sketch in SATA 14
Grant, Nicholas
  See Nicole, Christopher (Robin)
Grant, Richard 1948- 80
Grant, Skeeter
  See Spiegelman, Art
Grater, Michael 1923- 57
Gravel, Fern
  See Hall, James Norman
Gravelle, Karen 1942- 166
  Earlier sketch in SATA 78
Graves, Charles Parlin 1911-1972 4
Graves, Keith 191
  Earlier sketch in SATA 156
Graves, Robert 1895-1985 45
Graves, Robert von Ranke
  See Graves, Robert
Graves, Valerie
  See Bradley, Marion Zimmer
Gravett, Emily 1972(?)- 189
Gray, Betsy
  See Poole, Gray Johnson
Gray, Caroline
  See Nicole, Christopher (Robin)
Gray, Dianne E. 183
Gray, Elizabeth Janet
  See Vining, Elizabeth Gray
Gray, Genevieve S(tuck) 1920-1995 4
Gray, Harold (Lincoln) 1894-1968 33
  Brief entry 32
Gray, Jenny
  See Gray, Genevieve S(tuck)

Gray, John Lee
  See Jakes, John
Gray, Judith A. 1949- 93
Gray, Judith Anne
  See Gray, Judith A.
Gray, Keith 151
Gray, Kes 1960- 153
Gray, Les 1929- 82
Gray, Libba Moore 1937- 83
Gray, Luli 1945- 149
  Earlier sketch in SATA 90
Gray, Marian
  See Pierce, Edith Gray
Gray, Nicholas Stuart 1922-1981 4
  Obituary 27
Gray, Nigel 1941- 104
  Earlier sketch in SATA 33
Gray, (Lucy) Noel (Clervaux) 1898-1983 47
Gray, Patricia (Clark) 7
Gray, Patsey
  See Gray, Patricia (Clark)
Gray, Rita 184
Graydon, Shari 1958- 158
Grayland, V. Merle
  See Grayland, Valerie (Merle Spanner)
Grayland, Valerie (Merle Spanner) 7
Grayson, Devin (Kalile) 1970- 119
Grayson, Kristine
  See Rusch, Kristine Kathryn
Grayson, Paul 1946- 79
Graystone, Lynn
  See Brennan, Joseph Lomas
Great Comte, The
  See Hawkesworth, Eric
Greaves, Margaret 1914-1995 87
  Earlier sketch in SATA 7
Greaves, Nick 1955- 77
Gree, Alain 1936- 28
Green, Adam
  See Weisgard, Leonard (Joseph)
Green, Anne Canevari 1943- 62
Green, Brian
  See Card, Orson Scott
Green, Cliff(ord) 1934- 126
Green, Connie Jordan 1938- 80
Green, D.
  See Casewit, Curtis W(erner)
Green, Elizabeth Shippen 1871-1954 139
Green, Hannah
  See Greenberg, Joanne (Goldenberg)
Green, Jane 1937- 9
Green, John 1977(?)- 170
Green, Mary Moore 1906- 11
Green, Morton 1937- 8
Green, Norma B(erger) 1925- 11
Green, Phyllis 1932- 20
Green, Roger (Gilbert) Lancelyn 1918-1987 . 2
  Obituary 53
Green, (James Le)Roy 1948- 89
Green, Sheila Ellen 1934- 148
  Earlier sketches in SATA 8, 87
Green, Timothy 1953- 91
Greenaway, Kate 1846-1901 100
  See also YABC 2
  See also CLR 111
Greenbank, Anthony Hunt 1933- 39
Greenberg, David 1954- 171
Greenberg, David T.
  See Greenberg, David
Greenberg, Harvey R. 1935- 5
Greenberg, Jan 1942- 125
  Earlier sketch in SATA 61
Greenberg, Joanne (Goldenberg) 1932- 25
Greenberg, Melanie Hope 1954- 72
Greenberg, Polly 1932- 52
  Brief entry 43
Greenblat, Rodney Alan 1960- 106
Greenburg, Dan 1936- 175
  Earlier sketch in SATA 102

Greene, Bette 1934- 161
  Earlier sketches in SATA 8, 102
  See also CLR 140
  See also SAAS 16
Greene, Carla 1916- 67
  Earlier sketch in SATA 1
Greene, Carol 102
  Brief entry 44
  Earlier sketch in SATA 66
Greene, Constance C(larke) 1924- 72
  Earlier sketch in SATA 11
  See also CLR 62
  See also SAAS 11
Greene, Edgar
  See Papademetriou, Lisa
Greene, Ellin 1927- 23
Greene, Graham 1904-1991 20
Greene, Graham Henry
  See Greene, Graham
Greene, Jacqueline Dembar 1946- 131
  Earlier sketch in SATA 76
Greene, Laura Offenhartz 1935- 38
Greene, Meg
  See Malvasi, Meg Greene
Greene, Michele 1962- 178
Greene, Michele Dominguez
  See Greene, Michele
Greene, Rhonda Gowler 1955- 160
  Earlier sketch in SATA 101
Greene, Stephanie 1953- 173
  Earlier sketch in SATA 127
Greene, Wade 1933- 11
Greene, Yvonne
  See Flesch, Yolande (Catarina)
Greenfeld, Howard (Scheinman) 1928- 140
  Earlier sketch in SATA 19
Greenfeld, Josh(ua Joseph) 1928- 62
Greenfield, Eloise 1929- 155
  Earlier sketches in SATA 19, 61, 105
  See also CLR 38
  See also SAAS 16
Greenhaus, Thelma Nurenberg 1903-1984
  Obituary 45
Greenhut, Josh
  See Mercer, Sienna
Greening, Hamilton
  See Hamilton, Charles (Harold St. John)
Greenlaw, M. Jean 1941- 107
Greenleaf, Barbara Kaye 1942- 6
Greenleaf, Peter 1910-1997 33
Greenlee, Sharon 1935- 77
Greeno, Gayle 1949- 81
Greenseid, Diane 1948- 178
  Earlier sketch in SATA 93
Greenspun, Adele Aron 1938- 142
  Earlier sketch in SATA 76
Greenstein, Elaine 1959- 150
  Earlier sketch in SATA 82
Greenwald, Sheila
  See Green, Sheila Ellen
Greenwood, Barbara 1940- 129
  Earlier sketch in SATA 90
Greenwood, Mark 1958- 202
Greenwood, Pamela D. 1944- 115
Greer, Richard
  See Garrett, Randall
  and Silverberg, Robert
Gregg, Andrew K. 1929- 81
Gregg, Charles T(hornton) 1927- 65
Gregg, Walter H(arold) 1919- 20
Gregor, Arthur 1923- 36
Gregor, Lee
  See Pohl, Frederik
Gregori, Leon 1919- 15
Gregorian, Joyce Ballou 1946-1991 30
  Obituary 83
Gregorich, Barbara 1943- 184
  Earlier sketch in SATA 66
Gregorowski, Christopher 1940- 30
Gregory, Diana (Jean) 1933- 49
  Brief entry 42

Gregory, Harry
  See Gottfried, Theodore Mark
Gregory, Jean
  See Ure, Jean
Gregory, Kristiana 1951- 136
  Earlier sketch in SATA 74
Gregory, Nan 1944- 192
  Earlier sketch in SATA 148
Gregory, Philippa 1954- 122
Gregory, Stephen
  See Penzler, Otto
Gregory, Valiska 1940- 82
Greif, Jean-Jacques 1944- 195
Greisman, Joan Ruth 1937- 31
Grendon, Stephen
  See Derleth, August (William)
Grenville, Pelham
  See Wodehouse, P. G.
Gretz, Susanna 1937- 7
Gretzer, John 18
Grewdead, Roy
  See Gorey, Edward (St. John)
Grey, Carol
  See Lowndes, Robert A(ugustine) W(ard)
Grey, Christopher 191
Grey, Christopher Peter
  See Grey, Christopher
Grey, Jerry 1926- 11
Grey, Mini 205
  Earlier sketch in SATA 166
Greybeard the Pirate
  See Macintosh, Brownie
Grey Owl
  See Belaney, Archibald Stansfeld
Gri
  See Denney, Diana
Gribbin, John 1946- 159
Gribbin, John R.
  See Gribbin, John
Grice, Frederick 1910-1983 6
Grider, Dorothy 1915- 31
Gridley, Marion E(leanor) 1906-1974 35
  Obituary 26
Grieco-Tiso, Pina 1954- 108
Grieder, Walter 1924- 9
Griego, Tony A. 1955- 77
Griese, Arnold A(lfred) 1921- 9
Griessman, Annette 1962- 170
  Earlier sketch in SATA 116
Grieve, James 1934- 146
Grifalconi, Ann 1929- 133
  Earlier sketches in SATA 2, 66
  See also CLR 35
  See also SAAS 16
Griffin, Adele 1970- 195
  Earlier sketches in SATA 105, 153
Griffin, Elizabeth May 1985- 89
Griffin, Gillett Good 1928- 26
Griffin, Judith Berry 34
Griffin, Kitty 1951- 137
Griffin, Peni R. 1961- 193
  Earlier sketches in SATA 67, 99
Griffin, Steven A. 1953- 89
Griffin, Steven Arthur
  See Griffin, Steven A.
Griffin, W.E.B. 1929- 5
Griffith, Connie 1946- 89
Griffith, Gershom 1960- 85
Griffith, Helen V(irginia) 1934- 87
  Autobiography Feature 107
  Earlier sketch in SATA 39
Griffith, Jeannette
  See Eyerly, Jeannette
Griffith, Saul 1974- 200
Griffiths, Andy 1961- 196
  Earlier sketch in SATA 152
Griffiths, G(ordon) D(ouglas) 1910-1973
  Obituary 20

Griffiths, Helen 1939- 86
Earlier sketch in SATA 5
See also CLR 75
See also SAAS 5
Grigson, Jane (McIntire) 1928-1990 63
Grimes, Lee 1920- 68
Grimes, Nikki 1950- 174
Earlier sketches in SATA 93, 136
See also CLR 42
Grimly, Gris 186
Grimm, Jacob Ludwig Karl 1785-1863 22
See also CLR 112
Grimm, Wilhelm Karl 1786-1859 22
See also CLR 112
Grimm, William C(arey) 1907-1992 14
Grimm and Grim
See Grimm, Jacob Ludwig Karl
and Grimm, Wilhelm Karl
Grimm Brothers
See Grimm, Jacob Ludwig Karl
and Grimm, Wilhelm Karl
Grimsdell, Jeremy 1942- 83
Grimshaw, Nigel (Gilroy) 1925- 23
Grimsley, Gordon
See Groom, Arthur William
Grindley, Jane Sally
See Grindley, Sally
Grindley, Sally 1953- 148
Gringhuis, Dirk
See Gringhuis, Richard H.
Gringhuis, Richard H. 1918-1974 6
Obituary 25
Grinnell, David
See Wollheim, Donald A(llen)
Grinnell, George Bird 1849-1938 16
Grinspoon, David
See Grinspoon, David H.
Grinspoon, David H. 1959- 156
Grinspoon, David Harry
See Grinspoon, David H.
Gripe, Maria 1923- 74
Earlier sketch in SATA 2
See also CLR 5
Gripe, Maria Kristina
See Gripe, Maria
Grobler, Piet 1959- 201
Groch, Judith (Goldstein) 1929- 25
Grode, Redway
See Gorey, Edward (St. John)
Groener, Carl
See Lowndes, Robert A(ugustine) W(ard)
Groening, Matt 1954- 116
Earlier sketch in SATA 81
Grohmann, Susan 1948- 84
Grohskopf, Bernice 7
Grol, Lini R(icharda) 1913- 9
Grollman, Earl A. 1925- 22
Groom, Arthur William 1898-1964 10
Grooms, Duffy 1964- 169
Gross, Alan 1947- 54
Brief entry 43
Gross, Ernie 1913- 67
Gross, Philip 1952- 164
Earlier sketch in SATA 84
Gross, Philip John
See Gross, Philip
Gross, Ruth Belov 1929- 33
Gross, Sarah Chokla 1906-1976 9
Obituary 26
Grosser, Morton 1931- 74
Grosser, Vicky 1958- 83
Grossman, Bill 1948- 126
Earlier sketch in SATA 72
Grossman, Nancy 1940- 29
Grossman, Patricia 1951- 73
Grossman, Robert 1940- 11
Grote, JoAnn A. 1951- 113
Groten, Dallas 1951- 64
Groth, John (August) 1908-1988 21
Obituary 56

Groth-Fleming, Candace
See Fleming, Candace
Grove, Vicki 1948- 151
Autobiography Feature 151
Earlier sketch in SATA 122
Grover, Lorie Ann 1964- 168
Grover, Wayne 1934- 69
Groves, Georgina
See Symons, (Dorothy) Geraldine
Groves, Maketa 1950- 107
Groves, Seli 77
Grubb, Lisa 160
Gruber, Michael 1940- 173
Gruber, Terry (deRoy) 1953- 66
Gruelle, John 1880-1938 35
Brief entry 32
See also CLR 34
Gruelle, Johnny
See Gruelle, John
Gruenberg, Sidonie Matsner 1881-1974 2
Obituary 27
Gruhzit-Hoyt, Olga (Margaret) 1922- 127
Earlier sketch in SATA 16
Grummer, Arnold E(dward) 1923- 49
Grunewalt, Pine
See Kunhardt, Edith
Grunwell, Jeanne Marie 1971- 147
Grupper, Jonathan 137
Gryski, Camilla 1948- 72
Guarino, Dagmar
See Guarino, Deborah
Guarino, Deborah 1954- 68
Guay, Georgette (Marie Jeanne) 1952- 54
Guay, Rebecca 209
Guay-Mitchell, Rebecca
See Guay, Rebecca
Guback, Georgia 88
Guccione, Leslie Davis 1946- 111
Earlier sketch in SATA 72
Guck, Dorothy 1913-2002 27
Guerny, Gene
See Gurney, Gene
Guest, Elissa Haden 1953- 125
Guest, Jacqueline 1952- 135
Guevara, Susan 167
Earlier sketch in SATA 97
Gugler, Laurel Dee 95
Gugliotta, Bobette 1918-1994 7
Guianan, Eve 1965- 102
Guiberson, Brenda Z. 1946- 124
Earlier sketch in SATA 71
Guibert, Emmanuel 1964- 181
Guile, Melanie 1949- 152
Earlier sketch in SATA 104
Guillaume, Jeanette G. Flierl 1899-1990 8
Guillot, Rene 1900-1969 7
See also CLR 22
Guisewite, Cathy (Lee) 1950- 57
Gulbis, Stephen 1959- 142
Gulley, Judie 1942- 58
Gump, P. Q.
See Card, Orson Scott
Gundrey, Elizabeth 1924- 23
Gunn, James E. 1923- 35
Gunn, James Edwin
See Gunn, James E.
Gunn, Robin Jones 1955- 84
Gunnella 1956- 197
Gunning, Monica Olwen 1930- 161
Gunston, Bill
See Gunston, William Tudor
Gunston, William Tudor 1927- 9
Gunterman, Bertha Lisette 1886(?)-1975
Obituary 27
Gunther, John 1901-1970
Guravich, Dan 1918- 74
Gurko, Leo 1914- 9
Gurko, Miriam 1910(?)-1988 9
Obituary 58
Gurney, Gene 1924- 65

Gurney, James 1958- 120
Earlier sketch in SATA 76
Gurney, John Steven 1962- 143
Earlier sketch in SATA 75
Gustafson, Sarah R.
See Riedman, Sarah R(egal)
Gustafson, Scott 1956- 34
Gustavson, Adam 176
Guthrie, A(lfred) B(ertram), Jr. 1901-1991 .. 62
Obituary 67
Guthrie, Anne 1890-1979 28
Guthrie, Donna W. 1946- 105
Earlier sketch in SATA 63
Gutierrez, Akemi 172
Gutierrez, Rudy 203
Gutman, Bill 128
Brief entry 43
Earlier sketch in SATA 67
Gutman, Dan 1955- 188
Earlier sketches in SATA 77, 139
Gutman, Naham 1899(?)-1981
Obituary 25
Gutmann, Bessie Pease 1876-1960 73
Guy, Geoffrey 1942- 153
Guy, Ginger Foglesong 1954- 171
Guy, Rosa (Cuthbert) 1925- 122
Earlier sketches in SATA 14, 62
See also CLR 137
Guy, Susan 1948- 149
Guymer, (Wilhelmina) Mary 1909- 50
Guzman, Lila 1952- 168
Guzman, Rick 1957- 168
Gwaltney, Doris 1932- 181
Gwynne, Fred(erick Hubbard) 1926-1993 41
Brief entry 27
Obituary 75
Gwynne, Oscar A.
See Ellis, Edward S.
Gwynne, Oswald A.
See Ellis, Edward S.

H

Haab, Sherri 1964- 169
Earlier sketch in SATA 91
Haar, Jaap ter
See ter Haar, Jaap
Haarsma, P.J. 183
Haas, Carolyn Buhai 1926- 43
Haas, Dan 1957- 105
Haas, Dorothy F. 46
Brief entry 43
See also SAAS 17
Haas, Irene 1929- 96
Earlier sketch in SATA 17
Haas, James E(dward) 1943- 40
Haas, (Katherine) Jessie 1959- 135
Autobiography Feature 135
Earlier sketch in SATA 98
Haas, Merle S. 1896(?)-1985
Obituary 41
Habenstreit, Barbara 1937- 5
Haber, Karen 1955- 78
Haber, Louis 1910-1988 12
Hacker, Randi 1951- 185
Hacker, Randi Dawn
See Hacker, Randi
Hackett, John Winthrop 1910-1997 65
Hacks, Peter 1928-2003
Obituary 151
Haddix, Margaret Peterson 1964- 187
Earlier sketches in SATA 94, 125
Haddon, Mark 1962- 155
Hader, Berta (Hoerner) 1891(?)-1976 16
Hader, Elmer (Stanley) 1889-1973 16
Hadithi, Mwenye
See Hobson, Bruce
Hadley, Franklin
See Winterbotham, R(ussell) R(obert)

Hadley, Lee 1934-1995 89
  Brief entry 38
  Obituary 86
  Earlier sketch in SATA 47
  See also CLR 40
  See also SAAS 14
Haeffele, Deborah 1954- 76
Haenel, Wolfram 1956- 89
  See also CLR 64
Hafner, Marylin 1925- 179
  Earlier sketches in SATA 7, 121
Haft, Erin
  See Ehrenhaft, Daniel
Hager, Alan 1940- 176
Hager, Alice Rogers 1894-1969
  Obituary 26
Hager, Betty 1923- 89
Hager, Jenna Bush
  See Bush, Jenna
Hager, Sarah 171
Hager, Thomas 1953- 119
Hager, Tom
  See Hager, Thomas
Hagerup, Klaus 1946- 186
Haggard, H(enry) Rider 1856-1925 16
Haggerty, James J(oseph) 1920- 5
Hagon, Priscilla
  See Allan, Mabel Esther
Hague, (Susan) Kathleen 1949- 49
  Brief entry 45
Hague, Michael 1948- 185
  Brief entry 32
  Earlier sketches in SATA 48, 80, 129
Hague, Michael R.
  See Hague, Michael
Hahn, Emily 1905-1997 3
  Obituary 96
Hahn, Hannelore 8
Hahn, James (Sage) 1947- 9
Hahn, (Mona) Lynn 1949- 9
Hahn, Mary Downing 1937- 208
  Autobiography Feature 157
  Brief entry 44
  Earlier sketches in SATA 50, 81, 138, 157
  See also SAAS 12
Hahn, Michael T. 1953- 92
Haig-Brown, Roderick (Langmere)
  1908-1976 12
  See also CLR 31
Haight, Anne Lyon 1895-1977
  Obituary 30
Haight, Rip
  See Carpenter, John
Haight, Sandy 1949- 79
Haij, Vera
  See Jansson, Tove (Marika)
Haines, Gail Kay 1943- 11
Haines, Margaret Ann Beck
  See Beck, Peggy
Haining, Peter 1940-2007 14
  Obituary 188
Haining, Peter Alexander
  See Haining, Peter
Hains, Harriet
  See Watson, Carol
Hajdusiewicz, Babs Bell 163
Hakim, Joy 1931- 173
  Earlier sketch in SATA 83
Halacy, D. S., Jr. 1919-2002 36
  See also SAAS 8
Halacy, Dan
  See Halacy, D. S., Jr.
Halam, Ann
  See Jones, Gwyneth A(nn)
Haldane, Roger John 1945- 13
Hale, Arlene 1924-1982 49
Hale, Bruce 1957- 203
  Earlier sketch in SATA 123
Hale, Christy
  See Apostolou, Christine Hale
Hale, Edward Everett 1822-1909 16

Hale, Glenn
  See Walker, Robert W.
Hale, Helen
  See Mulcahy, Lucille Burnett
Hale, Irina 1932- 26
Hale, Kathleen 1898-2000 66
  Obituary 121
  Earlier sketch in SATA 17
Hale, Linda (Howe) 1929- 6
Hale, Lucretia P.
  See Hale, Lucretia Peabody
Hale, Lucretia Peabody 1820-1900 26
  See also CLR 105
Hale, Marian 194
Hale, Nancy 1908-1988 31
  Obituary 57
Hale, Shannon 200
  Earlier sketch in SATA 158
Haley, Amanda 205
Haley, Gail E(inhart) 1939- 161
  Autobiography Feature 161
  Brief entry 28
  Earlier sketches in SATA 43, 78, 136
  See also CLR 21
  See also SAAS 13
Haley, Neale 52
Halfmann, Janet 1944- 208
Hall, Adam
  See Trevor, Elleston
Hall, Adele 1910- 7
Hall, Anna Gertrude 1882-1967 8
Hall, August 207
Hall, Barbara 1961- 68
Hall, Becky 1950- 186
Hall, Beverly B. 1918- 95
Hall, Borden
  See Yates, Raymond F(rancis)
Hall, Brian P(atrick) 1935- 31
Hall, Cameron
  See del Rey, Lester
Hall, Caryl
  See Hansen, Caryl (Hall)
Hall, Donald 1928- 97
  Earlier sketch in SATA 23
Hall, Donald Andrew, Jr.
  See Hall, Donald
Hall, Douglas 1931- 43
Hall, Elizabeth 1929- 77
Hall, Elvajean 1910-1984 6
Hall, Francie 1940- 166
Hall, James Norman 1887-1951 21
Hall, Jesse
  See Boesen, Victor
Hall, Katy
  See McMullan, Kate
Hall, Kirsten Marie 1974- 67
Hall, Lynn 1937- 79
  Earlier sketches in SATA 2, 47
  See also SAAS 4
Hall, Malcolm 1945- 7
Hall, Marcellus 203
Hall, Marjory
  See Yeakley, Marjory Hall
Hall, Melanie W. 1949- 169
  Earlier sketches in SATA 78, 116
Hall, Patricia 1940- 136
Hall, Rosalys Haskell 1914- 7
Hall, Willis 1929-2005 66
Hallard, Peter
  See Catherall, Arthur
Hallas, Richard
  See Knight, Eric
Hall-Clarke, James
  See Rowland-Entwistle, (Arthur) Theodore
  (Henry)
Hallensleben, Georg 1958- 173
Haller, Dorcas Woodbury 1946- 46
Hallett, Mark 1947- 83
Halliburton, Richard 1900-1939(?) 81
Halliburton, Warren J. 1924- 19

Halliday, Brett
  See Dresser, Davis
  and Johnson, (Walter) Ryerson
  and Terrall, Robert
Halliday, William R(oss) 1926- 52
Hallin, Emily Watson 1916-1995 6
Hallinan, P(atrick) K(enneth) 1944- 39
  Brief entry 37
Hallman, Ruth 1929- 43
  Brief entry 28
Hallowell, Tommy
  See Hill, Thomas
Hall-Quest, (Edna) Olga W(ilbourne)
  1899-1986 11
  Obituary 47
Halls, Kelly Milner 1957- 131
Hallstead, William F(inn III) 1924- 11
Hallward, Michael 1889-1982 12
Halperin, Michael 156
Halperin, Wendy Anderson 1952- 200
  Earlier sketches in SATA 80, 125
Halpern, Julie 1975- 198
Halpin, Brendan 1968- 193
Halpin, Marlene 1927- 88
Halsell, Grace (Eleanor) 1923-2000 13
Halsey, Megan 185
Halsted, Anna Roosevelt 1906-1975
  Obituary 30
Halter, Jon C(harles) 1941- 22
Halverson, Deborah 202
Halvorson, Marilyn 1948- 123
Hamalian, Leo 1920- 41
Hamberger, John 1934- 14
Hamblin, Dora Jane 1920- 36
Hambly, Barbara 1951- 108
Hambly, Barbara Joan
  See Hambly, Barbara
Hamer, Martyn
  See Eldin, Peter
Hamerstrom, Frances 1907-1998 24
Hamil, Thomas Arthur 1928- 14
Hamill, Ethel
  See Webb, Jean Francis (III)
Hamilton, (John) Alan 1943- 66
Hamilton, Alice
  See Cromie, Alice Hamilton
Hamilton, Anita 1919- 92
Hamilton, Buzz
  See Hemming, Roy G.
Hamilton, Carol (Jean Barber) 1935- 94
Hamilton, Charles (Harold St. John)
  1876-1961 13
Hamilton, Charles 1913-1996 65
  Obituary 93
Hamilton, Clive
  See Lewis, C. S.
Hamilton, Dorothy (Drumm) 1906-1983 12
  Obituary 35
Hamilton, Edith 1867-1963 20
Hamilton, Edmond 1904-1977 118
Hamilton, (Muriel) Elizabeth (Mollie)
  1906- 23
Hamilton, Emma Walton 1962- 177
Hamilton, Franklin
  See Silverberg, Robert
Hamilton, Gail
  See Corcoran, Barbara (Asenath)
  and Dodge, Mary Abigail
Hamilton, Kersten 1958- 204
  Earlier sketch in SATA 134
Hamilton, K.R.
  See Hamilton, Kersten
Hamilton, Martha 1953- 183
  Earlier sketch in SATA 123
Hamilton, Mary (E.) 1927- 55
Hamilton, Mollie
  See Kaye, M.M.
Hamilton, Morse 1943-1998 101
  Earlier sketch in SATA 35
Hamilton, Peter F. 1960- 109

Author Index

Hamilton, Priscilla
  See Gellis, Roberta
Hamilton, Ralph
  See Stratemeyer, Edward L.
Hamilton, Virginia 1936-2002 .... *123*
  Obituary *132*
  Earlier sketches in SATA *4, 56, 79*
  See also CLR *127*
Hamilton, Virginia Esther
  See Hamilton, Virginia
Hamilton-Paterson, James 1941- *82*
Hamlet, Ova
  See Lupoff, Richard A(llen)
Hamley, D. C.
  See Hamley, Dennis
Hamley, Dennis 1935- *69*
  Earlier sketch in SATA *39*
  See also CLR *47*
  See also SAAS *22*
Hamley, Dennis C.
  See Hamley, Dennis
Hamlin, Peter J. 1970- *84*
Hamm, Diane Johnston 1949- *78*
Hammer, Charles 1934- *58*
Hammer, Richard 1928- *6*
Hammerman, Gay M(orenus) 1926- *9*
Hammill, Matt 1982- *206*
Hammond, Andrew 1970- *181*
Hammond, Ralph
  See Hammond Innes, Ralph
Hammond, Winifred G(raham) 1899-1992 ... *29*
  Obituary *107*
Hammond Innes, Ralph 1913-1998 .... *116*
Hammontree, Marie (Gertrude) 1913- *13*
Hample, Zack 1977- *161*
Hampshire, Joyce Gregorian
  See Gregorian, Joyce Ballou
Hampshire, Susan 1942- *98*
Hampson, (Richard) Denman 1929- *15*
Hampson, Frank 1918(?)-1985
  Obituary *46*
Hampton, Wilborn 1940- *196*
  Earlier sketch in SATA *156*
Hamre, Leif 1914- *5*
Hamsa, Bobbie 1944- *52*
  Brief entry *38*
Han, Jenny 1981- *175*
Han, Lu
  See Stickler, Soma Han
Han, Soma
  See Stickler, Soma Han
Han, Suzanne Crowder 1953- *89*
Hancock, Mary A. 1923- *31*
Hancock, Sibyl 1940- *9*
Hand, Elizabeth 1957- *167*
  Earlier sketch in SATA *118*
Handford, Martin (John) 1956- *64*
  See also CLR *22*
Handforth, Thomas (Schofield) 1897-1948 .. *42*
Handler, Daniel
  See Snicket, Lemony
Handville, Robert (Tompkins) 1924- *45*
Hane, Roger 1940-1974
  Obituary *20*
Hanel, Wolfram
  See Haenel, Wolfram
Haney, Lynn 1941- *23*
Hanff, Helene 1916-1997 .... *97*
  Earlier sketch in SATA *11*
Hanft, Josh 1956- *197*
Hanft, Joshua E.
  See Hanft, Josh
Hanley, Boniface Francis 1924- *65*
Hanlon, Emily 1945- *15*
Hann, Jacquie 1951- *19*
Hann, Judith 1942- *77*
Hanna, Bill
  See Hanna, William (Denby)
Hanna, Cheryl 1951- *84*
Hanna, Dan *200*
Hanna, Jack (Bushnell) 1947- *74*

Hanna, Nell(ie L.) 1908- *55*
Hanna, Paul R(obert) 1902-1988 .... *9*
Hanna, William (Denby) 1910-2001 .... *51*
  Obituary *126*
Hannam, Charles 1925- *50*
Hannan, Peter 1954- *187*
Hannigan, Katherine *170*
Hannon, Ezra
  See Hunter, Evan
Hann-Syme, Marguerite *127*
Hano, Arnold 1922- *12*
Hano, Renee Roth
  See Roth-Hano, Renee
Hanover, Terri
  See Huff, Tanya
Hansen, Ann Larkin 1958- *96*
Hansen, Brooks 1965- *104*
Hansen, Caryl (Hall) 1929- *39*
Hansen, Ian V. 1929- *113*
Hansen, Jennifer 1972- *156*
Hansen, Joyce 1942- *172*
  Autobiography Feature *172*
  Brief entry *39*
  Earlier sketches in SATA *46, 101*
  See also CLR *21*
  See also SAAS *15*
Hansen, Joyce Viola
  See Hansen, Joyce
Hansen, Mark Victor *112*
Hansen, Ron 1947- *56*
Hansen, Ronald Thomas
  See Hansen, Ron
Hanser, Richard (Frederick) 1909-1981 .... *13*
Hanson, Joan 1938- *8*
Hanson, Joseph E. 1894(?)-1971
  Obituary *27*
Hanson, Mary Elizabeth *188*
Hanson, Warren 1949- *155*
Hansson, Gunilla 1939- *64*
Hantman, Clea *200*
Harald, Eric
  See Boesen, Victor
Harcourt, Ellen Knowles 1890(?)-1984
  Obituary *36*
Hard, Charlotte (Ann) 1969- *98*
Hardcastle, Michael 1933- *47*
  Brief entry *38*
Harding, Lee 1937- *32*
  Brief entry *31*
Hardt, Helga Fleischhauer
  See Fleischhauer-Hardt, Helga
Hardwick, Richard Holmes, Jr. 1923- *12*
Hardy, Alice Dale *67*
  Earlier sketch in SATA *1*
Hardy, David A(ndrews) 1936- *9*
Hardy, Jon 1958- *53*
Hardy, LeAnne 1951- *154*
Hardy, Stuart
  See Schisgall, Oscar
Hare, Norma Q(uarles) 1924- *46*
  Brief entry *41*
Harel, Nira 1936- *154*
Harford, Henry
  See Hudson, W(illiam) H(enry)
Hargrave, Leonie
  See Disch, Thomas M.
Hargreaves, (Charles) Roger 1935-1988
  Obituary *56*
Hargrove, James 1947- *57*
  Brief entry *50*
Hargrove, Jim
  See Hargrove, James
Harik, Elsa
  See Marston, Elsa
Harik, Elsa M.
  See Marston, Elsa
Harik, Elsa Marston
  See Marston, Elsa
Hariton, Anca I. 1955- *79*
Hark, Mildred
  See McQueen, Mildred Hark

Harkaway, Hal
  See Stratemeyer, Edward L.
Harkins, Philip 1912-1997 .... *6*
  Obituary *129*
Harlan, Elizabeth 1945- *41*
  Brief entry *35*
Harlan, Glen
  See Cebulash, Mel
Harlan, Judith 1949- *135*
  Earlier sketch in SATA *74*
  See also CLR *81*
Harland, Richard 1947- *152*
Harlee, J. V.
  See Leese, Jennifer L.B.
Harler, Ann
  See Van Steenwyk, Elizabeth (Ann)
Harley, Avis *183*
Harley, Bill 1954- *208*
  Earlier sketch in SATA *87*
Harlow, Joan Hiatt 1932- *157*
Harman, Fred 1902(?)-1982
  Obituary *30*
Harman, Hugh 1903-1982
  Obituary *33*
Harmelink, Barbara (Mary) *9*
Harmer, Mabel 1894-1992 .... *45*
Harmon, Dan
  See Harmon, Daniel E(lton)
Harmon, Daniel E(lton) 1949- *157*
Harmon, Margaret 1906- *20*
Harmon, Michael 1969- *189*
Harmon, Michael B.
  See Harmon, Michael
Harmon, William (Ruth) 1938- *65*
Harnan, Terry 1920- *12*
Harness, Cheryl 1951- *178*
  Earlier sketch in SATA *131*
Harnett, Cynthia (Mary) 1893-1981 .... *5*
  Obituary *32*
Harper, Anita 1943- *41*
Harper, Betty 1946- *126*
Harper, Charise
  See Harper, Charise Mericle
Harper, Charise Mericle *179*
Harper, Elaine
  See Hallin, Emily Watson
Harper, Ellen
  See Noble, Marty
Harper, Jamie *174*
Harper, Jessica 1949- *148*
Harper, Jo 1932- *169*
  Earlier sketch in SATA *97*
Harper, Lee *201*
Harper, Mary Wood
  See Dixon, Jeanne
Harper, Piers 1966- *161*
  Earlier sketch in SATA *105*
Harper, Suzanne *194*
Harper, Wilhelmina 1884-1973 .... *4*
  Obituary *26*
Harrah, Madge 1931- *154*
Harrah, Michael 1940- *41*
Harrah, Monique
  See Harrah, Madge
Harrar, George E. 1949- *124*
Harrell, Beatrice Orcutt 1943- *93*
Harrell, Janice 1945- *70*
Harries, Joan 1922- *39*
Harrill, Ronald 1950- *90*
Harrington, Denis J(ames) 1932- *88*
Harrington, Evelyn Davis 1911- *5*
Harrington, Janice N. 1956- *187*
Harrington, Lyn
  See Harrington, Evelyn Davis
Harris, Alan 1944- *71*
Harris, Aurand 1915-1996 .... *37*
  Obituary *91*
Harris, Bob
  See Harris, Robert J.
Harris, Carol Flynn 1933- *135*

Harris, Catherine
  See Ainsworth, Catherine Harris
Harris, Christie
  See Harris, Christie (Lucy) Irwin
Harris, Christie (Lucy) Irwin 1907-2002 74
  Autobiography Feature 116
  Earlier sketch in SATA *6*
  See also CLR *47*
  See also SAAS *10*
Harris, Christine 1955- 105
Harris, Colver
  See Colver, Anne
Harris, David 1942- 118
Harris, David William
  See Harris, David
Harris, Dorothy Joan 1931- 153
  Earlier sketch in SATA *13*
Harris, Geraldine (Rachel) 1951- 54
Harris, Jacqueline L. 1929- 62
Harris, Janet 1932-1979 4
  Obituary 23
Harris, Jesse
  See Standiford, Natalie
Harris, Joan 1946- 146
Harris, Joe 1928- 201
Harris, Joel Chandler 1848-1908 100
  See also YABC *1*
  See also CLR *128*
Harris, John (Wyndham Parkes Lucas) Beynon
  1903-1969 118
Harris, Johnson
  See Harris, John (Wyndham Parkes Lucas)
  Beynon
Harris, Jonathan 1921-1997 52
Harris, Larry Vincent 1939- 59
Harris, Lavinia
  See St. John, Nicole
Harris, Leon A., Jr. 1926-2000 4
Harris, Lois V. 199
Harris, Lorle K(empe) 1912-2001 22
Harris, Marilyn
  See Springer, Marilyn Harris
Harris, Mark Jonathan 1941- 84
  Earlier sketch in SATA *32*
Harris, Mary K(athleen) 1905-1966 119
Harris, Robert J. 1955- 195
Harris, Robie H. 1940- 203
  Brief entry 53
  Earlier sketches in SATA *90, 147*
Harris, Robin
  See Shine, Deborah
Harris, Rosemary (Jeanne) 82
  Earlier sketch in SATA *4*
  See also CLR *30*
  See also SAAS *7*
Harris, Ruth Elwin 1935- 164
Harris, Sherwood 1932-2009 25
Harris, Steven Michael 1957- 55
Harris, Trudy 1949- 191
  Earlier sketch in SATA *128*
Harris-Filderman, Diane
  See Filderman, Diane E(lizabeth)
Harrison, C(hester) William 1913-1994 35
Harrison, Carol
  See Harrison, Carol Thompson
Harrison, Carol Thompson 113
Harrison, David L. 1937- 186
  Earlier sketches in SATA *26, 92, 150*
Harrison, Deloris 1938- 9
Harrison, Edward Hardy 1926- 56
Harrison, Elizabeth (Allen) Cavanna
  1909-2001 30
  Earlier sketch in SATA *1*
  See also SAAS *4*
Harrison, Harry 1925- 4
Harrison, Harry Max
  See Harrison, Harry
Harrison, Mette Ivie 1970- 202
  Earlier sketch in SATA *149*
Harrison, Michael 1939- 106
Harrison, Molly (Hodgett) 1909-2002 41

Harrison, Sarah 1946- 63
Harrison, Ted
  See Harrison, Edward Hardy
Harsh, Fred (T.) 1925- 72
Harshaw, Ruth H(etzel) 1890-1968 27
Harshman, Marc 1950- 109
  Earlier sketch in SATA *71*
Hart, Alexandra 1939- 14
Hart, Alison
  See Leonhardt, Alice
Hart, Bruce 1938-2006 57
  Brief entry 39
Hart, Carole 1943- 57
  Brief entry 39
Hart, Carolyn 1936- 74
Hart, Carolyn G.
  See Hart, Carolyn
Hart, Carolyn Gimpel
  See Hart, Carolyn
Hart, Jan Siegel 1940- 79
Hart, Joyce 1954- 148
Hart, Karen 185
Hart, Lenore 171
Hart, Philip S. 1944- 180
Hart, Virginia 1949- 83
Harte, Bret 1836(?)-1902 26
Harte, Francis Brett
  See Harte, Bret
Harter, Debbie 1963- 107
Hartfield, Claire 1957- 147
Hartinger, Brent 1964- 174
  Earlier sketch in SATA *145*
Hartland, Jessie 171
Hartley, Ellen (Raphael) 1915-1980 23
Hartley, Fred Allan III 1953- 41
Hartley, William B(rown) 1913-1980 23
Hartling, Peter
  See Hartling, Peter
Hartling, Peter 1933- 66
  See also CLR *29*
Hartman, Cassie 202
Hartman, Dan 1955- 202
Hartman, Evert 1937- 38
  Brief entry 35
Hartman, Jane E(vangeline) 1928- 47
Hartman, Louis F(rancis) 1901-1970 22
Hartman, Rachel 174
Hartman, Victoria 1942- 91
Hartnett, Sonya 1968- 176
  Earlier sketches in SATA *93, 130*
Hartshorn, Ruth M. 1928- 11
Hartung, Susan Kathleen 192
  Earlier sketch in SATA *150*
Hartwig, Manfred 1950- 81
Harvey, Brett 1936- 61
Harvey, Edith 1908(?)-1972
  Obituary 27
Harvey, Gill 189
Harvey, Karen D. 1935- 88
Harvey, Roland 1945- 179
  Earlier sketches in SATA *71, 123*
Harvey-Fitzhenry, Alyxandra 1974- 189
Harwick, B. L.
  See Keller, Beverly L(ou)
Harwin, Brian
  See Henderson, LeGrand
Harwood, Pearl Augusta (Bragdon)
  1903-1998 9
Haseley, Dennis 1950- 157
  Brief entry 44
  Earlier sketches in SATA *57, 105*
Hashmi, Kerri 1955- 108
Haskell, Arnold L(ionel) 1903-1981(?) 6
Haskins, James
  See Haskins, James S.
Haskins, James S. 1941-2005 132
  Autobiography Feature 132
  Earlier sketches in SATA *9, 69, 105*
  See also CLR *39*
  See also SAAS *4*

Haskins, Jim
  See Haskins, James S.
Hasler, Eveline 1933- 181
Hasler, Joan 1931- 28
Hass, Robert 1941- 94
Hassall, Joan 1906-1988 43
  Obituary 56
Hassett, Ann 1958- 162
Hassett, John 162
Hassler, Jon 1933-2008 19
  Obituary 191
Hassler, Jon Francis
  See Hassler, Jon
Hastings, Beverly
  See Barkin, Carol
  and James, Elizabeth
Hastings, Graham
  See Jeffries, Roderic
Hastings, Ian 1912- 62
Hastings, Victor
  See Disch, Thomas M.
Haszard, Patricia Moyes 1923-2000 63
Hatch, Lynda S. 1950- 90
Hathaway, Barbara 164
Hathorn, Elizabeth
  See Hathorn, Elizabeth Helen
Hathorn, Elizabeth Helen 1943- 156
  Autobiography Feature 156
  Earlier sketches in SATA *74, 120*
Hathorn, Libby 1943-
  See Hathorn, Elizabeth Helen
Hatkoff, Craig 1954- 192
Hatlo, Jimmy 1898-1963
  Obituary 23
Hatton, Caroline 1957- 205
Haugaard, Erik Christian 1923- 68
  Earlier sketch in SATA *4*
  See also CLR *11*
  See also SAAS *12*
Haugaard, Kay 117
Haugen, Hayley Mitchell 1968- 172
Haugen, Tormod 1945- 66
Hauman, Doris 1898-1984 32
Hauman, George 1890-1961 32
Hauptly, Denis J(ames) 1945- 57
Hauser, Jill Frankel 1950- 127
Hauser, Margaret L(ouise) 1909- 10
Hausherr, Rosmarie 1943- 86
Hausman, Gerald 1945- 180
  Earlier sketches in SATA *13, 90, 132*
  See also CLR *89*
Hausman, Gerry
  See Hausman, Gerald
Hauth, Katherine B. 1940- 99
Hautman, Pete 1952- 173
  Earlier sketches in SATA *82, 128*
Hautman, Peter Murray
  See Hautman, Pete
Hautzig, Deborah 1956- 106
  Earlier sketch in SATA *31*
Hautzig, Esther Rudomin 1930-2009 148
  Earlier sketches in SATA *4, 68*
  See also CLR *22*
  See also SAAS *15*
Havel, Geoff 1955- 152
Havel, Jennifer
  See Havill, Juanita
Havelin, Kate 1961- 143
Havighurst, Walter (Edwin) 1901-1994 1
  Obituary 79
Haviland, Virginia 1911-1988 6
  Obituary 54
Havill, Juanita 1949- 155
  Earlier sketch in SATA *74*
Hawes, Judy 1913- 4
Hawes, Louise 1943- 180
  Earlier sketch in SATA *60*
Hawke, Rosanne 1953- 165
  Earlier sketch in SATA *124*
Hawke, Rosanne Joy
  See Hawke, Rosanne

Hawkes, Kevin 1959- 201
  Earlier sketches in SATA *78, 150*
Hawkes, Nigel 1943- *119*
Hawkesworth, Eric 1921- *13*
Hawking, Lucy 1969- *197*
Hawkins, Arthur 1903-1985 .... *19*
Hawkins, Colin 1945- *162*
  Earlier sketch in SATA *112*
Hawkins, Jacqui *162*
  Earlier sketch in SATA *112*
Hawkins, Jimmy 1941- *188*
Hawkins, Laura 1951- *74*
Hawkins, (Helena Ann) Quail 1905-2002 ...... *6*
  Obituary *141*
Hawkinson, John (Samuel) 1912-1994 .... *4*
Hawkinson, Lucy (Ozone) 1924-1971 .... *21*
Hawks, Robert 1961- *85*
Hawley, Mabel C. *67*
  Earlier sketch in SATA *1*
Haworth, Danette *207*
Hawthorne, Captain R. M.
  See Ellis, Edward S.
Hawthorne, Nathaniel 1804-1864
  See YABC *2*
  See also CLR *103*
Hay, Jeff T. *154*
Hay, John 1915- *13*
Hay, Timothy
  See Brown, Margaret Wise
Hayashi, Leslie Ann 1954- *115*
Hayashi, Nancy 1939- *186*
  Earlier sketch in SATA *80*
Haycak, Cara 1961- *180*
Haycock, Kate 1962- *77*
Haycraft, Howard 1905-1991 .... *6*
  Obituary *70*
Haycraft, Molly Costain 1911- *6*
Hayden, Gwendolen Lampshire 1904- *35*
Hayden, Robert
  See Hayden, Robert Earl
Hayden, Robert C(arter), Jr. 1937- *47*
  Brief entry *28*
Hayden, Robert E.
  See Hayden, Robert Earl
Hayden, Robert Earl 1913-1980 .... *19*
  Obituary *26*
Hayden, Torey L. 1951- *163*
  Earlier sketch in SATA *65*
Hayden, Torey Lynn
  See Hayden, Torey L.
Hayes, Carlton J(oseph) H(untley)
  1882-1964 .... *11*
Hayes, Daniel 1952- *109*
  Earlier sketch in SATA *73*
Hayes, Geoffrey 1947- *207*
  Earlier sketches in SATA *26, 91*
Hayes, Joe 1945- *131*
  Earlier sketch in SATA *88*
Hayes, John F. 1904-1980 .... *11*
Hayes, Karel 1949- *207*
Hayes, Rosemary *158*
Hayes, Sarah 1945- *208*
Hayes, Sheila 1937- *51*
  Brief entry *50*
Hayes, Will *7*
Hayes, William D(imitt) 1913-1976 .... *8*
Haynes, Betsy 1937- *94*
  Brief entry *37*
  Earlier sketch in SATA *48*
  See also CLR *90*
Haynes, David 1955- *97*
Haynes, Linda
  See Swinford, Betty (June Wells)
Haynes, Mary 1938- *65*
Haynes, Max 1956- *72*
Hays, H(offmann) R(eynolds) 1904-1980 .... *26*
Hays, Thomas Anthony 1957- *84*
Hays, Tony
  See Hays, Thomas Anthony

Hays, Wilma Pitchford 1909- *28*
  Earlier sketch in SATA *1*
  See also CLR *59*
  See also SAAS *3*
Hayward, Linda 1943- *185*
  Brief entry *39*
  Earlier sketch in SATA *101*
Haywood, Carolyn 1898-1990 .... *75*
  Obituary *64*
  Earlier sketches in SATA *1, 29*
  See also CLR *22*
Hazell, Rebecca (Eileen) 1947- *141*
Hazen, Barbara Shook 1930- *178*
  Earlier sketches in SATA *27, 90*
Hazen, Lynn E. *202*
Head, Gay
  See Hauser, Margaret L(ouise)
Head, Tom 1978- *167*
Headley, Elizabeth
  See Harrison, Elizabeth (Allen) Cavanna
Headley, Justina Chen 1968- *176*
Headstrom, (Birger) Richard 1902-1985 .... *8*
Heady, Eleanor B(utler) 1917-1979 .... *8*
Heagy, William D. 1964- *76*
Heal, Edith 1903-1995 .... *7*
Heal, Gillian 1934- *89*
Heale, Jay (Jeremy Peter Wingfield) 1937- .. *84*
Healey, Brooks
  See Albert, Burton
Healey, Larry 1927- *44*
  Brief entry *42*
Heap, Sue 1954- *187*
  Earlier sketch in SATA *150*
Heaps, Willard A(llison) 1908-1987 .... *26*
Hearn, Diane Dawson 1952- *209*
  Earlier sketch in SATA *79*
Hearn, Emily
  See Valleau, Emily
Hearn, Julie 1958- *152*
Hearn, Lian
  See Rubinstein, Gillian
Hearn, Sneed
  See Gregg, Andrew K.
Hearne, Betsy 1942- *146*
  Earlier sketches in SATA *38, 95*
Heath, Charles D(ickinson) 1941- *46*
Heath, Veronica
  See Blackett, Veronica Heath
Heaven, Constance (Christina) 1911- *7*
Hebert-Collins, Sheila 1948- *111*
Hecht, George J(oseph) 1895-1980
  Obituary *22*
Hecht, Henri Joseph 1922- *9*
Hechtkopf, Henryk 1910- *17*
Heck, Bessie (Mildred) Holland 1911-1995 . *26*
Heck, Ed 1963- *173*
Heckert, Connie K(aye Delp) 1948- *82*
Hector, Julian *205*
Hedderwick, Mairi 1939- *145*
  Earlier sketches in SATA *30, 77*
Hedges, Sid(ney) G(eorge) 1897-1974 .... *28*
Hedrick, Irene Hope 1920- *175*
Heelan, Jamee Riggio 1965- *146*
Heerboth, Sharon
  See Leon, Sharon
Heffernan, John 1949- *168*
  Earlier sketch in SATA *121*
Heffron, Dorris 1944- *68*
Hefter, Richard 1942- *31*
Hegamin, Tonya C. 1975- *209*
Hegarty, Reginald Beaton 1906-1973 .... *10*
Hehenberger, Shelly 1968- *126*
Heidbreder, Robert 1947- *196*
  Earlier sketch in SATA *130*
Heidbreder, Robert K.
  See Heidbreder, Robert
Heide, Florence Parry 1919- *192*
  Earlier sketches in SATA *32, 69, 118*
  See also CLR *60*
  See also SAAS *6*
Heiderstadt, Dorothy 1907-2001 .... *6*

Heidi Louise
  See Erdrich, Louise
Heidler, David S(tephen) 1955- *132*
Heidler, Jeanne T. 1956- *132*
Heilbroner, Joan Knapp 1922- *63*
Heilbrun, Lois Hussey 1922(?)-1987
  Obituary *54*
Heiligman, Deborah 1958- *193*
  Earlier sketches in SATA *90, 144*
Heilman, Joan Rattner *50*
Heimann, Rolf 1940- *164*
  Earlier sketch in SATA *120*
Hein, Lucille Eleanor 1915-1994 .... *20*
Heine, Helme 1941- *135*
  Earlier sketch in SATA *67*
  See also CLR *18*
Heinlein, Robert A. 1907-1988 .... *69*
  Obituary *56*
  Earlier sketch in SATA *9*
  See also CLR *75*
Heinlein, Robert Anson
  See Heinlein, Robert A.
Heins, Ethel L(eah) 1918-1997 .... *101*
Heins, Paul 1909- *13*
Heintze, Carl 1922- *26*
Heinz, Bill
  See Heinz, W. C.
Heinz, Brian J. 1946- *181*
  Earlier sketch in SATA *95*
Heinz, Brian James
  See Heinz, Brian J.
Heinz, W. C. 1915-2008 .... *26*
Heinz, Wilfred Charles
  See Heinz, W. C.
Heinzen, Mildred
  See Masters, Mildred
Heisel, Sharon E(laine) 1941- *125*
  Earlier sketch in SATA *84*
Heitzmann, William Ray 1948- *73*
Heitzmann, Wm. Ray
  See Heitzmann, William Ray
Helakoski, Leslie *178*
Helberg, Shirley Adelaide Holden 1919- ... *138*
Helfer, Andrew *187*
Helfer, Ralph 1937- *177*
Helfman, Elizabeth S(eaver) 1911-2001 .... *3*
Helfman, Harry Carmozin 1910-1995 .... *3*
Helgerson, Joseph 1950- *181*
Hellard, Susan *182*
Hellberg, Hans-Eric 1927- *38*
Heller, Linda 1944- *46*
  Brief entry *40*
Heller, Mike
  See Hano, Arnold
Heller, Ruth M. 1924- *112*
  Earlier sketch in SATA *66*
Hellman, Hal
  See Hellman, Harold
Hellman, Harold 1927- *4*
Helman, Andrea (Jean) 1946- *160*
  Earlier sketch in SATA *107*
Helmer, Diana Star 1962- *86*
Helmer, Marilyn *160*
  Earlier sketch in SATA *112*
Helps, Racey 1913-1971 .... *2*
  Obituary *25*
Helquist, Brett *187*
  Earlier sketch in SATA *146*
Helweg, Hans H. 1917- *50*
  Brief entry *33*
Helyar, Jane Penelope Josephine 1933- *5*
  Autobiography Feature *138*
  See also SAAS *2*
Hemmant, Lynette 1938- *69*
Hemming, Roy G. 1928-1995 .... *11*
  Obituary *86*
Hemphill, Helen 1955- *179*
Hemphill, Kris (Harrison) 1963- *118*
Hemphill, Martha Locke 1904-1973 .... *37*
Hemphill, Stephanie *190*
Hemstock, Gillian 1956- *173*

Henba, Bobbie 1926- 87
Henbest, Nigel 1951- 55
  Brief entry 52
Henderley, Brooks 1
Henderson, Aileen Kilgore 1921- 178
Henderson, Aileen Mary
  See Fox, Aileen
Henderson, Gordon 1950- 53
Henderson, Kathy 1949- 155
  Brief entry 53
  Earlier sketches in SATA 55, 95
Henderson, Lauren 1966- 201
Henderson, LeGrand 1901-1965 9
Henderson, Nancy Wallace 1916- 22
Henderson, Zenna (Chlarson) 1917-1983 5
Hendrickson, Walter Brookfield, Jr. 1936- 9
Hendrix, John 1976- 208
Hendry, Diana 1941- 106
  Earlier sketch in SATA 68
Hendry, Frances Mary 1941- 171
  Earlier sketch in SATA 110
Hendry, Linda (Gail) 1961- 83
Heneghan, James 1930- 160
  Earlier sketches in SATA 53, 97
Henkes, Kevin 1960- 207
  Earlier sketches in SATA 43, 76, 108, 154
  See also CLR 108
Hennessy, Barbara G.
  See Hennessy, B.G.
Hennessy, Barbara Gulbrandsen
  See Hennessy, B.G.
Hennessy, B.G. 1951- 175
Henney, Carolee Wells 1928- 102
Henriod, Lorraine 1925- 26
Henriquez, Emile F. 1937- 170
  Earlier sketch in SATA 89
Henry, April 1959- 174
Henry, Ernest 1948- 107
Henry, Joanne Landers 1927- 6
Henry, Maeve 1960- 75
Henry, Marguerite 1902-1997 100
  Obituary 99
  See also CLR 4
  See also SAAS 7
Henry, Marie H. 1935- 65
Henry, Marilyn 1939- 117
Henry, Marion
  See del Rey, Lester
Henry, O. 1862-1910
  See YABC 2
Henry, Oliver
  See Henry, O.
Henry, T. E.
  See Rowland-Entwistle, (Arthur) Theodore
  (Henry)
Henschel, Elizabeth Georgie 56
Henson, Heather 206
Henson, James Maury
  See Henson, Jim
Henson, Jim 1936-1990 43
  Obituary 65
Henstra, Friso 1928- 73
  Earlier sketch in SATA 8
  See also SAAS 14
Hentoff, Nat(han Irving) 1925- 133
  Brief entry 27
  Earlier sketches in SATA 42, 69
  See also CLR 52
Henty, G(eorge) A(lfred) 1832-1902 64
  See also CLR 76
Heo, Yumi 1964- 206
  Earlier sketches in SATA 94, 146
Hepler, Heather 177
Herald, Kathleen
  See Peyton, Kathleen Wendy
Herb, Angela M. 1970- 92
Herbert, Cecil
  See Hamilton, Charles (Harold St. John)
Herbert, Don 1917-2007 2
  Obituary 184

Herbert, Donald Jeffrey
  See Herbert, Don
Herbert, Frank 1920-1986 37
  Obituary 47
  Earlier sketch in SATA 9
Herbert, Frank Patrick
  See Herbert, Frank
Herbert, Helen (Jean) 1947- 57
Herbert, Janis 1956- 139
Herbert, Wally 1934-2007 23
Herbert, Walter William
  See Herbert, Wally
Herbst, Judith 1947- 74
Herda, D.J. 1948- 80
Herge
  See Remi, Georges
Heritage, Martin
  See Horler, Sydney
Herkimer, L(awrence) R(ussell) 1925(?)- 42
Herlihy, Dirlie Anne 1935- 73
Herman, Charlotte 1937- 203
  Earlier sketches in SATA 20, 99
Hermanson, Dennis (Everett) 1947- 10
Hermes, Jules 1962- 92
Hermes, Patricia 1936- 191
  Earlier sketches in SATA 31, 78, 141
Hermes, Patricia Mary
  See Hermes, Patricia
Hernandez, Natalie Nelson 1929- 123
Herndon, Ernest 91
Herold, Ann Bixby 1937- 72
Herrera, Juan Felipe 1948- 127
Herrick, Steven 1958- 209
  Earlier sketches in SATA 103, 156
Herriman, George (Joseph) 1880-1944 140
Herriot, James 1916-1995
  See Wight, James Alfred
Herrmanns, Ralph 1933- 11
Herrold, Tracey
  See Dils, Tracey E.
Herron, Carolivia 1947- 203
Herron, Edward A(lbert) 1912- 4
Herschler, Mildred Barger 130
Hersey, John 1914-1993 25
  Obituary 76
Hersey, John Richard
  See Hersey, John
Hershberger, Priscilla (Gorman) 1951- 81
Hershenhorn, Esther 1945- 151
Hershey, Kathleen M. 1934- 80
Hershey, Mary 173
Hersom, Kathleen 1911- 73
Hertz, Grete Janus 1915- 23
Herzig, Alison Cragin 1935- 87
Herzog, Brad 1968- 131
Heslewood, Juliet 1951- 82
Hess, Lilo 1916- 4
Hess, Paul 1961- 134
Hesse, Hermann 1877-1962 50
Hesse, Karen 1952- 158
  Autobiography Feature 113
  Earlier sketches in SATA 74, 103
  See also CLR 141
  See also SAAS 25
Hest, Amy 1950- 193
  Earlier sketches in SATA 55, 82, 129
Heuer, Karsten 1968(?)- 202
Heuer, Kenneth John 1927- 44
Heuman, William 1912-1971 21
Heuston, Kimberley 1960- 167
Heuston, Kimberley Burton
  See Heuston, Kimberley
Hewes, Agnes Danforth 1874-1963 35
Hewett, Anita 1918-1989 13
Hewett, Joan 1930- 140
  Earlier sketch in SATA 81
Hewett, Richard 1929- 81
Hewitson, Jennifer 1961- 97
Hewitt, Margaret 1961- 84
Hewitt, Sally 1949- 127

Hext, Harrington
  See Phillpotts, Eden
Hey, Nigel S(tewart) 1936- 20
Heyduck-Huth, Hilde 1929- 8
Heyer, Carol 1950- 130
  Earlier sketch in SATA 74
Heyer, Marilee 1942- 102
  Earlier sketch in SATA 64
Heyerdahl, Thor 1914-2002 52
  Earlier sketch in SATA 2
Heyes, (Nancy) Eileen 1956- 150
  Earlier sketch in SATA 80
Heyliger, William 1884-1955
  See YABC 1
Heyman, Ken(neth Louis) 1930- 114
  Earlier sketch in SATA 34
Heyward, (Edwin) DuBose 1885-1940 21
Heywood, Karen 1946- 48
Hezlep, William (Earl) 1936- 88
Hiaasen, Carl 1953- 208
Hibbert, Arthur Raymond
  See Hibbert, Christopher
Hibbert, Christopher 1924-2008 4
  Obituary 201
Hibbert, Eleanor Alice Burford 1906-1993 2
  Obituary 74
Hickman, Estella (Lee) 1942- 111
Hickman, Janet 1940- 127
  Earlier sketch in SATA 12
Hickman, Martha Whitmore 1925- 26
Hickman, Pamela 1958- 186
  Earlier sketch in SATA 128
Hickock, Will
  See Harrison, C(hester) William
Hickok, Lorena A. 1893-1968 20
Hickox, Rebecca (Ayres) 116
Hicks, Barbara Jean 1953- 165
Hicks, Betty 191
Hicks, Clifford B. 1920- 50
Hicks, Eleanor B.
  See Coerr, Eleanor (Beatrice)
Hicks, Harvey
  See Stratemeyer, Edward L.
Hicks, Peter 1952- 111
Hicyilmaz, Gaye 1947- 157
  Earlier sketch in SATA 77
Hieatt, Constance B(artlett) 1928- 4
Hiebert, Ray Eldon 1932- 13
Higdon, Hal 1931- 4
Higginbottom, David 1923- 87
  Earlier sketch in SATA 25
Higginbottom, J(effrey) Winslow 1945- 29
Higgins, Joanna 1945- 125
Higgins, Simon (Richard) 1958- 105
Higginsen, Vy 79
High, Linda Oatman 1958- 188
  Autobiography Feature 188
  Earlier sketches in SATA 94, 145
High, Philip E. 1914- 119
High, Philip Empson
  See High, Philip E.
Higham, David (Michael) 1949- 50
Higham, Jon Atlas
  See Higham, Jonathan Huw
Higham, Jonathan Huw 1960- 59
Highet, Helen
  See MacInnes, Helen (Clark)
Hightman, Jason 1971(?)- 189
Hightman, J.P.
  See Hightman, Jason
Hightower, Florence Cole 1916-1981 4
  Obituary 27
Highwater, Jamake (Mamake)
  1942(?)-2001 69
  Brief entry 30
  Earlier sketch in SATA 32
  See also CLR 17
Hilb, Nora 1953- 178
Hildebrandt, Greg 1939- 172
  Brief entry 33
  Earlier sketch in SATA 55

Hildebrandt, Tim 1939-2006 55
   Brief entry 33
Hildebrandt, Timothy
   See Hildebrandt, Tim
Hildebrandts, The
   See Hildebrandt, Greg
   and Hildebrandt, Tim
Hilder, Rowland 1905-1993 36
   Obituary 77
Hildick, E. W.
   See Hildick, Wallace
Hildick, Wallace 1925-2001 68
   Earlier sketch in SATA *2*
   See also SAAS *6*
Hilgartner, Beth 1957- 58
Hill, Alexis
   See Craig, Mary (Francis) Shura
   and Glick, Ruth (Burtnick)
Hill, Anthony R. 1942- 164
   Earlier sketch in SATA *91*
Hill, Anthony Robert
   See Hill, Anthony R.
Hill, David 1942- 152
   Earlier sketch in SATA *103*
Hill, Donna (Marie) 1921- 124
   Earlier sketch in SATA *24*
Hill, Douglas 1935-2007 78
   Earlier sketch in SATA *39*
Hill, Douglas Arthur
   See Hill, Douglas
Hill, Elizabeth Starr 1925- 143
   Earlier sketch in SATA *24*
Hill, Eric 1927- 133
   Brief entry 53
   Earlier sketch in SATA *66*
   See also CLR *13*
Hill, Gordon
   See Eldin, Peter
Hill, Grace Brooks 67
   Earlier sketch in SATA *1*
Hill, Grace Livingston 1865-1947
   See YABC *2*
Hill, Helen M(orey) 1915- 27
Hill, John
   See Koontz, Dean
Hill, Johnson
   See Kunhardt, Edith
Hill, Judy I. R.
   See Roberts, Judy I.
Hill, Kathleen Louise 1917- 4
Hill, Kay
   See Hill, Kathleen Louise
Hill, Kirkpatrick 1938- 188
   Earlier sketches in SATA *72, 126*
Hill, Laban
   See Hill, Laban Carrick
Hill, Laban Carrick 170
Hill, Lee Sullivan 1958- 96
Hill, Lorna 1902-1991 12
Hill, Margaret (Ohler) 1915- 36
Hill, Meg
   See Hill, Margaret (Ohler)
Hill, Meredith
   See Craig, Mary (Francis) Shura
Hill, Monica
   See Watson, Jane Werner
Hill, Pamela Smith 1954- 112
Hill, Ralph Nading 1917-1987 65
Hill, Robert W(hite) 1919-1982 12
   Obituary 31
Hill, Ruth A.
   See Viguers, Ruth Hill
Hill, Ruth Livingston
   See Munce, Ruth Hill
Hill, Stuart 1958- 186
Hill, Susan 1942- 183
Hill, Susan Elizabeth
   See Hill, Susan
Hill, Susanna Leonard 1965- 193
Hill, Thomas 1960- 82
Hillcourt, William 1900-1992 27

Hillenbrand, Will 1960- 147
   Earlier sketch in SATA *84*
Hiller, Ilo (Ann) 1938- 59
Hillerman, Anthony Grove
   See Hillerman, Tony
Hillerman, Tony 1925-2008 6
   Obituary 198
Hillert, Margaret 1920- 91
   Earlier sketch in SATA *8*
Hilliard, Richard 183
Hillman, Ben 1957- 202
Hillman, Elizabeth 1942- 75
Hillman, John 1952- 120
Hillman, Martin
   See Hill, Douglas
Hillman, Priscilla 1940- 48
   Brief entry 39
Hillman, Shane 200
Hills, C.A.R. 1955- 39
Hills, Charles Albert Reis
   See Hills, C.A.R.
Hills, Tad 173
Hilton, Irene Pothus -1979 7
Hilton, James 1900-1954 34
Hilton, Margaret Lynette 1946- 105
   Earlier sketch in SATA *68*
   See also CLR *25*
   See also SAAS *21*
Hilton, Nette
   See Hilton, Margaret Lynette
Hilton, Ralph 1907-1982 8
Hilton, Suzanne 1922- 4
Hilton-Bruce, Anne
   See Hilton, Margaret Lynette
Him, George 1937-1982
   Obituary 30
Himelblau, Linda -2005 179
Himelstein, Shmuel 1940- 83
Himler, Ann 1946- 8
Himler, Ronald 1937- 183
   Earlier sketches in SATA *6, 92, 137*
Himler, Ronald Norbert
   See Himler, Ronald
Himmelman, John C(arl) 1959- 159
   Earlier sketches in SATA *47, 94*
Hinckley, Helen
   See Jones, Helen Hinckley
Hind, Dolores (Ellen) 1931- 53
   Brief entry 49
Hindin, Nathan
   See Bloch, Robert (Albert)
Hindley, Judy 1940- 179
   Earlier sketch in SATA *120*
Hinds, P(atricia) Mignon 98
Hine, Sesyle Joslin 1929- 2
Hines, Anna Grossnickle 1946- 209
   Brief entry 45
   Earlier sketches in SATA *51, 95, 141*
   See also SAAS *16*
Hines, Gary (Roger) 1944- 136
   Earlier sketch in SATA *74*
Hinojosa, Maria (de Lourdes) 1961- 88
Hinton, Nigel 1941- 166
Hinton, S. E. 1950- 160
   Earlier sketches in SATA *19, 58, 115*
   See also CLR *23*
Hinton, Sam 1917-2009 43
Hinton, Susan Eloise
   See Hinton, S. E.
Hintz, Martin 1945- 128
   Brief entry 39
   Earlier sketch in SATA *47*
Hintz, Stephen V. 1975- 129
Hippopotamus, Eugene H.
   See Kraus, (Herman) Robert
Hirano, Cathy 1957- 68
Hirao, Amiko 203
Hirsch, Karen 1941- 61
Hirsch, Odo 157
   Earlier sketch in SATA *111*
Hirsch, Phil 1926- 35

Hirsch, S. Carl 1913-1990 2
   See also SAAS *7*
Hirschfelder, Arlene B. 1943- 138
   Earlier sketch in SATA *80*
Hirschi, Ron 1948- 192
   Earlier sketches in SATA *56, 95*
Hirschmann, Linda (Ann) 1941- 40
Hirsh, Marilyn 1944-1988 7
   Obituary 58
Hirshberg, Al(bert Simon) 1909-1973 38
Hiscock, Bruce 1940- 204
   Earlier sketches in SATA *57, 137*
Hiser, Constance 1950- 71
Hiser, Iona Seibert -1998 4
Hislop, Julia Rose Catherine 1962- 74
Hissey, Jane 1952- 130
   Autobiography Feature 130
   Earlier sketches in SATA *58, 103*
Hissey, Jane Elizabeth
   See Hissey, Jane
Hitchcock, Alfred (Joseph) 1899-1980 27
   Obituary 24
Hite, Sid 1954- 175
   Earlier sketches in SATA *75, 136*
Hitte, Kathryn 1919- 16
Hitz, Demi 1942- 152
   Earlier sketches in SATA *11, 66, 102*
   See also CLR *58*
Hitzeroth, Deborah L. 1961- 78
Hnizdovsky, Jacques 1915- 32
Ho, Louise 185
Ho, Minfong 1951- 151
   Earlier sketches in SATA *15, 94*
   See also CLR *28*
Hoagland, Edward (Morley) 1932- 51
Hoare, Robert J(ohn) 1921-1975 38
Hoban, Lillian 1925-1998 69
   Obituary 104
   Earlier sketch in SATA *22*
   See also CLR *67*
Hoban, Russell 1925- 136
   Earlier sketches in SATA *1, 40, 78*
   See also CLR *139*
Hoban, Russell Conwell
   See Hoban, Russell
Hoban, Tana 1917(?)-2006 104
   Obituary 173
   Earlier sketches in SATA *22, 70*
   See also CLR *76*
   See also SAAS *12*
Hobart, Lois (Elaine) 7
Hobbie, Holly 1944- 178
   See also CLR *88*
Hobbie, Jocelyn 190
Hobbie, Nathaniel 196
Hobbs, Leigh 1953- 166
Hobbs, Valerie 1941- 193
   Autobiography Feature 145
   Earlier sketches in SATA *93, 145*
   See also CLR *148*
Hobbs, Will 1947- 177
   Autobiography Feature 127
   Earlier sketches in SATA *72, 110*
   See also CLR *59*
Hobbs, William Carl
   See Hobbs, Will
Hoberman, Mary Ann 1930- 158
   Earlier sketches in SATA *5, 72, 111*
   See also CLR *22*
   See also SAAS *18*
Hobson, Bruce 1950- 62
Hobson, Burton (Harold) 1933- 28
Hobson, Laura Z(ametkin) 1900-1986 52
Hobson, Sally 1967- 172
   Earlier sketch in SATA *84*
Hoce, Charley E. 174
Hochman, David 202
Hochschild, Arlie Russell 1940- 11
Hockaby, Stephen
   See Mitchell, Gladys (Maude Winifred)

Hockenberry, Hope
    See Newell, Hope Hockenberry
Hodge, Deborah 1954- 163
    Earlier sketch in SATA 122
Hodge, P. W.
    See Hodge, Paul W(illiam)
Hodge, Paul W(illiam) 1934- 12
Hodgell, P(atricia) C(hristine) 1951- 42
Hodges, C. Walter 1909-2004 2
    Obituary 158
Hodges, Carl G. 1902-1964 10
Hodges, Cyril Walter
    See Hodges, C. Walter
Hodges, Elizabeth Jamison 1
Hodges, Margaret 1911-2005 167
    Obituary 172
    Earlier sketches in SATA 1, 33, 75, 117
    See also SAAS 9
Hodges, Margaret Moore
    See Hodges, Margaret
Hodgetts, Blake Christopher 1967- 43
Hodgkins, Fran 1964- 199
Hodgkinson, Leigh 1975- 202
Hodgman, Ann 1956- 198
Hodgson, Harriet (W.) 1935- 84
Hoehne, Marcia 1951- 89
Hoellwarth, Cathryn Clinton
    See Clinton, Cathryn
Hoestlandt, Jo 1948- 94
Hoestlandt, Jocelyne
    See Hoestlandt, Jo
Hoexter, Corinne K. 1927- 6
Hoeye, Michael 1947- 136
Hoff, Carol 1900-1979 11
Hoff, Mary (King) 1956- 157
    Earlier sketch in SATA 74
Hoff, Syd(ney) 1912-2004 138
    Obituary 154
    Earlier sketches in SATA 9, 72
    See also CLR 83
    See also SAAS 4
Hoffman, Edwin D. 49
Hoffman, Elizabeth P(arkinson) 1921-2003
    Obituary 153
Hoffman, Mary 1945- 144
    Earlier sketches in SATA 59, 97
    See also SAAS 24
Hoffman, Mat 1972- 150
Hoffman, Nina Kiriki 1955- 160
Hoffman, Phyllis M(iriam) 1944- 4
Hoffman, Rosekrans 1926- 15
Hoffmann, E(rnst) T(heodor) A(madeus)
    1776-1822 27
    See also CLR 133
Hoffmann, Felix 1911-1975 9
Hoffmann, Heinrich 1809-1894
    See CLR 122
Hoffmann, Margaret Jones 1910- 48
Hoffmann, Peggy
    See Hoffmann, Margaret Jones
Hofher, Catherine Baxley 1954- 130
Hofher, Cathy
    See Hofher, Catherine Baxley
Hofmeyr, Dianne (Louise) 138
Hofsepian, Sylvia A. 1932- 74
Hofsinde, Robert 1902-1973 21
Hogan, Bernice Harris 1929- 12
Hogan, Inez 1895-1973 2
Hogan, James P(atrick) 1941- 81
Hogan, Jamie 192
Hogan, Linda 1947- 132
Hogarth, Burne 1911-1996 89
    Earlier sketch in SATA 63
Hogarth, Grace (Weston Allen) 1905-1995 .. 91
Hogarth, Jr.
    See Kent, Rockwell
Hogarth, (Arthur) Paul 1917-2001 41
Hogg, Garry 1902-1976 2
Hogg, Gary 1957- 172
    Earlier sketch in SATA 105
Hogner, Dorothy Childs 4

Hogner, Nils 1893-1970 25
Hogrogian, Nonny 1932- 74
    Autobiography Feature 127
    Earlier sketch in SATA 7
    See also CLR 95
    See also SAAS 1
Hoh, Diane 1937- 102
    Brief entry 48
    Earlier sketch in SATA 52
Hoke, Helen
    See Watts, Helen L. Hoke
Hoke, Helen L.
    See Watts, Helen L. Hoke
Hoke, John (Lindsay) 1925- 7
Hokenson, Terry 1948- 193
Hol, Coby 1943- 126
Holabird, Katharine 1948- 135
    Earlier sketch in SATA 62
Holaday, Bobbie 1922- 153
Holbeach, Henry
    See Rands, William Brighty
Holberg, Ruth L(angland) 1889-1984 1
Holbrook, Kathy 1963- 107
Holbrook, Peter
    See Glick, Carl (Cannon)
Holbrook, Sabra
    See Erickson, Sabra Rollins
Holbrook, Sara 131
Holbrook, Stewart Hall 1893-1964 2
Holcomb, Jerry (Leona) Kimble 1927- 113
Holcomb, Nan
    See McPhee, Norma H.
Holden, Elizabeth Rhoda
    See Lawrence, Louise
Holding, James (Clark Carlisle, Jr.)
    1907-1997 3
Hole, Stian 1969- 204
Holeman, Linda 1949- 136
    Autobiography Feature 136
    Earlier sketch in SATA 102
Holinger, William (Jacques) 1944- 90
Holisher, Desider 1901-1972 6
Holl, Adelaide Hinkle 1910- 8
Holl, Kristi D(iane) 1951- 51
Holland, Gay W. 1941- 128
Holland, Isabelle (Christian) 1920-2002 70
    Autobiography Feature 103
    Obituary 132
    Earlier sketch in SATA 8
    See also CLR 57
Holland, Janice 1913-1962 18
Holland, John L(ewis) 1919- 20
Holland, Joyce
    See Morice, Dave
Holland, Julia 1954- 106
Holland, Lynda (H.) 1959- 77
Holland, Lys
    See Gater, Dilys
Holland, Marion 1908-1989 6
    Obituary 61
Hollander, John 1929- 13
Hollander, Nicole 1940(?)- 101
Hollander, Paul
    See Silverberg, Robert
Hollander, Phyllis 1928- 39
Hollander, Zander 1923- 63
Holldobler, Turid 1939- 26
Holliday, Joe
    See Holliday, Joseph
Holliday, Joseph 1910- 11
Holling, Holling C(lancy) 1900-1973 15
    Obituary 26
    See also CLR 50
Hollingsworth, Alvin C(arl) 1930- 39
Hollingsworth, Mary 1947- 166
    Earlier sketch in SATA 91
Holloway, Teresa (Bragunier) 1906- 26
Hollyer, Belinda 204
Holm, (Else) Anne (Lise) 1922-1998 1
    See also CLR 75
    See also SAAS 7

Holm, Jennifer L. 1968(?)- 183
    Earlier sketches in SATA 120, 163
Holm, Matthew 1974- 174
Holm, Sharon Lane 1955- 114
    Earlier sketch in SATA 78
Holman, Felice 1919- 82
    Earlier sketch in SATA 7
    See also SAAS 17
Holm and Hamel
    See Holm, Jennifer L.
Holmberg, Bo R. 1945- 203
Holme, Bryan 1913-1990 26
    Obituary 66
Holmes, Barbara Ware 1945- 127
    Earlier sketch in SATA 65
Holmes, Elizabeth 1957- 191
Holmes, Elizabeth Ann
    See Holmes, Elizabeth
Holmes, John
    See Souster, (Holmes) Raymond
Holmes, Marjorie (Rose) 1910-2002 43
Holmes, Martha 1961- 72
Holmes, Mary Tavener 1954- 199
Holmes, Mary Z(astrow) 1943- 80
Holmes, Oliver Wendell 1809-1894 34
Holmes, Peggy 1898- 60
Holmes, Raymond
    See Souster, (Holmes) Raymond
Holmes, Rick
    See Hardwick, Richard Holmes, Jr.
Holmes, Sara Lewis 186
Holmgren, Helen Jean 1930- 45
Holmgren, Sister George Ellen
    See Holmgren, Helen Jean
Holmgren, Virginia C(unningham) 1909- 26
Holmquist, Eve 1921- 11
Holt, Kimberly Willis 1960- 179
    Earlier sketch in SATA 122
Holt, Margaret 1937- 4
Holt, Margaret Van Vechten (Saunders)
    1899-1963 32
Holt, Michael (Paul) 1929- 13
Holt, Rackham
    See Holt, Margaret Van Vechten (Saunders)
Holt, Rochelle L.
    See DuBois, Rochelle Holt
Holt, Stephen
    See Thompson, Harlan
Holt, Victoria
    See Hibbert, Eleanor Alice Burford
Holton, Leonard
    See Wibberley, Leonard
Holtz, Thomas R., Jr. 1965- 203
Holtze, Sally Holmes 1952- 64
Holtzman, Jerome 1926-2008 57
    Obituary 194
Holub, Joan 1956- 149
    Earlier sketch in SATA 99
Holub, Josef 1926- 175
Holubitsky, Katherine 1955- 165
    Earlier sketch in SATA 121
Holyer, Erna Maria 1925- 22
Holyer, Ernie
    See Holyer, Erna Maria
Holz, Loretta (Marie) 1943- 17
Homel, David 1952- 97
Homze, Alma C. 1932- 17
Honey, Elizabeth 1947- 137
    Autobiography Feature 137
    Earlier sketch in SATA 112
Honeycutt, Natalie 1945- 97
Hong, Lily Toy 1958- 76
Hong, Maxine Ting Ting
    See Kingston, Maxine Hong
Honig, Donald 1931- 18
Honness, Elizabeth H. 1904- 2
Hoobler, Dorothy 1941- 161
    Earlier sketches in SATA 28, 109
Hoobler, Thomas 161
    Earlier sketches in SATA 28, 109
Hood, Joseph F. 1925- 4

Hood, Robert E. 1926- 21
Hood, Sarah
    See Killough, (Karen) Lee
Hook, Brendan 1963- 105
Hook, Frances 1912-1983 27
Hook, Geoffrey R(aynor) 1928- 103
Hook, Jeff
    See Hook, Geoffrey R(aynor)
Hook, Martha 1936- 27
Hooker, Richard
    See Heinz, W. C.
Hooker, Ruth 1920-1998 21
hooks, bell 1952(?)- 170
    Earlier sketch in SATA 115
Hooks, William H(arris) 1921- 94
    Earlier sketch in SATA 16
Hoon, Patricia Easterly 1954- 90
Hooper, Byrd
    See St. Clair, Byrd Hooper
Hooper, Mary 1948- 205
    Earlier sketch in SATA 160
Hooper, Maureen Brett 1927- 76
Hooper, Meredith 1939- 159
    Earlier sketches in SATA 28, 101
Hooper, Meredith Jean
    See Hooper, Meredith
Hooper, Patricia 1941- 95
Hoopes, Lyn Littlefield 1953- 49
    Brief entry 44
Hoopes, Ned E(dward) 1932- 21
Hoopes, Roy 1922-2009 11
Hoose, Phillip M. 1947- 137
Hoover, H(elen) M(ary) 1935- 132
    Brief entry 33
    Earlier sketches in SATA 44, 83
    See also SAAS 8
Hoover, Helen (Drusilla Blackburn)
    1910-1984 12
    Obituary 39
Hope, Christopher 1944- 62
Hope, Christopher David Tully
    See Hope, Christopher
Hope, Laura Lee
    See Goulart, Ron
    and Stanley, George Edward
Hope Simpson, Jacynth 1930- 12
Hopf, Alice (Martha) L(ightner) 1904-1988 ... 5
    Obituary 55
Hopkins, A. T.
    See Turngren, Annette
Hopkins, C. M.
    See Hopkins, Cathy
Hopkins, Cathy 1953- 165
Hopkins, Cathy M.
    See Hopkins, Cathy
Hopkins, Clark 1895-1976
    Obituary 34
Hopkins, Ellen 1955- 128
    See Hopkins, Ellen L.
Hopkins, Ellen L.
    See Hopkins, Ellen
Hopkins, Jackie
    See Hopkins, Jackie Mims
Hopkins, Jackie Mims 1952- 178
    Earlier sketch in SATA 92
Hopkins, Joseph G(erard) E(dward) 1909- ... 11
Hopkins, (Hector) Kenneth 1914-1988
    Obituary 58
Hopkins, Lee Bennett 1938- 168
    Earlier sketches in SATA 3, 68, 125
    See also CLR 44
    See also SAAS 4
Hopkins, Lyman
    See Folsom, Franklin (Brewster)
Hopkins, Marjorie 1911-1999 9
Hopkins, Mary R(ice) 1956- 97
Hopkinson, Amanda 1948- 84
Hopkinson, Deborah 1952- 180
    Autobiography Feature 180
    Earlier sketches in SATA 76, 108, 159
    See also CLR 118

Hopman, Philip 1961- 177
Hoppe, Joanne 1932- 42
Hoppe, Matthias 1952- 76
Hoppe, Paul 209
Hopper, Nancy J. 1937- 38
    Brief entry 35
Hopping, Lorraine Jean
    See Egan, Lorraine Hopping
Horacek, Petr 163
Horenstein, Henry 1947- 108
Horgan, Paul (George Vincent O'Shaughnessy)
    1903-1995 13
    Obituary 84
Horlak, E.E.
    See Tepper, Sheri S.
Horler, Sydney 1888-1954 102
Horn, Sandra Ann 1944- 154
Hornblow, Arthur, Jr. 1893-1976 15
Hornblow, Leonora 1920-2005 18
    Obituary 171
Hornblow, Leonora Schinasi
    See Hornblow, Leonora
Horne, Constance 1927- 149
Horne, Richard 1960-2007 169
    Obituary 180
    Earlier sketch in SATA 111
Horne, Richard Henry Hengist
    1802(?)-1884 29
Horner, Althea (Jane) 1926- 36
Horner, Dave 1934- 12
Horner, Jack
    See Horner, John R(obert)
Horner, John R(obert) 1946- 106
Hornik, Laurie Miller 159
Horniman, Joanne 1951- 167
    Earlier sketch in SATA 98
Hornos, Axel 1907-1994 20
Hornstein, Reuben Aaron 1912- 64
Horowitz, Anthony 1955- 195
    Earlier sketch in SATA 137
Horowitz, Dave 1970- 204
    Earlier sketch in SATA 172
Horowitz, Ruth 1957- 136
Horrocks, Anita 1958- 169
Horse, Harry
    See Horne, Richard
Horsfield, Alan 1939- 153
Hort, Lenny 179
Horton, James O. 1943- 173
Horton, James Oliver
    See Horton, James O.
Horton, Madelyn (Stacey) 1962- 77
Horvath, Betty 1927- 4
Horvath, David 1972(?)- 192
Horvath, Polly 1957- 194
    Earlier sketches in SATA 85, 140
    See also CLR 90
Horwich, Frances R(appaport) 1908-2001 11
    Obituary 130
Horwitz, Elinor Lander 45
    Brief entry 33
Horwood, William 1944- 85
Hosford, Dorothy (Grant) 1900-1952 22
Hosford, Jessie 1892-1990 5
Hoshi, Shin'ichi 1926- 101
Hoshino, Felicia 1968- 189
Hoskyns-Abrahall, Clare (Constance
    Drury) 13
Hosler, Danamarie 1978- 184
Hossack, Sylvia 1939- 83
Hossack, Sylvie Adams
    See Hossack, Sylvia
Hosseini, Khaled 1965- 156
Hossell, Karen Price
    See Price, Karen
Hosta, Dar 192
Hostetler, Marian 1932- 91
Houck, Carter 1924- 22
Hough, Charlotte 1924-2008 9
    Obituary 202

Hough, Helen Charlotte
    See Hough, Charlotte
Hough, Judy Taylor 1932- 63
    Brief entry 51
    Earlier sketch in SATA 56
Hough, Richard (Alexander) 1922-1999 ... 17
Houghton, Eric 1930- 7
Houk, Randy 1944- 97
Houlehen, Robert J. 1918- 18
Houlton, Peggy Mann 1925(?)-1990 6
Household, Geoffrey (Edward West)
    1900-1988 14
    Obituary 59
Housman, Laurence 1865-1959 25
Houston, Dick 1943- 74
Houston, Gloria 138
    Autobiography Feature 138
    Earlier sketch in SATA 81
Houston, James A(rchibald) 1921-2005 74
    Obituary 163
    Earlier sketch in SATA 13
    See also CLR 3
    See also SAAS 17
Houston, James D. 1933-2009 78
    Obituary 203
Houston, James Dudley
    See Houston, James D.
Houston, James Dudley
    See Houston, James D.
Houston, Jeanne Toyo Wakatsuki
    See Houston, Jeanne Wakatsuki
Houston, Jeanne Wakatsuki 1934- 168
    Autobiography Feature 168
    Earlier sketch in SATA 78
Houston, Juanita C. 1921- 129
Houton, Kathleen
    See Kilgore, Kathleen
Houts, Amy F. 164
Hovey, Kate 158
Howard, Alan 1922- 45
Howard, Alyssa
    See Buckholtz, Eileen (Garber)
    and Glick, Ruth (Burtnick)
    and Titchener, Louise
Howard, Arthur 1948- 165
Howard, Arthur Charles
    See Howard, Arthur
Howard, Elizabeth Fitzgerald 1927- 119
    Earlier sketch in SATA 74
Howard, Ellen 1943- 184
    Earlier sketches in SATA 67, 99
Howard, Jane R(uble) 1924- 87
Howard, Norman Barry 1949- 90
Howard, P. M.
    See Howard, Pauline Rodriguez
Howard, Paul 1967- 190
    Earlier sketch in SATA 118
Howard, Pauline Rodriguez 1951- 124
Howard, Prosper
    See Hamilton, Charles (Harold St. John)
Howard, Robert West 1908-1988 5
Howard, Todd 1964- 135
Howard, Tristan
    See Currie, Stephen
Howard, Vernon (Linwood) 1918-1992 40
    Obituary 73
Howard, Warren F.
    See Pohl, Frederik
Howarth, Daniel 188
Howarth, David (Armine) 1912-1991 6
    Obituary 68
Howarth, Lesley 1952- 94
Howe, Deborah 1946-1978 29
Howe, James 1946- 161
    Earlier sketches in SATA 29, 71, 111
    See also CLR 9
Howe, John F. 1957- 79
Howe, Norma 1930- 126
Howell, Pat 1947- 15
Howell, S.
    See Styles, (Frank) Showell

Howell, Virginia
   See Ellison, Virginia H(owell)
Howes, Barbara 1914-1996 5
Howie, Diana 1945- 122
Howie, Diana Melson
   See Howie, Diana
Howker, Janni 1957- 72
   Brief entry 46
   See also CLR 14
   See also SAAS 13
Howland, Ethan 1963- 131
Hoy, Linda 1946- 65
Hoy, Nina
   See Roth, Arthur J(oseph)
Hoyle, Geoffrey 1942- 18
Hoyt, Ard 190
Hoyt, Edwin P(almer), Jr. 1923- 28
Hoyt, Erich 1950- 140
   Earlier sketch in SATA 65
Hoyt, Olga
   See Gruhzit-Hoyt, Olga (Margaret)
Hrdlitschka, Shelley 1956- 167
   Earlier sketch in SATA 111
Hrdlitschka, Shelley Joanne
   See Hrdlitschka, Shelley
Htin Aung, U.
   See Aung, (Maung) Htin
Hu, Ying-Hwa 173
Huang, Benrei 1959- 86
Hubalek, Linda K. 1954- 111
Hubbard, Crystal 209
Hubbard, Margaret Ann
   See Priley, Margaret (Ann) Hubbard
Hubbard, Michelle Calabro 1953- 122
Hubbard, Patricia 1945- 124
Hubbard, Woodleigh Marx 160
   Earlier sketch in SATA 98
Hubbell, Patricia 1928- 186
   Earlier sketches in SATA 8, 132
Hubery, Julia 195
Hubley, Faith Elliot 1924-2001 48
   Obituary 133
Hubley, John 1914-1977 48
   Obituary 24
Huck, Charlotte S. 1922- 136
   Earlier sketch in SATA 82
Hudak, Michal 1956- 143
Hudson, Cheryl Willis 1948- 160
   Earlier sketch in SATA 81
Hudson, Jan 1954-1990 77
   See also CLR 40
Hudson, Jeffery
   See Crichton, Michael
Hudson, Jeffrey
   See Crichton, Michael
Hudson, (Margaret) Kirsty 1947- 32
Hudson, Margaret
   See Shuter, Jane (Margaret)
Hudson, W(illiam) H(enry) 1841-1922 35
Hudson, Wade 1946- 162
   Earlier sketch in SATA 74
Huelsmann, Eva 1928- 16
Huerlimann, Bettina 1909-1983 39
   Obituary 34
Huerlimann, Ruth 1939- 32
   Brief entry 31
Huff, Barbara A. 1929- 67
Huff, Tanya 1957- 171
   Earlier sketch in SATA 85
Huff, Tanya Sue
   See Huff, Tanya
Huff, T.S.
   See Huff, Tanya
Huff, Vivian 1948- 59
Huffaker, Sandy 1943- 10
Huffman, Tom 24
Huggins, Nathan Irvin 1927-1989 63
Huggins, Peter 1951- 178
Hughes, Carol 1955- 108

Hughes, Dean 1943- 139
   Earlier sketches in SATA 33, 77
   See also CLR 76
Hughes, Eden
   See Griffin, W.E.B.
Hughes, Edward James
   See Hughes, Ted
Hughes, James Langston
   See Hughes, Langston
Hughes, Langston 1902-1967 33
   Earlier sketch in SATA 4
   See also CLR 17
Hughes, Libby 71
Hughes, Matilda
   See MacLeod, Charlotte (Matilda)
Hughes, Monica 1925-2003 162
   Earlier sketches in SATA 15, 70, 119
   See also CLR 60
   See also SAAS 11
Hughes, Monica Ince
   See Hughes, Monica
Hughes, Pat 197
Hughes, Richard (Arthur Warren)
   1900-1976 8
   Obituary 25
Hughes, Sara
   See Saunders, Susan
Hughes, Shirley 1927- 159
   Earlier sketches in SATA 16, 70, 110
   See also CLR 15
Hughes, Ted 1930-1998 49
   Brief entry 27
   Obituary 107
   See also CLR 131
Hughes, Thomas 1822-1896 31
Hughes, Virginia
   See Campbell, Hope
Hughes, Walter (Llewellyn) 1910-1993 26
Hughey, Roberta 1942- 61
Hugo, Pierre Brackers de
   See Brackers de Hugo, Pierre
Hugo, Victor 1802-1885 47
Hugo, Victor Marie
   See Hugo, Victor
Huline-Dickens, Frank William 1931- 34
Huling, Jan 172
Huliska-Beith, Laura 175
Hull, Eleanor (Means) 1913- 21
Hull, Eric Traviss
   See Harnan, Terry
Hull, H. Braxton
   See Jacobs, Helen Hull
Hull, Jesse Redding
   See Hull, Jessie Redding
Hull, Jessie Redding 1932- 51
Hull, Katharine 1921-1977 23
Hull, Lise (E.) 1954- 148
Hull, Maureen 1949- 142
Hulme, Joy N. 1922- 161
   Earlier sketches in SATA 74, 112
Hults, Dorothy Niebrugge 1898-2000 6
Humble, Richard 1945- 60
Hume, Lachie 189
Hume, Lotta Carswell 7
Hume, Ruth Fox 1922-1980 26
   Obituary 22
Hume, Stephen Eaton 1947- 136
Hummel, Berta 1909-1946 43
Hummel, Sister Maria Innocentia
   See Hummel, Berta
Humphrey, Carol Sue 1956- 167
Humphrey, Henry (III) 1930- 16
Humphrey, Kate
   See Forsyth, Kate
Humphrey, Sandra McLeod 1936- 95
Humphreys, Martha 1943- 71
Humphreys, Susan L.
   See Lowell, Susan
Hundal, Nancy 1957- 128
Huneck, Stephen 1949- 183
   Earlier sketch in SATA 129

Hungerford, Hesba Fay
   See Brinsmead, H(esba) F(ay)
Hungerford, Pixie
   See Brinsmead, H(esba) F(ay)
Hunkin, Timothy Mark Trelawney 1950- 53
Hunt, Angela Elwell 1957- 159
   Earlier sketch in SATA 75
Hunt, Bernice 1920- 4
Hunt, Francesca
   See Holland, Isabelle (Christian)
Hunt, Irene 1907-2001 91
   Earlier sketch in SATA 2
   See also CLR 1
Hunt, Janie Louise 1963- 102
Hunt, Jonathan 1966- 84
Hunt, Joyce 1927- 31
Hunt, Linda 1940- 39
Hunt, Lisa B(ehnke) 1967- 84
Hunt, Mabel Leigh 1892-1971 1
   Obituary 26
Hunt, Morton M(agill) 1920- 22
Hunt, Nigel
   See Greenbank, Anthony Hunt
Hunt, Peter (Leonard) 1945- 76
Hunter, Anne B. 1966- 118
Hunter, Bernice Thurman 1922-2002 85
   Brief entry 45
Hunter, Bobbi Dooley 1945- 89
Hunter, Captain Marcy
   See Ellis, Edward S.
Hunter, Chris
   See Fluke, Joanne
Hunter, Clingham M.D.
   See Adams, William Taylor
Hunter, Edith Fisher 1919- 31
Hunter, Erin
   See Cary, Kate
Hunter, Evan 1926-2005 25
   Obituary 167
Hunter, George E.
   See Ellis, Edward S.
Hunter, Hilda 1921- 7
Hunter, Jana
   See Hunter, Jana Novotny
Hunter, Jana Novotny 190
Hunter, Jim 1939- 65
Hunter, Kristin
   See Lattany, Kristin Hunter
Hunter, Leigh
   See Etchison, Birdie L(ee)
Hunter, Lieutenant Ned
   See Ellis, Edward S.
Hunter, Mel 1927-2004 39
Hunter, Mollie 1922- 139
   Autobiography Feature 139
   Earlier sketches in SATA 2, 54, 106
   See also CLR 25
   See also SAAS 7
Hunter, Ned
   See Ellis, Edward S.
Hunter, Norman (George Lorimer)
   1899-1995 84
   Earlier sketch in SATA 26
Hunter, Ryan Ann
   See Greenwood, Pamela D.
   and Macalaster, Elizabeth G.
Hunter, Sara Hoagland 1954- 98
Hunter Blair, Pauline
   See Clarke, Pauline
Huntington, Amy 1956- 180
   Earlier sketch in SATA 138
Huntington, Geoffrey 145
Huntington, Harriet E(lizabeth) 1909- 1
Huntsberry, William E(mery) 1916- 5
Hurd, Clement (G.) 1908-1988 64
   Obituary 54
   Earlier sketch in SATA 2
   See also CLR 49

Hurd, Edith Thacher 1910-1997 .... *64*
  Obituary *95*
  Earlier sketch in SATA *2*
  See also CLR *49*
  See also SAAS *13*
Hurd, (John) Thacher 1949- *94*
  Autobiography Feature *123*
  Brief entry *45*
  Earlier sketch in SATA *46*
Hurley, Jo
  See Dower, Laura
Hurley, Tonya *207*
Hurlimann, Bettina
  See Huerlimann, Bettina
Hurlimann, Ruth
  See Huerlimann, Ruth
Hurmence, Belinda 1921- *77*
  See also CLR *25*
  See also SAAS *20*
Hurst, Carol Otis 1933-2007 .... *185*
  Earlier sketch in SATA *130*
Hurt-Newton, Tania 1968- *84*
  Hurwin, Davida Wills 1950- *180*
Hurwitz, Johanna 1937- *175*
  Earlier sketches in SATA *20, 71, 113*
  See also SAAS *18*
Hurwood, Bernhardt J. 1926-1987 .... *12*
  Obituary *50*
Husain, Shahrukh 1950- *108*
Huser, Glen 1943- *151*
Hutchens, Paul 1902-1977 .... *31*
Hutchins, Carleen M.
  See Hutchins, Carleen Maley
Hutchins, Carleen Maley 1911-2009 .... *9*
  Obituary *206*
Hutchins, Hazel J. 1952- *175*
  Brief entry *51*
  Earlier sketches in SATA *81, 135*
  See also SAAS *24*
Hutchins, Pat 1942- *178*
  Earlier sketches in SATA *15, 70, 111*
  See also CLR *20*
  See also SAAS *16*
Hutchins, Ross Elliott 1906- *4*
Hutchison, Linda 1942- *152*
Huthmacher, J. Joseph 1929- *5*
Hutto, Nelson (Allen) 1904-1985 .... *20*
Hutton, Kathryn 1915- *89*
Hutton, Sam
  See Jones, Allan Frewin
Hutton, Warwick 1939-1994 .... *20*
  Obituary *83*
  See also SAAS *17*
Huxley, Aldous 1894-1963 .... *63*
Huxley, Aldous Leonard
  See Huxley, Aldous
Huxley, Elspeth (Josceline Grant)
  1907-1997 .... *62*
  Obituary *95*
Hyde, Catherine R.
  See Hyde, Catherine Ryan
Hyde, Catherine Ryan 1955- *141*
Hyde, Dayton O(gden) *9*
Hyde, Hawk
  See Hyde, Dayton O(gden)
Hyde, Jeannette
  See Eyerly, Jeannette
Hyde, Margaret O. 1917- *139*
  Earlier sketches in SATA *1, 42, 76*
  See also CLR *23*
  See also SAAS *8*
Hyde, Margaret Oldroyd
  See Hyde, Margaret O.
Hyde, Shelley
  See Reed, Kit
Hyde, Wayne Frederick 1922- *7*
Hylander, Clarence J(ohn) 1897-1964 .... *7*
Hyman, Robin P(hilip) 1931- *12*

Hyman, Trina Schart 1939-2004 .... *95*
  Obituary *158*
  Earlier sketches in SATA *7, 46*
  See also CLR *50*
Hymes, Lucia M(anley) 1907-1998 .... *7*
Hyndman, Jane Andrews Lee 1912-1978 ..... *46*
  Obituary *23*
  Earlier sketch in SATA *1*
Hyndman, Robert Utley 1906-1973 .... *18*
Hynes, Pat *98*

I

Iannone, Jeanne
  See Balzano, Jeanne (Koppel)
Ibatoulline, Bagram 1965(?)- *174*
Ibbitson, John Perrie 1955- *102*
Ibbotson, Eva 1925- *156*
  Earlier sketches in SATA *13, 103*
Ibbotson, M. C(hristine) 1930- *5*
Icenoggle, Jodi 1967- *168*
Icenoggle, Jodi O.
  See Icenoggle, Jodi
Ichikawa, Satomi 1949- *208*
  Brief entry *36*
  Earlier sketches in SATA *47, 78, 146*
  See also CLR *62*
Iggulden, Hal 1972- *196*
Ignoffo, Matthew 1945- *92*
Igus, Toyomi 1953- *112*
  Earlier sketch in SATA *76*
Ihimaera, Witi (Tame) 1944- *148*
Ikeda, Daisaku 1928- *77*
Ilowite, Sheldon A. 1931- *27*
Ilsey, Dent
  See Chapman, John Stanton Higham
Ilsley, Dent
  See Chapman, John Stanton Higham
Ilsley, Velma (Elizabeth) 1918- *12*
Imai, Ayano 1980- *190*
Imai, Miko 1963- *90*
Imershein, Betsy 1953- *62*
Immel, Mary Blair 1930- *28*
Immell, Myra H. 1941- *92*
Impey, Rose 1947- *152*
  Earlier sketch in SATA *69*
Ingelow, Jean 1820-1897 .... *33*
Ingermanson, Randall 1958- *134*
Ingermanson, Randy
  See Ingermanson, Randall
Ingersoll, Norman 1928- *79*
Ingham, Colonel Frederic
  See Hale, Edward Everett
Ingman, Bruce 1963- *182*
  Earlier sketch in SATA *134*
Ingman, Nicholas 1948- *52*
Ingold, Jeanette *128*
Ingpen, Robert 1936- *166*
  Earlier sketch in SATA *109*
Ingpen, Robert Roger
  See Ingpen, Robert
Ingraham, Erick 1950- *145*
Ingraham, Leonard W(illiam) 1913-2003 .... *4*
Ingram, Scott 1948- *167*
  Earlier sketch in SATA *92*
Ingram, W. Scott
  See Ingram, Scott
Ingrams, Doreen 1906-1997 .... *97*
  Earlier sketch in SATA *20*
Ingrid, Charles
  See Salsitz, Rhondi Vilott
Ingves, Gunilla (Anna Maria Folkesdotter)
  1939- *101*
Inkpen, Mick 1952- *154*
  Earlier sketch in SATA *99*
Innes, (Ralph) Hammond
  See Hammond Innes, Ralph
Innes, Ralph Hammond
  See Hammond Innes, Ralph

Innocenti, Roberto 1940- *159*
  Earlier sketch in SATA *96*
  See also CLR *126*
Innocenti and Gallaz
  See Gallaz, Christophe
  and Innocenti, Roberto
Inyart, Gene
  See Namovicz, Gene Inyart
Ionesco, Eugene 1909-1994 .... *7*
  Obituary *79*
Ipcar, Dahlov (Zorach) 1917- *147*
  Autobiography Feature *147*
  Earlier sketches in SATA *1, 49*
  See also SAAS *8*
Ireland, Karin *151*
  Earlier sketch in SATA *101*
Ironside, Jetske 1940- *60*
Irvin, Fred 1914- *15*
Irvine, Georgeanne 1955- *72*
Irvine, Joan 1951- *80*
Irving, Alexander
  See Hume, Ruth Fox
Irving, Robert
  See Adler, Irving
Irving, Washington 1783-1859
  See YABC *2*
  See also CLR *97*
Irwin, Ann(abelle Bowen) 1915-1998 .... *89*
  Brief entry *38*
  Obituary *106*
  Earlier sketch in SATA *44*
  See also CLR *40*
  See also SAAS *14*
Irwin, Constance (H.) Frick 1913-1995 .... *6*
Irwin, Hadley
  See Hadley, Lee
  and Irwin, Ann(abelle Bowen)
Irwin, Keith Gordon 1885-1964 .... *11*
Isaac, Joanne 1934- *21*
Isaacs, Anne 1949- *185*
  Earlier sketch in SATA *90*
Isaacs, Jacob
  See Kranzler, George G(ershon)
Isaacson, Philip M(arshal) 1924- *87*
Isadora, Rachel 1953(?)- *204*
  Brief entry *32*
  Earlier sketches in SATA *54, 79, 121, 165*
  See also CLR *7*
Isbell, Rebecca T(emple) 1942- *125*
Isham, Charlotte H(ickock) 1912- *21*
Ishida, Jui *176*
Ish-Kishor, Judith 1892-1972 .... *11*
Ish-Kishor, Sulamith 1896-1977 .... *17*
Ishmael, Woodi 1914-1995 .... *31*
  Obituary *109*
Isle, Sue 1963- *105*
Israel, Elaine 1945- *12*
Israel, Marion Louise 1882-1973
  Obituary *26*
Iterson, S(iny) R(ose) Van
  See Van Iterson, S(iny) R(ose)
Ivanko, John D. 1966- *111*
Ivanko, John Duane
  See Ivanko, John D.
Iversen, Jeremy 1980(?)- *174*
Iversen, Jeremy Watt
  See Iversen, Jeremy
Iverson, Carol (L.) 1941- *145*
Iverson, Diane 1950- *122*
Iverson, Eric G.
  See Turtledove, Harry
Ivery, Martha M. 1948- *124*
Ives, David 1951- *173*
Ives, Morgan
  See Bradley, Marion Zimmer
Iwai, Melissa *183*
Iwamatsu, Jun Atsushi 1908-1994 .... *81*
  Earlier sketch in SATA *14*
  See also CLR *4*
Iwasaki (Matsumoto), Chihiro 1918-1974
  See CLR *18*

J

Jablonski, Carla *184*
Jac, Lee
  See Morton, Lee Jack, Jr.
Jacka, Martin 1943- *72*
Jackson, Alison 1953- *160*
  Earlier sketches in SATA *73, 108*
Jackson, Anne 1896(?)-1984
  Obituary *37*
Jackson, Barry
  See Jackson, Barry E.
Jackson, Barry E. *200*
Jackson, C(aary) Paul 1902-1991 .... *6*
Jackson, Caary
  See Jackson, C(aary) Paul
Jackson, Charlotte E. (Cobden) 1903(?)-1989
  Obituary *62*
Jackson, Dave
  See Jackson, J. David
Jackson, Donna M. 1959- *206*
Jackson, Ellen B. 1943- *167*
  Earlier sketches in SATA *75, 115*
Jackson, Garnet Nelson 1944- *87*
Jackson, Geoffrey (Holt Seymour) 1915-1987
  Obituary *53*
Jackson, Gina
  See Fluke, Joanne
Jackson, Guida M. 1930- *71*
Jackson, J. David 1944- *91*
Jackson, Jacqueline 1928- *65*
Jackson, Jacqueline Dougan
  See Jackson, Jacqueline
Jackson, Jesse 1908-1983 .... *29*
  Obituary *48*
  Earlier sketch in SATA *2*
  See also CLR *28*
Jackson, Marjorie 1928- *127*
Jackson, Melanie 1956- *141*
Jackson, Mike 1946- *91*
Jackson, Neta J. 1944- *91*
Jackson, O. B.
  See Jackson, C(aary) Paul
Jackson, Rob 1961- *176*
Jackson, Robert B(lake) 1926- *8*
Jackson, Robert Bradley
  See Jackson, Rob
Jackson, Sally
  See Kellogg, Jean (Defrees)
Jackson, Shirley 1919-1965 .... *2*
Jackson, Woody 1948- *92*
Jackson Issa, Kai *205*
Jacob, Helen Pierce 1927- *21*
Jacobin
  See Bisson, Terry
Jacobs, Deborah Lynn *187*
Jacobs, Flora Gill 1918-2006 .... *5*
  Obituary *178*
Jacobs, Francine 1935- *150*
  Brief entry *42*
  Earlier sketch in SATA *43*
Jacobs, Frank 1929- *30*
Jacobs, Helen Hull 1908-1997 .... *12*
Jacobs, Joseph 1854-1916 .... *25*
Jacobs, Judy 1952- *69*
Jacobs, Laurie A. 1956- *89*
Jacobs, Leah
  See Gellis, Roberta
Jacobs, Leland Blair 1907-1992 .... *20*
  Obituary *71*
Jacobs, Linda
  See Altman, Linda Jacobs
Jacobs, Lou(is), Jr. 1921- *2*
Jacobs, Shannon K. 1947- *77*
Jacobs, Susan
  See Quinn, Susan
Jacobs, William Jay 1933- *89*
  Earlier sketch in SATA *28*
Jacobsen, Laura *177*
Jacobson, Daniel 1923- *12*

Jacobson, Jennifer
  See Jacobson, Jennifer Richard
Jacobson, Jennifer Richard 1958- *170*
Jacobson, Morris K(arl) 1906- *21*
Jacobson, Rick *170*
Jacopetti, Alexandra
  See Hart, Alexandra
Jacques, Brian 1939- *176*
  Earlier sketches in SATA *62, 95, 138*
  See also CLR *21*
Jacques, Robin 1920-1995 .... *32*
  Brief entry *30*
  Obituary *86*
  See also SAAS *5*
Jaekel, Susan M. 1948- *89*
Jaffe, Michele *179*
Jaffe, Michele Sharon
  See Jaffe, Michele
Jaffee, Al(lan) 1921- *66*
  Earlier sketch in SATA *37*
Jagendorf, Moritz (Adolf) 1888-1981 .... *2*
  Obituary *24*
Jahn, Joseph Michael
  See Jahn, Michael
Jahn, Michael 1943- *28*
Jahn, Mike
  See Jahn, Michael
Jahn-Clough, Lisa 1967- *193*
  Earlier sketches in SATA *88, 152*
Jahsmann, Allan Hart 1916- *28*
Jakes, John 1932- *62*
Jakes, John William
  See Jakes, John
James, Andrew
  See Kirkup, James
James, Ann 1952- *168*
  Earlier sketches in SATA *82, 117*
James, Betsy *183*
James, Brian 1976- *140*
James, Bronte
  See Nash, Renea Denise
James, Captain Lew
  See Stratemeyer, Edward L.
James, Charlie 1961- *185*
James, Curtis E. *182*
James, Dynely
  See Mayne, William (James Carter)
James, Edwin
  See Gunn, James E.
James, Elizabeth 1942- *97*
  Earlier sketches in SATA *39, 45, 52*
James, Emily
  See Standiford, Natalie
James, Gordon C. 1973- *195*
James, Harry Clebourne 1896-1978 .... *11*
James, J. Alison 1962- *146*
  Earlier sketch in SATA *83*
James, Josephine
  See Sterne, Emma Gelders
James, Mary
  See Meaker, Marijane
James, Matt *201*
James, Philip
  See del Rey, Lester
  and Moorcock, Michael
James, Robin 1953- *50*
James, Robin Irene
  See James, Robin
James, Simon *202*
  See Kunen, James Simon
James, T. F.
  See Fleming, Thomas
James, Tegan
  See Odgers, Sally Farrell
James, Will(iam Roderick) 1892-1942 .... *19*
Jameson, W. C. 1942- *93*
Jamieson, Ian R.
  See Goulart, Ron
Jamiolkowski, Raymond M. 1953- *81*
Jane, Mary Childs 1909- *6*
Jane, Pamela *158*

Janeczko, Paul B(ryan) 1945- *155*
  Earlier sketches in SATA *53, 98*
  See also CLR *47*
  See also SAAS *18*
Janes, Edward C. 1908-1984 .... *25*
Janes, J(oseph) Robert 1935- *148*
  Brief entry *50*
  Earlier sketch in SATA *101*
Janeway, Elizabeth (Hall) 1913-2005 .... *19*
Janger, Kathleen N. 1940- *66*
Jango-Cohen, Judith 1955- *208*
Janice
  See Brustlein, Janice Tworkov
Janisch, Heinz 1960- *181*
Janosch
  See Eckert, Horst
Janover, Caroline (Davis) 1943- *141*
  Earlier sketch in SATA *89*
Janovitz, Marilyn *194*
Jansen, Jared
  See Cebulash, Mel
Janson, Dora Jane (Heineberg) 1916- *31*
Janson, H(orst) W(oldemar) 1913-1982 .... *9*
Jansson, Tove (Marika) 1914-2001 .... *41*
  Earlier sketch in SATA *3*
  See also CLR *125*
Janus, Grete
  See Hertz, Grete Janus
Jaques, Faith 1923-1997 .... *97*
  Earlier sketches in SATA *21, 69*
Jaquith, Priscilla 1908- *51*
Jaramillo, Mari-Luci 1928- *139*
Jarman, Julia 1946- *198*
  Earlier sketch in SATA *133*
Jarman, Rosemary Hawley 1935- *7*
Jarrell, Mary Von Schrader 1914- *35*
Jarrell, Randall 1914-1965 .... *7*
  See also CLR *111*
Jarrett, Clare 1952- *201*
Jarrett, Roxanne
  See Werner, Herma
Jarrow, Gail 1952- *185*
  Earlier sketch in SATA *84*
Jarvis, E.K.
  See Ellison, Harlan
  and Silverberg, Robert
Jarvis, Robin 1963- *181*
Jaskol, Julie 1958- *127*
Jasner, W. K.
  See Watson, Jane Werner
Jassem, Kate
  See Oppenheim, Joanne
Jauss, Anne Marie 1902(?)-1991 .... *10*
  Obituary *69*
Javernick, Ellen 1938- *89*
Jay, Alison *196*
Jayne, Lieutenant R. H.
  See Ellis, Edward S.
Jaynes, Clare
  See Mayer, Jane Rothschild
Jeake, Samuel, Jr.
  See Aiken, Conrad
Jean-Bart, Leslie 1954- *121*
Jeapes, Ben 1965- *174*
Jecan, Gavriel 1962- *200*
Jefferds, Vincent H(arris) 1916- *59*
  Brief entry *49*
Jefferies, (John) Richard 1848-1887 .... *16*
Jeffers, Dawn *189*
Jeffers, Oliver 1977- *175*
Jeffers, Susan 1942- *202*
  Earlier sketches in SATA *17, 70, 129, 137*
  See also CLR *30*
Jefferson, Sarah
  See Farjeon, (Eve) Annabel
Jeffries, Roderic 1926- *4*
Jeffries, Roderic Graeme
  See Jeffries, Roderic
Jenkin-Pearce, Susie 1943- *80*
Jenkins, A.M. 1961- *174*

Jenkins, Amanda McRaney
    See Jenkins, A.M.
Jenkins, Debra Reid
    See Reid Jenkins, Debra
Jenkins, Emily 1967- *174*
    Earlier sketch in SATA *144*
Jenkins, Jean 98
Jenkins, Jerry B. 1949- *149*
Jenkins, Jerry Bruce
    See Jenkins, Jerry B.
Jenkins, Leonard *189*
Jenkins, Marie M(agdalen) 1909- 7
Jenkins, Patrick 1955- 72
Jenkins, Steve 1952- *188*
    Earlier sketch in SATA *154*
Jenkins, William A(twell) 1922-1998 9
Jenkyns, Chris 1924- 51
Jennings, Christopher S. 1971(?)- *201*
Jennings, Coleman A(lonzo) 1933- *64*
Jennings, C.S.
    See Jennings, Christopher S.
Jennings, Dana Andrew 1957- 93
Jennings, Elizabeth (Joan) 1926-2001 66
Jennings, Gary 1928-1999 9
    Obituary *117*
Jennings, Gary Gayne
    See Jennings, Gary
Jennings, Patrick 1962- *205*
    Earlier sketches in SATA *96, 160*
Jennings, Paul 1943- *165*
    Earlier sketch in SATA *88*
    See also CLR *40*
Jennings, Richard W. 1945- *185*
    Earlier sketch in SATA *136*
Jennings, Robert
    See Hamilton, Charles (Harold St. John)
Jennings, S. M.
    See Meyer, Jerome Sydney
Jennings, Sharon 1954- 95
Jennings, Sharon Elizabeth
    See Jennings, Sharon
Jennison, C. S.
    See Starbird, Kaye
Jennison, Keith Warren 1911-1995 .... *14*
Jensen, Kathryn 1949- 81
Jensen, Kristine Mary 1961- 78
Jensen, Niels 1927- 25
Jensen, Vickie (Dee) 1946- 81
Jensen, Virginia Allen 1927- 8
Jenson-Elliott, Cynthia L(ouise) 1962- *143*
Jeram, Anita 1965- *154*
    Earlier sketches in SATA *71, 102*
Jerman, Jerry 1949- 89
Jernigan, E. Wesley 1940- 85
Jernigan, Gisela (Evelyn) 1948- 85
Jeschke, Susan 1942- 42
    Brief entry 27
Jessel, Camilla (Ruth) 1937- *143*
    Earlier sketch in SATA *29*
Jessell, Tim *177*
Jessey, Cornelia
    See Sussman, Cornelia Silver
Jewel
    See Kilcher, Jewel
Jewell, Nancy 1940- *109*
    Brief entry 41
Jewett, Eleanore Myers 1890-1967 5
Jewett, Sarah Orne 1849-1909 15
Jewett, Theodora Sarah Orne
    See Jewett, Sarah Orne
Jezard, Alison 1919- 57
    Brief entry 34
Jiang, Cheng An 1943- *109*
Jiang, Ji-li 1954- *101*
Jiang, Zheng An
    See Jiang, Cheng An
Jiler, John 1946- 42
    Brief entry 35
Jimenez, Francisco 1943- *108*
Jinks, Catherine 1963- *207*
    Earlier sketches in SATA *94, 155*

Jobb, Jamie 1945- 29
Jobling, Curtis *131*
Jocelyn, Ann Henning 1948- 92
Jocelyn, Marthe 1956- *198*
    Earlier sketches in SATA *118, 163*
Joerns, Consuelo 44
    Brief entry *33*
Joey D
    See Macaulay, Teresa (E.)
Johansen, Krista V.
    See Johansen, K.V.
Johansen, K.V 1968- *186*
Johansen, K.V. 1968- *186*
    Earlier sketch in SATA *129*
Johansson, Philip *163*
John, Antony 1972- *206*
John, Joyce 59
Johns, Avery
    See Cousins, Margaret
Johns, Elizabeth 1943- 88
Johns, Janetta
    See Quin-Harkin, Janet
Johns, Linda 1945- *173*
Johns, W(illiam) E(arle) 1893-1968 55
Johns, Captain W. E.
    See Johns, W(illiam) E(arle)
Johnson, A.
    See Johnson, Annabell
Johnson, A. E.
    See Johnson, Annabell
    and Johnson, Edgar (Raymond)
Johnson, Angela 1961- *188*
    Earlier sketches in SATA *69, 102, 150*
    See also CLR *33*
Johnson, Annabel
    See Johnson, Annabell
Johnson, Annabell 1921- 72
    Earlier sketch in SATA *2*
Johnson, Art 1946- *123*
Johnson, B. F. 1920- *1*
Johnson, Benjamin F., of Boone
    See Riley, James Whitcomb
Johnson, Bettye 1858-1919
    See Rogers, Bettye
Johnson, Caryn
    See Goldberg, Whoopi
Johnson, Caryn E.
    See Goldberg, Whoopi
Johnson, Caryn Elaine
    See Goldberg, Whoopi
Johnson, Charles R. 1925- *11*
Johnson, Charlotte Buel
    See von Wodtke, Charlotte Buel Johnson
Johnson, Chuck
    See Johnson, Charles R.
Johnson, Crockett
    See Leisk, David (Johnson)
Johnson, D(ana) William 1945- 23
Johnson, Daniel Shahid 1954- 73
Johnson, David
    See Johnson, David A.
Johnson, David A. 1951- *191*
Johnson, D.B. 1944- *183*
    Earlier sketch in SATA *146*
Johnson, Dianne 1960- *130*
Johnson, Dinah
    See Johnson, Dianne
Johnson, Dolores 1949- 69
Johnson, Donald B.
    See Johnson, D.B.
Johnson, Dorothy M(arie) 1905-1984 6
    Obituary 40
Johnson, E(ugene) Harper 44
Johnson, Edgar (Raymond) 1912-1990 72
    Earlier sketch in SATA *2*
Johnson, Eleanor Murdock 1892-1987
    Obituary 54
Johnson, Elizabeth 1911-1984 7
    Obituary 39

Johnson, Eric W(arner) 1918-1994 ....
    Obituary 82
    Earlier sketch in SATA *8*
Johnson, Evelyne 1922- 20
Johnson, Fred 19(?)-1982 63
Johnson, Gaylord 1884-1972 7
Johnson, Gerald White 1890-1980 19
    Obituary 28
Johnson, Harper
    See Johnson, E(ugene) Harper
Johnson, Harriett 1908-1987
    Obituary 53
Johnson, James Ralph 1922- *1*
Johnson, James Weldon 1871-1938 31
    See also CLR *32*
Johnson, Jane 1951- 48
Johnson, Joan J. 1942- 59
Johnson, John E(mil) 1929- 34
Johnson, Johnny 1901-1995
    See Johnson, (Walter) Ryerson
Johnson, Kathleen Jeffrie 1950- *186*
Johnson, La Verne B(ravo) 1925- 13
Johnson, Layne *187*
Johnson, Lee Kaiser 1962- 78
Johnson, Lissa H(alls) 1955- 65
Johnson, Lois Smith 1894-1993 6
Johnson, Lois Walfrid 1936- *130*
    Earlier sketches in SATA *22, 91*
Johnson, Margaret S(weet) 1893-1964 35
Johnson, Marguerite Annie
    See Angelou, Maya
Johnson, Mary Frances K. 1929(?)-1979
    Obituary 27
Johnson, Maud Battle 1918(?)-1985
    Obituary 46
Johnson, Maureen 1973- *200*
Johnson, Meredith Merrell 1952- *104*
Johnson, Milton 1932- 31
Johnson, Neil 1954- *135*
    Earlier sketch in SATA *73*
Johnson, Pamela 1949- 71
Johnson, Patricia Polin 1956- 84
Johnson, Paul Brett 1947- *132*
    Earlier sketch in SATA *83*
Johnson, Rebecca L. 1956- *147*
    Earlier sketch in SATA *67*
Johnson, Rick L. 1954- 79
Johnson, (Walter) Ryerson 1901-1995 10
    Obituary *106*
Johnson, Scott 1952- *119*
    Earlier sketch in SATA *76*
Johnson, Sherrie 1948- 87
Johnson, Shirley K(ing) 1927- 10
Johnson, Siddie Joe 1905-1977
    Obituary 20
Johnson, Spencer 1938- *145*
    Brief entry 38
Johnson, Stacie
    See Myers, Walter Dean
Johnson, Stephen T. 1964- *189*
    Earlier sketches in SATA *84, 141*
Johnson, Steve 1960- *177*
Johnson, Sue Kaiser 1963- 78
Johnson, Sylvia A. *166*
    Brief entry 52
    Earlier sketch in SATA *104*
Johnson, William R. 38
Johnson, William Weber 1909-1992 7
Johnson-Feelings, Dianne
    See Johnson, Dianne
Johnston, Agnes Christine
    See Dazey, Agnes J(ohnston)
Johnston, Annie Fellows 1863-1931 37
Johnston, Dorothy Grunbock 1915-1979 54
Johnston, Ginny 1946- 60
Johnston, H(ugh) A(nthony) S(tephen)
    1913-1967 .... *14*
Johnston, Janet 1944- 71
Johnston, Jeffry W. *188*
Johnston, Johanna 1914(?)-1982 12
    Obituary 33

Johnston, Julie 1941- *110*
   Autobiography Feature *128*
   Earlier sketch in SATA *78*
   See also CLR *41*
   See also SAAS *24*
Johnston, Lynn 1947- *118*
Johnston, Lynn Beverley
   See Johnston, Lynn
Johnston, Mark *194*
Johnston, Norma
   See St. John, Nicole
Johnston, Portia
   See Takakjian, Portia
Johnston, Susan Taylor 1942- *180*
   Earlier sketches in SATA *8, 83, 128*
Johnston, Tim(othy Patrick) 1962- *146*
Johnston, Tony
   See Johnston, Susan Taylor
Joinson, Carla *160*
Jolin, Paula *186*
Jonas, Ann 1932- *135*
   Brief entry *42*
   Earlier sketch in SATA *50*
   See also CLR *74*
Jonell, Lynne 1956- *196*
   Earlier sketch in SATA *109*
Jones, Adrienne 1915-2000 .... *82*
   Earlier sketch in SATA *7*
   See also SAAS *10*
Jones, Allan Frewin 1954- *204*
Jones, Annabel
   See Lewis, Mary
Jones, Betty Millsaps 1940- *54*
Jones, Carol 1942- *153*
   Earlier sketch in SATA *79*
Jones, Carrie 1971- *191*
Jones, Charles M. 1912-2002 .... *53*
   Obituary *133*
Jones, Charlotte Foltz 1945- *122*
   Earlier sketch in SATA *77*
Jones, Chuck
   See Jones, Charles M.
Jones, Constance *112*
Jones, Constance A.
   See Jones, Constance
Jones, David 1956- *202*
Jones, Diana Wynne 1934- *160*
   Earlier sketches in SATA *9, 70, 108*
   See also CLR *120*
   See also SAAS *7*
Jones, Douglas B. *202*
Jones, Douglas C(lyde) 1924-1998 .... *52*
Jones, Elizabeth McDavid *155*
Jones, Elizabeth Orton 1910-2005 .... *18*
   Obituary *164*
Jones, Evan 1915-1996 .... *3*
Jones, Frewin
   See Jones, Allan Frewin
Jones, Geraldine
   See McCaughrean, Geraldine
Jones, Gillingham
   See Hamilton, Charles (Harold St. John)
Jones, Gwyneth A(nn) 1952- *159*
Jones, Harold 1904-1992 .... *14*
   Obituary *72*
Jones, Helen Hinckley 1903-1991 .... *26*
Jones, Helen L(ouise) 1903-1973
   Obituary *22*
Jones, Hettie 1934- *42*
   Brief entry *27*
Jones, Hortense P. 1918- *9*
Jones, J. Sydney 1948- *101*
Jones, Jasmine
   See Papademetriou, Lisa
Jones, Jennifer (Berry) 1947- *90*
Jones, Jessie Mae Orton 1887(?)-1983
   Obituary *37*
Jones, John R(obert) 1926- *76*
Jones, Jon Sydney
   See Jones, J. Sydney
Jones, Kimberly K. 1957- *187*

Jones, Marcia Thornton 1958- *115*
   Earlier sketch in SATA *73*
Jones, Martha T(annery) 1931- *130*
Jones, Mary Alice 1898(?)-1980 .... *6*
Jones, McClure *34*
Jones, Noah Z. *182*
Jones, Patrick 1961- *136*
Jones, Penelope 1938- *31*
Jones, Rebecca C(astaldi) 1947- *99*
   Earlier sketch in SATA *33*
Jones, Robin D(orothy) 1959- *80*
Jones, Sanford W.
   See Thorn, John
Jones, Sylvie *185*
Jones, Sylvie Michelle
   See Jones, Sylvie
Jones, Terence Graham Parry 1942- *127*
   Brief entry *51*
   Earlier sketch in SATA *67*
Jones, Terry
   See Jones, Terence Graham Parry
Jones, Tim Wynne
   See Wynne-Jones, Tim
Jones, Traci L. *186*
Jones, V. M. 1958- *147*
Jones, Veda Boyd 1948- *119*
Jones, Victoria Mary
   See Jones, V. M.
Jones, Volcano
   See Mitchell, Adrian
Jones, Weyman (B.) 1928- *4*
   See also SAAS *11*
Jones, William Glynne
   See Glynne-Jones, William
Jonk, Clarence 1906-1987 .... *10*
Jonsberg, Barry 1951- *168*
Joos, Francoise 1956- *78*
Joos, Frederic 1953- *78*
Joosse, Barbara M. 1949- *164*
   Earlier sketches in SATA *52, 96*
Joosse, Barbara Monnot
   See Joosse, Barbara M.
Jordan, Alexis Hill
   See Glick, Ruth (Burtnick)
   and Titchener, Louise
Jordan, Anne Devereaux 1943- *80*
Jordan, Chris
   See Philbrick, Rodman
Jordan, Deloris *191*
Jordan, Don
   See Howard, Vernon (Linwood)
Jordan, Hope Dahle 1905-1995 .... *15*
Jordan, Jael (Michal) 1949- *30*
Jordan, June 1936-2002 .... *136*
   Earlier sketch in SATA *4*
   See also CLR *10*
Jordan, June Meyer
   See Jordan, June
Jordan, Lee
   See Scholefield, Alan
Jordan, Martin George 1944- *84*
Jordan, Robert 1948-2007 .... *95*
Jordan, Robert K.
   See Jordan, Robert
Jordan, Rosa 1939- *191*
Jordan, Roslyn M. *189*
Jordan, Sherryl 1949- *122*
   Earlier sketch in SATA *71*
   See also SAAS *23*
Jordan, Shirley 1930- *154*
Jordan, Tanis 1946- *84*
Jorgensen, Ivar
   See Ellison, Harlan
   and Garrett, Randall
Jorgensen, Mary Venn -1995 .... *36*
Jorgensen, Norman 1954- *157*
Jorgenson, Ivar
   See Silverberg, Robert
Jorisch, Stephane *178*
Joseph, Anne
   See Coates, Anna

Joseph, James (Herz) 1924- *53*
Joseph, Joan 1939- *34*
Joseph, Joseph M(aron) 1903-1979 .... *22*
Joseph, Patrick
   See O'Malley, Kevin
Josephs, Rebecca
   See Talbot, Toby
Josephson, Judith Pinkerton 1943- *198*
Josh
   See Twain, Mark
Joshua, Peter
   See Stone, Peter
Joslin, Mary 1953- *176*
Joslin, Sesyle
   See Hine, Sesyle Joslin
Joubert, Beverly 1957- *204*
Joubert, Dereck *204*
Journet, Mireille
   See Marokvia, Mireille
Joyce, Bill
   See Joyce, William
Joyce, J(ames) Avery 1902-1987 .... *11*
   Obituary *50*
Joyce, Peter 1937- *127*
Joyce, William 1957- *118*
   Brief entry *46*
   Earlier sketch in SATA *72*
   See also CLR *26*
Joyner, Jerry 1938- *34*
Juan, Ana 1961- *179*
Jubert, Herve *185*
Juby, Susan 1969- *202*
   Earlier sketch in SATA *156*
Jucker, Sita 1921- *5*
Judah, Aaron 1923- *118*
Judd, Cyril
   See Kornbluth, C(yril) M.
   and Merril, Judith
   and Pohl, Frederik
Judd, Denis (O'Nan) 1938- *33*
Judd, Frances K.
   See Benson, Mildred
Jude, Conny *81*
Judge, Lita *192*
Judson, Clara Ingram 1879-1960 .... *38*
   Brief entry *27*
Judy, Stephen
   See Tchudi, Stephen N.
Judy, Stephen N.
   See Tchudi, Stephen N.
Juhasz, Victor 1954- *177*
Jukes, Mavis 1947- *111*
   Brief entry *43*
   Earlier sketch in SATA *72*
   See also SAAS *12*
Jules, Jacqueline 1956- *183*
   Earlier sketch in SATA *148*
Julesberg, Elizabeth Rider Montgomery
   1902-1985 .... *34*
   Obituary *41*
   Earlier sketch in SATA *3*
Julian, Jane
   See Wiseman, David
Jumpp, Hugo
   See MacPeek, Walter G.
Jungman, Ann *165*
Jupo, Frank J. 1904-1981 .... *7*
Jurmain, Suzanne 1945- *169*
   Earlier sketch in SATA *72*
Jurmain, Suzanne Tripp
   See Jurmain, Suzanne
Juster, Norton 1929- *132*
   Earlier sketch in SATA *3*
   See also CLR *112*
Justus, May 1898-1989 .... *1*
   Obituary *106*
Juvenilia
   See Taylor, Ann

K

Kaaberbol, Lene
  See Kaaberbol, Lene
Kaaberbol, Lene 1960- *159*
Kabdebo, Tamas
  See Kabdebo, Thomas
Kabdebo, Thomas 1934- *10*
Kabibble, Osh
  See Jobb, Jamie
Kacer, Kathy 1954- *184*
  Earlier sketch in SATA *142*
Kaczman, James *156*
Kadair, Deborah Ousley *184*
Kadesch, Robert R(udstone) 1922- *31*
Kadohata, Cynthia 1956(?)- *180*
  Earlier sketch in SATA *155*
  See also CLR *121*
Kaempfert, Wade
  See del Rey, Lester
Kaestner, Erich 1899-1974 .... *14*
  See also CLR *4*
Kahl, Jonathan (D.) 1959- *77*
Kahl, M(arvin) P(hilip) 1934- *37*
Kahl, Virginia (Caroline) 1919-2004 .... *48*
  Brief entry *38*
  Obituary *158*
Kahn, Joan 1914-1994 .... *48*
  Obituary *82*
Kahn, Katherine Janus 1942- *167*
  Earlier sketch in SATA *90*
Kahn, Peggy
  See Katz, Bobbi
Kahn, Roger 1927- *37*
Kahukiwa, Robyn 1940- *134*
Kains, Josephine
  See Goulart, Ron
Kaizuki, Kiyonori 1950- *72*
Kakimoto, Kozo 1915- *11*
Kalashnikoff, Nicholas 1888-1961 .... *16*
Kalb, Jonah 1926- *23*
Kalbacken, Joan 1925- *96*
Kalechofsky, Roberta 1931- *92*
Kaler, James Otis 1848-1912 .... *15*
Kalis, Jennifer *207*
Kalish, Claire M. 1947- *92*
Kallen, Stuart A(rnold) 1955- *126*
  Earlier sketch in SATA *86*
Kallevig, Christine Petrell 1955- *164*
Kalman, Bobbie 1947- *63*
Kalman, Maira 1949- *137*
  Earlier sketch in SATA *96*
  See also CLR *32*
Kalnay, Francis 1899-1992 .... *7*
Kaloustian, Rosanne 1955- *93*
Kalow, Gisela 1946- *32*
Kalstein, Dave *175*
Kamen, Gloria 1923- *98*
  Earlier sketch in SATA *9*
Kamerman, Sylvia E.
  See Burack, Sylvia K.
Kamm, Josephine (Hart) 1905-1989 .... *24*
Kammerman, Sylvia K.
  See Burack, Sylvia K.
Kandel, Michael 1941- *93*
Kandell, Alice S. 1938- *35*
Kane, Bob 1916-1998 .... *120*
Kane, Henry Bugbee 1902-1971 .... *14*
Kane, L. A.
  See Mannetti, Lisa
Kane, Robert W. 1910- *18*
Kane, Wilson
  See Bloch, Robert (Albert)
Kanefield, Teri 1960- *135*
Kaner, Etta 1947- *198*
  Earlier sketch in SATA *126*
Kanetzke, Howard W(illiam) 1932- *38*
Kangas, Juli 1958- *200*
Kann, Elizabeth *180*
Kann, Victoria *180*
Kanninen, Barbara *196*

Kanninen, Barbara J.
  See Kanninen, Barbara
Kanoza, Muriel Canfield
  See Canfield, Muriel
Kantner, Seth 1965- *179*
Kanzawa, Toshiko
  See Furukawa, Toshi
Kanzler, John 1963- *188*
Kaplan, Andrew 1960- *78*
Kaplan, Anne Bernays
  See Bernays, Anne
Kaplan, Bess 1927- *22*
Kaplan, Boche 1926- *24*
Kaplan, Elizabeth 1956- *83*
Kaplan, Elizabeth A.
  See Kaplan, Elizabeth
Kaplan, Irma 1900- *10*
Kaplan, Jean Caryl Korn 1926- *10*
Kaplow, Robert 1954- *70*
Karageorge, Michael
  See Anderson, Poul
Karas, G. Brian 1957- *178*
Karas, George Brian
  See Karas, G. Brian
Karasz, Ilonka 1896-1981
  Obituary *29*
Karen, Ruth 1922-1987 .... *9*
  Obituary *54*
Kark, Nina Mary
  See Bawden, Nina
Karl, Herb 1938- *73*
Karl, Jean E(dna) 1927-2000 .... *122*
  Earlier sketch in SATA *34*
  See also SAAS *10*
Karlin, Bernie 1927- *68*
Karlin, Eugene 1918- *10*
Karlin, Nurit *103*
  Earlier sketch in SATA *63*
Karnes, Frances A. 1937- *110*
Karp, Naomi J. 1926- *16*
Karpinski, J. Rick
  See Karpinski, John Eric
Karpinski, John Eric 1952- *81*
Karpinski, Rick
  See Karpinski, John Eric
Karr, Kathleen 1946- *127*
  Earlier sketch in SATA *82*
Karr, Phyllis Ann 1944- *119*
Karwoski, Gail 1949- *127*
Karwoski, Gail Langer
  See Karwoski, Gail
Kashiwagi, Isami 1925- *10*
Kaslik, Ibi
  See Kaslik, Ibolya Emma
Kaslik, Ibolya Emma 1973- *185*
Kassem, Lou 1931- *62*
  Brief entry *51*
Kastel, Warren
  See Silverberg, Robert
Kastner, Erich
  See Kaestner, Erich
Kastner, Jill (Marie) 1964- *117*
  Earlier sketch in SATA *70*
Kasuya, Masahiro 1937- *51*
Kasza, Keiko 1951- *191*
  Earlier sketch in SATA *124*
Kataphusin
  See Ruskin, John
Katchen, Carole 1944- *9*
Katcher, Brian 1975- *203*
Kathryn
  See Searle, Kathryn Adrienne
Kato, Aya 1982- *202*
Katona, Robert 1949- *21*
Katsarakis, Joan Harries
  See Harries, Joan
Katz, Alan *185*
Katz, Avi 1949- *199*
Katz, Avner 1939- *103*
Katz, Bobbi 1933- *179*
  Earlier sketch in SATA *12*

Katz, Fred(eric Phillip) 1938- *6*
Katz, Jane B(resler) 1934- *33*
Katz, Karen 1947- *195*
  Earlier sketch in SATA *158*
Katz, Marjorie P.
  See Weiser, Marjorie P(hillis) K(atz)
Katz, Susan 1945- *156*
Katz, Welwyn Wilton 1948- *96*
  Autobiography Feature *118*
  Earlier sketch in SATA *62*
  See also CLR *45*
Katz, William 1940- *98*
Katz, William Loren 1927- *13*
Kaufman, Bel *57*
Kaufman, Jeff 1955- *84*
Kaufman, Joe 1911-2001 .... *33*
Kaufman, Joseph
  See Kaufman, Joe
Kaufman, Mervyn D. 1932- *4*
Kaufmann, Angelika 1935- *15*
Kaufmann, John 1931- *18*
Kaula, Edna Mason 1906-1987 .... *13*
Kaur Khalsa, Dayal
  See Khalsa, Dayal Kaur
Kavaler, Lucy 1930- *23*
Kavanagh, Jack 1920- *85*
Kavanagh, P(atrick) J(oseph Gregory)
  1931- *122*
Kavanaugh, Ian
  See Webb, Jean Francis (III)
Kay, Alan N. 1965- *144*
Kay, Elizabeth 1949- *165*
Kay, Guy Gavriel 1954- *167*
  Earlier sketch in SATA *121*
Kay, Helen
  See Goldfrank, Helen Colodny
Kay, Jackie 1961- *165*
  Earlier sketch in SATA *97*
Kay, Jacqueline Margaret
  See Kay, Jackie
Kay, Julia *205*
Kay, Mara *13*
Kay, Verla 1946- *120*
Kaye, Danny 1913-1987
  Obituary *50*
Kaye, Geraldine (Hughesdon) 1925- *85*
  Earlier sketch in SATA *10*
Kaye, Judy
  See Baer, Judy
Kaye, Marilyn 1949- *110*
  Earlier sketch in SATA *56*
Kaye, Mary Margaret
  See Kaye, M.M.
Kaye, M.M. 1908-2004 .... *62*
  Obituary *152*
Kaye, Mollie
  See Kaye, M.M.
Kaye, Peggy 1948- *143*
Keach, James P. 1950- *125*
Keams, Geri 1951- *117*
Keane, Bil 1922- *4*
Keaney, Brian 1954- *188*
  Earlier sketch in SATA *106*
Kearney, Meg 1964- *178*
Kearny, Jillian
  See Goulart, Ron
Keating, Bern
  See Keating, Leo Bernard
Keating, Frank 1944- *143*
Keating, Lawrence A. 1903-1966 .... *23*
Keating, Leo Bernard 1915- *10*
Keats, Emma 1899(?)-1979(?) *68*
Keats, Ezra Jack 1916-1983 .... *57*
  Obituary *34*
  Earlier sketch in SATA *14*
  See also CLR *35*
Keefer, Catherine
  See Ogan, George F.
  and Ogan, Margaret E. (Nettles)
Keefer, Janice Kulyk
  See Kulyk Keefer, Janice

Keegan, Marcia 1943- 104
Earlier sketch in SATA 9
Keehn, Sally M. 1947- 165
Earlier sketch in SATA 87
Keel, Frank
See Keeler, Ronald F(ranklin)
Keeler, Patricia 183
Keeler, Patricia A.
See Keeler, Patricia
Keeler, Ronald F(ranklin) 1913-1983 47
Keely, Jack 1951- 119
Keen, Martin L. 1913-1992 4
Keenan, Sheila 1953- 95
Keene, Ann T(odd) 1940- 86
Keene, Carolyn
See Benson, Mildred
and Goulart, Ron
and Lerangis, Peter
and McFarlane, Leslie
and Stanley, George Edward
and Stratemeyer, Edward L.
Keens-Douglas, Richardo 1953- 154
Earlier sketch in SATA 95
Keep, Linda Lowery
See Lowery, Linda
Keep, Richard 1949- 170
Keep, Richard Cleminson
See Keep, Richard
Keeping, Charles (William James)
1924-1988 69
Obituary 56
Earlier sketch in SATA 9
See also CLR 34
Keeshan, Robert J. 1927-2004 32
Obituary 151
Kehlenbeck, Angela 1959- 186
Kehret, Peg 1936- 149
Autobiography Feature 149
Earlier sketches in SATA 73, 108
Keillor, Garrison 1942- 58
Keillor, Gary Edward
See Keillor, Garrison
Keir, Christine
See Pullein-Thompson, Christine
Keister, Douglas 1948- 88
Keith, Doug 1952- 81
Keith, Eros 1942- 52
Keith, Hal 1934- 36
Keith, Harold (Verne) 1903-1998 74
Earlier sketch in SATA 2
Keith, Robert
See Applebaum, Stan
Keleinikov, Andrei 1924- 65
Kelemen, Julie 1959- 78
Kelen, Emery 1896-1978 13
Obituary 26
Kelleam, Joseph E(veridge) 1913-1975 31
Kelleher, Anne 1959- 97
Kelleher, Annette 1950- 122
Kelleher, Daria Valerian 1955- 79
Kelleher, Victor (Michael Kitchener)
1939- 129
Brief entry 52
Earlier sketch in SATA 75
See also CLR 36
Keller, Beverly L(ou) 91
Earlier sketch in SATA 13
Keller, Charles 1942- 82
Earlier sketch in SATA 8
Keller, Debra 1958- 94
Keller, Dick 1923- 36
Keller, Emily 96
Keller, Gail Faithfull
See Faithfull, Gail
Keller, Holly 1942- 157
Brief entry 42
Earlier sketches in SATA 76, 108
See also CLR 45
Keller, Irene (Barron) 1927-2002 36
Obituary 139
Keller, Laurie 1961(?)- 196

Kelley, Ellen A. 185
Kelley, Ellen Chavez
See Kelley, Ellen A.
Kelley, Gary 1945- 183
Kelley, Leo P(atrick) 1928- 32
Brief entry 31
Kelley, Patrick (G.) 1963- 129
Kelley, Patte 1947- 93
Kelley, True 1946- 179
Kelley, True (Adelaide) 1946- 130
Brief entry 39
Earlier sketches in SATA 41, 92
Kelley, True Adelaide
See Kelley, True
Kellin, Sally Moffet 1932- 9
Kelling, Furn L. 1914-2000 37
Kellogg, Gene
See Kellogg, Jean (Defrees)
Kellogg, Jean (Defrees) 1916-1978 10
Kellogg, Steven 1941- 177
Earlier sketches in SATA 8, 57, 130
See also CLR 6
Kellogg, Steven Castle
See Kellogg, Steven
Kellow, Kathleen
See Hibbert, Eleanor Alice Burford
Kelly, C. M. O.
See Gibbs, (Cecilia) May
Kelly, Clint 1950- 140
Kelly, Eric P(hilbrook) 1884-1960
See YABC 1
Kelly, Fiona
See Coleman, Michael
and Hendry, Frances Mary
and Jones, Allan Frewin
and Oldfield, Jenny
and Welford, Sue
Kelly, Irene 1957- 147
Kelly, Jeff
See Kelly, Jeffrey
Kelly, Jeffrey 1946- 65
Kelly, Joanne (W.) 1934- 87
Kelly, Kate 1958- 91
Kelly, Kathleen M. 1964- 71
Kelly, Katy 1955- 169
Kelly, Lauren
See Oates, Joyce Carol
Kelly, Laurene 1954- 123
Kelly, Martha Rose 1914-1983 37
Kelly, Marty
See Kelly, Martha Rose
Kelly, Mij 166
Kelly, Ralph
See Geis, Darlene Stern
Kelly, Regina Z(immerman) 1898-1986 5
Kelly, Rosalie (Ruth) 43
Kelly, Tom 1961- 191
Kelly, Walt(er Crawford) 1913-1973 18
Kelsey, Alice Geer 1896-1982 1
Kelsey, Elin 1961- 159
Kemly, Kathleen 1958- 197
Kemnitz, Thomas Milton, Jr. 1984- 152
Kemnitz, Tom, Jr.
See Kemnitz, Thomas Milton, Jr.
Kemp, Gene 1926- 75
Earlier sketch in SATA 25
See also CLR 29
Kempner, Mary Jean 1913-1969 10
Kempter, Christa 1945- 187
Kempton, Jean Welch 1914- 10
Kenah, Katharine 1949- 182
Kenda, Margaret 1942- 71
Kendall, Carol (Seeger) 1917- 74
Earlier sketch in SATA 11
See also SAAS 7
Kendall, Katherine
See Applegate, Katherine
Kendall, Lace
See Stoutenburg, Adrien (Pearl)
Kendall, Martha E. 87
Kendall, Russ 1957- 83

Kenealy, James P. 1927- 52
Brief entry 29
Kenealy, Jim
See Kenealy, James P.
Kennaway, Adrienne 1945- 171
Earlier sketch in SATA 60
Kennedy, Anne 1955- 198
Kennedy, Anne Vittur
See Kennedy, Anne
Kennedy, Brendan 1970- 57
Kennedy, Dana Forrest 1917- 74
Kennedy, Dorothy M(intzlaff) 1931- 53
Kennedy, Doug 1963- 189
Earlier sketch in SATA 122
Kennedy, Frances 1937- 192
Kennedy, John F. 1917-1963 11
Kennedy, John Fitzgerald
See Kennedy, John F.
Kennedy, Joseph Charles 1929- 130
Autobiography Feature 130
Earlier sketches in SATA 14, 86
See also CLR 27
See also SAAS 22
See Kennedy, X. J.
Kennedy, Kim 189
Kennedy, Pamela (J.) 1946- 87
Kennedy, Paul E(dward) 1929- 113
Earlier sketch in SATA 33
Kennedy, Richard (Pitt) 1910-1989
Obituary 60
Kennedy, (Jerome) Richard 1932- 22
Kennedy, Robert 1938- 63
Kennedy, T.A. 1953- 42
Brief entry 35
Kennedy, Teresa
See Kennedy, T.A.
Kennedy, Teresa A.
See Kennedy, T.A.
Kennedy, William 1928- 57
Kennedy, William Joseph
See Kennedy, William
Kennedy, X. J.
See CLR 27
See also SAAS 22
See Kennedy, Joseph Charles
Kennell, Ruth Epperson 1893-1977 6
Obituary 25
Kennemore, Tim 1957- 133
Kennen, Ally 190
Kennett, David 1959- 206
Earlier sketch in SATA 121
Kennison, Ruth 202
Kenny, Ellsworth Newcomb 1909-1971
Obituary 26
Kenny, Herbert Andrew 1912-2002 13
Kenny, Jude
See Daly, Jude
Kenny, Kathryn
See Bowden, Joan Chase
and Krull, Kathleen
and Sanderlin, Owenita (Harrah)
and Stack, Nicolete Meredith
Kenny, Kevin
See Krull, Kathleen
Kensinger, George
See Fichter, George S.
Kensington, Kathryn Wesley
See Rusch, Kristine Kathryn
Kent, Alexander
See Reeman, Douglas Edward
Kent, David
See Lambert, David
Kent, Deborah Ann 1948- 155
Brief entry 41
Earlier sketches in SATA 47, 104
Kent, Jack
See Kent, John Wellington
Kent, John Wellington 1920-1985 24
Obituary 45
Kent, Lisa 1942- 90

Kent, Mallory
   See Lowndes, Robert A(ugustine) W(ard)
Kent, Margaret 1894- 2
Kent, Rockwell 1882-1971 6
Kent, Rose 188
Kent, Sherman 1903-1986 20
   Obituary 47
Kenward, Jean 1920- 42
Kenworthy, Leonard S. 1912-1991 6
Kenyon, Karen (Smith) 1938- 145
Kenyon, Kate
   See Adorjan, Carol (Madden)
   and Ransom, Candice F.
Kenyon, Ley 1913-1990 6
Keown, Elizabeth 78
Kepes, Juliet A(ppleby) 1919-1999 13
Kephart, Beth 1960- 196
Kerby, Mona 1951- 202
   Earlier sketch in SATA 75
Kerigan, Florence 1896-1984 12
Kerley, Barbara 1960- 191
   Earlier sketch in SATA *138*
Kerman, Gertrude
   See Furman, Gertrude Lerner Kerman
Kerns, Thelma 1929- 116
Kerr, Anne Louise
   See Mackey, Weezie Kerr
Kerr, Bob 1951- 120
Kerr, Jessica 1901-1991 13
Kerr, (Anne-)Judith 1923-1970 24
Kerr, M. E.
   See Meaker, Marijane
Kerr, P.B.
   See Kerr, Philip
Kerr, Philip 1956- 168
Kerr, Phyllis Forbes 1942- 72
Kerr, Tom 1950- 77
Kerrin, Jessica Scott 174
Kerry, Frances
   See Kerigan, Florence
Kerry, Lois
   See Duncan, Lois
Kershen, (L.) Michael 1982- 82
Kerven, Rosalind 1954- 83
Ker Wilson, Barbara 1929- 121
   Earlier sketches in SATA *20, 70*
   See also SAAS *18*
Keselman, Gabriela 1953- 128
Kesey, Ken 1935-2001 66
   Obituary 131
Kesey, Ken Elton
   See Kesey, Ken
Kesler, Jay 1935- 65
Kessel, Joyce Karen 1937- 41
Kessler, Cristina 190
Kessler, Ethel 1922- 44
   Brief entry 37
Kessler, Leonard P. 1921- 14
Kessler, Liz 1966- 206
Kest, Kristin 1967- 168
   Earlier sketch in SATA *118*
Kesteven, G. R.
   See Crosher, G. R.
Ketcham, Hank
   See Ketcham, Henry King
Ketcham, Henry King 1920-2001 28
   Brief entry 27
   Obituary 128
Ketcham, Sallie 1963- 124
Ketchum, Liza 1946-
   See Murrow, Liza Ketchum
Ketner, Mary Grace 1946- 75
Kettelkamp, Larry (Dale) 1933- 2
   See also SAAS *3*
Ketteman, Helen 1945- 167
   Earlier sketches in SATA *73, 115*
Kettle, Peter
   See Glover, Denis (James Matthews)
Kevles, Bettyann Holtzmann 1938- 23
Key, Alexander (Hill) 1904-1979 8
   Obituary 23

Key, Samuel M.
   See de Lint, Charles
Key, Watt 1970- 189
Keyes, Daniel 1927- 37
Keyes, Diane 207
Keyes, Fenton 1915-1999 34
Keyes, Greg 1963- 116
Keyes, J. Gregory
   See Keyes, Greg
Keyser, Marcia 1933- 42
Keyser, Sarah
   See McGuire, Leslie (Sarah)
Khalid, Mohamed Nor
   See Lat
Khalsa, Dayal Kaur 1943-1989 62
   See also CLR *30*
Khan, Rukhsana 1962- 165
   Earlier sketch in SATA *118*
Khanshendel, Chiron
   See Rose, Wendy
Kheirabadi, Masoud 1951- 158
Khemir, Sabiha 87
Kherdian, David 1931- 74
   Autobiography Feature 125
   Earlier sketch in SATA *16*
   See also CLR *24*
Khing, T.T. 1933- 192
Kibbe, Pat (Hosley) 60
Kidd, Diana 1933-2000 150
Kidd, Richard 1952-2008 152
   Obituary 194
Kidd, Ronald 1948- 173
   Earlier sketches in SATA *42, 92*
Kiddell, John 1922- 3
Kiddell-Monroe, Joan 1908-1972 55
Kidwell, Carl 1910- 43
Kiefer, Irene 1926- 21
Kiefer, Kathleen Balmes 1957- 142
Kiepper, Shirley Morgan 1933- 10
Kierstead, Vera M.
   See Kierstead-Farber, Vera M.
Kierstead-Farber, Vera M. 1913- 121
Kierstead-Farber, Vera May
   See Kierstead-Farber, Vera M.
Kiesel, Stanley 1925- 35
Kiesler, Kate (A.) 1971- 152
   Earlier sketch in SATA *90*
Kihn, Greg 1952- 110
Kikukawa, Cecily H(arder) 1919- 44
   Brief entry 35
Kilcher, Jewel 1974- 109
Kile, Joan 1940- 78
Kilgore, Kathleen 1946- 42
Kilian, Crawford 1941- 35
Killdeer, John
   See Mayhar, Ardath
Killien, Christi 1956- 73
Killilea, Marie (Lyons) 1913-1991 2
Killingback, Julia 1944- 63
Killough, (Karen) Lee 1942- 64
Kilpatrick, Don 206
Kilreon, Beth
   See Walker, Barbara (Jeanne) K(erlin)
Kilworth, Garry 1941- 94
Kilworth, Garry D.
   See Kilworth, Garry
Kilworth, Garry Douglas
   See Kilworth, Garry
Kim, David 1977- 201
Kim, Helen 1899-1970 98
Kim, Joung Un 1970- 205
Kimball, Gayle 1943- 90
Kimball, Violet T(ew) 1932- 126
Kimball, Yeffe 1914-1978 37
Kimber, Murray 1964- 171
Kimble, Warren 176
Kimbrough, Emily 1899-1989 2
   Obituary 59
Kimeldorf, Martin 1948- 121
Kimeldorf, Martin R.
   See Kimeldorf, Martin

Kimenye, Barbara 1940(?)- 121
Kimmel, Elizabeth Cody 209
   Earlier sketch in SATA *170*
Kimmel, Eric A. 1946- 208
   Earlier sketches in SATA *13, 80, 125, 176*
Kimmel, Margaret Mary 1938- 43
   Brief entry 33
Kimmelman, Burt 1947- 180
Kimmelman, Leslie (Grodinsky) 1958- 156
   Earlier sketch in SATA *85*
Kincaid, Jamaica 1949-
   See CLR *63*
Kincher, Jonni 1949- 79
Kindl, Patrice 1951- 128
   Earlier sketch in SATA *82*
   See also CLR *132*
Kindred, Wendy (Good) 1937- 7
Kinerk, Robert 199
Kines, Pat Decker 1937- 12
King, Adam
   See Hoare, Robert J(ohn)
King, Alison
   See Martini, Teri
King, (Maria) Anna 1964- 72
King, Billie Jean 1943- 12
King, Christopher (L.) 1945- 84
King, (David) Clive 1924- 144
   Earlier sketch in SATA *28*
King, Colin 1943- 76
King, Cynthia 1925- 7
King, Daniel (John) 1963- 130
King, Daren 1972- 197
King, Elizabeth 1953- 83
King, Frank O. 1883-1969
   Obituary 22
King, Frank R. 1904-1999 127
King, Jane
   See Currie, Stephen
King, Jeanette (Margaret) 1959- 105
King, Larry L. 1929- 66
King, Laurie R. 1952- 88
King, Marian 1900(?)-1986 23
   Obituary 47
King, Martin Luther, Jr. 1929-1968 14
King, Mary Ellen 1958- 93
King, Paul
   See Drackett, Phil(ip Arthur)
King, Paula
   See Downing, Paula E.
King, Stephen 1947- 161
   Earlier sketches in SATA *9, 55*
   See also CLR *124*
King, Stephen Edwin
   See King, Stephen
King, Stephen Michael 157
King, Steve
   See King, Stephen
King, Thomas 1943- 96
King, Thomas Hunt
   See King, Thomas
King, Tony 1947- 39
King, Willie Christine
   See Farris, Christine King
Kingfisher, Rupert 209
Kingman, Dong (Moy Shu) 1911-2000 44
Kingman, Lee
   See Natti, Lee
Kingsland, Leslie William 1912- 13
Kingsley, Charles 1819-1875
   See YABC *2*
   See also CLR *77*
Kingsley, Emily Perl 1940- 33
Kingsley, Kaza 193
King-Smith, Dick 1922- 192
   Brief entry 38
   Earlier sketches in SATA *47, 80, 135*
   See also CLR *40*
Kingston, Maxine Hong 1940- 53
Kingston, Maxine Ting Ting Hong
   See Kingston, Maxine Hong
Kinney, C. Cle(land) 1915- 6

Kinney, Harrison 1921- 13
Kinney, Jean Stout 1912- 12
Kinney, Jeff 1971- 187
Kinsey, Elizabeth
See Clymer, Eleanor
Kinsey, Helen 1948- 82
Kinsey-Warnock, Natalie 1956- 167
Earlier sketches in SATA *71, 116*
Kinzel, Dorothy 1950- 57
Kinzel, Dottie
See Kinzel, Dorothy
Kipling, Joseph Rudyard
See Kipling, Rudyard
Kipling, Rudyard 1865-1936 100
See also YABC *2*
See also CLR *65*
Kippax, Frank
See Needle, Jan
Kirby, David K. 1944- 78
Kirby, David Kirk
See Kirby, David K.
Kirby, Margaret
See Bingley, Margaret (Jane Kirby)
Kirby, Susan E. 1949- 62
Kirk, Connie Ann 1957- 167
Kirk, Daniel 1952- 196
Earlier sketches in SATA *107, 153*
Kirk, David 1955- 161
Earlier sketch in SATA *117*
Kirk, Heather 1949- 166
Kirk, Ruth (Kratz) 1925- 5
Kirkham, Dinah
See Card, Orson Scott
Kirkland, Will
See Hale, Arlene
Kirkpatrick, Katherine (Anne) 1964- 113
Kirkup, James 1918-2009 12
Kirkus, Virginia
See Glick, Virginia Kirkus
Kirkwood, Kathryn
See Fluke, Joanne
Kirshenbaum, Binnie 79
Kirshner, David S. 1958- 123
Kirtland, G. B.
See Hine, Sesyle Joslin
and Hine, Al(fred Blakelee)
Kirwan, Wednesday 198
Kish, Eleanor M(ary) 1924- 73
Kish, Ely
See Kish, Eleanor M(ary)
Kishida, Eriko 1929- 12
Kisinger, Grace Gelvin (Maze) 1913-1965 .. 10
Kissel, Richard 209
Kissin, Eva H. 1923- 10
Kissinger, Rosemary K.
See Updyke, Rosemary K.
Kistler, John M. 1967- 160
Kitamura, Satoshi 1956- 201
Earlier sketches in SATA *62, 98, 143*
See also CLR *60*
Kitchen, Bert
See Kitchen, Herbert Thomas
Kitchen, Herbert Thomas 1940- 70
Kite, L. Patricia
See Kite, Pat
Kite, Pat 1940- 78
Kitt, Tamara
See de Regniers, Beatrice Schenk (Freedman)
Kittinger, Jo S(usenbach) 1955- 148
Earlier sketch in SATA *96*
Kituomba
See Odaga, Asenath (Bole)
Kitzinger, Sheila 1929- 57
Kiwak, Barbara 1966- 103
Kjelgaard, James Arthur 1910-1959 17
See also CLR *81*
See Kjelgaard, Jim
Kjelgaard, Jim
See Kjelgaard, James Arthur
Kjelle, Marylou Morano 1954- 146
Klages, Ellen 1954- 196

Klagsbrun, Francine (Lifton) 36
Klaits, Barrie 1944- 52
Klam, Cheryl 191
Klaperman, Gilbert 1921- 33
Klaperman, Libby Mindlin 1921-1982 33
Obituary 31
Klass, David 1960- 207
Earlier sketches in SATA *88, 142*
Klass, Morton 1927-2001 11
Klass, Sheila Solomon 1927- 99
Autobiography Feature 126
Earlier sketch in SATA *45*
See also SAAS *26*
Klause, Annette Curtis 1953- 175
Earlier sketch in SATA *79*
See also CLR *104*
Klaveness, Jan O'Donnell 1939- 86
Kleberger, Ilse 1921- 5
Kleeberg, Irene (Flitner) Cumming 1932- 65
Klein, Aaron E. 1930-1998 45
Brief entry 28
Klein, Bill 1945- 89
Klein, David 1919-2001 59
Klein, Frederick C. 1938- 154
Klein, H(erbert) Arthur 8
Klein, James 1932- 115
Klein, Leonore (Glotzer) 1916- 6
Klein, Mina C(ooper) 1906-1979 8
Klein, Norma 1938-1989 57
Earlier sketch in SATA *7*
See also CLR *19*
See also SAAS *1*
Klein, Rachel S. 1953- 105
Klein, Robin 1936- 164
Brief entry 45
Earlier sketches in SATA *55, 80*
See also CLR *21*
Klemin, Diana 65
Klemm, Barry 1945- 104
Klemm, Edward G., Jr. 1910-2001 30
Klemm, Roberta K(ohnhorst) 1884-1975 30
Kleven, Elisa 1958- 173
Earlier sketch in SATA *76*
See also CLR *85*
Klevin, Jill Ross 1935- 39
Brief entry 38
Kliban, B(ernard) 1935-1990 35
Obituary 66
Klier, Kimberly Wagner 208
Klimowicz, Barbara 1927- 10
Kline, Christina Baker 1964- 101
Kline, James
See Klein, James
Kline, Jim
See Kline, Jim
Kline, Lisa Williams 1954- 143
Kline, Suzy 1943- 193
Autobiography Feature 193
Brief entry 48
Earlier sketches in SATA *67, 99, 152*
Kliros, Thea 1935- 106
Klise, Kate 181
Klise, M. Sarah 1961- 180
Earlier sketch in SATA *128*
Klots, Alexander Barrett 1903-1989
Obituary 62
Klug, Ron(ald) 1939- 31
Knaak, Richard A. 1961- 166
Earlier sketch in SATA *86*
Knaak, Richard Allen
See Knaak, Richard A.
Knapman, Timothy 200
Knapp, Edward
See Kunhardt, Edith
Knapp, Ron 1952- 34
Knebel, Fletcher 1911-1993 36
Obituary 75
Kneeland, Linda Clarke 1947- 94
Knickerbocker, Diedrich
See Irving, Washington

Knifesmith
See Cutler, Ivor
Knigge, Robert (R.) 1921(?)-1987 50
Knight, Anne (Katherine) 1946- 34
Knight, Brenda 112
Knight, Christopher G. 1943- 96
Knight, Damon (Francis) 1922-2002 9
Obituary 139
Knight, David C(arpenter) 1925-1984 14
See also CLR *38*
Knight, Eric 1897-1943 18
Knight, Eric Mowbray
See Knight, Eric
Knight, Francis Edgar 1905- 14
Knight, Frank
See Knight, Francis Edgar
Knight, Hilary 1926- 132
Earlier sketches in SATA *15, 69*
Knight, Joan (MacPhail) 159
Earlier sketch in SATA *82*
Knight, Joan
See Knight, Joan (MacPhail)
Knight, Kathryn Lasky
See Lasky, Kathryn
Knight, Mallory T.
See Hurwood, Bernhardt J.
Knight, Ruth Adams 1898-1974
Obituary 20
Knight, Theodore O. 1946- 77
Knobloch, Dorothea 1951- 88
Knoepfle, John (Ignatius) 1923- 66
Knorr, Laura 1971- 200
Knott, Bill
See Knott, William C(ecil, Jr.)
Knott, William C(ecil, Jr.) 1927- 3
Knotts, Howard (Clayton, Jr.) 1922- 25
Knowles, Anne 1933- 37
Knowles, Jo 1970- 197
Knowles, Johanna Beth
See Knowles, Jo
Knowles, John 1926-2001 89
Obituary 134
Earlier sketch in SATA *8*
See also CLR *98*
Knox, Calvin M.
See Silverberg, Robert
Knox, (Mary) Eleanor Jessie 1909-2000 59
Earlier sketch in SATA *30*
Knox, Elizabeth 1959- 176
Knox, Elizabeth Fiona
See Knox, Elizabeth
Knox, James
See Brittain, William
Knox, Jolyne 1937- 76
Knudsen, James 1950- 42
Knudsen, Michelle 171
Knudson, Mike 1965- 209
Knudson, R. R.
See Knudson, Rozanne
Knudson, Richard L(ewis) 1930- 34
Knudson, Rozanne 1932-2008 79
Earlier sketch in SATA *7*
See also SAAS *18*
Knutson, Barbara 1959-2005 166
Knutson, Kimberley 115
Knye, Cassandra
See Disch, Thomas M.
Kobayashi, Masako Matsuno 1935- 6
Koch, Dorothy Clarke 1924- 6
Koch, Kenneth 1925-2002 65
Koch, Kenneth Jay
See Koch, Kenneth
Koch, Phyllis (Mae) McCallum 1911- 10
Kochalka, James 1967- 196
Kocsis, J. C.
See Paul, James
Koda-Callan, Elizabeth 1944- 140
Earlier sketch in SATA *67*
Kodman, Stanislawa 201
Koehler, Phoebe 1955- 85

Koehler-Pentacoff, Elizabeth 1957- *160*
  Earlier sketch in SATA *96*
Koehn, Ilse
  See Van Zwienen, Ilse Charlotte Koehn
Koeller, Carol *192*
Koenig, Viviane 1950- *80*
Koering, Ursula 1921-1976 .... *64*
Koerner, W(illiam) H(enry) D(avid)
  1878-1938 .... *21*
Koertge, Ron 1940- *209*
  Earlier sketches in SATA *53, 92, 131*
Koestler-Grack, Rachel A. 1973- *156*
Koff, Richard Myram 1926- *62*
Koffinke, Carol 1949- *82*
Kogan, Deborah
  See Kogan Ray, Deborah
Kogan Ray, Deborah 1940- *203*
  Earlier sketches in SATA *8, 50, 161*
Kogawa, Joy 1935- *99*
Kogawa, Joy Nozomi
  See Kogawa, Joy
Kogler, Jennifer Anne 1982(?)- *174*
Kohara, Kazuno *207*
Kohl, Herbert 1937- *47*
Kohl, Herbert R.
  See Kohl, Herbert
Kohl, MaryAnn F(aubion) 1947- *144*
  Earlier sketch in SATA *74*
Kohler, Julilly H(ouse) 1908-1976
  Obituary *20*
Kohn, Bernice
  See Hunt, Bernice
Kohn, Rita (T.) 1933- *89*
Kohner, Frederick 1905-1986 .... *10*
  Obituary *48*
Koide, Tan 1938-1986 .... *50*
Koike, Kay 1940- *72*
Koja, Kathe 1960- *199*
  Earlier sketch in SATA *155*
Koja, Stephan *198*
Kolar, Bob 1960(?)- *206*
Kolb, Larry J. 1953- *175*
Kolba, St. Tamara *22*
Kolibalova, Marketa
  See Kolibalova, Marketa
Kolibalova, Marketa 1953- *126*
Koller, Jackie French 1948- *157*
  Earlier sketches in SATA *72, 109*
  See also CLR *68*
Kolodny, Nancy J. 1946- *76*
Kolosov, Jacqueline 1967- *199*
Komaiko, Leah 1954- *164*
  Earlier sketch in SATA *97*
Komisar, Lucy 1942- *9*
Komoda, Beverly 1939- *25*
Komoda, Kiyo 1937- *9*
Kompaneyets, Marc 1974- *169*
Komroff, Manuel 1890-1974 .... *2*
  Obituary *20*
Konigsberg, Bill 1970- *207*
Konigsburg, E.L. 1930- *194*
  Earlier sketches in SATA *4, 48, 94, 126*
  See also CLR *81*
Konigsburg, Elaine Lobl
  See Konigsburg, E.L.
Koning, Hans 1921-2007 .... *5*
  Obituary *182*
Koningsberger, Hans
  See Koning, Hans
Konkle, Janet Everest 1917- *12*
Kono, Erin Eitter 1973- *177*
Konzak, Burt 1946- *151*
Koob, Theodora (J. Foth) 1918- *23*
Kooiker, Leonie
  See Kooyker-Romijn, Johanna Maria
Koons, James
  See Pernu, Dennis
Koontz, Dean 1945- *165*
  Earlier sketch in SATA *92*
Koontz, Dean R.
  See Koontz, Dean

Koontz, Dean Ray
  See Koontz, Dean
Koontz, Robin Michal 1954- *136*
  Earlier sketch in SATA *70*
Kooyker, Leonie
  See Kooyker-Romijn, Johanna Maria
Kooyker-Romijn, Johanna Maria 1927- *48*
Kooyker-Romyn, Johanna Maria
  See Kooyker-Romijn, Johanna Maria
Kopelke, Lisa 1963- *154*
Kopper, Lisa (Esther) 1950- *105*
  Brief entry *51*
Koppes, Steven N. 1957- *169*
Koppes, Steven Nelson
  See Koppes, Steven N.
Korach, Mimi 1922- *9*
Koralek, Jenny 1934- *140*
  Earlier sketch in SATA *71*
Korczak, Janusz
  See Goldszmit, Henryk
Koren, Edward (Benjamin) 1935- *148*
  Earlier sketch in SATA *5*
Koren, Edward 1935- *206*
Korinets, Iurii Iosifovich
  See Korinetz, Yuri (Iosifovich)
Korinetz, Yuri (Iosifovich) 1923- *9*
  See also CLR *4*
Korman, Bernice 1937- *78*
Korman, Gordon 1963- *167*
  Brief entry *41*
  Earlier sketches in SATA *49, 81, 119*
  See also CLR *25*
Korman, Gordon Richard
  See Korman, Gordon
Korman, Justine 1958- *70*
Kornblatt, Marc 1954- *147*
  Earlier sketch in SATA *84*
Kornprobst, Jacques 1937- *177*
Korte, Gene J. 1950- *74*
Korthues, Barbara 1971- *203*
Korty, Carol 1937- *15*
Koscielniak, Bruce 1947- *153*
  Earlier sketches in SATA *67, 99*
Koshin, Alexander (A.) 1952- *86*
Kositsky, Lynne 1947- *158*
Koskenmaki, Rosalie
  See Maggio, Rosalie
Koss, Amy Goldman 1954- *158*
  Earlier sketch in SATA *115*
Kossin, Sandy (Sanford) 1926- *10*
Kossman, Nina 1959- *84*
Kostecki-Shaw, Jenny Sue *203*
Kostick, Conor 1964- *186*
Kotzwinkle, William 1938- *146*
  Earlier sketches in SATA *24, 70*
  See also CLR *6*
Kouhi, Elizabeth 1917- *54*
  Brief entry *49*
Kouts, Anne 1945- *8*
Koutsky, Jan Dale 1955- *146*
Kovacs, Deborah 1954- *132*
  Earlier sketch in SATA *79*
Kovalski, Maryann 1951- *175*
  Earlier sketches in SATA *58, 97*
  See also CLR *34*
  See also SAAS *21*
Kowalski, Kathiann M. 1955- *151*
  Earlier sketch in SATA *96*
Kozjan, Drazen *209*
Kraft, Betsy Harvey 1937- *157*
Kraft, Erik P. *193*
Krahn, Fernando 1935- *49*
  Brief entry *31*
  See also CLR *3*
Krakauer, Hoong Yee Lee 1955- *86*
Krakauer, Jon 1954- *108*
Kramer, George
  See Heuman, William
Kramer, Nora 1896(?)-1984 .... *26*
  Obituary *39*
Kramer, Remi (Thomas) 1935- *90*

Krantz, Hazel (Newman) *12*
Kranzler, George G(ershon) 1916- *28*
Kranzler, Gershon
  See Kranzler, George G(ershon)
Krasilovsky, Phyllis 1926- *38*
  Earlier sketch in SATA *1*
  See also CLR *83*
  See also SAAS *5*
Krasne, Betty
  See Levine, Betty K(rasne)
Krasner, Steven 1953- *154*
Krasno, Rena 1923- *104*
Kratman, Tom *175*
Kraus, Joanna Halpert 1937- *87*
Kraus, (Herman) Robert 1925-2001 .... *93*
  Obituary *130*
  Earlier sketches in SATA *4, 65*
  See also SAAS *11*
Krauss, Ruth (Ida) 1911-1993 .... *30*
  Obituary *75*
  Earlier sketch in SATA *1*
  See also CLR *42*
Krautter, Elisa (Bialk) 1912(?)-1990 .... *1*
  Obituary *65*
Krautwurst, Terry 1946- *79*
Kray, Robert Clement 1930- *82*
Krech, Bob 1956- *185*
Krech, Robert
  See Krech, Bob
Kredel, Fritz 1900-1973 .... *17*
Kreikemeier, Gregory Scott 1965- *85*
Kreloff, Elliot *189*
Krementz, Jill 1940- *134*
  Earlier sketches in SATA *17, 71*
  See also CLR *5*
  See also SAAS *8*
Kremer, Marcie
  See Sorenson, Margo
Krenina, Katya 1968- *101*
Krensky, Stephen 1953- *188*
  Brief entry *41*
  Earlier sketches in SATA *47, 93, 136*
Krensky, Stephen Alan
  See Krensky, Stephen
Kresh, Paul 1919-1997 .... *61*
  Obituary *94*
Kress, Nancy 1948- *147*
  Autobiography Feature *147*
  Earlier sketch in SATA *85*
Kricher, John C. 1944- *113*
Krieger, Melanie *96*
Krinitz, Esther Nisenthal 1927-2001 .... *194*
Kripke, Dorothy Karp *30*
Krisher, Trudy 1946- *160*
  Earlier sketch in SATA *86*
Krisher, Trudy B.
  See Krisher, Trudy
Krishnaswami, Uma 1956- *182*
  Earlier sketch in SATA *144*
Kristof, Jane 1932- *8*
Kroeber, Theodora (Kracaw) 1897-1979 .... *1*
Kroeger, Mary Kay 1950- *92*
Krohn, Katherine E(lizabeth) 1961- *125*
  Earlier sketch in SATA *84*
Kroll, Francis Lynde 1904-1973 .... *10*
Kroll, Steven 1941- *135*
  Autobiography Feature *135*
  Earlier sketches in SATA *19, 66, 125*
  See also SAAS *7*
Kroll, Virginia L. 1948- *168*
  Earlier sketches in SATA *76, 114*
Kroll, Virginia Louisa
  See Kroll, Virginia L.
Kromhout, Rindert 1958- *189*
Krommes, Beth 1956- *208*
  Earlier sketches in SATA *128, 181*
Kronenwetter, Michael 1943- *62*
Kroniuk, Lisa
  See Berton, Pierre (Francis de Marigny)

Kropp, Paul 1948- *38*
   Brief entry *34*
   See also CLR 96
Kropp, Paul Stephan
   See Kropp, Paul
Krosoczka, Jarrett J. 1977- *200*
   Earlier sketch in SATA *155*
Krovatin, Christopher 1985- *171*
Kruess, James
   See Kruss, James
Kruglik, Gerald *187*
Krull, Kathleen 1952- *184*
   Autobiography Feature *106*
   Brief entry *39*
   Earlier sketches in SATA *52, 80, 149*
   See also CLR 44
Krumgold, Joseph (Quincy) 1908-1980 .... *48*
   Obituary *23*
   Earlier sketch in SATA *1*
Krupinski, Loretta 1940- *161*
   Earlier sketches in SATA *67, 102*
Krupnick, Karen 1947- *89*
Krupp, E(dwin) C(harles) 1944- *123*
   Earlier sketch in SATA *53*
Krupp, Robin Rector 1946- *53*
Krush, Beth 1918- *18*
Krush, Joe 1918-
   See Krush, Joseph P.
Krush, Joseph P. 1918- *18*
Kruss, James 1926-1997 .... *8*
   See also CLR 9
Kruusval, Catarina 1951- *201*
Krykorka, Vladyana 1945- *96*
Krystoforski, Andrej 1943- *196*
Kubie, Eleanor Gottheil
   See Kubie, Nora Gottheil Benjamin
Kubie, Nora Benjamin
   See Kubie, Nora Gottheil Benjamin
Kubie, Nora Gottheil Benjamin 1899-1988 . *39*
   Obituary *59*
Kubinyi, Laszlo 1937- *94*
   Earlier sketch in SATA *17*
Kudlinski, Kathleen V. 1950- *150*
Kuehnert, Stephanie 1979- *205*
Kuenstler, Morton 1927- *10*
Kuh, Charlotte 1892(?)-1985
   Obituary *43*
Kuharski, Janice 1947- *128*
Kuhn, Dwight *199*
Kuijer, Guus 1942- *179*
Kujoth, Jean Spealman 1935-1975
   Obituary *30*
Kuklin, Susan 1941- *163*
   Earlier sketches in SATA *63, 95*
   See also CLR 51
Kulikov, Boris 1966- *205*
   Earlier sketch in SATA *170*
Kulka, Joe *188*
Kulling, Monica 1952- *89*
Kullman, Harry 1919-1982 .... *35*
Kulyk Keefer, Janice 1952- *132*
Kumin, Maxine 1925- *12*
Kumin, Maxine Winokur
   See Kumin, Maxine
Kunhardt, Dorothy (Meserve) 1901-1979 .... *53*
   Obituary *22*
Kunhardt, Edith 1937- *67*
Kunjufu, Jawanza 1953- *73*
Kunstler, Morton
   See Kuenstler, Morton
Kuntz, J(ohn) L. 1947- *91*
Kuntz, Jerry 1956- *133*
Kupferberg, Herbert 1918-2001 .... *19*
Kuratomi, Chizuko 1939- *12*
   See also CLR 32
Kurczok, Belinda 1978- *121*
Kurelek, William 1927-1977 .... *8*
   Obituary *27*
   See also CLR 2
Kurian, George 1928- *65*
Kurjian, Judi(th M.) 1944- *127*

Kurland, Gerald 1942- *13*
Kurland, Michael 1938- *118*
   Earlier sketch in SATA *48*
Kurland, Michael Joseph
   See Kurland, Michael
Kuroi, Ken 1947- *120*
Kurokawa, Mitsuhiro 1954- *88*
Kurten, Bjorn (Olof) 1924-1988 .... *64*
Kurtz, Jane 1952- *139*
   Earlier sketch in SATA *91*
   See also CLR 123
Kurtz, Katherine 1944- *182*
   Earlier sketches in SATA *76, 126*
Kurtz, Katherine Irene
   See Kurtz, Katherine
Kurz, Rudolf 1952- *95*
Kushner, Donn (J.) 1927- *52*
   See also CLR 55
Kushner, Ellen 1955- *202*
   Earlier sketch in SATA *98*
Kushner, Ellen Ruth
   See Kushner, Ellen
Kushner, Jill Menkes 1951- *62*
Kushner, Lawrence 1943- *169*
   Earlier sketch in SATA *83*
Kushner, Tony 1956- *160*
Kuskin, Karla 1932-2009 .... *164*
   Obituary *206*
   Earlier sketches in SATA *2, 68, 111*
   See also CLR 4
   See also SAAS 3
Kuskin, Karla Seidman
   See Kuskin, Karla
Kusugak, Michael 1948- *143*
Kusugak, Michael Arvaarluk
   See Kusugak, Michael
Kutner, Merrily 1948- *196*
Kuttner, Paul 1922- *18*
Kuyper, Sjoerd 1952- *177*
Kuzma, Kay 1941- *39*
Kvale, Velma R(uth) 1898-1979 .... *8*
Kvasnosky, Laura McGee 1951- *182*
   Earlier sketches in SATA *93, 142*
Kwasney, Michelle D. 1960- *162*
Kyle, Benjamin
   See Gottfried, Theodore Mark
Kyle, Elisabeth
   See Dunlop, Agnes M. R.
Kyte, Kathy S. 1946- *50*
   Brief entry *44*

L

L., Barry
   See Longyear, Barry B(rookes)
L., Tommy
   See Lorkowski, Thomas V(incent)
Labouisse, Eve Curie
   See Curie, Eve
Labouisse, Eve Denise
   See Curie, Eve
Lace, William W. 1942- *126*
Lacey, Joshua
   See Doder, Josh
Lachner, Dorothea
   See Knobloch, Dorothea
Lachtman, Ofelia Dumas 1919- *179*
Lackey, Mercedes R. 1950- *127*
   Earlier sketch in SATA *81*
Lackey, Mercedes Ritchie
   See Lackey, Mercedes R.
Lacoe, Addie *78*
Lacombe, Benjamin 1982- *198*
Lacome, Julie 1961- *174*
   Earlier sketch in SATA *80*
Lacy, Leslie Alexander 1937- *6*
Ladd, Cheryl (Jean) 1951- *113*
Ladd, London 1972(?)- *206*
Ladd, Louise 1943- *97*

Ladd, Veronica
   See Miner, Jane Claypool
Laden, Nina 1962- *148*
   Earlier sketch in SATA *85*
Lader, Lawrence 1919-2006 .... *6*
   Obituary *178*
LaDoux, Rita C. 1951- *74*
Lady, A
   See Taylor, Ann
Lady Mears
   See Tempest, Margaret Mary
Lady of Quality, A
   See Bagnold, Enid
La Farge, Oliver 1901-1963 .... *19*
La Farge, Oliver Hazard Perry
   See La Farge, Oliver
La Farge, Phyllis *14*
LaFave, Kim *196*
LaFaye, A. 1970- *156*
   Earlier sketch in SATA *105*
LaFaye, Alexandria R.T.
   See LaFaye, A.
LaFevers, R.L. *191*
LaFevers, Robin L.
   See LaFevers, R.L.
Laffin, John (Alfred Charles) 1922- *31*
LaFontaine, Bruce 1948- *176*
   Earlier sketch in SATA *114*
La Fontaine, Jean de 1621-1695 .... *18*
Lafrance, Marie 1955- *197*
Lager, Claude
   See Lapp, Christiane (Germain)
Lager, Marilyn 1939- *52*
Lagercrantz, Rose (Elsa) 1947- *39*
Lagerloef, Selma
   See Lagerlof, Selma
Lagerlof, Selma 1858-1940 .... *15*
   See also CLR 7
Laguna, Sofie 1968- *158*
LaHaye, Tim F. 1926- *149*
LaHaye, Timothy F.
   See LaHaye, Tim F.
Laidlaw, Rob *205*
Laiken, Deirdre S(usan) 1948- *48*
   Brief entry *40*
Laimgruber, Monika 1946- *11*
Lain, Anna
   See Lamb, Nancy
Laing, Alexander (Kinnan) 1903-1976 .... *117*
Laing, Martha 1951- *39*
Laird, Christa 1944- *108*
   Autobiography Feature *120*
   See also SAAS 26
Laird, Elizabeth (Mary Risk) 1943- *159*
   Earlier sketches in SATA *77, 114*
   See also CLR 65
Laird, Jean E(louise) 1930- *38*
Laite, Gordon 1925- *31*
Lake, Harriet
   See Taylor, Paula (Wright)
Lakin, Patricia 1944- *190*
Laklan, Carli 1907-1988 .... *5*
Laliberte, Louise-Andree 1958- *169*
Lalicki, Barbara *61*
Lalicki, Tom 1949- *186*
Lally, Soinbhe 1945- *119*
LaMarche, Jim *162*
Lamb, Albert *187*
Lamb, Beatrice Pitney 1904-1997 .... *21*
Lamb, Charles 1775-1834 .... *17*
Lamb, Elizabeth Searle 1917- *31*
Lamb, G(eoffrey) F(rederick) *10*
Lamb, Harold (Albert) 1892-1962 .... *53*
Lamb, Lynton (Harold) 1907-1977 .... *10*
Lamb, Mary Ann 1764-1847 .... *17*
Lamb, Nancy 1939- *80*
Lamb, Robert (Boyden) 1941- *13*
Lamba, Marie *195*
Lambert, David 1932- *84*
   Brief entry *49*

Lambert, David Compton
  See Lambert, David
Lambert, Janet 1895(?)-1973 25
Lambert, Martha L. 113
Lambert, Saul 1928- 23
Lambert, Stephen 174
Lamburn, Richmal Crompton 1890-1969 5
Lamensdorf, Len 1930- 120
Lamensdorf, Leonard
  See Lamensdorf, Len
Laminack, Lester L. 1956- 163
  Earlier sketch in SATA 120
Lamont, Priscilla 200
Lamorisse, Albert (Emmanuel) 1922-1970 ... 23
Lampert, Emily 1951- 52
  Brief entry 49
Lamplugh, Lois 1921- 17
Lampman, Evelyn Sibley 1907-1980 87
  Obituary 23
  Earlier sketch in SATA 4
Lamprey, Louise 1869-1951
  See YABC 2
Lampton, Chris
  See Lampton, Christopher F.
Lampton, Christopher
  See Lampton, Christopher F.
Lampton, Christopher F. 67
  Brief entry 47
Lamstein, Sarah 1943- 174
  Earlier sketch in SATA 126
Lamstein, Sarah Marwil
  See Lamstein, Sarah
Lanagan, Margo 1960- 201
  Earlier sketch in SATA 163
Lancaster, Bruce 1896-1963 9
Lancaster, Matthew 1973(?)-1983
  Obituary 45
Lance, Kathryn 1943- 76
Land, Barbara (Neblett) 1923- 16
Land, Jane
  See Borland, Kathryn Kilby
  and Speicher, Helen Ross S(mith)
Land, Myrick (Ebben) 1922-1998 15
Land, Ross
  See Borland, Kathryn Kilby
  and Speicher, Helen Ross S(mith)
Landau, Elaine 1948- 141
  Earlier sketches in SATA 10, 94
Landau, Jacob 1917- 38
Landeck, Beatrice 1904-1978 15
Landin, Les 1923- 2
Landis, J(ames) D(avid) 1942- 60
  Brief entry 52
Landis, James D.
  See Landis, J(ames) D(avid)
Landis, Jill Marie 1948- 101
Landman, Tanya 207
Landmann, Bimba 1968- 176
Landon, Dena 1978(?)- 168
Landon, Lucinda 1950- 56
  Brief entry 51
Landon, Margaret (Dorothea Mortenson)
  1903-1993 50
Landry, Leo 202
Landshoff, Ursula 1908-1989 13
Landstrom, Lena 1943- 206
  Earlier sketch in SATA 146
Landstrom, Olof 1943- 146
Lane, Carolyn 1926-1993 10
Lane, Connie
  See Laux, Constance
Lane, Dakota 1959- 166
  Earlier sketch in SATA 105
Lane, Jerry
  See Martin, Patricia Miles
Lane, John (Richard) 1932- 15
Lane, Leena 199
Lane, Margaret 1907-1994 65
  Brief entry 38
  Obituary 79

Lane, Rose Wilder 1887-1968 29
  Brief entry 28
Lanes, Selma Gordon 1929- 3
Lanfredi, Judy 1964- 83
Lang, Andrew 1844-1912 16
  See also CLR 101
Lang, Aubrey 169
Lang, Lang 1982- 208
Lang, Paul 1948- 83
Lang, Susan S. 1950- 68
Lang, T.T.
  See Taylor, Theodore
Langart, Darrell T.
  See Garrett, Randall
Langdo, Bryan 1973- 191
  Earlier sketch in SATA 138
Lange, John
  See Crichton, Michael
Lange, Karen E. 190
Lange, Suzanne 1945- 5
Langley, Andrew 1949- 166
  Earlier sketch in SATA 104
Langley, Charles P(itman) III 1949- 103
Langley, Jonathan 1952- 122
Langley, Noel 1911-1980
  Obituary 25
Langley, Wanda 173
Langner, Nola
  See Malone, Nola Langner
Langone, John (Michael) 1929- 46
  Brief entry 38
Langreuter, Jutta 1944- 122
Langrish, Katherine 177
Langsen, Richard C. 1953- 95
Langstaff, John 1920-2005 68
  Obituary 172
  Earlier sketch in SATA 6
  See also CLR 3
Langstaff, John Meredith
  See Langstaff, John
Langstaff, Launcelot
  See Irving, Washington
Langston, Laura 1958- 186
Langton, Jane 1922- 200
  Autobiography Feature 140
  Earlier sketches in SATA 3, 68, 129, 140
  See also CLR 33
  See also SAAS 5
Lanier, Sidney 1842-1881 18
Lanier, Sterling E. 1927-2007 109
Lanier, Sterling Edmund
  See Lanier, Sterling E.
Lanino, Deborah 1964- 123
Lankford, Mary D. 1932- 112
  Earlier sketch in SATA 77
Lannin, Joanne 1951- 121
Lannin, Joanne A.
  See Lannin, Joanne
Lansdale, Joe R. 1951- 116
Lansdale, Joe Richard
  See Lansdale, Joe R.
Lansing, Alfred 1921-1975 35
Lansing, Karen E. 1954- 71
Lansky, Vicki 1942- 177
Lanthier, Jennifer 1964- 204
Lantier-Sampon, Patricia 1952- 92
Lantz, Fran
  See Lantz, Francess L(in)
Lantz, Francess L(in) 1952-2004 153
  Autobiography Feature 153
  Obituary 159
  Earlier sketches in SATA 63, 109
Lantz, Paul 1908- 45
Lantz, Walter 1900-1994 37
  Obituary 79
Lanza, Barbara 1945- 101
Lapp, Christiane (Germain) 1948- 74
Lappin, Peter 1911-1999 32
Larbalestier, Justine 178
Lardy, Philippe 1963- 168
LaReau, Jenna 181

LaReau, Kara 181
Larios, Julie 1949- 178
Larios, Julie Hofstrand
  See Larios, Julie
Larkin, Amy
  See Burns, Olive Ann
Larkin, Maia
  See Wojciechowska, Maia (Teresa)
Larkspur, Penelope
  See Wyatt, Valerie
Laroche, Giles 1956- 126
  Earlier sketch in SATA 71
LaRochelle, David 1960- 171
  Earlier sketch in SATA 115
Larom, Henry V. 1903(?)-1975
  Obituary 30
LaRose, Linda 125
Larrabee, Lisa 1947- 84
Larrecq, John M(aurice) 1926-1980 44
  Obituary 25
Larrick (Crosby), Nancy 1910-2004 4
Larsen, Anita 1942- 78
Larsen, Egon 1904- 14
Larsen, Rebecca 1944- 54
Larson, Eve
  See St. John, Wylly Folk
Larson, Gary 1950- 57
Larson, Hope 1982- 205
Larson, Ingrid D(ana) 1965- 92
Larson, Jean Russell 1930- 121
Larson, Kirby 1954- 181
  Earlier sketch in SATA 96
Larson, Norita D(ittberner) 1944- 29
Larson, William H. 1938- 10
Larsson, Carl (Olof) 1853-1919 35
LaSalle, Charles A.
  See Ellis, Edward S.
LaSalle, Charles E.
  See Ellis, Edward S.
Lasell, Elinor H. 1929- 19
Lasell, Fen H.
  See Lasell, Elinor H.
Lasenby, Jack 1931- 172
  Earlier sketches in SATA 65, 103
Laser, Michael 1954- 117
Lash, Joseph P. 1909-1987 43
Lasher, Faith B. 1921- 12
Lasker, David 1950- 38
Lasker, Joe
  See Lasker, Joseph Leon
Lasker, Joseph Leon 1919- 83
  Earlier sketch in SATA 9
  See also SAAS 17
Laski, Marghanita 1915-1988 55
Laskin, Pamela L. 1954- 75
Lasky, Kathryn 1944- 157
  Earlier sketches in SATA 13, 69, 112
  See also CLR 140
Lasky Knight, Kathryn
  See Lasky, Kathryn
Lass, Bonnie 131
Lassalle, C. E.
  See Ellis, Edward S.
Lassiter, Mary
  See Hoffman, Mary
Lassiter, Rhiannon 1977- 157
Lat 1951- 196
Latham, Barbara 1896- 16
Latham, Frank B(rown) 1910-2000 6
Latham, Jean Lee 1902-1995 68
  Earlier sketch in SATA 2
  See also CLR 50
Latham, Mavis
  See Clark, Mavis Thorpe
Latham, Philip
  See Richardson, Robert S(hirley)
Lathrop, Dorothy P(ulis) 1891-1980 14
  Obituary 24
Lathrop, Francis
  See Leiber, Fritz (Reuter, Jr.)
Latimer, Jim 1943- 80

Latta, Rich
  See Latta, Richard
Latta, Richard 1946- 113
Latta, Sara L. 1960- 174
Lattany, Kristin
  See Lattany, Kristin Hunter
Lattany, Kristin (Eggleston) Hunter 1931- . 154
  Autobiography Feature 154
  Earlier sketch in SATA *132*
Lattany, Kristin Hunter 1931- 132
  Earlier sketch in SATA *12*
  See also CLR *3*
  See also SAAS *10*
Lattimore, Eleanor Frances 1904-1986 7
  Obituary 48
Lattin, Ann
  See Cole, Lois Dwight
Lauber, Patricia (Grace) 1924- 138
  Earlier sketches in SATA *1, 33, 75*
  See also CLR *16*
Laugesen, Malene 207
Laugesen, Malene Reynolds
  See Laugesen, Malene
Laugesen, Mary E(akin) 1906-1995 5
Laughbaum, Steve 1945- 12
Laughlin, Florence Young 1910-2001 3
Laughlin, Rosemary 1941- 123
Launder, Sally 206
Laure, Ettagale
  See Blauer, Ettagale
Laure, Jason 1940- 50
  Brief entry 44
Laurence, Ester Hauser 1935- 7
Laurence, Jean Margaret Wemyss
  See Laurence, Margaret
Laurence, Margaret 1926-1987
  Obituary 50
Laurie, Rona 1916- 55
Laurin, Anne
  See McLaurin, Anne
Lauritzen, Jonreed 1902-1979 13
Lauscher, Hermann
  See Hesse, Hermann
Lauture, Denize 1946- 86
Laux, Connie
  See Laux, Constance
Laux, Constance 1952- 97
Laux, Dorothy 1920- 49
Lavallee, Barbara 1941- 166
  Earlier sketch in SATA *74*
Lavender, David (Sievert) 1910-2003 97
  Obituary 145
  Earlier sketch in SATA *64*
Lavender, William D. 1921- 143
Laverne, Christine 175
Lavert, Gwendolyn Battle 1951-
  See Battle-Lavert, Gwendolyn
Laverty, Donald
  See Blish, James
  and Knight, Damon (Francis)
Lavigne, Louis-Dominique 107
Lavine, David 1928- 31
Lavine, Sigmund Arnold 1908-1986 82
  Earlier sketch in SATA *3*
  See also CLR *35*
Lavond, Paul Dennis
  See Kornbluth, C(yril) M.
  and Lowndes, Robert A(ugustine) W(ard)
  and Pohl, Frederik
Lawford, Paula Jane 1960- 57
  Brief entry 53
Lawhead, Stephen R. 1950- 109
Lawhead, Steve
  See Lawhead, Stephen R.
Lawlor, Laurie 1953- 137
  Earlier sketch in SATA *80*
Lawlor, William
  See Lawlor, William T.
Lawlor, William T. 1951- 183
Lawrence, Ann (Margaret) 1942-1987 41
  Obituary 54

Lawrence, Caroline 1954- 203
Lawrence, Iain 1955- 183
  Earlier sketch in SATA *135*
Lawrence, J. T.
  See Rowland-Entwistle, (Arthur) Theodore
  (Henry)
Lawrence, Jerome 1915-2004 65
Lawrence, John 1933- 30
Lawrence, Josephine 1890(?)-1978
  Obituary 24
Lawrence, Louise 1943- 119
  Earlier sketches in SATA *38, 78*
Lawrence, Louise de Kiriline 1894-1992 13
Lawrence, Lynn
  See Garland, Sherry
Lawrence, Margery H. 1889-1969 120
Lawrence, Michael 1943- 132
Lawrence, Mildred Elwood 1907-1997 3
Lawrence, R(onald) D(ouglas) 1921- 55
Lawrinson, Julia 1969- 141
Lawson, Amy
  See Gordon, Amy
Lawson, Carol (Antell) 1946- 42
Lawson, Don(ald Elmer) 1917-1990 9
Lawson, Joan 1906- 55
Lawson, Julie 1947- 126
  Earlier sketch in SATA *79*
  See also CLR *89*
Lawson, Marion Tubbs 1896-1994 22
Lawson, Robert 1892-1957 100
  See also YABC *2*
  See also CLR *73*
Lawton, Clive A. 1951- 145
Laxdal, Vivienne 1962- 112
Laybourn, Emma 193
Laycock, George (Edwin) 1921- 5
Layne, Laura
  See Knott, William C(ecil, Jr.)
Layne, Steven L. 171
Layton, Neal 1971- 187
  Earlier sketch in SATA *152*
Layton, Neal Andrew
  See Layton, Neal
Lazare, Gerald John 1927- 44
Lazare, Jerry
  See Lazare, Gerald John
Lazarevich, Mila 1942- 17
Lazarus, Keo Felker 1913-1993 21
  Obituary 129
Lea, Alec 1907- 19
Lea, Bob 1952- 203
Lea, Joan
  See Neufeld, John (Arthur)
Leach, Maria 1892-1977 39
  Brief entry 28
Leacock, Elspeth 1946- 131
Leacroft, Helen (Mabel Beal) 1919- 6
Leacroft, Richard (Vallance Becher) 1914- 6
Leaf, Margaret P. 1909(?)-1988
  Obituary 55
Leaf, (Wilbur) Munro 1905-1976 20
  See also CLR *25*
Leaf, VaDonna Jean 1929- 26
Leah, Devorah
  See Devorah-Leah
Leakey, Richard E(rskine Frere) 1944- 42
Leander, Ed
  See Richelson, Geraldine
Lear, Edward 1812-1888 100
  Earlier sketch in SATA *18*
  See also CLR *75*
Lears, Laurie 1955- 127
Leasor, James 1923-2007 54
Leasor, Thomas James
  See Leasor, James
Leavitt, Jerome E(dward) 1916- 23
Leavitt, Martine 1953- 170
LeBar, Mary E(velyn) 1910-1982 35
LeBlanc, Annette M. 1965- 68
LeBlanc, L(ee) 1913- 54
LeBox, Annette 1943- 145

Lebrun, Claude 1929- 66
Le Cain, Errol (John) 1941-1989 68
  Obituary 60
  Earlier sketch in SATA *6*
Lechner, Jack 201
Lechner, John 1966- 200
Lecourt, Nancy (Hoyt) 1951- 73
Ledbetter, Suzann 1953- 119
Leder, Jane Mersky 1945- 61
  Brief entry 51
Lederer, Muriel 1929- 48
Lederer, William J. 1912-2009 62
Lederer, William Julius
  See Lederer, William J.
Lee, Amanda
  See Baggett, Nancy
  and Buckholtz, Eileen (Garber)
  and Glick, Ruth (Burtnick)
Lee, Benjamin 1921- 27
Lee, Betsy 1949- 37
Lee, Carol
  See Fletcher, Helen Jill
Lee, Carol Ann 1969- 185
Lee, Chinlun 182
Lee, Cora
  See Anderson, Catherine Corley
Lee, Dennis (Beynon) 1939- 102
  Earlier sketch in SATA *14*
  See also CLR *3*
Lee, Dom 1959- 146
  Autobiography Feature 121
  Earlier sketch in SATA *83*
  See also SAAS *26*
Lee, Doris Emrick 1905-1983 44
  Obituary 35
Lee, Edward
  See Lee, J. Edward
Lee, Elizabeth Rogers 1940- 90
Lee, Harper 1926- 11
Lee, Hector Viveros 1962- 115
Lee, Howard N.
  See Goulart, Ron
Lee, Huy Voun 1969- 129
Lee, J. Edward 1953- 130
Lee, Jeanne M. 1943- 138
Lee, John R(obert) 1923-1976 27
Lee, Jordan
  See Scholefield, Alan
Lee, Joseph Edward
  See Lee, J. Edward
Lee, Julian
  See Latham, Jean Lee
Lee, Linda
  See Eyerly, Jeannette
Lee, Liz
  See Lee, Elizabeth Rogers
Lee, Lucy
  See Talbot, Charlene Joy
Lee, Lyn 1953- 128
Lee, Manning de Villeneuve 1894-1980 37
  Obituary 22
Lee, Marian
  See Clish, (Lee) Marian
Lee, Marie G. 1964- 178
  Earlier sketches in SATA *81, 130*
Lee, Marie Myung-Ok
  See Lee, Marie G.
Lee, Mary Price 1934- 82
  Earlier sketch in SATA *8*
Lee, Mildred
  See Scudder, Mildred Lee
Lee, Nelle Harper
  See Lee, Harper
Lee, Richard S. 1927- 82
Lee, Robert C. 1931- 20
Lee, Robert Edwin 1918-1994 65
  Obituary 82
Lee, Robert J. 1921- 10
Lee, Roy
  See Hopkins, Clark
Lee, Sally 1943- 67

Lee, Suzy 193
Lee, Tammie
  See Townsend, Thomas L.
Lee, Tanith 1947- 185
  Earlier sketches in SATA 8, 88, 134
Lee, Virginia 1976- 208
Leech, Ben
  See Bowkett, Stephen
Leeds, Contance 188
Leedy, Loreen 1959- 175
  Brief entry 50
  Earlier sketches in SATA 54, 84, 128
Leedy, Loreen Janelle
  See Leedy, Loreen
Lee-Hostetler, Jeri 1940- 63
Leekley, Thomas B(riggs) 1910-2001 23
Leeming, Jo Ann
  See Leeming, Joseph
Leeming, Joseph 1897-1968 26
Leemis, Ralph B. 1954- 72
Leese, Jennifer L.B. 1970- 163
Leeson, Muriel 1920- 54
Leeson, R. A.
  See Leeson, Robert (Arthur)
Leeson, Robert (Arthur) 1928- 76
  Earlier sketch in SATA 42
Lee Tae-Jun 1904-1956(?) 194
Lee-Tai, Amy 1964- 189
Leffland, Ella 1931- 65
Leffler, Silke 197
Lefler, Irene (Whitney) 1917- 12
LeFrak, Karen 182
Le Gallienne, Eva 1899-1991 9
  Obituary 68
Legg, Gerald 1947- 143
Legg, Sarah Martha Ross Bruggeman (?)-1982
  Obituary 40
LeGrand
  See Henderson, LeGrand
Le Guin, Ursula K. 1929- 194
  Earlier sketches in SATA 4, 52, 99, 149
  See also CLR 91
Le Guin, Ursula Kroeber
  See Le Guin, Ursula K.
Legum, Colin 1919-2003 10
Lehman, Barbara 1963- 170
  Earlier sketch in SATA 115
Lehman, Bob 91
Lehman, Elaine 91
Lehmann, Debra Lynn
  See Vanasse, Deb
Lehn, Cornelia 1920- 46
Lehne, Judith Logan 1947- 93
Lehr, Delores 1920- 10
Lehr, Norma 1930- 71
Leiber, Fritz (Reuter, Jr.) 1910-1992 45
  Obituary 73
Leibold, Jay 1957- 57
  Brief entry 52
Leichman, Seymour 1933- 5
Leick, Bonnie 205
Leigh, Nila K. 1981- 81
Leigh, Tom 1947- 46
Leigh-Pemberton, John 1911-1997 35
Leighton, Clare (Veronica Hope)
  1899-1989 37
Leighton, Margaret (Carver) 1896-1987 1
  Obituary 52
Leiner, Al(an) 1938- 83
Leiner, Katherine 1949- 93
Leipold, L. Edmond 1902-1983 16
Leisk, David (Johnson) 1906-1975 30
  Obituary 26
  Earlier sketch in SATA 1
  See also CLR 98
Leister, Mary 1917- 29
Leitch, Patricia 1933- 98
  Earlier sketch in SATA 11
Leitner, Isabella 1924- 86
Lekich, John 202
Leland, Bob 1956- 92

Leland, Robert E.
  See Leland, Bob
Lematre, Pascal 1967- 176
Lember, Barbara Hirsch 1941- 92
LeMieux, A.C. 1954- 125
  Earlier sketch in SATA 90
LeMieux, Anne
  See LeMieux, A.C.
LeMieux, Anne Connelly
  See LeMieux, A.C.
Lemieux, Michele 1955- 139
Lemke, Horst 1922- 38
Lenain, Thierry 1959- 201
Lenanton, Carola Mary Anima Oman
  See Oman, Carola (Mary Anima)
Lenard, Alexander 1910-1972
  Obituary 21
Lendroth, Susan 207
L'Engle, Madeleine 1918-2007 128
  Obituary 186
  Earlier sketches in SATA 1, 27, 75
  See also CLR 57
  See also SAAS 15
L'Engle, Madeleine Camp Franklin
  See L'Engle, Madeleine
Lengyel, Cornel Adam 1915- 27
Lengyel, Emil 1895-1985 3
  Obituary 42
Lennon, John 1940-1980 114
Lennon, John Ono
  See Lennon, John
Leno, Jay 1950- 154
LeNoir, Janice 1941- 89
Lens, Sidney 1912-1986 13
  Obituary 48
Lenski, Lois 1893-1974 100
  Earlier sketches in SATA 1, 26
  See also CLR 26
Lent, Blair 1930-2009 133
  Obituary 200
  Earlier sketch in SATA 2
Lent, Henry Bolles 1901-1973 17
Lent, John 1948- 108
Leodhas, Sorche Nic
  See Alger, Leclaire (Gowans)
Leokum, Arkady 1916(?)- 45
Leon, Sharon 1959- 79
Leonard, Alison 1944- 70
Leonard, Anna
  See Gilman, Laura Anne
Leonard, Constance (Brink) 1923- 42
  Brief entry 40
Leonard, Dutch
  See Leonard, Elmore
Leonard, Elmore 1925- 163
Leonard, Elmore John, Jr.
  See Leonard, Elmore
Leonard, Jonathan N(orton) 1903-1975 36
Leonard, Laura 1923- 75
Leonard, Tom 1955- 207
Leonetti, Mike 1958- 202
Leong, Gor Yun
  See Ellison, Virginia H(owell)
Leonhardt, Alice 1950- 152
Lerangis, Peter 1955- 171
  Earlier sketch in SATA 72
Lerner, Aaron 1920-2007 35
  Obituary 179
Lerner, Aaron Bunsen
  See Lerner, Aaron
Lerner, Carol 1927- 86
  Earlier sketch in SATA 33
  See also CLR 34
  See also SAAS 12
Lerner, Gerda 1920- 65
Lerner, Harriet 1944- 101
Lerner, Marguerite Rush 1924-1987 11
  Obituary 51
Lerner, Sharon (Ruth) 1938-1982 11
  Obituary 29

Leroe, Ellen W(hitney) 1949- 99
  Brief entry 51
  Earlier sketch in SATA 61
Leroux, Gaston 1868-1927 65
Leroux-Hugon, Helene 1955- 132
LeRoy, Gen 52
  Brief entry 36
Lerrigo, Marion Olive 1898-1968
  Obituary 29
LeShan, Eda J(oan) 1922-2002 21
  See also CLR 6
LeSieg, Theo.
  See Dr. Seuss
Lesinski, Jeanne M. 1960- 120
Leslie, Robert Franklin 1911-1990 7
Leslie, Roger 1961- 168
Leslie, Roger James
  See Leslie, Roger
Leslie, Sarah
  See McGuire, Leslie (Sarah)
LeSourd, Catherine
  See Marshall, (Sarah) Catherine (Wood)
Lessac, Frane
  See Lessac, Frane
Lessac, Frane 1954- 209
  Earlier sketches in SATA 61, 148
Lessem, Dino Don
  See Lessem, Don
Lessem, Don 1951- 182
  Earlier sketches in SATA 97, 155
Lesser, Margaret 1899(?)-1979
  Obituary 22
Lesser, Rika 1953- 53
Lester, Alison 1952- 129
  Earlier sketches in SATA 50, 90
Lester, Helen 1936- 189
  Earlier sketches in SATA 46, 92, 145
Lester, Julius 1939- 157
  Earlier sketches in SATA 12, 74, 112
  See also CLR 143
Lester, Julius Bernard
  See Lester, Julius
Lester, Mike 1955- 206
  Earlier sketch in SATA 131
Le Sueur, Meridel 1900-1996 6
Lethcoe, Jason 191
Le Tord, Bijou 1945- 95
  Earlier sketch in SATA 49
Letts, Billie 1938- 121
Letts, Elizabeth
  See Alalou, Elizabeth
Leuck, Laura 1962- 192
  Earlier sketches in SATA 85, 146
Leutscher, Alfred (George) 1913- 23
Levai, Blaise 1919- 39
Levenkron, Steven 1941- 86
Leverich, Kathleen 1948- 103
LeVert, (William) John 1946- 55
Levete, Sarah 1961- 153
Levin, Betty 1927- 201
  Earlier sketches in SATA 19, 84, 137
  See also SAAS 11
Levin, Ira 1929-2007 66
  Obituary 187
Levin, Ira Marvin
  See Levin, Ira
Levin, Marcia Obrasky 1918- 13
Levin, Meyer 1905-1981 21
  Obituary 27
Levin, Miriam (Ramsfelder) 1962- 97
Levine, Abby 1943- 54
  Brief entry 52
Levine, Betty K(rasne) 1933- 66
Levine, David 1926-2009 43
  Brief entry 35
Levine, Edna S(imon) 35
Levine, Ellen 1939- 190
Levine, Evan 1962- 77
  Earlier sketch in SATA 74

Levine, Gail Carson 1947- 195
Earlier sketches in SATA *98, 161*
See also CLR *85*
Levine, I(srael) E. 1923-2003 .... *12*
Obituary *146*
Levine, Joan Goldman *11*
Levine, Joseph 1910- *33*
Levine, Marge 1934- *81*
Levine, Rhoda *14*
Levine, Sarah 1970- *57*
Levine, Shar 1953- *131*
Levine-Freidus, Gail
See Provost, Gail Levine
Levinson, Nancy Smiler 1938- *140*
Earlier sketches in SATA *33, 80*
Levinson, Riki *99*
Brief entry *49*
Earlier sketch in SATA *52*
Levithan, David 1972- *166*
Levitin, Sonia 1934- *192*
Autobiography Feature *131*
Earlier sketches in SATA *4, 68, 119, 131*
See also CLR *53*
See also SAAS *2*
Levitt, Sidney (Mark) 1947- *68*
Levon, O. U.
See Kesey, Ken
Levoy, Myron *49*
Brief entry *37*
Levy, Barrie *112*
Levy, Constance 1931- *140*
Earlier sketch in SATA *73*
See also SAAS *22*
Levy, Elizabeth 1942- *169*
Earlier sketches in SATA *31, 69, 107*
See also SAAS *18*
Levy, Janice *172*
Levy, Marilyn 1937- *67*
Levy, Nathan 1945- *63*
Levy, Robert 1945- *82*
Lewees, John
See Stockton, Francis Richard
Lewin, Betsy 1937- *169*
Autobiography Feature *115*
Earlier sketches in SATA *32, 90*
Lewin, Hugh 1939- *72*
Brief entry *40*
See also CLR *9*
Lewin, Ted 1935- *195*
Autobiography Feature *115*
Earlier sketches in SATA *21, 76, 119, 165*
Lewis, Alice C. 1936- *46*
Lewis, Alice Hudson 1895(?)-1971
Obituary *29*
Lewis, Amanda 1955- *80*
Lewis, Anthony 1927- *27*
Lewis, Anthony 1966- *120*
Lewis, Barbara A. 1943- *73*
Lewis, Beverly 1949- *80*
Lewis, Brenda Ralph 1932- *72*
Lewis, Brian 1963- *128*
Lewis, C. S. 1898-1963 .... *100*
Earlier sketch in SATA *13*
See also CLR *109*
Lewis, Claudia (Louise) 1907-2001 .... *5*
Lewis, Clive Staples
See Lewis, C. S.
Lewis, Cynthia Copeland 1960- *111*
Lewis, E. M. *123*
Earlier sketch in SATA *20*
Lewis, Earl Bradley
See Lewis, E.B.
Lewis, E.B. 1956- *168*
Earlier sketches in SATA *93, 124*
Lewis, Elizabeth Foreman 1892-1958 .... *121*
See also YABC *2*
Lewis, Francine
See Wells, Helen
Lewis, Harry Sinclair
See Lewis, Sinclair

Lewis, Hilda (Winifred) 1896-1974
Obituary *20*
Lewis, J. Patrick 1942- *205*
Earlier sketches in SATA *69, 104, 162*
Lewis, Jack P(earl) 1919- *65*
Lewis, Jean 1924- *61*
Lewis, Jon Samuel
See Lewis, J.S.
Lewis, Joseph Anthony
See Lewis, Anthony
Lewis, J.S. 1972- *203*
Lewis, Julinda
See Lewis-Ferguson, Julinda
Lewis, Kevin *173*
Lewis, Kim 1951- *136*
Earlier sketch in SATA *84*
Lewis, Linda (Joy) 1946- *67*
Lewis, Lucia Z.
See Anderson, Lucia (Lewis)
Lewis, Marjorie 1929- *40*
Brief entry *35*
Lewis, Mary 1907(?)-1988 .... *64*
Obituary *56*
Lewis, Mervyn
See Frewer, Glyn (M.)
Lewis, Michael
See Untermeyer, Louis
Lewis, Naomi 1911-2009 .... *144*
Earlier sketch in SATA *76*
Lewis, Paeony 1960- *173*
Lewis, Paul
See Gerson, Noel Bertram
Lewis, Richard 1935- *3*
Lewis, Richard 1956- *209*
Lewis, Rob 1962- *72*
Lewis, Roger
See Zarchy, Harry
Lewis, Rose *209*
Lewis, Rose A.
See Lewis, Rose
Lewis, Shannon
See Llywelyn, Morgan
Lewis, Shari 1934-1998 .... *35*
Brief entry *30*
Obituary *104*
Lewis, Sylvan R.
See Aronson, Virginia
Lewis, Thomas P(arker) 1936- *27*
Lewis, Wendy A. 1966- *150*
Lewis-Ferguson, Julinda 1955- *85*
Lewison, Wendy Cheyette *177*
Lewiton, Mina 1904-1970 .... *2*
Lew-Vriethoff, Joanne *186*
Lexau, Joan M. *130*
Earlier sketches in SATA *1, 36*
Ley, Willy 1906-1969 .... *2*
Leydon, Rita (Floden) 1949- *21*
Leyland, Eric (Arthur) 1911- *37*
L'Hommedieu, Dorothy Keasley 1885-1961
Obituary *29*
Li, Xiao Jun 1952- *86*
Liao, Jimmy 1958- *202*
Liatsos, Sandra Olson 1942- *103*
Libby, Alisa M. *189*
Libby, Barbara M. *153*
Libby, Bill
See Libby, William M.
Libby, William M. 1927-1984 .... *5*
Obituary *39*
Liberty, Gene 1924- *3*
Lichtenheld, Tom *208*
Earlier sketch in SATA *152*
Lichtman, Wendy 1946- *193*
Liddell, Kenneth 1912-1975 .... *63*
Lidz, Jane *120*
Lieberman, E(dwin) James 1934- *62*
Liebers, Arthur 1913-1984 .... *12*
Lieblich, Irene 1923- *22*
Liers, Emil E(rnest) 1890-1975 .... *37*
Lies, Brian 1963- *190*
Earlier sketch in SATA *131*

Liestman, Vicki 1961- *72*
Lietz, Gerald S. 1918- *11*
Life, Kay (Guinn) 1930- *83*
Lifton, Betty Jean *118*
Earlier sketch in SATA *6*
Lifton, Robert Jay 1926- *66*
Lightburn, Ron 1954- *91*
Lightburn, Sandra 1955- *91*
Lightner, A. M.
See Hopf, Alice (Martha) L(ightner)
Lightner, Alice
See Hopf, Alice (Martha) L(ightner)
Lignell, Lois 1911- *37*
Liles, Maurine Walpole 1935- *81*
Lillegard, Dee *184*
Lilley, Stephen R. 1950- *97*
Lilley, Stephen Ray
See Lilley, Stephen R.
Lillington, Kenneth (James) 1916-1998 .... *39*
Lilly, Nate *182*
Lilly, Ray
See Curtis, Richard
Lim, John 1932- *43*
Liman, Ellen (Fogelson) 1936- *22*
Limb, Sue 1946- *203*
Earlier sketch in SATA *158*
Limburg, Peter R(ichard) 1929- *13*
Lin, Grace 1974- *198*
Earlier sketches in SATA *111, 162*
Lincoln, C(harles) Eric 1924-2000 .... *5*
Lincoln, Christopher 1952- *208*
Lincoln, Hazel *187*
Lincoln, James
See Bates, Katharine Lee
Lindbergh, Anne
See Sapieyevski, Anne Lindbergh
Lindbergh, Anne Morrow 1906-2001 .... *33*
Obituary *125*
Lindbergh, Anne Spencer Morrow
See Lindbergh, Anne Morrow
Lindbergh, Charles A(ugustus, Jr.)
1902-1974 .... *33*
Lindbergh, Reeve 1945- *163*
Earlier sketch in SATA *116*
Lindblom, Steven (Winther) 1946- *94*
Brief entry *39*
Earlier sketch in SATA *42*
Linde, Gunnel 1924- *5*
Lindenbaum, Pija 1955- *183*
Earlier sketches in SATA *77, 144*
Lindgren, Astrid (Anna Emilia Ericsson)
1907-2002 .... *38*
Obituary *128*
Earlier sketch in SATA *2*
See also CLR *119*
Lindgren, Barbro 1937- *207*
Brief entry *46*
Earlier sketches in SATA *63, 120*
See also CLR *86*
Lindman, Maj (Jan) 1886-1972 .... *43*
Lindop, Edmund 1925- *5*
Lindquist, Jennie Dorothea 1899-1977 .... *13*
Lindquist, Rowena Cory 1958- *98*
Lindquist, Willis 1908-1988 .... *20*
Lindsay, Nicholas Vachel
See Lindsay, Vachel
Lindsay, Norman Alfred William
1879-1969 .... *67*
See also CLR *8*
Lindsay, Vachel 1879-1931 .... *40*
Lindsey, Kathleen D(orothy) 1949- *153*
Line, David
See Davidson, Lionel
Line, Les 1935- *27*
Lines, Kathleen Mary 1902-1988
Obituary *61*
Linfield, Esther *40*

Lingard, Joan (Amelia) 1932- 130
    Autobiography Feature 130
    Earlier sketches in SATA 8, 74, 114
    See also CLR 89
    See also SAAS 5
Link, Martin 1934- 28
Linn, Margot
    See Ziefert, Harriet
Linnea, Sharon 1956- 82
Lion, Melissa 1976- 176
Lionni, Leo(nard) 1910-1999 72
    Obituary 118
    Earlier sketch in SATA 8
    See also CLR 71
Lipinsky de Orlov, Lino S. 1908- 22
Lipkind, William 1904-1974 15
Lipman, David 1931-2008 21
Lipman, Matthew 1923- 14
Lipp, Frederick 204
Lippincott, Bertram 1898(?)-1985
    Obituary 42
Lippincott, Gary A. 1953- 119
    Earlier sketch in SATA 73
Lippincott, Joseph W(harton) 1887-1976 17
Lippincott, Sarah Lee 1920- 22
Lippman, Peter J. 1936- 31
Lipsyte, Robert 1938- 198
    Earlier sketches in SATA 5, 68, 113, 161
    See also CLR 76
Lipsyte, Robert Michael
    See Lipsyte, Robert
Lisandrelli, Elaine Slivinski 1951- 94
Lisker, Sonia O. 1933- 44
Lisle, Holly 1960- 208
    Earlier sketch in SATA 98
Lisle, Janet Taylor 1947- 150
    Brief entry 47
    Earlier sketches in SATA 59, 96
    See also SAAS 14
Lisle, Rebecca 162
Lisle, Seward D.
    See Ellis, Edward S.
Lisowski, Gabriel 1946- 47
    Brief entry 31
Liss, Howard 1922-1995 4
    Obituary 84
Lissiat, Amy
    See Thompson, Colin
Lisson, Deborah 1941- 110
    Earlier sketch in SATA 71
List, Ilka Katherine 1935- 6
Liston, Robert A. 1927- 5
Litchfield, Ada B(assett) 1916-1999 5
Litchfield, Jo 1973- 116
Lithgow, John 1945- 145
Lithgow, John Arthur
    See Lithgow, John
Litowinsky, Olga (Jean) 1936- 26
Littke, Lael J. 1929- 140
    Earlier sketches in SATA 51, 83
Little, A. Edward
    See Klein, Aaron E.
Little, Douglas 1942- 96
Little, (Flora) Jean 1932- 149
    Earlier sketches in SATA 2, 68, 106
    See also CLR 4
    See also SAAS 17
Little, Lessie Jones 1906-1986 60
    Obituary 50
Little, Mary E. 1912-1999 28
Littlechild, George 1958- 85
Littledale, Freya (Lota) 1929-1992 74
    Earlier sketch in SATA 2
Littlefield, Bill 1948- 83
Littlefield, Holly 1963- 97
Littlesugar, Amy 1953- 176
    Earlier sketch in SATA 122
Littleton, Mark R. 1950- 142
    Earlier sketch in SATA 89
Littman, Sarah Darer 175
Litty, Julie 1971- 181

Litzinger, Rosanne 1948- 196
Lively, Penelope 1933- 164
    Earlier sketches in SATA 7, 60, 101
    See also CLR 7
Lively, Penelope Margaret
    See Lively, Penelope
Liverakos, L. A.
    See Gilman, Laura Anne
Liversidge, (Henry) Douglas 1913- 8
Livesey, Claire (Warner) 1927- 127
Livingston, Carole 1941- 42
Livingston, (M.) Irene 1932- 150
Livingston, Myra Cohn 1926-1996 68
    Obituary 92
    Earlier sketch in SATA 5
    See also CLR 7
    See also SAAS 1
Livingston, Richard R(oland) 1922- 8
Livo, Norma J. 1929- 76
Liwska, Renata 199
Ljungkvist, Laura 180
Llerena Aguirre, Carlos 1952- 19
Llerena Aguirre, Carlos Antonio
    See Llerena Aguirre, Carlos
Llewellyn, Claire 1954- 196
    Earlier sketches in SATA 77, 143
Llewellyn, Grace 1964- 110
Llewellyn, Richard
    See Llewellyn Lloyd, Richard Dafydd Vivian
Llewellyn, Sam 1948- 185
    Earlier sketch in SATA 95
Llewellyn Lloyd, Richard Dafydd Vivian
    1906-1983 11
    Obituary 37
Llewelyn, T. Harcourt
    See Hamilton, Charles (Harold St. John)
Lloyd, Alan
    See Lloyd, A.R.
Lloyd, Alan Richard
    See Lloyd, A.R.
Lloyd, A.R. 1927- 168
    Earlier sketch in SATA 97
Lloyd, David
    See Lloyd, David T.
Lloyd, David T. 1954- 167
Lloyd, E. James
    See James, Elizabeth
Lloyd, Errol 1943- 22
Lloyd, Hugh
    See Fitzhugh, Percy Keese
Lloyd, James
    See James, Elizabeth
Lloyd, Megan 1958- 189
    Earlier sketches in SATA 77, 117
Lloyd, Norman 1909-1980
    Obituary 23
Lloyd, (Mary) Norris 1908-1993 10
    Obituary 75
Lloyd, Sam 183
Lloyd-Jones, Sally 1960- 179
Lloyd Webber, Andrew 1948- 56
Llywelyn, Morgan 1937- 109
Lo, Ginnie 165
Lo, Virginia M.
    See Lo, Ginnie
Lobato, Jose Bento Monteiro 1882-1948 ... 114
Lobel, Anita (Kempler) 1934- 162
    Earlier sketches in SATA 6, 55, 96
Lobel, Arnold (Stark) 1933-1987 55
    Obituary 54
    Earlier sketch in SATA 6
    See also CLR 5
Lobel, Gillian 181
Lobsenz, Amelia 12
Lobsenz, Norman M(itchell) 1919- 6
Lochak, Michele 1936- 39
Lochlons, Colin
    See Jackson, C(aary) Paul
Locke, Clinton W. 1
Locke, Elsie (Violet) 1912-2001 87
Locke, Gary 1963- 197

Locke, Lucie 1904-1989 10
Locke, Robert 1944- 63
    See also CLR 39
Locker, Thomas 1937- 109
    Earlier sketch in SATA 59
    See also CLR 14
Lockhart, E.
    See Jenkins, Emily
Lockridge, Hildegarde (Dolson)
    1908-1981 121
    Earlier sketch in SATA 5
Lockwood, Mary
    See Spelman, Mary
Lodge, Bernard 1933- 107
    Earlier sketch in SATA 33
Lodge, Jo 1966- 173
    Earlier sketch in SATA 112
Loeb, Jeffrey 1946- 57
Loeb, Robert H., Jr. 1917- 21
Loefgren, Ulf 1931- 3
Loehfelm, Bill 1969- 153
Loehr, Mallory 184
Loehr, Patrick 1968(?)- 194
Loeper, John J(oseph) 1929- 118
    Earlier sketch in SATA 10
Loescher, Ann Dull 1942- 20
Loescher, Gil(burt Damian) 1945- 20
Loewer, Jean Jenkins
    See Jenkins, Jean
Loewer, (Henry) Peter 1934- 98
LoFaro, Jerry 1959- 77
Lofo
    See Heimann, Rolf
Lofthouse, Liz 199
Lofting, Hugh (John) 1886-1947 100
    Earlier sketch in SATA 15
    See also CLR 143
Lofts, Norah (Robinson) 1904-1983 8
    Obituary 36
Logan, Jake
    See Knott, William C(ecil, Jr.)
    and Krepps, Robert W(ilson)
    and Pearl, Jacques Bain
    and Riefe, Alan
    and Rifkin, Shepard
    and Smith, Martin Cruz
Logan, Mark
    See Nicole, Christopher (Robin)
Logan, Rochelle 1954- 169
Logston, Anne 1962- 112
Logue, Christopher 1926- 23
Logue, Mary 1952- 161
    Earlier sketch in SATA 112
Logue, Mary Louise
    See Logue, Mary
Loh, Morag 1935- 73
Lohans, Alison 1949- 101
Loizeaux, William 185
Loken, Newton Clayton 1919- 26
Lomas, Steve
    See Brennan, Joseph Lomas
Lomask, Milton (Nachman) 1909-1991 20
Lombard, Jenny 178
Lombino, Salvatore
    See Hunter, Evan
LoMonaco, Palmyra 1932- 102
London, Jack 1876-1916 18
    See also CLR 108
London, Jane
    See Geis, Darlene Stern
London, John Griffith
    See London, Jack
London, Jonathan (Paul) 1947- 157
    Earlier sketches in SATA 74, 113
Lonergan, (Pauline) Joy (MacLean) 1909- ... 10
Lonette, Reisie (Dominee) 1924- 43
Long, Cathryn J. 1946- 89
Long, Earlene (Roberta) 1938- 50
Long, Emmett
    See Leonard, Elmore
Long, Ethan 1968(?)- 182

Long, Helen Beecher *1*
Long, Judith Elaine 1953- *20*
Long, Judy
  See Long, Judith Elaine
Long, Kim 1949- *69*
Long, Laura Mooney 1892-1967
  Obituary *29*
Long, Laurel *203*
Long, Loren 1966(?)- *188*
  Earlier sketch in SATA *151*
Long, Melinda 1960- *152*
Long, Sylvia 1948- *179*
  Earlier sketch in SATA *120*
Longbeard, Frederick
  See Longyear, Barry B(rookes)
Longfellow, Henry Wadsworth 1807-1882 ... *19*
  See also CLR *99*
Longfellow, Layne (A.) 1937- *102*
Longman, Harold S. 1919- *5*
Longsworth, Polly 1933- *28*
Longtemps, Kenneth 1933- *17*
Longway, A. Hugh
  See Lang, Andrew
Longyear, Barry B(rookes) 1942- *117*
Look, Lenore *180*
Loomans, Diane 1955- *90*
Loomis, Christine *160*
  Earlier sketch in SATA *113*
Loomis, Jennifer A. 1942- *101*
Loomis, Robert D. *5*
Lopez, Angelo (Cayas) 1967- *83*
Lopez, Barry 1945- *67*
Lopez, Barry Holstun
  See Lopez, Barry
Lopez, Jack 1950- *178*
Lopez, Loretta 1963- *190*
Lopez, Lorraine 1956- *181*
Lopez, Lorraine M.
  See Lopez, Lorraine
Lopez, Rafael 1961(?)- *198*
Lopshire, Robert M(artin) 1927- *6*
Loraine, Connie
  See Reece, Colleen L.
Lorbiecki, Marybeth 1959- *172*
  Earlier sketch in SATA *121*
Lord, Athena V. 1932- *39*
Lord, Beman 1924-1991 .... *5*
  Obituary *69*
Lord, Bette Bao 1938- *58*
Lord, Cynthia *182*
Lord, Doreen Mildred Douglas
  See Lord, Douglas
Lord, Douglas 1904-1992 .... *12*
Lord, Janet *204*
Lord, John Vernon 1939- *21*
Lord, Michele *201*
Lord, Nancy
  See Titus, Eve
Lord, Patricia C. 1927-1988
  Obituary *58*
Lord, Walter 1917-2002 .... *3*
Lorde, Diana
  See Reno, Dawn E(laine)
Lorenz, Albert 1941- *115*
Lorenzini, Carlo
  See Collodi, Carlo
Lorey, Dean 1967- *193*
Lorimer, Janet 1941- *60*
Loring, Emilie (Baker) 1864(?)-1951 .... *51*
Lorkowski, Thomas V(incent) 1950- *92*
Lorkowski, Tom
  See Lorkowski, Thomas V(incent)
Lorraine, Walter (Henry) 1929- *16*
Lorrimer, Claire
  See Clark, Patricia Denise
Loss, Joan 1933- *11*
Lothrop, Harriet Mulford Stone 1844-1924 . *20*
Lottridge, Celia Barker 1936- *157*
  Earlier sketch in SATA *112*
LoTurco, Laura 1963- *84*
Lotz, Wolfgang 1912-1981 .... *65*

Louie, Ai-Ling 1949- *40*
  Brief entry *34*
Louis, Catherine 1963- *186*
Louis, Pat
  See Francis, Dorothy
Louisburgh, Sheila Burnford
  See Burnford, Sheila (Philip Cochrane Every)
Louise, Anita
  See Riggio, Anita
Louise, Tina 1934- *191*
Lourie, Helen
  See Storr, Catherine (Cole)
Lourie, Peter 1952- *183*
  Earlier sketches in SATA *82, 142*
Lourie, Peter King
  See Lourie, Peter
Love, Ann 1947- *168*
  Earlier sketch in SATA *79*
Love, D. Anne 1949- *180*
  Earlier sketches in SATA *96, 145*
Love, Douglas 1967- *92*
Love, Judith Dufour
  See Love, Judy
Love, Judy *188*
Love, Katherine (Isabel) 1907- *3*
Love, Kathleen Ann
  See Love, Ann
Love, Sandra (Weller) 1940- *26*
Lovejoy, Jack 1937- *116*
Lovelace, Delos Wheeler 1894-1967 .... *7*
Lovelace, Maud Hart 1892-1980 .... *2*
  Obituary *23*
Lovell, Ingraham
  See Bacon, Josephine Dodge (Daskam)
Loverseed, Amanda (Jane) 1965- *75*
Lovett, Margaret (Rose) 1915- *22*
Low, Alice 1926- *156*
  Earlier sketches in SATA *11, 76*
Low, Elizabeth Hammond 1898-1991 .... *5*
Low, Joseph 1911-2007 .... *14*
Low, Penelope Margaret
  See Lively, Penelope
Low, William *177*
Lowe, Helen 1961- *206*
Lowe, Jay, Jr.
  See Loeper, John J(oseph)
Lowell, Pamela *187*
Lowell, Susan 1950- *206*
  Earlier sketches in SATA *81, 127*
Lowenstein, Dyno 1914-1996 .... *6*
Lowenstein, Sallie 1949- *116*
Lowery, Linda 1949- *151*
  Earlier sketch in SATA *74*
Lowitz, Anson C. 1901(?)-1978 .... *18*
Lowitz, Sadyebeth Heath 1901-1969 .... *17*
Lowndes, Robert A(ugustine) W(ard)
  1916-1998 .... *117*
Lowrey, Janette Sebring 1892-1986 .... *43*
Lowry, Lois 1937- *177*
  Autobiography Feature *127*
  Earlier sketches in SATA *23, 70, 111*
  See also CLR *72*
  See also SAAS *3*
Lowry, Lois Hammersberg
  See Lowry, Lois
Lowry, Peter 1953- *7*
Lowther, George F. 1913-1975
  Obituary *30*
Loyie, Larry 1933- *150*
Lozansky, Edward D. 1941- *62*
Lozier, Herbert 1915- *26*
Lubar, David 1954- *190*
  Earlier sketch in SATA *133*
Lubell, Cecil 1912-2000 .... *6*
Lubell, Winifred (A. Milius) 1914- *6*
Lubin, Leonard
  See Lubin, Leonard B.
Lubin, Leonard B. 1943-1994 .... *45*
  Brief entry *37*
Lubka, S. Ruth 1948- *154*
Lubner, Susan *185*

Luby, Thia 1954- *124*
Lucado, Max (Lee) 1955- *104*
Lucas, Cedric 1962- *101*
Lucas, David 1966- *208*
Lucas, E(dward) V(errall) 1868-1938 .... *20*
Lucas, Eileen 1956- *113*
  Earlier sketch in SATA *76*
Lucas, George 1944- *56*
Lucas, Jerry 1940- *33*
Lucas, Margeaux *186*
Lucas, Victoria
  See Plath, Sylvia
Lucashenko, Melissa 1967- *104*
Luccarelli, Vincent 1923- *90*
Luce, Celia (Geneva Larsen) 1914- *38*
Luce, Willard (Ray) 1914-1990 .... *38*
Lucht, Irmgard 1937- *82*
Lucke, Deb *202*
Luckett, Dave 1951- *167*
  Earlier sketch in SATA *106*
Luckhardt, Mildred Corell 1898-1990 .... *5*
Ludden, Allen (Ellsworth) 1918(?)-1981
  Obituary *27*
Ludel, Jacqueline 1945- *64*
Ludlow, Geoffrey
  See Meynell, Laurence Walter
Ludlum, Mabel Cleland
  See Widdemer, Mabel Cleland
Ludwig, Helen *33*
Ludwig, Lyndell 1923- *63*
Ludwig, Trudy 1959- *209*
  Earlier sketch in SATA *166*
Lueders, Edward (George) 1923- *14*
Luenn, Nancy 1954- *79*
  Earlier sketch in SATA *51*
Lufkin, Raymond H. 1897- *38*
Lugard, Flora Louisa Shaw 1852-1929 .... *21*
Luger, Harriett Mandelay 1914- *23*
Luhrmann, Winifred B(ruce) 1934- *11*
Luis, Earlene W. 1929- *11*
Lujan, Jorge *201*
Luke, Pauline *178*
Luke, Pauline R.
  See Luke, Pauline
Lum, Peter
  See Crowe, (Bettina) Peter Lum
Lumry, Amanda (R.) *159*
Lund, Deb *157*
Lund, Doris Herold 1919- *12*
Lunde, Darrin *202*
Lung, Chang
  See Jordan, Robert
Lunge-Larsen, Lise 1955- *184*
  Earlier sketch in SATA *138*
Lunn, Carolyn (Kowalczyk) 1960- *67*
Lunn, Janet (Louise Swoboda) 1928- *110*
  Earlier sketches in SATA *4, 68*
  See also CLR *18*
  See also SAAS *12*
Lunsford, Cin Forshay
  See Forshay-Lunsford, Cin
Lupica, Michael
  See Lupica, Mike
Lupica, Michael Thomas
  See Lupica, Mike
Lupica, Mike 1952- *177*
Lupoff, Dick
  See Lupoff, Richard A(llen)
Lupoff, Richard A(llen) 1935- *60*
Lurie, Alison 1926- *112*
  Earlier sketch in SATA *46*
Lurie, Morris 1938- *72*
Lussert, Anneliese 1929- *101*
Lusted, Marcia Amidon 1962- *143*
Lustig, Arnost 1926- *56*
Lustig, Loretta 1944- *46*
Luthardt, Kevin 1973- *172*
Luther, Frank 1905-1980
  Obituary *25*
Luther, Rebekah (Lyn) S(tiles) 1960- *90*

Luttmann, Gail
    See Damerow, Gail
Luttrell, Guy L. 1938- 22
Luttrell, Ida (Alleene) 1934- 91
    Brief entry 35
    Earlier sketch in SATA 40
Luttrell, William (J. III) 1954- 149
Lutz, John 1939- 180
Lutz, John Thomas
    See Lutz, John
Lutz, Norma Jean 1943- 122
Lutzeier, Elizabeth 1952- 72
Lutzker, Edythe 1904-1991 5
Luxbacher, Irene M. 1970- 153
Luzadder, Patrick 1954- 89
Luzzati, Emanuele 1921-2007 7
Luzzatto, Paola Caboara 1938- 38
Ly, Many 1977- 208
Lybbert, Tyler 1970- 88
Lydon, Michael 1942- 11
Lyfick, Warren
    See Reeves, Lawrence F.
Lyle, Katie Letcher 1938- 8
Lynch, Chris 1962- 209
    Earlier sketches in SATA 95, 131, 171
    See also CLR 58
Lynch, Jay 1945- 204
Lynch, Lorenzo 1932- 7
Lynch, Marietta 1947- 29
Lynch, P(atrick) J(ames) 1962- 122
    Earlier sketch in SATA 79
Lynch, Patricia (Nora) 1898-1972 9
Lynds, Dennis 1924-2005 47
    Brief entry 37
Lyne, Alison Davis 188
Lyngseth, Joan
    See Davies, Joan
Lynn, Elizabeth A(nne) 1946- 99
Lynn, Mary
    See Brokamp, Marilyn
Lynn, Patricia
    See Watts, Mabel Pizzey
Lynn, Tracy 175
Lyon, Elinor 1921-2008 6
    Obituary 192
Lyon, Elinor Bruce
    See Lyon, Elinor
Lyon, George Ella 1949- 207
    Autobiography Feature 148
    Earlier sketches in SATA 68, 119, 148
Lyon, Lyman R.
    See de Camp, L. Sprague
Lyons, Dorothy M(arawee) 1907-1997 3
Lyons, Grant 1941- 30
Lyons, Marcus
    See Blish, James
Lyons, Mary E. 1947- 195
    Autobiography Feature 195
    Earlier sketches in SATA 93, 142
Lyons, Mary Evelyn
    See Lyons, Mary E.
Lystad, Mary (Hanemann) 1928- 11
Lytle, Elizabeth Stewart 1949- 79
Lytle, Robert A. 1944- 119
Lyttle, Richard B(ard) 1927- 23
Lytton of Knebworth, Baron
    See Bulwer-Lytton, Edward

M

Ma, Wenhai 1954- 84
Maar, Leonard (Frank, Jr.) 1927- 30
Maartens, Maretha 1945- 73
Maas, Selve -1997 14
Maass, Robert 195
Mabie, Grace
    See Mattern, Joanne

Mac
    See MacManus, Seumas
    and Maccari, Ruggero
Macalaster, Elizabeth G. 1951- 115
MacAlister, Katie 159
MacAllan, Andrew
    See Leasor, James
MacAodhagain, Eamon
    See Egan, E(dward) W(elstead)
MacArthur-Onslow, Annette Rosemary
    1933- 26
Macaulay, David (Alexander) 1946- 137
    Brief entry 27
    Earlier sketches in SATA 46, 72
    See also CLR 14
Macaulay, Teresa (E.) 1947- 95
Macavinta, Courtney 176
MacBeth, George (Mann) 1932-1992 4
    Obituary 70
MacBride, Roger Lea 1929-1995 85
MacCarter, Don 1944- 91
MacClintock, Dorcas 1932- 8
MacCready, Robin Merrow 1959(?)- 190
MacCullough, Carolyn 174
MacDonald, Alan 1958- 192
MacDonald, Amy 1951- 156
    Autobiography Feature 156
    Earlier sketches in SATA 76, 136
MacDonald, Anne Elizabeth Campbell Bard
    -1958
    See MacDonald, Betty
MacDonald, Anson
    See Heinlein, Robert A.
MacDonald, Betty 1908-1958
    See YABC 1
Macdonald, Blackie
    See Emrich, Duncan (Black Macdonald)
Macdonald, Caroline 1948- 86
    Obituary 111
    See also CLR 60
Macdonald, Dwight 1906-1982 29
    Obituary 33
MacDonald, George 1824-1905 100
    Earlier sketch in SATA 33
    See also CLR 67
MacDonald, Golden
    See Brown, Margaret Wise
Macdonald, Guy 195
Macdonald, James D. 1954- 67
    Earlier sketches in SATA 81, 114, 165, 1
Macdonald, Marcia
    See Hill, Grace Livingston
MacDonald, Margaret Read 1940- 194
    Earlier sketches in SATA 94, 164
Macdonald, Marianne 1934- 113
Macdonald, Mary
    See Gifford, Griselda
Macdonald, Maryann 1947- 189
    Earlier sketch in SATA 72
MacDonald, Ross 1957- 201
Macdonald, Shelagh 1937- 25
MacDonald, Suse 1940- 193
    Brief entry 52
    Earlier sketches in SATA 54, 109
Macdonald, Zillah K(atherine) 1885-1979 ... 11
MacDonnell, Megan
    See Stevens, Serita
MacDougal, John
    See Blish, James
Mace, Elisabeth 1933- 27
Mace, Varian 1938- 49
MacEachern, Stephen 206
MacEwen, Gwendolyn (Margaret)
    1941-1987 50
    Obituary 55
Macfarlan, Allan A. 1892-1982 35
MacFarlane, Iris 1922- 11
MacGill-Callahan, Sheila 1926-2000 78
MacGregor, Carol Lynn 153
MacGregor, Ellen 1906-1954 39
    Brief entry 27

MacGregor-Hastie, Roy (Alasdhair Niall)
    1929- 3
MacGrory, Yvonne 1948- 142
Machado, Ana Maria 1941- 150
MacHale, D.J. 1956- 175
MacHale, Donald James
    See MacHale, D.J.
Machetanz, Frederick 1908- 34
Machin, Sue
    See Williams, Sue
Machin Goodall, Daphne (Edith) 37
Macht, Norm
    See Macht, Norman L.
Macht, Norman L. 1929- 122
Macht, Norman Lee
    See Macht, Norman L.
MacInnes, Helen (Clark) 1907-1985 22
    Obituary 44
Macintosh, Brownie 1950- 98
MacIntyre, Elisabeth 1916- 17
MacIntyre, Rod
    See MacIntyre, R.P.
MacIntyre, R.P. 1947- 203
MacIntyre, R.P. 1947- 203
MacIntyre, Wendy 1947- 196
Mack, Jeff 194
Mack, L.V.
    See Kimmelman, Burt
Mack, Stan(ley) 17
Mack, Todd 168
Mack, Tracy 1968- 183
    Earlier sketch in SATA 128
Mackall, Dandi D.
    See Mackall, Dandi Daley
Mackall, Dandi Daley 1949- 182
    Earlier sketches in SATA 118, 177
Mackay, Claire 1930- 97
    Autobiography Feature 124
    Earlier sketch in SATA 40
    See also CLR 43
Mackay, Constance D'Arcy (?)-1966 125
Mackay, Donald 1914-2005 81
    Obituary 173
Mackay, Donald Alexander
    See Mackay, Donald
MacKaye, Percy (Wallace) 1875-1956 32
Mackel, Kathryn 1950- 162
Mackel, Kathy
    See Mackel, Kathryn
MacKellar, William 1914- 4
Macken, JoAnn Early 1953- 201
Macken, Walter 1915-1967 36
MacKenzie, Jill (Kelly) 1947- 75
Mackenzie, Robert 1974- 204
Mackey, Ernan
    See McInerny, Ralph
Mackey, Weezie Kerr 188
Mackie, Maron
    See McNeely, Jeannette
Mackin, Edward
    See McInerny, Ralph
MacKinnon, Bernie 1957- 69
MacKinnon Groomer, Vera 1915- 57
MacKinstry, Elizabeth 1879-1956 42
Mackler, Carolyn 1973- 156
MacLachlan, Emily
    See Charest, Emily MacLachlan
MacLachlan, Patricia 1938- 168
    Brief entry 42
    Earlier sketches in SATA 62, 107
    See also CLR 14
MacLane, Jack
    See Crider, Bill
MacLean, Alistair 1922(?)-1987 23
    Obituary 50
MacLean, Alistair Stuart
    See MacLean, Alistair
Maclean, Art
    See Shirreffs, Gordon D(onald)
MacLean, Christine Kole 1962- 177
MacLean, Glynne 1964- 150

MacLeod, Beatrice 1910- *162*
  Earlier sketch in SATA *10*
MacLeod, Beatrice Beach
  See MacLeod, Beatrice
MacLeod, Charlotte (Matilda) 1922-2005 .... *28*
  Obituary *160*
MacLeod, Doug 1959- *201*
  Earlier sketch in SATA *60*
MacLeod, Elizabeth *184*
  Earlier sketch in SATA *158*
MacLeod, Ellen Jane (Anderson) 1916- *14*
MacManus, James
  See MacManus, Seumas
MacManus, Seumas 1869-1960 .... *25*
MacMaster, Eve (Ruth) B(owers) 1942- *46*
MacMillan, Annabelle
  See Quick, Annabelle
MacMillan, Dianne M(arie) 1943- *125*
  Earlier sketch in SATA *84*
Macnaughton, Tina *182*
Macneill, Janet
  See McNeely, Jeannette
MacPeek, Walter G. 1902-1973 .... *4*
  Obituary *25*
MacPhail, Catherine 1946- *197*
  Earlier sketch in SATA *130*
MacPherson, Margaret 1908-2001 .... *9*
  See also SAAS *4*
MacPherson, Thomas George 1915-1976
  Obituary *30*
MacPherson, Winnie 1930- *107*
MacRae, Tom 1980- *181*
Macrae, Travis
  See Feagles, Anita M(acRae)
MacRaois, Cormac 1944- *72*
Macumber, Mari
  See Sandoz, Mari(e Susette)
Macy, Sue 1954- *134*
  Earlier sketch in SATA *88*
Madaras, Lynda 1947- *151*
Madden, Don 1927- *3*
Madden, Kerry 1961- *168*
Madden-Lunsford, Kerry
  See Madden, Kerry
Maddern, Eric 1950- *166*
Maddigan, Beth 1967- *174*
Maddison, Angela Mary 1923- *10*
  See also CLR *24*
Maddock, Reginald (Bertram) 1912-1994 .... *15*
Madenski, Melissa (Ann) 1949- *77*
Madian, Jon 1941- *9*
Madison, Alan *182*
Madison, Arnold 1937- *6*
Madison, Winifred *5*
Madonna 1958- *149*
Madsen, Gunnar *171*
Madsen, Jim 1964- *202*
Madsen, Ross Martin 1946- *82*
Madsen, Susan A. 1954- *90*
Madsen, Susan Arrington
  See Madsen, Susan A.
Maehlqvist, Stefan 1943- *30*
Maestro, Betsy (Crippen) 1944- *106*
  Brief entry *30*
  Earlier sketch in SATA *59*
  See also CLR *45*
Maestro, Giulio 1942- *106*
  Earlier sketches in SATA *8, 59*
  See also CLR *45*
Maeterlinck, Maurice 1862-1949 .... *66*
Magee, Doug 1947- *78*
Magee, Wes 1939- *64*
Maggio, Rosalie 1943- *69*
Magid, Ken(neth Marshall) *65*
Magnus, Erica 1946- *77*
Magoon, Scott *182*
Magorian, James 1942- *92*
  Earlier sketch in SATA *32*
Magorian, Michelle 1947- *128*
  Earlier sketch in SATA *67*

Magorian, Michelle Jane
  See Magorian, Michelle
Magovern, Peg *103*
Maguire, Anne
  See Nearing, Penny
Maguire, Gregory 1954- *200*
  Autobiography Feature *200*
  Earlier sketches in SATA *28, 84, 129*
  See also SAAS *22*
Maguire, Gregory Peter
  See Maguire, Gregory
Maguire, Jack 1920-2000 .... *74*
Maguire, Jesse
  See Smith, Sherwood
Maguire, Jessie
  See Smith, Sherwood
Maher, Ramona 1934- *13*
Mahlqvist, Stefan
  See Maehlqvist, Stefan
Mahon, Julia C(unha) 1916- *11*
Mahony, Elizabeth Winthrop
  See Winthrop, Elizabeth
Mahood, Kenneth 1930- *24*
Mahy, Margaret 1936- *171*
  Earlier sketches in SATA *14, 69, 119*
  See also CLR *78*
Mahy, Margaret May
  See Mahy, Margaret
Maiden, Cecil (Edward) 1902-1981 .... *52*
Maidoff, Ilka
  See List, Ilka Katherine
Maifair, Linda Lee 1947- *83*
Maik, Henri
  See Hecht, Henri Joseph
Maillu, David G(ian) 1939- *111*
Maine, Trevor
  See Catherall, Arthur
Mains, Randolph P. 1946- *80*
Maione, Heather *189*
Maiorano, Robert 1946- *43*
Maisner, Heather 1947- *89*
Maison, Della
  See Katz, Bobbi
Maitland, Antony Jasper 1935- *25*
Maitland, Barbara *102*
Mai-Wyss, Tatjana 1972- *187*
Major, Kevin (Gerald) 1949- *134*
  Earlier sketches in SATA *32, 82*
  See also CLR *11*
Majure, Janet 1954- *96*
Makhijani, Pooja *188*
Makie, Pam 1943- *37*
Makowski, Silk
  See Makowski, Silvia Ann
Makowski, Silvia Ann 1940- *101*
Malam, John 1957- *152*
  Earlier sketch in SATA *89*
Maland, Nick *195*
Malcolm, Dan
  See Silverberg, Robert
Malcolm, Jahnna N.
  See Beecham, Jahnna
Malcolmson, Anne
  See von Storch, Anne B.
Malcolmson, David 1899-1978 .... *6*
Maletta, Dr. Arlene
  See Feltenstein, Arlene (H.)
Maley, Carleen
  See Hutchins, Carleen Maley
Mali, Jane Lawrence 1937-1995 .... *51*
  Brief entry *44*
  Obituary *86*
Malkin, Nina 1959(?)- *179*
Mallett, Jerry J. 1939- *76*
Malley, Gemma *198*
Malley, G.R.
  See Malley, Gemma
Mallory, Kenneth 1945- *185*
  Earlier sketch in SATA *128*
Mallowan, Agatha Christie
  See Christie, Agatha

Malmberg, Carl 1904-1979 .... *9*
Malmgren, Dallin 1949- *65*
Malo, John W. 1911-2000 .... *4*
Malone, James Hiram 1930- *84*
Malone, Nola Langner 1930-2003 .... *8*
  Obituary *151*
Malone, Patricia 1932- *155*
Malone, Peter 1953- *191*
Maloney, Pat
  See Markun, Patricia Maloney
Malory, Sir Thomas 1410(?)-1471(?) *59*
  Brief entry *33*
Maltese, Michael 1909(?)-1981
  Obituary *24*
Malvasi, Meg Greene *143*
Malvern, Corinne 1905-1956 .... *34*
Malvern, Gladys (?)-1962 .... *23*
Mama G.
  See Davis, Grania
Mammano, Julie 1962- *202*
  Earlier sketch in SATA *107*
Mamonova, Tatyana 1943- *93*
Manchel, Frank 1935- *10*
Manchess, Gregory 1955- *203*
Manchester, William (Raymond)
  1922-2004 .... *65*
Mandabach, Brian 1962(?)- *197*
Mandel, Brett H. 1969- *108*
Mandel, Peter 1957- *87*
Mandel, Sally (Elizabeth) 1944- *64*
Mandell, Muriel (Hortense Levin) 1921- *63*
Manders, John 1957- *175*
Manes, Stephen 1949- *99*
  Brief entry *40*
  Earlier sketch in SATA *42*
Manfred, Frederick (Feikema) 1912-1994 .... *30*
Mangin, Marie France 1940- *59*
Mangione, Gerlando 1909-1998 .... *6*
  Obituary *104*
Mangione, Jerre
  See Mangione, Gerlando
Mango, Karin N. 1936- *52*
Mangurian, David 1938- *14*
Mania, Cathy 1950- *102*
Mania, Robert 1952- *102*
Mania, Robert C., Jr.
  See Mania, Robert
Maniatty, Taramesha 1978- *92*
Maniscalco, Joseph 1926- *10*
Manley, Deborah 1932- *28*
Manley, Seon 1921- *15*
  See also CLR *3*
  See also SAAS *2*
Mann, Elizabeth 1948- *153*
Mann, Josephine
  See Pullein-Thompson, Josephine (Mary
    Wedderburn)
Mann, Kenny 1946- *91*
Mann, Pamela 1946- *91*
Mann, Patrick
  See Waller, Leslie
Mann, Peggy
  See Houlton, Peggy Mann
Mannetti, Lisa 1953- *57*
  Brief entry *51*
Mannheim, Grete (Salomon) 1909-1986 ...... *10*
Manniche, Lise 1943- *31*
Manning, Jane K. *185*
Manning, Mick 1959- *176*
Manning, Rosemary 1911-1988 .... *10*
Manning, Sarra *162*
Manning-Sanders, Ruth (Vernon)
  1895(?)-1988 .... *73*
  Obituary *57*
  Earlier sketch in SATA *15*
Mannion, Diane
  See Paterson, Diane
Mannis, Celeste Davidson *173*
Mannon, Warwick
  See Hopkins, (Hector) Kenneth
Manos, Helen *199*

Mansir, A. Richard 1932- *170*
Manson, Ainslie Kertland 1938- *115*
Manson, Beverlie 1945- 57
  Brief entry 44
Manthorpe, Helen 1958- *122*
Mantinband, Gerda (B.) 1917- 74
Manton, Jo
  See Gittings, Jo (Grenville) Manton
Manuel, Lynn 1948- *179*
  Earlier sketch in SATA *99*
Manushkin, Fran 1942- 205
  Earlier sketches in SATA *7, 54, 93, 166*
Manushkin, Frances
  See Manushkin, Fran
Man Without a Spleen, A
  See Chekhov, Anton
Manzano, Sonia 1950- *167*
Mapes, Mary A.
  See Ellison, Virginia H(owell)
Maple, Marilyn 1931- 80
Mappin, Strephyn 1956- *109*
Mara, Barney
  See Roth, Arthur J(oseph)
Mara, Jeanette
  See Cebulash, Mel
Mara, Rachna
  See Gilmore, Rachna
Marais, Josef 1905-1978
  Obituary 24
Marasmus, Seymour
  See Rivoli, Mario
Marbach, Ethel
  See Pochocki, Ethel (Frances)
Marcal, Annette B.
  See Callaway, Bernice (Anne)
Marcelino
  See Agnew, Edith J(osephine)
Marcellino, Fred 1939-2001 .... *118*
  Obituary *127*
  Earlier sketch in SATA *68*
March, Carl
  See Fleischman, Sid
Marchant, Bessie 1862-1941
  See YABC 2
Marchant, Catherine
  See Cookson, Catherine (McMullen)
Marcher, Marion Walden 1890-1987 .... *10*
Marchesi, Stephen 1951- *114*
Marchesi, Steve
  See Marchesi, Stephen
  and Older, Effin
  and Older, Jules
Marchetta, Melina 1965- *170*
Marciano, John Bemelmans 1970- *167*
  Earlier sketch in SATA *118*
  See also CLR *93*
Marco, Lou
  See Gottfried, Theodore Mark
Marcus, Leonard S. 1950- *187*
  Earlier sketch in SATA *133*
Marcus, Paul 1953- 82
Marcus, Rebecca B(rian) 1907- 9
Marcuse, Aida E. 1934- 89
Marek, Margot L. 1934(?)-1987
  Obituary 54
Maren, Julie 1970- *199*
Margaret, Karla
  See Andersdatter, Karla M(argaret)
Margolin, Harriet
  See Ziefert, Harriet
Margolis, Jeffrey A. 1948- *108*
Margolis, Leslie *187*
Margolis, Richard J(ules) 1929-1991 86
  Obituary 67
  Earlier sketch in SATA *4*
Margolis, Vivienne 1922- 46
Mariana
  See Foster, Marian Curtis
Marie, Geraldine 1949- 61
Mariner, Scott
  See Pohl, Frederik

Marino, Dorothy Bronson 1912- 14
Marino, Jan 1936- *114*
Marino, Nick
  See Deming, Richard
Marino, Peter 1960- *179*
Mario, Anna
  See Odgers, Sally Farrell
Marion, Henry
  See del Rey, Lester
Maris, Ron 71
  Brief entry 45
Mark, Jan 1943-2006 .... *164*
  Obituary *173*
  Earlier sketches in SATA *22, 69, 114*
  See also CLR *11*
Mark, Janet Marjorie
  See Mark, Jan
Mark, Joan T. 1937- *122*
Mark, Pauline (Dahlin) 1913-1997 14
Mark, Polly
  See Mark, Pauline (Dahlin)
Mark, Ted
  See Gottfried, Theodore Mark
Markel, Michelle *169*
Marker, Sherry 1941- 76
Markert, Jennifer 1965- 83
Markert, Jenny
  See Markert, Jennifer
Markham, Lynne 1947- *102*
Markham, Marion M. 1929- 60
Markham, Wendy
  See Staub, Wendy Corsi
Markins, W. S.
  See Jenkins, Marie M(agdalen)
Markle, Sandra L. 1946- *185*
  Brief entry 41
  Earlier sketches in SATA *57, 92, 148*
Markle, Sandra Lee
  See Markle, Sandra L.
Marko, Katherine D(olores) 28
Markoosie
  See Patsauq, Markoosie
Marks, Alan 1957- *187*
  Earlier sketches in SATA *77, 151*
Marks, Burton 1930- 47
  Brief entry 43
Marks, Graham *158*
Marks, Hannah K.
  See Trivelpiece, Laurel
Marks, J.
  See Highwater, Jamake (Mamake)
Marks, J(ames) M(acdonald) 1921- 13
Marks, Laurie J. 1957- 68
Marks, Margaret L. 1911(?)-1980
  Obituary 23
Marks, Mickey Klar -1986 12
Marks, Peter
  See Smith, Robert Kimmel
Marks, Rita 1938- 47
Marks, Stan(ley) 14
Marks-Highwater, J.
  See Highwater, Jamake (Mamake)
Markun, Patricia Maloney 1924- 15
Markusen, Bruce (Stanley Rodriguez)
  1965- *141*
Marley, Louise 1952- *173*
  Earlier sketch in SATA *120*
Marlin, Hilda
  See Van Stockum, Hilda
Marlow, Layne *204*
Marlow, Max
  See Nicole, Christopher (Robin)
Marlow, Susan K. 1953- *178*
Marlowe, Amy Bell 67
  Earlier sketch in SATA *1*
Marlowe, Jack
  See Deary, Terry
Marney, Dean 1952- 90
Marokvia, Artur 1909- 31
Marokvia, Mireille 1908-2008 5
  Obituary *197*

Marokvia, Mireille Journet
  See Marokvia, Mireille
Marol, Jean-Claude 1946- *125*
Marr, John S(tuart) 1940- 48
Marr, Melissa 1972- *189*
Marric, J. J.
  See Butler, William Vivian
  and Creasey, John
Marrin, Albert 1936- *193*
  Brief entry 43
  Earlier sketches in SATA *53, 90, 126*
  See also CLR *53*
Marriott, Alice Lee 1910-1992 31
  Obituary 71
Marriott, Janice 1946- *134*
Marriott, Pat(ricia) 1920- 35
Marroquin, Patricio
  See Markun, Patricia Maloney
Mars, W. T.
  See Mars, Witold Tadeusz J.
Mars, Witold Tadeusz J. 1912-1985 3
Marsden, Carolyn 1950- *175*
  Earlier sketch in SATA *140*
Marsden, John 1950- *146*
  Earlier sketches in SATA *66, 97*
  See also CLR *34*
  See also SAAS *22*
Marsh, Carole 1946- *127*
Marsh, Dave 1950- 66
Marsh, J. E.
  See Marshall, Evelyn
Marsh, James 1946- 73
Marsh, Jean
  See Marshall, Evelyn
Marsh, Joan F. 1923- 83
Marsh, Paul
  See Hopkins, (Hector) Kenneth
Marsh, Valerie 1954- 89
Marshall, Anthony D(ryden) 1924- 18
Marshall, Bonnie C. 1941- *141*
  Earlier sketch in SATA *18*
Marshall, Bridget M(ary) 1974- *103*
Marshall, (Sarah) Catherine (Wood)
  1914-1983 2
  Obituary 34
Marshall, Douglas
  See McClintock, Marshall
Marshall, Edmund
  See Hopkins, (Hector) Kenneth
Marshall, Edward
  See Marshall, James
Marshall, Evelyn 1897-1991 11
Marshall, Felicity 1950- *116*
Marshall, Garry 1934- 60
Marshall, H. H.
  See Jahn, Michael
Marshall, James 1942-1992 75
  Earlier sketches in SATA *6, 51*
  See also CLR *21*
Marshall, James Edward
  See Marshall, James
Marshall, James Vance
  See Payne, Donald Gordon
Marshall, Janet (Perry) 1938- 97
Marshall, Jeff
  See Laycock, George (Edwin)
Marshall, Kim
  See Marshall, Michael (Kimbrough)
Marshall, Michael (Kimbrough) 1948- 37
Marshall, Percy
  See Young, Percy M(arshall)
Marshall, S(amuel) L(yman) A(twood)
  1900-1977 21
Marsoli, Lisa Ann 1958- *101*
  Brief entry 53
Marsten, Richard
  See Hunter, Evan
Marston, Elsa 1933- *156*
Marston, Hope Irvin 1935- *127*
  Earlier sketch in SATA *31*
Marszalek, John F. 1939- *167*

Marszalek, John Francis, Jr.
  See Marszalek, John F.
Marszalek, John Francis 1939-
  See Marszalek, John F.
Martchenko, Michael 1942- 154
  Earlier sketches in SATA *50, 95*
Martel, Aimee
  See Thurlo, Aimee
  and Thurlo, David
Martel, Suzanne 1924- 99
Martignoni, Margaret E. 1908(?)-1974
  Obituary 27
Martin, Ann M. 1955- 192
  Brief entry 41
  Earlier sketches in SATA *44, 70, 126*
  See also CLR *32*
Martin, Bill, Jr. 1916-2004 145
  Brief entry 40
  Earlier sketches in SATA *40, 67*
  See also CLR *97*
Martin, Charles E(lmer)
  See Mastrangelo, Charles E(lmer)
Martin, Christopher
  See Hoyt, Edwin P(almer), Jr.
Martin, C.K. Kelly 207
Martin, Claire 1933- 76
Martin, Courtney Autumn 1984- 205
Martin, David Stone 1913-1992 39
Martin, Del 1921-2008 47
Martin, Donald
  See Honig, Donald
Martin, Dorothy
  See Martin, Del
Martin, Dorothy L.
  See Martin, Del
Martin, Eugene 1
Martin, Eva M. 1939- 65
Martin, Frances M(cEntee) 1906-1998 36
Martin, Francesca 1947- 101
Martin, Fred 1948- 119
Martin, Fredric
  See Christopher, Matt(hew Frederick)
Martin, George Raymond Richard
  See Martin, George R.R.
Martin, George R.R. 1948- 118
Martin, J(ohn) P(ercival) 1880(?)-1966 15
Martin, Jacqueline Briggs 1945- 188
  Earlier sketches in SATA *98, 149*
Martin, Jane Read 1957- 84
Martin, Jeremy
  See Levin, Marcia Obrasky
Martin, Les
  See Schulman, L(ester) M(artin)
Martin, Linda 1961- 82
Martin, Lynne 1923- 21
Martin, Marcia
  See Levin, Marcia Obrasky
Martin, Marvin 1926- 126
Martin, Melanie
  See Pellowski, Michael (Joseph)
Martin, Nancy
  See Salmon, Annie Elizabeth
Martin, Patricia 200
Martin, Patricia A.
  See Martin, Patricia
Martin, Patricia Miles 1899-1986 43
  Obituary 48
  Earlier sketch in SATA *1*
Martin, Peter
  See Chaundler, Christine
Martin, Rafe 1946- 175
Martin, Rene 1891-1977 42
  Obituary 20
Martin, Rupert (Claude) 1905- 31
Martin, S. R.
  See Mappin, Strephyn
Martin, Stefan 1936- 32
Martin, Vicky
  See Storey, Victoria Carolyn
Martin, Webber
  See Silverberg, Robert

Martin, Wendy
  See Martini, Teri
Martin, William Ivan, Jr.
  See Martin, Bill, Jr.
Martineau, Diane 1940- 178
Martineau, Harriet 1802-1876
  See YABC *2*
Martinet, Jeanne 1958- 80
Martinez, Agnes 167
Martinez, Arturo O. 1933- 192
Martinez, Ed(ward) 1954- 98
Martinez, Elizabeth Coonrod 1954- 85
Martinez, Victor 1954- 95
Martini, Teri 1930- 3
Martini, Therese
  See Martini, Teri
Martino, Alfred C. 1964- 174
Martinson, Janis
  See Herbert, Janis
Marton, Jirina 1946- 144
  Earlier sketch in SATA *95*
Marton, Pierre
  See Stone, Peter
Martson, Del
  See Lupoff, Richard A(llen)
Martyr, Paula (Jane)
  See Lawford, Paula Jane
Maruki, Toshi 1912-2000 112
  See also CLR *19*
Marvin, Isabel R(idout) 1924- 84
Marx, Patricia Windschill
  See Marx, Trish
Marx, Robert F(rank) 1936- 24
Marx, Trish 1948- 202
  Earlier sketches in SATA *112, 160*
Marzani, Carl (Aldo) 1912-1994 12
Marzollo, Jean 1942- 190
  Autobiography Feature 190
  Earlier sketches in SATA *29, 77, 130*
  See also SAAS *15*
Masefield, John (Edward) 1878-1967 19
Masoff, Joy 1951- 118
Mason, Adrienne 1962- 163
Mason, Cherie 170
Mason, Edwin A. 1905-1979
  Obituary 32
Mason, Ernst
  See Pohl, Frederik
Mason, F(rancis) van Wyck 1901-1978 3
  Obituary 26
Mason, Frank W.
  See Mason, F(rancis) van Wyck
Mason, George Frederick 1904-2000 14
Mason, Miriam E(vangeline) 1900-1973 2
  Obituary 26
Mason, Prue 195
Mason, Simon 1962- 178
Mason, Tally
  See Derleth, August (William)
Mason, Van Wyck
  See Mason, F(rancis) van Wyck
Mass, Wendy 1967- 196
  Earlier sketch in SATA *158*
Mass, William
  See Gibson, William
Masselman, George 1897-1971 19
Massie, Dianne Redfield 1938- 125
  Earlier sketch in SATA *16*
Massie, Elizabeth 108
Masson, Sophie 1959- 179
  Earlier sketch in SATA *133*
Masters, Anthony (Richard) 1940-2003 112
  Obituary 145
Masters, Kelly R(ay) 1897-1987 3
Masters, Mildred 1932- 42
Masters, William
  See Cousins, Margaret
Masters, Zeke
  See Bensen, Donald R.
  and Goulart, Ron

Mastrangelo, Charles E(lmer) 1910-1995 70
  Earlier sketch in SATA *69*
Masuda, Takeshi 1944- 56
Matas, Carol 1949- 194
  Autobiography Feature 112
  Earlier sketch in SATA *93*
  See also CLR *52*
Matchette, Katharine E. 1941- 38
Math, Irwin 1940- 42
Mathabane, Mark 1960- 123
Mather, Kirtley F(letcher) 1888-1978 65
Mathers, Petra 1945- 176
  Earlier sketch in SATA *119*
  See also CLR *76*
Matheson, Richard (Christian) 1953- 119
Matheson, Shirlee Smith 1942- 155
Mathews, Eleanor
  See Mathews, Ellie
Mathews, Ellie 1946(?)- 193
Mathews, Janet 1914-1992 41
Mathews, Judith
  See Goldberger, Judith M.
Mathews, Louise
  See Tooke, Louise Mathews
Mathiesen, Egon 1907-1976
  Obituary 28
Mathieu, Joe 1949- 185
  Brief entry 36
  Earlier sketches in SATA *43, 94*
Mathieu, Joseph P.
  See Mathieu, Joe
Mathis, Sharon Bell 1937- 58
  Earlier sketch in SATA *7*
  See also CLR *147*
  See also SAAS *3*
Matlin, Marlee 1965- 181
Matlin, Marlee Beth
  See Matlin, Marlee
Matloff, Gregory 1945- 73
Matott, Justin 1961- 109
Matranga, Frances Carfi 1922- 78
Matray, James I. 1948- 161
Matray, James Irving
  See Matray, James I.
Matson, Emerson N(els) 1926- 12
Matsui, Tadashi 1926- 8
Matsuno, Masako
  See Kobayashi, Masako Matsuno
Matsuoka, Mei 1981- 192
Matte, (Encarnacion) L'Enc 1936- 22
Mattern, Joanne 1963- 122
Matheson, Jenny 180
Matthew, James
  See Barrie, J. M.
Matthews, Aline
  See De Wire, Elinor
Matthews, Andrew 1948- 138
Matthews, Caitlin 1952- 122
Matthews, Downs 1925- 71
Matthews, Elizabeth 1978- 194
Matthews, Ellen
  See Bache, Ellyn
Matthews, Ellen 1950- 28
Matthews, Harold Downs
  See Matthews, Downs
Matthews, Jacklyn Meek
  See Meek, Jacklyn O'Hanlon
Matthews, John (Kentigern) 1948- 116
Matthews, Laura S.
  See Matthews, L.S.
Matthews, Liz
  See Pellowski, Michael (Joseph)
Matthews, L.S. 183
Matthews, Morgan
  See Pellowski, Michael (Joseph)
Matthews, Nicola
  See Browne, N.M.
Matthews, Patricia 1927-2006 28
Matthews, Patricia Anne
  See Matthews, Patricia
Matthews, Tina 1961- 190

Matthews, Tom L.
  See Lalicki, Tom
Matthews, William Henry III 1919- 45
  Brief entry 28
Matthiessen, Peter 1927- 27
Mattingley, Christobel (Rosemary) 1931- 85
  Earlier sketch in SATA *37*
  See also CLR *24*
  See also SAAS *18*
Matulay, Laszlo 1912- 43
Matus, Greta 1938- 12
Maugham, W. S.
  See Maugham, W. Somerset
Maugham, W. Somerset 1874-1965 54
Maugham, William S.
  See Maugham, W. Somerset
Maugham, William Somerset
  See Maugham, W. Somerset
Maurer, Diane Philippoff
  See Maurer-Mathison, Diane V(ogel)
Maurer, Diane Vogel
  See Maurer-Mathison, Diane V(ogel)
Maurer-Mathison, Diane V(ogel) 1944- 89
Mauser, Pat Rhoads
  See McCord, Patricia
Mauser, Patricia Rhoads
  See McCord, Patricia
Maves, Mary Carolyn 1916- 10
Maves, Paul B(enjamin) 1913-1994 10
Mavor, Salley 1955- 125
Mawicke, Tran 1911- 15
Max 1906-1989
  See Diop, Birago (Ismael)
Max, Peter 1939- 45
Maxon, Anne
  See Best, (Evangel) Allena Champlin
Maxwell, Arthur S. 1896-1970 11
Maxwell, Edith 1923- 7
Maxwell, Gavin 1914-1969 65
Maxwell, Katie
  See MacAlister, Katie
Maxwell, William (Keepers, Jr.) 1908-2000
  Obituary 128
Maxwell-Hyslop, Miranda 1968- 154
May, Charles Paul 1920- 4
May, Elaine Tyler 1947- 120
May, J. C.
  See May, Julian
May, Julian 1931- 11
May, Robert Lewis 1905-1976
  Obituary 27
May, Robert Stephen 1929-1996 46
May, Robin
  See May, Robert Stephen
Mayall, Beth 171
Mayberry, Florence V(irginia) Wilson 10
Maybury, Richard J. 1946- 72
Maybury, Rick
  See Maybury, Richard J.
Mayer, Agatha
  See Maher, Ramona
Mayer, Albert Ignatius, Jr. 1906-1994
  Obituary 29
Mayer, Ann M(argaret) 1938- 14
Mayer, Bill 200
Mayer, Danuta 1958- 117
Mayer, Hannelore Valencak 1929- 42
Mayer, Jane Rothschild 1903-2001 38
Mayer, Marianna 1945- 132
  Earlier sketches in SATA *32, 83*
Mayer, Mercer 1943- 137
  Earlier sketches in SATA *16, 32, 73, 129*
  See also CLR *11*
Mayerson, Charlotte Leon 36
Mayerson, Evelyn Wilde 1935- 55
Mayfield, Katherine 1958- 118
Mayfield, Sue 1963- 146
  Earlier sketch in SATA *72*
Mayhar, Ardath 1930- 38
Mayhew, James 1964- 204
  Earlier sketches in SATA *85, 149*

Maynard, Olga 1920- 40
Mayne, William (James Carter) 1928- 122
  Earlier sketches in SATA *6, 68*
  See also CLR *123*
  See also SAAS *11*
Maynes, J. O. Rocky, Jr.
  See Maynes, J. Oscar, Jr.
Maynes, J. Oscar, Jr. 1929- 38
Mayo, Gretchen Will 1936- 163
  Earlier sketch in SATA *84*
Mayo, Margaret 1935- 165
  Earlier sketches in SATA *38, 96*
Mayo, Margaret Mary
  See Mayo, Margaret
Mayr, Diane 1949- 197
Mays, Lucinda L(a Bella) 1924- 49
Mays, (Lewis) Victor (Jr.) 1927- 5
Mazer, Anne 1953- 192
  Earlier sketches in SATA *67, 105*
Mazer, Harry 1925- 167
  Earlier sketches in SATA *31, 67, 105*
  See also CLR *16*
  See also SAAS *11*
Mazer, Norma Fox 1931-2009 198
  Earlier sketches in SATA *24, 67, 105, 168*
  See also CLR *23*
  See also SAAS *1*
Mazille, Capucine 1953- 96
Mazza, Adriana 1928- 19
Mazzio, Joann 1926- 74
Mbugua, Kioi Wa 1962- 83
McAfee, Carol 1955- 81
McAllister, Amanda
  See Dowdell, Dorothy (Florence) Karns
  and Hager, Jean
  and Meaker, Eloise
McAllister, Angela 182
McAllister, Margaret I. 1956- 169
  Earlier sketch in SATA *117*
McAllister, M.I.
  See McAllister, Margaret I.
McArdle, Paula 1971- 198
McArthur, Nancy 96
McAvoy, Jim 1972- 142
McBain, Ed
  See Hunter, Evan
McBain, Georgina 189
McBratney, Sam 1943- 203
  Earlier sketches in SATA *89, 164*
  See also CLR *44*
McBrier, Michael
  See Older, Effin
  and Older, Jules
McCafferty, Jim 1954- 84
McCaffery, Janet 1936- 38
McCaffrey, Anne 1926- 152
  Autobiography Feature 152
  Earlier sketches in SATA *8, 70, 116*
  See also CLR *130*
  See also SAAS *11*
McCaffrey, Anne Inez
  See McCaffrey, Anne
McCaffrey, Mary
  See Szudek, Agnes S(usan) P(hilomena)
McCain, Becky Ray 1954- 138
McCain, Murray (David, Jr.) 1926-1981 7
  Obituary 29
McCall, Bruce 1935(?)- 209
McCall, Edith (Sansom) 1911- 6
McCall, Virginia Nielsen 1909-2000 13
McCall, Wendell
  See Pearson, Ridley
McCall Smith, Alexander
  See Smith, Alexander McCall
McCallum, Phyllis
  See Koch, Phyllis (Mae) McCallum
McCallum, Stephen 1960- 91
McCampbell, Darlene Z. 1942- 83
McCann, Edson
  See del Rey, Lester
  and Pohl, Frederik

McCann, Gerald 1916- 41
McCann, Helen 1948- 75
McCannon, Dindga 41
McCants, William D. 1961- 82
McCarter, Neely Dixon 1929- 47
McCarthy, Agnes 1933- 4
McCarthy, Colin (John) 1951- 77
McCarthy, Mary 1951- 203
McCarthy, Meghan 199
  Earlier sketch in SATA *168*
McCarthy, Ralph F. 1950- 139
McCarthy-Tucker, Sherri N. 1958- 83
McCarty, Peter 1966- 182
McCarty, Rega Kramer 1904-1986 10
McCaslin, Nellie 1914-2005 12
McCaughrean, Geraldine 1951- 173
  Earlier sketches in SATA *87, 139*
  See also CLR *38*
McCaughren, Tom 1936- 75
McCauley, Adam 1965- 209
  Earlier sketch in SATA *128*
McCay, (Zenas) Winsor 1869-1934 134
  Earlier sketch in SATA *41*
McClafferty, Carla Killough 1958- 137
McClary, Jane Stevenson 1919-1990
  Obituary 64
McCleery, Patsy R. 1925- 133
  Earlier sketch in SATA *88*
McClements, George 196
McClintock, Barbara 1955- 146
  Earlier sketches in SATA *57, 95*
McClintock, Marshall 1906-1967 3
McClintock, May Garelick
  See Garelick, May
McClintock, Mike
  See McClintock, Marshall
McClintock, Norah 178
McClintock, Theodore 1902-1971 14
McClinton, Leon 1933- 11
McCloskey, Kevin 1951- 79
McCloskey, (John) Robert 1914-2003 100
  Obituary 146
  Earlier sketches in SATA *2, 39*
  See also CLR *7*
McCloy, James F(loyd) 1941- 59
McClung, Robert M(arshall) 1916- 135
  Earlier sketches in SATA *2, 68*
  See also CLR *11*
  See also SAAS *15*
McClure, Gillian Mary 1948- 31
McColley, Kevin 1961- 80
  See also SAAS *23*
McConduit, Denise Walter 1950- 89
McConnell, James Douglas Rutherford
  1915-1988 40
  Obituary 56
McCord, Anne 1942- 41
McCord, David (Thompson Watson)
  1897-1997 18
  Obituary 96
  See also CLR *9*
McCord, Jean 1924- 34
McCord, Pat Mauser
  See McCord, Patricia
McCord, Patricia 1943- 159
  Earlier sketch in SATA *37*
McCord, Patricia Sue Rhoads Mauser
  See McCord, Patricia
McCormick, Brooks
  See Adams, William Taylor
McCormick, Dell J. 1892-1949 19
McCormick, (George) Donald (King)
  1911-1998 14
McCormick, Edith (Joan) 1934- 30
McCormick, Kimberly A. 1960- 153
McCormick, Patricia 1956- 181
  Earlier sketch in SATA *128*
McCourt, Edward (Alexander) 1907-1972
  Obituary 28
McCourt, Lisa 1964- 159
  Earlier sketch in SATA *117*

McCourt, Malachy 1931- *126*
McCoy, Iola Fuller *3*
McCoy, J(oseph) J(erome) 1917- *8*
McCoy, Karen Kawamoto 1953- *82*
McCoy, Lois (Rich) 1941- *38*
McCrady, Lady 1951- *16*
McCrea, James (Craig, Jr.) 1920- *3*
McCrea, Ruth (Pirman) 1921- *3*
McCreigh, James
    See Pohl, Frederik
McCrumb, Sharyn 1948- *109*
McCue, Lisa 1959- *177*
    Earlier sketch in SATA *65*
McCue, Lisa Emiline
    See McCue, Lisa
McCullen, Andrew
    See Arthur, Robert, (Jr.)
McCullers, Carson 1917-1967 .... *27*
McCullers, Lula Carson Smith
    See McCullers, Carson
McCulloch, Derek (Ivor Breashur) 1897-1967
    Obituary *29*
McCulloch, John Tyler
    See Burroughs, Edgar Rice
McCulloch, Sarah
    See Ure, Jean
McCullough, David 1933- *62*
McCullough, David Gaub
    See McCullough, David
McCullough, Frances Monson 1938- *8*
McCullough, Sharon Pierce 1943- *131*
McCully, Emily Arnold
    See Arnold, Emily
McCune, Dan
    See Haas, Dorothy F.
McCunn, Ruthanne Lum 1946- *63*
McCurdy, Michael (Charles) 1942- *147*
    Earlier sketches in SATA *13, 82*
McCutcheon, Elsie (Mary Jackson) 1937- ... *60*
McCutcheon, John 1952- *97*
McDaniel, Becky Bring 1953- *61*
McDaniel, Lurlene 1944- *146*
    Earlier sketch in SATA *71*
McDaniels, Pellom III 1968- *121*
McDaniels, Preston 1952- *192*
McDearmon, Kay *20*
McDermott, Beverly Brodsky 1941- *11*
McDermott, Eleni *156*
McDermott, Gerald (Edward) 1941- *163*
    Earlier sketches in SATA *16, 74*
    See also CLR *9*
McDermott, Michael 1962- *76*
McDevitt, Jack 1935- *155*
    Earlier sketch in SATA *94*
McDevitt, John Charles
    See McDevitt, Jack
McDole, Carol
    See Farley, Carol (J.)
McDonald, Collin 1943- *79*
McDonald, Gerald D(oan) 1905-1970 .... *3*
McDonald, Jamie
    See Heide, Florence Parry
McDonald, Janet 1953-2007 .... *204*
    Earlier sketch in SATA *148*
McDonald, Jill (Masefield) 1927-1982 .... *13*
    Obituary *29*
McDonald, Joyce 1946- *164*
    Earlier sketch in SATA *101*
McDonald, Lucile Saunders 1898-1992 .... *10*
McDonald, Mary Ann 1956- *84*
McDonald, Megan 1958- *202*
    Autobiography Feature *151*
    Earlier sketches in SATA *67, 99, 148, 151*
    See also CLR *94*
McDonald, Meme 1954- *112*
McDonald, Mercedes 1956- *169*
    Earlier sketch in SATA *97*
McDonald, Rae A. 1952- *201*
McDonell, Chris 1960- *138*
McDonnell, Christine 1949- *115*
    Earlier sketch in SATA *34*

McDonnell, Flora (Mary) 1963- *146*
    Earlier sketch in SATA *90*
McDonnell, Kathleen 1947- *186*
McDonnell, Lois Eddy 1914-2001 .... *10*
McDonnell, Patrick 1956- *179*
McDonough, Yona Zeldis 1957- *73*
McElligott, Matt 1968- *196*
    Earlier sketch in SATA *135*
McElligott, Matthew
    See McElligott, Matt
McElmeel, Sharron L. 1942- *128*
McElmurry, Jill 1968- *198*
    Earlier sketch in SATA *159*
McElrath, William N. 1932- *65*
McElrath-Eslick, Lori 1960- *204*
    Earlier sketch in SATA *96*
McEntee, Dorothy (Layng) 1902- *37*
McEwen, Katherine *183*
McEwen, Robert (Lindley) 1926-1980
    Obituary *23*
McFadden, Kevin Christopher
    See Pike, Christopher
McFall, Christie 1918- *12*
McFall, Gardner 1952- *183*
McFarlan, Donald M(aitland) 1915- *59*
McFarland, Henry "Hammer"
    See McFarland, Henry O.
McFarland, Henry O. 1934- *143*
McFarland, Kenton D(ean) 1920- *11*
McFarland, Martha
    See Smith-Ankrom, M. E.
McFarlane, Leslie 1902-1977 .... *100*
    Earlier sketches in SATA *31, 1, 65, 67*
    See also CLR *118*
McFarlane, Leslie Charles
    See McFarlane, Leslie
McFarlane, Peter (William) 1940- *95*
McFarlane, Sheryl P. 1954- *86*
McFarlane, Todd 1961- *117*
McGaw, Jessie Brewer 1913-1997 .... *10*
McGee, Barbara 1943- *6*
McGee, Marni *163*
McGhee, Alison 1960- *196*
McGiffin, (Lewis) Lee (Shaffer) 1908-1978 ... *1*
McGill, Alice *159*
McGill, Ormond 1913- *92*
McGinley, Jerry 1948- *116*
McGinley, Phyllis 1905-1978 .... *44*
    Obituary *24*
    Earlier sketch in SATA *2*
McGinnis, Lila S(prague) 1924- *44*
McGinty, Alice B. 1963- *202*
    Earlier sketch in SATA *134*
McGivern, Justin 1985- *129*
McGivern, Maureen Daly
    See Daly, Maureen
McGivern, Maureen Patricia Daly
    See Daly, Maureen
McGough, Elizabeth (Hemmes) 1934- *33*
McGovern, Ann 1930- *132*
    Earlier sketches in SATA *8, 69, 70*
    See also CLR *50*
    See also SAAS *17*
McGowen, Thomas E. 1927- *109*
    Earlier sketch in SATA *2*
McGowen, Tom
    See McGowen, Thomas E.
McGrady, Mike 1933- *6*
McGrath, Barbara Barbieri 1953- *169*
    Earlier sketch in SATA *108*
McGrath, Robin 1949- *121*
McGrath, Thomas (Matthew) 1916-1990 ..... *41*
    Obituary *66*
McGraw, Eloise Jarvis 1915-2000 .... *67*
    Obituary *123*
    Earlier sketch in SATA *1*
    See also SAAS *6*
McGraw, William Corbin 1916-1999 .... *3*
McGreal, Elizabeth
    See Yates, Elizabeth
McGregor, Barbara 1959- *82*

McGregor, Craig 1933- *8*
McGregor, Iona 1929- *25*
McGrory, Anik *193*
McGuffey, Alexander Hamilton 1816-1896 . *60*
McGuigan, Mary Ann 1949- *106*
McGuire, Edna 1899- *13*
McGuire, Leslie (Sarah) 1945- *94*
    Brief entry *45*
    Earlier sketch in SATA *52*
McGuire, Robert *187*
McGuirk, Leslie (A.) 1960- *152*
McGurk, Slater
    See Roth, Arthur J(oseph)
McHargue, Georgess 1941- *77*
    Earlier sketch in SATA *4*
    See also CLR *2*
    See also SAAS *5*
McHenry, E.B. 1963(?)- *193*
McHugh, (Berit) Elisabet 1941- *55*
    Brief entry *44*
McIlvaine, Jane
    See McClary, Jane Stevenson
McIlwraith, Maureen Mollie Hunter
    See Hunter, Mollie
McInerney, Judith W(hitelock) 1945- *49*
    Brief entry *46*
McInerny, Ralph 1929- *93*
McInerny, Ralph Matthew
    See McInerny, Ralph
McKaughan, Larry (Scott) 1941- *75*
McKay, Donald 1895- *45*
McKay, Hilary 1959- *208*
    Earlier sketches in SATA *92, 145*
    See also SAAS *23*
McKay, Hilary Jane
    See McKay, Hilary
McKay, Lawrence, Jr. 1948- *114*
McKay, Robert W. 1921- *15*
McKay, Sharon E. 1954- *165*
McKay, Simon
    See Nicole, Christopher (Robin)
McKean, Dave 1963- *197*
McKean, David Jeff
    See McKean, Dave
McKeating, Eileen 1957- *81*
McKee, David (John) 1935- *158*
    Earlier sketches in SATA *70, 107*
    See also CLR *38*
McKee, Tim 1970- *111*
McKeever, Marcia
    See Laird, Jean E(louise)
McKelvey, Carole A. 1942- *78*
McKelvy, Charles 1950- *124*
McKendrick, Melveena (Christine) 1941- *55*
McKendry, Joe 1972- *170*
McKenna, Colleen O'Shaughnessy 1948- .. *136*
    Earlier sketch in SATA *76*
McKenzie, Dorothy Clayton 1910-1981
    Obituary *28*
McKenzie, Ellen Kindt 1928- *80*
McKernan, Victoria 1957- *171*
McKie, Robin *112*
McKillip, Patricia A. 1948- *174*
    Earlier sketches in SATA *30, 80, 126*
McKillip, Patricia Anne
    See McKillip, Patricia A.
McKim, Audrey Margaret 1909-1999 .... *47*
McKimmie, Chris *194*
McKinley, Jennifer Carolyn Robin
    See McKinley, Robin
McKinley, Robin 1952- *195*
    Brief entry *32*
    Earlier sketches in SATA *50, 89, 130*
    See also CLR *127*
McKinney, Barbara Shaw 1951- *116*
McKinney, Nadine 1938- *91*
McKinty, Adrian *186*
McKissack, Fredrick L. 1939- *162*
    Brief entry *53*
    Earlier sketches in SATA *73, 117*
    See also CLR *55*

McKissack, Fredrick Lemuel
    See McKissack, Fredrick L.
McKissack, Patricia C. 1944- *195*
    Earlier sketches in SATA *51, 73, 117, 162*
    See also CLR *129*
McKissack, Patricia L'Ann Carwell
    See McKissack, Patricia C.
McKissack and McKissack
    See McKissack, Fredrick L.
    and McKissack, Patricia C.
McKown, Robin (?)-1976 .... *6*
McKy, Katie 1956- *184*
McLaren, Clemence 1938- *158*
    Earlier sketch in SATA *105*
McLaughlin, Frank 1934- *73*
McLaughlin, Lauren *209*
McLaurin, Anne 1953- *27*
McLean, Andrew 1946- *172*
    Earlier sketch in SATA *113*
McLean, J. Sloan
    See Gillette, Virginia M(ary)
    and Wunsch, Josephine (McLean)
McLean, Jacqueline
    See Kolosov, Jacqueline
McLean, Janet 1946- *113*
McLean, Kathryn (Anderson) 1909-1966 .... *9*
McLean, Virginia Overton 1946- *90*
McLean-Carr, Carol 1948- *122*
McLeish, Kenneth 1940-1997 .... *35*
McLenighan, Valjean 1947- *46*
    Brief entry *40*
McLennan, Connie *171*
McLennan, Will
    See Wisler, G(ary) Clifton
McLeod, Bob 1951- *173*
McLeod, Chum 1955- *95*
McLeod, Emilie Warren 1926-1982 .... *23*
    Obituary *31*
McLeod, Kirsty
    See Hudson, (Margaret) Kirsty
McLeod, Margaret Vail
    See Holloway, Teresa (Bragunier)
McLerran, Alice 1933- *137*
    Earlier sketch in SATA *68*
McLimans, David 1949- *182*
McLoughlin, John C. 1949- *47*
McMahon, Bob 1956- *208*
McManus, Patrick F. 1933- *46*
McManus, Patrick Francis
    See McManus, Patrick F.
McMeekin, Clark
    See McMeekin, Isabel McLennan
McMeekin, Isabel McLennan 1895-1973 .... *3*
McMenemy, Sarah 1965- *156*
McMillan, Bruce 1947- *192*
    Earlier sketches in SATA *22, 70, 129*
    See also CLR *47*
McMillan, Naomi
    See Grimes, Nikki
McMorey, James L.
    See Moyer, Terry J.
McMorrow, Annalisa 1969- *104*
McMullan, Jim 1934- *150*
    Earlier sketch in SATA *87*
McMullan, K. H.
    See McMullan, Kate
McMullan, Kate 1947- *189*
    Brief entry *48*
    Earlier sketches in SATA *52, 87, 132*
McMullan, Kate Hall
    See McMullan, Kate
McMullen, Margaret 1960- *203*
McMurtrey, Martin A(loysius) 1921- *21*
McNabb, Linda 1963- *147*
McNair, Kate *3*
McNair, Sylvia 1924-2002 .... *74*
McNamara, Margaret C(raig) 1915-1981
    Obituary *24*
McNaught, Harry *32*

McNaughton, Colin 1951- *134*
    Earlier sketches in SATA *39, 92*
    See also CLR *54*
McNaughton, Janet 1953- *162*
    Earlier sketch in SATA *110*
McNeal, Laura *194*
McNeal, Tom *194*
McNeely, Jeannette 1918- *25*
McNeer, May (Yonge) 1902-1994 .... *81*
    Earlier sketch in SATA *1*
McNeese, Tim 1953- *139*
McNeill, Janet
    See Alexander, Janet
McNicholas, Shelagh *191*
McNickle, D'Arcy 1904-1977
    Obituary *22*
McNickle, William D'Arcy
    See McNickle, D'Arcy
McNicoll, Sylvia (Marilyn) 1954- *113*
    See also CLR *99*
McNulty, Faith 1918-2005 .... *168*
    Earlier sketches in SATA *12, 84, 139*
McPhail, David 1940- *183*
    Brief entry *32*
    Earlier sketches in SATA *47, 81, 140*
McPhail, David M.
    See McPhail, David
McPhail, David Michael
    See McPhail, David
McPhee, Norma H. 1928- *95*
McPhee, Richard B(yron) 1934- *41*
McPherson, James M. 1936- *141*
    Earlier sketch in SATA *16*
McPherson, James Munro
    See McPherson, James M.
McQueen, Lucinda 1950- *58*
    Brief entry *48*
McQueen, Mildred Hark 1908-1978 .... *12*
McQuillan, Mary *200*
McRae, Russell (William) 1934- *63*
McShean, Gordon 1936- *41*
Mc Swigan, Marie 1907-1962 .... *24*
McTavish, Sandy
    See Eyerly, Jeannette
McVeity, Jen *148*
McVey, Vicki 1946- *80*
McVicker, Charles (Taggart) 1930- *39*
McVicker, Chuck
    See McVicker, Charles (Taggart)
McWhirter, A(lan) Ross 1925-1975 .... *37*
    Obituary *31*
McWhirter, Norris (Dewar) 1925-2004 .... *37*
McWilliams, Karen 1943- *65*
Mdurvwa, Hajara E. 1962- *92*
Meacham, Margaret 1952- *203*
    Earlier sketch in SATA *95*
Meachum, Virginia 1918- *133*
    Earlier sketch in SATA *87*
Mead, Alice 1952- *146*
    Earlier sketch in SATA *94*
Mead, Margaret 1901-1978
    Obituary *20*
Mead, Russell (M., Jr.) 1935- *10*
Mead, Stella (?)-1981
    Obituary *27*
Meade, Ellen
    See Roddick, Ellen
Meade, Holly *207*
Meade, Marion 1934- *127*
    Earlier sketch in SATA *23*
Meader, Stephen W(arren) 1892-1977 .... *1*
Meadmore, Susan
    See Sallis, Susan (Diana)
Meadow, Charles T(roub) 1929- *23*
Meadowcroft, Enid LaMonte
    See Wright, Enid Meadowcroft (LaMonte)
Meadows, Graham (W.) 1934- *161*
Meadows, Michelle *202*
Meaker, M. J.
    See Meaker, Marijane

Meaker, Marijane 1927- *160*
    Autobiography Feature *111*
    Earlier sketches in SATA *20, 61, 99*
    See also CLR *29*
    See also SAAS *1*
Meaker, Marijane Agnes
    See Meaker, Marijane
Means, Florence Crannell 1891-1980 .... *1*
    Obituary *25*
    See also CLR *56*
Mearian, Judy Frank 1936- *49*
Mecca, Judy Truesdell 1955- *127*
Mechling, Lauren 1978(?)- *194*
Mechling, Lauren 1978(?)- *194*
Mechner, Jordan 1964- *205*
Medary, Marjorie 1890-1980 .... *14*
Meddaugh, Susan 1944- *176*
    Earlier sketches in SATA *29, 84, 125*
Medearis, Angela Shelf 1956- *123*
    Earlier sketch in SATA *72*
Medearis, Mary 1915- *5*
Medina, Jane 1953- *167*
    Earlier sketch in SATA *122*
Medina, Nico 1982- *193*
Medlicott, Mary 1946- *88*
Mee, Charles L., Jr. 1938- *72*
    Earlier sketch in SATA *8*
Meehl, Brian *204*
Meek, Jacklyn O'Hanlon 1933- *51*
    Brief entry *34*
Meek, S(terner St.) P(aul) 1894-1972
    Obituary *28*
Meeker, Clare Hodgson 1952- *96*
Meeker, Oden 1919(?)-1976 .... *14*
Meeker, Richard
    See Brown, Fornan
Meeks, Esther MacBain *1*
Meggs, Libby Phillips 1943- *130*
Mehdevi, Alexander (Sinclair) 1947- *7*
Mehdevi, Anne (Marie) Sinclair 1947- *8*
Meidell, Sherry 1951- *73*
Meier, Minta 1906- *55*
Meighan, Donald Charles 1929- *30*
Meigs, Cornelia Lynde 1884-1973 .... *6*
    See also CLR *55*
Meilach, Dona Z(weigoron) 1926- *34*
Meilman, Philip W(arren) 1951- *79*
Meinstereifel, Ronald L. 1960- *134*
Meisel, Paul *184*
Meister, Cari *204*
Melanson, Luc *198*
Melcher, Daniel 1912-1985
    Obituary *43*
Melcher, Frederic Gershom 1879-1963
    Obituary *22*
Melcher, Marguerite Fellows 1879-1969 ...... *10*
Meldrum, Christina *206*
Melendez, Francisco 1964- *72*
Melhuish, Eva *199*
Melin, Grace Hathaway 1892-1973 .... *10*
Mellersh, H(arold) E(dward) L(eslie)
    1897- *10*
Melling, David *186*
Melmoth, Sebastian
    See Wilde, Oscar
Melnikoff, Pamela (Rita) *97*
Meltzer, Amy 1968- *202*
Meltzer, Milton 1915-2009 .... *201*
    Autobiography Feature *124*
    Earlier sketches in SATA *1, 50, 80, 128*
    See also CLR *13*
    See also SAAS *1*
Melville, Anne
    See Potter, Margaret
Melville, Herman 1819-1891 .... *59*
Melwood, Mary
    See Lewis, E. M.
Melzack, Ronald 1929- *5*
Memling, Carl 1918-1969 .... *6*
Menchin, Scott *188*

Mendel, Jo
  See Bond, Gladys Baker
  and Gilbertson, Mildred Geiger
Mendelson, Steven T. 1958-1995 86
Mendelson-Stevens, Serita Deborah
  See Stevens, Serita
Mendes, Valerie 1939- 157
Mendez, Raymond A. 1947- 66
Mendonca, Susan
  See Smith, Susan Vernon
Mendoza, George 1934- 41
  Brief entry 39
  See also SAAS 7
Menendez, Shirley (C.) 1937- 146
Meng, Cece 194
Meng, Heinz (Karl) 1924- 13
Mennen, Ingrid 1954- 85
Menotti, Gian Carlo 1911-2007 29
  Obituary 180
Menuhin, Sir Yehudi 1916-1999 40
  Obituary 113
Menville, Douglas 1935- 64
Menzel, Barbara Jean 1946- 63
Menzel, Peter 1948- 207
Mercati, Cynthia 164
Mercati, Cynthia J.
  See Mercati, Cynthia
Mercer, Charles (Edward) 1917-1988 16
  Obituary 61
Mercer, Jessie 21
Mercer, Sienna 192
Meredith, Arnold
  See Hopkins, (Hector) Kenneth
Meredith, David William
  See Miers, Earl Schenck
Meringoff, Laurene Krasny
  See Brown, Laurene Krasny
Meriwether, Louise 1923- 52
  Brief entry 31
Merlin, Arthur
  See Blish, James
Merlin, Christina
  See Heaven, Constance (Christina)
Merriam, Eve 1916-1992 73
  Earlier sketches in SATA 3, 40
  See also CLR 14
Merrill, Jane 1946- 42
Merrill, Jane Merrill
  See Merrill, Jane
Merrill, Jean (Fairbanks) 1923- 82
  Earlier sketch in SATA 1
  See also CLR 52
Merrill, Phil
  See Merrill, Jane
Merriman, Alex
  See Silverberg, Robert
Merriman, Rachel 1971- 149
  Earlier sketch in SATA 98
Merrit, Elizabeth
  See Goudge, Eileen
Merski, Patricia K.
  See Merski, P.K.
Merski, P.K. 172
Mertz, Barbara
  See Peters, Elizabeth
Mertz, Barbara Gross
  See Peters, Elizabeth
Merveille, David 200
Merz, Jennifer J. 196
Meschel, Susan V. 1936- 83
Messenger, Charles (Rynd Milles) 1942- 59
Messick, Dale 1906-2005 64
  Brief entry 48
Messier, Claire 1956- 103
Messieres, Nicole de
  See de Messieres, Nicole
Messinger, Carla 198
Messmer, Otto 1892(?)-1983 37
Mesta, Gabriel
  See Moesta, Rebecca
Metcalf, Doris H(unter) 91

Metcalf, Suzanne
  See Baum, L. Frank
Metos, Thomas H(arry) 1932- 37
Metter, Bert(ram Milton) 1927- 56
Metzenthen, David 1958- 167
  Earlier sketch in SATA 106
Meunier, Brian 1954- 195
Meyer, Barbara 1939- 77
Meyer, Carolyn 1935- 142
  Autobiography Feature 142
  Earlier sketches in SATA 9, 70, 118
  See also SAAS 9
Meyer, Carolyn Mae
  See Meyer, Carolyn
Meyer, Edith Patterson 1895-1993 5
Meyer, F(ranklyn) E(dward) 1932- 9
Meyer, Jean Shepherd 11
Meyer, Jerome Sydney 1895-1975 3
  Obituary 25
Meyer, June
  See Jordan, June
Meyer, Kerstin 1966- 190
Meyer, L. A.
  See Meyer, Louis A(lbert), Jr.
Meyer, Louis A(lbert), Jr. 1942- 144
  Earlier sketch in SATA 12
Meyer, Renate 1930- 6
Meyer, Stephenie 1973- 193
  See also CLR 142
Meyer, Susan E. 1940- 64
Meyerhoff, Jenny 1972- 208
Meyers, Susan 1942- 164
  Earlier sketches in SATA 19, 108
Meynell, Laurence Walter 1899-1989
  Obituary 61
Meynier, Yvonne (Pollet) 1908- 14
Mezey, Robert 1935- 33
Micale, Albert 1913- 22
Michael, James
  See Scagnetti, Jack
Michael, Livi 1960- 172
Michael, Manfred
  See Winterfeld, Henry
Michael, Olivia
  See Michael, Livi
Michaels, Barbara
  See Peters, Elizabeth
Michaels, Jamie 195
Michaels, Joanne Louise
  See Teitelbaum, Michael
Michaels, Kristin
  See Williams, Jeanne
Michaels, Molly
  See Untermeyer, Louis
Michaels, Neal
  See Teitelbaum, Michael
Michaels, Rune 194
Michaels, Ski
  See Pellowski, Michael (Joseph)
Michaels, Steve 1955- 71
Michaels, William M. 1917- 77
Michel, Anna 1943- 49
  Brief entry 40
Michel, Francois 1948- 82
Michelin, Linda 183
Michelson, Richard 198
  Earlier sketch in SATA 173
Micich, Paul 74
Micklish, Rita 1931- 12
Micklos, John, Jr. 1956- 173
  Earlier sketch in SATA 129
Micklos J., John, Jr. 1956-
  See Micklos, John, Jr.
Micucci, Charles (Patrick, Jr.) 1959- 144
  Earlier sketch in SATA 82
Middleton, Haydn 1955- 152
  Earlier sketch in SATA 85
Miers, Earl Schenck 1910-1972 1
  Obituary 26
Migdale, Lawrence 1951- 89
Miglio, Paige 1966- 201

Mikaelsen, Ben 1952- 173
  Earlier sketches in SATA 73, 107
Mikaelsen, Benjamin John
  See Mikaelsen, Ben
Miklowitz, Gloria D. 1927- 129
  Earlier sketches in SATA 4, 68
  See also SAAS 17
Mikolaycak, Charles 1937-1993 78
  Obituary 75
  Earlier sketch in SATA 9
  See also SAAS 4
Mild, Warren (Paul) 1922- 41
Milelli, Pascal 1965- 135
Miles, Betty 1928- 78
  Earlier sketch in SATA 8
  See also SAAS 9
Miles, Miska
  See Martin, Patricia Miles
Miles, (Mary) Patricia 1930- 29
Miles, Patricia A.
  See Martin, Patricia Miles
Miles, Victoria 1966- 188
Milgrim, David 187
  Earlier sketch in SATA 158
Milgrom, Harry 1912-1978 25
Milhous, Katherine 1894-1977 15
Milich, Zoran 174
Milios, Rita 1949- 79
Militant
  See Sandburg, Carl
Millais, Raoul 1901- 77
Millar, Barbara F. 1924- 12
Millar, Margaret (Ellis Sturm) 1915-1994 61
  Obituary 79
Millard, Glenda 203
Millard, Kerry 204
Millbank, Captain H. R.
  See Ellis, Edward S.
Millen, C(ynthia) M. 1955- 114
Miller, Albert G(riffith) 1905-1982 12
  Obituary 31
Miller, Alice Ann 1958- 150
Miller, Alice P(atricia McCarthy) 22
Miller, Debbie 1951- 160
  Earlier sketch in SATA 103
Miller, Debbie S.
  See Miller, Debbie
Miller, Deborah Uchill 1944- 61
Miller, Don 1923- 15
Miller, Doris R.
  See Mosesson, Gloria R(ubin)
Miller, Eddie
  See Miller, Edward
Miller, Edna Anita 1920- 29
Miller, Edward 1905-1974 8
Miller, Edward 1964- 183
Miller, Elizabeth 1933- 41
Miller, Ellanita 1957- 87
Miller, Eugene 1925- 33
Miller, Frances A. 1937- 52
  Brief entry 46
Miller, Helen M(arkley) -1984 5
Miller, Helen Topping 1884-1960
  Obituary 29
Miller, Jane (Judith) 1925-1989 15
Miller, Jewel 1956- 73
Miller, John
  See Samachson, Joseph
Miller, Judi 117
Miller, Kate 1948- 193
Miller, Kirsten 1973- 185
Miller, Louise (Rolfe) 1940- 76
Miller, M. L. 85
Miller, Madge 1918- 63
Miller, Margaret J.
  See Dale, Margaret J(essy) Miller
Miller, Marilyn (Jean) 1925- 33
Miller, Marvin 65
Miller, Mary
  See Northcott, (William) Cecil
Miller, Mary Beth 1942- 9

Miller, Mary Beth 1964- *185*
Miller, Maryann 1943- *73*
Miller, Natalie 1917-1976 .... *35*
Miller, Robert H. 1944- *91*
Miller, Ron 1947- *185*
Miller, Ruth White
  See White, Ruth C.
Miller, Sandra
  See Miller, Sandy
Miller, Sandra Peden
  See Miller, Sandy
Miller, Sandy 1948- *41*
  Brief entry *35*
Miller, Sarah 1969- *175*
Miller, Virginia
  See Austin, Virginia
Miller, William R. 1959- *116*
Milligan, Bryce 1953- *170*
Milligan, Spike
  See Milligan, Terence Alan
Milligan, Terence Alan 1918-2002 .... *29*
  Obituary *134*
  See also CLR *92*
Millington, Ada
  See Deyneka, Anita
Millman, Isaac 1933- *140*
Mills, Adam
  See Stanley, George Edward
Mills, Claudia 1954- *191*
  Brief entry *41*
  Earlier sketches in SATA *44, 89, 145*
Mills, Elaine (Rosemary) 1941- *72*
Mills, G. Riley *196*
Mills, Joyce C. 1944- *102*
Mills, Judith Christine 1956- *130*
Mills, Yaroslava Surmach 1925- *35*
Millspaugh, Ben P. 1936- *77*
Millstead, Thomas E. *30*
Millward, Gwen *202*
Milne, A. A. 1882-1956 .... *100*
  See also YABC *1*
  See also CLR *108*
Milne, Alan Alexander
  See Milne, A. A.
Milne, Lorus J. *5*
  See also CLR *22*
  See also SAAS *18*
Milne, Margery *5*
  See also CLR *22*
  See also SAAS *18*
Milne, Terry
  See Milne, Theresa Ann
Milne, Theresa Ann 1964- *84*
Milnes, Irma McDonough 1924- *101*
Milonas, Rolf
  See Myller, Rolf
Milone, Karen
  See Dugan, Karen
Milone-Dugan, Karen
  See Dugan, Karen
Milord, Susan 1954- *200*
  Earlier sketches in SATA *74, 147*
Milotte, Alfred G(eorge) 1904-1989 .... *11*
  Obituary *62*
Milstein, Linda 1954- *80*
Milton, Ann *134*
Milton, Hilary (Herbert) 1920- *23*
Milton, John R(onald) 1924- *24*
Milton, Joyce 1946- *101*
  Brief entry *41*
  Earlier sketch in SATA *52*
Milverton, Charles A.
  See Penzler, Otto
Milway, Katie Smith 1960- *203*
Minahan, John A. 1956- *92*
Minar, Barbra (Goodyear) 1940- *79*
Minard, Rosemary 1939- *63*
Minarik, Else Holmelund 1920- *127*
  Earlier sketch in SATA *15*
  See also CLR *33*

Miner, Jane Claypool 1933- *103*
  Brief entry *37*
  Earlier sketch in SATA *38*
Miner, Lewis S. 1909-1971 .... *11*
Mines, Jeanette 1948- *61*
Mines, Jeanette Marie
  See Mines, Jeanette
Minier, Nelson
  See Stoutenburg, Adrien (Pearl)
Minnitt, Ronda Jacqueline
  See Armitage, David
Minor, Wendell 1944- *199*
  Earlier sketches in SATA *78, 109, 164*
Minter, Daniel 1961- *176*
Mintonye, Grace *4*
Miranda, Anne 1954- *109*
  Earlier sketch in SATA *71*
Miranda, Inaki 1983(?)- *207*
Mirocha, Paul *192*
Mirsky, Jeannette 1903-1987 .... *8*
  Obituary *51*
Mirsky, Reba Paeff 1902-1966 .... *1*
Misako Rocks! *192*
Mishica, Clare 1960- *91*
Miskovits, Christine 1939- *10*
Miss Frances
  See Horwich, Frances R(appaport)
Miss Read
  See Saint, Dora Jessie
Mister Rogers
  See Rogers, Fred McFeely
Mitchard, Jacquelyn 1956- *168*
  Earlier sketch in SATA *98*
Mitchell, Adrian 1932-2008 .... *166*
  Obituary *200*
  Earlier sketch in SATA *104*
Mitchell, Allison
  See Griffin, W.E.B.
Mitchell, Betty Jo
  See Mitchell, B.J.
Mitchell, B.J. 1931- *120*
Mitchell, Clyde
  See Ellison, Harlan
  and Silverberg, Robert
Mitchell, Cynthia 1922- *29*
Mitchell, (Sibyl) Elyne (Keith) 1913- *10*
Mitchell, Gladys (Maude Winifred)
  1901-1983 .... *46*
  Obituary *35*
Mitchell, Jay
  See Roberson, Jennifer
Mitchell, Joyce Slayton 1933- *142*
  Brief entry *43*
  Earlier sketch in SATA *46*
Mitchell, K. L.
  See Lamb, Elizabeth Searle
Mitchell, Kathy 1948- *59*
Mitchell, Lori 1961- *128*
Mitchell, Margaree King 1953- *84*
Mitchell, Marianne 1947- *145*
Mitchell, Rhonda *89*
Mitchell, Stephen 1943- *199*
Mitchell, Todd 1974- *191*
Mitchell, Yvonne 1925-1979
  Obituary *24*
Mitchelson, Mitch
  See Mitchelson, Peter Richard
Mitchelson, Peter Richard 1950- *104*
Mitchison, Naomi (Margaret Haldane)
  1897-1999 .... *24*
  Obituary *112*
Mitchnik, Helen 1901-1982 .... *41*
  Brief entry *35*
Mitchum, Hank
  See Knott, William C(ecil, Jr.)
  and Murray, Stuart A. P.
  and Newton, D(wight) B(ennett)
  and Sherman, Jory (Tecumseh)
Mitgutsch, Ali 1935- *76*
Mitsuhashi, Yoko *45*
  Brief entry *33*

Mitton, Jacqueline 1948- *162*
  Earlier sketches in SATA *66, 115*
Mitton, Simon 1946- *66*
Mitton, Tony 1951- *203*
  Earlier sketches in SATA *104, 149*
Miura, Taro 1968- *181*
Mizner, Elizabeth Howard 1907- *27*
Mizumura, Kazue *18*
Mlynowski, Sarah 1977(?)- *180*
Mobin-Uddin, Asma *172*
Mobley, Joe A. 1945- *91*
Moche, Dinah (Rachel) L(evine) 1936- *44*
  Brief entry *40*
Mochi, Ugo (A.) 1889-1977 .... *38*
Mochizuki, Ken 1954- *146*
  Earlier sketch in SATA *81*
  See also SAAS *22*
Modarressi, Mitra 1967- *200*
  Earlier sketch in SATA *126*
Modell, Frank B. 1917- *39*
  Brief entry *36*
Modesitt, Jeanne 1953- *143*
  Earlier sketch in SATA *92*
Modesitt, L.E., Jr. 1943- *164*
  Earlier sketch in SATA *91*
Modesitt, Leland Exton, Jr.
  See Modesitt, L.E., Jr.
Modrell, Dolores 1933- *72*
Moe, Barbara 1937- *20*
Moe, Jorgen (Ingebretsen) 1813-1882
  See CLR *104*
Moed-Kass, Pnina *169*
Moerbeek, Kees 1955- *98*
Moeri, Louise 1924- *93*
  Earlier sketch in SATA *24*
  See also SAAS *10*
Moesta, Rebecca 1956- *182*
Moffett, Jami 1952- *84*
Moffett, Mark W. 1957(?)- *203*
Moffett, Martha (Leatherwood) 1934- *8*
Mogensen, Suzanne A(ncher) 1946- *129*
Mohammed, Khadra *197*
Mohn, Peter B(urnet) 1934- *28*
Mohn, Viola Kohl 1914- *8*
Mohr, Nicholasa 1938- *97*
  Autobiography Feature *113*
  Earlier sketch in SATA *8*
  See also CLR *22*
  See also SAAS *8*
Mok, Esther 1953- *93*
Molan, Christine 1943- *84*
Molarsky, Osmond 1909- *16*
Moldon, Peter L(eonard) 1937- *49*
Mole, John 1941- *103*
  Earlier sketch in SATA *36*
  See also CLR *61*
Molesworth, Mary Louisa 1839-1921 .... *98*
Molin, Charles
  See Mayne, William (James Carter)
Molina, Silvia 1946- *97*
Molk, Laurel 1957- *162*
  Earlier sketch in SATA *92*
Mollel, Tololwa M. 1952- *88*
Molloy, Anne Baker 1907-1999 .... *32*
Molloy, Michael (John) 1940- *162*
Molloy, Paul (George) 1924- *5*
Moloney, James 1954- *202*
  Autobiography Feature *144*
  Earlier sketches in SATA *94, 144*
Momaday, N. Scott 1934- *48*
  Brief entry *30*
Momaday, Navarre Scott
  See Momaday, N. Scott
Monaco, Octavia 1963- *169*
Monagle, Bernie 1957- *121*
Moncure, Jane Belk 1926- *23*
Monjo, F(erdinand) N(icholas III)
  1924-1978 .... *16*
  See also CLR *2*
Monk, Isabell 1952- *136*
Monks, Lydia *189*

Monroe, Lyle
  See Heinlein, Robert A.
Monroe, Marion
  See Cox, Marion Monroe
Monroy, Manuel 1970- 196
Monsell, Helen Albee 1895-1971 24
Monson-Burton, Marianne 1975- 139
Montana, Bob 1920-1975
  Obituary 21
Montanari, Eva 1977- 209
Montecalvo, Janet 177
Montenegro, Laura Nyman 1953- 95
Montero, Gloria 1933- 109
Montes, Marisa 1951- 144
Montgomerie, Norah (Mary) 1913- 26
Montgomery, Constance
  See Cappel, Constance
Montgomery, Elizabeth
  See Julesberg, Elizabeth Rider Montgomery
Montgomery, Elizabeth Rider
  See Julesberg, Elizabeth Rider Montgomery
Montgomery, Hugh (Edward) 1962- 146
Montgomery, L. M. 1874-1942 100
  See also YABC *1*
  See also CLR *145*
Montgomery, Lucy Maud
  See Montgomery, L. M.
Montgomery, Michael G. 1952- 208
Montgomery, Raymond A. (Jr.) 1936- 39
Montgomery, Rutherford George 1894-1985 . 3
Montgomery, Sy 1958- 184
  Autobiography Feature 132
  Earlier sketches in SATA *114, 132*
Montgomery, Vivian 36
Monthei, Betty 179
Montijo, Rhode 179
Montileaux, Donald F. 1948- 183
Montpetit, Charles 1958- 101
Montresor, Beni 1926-2001 38
  Earlier sketch in SATA *3*
  See also SAAS *4*
Montserrat, Pep 181
Monty Python
  See Chapman, Graham
  and Cleese, John (Marwood)
  and Gilliam, Terry
  and Idle, Eric
  and Jones, Terence Graham Parry
  and Palin, Michael
Moodie, Craig 1956- 172
Moodie, Fiona 1952- 133
Moody, Minerva
  See Alcott, Louisa May
Moody, Ralph Owen 1898-1982 1
Moon, Carl 1879(?)-1948 25
Moon, Grace (Purdie) 1877(?)-1947 25
Moon, Lily
  See Warnes, Tim
Moon, Nicola 1952- 147
  Earlier sketch in SATA *96*
Moon, Pat 1946- 113
Moon, Sheila 1910-1991 5
  Obituary 114
Moon, Sheila Elizabeth
  See Moon, Sheila
Mooney, Bel 1946- 95
Mooney, Bill 1936- 122
Mooney, Elizabeth C(omstock) 1918-1986
  Obituary 48
Mooney, William
  See Mooney, Bill
Moor, Emily
  See Deming, Richard
Moorcock, Michael 1939- 166
  Earlier sketch in SATA *93*
Moorcock, Michael John
  See Moorcock, Michael
Moore, Anne Carroll 1871-1961 13
Moore, Cheri
  See Ladd, Cheryl (Jean)
Moore, Clement Clarke 1779-1863 18

Moore, Cyd 1957- 186
  Earlier sketches in SATA *83, 133*
Moore, Don W. 1905(?)-1986
  Obituary 48
Moore, Elaine 1944- 86
Moore, Eva 1942- 103
  Earlier sketch in SATA *20*
Moore, Ishbel (Lindsay) 1954- 140
Moore, Jack (William) 1941- 46
  Brief entry 32
Moore, Janet Gaylord 1905-1992 18
Moore, Jim 1946- 42
Moore, John Travers 1908- 12
Moore, Lilian 1909-2004 137
  Obituary 155
  Earlier sketch in SATA *52*
  See also CLR *15*
Moore, Liz
  See Moore, M. Elizabeth
Moore, M. Elizabeth 1959- 156
Moore, Margaret R(umberger) 1903- 12
Moore, Margie 176
Moore, Marianne 1887-1972 20
Moore, Marianne Craig
  See Moore, Marianne
Moore, Patrick (Alfred Caldwell) 1923- 49
  Brief entry 39
  See also SAAS *8*
Moore, Patrick 1959- 184
Moore, Perry 193
Moore, Peter 1963- 175
Moore, Peter G.
  See Moore, Peter
Moore, Ray (S.) 1905(?)-1984
  Obituary 37
Moore, Regina
  See Dunne, Mary Collins
Moore, Rosalie (Gertrude) 1910-2001 9
Moore, Ruth (Ellen) 1908-1989 23
Moore, Ruth Nulton 1923- 38
Moore, S(arah) E. 23
Moore, Sarah Margaret
  See Hodges, Margaret
Moore, Tara 1950- 61
Moore, Yvette 1958- 154
  Earlier sketches in SATA *69, 70*
Moores, Dick
  See Moores, Richard (Arnold)
Moores, Richard (Arnold) 1909-1986
  Obituary 48
Mooser, Stephen 1941- 75
  Earlier sketch in SATA *28*
Mora, Francisco X(avier) 1952- 90
Mora, Pat 1942- 186
  Earlier sketches in SATA *92, 134*
  See also CLR *58*
Mora, Patricia
  See Mora, Pat
Morais, Flavio 207
Morales, Yuyi 180
  Earlier sketch in SATA *154*
Moran, Tom 1943- 60
Moranville, Sharelle Byars 196
  Earlier sketch in SATA *152*
Moray Williams, Ursula 1911-2006 3
  Obituary 177
  See also SAAS *9*
Mordvinoff, Nicolas 1911-1973 17
More, Caroline
  See Cone, Molly (Lamken)
  and Strachan, Margaret Pitcairn
Moreno, Rene King 190
Moreton, Andrew Esq.
  See Defoe, Daniel
Morey, Charles
  See Fletcher, Helen Jill
Morey, Walt(er Nelson) 1907-1992 51
  Obituary 70
  Earlier sketch in SATA *3*
  See also SAAS *9*
Morgan, Alfred P(owell) 1889-1972 33

Morgan, Alison (Mary) 1930- 85
  Earlier sketch in SATA *30*
Morgan, Anne 1954- 121
Morgan, Christopher 1956- 199
Morgan, Clay 1950- 198
Morgan, Douglas
  See Macdonald, James D.
Morgan, Ellen
  See Bumstead, Kathleen Mary
Morgan, Geoffrey 1916- 46
Morgan, Helen (Gertrude Louise)
  1921-1990 29
Morgan, Jane
  See Cooper, James Fenimore
  and Franklin, Jane (Morgan)
  and Moren, Sally M(oore)
Morgan, Lenore H. 1908-1976 8
Morgan, Mary 1957- 114
  Earlier sketch in SATA *81*
Morgan, McKayla
  See Basile, Gloria Vitanza
Morgan, Michaela
  See Basile, Gloria Vitanza
Morgan, Nicola 1961- 161
Morgan, Nina 1953- 110
Morgan, Pierr 1952- 122
  Earlier sketch in SATA *77*
Morgan, Robin (Evonne) 1941- 80
Morgan, Roxanne
  See Gentle, Mary
Morgan, Sarah (Nicola) 1959- 68
Morgan, Shirley
  See Kiepper, Shirley Morgan
Morgan, Stacy T(owle) 1959- 104
Morgan, Stevie
  See Davies, Nicola
Morgan, Tom 1942- 42
Morgan, Wendy
  See Staub, Wendy Corsi
Morgan-Vanroyen, Mary
  See Morgan, Mary
Morgenstern, Susie Hoch 1945- 133
Mori, Hana 1909-1990(?) 88
Mori, Kyoko 1957- 122
  Autobiography Feature 126
  See also CLR *64*
  See also SAAS *26*
Moriarty, Jaclyn 162
Moriarty, William J. 1930- 127
Morice, Dave 1946- 93
Morin, Isobel V. 1928- 110
Morine, Hoder
  See Conroy, John Wesley
Morley, Taia 199
Morley, Wilfred Owen
  See Lowndes, Robert A(ugustine) W(ard)
Morningstar, Mildred (Whaley) 1912-1997 .. 61
  Obituary 114
Morozumi, Atsuko 110
Morpurgo, Michael 1943- 184
  Earlier sketches in SATA *93, 143*
  See also CLR *51*
Morrah, Dave
  See Morrah, David Wardlaw, Jr.
Morrah, David Wardlaw, Jr. 1914-1991 10
Morreale-de la Garza, Phyllis
  See De la Garza, Phyllis
Morressy, John 1930-2006 23
Morrill, Leslie H(olt) 1934-2003 48
  Brief entry 33
  Obituary 148
  See also SAAS *22*
Morris, Chris(topher Crosby) 1946- 66
Morris, Deborah 1956- 91
Morris, Desmond 1928- 14
Morris, Desmond John
  See Morris, Desmond
Morris, Don 1954- 83
Morris, Gerald 1963- 207
  Earlier sketches in SATA *107, 150*

Morris, Gerald Paul
  See Morris, Gerald
Morris, Gilbert (Leslie) 1929- *104*
Morris, Jackie *202*
  Earlier sketch in SATA *151*
Morris, Janet (Ellen) 1946- *66*
Morris, Jay
  See Tatham, Julie Campbell
Morris, (Margaret) Jean 1924- *98*
Morris, Jeffrey B(randon) 1941- *92*
Morris, Jennifer E. 1969- *179*
Morris, Jill 1936- *165*
  Earlier sketch in SATA *119*
Morris, Juddi *85*
Morris, Judy K. 1936- *61*
Morris, Oradel Nolen *128*
Morris, Robert A(da) 1933- *7*
Morris, William 1913-1994 .... *29*
Morrison, Bill 1935- *66*
  Brief entry *37*
Morrison, Chloe Anthony Wofford
  See Morrison, Toni
Morrison, Dorothy Nafus *29*
Morrison, Frank 1971- *185*
Morrison, Gordon 1944- *183*
  Earlier sketches in SATA *87, 128*
Morrison, Joan 1922- *65*
Morrison, Lillian 1917- *108*
  Earlier sketch in SATA *3*
Morrison, Lucile Phillips 1896- *17*
Morrison, Martha A. 1948- *77*
Morrison, Meighan 1966- *90*
Morrison, P.R. *196*
Morrison, Richard
  See Lowndes, Robert A(ugustine) W(ard)
Morrison, Robert
  See Lowndes, Robert A(ugustine) W(ard)
Morrison, Roberta
  See Webb, Jean Francis (III)
Morrison, Susan Dudley
  See Gold, Susan Dudley
Morrison, Taylor 1971- *187*
  Earlier sketches in SATA *95, 159*
Morrison, Toni 1931- *144*
  Earlier sketch in SATA *57*
  See also CLR *99*
Morrison, Velma Ford 1909- *21*
Morrison, Wilbur Howard 1915- *64*
Morrison, William
  See Samachson, Joseph
Morriss, James E(dward) 1932- *8*
Morrissey, Dean *183*
Morrow, Barbara Olenyik 1952- *167*
Morrow, Betty
  See Bacon, Elizabeth
Morse, C. Scott
  See Morse, Scott
Morse, Carol
  See Yeakley, Marjory Hall
Morse, C.S.
  See Morse, Scott
Morse, Dorothy B(ayley) 1906-1979
  Obituary *24*
Morse, Flo 1921- *30*
Morse, Scott 1973- *200*
Morse, Tony 1953- *129*
Mort, Vivian
  See Cromie, Alice Hamilton
Mortensen, Denise Dowling *179*
Mortimer, Anne 1958- *206*
  Earlier sketch in SATA *116*
Mortimer, Mary H.
  See Coury, Louise Andree
Morton, Alexandra (Hubbard) 1957- *144*
Morton, Anthony
  See Arthur, Robert, (Jr.)
Morton, Jane 1931- *50*
Morton, Joseph C. 1932- *156*
Morton, Lee Jack, Jr. 1928- *32*
Morton, Miriam 1918(?)-1985 .... *9*
  Obituary *46*

Mosatche, Harriet
  See Mosatche, Harriet
Mosatche, Harriet 1949- *122*
Moscow, Alvin 1925- *3*
Mosel, Arlene (Tichy) 1921-1996 .... *7*
Moseley, James W(illett) 1931- *139*
Moseng, Elisabeth 1967- *90*
Moser, Barry 1940- *185*
  Earlier sketches in SATA *56, 79, 138*
  See also CLR *49*
  See also SAAS *15*
Moser, Don(ald Bruce) 1932- *31*
Moser, Laura *194*
Moser, Lisa *192*
Moses, Sheila P. 1961- *168*
Moses, Will 1956- *178*
  Earlier sketch in SATA *120*
Mosesson, Gloria R(ubin) *24*
Mosher, Richard 1949- *120*
Moskin, Marietta D(unston) 1928- *23*
Moskof, Martin Stephen 1930- *27*
Mosley, Francis 1957- *57*
Moss, Don(ald) 1920- *11*
Moss, Elaine (Dora) 1924- *57*
  Brief entry *31*
Moss, Jeff(rey) 1942-1998 .... *73*
  Obituary *106*
Moss, Marissa 1959- *163*
  Earlier sketches in SATA *71, 104*
  See also CLR *134*
Moss, Miriam 1955- *202*
  Earlier sketches in SATA *76, 140*
Moss, Thylias 1954- *108*
Moss, Thylias Rebecca Brasier
  See Moss, Thylias
Most, Bernard 1937- *134*
  Brief entry *40*
  Earlier sketches in SATA *48, 91*
Mosz, Gosia 1972- *194*
Mott, Evelyn Clarke 1962- *133*
  Earlier sketch in SATA *75*
Motz, Lloyd 1909-2004 .... *20*
Mould, Chris *205*
Mould, Edwin
  See Whitlock, Ralph
Mouly, Francoise *155*
Mountain, Robert
  See Montgomery, Raymond A. (Jr.)
Mountfield, David
  See Grant, Neil
Mourlevat, Jean-Claude 1952- *187*
Mourning, Tuesday *206*
Moussard, Jacqueline 1924- *24*
Mowat, Claire 1933- *123*
Mowat, Claire Angel Wheeler
  See Mowat, Claire
Mowat, Farley 1921- *55*
  Earlier sketch in SATA *3*
  See also CLR *20*
Mowat, Farley McGill
  See Mowat, Farley
Mowll, Joshua 1970(?)- *188*
Mowry, Jess 1960- *131*
  Autobiography Feature *131*
  Earlier sketch in SATA *109*
  See also CLR *65*
Moxley, Sheila 1966- *96*
Moyer, Terry J. 1937- *94*
Moyes, Patricia
  See Haszard, Patricia Moyes
Moyler, Alan (Frank Powell) 1926- *36*
Mozelle, Shirley *179*
Mozley, Charles 1915- *43*
  Brief entry *32*
Mphahlele, Es'kia 1919-2008 .... *119*
  Obituary *198*
Mphahlele, Ezekiel
  See Mphahlele, Es'kia
Mphahlele, Zeke
  See Mphahlele, Es'kia

Mr. McGillicuddy
  See Abisch, Roslyn Kroop
Mr. Sniff
  See Abisch, Roslyn Kroop
Mr. Tivil
  See Lorkowski, Thomas V(incent)
Mr. Wizard
  See Herbert, Don
Mrs. Fairstar
  See Horne, Richard Henry Hengist
Muchamore, Robert 1972- *175*
Muchmore, Jo Ann 1937- *103*
Mude, O.
  See Gorey, Edward (St. John)
Mudgeon, Apeman
  See Mitchell, Adrian
Mueller, Jorg 1942- *67*
  See also CLR *43*
Mueller, Miranda R. *201*
Mueller, Virginia 1924- *28*
Muggs
  See Watkins, Lois
Muir, Diana
  See Appelbaum, Diana Muir Karter
Muir, Frank (Herbert) 1920-1998 .... *30*
Muir, Helen 1937- *65*
Mukerji, Dhan Gopal 1890-1936 .... *40*
  See also CLR *10*
Mulcahy, Lucille Burnett *12*
Mulford, Philippa G. 1948- *112*
  Earlier sketch in SATA *43*
Mulford, Philippa Greene
  See Mulford, Philippa G.
Mulgan, Catherine 1931- *24*
Mulila, Vigad G.
  See Maillu, David G(ian)
Mull, Brandon 1974- *190*
Mullen, Michael 1937- *122*
Muller, Billex
  See Ellis, Edward S.
Muller, Jorg
  See Mueller, Jorg
Muller, (Lester) Robin 1953- *86*
Mullin, Caryl Cude 1969- *130*
Mullins, Edward S(wift) 1922- *10*
Mullins, Hilary 1962- *84*
Mulock, Dinah Maria
  See Craik, Dinah Maria (Mulock)
Mulvihill, William Patrick 1923- *8*
Mumford, Ruth
  See Dallas, Ruth
Mumy, Bill 1954- *112*
Mun
  See Leaf, (Wilbur) Munro
Munari, Bruno 1907-1998 .... *15*
  See also CLR *9*
Munce, Ruth Hill 1898- *12*
Mundy, Simon 1954- *64*
Mundy, Simon Andrew James Hainault
  See Mundy, Simon
Munger, Nancy *170*
Munowitz, Ken 1935-1977 .... *14*
Munoz, Claudio *208*
Munoz, William 1949- *92*
  Earlier sketch in SATA *42*
Munro, Alice 1931- *29*
Munro, Alice Anne
  See Munro, Alice
Munro, Eleanor 1928- *37*
Munro, Roxie 1945- *184*
  Earlier sketches in SATA *58, 136*
Munsch, Bob
  See Munsch, Robert (Norman)
Munsch, Robert (Norman) 1945- *120*
  Brief entry *48*
  Earlier sketches in SATA *50, 83*
  See also CLR *19*
Munsinger, Lynn 1951- *177*
  Earlier sketches in SATA *33, 94*
Munson, Derek 1970- *139*

Munson, R. W.
  See Karl, Jean E(dna)
Munson-Benson, Tunie 1946- 15
Munsterberg, Peggy 1921- 102
Muntean, Michaela 182
Munthe, Nelly 1947- 53
Munves, James (Albert) 1922- 30
Munzer, Martha E. 1899-1999 4
Murawski, Darlyne A. 193
Murch, Mel
  See Manes, Stephen
Murdoch, David H(amilton) 1937- 96
Murdoch, Patricia 1957- 192
Murdock, Catherine Gilbert 185
Murhall, J(acqueline) J(ane) 1964- 143
Murphy, Barbara Beasley 1933- 130
  Earlier sketch in SATA 5
Murphy, Claire Rudolf 1951- 137
  Earlier sketch in SATA 76
Murphy, E(mmett) Jefferson 1926- 4
Murphy, Jill (Frances) 1949- 142
  Earlier sketches in SATA 37, 70
  See also CLR 39
Murphy, Jim 1947- 185
  Brief entry 32
  Earlier sketches in SATA 37, 77, 124
  See also CLR 53
Murphy, Joseph E., Jr. 1930- 65
Murphy, Kelly 1977- 190
  Earlier sketch in SATA 143
Murphy, Louise 1943- 155
Murphy, Mary 1961- 196
Murphy, Pat
  See Murphy, E(mmett) Jefferson
Murphy, Patricia J. 1963- 132
Murphy, Rita 180
Murphy, Robert (William) 1902-1971 10
Murphy, Shirley Rousseau 1928- 126
  Earlier sketches in SATA 36, 71
  See also SAAS 18
Murphy, Stuart J. 1942- 157
  Earlier sketch in SATA 115
Murphy, Thomas Basil, Jr. 1935- 191
Murphy, Tim
  See Murphy, Jim
Murphy, Tom
  See Murphy, Thomas Basil, Jr.
Murray, John 1923- 39
Murray, Kirsty 1960- 165
  Earlier sketch in SATA 108
Murray, Marguerite 1917- 63
Murray, Marian 5
Murray, Martine 1965- 125
Murray, (Judith) Michele (Freedman)
  1933-1974 7
Murray, Ossie 1938- 43
Murray, Peter
  See Hautman, Pete
Murrow, Liza Ketchum 1946- 132
  Earlier sketch in SATA 78
Musgrave, Florence 1902-1999 3
Musgrove, Margaret W(ynkoop) 1943- 124
  Earlier sketch in SATA 26
Musgrove, Marianne 207
Mussey, Virginia Howell
  See Ellison, Virginia H(owell)
Mussey, Virginia T.H.
  See Ellison, Virginia H(owell)
Mussi, Sarah 206
Mutel, Cornelia F. 1947- 74
Muth, Jon J. 206
  Earlier sketch in SATA 165
Mutz
  See Kuenstler, Morton
Mwangi, Meja 1948- 174
My Brother's Brother
  See Chekhov, Anton
Myers, Anna 160
Myers, Arthur 1917- 91
  Earlier sketch in SATA 35

Myers, Bernice 81
  Earlier sketch in SATA 9
Myers, Caroline Elizabeth Clark
  1887-1980 28
Myers, Christopher 1975- 183
  See also CLR 97
Myers, Edward 1950- 172
  Earlier sketch in SATA 96
Myers, Elisabeth P(erkins) 1918- 36
Myers, (Mary) Hortense (Powner)
  1913-1987 10
Myers, Jack 1913-2006 83
  Obituary 178
Myers, Jack Edgar
  See Myers, Jack
Myers, Lou 1915-2005 81
  Obituary 171
Myers, Louis
  See Myers, Lou
Myers, R.E. 1924- 119
Myers, Robert Eugene
  See Myers, R.E.
Myers, Tim 1953- 176
  Earlier sketch in SATA 147
Myers, Timothy Joseph
  See Myers, Tim
Myers, Walter Dean 1937- 193
  Brief entry 27
  Earlier sketches in SATA 41, 71, 109, 157
  See also CLR 110
  See also SAAS 2
Myers, Walter M.
  See Myers, Walter Dean
Myller, Rolf 1926-2006 27
  Obituary 175
Myra, Harold L(awrence) 1939- 46
  Brief entry 42
Myracle, Lauren 1969- 204
  Earlier sketch in SATA 162
Myrus, Donald (Richard) 1927- 23
Mysterious Traveler, The
  See Arthur, Robert, (Jr.)

N

Na, An 149
Naaslund, Goorel Kristina 1940- 170
Nadel, Laurie 1948- 74
Naden, Corinne J. 1930- 166
  Earlier sketch in SATA 79
Nadimi, Suzan 188
Nagda, Ann Whitehead 199
Nagel, Andreas Fischer
  See Fischer-Nagel, Andreas
Nagel, Heiderose Fischer
  See Fischer-Nagel, Heiderose
Nagle, Shane 176
Naidoo, Beverley 1943- 180
  Earlier sketches in SATA 63, 135
  See also CLR 29
Nakae, Noriko 1940- 59
Nakata, Hiroe 205
Nakatani, Chiyoko 1930-1981 55
  Brief entry 40
  See also CLR 30
Nally, Susan W. 1947- 90
Namioka, Lensey 1929- 157
  Autobiography Feature 116
  Earlier sketches in SATA 27, 89
  See also CLR 48
  See also SAAS 24
Namovicz, Gene Inyart 1927- 6
Nanji, Shenaaz 1954- 204
  Earlier sketch in SATA 131
Nanogak Agnes 1925- 61
Napier, Mark
  See Laffin, John (Alfred Charles)

Napoli, Donna Jo 1948- 190
  Earlier sketches in SATA 92, 137
  See also CLR 51
  See also SAAS 23
Napp, Daniel 1974- 204
Narahashi, Keiko 1959- 115
  Earlier sketch in SATA 79
Narayan, R. K. 1906-2001 62
Narayan, Rasipuram Krishnaswami
  See Narayan, R. K.
Nascimbene, Yan 1949- 173
  Earlier sketch in SATA 133
Nash, Bruce M(itchell) 1947- 34
Nash, Fredric Ogden
  See Nash, Ogden
Nash, Linell
  See Smith, Linell Nash
Nash, Mary (Hughes) 1925- 41
Nash, Ogden 1902-1971 46
  Earlier sketch in SATA 2
Nash, Renea Denise 1963- 81
Nast, Elsa Ruth
  See Watson, Jane Werner
Nast, Thomas 1840-1902 51
  Brief entry 33
Nastick, Sharon 1954- 41
Natale, Vince 196
Natarajan, Srividya 187
Nathan, Adele (Gutman) 1900(?)-1986
  Obituary 48
Nathan, Amy 155
  Earlier sketch in SATA 104
Nathan, Dorothy (Goldeen) (?)-1966 15
Nathan, Robert (Gruntal) 1894-1985 6
  Obituary 43
Nathanson, Laura Walther 1941- 57
Natti, Lee 1919- 67
  Earlier sketch in SATA 1
  See also SAAS 3
Natti, Susanna 1948- 125
  Earlier sketch in SATA 32
Nau, Thomas 186
Naughtie, Eleanor
  See Updale, Eleanor
Naughton, Bill
  See Naughton, William John (Francis)
Naughton, James Franklin 1957- 85
Naughton, Jim
  See Naughton, James Franklin
Naughton, William John (Francis)
  1910-1992 86
Navarra, John Gabriel 1927- 8
Naylor, Penelope 1941- 10
Naylor, Phyllis 1933- 152
  Autobiography Feature 152
  Earlier sketches in SATA 12, 66, 102
  See also CLR 135
  See also SAAS 10
  See Naylor, Phyllis Reynolds
Naylor, Phyllis Reynolds 1933- 209
  See Naylor, Phyllis
Nazarian, Nikki
  See Nichols, Cecilia Fawn
Nazaroff, Alexander I(vanovich) 1898-1981 .. 4
Nazoa, Aquiles 1920-1976 198
Neal, Harry Edward 1906-1993 5
  Obituary 76
Neal, Michael
  See Teitelbaum, Michael
Nearing, Penny 1916- 47
  Brief entry 42
Nebel, Gustave E. 45
  Brief entry 33
Nebel, Mimouca
  See Nebel, Gustave E.
Nee, Kay Bonner 10
Needham, Kate 1962- 95
Needle, Jan 1943- 98
  Earlier sketch in SATA 30
  See also CLR 43
  See also SAAS 23

Needleman, Jacob 1934- 6
Neel, David 1960- 82
Neel, Preston 1959- 93
Negri, Rocco 1932- 12
Negrin, Fabian 1963- 189
Neidigh, Sherry 1956- 204
Neier, Aryeh 1937- 59
Neigoff, Anne 13
Neigoff, Mike 1920- 13
Neilan, Eujin Kim 1969- 200
Neilson, Frances Fullerton (Jones)
    1910-2001 14
Neimark, Anne E. 1935- 145
    Earlier sketch in SATA 4
Neimark, Paul G. 1934- 80
    Brief entry 37
Neitzel, Shirley 1941- 134
    Earlier sketch in SATA 77
Nell
    See Hanna, Nell(ie L.)
Nelscott, Kris
    See Rusch, Kristine Kathryn
Nelson, Blake 1960- 177
Nelson, Catherine Chadwick 1926- 87
Nelson, Cordner 1918-2009 54
    Brief entry 29
Nelson, Cordner Bruce
    See Nelson, Cordner
Nelson, Drew 1952- 77
Nelson, Esther L. 1928- 13
Nelson, Jim A.
    See Stotter, Mike
Nelson, Julie L. 1970- 117
Nelson, Kadir 181
    Earlier sketch in SATA 154
Nelson, Kris
    See Rusch, Kristine Kathryn
Nelson, Lawrence E(rnest) 1928-1977
    Obituary 28
Nelson, Marilyn 1946- 60
    Autobiography Feature 180
Nelson, Mary Carroll 1929- 23
Nelson, O. Terry 1941- 62
Nelson, Peter N. 1953- 73
Nelson, R. A. 197
Nelson, Richard K(ing) 1941- 65
Nelson, Robin Laura 1971- 141
Nelson, Roy Paul 1923- 59
Nelson, S.D. 181
Nelson, Sharlene (P.) 1933- 96
Nelson, Suzanne 1976- 184
Nelson, Ted (W.) 1931- 96
Nelson, Theresa 1948- 143
    Autobiography Feature 143
    Earlier sketch in SATA 79
Nemeth, Sally 187
Neri, G. 197
Neri, Greg
    See Neri, G.
Neri, Gregory
    See Neri, G.
Nerlove, Miriam 1959- 53
    Brief entry 49
Nesbit, E. 1858-1924 100
    See also YABC 1
    See also CLR 70
Nesbit, Edith
    See Nesbit, E.
Nesbit, Troy
    See Folsom, Franklin (Brewster)
Nespojohn, Katherine V(eronica) 1912-1975 . 7
Ness, Evaline (Michelow) 1911-1986 26
    Obituary 49
    Earlier sketch in SATA 1
    See also CLR 6
    See also SAAS 1
Ness, Patrick 1971- 207
Nestor, Larry 1940- 149
Nestor, William P(rodromos) 1947- 49
Nethery, Mary 93
Neubecker, Robert 170

Neuberger, Julia (Babette Sarah) 1950- 142
    Earlier sketch in SATA 78
Neufeld, John (Arthur) 1938- 131
    Autobiography Feature 131
    Earlier sketches in SATA 6, 81
    See also CLR 52
    See also SAAS 3
Neuhaus, David 1958- 83
Neumeyer, Peter F(lorian) 1929- 13
Neurath, Marie (Reidemeister) 1898-1986 1
Neuschwander, Cindy 1953- 157
    Earlier sketch in SATA 107
Neusner, Jacob 1932- 38
Neville, Charles
    See Bodsworth, (Charles) Fred(erick)
Neville, Emily Cheney 1919- 1
    See also SAAS 2
Neville, Mary
    See Woodrich, Mary Neville
Nevins, Albert (Francis) J(erome)
    1915-1997 20
Nevius, Carol 1955- 186
Newberger, Devra
    See Speregen, Devra Newberger
Newberry, Clare Turlay 1903-1970 1
    Obituary 26
Newbery, John 1713-1767 20
    See also CLR 147
Newbery, Linda 1952- 184
    Earlier sketch in SATA 142
Newbigging, Martha 198
Newbold, Greg 199
Newcomb, Ellsworth
    See Kenny, Ellsworth Newcomb
Newcombe, Eugene A. 1923-1990 45
    Brief entry 33
Newcombe, Jack
    See Newcombe, Eugene A.
Newcome, Robert 1955- 91
Newcome, Zita 1959- 88
Newell, Crosby
    See Bonsall, Crosby Barbara (Newell)
Newell, Edythe W(eatherford) 1910-1989 11
Newell, Hope Hockenberry 1896-1965 24
Newfeld, Frank 1928- 26
Newgarden, Mark 1959- 194
Newlon, (Frank) Clarke 1905(?)-1982 6
    Obituary 33
Newman, Barbara Johansen 191
Newman, C.J.
    See Newman, Coleman J.
Newman, Coleman J. 1935- 82
Newman, Daisy 1904-1994 27
    Obituary 78
Newman, Gerald 1939- 46
    Brief entry 42
Newman, Jerry
    See Newman, Coleman J.
Newman, Leslea 1955- 134
    Earlier sketches in SATA 71, 128
Newman, Margaret
    See Potter, Margaret
Newman, Marjorie 146
Newman, Matthew (Harrison) 1955- 56
Newman, Nanette 1934- 162
Newman, Robert (Howard) 1909-1988 87
    Obituary 60
    Earlier sketch in SATA 4
Newman, Shirlee P(etkin) 144
    Earlier sketches in SATA 10, 90
Newsom, Carol 1948- 92
    Earlier sketch in SATA 40
Newsom, Tom 1944- 80
Newth, Mette 1942- 140
Newton, David E(dward) 1933- 67
Newton, James R(obert) 1935- 23
Newton, Jill 1964- 200
Newton, Robert 1965- 191
Newton, Suzanne 1936- 77
    Earlier sketch in SATA 5

Newton, Vanessa
    See Newton, Vanessa Brantley
Newton, Vanessa Brantley 1962(?)- 206
Ney, John 1923- 43
    Brief entry 33
Nez, John 155
Ng, Franklin 82
Nguyen, Vincent 187
Nichol, B(arrie) P(hillip) 1944-1988 66
Nicholas, Louise D.
    See Watkins, Dawn L.
Nicholls, Judith (Ann) 1941- 61
Nicholls, Sally 1983- 209
Nichols, Cecilia Fawn 1906-1987 12
Nichols, Grace 1950- 164
    Earlier sketch in SATA 98
Nichols, Janet (Louise) 1952- 67
Nichols, Judy 1947- 124
Nichols, Leigh
    See Koontz, Dean
Nichols, Paul
    See Hawks, Robert
Nichols, Peter
    See Youd, Samuel
Nichols, (Joanna) Ruth 1948- 15
    See also CLR 149
Nichols, Travis 206
Nicholson, C. R.
    See Nicole, Christopher (Robin)
Nicholson, Christina
    See Nicole, Christopher (Robin)
Nicholson, Joyce Thorpe 1919- 35
Nicholson, Lois P. 1949- 88
Nicholson, Robin
    See Nicole, Christopher (Robin)
Nicholson, William 180
Nicholson, William 1872-1949
    See CLR 76
Nickel, Barbara 1966- 188
Nickell, Joe 1944- 167
    Earlier sketch in SATA 73
Nickelsburg, Janet 1893-1983 11
Nickerson, Betty 1922- 14
Nickerson, Elizabeth
    See Nickerson, Betty
Nickl, Barbara (Elisabeth) 1939- 56
Nicklaus, Carol 62
    Brief entry 33
Nickle, John 181
Nickless, Will 1902-1979(?) 66
Nic Leodhas, Sorche
    See Alger, Leclaire (Gowans)
Nicol, Ann
    See Turnbull, Ann
Nicolas
    See Mordvinoff, Nicolas
Nicolay, Helen 1866-1954
    See YABC 1
Nicole, Christopher (Robin) 1930- 5
Nicoll, Helen 1937- 87
Nicolson, Cynthia Pratt 1949- 141
Ni Dhuibhne, Eilis 1954- 91
Niehaus, Paddy Bouma
    See Bouma, Paddy
Nields, Nerissa 1967- 166
Nielsen, Kay (Rasmus) 1886-1957 16
    See also CLR 16
Nielsen, Laura F. 1960- 93
Nielsen, Laura Farnsworth
    See Nielsen, Laura F.
Nielsen, Nancy J. 1951- 77
Nielsen, Susin 1964- 195
Nielsen, Virginia
    See McCall, Virginia Nielsen
Nielsen-Fernlund, Susin
    See Nielsen, Susin
Niemann, Christoph 1970- 191
Nieuwsma, Milton J(ohn) 1941- 142
Nightingale, Sandy 1953- 76
Nikolajeva, Maria 1952- 127

Nikola-Lisa, W. 1951- *180*
  Earlier sketch in SATA *71*
Niland, Deborah 1951- *172*
  Earlier sketch in SATA *27*
Niland, Kilmeny *75*
Nilsen, Anna 1948- *174*
  Earlier sketch in SATA *96*
Nilsson, Eleanor 1939- *117*
  Earlier sketch in SATA *81*
  See also SAAS *23*
Nilsson, Per 1954- *159*
Nimmo, Jenny 1944- *144*
  Earlier sketch in SATA *87*
  See also CLR *44*
Nishimura, Kae *196*
Niven, Larry 1938- *171*
  Earlier sketch in SATA *95*
Niven, Laurence VanCott
  See Niven, Larry
Nivola, Claire A. 1947- *208*
  Earlier sketches in SATA *84, 140*
Nix, Garth 1963- *143*
  Earlier sketch in SATA *97*
  See also CLR *68*
Nixon, Hershell Howard 1923- *42*
Nixon, Joan Lowery 1927-2003 .... *115*
  Obituary *146*
  Earlier sketches in SATA *8, 44, 78*
  See also CLR *24*
  See also SAAS *9*
Nixon, K.
  See Nixon, Kathleen Irene (Blundell)
Nixon, Kathleen Irene (Blundell)
  1894-1988(?) *14*
  Obituary *59*
Nobati, Eugenia 1968- *201*
Nobisso, Josephine 1953- *121*
  Earlier sketch in SATA *78*
Noble, Iris (Davis) 1922-1986 .... *5*
  Obituary *49*
Noble, Marty 1947- *125*
  Earlier sketch in SATA *97*
Noble, Trinka Hakes 1944- *197*
  Brief entry *37*
  Earlier sketch in SATA *123*
Nobleman, Marc Tyler 1972- *203*
Noda, Takayo 1961- *168*
Nodelman, Perry 1942- *101*
Nodset, Joan L.
  See Lexau, Joan M.
Noel Hume, Ivor 1927- *65*
Noestlinger, Christine
  See Nostlinger, Christine
Noguere, Suzanne 1947- *34*
Nolan, Dennis 1945- *166*
  Brief entry *34*
  Earlier sketches in SATA *42, 92*
Nolan, Han 1956- *157*
  Earlier sketch in SATA *109*
Nolan, Janet 1956- *191*
  Earlier sketch in SATA *145*
Nolan, Jeannette Covert 1897-1974 .... *2*
  Obituary *27*
Nolan, Paul T(homas) 1919- *48*
Nolan, William F. 1928- *88*
  Brief entry *28*
Nolan, William Francis
  See Nolan, William F.
Nolen, Jerdine 1953- *157*
  Earlier sketch in SATA *105*
Noll, Sally 1946- *82*
Noonan, Brandon 1979- *184*
Noonan, Diana 1960- *146*
Noonan, Julia 1946- *148*
  Earlier sketches in SATA *4, 95*
Norac, Carl 1960- *166*
Norcross, John
  See Conroy, John Wesley
Nordan, Robert W(arren) 1934-2004 .... *133*
Nordhoff, Charles Bernard 1887-1947 .... *23*
Nordlicht, Lillian *29*

Nordstrom, Ursula 1910-1988 .... *3*
  Obituary *57*
Nordtvedt, Matilda 1926- *67*
Norling, Beth 1969- *149*
Norman, Charles 1904-1996 .... *38*
  Obituary *92*
Norman, Howard
  See Norman, Howard A.
Norman, Howard A. 1949- *81*
Norman, James
  See Schmidt, James Norman
Norman, Jay
  See Arthur, Robert, (Jr.)
Norman, Lilith 1927- *120*
  Earlier sketch in SATA *86*
Norman, Mary 1931- *36*
Norman, Steve
  See Pashko, Stanley
Norment, Lisa 1966- *91*
Norris, Gunilla Brodde 1939- *20*
North, Andrew
  See Norton, Andre
North, Anthony
  See Koontz, Dean
North, Captain George
  See Stevenson, Robert Louis
North, Captain George
  See Stevenson, Robert Louis
North, Howard
  See Trevor, Elleston
North, Joan 1920- *16*
North, Milou
  See Erdrich, Louise
North, Robert
  See Withers, Carl A.
North, Sara
  See Bonham, Barbara Thomas
  and Hager, Jean
North, Sherry *201*
North, Sterling 1906-1974 .... *45*
  Obituary *26*
  Earlier sketch in SATA *1*
Northcott, (William) Cecil 1902-1987
  Obituary *55*
Northeast, Brenda V(ictoria) 1948- *106*
Northmore, Elizabeth Florence 1906-1974 . *122*
Norton, Alice Mary
  See Norton, Andre
Norton, Andre 1912-2005 .... *91*
  Earlier sketches in SATA *1, 43*
  See also CLR *50*
Norton, Browning
  See Norton, Frank R. B(rowning)
Norton, Frank R. B(rowning) 1909-1989 ..... *10*
Norton, Mary 1903-1992 .... *60*
  Obituary *72*
  Earlier sketch in SATA *18*
  See also CLR *140*
Nosredna, Trebor
  See Anderson, Bob
Nostlinger, Christine 1936- *162*
  Brief entry *37*
  Earlier sketch in SATA *64*
  See also CLR *12*
Nourse, Alan E(dward) 1928-1992 .... *48*
  See also CLR *33*
Novak, Matt 1962- *204*
  Brief entry *52*
  Earlier sketches in SATA *60, 104, 165*
Novelli, Luca 1947- *61*
Nowell, Elizabeth Cameron *12*
Noyes, Deborah 1965- *194*
  Earlier sketch in SATA *145*
Nugent, Cynthia 1954- *205*
Nugent, Nicholas 1949- *73*
Numeroff, Laura 1953- *206*
  Earlier sketches in SATA *28, 90, 142*
  See also CLR *85*
Numeroff Joffe, Laura
  See Numeroff, Laura

Nunes, Lygia Bojunga 1932- *154*
  Earlier sketch in SATA *75*
Nunn, Laura (Donna) Silverstein 1968- *124*
Nurenberg, Thelma
  See Greenhaus, Thelma Nurenberg
Nurnberg, Maxwell 1897-1984 .... *27*
  Obituary *41*
Nussbaumer, Paul (Edmund) 1934- *16*
Nutt, Ken 1951- *163*
  Earlier sketch in SATA *97*
Nuttall-Smith, Margaret Emily Noel 1919- .. *26*
Nuygen, Mathieu 1967- *80*
Nuzum, K. A. *195*
Nuzum, Kathy A.
  See Nuzum, K. A.
Nyberg, (Everett Wayne) Morgan 1944- *87*
Nyce, (Nellie) Helene von Strecker
  1885-1969 .... *19*
Nyce, Vera 1862-1925 .... *19*
Nye, Naomi Shihab 1952- *198*
  Earlier sketches in SATA *86, 147*
  See also CLR *59*
Nye, Robert 1939- *6*
Nyeu, Tao *206*
Nyikos, Stacy A. 1969- *164*
Nystrom, Carolyn 1940- *130*
  Earlier sketch in SATA *67*

O

O. Henry
  See Henry, O.
Oakes, Elizabeth H. 1964- *132*
Oakes, Vanya 1909-1983 .... *6*
  Obituary *37*
Oakley, Don(ald G.) 1927- *8*
Oakley, Graham 1929- *84*
  Earlier sketch in SATA *30*
  See also CLR *7*
Oakley, Helen (McKelvey) 1906- *10*
Oana, Katherine 1929- *53*
  Brief entry *37*
Oates, Eddie H. 1943- *88*
Oates, Joyce Carol 1938- *159*
Oates, Stephen B(aery) 1936- *59*
Obed, Ellen Bryan 1944- *74*
Oberle, Joseph 1958- *69*
Oberman, Sheldon 1949-2004 .... *85*
  Autobiography Feature *114*
  Obituary *153*
  See also CLR *54*
  See also SAAS *26*
Obligado, Lilian (Isabel) 1931- *61*
  Brief entry *45*
Obrant, Susan 1946- *11*
O'Brian, E.G.
  See Clarke, Arthur C.
O'Brien, Anne Sibley 1952- *80*
  Brief entry *48*
  Earlier sketch in SATA *53*
O'Brien, E.G.
  See Clarke, Arthur C.
O'Brien, Esse Forrester 1895(?)-1975
  Obituary *30*
O'Brien, Patrick 1960- *193*
O'Brien, Robert C.
  See Conly, Robert Leslie
O'Brien, Thomas C(lement) 1938- *29*
O'Callaghan, Julie 1954- *113*
O'Callahan, Jay 1938- *88*
O'Carroll, Ryan
  See Markun, Patricia Maloney
Ochiltree, Dianne 1953- *117*
Ockham, Joan Price
  See Price, Joan
O'Connell, Margaret F(orster) 1935-1977 .... *30*
  Obituary *30*
O'Connell, Peg
  See Ahern, Margaret McCrohan

O'Connell, Rebecca 1968- *130*
O'Connor, Barbara 1950- *193*
  Earlier sketch in SATA *154*
O'Connor, Francine M(arie) 1930- *90*
O'Connor, Genevieve A. 1914- *75*
O'Connor, George *183*
O'Connor, Ian 1965- *188*
O'Connor, Jane 1947- *186*
  Brief entry *47*
  Earlier sketches in SATA *59, 103, 150*
O'Connor, Karen 1938- *89*
  Earlier sketch in SATA *34*
O'Connor, Patrick
  See Wibberley, Leonard
O'Connor, Richard 1915-1975
  Obituary *21*
O'Conor, Jane 1958- *78*
Odaga, Asenath (Bole) 1937- *130*
  Earlier sketch in SATA *67*
  See also SAAS *19*
O Danachair, Caoimhin
  See Danaher, Kevin
Odanaka, Barbara *159*
O'Daniel, Janet 1921- *24*
O'Day, Cathy
  See Crane, Barbara (Joyce)
O'Dell, Scott 1898-1989 .... *134*
  Earlier sketches in SATA *12, 60*
  See also CLR *126*
Odenwald, Robert P(aul) 1899-1965 .... *11*
Odgers, Sally
  See Odgers, Sally Farrell
Odgers, Sally Farrell 1957- *139*
  Earlier sketch in SATA *72*
Odone, Jamison 1980- *209*
O'Donnell, Dick
  See Lupoff, Richard A(llen)
  and Thompson, Don(ald Arthur)
O'Donnell, Liam 1970- *209*
Odriozola, Elena *186*
Oechsli, Kelly 1918-1999 .... *5*
Oesterle, Virginia Rorby
  See Rorby, Ginny
Ofek, Uriel 1926- *36*
  See also CLR *28*
Ofer, Avi 1975- *207*
Offenbacher, Ami 1958- *91*
Offit, Sidney 1928- *10*
Ofosu-Appiah, L(awrence) H(enry) 1920- ... *13*
Ogan, George F. 1912-1983 .... *13*
Ogan, M. G.
  See Ogan, George F.
  and Ogan, Margaret E. (Nettles)
Ogan, Margaret E. (Nettles) 1923-1979 .... *13*
Ogburn, Charlton (Jr.) 1911-1998 .... *3*
  Obituary *109*
Ogburn, Jacqueline K. *162*
Ogilvie, Elisabeth May 1917-2006 .... *40*
  Brief entry *29*
  Obituary *176*
Ogilvy, Gavin
  See Barrie, J. M.
Ogilvy, Ian 1943- *177*
Ogilvy, Ian Raymond
  See Ogilvy, Ian
Ogle, Lucille Edith 1904-1988
  Obituary *59*
Ogletree, Charles J. 1952- *175*
O'Green, Jennifer
  See Roberson, Jennifer
O'Green, Jennifer Roberson
  See Roberson, Jennifer
O'Hagan, Caroline 1946- *38*
O'Hanlon, Jacklyn
  See Meek, Jacklyn O'Hanlon
O'Hara, Elizabeth
  See Ni Dhuibhne, Eilis
O'Hara, Kenneth
  See Morris, (Margaret) Jean
O'Hara, Mary
  See Alsop, Mary O'Hara

O'Hara (Alsop), Mary
  See Alsop, Mary O'Hara
O'Hare, Jeff(rey A.) 1958- *105*
Ohi, Ruth 1964- *95*
Ohiyesa
  See Eastman, Charles A(lexander)
Ohlsson, Ib 1935- *7*
Ohmi, Ayano 1959- *115*
Ohtomo, Yasuo 1946- *37*
o huigin, sean 1942- *138*
  See also CLR *75*
Oiseau
  See Moseley, James W(illett)
Oke, Janette 1935- *97*
O'Keefe, Susan Heyboer *176*
  Earlier sketch in SATA *133*
O'Keeffe, Frank 1938- *99*
O'Kelley, Mattie Lou 1908-1997 .... *97*
  Earlier sketch in SATA *36*
Okimoto, Jean Davies 1942- *103*
  Earlier sketch in SATA *34*
Okomfo, Amasewa
  See Cousins, Linda
olafsdottir, Gudrun Elin
  See Gunnella
Olaleye, Isaac O. 1941- *96*
  See also SAAS *23*
Olcott, Frances Jenkins 1872(?)-1963 .... *19*
Old, Wendie C(orbin) 1943- *154*
Old Boy
  See Hughes, Thomas
Oldenburg, E(gbert) William 1936-1974 ...... *35*
Older, Effin 1942- *114*
Older, Jules 1940- *156*
  Earlier sketch in SATA *114*
Oldfield, Jenny 1949- *140*
Oldfield, Margaret J(ean) 1932- *56*
Oldfield, Pamela 1931- *86*
Oldham, June *70*
Oldham, Mary 1944- *65*
Olds, Elizabeth 1896-1991 .... *3*
  Obituary *66*
Olds, Helen Diehl 1895-1981 .... *9*
  Obituary *25*
Oldstyle, Jonathan
  See Irving, Washington
O'Leary, Brian (Todd) 1940- *6*
O'Leary, Chris *208*
O'Leary, Patsy B(aker) 1937- *97*
Oleynikov, Igor 1953- *202*
Oliphant, B.J.
  See Tepper, Sheri S.
Oliver, Burton
  See Burt, Olive Woolley
Oliver, Chad
  See Oliver, Symmes C.
Oliver, John Edward 1933- *21*
Oliver, Lin *202*
Oliver, Marilyn Tower 1935- *89*
Oliver, Narelle 1960- *197*
  Earlier sketch in SATA *152*
Oliver, Shirley (Louise Dawkins) 1958- *74*
Oliver, Symmes C. 1928-1993 .... *101*
Oliviero, Jamie 1950- *84*
Olmsted, Lorena Ann 1890-1989 .... *13*
Olney, Ross R. 1929- *13*
Olschewski, Alfred (Erich) 1920- *7*
Olsen, Barbara *148*
Olsen, Carol 1945- *89*
Olsen, Ib Spang 1921- *81*
  Earlier sketch in SATA *6*
Olsen, Violet (Mae) 1922-1991 .... *58*
Olson, Arielle North 1932- *67*
Olson, David J. 1974- *198*
Olson, Gene 1922- *32*
Olson, Gretchen *187*
Olson, Helen Kronberg *48*
Olson, Kay Melchisedech 1948- *175*
Olson, Marianne
  See Mitchell, Marianne
Olson-Brown, Ellen 1967- *183*

Olten, Manuela 1970- *197*
Olugebefola, Ademole 1941- *15*
Oluonye, Mary N(kechi) 1955- *111*
Om
  See Gorey, Edward (St. John)
O'Malley, Donough *208*
O'Malley, Kevin 1961- *191*
  Earlier sketch in SATA *157*
Oman, Carola (Mary Anima) 1897-1978 ..... *35*
O'Mara, Carmel 1965- *166*
O'Mara-Horwitz, Carmel
  See O'Mara, Carmel
O'Meara, Walter (Andrew) 1897-1989 .... *65*
Ommanney, F(rancis) D(ownes) 1903-1980 . *23*
O Mude
  See Gorey, Edward (St. John)
Oneal, Elizabeth 1934- *82*
  Earlier sketch in SATA *30*
  See also CLR *13*
O'Neal, Katherine Pebley 1957- *204*
O'Neal, Reagan
  See Jordan, Robert
O'Neal, Regan
  See Jordan, Robert
Oneal, Zibby
  See Oneal, Elizabeth
O'Neill, Amanda 1951- *111*
O'Neill, Catharine *203*
O'Neill, Gerard K(itchen) 1927-1992 .... *65*
O'Neill, Judith (Beatrice) 1930- *34*
O'Neill, Mary L(e Duc) 1908(?)-1990 .... *2*
  Obituary *64*
O'Neill, Reagan
  See Jordan, Robert
Onslow, Annette Rosemary MacArthur
  See MacArthur-Onslow, Annette Rosemary
Onslow, John 1906-1985
  Obituary *47*
Onyefulu, Ifeoma 1959- *157*
  Earlier sketches in SATA *81, 115*
Opie, Iona (Margaret Balfour) 1923- *118*
  Earlier sketches in SATA *3, 63*
  See also SAAS *6*
Opie, Peter (Mason) 1918-1982 .... *118*
  Obituary *28*
  Earlier sketches in SATA *3, 63*
Oppel, Kenneth 1967- *199*
  Earlier sketches in SATA *99, 153*
Oppel, Kenneth Kerry
  See Oppel, Kenneth
Oppenheim, Joanne 1934- *174*
  Earlier sketches in SATA *5, 82, 136*
Oppenheim, Shulamith Levey 1928- *177*
Oppenheimer, Joan L(etson) 1925- *28*
Oppong, Joseph Ransford 1953- *160*
Optic, Oliver
  See Adams, William Taylor
  and Stratemeyer, Edward L.
Oram, Hiawyn 1946- *101*
  Earlier sketch in SATA *56*
Orbach, Ruth Gary 1941- *21*
Orback, Craig *197*
Orczy, Emma
  See Orczy, Baroness Emmuska
Orczy, Emma Magdalena Rosalia Maria Josefa
  See Orczy, Baroness Emmuska
Orczy, Emmuska
  See Orczy, Baroness Emmuska
Orczy, Baroness Emmuska 1865-1947 .... *40*
Orde, A.J.
  See Tepper, Sheri S.
O'Reilly, Jackson
  See Jordan, Robert
Orenstein, Denise Gosliner 1950- *157*
Orgad, Dorit 1936- *199*
Orgel, Doris 1929- *148*
  Earlier sketches in SATA *7, 85*
  See also CLR *48*
  See also SAAS *19*
Orgill, Roxane *198*

Oriolo, Joe
See Oriolo, Joseph D.
Oriolo, Joseph D. 1913-1985
Obituary *46*
Orlean, Susan 1955- *209*
Orleans, Ilo 1897-1962 .... *10*
Orlev, Uri 1931- *135*
Earlier sketch in SATA *58*
See also CLR *30*
See also SAAS *19*
Ormai, Stella *57*
Brief entry *48*
Ormerod, Jan 1946- *132*
Brief entry *44*
Earlier sketches in SATA *55, 70*
See also CLR *20*
Ormes, Jackie
See Ormes, Zelda J.
Ormes, Zelda J. 1914-1986
Obituary *47*
Ormondroyd, Edward 1925- *14*
Ormsby, Virginia H(aire) 1906-1990 .... *11*
Orona-Ramirez, Kristy 1964- *189*
Orozco, Jose-Luis 1948- *179*
Orr, Katherine S(helley) 1950- *72*
Orr, Wendy 1953- *206*
Earlier sketches in SATA *90, 141*
Orris
See Ingelow, Jean
Orth, Richard
See Gardner, Richard (M.)
Ortiz Cofer, Judith
See Cofer, Judith Ortiz
Orwell, George 1903-1950 .... *29*
See also CLR *68*
Orwin, Joanna 1944- *141*
Osborn, Elinor 1939- *145*
Osborn, Kathy 1955(?)- *199*
Osborn, Lois D(orothy) 1915- *61*
Osborne, Charles 1927- *59*
Osborne, Chester G(orham) 1915-1987 .... *11*
Osborne, David
See Silverberg, Robert
Osborne, George
See Silverberg, Robert
Osborne, Leone Neal 1914-1996 .... *2*
Osborne, Mary Pope 1949- *144*
Earlier sketches in SATA *41, 55, 98*
See also CLR *88*
Osceola
See Blixen, Karen
Osgood, William E(dward) 1926- *37*
O'Shaughnessy, Darren
See Shan, Darren
O'Shaughnessy, Ellen Cassels 1937- *78*
O'Shea, Catherine Patricia Shiels
See O'Shea, Pat
O'Shea, Pat 1931-2007 .... *87*
See also CLR *18*
Osmond, Edward 1900- *10*
Ossoli, Sarah Margaret
See Fuller, Margaret
Ostendorf, (Arthur) Lloyd, (Jr.) 1921-2000 .. *65*
Obituary *125*
Ostow, Micol 1976- *170*
Otfinoski, Steven 1949- *116*
Earlier sketch in SATA *56*
Otis, James
See Kaler, James Otis
O'Toole, Thomas 1941- *71*
O'Trigger, Sir Lucius
See Horne, Richard Henry Hengist
Otten, Charlotte
See Otten, Charlotte F.
Otten, Charlotte F. 1926- *98*
Otten, Charlotte Fennema
See Otten, Charlotte F.
Ottley, Matt 1962- *171*
Earlier sketch in SATA *102*
Ottley, Reginald Leslie 1909-1985 .... *26*
See also CLR *16*

Otto, Margaret Glover 1909-1976
Obituary *30*
Otto, Svend
See Soerensen, Svend Otto
Oughton, Jerrie (Preston) 1937- *131*
Earlier sketch in SATA *76*
Oughton, (William) Taylor 1925- *104*
Ouida
See De La Ramee, Marie Louise
Ousley, Odille 1896-1976 .... *10*
Outcalt, Todd 1960- *123*
Overmyer, James E. 1946- *88*
Overton, Jenny (Margaret Mary) 1942- *52*
Brief entry *36*
Owen, Ann
See Qualey, Marsha
Owen, Annie 1949- *75*
Owen, Caroline Dale
See Snedeker, Caroline Dale (Parke)
Owen, Clifford
See Hamilton, Charles (Harold St. John)
Owen, Dilys
See Gater, Dilys
Owen, (Benjamin) Evan 1918-1984 .... *38*
Owen, (John) Gareth 1936-2002 .... *162*
Earlier sketch in SATA *83*
See also CLR *31*
See also SAAS *14*
Owen, James A. *185*
Owens, Bryant 1968- *116*
Owens, Dana Elaine
See Queen Latifah
Owens, Gail 1939- *54*
Owens, Mary Beth *191*
Owens, Thomas S(heldon) 1960- *86*
Owens, Tom
See Owens, Thomas S(heldon)
Oxenbury, Helen 1938- *149*
Earlier sketches in SATA *3, 68*
See also CLR *70*
Oxendine, Bess Holland 1933- *90*
Oz, Frank (Richard) 1944- *60*
Ozer, Jerome S. 1927- *59*

P

Paananen, Eloise (Katherine) 1923-1993 .... *9*
Pace, Lorenzo 1943- *131*
Pace, Mildred Mastin 1907- *46*
Brief entry *29*
Pachter, Hedwig (?)-1988 .... *63*
Pack, Janet 1952- *77*
Pack, Robert 1929- *118*
Packard, Edward 1931- *148*
Earlier sketches in SATA *47, 90*
Packer, Kenneth L. 1946- *116*
Packer, Vin
See Meaker, Marijane
Pad, Peter
See Stratemeyer, Edward L.
Page, Eileen
See Heal, Edith
Page, Eleanor
See Coerr, Eleanor (Beatrice)
Page, Gail 1950- *205*
Page, Jake 1936- *81*
Page, James Keena, Jr.
See Page, Jake
Page, Lou Williams 1912-1997 .... *38*
Page, Mary
See Heal, Edith
Page, Robin 1943- *154*
Pagnucci, Susan 1944- *90*
Pahlen, Kurt 1907-2003
Obituary *147*
Pahz, Cheryl
See Pahz, Cheryl Suzanne
Pahz, Cheryl Suzanne 1949- *11*
Pahz, James Alon 1943- *11*

Paice, Margaret 1920- *10*
Paige, Harry W(orthington) 1922- *41*
Brief entry *35*
Paige, Richard
See Koontz, Dean
Paige, Robin
See Albert, Susan Wittig
Paine, Penelope Colville 1946- *87*
Paine, Roberta M. 1925- *13*
Paisley, Tom 1932- *11*
See also CLR *3*
Palatini, Margie *207*
Earlier sketches in SATA *134, 174*
Palazzo, Anthony D.
See Palazzo, Tony
Palazzo, Tony 1905-1970 .... *3*
Palder, Edward L. 1922- *5*
Palecek, Josef 1932- *56*
Palecek, Libuse 1937- *89*
Palen, Debbie *195*
Palin, Michael 1943- *67*
Palin, Michael Edward
See Palin, Michael
Palladini, David (Mario) 1946- *40*
Brief entry *32*
Pallas, Norvin 1918-1983 .... *23*
Pallister, John C(lare) 1891-1980
Obituary *26*
Pallotta, Gerard Larry
See Pallotta, Jerry
Pallotta, Jerry 1953- *186*
Pallotta-Chiarolli, Maria 1960- *117*
Palmer, Bernard (Alvin) 1914-1998 .... *26*
Palmer, C. Everard 1930- *14*
Palmer, (Ruth) Candida 1926- *11*
Palmer, Cyril Everard
See Palmer, C. Everard
Palmer, Don
See Benson, Mildred
Palmer, Hap 1942- *68*
Palmer, Heidi 1948- *15*
Palmer, Helen Marion
See Geisel, Helen
Palmer, Jessica 1953- *120*
Palmer, Judd 1972- *153*
Palmer, Juliette 1930- *15*
Palmer, Kate Salley 1946- *97*
Palmer, Maria
See Strachan, Ian
Palmer, Maria
See Brennan, Herbie
Palmer, Robin 1909-2000 .... *43*
Palmero Caceres, Ana *198*
Palmisciano, Diane *202*
Paltrowitz, Donna 1950- *61*
Brief entry *50*
Paltrowitz, Donna Milman
See Paltrowitz, Donna
Paltrowitz, Stuart 1946- *61*
Brief entry *50*
Pamela, Todd 1950- *124*
Pamintuan, Macky *178*
Panagopoulos, Janie Lynn *149*
Panati, Charles 1943- *65*
Panchyk, Richard 1970- *138*
Panetta, George 1915-1969 .... *15*
Panetta, Joseph N. 1953- *96*
Pang, YaWen Ariel *206*
Panik, Sharon 1952- *82*
Panowski, Eileen Thompson 1920- *49*
Pansy
See Alden, Isabella (Macdonald)
Pantell, Dora (Fuchs) *39*
Panter, Carol 1936- *9*
Paolini, Christopher 1983- *157*
See also CLR *102*
Papademetriou, Lisa *175*
Paparone, Pam *185*
Paparone, Pamela
See Paparone, Pam

Papas, Bill
  See Papas, William
Papas, William 1927-2000 50
Papashvily, George 1898-1978 17
Papashvily, Helen (Waite) 1906-1996 17
Pape, D. L.
  See Pape, Donna (Lugg)
Pape, Donna (Lugg) 1930- 82
  Earlier sketch in SATA 2
Paperny, Myra (Green) 1932- 51
  Brief entry 33
Papp, Robert 1967- 205
Paradis, Adrian A(lexis) 1912- 67
  Earlier sketch in SATA 1
  See also SAAS 8
Paradis, Marjorie Bartholomew
  1886(?)-1970 17
Paradiz, Valerie 1963- 176
Paratore, Coleen
  See Paratore, Coleen Murtagh
Paratore, Coleen Murtagh 1958- 200
Parenteau, Shirley 1935- 199
  Brief entry 40
  Earlier sketch in SATA 47
Parish, Margaret 1927-1988 73
  Obituary 59
  Earlier sketch in SATA 17
  See also CLR 22
Parish, Margaret Holt
  See Holt, Margaret
Parish, Peggy
  See Parish, Margaret
Park, Barbara 1947- 123
  Brief entry 35
  Earlier sketches in SATA 40, 78
  See also CLR 34
Park, Bill
  See Park, W(illiam) B(ryan)
Park, Frances 1955- 171
Park, Ginger 173
Park, Janie Jaehyun 150
Park, Jordan
  See Kornbluth, C(yril) M.
  and Pohl, Frederik
Park, Linda Sue 1960- 200
  Earlier sketches in SATA 127, 173
  See also CLR 84
Park, Nick 1958- 113
Park, (Rosina) Ruth (Lucia) 1923(?)- 93
  Earlier sketch in SATA 25
  See also CLR 51
Park, W(illiam) B(ryan) 1936- 22
Parke, Marilyn 1928- 82
Parker, Barbara Keevil 1938- 157
Parker, Daniel
  See Ehrenhaft, Daniel
Parker, Elinor Milnor 1906- 3
Parker, Julie F. 1961- 92
Parker, Kim 1963- 174
Parker, Kristy 1957- 59
Parker, Lois M(ay) 1912-1996 30
Parker, Margot M. 1937- 52
Parker, Marjorie Blain 1960- 205
  Earlier sketch in SATA 145
Parker, Mary Jessie 1948- 71
Parker, Nancy Winslow 1930- 132
  Earlier sketches in SATA 10, 69
  See also SAAS 20
Parker, Richard 1915-1990 14
Parker, Robert
  See Boyd, Waldo T.
  and Parker, Robert Andrew
Parker, Robert Andrew 1927- 200
Parker, Toni Trent 1947-2005 142
  Obituary 169
Parker-Rees, Guy 193
Parkes, Lucas
  See Harris, John (Wyndham Parkes Lucas)
  Beynon
Parkhill, John
  See Cox, William R(obert)

Parkins, David 1955- 176
Parkinson, Ethelyn M(inerva) 1906-1999 11
Parkinson, Kathryn N. 1954- 71
Parkinson, Kathy
  See Parkinson, Kathryn N.
Parkinson, Siobhan
  See Parkinson, Siobhan
Parkinson, Siobhan 1954- 178
Parks, Deborah A. 1948- 133
  Earlier sketch in SATA 91
Parks, Edd Winfield 1906-1968 10
Parks, Gordon 1912-2006 108
  Obituary 175
  Earlier sketch in SATA 8
Parks, Gordon Roger Alexander
  See Parks, Gordon
Parks, Peggy J. 1951- 143
Parks, PJ
  See Parks, Peggy J.
Parks, Rosa 1913-2005 83
  Obituary 169
Parks, Rosa Louise Lee
  See Parks, Rosa
Parks, Van Dyke 1943- 62
Parley, Peter
  See Goodrich, Samuel Griswold
Parlin, John
  See Graves, Charles Parlin
Parme, Fabrice 1966- 191
Parnall, Peter 1936- 69
  Earlier sketch in SATA 16
  See also SAAS 11
Parotti, Phillip (Elliott) 1941- 109
Parr, Ann 1943- 144
Parr, Danny
  See Parr, Ann
Parr, Letitia (Evelyn) 1906-1985(?) 37
Parr, Lucy 1924- 10
Parr, Todd 179
  Earlier sketch in SATA 134
Parrish, Anne 1888-1957 27
Parrish, Mary
  See Cousins, Margaret
Parrish, Maxfield
  See Parrish, (Frederick) Maxfield
Parrish, (Frederick) Maxfield 1870-1966 14
Parry, Marian 1924- 13
Parson Lot
  See Kingsley, Charles
Parsons, Alexandra 1947- 92
Parsons, Ellen
  See Dragonwagon, Crescent
Parsons, Garry 197
Parsons, Martin 1951- 116
Parsons, Martin Leslie
  See Parsons, Martin
Parsons, Tom
  See MacPherson, Thomas George
Parsons-Yazzi, Evangeline 172
Partch, Virgil Franklin II 1916-1984 39
  Obituary 39
Parton, Dolly 1946- 94
Parton, Dolly Rebecca
  See Parton, Dolly
Partridge, Benjamin W., Jr. 1915-2005 28
  Obituary 163
Partridge, Benjamin Waring, Jr.
  See Partridge, Benjamin W., Jr.
Partridge, Cora Cheney
  See Cheney, Cora
Partridge, Elizabeth 134
Partridge, Jenny (Lilian) 1947- 52
  Brief entry 37
Pasachoff, Naomi 1947- 147
Pascal, David 1918- 14
Pascal, Francine 1938- 143
  Brief entry 37
  Earlier sketches in SATA 51, 80
  See also CLR 25
Paschal, Nancy
  See Trotter, Grace V(iolet)

Paschkis, Julie 1957- 177
Pascudniak, Pascal
  See Lupoff, Richard A(llen)
Pashko, Stanley 1913-1982 29
Passailaigue, Thomas E.
  See Paisley, Tom
Pastel, Elyse 201
Pateman, Robert 1954- 84
Patent, Dorothy Hinshaw 1940- 162
  Autobiography Feature 162
  Earlier sketches in SATA 22, 69, 120
  See also CLR 19
  See also SAAS 13
Paterson, A(ndrew) B(arton) 1864-1941 97
Paterson, Banjo
  See Paterson, A(ndrew) B(arton)
Paterson, Diane 1946- 177
  Brief entry 33
  Earlier sketch in SATA 59
Paterson, John (Barstow) 1932- 114
Paterson, Katherine 1932- 204
  Earlier sketches in SATA 13, 53, 92, 133
  See also CLR 127
Paterson, Katherine Womeldorf
  See Paterson, Katherine
Patience, John 1949- 90
Patneaude, David 1944- 159
  Earlier sketch in SATA 85
Paton, Alan 1903-1988 11
  Obituary 56
Paton, Alan Stewart
  See Paton, Alan
Paton, Jane (Elizabeth) 1934- 35
Paton, Priscilla 1952- 98
Paton Walsh, Gillian
  See Paton Walsh, Jill
Paton Walsh, Jill 1937- 190
  Autobiography Feature 190
  Earlier sketches in SATA 4, 72, 109
  See also CLR 128
  See also SAAS 3
Patricelli, Leslie 207
Patrick, Susan
  See Clark, Patricia Denise
Patron, Susan 1948- 182
  Earlier sketch in SATA 76
Patsauq, Markoosie 1942-
  See CLR 23
Patschke, Steve 1955- 125
Patten, Brian 1946- 152
  Earlier sketch in SATA 29
Patterson, Charles 1935- 59
Patterson, Geoffrey 1943- 54
  Brief entry 44
Patterson, James 1947- 197
  Earlier sketch in SATA 164
Patterson, James B.
  See Patterson, James
Patterson, Lillie G. -1999 88
  Earlier sketch in SATA 14
Patterson, Nancy Ruth 1944- 148
  Earlier sketch in SATA 72
Pattison, Darcy (S.) 1954- 126
  Earlier sketch in SATA 72
Pattou, Edith 164
Patz (Blaustein), Nancy 154
Paul, Aileen 1917- 12
Paul, Alison 196
Paul, Ann Whitford 1941- 209
  Earlier sketches in SATA 76, 110, 168
Paul, David (Tyler) 1934-1988
  Obituary 56
Paul, Dominique 1973- 184
Paul, Elizabeth
  See Crow, Donna Fletcher
Paul, Hamish Vigne Christie 1951- 151
  See also CLR 87
Paul, James 1936- 23
Paul, Korky
  See Paul, Hamish Vigne Christie

Paul, Robert
  See Roberts, John G(aither)
Paul, Tessa 1944- *103*
Pauley, Kimberly 1973- *208*
Pauli, Hertha (Ernestine) 1909-1973 .... *3*
  Obituary *26*
Paull, Grace A. 1898- *24*
Paulsen, Gary 1939- *189*
  Earlier sketches in SATA *22, 50, 54, 79, 111,*
   158
  See also CLR *82*
Paulson, Jack
  See Jackson, C(aary) Paul
Pauquet, Gina Ruck
  See Ruck-Pauquet, Gina
Pausacker, Jenny 1948- *72*
  See also SAAS *23*
Pausewang, Gudrun 1928- *165*
  Earlier sketch in SATA *104*
Pavel, Frances 1907- *10*
Paver, Michelle *170*
Paxton, Thomas R. 1937- *70*
Paxton, Tom
  See Paxton, Thomas R.
Paye, Won-Ldy *185*
Payne, Alan
  See Jakes, John
Payne, Bernal C., Jr. 1941- *60*
Payne, C. Douglas
  See Payne, C.D.
Payne, C.D. 1949- *133*
Payne, C.F. 1956- *179*
Payne, Chris Fox
  See Payne, C.F.
Payne, Donald Gordon 1924- *37*
Payne, Emmy
  See West, Emily Govan
Payne, Nina *135*
Payne, Rachel Ann
  See Jakes, John
Payson, Dale 1943- *9*
Payzant, Charles *18*
Paz, A.
  See Pahz, James Alon
Paz, Natalia Toledo
  See Toledo, Natalia
Paz, Zan
  See Pahz, Cheryl Suzanne
Peace, Mary
  See Finley, Mary Peace
Peacock, Shane 1957- *192*
Peake, Mervyn 1911-1968 .... *23*
Peale, Norman Vincent 1898-1993 .... *20*
  Obituary *78*
Pearce, Ann Philippa
  See Pearce, Philippa
Pearce, Emily Smith 1975- *199*
Pearce, Jacqueline 1962- *146*
Pearce, Margaret *104*
Pearce, Philippa 1920-2006 .... *129*
  Obituary *179*
  Earlier sketches in SATA *1, 67*
  See also CLR *9*
Peare, Catherine Owens 1911- *9*
Pearle, Ida *207*
Pearsall, Shelley 1966- *190*
Pearson, Gayle 1947- *119*
  Earlier sketch in SATA *53*
Pearson, Jean Mary
  See Gardam, Jane
Pearson, Kit 1947- *77*
  Autobiography Feature *117*
  See also CLR *26*
Pearson, Mary E. 1955- *134*
Pearson, Ridley 1953- *182*
Pearson, Susan 1946- *166*
  Brief entry *27*
  Earlier sketches in SATA *39, 91*
Pearson, Tracey Campbell 1956- *155*
  Earlier sketch in SATA *64*

Pease, (Clarence) Howard 1894-1974 .... *2*
  Obituary *25*
Peavy, Linda 1943- *54*
Peck, Anne Merriman 1884-1976 .... *18*
Peck, Beth 1957- *190*
  Earlier sketch in SATA *79*
Peck, Jan *159*
Peck, Jeanie J. 1967- *147*
Peck, Marshall III 1951- *92*
Peck, Richard 1934- *190*
  Autobiography Feature *110*
  Earlier sketches in SATA *18, 55, 97, 110, 158*
  See also CLR *142*
  See also SAAS *2*
Peck, Richard Wayne
  See Peck, Richard
Peck, Robert Newton 1928- *156*
  Autobiography Feature *108*
  Earlier sketches in SATA *21, 62, 111*
  See also CLR *45*
  See also SAAS *1*
Peck, Sylvia 1953- *133*
Peck-Whiting, Jeanie J.
  See Peck, Jeanie J.
Peddicord, Jane Ann *199*
Pedersen, Janet *193*
Pederson, Sharleen
  See Collicott, Sharleen
Pedler, Caroline *197*
Peebles, Anne
  See Galloway, Priscilla
Peek, Merle 1938- *39*
Peel, John 1954- *79*
Peel, Norman Lemon
  See Hirsch, Phil
Peeples, Edwin A(ugustus, Jr.) 1915-1994 ..... *6*
Peers, Judi 1956- *119*
Peers, Judith May West
  See Peers, Judi
Peet, Bill
  See Peet, William Bartlett
Peet, Creighton B. 1899-1977 .... *30*
Peet, Mal *171*
Peet, Malcolm
  See Peet, Mal
Peet, William Bartlett 1915-2002 .... *78*
  Obituary *137*
  Earlier sketches in SATA *2, 41*
  See also CLR *12*
Peguero, Leone *116*
Pelaez, Jill 1924- *12*
Pelham, David 1938- *70*
Pell, Ed(ward) 1950- *157*
Pelletier, Andrew T. *195*
Pelletier, Andrew Thomas
  See Pelletier, Andrew T.
Pellowski, Anne 1933- *20*
Pellowski, Michael (Joseph) 1949- *151*
  Brief entry *48*
  Earlier sketch in SATA *88*
Pellowski, Michael Morgan
  See Pellowski, Michael (Joseph)
Pelta, Kathy 1928- *18*
Peltier, Leslie C(opus) 1900-1980 .... *13*
Pemberton, Bonnie *191*
Pemberton, John Leigh
  See Leigh-Pemberton, John
Pembury, Bill
  See Groom, Arthur William
Pemsteen, Hans
  See Manes, Stephen
Pendennis, Arthur Esquir
  See Thackeray, William Makepeace
Pender, Lydia Podger 1907- *61*
Pendery, Rosemary (Schmitz) *7*
Pendle, Alexy 1943- *29*
Pendle, George 1906-1977
  Obituary *28*

Pendleton, Don
  See Cunningham, Chet
  and Garside, Jack
  and Jagninski, Tom
  and Krauzer, Steven M(ark)
  and Obstfeld, Raymond
Pendleton, Thomas 1965- *206*
Pendziwol, Jean E. 1965- *177*
Pene du Bois, William (Sherman)
  1916-1993 .... *68*
  Obituary *74*
  Earlier sketch in SATA *4*
  See also CLR *1*
Penn, Audrey 1950- *22*
Penn, Ruth Bonn
  See Rosenberg, Eth Clifford
Pennac, Daniel 1944- *155*
Pennage, E. M.
  See Finkel, George (Irvine)
Penner, Fred 1946- *169*
  Earlier sketch in SATA *67*
Penner, Frederick Ralph Cornelius
  See Penner, Fred
Penney, Grace Jackson 1904-2000 .... *35*
Penney, Ian 1960- *76*
Penney, Sue 1957- *152*
  Earlier sketch in SATA *102*
Pennington, Eunice 1923- *27*
Pennington, Lillian Boyer 1904-2003 .... *45*
Pennypacker, Sara 1951- *187*
Penrose, Gordon 1925- *66*
Penson, Mary E. 1917- *78*
Penzler, Otto 1942- *38*
Pepe, Phil 1935- *20*
Pepe, Philip
  See Pepe, Phil
Peppe, Rodney (Darrell) 1934- *74*
  Earlier sketch in SATA *4*
  See also SAAS *10*
Pepper, Frank S. 1910-1988
  Obituary *61*
Percy, Charles Henry
  See Smith, Dorothy Gladys
Percy, Rachel 1930- *63*
Perdrizet, Marie-Pierre 1952- *79*
Perenyi, Constance 1954- *93*
Perenyi, Constance Marie
  See Perenyi, Constance
Perera, Hilda 1926- *105*
Perera, Thomas Biddle 1938- *13*
Peretti, Frank E. 1951- *141*
  Earlier sketch in SATA *80*
Perez, L. King 1940- *199*
Perez, Lana
  See Perez, Marlene
Perez, Lucia Angela 1973- *182*
Perez, Marlene *170*
Pericoli, Matteo 1968- *178*
Perkins, Al(bert Rogers) 1904-1975 .... *30*
Perkins, Lucy Fitch 1865-1937 .... *72*
Perkins, Lynne Rae 1956- *172*
  Earlier sketch in SATA *131*
Perkins, (Richard) Marlin 1905-1986 .... *21*
  Obituary *48*
Perkins, Mitali 1963- *188*
  Earlier sketch in SATA *88*
Perks, Anne-Marie 1955- *122*
Perl, Erica S. *188*
Perl, Lila *72*
  Earlier sketch in SATA *6*
Perl, Susan 1922-1983 .... *22*
  Obituary *34*
Perlman, Rhea 1948- *183*
Perlmutter, O(scar) William 1920-1975 .... *8*
Pernu, Dennis 1970- *87*
Perrault, Charles 1628-1703 .... *25*
  See also CLR *134*
Perret, Delphine 1980- *190*
Perret, Gene (Richard) 1937- *76*
Perrine, Mary 1913-1976 .... *2*
Perrins, Lesley 1953- *56*

Perrow, Angeli 1954- *121*
Perry, Andrea 1956- *190*
  Earlier sketch in SATA *148*
Perry, Barbara Fisher
  See Fisher, Barbara
Perry, Elizabeth 1959- *174*
Perry, Elizabeth Goodwin
  See Perry, Elizabeth
Perry, Marie Fritz *165*
Perry, Patricia 1949- *30*
Perry, Phyllis J(ean) 1933- *152*
  Earlier sketches in SATA *60, 101*
Perry, Ritchie (John Allen) 1942- *105*
Perry, Roger 1933- *27*
Perry, Steve(n Carl) 1947- *76*
Pershall, Mary K. 1951- *172*
  Earlier sketch in SATA *70*
Pershing, Marie
  See Schultz, Pearle Henriksen
Perske, Robert 1927- *57*
Persun, Morgan Reed
  See Watkins, Dawn L.
Petach, Heidi *149*
Peter
  See Stratemeyer, Edward L.
Peters, Alexander
  See Hollander, Zander
Peters, Andrew Fusek 1965- *169*
  Earlier sketch in SATA *107*
Peters, Caroline
  See Betz, Eva Kelly
Peters, David
  See David, Peter
Peters, Elizabeth 1927- *49*
Peters, Emma
  See Price, Karen
Peters, Gabriel
  See Matott, Justin
Peters, Julie Anne 1952- *197*
  Earlier sketches in SATA *82, 128*
Peters, Linda
  See Catherall, Arthur
Peters, Lisa Westberg 1951- *161*
  Earlier sketches in SATA *74, 115*
Peters, Patricia 1953- *84*
Peters, Russell M. 1929- *78*
Peters, S. H.
  See Henry, O.
  and Proffitt, Nicholas
Petersen, David 1946- *109*
  Earlier sketch in SATA *62*
Petersen, Gwenn Boardman 1924- *12*
Petersen, P(eter) J(ames) 1941- *118*
  Brief entry *43*
  Earlier sketches in SATA *48, 83*
Petersen, Palle 1943- *85*
Petersham, Maud 1890-1971 .... *17*
  See also CLR *24*
Petersham, Maud Sylvia Fuller
  See Petersham, Maud
Petersham, Miska 1888-1960 .... *17*
  See also CLR *24*
Peterson, Cris 1952- *174*
  Earlier sketches in SATA *84, 145*
Peterson, Dawn 1934- *86*
Peterson, Esther (Allen) 1934- *35*
Peterson, Hans 1922- *8*
Peterson, Harold L(eslie) 1922-1978 .... *8*
Peterson, Helen Stone 1910- *8*
Peterson, Jean Sunde 1941- *108*
Peterson, Jeanne Whitehouse 1939- *159*
  Earlier sketch in SATA *29*
Peterson, Kathleen B. 1951- *119*
Peterson, Lorraine 1940- *56*
  Brief entry *44*
Peterson, Shelley 1952- *146*
Peterson, Will
  See Cocks, Peter
Petie, Haris
  See Petty, Roberta
Petricic, Dusan 1946- *176*

Petrides, Heidrun 1944- *19*
Petrie, Catherine 1947- *52*
  Brief entry *41*
Petrone, Valeria *186*
Petrosino, Tamara *193*
Petroski, Catherine (Ann Groom) 1939- *48*
Petrovich, Michael B(oro) 1922- *40*
Petrovskaya, Kyra
  See Wayne, Kyra Petrovskaya
Petruccio, Steven James 1961- *67*
Petry, Ann 1908-1997 .... *5*
  Obituary *94*
  See also CLR *12*
Petry, Ann Lane
  See Petry, Ann
Pettit, Jayne 1932- *108*
Petty, J.T. 1977- *189*
Petty, Kate 1951-2007 .... *204*
Petty, Roberta 1915- *10*
Pevsner, Stella *131*
  Earlier sketches in SATA *8, 77*
  See also SAAS *14*
Peyo
  See Culliford, Pierre
Peyton, K. M.
  See Peyton, Kathleen Wendy
Peyton, Kathleen Wendy 1929- *157*
  Earlier sketches in SATA *15, 62*
  See also CLR *3*
  See also SAAS *17*
Pfanner, (Anne) Louise 1955- *68*
Pfeffer, Susan Beth 1948- *180*
  Earlier sketches in SATA *4, 83*
  See also CLR *11*
  See also SAAS *17*
Pfeffer, Wendy 1929- *204*
  Earlier sketches in SATA *78, 142*
Pfeiffer, Janet (B.) 1949- *96*
Pfister, Marcus *207*
  Earlier sketches in SATA *83, 150*
  See also CLR *42*
Pfitsch, Patricia Curtis 1948- *148*
Pflieger, Pat 1955- *84*
Pham, LeUyen 1973- *201*
  Earlier sketch in SATA *175*
Phelan, Mary Kay 1914- *3*
Phelan, Matt 1970- *172*
Phelan, Terry Wolfe 1941- *56*
Phelps, Ethel Johnston 1914-1984 .... *35*
Philbrick, Rodman 1951- *163*
Philbrick, W. R.
  See Philbrick, Rodman
Philbrick, W. Rodman
  See Philbrick, Rodman
Philbrook, Clem(ent E.) 1917- *24*
Phillips, Aileen Paul
  See Paul, Aileen
Phillips, Betty Lou
  See Phillips, Elizabeth Louise
Phillips, Bob 1940- *95*
Phillips, Douglas A. 1949- *161*
Phillips, Elizabeth Louise *58*
  Brief entry *48*
Phillips, Irv(ing W.) 1905-2000 .... *11*
  Obituary *125*
Phillips, Jack
  See Sandburg, Carl
Phillips, Leon
  See Gerson, Noel Bertram
Phillips, Loretta (Hosey) 1893-1987 .... *10*
Phillips, Louis 1942- *102*
  Earlier sketch in SATA *8*
Phillips, Mark
  See Garrett, Randall
  and Janifer, Laurence M(ark)
Phillips, Mary Geisler 1881-1964 .... *10*
Phillips, Michael
  See Nolan, William F.
Phillips, (Woodward) Prentice 1894-1981 .... *10*
Phillpotts, Eden 1862-1960 .... *24*

Phin
  See Thayer, Ernest Lawrence
Phipson, Joan
  See Fitzhardinge, Joan Margaret
Phiz
  See Browne, Hablot Knight
Phleger, Fred B. 1909-1993 .... *34*
Phleger, Marjorie Temple 1908(?)-1986 .... *1*
  Obituary *47*
Piaget, Jean 1896-1980
  Obituary *23*
Piatti, Celestino 1922- *16*
Picard, Barbara Leonie 1917- *89*
  Earlier sketch in SATA *2*
  See also SAAS *10*
Pichon, Liz *174*
Pickard, Charles 1932- *36*
Pickering, James Sayre 1897-1969 .... *36*
  Obituary *28*
Pickering, Jimmy *195*
Pickering, Robert B. 1950- *93*
Pielichaty, Helena 1955- *142*
Pienkowski, Jan (Michal) 1936- *131*
  Earlier sketches in SATA *6, 58*
  See also CLR *6*
Pierce, Edith Gray 1893-1977 .... *45*
Pierce, Katherine
  See St. John, Wylly Folk
Pierce, Meredith Ann 1958- *127*
  Brief entry *48*
  Earlier sketch in SATA *67*
  See also CLR *20*
Pierce, Ruth (Ireland) 1936- *5*
Pierce, Sharon
  See McCullough, Sharon Pierce
Pierce, Tamora 1954- *187*
  Brief entry *49*
  Earlier sketches in SATA *51, 96, 153*
Pierce, Terry *178*
Pierik, Robert 1921- *13*
Piernas-Davenport, Gail *199*
Piers, Robert
  See Anthony, Piers
Pig, Edward
  See Gorey, Edward (St. John)
Pike, Bob
  See Pike, Robert W(ilson)
Pike, Christopher 1954(?)- *156*
  Earlier sketch in SATA *68*
  See also CLR *29*
Pike, Deborah 1951- *89*
Pike, E(dgar) Royston 1896-1980 .... *22*
  Obituary *56*
Pike, R. William 1956- *92*
Pike, Robert W(ilson) 1931- *102*
Pilarski, Laura 1926- *13*
Pilgrim, Anne
  See Allan, Mabel Esther
Pilkey, Dav 1966- *166*
  Earlier sketches in SATA *68, 115*
  See also CLR *48*
Pilkey, David Murray, Jr.
  See Pilkey, Dav
Pilkington, Francis Meredyth 1907-1993 .... *4*
Pilkington, Roger (Windle) 1915-2003 .... *10*
  Obituary *144*
Pilutti, Deb *208*
Pin, Isabel 1975- *183*
Pinchot, David 1914(?)-1983
  Obituary *34*
Pincus, Harriet 1938- *27*
Pinczes, Elinor J(ane) 1940- *81*
Pine, Nicholas 1951- *91*
Pine, Tillie S(chloss) 1896-1999 .... *13*
Pini, Richard (Alan) 1950- *89*
Pini, Wendy 1951- *89*
Pinkerton, Kathrene Sutherland (Gedney)
  1887-1967
  Obituary *26*
Pinkett, Jada
  See Smith, Jada Pinkett

Pinkney, Andrea Davis 1963- *160*
    Earlier sketch in SATA *113*
Pinkney, Brian 1961- *206*
    Earlier sketches in SATA *74, 148*
    See also CLR *54*
Pinkney, Gloria Jean 1941- *85*
Pinkney, J. Brian
    See Pinkney, Brian
Pinkney, Jerry 1939- *198*
    Autobiography Feature *198*
    Brief entry *32*
    Earlier sketches in SATA *41, 71, 107, 151*
    See also CLR *43*
    See also SAAS *12*
Pinkney, John *97*
Pinkney, Sandra L. *193*
    Earlier sketch in SATA *128*
Pinkwater, D. Manus
    See Pinkwater, Daniel
Pinkwater, Daniel 1941- *158*
    Earlier sketches in SATA *8, 46, 76, 114*
    See also CLR *4*
    See also SAAS *3*
Pinkwater, Daniel M.
    See Pinkwater, Daniel
Pinkwater, Daniel Manus
    See Pinkwater, Daniel
Pinkwater, Jill *188*
Pinkwater, Manus
    See Pinkwater, Daniel
Pinner, Joma
    See Werner, Herma
Pinto, Sara *200*
Pioneer
    See Yates, Raymond F(rancis)
Piowaty, Kim Kennelly 1957- *49*
Piper, Roger
    See Fisher, John
Pirner, Connie White 1955- *72*
Piro, Richard 1934- *7*
Pirot, Alison Lohans
    See Lohans, Alison
Pirotta, Saviour *184*
Pirsig, Robert M(aynard) 1928- *39*
Pita
    See Rendon, Maria
Pitcher, C.
    See Pitcher, Caroline
Pitcher, Caroline 1948- *128*
Pitcher, Caroline Nell
    See Pitcher, Caroline
Pitman, (Isaac) James 1901-1985
    Obituary *46*
Pitre, Felix 1949- *84*
Pitrone, Jean Maddern 1920- *4*
Pittman, Helena Clare 1945- *71*
Pitz, Henry C(larence) 1895-1976 .... *4*
    Obituary *24*
Pitzer, Susanna 1958- *181*
Piven, Hanoch 1963- *173*
Pixley, Marcella *194*
Pizer, Vernon 1918- *21*
Place, Marian T(empleton) 1910- *3*
Place, Robin (Mary) 1926- *71*
Plaidy, Jean
    See Hibbert, Eleanor Alice Burford
Plain, Belva 1919- *62*
Plaine, Alfred R. 1898(?)-1981
    Obituary *29*
Plath, Sylvia 1932-1963 .... *96*
Platt, Chris 1959- *185*
Platt, Kin 1911- *86*
    Earlier sketch in SATA *21*
    See also SAAS *17*
Platt, Randall 1948- *95*
Platt, Randall Beth
    See Platt, Randall
Platt, Richard 1953- *166*
    Earlier sketch in SATA *120*
Playfellow, Robin
    See Ellis, Edward S.

Playsted, James
    See Wood, James Playsted
Plecas, Jennifer 1966- *149*
    Earlier sketch in SATA *84*
Plimpton, George 1927-2003 .... *10*
    Obituary *150*
Plimpton, George Ames
    See Plimpton, George
Plomer, William Charles Franklin
    1903-1973 .... *24*
Plotz, Helen Ratnoff 1913-2000 .... *38*
Plourde, Lynn 1955- *168*
    Earlier sketch in SATA *122*
Plowden, David 1932- *52*
Plowden, Martha Ward 1948- *98*
Plowhead, Ruth Gipson 1877-1967 .... *43*
Plowman, Stephanie 1922- *6*
Pluckrose, Henry (Arthur) 1931- *141*
    Earlier sketch in SATA *13*
Plum, J.
    See Wodehouse, P. G.
Plum, Jennifer
    See Kurland, Michael
Plumb, Charles P. 1900(?)-1982
    Obituary *29*
Plume, Ilse *170*
    Brief entry *43*
Plumme, Don E.
    See Katz, Bobbi
Plummer, Margaret 1911- *2*
Plum-Ucci, Carol *184*
Pochocki, Ethel (Frances) 1925- *76*
Podendorf, Illa (E.) 1903(?)-1983 .... *18*
    Obituary *35*
Podwal, Mark 1945- *160*
    Earlier sketch in SATA *101*
Podwal, Mark H.
    See Podwal, Mark
Poe, Edgar Allan 1809-1849 .... *23*
Poe, Ty (Christopher) 1975- *94*
Pogany, William Andrew 1882-1955 .... *44*
    Brief entry *30*
Pogany, Willy
    See Pogany, William Andrew
Pohl, Frederik 1919- *24*
Pohlmann, Lillian (Grenfell) 1902-1997 .... *11*
Pohrt, Tom 1953- *195*
    Earlier sketches in SATA *67, 152*
Pointon, Robert
    See Rooke, Daphne
Points, Larry G. 1945- *177*
    Earlier sketch in SATA *133*
Points, Larry Gene
    See Points, Larry G.
Pokeberry, P.J.
    See Mitchell, B.J.
POLA
    See Watson, Pauline
Polacco, Patricia 1944- *180*
    Earlier sketches in SATA *74, 123*
    See also CLR *40*
Polacco, Patricia Ann
    See Polacco, Patricia
Polak, Monique 1960- *178*
Polatnick, Florence T. 1923- *5*
Polder, Markus
    See Kruss, James
Polese, Carolyn 1947- *58*
Polese, James 1914- *87*
Polette, Nancy (Jane) 1930- *42*
Polhamus, Jean Burt 1928- *21*
Policoff, Stephen Phillip 1948- *77*
Polikoff, Barbara G. 1929- *162*
    Earlier sketch in SATA *77*
Polikoff, Barbara Garland
    See Polikoff, Barbara G.
Polisar, Barry Louis 1954- *134*
    Earlier sketch in SATA *77*

Politi, Leo 1908-1996 .... *47*
    Obituary *88*
    Earlier sketch in SATA *1*
    See also CLR *29*
Polking, Kirk 1925- *5*
Pollack, Jill S. 1963- *88*
Pollack, Merrill S. 1924-1988
    Obituary *55*
Polland, Barbara K(ay) 1939- *44*
Polland, Madeleine A(ngela Cahill) 1918- ... *68*
    Earlier sketch in SATA *6*
    See also SAAS *8*
Pollema-Cahill, Phyllis 1958- *123*
Pollock, Bruce 1945- *46*
Pollock, Mary
    See Blyton, Enid
Pollock, Penny 1935- *137*
    Brief entry *42*
    Earlier sketch in SATA *44*
Pollowitz, Melinda Kilborn 1944- *26*
Polner, Murray 1928- *64*
Polonsky, Arthur 1925- *34*
Polseno, Jo *17*
Pomaska, Anna 1946- *117*
Pomerantz, Charlotte 1930- *177*
    Earlier sketches in SATA *20, 80*
Pomeroy, Pete
    See Roth, Arthur J(oseph)
Pond, Alonzo W(illiam) 1894-1986 .... *5*
Pontiflet, Ted 1932- *32*
Poole, Gray Johnson 1906- *1*
Poole, Josephine
    See Helyar, Jane Penelope Josephine
Poole, (Jane Penelope) Josephine
    See Helyar, Jane Penelope Josephine
Poole, Lynn 1910-1969 .... *1*
Poole, Peggy 1925- *39*
Poortvliet, Rien 1932- *65*
    Brief entry *37*
Pope, Elizabeth Marie 1917-1992 .... *38*
    Brief entry *36*
Pope, Kevin 1958- *183*
Popescu, Christine
    See Pullein-Thompson, Christine
Poploff, Michelle 1956- *67*
Popp, K. Wendy *91*
Poppel, Hans 1942- *71*
Porfirio, Guy 1958- *197*
Portal, Colette 1936- *6*
Porte, Barbara Ann 1943- *152*
    Brief entry *45*
    Earlier sketches in SATA *57, 93*
Porter, A(nthony) P(eyton) 1945- *68*
Porter, Connie (Rose) 1959(?)- *129*
    Earlier sketch in SATA *81*
Porter, Donald Clayton
    See Gerson, Noel Bertram
Porter, Eleanor H(odgman) 1868-1920
    See CLR *110*
Porter, Gene Stratton
    See Stratton-Porter, Gene
Porter, Janice Lee 1953- *108*
    Earlier sketch in SATA *68*
Porter, Katherine Anne 1890-1980 .... *39*
    Obituary *23*
Porter, Kathryn
    See Swinford, Betty (June Wells)
Porter, Pamela 1956- *193*
Porter, Sheena 1935- *24*
    See also SAAS *10*
Porter, Sue
    See Limb, Sue
Porter, Sue 1951- *76*
Porter, Tracey *191*
Porter, William Sydney
    See Henry, O.
Portis, Antoinette *189*
Porto, Tony 1960- *153*
Portteus, Eleanora Marie Manthei (?)-1983
    Obituary *36*
Posada, Mia *187*

Posell, Elsa Z(eigerman) -1995 3
Posten, Margaret L(ois) 1915- 10
Posthuma, Sieb 1960- 150
Postier, Jim 1965- 202
Potok, Chaim 1929-2002 106
   Obituary 134
   Earlier sketch in SATA *33*
   See also CLR *92*
Potok, Herbert Harold
   See Potok, Chaim
Potok, Herman Harold
   See Potok, Chaim
Potter, Beatrix 1866-1943 132
   Earlier sketch in SATA *100*
   See also YABC *1*
   See also CLR *73*
Potter, Giselle 187
   Earlier sketch in SATA *150*
Potter, Helen Beatrix
   See Potter, Beatrix
Potter, Margaret 1926-1998 21
   Obituary 104
Potter, Marian 1915- 9
Potter, Miriam Clark 1886-1965 3
Poulin, Stephane 1961- 98
   See also CLR *28*
Poulton, Kimberly 1957(?)- 136
Pournelle, Jerry (Eugene) 1933- 161
   Earlier sketches in SATA *26, 91*
Povelite, Kay 1955- 102
Pow, Tom 1950- 163
Powe-Allred, Alexandra
   See Allred, Alexandra Powe
Powell, A. M.
   See Morgan, Alfred P(owell)
Powell, Consie 174
Powell, E. Sandy 1947- 72
Powell, E.S.
   See Powell, E. Sandy
Powell, Pamela 1960- 78
Powell, Patricia Hruby 1951- 136
Powell, Randy 1956- 118
Powell, Richard Stillman
   See Barbour, Ralph Henry
Powell, Robert (Stephenson Smyth) Baden
   See Baden-Powell, Robert (Stephenson
   Smyth)
Powell, Stephanie 1953- 93
Power, Margaret (M.) 1945- 125
   Earlier sketch in SATA *75*
Powers, Anne
   See Schwartz, Anne Powers
Powers, Bill 1931- 52
   Brief entry 31
Powers, Daniel 1959- 164
Powers, J. L. 195
Powers, Jessica
   See Powers, J. L.
Powers, Jessica Lynn
   See Powers, J. L.
Powers, Margaret
   See Heal, Edith
Powers, Tim 1952- 107
Powers, Timothy Thomas
   See Powers, Tim
Powledge, Fred 1935- 37
Poydar, Nancy 190
Poynter, Margaret 1927- 27
Prachaticka, Marketa
   See Kolibalova, Marketa
Prachatika, Marketa
   See Kolibalova, Marketa
Prager, Arthur 44
Prager, Ellen J. 1962- 136
Prange, Beckie 172
Prap, Lila 1955- 177
Praprotnik-Zupancic, Lilijana
   See Prap, Lila
Pratchett, Terence David John
   See Pratchett, Terry

Pratchett, Terry 1948- 185
   Earlier sketches in SATA *82, 139*
   See also CLR *64*
Prater, John 1947- 149
   Earlier sketches in SATA *72, 103*
Prato, Rodica 184
Pratt, (Murray) Fletcher 1897-1956 102
Pratt, Kristin Joy 1976- 87
Pratt, Pierre 1962- 208
   Earlier sketches in SATA *95, 166*
Preiss, Byron 1953-2005 166
   Brief entry 42
   Earlier sketch in SATA *47*
Preiss, Byron Cary
   See Preiss, Byron
Preller, James 1961- 209
   Earlier sketch in SATA *88*
Prelutsky, Jack 1940- 171
   Earlier sketches in SATA *22, 66, 118*
   See also CLR *115*
Prentice, Amy
   See Kaler, James Otis
Prescott, Casey
   See Morris, Chris(topher Crosby)
Presnall, Judith (Ann) Janda 1943- 96
Pressler, Mirjam 1940- 155
Preston, Douglas 1956- 113
Preston, Edna Mitchell 40
Preston, Lillian Elvira 1918- 47
Preus, Margi 209
Preussler, Otfried 1923- 24
Prevert, Jacques (Henri Marie) 1900-1977
   Obituary 30
Prevost, Guillaume 1964- 192
Prevost, Mikela 203
Price, Beverley Joan 1931- 98
Price, Charlie 187
Price, Christine (Hilda) 1928-1980 3
   Obituary 23
Price, Garrett 1896-1979
   Obituary 22
Price, Jennifer
   See Hoover, Helen (Drusilla Blackburn)
Price, Joan 1931- 124
Price, Jonathan (Reeve) 1941- 46
Price, Karen 1957- 125
Price, Kathy Z. 1957- 172
Price, Lucie Locke
   See Locke, Lucie
Price, Olive 1903-1991 8
Price, Susan 1955- 128
   Earlier sketches in SATA *25, 85*
Price, Willard 1887-1983 48
   Brief entry 38
Price-Groff, Claire 127
Priceman, Marjorie 1958- 168
   Earlier sketches in SATA *81, 120*
Prichard, Katharine Susannah 1883-1969 66
Prideaux, Tom 1908-1993 37
   Obituary 76
Priestley, Alice 1962- 95
Priestley, Chris 1958- 198
Priestley, Lee (Shore) 1904-1999 27
Priestly, Doug 1954- 122
Priestly, Douglas Michael
   See Priestly, Doug
Prieto, Mariana Beeching 1912-1999 8
Priley, Margaret (Ann) Hubbard 1909-1992
   Obituary 130
Primavera, Elise 1954- 185
   Brief entry 48
   Earlier sketches in SATA *58, 109*
Prime, Derek (James) 1931- 34
Prince, Alison (Mary) 1931- 86
   Earlier sketch in SATA *28*
Prince, April Jones 1975- 180
Prince, J(ack) H(arvey) 1908- 17
Prince, Joshua 188
Prince, Maggie 102
Prineas, Sarah 204
Pringle, Eric 138

Pringle, Laurence 1935- 201
   Autobiography Feature 201
   Earlier sketches in SATA *4, 68, 104, 154*
   See also CLR *57*
   See also SAAS *6*
Pringle, Laurence Patrick
   See Pringle, Laurence
Prinz, Yvonne 1960- 175
Prior, Natalie Jane 1963- 106
Pritchett, Elaine H(illyer) 1920- 36
Pritchett, Laura 1971- 178
Pritchett, Laura Rose
   See Pritchett, Laura
Pritts, Kim Derek 1953- 83
Prochazkova, Iva 1953- 68
Proctor, Everitt
   See Montgomery, Rutherford George
Proeysen, Alf 1914-1970 67
   See also CLR *24*
Professor Scribbler
   See Hollingsworth, Mary
Proimos, James 1955- 173
Prose, Francine 1947- 198
   Earlier sketches in SATA *101, 149*
Protopopescu, Orel 186
Protopopescu, Orel Odinov
   See Protopopescu, Orel
Provensen, Alice 1918- 147
   Earlier sketches in SATA *9, 70*
   See also CLR *11*
Provensen, Martin 1916-1987 70
   Obituary 51
   Earlier sketch in SATA *9*
   See also CLR *11*
Provensen, Martin Elias
   See Provensen, Martin
Provenzo, Eugene (F., Jr.) 1949- 142
   Earlier sketch in SATA *78*
Provist, d'Alain 1906-1989
   See Diop, Birago (Ismael)
Provost, Gail Levine 1944- 65
Provost, Gary (Richard) 1944-1995 66
Proysen, Alf
   See Proeysen, Alf
Pruett, Candace (J.) 1968- 157
Pryor, Bonnie H. 1942- 69
Pryor, Boori (Monty) 1950- 112
Pryor, Helen Brenton 1897-1972 4
Pryor, Michael 1957- 153
Pucci, Albert John 1920- 44
Pudney, John (Sleigh) 1909-1977 24
Pugh, Ellen (Tiffany) 1920- 7
Pullein-Thompson, Christine 1925-2005 82
   Obituary 172
   Earlier sketch in SATA *3*
Pullein-Thompson, Diana
   See Farr, Diana
Pullein-Thompson, Joanna Maxwell
   1898-1961 82
Pullein-Thompson, Josephine (Mary
   Wedderburn) 82
   Earlier sketch in SATA *3*
Pullen, Zachary 189
Pullman, Philip 1946- 198
   Earlier sketches in SATA *65, 103, 150*
   See also CLR *84*
   See also SAAS *17*
Pullman, Philip Nicholas
   See Pullman, Philip
Pulver, Harry, Jr. 1960- 129
Pulver, Robin 1945- 208
   Earlier sketches in SATA *76, 133*
Puner, Helen W(alker) 1915-1989 37
   Obituary 63
Purdy, Carol 1943- 120
   Earlier sketch in SATA *66*
Purdy, Susan G(old) 1939- 8
Purkiss, Diane 1961- 194
Purmell, Ann 1953- 206
   Earlier sketch in SATA *147*
Purnell, Idella 1901-1982 120

Purscell, Phyllis 1934- 7
Purtill, Richard L. 1931- 53
Pushker, Gloria 1927- 162
    Earlier sketch in SATA 75
Pushker, Gloria Teles
    See Pushker, Gloria
Pushkin, Aleksandr Sergeevich
    See Pushkin, Alexander
Pushkin, Alexander 1799-1837 61
Putnam, Alice 1916- 61
Putnam, Arthur Lee
    See Alger, Horatio, Jr.
Putnam, Peter B(rock) 1920-1998 30
    Obituary 106
Puttapipat, Niroot 199
Puttock, Simon 178
Puvilland, Alex 205
Puvilland, Alexandre
    See Puvilland, Alex
Puybaret, Eric 1976- 195
Pyle, Howard 1853-1911 100
    Earlier sketch in SATA 16
    See also CLR 117
Pyle, Katharine 1863-1938 66
Pyne, Mable Mandeville 1903-1969 9
Pyrnelle, Louise-Clarke 1850-1907 114

Q

Quackenbush, Robert M(ead) 1929- 133
    Autobiography Feature 133
    Earlier sketches in SATA 7, 70
    See also CLR 122
    See also SAAS 7
Qualey, Marsha 1953- 124
    Earlier sketch in SATA 79
Qualls, Sean 177
Quammen, David 1948- 7
Quark, Jason
    See Eldin, Peter
Quarles, Benjamin 1904-1996 12
Quarles, Benjamin Arthur
    See Quarles, Benjamin
Quatermass, Martin
    See Carpenter, John
Quattlebaum, Mary 1958- 185
    Earlier sketches in SATA 88, 134
Quay, Emma 173
    Earlier sketch in SATA 119
Queen, Ellery
    See Deming, Richard
    and Dannay, Frederic
    and Davidson, Avram (James)
    and Fairman, Paul W.
    and Flora, Fletcher
    and Holding, James (Clark Carlisle, Jr.)
    and Hoch, Edward D.
    and Kane, Henry
    and Lee, Manfred B.
    and Marlowe, Stephen
    and Powell, (Oval) Talmage
    and Sheldon, Walter J(ames)
    and Sturgeon, Theodore (Hamilton)
    and Tracy, Don(ald Fiske)
    and Vance, Jack
Queen Latifah 1970- 185
Quennell, Marjorie Courtney 1884-1972 29
Quentin
    See Sheldon, David
Quentin, Brad
    See Bisson, Terry
Quest, (Edna) Olga W(ilbourne) Hall
    See Hall-Quest, (Edna) Olga W(ilbourne)
Quick, Annabelle 1922-1986 2
Quigg, Jane (Hulda) (?)-1986
    Obituary 49
Quill, Monica
    See McInerny, Ralph

Quin-Harkin, Janet 1941- 165
    Earlier sketches in SATA 18, 90, 119
Quin-Harkin, Janet Elizabeth
    See Quin-Harkin, Janet
Quinlan, Susan E. 1954- 88
Quinlan, Susan Elizabeth
    See Quinlan, Susan E.
Quinn, Elisabeth 1881-1962 22
Quinn, Pat 1947- 130
Quinn, Patrick 1950- 73
Quinn, Rob 1972- 138
Quinn, Susan 1940- 30
Quinn, Susan Taft
    See Quinn, Susan
Quinn, Theodora K.
    See Kroeber, Theodora (Kracaw)
Quinn, Vernon
    See Quinn, Elisabeth
Quirk, Anne (E.) 1956- 99
Quixley, Jim 1931- 56
Quyth, Gabriel
    See Jennings, Gary

R

Ra, Carol F. 1939- 76
Raab, Evelyn 1951- 129
Rabb, Margo 1972- 188
Rabb, M.E.
    See Rabb, Margo
Rabe, Berniece (Louise) 1928- 148
    Autobiography Feature 148
    Earlier sketches in SATA 7, 77
    See also SAAS 10
Rabe, Olive H(anson) (?)-1968 13
Rabin, Staton 1958- 162
    Earlier sketch in SATA 84
Rabinowich, Ellen 1946- 29
Rabinowitz, Sandy 1954- 52
    Brief entry 39
Rachlin, Carol K(ing) 1919- 64
Rachlin, Harvey 1951- 47
Rachlin, Harvey Brant
    See Rachlin, Harvey
Rachlin, Nahid 64
Rachlis, Eugene (Jacob) 1920-1986
    Obituary 50
Rackham, Arthur 1867-1939 100
    Earlier sketch in SATA 15
    See also CLR 57
Racoma, Robin Yoko 1953- 207
Raczka, Bob 1963- 191
    Earlier sketch in SATA 163
Radencich, Marguerite C. 1952-1998 79
Rader, Laura 197
Radford, Ruby L(orraine) 1891-1971 6
Radin, Ruth Yaffe 1938- 107
    Brief entry 52
    Earlier sketch in SATA 56
Radlauer, David 1952- 28
Radlauer, Edward 1921- 15
Radlauer, Ruth Shaw 1926- 98
    Earlier sketch in SATA 15
Radley, Gail 1951- 112
    Earlier sketch in SATA 25
Radunsky, Vladimir 177
Rae, Gwynedd 1892-1977 37
Raebeck, Lois 1921- 5
Rael, Elsa Okon 1927-
    See CLR 84
Raffi
    See Cavoukian, Raffi
Raftery, Gerald (Bransfield) 1905-1986 11
Ragan-Reid, Gale 1956- 90
Rahaman, Vashanti 1953- 98
Rahn, Joan Elma 1929- 27
Rai, Bali 1971- 152
Raible, Alton (Robert) 1918- 35
Raiff, Stan 1930- 11

Raines, Shirley C(arol) 1945- 128
Rainey, W. B.
    See Blassingame, Wyatt Rainey
Rake, Jody 1961- 157
Rallison, Janette 1966- 183
Ralston, Jan
    See Dunlop, Agnes M. R.
Rama, Sue 190
Ramal, Walter
    See de la Mare, Walter (John)
Ramanujan, A(ttipat) K(rishnaswami)
    1929-1993 86
Rame, David
    See Divine, Arthur Durham
Ramirez, Jose 1967- 198
Ramirez, Orlando L. 1972- 194
Ramos, Jorge 1958- 205
Ramstad, Ralph L. 1919- 115
Rana, Indi
    See Rana, Indira Higham
Rana, Indira Higham 1944- 82
Rana, J.
    See Bhatia, Jamunadevi
Ranadive, Gail 1944- 10
Rand, Ann (Binkley) 30
Rand, Gloria 1925- 156
    Earlier sketch in SATA 101
Rand, Paul 1914-1996 6
Randall, Carrie
    See Ransom, Candice F.
Randall, David 1972- 167
Randall, Florence Engel 1917-1997 5
Randall, Janet
    See Young, Janet Randall
    and Young, Robert W(illiam)
Randall, Robert
    See Garrett, Randall
    and Silverberg, Robert
Randall, Ruth (Elaine) Painter 1892-1971 3
Randell, Beverley
    See Price, Beverley Joan
Randle, Kristen D. 1952- 92
    Autobiography Feature 119
    See also SAAS 24
Randle, Kristen Downey
    See Randle, Kristen D.
Randolph, Boynton M.D.
    See Ellis, Edward S.
Randolph, Ellen
    See Rawn, Melanie
Randolph, Geoffrey
    See Ellis, Edward S.
Randolph, J. H.
    See Ellis, Edward S.
Randolph, Lieutenant J. H.
    See Ellis, Edward S.
Rands, William Brighty 1823-1882 17
Raney, Ken 1953- 74
Rankin, Joan 1940- 148
    Earlier sketch in SATA 88
Rankin, Laura 1953(?)- 176
Ranney, Agnes V. 1916-1985 6
Ransom, Candice F. 1952- 183
    Brief entry 49
    Earlier sketches in SATA 52, 89, 135
Ransom, Jeanie Franz 1957- 187
Ransome, Arthur (Michell) 1884-1967 22
    See also CLR 8
Ransome, James E. 1961- 178
    Earlier sketches in SATA 76, 123
    See also CLR 86
Rant, Tol E.
    See Longyear, Barry B(rookes)
Raphael, Elaine
    See Bolognese, Elaine
Raposo, Joseph Guilherme 1938-1989
    Obituary 61
Rapp, Adam 1968- 148
Rappaport, Doreen 151
Rappaport, Eva 1924- 6

Rappoport, Ken 1935- 167
  Earlier sketch in SATA 89
Rarick, Carrie 1911-2002 41
Raschka, Chris 1959- 207
  Earlier sketches in SATA 80, 117, 166
Raschka, Christopher
  See Raschka, Chris
Rascol, Sabina I. 159
Rash, Andy 162
Raskin, Edith Lefkowitz 1908-1987 9
Raskin, Ellen 1928-1984 139
  Earlier sketches in SATA 2, 38
  See also CLR 12
Raskin, Joseph 1897-1982 12
  Obituary 29
Rathjen, Carl Henry 1909-1984 11
Rathmann, Peggy 1953- 157
  Earlier sketch in SATA 94
  See also CLR 77
Ratliff, Thomas M. 1948- 118
Ratner, Sue Lynn
  See Alexander, Sue
Rattigan, Jama Kim 1951- 99
Ratto, Linda Lee 1952- 79
Rattray, Simon
  See Trevor, Elleston
Ratz de Tagyos, Paul 1958- 198
  Earlier sketch in SATA 76
Rau, Dana Meachen 1971- 167
  Earlier sketch in SATA 94
Rau, Margaret 1913- 168
  Earlier sketch in SATA 9
  See also CLR 8
Rauch, Mabel Thompson 1888-1972
  Obituary 26
Raucher, Herman 1928- 8
Raude, Karina 199
Rauh, Sherry
  See North, Sherry
Raum, Elizabeth 1949- 155
Raven, Margot Theis 184
RavenWolf, Silver 1956- 155
Ravielli, Anthony 1916-1997 3
  Obituary 95
Ravilious, Robin 1944- 77
Ravishankar, Anushka 1961- 200
Rawding, F(rederick) W(illiam) 1930- 55
Rawlings, Marjorie Kinnan 1896-1953 100
  See also YABC 1
  See also CLR 63
Rawlins, Donna 1956- 206
Rawlinson, Julia 175
Rawls, (Woodrow) Wilson 1913-1984 22
  See also CLR 81
Rawlyk, George Alexander 1935- 64
Rawn, Melanie 1954- 98
Rawn, Melanie Robin
  See Rawn, Melanie
Rawson, Katherine 1955- 190
Ray, Carl 1943-1978 63
Ray, Deborah
  See Kogan Ray, Deborah
Ray, Delia 1963- 179
  Earlier sketch in SATA 70
Ray, Irene
  See Sutton, Margaret Beebe
Ray, Jane 1960- 196
  Earlier sketches in SATA 72, 152
Ray, JoAnne 1935- 9
Ray, Mary (Eva Pedder) 1932- 127
  Earlier sketch in SATA 2
Ray, Mary Lyn 1946- 154
  Earlier sketch in SATA 90
Rayban, Chloe 1944- 167
Rayevsky, Robert 1955- 190
  Earlier sketch in SATA 81
Raymond, James Crossley 1917-1981
  Obituary 29
Raymond, Robert
  See Alter, Robert Edmond
Rayner, Catherine 204

Rayner, Hugh 151
Rayner, Mary 1933- 87
  Earlier sketch in SATA 22
  See also CLR 41
Rayner, Shoo
  See Rayner, Hugh
Rayner, William 1929- 55
  Brief entry 36
Raynor, Dorka 28
Rayson, Steven 1932- 30
Razzell, Arthur (George) 1925- 11
Razzell, Mary (Catherine) 1930- 102
Razzi, James 1931- 10
Read, Elfreida 1920- 2
Read, Nicholas 1956- 146
Read, Piers Paul 1941- 21
Reade, Deborah 1949- 69
Reader, Dennis 1929- 71
Reading, Richard P(atrick) 1962- 161
Readman, Jo 1958- 89
Ready, Kirk L(ewis) 1943- 39
Reaney, James 1926-2008 43
Reaney, James Crerar
  See Reaney, James
Reardon, Joyce
  See Pearson, Ridley
Reaver, Chap 1935-1993 69
  Obituary 77
Reaver, Herbert R.
  See Reaver, Chap
Reaves, J. Michael
  See Reaves, (James) Michael
Reaves, (James) Michael 1950- 99
Reber, Deborah 189
Recorvits, Helen 191
Redding, Robert Hull 1919- 2
Redekopp, Elsa 61
Redlich, Ben 1977- 181
Redsand, Anna 1948- 184
Redway, Ralph
  See Hamilton, Charles (Harold St. John)
Redway, Ridley
  See Hamilton, Charles (Harold St. John)
Reece, Colleen L. 1935- 116
Reece, Gabrielle 1970- 108
Reed, Betty Jane 1921- 4
Reed, Dallas
  See Pendleton, Thomas
Reed, E.
  See Evans, Mari
Reed, Gwendolyn E(lizabeth) 1932- 21
Reed, Kit 1932- 184
  Autobiography Feature 184
  Earlier sketches in SATA 34, 116
Reed, Lynn Rowe 171
Reed, Neil 1961- 99
Reed, Talbot Baines 1852-1893
  See CLR 76
Reed, Thomas (James) 1947- 34
Reed, William Maxwell 1871-1962 15
Reeder, Carolyn 1937- 97
  Earlier sketch in SATA 66
  See also CLR 69
Reeder, Colin (Dawson) 1938- 74
Reeder, Colonel Red
  See Reeder, Russell P(otter), Jr.
Reeder, Russell P(otter), Jr. 1902-1998 4
  Obituary 101
Reeder, Stephanie Owen 1951- 102
Reed-Jones, Carol 1955- 112
Reef, Catherine 1951- 189
  Earlier sketches in SATA 73, 128
Reekie, Jocelyn (Margaret) 1947- 145
Reeman, Douglas Edward 1924- 63
  Brief entry 28
Rees, Celia 1949- 124
Rees, David (Bartlett) 1936-1993 69
  Obituary 76
  Earlier sketch in SATA 36
  See also SAAS 5
Rees, Douglas 1947- 169

Rees, Ennis (Samuel, Jr.) 1925- 3
Rees, (George) Leslie (Clarence)
  1905-2000 105
  Obituary 135
Reese, Bob
  See Reese, Robert A.
Reese, Carolyn Johnson 1938- 64
Reese, Della 1931(?)- 114
Reese, Lyn
  See Reese, Carolyn Johnson
Reese, Robert A. 1938- 60
  Brief entry 53
Reese, (John) Terence 1913-1996 59
Reeve, Joel
  See Cox, William R(obert)
Reeve, Kirk 1934- 117
Reeve, Philip 201
  Earlier sketch in SATA 170
Reeve, Rosie 188
  Earlier sketch in SATA 186
Reeves, Faye Couch 1953- 76
Reeves, James
  See Reeves, John Morris
Reeves, Jeni 1947- 111
Reeves, John Morris 1909-1978 87
  Earlier sketch in SATA 15
Reeves, Joyce 1911- 17
Reeves, Lawrence F. 1926- 29
Reeves, Ruth Ellen
  See Ranney, Agnes V.
Regan, Dian Curtis 1950- 149
  Autobiography Feature 149
  Earlier sketches in SATA 75, 133
Regehr, Lydia 1903-1991 37
Reger, James P. 1952- 106
Reggiani, Renee 1925- 18
Rehm, Karl M. 1935- 72
Reich, Ali
  See Katz, Bobbi
Reich, Susanna 1954- 113
Reiche, Dietlof 1941- 159
Reichert, Edwin C(lark) 1909-1988
  Obituary 57
Reichert, Mickey Zucker
  See Reichert, Miriam Zucker
Reichert, Miriam Zucker 1962- 85
Reichert, Renee 172
Reichhold, Jane(t E.) 1937- 147
Reid, Alastair 1926- 46
Reid, Barbara 1922- 21
Reid, Barbara (Jane) 1957- 93
  See also CLR 64
Reid, Desmond
  See Moorcock, Michael
  and McNeilly, Wilfred (Glassford)
Reid, Eugenie Chazal 1924- 12
Reid, John Calvin 21
Reid, (Thomas) Mayne 1818-1883 24
Reid, Meta Mayne 1905-1991 58
  Brief entry 36
Reid, Robin (Nicole) 1969- 145
Reid Banks, Lynne 1929- 165
  Earlier sketches in SATA 22, 75, 111
  See also CLR 86
Reider, Katja 1960- 126
Reid Jenkins, Debra 1955- 87
Reiff, Stephanie Ann 1948- 47
  Brief entry 28
Reig, June 1933- 30
Reigot, Betty Polisar 1924- 55
  Brief entry 41
Reilly, Joan 195
Reim, Melanie (K.) 1956- 104
Reinach, Jacquelyn (Krasne) 1930-2000 28
Reiner, Carl 1922- 151
Reiner, William B(uck) 1910-1976 46
  Obituary 30
Reinfeld, Fred 1910-1964 3
Reinhardt, Dana 1971- 175
Reinhart, Matthew 1971- 197
  Earlier sketch in SATA 161

Reiniger, Lotte 1899-1981 .... *40*
    Obituary *33*
Reinsma, Carol 1949- *91*
Reinstedt, Randall A. 1935- *101*
Reinstedt, Randy
    See Reinstedt, Randall A.
Reisberg, Mira 1955- *82*
Reisberg, Veg
    See Reisberg, Mira
Reiser, Lynn 1944- *180*
    Earlier sketches in SATA *81, 138*
Reiser, Lynn Whisnant
    See Reiser, Lynn
Reisgies, Teresa (Maria) 1966- *74*
Reiss, Johanna (de Leeuw) 1929(?)- *18*
    See also CLR *19*
Reiss, John J. *23*
Reiss, Kathryn 1957- *144*
    Earlier sketch in SATA *76*
Reit, Seymour Victory 1918-2001 .... *21*
    Obituary *133*
Reit, Sy
    See Reit, Seymour Victory
Relf, Patricia 1954- *134*
    Earlier sketch in SATA *71*
Remi, Georges 1907-1983 .... *13*
    Obituary *32*
    See also CLR *114*
Remington, Frederic S(ackrider)
    1861-1909 .... *41*
Remkiewicz, Frank 1939- *152*
    Earlier sketch in SATA *77*
Rempt, Fiona 1973- *198*
Remy, Georges
    See Remi, Georges
Renaud, Bernadette 1945- *66*
Renault, Mary 1905-1983 .... *23*
    Obituary *36*
Rendell, Joan *28*
Rendina, Laura (Jones) Cooper 1902- *10*
Rendon, Marcie R. 1952- *97*
Rendon, Maria 1965- *116*
Renee, Janina 1956- *140*
Renfro, Ed 1924- *79*
Renick, Marion (Lewis) 1905-1983 .... *1*
Renier, Aaron 1977- *202*
Renken, Aleda 1907- *27*
Renlie, Frank H. 1936- *11*
Rennert, Richard Scott 1956- *67*
Rennison, Louise 1951- *149*
Reno, Dawn E(laine) 1953- *130*
Rensie, Willis
    See Eisner, Will
Renton, Cam
    See Armstrong, Richard
Renvoize, Jean *5*
Resau, Laura 1973- *190*
Resciniti, Angelo G. 1952- *75*
Resnick, Michael David
    See Resnick, Mike
Resnick, Mike 1942- *159*
    Earlier sketches in SATA *38, 106*
Resnick, Seymour 1920- *23*
Retla, Robert
    See Alter, Robert Edmond
Rettig, Liz *199*
Rettstatt, Chris
    See Ashland, Monk
Reuter, Bjarne (B.) 1950- *142*
    Earlier sketch in SATA *68*
Reuter, Carol (Joan) 1931- *2*
Revena
    See Wright, Betty Ren
Revsbech, Vicki
    See Liestman, Vicki
Rex, Adam *186*
Rex, Michael *191*
Rey, H. A. 1898-1977 .... *100*
    Earlier sketches in SATA *1, 26, 69*
    See also CLR *93*

Rey, Hans Augusto
    See Rey, H. A.
Rey, Luis V. 1955- *201*
Rey, Margret 1906-1996 .... *86*
    Obituary *93*
    Earlier sketch in SATA *26*
    See also CLR *93*
Rey, Margret Elisabeth
    See Rey, Margret
Reyher, Becky
    See Reyher, Rebecca Hourwich
Reyher, Rebecca Hourwich 1897-1987 .... *18*
    Obituary *50*
Reynold, Ann
    See Bernardo, Anilu
Reynolds, Aaron 1970- *197*
Reynolds, Adrian 1963- *192*
Reynolds, C. Buck 1957- *107*
Reynolds, Dickson
    See Reynolds, Helen Mary Greenwood Camp-
    bell
Reynolds, Helen Mary Greenwood Campbell
    1884-1969
    Obituary *26*
Reynolds, Jan 1956- *180*
Reynolds, John
    See Whitlock, Ralph
Reynolds, Madge
    See Whitlock, Ralph
Reynolds, Malvina 1900-1978 .... *44*
    Obituary *24*
Reynolds, Marilyn 1935- *121*
    See also SAAS *23*
Reynolds, Marilyn M.
    See Reynolds, Marilyn
Reynolds, Marilynn 1940- *141*
    Earlier sketch in SATA *80*
Reynolds, Pamela 1923- *34*
Reynolds, Peter H. 1961- *128*
Reynolds, Peter J. 1961- *179*
Reynolds, Susan *179*
Rhine, Richard
    See Silverstein, Alvin
    and Silverstein, Virginia B.
Rhoades, Diane 1952- *90*
Rhodes, Bennie (Loran) 1927- *35*
Rhodes, Donna McKee 1962- *87*
Rhodes, Frank Harold Trevor 1926- *37*
Rhue, Morton
    See Strasser, Todd
Rhyne, Nancy 1926- *66*
Rhynes, Martha E. 1939- *141*
Ribbons, Ian 1924- *37*
    Brief entry *30*
    See also SAAS *3*
Ricciuti, Edward R(aphael) 1938- *10*
Rice, Alice (Caldwell) Hegan 1870-1942 ...... *63*
Rice, Bebe Faas 1932- *89*
Rice, Charles D(uane) 1910-1971
    Obituary *27*
Rice, Dale R. 1948- *42*
Rice, Dale Richard
    See Rice, Dale R.
Rice, Dick
    See Rice, R. Hugh
Rice, Earle (Wilmont), Jr. 1928- *151*
    Earlier sketch in SATA *92*
Rice, Edward 1918-2001 .... *47*
    Brief entry *42*
Rice, Elizabeth 1913-1976 .... *2*
Rice, Eve 1951- *91*
    Earlier sketch in SATA *34*
Rice, Eve Hart
    See Rice, Eve
Rice, Inez 1907- *13*
Rice, James 1934- *93*
    Earlier sketch in SATA *22*
Rice, John F. 1958- *82*
Rice, R. Hugh 1929- *115*
Rice, Richard H.
    See Rice, R. Hugh

Rich, Barbara
    See Graves, Robert
Rich, Elaine Sommers 1926- *6*
Rich, Josephine Bouchard 1912- *10*
Rich, Louise Dickinson 1903-1991 .... *54*
    Obituary *67*
Richard, Adrienne 1921- *5*
    See also SAAS *9*
Richard, James Robert
    See Bowen, Robert Sydney
Richards, Chuck 1957- *170*
Richards, Frank
    See Hamilton, Charles (Harold St. John)
Richards, Hilda
    See Hamilton, Charles (Harold St. John)
Richards, Jackie 1925- *102*
Richards, Jean 1940- *135*
Richards, Justin *169*
Richards, Kay
    See Baker, Susan (Catherine)
Richards, Laura E(lizabeth Howe) 1850-1943
    See YABC *1*
    See also CLR *54*
Richards, Leigh
    See King, Laurie R.
Richards, Marlee
    See Brill, Marlene Targ
Richards, Norman 1932- *48*
Richards, R(onald) C(harles) W(illiam)
    1923- *59*
    Brief entry *43*
Richards, Walter Alden (Jr.) 1907-1988
    Obituary *56*
Richardson, Andrew (William) 1986- *120*
Richardson, Carol 1932- *58*
Richardson, Frank Howard 1882-1970
    Obituary *27*
Richardson, Grace Lee
    See Dickson, Naida
Richardson, Jean (Mary) *59*
Richardson, Judith Benet 1941- *77*
Richardson, Nigel 1957- *187*
Richardson, Robert S(hirley) 1902-1981 .... *8*
Richardson, Sandy 1949- *116*
Richardson, V.A. *189*
Richardson, Willis 1889-1977 .... *60*
Richelson, Geraldine 1922- *29*
Richemont, Enid 1940- *82*
Richler, Mordecai 1931-2001 .... *98*
    Brief entry *27*
    Earlier sketch in SATA *44*
    See also CLR *17*
Richman, Sophia 1941- *142*
Rich-McCoy, Lois
    See McCoy, Lois (Rich)
Richmond, Robin 1951- *75*
Richoux, Pat(ricia) 1927- *7*
Richter, Alice 1941- *30*
Richter, Conrad (Michael) 1890-1968 .... *3*
Richter, Hans Peter 1925-1993 .... *6*
    See also CLR *21*
    See also SAAS *11*
Richter, Jutta 1955- *184*
Rickard, Graham 1949- *71*
Rico, Don(ato) 1917-1985
    Obituary *43*
Riddell, Chris 1962- *166*
    Earlier sketch in SATA *114*
Riddell, Christopher Barry
    See Riddell, Chris
Riddell, Edwina 1955- *82*
Ridden, Brian (John) 1934- *123*
Riddle, Tohby 1965- *151*
    Earlier sketch in SATA *74*
Riddleburger, Sam *202*
Riddles, Libby 1956- *140*
Rideout, Sandy *194*
Ridge, Antonia (Florence) (?)-1981 .... *7*
    Obituary *27*
Ridge, Martin 1923-2003 .... *43*

Ridley, Philip .... _171_
  Earlier sketch in SATA _88_
Ridlon, Marci
  See Balterman, Marcia Ridlon
Riedman, Sarah R(egal) 1902-1995 .... _1_
Riehecky, Janet 1953- .... _164_
Ries, Lori .... _185_
Riesenberg, Felix, Jr. 1913-1962 .... _23_
Rieu, E(mile) V(ictor) 1887-1972 .... _46_
  Obituary .... _26_
Riffenburgh, Beau 1955- .... _175_
Rigg, Sharon
  See Creech, Sharon
Riggio, Anita 1952- .... _148_
  Earlier sketch in SATA _73_
Riggs, Shannon .... _190_
Riggs, Sidney Noyes 1892-1975
  Obituary .... _28_
Riggs, Stephanie 1964- .... _138_
Riglietti, Serena 1969- .... _189_
Rigney, James Oliver, Jr.
  See Jordan, Robert
Rikhoff, Jean 1928- .... _9_
Rikki
  See Ducornet, Erica
Riley, James A. 1939- .... _97_
Riley, James Whitcomb 1849-1916 .... _17_
Riley, Jocelyn 1949- .... _60_
  Brief entry .... _50_
Riley, Jocelyn Carol
  See Riley, Jocelyn
Riley, Linda Capus 1950- .... _85_
Riley, Martin 1948- .... _81_
Rimbauer, Steven
  See Pearson, Ridley
Rimes, (Margaret) LeAnn 1982- .... _154_
Rinaldi, Ann 1934- .... _202_
  Brief entry .... _50_
  Earlier sketches in SATA _51, 78, 117, 161_
  See also CLR _46_
Rinard, Judith E(llen) 1947- .... _140_
  Earlier sketch in SATA _44_
Rinder, Lenore 1949- .... _92_
Ring, Elizabeth 1920- .... _79_
Ringdahl, Mark
  See Longyear, Barry B(rookes)
Ringgold, Faith 1930- .... _187_
  Earlier sketches in SATA _71, 114_
  See also CLR _30_
Ringi, Kjell (Arne Soerensen) 1939- .... _12_
Rinkoff, Barbara Jean (Rich) 1923-1975 .... _4_
  Obituary .... _27_
Rinn, Miriam 1946- .... _127_
Riordan, James 1936- .... _95_
Riordan, Rick .... _208_
  Earlier sketch in SATA _174_
Rios, Tere
  See Versace, Marie Teresa Rios
Ripken, Cal, Jr. 1960- .... _114_
Ripken, Calvin Edward, Jr.
  See Ripken, Cal, Jr.
Ripley, Catherine 1957- .... _82_
Ripley, Elizabeth Blake 1906-1969 .... _5_
Ripper, Charles L(ewis) 1929- .... _3_
Ripper, Chuck
  See Ripper, Charles L(ewis)
Riq
  See Atwater, Richard (Tupper)
Rish, David 1955- .... _110_
Riskind, Mary 1944- .... _60_
Rissinger, Matt 1956- .... _93_
Rissman, Art
  See Sussman, Susan
Rissman, Susan
  See Sussman, Susan
Ritchie, Barbara Gibbons .... _14_
Ritter, Felix
  See Kruss, James
Ritter, John H. 1951- .... _137_
  Earlier sketch in SATA _129_

Ritter, Lawrence S(tanley) 1922-2004 .... _58_
  Obituary .... _152_
Ritthaler, Shelly 1955- .... _91_
Ritts, Paul 1920(?)-1980
  Obituary .... _25_
Ritz, Karen 1957- .... _202_
  Earlier sketch in SATA _80_
Rivera, Geraldo (Miguel) 1943- .... _54_
  Brief entry .... _28_
Rivers, Elfrida
  See Bradley, Marion Zimmer
Rivers, Karen 1970- .... _131_
Riverside, John
  See Heinlein, Robert A.
Rivkin, Ann 1920- .... _41_
Rivoli, Mario 1943- .... _10_
Roach, Marilynn K. 1946- .... _9_
Roach, Marilynne Kathleen
  See Roach, Marilynne K.
Roach, Portia
  See Takakjian, Portia
Robb, Don 1937- .... _194_
Robb, Laura 1937- .... _95_
Robberecht, Thierry 1960- .... _182_
Robbins, Frank 1917-1994(?) .... _42_
  Brief entry .... _32_
Robbins, Ken 1945- .... _147_
  Brief entry .... _53_
  Earlier sketch in SATA _94_
Robbins, Raleigh
  See Hamilton, Charles (Harold St. John)
Robbins, Ruth 1917(?)- .... _14_
Robbins, Tony
  See Pashko, Stanley
Robbins, Wayne
  See Cox, William R(obert)
Robel, S. L.
  See Fraustino, Lisa Rowe
Roberson, Jennifer 1953- .... _72_
Roberson, John R(oyster) 1930- .... _53_
Robert, Adrian
  See St. John, Nicole
Roberts, Bethany .... _202_
  Earlier sketch in SATA _133_
Roberts, Bruce (Stuart) 1930- .... _47_
  Brief entry .... _39_
Roberts, Charles G(eorge) D(ouglas)
  1860-1943 .... _88_
  Brief entry .... _29_
  See also CLR _33_
Roberts, David
  See Cox, John Roberts
Roberts, David 1970- .... _191_
Roberts, Diane 1937- .... _184_
Roberts, Elizabeth 1944- .... _80_
Roberts, Elizabeth Madox 1886-1941 .... _33_
  Brief entry .... _27_
  See also CLR _100_
Roberts, Jim
  See Bates, Barbara S(nedeker)
Roberts, John G(aither) 1913-1993 .... _27_
Roberts, Judy I. 1957- .... _93_
Roberts, Katherine 1962- .... _152_
Roberts, M. L.
  See Mattern, Joanne
Roberts, Nancy Correll 1924- .... _52_
  Brief entry .... _28_
Roberts, Priscilla 1955- .... _184_
Roberts, Terence
  See Sanderson, Ivan T(erence)
Roberts, Willo Davis 1928-2004 .... _150_
  Autobiography Feature .... _150_
  Obituary .... _160_
  Earlier sketches in SATA _21, 70, 133_
  See also CLR _95_
  See also SAAS _8_
Robertson, Barbara (Anne) 1931- .... _12_
Robertson, Don 1929-1999 .... _8_
  Obituary .... _113_
Robertson, Dorothy Lewis 1912- .... _12_

Robertson, Ellis
  See Ellison, Harlan
  and Silverberg, Robert
Robertson, James I., Jr. 1930- .... _182_
Robertson, James Irvin
  See Robertson, James I., Jr.
Robertson, Janet (E.) 1935- .... _68_
Robertson, Jennifer Sinclair 1942-1998 .... _12_
Robertson, Jenny
  See Robertson, Jennifer Sinclair
Robertson, Keith (Carlton) 1914-1991 .... _85_
  Obituary .... _69_
  Earlier sketch in SATA _1_
  See also SAAS _15_
Robertson, Mark
  See Robertson, M.P.
Robertson, M.P. 1965- .... _197_
Robertson, Stephen
  See Walker, Robert W.
Robertus, Polly M. 1948- .... _73_
Robeson, Kenneth
  See Dent, Lester
  and Goulart, Ron
Robeson, Kenneth
  See Johnson, (Walter) Ryerson
Robinet, Harriette Gillem 1931- .... _104_
  Earlier sketch in SATA _27_
  See also CLR _64_
Robins, Deri 1958- .... _166_
  Earlier sketch in SATA _117_
Robins, Patricia
  See Clark, Patricia Denise
Robins, Rollo, Jr.
  See Ellis, Edward S.
Robins, Seelin
  See Ellis, Edward S.
Robinson, Adjai 1932- .... _8_
Robinson, Aminah Brenda Lynn 1940- ...... _159_
  Earlier sketch in SATA _77_
Robinson, Barbara (Webb) 1927- .... _84_
  Earlier sketch in SATA _8_
Robinson, C(harles) A(lexander), Jr.
  1900-1965 .... _36_
Robinson, Charles 1870-1937 .... _17_
Robinson, Charles 1931- .... _6_
Robinson, Dorothy W. 1929- .... _54_
Robinson, Elizabeth Keeler 1959- .... _204_
Robinson, Eve
  See Tanselle, Eve
Robinson, Glen 1953- .... _92_
Robinson, Glendal P.
  See Robinson, Glen
Robinson, Jan M. 1933- .... _6_
Robinson, Jean O. 1934- .... _7_
Robinson, Joan (Mary) G(ale Thomas)
  1910-1988 .... _7_
Robinson, Kim Stanley 1952- .... _109_
Robinson, Lee 1948- .... _110_
Robinson, Lloyd
  See Silverberg, Robert
Robinson, Lynda S(uzanne) 1951- .... _107_
Robinson, Marileta 1942- .... _32_
Robinson, Maudie Millian Oller 1914- .... _11_
Robinson, Maurice R(ichard) 1895-1982
  Obituary .... _29_
Robinson, Nancy K(onheim) 1942-1994 ...... _91_
  Brief entry .... _31_
  Obituary .... _79_
  Earlier sketch in SATA _32_
Robinson, Ray 1920- .... _23_
Robinson, Raymond Kenneth
  See Robinson, Ray
Robinson, Shari
  See McGuire, Leslie (Sarah)
Robinson, Sharon 1950- .... _197_
  Earlier sketch in SATA _162_
Robinson, Spider 1948- .... _118_
Robinson, Sue
  See Robinson, Susan Maria
Robinson, Susan Maria 1955- .... _105_

Robinson, Susan Patricia
  See Gates, Susan
Robinson, Suzanne
  See Robinson, Lynda S(uzanne)
Robinson, T(homas) H(eath) 1869-1950 ...... *17*
Robinson, Tim 1963- *205*
Robinson, (Wanda) Veronica 1926- *30*
Robinson, W(illiam) Heath 1872-1944 .... *17*
Robison, Bonnie 1924- *12*
Robison, Nancy L(ouise) 1934- *32*
Robles, Harold E. 1948- *87*
Robottom, John 1934- *7*
Robson, Eric 1939- *82*
Roca, Francois 1971- *200*
Rocco, John 1967- *188*
Roche, A. K.
  See Abisch, Roslyn Kroop
  and Kaplan, Boche
Roche, Denis 1967- *196*
  Earlier sketch in SATA *99*
Roche, Denis Mary
  See Roche, Denis
Roche, Luane 1937- *170*
Roche, P(atricia) K. 1935- *57*
  Brief entry *34*
Roche, Terry
  See Poole, Peggy
Rochman, Hazel 1938- *105*
Rock, Lois
  See Joslin, Mary
Rock, Maxine 1940- *108*
Rocker, Fermin 1907- *40*
Rocklin, Joanne 1946- *134*
  Earlier sketch in SATA *86*
Rockwell, Anne F. 1934- *194*
  Earlier sketches in SATA *33, 71, 114, 162*
  See also SAAS *19*
Rockwell, Anne Foote
  See Rockwell, Anne F.
Rockwell, Bart
  See Pellowski, Michael (Joseph)
Rockwell, Harlow 1910-1988 .... *33*
  Obituary *56*
Rockwell, Lizzy 1961- *185*
Rockwell, Norman (Percevel) 1894-1978 .... *23*
Rockwell, Thomas 1933- *70*
  Earlier sketch in SATA *7*
  See also CLR *6*
Rockwood, Joyce 1947- *39*
Rockwood, Roy
  See McFarlane, Leslie
  and Stratemeyer, Edward L.
Rodanas, Kristina 1952- *155*
Rodari, Gianni 1920-1980
  See CLR *24*
Rodd, Kathleen Tennant
  See Rodd, Kylie Tennant
Rodd, Kylie Tennant 1912-1988 .... *57*
  Obituary *55*
  Earlier sketch in SATA *6*
Rodda, Emily 1948- *146*
  Earlier sketch in SATA *97*
  See also CLR *32*
Roddenberry, Eugene Wesley 1921-1991 ..... *45*
  Obituary *69*
Roddenberry, Gene
  See Roddenberry, Eugene Wesley
Roddick, Ellen 1936- *5*
Roddie, Shen *153*
Roddy, Lee 1921- *57*
Rodenas, Paula *73*
Rodgers, Frank 1944- *69*
Rodgers, Mary 1931- *130*
  Earlier sketch in SATA *8*
  See also CLR *20*
Rodman, Emerson
  See Ellis, Edward S.
Rodman, Eric
  See Silverberg, Robert
Rodman, Maia
  See Wojciechowska, Maia (Teresa)

Rodman, Mary Ann *185*
Rodman, (Cary) Selden 1909-2002 .... *9*
Rodowsky, Colby 1932- *164*
  Earlier sketches in SATA *21, 77, 120*
  See also SAAS *22*
Rodowsky, Colby F.
  See Rodowsky, Colby
Rodriguez, Alejo 1941- *83*
Rodriguez, Alex 1975- *189*
Rodriguez, Christina 1981- *177*
Rodriguez, Edel 1971- *196*
Rodriguez, Luis J. 1954- *125*
Rodriguez, Rachel *180*
Rodriguez, Rachel Victoria
  See Rodriguez, Rachel
Roeder, Virginia Marsh 1926- *98*
Roehrig, Catharine H. 1949- *67*
Roennfeldt, Robert 1953- *78*
Roessel-Waugh, C. C.
  See Waugh, Carol-Lynn Rossel
  and Waugh, Charles G(ordon)
Roets, Lois F. 1937- *91*
Roever, J(oan) M(arilyn) 1935- *26*
Rofes, Eric 1954-2006 .... *52*
Rofes, Eric Edward 1954-2006
  See Rofes, Eric
Roffey, Maureen 1936- *33*
Rogak, Lisa 1962- *80*
Rogak, Lisa Angowski
  See Rogak, Lisa
Rogan, S. Jones *199*
Rogan, Sally Jones
  See Rogan, S. Jones
Rogasky, Barbara 1933- *144*
  Earlier sketch in SATA *86*
Rogers, (Thomas) Alan (Stinchcombe)
  1937- *81*
  Earlier sketch in SATA *2*
Rogers, Bettye 1858-1919 .... *103*
Rogers, Cindy 1950- *89*
Rogers, Emma 1951- *74*
Rogers, Frances 1888-1974 .... *10*
Rogers, Fred McFeely 1928-2003 .... *33*
  Obituary *138*
Rogers, Hal
  See Sirimarco, Elizabeth
Rogers, Jean 1919- *55*
  Brief entry *47*
Rogers, Matilda 1894-1976 .... *5*
  Obituary *34*
Rogers, Pamela 1927- *9*
Rogers, Paul 1950- *98*
  Earlier sketch in SATA *54*
Rogers, Robert
  See Hamilton, Charles (Harold St. John)
Rogers, Sherry *193*
Rogers, W(illiam) G(arland) 1896-1978 .... *23*
Rohan, M. S.
  See Rohan, Michael Scott
Rohan, Michael Scott 1951- *98*
Rohan, Mike Scott
  See Rohan, Michael Scott
Rohmann, Eric 1957- *171*
  See also CLR *100*
Rohmer, Harriet 1938- *56*
Rohrer, Doug 1962- *89*
Rojan
  See Rojankovsky, Feodor (Stepanovich)
Rojankovsky, Feodor (Stepanovich)
  1891-1970 .... *21*
Rojany, Lisa *94*
Rokeby-Thomas, Anna E(lma) 1911- *15*
Roland, Albert 1925-2002 .... *11*
Roland, Mary
  See Lewis, Mary
Roleff, Tamara L. 1959- *143*
Rolerson, Darrell A(llen) 1946- *8*
Roll, Winifred 1909-1998 .... *6*
Rollins, Charlemae Hill 1897-1979 .... *3*
  Obituary *26*
Rollock, Barbara T(herese) 1924- *64*

Rolston, Steve 1978- *209*
Romack, Janice Reed
  See LeNoir, Janice
Romain, Trevor *134*
Romanenko, Vitaly 1962- *101*
Romano, Clare 1922- *111*
  Earlier sketch in SATA *48*
Romano, Louis G. 1921- *35*
Romano, Melora A. 1966- *118*
Romano, Ray 1957- *170*
Romano, Raymond
  See Romano, Ray
Romijn, Johanna Maria Kooyker
  See Kooyker-Romijn, Johanna Maria
Romyn, Johanna Maria Kooyker
  See Kooyker-Romijn, Johanna Maria
Rong, Yu 1970- *174*
Rongen, Bjoern 1906- *10*
Rongen, Bjorn
  See Rongen, Bjoern
Ronson, Mark
  See Alexander, Marc
Rood, Ronald (N.) 1920- *12*
Rook, Sebastian
  See Jeapes, Ben
Rooke, Daphne 1914-2009 .... *12*
Rooke, Daphne Marie
  See Rooke, Daphne
Roop, Connie 1951- *167*
  Brief entry *49*
  Earlier sketches in SATA *54, 116*
Roop, Constance Betzer
  See Roop, Connie
Roop, Peter 1951- *167*
  Brief entry *49*
  Earlier sketches in SATA *54, 116*
Roop, Peter G.
  See Roop, Peter
Roop, Peter Geiger
  See Roop, Peter
Roos, Stephen 1945- *128*
  Brief entry *41*
  Earlier sketches in SATA *47, 77*
Roose-Evans, James 1927- *65*
Roosevelt, Eleanor 1884-1962 .... *50*
Root, Barry *182*
Root, Betty *84*
Root, Kimberly Bulcken *192*
Root, Phyllis 1949- *184*
  Brief entry *48*
  Earlier sketches in SATA *55, 94, 145*
Root, Shelton L., Jr. 1923-1986
  Obituary *51*
Roper, Laura (Newbold) Wood 1911-2003 .. *34*
  Obituary *150*
Roper, Robert 1946- *142*
  Earlier sketch in SATA *78*
Roraback, Robin (Ellan) 1964- *111*
Rorby, Ginny 1944- *94*
Rorer, Abigail 1949- *85*
Rosaler, Maxine *208*
Rosamel, Godeleine de 1968- *151*
Roscoe, D(onald) T(homas) 1934- *42*
Rose, Anne *8*
Rose, Deborah Lee 1955- *185*
  Earlier sketches in SATA *71, 124*
Rose, Elizabeth (Jane Pretty) 1933- *68*
  Brief entry *28*
Rose, Florella
  See Carlson, Vada F.
Rose, Gerald (Hembdon Seymour) 1935- *68*
  Brief entry *30*
Rose, Malcolm 1953- *168*
  Earlier sketch in SATA *107*
Rose, Nancy A.
  See Sweetland, Nancy A(nn)
Rose, Ted 1940- *93*
Rose, Wendy 1948- *12*
Rosen, Elizabeth 1961- *205*
Rosen, Lillian (Diamond) 1928- *63*
Rosen, Marvin 1933- *161*

Rosen, Michael 1946- *181*
  Brief entry *40*
  Earlier sketches in SATA *48, 84, 137*
  See also CLR *45*
Rosen, Michael J. 1954- *199*
  Earlier sketch in SATA *86*
Rosen, Michael Wayne
  See Rosen, Michael
Rosen, Sidney 1916- *1*
Rosen, Winifred 1943- *8*
Rosenbaum, Maurice 1907-1987 .... *6*
Rosenberg, Amye 1950- *74*
Rosenberg, Dorothy 1906- *40*
Rosenberg, Eth Clifford 1915- *92*
  See also SAAS *22*
Rosenberg, Jane 1949- *58*
Rosenberg, Liz 1958- *129*
  Earlier sketch in SATA *75*
Rosenberg, Maxine B(erta) 1939- *93*
  Brief entry *47*
  Earlier sketch in SATA *55*
Rosenberg, Nancy (Sherman) 1931- *4*
Rosenberg, Sharon 1942- *8*
Rosenberry, Vera 1948- *144*
  Earlier sketch in SATA *83*
Rosenblatt, Arthur
  See Rosenblatt, Arthur S.
Rosenblatt, Arthur S. 1938- *68*
  Brief entry *45*
Rosenblatt, Lily 1956- *90*
Rosenbloom, Joseph 1928- *21*
Rosenblum, Richard 1928- *11*
Rosenburg, John M. 1918- *6*
Rosenfeld, Dina 1962- *99*
Rosenstiehl, Agnes 1941- *203*
Rosenthal, Amy Krouse 1965- *177*
Rosenthal, Betsy R. 1957- *178*
Rosenthal, Harold 1914-1999 .... *35*
Rosenthal, M(acha) L(ouis) 1917-1996 .... *59*
Rosenthal, Marc 1949- *193*
Rosenthal, Mark A(lan) 1946- *64*
Rosing, Norbert 1953- *196*
Rosman, Steven M 1956- *81*
Rosman, Steven Michael
  See Rosman, Steven M
Rosoff, Meg 1956- *209*
  Earlier sketch in SATA *160*
Ross, Alan
  See Warwick, Alan R(oss)
Ross, Christine 1950- *172*
  Earlier sketch in SATA *83*
Ross, Clare
  See Romano, Clare
Ross, Dana Fuller
  See Cockrell, Amanda
  and Gerson, Noel Bertram
Ross, Dave
  See Ross, David
Ross, David 1896-1975 .... *49*
  Obituary *20*
Ross, David 1949- *133*
  Earlier sketch in SATA *32*
Ross, Deborah J.
  See Wheeler, Deborah
Ross, Diana
  See Denney, Diana
Ross, Edward S(hearman) 1915- *85*
Ross, Eileen 1950- *115*
Ross, Frank (Xavier), Jr. 1914- *28*
Ross, Jane 1961- *79*
Ross, John 1921- *45*
Ross, Judy 1942- *54*
Ross, Katharine Reynolds
  See Ross, Kathy
Ross, Kathy 1948- *169*
  Earlier sketch in SATA *89*
Ross, Kent 1956- *91*
Ross, Lillian Hammer 1925- *72*
Ross, Michael Elsohn 1952- *170*
  Earlier sketches in SATA *80, 127*

Ross, Pat(ricia Kienzle) 1943- *53*
  Brief entry *48*
Ross, Ramon R(oyal) 1930- *62*
Ross, Stewart 1947- *134*
  Earlier sketch in SATA *92*
  See also SAAS *23*
Ross, Tom 1958- *84*
Ross, Tony 1938- *176*
  Earlier sketches in SATA *17, 65, 130*
Ross, Wilda 1915- *51*
  Brief entry *39*
Rossel, Seymour 1945- *28*
Rossell, Judith 1953- *187*
Rossel-Waugh, C. C.
  See Waugh, Carol-Lynn Rossel
Rossetti, Christina 1830-1894 .... *20*
  See also CLR *115*
Rossetti, Christina Georgina
  See Rossetti, Christina
Rossi, Joyce 1943- *116*
Rossotti, Hazel Swaine 1930- *95*
Rostkowski, Margaret I. 1945- *59*
Roth, Arnold 1929- *21*
Roth, Arthur J(oseph) 1925-1993 .... *43*
  Brief entry *28*
  Obituary *75*
  See also SAAS *11*
Roth, David 1940- *36*
Roth, Julie Jersild *180*
Roth, Matthue 1978(?)- *174*
Roth, Roger *190*
Roth, Stephanie *202*
Roth, Susan L. *181*
  Earlier sketch in SATA *134*
Rothberg, Abraham 1922- *59*
Roth-Hano, Renee 1931- *85*
Rothkopf, Carol Z. 1929- *4*
Rothman, Joel 1938- *7*
Rotner, Shelley 1951- *169*
  Earlier sketch in SATA *76*
Rottman, S.L. 1970- *157*
  Earlier sketch in SATA *106*
Rottman, Susan Lynn
  See Rottman, S.L.
Roueche, Berton 1911-1994 .... *28*
Roughsey, Dick 1921(?)-1985 .... *35*
  See also CLR *41*
Roughsey, Goobalathaldin
  See Roughsey, Dick
Rounds, Glen (Harold) 1906-2002 .... *112*
  Obituary *141*
  Earlier sketches in SATA *8, 70*
Rourke, Constance Mayfield 1885-1941
  See YABC *1*
Rovetch, Gerda 1925(?)- *202*
Rovetch, L. Bob
  See Rovetch, Lissa
Rovetch, Lissa *201*
Rowan, Deirdre
  See Williams, Jeanne
Rowe, Jennifer
  See Rodda, Emily
Rowe, John A. 1949- *198*
  Earlier sketch in SATA *146*
Rowe, Viola Carson 1903-1969
  Obituary *26*
Rowh, Mark 1952- *90*
Rowland, Florence Wightman 1900-1997 .... *8*
  Obituary *108*
Rowland-Entwistle, (Arthur) Theodore (Henry)
  1925- *94*
  Earlier sketch in SATA *31*
Rowling, J. K. 1965- *174*
  Earlier sketch in SATA *109*
  See also CLR *112*
Rowling, Joanne Kathleen
  See Rowling, J. K.
Rowsome, Frank (Howard), Jr. 1914-1983 .. *36*
Roy, Gabrielle 1909-1983 .... *104*
Roy, Jacqueline 1954- *74*

Roy, Jennifer
  See Roy, Jennifer Rozines
Roy, Jennifer Rozines 1967- *178*
Roy, Jessie Hailstalk 1895-1986
  Obituary *51*
Roy, Liam
  See Scarry, Patricia (Murphy)
Roy, Ron(ald) 1940- *110*
  Brief entry *35*
  Earlier sketch in SATA *40*
Roybal, Laura 1956- *85*
Roybal, Laura Husby
  See Roybal, Laura
Royds, Caroline 1953- *55*
Royston, Angela 1945- *169*
  Earlier sketch in SATA *120*
Rozakis, Laurie E. 1952- *84*
Rozen, Anna 1960- *206*
Rubel, Nicole 1953- *181*
  Earlier sketches in SATA *18, 95, 135*
Rubin, Eva Johanna 1925- *38*
Rubin, Susan Goldman 1939- *182*
  Earlier sketches in SATA *84, 132*
Rubin, Vicky 1964- *193*
Rubinetti, Donald 1947- *92*
Rubinstein, Gillian 1942- *158*
  Autobiography Feature *116*
  Earlier sketches in SATA *68, 105*
  See also CLR *35*
  See also SAAS *25*
Rubinstein, Gillian Margaret
  See Rubinstein, Gillian
Rubinstein, Patricia -2003
  See Forest, Antonia
Rubinstein, Patricia Giulia Caulfield Kate
  See Forest, Antonia
Rubinstein, Robert E(dward) 1943- *49*
Rublowsky, John M(artin) 1928- *62*
Rubright, Lynn 1936- *171*
Ruby, Laura *181*
  Earlier sketch in SATA *155*
Ruby, Lois 1942- *184*
  Autobiography Feature *105*
  Brief entry *34*
  Earlier sketches in SATA *35, 95*
Ruby, Lois F.
  See Ruby, Lois
Ruchlis, Hy(man) 1913-1992 .... *3*
  Obituary *72*
Rucker, Mike 1940- *91*
Ruckman, Ivy 1931- *93*
  Earlier sketch in SATA *37*
Ruck-Pauquet, Gina 1931- *40*
  Brief entry *37*
Ruditis, Paul *190*
Rudley, Stephen 1946- *30*
Rudolph, Marguerita 1908- *21*
Rudomin, Esther
  See Hautzig, Esther Rudomin
Rue, Leonard Lee III 1926- *142*
  Earlier sketch in SATA *37*
Rueda, Claudia *183*
Ruedi, Norma Paul
  See Ainsworth, Norma
Ruelle, Karen Gray 1957- *209*
  Earlier sketches in SATA *84, 126*
Ruemmler, John D(avid) 1948- *78*
Ruepp, Krista 1947- *143*
Ruffell, Ann 1941- *30*
Ruffins, Reynold 1930- *125*
  Earlier sketch in SATA *41*
Rugg, Jim *206*
Rugoff, Milton 1913- *30*
Ruhen, Olaf 1911-1989 .... *17*
Rukeyser, Muriel 1913-1980
  Obituary *22*
Rumbaut, Hendle 1949- *84*
Rumford, James 1948- *193*
  Earlier sketch in SATA *116*
Rumsey, Marian (Barritt) 1928- *16*

Rumstuckle, Cornelius
  See Brennan, Herbie
Runnerstroem, Bengt Arne 1944- 75
Runyan, John
  See Palmer, Bernard (Alvin)
Runyon, Catherine 1947- 62
Ruoff, A. LaVonne Brown 1930- 76
Rupp, Rebecca 185
Rusch, Elizabeth 1966- 198
Rusch, Kris
  See Rusch, Kristine Kathryn
Rusch, Kristine Kathryn 1960- 113
Rush, Alison 1951- 41
Rush, Peter 1937- 32
Rushdie, Ahmed Salman
  See Rushdie, Salman
Rushdie, Salman 1947-
  See CLR 125
Rushford, Patricia H(elen) 1943- 134
Rushmore, Helen 1898-1994 3
Rushmore, Robert (William) 1926-1986 8
  Obituary 49
Ruskin, Ariane
  See Batterberry, Ariane Ruskin
Ruskin, John 1819-1900 24
Russ, Lavinia (Faxon) 1904-1992 74
Russell, Charlotte
  See Rathjen, Carl Henry
Russell, Ching Yeung 1946- 107
Russell, Don(ald Bert) 1899-1986
  Obituary 47
Russell, Franklin (Alexander) 1926- 11
Russell, Gertrude Barrer
  See Barrer-Russell, Gertrude
Russell, Helen Ross 1915- 8
Russell, James 1933- 53
Russell, Jim
  See Russell, James
Russell, Joan Plummer 1930- 139
Russell, P(hilip) Craig 1951- 162
  Earlier sketch in SATA 80
Russell, Patrick
  See Sammis, John
Russell, Paul (Gary) 1942- 57
Russell, Sarah
  See Laski, Marghanita
Russell, Sharman Apt 1954- 123
Russell, Solveig Paulson 1904-1985 3
Russo, Marisabina 1950- 188
  Earlier sketches in SATA 106, 151
Russo, Monica J. 1950- 83
Russo, Susan 1947- 30
Russon, Penni 1974- 179
Rutgers van der Loeff, An
  See Rutgers van der Loeff-Basenau, An(na)
    Maria Margaretha
Rutgers van der Loeff-Basenau, An(na) Maria
  Margaretha 1910- 22
Ruth, Rod 1912-1987 9
Rutherford, Douglas
  See McConnell, James Douglas Rutherford
Rutherford, Meg 1932- 34
Ruthin, Margaret
  See Catherall, Arthur
Rutledge, Jill Zimmerman 1951- 155
Rutz, Viola Larkin 1932- 12
Ruurs, Margriet 1952- 147
  Earlier sketch in SATA 97
Ruzicka, Rudolph 1883-1978
  Obituary 24
Ruzzier, Sergio 1966- 159
, Ryan
  See Ryan, John
Ryan, Betsy
  See Ryan, Elizabeth (Anne)
Ryan, Cheli Duran 20
Ryan, Darlene 1958- 176
Ryan, Elizabeth (Anne) 1943- 30
Ryan, Jeanette
  See Mines, Jeanette
Ryan, John 1921-2009 22

Ryan, Margaret 1950- 166
  Earlier sketch in SATA 78
Ryan, Mary E. 1953- 61
Ryan, Mary Elizabeth
  See Ryan, Mary E.
Ryan, Pam Munoz 1951- 197
  Earlier sketch in SATA 134
Ryan, Patrick 1957- 138
Ryan, Peter (Charles) 1939- 15
Ryan-Lush, Geraldine 1949- 89
Rybakov, Anatoli (Naumovich) 1911-1998 .. 79
  Obituary 108
Rybakov, Anatolii (Naumovich)
  See Rybakov, Anatoli (Naumovich)
Rybolt, Thomas R. 1954- 62
Rybolt, Thomas Roy
  See Rybolt, Thomas R.
Rybolt, Tom
  See Rybolt, Thomas R.
Rydberg, Ernest E(mil) 1901-1993 21
Rydberg, Lou(isa Hampton) 1908- 27
Rydell, Katy 1942- 91
Rydell, Wendell
  See Rydell, Wendy
Rydell, Wendy 4
Ryden, Hope 91
  Earlier sketch in SATA 8
Ryder, Joanne (Rose) 1946- 163
  Brief entry 34
  Earlier sketches in SATA 65, 122
  See also CLR 37
Ryder, Pamela
  See Lamb, Nancy
Rye, Anthony
  See Youd, Samuel
Rylant, Cynthia 1954- 195
  Brief entry 44
  Earlier sketches in SATA 50, 76, 112, 160
  See also CLR 86
  See also SAAS 13
Rymer, Alta May 1925- 34
Rymond, Lynda Gene 199

S

S. L. C.
  See Twain, Mark
S., Svend Otto
  See Soerensen, Svend Otto
Saaf, Donald W(illiam) 1961- 124
Saal, Jocelyn
  See Sachs, Judith
Sabbeth, Carol (Landstrom) 1957- 125
Saberhagen, Fred 1930-2007 89
  Obituary 184
  Earlier sketch in SATA 37
Saberhagen, Fred T.
  See Saberhagen, Fred
Saberhagen, Fred Thomas
  See Saberhagen, Fred
Saberhagen, Frederick Thomas
  See Saberhagen, Fred
Sabin, Edwin L(egrand) 1870-1952
  See YABC 2
Sabin, Francene 27
Sabin, Lou
  See Sabin, Louis
Sabin, Louis 1930- 27
Sabre, Dirk
  See Laffin, John (Alfred Charles)
Sabuda, Robert (James) 1965- 120
  Earlier sketch in SATA 81
Sabuda, Robert 1965- 170
Sabuda, Robert James
  See Sabuda, Robert
Sachar, Louis 1954- 154
  Brief entry 50
  Earlier sketches in SATA 63, 104
  See also CLR 79

Sachs, Elizabeth-Ann 1946- 48
Sachs, Judith 1947- 52
  Brief entry 51
Sachs, Marilyn 1927- 164
  Autobiography Feature 110
  Earlier sketches in SATA 3, 68
  See also CLR 2
  See also SAAS 2
Sachs, Marilyn Stickle
  See Sachs, Marilyn
Sackett, S(amuel) J(ohn) 1928- 12
Sackson, Sid 1920- 16
Sacre, Antonio 1968- 152
Saddler, Allen
  See Richards, R(onald) C(harles) W(illiam)
Saddler, K. Allen
  See Richards, R(onald) C(harles) W(illiam)
Sadie, Stanley 1930-2005 14
Sadie, Stanley John
  See Sadie, Stanley
Sadiq, Nazneen 1944- 101
Sadler, Catherine Edwards 1952- 60
  Brief entry 45
Sadler, Marilyn (June) 1950- 79
Sadler, Mark
  See Lynds, Dennis
Saffer, Barbara 144
Sagan, Carl 1934-1996 58
  Obituary 94
Sagan, Carl Edward
  See Sagan, Carl
Sage, Angie 1952- 197
Sage, Juniper
  See Brown, Margaret Wise
  and Hurd, Edith Thacher
Sagsoorian, Paul 1923- 12
Said, S.F. 1967- 174
Saidman, Anne 1952- 75
Saint, Dora Jessie 1913- 10
St. Anthony, Jane 175
St. Antoine, Sara L. 1966- 84
St. Clair, Byrd Hooper 1905-1976
  Obituary 28
Saint-Exupery, Antoine de 1900-1944 20
  See also CLR 142
Saint-Exupery, Antoine Jean Baptiste Marie
  Roger de
  See Saint-Exupery, Antoine de
St. George, Judith 1931- 161
  Earlier sketches in SATA 13, 99
  See also CLR 57
  See also SAAS 12
St. George, Judith Alexander
  See St. George, Judith
St. James, Blakely
  See Gottfried, Theodore Mark
  and Platt, Charles
St. James, Blakely
  See Griffin, W.E.B.
St. James, Sierra
  See Rallison, Janette
Saint James, Synthia 1949- 152
  Earlier sketch in SATA 84
St. John, Nicole 143
  Autobiography Feature 143
  Earlier sketches in SATA 29, 89
  See also CLR 46
  See also SAAS 7
St. John, Patricia Mary 1919-1993
  Obituary 79
St. John, Philip
  See del Rey, Lester
St. John, Wylly Folk 1908-1985 10
  Obituary 45
St. Max, E. S.
  See Ellis, Edward S.
St. Meyer, Ned
  See Stratemeyer, Edward L.
St. Mox, E. A.
  See Ellis, Edward S.

St. Myer, Ned
    See Stratemeyer, Edward L.
St. Tamara
    See Kolba, St. Tamara
Saito, Michiko
    See Fujiwara, Michiko
Sakaki, Ichiro 1969- 192
Sakamoto, Miki 198
Sakers, Don 1958- 72
Sakharnov, S.
    See Sakharnov, Svyatoslav
Sakharnov, Svyatoslav 1923- 65
Sakharnov, Svyatoslav Vladimirovich
    See Sakharnov, Svyatoslav
Saksena, Kate 148
Sakurai, Gail 1952- 153
    Earlier sketch in SATA 87
Salamanca, Lucy
    See del Barco, Lucy Salamanca
Salassi, Otto R(ussell) 1939-1993 38
    Obituary 77
Salat, Cristina 82
Saldana, Rene, Jr. 186
Saldutti, Denise 1953- 39
Sale, Tim 1956- 153
Salem, Kay 1952- 92
Salerno, Steven 176
Salinger, J.D. 1919-2010 67
    See also CLR 18
Salinger, Jerome David
    See Salinger, J.D.
Salisbury, Graham 1944- 195
    Earlier sketches in SATA 76, 108, 161
Salisbury, Joyce E(llen) 1944- 138
Salkey, (Felix) Andrew (Alexander)
    1928-1995 118
    Earlier sketch in SATA 35
Salley, Coleen 166
Sallis, Susan (Diana) 1929- 55
Salmieri, Daniel 1983- 208
Salmon, Annie Elizabeth 1899- 13
Salonen, Roxane Beauclair 1968- 184
Salsi, Lynn 1947- 130
Salsitz, R. A. V.
    See Salsitz, Rhondi Vilott
Salsitz, Rhondi Vilott 115
Salten, Felix
    See Salzmann, Siegmund
Salter, Cedric
    See Knight, Francis Edgar
Saltman, Judith 1947- 64
Saltzberg, Barney 1955- 194
    Earlier sketch in SATA 135
Saltzman, David (Charles Laertes)
    1967-1990 86
Salvadori, Mario (George) 1907-1997 97
    Earlier sketch in SATA 40
Salwood, F.K.
    See Kilworth, Garry
Salzer, L. E.
    See Wilson, Lionel
Salzman, Marian 1959- 77
Salzmann, Siegmund 1869-1945 25
Samachson, Dorothy (Mirkin) 1914-1997 3
Samachson, Joseph 1906-1980 3
    Obituary 52
Sammis, John 1942- 4
Sampson, Emma (Keats) Speed 1868-1947 . 68
Sampson, Fay (Elizabeth) 1935- 151
    Brief entry 40
    Earlier sketch in SATA 42
Sampson, Michael 1952- 143
    Earlier sketch in SATA 95
Samson, Anne S(tringer) 1933- 2
Samson, Joan 1937-1976 13
Samson, Suzanne M. 1959- 91
Samuels, Barbara 199
Samuels, Charles 1902-1982 12
Samuels, Cynthia K(alish) 1946- 79
Samuels, Gertrude 1910(?)-2003 17
    Obituary 147

Sanborn, Duane 1914-1996 38
Sancha, Sheila 1924- 38
Sanchez, Alex 1957- 151
Sanchez, Anita 1956- 209
Sanchez, Sonia 1934- 136
    Earlier sketch in SATA 22
    See also CLR 18
Sanchez-Silva, Jose Maria 1911- 132
    Earlier sketch in SATA 16
    See also CLR 12
Sand, George X. 45
Sandak, Cass R(obert) 1950-2001 51
    Brief entry 37
Sandberg, (Karin) Inger 1930- 15
Sandberg, Karl C. 1931- 35
Sandberg, Lasse (E. M.) 1924- 15
Sandburg, Carl 1878-1967 8
    See also CLR 67
Sandburg, Carl August
    See Sandburg, Carl
Sandburg, Charles
    See Sandburg, Carl
Sandburg, Charles A.
    See Sandburg, Carl
Sandburg, Helga 1918- 3
    See also SAAS 10
Sandell, Lisa Ann 1977- 175
Sander, Heather L. 1947- 157
Sanderlin, George 1915- 4
Sanderlin, Owenita (Harrah) 1916- 11
Sanders, Betty Jane
    See Monthei, Betty
Sanders, Nancy I. 1960- 141
    Earlier sketch in SATA 90
Sanders, Scott Russell 1945- 109
    Earlier sketch in SATA 56
Sanders, Winston P.
    See Anderson, Poul
Sanderson, Irma 1912- 66
Sanderson, Ivan T(erence) 1911-1973 6
Sanderson, Margaret Love
    See Keats, Emma
    and Sampson, Emma (Keats) Speed
Sanderson, Ruth 1951- 172
    Earlier sketches in SATA 41, 109
Sanderson, Ruth L.
    See Sanderson, Ruth
Sandin, Joan 1942- 197
    Earlier sketches in SATA 12, 94, 153
Sandison, Janet
    See Cameron, Elizabeth Jane
Sandler, Martin W. 160
Sandom, J. Gregory
    See Welsh, T.K.
Sandom, J.G.
    See Welsh, T.K.
Sandoz, Mari(e Susette) 1900-1966 5
Sanford, Agnes (White) 1897-1976 61
Sanford, Doris 1937- 69
Sanford, Rose
    See Simmonds, Posy
Sanger, Amy Wilson 1967- 205
Sanger, Marjory Bartlett 1920- 8
San Jose, Christine 1929- 167
Sankey, Alice (Ann-Susan) 1910- 27
San Souci, Daniel 192
    Earlier sketch in SATA 96
San Souci, Robert D. 1946- 158
    Earlier sketches in SATA 40, 81, 117
    See also CLR 43
Santamaria, Benjamin 1955- 184
Santat, Dan 188
Santesson, Hans Stefan 1914(?)-1975
    Obituary 30
Santiago, Esmeralda 1948- 129
Santore, Charles 1935- 200
Santos, Helen
    See Griffiths, Helen
Santrey, Louis
    See Sabin, Louis
Santucci, Barbara 1948- 130

Sapergia, Barbara 1943- 181
Sapieyevski, Anne Lindbergh 1940-1993 81
    Brief entry 32
    Earlier sketches in SATA 35, 78
Saport, Linda 1954- 123
Sapp, Allen 1929- 151
Sarac, Roger
    See Caras, Roger A(ndrew)
Sarah, Duchess of York
    See Ferguson, Sarah
Sarasin, Jennifer
    See Sachs, Judith
Sardinha, Rick 192
Sarg, Anthony Frederick
    See Sarg, Tony
Sarg, Tony 1882-1942
    See YABC 1
Sargent, Pamela 1948- 78
    Earlier sketch in SATA 29
Sargent, Robert 1933- 2
Sargent, Sarah 1937- 44
    Brief entry 41
Sargent, Shirley 1927-2004 11
Sarnoff, Jane 1937- 10
Saroff, Phyllis V. 202
Saroyan, William 1908-1981 23
    Obituary 24
Sarton, Eleanor May
    See Sarton, May
Sarton, May 1912-1995 36
    Obituary 86
Sasaki, Chris 182
Sasaki, Ellen Joy 206
Saseen, Sharon (Dillon) 1949- 59
Sasek, Miroslav 1916-1980 16
    Obituary 23
    See also CLR 4
Sasso, Sandy Eisenberg 1947- 162
    Earlier sketches in SATA 86, 116
Sathre, Vivian 1952- 133
    Earlier sketch in SATA 79
Satterfield, Charles
    See del Rey, Lester
    and Pohl, Frederik
Sattgast, L. J.
    See Sattgast, Linda J.
Sattgast, Linda J. 1953- 91
Sattler, Helen Roney 1921-1992 74
    Earlier sketch in SATA 4
    See also CLR 24
Sauer, Julia Lina 1891-1983 32
    Obituary 36
Sauerwein, Leigh 1944- 155
Saul, Carol P. 1947- 117
    Earlier sketch in SATA 78
Saul, John III
    See Saul, John
Saul, John 1942- 98
Saul, John W.
    See Saul, John
Saul, John W. III
    See Saul, John
Saul, John Woodruff III
    See Saul, John
Saul, (Ellen) Wendy 1946- 42
Saulnier, Karen Luczak 1940- 80
Saunders, Caleb
    See Heinlein, Robert A.
Saunders, Dave 1939- 85
Saunders, Julie 1939- 85
Saunders, (William) Keith 1910-1994 12
Saunders, Rubie (Agnes) 1929- 21
Saunders, Steven
    See Jones, Allan Frewin
Saunders, Susan 1945- 96
    Brief entry 41
    Earlier sketch in SATA 46
Saunders-Smith, Gail 1952- 169
Sauvain, Philip Arthur 1933- 111
Savadier, Elivia 1950- 164
    Earlier sketch in SATA 79

Savage, Alan
    See Nicole, Christopher (Robin)
Savage, Blake
    See Goodwin, Harold L(eland)
Savage, Candace 1949- 142
Savage, Deborah 1955- 76
Savage, Jeff 1961- 97
Savage, Katharine James 1905-1989
    Obituary 61
Savage, Stephen 1965- 194
Savage, Thomas 1915-2003
    Obituary 147
Savageau, Cheryl 1950- 96
Savery, Constance (Winifred) 1897-1999 1
Saville, Andrew
    See Taylor, Andrew
Saville, (Leonard) Malcolm 1901-1982 23
    Obituary 31
Saviozzi, Adriana
    See Mazza, Adriana
Savitt, Sam 1917-2000 8
    Obituary 126
Savitz, Harriet May 1933- 72
    Earlier sketch in SATA 5
    See also SAAS 26
Sawicki, Mary 1950- 90
Sawyer, (Frederick) Don(ald) 1947- 72
Sawyer, Kem Knapp 1953- 84
Sawyer, Robert J. 1960- 149
    Earlier sketch in SATA 81
Sawyer, Robert James
    See Sawyer, Robert J.
Sawyer, Ruth 1880-1970 17
    See also CLR 36
Saxby, H.M.
    See Saxby, (Henry) Maurice
Saxby, (Henry) Maurice 1924- 71
Saxon, Andrew
    See Arthur, Robert, (Jr.)
Saxon, Antonia
    See Sachs, Judith
Say, Allen 1937- 161
    Earlier sketches in SATA 28, 69, 110
    See also CLR 135
Sayers, Frances Clarke 1897-1989 3
    Obituary 62
Sayles, Elizabeth 1956- 163
    Earlier sketch in SATA 108
Saylor-Marchant, Linda 1963- 82
Sayre, April Pulley 1966- 191
    Earlier sketches in SATA 88, 131
Sazer, Nina 1949- 13
Scabrini, Janet 1953- 13
Scagell, Robin 1946- 107
Scagnetti, Jack 1924- 7
Scamander, Newt
    See Rowling, J. K.
Scamell, Ragnhild 1940- 180
    Earlier sketch in SATA 77
Scanlon, Marion Stephany 11
Scannel, John Vernon
    See Scannell, Vernon
Scannell, Vernon 1922-2007 59
    Obituary 188
Scarborough, Elizabeth
    See Scarborough, Elizabeth Ann
Scarborough, Elizabeth Ann 1947- 171
    Earlier sketch in SATA 98
Scarf, Maggi
    See Scarf, Maggie
Scarf, Maggie 1932- 5
Scariano, Margaret M. 1924- 86
Scarlett, Susan
    See Streatfeild, Noel
Scarry, Huck
    See Scarry, Richard McClure, Jr.
Scarry, Patricia (Murphy) 1924- 2
Scarry, Patsy
    See Scarry, Patricia (Murphy)

Scarry, Richard (McClure) 1919-1994 75
    Obituary 90
    Earlier sketches in SATA 2, 35
    See also CLR 41
Scarry, Richard McClure, Jr. 1953- 35
Schachner, Judith Byron 1951- 178
    Earlier sketch in SATA 88
Schachner, Judy
    See Schachner, Judith Byron
Schachtel, Roger 1949- 38
Schachtel, Roger Bernard
    See Schachtel, Roger
Schade, Susan 189
Schaedler, Sally 116
Schaefer, Carole Lexa 173
Schaefer, Jack (Warner) 1907-1991 66
    Obituary 65
    Earlier sketch in SATA 3
Schaefer, Lola M. 1950- 183
    Earlier sketches in SATA 91, 144
Schaeffer, Mead 1898- 21
Schaeffer, Susan Fromberg 1941- 22
Schaer, Brigitte 1958- 112
Schaller, George
    See Schaller, George B.
Schaller, George B. 1933- 30
Schaller, George Beals
    See Schaller, George B.
Schanzer, Rosalyn (Good) 1942- 138
    Earlier sketch in SATA 77
Schatell, Brian 66
    Brief entry 47
Schechter, Betty (Goodstein) 1921- 5
Schechter, Simone
    See Elkeles, Simone
Schecter, Ellen 1944- 85
Scheeder, Louis 1946- 141
Scheer, Julian (Weisel) 1926-2001 8
Scheffer, Victor B(lanchard) 1906- 6
Scheffler, Axel 1957- 180
Scheffler, Ursel 1938- 81
Scheffrin-Falk, Gladys 1928- 76
Scheidl, Gerda Marie 1913- 85
Scheier, Michael 1943- 40
    Brief entry 36
Schell, Mildred 1922- 41
Schell, Orville (Hickok) 1940- 10
Scheller, Melanie 1953- 77
Schellie, Don 1932- 29
Schembri, Jim 1962- 124
Schembri, Pamela 1969- 195
Schemm, Mildred Walker 1905-1998 21
    Obituary 103
Schenker, Dona 1947- 133
    Earlier sketch in SATA 68
Scher, Paula 1948- 47
Scherer, Jeffrey 194
Scherf, Margaret 1908-1979 10
Schermer, Judith (Denise) 1941- 30
Schertle, Alice 1941- 192
    Earlier sketches in SATA 36, 90, 145
Schick, Alice 1946- 27
Schick, Eleanor 1942- 144
    Earlier sketches in SATA 9, 82
Schick, Joel 1945- 31
    Brief entry 30
Schields, Gretchen 1948- 75
Schiff, Ken(neth Roy) 1942- 7
Schiller, Andrew 1919- 21
Schiller, Barbara (Heyman) 1928- 21
Schiller, Pamela (Byrne) 127
Schindel, John 1955- 115
    Earlier sketch in SATA 77
Schindelman, Joseph 1923- 67
    Brief entry 32
Schindler, S.D. 1952- 198
    Brief entry 50
    Earlier sketches in SATA 75, 118, 171
Schindler, Steven V.
    See Schindler, S.D.
Schinto, Jeanne 1951- 93

Schisgall, Oscar 1901-1984 12
    Obituary 38
Schlaepfer, Gloria G. 1931- 154
Schlee, Ann 1934- 44
    Brief entry 36
Schleichert, Elizabeth 1945- 77
Schlein, Miriam 1926-2004 130
    Obituary 159
    Earlier sketches in SATA 2, 87
    See also CLR 41
Schlesinger, Arthur M., Jr. 1917-2007 61
    Obituary 181
    See Schlesinger, Arthur Meier
Schlesinger, Arthur Meier 1888-1965
Schlessinger, Laura (Catherine) 1947- 160
    Earlier sketch in SATA 110
Schlitz, Laura Amy 184
Schloat, G. Warren, Jr. 1914-2000 4
Schmatz, Pat 197
Schmid, Eleonore 1939- 126
    Earlier sketches in SATA 12, 84
Schmid, Susan Maupin 208
Schmiderer, Dorothy 1940- 19
Schmidt, Annie M. G. 1911-1995 67
    Obituary 91
    See also CLR 22
Schmidt, C.A. 196
Schmidt, Diane 1953- 70
Schmidt, Elizabeth 1915- 15
Schmidt, Gary D. 1957- 193
    Earlier sketches in SATA 93, 135
Schmidt, James Norman 1912-1983 21
Schmidt, Karen Lee 1953- 185
    Earlier sketch in SATA 94
Schmidt, Lynette 1952- 76
Schmitz, Tamara 207
Schneider, Antonie 1954- 167
    Earlier sketch in SATA 89
Schneider, Christine M. 1972(?)- 171
    Earlier sketch in SATA 120
Schneider, Dick
    See Schneider, Richard H.
Schneider, Elisa
    See Kleven, Elisa
Schneider, Herman 1905-2003 7
    Obituary 148
Schneider, Howie -2007 181
Schneider, Josh 1980- 196
Schneider, Laurie
    See Adams, Laurie
Schneider, Nina 1913-2007 2
    Obituary 186
Schneider, Nina Zimet
    See Schneider, Nina
Schneider, Rex 1937- 44
Schneider, Richard H. 1922- 171
Schneider, Richard Henry
    See Schneider, Richard H.
Schneider, Robyn 1986- 187
Schnirel, James R. 1931- 14
Schnitter, Jane T. 1958- 88
Schnitzlein, Danny 134
Schnur, Steven 1952- 144
    Earlier sketch in SATA 95
Schnurre, Wolfdietrich 1920-1989
    Obituary 63
Schoberle, Cecile 1949- 80
Schock, Pauline 1928- 45
Schoell, William 1951- 160
Schoen, Barbara (Taylor) 1924-1993 13
Schoenherr, Ian 177
Schoenherr, John (Carl) 1935- 66
    Earlier sketch in SATA 37
    See also SAAS 13
Schofield, Sandy
    See Rusch, Kristine Kathryn
Scholastica, Sister Mary
    See Jenkins, Marie M(agdalen)
Scholefield, A. T.
    See Scholefield, Alan
Scholefield, Alan 1931- 66

Scholefield, Edmund O.
  See Griffin, W.E.B.
Scholey, Arthur 1932- 28
Scholz, Jackson Volney 1897-1986
  Obituary 49
Schone, Virginia 22
Schongut, Emanuel 1936- *184*
  Brief entry 36
  Earlier sketch in SATA *52*
Schoonover, Frank (Earle) 1877-1972 24
Schoor, Gene 1921- 3
Schories, Pat 1952- *164*
  Earlier sketch in SATA *116*
Schorr, Melissa 1972- *194*
Schorr, Melissa Robin
  See Schorr, Melissa
Schott, Jane A. 1946- *172*
Schotter, Roni *190*
  Earlier sketches in SATA *105, 149*
Schraff, Anne E(laine) 1939- 92
  Earlier sketch in SATA *27*
Schram, Peninnah 1934- *119*
Schrank, Joseph 1900-1984
  Obituary 38
Schrecengost, Maity 1938- *118*
Schrecengost, S. Maitland
  See Schrecengost, Maity
Schreck, Karen
  See Schreck, Karen Halvorsen
Schreck, Karen Halvorsen 1962- *185*
Schrecker, Judie 1954- 90
Schreiber, Elizabeth Anne (Ferguson)
  1947- *13*
Schreiber, Ralph W(alter) 1942- *13*
Schreiner, Samuel A(gnew), Jr. 1921- 70
Schroeder, Alan 1961- 98
  Earlier sketch in SATA *66*
Schroeder, Binette
  See Nickl, Barbara (Elisabeth)
Schroeder, Russell (K.) 1943- *146*
Schroeder, Ted 1931(?)-1973
  Obituary 20
Schubert, Dieter 1947- *101*
  Earlier sketch in SATA *62*
Schubert, Leda 1950(?)- *181*
Schubert-Gabrys, Ingrid 1953- *101*
  Earlier sketch in SATA *62*
Schuelein-Steel, Danielle
  See Steel, Danielle
Schuelein-Steel, Danielle Fernande
  See Steel, Danielle
Schuerger, Michele R. *110*
Schuett, Stacey 1960- *168*
  Earlier sketch in SATA *75*
Schulke, Flip Phelps Graeme 1930- 57
Schulman, Arlene 1961- *105*
Schulman, Janet 1933- *208*
  Earlier sketches in SATA *22, 137*
Schulman, L(ester) M(artin) 1934- *13*
Schulte, Elaine L(ouise) 1934- 36
Schultz, Betty K(epka) 1932- *125*
Schultz, Gwendolyn 21
Schultz, James Willard 1859-1947
  See YABC *1*
Schultz, Pearle Henriksen 1918- 21
Schulz, Charles M. 1922-2000 .... *10*
  Obituary *118*
Schulz, Charles Monroe
  See Schulz, Charles M.
Schumacher, Julie 1958- *191*
Schumaker, Ward 1943- 96
Schuman, Michael A. 1953- *134*
  Earlier sketch in SATA *85*
Schur, Maxine
  See Schur, Maxine Rose
Schur, Maxine Rose 1948- *135*
  Autobiography Feature *135*
  Brief entry 49
  Earlier sketches in SATA *53, 98*
Schurfranz, Vivian 1925- *13*
Schutzer, A. I. 1922- *13*

Schuyler, Pamela R. 1948- 30
Schwabach, Karen *185*
Schwager, Tina 1964- *110*
Schwandt, Stephen (William) 1947- 61
Schwark, Mary Beth 1954- 51
Schwartz, Alvin 1927-1992 56
  Obituary 71
  Earlier sketch in SATA *4*
  See also CLR *89*
Schwartz, Amy 1954- *189*
  Brief entry 41
  Earlier sketches in SATA *47, 83, 131*
  See also CLR *25*
  See also SAAS *18*
Schwartz, Anne Powers 1913-1987 10
Schwartz, Carol 1954- 77
Schwartz, Charles W(alsh) 1914- 8
Schwartz, David M. 1951- *110*
  Earlier sketch in SATA *59*
Schwartz, David Martin
  See Schwartz, David M.
Schwartz, Elizabeth Reeder 1912- 8
Schwartz, Ellen 1949- *117*
Schwartz, Jerome L.
  See Lawrence, Jerome
Schwartz, Joel L. 1940- 54
  Brief entry 51
Schwartz, Joyce R. 1950- 93
Schwartz, Julius 1907-2004 45
Schwartz, Perry 1942- 75
Schwartz, Sheila (Ruth) 1929- 27
Schwartz, Stephen (Lawrence) 1948- 19
Schwartz, Virginia Frances 1950- *184*
  Earlier sketch in SATA *131*
Schwarz, Silvia Tessa Viviane
  See Schwarz, Viviane
Schwarz, Viviane 1977- *204*
Schwarz, (Silvia Tessa) Viviane 1977- *141*
Schweitzer, Byrd Baylor
  See Baylor, Byrd
Schweitzer, Iris 59
  Brief entry 36
Schweninger, Ann 1951- *168*
  Earlier sketches in SATA *29, 98*
Schwerin, Doris H(alpern) 1922- 64
Schy, Yael *197*
Scieszka, Jon 1954- *199*
  Earlier sketches in SATA *68, 105, 160*
  See also CLR *107*
Scillian, Devin *199*
  Earlier sketch in SATA *128*
Scioscia, Mary (Hershey) 1926- 63
Sciurba, Katie 1957- *196*
Scofield, Penrod 1933- 62
  Obituary 78
Scoggin, Margaret C(lara) 1905-1968 47
  Brief entry 28
Scoltock, Jack 1942- *141*
  Earlier sketch in SATA *72*
Scoppettone, Sandra 1936- 92
  Earlier sketch in SATA *9*
Scot, Michael
  See Rohan, Michael Scott
Scot-Bernard, P.
  See Bernard, Patricia
Scotland, Jay
  See Jakes, John
Scott, Alastair
  See Allen, Kenneth S.
Scott, Ann Herbert 1926- *140*
  Autobiography Feature *140*
  Brief entry 29
  Earlier sketches in SATA *56, 94*
Scott, Bill
  See Scott, William N(eville)
Scott, Bill 1920(?)-1985
  Obituary 46
Scott, Cora Annett (Pipitone) 1931- 11
Scott, Dan
  See Barker, S. Omar

Scott, Elaine 1940- *198*
  Earlier sketches in SATA *36, 90, 164*
Scott, Elizabeth 1972- *194*
Scott, Jack Denton 1915-1995 83
  Earlier sketch in SATA *31*
  See also CLR *20*
  See also SAAS *14*
Scott, Jane (Harrington) 1931- 55
Scott, Jessica
  See De Wire, Elinor
Scott, John 1912-1976 14
Scott, John Anthony 1916- 23
Scott, John M(artin) 1913- 12
Scott, Mary
  See Mattern, Joanne
Scott, Melissa 1960- *109*
Scott, Richard
  See Rennert, Richard Scott
Scott, Roney
  See Gault, William Campbell
Scott, Sally 1909-1978 43
Scott, Sally 1948- 44
Scott, Sally Elisabeth
  See Scott, Sally
Scott, W. N.
  See Scott, William N(eville)
Scott, Sir Walter 1771-1832
  See YABC *2*
Scott, Warwick
  See Trevor, Elleston
Scott, William N(eville) 1923- 87
Scotti, Anna
  See Coates, Anna
Scotton, Rob 1960- *177*
Scribner, Charles, Jr. 1921-1995 .... *13*
  Obituary 87
Scribner, Joanne L. 1949- 33
Scribner, Kimball 1917- 63
Scrimger, Richard 1957- *164*
  Earlier sketch in SATA *119*
Scrimsher, Lila Gravatt 1897-1974
  Obituary 28
Scroder, Walter K. 1928- 82
Scroggs, Kirk *187*
Scruggs, Sandy 1961- 89
Scudder, Brooke 1959- *154*
Scudder, Mildred Lee 1908- 6
  See also SAAS *12*
Scull, Marie-Louise 1943-1993 77
Scuro, Vincent 1951- 21
Seabrooke, Brenda 1941- *148*
  Earlier sketches in SATA *30, 88*
Seaman, Augusta Huiell 1879-1950 31
Seamands, Ruth 1916- 9
Searcy, Margaret Zehmer 1926- 54
  Brief entry 39
Searight, Mary W(illiams) 1918- 17
Searle, Kathryn Adrienne 1942- 10
Searle, Ronald (William Fordham) 1920- 70
  Earlier sketch in SATA *42*
Sears, Stephen W. 1932- 4
Seaskull, Cecil
  See Castellucci, Cecil
Sebastian, Lee
  See Silverberg, Robert
Sebestyen, Igen
  See Sebestyen, Ouida
Sebestyen, Ouida 1924- *140*
  Earlier sketch in SATA *39*
  See also CLR *17*
  See also SAAS *10*
Sebrey, Mary Ann 1951- 62
Sechrist, Elizabeth Hough 1903-1991 2
Sedges, John
  See Buck, Pearl S.
Sedgwick, Marcus 1968- *197*
  Earlier sketch in SATA *160*
Seed, Cecile Eugenie 1930- 86
  Earlier sketch in SATA *8*
  See also CLR *76*

Seed, Jenny
  See Seed, Cecile Eugenie
Seed, Sheila Turner 1937(?)-1979
  Obituary 23
Seeger, Elizabeth 1889-1973
  Obituary 20
Seeger, Laura Vaccaro 200
  Earlier sketch in SATA 172
Seeger, Pete 1919- 139
  Earlier sketch in SATA 13
Seeger, Peter R.
  See Seeger, Pete
Seeley, Laura L. 1958- 71
Seever, R.
  See Reeves, Lawrence F.
Sefozo, Mary 1925- 82
Sefton, Catherine
  See Waddell, Martin
Segal, John 178
Segal, Joyce 1940- 35
Segal, Lore 1928- 163
  Earlier sketches in SATA 4, 66
  See also SAAS 11
Segal, Lore Groszmann
  See Segal, Lore
Segar, E(lzie) C(risler) 1894-1938 61
Segovia, Andres 1893(?)-1987
  Obituary 52
Seguin, Marilyn W(eymouth) 1951- 91
Seguin-Fontes, Marthe 1924- 109
Seibold, J. Otto 1960- 196
  Earlier sketches in SATA 83, 149
  See also SAAS 22
Seidel, Ross 95
Seidelman, James Edward 1926- 6
Seiden, Art(hur) 107
  Brief entry 42
Seidensticker, John 1944- 200
Seidler, Ann (G.) 1925- 131
Seidler, Tor 1952- 149
  Brief entry 46
  Earlier sketches in SATA 52, 98
Seidman, Karla
  See Kuskin, Karla
Seidman, Laurence Ivan 1925- 15
Seigel, Kalman 1917-1998 12
  Obituary 103
Seignobosc, Francoise 1897-1961 21
Seinfeld, Jerry 1954- 146
Seitz, Jacqueline 1931- 50
Seixas, Judith S. 1922- 17
Sejima, Yoshimasa 1913- 8
Selberg, Ingrid (Maria) 1950- 68
Selden, George
  See Thompson, George Selden
Selden, Neil R(oy) 1931- 61
Self, Margaret Cabell 1902-1996 24
Selfors, Suzanne 1963- 193
Selick, Henry 1952- 183
Selig, Sylvie 1942- 13
Selkirk, Jane
  See Chapman, John Stanton Higham
Sellers, Naomi
  See Flack, Naomi John White
Selman, LaRue W. 1927- 55
Selsam, Millicent E(llis) 1912-1996 29
  Obituary 92
  Earlier sketch in SATA 1
  See also CLR 1
Seltzer, Meyer 1932- 17
Seltzer, Richard 1946- 41
Seltzer, Richard Warren, Jr.
  See Seltzer, Richard
Selvadurai, Shyam 1965(?)- 171
Selway, Martina 1940- 169
  Earlier sketch in SATA 74
Selzer, Adam 1980- 192
Selznick, Brian 1966- 171
  Earlier sketches in SATA 79, 117
Semel, Nava 1954- 107

Semloh
  See Holmes, Peggy
Sendak, Jack 1924(?)-1995 28
Sendak, Maurice 1928- 165
  Earlier sketches in SATA 1, 27, 113
  See also CLR 131
Sendak, Maurice Bernard
  See Sendak, Maurice
Sender, Ruth M(insky) 1926- 62
Sengler, Johanna 1924- 18
Senisi, Ellen B. 1951- 116
Senisi, Ellen Babinec
  See Senisi, Ellen B.
Senn, J(oyce) A(nn) 1941- 115
Senn, Steve 1950- 60
  Brief entry 48
Sensel, Joni 1962- 204
Serafini, Frank 201
Serage, Nancy 1924- 10
Seredy, Kate 1899-1975 1
  Obituary 24
  See also CLR 10
Serfozo, Mary 1925- 194
Seroff, Victor I(ilyitch) 1902-1979 12
  Obituary 26
Serra, Sebastia 1966- 202
Serraillier, Ian (Lucien) 1912-1994 73
  Obituary 83
  Earlier sketch in SATA 1
  See also CLR 2
  See also SAAS 3
Serros, Michele 175
Serros, Michele M.
  See Serros, Michele
Servello, Joe 1932- 10
Service, Pamela F. 1945- 64
Service, Robert
  See Service, Robert W.
Service, Robert W. 1874(?)-1958 20
Serwadda, W(illiam) Moses 1931- 27
Serwer-Bernstein, Blanche L(uria)
  1910-1997 10
Sescoe, Vincent E. 1938- 123
Seth, Mary
  See Lexau, Joan M.
Seton, Anya 1904(?)-1990 3
  Obituary 66
Seton, Ernest (Evan) Thompson 1860-1946 . 18
  See also CLR 59
Seton-Thompson, Ernest
  See Seton, Ernest (Evan) Thompson
Seuling, Barbara 1937- 193
  Earlier sketches in SATA 10, 98, 145
  See also SAAS 24
Seuss, Dr.
  See Dr. Seuss
Severn, Bill
  See Severn, William Irving
Severn, David
  See Unwin, David S(torr)
Severn, William Irving 1914- 1
Sewall, Marcia 1935- 119
  Earlier sketches in SATA 37, 69
Seward, Prudence 1926- 16
Sewell, Anna 1820-1878 100
  Earlier sketch in SATA 24
  See also CLR 17
Sewell, Helen (Moore) 1896-1957 38
Sexton, Anne 1928-1974 10
Sexton, Anne Harvey
  See Sexton, Anne
Seymour, Alta Halverson 10
Seymour, Jane 1951- 139
Seymour, Tres 1966- 164
  Earlier sketch in SATA 82
Sfar, Joann 1971- 182
Shachtman, Tom 1942- 49
Shackleton, C.C.
  See Aldiss, Brian W.
Shader, Rachel
  See Sofer, Barbara

Shadow, Jak
  See Sutherland, Jon
Shadyland, Sal
  See Cooper, Louise
Shafer, Audrey 183
Shafer, Robert E(ugene) 1925- 9
Shaffer, Terea 1968- 79
Shahan, Sherry 1949- 134
  Earlier sketch in SATA 92
Shahn, Ben(jamin) 1898-1969
  Obituary 21
Shahn, Bernarda Bryson
  See Bryson, Bernarda
Shaik, Fatima 114
Shalant, Phyllis 1949- 150
Shan, Darren 1972- 199
  Earlier sketches in SATA 129, 168
Shan, D.B.
  See Shan, Darren
Shanahan, Lisa 199
Shanberg, Karen
  See Shragg, Karen (I.)
Shane, Harold Gray 1914-1993 36
  Obituary 76
Shange, Ntozake 1948- 157
Shanks, Ann Zane (Kushner) 10
Shannon, David 1959- 152
  Earlier sketch in SATA 107
  See also CLR 87
Shannon, George 1952- 202
  Earlier sketches in SATA 35, 94, 143
Shannon, George William Bones
  See Shannon, George
Shannon, Jacqueline 63
Shannon, Margaret
  See Silverwood, Margaret Shannon
Shannon, Monica 1905(?)-1965 28
Shannon, Terry
  See Mercer, Jessie
Shannon, Terry Miller 1951- 148
Shapiro, Irwin 1911-1981 32
Shapiro, Jody Fickes 1940- 193
Shapiro, Karen Jo 1964- 186
Shapiro, Michelle 1961- 196
Shapiro, Milton J. 1926- 32
Shapiro, Tricia
  See Andryszewski, Tricia
Shapp, Charles M(orris) 1906-1989
  Obituary 61
Shapp, Martha Glauber 1910- 3
Sharenow, Robert 193
Sharfman, Amalie 14
Sharma, Partap 1939- 15
Sharma, Rashmi
  See Singh, Rashmi Sharma
Sharman, Alison
  See Leonard, Alison
Sharmat, Marjorie Weinman 1928- 133
  Earlier sketches in SATA 4, 33, 74
Sharmat, Mitchell 1927- 127
  Earlier sketch in SATA 33
Sharp, Anne Wallace 1947- 144
Sharp, Luke
  See Alkiviades, Alkis
Sharp, Margery 1905-1991 29
  Obituary 67
  Earlier sketch in SATA 1
  See also CLR 27
Sharp, Zerna A. 1889-1981
  Obituary 27
Sharpe, Jon
  See Duncan, Alice
  and Knott, William C(ecil, Jr.)
  and Messman, Jon
Sharpe, Mitchell R(aymond) 1924- 12
Sharpe, Susan 1946- 71
Sharratt, Nick 1962- 199
  Earlier sketches in SATA 104, 153
Shasha, Mark 1961- 80
Shattuck, Roger 1923-2005 64
  Obituary 174

Shattuck, Roger Whitney
 See Shattuck, Roger
Shaw, Arnold 1909-1989 4
 Obituary 63
Shaw, Carolyn V. 1934- 91
Shaw, Charles (Green) 1892-1974 13
Shaw, Evelyn S. 1927- 28
Shaw, Flora Louisa
 See Lugard, Flora Louisa Shaw
Shaw, Janet 1937- 146
 Earlier sketch in SATA 61
 See also CLR 96
Shaw, Janet Beeler
 See Shaw, Janet
Shaw, Lisa
 See Rogak, Lisa
Shaw, Margret 1940- 68
Shaw, Mary 1965- 180
Shaw, Nancy 1946- 162
 Earlier sketch in SATA 71
Shaw, Ray 7
Shaw, Richard 1923- 12
Shawn, Frank S.
 See Goulart, Ron
Shay, Art
 See Shay, Arthur
Shay, Arthur 1922- 4
Shay, Lacey
 See Shebar, Sharon Sigmond
Shea, Bob 188
Shea, George 1940- 54
 Brief entry 42
Shea, Pegi Deitz 1960- 172
 Earlier sketches in SATA 77, 137
Shearer, Alex 1949- 204
Shearer, John 1947- 43
 Brief entry 27
 See also CLR 34
Shearer, Ted 1919- 43
Shearing, Leonie 1972- 184
Sheban, Chris 182
Shebar, Sharon Sigmond 1945- 36
Shecter, Ben 1935- 16
Shedd, Warner 1934- 147
 Earlier sketch in SATA 87
Sheedy, Alexandra Elizabeth 1962- 39
 Earlier sketch in SATA 19
Sheehan, Ethna 1908-2000 9
Sheehan, Patty 1945- 77
Sheehan, Sean 1951- 154
 Earlier sketch in SATA 86
Sheen, Barbara 1949- 143
Shefelman, Janice 1930- 205
 Earlier sketches in SATA 58, 129
Shefelman, Janice Jordan
 See Shefelman, Janice
Shefelman, Tom 1927- 204
 Earlier sketch in SATA 58
Sheffer, H. R.
 See Abels, Harriette S(heffer)
Sheffield, Charles 1935-2002 109
Sheffield, Janet N. 1926- 26
Sheikh, Nazneen
 See Sadiq, Nazneen
Sheinkin, Steve 1968- 204
Shekerjian, Regina Tor 16
Shelby, Anne 1948- 85
 Autobiography Feature 121
 See also SAAS 26
Sheldon, Ann
 See Antle, Nancy
Sheldon, Ann 67
 Earlier sketch in SATA 1
Sheldon, Aure 1917-1976 12
Sheldon, David 185
Sheldon, Deyan 181
Sheldon, John
 See Bloch, Robert (Albert)
Sheldon, Muriel 1926- 45
 Brief entry 39
Shell, Barry 1951- 176

Shelley, Frances
 See Wees, Frances Shelley
Shelley, John 1959- 202
Shelley, Mary
 See Shelley, Mary Wollstonecraft
Shelley, Mary Wollstonecraft 1797-1851 29
 See also CLR 133
Shelton, William Roy 1919-1995 5
 Obituary 129
Shemie, Bonnie (Jean Brenner) 1949- 96
Shemin, Margaretha (Hoeneveld) 1928- 4
Shen, Michele 1953- 173
Shenker, Michele
 See Shen, Michele
Shenton, Edward 1895-1977 45
Shepard, Aaron 1950- 187
 Earlier sketches in SATA 75, 113
Shepard, Ernest Howard 1879-1976 100
 Obituary 24
 Earlier sketches in SATA 3, 33
 See also CLR 27
Shepard, James R.
 See Shepard, Jim
Shepard, Jim 1956- 164
 Earlier sketch in SATA 90
Shepard, Mary
 See Knox, (Mary) Eleanor Jessie
Shephard, Esther 1891-1975 5
 Obituary 26
Shepherd, Amanda 201
Shepherd, Donna Walsh
 See Walsh Shepherd, Donna
Shepherd, Elizabeth 4
Shepherd, Irana 173
Shepherd, Roni
 See Shepherd, Irana
Sheppard, Kate 195
Shepperson, Rob 178
Sherburne, Zoa (Lillian Morin) 1912-1995 3
 See also SAAS 18
Sherk-Savage, Candace
 See Savage, Candace
Sherlock, Patti 71
Sherman, D(enis) R(onald) 1934- 48
 Brief entry 29
Sherman, Diane (Finn) 1928- 12
Sherman, Elizabeth
 See Friskey, Margaret (Richards)
Sherman, Harold (Morrow) 1898-1987 37
 Obituary 137
Sherman, Josepha 163
 Earlier sketch in SATA 75
Sherman, Michael
 See Lowndes, Robert A(ugustine) W(ard)
Sherman, Nancy
 See Rosenberg, Nancy (Sherman)
Sherman, Pat 174
Sherman, Peter Michael
 See Lowndes, Robert A(ugustine) W(ard)
Sherrard, Valerie (Anne) 1957- 141
Sherrod, Jane
 See Singer, Jane Sherrod
Sherry, Clifford J. 1943- 84
Sherry, (Dulcie) Sylvia 1932- 122
 Earlier sketch in SATA 8
Sherwan, Earl 1917- 3
Sherwood, Jonathan
 See London, Jonathan (Paul)
Sheth, Kashmira 186
Shetterly, Will 1955- 78
 Autobiography Feature 106
Shetterly, William Howard
 See Shetterly, Will
Shiefman, Vicky 1942- 22
Shields, Brenda Desmond (Armstrong)
 1914- 37
Shields, Carol Diggory 174
Shields, Charles 1944- 10
Shields, Gillian 203
Shiels, Barbara
 See Adams, Barbara Johnston

Shiffman, Lena 1957- 101
Shiina, Makoto 1944- 83
Shimin, Symeon 1902-1984 13
Shimko, Bonnie 1941- 191
Shine, Andrea 1955- 104
Shine, Deborah 1932- 71
Shinn, Everett 1876-1953 21
Shinn, Sharon 1957- 164
 Earlier sketch in SATA 110
Shippen, Katherine B(inney) 1892-1980 1
 Obituary 23
 See also CLR 36
Shippey, T. A. 1943- 143
Shippey, Thomas Alan
 See Shippey, T. A.
Shipton, Eric Earle 1907-1977 10
Shipton, Paul 1963- 196
Shiraz, Yasmin 173
Shirer, William L(awrence) 1904-1993 45
 Obituary 78
Shirley, Debra 203
Shirley, Gayle C 1955- 96
Shirley, Gayle Corbett
 See Shirley, Gayle C
Shirley, Jean 1919- 70
Shirreffs, Gordon D(onald) 1914-1996 11
Shirts, Morris A(lpine) 1922- 63
Shlichta, Joe 1968- 84
Shmurak, Carole B. 1944- 118
Sholokhov, Mikhail 1905-1984
 Obituary 36
Sholokhov, Mikhail Aleksandrovich
 See Sholokhov, Mikhail
Shore, Diane Z. 179
Shore, Diane ZuHone
 See Shore, Diane Z.
Shore, June Lewis 30
Shore, Nancy 1960- 124
Shore, Robert 1924- 39
Short, Michael 1937- 65
Short, Roger
 See Arkin, Alan
Shortall, Leonard W. 19
Shortt, Tim(othy Donald) 1961- 96
Shotwell, Louisa Rossiter 1902-1993 3
Shoup, Barbara 1947- 156
 Earlier sketch in SATA 86
 See also SAAS 24
Shoveller, Herb 184
Showalter, Jean B(reckinridge) 12
Showell, Ellen Harvey 1934- 33
Showers, Paul C. 1910-1999 92
 Obituary 114
 Earlier sketch in SATA 21
 See also CLR 6
 See also SAAS 7
Shpakow, Tanya 1959(?)- 94
Shpitalnik, Vladimir 1964- 83
Shragg, Karen (I.) 1954- 142
Shreeve, Elizabeth 1956- 156
Shreve, Susan
 See Shreve, Susan Richards
Shreve, Susan Richards 1939- 152
 Brief entry 41
 Earlier sketches in SATA 46, 95
Shriver, Jean Adair 1932- 75
Shriver, Maria 1955- 134
Shriver, Maria Owings
 See Shriver, Maria
Shrode, Mary
 See Hollingsworth, Mary
Shtainmets, Leon 32
Shub, Elizabeth 1915(?)-2004 5
Shuken, Julia 1948- 84
Shulevitz, Uri 1935- 165
 Earlier sketches in SATA 3, 50, 106
 See also CLR 61
Shulman, Alix Kates 1932- 7
Shulman, Dee 1957- 146
Shulman, Irving 1913-1995 13
Shulman, Lisa 202

Shulman, Mark 1962- *184*
Shulman, Max 1919-1988
  Obituary *59*
Shulman, Milton 1913-2004
  Obituary *154*
Shulman, Neil B(arnett) 1945- *89*
Shumsky, Zena
  See Collier, Zena
Shura, Mary Francis
  See Craig, Mary (Francis) Shura
Shusterman, Neal 1962- *201*
  Autobiography Feature *140*
  Earlier sketches in SATA *85, 121, 140*
Shuter, Jane (Margaret) 1955- *151*
  Earlier sketch in SATA *90*
Shuttlesworth, Dorothy Edwards *3*
Shwartz, Susan (Martha) 1949- *94*
Shyer, Christopher 1961- *98*
Shyer, Marlene Fanta *13*
Siberell, Anne *29*
Sibley, Don 1922- *12*
Siburt, Ruth 1951- *121*
Siculan, Daniel 1922- *12*
Siddon, Barbara
  See Bradford, Barbara Taylor
Sidgwick, Ethel 1877-1970 .... *116*
Sidjakov, Nicolas 1924- *18*
Sidman, Joyce 1956- *181*
  Earlier sketch in SATA *145*
Sidney, Frank
  See Warwick, Alan R(oss)
Sidney, Margaret
  See Lothrop, Harriet Mulford Stone
Siebert, Diane 1948- *189*
Siegal, Aranka 1930- *88*
  Brief entry *37*
Siegel, Beatrice *36*
Siegel, Helen
  See Siegl, Helen
Siegel, Robert 1939- *39*
Siegel, Robert Harold
  See Siegel, Robert
Siegel, Siena Cherson 1967(?)- *185*
Siegelson, Kim L. 1962- *114*
Sieger, Ted 1958- *189*
Siegl, Helen 1924- *34*
Siepmann, Mary Aline
  See Wesley, Mary (Aline)
Sierra, Judy 1945- *195*
  Earlier sketches in SATA *104, 162*
Sieswerda, Paul L. 1942- *147*
Sievert, Terri
  See Dougherty, Terri (L.)
Silas
  See McCay, (Zenas) Winsor
Silcock, Sara Lesley 1947- *12*
Silin-Palmer, Pamela *184*
Sill, Cathryn 1953- *141*
  Earlier sketch in SATA *74*
Sill, John 1947- *140*
  Earlier sketch in SATA *74*
Sillitoe, Alan 1928- *61*
Sills, Leslie (Elka) 1948- *129*
Silly, E. S.
  See Kraus, (Herman) Robert
Silsbe, Brenda 1953- *73*
Silva, Joseph
  See Goulart, Ron
Silver, Ruth
  See Chew, Ruth
Silverberg, Robert 1935- *91*
  Autobiography Feature *104*
  Earlier sketch in SATA *13*
  See also CLR *59*
Silverman, Erica 1955- *165*
  Earlier sketches in SATA *78, 112*
Silverman, Janis L. 1946- *127*
Silverman, Mel(vin Frank) 1931-1966 .... *9*
Silverman, Robin L. 1954- *96*
Silverman, Robin Landew
  See Silverman, Robin L.

Silverstein, Alvin 1933- *124*
  Earlier sketches in SATA *8, 69*
  See also CLR *25*
Silverstein, Herma 1945- *106*
Silverstein, Robert Alan 1959- *124*
  Earlier sketch in SATA *77*
Silverstein, Shel 1932-1999 .... *92*
  Brief entry *27*
  Obituary *116*
  Earlier sketch in SATA *33*
  See also CLR *96*
Silverstein, Sheldon Allan
  See Silverstein, Shel
Silverstein, Virginia B. 1937- *124*
  Earlier sketches in SATA *8, 69*
  See also CLR *25*
Silverstein, Virginia Barbara Opshelor
  See Silverstein, Virginia B.
Silverthorne, Elizabeth 1930- *35*
Silverwood, Margaret Shannon 1966- *137*
  Earlier sketch in SATA *83*
Silvey, Diane F. 1946- *135*
Sim, David 1953- *162*
Sim, Dorrith M. 1931- *96*
Simak, Clifford D(onald) 1904-1988
  Obituary *56*
Simard, Remy 1959- *168*
Simmie, Lois (Ann) 1932- *106*
Simmonds, Posy 1945- *130*
  See also CLR *23*
Simmonds, Rosemary Elizabeth
  See Simmonds, Posy
Simmons, Andra 1939- *141*
Simmons, Elly 1955- *134*
Simmons, Michael 1970- *185*
Simms, Laura 1947- *117*
Simner, Janni Lee *113*
Simon, Charlie May
  See Fletcher, Charlie May Hogue
Simon, Francesca 1955- *111*
Simon, Gabriel 1972- *118*
Simon, Hilda Rita 1921- *28*
  See also CLR *39*
Simon, Howard 1903-1979 .... *32*
  Obituary *21*
Simon, Joe
  See Simon, Joseph H.
Simon, Joseph H. 1913- *7*
Simon, Martin P(aul William) 1903-1969 .... *12*
Simon, Mina Lewiton
  See Lewiton, Mina
Simon, Norma (Feldstein) 1927- *129*
  Earlier sketches in SATA *3, 68*
Simon, Seymour 1931- *202*
  Earlier sketches in SATA *4, 73, 138*
  See also CLR *63*
Simon, Shirley (Schwartz) 1921- *11*
Simon, Solomon 1895-1970 .... *40*
Simonetta, Linda 1948- *14*
Simonetta, Sam 1936- *14*
Simons, Barbara B(rooks) 1934- *41*
Simont, Marc 1915- *126*
  Earlier sketches in SATA *9, 73*
Simpson, Colin 1908-1983 .... *14*
Simpson, Harriette
  See Arnow, Harriette (Louisa) Simpson
Simpson, Jacynth Hope
  See Hope Simpson, Jacynth
Simpson, Lesley 1963- *150*
Simpson, Margaret 1943- *128*
Simpson, Myrtle L(illias) 1931- *14*
Sims, Blanche *168*
  Earlier sketch in SATA *75*
Sims, Blanche L.
  See Sims, Blanche
Simundsson, Elva 1950- *63*
Sinclair, Clover
  See Gater, Dilys
Sinclair, Emil
  See Hesse, Hermann
Sinclair, Jeff 1958- *77*

Sinclair, Olga 1923- *121*
Sinclair, Rose
  See Smith, Susan Vernon
Sinclair, Upton 1878-1968 .... *9*
Sinclair, Upton Beall
  See Sinclair, Upton
Singer, A.L.
  See Lerangis, Peter
Singer, Arthur 1917-1990 .... *64*
Singer, Isaac
  See Singer, Isaac Bashevis
Singer, Isaac Bashevis 1904-1991 .... *27*
  Obituary *68*
  Earlier sketch in SATA *3*
  See also CLR *1*
Singer, Jane Sherrod 1917-1985 .... *4*
  Obituary *42*
Singer, Julia 1917- *28*
Singer, Kurt D. 1911-2005 .... *38*
  Obituary *172*
Singer, Marilyn 1948- *201*
  Autobiography Feature *158*
  Brief entry *38*
  Earlier sketches in SATA *48, 80, 125, 158*
  See also CLR *48*
  See also SAAS *13*
Singer, Muff 1942-2005 .... *104*
  Obituary *160*
Singer, Nicky 1956- *194*
Singer, Susan (Mahler) 1941- *9*
Singh, Rashmi Sharma 1952- *90*
Singleton, Linda Joy 1957- *166*
  Earlier sketch in SATA *88*
Singleton, L.J.
  See Singleton, Linda Joy
Sinykin, Sheri
  See Sinykin, Sheri Cooper
Sinykin, Sheri Cooper 1950- *142*
  Autobiography Feature *142*
  Earlier sketches in SATA *72, 133*
Sinykin, Sheril Terri Cooper
  See Sinykin, Sheri Cooper
Sipiera, Paul P., (Jr.) 1948- *144*
  Earlier sketch in SATA *89*
Siracusa, Catherine (Jane) 1947- *82*
Sirett, Dawn (Karen) 1966- *88*
Sirimarco, Elizabeth 1966- *158*
Sirof, Harriet 1930- *94*
  Earlier sketch in SATA *37*
Sirois, Allen L. 1950- *76*
Sirvaitis (Chernyaev), Karen (Ann) 1961- ... *79*
Sis, Peter 1949- *192*
  Earlier sketch in SATA *149*
  See also CLR *110*
Sisson, Rosemary Anne 1923- *11*
Sister Mary Terese
  See Donze, Mary Terese
Sita, Lisa 1962- *87*
Sitarski, Anita *200*
Sitomer, Alan Lawrence *174*
Sitomer, Harry 1903-1985 .... *31*
Sitomer, Mindel 1903-1987 .... *31*
Sittenfeld, Curtis 1975(?)- *164*
Sive, Helen R(obinson) 1951- *30*
Sivulich, Sandra (Jeanne) Stroner 1941- *9*
Siy, Alexandra *193*
Skarmeta, Antonio 1940- *57*
Skeers, Linda 1958- *207*
Skelly, James R(ichard) 1927- *17*
Skelton, Matthew 1971- *185*
Skinner, Constance Lindsay 1877-1939
  See YABC *1*
Skinner, Cornelia Otis 1901-1979 .... *2*
Skipper, G. C. 1939- *46*
  Brief entry *38*
Sklansky, Amy E. 1971- *204*
Sklansky, Amy E(dgar) 1971- *145*
Skofield, James *95*
  Brief entry *44*
Skold, Betty Westrom 1923- *41*
Skorpen, Liesel Moak 1935- *3*

Skott, Maria
  See Nikolajeva, Maria
Skrypuch, Marsha Forchuk 1954- *134*
Skultety, Nancy Laney 1960- *175*
Skurzynski, Gloria 1930- *145*
  Autobiography Feature *145*
  Earlier sketches in SATA *8, 74, 122*
  See also SAAS *9*
Skurzynski, Gloria Joan
  See Skurzynski, Gloria
Skutch, Robert 1925- *89*
Skye, Maggie
  See Werner, Herma
Skye, Obert *200*
  Earlier sketch in SATA *170*
Slack, Michael 1969- *189*
Slackman, Charles B. 1934- *12*
Slade, Arthur G. 1967- *149*
  Earlier sketch in SATA *106*
Slade, Arthur Gregory
  See Slade, Arthur G.
Slade, Christian 1974- *193*
Slade, Richard 1910-1971 .... *9*
Slangerup, Erik Jon 1969- *130*
Slate, Joseph 1928- *174*
  Earlier sketches in SATA *38, 122*
Slate, Joseph Frank
  See Slate, Joseph
Slater, Dashka 1963- *179*
Slater, Ray
  See Lansdale, Joe R.
Slaughter, Hope 1940- *84*
Slaughter, Jean
  See Doty, Jean Slaughter
Slaughter, Tom 1955- *152*
Slavicek, Louise Chipley 1956- *144*
Slavin, Bill 1959- *199*
  Earlier sketches in SATA *76, 148*
Slaymaker, Melissa Eskridge 1958- *158*
Sleator, William 1945- *208*
  Earlier sketches in SATA *3, 68, 118, 161*
  See also CLR *128*
Sleator, William Warner III
  See Sleator, William
Slegers, Liesbet 1975- *154*
Sleigh, Barbara 1906-1982 .... *86*
  Obituary *30*
  Earlier sketch in SATA *3*
Slepian, Jan 1921- *85*
  Brief entry *45*
  Earlier sketch in SATA *51*
  See also SAAS *8*
Slepian, Janice B.
  See Slepian, Jan
Slicer, Margaret O. 1920- *4*
Slier, Debby
  See Shine, Deborah
Sloan, Brian 1966- *172*
Sloan, Carolyn 1937- *116*
  Earlier sketch in SATA *58*
Sloan, Glenna (Davis) 1930- *120*
Sloane, Eric 1910(?)-1985 .... *52*
  Obituary *42*
Sloane, Todd 1955- *88*
Sloat, Teri 1948- *164*
  Earlier sketches in SATA *70, 106*
Slobodkin, Florence Gersh 1905-1994 .... *5*
  Obituary *107*
Slobodkin, Louis 1903-1975 .... *26*
  Earlier sketch in SATA *1*
Slobodkina, Esphyr 1908-2002 .... *1*
  Obituary *135*
  See also SAAS *8*
Sloggett, Nellie 1851-1923 .... *44*
Slonim, David 1966- *207*
Sloss, Lesley Lord 1965- *72*
Slote, Alfred 1926- *72*
  Earlier sketch in SATA *8*
  See also CLR *4*
  See also SAAS *21*
Slote, Elizabeth 1956- *80*

Small, Charlie
  See Ward, Nick
Small, David 1945- *183*
  Brief entry *46*
  Earlier sketches in SATA *50, 95, 126*
  See also CLR *53*
Small, Ernest
  See Lent, Blair
Small, Mary 1932- *165*
Small, Terry 1942- *75*
Smallcomb, Pam 1954- *159*
Smallman, Steve *197*
Smalls, Irene
  See Smalls-Hector, Irene
Smalls-Hector, Irene 1950- *146*
  Earlier sketch in SATA *73*
  See also CLR *103*
Smallwood, Norah (Evelyn) 1910(?)-1984
  Obituary *41*
Smaridge, Norah (Antoinette) 1903-1994 ...... *6*
Smath, Jerry 1933- *198*
Smee, Nicola 1948- *167*
  Earlier sketch in SATA *76*
Smiley, Virginia Kester 1923- *2*
Smit, Noelle 1972- *199*
Smith, Alexander McCall 1948- *179*
  Earlier sketch in SATA *73*
Smith, Andrew 1959- *209*
Smith, Andrew Anselmo
  See Smith, Andrew
Smith, Andy J. 1975- *207*
Smith, Anne Warren 1938- *41*
  Brief entry *34*
Smith, Barry (Edward Jervis) 1943- *75*
Smith, Beatrice S(chillinger) *12*
Smith, Betsy Covington 1937- *55*
  Earlier sketch in SATA *43*
Smith, Betty (Wehner) 1904-1972 .... *6*
Smith, Bradford 1909-1964 .... *5*
Smith, Brenda 1946- *82*
Smith, C. Pritchard
  See Hoyt, Edwin P(almer), Jr.
Smith, Caesar
  See Trevor, Elleston
Smith, Cat Bowman 1939- *201*
Smith, Charles R., Jr. 1969- *203*
  Earlier sketch in SATA *159*
Smith, Craig 1955- *172*
  Earlier sketches in SATA *81, 117*
Smith, Cynthia Leitich 1967- *152*
Smith, Datus C(lifford), Jr. 1907-1999 .... *13*
  Obituary *116*
Smith, Debra 1955- *89*
Smith, Derek 1943- *141*
Smith, Dick King
  See King-Smith, Dick
Smith, Dodie
  See Smith, Dorothy Gladys
Smith, Doris Buchanan 1934-2002 .... *75*
  Obituary *140*
  Earlier sketch in SATA *28*
  See also SAAS *10*
Smith, Dorothy Gladys 1896-1990 .... *82*
  Obituary *65*
Smith, Dorothy Stafford 1905- *6*
Smith, Duane 1974- *202*
Smith, E(lmer) Boyd 1860-1943
  See YABC *1*
Smith, E(dric) Brooks 1917- *40*
Smith, Elwood H. 1941- *203*
Smith, Emma 1923- *52*
  Brief entry *36*
Smith, (Katherine) Eunice (Young)
  1902-1993 .... *5*
Smith, Frances C(hristine) 1904-1986 .... *3*
Smith, Gary R. 1932- *14*
Smith, Geof 1969- *102*
Smith, George Harmon 1920- *5*
Smith, Gordon 1951- *184*
Smith, Greg Leitich *152*

Smith, H(arry) Allen 1907-1976
  Obituary *20*
Smith, Helene 1937- *142*
Smith, Hope Anita *202*
Smith, Howard E(verett), Jr. 1927- *12*
Smith, Hugh L(etcher) 1921-1968 .... *5*
Smith, Imogene Henderson 1922- *12*
Smith, Jacqueline B. 1937- *39*
Smith, Jada Pinkett 1971- *161*
Smith, James D. 1955- *176*
Smith, James Noel 1950- *193*
Smith, Janet (Buchanan) Adam
  See Adam Smith, Janet (Buchanan)
Smith, Janice Lee 1949- *155*
  Earlier sketch in SATA *54*
Smith, Jean
  See Smith, Frances C(hristine)
Smith, Jean Pajot 1945- *10*
Smith, Jeff 1958- *161*
  Earlier sketch in SATA *93*
Smith, Jeff Allen
  See Smith, Jeff
Smith, Jenny 1963- *90*
Smith, Jessie
  See Kunhardt, Edith
Smith, Jessie Willcox 1863-1935 .... *21*
  See also CLR *59*
Smith, Joan (Mary) 1933- *54*
  Brief entry *46*
Smith, Johnston
  See Crane, Stephen
Smith, Jos A. 1936- *181*
  Earlier sketches in SATA *73, 120*
Smith, Joseph Arthur
  See Smith, Jos A.
Smith, Judie R. 1936- *80*
Smith, Lafayette
  See Higdon, Hal
Smith, Lane 1959- *179*
  Earlier sketches in SATA *76, 131*
  See also CLR *47*
Smith, Lee
  See Albion, Lee Smith
Smith, Lendon H(oward) 1921- *64*
Smith, Lillian H(elena) 1887-1983
  Obituary *32*
Smith, Linda 1949- *177*
Smith, Linell Nash 1932- *2*
Smith, Lucia B. 1943- *30*
Smith, Maggie 1965- *190*
Smith, Margaret Emily Noel Nuttall
  See Nuttall-Smith, Margaret Emily Noel
Smith, Marion Hagens 1913- *12*
Smith, Marion Jaques 1899-1987 .... *13*
Smith, Mary Ellen *10*
Smith, Marya 1945- *78*
Smith, Mike
  See Smith, Mary Ellen
Smith, Nancy Covert 1935- *12*
Smith, Norman F. 1920- *70*
  Earlier sketch in SATA *5*
Smith, Patricia Clark 1943- *96*
Smith, Pauline C.
  See Arthur, Robert, (Jr.)
Smith, Pauline C(oggeshall) 1908-1994 .... *27*
Smith, Philip Warren 1936- *46*
Smith, R. Alexander McCall
  See Smith, Alexander McCall
Smith, Rebecca 1946- *123*
Smith, Robert Kimmel 1930- *77*
  Earlier sketch in SATA *12*
Smith, Robert Paul 1915-1977 .... *52*
  Obituary *30*
Smith, Roland 1951- *193*
  Earlier sketches in SATA *115, 161*
Smith, Rosamond
  See Oates, Joyce Carol
Smith, Ruth Leslie 1902- *2*
Smith, Samantha 1972-1985
  Obituary *45*
Smith, Sandra Lee 1945- *75*

Smith, Sarah Stafford
  See Smith, Dorothy Stafford
Smith, Sharon 1947- 82
Smith, Sherri L. 1971- 156
Smith, Sherwood 1951- 206
  Autobiography Feature 206
  Earlier sketches in SATA *82, 140*
Smith, Shirley Raines
  See Raines, Shirley C(arol)
Smith, Susan Carlton 1923- 12
Smith, Susan Mathias 1950- 43
  Brief entry 35
Smith, Susan Vernon 1950- 48
  Brief entry 45
Smith, Tim(othy R.) 1945- 151
Smith, Ursula 1934- 54
Smith, Vian (Crocker) 1920-1969 11
Smith, Wanda VanHoy 1926- 65
Smith, Ward
  See Goldsmith, Howard
Smith, William A. 1918- 10
Smith, William Jay 1918- 154
  Autobiography Feature 154
  Earlier sketches in SATA *2, 68*
  See also SAAS *22*
Smith, Winsome 1935- 45
Smith, Z.Z.
  See Westheimer, David
Smith-Ankrom, M. E. 1942- 130
Smith-Griswold, Wendy 1955- 88
Smith-Rex, Susan J. 1950- 94
Smithsen, Richard
  See Pellowski, Michael (Joseph)
Smits, Teo
  See Smits, Theodore R(ichard)
Smits, Theodore R(ichard) 1905-1996 45
  Brief entry 28
Smolinski, Dick 1932- 86
Smothers, Ethel Footman 1944- 149
  Earlier sketch in SATA *76*
Smucker, Anna Egan 1948- 209
Smucker, Barbara 1915-2003 130
  Earlier sketches in SATA *29, 76*
  See also CLR *10*
  See also SAAS *11*
Smucker, Barbara Claassen
  See Smucker, Barbara
Smyth, Iain 1959- 105
Snedeker, Caroline Dale (Parke) 1871-1956
  See YABC *2*
Sneed, Brad 191
Sneider, Marian 1932-2005 197
Snell, Nigel (Edward Creagh) 1936- 57
  Brief entry 40
Snellgrove, L(aurence) E(rnest) 1928- 53
Snelling, Dennis (Wayne) 1958- 84
Sneve, Virginia Driving Hawk 1933- 95
  Earlier sketch in SATA *8*
  See also CLR *2*
Snicket, Lemony 1970- 187
  Earlier sketch in SATA *126*
  See also CLR *79*
Sniegoski, Thomas E. 195
Sniegoski, Tom
  See Sniegoski, Thomas E.
Snodgrass, Mary Ellen 1944- 75
Snodgrass, Quentin Curtius
  See Twain, Mark
Snodgrass, Thomas Jefferson
  See Twain, Mark
Snook, Barbara (Lillian) 1913-1976 34
Snow, Alan 1959- 190
Snow, Carol 1965- 208
Snow, Donald Clifford 1917-1979 16
Snow, Dorothea J(ohnston) 1909- 9
Snow, Richard F(olger) 1947- 52
  Brief entry 37
Snyder, Anne 1922-2001 4
  Obituary 125
Snyder, Bernadette McCarver 1930- 97
Snyder, Carol 1941- 35

Snyder, Gerald S(eymour) 1933- 48
  Brief entry 34
Snyder, Jerome 1916-1976
  Obituary 20
Snyder, Laurel 1974- 209
Snyder, Midori 1954- 106
Snyder, Paul A. 1946- 125
Snyder, Zilpha Keatley 1927- 163
  Autobiography Feature 163
  Earlier sketches in SATA *1, 28, 75, 110*
  See also CLR *121*
  See also SAAS *2*
Snyderman, Reuven K. 1922- 5
So, Meilo 162
Sobel, June 1950- 149
Soble, Jennie
  See Cavin, Ruth (Brodie)
Sobol, Donald J. 1924- 132
  Earlier sketches in SATA *1, 31, 73*
  See also CLR *4*
Sobol, Harriet Langsam 1936- 47
  Brief entry 34
Sobol, Rose 1931- 76
Sobott-Mogwe, Gaele 1956- 97
Soderlind, Arthur E(dwin) 1920- 14
Soentpiet, Chris K. 1970- 159
  Earlier sketch in SATA *97*
Soerensen, Svend Otto 1916- 67
Sofer, Barbara 1949- 109
Sofer, Rachel
  See Sofer, Barbara
Softly, Barbara Frewin 1924- 12
Sogabe, Aki 207
Soglow, Otto 1900-1975
  Obituary 30
Sohl, Frederic J(ohn) 1916- 10
Sohr, Daniel 1973- 190
Sokol, Bill
  See Sokol, William
Sokol, William 1923- 37
Sokolov, Kirill 1930- 34
Solbert, Romaine G. 1925- 2
Solbert, Ronni
  See Solbert, Romaine G.
Solheim, James 133
Solomon, Heather M. 188
Solomon, Joan 1930- 51
  Brief entry 40
Solomons, Ikey Esquir
  See Thackeray, William Makepeace
Solonevich, George 1915-2003 15
Solot, Mary Lynn 1939- 12
Soman, David 1965- 200
Somerlott, Robert 1928-2001 62
Somers, Kevin 205
Somervill, Barbara A(nn) 1948- 140
Sommer, Angela
  See Sommer-Bodenburg, Angela
Sommer, Carl 1930- 175
  Earlier sketch in SATA *126*
Sommer, Elyse 1929- 7
Sommer, Robert 1929- 12
Sommer-Bodenburg, Angela 1948- 113
  Earlier sketch in SATA *63*
Sommerdorf, Norma 1926- 131
Sommerdorf, Norma Jean
  See Sommerdorf, Norma
Sommerfelt, Aimee 1892-1975 5
Son, John 160
Sones, Sonya 131
Sonneborn, Ruth (Cantor) 1899-1974 4
  Obituary 27
Sonnenblick, Jordan 1969- 185
  See also CLR *144*
Sonnenmark, Laura A. 1958- 73
Soo, Kean 201
Sopko, Eugen 1949- 58
Sorel, Edward 1929- 126
  Brief entry 37
  Earlier sketch in SATA *65*

Sorensen, Henri 1950- 115
  Earlier sketch in SATA *77*
Sorensen, Svend Otto
  See Soerensen, Svend Otto
Sorensen, Virginia 1912-1991 2
  Obituary 72
  See also SAAS *15*
Sorenson, Jane 1926- 63
Sorenson, Margo 1946- 96
Sorley Walker, Kathrine 41
Sorra, Kristin 185
Sorrells, Walter 177
Sorrentino, Joseph N. 1937- 6
Sortor, June Elizabeth 1939- 12
Sortor, Toni
  See Sortor, June Elizabeth
Sosa, Hernan 1977- 203
Soskin, V. H.
  See Ellison, Virginia H(owell)
Soto, Gary 1952- 174
  Earlier sketches in SATA *80, 120*
  See also CLR *38*
Sotomayor, Antonio 1902-1985 11
Souci, Robert D. San
  See San Souci, Robert D.
Soudley, Henry
  See Wood, James Playsted
Souhami, Jessica 176
Soule, Gardner (Bosworth) 1913-2000 14
Soule, Jean Conder 1919- 10
Souster, (Holmes) Raymond 1921- 63
South, Sheri Cobb 1959- 82
Southall, Ivan 1921-2008 134
  Autobiography Feature 134
  Earlier sketches in SATA *3, 68*
  See also CLR *2*
  See also SAAS *3*
Southall, Ivan Francis
  See Southall, Ivan
Southey, Robert 1774-1843 54
Southgate, Vera 54
Souza, Janet
  See Tashjian, Janet
Sovak, Jan 1953- 115
Sowden, Celeste
  See Walters, Celeste
Sowter, Nita 69
Spafford, Suzy 1945- 160
Spagnoli, Cathy 1950- 134
  Earlier sketch in SATA *79*
Spain, Sahara Sunday 1991- 133
Spain, Susan Rosson 185
Spalding, Andrea 1944- 150
  Earlier sketch in SATA *101*
Spalenka, Greg 1958- 198
Spanfeller, James J. 1930- 19
  See also SAAS *8*
Spanfeller, Jim
  See Spanfeller, James J.
Spangenberg, Judith Dunn 1942- 5
Spanyol, Jessica 1965- 206
  Earlier sketch in SATA *137*
Spar, Jerome 1918- 10
Sparks, Barbara 1942- 78
Sparks, Beatrice (Mathews) 1918- 44
  Brief entry 28
  See also CLR *139*
Sparks, Mary W. 1920- 15
Spaulding, Douglas
  See Bradbury, Ray
Spaulding, Leonard
  See Bradbury, Ray
Spaulding, Norma 107
Speare, Elizabeth George 1908-1994 62
  Obituary 83
  Earlier sketch in SATA *5*
  See also CLR *8*
Spearing, Judith (Mary Harlow) 1922- 9
Spears, Rick 182
Speck, Katie 196
Speck, Nancy 1959- 104

Specking, Inez 1890-1960(?) 11
Speed, Nell
    See Keats, Emma
    and Sampson, Emma (Keats) Speed
Speed, Nell (Ewing) 1878-1913 68
Speer, Bonnie Stahlman 1929- 113
Speer-Lyon, Tammie L. 1965- 89
Speicher, Helen Ross S(mith) 1915- 8
Speir, Nancy 1958- 81
Spellman, John W(illard) 1934- 14
Spellman, Roger G.
    See Cox, William R(obert)
Spelman, Cornelia Maude 1946- 144
    Earlier sketch in SATA 96
Spelman, Mary 1934- 28
Spelvin, George
    See Lerangis, Peter
    and Phillips, David Atlee
Spence, Cynthia
    See Eble, Diane
Spence, Eleanor (Rachel) 1928- 21
    See also CLR 26
Spence, Geraldine 1931- 47
Spencer, Ann 1918- 10
Spencer, Britt 206
Spencer, Cornelia
    See Yaukey, Grace S(ydenstricker)
Spencer, Donald D(ean) 1931- 41
Spencer, Elizabeth 1921- 14
Spencer, Leonard G.
    See Garrett, Randall
    and Silverberg, Robert
Spencer, William 1922- 9
Spencer, Zane A(nn) 1935- 35
Sper, Emily 1957- 142
Speregen, Devra Newberger 1964- 84
Sperling, Dan(iel Lee) 1949- 65
Sperry, Armstrong W. 1897-1976 1
    Obituary 27
Sperry, Raymond
    See Garis, Howard R.
Sperry, Raymond, Jr. 1
Spetter, Jung-Hee 1969- 134
Spicer, Dorothy Gladys -1975 32
Spiegel, Beth 184
Spiegelman, Art 1948- 158
    Earlier sketch in SATA 109
Spiegelman, Judith M. 5
Spielberg, Steven 1947- 32
Spier, Peter (Edward) 1927- 54
    Earlier sketch in SATA 4
    See also CLR 5
Spilhaus, Athelstan (Frederick) 1911-1998 .. 13
    Obituary 102
Spilka, Arnold 1917- 6
Spillane, Frank Morrison
    See Spillane, Mickey
Spillane, Mickey 1918-2006 66
    Obituary 176
Spinelli, Eileen 1942- 186
    Earlier sketches in SATA 38, 101, 150
Spinelli, Jerry 1941- 195
    Earlier sketches in SATA 39, 71, 110, 158
    See also CLR 82
Spink, Reginald (William) 1905-1994 11
Spinka, Penina Keen 1945- 72
Spinner, Stephanie 1943- 132
    Earlier sketches in SATA 38, 91
Spinossimus
    See White, William, Jr.
Spiotta-DiMare, Loren 173
Spires, Ashley 1978- 183
Spires, Elizabeth 1952- 111
    Earlier sketch in SATA 71
Spiridellis, Gregg 1971(?)- 199
Spirin, Gennadii
    See Spirin, Gennady
Spirin, Gennadij
    See Spirin, Gennady

Spirin, Gennady 1948- 204
    Earlier sketches in SATA 95, 134
    See also CLR 88
Spiro, Ruth 208
Spivak, Dawnine 101
Spizman, Robyn Freedman 194
Spohn, David 1948- 72
Spohn, Kate 1962- 147
    Earlier sketch in SATA 87
Spollen, Christopher 1952- 12
Spooner, Michael (Tim) 1954- 92
Spowart, Robin 1947- 177
    Earlier sketch in SATA 82
Spradlin, Michael P. 204
Sprague, Gretchen 1926-2003 27
Spranger, Nina 1969- 203
Sprengel, Artie
    See Lerangis, Peter
Sprigge, Elizabeth (Miriam Squire)
    1900-1974 10
Spring, (Robert) Howard 1889-1965 28
Springer, Margaret 1941- 78
Springer, Marilyn Harris 1931- 47
Springer, Nancy 1948- 172
    Earlier sketches in SATA 65, 110
Springstubb, Tricia 1950- 78
    Brief entry 40
    Earlier sketch in SATA 46
Spudvilas, Anne 1951- 199
    Earlier sketch in SATA 94
Spurll, Barbara 1952- 78
Spurr, Elizabeth 172
Spykman, E(lizabeth) C(hoate) 1896-1965 .. 10
    See also CLR 35
Spyri, Johanna (Heusser) 1827-1901 100
    Earlier sketch in SATA 19
    See also CLR 115
Squires, Phil
    See Barker, S. Omar
Srba, Lynne 98
Sreenivasan, Jyotsna 1964- 101
S-Ringi, Kjell
    See Ringi, Kjell (Arne Soerensen)
Staake, Bob 1957- 209
Stacey, Cherylyn 1945- 96
Stacy, Donald
    See Pohl, Frederik
Stadler, John 204
Stadtler, Bea 1921- 17
Stafford, Jean 1915-1979
    Obituary 22
Stafford, Liliana 1950- 141
Stafford, Paul 1966- 116
Stahl, Ben(jamin) 1910-1987 5
    Obituary 54
Stahl, Hilda 1938-1993 48
    Obituary 77
Stahler, David, Jr. 162
Stainton, Sue 187
Stair, Gobin (John) 1912- 35
Stalder, Valerie 27
Stamaty, Mark Alan 1947- 12
Stambler, Irwin 1924- 5
Stampler, Ann Redisch 209
Standiford, Natalie 1961- 169
    Earlier sketch in SATA 81
Stanek, Lou Willett 1931- 63
Stang, Judit 1921-1977 29
Stang, Judy
    See Stang, Judit
Stangl, (Mary) Jean 1928- 67
Stanhope, Eric
    See Hamilton, Charles (Harold St. John)
Stankevich, Boris 1928- 2
Stanley, Diane 1943- 164
    Brief entry 32
    Earlier sketches in SATA 37, 80, 115
    See also CLR 46
    See also SAAS 15
Stanley, Elizabeth 1947- 206

Stanley, George Edward 1942- 67
    Earlier sketches in SATA 53, 111, 157, 1
Stanley, Jerry 1941- 127
    Earlier sketch in SATA 79
Stanley, Mandy 165
Stanley, Robert
    See Hamilton, Charles (Harold St. John)
Stanley, Sanna 1962- 145
Stanli, Sue
    See Meilach, Dona Z(weigoron)
Stanstead, John
    See Groom, Arthur William
Stanton, Karen 1960- 190
Stanton, Schuyler
    See Baum, L. Frank
Staples, Suzanne Fisher 1945- 207
    Earlier sketches in SATA 70, 105, 151
    See also CLR 137
Stapleton, Marjorie (Winifred) 1932- 28
Stapp, Arthur D(onald) 1906-1972 4
Starbird, Kaye 1916- 6
    See also CLR 60
Stark, Evan 1942- 78
Stark, James
    See Goldston, Robert (Conroy)
Stark, Ken 1943- 199
Stark, Ulf 1944- 124
Starke, Ruth (Elaine) 1946- 129
Starkey, Marion L(ena) 1901-1991 13
Starr, Ward
    See Manes, Stephen
Starret, William
    See McClintock, Marshall
Starr Taylor, Bridget 1959- 99
Stasiak, Krystyna 49
Staub, Frank 1949- 116
Staub, Frank Jacob
    See Staub, Frank
Staub, Wendy Corsi 1964- 114
Stauffacher, Sue 1961- 199
    Earlier sketch in SATA 155
Stauffer, Don
    See Berkebile, Fred D(onovan)
Staunton, Schuyler
    See Baum, L. Frank
Staunton, Ted 1956- 167
    Earlier sketch in SATA 112
Stead, Rebecca 1968(?)- 188
Steadman, Ralph 1936- 123
    Earlier sketch in SATA 32
Steadman, Ralph Idris
    See Steadman, Ralph
Stearman, Kaye 1951- 118
Stearns, Monroe (Mather) 1913-1987 5
    Obituary 55
Steckler, Arthur 1921-1985 65
Steding, Laurie 1953- 119
Steel, Danielle 1947- 66
Steel, Danielle Fernande
    See Steel, Danielle
Steele, Addison II
    See Lupoff, Richard A(llen)
Steele, Alexander 1958- 116
Steele, Henry Maxwell
    See Steele, Max
Steele, Mary 1930- 94
Steele, Mary Q(uintard Govan) 1922-1992 .. 51
    Obituary 72
    Earlier sketch in SATA 3
Steele, Max 1922-2005 168
    Earlier sketch in SATA 10
Steele, Philip 1948- 140
    Earlier sketch in SATA 81
Steele, William O(wen) 1917-1979 51
    Obituary 27
    Earlier sketch in SATA 1
Steelhammer, Ilona 1952- 98
Steelsmith, Shari 1962- 72
Stefanik, Alfred T. 1939- 55

Steffanson, Con
See Cassiday, Bruce (Bingham)
and Goulart, Ron
Steffens, Bradley 1955- 166
Earlier sketch in SATA 77
Steffensmeier, Alexander 1977- 195
Stegeman, Janet Allais 1923- 49
Brief entry 49
Steggall, Susan 1967- 182
Steig, William 1907-2003 111
Obituary 149
Earlier sketches in SATA 18, 70
See also CLR 103
Steig, William H.
See Steig, William
Stein, David Ezra 180
Stein, M(eyer) L(ewis) 1920- 6
Stein, Mathilde 1969- 195
Stein, Mini 2
Stein, R(ichard) Conrad 1937- 154
Earlier sketches in SATA 31, 82
Stein, Wendy 1951- 77
Steinbeck, John 1902-1968 9
Steinbeck, John Ernst
See Steinbeck, John
Steinberg, Alfred 1917-1995 9
Steinberg, David 1962- 200
Steinberg, D.J.
See Steinberg, David
Steinberg, Fannie 1899-1990 43
Steinberg, Fred J. 1933- 4
Steinberg, Phillip Orso 1921- 34
Steinberg, Rafael (Mark) 1927- 45
Steinberg, Saul 1914-1999 67
Steincrohn, Maggie
See Davis, Maggie S.
Steiner, Barbara A(nnette) 1934- 83
Earlier sketch in SATA 13
See also SAAS 13
Steiner, Charlotte 1900-1981 45
Steiner, George 1929- 62
Steiner, Joan 199
Earlier sketch in SATA 110
Steiner, Jorg
See Steiner, Jorg
Steiner, Jorg 1930- 35
Steiner, K. Leslie
See Delany, Samuel R., Jr.
Steiner, Stan(ley) 1925-1987 14
Obituary 50
Steins, Richard 1942- 79
Stem, Jacqueline 1931- 110
Stemple, Jason 179
Steneman, Shep 1945- 132
Stengel, Joyce A. 1938- 158
Stephanie, Gordon
See Gordon, Stephanie Jacob
Stephens, Alice Barber 1858-1932 66
Stephens, Casey
See Wagner, Sharon B.
Stephens, Henrietta Henkle 1909-1993 6
Stephens, J.B.
See Lynn, Tracy
Stephens, Mary Jo 1935- 8
Stephens, Rebecca 1961- 141
Stephens, Reed
See Donaldson, Stephen R.
Stephens, Suzanne
See Kirby, Susan E.
Stephens, William M(cLain) 1925- 21
Stephensen, A. M.
See Manes, Stephen
Stephenson, Lynda 1941- 179
Stephenson, Lynda A.
See Stephenson, Lynda
Stepp, Ann 1935- 29
Stepto, Michele 1946- 61
Steptoe, Javaka 1971- 151
Steptoe, John (Lewis) 1950-1989 63
Earlier sketch in SATA 8
See also CLR 12

Sterling, Brett
See Bradbury, Ray
and Hamilton, Edmond
and Samachson, Joseph
Sterling, Dorothy 1913-2008 83
Autobiography Feature 127
Obituary 200
Earlier sketch in SATA 1
See also CLR 1
See also SAAS 2
Sterling, Helen
See Watts, Helen L. Hoke
Sterling, Philip 1907-1989 8
Obituary 63
Sterling, Shirley (Anne) 1948- 101
Stern, Ellen Norman 1927- 26
Stern, Judith M. 1951- 75
Stern, Madeleine
See Stern, Madeleine B.
Stern, Madeleine B. 1912-2007 14
Stern, Madeleine Bettina
See Stern, Madeleine B.
Stern, Maggie 1953- 156
Stern, Philip Van Doren 1900-1984 13
Obituary 39
Stern, Simon 1943- 15
Sterne, Emma Gelders 1894- 6
Steurt, Marjorie Rankin 1888-1978 10
Stevens, April 1963- 208
Stevens, Bryna 1924- 65
Stevens, Carla M(cBride) 1928- 13
Stevens, Chambers 1968- 128
Stevens, Diane 1939- 94
Stevens, Franklin 1933- 6
Stevens, Greg
See Cook, Glen
Stevens, Gwendolyn 1944- 33
Stevens, Helen 209
Stevens, Jan Romero 1953- 95
Stevens, Janet 1953- 193
Earlier sketches in SATA 90, 148
Stevens, Kathleen 1936- 49
Stevens, Leonard A. 1920- 67
Stevens, Lucile Vernon 1899-1994 59
Stevens, Margaret Dean
See Aldrich, Bess Streeter
Stevens, Patricia Bunning 1931- 27
Stevens, Peter
See Geis, Darlene Stern
Stevens, Serita 1949- 70
Stevens, Serita Deborah
See Stevens, Serita
Stevens, Serita Mendelson
See Stevens, Serita
Stevens, Shira
See Stevens, Serita
Stevenson, Anna (M.) 1905- 12
Stevenson, Augusta 1869(?)-1976 2
Obituary 26
Stevenson, Burton Egbert 1872-1962 25
Stevenson, Drew 1947- 60
Stevenson, Emma 207
Stevenson, Harvey 1960- 148
Earlier sketch in SATA 80
Stevenson, James 1929- 195
Brief entry 34
Earlier sketches in SATA 42, 71, 113, 161
See also CLR 17
Stevenson, Janet 1913- 8
Stevenson, Robert Louis 1850-1894 100
See also YABC 2
See also CLR 107
Stevenson, Robert Louis Balfour
See Stevenson, Robert Louis
Stevenson, Sucie
See Stevenson, Sucie
Stevenson, Sucie 1956- 194
Earlier sketch in SATA 104
Stewart, A(gnes) C(harlotte) 15
Stewart, Amber 181

Stewart, Chantal 1945- 173
Earlier sketch in SATA 121
Stewart, Charles
See Zurhorst, Charles (Stewart, Jr.)
Stewart, Eleanor
See Porter, Eleanor H(odgman)
Stewart, Elisabeth J(ane) 1927- 93
Stewart, Elizabeth Laing 1907- 6
Stewart, Gail B. 1949- 141
Stewart, George Rippey 1895-1980 3
Obituary 23
Stewart, Jennifer J(enkins) 1960- 128
Stewart, Joel 151
Stewart, John 1920- 14
Stewart, Mary (Florence Elinor) 1916- 12
Stewart, Mary Rainbow
See Stewart, Mary (Florence Elinor)
Stewart, Melissa 1968- 209
Earlier sketches in SATA 111, 167
Stewart, Paul 1955- 199
Earlier sketches in SATA 114, 163
Stewart, Robert Neil 1891-1972 7
Stewart, Sarah 143
Stewart, Scott
See Zaffo, George J.
Stewart, W(alter) P. 1924- 53
Stewart, Whitney 1959- 167
Earlier sketch in SATA 92
Stewig, John Warren 1937- 162
Earlier sketches in SATA 26, 110
Stickler, Soma Han 1942- 128
Stidworthy, John 1943- 63
Stiegemeyer, Julie 180
Stier, Catherine 198
Stiles, Martha Bennett 108
Earlier sketch in SATA 6
Still, James 1906-2001 29
Obituary 127
Stille, Darlene R. 1942- 170
Earlier sketch in SATA 126
Stille, Darlene Ruth
See Stille, Darlene R.
Stillerman, Marci 104
Stillerman, Robbie 1947- 12
Stilley, Frank 1918- 29
Stilton, Geronimo 158
Stimpson, Gerald
See Mitchell, Adrian
Stine, Catherine 165
Stine, G(eorge) Harry 1928-1997 136
Earlier sketch in SATA 10
Stine, Jovial Bob
See Stine, R.L.
Stine, R.L. 1943- 194
Earlier sketches in SATA 31, 76, 129
See also CLR 111
Stine, Robert Lawrence
See Stine, R.L.
Stinetorf, Louise (Allender) 1900-1992 10
Stinson, Kathy 1952- 98
Stirling, Arthur
See Sinclair, Upton
Stirling, Ian 1941- 77
Stirling, Nora B(romley) 1900-1997 3
Stirnweis, Shannon 1931- 10
Stobbs, William 1914-2000 17
Obituary 120
Stock, Carolmarie 1951- 75
Stock, Catherine 1952- 158
Earlier sketches in SATA 65, 114
Stockdale, Susan 1954- 206
Earlier sketch in SATA 98
Stockham, Peter (Alan) 1928- 57
Stockton, Francis Richard 1834-1902 44
Brief entry 32
Stockton, Frank R.
See Stockton, Francis Richard
Stockwell-Moniz, Marc J. 1954- 164
Stoddard, Edward G. 1923- 10
Stoddard, Hope 1900-1987 6

Stoddard, Sandol 1927- 98
  Earlier sketch in SATA *14*
Stoehr, Shelley 1969- 107
Stoeke, Janet Morgan 1957- 202
  Earlier sketches in SATA *90, 136*
Stohner, Anu 1952- 179
Stoiko, Michael 1919- 14
Stojic, Manya 1967- 156
Stoker, Abraham
  See Stoker, Bram
Stoker, Bram 1847-1912 29
Stokes, Cedric
  See Beardmore, George
Stokes, Jack (Tilden) 1923- 13
Stokes, Olivia Pearl 1916- 32
Stolarz, Laurie Faria 203
Stolz, Mary 1920-2006 133
  Obituary 180
  Earlier sketches in SATA *10, 71*
  See also SAAS *3*
Stolz, Mary Slattery
  See Stolz, Mary
Stone, Alan
  See Svenson, Andrew E(dward)
Stone, David K(arl) 1922- 9
Stone, David Lee 1978- 166
Stone, Eugenia 1879-1971 7
Stone, Gene
  See Stone, Eugenia
Stone, Helen V(irginia) 6
Stone, Idella Purnell
  See Purnell, Idella
Stone, Ikey
  See Purnell, Idella
Stone, Irving 1903-1989 3
  Obituary 64
Stone, Jeff 178
Stone, Jon 1931-1997 39
  Obituary 95
Stone, Josephine Rector
  See Dixon, Jeanne
Stone, Kyle M. 1972- 202
Stone, Lesley
  See Trevor, Elleston
Stone, Peter 1930-2003 65
  Obituary 143
Stone, Phoebe 205
  Earlier sketch in SATA *134*
Stone, Raymond 1
Stone, Rosetta
  See Dr. Seuss
Stone, Tanya Lee 1965- 182
Stonehouse, Bernard 1926- 140
  Earlier sketches in SATA *13, 80*
Stones, (Cyril) Anthony 1934- 72
Stong, Phil(ip Duffield) 1899-1957 32
Stoops, Erik D(aniel) 1966- 142
  Earlier sketch in SATA *78*
Stoppelmoore, Cheryl Jean
  See Ladd, Cheryl (Jean)
Stops, Sue 1936- 86
Storace, Patricia 193
Storad, Conrad J. 1957- 119
Storey, Margaret 1926- 9
Storey, Victoria Carolyn 1945- 16
Storme, Peter
  See Stern, Philip Van Doren
Storr, Catherine (Cole) 1913-2001 87
  Obituary 122
  Earlier sketch in SATA *9*
Story, Josephine
  See Loring, Emilie (Baker)
Stotko, Mary-Ann 1960- 154
Stott, Dorothy (M.) 1958- 99
  Earlier sketch in SATA *67*
Stott, Dot
  See Stott, Dorothy (M.)
Stotter, Mike 1957- 108
Stout, William 1949- 132
Stoutenburg, Adrien (Pearl) 1916-1982 3
Stoutland, Allison 1963- 130

Stover, Allan C(arl) 1938- 14
Stover, Jill (Griffin) 1958- 82
Stover, Marjorie Filley 1914- 9
Stowe, Harriet Beecher 1811-1896
  See YABC *1*
  See also CLR *131*
Stowe, Harriet Elizabeth Beecher
  See Stowe, Harriet Beecher
Stowe, Leland 1899-1994 60
  Obituary 78
Stowe, Rosetta
  See Ogan, George F.
  and Ogan, Margaret E. (Nettles)
Stower, Adam 195
Strachan, Bruce 1959- 205
Strachan, Ian 1938- 85
Strachan, Linda 167
Strachan, Margaret Pitcairn 1908-1998 14
Strahinich, H. C.
  See Strahinich, Helen C.
Strahinich, Helen C. 1949- 78
Strait, Treva Adams 1909-2002 35
Strand, Mark 1934- 41
Strange, Philippa
  See Coury, Louise Andree
Stranger, Joyce
  See Wilson, Joyce M.
Strangis, Joel 1948- 124
Strannigan, Shawn 1956- 93
Strannigan, Shawn Alyne
  See Strannigan, Shawn
Strasser, Todd 1950- 153
  Earlier sketches in SATA *41, 45, 71, 107*
  See also CLR *11*
Stratemeyer, Edward L. 1862-1930 100
  Earlier sketches in SATA *1, 67*
  See Adams, Harrison
Stratford, Philip 1927- 47
Stratton, Allan 1951- 178
Stratton, J. M.
  See Whitlock, Ralph
Stratton, Thomas
  See Coulson, Robert S(tratton)
  and DeWeese, Thomas Eugene
Stratton-Porter, Gene 1863-1924 15
  See also CLR *87*
Strauss, Gwen 1963- 77
Strauss, Joyce 1936- 53
Strauss, Linda Leopold 1942- 127
Strauss, Susan (Elizabeth) 1954- 75
Strayer, E. Ward
  See Stratemeyer, Edward L.
Streano, Vince(nt Catello) 1945- 20
Streatfeild, Mary Noel
  See Streatfeild, Noel
Streatfeild, Noel 1897(?)-1986 20
  Obituary 48
  See also CLR *83*
Street, Janet Travell 1959- 84
Street, Julia Montgomery 1898-1993 11
Streissguth, Thomas 1958- 116
Strelkoff, Tatiana 1957- 89
Stren, Patti 1949- 88
  Brief entry 41
  See also CLR *5*
Strete, Craig Kee 1950- 96
  Earlier sketch in SATA *44*
Stretton, Barbara (Humphrey) 1936- 43
  Brief entry 35
Strickland, Brad 1947- 200
  Earlier sketches in SATA *83, 137, 142*
Strickland, Craig (A.) 1956- 102
Strickland, Dorothy S(alley) 1933- 89
Strickland, Michael R. 1965- 144
  Earlier sketch in SATA *83*
Strickland, Shadra 209
Strickland, Tessa 173
Strickland, William Bradley
  See Strickland, Brad
Striegel, Jana 1955- 140

Striegel-Wilson, Jana
  See Striegel, Jana
Striker, Lee
  See Clark, Margaret (D.)
Striker, Susan 1942- 63
Stringer, Lauren 1957- 183
  Earlier sketch in SATA *129*
Stroeyer, Poul 1923- 13
Stromoski, Rick 1958- 111
Strong, Charles
  See Epstein, Beryl
  and Epstein, Samuel
Strong, David
  See McGuire, Leslie (Sarah)
Strong, Jeremy 1949- 175
  Earlier sketches in SATA *36, 105*
Strong, J.J.
  See Strong, Jeremy
Strong, Pat
  See Hough, Richard (Alexander)
Strong, Stacie 1965- 74
Stroud, Bettye 1939- 165
  Earlier sketch in SATA *96*
Stroud, Jonathan 1970- 159
  Earlier sketch in SATA *102*
  See also CLR *134*
Stroyer, Poul
  See Stroeyer, Poul
Strug, Kerri 1977- 108
Stryer, Andrea Stenn 1938- 192
Stryker, Daniel
  See Morris, Chris(topher Crosby)
  and Stump, Jane Barr
Stuart, David
  See Hoyt, Edwin P(almer), Jr.
Stuart, Derek
  See Foster, John L(ouis)
Stuart, Forbes 1924- 13
Stuart, Ian
  See MacLean, Alistair
Stuart, Jesse (Hilton) 1906-1984 2
  Obituary 36
Stuart, Ruth McEnery 1849(?)-1917 116
Stuart, Sheila
  See Baker, Mary Gladys Steel
Stuart-Clark, Christopher (Anthony) 1940- .. 32
Stubis, Talivaldis 1926- 5
Stubley, Trevor (Hugh) 1932- 22
Stuchner, Joan Betty 209
Stucky, Naomi R. 1922- 72
Stucley, Elizabeth
  See Northmore, Elizabeth Florence
Stultifer, Morton
  See Curtis, Richard
Sture-Vasa, Mary
  See Alsop, Mary O'Hara
Sturges, Philemon 174
Sturtevant, Katherine 1950- 180
  Earlier sketch in SATA *130*
Sturton, Hugh
  See Johnston, H(ugh) A(nthony) S(tephen)
Sturtzel, Howard A(llison) 1894-1985 1
Sturtzel, Jane Levington 1903-1996 1
Stutley, D(oris) J(ean) 1959- 142
Stutson, Caroline 1940- 104
Stuve-Bodeen, Stephanie 1965- 158
  Earlier sketch in SATA *114*
Stux, Erica 1929- 140
Styles, (Frank) Showell 1908- 10
Stynes, Barbara White 133
Suarez, Maribel 1952- 201
Suba, Susanne 4
Subond, Valerie
  See Grayland, Valerie (Merle Spanner)
Sudbery, Rodie 1943- 42
Sudyka, Diana 208
Sue, Majella Lue 209
Suen, Anastasia 1956(?)- 157
Sufrin, Mark 1925- 76
Sugarman, Joan G. 1917- 64
Sugarman, Tracy 1921- 37

Sugita, Yutaka 1930- 36
Suhl, Yuri (Menachem) 1908-1986 8
  Obituary 50
  See also CLR 2
  See also SAAS 1
Suhr, Joanne 129
Suid, Murray 1942- 27
Sullivan, Edward T. 206
Sullivan, George (Edward) 1927- 147
  Earlier sketches in SATA *4, 89*
Sullivan, Jacqueline Levering 203
Sullivan, Jody
  See Rake, Jody
Sullivan, Kathryn A. 1954- 141
Sullivan, Mary Ann 1954- 63
Sullivan, Mary W(ilson) 1907- 13
Sullivan, Pat
  See Messmer, Otto
Sullivan, Paul 1939- 106
Sullivan, Sarah G. 1953- 179
Sullivan, Silky
  See Makowski, Silvia Ann
Sullivan, Sue
  See Sullivan, Susan E.
Sullivan, Susan E. 1962- 123
Sullivan, Thomas Joseph, Jr. 1947- 16
Sullivan, Tom
  See Sullivan, Thomas Joseph, Jr.
Sully, Tom 1959- 104
Sumichrast, Jozef 1948- 29
Sumiko
  See Davies, Sumiko
Summerforest, Ivy B.
  See Kirkup, James
Summers, Barbara 1944- 182
Summers, James L(evingston) 1910-1973 57
  Brief entry 28
Summertree, Katonah
  See Windsor, Patricia
Summy, Barrie 208
Sun, Chyng Feng 1959- 90
Sunderlin, Sylvia (S.) 1911-1997 28
  Obituary 99
Sung, Betty Lee 26
Supeene, Shelagh Lynne 1952- 153
Supplee, Suzanne 204
Supraner, Robyn 1930- 101
  Earlier sketch in SATA *20*
Supree, Burt(on) 1941-1992 73
Surface, Mary Hall 1958- 126
Surge, Frank 1931- 13
Susac, Andrew 1929- 5
Susi, Geraldine Lee 1942- 98
Sussman, Cornelia Silver 1914-1999 59
Sussman, Irving 1908-1996 59
Sussman, Susan 1942- 48
Sutcliff, Rosemary 1920-1992 78
  Obituary 73
  Earlier sketches in SATA *6, 44*
  See also CLR *138*
Sutcliffe, Jane 1957- 138
Sutherland, Colleen 1944- 79
Sutherland, Efua (Theodora Morgue)
  1924-1996 25
Sutherland, Jon 1958- 167
Sutherland, Jonathan D.
  See Sutherland, Jon
Sutherland, Jonathan David
  See Sutherland, Jon
Sutherland, Margaret 1941- 15
Sutherland, Zena Bailey 1915-2002 37
  Obituary 137
Suttles, Shirley (Smith) 1922- 21
Sutton, Ann (Livesay) 1923- 31
Sutton, Eve(lyn Mary) 1906-1992 26
Sutton, Felix 1910(?)-1973 31
Sutton, Jane 1950- 52
  Brief entry 43
Sutton, Larry M(atthew) 1931- 29
Sutton, Margaret Beebe 1903-2001 1
  Obituary 131

Sutton, Myron Daniel 1925- 31
Sutton, Roger 1956- 93
Suzanne, Jamie
  See Hawes, Louise
  and Lantz, Francess L(in)
  and Singleton, Linda Joy
  and Zach, Cheryl (Byrd)
Suzuki, David 1936- 138
Suzuki, David Takayoshi
  See Suzuki, David
Svendsen, Mark 1962- 181
  Earlier sketch in SATA *120*
Svendsen, Mark Nestor
  See Svendsen, Mark
Svenson, Andrew E(dward) 1910-1975 2
  Obituary 26
Swaab, Neil 1978- 191
Swaim, Jessica 1950- 202
Swain, Carol 1962- 172
Swain, Gwenyth 1961- 134
  Earlier sketch in SATA *84*
Swain, Ruth
  See Swain, Ruth Freeman
Swain, Ruth Freeman 1951- 161
  Earlier sketch in SATA *119*
Swain, Su Zan (Noguchi) 1916- 21
Swallow, Pamela Curtis 178
Swamp, Jake 1941- 98
Swan, Susan 1944- 108
  Earlier sketch in SATA *22*
Swann, Brian (Stanley Frank) 1940- 116
Swann, E. L.
  See Lasky, Kathryn
Swann, Ruth Rice 1920- 84
Swanson, Diane 1944- 203
Swanson, Helen M(cKendry) 1919- 94
Swanson, June 1931- 76
Swanson, Susan Marie 209
Swanson, Wayne 1942- 167
Swarthout, Glendon (Fred) 1918-1992 26
Swarthout, Kathryn 1919- 7
Swayne, Sam(uel F.) 1907- 53
Swayne, Zoa (Lourana) 1905- 53
Sweat, Lynn 1934- 168
  Earlier sketch in SATA *57*
Swede, George 1940- 67
Sweeney, James B(artholomew) 1910-1999 . 21
Sweeney, Joyce 1955- 167
  Earlier sketches in SATA *65, 68, 108*
Sweeney, Joyce Kay
  See Sweeney, Joyce
Sweeney, Karen O'Connor
  See O'Connor, Karen
Sweeney, Matthew (Gerard) 1952- 156
Sweet, Melissa 1956- 172
Sweet, Sarah C.
  See Jewett, Sarah Orne
Sweetland, Nancy A(nn) 1934- 48
Swenson, Allan A(rmstrong) 1933- 21
Swenson, May 1919-1989 15
Swentzell, Rina 1939- 79
Swiatkowska, Gabi 1971(?)- 180
Swift, Bryan
  See Knott, William C(ecil, Jr.)
Swift, David
  See Kaufmann, John
Swift, Hildegarde Hoyt 1890(?)-1977
  Obituary 20
Swift, Jonathan 1667-1745 19
  See also CLR *53*
Swift, Merlin
  See Leeming, Joseph
Swiger, Elinor Porter 1927- 8
Swinburne, Laurence (Joseph) 1924- 9
Swinburne, Stephen R. 1952- 188
  Earlier sketch in SATA *150*
Swinburne, Steve
  See Swinburne, Stephen R.

Swindells, Robert (Edward) 1939- 150
  Brief entry 34
  Earlier sketches in SATA *50, 80*
  See also SAAS *14*
Swinford, Betty (June Wells) 1927- 58
Swinford, Bob
  See Swinford, Betty (June Wells)
Swithen, John
  See King, Stephen
Switzer, Ellen 1923- 48
Swope, Sam 156
Swope, Samuel
  See Swope, Sam
Sybesma, Jetske
  See Ironside, Jetske
Sydney, Frank
  See Warwick, Alan R(oss)
Sydor, Colleen 1960- 207
Sykes, Julie 1963- 202
Sylvada, Peter 1964- 202
Sylvester, Natalie G(abry) 1922- 22
Syme, (Neville) Ronald 1913-1992 87
  Earlier sketch in SATA *2*
Symes, R. F. 77
Symes, Ruth Louise 1962- 179
Symons, (Dorothy) Geraldine 1909- 33
Symons, Stuart
  See Stanley, George Edward
Symynkywicz, Jeffrey B. 1954- 87
Symynkywicz, Jeffrey Bruce
  See Symynkywicz, Jeffrey B.
Synge, (Phyllis) Ursula 1930- 9
Sypher, Lucy Johnston 1907- 7
Szasz, Suzanne (Shorr) 1915-1997 13
  Obituary 99
Szekeres, Cyndy 1933- 157
  Autobiography Feature 157
  Earlier sketches in SATA *5, 60, 131*
  See also SAAS *13*
Szekessy, Tanja 98
Szpura, Beata 1961- 93
Szudek, Agnes S(usan) P(hilomena) 57
  Brief entry 49
Szulc, Tad 1926-2001 26
Szydlow, Jarl
  See Szydlowski, Mary Vigliante
Szydlowski, Mary Vigliante 1946- 94
Szymanski, Lois 1957- 91

T

Taback, Simms 1932- 170
  Brief entry 36
  Earlier sketches in SATA *40, 104*
  See also CLR *100*
Taber, Gladys (Bagg) 1899-1980
  Obituary 22
Tabor, Nancy Maria Grande 1949- 161
  Earlier sketch in SATA *89*
Tabrah, Ruth Milander 1921- 14
Tackach, James 1953- 123
Tackach, James M.
  See Tackach, James
Tadgell, Nicole 1969- 177
Tafuri, Nancy 1946- 192
  Autobiography Feature 192
  Earlier sketches in SATA *39, 75, 130*
  See also CLR *74*
  See also SAAS *14*
Tagg, Christine Elizabeth 1962- 138
Tagliaferro, Linda 173
Taha, Karen T(erry) 1942- 156
  Earlier sketch in SATA *71*
Tai, Sharon O. 1963- 153
Tait, Douglas 1944- 12
Takabayashi, Mari 1960- 156
  Earlier sketch in SATA *115*
Takahashi, Hideko 209
Takahashi, Rumiko 1957- 163

Takakjian, Portia 1930- 15
Takashima, Misako
    See Misako Rocks!
Takashima, Shizuye 1928- 13
Takayama, Sandi 1962- 106
Takeda, Pete(r M.) 1964- 148
Tal, Eve 1947- 176
Talbert, Marc (Alan) 1953- 154
    Autobiography Feature 154
    Earlier sketches in SATA 68, 99
Talbot, Charlene Joy 1928- 10
Talbot, Toby 1928- 14
Talbott, Hudson 1949- 131
    Earlier sketch in SATA 84
Taliaferro, Dorothy L.
    See Martin, Del
Talifero, Gerald 1950- 75
Talker, T.
    See Rands, William Brighty
Tallarico, Tony 1933- 116
Tallcott, Emogene 10
Tallec, Olivier 1970- 197
Tallis, Robyn
    See Smith, Sherwood
Tallon, Robert 1939- 43
    Brief entry 28
Talmadge, Marian 14
Tamaki, Jillian 1980- 201
Tamar, Erika 1934- 150
    Earlier sketches in SATA 62, 101
Tamarin, Alfred H. 1913-1980 13
Tamburine, Jean 1930- 12
Tames, Richard (Lawrence) 1946- 102
    Earlier sketch in SATA 67
Tamminga, Frederick W(illiam) 1934- 66
Tammuz, Benjamin 1919-1989
    Obituary 63
Tan, Amy 1952- 75
Tan, Amy Ruth
    See Tan, Amy
Tan, Shaun 1974- 198
Tanaka, Beatrice 1932- 76
Tanaka, Shelley 136
Tang, Charles 1948- 81
Tang, Greg 172
Tang, You-Shan 1946- 53
Tania B.
    See Blixen, Karen
Tankard, Jeremy 1973- 191
Tannen, Mary 1943- 37
Tannenbaum, Beulah Goldstein 1916- 3
Tannenbaum, D(onald) Leb 1948- 42
Tanner, Jane 1946- 74
Tanner, Louise S(tickney) 1922-2000 9
Tanobe, Miyuki 1937- 23
Tanselle, Eve 1933- 125
Tapio, Pat Decker
    See Kines, Pat Decker
Tapp, Kathy Kennedy 1949- 88
    Brief entry 50
Tarbescu, Edith 1939- 107
Tarkington, (Newton) Booth 1869-1946 17
Tarpley, Natasha A(nastasia) 1971- 147
Tarr, Judith 1955- 149
    Earlier sketch in SATA 64
Tarry, Ellen 1906- 16
    See also CLR 26
    See also SAAS 16
Tarshis, Jerome 1936- 9
Tarshis, Lauren 187
Tarsky, Sue 1946- 41
Taschek, Karen 1956- 185
Tashjian, Janet 1956- 151
    Earlier sketch in SATA 102
Tashjian, Virginia A. 1921-2008 3
Tasker, James 1908- 9
Tate, Don(ald E.) 159
Tate, Eleanora E. 1948- 191
    Earlier sketches in SATA 38, 94
    See also CLR 37

Tate, Eleanora Elaine
    See Tate, Eleanora E.
Tate, Ellalice
    See Hibbert, Eleanor Alice Burford
Tate, Joan 1922- 86
    Earlier sketch in SATA 9
    See also SAAS 20
Tate, Mary Anne
    See Hale, Arlene
Tate, Nikki 134
Tate, Richard
    See Masters, Anthony (Richard)
Tate, Suzanne 1930- 91
Tatham, Betty 142
Tatham, Campbell
    See Elting, Mary
Tatham, Julie
    See Tatham, Julie Campbell
Tatham, Julie Campbell 1908-1999 80
Tavares, Matt 198
    Earlier sketch in SATA 159
Tavares, Victor 1971- 176
Taves, Isabella 1915- 27
Taylor, Alastair 1959- 130
Taylor, Andrew 1951- 70
Taylor, Andrew John Robert
    See Taylor, Andrew
Taylor, Ann 1782-1866 41
    Brief entry 35
Taylor, Audilee Boyd 1931- 59
Taylor, Barbara J. 1927- 10
Taylor, Ben
    See Strachan, Ian
Taylor, Brooke 205
Taylor, Carl 1937- 14
Taylor, Cheryl Munro 1957- 96
Taylor, Cora (Lorraine) 1936- 103
    Earlier sketch in SATA 64
    See also CLR 63
Taylor, Dave 1948- 78
Taylor, David
    See Taylor, Dave
Taylor, David 1900-1965 10
Taylor, Debbie A. 1955- 169
Taylor, Eleanor 1969- 206
Taylor, Elizabeth 1912-1975 13
Taylor, Florance Walton 9
Taylor, Florence M(arian Tompkins)
    1892-1983 9
Taylor, Gage 1942-2000 87
Taylor, Geoff 1946- 204
Taylor, G.P. 1958(?)- 156
Taylor, Graham Peter
    See Taylor, G.P.
Taylor, Herb(ert Norman, Jr.) 1942-1987 22
    Obituary 54
Taylor, J. David
    See Taylor, Dave
Taylor, Jane 1783-1824 41
    Brief entry 35
Taylor, Jerry D(uncan) 1938- 47
Taylor, John Robert
    See Taylor, Andrew
Taylor, Judy
    See Hough, Judy Taylor
Taylor, Kenneth N. 1917-2005 26
Taylor, Kenneth Nathaniel
    See Taylor, Kenneth N.
Taylor, Kim 180
Taylor, L(ester) B(arbour), Jr. 1932- 27
Taylor, Lois Dwight Cole
    See Cole, Lois Dwight
Taylor, Louise Todd 1939- 47
Taylor, Margaret 1950- 106
Taylor, Mark 1927- 32
    Brief entry 28
Taylor, Mildred D. 1943- 135
    See also CLR 144
    See also SAAS 5
Taylor, Mildred Delois
    See Taylor, Mildred D.

Taylor, Paula (Wright) 1942- 48
    Brief entry 33
Taylor, Robert Lewis 1912-1998 10
Taylor, Sean 1965- 192
Taylor, Sydney (Brenner) 1904(?)-1978 28
    Obituary 26
    Earlier sketch in SATA 1
Taylor, Theodore 1921-2006 128
    Obituary 177
    Earlier sketches in SATA 5, 54, 83
    See also CLR 30
    See also SAAS 4
Taylor, William 1938- 164
    Earlier sketches in SATA 78, 113
    See also CLR 63
Tazewell, Charles 1900-1972 74
Tchana, Katrin
    See Tchana, Katrin Hyman
Tchana, Katrin H.
    See Tchana, Katrin Hyman
Tchana, Katrin Hyman 1963- 177
    Earlier sketch in SATA 125
Tchekhov, Anton
    See Chekhov, Anton
Tchen, Richard 120
Tchudi, Stephen N. 1942- 55
Teague, Bob
    See Teague, Robert
Teague, Mark 1963- 205
    Earlier sketches in SATA 68, 99, 170
Teague, Mark Christopher
    See Teague, Mark
Teague, Robert 1929- 32
    Brief entry 31
Teal, Val 1902-1997 10
    Obituary 114
Teal, Valentine M.
    See Teal, Val
Teale, Edwin Way 1899-1980 7
    Obituary 25
Teasdale, Sara 1884-1933 32
Tebbel, John (William) 1912-2004 26
Teckentrup, Britta 1969- 200
Tedesco, P.R.
    See Naylor, Phyllis Reynolds
Teensma, Lynne Bertrand
    See Bertrand, Lynne
Tee-Van, Helen Damrosch 1893-1976 10
    Obituary 27
Tegner, Bruce 1928- 62
Teitelbaum, Michael 1953- 116
    Earlier sketch in SATA 59
Tejima
    See Tejima, Keizaburo
Tejima, Keizaburo 1931- 139
    See also CLR 20
Telander, Todd (G.) 1967- 88
Teleki, Geza 1943- 45
Telemaque, Eleanor Wong 1934- 43
Telescope, Tom
    See Newbery, John
Tellis, Annabel 1967- 191
Temkin, Sara Anne Schlossberg 1913-1996 . 26
Temko, Florence 13
Tempest, Margaret Mary 1892-1982
    Obituary 33
Templar, Maurice
    See Groom, Arthur William
Temple, Arthur
    See Northcott, (William) Cecil
Temple, Charles 1947- 79
Temple, Frances (Nolting) 1945-1995 85
Temple, Herbert 1919- 45
Temple, Paul
    See McConnell, James Douglas Rutherford
Temple, William F(rederick) 1914-1989 107
Tenggren, Gustaf 1896-1970 18
    Obituary 26
Tennant, Kylie
    See Rodd, Kylie Tennant
Tennant, Veronica 1947- 36

Tenneshaw, S.M.
 See Beaumont, Charles
 and Garrett, Randall
 and Silverberg, Robert
Tenniel, John 1820-1914 74
 Brief entry 27
 See also CLR 146
Tepper, Sheri S. 1929- 113
Terada, Alice M. 1928- 90
Terban, Marvin 1940- 54
 Brief entry 45
Teresi, Judith M.
 See Goldberger, Judith M.
ter Haar, Jaap 1922- 6
 See also CLR 15
Terhune, Albert Payson 1872-1942 15
Terkel, Susan N(eiburg) 1948- 103
 Earlier sketch in SATA 59
Terlouw, Jan (Cornelis) 1931- 30
Terrell, John Upton 1900-1988
 Obituary 60
Terrill, Beth 198
Terrill, Elizabeth
 See Terrill, Beth
Terris, Susan 1937- 77
 Earlier sketch in SATA 3
Terry, Luther L(eonidas) 1911-1985 11
 Obituary 42
Terry, Margaret
 See Dunnahoo, Terry Janson
Terry, Walter 1913-1982 14
Terry, Will 1966- 205
Terzian, James P. 1915- 14
Tessendorf, K(enneth) C(harles) 1925-2003 . 75
 Obituary 142
Tessler, Manya 200
Tessler, Stephanie Gordon
 See Gordon, Stephanie Jacob
Testa, Dom 208
Tester, Sylvia Root 1939- 64
 Brief entry 37
Tether, (Cynthia) Graham 1950- 46
 Brief entry 36
Tetzner, Lisa 1894-1963 169
Thach, James Otis 1969- 195
Thacher, Mary McGrath 1933- 9
Thackeray, William Makepeace 1811-1863 .. 23
Thaler, Michael C.
 See Thaler, Mike
Thaler, Mike 1936- 93
 Brief entry 47
 Earlier sketch in SATA 56
Thaler, Shmuel 1958- 126
 Earlier sketch in SATA 72
Thamer, Katie 1955- 42
Thane, Elswyth 1900-1984(?) 32
Tharp, Louise (Marshall) Hall 1898-1992 3
 Obituary 129
Tharp, Tim 1957- 189
Thayer, Ernest Lawrence 1863-1940 60
Thayer, Jane
 See Woolley, Catherine
Thayer, Marjorie 1908-1992 74
 Brief entry 37
Thayer, Peter
 See Wyler, Rose
Thelwell, Norman 1923-2004 14
Themerson, Stefan 1910-1988 65
Thermes, Jennifer 1966- 155
Theroux, Paul 1941- 109
 Earlier sketch in SATA 44
Theroux, Paul Edward
 See Theroux, Paul
Thesman, Jean 124
 Earlier sketch in SATA 74
The Tjong-Khing
 See Khing, T.T.
Thieda, Shirley Ann 1943- 13

Thiele, Colin 1920-2006 125
 Earlier sketches in SATA 14, 72
 See also CLR 27
 See also SAAS 2
Thiele, Colin Milton
 See Thiele, Colin
Thiesing, Lisa 1958- 159
 Earlier sketch in SATA 95
Thimmesh, Catherine 189
Thiry, Joan (Marie) 1926- 45
Thistlethwaite, Miles 1945- 12
Thollander, Earl 1922- 22
Thomas, Abigail 1941- 112
Thomas, Andrea
 See Hill, Margaret (Ohler)
Thomas, Art(hur Lawrence) 1952- 48
 Brief entry 38
Thomas, Carroll
 See Ratliff, Thomas M.
 and Shmurak, Carole B.
Thomas, Dylan 1914-1953 60
Thomas, Dylan Marlais
 See Thomas, Dylan
Thomas, Egbert S.
 See Ellis, Edward S.
Thomas, Estelle Webb 1899-1982 26
Thomas, Frances 1943- 171
 Earlier sketch in SATA 92
Thomas, H. C.
 See Keating, Lawrence A.
Thomas, Ianthe 1951- 139
 Brief entry 42
 See also CLR 8
Thomas, J. F.
 See Fleming, Thomas
Thomas, Jan 1958- 197
Thomas, Jane Resh 1936- 171
 Earlier sketches in SATA 38, 90
Thomas, Jerry D. 1959- 91
Thomas, Joan Gale
 See Robinson, Joan (Mary) G(ale Thomas)
Thomas, Joyce Carol 1938- 137
 Autobiography Feature 137
 Earlier sketches in SATA 40, 78, 123
 See also CLR 19
 See also SAAS 7
Thomas, Lee
 See Floren, Lee
 and Pendleton, Thomas
Thomas, Lowell Jackson, Jr. 1923- 15
Thomas, Margaret
 See Thomas, Peggy
Thomas, Meredith 1963- 119
Thomas, Michael
 See Wilks, Michael Thomas
Thomas, Middy 1931- 191
Thomas, Patricia 1934- 199
 Earlier sketch in SATA 51
Thomas, Peggy 174
Thomas, Rob 1965- 97
Thomas, Scott 1959- 147
Thomas, Velma Maia 1955- 171
Thomas, Vernon (Arthur) 1934- 56
Thomas, Victoria
 See DeWeese, Thomas Eugene
 and Kugi, Constance Todd
Thomasma, Kenneth R. 1930- 90
Thomassie, Tynia 1959- 92
Thompson, Brenda 1935- 34
Thompson, Carol 1951- 189
 Earlier sketch in SATA 85
Thompson, China
 See Lewis, Mary
Thompson, Colin 1942- 198
 Earlier sketches in SATA 95, 163
Thompson, David H(ugh) 1941- 17
Thompson, Eileen
 See Panowski, Eileen Thompson

Thompson, George Selden 1929-1989 73
 Obituary 63
 Earlier sketch in SATA 4
 See also CLR 8
Thompson, Harlan 1894-1987 10
 Obituary 53
Thompson, Hilary 1943- 56
 Brief entry 49
Thompson, Joanna Maxwell Pullein
 See Pullein-Thompson, Joanna Maxwell
Thompson, Julian F(rancis) 1927- 155
 Brief entry 40
 Earlier sketches in SATA 55, 99
 See also CLR 24
 See also SAAS 13
Thompson, K(athryn Carolyn) Dyble
 1952- 82
Thompson, Kate 1956- 204
Thompson, Kay 1912(?)-1998 16
 See also CLR 22
Thompson, Lauren 1962- 200
 Earlier sketches in SATA 132, 174
Thompson, Lauren Stevens
 See Thompson, Lauren
Thompson, Megan Lloyd
 See Lloyd, Megan
Thompson, Richard 1951- 184
Thompson, Ruth Plumly 1891-1976 66
Thompson, Sharon 1952- 119
Thompson, Sharon Elaine
 See Thompson, Sharon
Thompson, Stith 1885-1976 57
 Obituary 20
Thompson, Vivian L(aubach) 1911- 3
Thomson, Bill 1963- 187
Thomson, Celia
 See Lynn, Tracy
Thomson, David (Robert Alexander)
 1914-1988 40
 Obituary 55
Thomson, Melissa 1979- 205
Thomson, Pat 1939- 122
 Earlier sketch in SATA 77
Thomson, Peggy 1922- 31
Thomson, Sarah L. 178
Thon, Melanie Rae 1957- 132
Thong, Roseanne 174
Thorburn, John
 See Goldsmith, John Herman Thorburn
Thorn, John 1947- 59
Thorndyke, Helen Louise
 See Benson, Mildred
Thorne, Ian
 See May, Julian
Thorne, Jean Wright
 See May, Julian
Thornhill, Jan 1955- 148
 Earlier sketch in SATA 77
Thornton, Hall
 See Silverberg, Robert
Thornton, W. B.
 See Burgess, Thornton Waldo
Thornton, Yvonne S(hirley) 1947- 96
Thorpe, E(ustace) G(eorge) 1916- 21
Thorpe, J. K.
 See Nathanson, Laura Walther
Thorvall, Kerstin 1925- 13
Thorvall-Falk, Kerstin
 See Thorvall, Kerstin
Thrasher, Crystal (Faye) 1921- 27
Threadgall, Colin 1941- 77
Three Little Pigs
 See Lantz, Francess L(in)
Thum, Gladys 1920- 26
Thum, Marcella 28
 Earlier sketch in SATA 3
Thundercloud, Katherine
 See Witt, Shirley Hill
Thurber, James 1894-1961 13
Thurber, James Grover
 See Thurber, James

Thurlo, Aimee 161
Thurlo, David 161
Thurman, Judith 1946- 33
Thurman, Mark (Gordon Ian) 1948- 63
Thwaite, Ann (Barbara Harrop) 1932- 14
Tibbetts, Peggy 127
Tibbles, Jean-Paul 1958- 115
Tibo, Gilles 1951- 107
  Earlier sketch in SATA 67
Tiburzi, Bonnie 1948- 65
Ticheburn, Cheviot
  See Ainsworth, William Harrison
Tichenor, Tom 1923-1992 14
Tichnor, Richard 1959- 90
Tichy, William 1924- 31
Tickle, Jack
  See Chapman, Jane
Tiegreen, Alan F. 1935- 94
  Brief entry 36
Tierney, Frank M. 1930- 54
Tierney, Tom 1928- 113
Tiffault, Benette W. 1955- 77
Tiller, Ruth L. 1949- 83
Tilley, Debbie 190
Tilly, Nancy 1935- 62
Tilton, Madonna Elaine 1929- 41
Tilton, Rafael
  See Tilton, Madonna Elaine
Timberlake, Amy 156
Timberlake, Carolyn
  See Dresang, Eliza (Carolyn Timberlake)
Timmers, Leo 1970- 190
Timmins, William F(rederick) 10
Tinbergen, Niko(laas) 1907-1988
  Obituary 60
Tincknell, Cathy 194
Tiner, John Hudson 1944- 32
Tingle, Dolli (?)-
  See Brackett, Dolli Tingle
Tingle, Rebecca 174
Tingle, Tim 208
Tingum, Janice 1958- 91
Tinkelman, Murray 1933- 12
Tinkham, Kelly A. 188
Tinkle, (Julien) Lon 1906-1980 36
Tinling, Marion (Rose) 1904- 140
Tipene, Tim 1972- 141
Tippett, James S(terling) 1885-1958 66
Tirone Smith, Mary-Ann 1944- 143
Titlebaum, Ellen 195
Titler, Dale M(ilton) 1926- 35
  Brief entry 28
Titmarsh, Michael Angelo
  See Thackeray, William Makepeace
Titus, Eve 1922- 2
Tjia, Sherwin 1975- 204
Tjong Khing, The 1933- 76
Tobias, Katherine
  See Gottfried, Theodore Mark
Tobias, Tobi 1938- 82
  Earlier sketch in SATA 5
  See also CLR 4
Todd, Anne Ophelia
  See Dowden, Anne Ophelia Todd
Todd, Barbara 1961- 173
Todd, Barbara K(eith) 1917- 10
Todd, Chuck 195
Todd, H(erbert) E(atton) 1908-1988 84
  Earlier sketch in SATA 11
Todd, Loreto 1942- 30
Todd, Peter
  See Hamilton, Charles (Harold St. John)
Toews, Miriam 1964- 165
Tofel, Richard J. 1957- 140
Toft, Kim Michelle 1960- 170
Tokunbo, Dimitrea 187
Tolan, Stephanie S. 1942- 142
  Earlier sketches in SATA 38, 78
Toland, John (Willard) 1912-2004 38
Tolbert, Steve 1944- 143
Toledo, Francisco 1940- 198

Toledo, Natalia 1967- 197
Tolkien, J. R. R. 1892-1973 100
  Obituary 24
  Earlier sketches in SATA 2, 32
  See also CLR 56
Tolkien, John Ronald Reuel
  See Tolkien, J. R. R.
Toll, Emily
  See Cannon, Eileen E(mily)
Toll, Nelly S. 1935- 78
Tolland, W. R.
  See Heitzmann, William Ray
Tolles, Martha 1921- 76
  Earlier sketch in SATA 8
Tolliver, Ruby C(hangos) 1922- 110
  Brief entry 41
  Earlier sketch in SATA 55
Tolmie, Kenneth Donald 1941- 15
Tolstoi, Lev
  See Tolstoy, Leo
Tolstoy, Leo 1828-1910 26
Tolstoy, Count Leo
  See Tolstoy, Leo
Tolstoy, Leo Nikolaevich
  See Tolstoy, Leo
Tomalin, Ruth 29
Tomaselli, Rosa
  See Pausacker, Jenny
Tomecek, Steve 172
Tomes, Margot (Ladd) 1917-1991 70
  Brief entry 27
  Obituary 69
  Earlier sketch in SATA 36
Tomey, Ingrid 1943- 77
Tomfool
  See Farjeon, Eleanor
Tomic, Tomislav 1977- 202
Tomkins, Jasper
  See Batey, Tom
Tomline, F. Latour
  See Gilbert, W(illiam) S(chwenck)
Tomlinson, Heather 192
Tomlinson, Jill 1931-1976 3
  Obituary 24
Tomlinson, Reginald R(obert) 1885-1979(?)
  Obituary 27
Tomlinson, Theresa 1946- 165
  Earlier sketch in SATA 103
  See also CLR 60
Tommaso, Rich 1970(?)- 200
Tompert, Ann 1918- 139
  Earlier sketches in SATA 14, 89
Tompkins, Troy
  See Cle, Troy
Toner, Raymond John 1908-1986 10
Tong, Gary S. 1942- 66
Tong, Paul 188
Took, Belladonna
  See Chapman, Vera (Ivy May)
Tooke, Louise Mathews 1950- 38
Tooke, Susan 173
Toonder, Martin
  See Groom, Arthur William
Toothaker, Roy Eugene 1928- 18
Tooze, Ruth (Anderson) 1892-1972 4
Topek, Susan Remick 1955- 78
Topping, Audrey R(onning) 1928- 14
Tor, Regina
  See Shekerjian, Regina Tor
Torbert, Floyd James 1922- 22
Torgersen, Don Arthur 1934- 55
  Brief entry 41
Torley, Luke
  See Blish, James
Torrecilla, Pablo 1967- 206
Torres, Andres Segovia
  See Segovia, Andres
Torres, Daniel 1958- 102
Torres, John A. 1965- 163
  Earlier sketch in SATA 94

Torres, John Albert
  See Torres, John A.
Torres, Laura 1967- 146
  Earlier sketch in SATA 87
Torres, Leyla 1960- 155
Torrey, Rich
  See Torrey, Richard
Torrey, Richard 189
Torrie, Malcolm
  See Mitchell, Gladys (Maude Winifred)
Toten, Teresa 1955- 99
Totham, Mary
  See Breinburg, Petronella
Touponce, William F. 1948- 114
Tournier, Michel 1924- 23
Tournier, Michel Edouard
  See Tournier, Michel
Towle, Wendy 1963- 79
Towne, Mary
  See Spelman, Mary
Townley, Rod
  See Townley, Roderick
Townley, Roderick 1942- 177
Townsend, Brad W. 1962- 91
Townsend, John Rowe 1922- 132
  Autobiography Feature 132
  Earlier sketches in SATA 4, 68
  See also CLR 2
  See also SAAS 2
Townsend, Michael 1981- 194
Townsend, Sue
  See Townsend, Susan Lilian
Townsend, Susan Lilian 1946- 93
  Brief entry 48
  Earlier sketch in SATA 55
Townsend, Thomas L. 1944- 59
Townsend, Tom
  See Townsend, Thomas L.
Townsend, Wendy 1962- 201
Townson, Hazel 134
Toye, William Eldred 1926- 8
Traherne, Michael
  See Watkins-Pitchford, Denys James
Trahey, Jane 1923-2000 36
  Obituary 120
Trapani, Iza 1954- 116
  Earlier sketch in SATA 80
Trapp, Maria Augusta von
  See von Trapp, Maria Augusta
Travers, P(amela) L(yndon) 1899-1996 100
  Obituary 90
  Earlier sketches in SATA 4, 54
  See also CLR 93
  See also SAAS 2
Travis, Lucille 133
  Earlier sketch in SATA 88
Treadgold, Mary 1910- 49
Trease, (Robert) Geoffrey 1909-1998 60
  Obituary 101
  Earlier sketch in SATA 2
  See also CLR 42
  See also SAAS 6
Treat, Lawrence 1903-1998 59
Tredez, Alain 1926- 17
Tredez, Denise 1930- 50
Treece, Henry 1912-1966 2
  See also CLR 2
Tregarthen, Enys
  See Sloggett, Nellie
Tregaskis, Richard 1916-1973 3
  Obituary 26
Treherne, Katie Thamer 1955- 76
Trell, Max 1900-1996 14
  Obituary 108
Tremain, Ruthven 1922- 17
Trembath, Don 1963- 168
  Earlier sketch in SATA 96
Tremens, Del
  See MacDonald, Amy
Trent, Robbie 1894-1988 26

Trent, Timothy
  See Malmberg, Carl
Treseder, Terry Walton 1956- 68
Tresilian, (Cecil) Stuart 1891-(?) 40
Tresselt, Alvin 1916-2000 7
  See also CLR 30
Trevino, Elizabeth B(orton) de 1904- 29
  Earlier sketch in SATA 1
  See also SAAS 5
Trevor, Elleston 1920-1995 28
Trevor, Frances
  See Teasdale, Sara
Trevor, Glen
  See Hilton, James
Trevor, (Lucy) Meriol 1919-2000 113
  Obituary 122
  Earlier sketch in SATA 10
Trewellard, J.M. 195
Trewellard, Juliet
  See Trewellard, J.M.
Trez, Alain
  See Tredez, Alain
Trez, Denise
  See Tredez, Denise
Trezise, Percy 1923-
  See CLR 41
Trezise, Percy James
  See Trezise, Percy
Triggs, Tony D. 1946- 70
Trimble, Marshall I(ra) 1939- 93
Trimby, Elisa 1948- 47
  Brief entry 40
Tring, A. Stephen
  See Meynell, Laurence Walter
Tripp, Eleanor B(aldwin) 1936- 4
Tripp, Janet 1942- 108
Tripp, Jenny 188
Tripp, John
  See Moore, John Travers
Tripp, Nathaniel 1944- 101
Tripp, Paul 1916-2002 8
  Obituary 139
Tripp, Valerie 1951- 168
  Earlier sketch in SATA 78
Tripp, Wallace (Whitney) 1940- 31
Trivelpiece, Laurel 1926- 56
  Brief entry 46
Trivett, Daphne Harwood 1940- 22
Trivizas, Eugene 1946- 84
Trnka, Jiri 1912-1969 43
  Brief entry 32
Trollope, Anthony 1815-1882 22
Trost, Lucille W(ood) 1938- 149
  Earlier sketch in SATA 12
Trott, Betty 1933- 91
Trotter, Deborah W. 184
Trotter, Grace V(iolet) 1900-1991 10
Trottier, Maxine 1950- 175
  Earlier sketch in SATA 131
Troughton, Joanna (Margaret) 1947- 37
Trout, Kilgore
  See Farmer, Philip Jose
Trout, Richard E. 123
Trudeau, Garretson Beekman
  See Trudeau, G.B.
Trudeau, Garry
  See Trudeau, G.B.
Trudeau, Garry B.
  See Trudeau, G.B.
Trudeau, G.B. 1948- 168
  Earlier sketch in SATA 35
Trueit, Trudi
  See Trueit, Trudi Strain
Trueit, Trudi Strain 1963- 179
Trueman, Matthew 183
Trueman, Terry 1947- 178
  Earlier sketch in SATA 132
Truesdell, Judy
  See Mecca, Judy Truesdell
Truesdell, Sue
  See Truesdell, Susan G.

Truesdell, Susan G. 108
  Brief entry 45
Trumbauer, Lisa (Trutkoff) 1963- 149
Truss, Jan 1925- 35
Truss, Lynne 1955(?)- 194
Tryon, Leslie 194
  Earlier sketch in SATA 139
Tubb, Jonathan N. 1951- 78
Tubb, Kristin O'Donnell 1971- 209
Tubby, I. M.
  See Kraus, (Herman) Robert
Tucker, Caroline
  See Nolan, Jeannette Covert
Tudor, Edward
  See Browne, Anthony
Tudor, Tasha 1915-2008 160
  Obituary 205
  Earlier sketches in SATA 20, 69
  See also CLR 13
Tuerk, Hanne 1951- 71
Tugeau, Jeremy 199
Tulloch, Richard 1949- 180
  Earlier sketch in SATA 76
Tulloch, Richard George
  See Tulloch, Richard
Tulloch, Shirley 169
Tully, John (Kimberley) 1923- 14
Tumanov, Vladimir A. 1961- 138
Tung, Angela 1972- 109
Tunis, Edwin (Burdett) 1897-1973 28
  Obituary 24
  Earlier sketch in SATA 1
  See also CLR 2
Tunis, John R(oberts) 1889-1975 37
  Brief entry 30
Tunnell, Michael
  See Tunnell, Michael O.
Tunnell, Michael O. 1950- 157
  Earlier sketch in SATA 103
Tunnell, Michael O'Grady
  See Tunnell, Michael O.
Tunnicliffe, C(harles) F(rederick)
  1901-1979 62
Turck, Mary C. 1950- 144
Turk, Hanne
  See Tuerk, Hanne
Turk, Ruth 1917- 82
Turkle, Brinton 1915- 79
  Earlier sketch in SATA 2
Turlington, Bayly 1919-1977 5
  Obituary 52
Turnbull, Agnes Sligh 1888-1982 14
Turnbull, Ann 1943- 160
  Earlier sketch in SATA 18
Turnbull, Ann Christine
  See Turnbull, Ann
Turner, Alice K. 1940- 10
Turner, Ann 1945- 188
  Autobiography Feature 188
  Earlier sketches in SATA 14, 77, 113, 178
Turner, Ann Warren
  See Turner, Ann
Turner, Bonnie 1932- 75
Turner, Elizabeth 1774-1846
  See YABC 2
Turner, Glennette Tilley 1933- 183
  Earlier sketch in SATA 71
Turner, Josie
  See Crawford, Phyllis
Turner, Megan Whalen 1965- 174
  Earlier sketch in SATA 94
Turner, Philip (William) 1925- 83
  Earlier sketch in SATA 11
  See also CLR 89
  See also SAAS 6
Turner, Robyn 1947- 77
Turner, Sheila R.
  See Seed, Sheila Turner
Turngren, Annette 1902(?)-1980
  Obituary 23
Turngren, Ellen (?)-1964 3

Turska, Krystyna (Zofia) 1933- 31
  Brief entry 27
Turteltaub, H.N.
  See Turtledove, Harry
Turtledove, Harry 1949- 166
  Earlier sketch in SATA 116
Turtledove, Harry Norman
  See Turtledove, Harry
Tusa, Tricia 1960- 207
  Earlier sketches in SATA 72, 111
Tusiani, Joseph 1924- 45
Twain, Mark 1835-1910 100
  See also YABC 2
  See also CLR 66
Tweit, Susan J 1956- 94
Tweit, Susan Joan
  See Tweit, Susan J
Tweton, D. Jerome 1933- 48
Twinem, Neecy 1958- 92
Twohill, Maggie
  See Angell, Judie
Tworkov, Jack 1900-1982 47
  Obituary 31
Tyche
  See Papademetriou, Lisa
Tyers, Jenny 1969- 89
Tyers, Kathy 1952- 82
Tyler, Anne 1941- 173
  Earlier sketches in SATA 7, 90
Tyler, Linda
  See Tyler, Linda W(agner)
Tyler, Linda W(agner) 1952- 65
Tyler, Vicki 1952- 64
Tyne, Joel
  See Schembri, Jim
Tyrrell, Frances 1959- 107

U

Ubell, Earl 1926-2007 4
  Obituary 182
Uchida, Yoshiko 1921-1992 53
  Obituary 72
  Earlier sketch in SATA 1
  See also CLR 56
  See also SAAS 1
Udall, Jan Beaney 1938- 10
Uden, (Bernard Gilbert) Grant 1910- 26
Uderzo, Albert 1927-
  See CLR 37
Udovic, David 1950- 189
Udry, Janice May 1928- 152
  Earlier sketch in SATA 4
Uegaki, Chieri 1969- 153
Ueno, Noriko
  See Nakae, Noriko
Ugliano, Natascia 196
Uhlberg, Myron 174
Uhlig, Richard 1970- 195
Uhlig, Susan 1955- 129
Ulam, S(tanislaw) M(arcin) 1909-1984 51
Ullman, James Ramsey 1907-1971 7
Ulm, Robert 1934-1977 17
Ulmer, Louise 1943- 53
Ulmer, Wendy K. 1950- 201
Ulrich, Maureen 1958- 206
Ulyatt, Kenneth 1920- 14
Umansky, Kaye 1946- 188
  Earlier sketch in SATA 158
Unada
  See Gliewe, Unada (Grace)
Uncle Carter
  See Boucher, (Clarence) Carter
Uncle Eric
  See Maybury, Richard J.
Uncle Gus
  See Rey, H. A.
Uncle Mac
  See McCulloch, Derek (Ivor Breashur)

Uncle Ray
  See Coffman, Ramon Peyton
Uncle Shelby
  See Silverstein, Shel
Underhill, Alice Mertie (Waterman)
  1900-1971 10
Underhill, Liz 1948- 53
  Brief entry 49
Underwood, Deborah 1962- 206
Unger, Harlow G. 1931- 75
Unger, Harlow Giles
  See Unger, Harlow G.
Unger, Jim 1937- 67
Ungerer, (Jean) Thomas 1931- 106
  Earlier sketches in SATA 5, 33
  See also CLR 77
Ungerer, Tomi 1931-
  See Ungerer, (Jean) Thomas
Unkelbach, Kurt 1913-1992 4
Unnerstad, Edith (Totterman) 1900-1982 3
  See also CLR 36
Unobagha, Uzo 139
Unrau, Ruth 1922- 9
Unstead, R(obert) J(ohn) 1915-1988 12
  Obituary 56
Unsworth, Walt(er) 1928- 4
Untermeyer, Bryna Ivens 1909-1985 61
Untermeyer, Louis 1885-1977 37
  Obituary 26
  Earlier sketch in SATA 2
Unwin, David S(torr) 1918- 14
Unwin, Nora S(picer) 1907-1982 3
  Obituary 49
Unzner, Christa 1958- 141
  Earlier sketch in SATA 80
Unzner-Fischer, Christa
  See Unzner, Christa
Updale, Eleanor 1953- 175
Updyke, Rosemary K. 1924- 103
Upitis, Alvis 109
Urban, Helle (Denise) 1957- 149
Urban, Linda 199
Urbanovic, Jackie 189
Urbigkit, Cat 1965- 196
Ure, Jean 1943- 192
  Autobiography Feature 192
  Earlier sketches in SATA 48, 78, 129
  See also CLR 34
  See also SAAS 14
U'Ren, Andrea 1968- 142
Uris, Leon 1924-2003 49
  Obituary 146
Uris, Leon Marcus
  See Uris, Leon
Ursu, Anne 177
Ury, Allen B. 1954- 98
Uschan, Michael V. 1948- 129
Usher, Margo Scegge
  See McHargue, Georgess
Uslan, Michael E. 1951- 169
Uston, Ken(neth Senzo) 1935-1987 65
Uttley, Alice Jane 1884-1976 88
  Obituary 26
  Earlier sketch in SATA 3
Uttley, Alison
  See Uttley, Alice Jane
Utz, Lois (Marie) 1932-1986 5
  Obituary 50

V

Vaeth, J. Gordon 1921- 17
Vaeth, Joseph Gordon
  See Vaeth, J. Gordon
Vagin, Vladimir (Vasilevich) 1937- 142
Vail, Rachel 1966- 201
  Earlier sketch in SATA 94, 163
Vainio, Pirkko 1957- 123
  Earlier sketch in SATA 76

Valen, Nanine 1950- 21
Valencak, Hannelore
  See Mayer, Hannelore Valencak
Valens, Amy 1946- 70
Valens, E(vans) G(ladstone), Jr. 1920-1992 ... 1
Valentine, Johnny 72
Valerio, Geraldo 1970- 180
Valgardson, W. D. 1939- 151
  Earlier sketch in SATA 101
Valgardson, William Dempsey
  See Valgardson, W. D.
Valleau, Emily 1925- 51
Van Abbe, Salaman 1883-1955 18
Van Allsburg, Chris 1949- 156
  Earlier sketches in SATA 37, 53, 105
  See also CLR 113
Van Anrooy, Francine 1924- 2
Van Anrooy, Frans
  See Van Anrooy, Francine
Vanasse, Deb 1957- 170
Van Buren, David 203
Vance, Cynthia 207
Vance, Eleanor Graham 1908-1985 11
Vance, Gerald
  See Garrett, Randall
  and Silverberg, Robert
Vance, Marguerite 1889-1965 29
Vance-Abrams, Cynthia
  See Vance, Cynthia
VanCleave, Janice 1942- 116
  Autobiography Feature 123
  Earlier sketch in SATA 75
Vandenburg, Mary Lou 1943- 17
Vander Boom, Mae M. 14
Vander-Els, Betty 1936- 63
van der Heide, Iris 1970- 183
van der Linde, Laurel 1952- 78
van der Meer, Ron 1945- 98
van de Ruit, John 1975- 199
Van der Veer, Judy 1912-1982 4
  Obituary 33
Vanderwerff, Corrine 1939- 117
Vander Zee, Ruth 199
  Earlier sketch in SATA 159
Vande Velde, Vivian 1951- 141
  Earlier sketches in SATA 62, 95
  See also CLR 145
Vandivert, Rita (Andre) 1905-1986 21
Van Draanen, Wendelin 207
  Earlier sketch in SATA 122
Van Dusen, Chris 173
Van Duyn, Janet 1910- 18
Van Dyne, Edith
  See Baum, L. Frank
  and Sampson, Emma (Keats) Speed
  and van Zantwijk, Rudolf (Alexander
    Marinus)
Vane, Mitch
  See Vane, Mitchelle
Vane, Mitchelle 176
van Frankenhuyzen, Gijsbert 1951- 132
Van Genechten, Guido 1957- 165
van Haeringen, Annemarie 193
Van Hook, Beverly H. 1941- 99
Van Horn, William 1939- 43
van Hout, Mies 1962- 178
Van Iterson, S(iny) R(ose) 26
Van Kampen, Vlasta 1943- 163
  Earlier sketch in SATA 54
Van Laan, Nancy 1939- 105
van Lawick-Goodall, Jane
  See Goodall, Jane
Van Leeuwen, Jean 1937- 141
  Autobiography Feature 141
  Earlier sketches in SATA 6, 82, 132
  See also SAAS 8
van Lhin, Erik
  See del Rey, Lester
van Lieshout, Maria 201
Van Loon, Hendrik Willem 1882-1944 18
van Ommen, Sylvia 1978- 186

VanOosting, James 1951- 170
Van Orden, M(erton) D(ick) 1921- 4
Van Patter, Bruce 183
Van Reek, Wouter 204
Van Rensselaer, Alexander (Taylor Mason)
  1892-1962 14
Van Riper, Guernsey, Jr. 1909-1995 3
van Rossum, Heleen 1962- 174
Van Rynbach, Iris 1952- 102
Vansant, Rhonda Joy Edwards 1950- 92
Van Steenwyk, Elizabeth (Ann) 1928- 89
  Earlier sketch in SATA 34
Van Stockum, Hilda 1908-2006 5
  Obituary 179
van Straaten, Harmen 1961- 195
Van Tuyl, Barbara 1940- 11
van Vogt, A(lfred) E(lton) 1912-2000 14
  Obituary 124
Van Wassenhove, Sue 1951- 202
Van Woerkom, Dorothy (O'Brien)
  1924-1996 21
Van Wormer, Joe
  See Van Wormer, Joseph Edward
Van Wormer, Joseph Edward 1913-1998 35
Van Wright, Cornelius 173
Van Zwienen, Ilse Charlotte Koehn
  1929-1991 34
  Brief entry 28
  Obituary 67
Van Zyle, Jon 1942- 176
  Earlier sketch in SATA 84
Varela, Barry 180
Varga, Judy
  See Stang, Judit
Varley, Dimitry V. 1906-1984 10
Varley, Susan 1961- 134
  Earlier sketch in SATA 63
Varon, Sara 195
Vasileva, Tatiana
  See Wassiljewa, Tatjana
Vasiliev, Valery 1949- 80
Vasilieva, Tatiana
  See Wassiljewa, Tatjana
Vasiliu, Mircea 1920- 2
Vass, George 1927- 57
  Brief entry 31
Vaughan, Carter A.
  See Gerson, Noel Bertram
Vaughan, Harold Cecil 1923- 14
Vaughan, Marcia (K.) 1951- 159
  Earlier sketches in SATA 60, 95
Vaughan, Richard 1947- 87
Vaughan, Sam(uel) 1928- 14
Vaughn, Ruth 1935- 14
Vaught, Susan 1965- 195
Vaupel, Robin 198
Vautier, Ghislaine 1932- 53
Vavra, Robert James 1935- 8
Vecsey, George Spencer 1939- 9
Vedral, Joyce L(auretta) 1943- 65
Vega, Denise 174
Vega, Denise B.
  See Vega, Denise
Vega, Diego
  See Adkins, Jan
Veglahn, Nancy (Crary) 1937- 5
Vejjajiva, Jane 1963- 189
Velasquez, Eric 192
Velasquez, Gloria 1949- 113
Velasquez, Gloria 1949-
  See Velasquez, Gloria
Velthuijs, Max 1923-2005 110
  Obituary 160
  Earlier sketch in SATA 53
Venable, Alan (Hudson) 1944- 8
Venezia, Mike 1945- 150
Ventura, Anthony
  See Pellowski, Michael (Joseph)
Ventura, Piero (Luigi) 1937- 61
  Brief entry 43
  See also CLR 16

Vequin, Capini
  See Quinn, Elisabeth
Verba, Joan Marie 1953- 78
Verboven, Agnes 1951- 103
verDorn, Bethea (Stewart) 1952- 76
Vere, Ed 197
Verissimo, Erico (Lopes) 1905-1975 113
Verne, Jules 1828-1905 21
  See also CLR 88
Verne, Jules Gabriel
  See Verne, Jules
Verner, Gerald 1897(?)-1980
  Obituary 25
Verney, John 1913-1993 14
  Obituary 75
Verniero, Joan C. 1949- 181
Vernon, (Elda) Louise A(nderson) 1914- 14
Vernon, Rosemary
  See Smith, Susan Vernon
Vernon, Ursula 204
Vernor, D.
  See Casewit, Curtis W(erner)
Verr, Harry Coe
  See Kunhardt, Edith
Verral, Charles Spain 1904-1990 11
  Obituary 65
Verrillo, Erica 1953- 199
Verrillo, Erica F.
  See Verrillo, Erica
Verrone, Robert J. 1935(?)-1984
  Obituary 39
Versace, Marie Teresa Rios 1917- 2
Vertreace, Martha M(odena) 1945- 78
Vesey, A(manda) 1939- 62
Vesey, Mark (David) 1958- 123
Vesey, Paul
  See Allen, Samuel W(ashington)
Vestergaard, Hope 178
Vestly, Anne-Cath(arina) 1920- 14
  See also CLR 99
Vevers, (Henry) Gwynne 1916-1988 45
  Obituary 57
Viator, Vacuus
  See Hughes, Thomas
Viau, Nancy 208
Vicar, Henry
  See Felsen, Henry Gregor
Vick, Helen Hughes 1950- 88
Vicker, Angus
  See Felsen, Henry Gregor
Vickers, Sheena 1960- 94
Vickery, Kate
  See Kennedy, T.A.
Victor, Edward 1914- 3
Victor, Joan Berg 1942- 30
Vidrine, Beverly Barras 1938- 188
  Earlier sketch in SATA 103
Viereck, Ellen K. 1928- 14
Viereck, Phillip 1925- 3
Viertel, Janet 1915- 10
Vigliante, Mary
  See Szydlowski, Mary Vigliante
Vigna, Judith 1936- 102
  Earlier sketch in SATA 15
Viguers, Ruth Hill 1903-1971 6
Vila, Laura 207
Villareal, Ray 187
Villasenor, Edmund
  See Villasenor, Victor E.
Villasenor, Edmundo
  See Villasenor, Victor E.
Villasenor, Victor
  See Villasenor, Victor E.
Villasenor, Victor E. 1940- 171
Villasenor, Victor Edmundo
  See Villasenor, Victor E.
Villiard, Paul 1910-1974 51
  Obituary 20
Villiers, Alan (John) 1903-1982 10
Vilott, Rhondi
  See Salsitz, Rhondi Vilott

Vincent, Eric Douglas 1953- 40
Vincent, Erin 1969- 188
Vincent, Felix 1946- 41
Vincent, Gabrielle 1928-2000 121
  Earlier sketch in SATA 61
  See also CLR 13
Vincent, Mary Keith
  See St. John, Wylly Folk
Vincent, William R.
  See Heitzmann, William Ray
Vinegar, Tom
  See Gregg, Andrew K.
Vinest, Shaw
  See Longyear, Barry B(rookes)
Vinge, Joan (Carol) D(ennison) 1948- 113
  Earlier sketch in SATA 36
Vining, Elizabeth Gray 1902-1999 6
  Obituary 117
Vinson, Kathryn 1911-1995 21
Vinton, Iris 1906(?)-1988 24
  Obituary 55
Viola, Herman J(oseph) 1938- 126
Viorst, Judith 1931- 172
  Earlier sketches in SATA 7, 70, 123
  See also CLR 90
Vip
  See Partch, Virgil Franklin II
Vipont, Charles
  See Foulds, Elfrida Vipont
Vipont, Elfrida
  See Foulds, Elfrida Vipont
Viramontes, Helena Maria 1954-
  See CLR 285
Viscott, David S(teven) 1938-1996 65
Visser, W(illem) F(rederik) H(endrik)
  1900-1968 10
Vitale, Stefano 1958- 180
  Earlier sketch in SATA 114
Vivas, Julie 1947- 96
Vivelo, Jackie 1943- 63
Vivelo, Jacqueline J.
  See Vivelo, Jackie
Vivelo, Jacqueline Jean
  See Vivelo, Jackie
Vizzini, Ned 1981- 179
  Earlier sketch in SATA 125
Vlahos, Olivia 1924- 31
Vlasic, Bob
  See Hirsch, Phil
Voake, Charlotte 180
  Earlier sketch in SATA 114
Voake, Steve 1961- 178
Vo-Dinh, Mai 1933- 16
Vogel, Carole Garbuny 1951- 105
  Earlier sketch in SATA 70
Vogel, Ilse-Margret 1918- 14
Vogel, John H., Jr. 1950- 18
Vogt, Esther Loewen 1915-1999 14
Vogt, Gregory L. 94
Vogt, Marie Bollinger 1921- 45
Vohwinkel, Astrid 1969- 207
Voight, Virginia Frances 1909-1989 8
Voigt, Cynthia 1942- 160
  Brief entry 33
  Earlier sketches in SATA 48, 79, 116
  See also CLR 141
Voigt, Erna 1925- 35
Voigt-Rother, Erna
  See Voigt, Erna
Vojtech, Anna 1946- 108
  Earlier sketch in SATA 42
Vollstadt, Elizabeth Weiss 1942- 121
Volponi, Paul 175
Volting, Dr. R.E.
  See Lerangis, Peter
Von Ahnen, Katherine 1922- 93
von Buhler, Cynthia 185
Vondra, J. Gert
  See Vondra, Josef
Vondra, Josef 1941- 121

Vondra, Josef Gert
  See Vondra, Josef
Von Gunden, Kenneth 1946- 113
Von Hagen, Victor Wolfgang 1908-1985 29
von Klopp, Vahrah
  See Malvern, Gladys
von Schmidt, Eric 1931-2007 50
  Brief entry 36
  Obituary 181
von Storch, Anne B. 1910- 1
von Trapp, Maria Augusta 1905-1987 16
von Wodtke, Charlotte Buel Johnson
  1918-1982 46
von Ziegesar, Cecily 1970- 161
Vos, Ida 1931-2006 121
  Earlier sketch in SATA 69
  See also CLR 85
Vosburgh, Leonard (W.) 1912- 15
Votaw, Carol 1961- 201
Voyle, Mary
  See Manning, Rosemary
Vrettos, Adrienne Maria 187
Vriens, Jacques 1946- 151
Vugteveen, Verna Aardema
  See Aardema, Verna
Vulture, Elizabeth T.
  See Gilbert, Suzie
Vuong, Lynette Dyer 1938- 110
  Earlier sketch in SATA 60

W

Waas, Uli
  See Waas-Pommer, Ulrike
Waas-Pommer, Ulrike 1949- 85
Waber, Bernard 1924- 155
  Brief entry 40
  Earlier sketches in SATA 47, 95
  See also CLR 55
Wachtel, Shirley Russak 1951- 88
Wachter, Oralee (Roberts) 1935- 61
  Brief entry 51
Waddell, Evelyn Margaret 1918- 10
Waddell, Martin 1941- 129
  Autobiography Feature 129
  Earlier sketches in SATA 43, 81, 127
  See also CLR 31
  See also SAAS 15
Waddy, Lawrence (Heber) 1914- 91
Wade, Mary Dodson 1930- 151
  Earlier sketch in SATA 79
Wade, Suzanne
  See Kirby, Susan E.
Wade, Theodore E., Jr. 1936- 37
Wademan, Peter John 1946- 122
Wademan, Spike
  See Wademan, Peter John
Wadsworth, Ginger 1945- 157
  Earlier sketch in SATA 103
Wagenheim, Kal 1935- 21
Wagner, Michele R. 1975- 157
Wagner, Sharon B. 1936- 4
Wagoner, David (Russell) 1926- 14
Wahl, Jan (Boyer) 1933- 132
  Earlier sketches in SATA 2, 34, 73
  See also SAAS 3
Wahl, Mats 1945- 186
Waide, Jan 1952- 29
Wainscott, John Milton 1910-1981 53
Wainwright, Richard M. 1935- 91
Wainwright, Ruth
  See Symes, Ruth Louise
Wait, Lea 1946- 137
Waite, Judy 174
Waite, Judy Bernard
  See Bernard, Patricia
Waite, Michael
  See Waite, Michael P.
Waite, Michael P. 1960- 101

Waite, P(eter) B(usby) 1922- 64
Waites, Joan C. 187
Waitley, Douglas 1927- 30
Wakefield, Jean L.
    See Laird, Jean E(louise)
Wakin, Daniel (Joseph) 1961- 84
Wakin, Edward 1927- 37
Wakiyama, Hanako 1966- 192
Walck, Henry Z. 1908(?)-1984
    Obituary 40
Walden, Amelia Elizabeth 3
Walden, Mark 188
Waldherr, Kris 1963- 76
Waldman, Bruce 1949- 15
Waldman, Neil 1947- 203
    Earlier sketches in SATA 51, 94, 142
Waldrep, Richard 198
Waldron, Ann Wood 1924- 16
Waldron, Kathleen Cook 176
Wales, Dirk 1931- 205
Walgren, Judy 1963- 118
Walker, Addison
    See Walker, (Addison) Mort
Walker, Alice 1944- 31
Walker, Alice Malsenior
    See Walker, Alice
Walker, Barbara (Jeanne) K(erlin) 1921- 80
    Earlier sketch in SATA 4
Walker, Barbara M(uhs) 1928- 57
Walker, (James) Braz(elton) 1934-1983 45
Walker, David 1965- 197
Walker, David G(ordon) 1926- 60
Walker, David Harry 1911-1992 8
    Obituary 71
Walker, Diana 1925- 9
Walker, Diane Marie Catherine
    See Walker, Kate
Walker, Dick
    See Pellowski, Michael (Joseph)
Walker, Frank 1931-2000 36
Walker, Holly Beth
    See Bond, Gladys Baker
Walker, Kate 1950- 165
    Earlier sketch in SATA 82
Walker, Kathrine Sorley
    See Sorley Walker, Kathrine
Walker, Lou Ann 1952- 66
    Brief entry 53
Walker, Louise Jean 1891-1976
    Obituary 35
Walker, Mary Alexander 1927- 61
Walker, Mildred
    See Schemm, Mildred Walker
Walker, (Addison) Mort 1923- 8
Walker, Pamela 1948- 142
    Earlier sketch in SATA 24
Walker, Paul Robert 1953- 154
Walker, Robert W. 1948- 66
Walker, Sally M(acArt) 1954- 135
Walker, Stephen J. 1951- 12
Walker-Blondell, Becky 1951- 89
Wallace, Barbara Brooks 1922- 136
    Earlier sketches in SATA 4, 78
    See also CLR 150
    See also SAAS 17
Wallace, Beverly Dobrin 1921- 19
Wallace, Bill 1947- 169
    Brief entry 47
    Earlier sketches in SATA 53, 101
Wallace, Daisy
    See Cuyler, Margery
Wallace, Ian 1950- 141
    Earlier sketches in SATA 53, 56
    See also CLR 37
Wallace, John 1966- 155
    Earlier sketch in SATA 105
Wallace, John A(dam) 1915-2004 3
    Obituary 155
Wallace, Karen 1951- 188
    Earlier sketches in SATA 83, 139

Wallace, Nancy Elizabeth 1948- 186
    Earlier sketch in SATA 141
Wallace, Nigel
    See Hamilton, Charles (Harold St. John)
Wallace, Paula S. 153
Wallace, Rich 1957- 196
    Earlier sketches in SATA 117, 158
Wallace, Robert 1932-1999 47
    Brief entry 37
Wallace, Ruby Ann 1923(?)- 77
Wallace, William Keith
    See Wallace, Bill
Wallace-Brodeur, Ruth 1941- 169
    Brief entry 41
    Earlier sketches in SATA 51, 88
Wallenta, Adam 1974- 123
Waller, Leslie 1923-2007 20
Walley, Byron
    See Card, Orson Scott
Wallis, Diz 1949- 77
Wallis, G. McDonald
    See Campbell, Hope
Wallner, Alexandra 1946- 156
    Brief entry 41
    Earlier sketches in SATA 51, 98
Wallner, John C. 1945- 133
    Earlier sketches in SATA 10, 51
Wallower, Lucille 11
Walrod, Amy 1973(?)- 182
Walsh, Ann 1942- 176
    Earlier sketch in SATA 62
Walsh, Ellen Stoll 1942- 194
    Earlier sketches in SATA 49, 99, 147
Walsh, George Johnston 1889-1981 53
Walsh, Gillian Paton
    See Paton Walsh, Jill
Walsh, Jill Paton
    See Paton Walsh, Jill
Walsh, Joanna 1970- 182
Walsh, Lawrence 1942- 170
Walsh, Marissa 1972- 195
Walsh, Mary Caswell 1949- 118
Walsh, Mitzy
    See Walsh, Marissa
Walsh, Suella 170
Walsh, V. L.
    See Walsh, Vivian
Walsh, Vivian 1960- 120
Walsh Shepherd, Donna 1948- 78
Walter, Frances V. 1923- 71
Walter, Mildred Pitts 1922- 133
    Brief entry 45
    Earlier sketch in SATA 69
    See also CLR 61
    See also SAAS 12
Walter, Villiam Christian
    See Andersen, Hans Christian
Walter, Virginia
    See Walter, Virginia A.
Walter, Virginia A. 134
Walters, Audrey 1929- 18
Walters, Celeste 1938- 126
Walters, Eric 1957- 205
    Earlier sketches in SATA 99, 155
Walters, Eric Robert
    See Walters, Eric
Walters, Helen B. (?)-1987
    Obituary 50
Walters, Hugh
    See Hughes, Walter (Llewellyn)
Walther, Thomas A. 1950- 31
Walther, Tom
    See Walther, Thomas A.
Waltner, Elma 1912-1987 40
Waltner, Willard H. 1909- 40
Walton, Darwin McBeth 1926- 119
Walton, Fiona L. M. 1959- 89
Walton, Richard J. 1928- 4
Walton, Rick 1957- 204
    Earlier sketches in SATA 101, 151
Waltrip, Lela (Kingston) 1904-1995 9

Waltrip, Mildred 1911- 37
Waltrip, Rufus (Charles) 1898-1988 9
Walworth, Nancy Zinsser 1917- 14
Wangerin, Walter, Jr. 1944- 98
    Brief entry 37
    Earlier sketch in SATA 45
Waniek, Marilyn Nelson 1946-
    See Nelson, Marilyn
Wannamaker, Bruce
    See Moncure, Jane Belk
Warbler, J. M.
    See Cocagnac, Augustin Maurice(-Jean)
Warburg, Sandol Stoddard
    See Stoddard, Sandol
Ward, E. D.
    See Gorey, Edward (St. John)
    and Lucas, E(dward) V(errall)
Ward, Ed
    See Stratemeyer, Edward L.
Ward, Helen 1962- 206
    Earlier sketches in SATA 72, 144
Ward, Jay 1920-1989
    Obituary 63
Ward, Jennifer 1963- 146
Ward, John (Stanton) 1917- 42
Ward, Jonas
    See Ard, William
    and Cox, William R(obert)
    and Garfield, Brian (Francis Wynne)
Ward, Lynd (Kendall) 1905-1985 36
    Obituary 42
    Earlier sketch in SATA 2
Ward, Martha (Eads) 5
Ward, Melanie
    See Curtis, Richard
    and Lynch, Marilyn
Ward, Nicholas John
    See Ward, Nick
Ward, Nick 1955- 190
Ward, Tom
    See Stratemeyer, Edward L.
Wardell, Dean
    See Prince, J(ack) H(arvey)
Wardlaw, Lee 1955- 115
    Earlier sketch in SATA 79
Ware, Cheryl 1963- 101
Ware, Chris 1967- 140
Ware, Leon (Vernon) 1909-1976 4
Wargin, Kathy-jo 1964- 145
Warhola, James 1955- 187
Warner, Frank A. 67
    Earlier sketch in SATA 1
Warner, Gertrude Chandler 1890-1979 9
    Obituary 73
Warner, J(ohn) F. 1929- 75
Warner, Lucille Schulberg 30
Warner, Matt
    See Fichter, George S.
Warner, Oliver (Martin Wilson) 1903-1976 . 29
Warner, Sally 1946- 131
Warner, Sunny (B.) 1931- 108
Warnes, Tim 1971- 166
    Earlier sketch in SATA 116
Warnes, Timothy
    See Warnes, Tim
Warnick, Elsa 1942- 113
Warren, Andrea 1946- 98
Warren, Betsy
    See Warren, Elizabeth Avery
Warren, Billy
    See Warren, William Stephen
Warren, Cathy 1951- 62
    Brief entry 46
Warren, Elizabeth
    See Supraner, Robyn
Warren, Elizabeth Avery 1916- 46
    Brief entry 38
Warren, Jackie M. 1953- 135
Warren, Joshua P(aul) 1976- 107
Warren, Joyce W(illiams) 1935- 18
Warren, Mary Phraner 1929- 10

Warren, Robert Penn 1905-1989 46
  Obituary 63
Warren, Scott S. 1957- 79
Warren, William Stephen 1882-1968 9
Warrick, Patricia Scott 1925- 35
Warriner, John 1907(?)-1987
  Obituary 53
Warsh
  See Warshaw, Jerry
Warshaw, Jerry 1929- 30
Warshaw, Mary 1931- 89
Warshofsky, Fred 1931- 24
Warshofsky, Isaac
  See Singer, Isaac Bashevis
Wartski, Maureen (Ann Crane) 1940- 50
  Brief entry 37
Warwick, Alan R(oss) 1900-1973 42
Wa-Sha-Quon-Asin
  See Belaney, Archibald Stansfeld
Wa-sha-quon-asin
  See Belaney, Archibald Stansfeld
Washburn, Bradford 1910-2007 38
  Obituary 181
Washburn, Henry Bradford, Jr.
  See Washburn, Bradford
Washburn, Jan(ice) 1926- 63
Washburn, Lucia 193
Washburne, Carolyn Kott 1944- 86
Washburne, Heluiz Chandler 1892-1970 10
  Obituary 26
Washington, Booker T. 1856-1915 28
Washington, Donna L. 1967- 159
  Earlier sketch in SATA 98
Wasserman, Robin 1978- 207
Wasserstein, Wendy 1950-2006 94
  Obituary 174
Wassiljewa, Tatjana 1928- 106
Watanabe, Shigeo 1928- 131
  Brief entry 32
  Earlier sketch in SATA 39
  See also CLR 8
Waters, John F(rederick) 1930- 4
Waters, Summer
  See Sykes, Julie
Waters, Tony 1958- 75
Waterton, Betty 1923- 99
  Brief entry 34
  Earlier sketch in SATA 37
Waterton, Betty Marie
  See Waterton, Betty
Watkins, Dawn L. 126
Watkins, Gloria Jean
  See hooks, bell
Watkins, Lois 1930- 88
Watkins, Peter 1934- 66
Watkins, Yoko Kawashima 1933- 93
Watkins-Pitchford, Denys James
  1905-1990 87
  Obituary 66
  Earlier sketch in SATA 6
  See also SAAS 4
Watling, James 1933- 117
  Earlier sketch in SATA 67
Watson, Aldren A(uld) 1917- 42
  Brief entry 36
Watson, Amy Zakrzewski 1965- 76
Watson, B. S.
  See Teitelbaum, Michael
Watson, Carol 1949- 78
Watson, C.G. 193
Watson, Clyde 1947- 68
  Earlier sketch in SATA 5
  See also CLR 3
Watson, Helen Orr 1892-1978
  Obituary 24
Watson, James 1936- 106
  Earlier sketch in SATA 10
Watson, Jane Werner 1915- 54
  Earlier sketch in SATA 3
Watson, Jesse Joshua 199

Watson, John H.
  See Farmer, Philip Jose
Watson, Mary 1953- 117
Watson, N. Cameron 1955- 81
Watson, Nancy Dingman 32
Watson, Pauline 1925- 14
Watson, Richard F.
  See Silverberg, Robert
Watson, Richard Jesse 1951- 62
Watson, Sally (Lou) 1924- 3
Watson, Wendy (McLeod) 1942- 142
  Earlier sketches in SATA 5, 74
Watson Taylor, Elizabeth 1915- 41
Watt, Melanie 1975- 193
  Earlier sketch in SATA 136
Watt, Thomas 1935- 4
Wattenberg, Jane 174
Watterson, Bill 1958- 66
Watt-Evans, Lawrence 1954- 121
Watts, (Anna) Bernadette 1942- 103
  Earlier sketch in SATA 4
Watts, Ephraim
  See Horne, Richard Henry Hengist
Watts, Franklin (Mowry) 1904-1978 46
  Obituary 21
Watts, Helen L. Hoke 1903-1990
  Obituary 65
Watts, Irene N(aemi) 1931- 111
  Earlier sketch in SATA 56
Watts, Isaac 1674-1748 52
Watts, James K(ennedy) M(offitt) 1955- 59
Watts, Jeri Hanel 1957- 170
Watts, Julia 1969- 103
Watts, Leander 1956- 146
Watts, Leslie Elizabeth 1961- 168
Watts, Mabel Pizzey 1906-1994 11
Watts, Nigel 1957-1999 121
Waugh, C. C. Roessel
  See Waugh, Carol-Lynn Rossel
  and Waugh, Charles G(ordon)
Waugh, Carol-Lynn Rossel 1947- 41
Waugh, Dorothy -1996 11
Waugh, Sylvia 1935- 169
Waugh, Virginia
  See Sorensen, Virginia
Wax, Wendy A. 1963- 163
  Earlier sketch in SATA 73
Wayland, April Halprin 1954- 143
  Earlier sketch in SATA 78
  See also SAAS 26
Wayland, Patrick
  See O'Connor, Richard
Wayne, (Anne) Jenifer 1917-1982 32
Wayne, Kyra Petrovskaya 1918- 8
Wayne, Richard
  See Decker, Duane
Wayshak, Deborah Noyes
  See Noyes, Deborah
Waystaff, Simon
  See Swift, Jonathan
Weales, Gerald (Clifford) 1925- 11
Weary, Ogdred
  See Gorey, Edward (St. John)
Weatherford, Carole Boston 1956- 181
  Earlier sketch in SATA 138
Weatherill, Cat 203
Weatherly, Lee 1967- 192
Weatherly, Myra 1926- 130
Weatherly, Myra S.
  See Weatherly, Myra
Weaver, Harriett E. 1908-1993 65
Weaver, John L. 1949- 42
Weaver, Robyn
  See Conley, Robyn
Weaver, Robyn M.
  See Conley, Robyn
Weaver, Tess 197
Weaver, Ward
  See Mason, F(rancis) van Wyck
Weaver, Will 1950- 161
  Earlier sketches in SATA 88, 109

Weaver, William Weller
  See Weaver, Will
Weaver-Gelzer, Charlotte 1950- 79
Webb, Christopher
  See Wibberley, Leonard
Webb, Jacqueline
  See Pearce, Margaret
Webb, Jacquelyn
  See Pearce, Margaret
  and Pearce, Margaret
Webb, Jean Francis (III) 1910-1991 35
Webb, Kaye 1914- 60
Webb, Lois Sinaiko 1922- 82
Webb, Margot 1934- 67
Webb, Sharon 1936- 41
Webb, Sophie 1958- 135
Webber, Andrew Lloyd
  See Lloyd Webber, Andrew
Webber, Desiree Morrison 1956- 170
Webber, Irma E(leanor Schmidt)
  1904-1995 14
Weber, Alfons 1921- 8
Weber, Bruce 1942- 120
  Earlier sketch in SATA 73
Weber, Debora 1955- 58
Weber, EdNah New Rider 1919(?)- 168
Weber, Jill 1950- 209
  Earlier sketch in SATA 127
Weber, Judith E(ichler) 1938- 64
Weber, Ken(neth J.) 1940- 90
Weber, Lenora Mattingly 1895-1971 2
  Obituary 26
Weber, Michael 1945- 87
Weber, Sandra 1961- 158
Weber, William J(ohn) 1927- 14
Webster, Alice Jane Chandler 1876-1916 17
Webster, David 1930- 11
Webster, Frank V. 67
  Earlier sketch in SATA 1
Webster, Gary
  See Garrison, Webb B(lack)
Webster, James 1925-1981 17
  Obituary 27
Webster, Jean
  See Webster, Alice Jane Chandler
Wechsler, Doug 189
Wechsler, Herman J. 1904-1976
  Obituary 20
Wechter, Nell (Carolyn) Wise 1913-1989 .. 127
  Earlier sketch in SATA 60
Weck, Thomas L. 1942- 62
Wedd, Kate
  See Gregory, Philippa
Weddle, Ethel Harshbarger 1897-1996 11
Wedekind, Annie 204
Weeks, Sarah 194
  Earlier sketch in SATA 158
Weems, David B(urnola) 1922- 80
Wees, Frances Shelley 1902-1982 58
Weevers, Peter 1944- 59
Wegen, Ronald 1946-1985 99
Wegman, William (George) 1943- 135
  Earlier sketches in SATA 78, 129
Wegner, Fritz 1924- 20
Weidhorn, Manfred 1931- 60
Weidt, Maryann N. 1944- 85
Weigel, Jeff 1958- 170
Weigelt, Udo 1960- 201
  Earlier sketch in SATA 168
Weihs, Erika 1917- 107
  Earlier sketch in SATA 15
Weik, Mary Hays 1898(?)-1979 3
  Obituary 23
Weil, Ann Yezner 1908-1969 9
Weil, Lisl 1910- 7
Weilerstein, Sadie Rose 1894-1993 3
  Obituary 75
Weill, Cynthia 1959- 167
Wein, Elizabeth E. 1964- 151
  Earlier sketch in SATA 82

Wein, Elizabeth Eve
  See Wein, Elizabeth E.
Weinberg, Larry
  See Weinberg, Lawrence (E.)
Weinberg, Lawrence (E.) 92
  Brief entry 48
Weinberger, Tanya 1939- 84
Weiner, Sandra 1922- 14
Weingarten, Violet (Brown) 1915-1976 3
  Obituary 27
Weingartner, Charles 1922- 5
Weinheimer, Beckie 1958- 186
Weinstein, Ellen Slusky 1959- 200
Weinstein, Nina 1951- 73
Weinstock, Robert 1967- 204
Weir, Bob 1947- 76
Weir, Diana (R.) Loiewski 1958- 111
Weir, Joan S(herman) 1928- 99
Weir, LaVada 2
Weir, Rosemary (Green) 1905-1994 21
Weir, Wendy 1949- 76
Weis, Margaret 1948- 164
  Earlier sketches in SATA *38, 92*
Weisberger, Bernard A(llen) 1922- 21
Weisburd, Stefi 1957- 202
Weiser, Marjorie P(hillis) K(atz) 1934- 33
Weisgard, Leonard (Joseph) 1916-2000 85
  Obituary 122
  Earlier sketches in SATA *2, 30*
  See also SAAS *19*
Weiss, Adelle 1920- 18
Weiss, Ann E(dwards) 1943- 69
  Earlier sketch in SATA *30*
  See also SAAS *13*
Weiss, Edna
  See Barth, Edna
Weiss, Ellen 1953- 44
Weiss, Harvey 1922- 76
  Earlier sketches in SATA *1, 27*
  See also CLR *4*
  See also SAAS *19*
Weiss, Jaqueline Shachter 1926- 65
Weiss, Malcolm E. 1928- 3
Weiss, Margaret Edith
  See Weis, Margaret
Weiss, Miriam
  See Schlein, Miriam
Weiss, Mitch 1951- 183
  Earlier sketch in SATA *123*
Weiss, Nicki 1954- 86
  Earlier sketch in SATA *33*
Weiss, Renee Karol 1923- 5
Weissberger, Ela 1930- 181
Weissberger, Ela Stein
  See Weissberger, Ela
Weissenborn, Hellmuth 1898-1982
  Obituary 31
Weitzman, David L. 1936- 172
  Earlier sketch in SATA *122*
Wekesser, Carol A. 1963- 76
Welber, Robert 26
Welch, Amanda (Jane) 1945- 75
Welch, D'Alte Aldridge 1907-1970
  Obituary 27
Welch, Holly 206
Welch, Jean-Louise
  See Kempton, Jean Welch
Welch, Pauline
  See Bodenham, Hilda Morris
Welch, Ronald
  See Felton, Ronald Oliver
Welch, Sheila Kelly 1945- 130
Welch, Willy 1952- 93
Weldin, Frauke 1969- 188
Welford, Sue 1942- 75
Weller, George 1907-2002 31
  Obituary 140
Weller, George Anthony
  See Weller, George
Welling, Peter J. 1947- 135

Wellington, Monica 1957- 157
  Earlier sketches in SATA *67, 99*
Wellman, Alice 1900-1984 51
  Brief entry 36
Wellman, Manly Wade 1903-1986 6
  Obituary 47
Wellman, Paul I. 1898-1966 3
Wellman, Paul Iselin
  See Wellman, Paul I.
Wellman, Sam(uel) 1939- 122
Wells, H. G. 1866-1946 20
  See also CLR *133*
Wells, Helen
  See Campbell, Hope
Wells, Helen 1910-1986 49
  Earlier sketch in SATA *2*
Wells, Herbert George
  See Wells, H. G.
Wells, J. Wellington
  See de Camp, L. Sprague
Wells, June
  See Swinford, Betty (June Wells)
Wells, Robert
  See Welsch, Roger L(ee)
Wells, Robert E. 184
Wells, Rosemary 1943- 207
  Earlier sketches in SATA *18, 69, 114, 156*
  See also CLR *69*
  See also SAAS *1*
Wells, Susan (Mary) 1951- 78
Wels, Byron G(erald) 1924-1993 9
Welsbacher, Anne 1955- 89
Welsch, Roger L(ee) 1936- 82
Welsh, David
  See Hills, C.A.R.
Welsh, Mary Flynn 1910(?)-1984
  Obituary 38
Welsh, T.K. 1956- 184
Weltner, Linda R(iverly) 1938- 38
Welton, Jude 1955- 143
  Earlier sketch in SATA *79*
Welty, S. F.
  See Welty, Susan F.
Welty, Susan F. 1905- 9
Wemmlinger, Raymond 190
Wendelin, Rudolph 1910-2000 23
Weninger, Brigitte 1960- 189
Wentworth, Robert
  See Hamilton, Edmond
Werlin, Nancy 1961- 161
  Earlier sketches in SATA *87, 119*
Werner, Elsa Jane
  See Watson, Jane Werner
Werner, Herma 1926- 47
  Brief entry 41
Werner, Jane
  See Watson, Jane Werner
Werner, K.
  See Casewit, Curtis W(erner)
Wersba, Barbara 1932- 58
  Autobiography Feature 103
  Earlier sketch in SATA *1*
  See also CLR *78*
  See also SAAS *2*
Werstein, Irving 1914(?)-1971 14
Werth, Kurt 1896-1983 20
Wesley, Alison
  See Barnes, Michael
Wesley, Kathryn
  See Rusch, Kristine Kathryn
Wesley, Mary (Aline) 1912-2002 66
Wesley, Valerie Wilson 1947- 168
  Earlier sketch in SATA *106*
West, Andrew
  See Arthur, Robert, (Jr.)
West, Anna 1938- 40
West, Barbara
  See Price, Olive
West, Betty 1921- 11
West, Bruce 1951- 63

West, C. P.
  See Wodehouse, P. G.
West, Dorothy
  See Benson, Mildred
West, Emily Govan 1919- 38
West, Emmy
  See West, Emily Govan
West, James
  See Withers, Carl A.
West, Jerry
  See Svenson, Andrew E(dward)
West, (Mary) Jessamyn 1902-1984
  Obituary 37
West, John
  See Arthur, Robert, (Jr.)
West, Owen
  See Koontz, Dean
West, Ward
  See Borland, Harold Glen
Westall, Robert (Atkinson) 1929-1993 69
  Obituary 75
  Earlier sketch in SATA *23*
  See also CLR *13*
  See also SAAS *2*
Westaway, Jane 1948- 121
Westcott, Nadine Bernard 1949- 130
Westera, Marleen 1962- 187
Westerberg, Christine 1950- 29
Westerduin, Anne 1945- 105
Westerfeld, Scott 1963- 161
Westervelt, Virginia Veeder 1914-2005 10
Westheimer, David 1917-2005 14
  Obituary 170
Westheimer, David Kaplan
  See Westheimer, David
Westmacott, Mary
  See Christie, Agatha
Westman, Barbara 70
Westman, Paul (Wendell) 1956- 39
Westmoreland, William C. 1914-2005 63
Westmoreland, William Childs
  See Westmoreland, William C.
Weston, Allen
  See Hogarth, Grace (Weston Allen)
  and Norton, Andre
Weston, Carol 1956- 135
Weston, Carrie 190
Weston, John (Harrison) 1932- 21
Weston, Martha 1947- 119
  Earlier sketch in SATA *53*
Weston, Robert Paul 209
Westphal, Arnold Carl 1897- 57
Westrup, Hugh 102
Westwood, Jennifer 1940-2008 10
  Obituary 192
Wexler, Jerome (LeRoy) 1923- 14
Weyland, Jack 1940- 81
Weyn, Suzanne 1955- 164
  Earlier sketches in SATA *63, 101*
Weyr, Garret
  See Freymann-Weyr, (Rhoda) Garret
  (Michaela)
Wezyk, Joanna 1966- 82
Whaley, Joyce Irene 1923- 61
Whalin, W. Terry 1953- 93
Wharf, Michael
  See Weller, George
Wharmby, Margot 63
Wharton, Edith 1862-1937
  See CLR *136*
Wharton, Edith Newbold Jones
  See Wharton, Edith
Whatley, Bruce 1954- 177
Wheatley, Arabelle 1921- 16
Wheatley, Nadia 1949- 147
Wheeler, Cindy 1955- 49
  Brief entry 40
Wheeler, Deborah 1947- 83
Wheeler, Janet D. 1
Wheeler, Jill C. 1964- 136
  Earlier sketch in SATA *86*

Wheeler, Jody 1952- *148*
  Earlier sketch in SATA *84*
Wheeler, Lisa 1963- *200*
  Earlier sketch in SATA *162*
Wheeler, Opal 1898- *23*
Whelan, Elizabeth M(urphy) 1943- *14*
Whelan, Gloria 1923- *178*
  Earlier sketches in SATA *85, 128*
  See also CLR *90*
Whelan, Gloria Ann
  See Whelan, Gloria
Whipple, A(ddison) B(eecher) C(olvin)
  1918- *64*
Whipple, Cal
  See Whipple, A(ddison) B(eecher) C(olvin)
Whisp, Kennilworthy
  See Rowling, J. K.
Whistler, Reginald John 1905-1944 .... *30*
Whistler, Rex
  See Whistler, Reginald John
Whitaker, Zai *183*
Whitcher, Susan (Godsil) 1952- *96*
Whitcomb, Jon 1906-1988 .... *10*
  Obituary *56*
Whitcomb, Laura 1958- *171*
White, Anne Terry 1896-1980 .... *2*
White, Bessie (Felstiner) 1892(?)-1986
  Obituary *50*
White, Carolyn 1948- *130*
White, Dale
  See Place, Marian T(empleton)
White, Dori 1919- *10*
White, E. B. 1899-1985 .... *100*
  Obituary *44*
  Earlier sketches in SATA *2, 29*
  See also CLR *107*
White, Eliza Orne 1856-1947
  See YABC *2*
White, Elwyn Brooks
  See White, E. B.
White, Florence M(eiman) 1910- *14*
White, Laurence B(arton), Jr. 1935- *10*
White, Lee *176*
White, Martin 1943- *51*
White, Nancy 1942- *126*
White, Ramy Allison *67*
  Earlier sketch in SATA *1*
White, Robb 1909-1990 .... *83*
  Earlier sketch in SATA *1*
  See also CLR *3*
  See also SAAS *1*
White, Ruth C. 1942- *186*
  Autobiography Feature *186*
  Earlier sketches in SATA *39, 117, 165*
White, T(erence) H(anbury) 1906-1964 .... *12*
  See also CLR *139*
White, Tekla N. 1934- *115*
White, Timothy (Thomas Anthony)
  1952-2002 .... *60*
White, Tom 1923- *148*
White, William, Jr. 1934- *16*
Whitehead, Don(ald) F. 1908-1981 .... *4*
Whitehead, Jenny 1964- *191*
Whitehead, Kathy 1957- *176*
Whitehouse, Arch
  See Whitehouse, Arthur George Joseph
Whitehouse, Arthur George Joseph
  1895-1979 .... *14*
  Obituary *23*
Whitehouse, Elizabeth S(cott) 1893-1968 .... *35*
Whitehouse, Jeanne
  See Peterson, Jeanne Whitehouse
Whitelaw, Nancy 1933- *166*
  Earlier sketch in SATA *76*
Whitesel, Cheryl Aylward *162*
Whiting, Sue 1960- *205*
Whiting, Susan Allana
  See Whiting, Sue
Whitinger, R. D.
  See Place, Marian T(empleton)

Whitley, Mary Ann
  See Sebrey, Mary Ann
Whitley, Peggy 1938- *140*
Whitlock, Pamela 1921(?)-1982
  Obituary *31*
Whitlock, Ralph 1914-1995 .... *35*
Whitman, Alice
  See Marker, Sherry
Whitman, Candace 1958- *208*
Whitman, Sylvia (Choate) 1961- *135*
  Earlier sketch in SATA *85*
Whitman, Walt 1819-1892 .... *20*
Whitman, Walter
  See Whitman, Walt
Whitmore, Arvella 1922- *125*
Whitmore, Benette 1955- *203*
Whitney, Alex(andra) 1922- *14*
Whitney, David C(harles) 1921- *48*
  Brief entry *29*
Whitney, Kim Ablon *162*
Whitney, Phyllis A. 1903-2008 .... *30*
  Obituary *189*
  Earlier sketch in SATA *1*
  See also CLR *59*
Whitney, Phyllis Ayame
  See Whitney, Phyllis A.
Whitney, Sharon 1937- *63*
Whitney, Thomas P. 1917-2007 .... *25*
  Obituary *189*
Whitney, Thomas Porter
  See Whitney, Thomas P.
Whittington, Mary K(athrine) 1941- *75*
Whitworth, John 1945- *123*
Whybrow, Ian *202*
  Earlier sketch in SATA *132*
Whyte, Mal(colm Kenneth, Jr.) 1933- *62*
Whyte, Mary 1953- *148*
  Earlier sketch in SATA *94*
Whyte, Ron 1942(?)-1989
  Obituary *63*
Whytock, Cherry *177*
Wiater, Stanley 1953- *84*
Wibbelsman, Charles J(oseph) 1945- *59*
Wibberley, Leonard 1915-1983 .... *45*
  Obituary *36*
  Earlier sketch in SATA *2*
  See also CLR *3*
Wibberley, Leonard Patrick O'Connor
  See Wibberley, Leonard
Wiberg, Harald (Albin) 1908- *93*
  Brief entry *40*
Wick, Walter 1953- *148*
Wickberg, Susan
  See Rottman, S.L.
Wickens, Elaine *86*
Wicker, Ireene 1905(?)-1987
  Obituary *55*
Wickstrom, Sylvie 1960- *169*
Wickstrom, Thor 1960- *200*
Widdemer, Mabel Cleland 1902-1964 .... *5*
Widener, Terry 1950- *209*
  Earlier sketch in SATA *105*
Widerberg, Siv 1931- *10*
Wiebe, Rudy 1934- *156*
Wiebe, Rudy Henry
  See Wiebe, Rudy
Wieler, Diana (Jean) 1961- *109*
Wiener, Lori 1956- *84*
Wier, Ester (Alberti) 1910-2000 .... *3*
Wiese, Kurt 1887-1974 .... *36*
  Obituary *24*
  Earlier sketch in SATA *3*
  See also CLR *86*
Wiesel, Elie 1928- *56*
Wiesel, Eliezer
  See Wiesel, Elie
Wiesner, David 1956- *181*
  Earlier sketches in SATA *72, 117, 139*
  See also CLR *84*
Wiesner, Portia
  See Takakjian, Portia

Wiesner, William 1899-1984 .... *5*
Wiggers, Raymond 1952- *82*
Wiggin, Eric E. 1939- *167*
  Earlier sketch in SATA *88*
Wiggin, Eric Ellsworth 1939-
  See Wiggin, Eric E.
Wiggin (Riggs), Kate Douglas (Smith)
  1856-1923
  See YABC *1*
  See also CLR *52*
Wiggins, VeraLee (Chesnut) 1928-1995 .... *89*
Wight, James Alfred 1916-1995 .... *135*
  Brief entry *44*
  Earlier sketch in SATA *86*
  See also CLR *80*
Wignell, Edel 1936- *69*
Wijnberg, Ellen *85*
Wikland, Ilon 1930- *93*
  Brief entry *32*
Wikler, Madeline 1943- *114*
Wilber, Donald N(ewton) 1907-1997 .... *35*
Wilbur, C. Keith 1923- *27*
Wilbur, Frances 1921- *107*
Wilbur, Helen L. 1948- *204*
Wilbur, Richard 1921- *108*
  Earlier sketch in SATA *9*
Wilbur, Richard Purdy
  See Wilbur, Richard
Wilburn, Kathy 1948- *68*
Wilcox, Charlotte 1948- *72*
Wilcox, Leah 1975(?)- *207*
Wilcox, R(uth) Turner 1888-1970 .... *36*
Wilcox, Roger
  See Collins, Paul
Wild, Jocelyn 1941- *46*
Wild, Kate 1954- *192*
Wild, Margaret 1948- *197*
  Earlier sketch in SATA *151*
Wild, Robin (Evans) 1936- *46*
Wild, Robyn 1947- *117*
Wilde, D. Gunther
  See Hurwood, Bernhardt J.
Wilde, Oscar 1854(?)-1900 .... *24*
  See also CLR *114*
Wilde, Oscar Fingal O'Flahertie Willis
  See Wilde, Oscar
Wilder, Buck
  See Smith, Tim(othy R.)
Wilder, Laura Elizabeth Ingalls
  See Wilder, Laura Ingalls
Wilder, Laura Ingalls 1867-1957 .... *100*
  Earlier sketches in SATA *15, 29*
  See also CLR *111*
Wildsmith, Brian 1930- *124*
  Earlier sketches in SATA *16, 69*
  See also CLR *52*
  See also SAAS *5*
Wiles, Deborah *171*
Wilhelm, Doug 1952- *190*
Wilhelm, Hans 1945- *196*
  Autobiography Feature *196*
  Earlier sketches in SATA *58, 135*
  See also CLR *46*
  See also SAAS *21*
Wilkie, Katharine E(lliott) 1904-1980 .... *31*
Wilkin, Eloise 1904-1987 .... *49*
  Obituary *54*
Wilkins, Frances 1923- *14*
Wilkins, Kim *147*
Wilkins, Marilyn (Ruth) 1926- *30*
Wilkins, Marne
  See Wilkins, Marilyn (Ruth)
Wilkins, Mary Huiskamp 1926- *2*
  See also CLR *42*
Wilkins, Mary Huiskamp Calhoun
  See Wilkins, Mary Huiskamp
Wilkins, Rose *180*
Wilkinson, (Thomas) Barry 1923- *50*
  Brief entry *32*
Wilkinson, Beth 1925- *80*

Wilkinson, Brenda 1946- 91
  Earlier sketch in SATA 14
  See also CLR 20
Wilkinson, (John) Burke 1913-2000 4
Wilkinson, Sylvia 1940- 56
  Brief entry 39
Wilkon, Jozef 1930- 133
  Earlier sketches in SATA 31, 71
Wilkowski, Sue 193
Wilks, Michael Thomas 1947- 44
Wilks, Mike
  See Wilks, Michael Thomas
Will
  See Lipkind, William
Willard, Barbara (Mary) 1909-1994 74
  Earlier sketch in SATA 17
  See also CLR 2
  See also SAAS 5
Willard, Elizabeth Kimmel
  See Kimmel, Elizabeth Cody
Willard, Mildred Wilds 1911-1978 14
Willard, Nancy 1936- 191
  Brief entry 30
  Earlier sketches in SATA 37, 71, 127
  See also CLR 5
Willcox, Isobel 1907-1996 42
Willems, Mo 180
  Earlier sketch in SATA 154
  See also CLR 114
Willett, Edward 1959- 115
Willett, Edward C.
  See Willett, Edward
Willey, Bee 184
Willey, Margaret 1950- 86
Willey, Robert
  See Ley, Willy
Willhoite, Michael A. 1946- 71
William, Kate
  See Armstrong, Jennifer
Williams, Alex 1969- 209
Williams, Arlene 171
Williams, Barbara 1925- 107
  Earlier sketch in SATA 11
  See also CLR 48
  See also SAAS 16
Williams, Barbara 1937- 62
Williams, Beryl
  See Epstein, Beryl
Williams, Brian (Peter) 1943- 54
Williams, Carol Lynch 1959- 110
Williams, Charles
  See Collier, James Lincoln
Williams, Clyde C. 1881-1974 8
  Obituary 27
Williams, Coe
  See Harrison, C(hester) William
Williams, Colleen Madonna Flood 1963- .. 156
Williams, Cynthia G. 1958- 123
Williams, Dar 1967- 168
Williams, Donna Reilly 1945- 83
Williams, Dorothy
  See Williams, Marcia
Williams, Dorothy Snowden
  See Williams, Dar
Williams, Eric (Ernest) 1911-1983 14
  Obituary 38
Williams, Ferelith Eccles
  See Eccles Williams, Ferelith
Williams, Frances N.
  See Browin, Frances Williams
Williams, Garth (Montgomery) 1912-1996 .. 66
  Obituary 90
  Earlier sketch in SATA 18
  See also CLR 57
  See also SAAS 7
Williams, Guy R(ichard) 1920- 11
Williams, Hawley
  See Heyliger, William
Williams, Helen 1948- 77
Williams, J. R.
  See Williams, Jeanne

Williams, J. Walker
  See Wodehouse, P. G.
Williams, Jay 1914-1978 41
  Obituary 24
  Earlier sketch in SATA 3
  See also CLR 8
Williams, Jeanne 1930- 5
Williams, Jenny 1939- 60
Williams, Karen Lynn 1952- 99
  Earlier sketch in SATA 66
Williams, Kit 1946(?)- 44
  See also CLR 4
Williams, Laura E. 180
Williams, Laura Ellen
  See Williams, Laura E.
Williams, L.E.
  See Williams, Laura Ellen
Williams, Leslie 1941- 42
Williams, Linda 1948- 59
Williams, Louise Bonino 1904(?)-1984
  Obituary 39
Williams, Lynn
  See Hale, Arlene
Williams, Marcia 1945- 159
  Earlier sketches in SATA 71, 97
Williams, Marcia Dorothy
  See Williams, Marcia
Williams, Margery
  See Bianco, Margery Williams
Williams, Mark
  See Arthur, Robert, (Jr.)
Williams, Mark London 1959- 140
Williams, Maureen 1951- 12
Williams, Michael
  See St. John, Wylly Folk
Williams, Patrick J.
  See Griffin, W.E.B.
Williams, Pete
  See Faulknor, Cliff(ord Vernon)
Williams, S. P.
  See Hart, Virginia
Williams, Sam 177
  Earlier sketch in SATA 124
Williams, Selma R(uth) 1925- 14
Williams, Sherley Anne 1944-1999 78
  Obituary 116
Williams, Sheron 1955- 77
Williams, Shirley
  See Williams, Sherley Anne
Williams, Slim
  See Williams, Clyde C.
Williams, Sophy 1965- 135
Williams, Sue 1948-2007 208
Williams, Susan
  See Beckhorn, Susan Williams
Williams, Suzanne
  See Williams, Suzanne Morgan
Williams, Suzanne 1953- 202
  Earlier sketch in SATA 71
Williams, Suzanne M.
  See Williams, Suzanne Morgan
Williams, Suzanne Morgan 1949- 207
Williams, Ursula Moray
  See Moray Williams, Ursula
Williams, Vera B(aker) 1927- 102
  Brief entry 33
  Earlier sketch in SATA 53
  See also CLR 9
Williams-Andriani, Renee 1963- 98
Williams-Ellis, (Mary) Amabel (Nassau
  Strachey) 1894-1984 29
  Obituary 41
Williams-Garcia, Rita 1957- 160
  Earlier sketch in SATA 98
  See also CLR 36
Williamson, Gwyneth 1965- 109
Williamson, Henry (William) 1895-1977 37
  Obituary 30
Williamson, Joanne S(mall) 1926- 122
  Earlier sketch in SATA 3
Williamson, Melanie 196

Willis, Charles
  See Clarke, Arthur C.
Willis, Connie 1945- 110
  See also CLR 66
Willis, Jeanne 1959- 195
  Earlier sketches in SATA 61, 123
Willis, Jeanne Mary
  See Willis, Jeanne
Willis, Meredith Sue 1946- 101
Willis, Nancy Carol 1952- 139
  Earlier sketch in SATA 93
Willis, Paul J. 1955- 113
Willms, Russ 95
Willoughby, Lee Davis
  See Avallone, Michael (Angelo, Jr.)
  and Brandner, Gary (Phil)
  and Deming, Richard
  and DeAndrea, William L(ouis)
  and Laymon, Richard (Carl)
  and Streib, Dan(iel Thomas)
  and Toombs, John
  and Webb, Jean Francis (III)
Willson, Robina Beckles
  See Beckles Willson, Robina
Wilma, Dana
  See Faralla, Dana
Wilsdorf, Anne 1954- 191
Wilson, April 80
Wilson, Barbara Ker
  See Ker Wilson, Barbara
Wilson, Beth P(ierre) 8
Wilson, Budge 1927- 55
  Brief entry 51
Wilson, Carletta 1951- 81
Wilson, Carter 1941- 6
Wilson, Charles Morrow 1905-1977 30
Wilson, Christopher B. 1910(?)-1985
  Obituary 46
Wilson, Darryl B(abe) 1939- 90
Wilson, Diane Lee 172
Wilson, Dirk
  See Pohl, Frederik
Wilson, Dorothy Clarke 1904-2003 16
Wilson, Edward A(rthur) 1886-1970 38
Wilson, Ellen (Janet Cameron) (?)-1976 9
  Obituary 26
Wilson, Eric (H.) 1940- 34
  Brief entry 32
Wilson, Erica 51
Wilson, Forrest 1918- 27
Wilson, Gahan 1930- 35
  Brief entry 27
Wilson, Gina 1943- 85
  Brief entry 34
  Earlier sketch in SATA 36
Wilson, (Leslie) Granville 1912- 14
Wilson, Hazel (Hutchins) 1898-1992 3
  Obituary 73
Wilson, J(erry) M. 1964- 121
Wilson, Jacqueline 1945- 199
  Brief entry 52
  Earlier sketches in SATA 61, 102, 153
Wilson, John 1922- 22
Wilson, John 1951- 182
Wilson, John Alexander
  See Wilson, John
Wilson, Johnniece Marshall 1944- 75
Wilson, Jonathan 1950- 181
Wilson, Joyce M. 84
  Earlier sketch in SATA 21
  See also SAAS 24
Wilson, Karma 174
Wilson, Leslie 1952- 166
Wilson, Linda Miller 1936- 116
Wilson, Lionel 1924-2003 33
  Brief entry 31
  Obituary 144
Wilson, Marjorie
  See Wilson, Budge
Wilson, Martin 1973- 205
Wilson, Maurice (Charles John) 1914- 46

Wilson, Nancy Hope 1947- 138
    Earlier sketch in SATA *81*
Wilson, Nathan D.
    See Wilson, N.D.
Wilson, N.D. 1978- 194
Wilson, Nick
    See Ellis, Edward S.
Wilson, Phil 1948- 181
Wilson, Ron(ald William) 1941- 38
Wilson, Sarah 1934- 208
    Earlier sketches in SATA *50, 142*
Wilson, Tom 1931- 33
    Brief entry 30
Wilson, Troy 1970- 169
Wilson, Walt(er N.) 1939- 14
Wilson-Max, Ken 1965- 170
    Earlier sketch in SATA *93*
Wilton, Elizabeth 1937- 14
Wilton, Hal
    See Pepper, Frank S.
Wilwerding, Walter Joseph 1891-1966 9
Wimmer, Mike 1961- 194
    Earlier sketch in SATA *70*
Winborn, Marsha (Lynn) 1947- 75
Winch, John 1944- 165
    Earlier sketch in SATA *117*
Winchester, James H(ugh) 1917-1985 30
    Obituary 45
Winchester, Stanley
    See Youd, Samuel
Windawi, Thura al- 1983(?)- 165
Winders, Gertrude Hecker -1987 3
Windham, Basil
    See Wodehouse, P. G.
Windham, Kathryn T(ucker) 1918- 14
Windham, Sophie 184
Windling, Terri 1958- 151
Windrow, Martin
    See Windrow, Martin Clive
Windrow, Martin C.
    See Windrow, Martin Clive
Windrow, Martin Clive 1944- 68
Windsor, Claire
    See Hamerstrom, Frances
Windsor, Linda 1950- 124
Windsor, Patricia 1938- 78
    Earlier sketch in SATA *30*
    See also SAAS *19*
Wineman-Marcus, Irene 1952- 81
Winer, Yvonne 1934- 120
Winerip, Michael 175
Winfield, Arthur M.
    See Stratemeyer, Edward L.
Winfield, Edna
    See Stratemeyer, Edward L.
Winfield, Julia
    See Armstrong, Jennifer
Wing, Natasha 1960- 200
    Earlier sketch in SATA *82*
Wingerter, Linda S. 1973(?)- 207
Winick, Judd 1970- 124
Winks, Robin William 1930-2003 61
Winn, Alison
    See Wharmby, Margot
Winn, Chris 1952- 42
Winn, Janet Bruce 1928- 43
Winn, Marie 1936(?)- 38
Winnick, Karen B(eth) B(inkoff) 1946- 51
Winn-Lederer, Ilene 198
Winslow, Barbara 1947- 91
Winstead, Rosie 180
Winston, Clara 1921-1983 54
    Obituary 39
Winston, Richard 1917-1979 54
Winston, Sherri 1964(?)- 201
Winter, Janet 1926- 126
Winter, Jeanette 1939- 184
    Earlier sketch in SATA *151*
Winter, Jonah 1962- 179
Winter, Milo (Kendall) 1888-1956 21
Winter, Paula Cecelia 1929- 48

Winter, R. R.
    See Winterbotham, R(ussell) R(obert)
Winter, Susan 182
Winterbotham, R(ussell) R(obert)
    1904-1971 10
Winterbotham, Russ
    See Winterbotham, R(ussell) R(obert)
Winterfeld, Henry 1901-1990 55
Winters, J. C.
    See Cross, Gilbert B.
Winters, Jon
    See Cross, Gilbert B.
Winters, Katherine
    See Winters, Kay
Winters, Kay 1936- 153
    Earlier sketch in SATA *103*
Winters, Nina 1944- 62
Winters, Paul A. 1965- 106
Winterson, Jeanette 1959- 190
Winterton, Gayle
    See Adams, William Taylor
Winthrop, Elizabeth 1948- 164
    Autobiography Feature 116
    Earlier sketches in SATA *8, 76*
    See also CLR *89*
Winton, Ian (Kenneth) 1960- 76
Winton, Tim 1960- 98
Wintz-Litty, Julie
    See Litty, Julie
Wirt, Ann
    See Benson, Mildred
Wirt, Mildred A.
    See Benson, Mildred
Wirtenberg, Patricia Z. 1932-2007 10
Wirtenberg, Patricia Zarrella
    See Wirtenberg, Patricia Z.
Wirth, Beverly 1938- 63
Wirths, Claudine (Turner) G(ibson)
    1926-2000 104
    Earlier sketch in SATA *64*
Wise, Bill 1958- 191
Wise, Lenny
    See Wise, Leonard
Wise, Leonard 1940- 167
Wise, Leonard A.
    See Wise, Leonard
Wise, Leonard Allan
    See Wise, Leonard
Wise, William 1923- 163
    Earlier sketch in SATA *4*
Wise, Winifred E. 2
Wiseman, Ann (Sayre) 1926- 31
Wiseman, B(ernard) 1922-1995 4
Wiseman, David 1916- 43
    Brief entry 40
Wishinsky, Frieda 1948- 166
    Earlier sketches in SATA *70, 112*
Wisler, G(ary) Clifton 1950- 103
    Brief entry 46
    Earlier sketch in SATA *58*
Wismer, Donald (Richard) 1946- 59
Wisner, Bill
    See Wisner, William L.
Wisner, William L. 1914(?)-1983 42
Wisnewski, David 1953-2002
    See Wisniewski, David
Wisniewski, David 1953-2002 95
    Obituary 139
    See also CLR *51*
Wister, Owen 1860-1938 62
Witham, (Phillip) Ross 1917- 37
Withers, Carl A. 1900-1970 14
Withers, Pam 1956- 182
Withrow, Sarah 1966- 199
    Earlier sketch in SATA *124*
Witt, Dick 1948- 80
Witt, Shirley Hill 1934- 17
Wittanen, Etolin 1907- 55
Wittels, Harriet Joan 1938- 31
Wittig, Susan
    See Albert, Susan Wittig

Wittlinger, Ellen 1948- 189
    Autobiography Feature 128
    Earlier sketches in SATA *83, 122*
Wittman, Sally (Anne Christensen) 1941- 30
Witty, Paul 1898-1976 50
    Obituary 30
Wodehouse, P. G. 1881-1975 22
Wodehouse, Pelham Grenville
    See Wodehouse, P. G.
Wodge, Dreary
    See Gorey, Edward (St. John)
Woelfle, Gretchen 1945- 145
Wohlberg, Meg 1905-1990 41
    Obituary 66
Wohlrabe, Raymond A. 1900-1977 4
Wohnoutka, Mike 195
Wojciechowska, Maia (Teresa) 1927-2002 ... 83
    Autobiography Feature 104
    Obituary 134
    Earlier sketches in SATA *1, 28*
    See also CLR *1*
    See also SAAS *1*
Wojciechowski, Susan 126
    Earlier sketch in SATA *78*
Wojnarowski, Adrian 1970- 190
Wojtusik, Elizabeth 208
Wolcott, Patty 1929- 14
Wold, Allen L. 1943- 64
Wold, Jo Anne 1938- 30
Woldin, Beth Weiner 1955- 34
Wolf, Allan 1963- 192
Wolf, Bernard 1930- 102
    Brief entry 37
Wolf, Erica (Van Varick) 1978- 156
Wolf, Gita 1956- 101
Wolf, J. M.
    See Wolf, Joan M.
Wolf, Janet 1957- 78
Wolf, Joan M. 1966- 193
Wolf, Sallie 1950- 205
    Earlier sketch in SATA *80*
Wolfe, Art 1952- 76
Wolfe, Burton H. 1932- 5
Wolfe, Gene 1931- 165
    Earlier sketch in SATA *118*
Wolfe, Gene Rodman
    See Wolfe, Gene
Wolfe, Gillian 199
Wolfe, Louis 1905-1985 8
    Obituary 133
Wolfe, Rinna (Evelyn) 1925- 38
Wolfenden, George
    See Beardmore, George
Wolfer, Dianne 1961- 167
    Autobiography Feature 117
    Earlier sketch in SATA *104*
Wolff, Alexander (Nikolaus) 1957- 137
    Earlier sketch in SATA *63*
Wolff, Ashley 1956- 203
    Earlier sketches in SATA *50, 81, 155*
Wolff, Diane 1945- 27
Wolff, Ferida 1946- 164
    Earlier sketch in SATA *79*
Wolff, Jennifer Ashley
    See Wolff, Ashley
Wolff, Nancy 202
Wolff, Robert Jay 1905-1977 10
Wolff, Sonia
    See Levitin, Sonia
Wolff, Virginia Euwer 1937- 137
    Earlier sketch in SATA *78*
    See also CLR *62*
Wolfman, Judy 1933- 138
Wolfson, Evelyn 1937- 62
Wolitzer, Hilma 1930- 31
Wolkoff, Judie (Edwards) 93
    Brief entry 37
Wolkstein, Diane 1942- 138
    Earlier sketches in SATA *7, 82*
Wollheim, Donald A(llen) 1914-1990
    Obituary 69

Wolny, P.
  See Janeczko, Paul B(ryan)
Wolters, Richard A. 1920-1993 35
Wondriska, William 1931- 6
Wong, Jade Snow 1922-2006 112
  Obituary 175
Wong, Janet S. 1962- 148
  Earlier sketch in SATA 98
  See also CLR 94
Woo, Howie 1974- 207
Wood, Anne (Savage) 1937- 64
Wood, Audrey 198
  Brief entry 44
  Earlier sketches in SATA 50, 81, 139
  See also CLR 26
Wood, Catherine
  See Etchison, Birdie L(ee)
Wood, David 1944- 87
Wood, Don 1945- 50
  Brief entry 44
  See also CLR 26
Wood, Douglas 1951- 180
  Earlier sketches in SATA 81, 132
Wood, Douglas Eric
  See Wood, Douglas
Wood, Edgar A(llardyce) 1907-1998 14
Wood, Esther
  See Brady, Esther Wood
Wood, Frances Elizabeth 34
Wood, Frances M. 1951- 97
Wood, James Playsted 1905- 1
Wood, Jenny 1955- 88
Wood, John Norris 1930- 85
Wood, June Rae 1946- 120
  Earlier sketch in SATA 79
  See also CLR 82
Wood, Kerry
  See Wood, Edgar A(llardyce)
Wood, Kim Marie 134
Wood, Laura N.
  See Roper, Laura (Newbold) Wood
Wood, Linda C(arol) 1945- 59
Wood, Marcia 1956- 80
Wood, Marcia Mae
  See Wood, Marcia
Wood, Nancy
  See Wood, Nancy C.
Wood, Nancy C. 1936- 178
  Earlier sketch in SATA 6
Wood, Nuria
  See Nobisso, Josephine
Wood, Owen 1929- 64
Wood, Phyllis Anderson 1923- 33
  Brief entry 30
Wood, Richard 1949- 110
Wood, Tim(othy William Russell) 1946- 88
Wood, Wallace 1927-1981
  Obituary 33
Woodard, Carol 1929- 14
Woodburn, John Henry 1914- 11
Woodbury, David Oakes 1896-1981 62
Woodford, Peggy 1937- 25
Woodhouse, Barbara (Blackburn)
  1910-1988 63
Woodhull, Ann Love 194
Wooding, Chris 1977- 166
Wooding, Sharon
  See Wooding, Sharon L(ouise)
Wooding, Sharon L(ouise) 1943- 66
Woodman, Allen 1954- 76
Woodrich, Mary Neville 1915- 2
Woodruff, Elvira 1951- 162
  Earlier sketches in SATA 70, 106
Woodruff, Joan Leslie 1953- 104
Woodruff, Liza 1971(?)- 182
Woodruff, Marian
  See Goudge, Eileen
Woodruff, Noah 1977- 86
Woods, George A(llan) 1926-1988 30
  Obituary 57

Woods, Geraldine 1948- 111
  Brief entry 42
  Earlier sketch in SATA 56
Woods, Harold 1945- 56
  Brief entry 42
Woods, Lawrence
  See Lowndes, Robert A(ugustine) W(ard)
Woods, Margaret 1921- 2
Woods, Nat
  See Stratemeyer, Edward L.
Woods, Titania
  See Weatherly, Lee
Woodson, Jack
  See Woodson, John Waddie Jr.
Woodson, Jacqueline 1964- 189
  Earlier sketches in SATA 94, 139
  See also CLR 49
Woodson, Jacqueline Amanda
  See Woodson, Jacqueline
Woodson, John Waddie Jr. 1913- 10
Woodtor, Dee
  See Woodtor, Delores Parmer
Woodtor, Dee Parmer 1945(?)-2002
  See Woodtor, Delores Parmer
Woodtor, Delores Parmer 1945-2002 93
Wood-Trost, Lucille
  See Trost, Lucille W(ood)
Woodward, (Landon) Cleveland 1900-1986 . 10
  Obituary 48
Woodworth, Chris 1957- 168
Woodworth, Viki 1952- 127
Woody, Regina Jones 1894-1983 3
Woodyadd, Charlotte
  See Hough, Charlotte
Woog, Adam 1953- 125
  Earlier sketch in SATA 84
Wooldridge, Connie Nordhielm 1950- 143
  Earlier sketch in SATA 92
Wooldridge, Frosty 1947- 140
Wooldridge, Rhoda 1906-1988 22
Wooley, Susan Frelick 1945- 113
Woolf, Paula 1950- 104
Woolfe, Angela 1976- 169
Woolley, Catherine 1904-2005 3
  Obituary 166
Woolman, Steven 1969-2004 163
  Earlier sketch in SATA 90
Woolsey, Janette 1904-1989 3
  Obituary 131
Worcester, Donald E(mmet) 1915- 18
Word, Reagan 1944- 103
Work, Virginia 1946- 57
  Brief entry 45
Worline, Bonnie Bess 1914- 14
Wormell, Christopher 1955- 154
  Earlier sketch in SATA 103
Wormell, Mary 1959- 96
Wormser, Richard 1933- 106
  Autobiography Feature 118
  See also SAAS 26
Wormser, Sophie 1897-1979 22
Worth, Richard 1945- 59
  Brief entry 46
Worth, Valerie 1933-1994 81
  Earlier sketches in SATA 8, 70
  See also CLR 21
Worthington, Leonie 1956- 200
Wortis, Avi
  See Avi
Wortis, Edward Irving
  See Avi
Wosmek, Frances 1917- 29
Woychuk, Denis 1953- 71
Wrede, Patricia C(ollins) 1953- 146
  Earlier sketch in SATA 67
Wriggins, Sally Hovey 1922- 17
Wright, Alexandra 1979- 103
Wright, Betty Ren 1927- 109
  Brief entry 48
  Earlier sketch in SATA 63

Wright, Cliff 1963- 168
  Earlier sketch in SATA 76
Wright, Courtni
  See Wright, Courtni C(rump)
Wright, Courtni C(rump) 1950- 84
Wright, Courtni Crump
  See Wright, Courtni C(rump)
Wright, Dare 1914(?)-2001 21
  Obituary 124
Wright, David K. 1943- 112
  Earlier sketch in SATA 73
Wright, Elinor
  See Lyon, Elinor
Wright, Enid Meadowcroft (LaMonte)
  1898-1966 3
Wright, Esmond 1915-2003 10
Wright, Frances Fitzpatrick 1897-1982 10
Wright, J. B.
  See Barkan, Joanne
Wright, Judith 1915-2000 14
  Obituary 121
Wright, Judith Arundell
  See Wright, Judith
Wright, Katrina
  See Gater, Dilys
Wright, Kenneth
  See del Rey, Lester
Wright, Kit 1944- 87
Wright, Leslie B(ailey) 1959- 91
Wright, Michael 1954- 198
Wright, Nancy Means 38
Wright, R(obert) H(amilton) 1906- 6
Wright, Rachel 134
Wright, Susan Kimmel 1950- 97
Wrightfrierson
  See Wright-Frierson, Virginia (Marguerite)
Wright-Frierson, Virginia (Marguerite)
  1949- 110
  Earlier sketch in SATA 58
Wrightson, (Alice) Patricia 1921- 112
  Earlier sketches in SATA 8, 66
  See also CLR 14
  See also SAAS 4
Wroble, Lisa A. 1963- 134
Wrongo, I.B.
  See Katz, Alan
Wronker, Lili
  See Wronker, Lili Cassel
Wronker, Lili Cassel 1924- 10
Wryde, Dogear
  See Gorey, Edward (St. John)
Wu, Elizabeth
  See Wu, Liz
Wu, Liz 184
Wu, Norbert 1961- 155
  Earlier sketch in SATA 101
Wulf, Linda Press 205
Wulffson, Don 1943- 155
  Earlier sketches in SATA 32, 88
Wulffson, Don L.
  See Wulffson, Don
Wummer, Amy 1955- 201
Wunderli, Stephen 1958- 79
Wunsch, Josephine (McLean) 1914- 64
Wuorio, Eva-Lis 1918- 34
  Brief entry 28
Wurts, Janny 1953- 98
Wyatt, B. D.
  See Robinson, Spider
Wyatt, David 1968- 185
Wyatt, Jane
  See Bradbury, Bianca (Ryley)
Wyatt, Melissa 1963- 177
Wyatt, Valerie 209
Wyeth, Betsy James 1921- 41
Wyeth, N(ewell) C(onvers) 1882-1945 17
  See also CLR 106
Wyler, Rose 1909-2000 18
  Obituary 121
Wylie, Betty Jane 48

Wylie, Laura
  See Matthews, Patricia
Wylie, Laurie
  See Matthews, Patricia
Wyllie, Stephen 86
Wyman, Andrea 75
Wyman, Carolyn 1956- 83
Wymer, Norman (George) 1911- 25
Wynard, Talbot
  See Hamilton, Charles (Harold St. John)
Wyndham, John
  See Harris, John (Wyndham Parkes Lucas)
  Beynon
Wyndham, Lee
  See Hyndman, Jane Andrews Lee
Wyndham, Robert
  See Hyndman, Robert Utley
Wynne-Jones, Tim 1948- 186
  Autobiography Feature 136
  Earlier sketches in SATA 67, 96, 136
  See also CLR 58
Wynne-Jones, Timothy
  See Wynne-Jones, Tim
Wynter, Edward (John) 1914- 14
Wynyard, Talbot
  See Hamilton, Charles (Harold St. John)
Wyss, Johann David Von 1743-1818 29
  Brief entry 27
  See also CLR 92
Wyss, Thelma Hatch 1934- 202
  Earlier sketches in SATA 10, 140

X

Xavier, Father
  See Hurwood, Bernhardt J.
Xuan, YongSheng 1952- 116
  Autobiography Feature 119

Y

Yaccarino, Dan 192
  Earlier sketch in SATA 141
Yadin, (Rav-Aloof) Yigael 1917-1984 55
Yaffe, Alan
  See Yorinks, Arthur
Yagher, Kevin 1962- 143
Yakovetic, (Joseph Sandy) 1952- 59
Yakovetic, Joe
  See Yakovetic, (Joseph Sandy)
Yamada, Utako 1963- 188
Yamaguchi, Marianne (Illenberger) 1936- 7
Yamaka, Sara 1978- 92
Yamanaka, Lois-Ann 1961- 166
Yamasaki, Katie 206
Yancey, Diane 1951- 138
  Earlier sketch in SATA 81
Yancey, Richard 193
Yancey, Rick
  See Yancey, Richard
Yang, Belle 1960- 170
Yang, James 1960- 190
Yang, Jay 1941- 12
Yang, Mingyi 1943- 72
Yarbrough, Camille 1938- 79
  See also CLR 29
Yarbrough, Ira 1910(?)-1983
  Obituary 35
Yaroslava
  See Mills, Yaroslava Surmach
Yarrow, Peter 1938- 195
Yashima, Taro
  See Iwamatsu, Jun Atsushi
Yates, Elizabeth 1905-2001 68
  Obituary 128
  Earlier sketch in SATA 4
  See also SAAS 6
Yates, Janelle K(aye) 1957- 77

Yates, John 1939- 74
Yates, Kelly 1971- 208
Yates, Philip 1958- 149
  Earlier sketch in SATA 92
Yates, Raymond F(rancis) 1895-1966 31
Yaukey, Grace S(ydenstricker) 1899-1994 ... 80
  Earlier sketch in SATA 5
Yazzie, Johnson 1946- 205
Ye, Ting-xing 1952- 106
Yeahpau, Thomas M. 1975- 187
Yeakley, Marjory Hall 1908- 21
Yeatman, Linda 1938- 42
Yee, Brenda Shannon 133
Yee, Lisa 1959- 160
Yee, Paul (R.) 1956- 143
  Earlier sketches in SATA 67, 96
  See also CLR 44
Yee, Tammy 206
Yee, Wong Herbert 1953- 172
  Earlier sketches in SATA 78, 115
Yeh, Chun-Chan 1914- 79
Ye Junjian
  See Yeh, Chun-Chan
Yelchin, Eugene 1956- 196
Yenawine, Philip 1942- 85
Yensid, Retlaw
  See Disney, Walt(er Elias)
Yeo, Wilma (Lethem) 1918-1994 81
  Earlier sketch in SATA 24
Yeoman, John 1934- 80
  Earlier sketch in SATA 28
  See also CLR 46
Yep, Kathleen S. 203
Yep, Laurence 1948- 176
  Earlier sketches in SATA 7, 69, 123
  See also CLR 132
Yep, Laurence Michael
  See Yep, Laurence
Yepsen, Roger B(ennet), Jr. 1947- 59
Yerian, Cameron John 21
Yerian, Margaret A. 21
Yerxa, Leo 1947- 181
Yetska
  See Ironside, Jetske
Yezerski, Thomas F. 1969- 190
Yin 194
Ylvisaker, Anne 1965(?)- 172
Yoder, Carolyn P. 1953- 149
Yoder, Carolyn Patricia
  See Yoder, Carolyn P.
Yoder, Dorothy Meenen 1921- 96
Yoder, Dot
  See Yoder, Dorothy Meenen
Yoder, Walter D. 1933- 88
Yolen, Jane 1939- 194
  Autobiography Feature 111
  Earlier sketches in SATA 4, 40, 75, 112, 158
  See also CLR 149
  See also SAAS 1
Yolen, Jane Hyatt
  See Yolen, Jane
Yonezu, Yusuke 196
Yonge, Charlotte 1823-1901 17
Yonge, Charlotte Mary
  See Yonge, Charlotte
Yoo, Paula 1969(?)- 174
Yoo, Taeeun 191
Yoon, Salina 1972- 204
Yorinks, Adrienne 1956- 171
Yorinks, Arthur 1953- 200
  Earlier sketches in SATA 33, 49, 85, 144
  See also CLR 20
York, Alison
  See Nicole, Christopher (Robin)
York, Andrew
  See Nicole, Christopher (Robin)
York, Carol Beach 1928- 77
  Earlier sketch in SATA 6
York, Rebecca
  See Buckholtz, Eileen (Garber)
  and Glick, Ruth (Burtnick)

York, Simon
  See Heinlein, Robert A.
Yoshida, Toshi 1911- 77
Yoshikawa, Sachiko 181
Yost, Edna 1889-1971
  Obituary 26
Youd, C. S.
  See Youd, Samuel
Youd, Samuel 1922- 135
  Brief entry 30
  Earlier sketch in SATA 47
  See also CLR 2
  See also SAAS 6
Young, Amy L. 185
Young, Anne Mortimer
  See Mortimer, Anne
Young, Bob
  See Young, Robert W(illiam)
  and Young, James Robert
Young, Carol 1945- 102
Young, Catherine
  See Olds, Helen Diehl
Young, Clarence
  See Garis, Howard R.
  and Stratemeyer, Edward L.
Young, Collier
  See Bloch, Robert (Albert)
Young, Dan 1952- 126
Young, Dianne 1959- 88
Young, Dorothea Bennett 1924- 31
Young, Ed 1931- 173
  Earlier sketches in SATA 10, 74, 122
  See also CLR 27
Young, Ed Tse-chun
  See Young, Ed
Young, Edward
  See Reinfeld, Fred
Young, Elaine L.
  See Schulte, Elaine L(ouise)
Young, James
  See Graham, Ian
Young, Jan
  See Young, Janet Randall
Young, Janet 1957- 188
Young, Janet Randall 1919-1994 3
Young, Janet Ruth
  See Young, Janet
Young, Jeff C. 1948- 132
Young, John
  See Macintosh, Brownie
Young, Judy 1956- 207
  Earlier sketch in SATA 155
Young, Judy (Elaine) Dockrey 1949- 72
Young, Karen Romano 1959- 168
  Earlier sketch in SATA 116
Young, Ken 1956- 86
Young, Lois Horton 1911-1981 26
Young, Louisa 161
Young, Louise B. 1919- 64
Young, Margaret B. 1922-2009 2
Young, Margaret Buckner
  See Young, Margaret B.
Young, Mary 1940- 89
Young, Miriam 1913-1974 7
Young, Noela 1930- 89
Young, (Rodney Lee) Patrick (Jr.) 1937- 22
Young, Percy M(arshall) 1912-2004 31
  Obituary 154
Young, Richard Alan 1946- 72
Young, Robert W(illiam) 1916-1969 3
Young, Ross B. 1955- 150
Young, Ruth 1946- 67
Young, Sara
  See Pennypacker, Sara
Young, Scott A. 1918-2005 5
Young, Scott Alexander
  See Young, Scott A.
Young, Selina 1971-2006 201
Young, Vivien
  See Gater, Dilys
Younger, Barbara 1954- 108

Youngs, Betty 1934-1985 .... *53*
    Obituary *42*
Younkin, Paula 1942- *77*
Yount, Lisa (Ann) 1944- *124*
    Earlier sketch in SATA *74*
Yourgrau, Barry *179*
Yuditskaya, Tatyana 1964- *75*
Yumoto, Kazumi 1959- *153*

Z

Zach, Cheryl (Byrd) 1947- *98*
    Brief entry *51*
    Earlier sketch in SATA *58*
    See also SAAS *24*
Zacharias, Gary L. 1946- *153*
Zaffo, George J. (?)-1984 .... *42*
Zagarenski, Pamela 1969(?)- *183*
Zagwyn, Deborah Turney 1953- *138*
    Earlier sketch in SATA *78*
Zahares, Wade *193*
Zahn, Timothy 1951- *156*
    Earlier sketch in SATA *91*
Zaid, Barry 1938- *51*
Zaidenberg, Arthur 1908(?)-1990 .... *34*
    Obituary *66*
Zalben, Jane Breskin 1950- *170*
    Earlier sketches in SATA *7, 79, 120*
    See also CLR *84*
Zallinger, Jean (Day) 1918- *115*
    Earlier sketches in SATA *14, 80*
Zallinger, Peter Franz 1943- *49*
Zambreno, Mary Frances 1954- *140*
    Earlier sketch in SATA *75*
Zanderbergen, George
    See May, Julian
Zappa, Ahmet 1974- *180*
Zappa, Ahmet Emuukha Rodan
    See Zappa, Ahmet
Zappler, Lisbeth 1930- *10*
Zarchy, Harry 1912-1987 .... *34*
Zarin, Cynthia 1959- *192*
    Earlier sketch in SATA *108*
Zaring, Jane (Thomas) 1936- *40*
Zarins, Joyce Audy
    See dos Santos, Joyce Audy
Zaslavsky, Claudia 1917- *36*
Zaugg, Sandra L. 1938- *118*
Zaugg, Sandy
    See Zaugg, Sandra L.
Zaunders, Bo 1939- *137*
Zawadzki, Marek 1958- *97*
Zebra, A.
    See Scoltock, Jack
Zebrowski, George 1945- *67*
Zebrowski, George T.
    See Zebrowski, George
Zecca, Katherine *207*
Zeck, Gerald Anthony 1939- *40*
Zeck, Gerry
    See Zeck, Gerald Anthony
Zed, Dr.
    See Penrose, Gordon
Zei, Alki 1925- *24*
    See also CLR *6*
Zeier, Joan T(heresa) 1931- *81*

Zeinert, Karen 1942-2002 .... *137*
    Earlier sketch in SATA *79*
Zeises, Lara M. 1976- *184*
    Earlier sketch in SATA *145*
Zelazny, Roger 1937-1995 .... *57*
    Brief entry *39*
Zelazny, Roger Joseph
    See Zelazny, Roger
Zeldis, Malcah 1931- *146*
    Earlier sketch in SATA *86*
Zelinsky, Paul O. 1953- *154*
    Brief entry *33*
    Earlier sketches in SATA *49, 102*
    See also CLR *55*
Zellan, Audrey Penn
    See Penn, Audrey
Zemach, Harve
    See Fischtrom, Harvey
Zemach, Kaethe 1958- *149*
    Brief entry *39*
    Earlier sketch in SATA *49*
Zemach, Margot 1931-1989 .... *70*
    Obituary *59*
    Earlier sketch in SATA *21*
Zemach-Bersin, Kaethe
    See Zemach, Kaethe
Zeman, Ludmila 1947- *153*
Zepeda, Gwendolyn 1971- *206*
Zephaniah, Benjamin 1958- *189*
    Earlier sketches in SATA *86, 140*
Zephaniah, Benjamin Obadiah Iqbal
    See Zephaniah, Benjamin
Zephaniah, Benjamin Pbadiah Iqubal
    See Zephaniah, Benjamin
Zerman, Melvyn Bernard 1930- *46*
Zettner, Pat 1940- *70*
Zevin, Gabrielle *176*
Zhang, Christopher Zhong-Yuan 1954- *91*
Zhang, Song Nan 1942- *170*
    Earlier sketch in SATA *85*
Ziefert, Harriet 1941- *205*
    Earlier sketches in SATA *101, 154*
Ziegler, Jack (Denmore) 1942- *60*
Ziemienski, Dennis (Theodore) 1947- *10*
Ziliox, Marc
    See Fichter, George S.
Zillah
    See Macdonald, Zillah K(atherine)
Zim, Herbert S(pencer) 1909-1994 .... *30*
    Obituary *85*
    Earlier sketch in SATA *1*
    See also CLR *2*
    See also SAAS *2*
Zim, Sonia Bleeker 1909-1971 .... *2*
    Obituary *26*
Zima, Gordon 1920- *90*
Zimelman, Nathan 1921- *65*
    Brief entry *37*
Zimmer, Dirk 1943- *147*
    Earlier sketch in SATA *65*
Zimmer, Tracie Vaughn *169*
Zimmerman, Andrea 1950- *192*
    Earlier sketch in SATA *123*
Zimmerman, Andrea Griffing
    See Zimmerman, Andrea
Zimmerman, H. Werner 1951- *101*
Zimmerman, Heinz Werner
    See Zimmerman, H. Werner

Zimmerman, Naoma 1914-2004 .... *10*
Zimmermann, Arnold E. 1909- *58*
Zimmett, Debbie
    See Becker, Deborah Zimmett
Zimmy
    See Stratemeyer, Edward L.
Zimnik, Reiner 1930- *36*
    See also CLR *3*
Zindel, Bonnie 1943- *34*
Zindel, Lizabeth *187*
Zindel, Paul 1936-2003 .... *102*
    Obituary *142*
    Earlier sketches in SATA *16, 58*
    See also CLR *85*
Ziner, Feenie
    See Ziner, Florence
Ziner, Florence 1921- *5*
Zingara, Professor
    See Leeming, Joseph
Zinger, Yitskhok
    See Singer, Isaac Bashevis
Zion, Eugene 1913-1975 .... *18*
Zion, Gene
    See Zion, Eugene
Zoehfeld, Kathleen Weidner 1954- *193*
Zohorsky, Janet R. 1958- *148*
Zolkower, Edie Stoltz *171*
Zolkowski, Cathy (A.) 1969- *121*
Zollars, Jaime *191*
Zolotow, Charlotte 1915- *138*
    Earlier sketches in SATA *1, 35, 78*
    See also CLR *77*
Zolotow, Charlotte Gertrude Shapiro
    See Zolotow, Charlotte
Zolotow, Ellen
    See Dragonwagon, Crescent
Zonderman, Jon 1957- *92*
Zonia, Dhimitri 1921- *20*
Zonta, Pat 1951- *143*
Zubrowski, Bernard 1939- *90*
    Earlier sketch in SATA *35*
Zubrowski, Bernie
    See Zubrowski, Bernard
Zucker, Miriam S.
    See Reichert, Miriam Zucker
Zuckerman, Linda *190*
Zudeck, Darryl 1961- *61*
Zug, Mark *204*
Zupa, G. Anthony
    See Zeck, Gerald Anthony
Zupancic, Lilijana Praprotnik
    See Prap, Lila
Zurbo, Matt(hew) 1967- *98*
Zurhorst, Charles (Stewart, Jr.) 1913-1989 .. *12*
Zurlo, Tony 1941- *145*
Zuromskis, Diane
    See Stanley, Diane
Zuromskis, Diane Stanley
    See Stanley, Diane
Zusak, Markus 1975- *149*
Zwahlen, Diana 1947- *88*
Zweifel, Frances W. 1931- *14*
Zwerger, Lisbeth 1954- *194*
    Earlier sketches in SATA *66, 130*
    See also CLR *46*
    See also SAAS *13*
Zwinger, Ann (H.) 1925- *46*
Zymet, Cathy Alter 1965- *121*